W9-AWT-510

PRINCIPLES OF PSYCHOLOGY

SECOND EDITION

Richard H. Price
University of Michigan, Ann Arbor

Mitchell Glickstein
University College, London

David L. Horton
University of Maryland, College Park

Steven J. Sherman
Indiana University, Bloomington

Russell H. Fazio
Indiana University, Bloomington

Scott, Foresman and Company
Glenview, Illinois
London, England

Cover: Robert Drea for Scott, Foresman.

123456   VHJ   919089888786

Library of Congress Cataloging in Publication Data
Principles of psychology.
  Bibliography: p.
  Includes index.
  1. Psychology.   I. Price, Richard H.
BF121.P7   1987   150   86-29714
ISBN 0-673-18743-8

OVERVIEW

CONTENTS

PREFACE

One of the reasons psychology is exciting to teach and to learn is that it is a series of stories of discovery. In telling these stories to our students, we are presenting the science of psychology at its best. Seen this way, psychology can be enjoyed for its logic, its rigor, and its use of the scientific method. To be sure, the story of discovery in psychology is also a story of false starts and blind alleys that have tested the persistence and insight of those men and women who have contributed to the field through their research. We believe that psychology can be taught in all its complexity without sacrificing accuracy or understanding if we teach it by telling the story of discovery. It is this idea that has inspired us as we prepared the second edition of *Principles of Psychology*.

Our Goals in Preparing the Second Edition

As we reflected on what we had accomplished in the first edition of *Principles* and what we hoped to accomplish in the second, several major themes emerged. First, as with the first edition, we wanted to emphasize psychological research. In order to do this, we believed it crucial to draw on the expertise of active researchers to provide sound scholarship across the broad expanse of psychology. In addition, we wanted to add depth to several chapters while maintaining our orientation to comprehensive content. Third, we planned the format design and illustration for this edition to be even more inviting and engaging. Finally, we felt that this edition of *Principles* should have a special set of learning aids designed especially for it.

Research: The Story of Discovery

Psychology is a method of inquiry as well as a body of knowledge. In addition to describing what we know about behavior and mental processes, *Principles* explains precisely *how we know it*. For example, one of the most exciting new areas of psychological research focuses on the chemistry of the brain. *Principles* describes not only the newest findings about the ways in which these chemicals influence behavior, but also tells the fascinating story of how they were discovered in the first place. Such stories, interesting in their own right, demonstrate the fascinating processes of psychological research. By understanding these processes, students are more likely to retain important information and to achieve insight into psychology as a dynamic evolving science.

Both in the text and in special features, *Principles* tells the story of how important scientific discoveries in psychology have been made and shows their significance for current theory and research. For example, in the introductory chapter, we discuss the discovery of ''opiate receptors'' by Candace Pert and Solomon Snyder and consider its meaning for contemporary understanding of brain and behavior relationships. At the same time, we tell classical stories of discovery such as Paul Broca's discovery of the area of the brain that controls speech and Otto Lowi's dream that inspired the experiment uncovering evidence of neurotransmitters in 1921. Still other stories of discovery relate to the intense competition between contrasting learning and biological perspectives to explain phenomena such as learned helplessness.

The Author Team

Such is the breadth of modern psychology that no single author can hope to encompass all of its variety with the accuracy and authority that comes from sound scholarship and firsthand research. The principal authors represent a wide range of authority and expertise. They are: Richard H. Price of the University of Michigan (personality, intelligence, abnormal psychology, behavior change); Mitchell Glickstein of University College, London, England (physiological psychology, sensation, and perception); David L. Horton of the University of Maryland (learning, memory and cognition, language, statistics); Steven J. Sherman and Russell H. Fazio, both of Indiana University (social psychology, motivation and emotion); Julian M. Davidson of Stanford University (consciousness, sexual behavior); and David M. Brodzinsky of Rutgers University (development). Each of our authors is an active researcher who has also made contributions to psychology's story of discovery.

Coverage in the Second Edition

Our goal in the second edition was to provide as thorough a text as possible, a book with both breadth and depth, within the constraints of the introductory course. This means a sophisticated, straightforward text appropriate for psychology majors and comprehensive enough even for a two-semester course. Chapter 1 presents the story of discovery theme and describes the science and the scientists in psychology's history who have shaped modern day psychology. From that beginning, the entire range of topics traditional in the mainstream courses of psychology is then surveyed in this text.

In addition, *Principles* presents in unusual detail, several areas of investigation that reflect the widening scope of psychological research. An entire chapter, for example, is devoted to sexual behavior. We also paid particular attention to the rapid growth of psychobiological research in the past two decades. While Chapter 2 describes the basic structures of the nervous system, including the substrates of behavior at the cellular level, other chapters—for example, Sensation, Perception, Consciousness, and Abnormal Behavior—expand the discussion of the role of the brain.

Chapter 6 on Development has been extensively revised. The foundations of our understanding of development is provided covering physical, cognitive, social, and moral development through the entire life span. Considerable additional coverage has been given to adult development and development in aging to provide a life-span orientation to human development.

Format and Special Features

In thinking about presenting *Principles* to the student in the second edition, we wanted to discuss psychology in prose that is clear, interesting, and lucid without sacrificing depth or accuracy. The concepts and methods of psychology are often complex, and we do not pretend that they are always easily grasped. Yet the most rigorous of experiments and studies typically possess an essence of elegant simplicity. We illustrate this work not only with relevant examples taken from everyday life, but also from stories drawn from the human framework in which research is carried on.

To aid the student, we have begun each chapter with a brief outline of the main topics to be covered and ended it with a concisely detailed summary. Each chapter also contains two brief essays set off from the main text. One, labeled "Research," makes the methodology of psychology explicit and provides an up-close look at how psychologists work and think. It takes the reader step-by-step through an important experiment or study from the original hypothesis and how it was formulated to the results and the implications of the findings. Our discussion centers on studies and experiments that expand on chapter topics. For example, the "Research" essay in Chapter 5 (Conciousness) discusses the surprising recent study of the "near-death experience."

Chapter 13 (Intelligence) recalls in careful detail a classic study of environmental influence. In Chapter 16 (Environmental Influence) the reader is taken to the race track for a novel experiment on dissonance and the two dollar bettor.

The second essay, entitled "Focus," highlights a topic of special interest intended to supplement or amplify material in the main text. The focus may be on an important new finding as in Chapter 2 (The Nervous System)—"The Brain's Own Opiates"; an intriguing insight from animal research as in Chapter 4 (Sensation)—"Senses We Do Not Have"; a controversial issue as in Chapter 10 (Motivation and Emotion)—"The Effects of TV Violence"; or an unconventional approach to treatment as in Chapter 15 (Behavior Change)—"Therapy Through Folk Healing."

In addition, the illustration and design program for the second edition of *Principles* has been carefully structured to invite the reader into the content of each chapter, using illustrations and drawings to amplify and explain fundamental concepts discussed in the text.

Supplementary Materials

The needs of today's instructors and students demand not only a text with a solid base in scientific research, but also a full and broad array of ancillary materials to make teaching and learning more effective.

Coursepack is a combination study guide/anthology designed to assist students in learning the subject matter of psychology and to excite them about the subtleties of psyshological research. Written by William Buskist (Auburn University), Part I contains chapter outlines, learning objectives, identification exercises, suggested readings, and short-essay and multiple-choice drill questions; in addition, for each chapter a 20-item practice quiz (with the answer key in the *Instructor's Manual* only) can be assigned by the instructor for extra drill or as a pop quiz. Part II of *Coursepack* is the anthology; it includes a selection of brief essays on important issues in psychological research. These essays are not meant to be exhaustive but rather to stimulate students' interest and broaden their awareness of the role of research in psychology. Multiple-choice items follow each essay to check student learning. Most important, *Coursepack* is shrinkwrapped with each copy of the text—that means *every* student will have a copy of this innovative study aid.

In addition to *Coursepack,* there are available excellent resources specifically designed for the instructor. The *Instructor's Manual,* also prepared by William Buskist, is written especially for first-time instructors. It includes over 2000 multiple-choice items; annotated lecture outlines for each chapter, referenced to the text and to *Coursepack;* suggestions for teaching and organizing the course; and suggested readings. Available, too, are the following: two- and four-color transparencies/35mm slides; a videotape library consisting of short videotaped experiments, demonstrations, and high-interest features covering the broad spectrum of psychology; computerized test items; DIPLOMA, a computerized classroom management system; and SIMLABS, a set of computer-simulated laboratory experiments.

Acknowledgments

The writing and preparation of the second edition has required the effort and support of many individuals. Our appreciation is extended to those psychologists who have reviewed the manuscript in its several drafts and who have contributed to its improvement, coherence, and overall refinement. They were:

Richard Burns   Georgia Southwestern College
Peter Crane   University of Pittsburgh, Johnstown
Joseph Eubanks   San Antonio College
Phillip Freedman   University of Illinois, Chicago

Bruce Fretz   University of Maryland, College Park
Josh Gerow   Indiana University - Purdue University at Fort Wayne
Daniel Kaye   UCLA
Donald Kline   University of Notre Dame
John Kulig   Carthage College
Joan Lockhart   University of Washington, Seattle
Jane Ellen Maddy   University of Minnesota, Duluth
Gerald Miller   University of Texas, El Paso
Richard Sanders   University of North Carolina, Wilmington
David Schroeder   University of Arkansas
Joseph Stokes   University of Illinois, Chicago
A. Bond Woodruff   Northern Illinois University

A special note of appreciation is due to Alfred Kellam of the University of Michigan, a dedicated teacher of introductory psychology who aided substantially in the final revisions of many of the chapters in this edition. We also wish to thank our friends and colleagues, the competent and supportive people at Scott, Foresman whose aid and resourcefulness were so instrumental in completing the second edition. They are: Scott Hardy, Acquisitions Editor who engineered the entire process; Joanne Tinsley, Developmental Editor, and Elizabeth Fresen, Project Editor whose patience and commitment to detail and accuracy were so remarkable. In addition, we wish to thank Heidi Fieschko, who designed the text, and Sandy Schneider, Senior Picture Researcher. Each of these people at Scott, Foresman contributed their high standards of professionalism to this second edition of *Principles of Psychology*.

Richard H. Price

University of Michigan, Ann Arbor

PRINCIPLES OF PSYCHOLOGY

SECOND EDITION

1

Psychology: The Science and the Scientists

1

The Science and the Scientists

Approaches in Psychology

The Behavioral Approach
The Cognitive Approach
The Psychodynamic Approach
The Humanistic Approach
The Biological Approach
Contemporary Approaches and Psychological Science

Methods in Psychology

Correlational Research
Experimental Research
Comparing the Correlational and Experimental Methods

Summary

Focus: On the Frontiers of Research

Modern novelists often describe in minute detail practically everything the protagonist thinks, feels, and does during a single day. If you were to attempt such a narrative of 24 hours in your own life, the result might be as long as a novel such as James Joyce's *Ulysses*. As a matter of fact, themes woven through your narrative would resemble the chapter headings in our table of contents.

For example, your every breath and heartbeat are controlled by the nervous system (chapter 2). What you see and hear would be discussed under the titles of sensation and perception (chapters 3 and 4). Your dreams and daydreams would be described as states of consciousness (chapter 5). Your classroom performance would reflect processes of learning (chapter 7) and memory (chapter 8), along with motivation (chapter 10) and intelligence (chapter 13). Your relationships with others would represent social influence (chapter 16) and social interaction (chapter 17).

All of this and more—24 hours in your life, all of the years in all of our lives—is the province of psychology and the scope of this textbook. **Psychology** is the study of mind and behavior. It embraces a dozen or more areas of specialization as shown in Figure 1.1. What holds together the complex pluralism of psychology is the effort of psychologists to understand, predict, and control behavior.

This book reflects our conviction that psychology can be more fruitfully studied in terms of the processes psychologists use to learn about behavior rather than as an established and static body of truth. There are few immutable laws of behavior; theories and knowledge change in all sciences. Thus, where possible, our approach will be to focus on psychology as a method of inquiry, a way of thinking about problems and approaching them through observation and experiment. In addition to describing what we know about behavior and

Figure 1.1

Employment settings and specialty areas of APA members (based on Stapps & Fulcher, 1983).

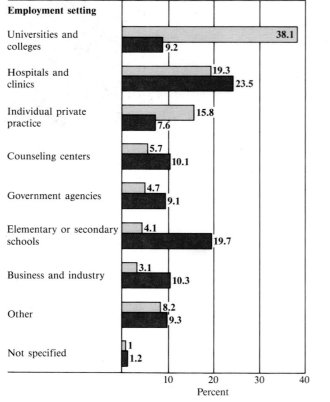

Employment settings for APA members with full-time positions
(Based on Stapp & Fulcher, 1983.)

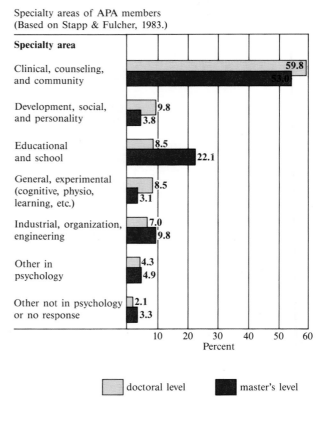

Specialty areas of APA members
(Based on Stapp & Fulcher, 1983.)

CHAPTER 1   THE SCIENCE AND THE SCIENTISTS

mental processes, we will explain how we know it. By understanding psychology as a process, you will be better able to achieve insights into this science of behavior.

Approaches in Psychology

There are several different approaches to the study of behavior and psychological processes. Each of these approaches looks at behavior from a different point of view, fixing attention on one particular aspect.

Before we describe these contemporary approaches in detail, let us look briefly at the roots of psychology, tracing some of the themes that persist in contemporary research. Although people have always attempted to understand behavior and the workings of the brain, the study of psychology as a distinct science is scarcely more than a century old. Most historians date the founding of scientific psychology to 1879, the year when Wilhelm Wundt established his psychology laboratory at the University of Leipzig in Germany.

The new discipline represented a convergence of two streams in philosophy and science. One was the tradition of empiricism with its emphasis on experience. **Empiricism,** proposed as a philosophy by John Locke in the seventeenth century, stressed experience of the world as the source of all knowledge. Because the world is communicated to people through the sensory organs, Wundt was interested in the relationship between the activation of the sense organs by physical events and the resulting psychological experiences.

The other tradition was the science of physiology, which in nineteenth-century Europe resulted in systematic explorations of the brain and nervous system. Wundt was himself a physiologist. The son of a Lutheran minister, and an indefatigable but irascible man (his name in an old German spelling means "sore" or "wounded"), Wundt wanted to study the contents of the mind. His experimental methods may seem naive now, but at least they were systematic. For example, Wundt established stringent guidelines for the use of self-observation, or introspection, in his laboratory experiments: (1) subjects were to control the onset of stimulation; (2) subjects were to be in a state of heightened readiness; (3) experiments were to be repeated several times; and (4) experiments were to involve the controlled manipulation of stimuli. These conditions represented significant advances over previous methods of psychological investigation in which important aspects of an experiment were often not held constant and replications were not deemed critical. Apparently, Wundt was somewhat fanatical about his requirements: Boring (1953) noted that Wundt's reaction time observers had to carry out about 10,000 trials—often consisting of carefully listening to metronome beats—before they were considered qualified to provide valid data.

In launching the new science, Wundt also founded the first school of psychological thought, which was later called **structuralism.** Through identification of the basic elements of mental experience—he considered them to be sensations, images, and feelings—Wundt and his followers sought to understand the structure of the mind.

During the next four decades, at least four other distinct schools of psychology arose to oppose structuralism. Each school had its own particular theoretical approach, methodology, and area of interests: **functionalism** was concerned with the use of the mind in the organism's adaptation to its environment; **behaviorism** rejected the study of the mind and focused on behavior; **Gestalt psychology** emphasized the wholeness and organization of mental experience; and the **psychodynamic approach** of Sigmund Freud looked beyond conscious awareness to unconscious desires and impulses.

Bitter rivalries often marked the differences among the five schools. Today many of these differences are largely of historical interest. But as we consider

John Locke

Wilhelm Wundt

John B. Watson

five contemporary approaches, we will see ways in which the earlier contending schools have influenced modern thought. Indeed, two of the schools—behaviorism and psychoanalysis—have survived with their theoretical perspectives and rivalries virtually intact.

We will now review five major contemporary approaches within the field of psychology. For each perspective, the theoretical principles and fundamental assumptions underlying that approach will be summarized. Also, the major contributions of a well-known psychologist who represents each approach will be described. It must be kept in mind that these perspectives are not mutually exclusive, nor does any single point of view constitute the "whole truth" with regard to a given psychological event. Rather, the synthesis of many divergent kinds of information is necessary in order to comprehend even apparently simple actions.

For example, let us consider the routine act of eating a sandwich for lunch. The biological psychologist's interest might be drawn to the neural mechanisms underlying the urge to eat, and how food intake leads to satiation. The behaviorist might feel compelled to assess the person's actions in the context of previous learning experiences and examine how environmental factors operate to maintain the eating response in its present form. In contrast, the cognitive psychologist might examine the thoughts, images, and mental representations that accompany the act of eating. A psychoanalyst might seek to discover the symbolic meanings consumption has for the individual. On the other hand, the humanistic psychologist might try to understand how eating fits into the person's view of self. In the chapters that follow, we will dissect a broad range of psychological phenomena in a similar fashion in order to gain a more thorough understanding and appreciation of the complexity of human experience.

The Behavioral Approach

Concerned chiefly with stimuli—events in the environment—and the resulting behavioral responses, the behavioral approach is sometimes called S-R psychology (for stimulus-response). Behavior is viewed as a series of learned responses and is limited to observable actions. In effect, behaviorists consider mental activities and conscious experiences as if they were events occurring in a "black box" and disregard them in favor of observable responses. What goes on inside the black box cannot be objectively observed or measured, it is argued—only what goes in (the environmental stimuli) and what comes out (the behavioral response) can be observed and measured.

Behaviorism has dominated American psychology for most of the seven decades since it was formulated by John B. Watson of Johns Hopkins University in 1913. Watson was greatly influenced by the work of the Russian Ivan Pavlov, who had conditioned dogs to salivate at the sound of a bell. Behavior, Watson said, was a succession of conditioned responses to environmental stimuli. Such stimuli are objectively observable and measurable, Watson pointed out, unlike subjective mental processes. He defined the new goal of psychology as "the prediction and control of behavior" (Watson, 1913).

In 1924 in his book *Behaviorism,* Watson, a skillful and enthusiastic propagandist who later became a successful advertising executive, hinted at the awesome potential of behavioral psychology:

"I should like to go one step further now and say, 'Give me a dozen healthy infants, well formed, and my own specified world to bring them up in, and I'll guarantee to take anyone at random and train him to become any type of specialist I might select—doctor, lawyer, artist, merchant-chief, and yes, even beggarman and thief, regardless of his talents, penchants, tendencies, abilities, vocations, and race of his ancestors.' I am going beyond my facts and I admit it. . . . Please note that when this experiment is made I am to be allowed to specify the way the children are to be brought up and the type of world they have to live in."

Watson's strident behaviorism has been qualified by a number of later researchers, principally Edward Tolman, Clark Hull, and B. F. Skinner. Tolman and Hull made behaviorism less simplistic. Specifically, Tolman demonstrated how a behavioral model could be developed to handle cognitive constructs—what goes on in the black box (Tolman, 1932, 1938, 1948). Hull showed how theoretical constructs could be measured. Hull's theoretical efforts remain the most ambitious attempt to explain all behavior—animal and human—with a single model (Hull, 1943, 1951, 1952).

Today's behaviorists have continued to move away from the strict behaviorism of Watson and have increasingly acknowledged the role of private "mediating events" such as thoughts and images. Other psychologists known as social learning theorists emphasize the critical importance of imitation in the process of socialization. Thus, many behaviorists have allowed the return, if only in a limited way, of internal experiences to their domain of study.

The behavioral perspective remains a strong influence in modern psychology. Let us now look at the behavioral approach in more detail by examining the life and work of B. F. Skinner, one of its leading proponents.

B. F. Skinner: Of Pigeons and People

B. F. Skinner is probably American's best-known psychologist. His name has become synonymous with an approach to learning—in animals and in humans—that is formally called operant conditioning. The essence of Skinner's approach, which has long been a dominant force in American psychology, is the assertion that behavior is shaped not from within the organism but from without—by reinforcements (Skinner, 1938).

Growing up early in this century in Susquehanna, Pennsylvania, Skinner was intrigued by animal behavior, mechanical gadgetry, and writing—three interests that would mark his career. At Hamilton College he majored in English but was fascinated by the writings of John B. Watson, the founder of the behaviorist movement, which held that the environment alone determined behavior. After two years during which Skinner later said he "failed as a writer," he entered the doctoral program in psychology at Harvard University.

At the University of Minnesota, Indiana University, and finally back at Harvard, Skinner conducted his famous laboratory experiments in learning

The Skinner box is a soundproof enclosure with a food dispenser. Food is used to reward the animal at first for lever pressing and later for more complex actions.

through operant conditioning (operant because the organism operates upon the environment). In these experiments, Skinner demonstrated how pigeons and rats could be conditioned by systematic rewards. The animals were placed in a special apparatus Skinner had designed. Now known as the Skinner box, or operant chamber, it was a soundproof enclosure with a food dispenser that a rat could operate by pressing a lever and a pigeon could operate by pecking a key. Food was used to reward the animals, at first for lever pressing or key pecking and later for more complex actions (Skinner, 1956).

By rewarding parts of a desired behavioral sequence, Skinner was able to condition his animals to perform seemingly extraordinary feats. He taught pigeons to play a kind of Ping-Pong and to dance with each other, and during World War II he even worked out a scheme to guide missiles by the pecking of pigeons (Edson, 1975). Although the plan was not put to use, Skinner convincingly demonstrated that he could indeed train pigeons to guide missiles.

From his work with animals Skinner concluded that all behavior could be explained in terms of the contingencies of reinforcement—when and how the subject is rewarded for what action. This perspective has had enormous influence on the study of psychology and on learning theory in particular. It has also resulted in widespread practical applications. These include teaching machines, which provide immediate reinforcement during learning, and programs of behavior modification in which systematic rewards are aimed at changing the behavior, for example, of prison inmates and mental patients (Skinner, 1953).

Skinner has reached a wide audience with his ideas about controlling behavior in two popular and highly controversial books. *Walden Two*, published in 1948, is a fictional account of a utopian community based on the benevolent control of people through the principles of operant conditioning. In his nonfiction version of behavioral control, *Beyond Freedom and Dignity,* published in 1971, Skinner argues that none of us has real freedom of choice. Because we are already being shaped by external influences that tend to be haphazard, Skinner says, we should utilize the principles of systematic behavioral control in order to attain the good of all, thereby creating a world free of war, pollution, and other threats to survival.

The Cognitive Approach

The cognitive approach stresses the importance of what intervenes between stimulus and response—the psychological processes themselves. In this view, behavior is the outward manifestation of internal psychological processes. As we have seen, psychology as a science began with Wundt's attempt to analyze mental processes, which also was the focus of the functionalist and Gestalt schools. The best known of the early American psychologists, William James, brother of novelist Henry James, was particularly concerned with the study of consciousness. To James, the mind was a continuous, ongoing "stream of consciousness" that could not be analyzed into elementary building blocks. His method, like Wundt's, was simple introspection—looking inward to examine one's own mental and emotional states.

In recent years, after decades of dominance by the behavioral tradition, American psychology has begun looking inward again at such cognitive functions as perception, thinking, memory, and consciousness.

More relevant to cognitive theorists is the information-processing model provided by the modern computer. Many cognitive theorists view psychological processes as a kind of information processing, which receives inputs from stimuli, retrieves stored-up memories, makes comparisons and decisions to solve problems, and produces outputs in the form of behavioral responses.

When we see an old friend, our brains actively process pinpoints of light and transform them into an image. The image is recognizable because we are able to match it with stored memories.

This rather abstract information-processing concept becomes more concrete if we look at perception. When we see an old friend, we are not passive receivers of an image from the physical world. The stimulus, or input, in fact, consists of nothing more than pinpoints of light. Our brains actively process these pinpoints of light and transform them into an image. The image is recognizable as an old friend because we are able to match it with stored memories. Retrieval from storage occurs here, along with some sort of comparison process. Further processing and decision making that lead to the response: we say "hello" to our old friend.

One of the great pioneers in the cognitive tradition, Jean Piaget has proposed detailed theories about the nature of cognition as it develops in the child. This developmental view of cognition has had a profound effect on our ideas about both the nature of thought and the course of development. Let us consider Piaget and his ideas in more detail.

Jean Piaget: How Children Think

When Jean Piaget died in 1980 at age 84, he had established a formidable reputation as the most influential theorist in the history of developmental psychology. Developmental psychologists study the factors that shape changes in behavior from infancy through adulthood. For nearly six decades, Piaget investigated how children think, illuminating the ways in which their thoughts differ from adult reasoning and showing the progressive stages in the process of mental growth.

Piaget himself was something of a prodigy. At age 10 he published his first scientific paper on mollusks (marine invertebrates such as oysters). Later he was offered a curatorship in a museum in Geneva but had to turn it down because he was still in high school. By age 22 he had his doctorate in biology but was switching his intended field of research from mollusks to children. While studying at the Sorbonne in Paris, he worked with children in the laboratory of Theophile Simon, the codeveloper of early intelligence tests, and there Piaget evolved some of the methods that would characterize his later research. He returned to Geneva to teach and to seek among children a sort of "embryology" of intelligence—an understanding of how thinking grows and develops—as does an embryo.

Piaget's research methods differed from those of most psychologists. He watched and listened to children, including his own two young daughters. He

Jean Piaget watched and listened to children, and, from his observations, distilled a whole new perspective on cognitive development.

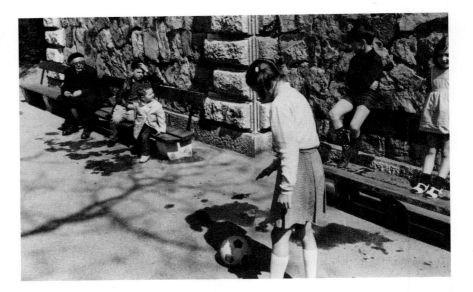

Jean Piaget watched and listened to children, and, from his observations, distilled a whole new perspective on cognitive development.

played with children, getting down on his knees to shoot marbles or join in other games, sharing the child's view of the world. He constantly asked children questions and, by asking more questions, attempted to understand the thought processes behind their answers. He also devised simple experiments but had little use for the scientific controls or statistical measurements that characterize much of modern psychology.

From his observations, Piaget distilled a whole new perspective on cognitive development, the ways in which children learn to think (Piaget, 1926/1959). Children do not think like miniature adults, as many people believe. He demonstrated, for example, that infants do not possess a characteristic that psychologists call object permanency—if an object is no longer in sight, infants act as if it no longer exists (Piaget, 1963/1974). Similarly, not until about age seven do children develop the notion of conservation of quantities—comprehension that the quantity of a liquid, for example, does not change when it is poured into differently shaped vessels.

Piaget formulated his findings into a theory that intellectual development proceeds in an orderly schedule of four stages. According to Piaget, this sequence is universal and invariable, the result of genetic programming and of the child's interaction with the environment. The four stages range from the infant's exploration of simple physical objects to the adolescent's development of abstract reasoning (Piaget, 1962).

Piaget's work, set forth in more than 60 books, has had important implications for the education of children. His theory of the four stages of mental growth suggests limitations: learning must be geared to what a child can comprehend at a given age. On the other hand, his emphasis on the child as an active problem solver who is constantly acting upon the environment suggests new possibilities; for example, it has helped popularize the so-called discovery method of education whereby children learn by doing. Perhaps most important, Piaget demonstrated that practically all children will inevitably develop intellectually and learn—sometimes in spite of the educational system available to them.

The Psychodynamic Approach

The psychodynamic approach suggests that human behavior is the result of a complex interplay of psychological processes, both conscious and those beyond the horizon of our awareness. This position emphasizes the struggle be-

Piaget's four stages of intellectual development range from the infant's exploration of simple physical objects to the adolescent's development of abstract reasoning.

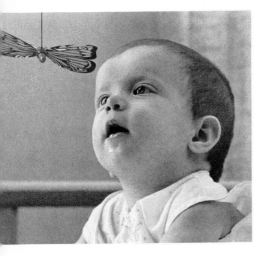

CHAPTER 1   THE SCIENCE AND THE SCIENTISTS

tween the rational and irrational aspects of one's personality, and assumes that conflict, in varying degrees, is intrinsic to the human condition.

According to this view, tension results when basic instincts that press for unrestricted, immediate gratification come into conflict with societal restrictions to inhibit our desires and conform to external demands. These primal impulses must be tamed by increasingly elaborate psychic mechanisms that ultimately relegate primitive urges, wishes, and fantasies to the realm of the unconscious, from which they exert their effect upon overt behavior indirectly or in symbolic fashion. We humans are viewed as forever embroiled in a struggle to gain control over aspects of our psychological selves into which we have little insight and which often represent the more savage elements of our characters.

The psychodynamic approach has been broadly applied in the treatment of people experiencing various forms of emotional distress. As a consequence of this decidedly clinical orientation, its principal theoretical underpinnings have come primarily from the observation of people undergoing intensive treatment and from their case histories.

The originator of the psychodynamic approach was Sigmund Freud, a Viennese physician. Although Freudian psychoanalysis launched the psychodynamic movement, the two terms are not synonymous. The psychodynamic perspective also embraces the theories of disciples who later broke with Freud, most prominently the Swiss psychologist Carl Jung. Differing with Freud on the importance of sexual motives (Jung thought them less significant), Jung established his own movement called analytical psychology, which draws heavily on the insights of myth, literature, and art (Jung, 1954–1979). Other followers of Freud such as Erich Fromm and Karen Horney (sometimes called neo-Freudians) modified psychoanalytic theory to take into account the role of social and cultural factors.

The psychodynamic approach has been used not only in understanding abnormal behavior but also by historians, biographers, and literary critics as a conceptual tool for understanding the formative experiences of historical figures. The writing of psychohistory—as practiced, for example, by Erik Erikson in his biography, *Gandhi's Truth* (1969)—has stimulated a major intellectual movement in this direction.

In addition, psychodynamic concepts have also been used to explain normal behavior. For example, slips of the tongue (Freudian slips) and symbolism in dreams can be understood within a psychodynamic framework as revealing hidden ideas and conflicts. Similarly, forgetting a certain fact or misplacing an item of importance may, within this model, reflect the influence of unconscious motives and desires.

In later chapters we will see the widespread influence of the psychodynamic approach. This viewpoint has shaped theories of developmental psychology, personality, abnormal behavior, and psychological treatment. Perhaps the best way to understand the psychodynamic approach is to examine the work of its founder, Sigmund Freud.

Sigmund Freud

Sigmund Freud: Uncovering the Unconscious

Love/sex fuse

In the late 1880s, Freud was treating patients who suffered from hysteria, a disorder in which people displayed physical symptoms, such as temporary paralysis, that had no apparent physiological basis. Freud and his colleague Josef Breuer used hypnosis as a means of trying to retrieve lost memories and experiences from their patients (Breuer & Freud, 1895/1966; Freud, 1905/1953). To Freud's surprise, the patients revealed past experiences and early traumas that appeared to be symbolically related to their symptoms of paralysis. From these early observations and later analyses of dream content, Freud developed the idea that much of the psychological life of the individual was unconscious—inaccessible to the individual by ordinary means.

Jean-Paul Sartre

Freud eventually became disenchanted with hypnosis and began to instruct his patients to say aloud whatever thoughts came to mind no matter how insignificant or bizarre they might seem. This process was termed **free association.** Freud hypothesized that repressed memories could be unearthed by following the elaborate associative linkages provided by the patient's unedited flow of material. Freud tried to interpret these connections between ideas in the hope of ultimately identifying, clarifying, and thus neutralizing the negative effects of traumatic childhood memories.

To his dismay, Freud quickly found himself frustrated by his patients' often subtle refusal to adhere to the fundamental role of free association; powerful *resistances* were blocking the road to insight. Freud concluded that forces were at work to reduce the patient's self-awareness and prolong neurotic misery. Put another way, suffering itself seemed to provide the person with sufficient ''gain'' to resist the analyst's best efforts. Freud then set about to decipher this network of resistances and discover how unconscious mechanisms were employed to obstruct the person's movement toward health.

Freud generalized his theoretical constructs to include behavior of normal persons as well. The concept of the unconscious and the idea that each of us experiences conflicting inner motives and drives that we must reconcile are two cornerstones of Freud's theory of psychological life.

Aside from his emphasis on the unconscious aspects of mental life and the methods by which emotional distress may be delineated, Freud is probably best known for his psychosexual theory of human development. He believed that everyone is born with an innate sexual instinct that produces a fairly regular sequence of psychological and sexual (psychosexual) development in children. Freud saw people's character as developing out of the ways in which their psychosexual development was handled. These concepts have influenced the modern study of personality and, in particular, the treatment of the emotionally disturbed.

The Humanistic Approach

Of all the viewpoints in psychology, the humanistic approach is the most difficult to encapsulate. In large part, it represents a reaction against what is perceived as the deterministic emphasis of the other approaches: against the view of human beings as simple stimulus-response machines, supercomputers, or helpless creatures of unconscious forces. It opposes the reduction of behavior to mechanistic processes and affirms the unique wholeness of each human being. In this view, the key to understanding a person's thoughts and actions is an appreciation of his or her subjective experience—the individual's own perception and interpretation of external events and personal goals.

The humanistic stress on the wholeness of human experience stems in some measure from the earlier school of Gestalt theorists who insisted that the psychological experience is greater than the sum of its parts. A more important influence, however, has been exerted by the philosophy of existentialism as manifested in the writings of the Danish theologian Sören Kierkegaard and the French author Jean-Paul Sartre.

The leading contemporary force in humanistic psychology is Carl Rogers. His model of human behavior emphasizes the essential goodness within people and their continuing struggle to maximize their potential. Rogers' client-centered, nondirective therapy has helped shape the course of clinical psychology and of counseling. Other humanistic theorists have included the existential psychologists Rollo May and Abraham Maslow, who developed the concept of self-actualization to describe what Rogers calls the highest human motivation—the need to fulfill one's individual potential.

The methods of the humanistic approach are highly intuitive; some psychologists would call them unscientific and unsystematic. Perhaps the greatest

Rollo May

impact has been felt outside the formal discipline of psychology. In the human potential movement, the approach's antimaterialism, essential optimism, and refusal to impose theoretical preconceptions have appealed to millions of people in search of self-fulfillment. Let us turn now to look more closely at the humanistic approach through the work of Carl Rogers.

Carl Rogers: Empathy and Becoming

The approach to behavior advocated by Carl Rogers differ sharply from that of his frequent and friendly antagonist, Skinner. Whereas Skinner is an experimental psychologist, deriving his ideas originally from carefully controlled laboratory studies, Rogers represents an area of research and practice in which intuition often plays a decisive role. Rogers is a clinical psychologist whose theories have greatly influenced the study of personality and the treatment of emotional disturbances.

Carl Rogers

Rogers' own career has been marked by the processes of change and growth that characterize his views of the human organism. He grew up in an intensely religious family, spending his adolescent years on the Illinois farm that his father, a successful building contractor, operated as an experiment in scientific agriculture. Young Rogers enrolled at the University of Wisconsin in 1919, intending to major in agriculture. He soon switched to a preministry curriculum and, after graduation, attended Union Theological Seminary. Rogers later wrote that many of the students, himself included, "thought their way right out of religious work" (Rogers, 1961). Rogers already had taken several psychology courses at nearby Columbia University, and he transferred there, completing a doctorate in clinical psychology.

During the 1930s, Rogers worked with delinquent and deprived children for a community agency in Rochester, New York. Guided by the principle that "man's ultimate reliance is upon his own experience," he chafed under the prevailing tenets of clinical treatment, especially the Freudian emphasis on the therapist as an interpreter of the patient's problems. Increasingly, he relied on the client to determine the direction therapy would take. His work led him to formulate a new approach to clinical treatment.

Rogers' approach, nondirective or client-centered therapy, was set forth in 1942 in his book *Counseling and Psychotherapy*. This approach—as refined in research and teaching at Ohio State University, the University of Chicago, and the University of Wisconsin—was a marked departure from orthodox views and made Rogers the subject of considerable controversy. In client-centered therapy, no formal guidance is provided the client. The therapist attempts to empathize with clients and to help them clarify their own feelings. The task of the therapist is to facilitate an inner force for growth—what Rogers calls the "self-directed process of becoming"—but not to try to shape it.

In the 1960s, Rogers became interested in a phenomenon that he had first experimented with 15 years earlier at the University of Chicago—the group encounter. He helped popularize this method through books, television, and even a documentary movie, which won an Academy Award. This deviation from the mainstream of psychology brought further criticism that Rogers' humanistic approach was unscientific. Even his critics, however, concede that Rogers' ideas and his personal example have helped extend the scope of clinical psychology and fostered an expansion of counseling services.

The Biological Approach

The roots of the biological approach can be traced to the surge of physiological research that occurred in the second half of the nineteenth century. It was during this period that physiologists were first able to localize, in particular areas of the brain, structures that mediate behavior, such as speech and voluntary movement. In the late 1860s, for example, two Prussian physicians, Ed-

13

Researchers study perception by recording electrical activity in the brain.

ward Hitzig and Gustav Fritsch, inserted wires into the cortical surface of a dog's brain and found that passing electric current through the wires caused the animal's limbs to move. Thus they discovered the motor cortex, which plays a major role in voluntary movement in both animals and humans. In subsequent experiments involving electrical stimulation of the brain, physiological psychologists have found areas that elicit a variety of emotion and feelings, including pleasure and pain.

In recent years, the chemistry of the brain has become a significant area of research (see Focus, p.25). The study of neural chemistry is turning up clues to the biological correlates of pain, anxiety, depression, and schizophrenia. Psychoactive drugs, such as the major tranquilizers, which helped spur research into the chemistry of behavior, have proved helpful in alleviating the symptoms of mental illness.

In addition, the biological approach investigates possible genetic bases of behavior—inborn predispositions toward a given level of intelligence, for example, or the genetic basis of schizophrenia. Nonetheless, biological researchers aim basically at supplementing, rather than supplanting, the other perspectives in psychology. For example, the new biological hypothesis that schizophrenia is associated with an excess of a chemical neurotransmitter called dopamine, does not necessarily rule out a behavioral hypothesis that schizophrenia is the result of environmental determinants. It is quite possible that neural chemistry is somehow affected by the early childhood traumas stressed by the psychodynamic perspective, or by the learning experiences emphasized by the behavioral point of view.

Today, researchers are able to investigate the neural basis of perception and other processes by recording the naturally occurring electrical activity in single cells of the brain. Other research has begun exploring the neural processes of various levels of consciousness such as sleep, dreams, and drug states. Roger Sperry's work helps us gain an appreciation of how the biological approach has changed our thinking about psychological processes.

Roger Sperry: How the Brain Is "Wired"

Roger Sperry has spent more than four decades studying the relationships between behavior and the intricate and interconnecting patterns that link the brain's nerve cells. In the early 1940s, he provided new insights into how the interconnections developed; a decade later he began a series of important experiments that illuminated the differing functions of the brain's two hemispheres (Sperry, 1961).

Sperry, a native of Hartford, Connecticut, majored in English at Oberlin College. Influenced by his undergraduate courses in psychology, he went on to take a master's degree in psychology at Oberlin and then a doctorate in zoology at the University of Chicago. At Chicago, he came under the influence of a distinguished brain researcher, Paul Weiss, and began the study of how vision is organized in amphibians such as the newt and frog.

Amphibians were the appropriate animals for his experiments because, unlike mammals, their nerve cells regenerate, or grow back, after injury. Sperry's method was a typical one in physiological psychology—manipulate nerve tissue and then observe the behavioral effects of this intervention. The focus of his experiments was the optic nerve, a bundle of many thousands of individual nerve cell fibers that connect the eye and the brain. In one experiment, Sperry severed the optic nerve and then waited for it to regenerate; the nerve grew back in its original position, restoring normal sight. Then, he cut the optic nerve and placed an obstacle in its path; the nerve grew back in the same position even though it had to twist and turn to avoid the obstacle. Finally, he cut the optic nerve and removed the eye from the socket of the animal, rotated it 180 degrees and then replaced it; once again the nerve grew back in its original position, although the animal now saw in reverse (Sperry, 1968). These experiments demonstrated that little is left to chance or experience in the organization and development of the brain's wiring patterns; these patterns appear to be laid down with fine precision by heredity.

In the early 1950s, first at the University of Chicago and then at the California Institute of Technology, Sperry conducted his famed "split-brain" experiments and made his second major set of findings (Sperry, 1968). The purpose was to investigate the function of the corpus callosum, a band of nerve fibers that connects the two hemispheres of the brain. In the beginning, Sperry and his colleagues worked with experimental animals, severing the corpus callosum and rearranging the fibers of the optic nerve so that the visual input from one eye could be isolated in one hemisphere. Later, they studied human subjects who, in order to prevent severe epileptic seizures from being transmitted from one hemisphere to the other, had undergone surgery to sever the corpus callosum.

Through experiments Sperry found that each of the hemispheres is highly specialized for the processing of information. In most of us, the left hemisphere is the principal seat of language and mathematical skills and of logical reasoning; the right hemisphere, by contrast, seems to be superior at such tasks as spatial perception. Furthermore, Sperry discovered that each hemisphere can work independently and has separate consciousness and emotions. Sperry's split-brain work triggered a surge of research into hemispheric specialization and focused interest on that most tantalizing mystery of neuropsychology—how the physiology of the brain generates consciousness.

Roger Sperry

The left hemisphere is the seat of language, mathematical skills, and logical reasoning; the right hemisphere seems to be superior at such tasks as spatial perception.

Contemporary Approaches and Psychological Science

Each of the approaches we have examined here—behavioral, cognitive, psychodynamic, humanistic, and biological—emphasizes a particular aspect of thought and action and, of necessity, relegates other aspects of behavior to the background. Throughout our discussion of different topics we will see these approaches reemerge. In some cases, the biological perspective will be most salient as, for example, in the study of the senses. In others, a combination of views will contribute to our understanding, as in the case of exploring development over the lifespan or in understanding the causes of abnormal behavior.

Like explorers, researchers use a variety of conceptual maps to explore new territory. We can think of the approaches to human behavior we have

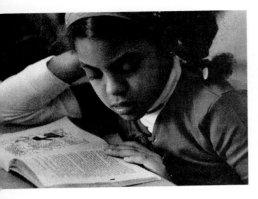

Reading habits are a possible influence on language development. The size of the vocabularies of children may depend on differences in exposure to printed language.

described so far as conceptual maps, too—sometimes in agreement, sometimes in conflict. In still other cases these approaches will describe completely different parts of the territory of human mind and behavior. These approaches will continue to evolve, illuminating our understanding and helping us to ask still more penetrating questions. At the same time, our confidence in the usefulness of these approaches will depend on the evidence we can accumulate to test their validity. How we collect that evidence and how we interpret it is a critical aspect of the enterprise of scientific psychology. Let us now turn to a discussion of those methods.

Methods in Psychology

Like all scientists, psychologist are stalkers of facts. But as Sir Peter Medawar, the British Nobel laureate in biology, has pointed out in his book, *Advice to a Young Scientist,* the scientist is less a hunter of facts than a "seeker after truth." Scientists look for the relationships among facts and try to conceive possible links between cause and effect. "Every discovery," writes Medawar, "every enlargement of the understanding begins as an imaginative preconception of what the truth might be" (Medawar, 1979).

The beginning point for the psychologist then is "an imaginative preconception of what the truth might be," in short, the **hypothesis,** or testable educated guess. The hypothesis may be derived from a larger psychological framework, such as Freud's theory of psychosexual development, or it may stem from a particular interest of the psychologist. For example, while working in the Binet laboratory in Paris, Piaget became interested in the similarity of incorrect responses on intelligence tests made by children of the same age, and how the responses differed in form from errors made by older or younger children. The understanding of these developmental differences in thinking became the focus of Piaget's subsequent investigations. In other instances, the hypothesis may deal less with specific questions than with a broad area of inquiry, as in Skinner's elaborate research on operant responding and the environmental determinants of behavior.

The particular characteristics of a phenomenon with which the researcher is concerned are called variables; they can take on different, or variable, values. The researcher seeks evidence of a relationship between two or more variables. As an example, if we wanted to study the influence of one variable, reading habits, on another variable, language development, we could compare two groups of children: a group of eight-year-olds who read a great deal and a group of eight-year-olds who read considerably less. We could then measure the size of the vocabularies of the children in each group. Differences in vocabulary size may depend, at least in part, on differences in exposure to printed language. Of course, reading habits are only one possible influence on language development. The verbal behavior of parents, language exposure in school, and even television, may have influence on vocabulary size as well. Ultimately, an investigator may come to see reading behavior as only one aspect of a broader concept, such as language environment, that may affect language development.

Our hypothesis, then, would have been that there is a relationship between reading habits and vocabulary size. The hypothesis states an inferred relationship between variables. A **theory** is simply a systematic explanation that consists of a group of unified hypotheses. In our example, the theory might involve the relationship between language environments and language development.

Psychologists must often define complex theoretical concepts in a way that allows them to be measured and tested. This is known as formulating an **operational definition.** For example, the theoretical construct of "achievement motivation" is frequently measured by analyzing the content of stories a person tells in response to a series of ambiguous pictures. If the stories depict characters striving to be successful; it is generally assumed that the subject producing such material has incorporated his or her high need to achieve into the answer. This, the content of a subject's stories constitutes the actual behavior that presumably reflects the individual's degree of achievement motivation.

Although operational definitions are needed in order to conduct empirical research, important ideas may be lost in the "translation" from lofty concepts to specific questions. For instance, the famous historian E. B. Boring's remark that "intelligence is what intelligence tests measure" typifies an operational approach to understanding intelligence, and illustrates how narrowing such a definition can become.

In formulating and testing hypotheses about behavior, the psychologist can use a number of different research methods. These methods can be classified into two basic categories, correlational and experimental.

Correlational Research

Correlational research techniques analyze relationships between variables through observing people or animals, asking people questions, or gathering data from existing documentary sources such as books and previous studies. Psychologists sometimes use a statistical measurement called the coefficient of correlation to measure the degree of relationship (see Appendix). A positive correlation exists if high scores on one set of variables tend to go with high scores on the other set of variables or when low scores on two sets of variables tend to go together. For example, a strong positive correlation has been found between scores on the Scholastic Achievement Test (SAT) given to college-bound high school students and their academic performance in college. People with high SAT scores generally perform well in college. A perfect positive correlation is designated as plus 1.00. If there is no relationship at all between the two variables, the correlation is said to be .00. If, on the other hand, there is an inverse relationship—that is, when high scores from one set of variables go with low scores from the other set or vice versa—the correlation is described as negative. A perfect negative correlation is minus 1.00.

Correlational studies are useful when we want to examine complex situations in which the factors of interest such as age, educational level, or income cannot be directly manipulated by the experimenter. Thus, our interest is in the association among variables. However, once such a relationship between variables is discovered, we must resist making a causal inference or assuming that one factor produced or caused the other to occur. As an example, assume that most teenagers who smoke marijuana show a preference for punk rock music—a positive correlation. This does not mean that smoking marijuana causes the preference for punk music. Neither can it be said that listening to this type of music causes one to smoke marijuana. Perhaps there is a third factor affecting both activities simultaneously, such as the influence of peer pressure or aspects of the social milieu. This example illustrates the fact that simply because two events are highly associated we cannot infer that the first event causes the second to happen. Correlational results provide clues regarding probable causal relationships between events or behaviors, although firm conclusions about what actually caused the relationship to occur can rarely be made.

Observation

All of us are observers of behavior and of our own inner processes. We are constantly making mental notes about these observations and inferring hypotheses from them. For example, one variable in a fellow student's behavior may be a tendency to do extremely well on classroom examinations. We ask ourselves why and look for a possible cause for this effect. If we observe the student spending a lot of time studying, we may conclude that there is a direct relationship between that student's grades and the time spent studying. If, on the other hand, we see that student often at parties and other campus events, we may assume that the other variable resides not in amount of effort but in another condition: the student is highly intelligent, perhaps, or simply very gifted at taking tests.

Psychologists use the **observational method** but in a much more systematic way than laypeople. For one thing, they attempt to maintain an objective attitude, putting aside personal biases and preconceptions. They also attempt to observe with precision, attending closely to the events before them and resisting the temptation to be diverted from the data by premature speculation about cause and effect.

Psychological observation may be as informal as merely being in a setting and making mental notes. The psychologist may even be a participant, as when Piaget got down on his knees and played marbles with the groups of Swiss children he was studying. More often, the investigator remains inconspicuous and records observations in an orderly manner, perhaps with the help of rating scales that permit statistical measurement of the behavior in question. Psychologists who study perception sometimes use introspection, or self-observation.

Highly formal observations typically take place in the psychologist's laboratory. For example, a developmental psychologist studying spontaneous aggression in young children might be stationed behind a one-way mirror that permits the researcher to see without being seen. Laboratories may also be equipped with videotaping equipment to record events or with elaborate electronic devices to monitor physiological changes in the subjects being observed. Thus, observation can range from the most naturalistic of situations—standing

Stationed behind a one-way mirror, developmental psychologists study spontaneous aggression in young children.

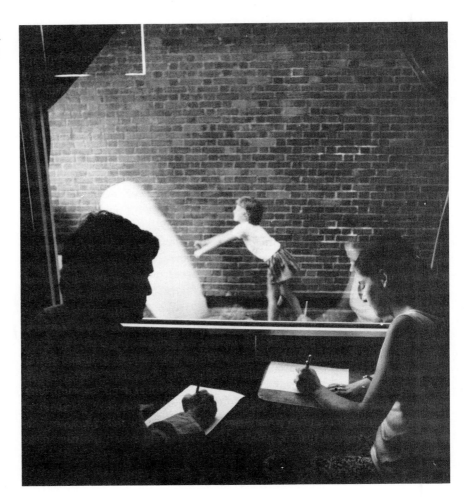

CHAPTER 1 THE SCIENCE AND THE SCIENTISTS

on a street corner and closely watching the behavior of motorists at a stop-light—to laboratory situations in which sophisticated equipment and recording devices may be used.

Asking People

Psychologists can observe behavior and their own mental processes, but they can also ask others. This method comprises a formidable array of correlational research methods: tests, interviews, questionnaires, and surveys.

1. **Tests.** Testing is such an important part of modern psychology that it comprises a special branch of study called **psychometrics.** Psychologists have devised tests to measure all kinds of abilities, interests, attitudes, traits, and behavioral tendencies. These measurements are often helpful in detecting the differences among individuals. The most familiar of such measurements is the general intelligence quotient, or IQ, test. In the diagnosis and treatment of clients in clinical psychology, tests may also be especially useful. One well-known test in clinical psychology is the Rorschach technique, which requires an individual to describe what he or she sees in an ambiguous series of ink-blots. From these descriptions, the clinician then attempts to draw inferences about clients' needs and impulses.

2. **Interviews.** The most direct technique for asking people is the interview, which allows a human give-and-take interaction between psychologist and subject. Some interviews, especially those with clients in clinical psychology, are structured along a predetermined course. Other interviews are less formal, allowing the psychologist to pursue insights as they develop.

3. **Questionnaires.** The questionnaire can provide valuable data for the researcher. This is particularly true in **longitudinal studies** that investigate behavior of the same subjects over a lengthy period of time. One of the most notable longitudinal studies in psychology is the investigation of a group of intellectually gifted children, which was begun in California in 1921 by Louis Terman. Questionnaires mailed to these subjects periodically have enabled several generations of researchers at Stanford University to keep abreast of the subjects' career achievements and personal lives.

4. **Surveys.** The advantage of the survey is that the opinions, attitudes, and experiences of large numbers of people can be assessed. The survey may be in the form of a brief written questionnaire or of an interview conducted by a carefully trained person. As in the questionnaire, the queries must be constructed in such a way as to avoid creating a bias in the answers. The respondents must be chosen so as to be representative of the population being sampled. Political polls are a familiar example of the survey method. The classic example of the political poll that went awry because of an imbalance in the sample was the survey conducted by *Literary Digest,* a national magazine, during the 1936 presidential election campaign. The Republican candidate, Alfred Landon, won the poll hands down. Only after Franklin Roosevelt swept the election, winning every state except Maine and Vermont, did the basic flaw of the magazine's survey become apparent. The survey was conducted by telephone. In those days only citizens with substantial income could afford a telephone and, as many other surveys have shown, upper-income people tend to vote Republican (Link, 1980).

When psychologists use the research method of asking people, they frequently draw on a sample of a population. A **population** is an entire group—for example, the population of California is made up of all the people living in that state. In statistical research a population might be made up of all the residents of California under age 20 who suffer from epilepsy. A population could be all the verbs in English or all the temperatures recorded in Chicago in a given year.

Interviews allow a human give-and-take interaction between psychologists and their subject.

Survey respondents must be chosen so as to be representative of the population being sampled.

Typically, researchers cannot query an entire population, so they choose a **random** (representative) **sample** of the population in question. Results from a study of a sample are projected to be representative—within the boundaries of sampling errors—of the population as a whole.

Case Histories

A familiar technique in clinical psychology is the compilation of the **case history,** which is a kind of psychological biography of the client. The history may combine several of the correlational techniques we have described previously—observation, tests, interviews, questionnaires, and surveys. In addition, the researcher may seek data by examining diaries, books, and other available documents.

Clinicians who compile such case histories are in the position of detectives seeking clues to the solution of a mystery. They look for those variables that seem to have a correlation with the behavior that is troubling the client. For the Freudian analyst, these clues are likely to reside in the early experiences of the client. The most famous case history in all of psychology was written by Freud himself (Breuer & Freud, 1895/1966; Freud, 1905/1953). It was a biography of his first patient, ''Anna O,'' whose symptoms of paralysis, Freud inferred, were associated with impulses previously out of her conscious awareness. This hypothesis was instrumental in Freud's formulation of psychoanalytic theory.

The case history is an important tool often used by clinical psychologists. The case history of the woman pictured here was the subject of a 1957 book by two therapists, Thigpen and Cleckley, called The Three Faces of Eve. *The paintings shown here were each done by a different personality.*

CHAPTER 1   THE SCIENCE AND THE SCIENTISTS

The case history also is valuable in other approaches to personality and abnormal behavior. The humanistic theorist Rogers relied on a combination of observations, tests, interviews, and case histories in developing his method of client-centered therapy and in verifying its efficacy.

Archival Studies

A research method closely related to the clinical case history is the **archival study.** Instead of focusing on one person, the archival study typically attempts to find historical data that sheds light on a particular kind of behavior. For example, in testing the hypothesis that frustration leads to aggression, William Hovland and Robert Sears studied archival records describing the price of cotton and the number of lynchings in the American South during the period 1882–1930. They reasoned that low cotton prices—an indicator of a depressed agricultural economy—would cause frustration and, hence, aggression. And, in fact, they found a significant negative correlation: as cotton prices went down during that period, the number of lynchings increased (Hovland & Sears, 1940).

Of course, other factors may have influenced the number of lynchings—race relations, migration patterns, even economic factors other than cotton prices. This is called a confounding effect: two variables may be correlated with each other because of the effect a third variable has on both of them. As we shall see in the next section, experiments are designed to reduce, as far as possible, the effects of such third or confounding variables.

Experimental Research

The experimental method differs from correlational techniques in an essential way that can be summed up in one word—manipulation. Experiments allow the researcher to systematically manipulate the variables under study in order to arrive at a clear conclusion of cause and effect.

An eminent social psychologist often cited for his ingenuity in designing and staging experiments is Stanley Schachter of Columbia University. His explorations on the effects of social context have ranged from the experience of deviants in a group to eating behavior and obesity. In a classic experiment, Schachter (1959) sought to investigate the circumstances under which people affiliate, or seek out one another. Schachter began with the question: What factors increase or decrease the tendency of people to seek out others? One possible clue, Schachter decided, might be provided by the case histories of people who were deprived of social contact and the opportunity to affiliate—prisoners in solitary confinement, shipwrecked sailors, and volunteers in isolation experiments. In virtually all instances of long-term isolation, people reported feelings of fear and anxiety. This suggested to Schachter a close link between fear and affiliation: if isolation results in fear, perhaps affiliation reduces fear. By this reasoning, Schachter constructed a specific hypothesis: Persons with high fear will tend to affiliate more than those with low fear. To test his hypothesis, Schachter designed an experiment in which he could manipulate the degree of fear experienced by his subjects and then record their subsequent tendency to affiliate.

Schachter had to turn to the experimental method to gain control over the variables. The simplest experimental research involves only two variables. One is the **independent variable,** the condition manipulated by the experimenter: it is independent because the experimenter controls and manipulates it. In Schachter's affiliation experiment, the independent variable was fear: by employing the ruse that some subjects would receive painful electric shocks, he created high fear in some subjects and low fear in others. The other variable is the response being measured: it is called the **dependent variable** because, under the hypothesis being tested, its value is presumed to be dependent upon the independent variable. Schachter's dependent variable was affiliation: he hypothesized that an increase in the independent variable, fear, would result in an increase in the dependent variable, affiliation, which it did. In short, Schachter was able to establish a cause, fear, and an effect, affiliation. More complex experiments may involve several independent and dependent variables and require sophisticated statistical analysis.

Schachter's particular experiment involved people, but many involve animals. In B. F. Skinner's work with pigeons, the independent variable was reinforcement—a fixed amount of access time to food delivered to the bird on a certain schedule—and the dependent variable was the rate at which the animal learned to perform a given task such as pecking a key.

Comparative psychologists study animals because they are often interested in the evolution of behavior. For psychologists whose primary interest is human behavior, animals have several advantages in experimental research. Animal behavior is usually less complex and thus easier to observe and measure. Moreover, animals can be manipulated in ways that would be either impractical or unethical in the case of humans. With rats, for example, the researcher can control practically every variable over the animal's entire life leading up to the experiment. Diet, climate, exposure to other rats, even heredity—all can be manipulated. And because the rat's life span is relatively short, the effects of genetic or environmental influences can be investigated by one researcher over several generations.

Without animals, experimental research in neuropsychology would be virtually impossible. While taking care not to cause unnecessary pain, researchers physically manipulate the brain of a laboratory animal in ways that would be unthinkable in human subjects—cutting nerve tissue, stimulating it electrically, altering it chemically, probing it with microelectrodes, and then often sacrificing the animal for postmortem studies.

How much of the data gleaned from animal experiments can be generalized to human behavior and psychological processes is a continuing issue in psychology. This issue can be assessed only on a case-by-case basis. In the case of neuropsychology, most findings can reasonably be generalized to humans because, at the basic level of the nerve cell, the physiology and chemistry of the brain of lower animals and humans are very similar. Most psychologists

Animal behavior is usually less complex and thus easier to observe and measure. Researchers can control practically every variable over the animal's entire life leading up to the experiment.

CHAPTER 1   THE SCIENCE AND THE SCIENTISTS

agree that the principles of operant conditioning formulated by Skinner from his experiments with rats have at least some limited application to human beings. On the other hand, the frenzied responses of rats to intense overcrowding in laboratory experiments may have little to tell us about how humans, with their enormous ability to adapt to the environment, respond to the high population density of big cities such as New York and Tokyo.

Experimental Safeguards

How can psychologists be reasonably certain that their experiments keep constant all factors except the variables they want to manipulate? The experimental method provides a number of possible safeguards; among them are the control group, random assignment, the ''blind'' techniques, and replication.

The research of Albert Bandura (1971) at Stanford University on the importance of observational learning or modeling in shaping aggressive behavior in children illustrates how the experimental method involves the controlled manipulation of specific variables while others are kept constant.

In his early work, Bandura conducted field studies in which he observed the families of juvenile delinquents. The findings suggested to him that the parents in such families often served as models of aggression and that their children simply learned by example. This led Bandura to hypothesize that children can acquire aggressive behaviors by observing an aggressive adult model. Beginning in the late 1950s, Bandura put this idea to the test in a series of now classic experiments in which children were exposed to adult models who behaved aggressively.

1. **The control group.** When Bandura exposed a group of young children to an aggressive model and then measured their responses, he needed to ensure that the results could be traced to the variable of the model's behavior and not to some other factor. Consequently, he used a **control group** of youngsters who underwent the same experimental procedure, except that the model they saw did not exhibit aggressive behavior. This control group provided a baseline against which to compare the experimental group.

Actually, Bandura employed two control groups. In addition to the two conditions we have recalled—aggressive model and nonaggressive model—there was a third condition in which a group of children was not exposed to any model. In Bandura's experiment, it was conceivable that exposure to any model—aggressive or not—might somehow cause the children to respond aggressively. By setting up a condition in which the children received no exposure to any model, Bandura thus had a second baseline against which to measure the behavior of subjects in the group who were exposed to the nonaggressive model.

Bandura's hypothesis was confirmed: Children who had observed aggressive models tended to be much more aggressive than those who had not. From the models, the children had learned distinctly new ways of being aggressive. Later experiments carried out by Bandura and his colleagues demonstrated that this learning process can occur whether the aggressive models were actually present, or merely shown in a film or on a television screen (Bandura, 1963, 1976).

2. **Random assignment.** There is the possibility that subjects in an experiment already possess the behavioral tendency that is being measured. A number of children in Bandura's experimental group might have been aggressive to begin with; Schachter's subjects in the high-fear condition may have sought out the company of others simply because they happened to be more gregarious than those in the low-fear condition; laboratory rats, through heredity or previous learning, may already have been skillful at running a maze. To prevent such other variables from influencing results, psychologists may first try to

match the subjects in the various experimental conditions by sex, age, or other characteristics that might influence the results: Schachter used only college-age males to eliminate possible variables associated with age or sex. Then to reduce the biasing effects of any other confounding variables, the researcher assigns the subjects to the various experimental conditions by methods of chance—a flip of the coin or random number tables, for example. Thus **random assignment** serves to neutralize the variables that are not being manipulated in the experiment.

3. **"Blind" techniques.** Researchers are human. They often have a vested interest in finding certain results in an experiment: they may want to find evidence for a pet theory. Even when researchers strive to avoid showing bias, they may nonetheless communicate subtle cues to the subjects. Simple tone of voice may suggest to subjects the expectations of the experimenters. And in order to please the experimenters—or to confound them—the subjects may alter their behavior accordingly, thus influencing the results.

Even rats may respond to the experimenter's expectations. It has been shown that when the experimenters think rats are bright, they learn faster than when the experimenters think they are dull. The most likely explanation is that the experimenters who harbor higher expectations for the "smart" rats tend to handle them in different ways than they handle dull rats.

To prevent this sort of influence, a techniques can be used so that the experimenter carrying out the research is kept ignorant, or "blind," about the nature of each experimental condition or group. In human drug experiments, a **double-blind technique** is often used; neither the person administering the drug nor the patients know which group is getting the drug and which is getting an inert substance or placebo.

4. **Replication**. The ultimate safeguard in the experimental method is the ability of other researchers to duplicate the results. If any researchers can perform the experiment in the same manner and obtain the same results, the experiment is said to be replicable. This process helps rule out any flaws in experimental design, bias on the part of the researcher, mistakes in recording the results, and even the possiblity of fraud. If an experiment can be repeated successfully, the reliability of the results is established beyond reasonable doubt. Failure to achieve reliable replication is one of the key reasons research into paranormal phenomena, such as extrasensory perception, is disregarded by many psychologists.

Comparing the Correlational and Experimental Methods

Most psychologists consider the experiment the most powerful tool in exploring behavior. Its great advantage is in the control that enables researchers to establish reliable linkage between cause and effect. The correlational approach, by definition, allows the researcher only to find relationships between variables. If variable A increases when variable B increases, there is a positive correlation, but is there cause and effect and, if so, which is cause and which is effect?

This essential contrast between the experimental and the correlational methods is dramatically illustrated in studies of the effect of television violence on children's behavior. The Bandura experiments in observational learning show cause and effect: young subjects exposed to a film depicting an aggressive model are more aggressive afterward than children exposed to a film of a nonaggressive model. Because the children were randomly assigned to the experimental and control groups, any already existing differences in character traits related to aggression presumably were controlled in examining group differences. By contrast, field studies that find—through tests, interviews, and ques-

FOCUS

Many psychologists labor in the laboratory for decades before diligence, creative insight, and, perhaps, a measure of luck combine to provide an important contribution to the study of behavior. Others make their mark very early. A notable case of the latter is Candace Pert, a researcher who, while still in her twenties, helped pave the way for the remarkable discovery that the brain secretes its own painkillers.

Pert arrived at the frontiers of scientific research in a roundabout manner. She was working as a typist for a psychology professor at Hofstra University when she met her future husband, Agu Pert, a graduate student in brain research. At his urging she majored in biology at Bryn Mawr College and then began graduate work in 1970 at Johns Hopkins University.

Pert decided to a specialize in the chemistry of behavior, a relatively new discipline in the branch of psychology known as physiological psychology, or neuropsychology. This fast-growing field of research now embraces several subareas, including neurophysiology, neuroanatomy, neurochemistry, and neuropharmacology. The goal is to understand the precise relationships between specific behaviors and psychological processes and the physical functioning of the brain and nervous system.

The study of the chemistry of behavior has produced some of the most exciting scientific discoveries of the past two decades. The principal focus is approximately 20 chemicals that are crucial to the process by which electrical impulses are propa-

gated in the nerve cells of the brain. Several of these chemicals, which are called neurotransmitters, have been implicated in mental disorders such as schizophrenia and depression.

For her doctoral dissertation at Johns Hopkins, Pert investigated the effects of morphine on the chemical neurotransmitters (Pert & Snyder, 1973; Snyder, 1977). It was suspected that morphine and other opiates exerted their psychological effects—a feeling of euphoria and the easing of pain—by interfering with the normal functioning of neurotransmitters. One possibility was that the opiates actually simulated the action of the neurotransmitters by occupying the receptor sites on the surface of nerve cells where neurotransmitters normally bind to the cells, as in the manner of a key fitting into a lock.

Working with Solomon Snyder, a noted neuropharmacologist, Pert set out to locate the actual receptor sites that morphine was thought to occupy. Pert and Snyder made use of a recently devised experimental technique called radioactive labeling. They injected into experimental animals morphine that contained a radioactive substance. The morphine

with its radioactive "label" was taken up by the nerve tissue in the animal's brain. Then, at postmortem, the tissue was viewed with a device that reveals radioactivity.

The morphine concentrated on nerve cell receptors in two different areas of the brain. One area is involved in the regulation of mood; the other is involved in sensations of chronic pain. Pert and Snyder called these nerve cell sites "opiate receptors" and concluded it was here that morphine bound to the nerve cells, presumably acting as an artificial neurotransmitter.

The discovery of the opiate receptors set the stage for highly important research by other neuroscientists. Why does the brain contain specialized receptors for opiates? One possible answer is that the brain must have its own naturally occurring painkillers. And, in fact, researchers soon discovered several such endogenous chemical compounds, which are called endorphins—from the Greek for "the morphine within." What began as a doctoral dissertation by Pert has launched several promising lines of research, including attempts by other scientists to synthesize a nonaddictive painkiller.

Pert is continuing her investigation of the brain's receptor sites as a researcher at the National Institute of Mental Health. Her work there includes the "mapping" of the sites where molecules of drugs, such as tranquilizers and marijuana, are believed to bind to particular receptors—work she hopes may lead eventually to better ways of treating mental illness. ∎

tionnaires—a correlation between watching violence on television and behaving aggressively must contend with a basic uncertainty: Which is cause and which is effect? Perhaps children who watch television violence tend to be more aggressive in the first place. In such a case, the presumed effect—aggressive behavior—would actually be the cause; the presumed cause—watching television violence—would actually be the effect.

The contrast between experimental and correlational methods is dramatically illustrated in studies of the effect of television violence on children's behavior.

Why, then, bother with the correlational techniques? First, they provide a much more efficient means of gathering a great deal of data on a number of variables in a relatively short time. Second, they enable psychologists to study problems where the experimental method is not applicable because of ethical or practical considerations. Third, people studied by the correlational method often are more representative of a large sample of the population than are subjects in experiments. It has been said that much of experimental psychology has been built on the laboratory rat and the college sophomore: both are frequently used in experiments simply because they are readily available for study. Finally, correlational techniques typically study behavior in real-live situations, whereas experiments, despite the efforts of researchers to create the illusion of reality, risk being artificial. Even when subjects are successfully deceived about the true purpose of an experiment in social psychology, for example, they know they are being studied and thus are less likely to act naturally or spontaneously.

In summary, both methods of research have their advantages and disadvantages. Both are necessary in psychologicl research, and throughout this book we will draw upon the findings of both methods. Which method is preferable depends largely upon the problems being studied and the aims of the researcher. Ideally, the two methods complement each other: the correlational method is a rich source of ideas that can then be put to the test in experiments. In the final analysis, the experiment is only a technique; how well it serves the study of psychology depends on the quality of ideas being tested.

Summary

1. Psychology is the study of behavior of organisms. Psychology is not one science but many, all examining behavior in different ways. Psychology is best seen in terms of processes rather than as an established and static body of knowledge. This text focuses on psychology as a method of inquiry about behavior—a way of thinking about problems and approaching them through observation and experiment.

2. The discipline of psychology is scarcely a century old, dating from Wilhelm Wundt's establishment of his laboratory at the University of Leipzig in 1879. Psychology represented a convergence of the tradition of empiricism with its emphasis on experience and the burgeoning science of physiology. Wundt's school of thought, later called structuralism, sought to identify the basic elements of psychological experience in order to understand the structure of the mind. The next 40 years saw the growth of other theories and schools of psychological thought. Functionalism was concerned with the use of the mind rather than its contents; behaviorism rejected the study of the mind and focused on behavior; Gestalt psychology emphasized the wholeness and organizations of mental experience; the psychoanalysis of Sigmund Freud looked beyond conscious awareness to unconscious desires and impulses. Today, we group the study of behavior into five broad approaches.

3. The behavioral approach is concerned chiefly with stimuli—events in the environment—and the resulting behavioral responses. Behaviorism, which was formulated by John B. Watson, sees psychological processes as a "black box." What goes on inside the black box cannot be objectively observed or measured—only what goes in (the environmental stimuli) and what comes out (the behavioral response). Behaviorism was modified by later researchers—principally B. F. Skinner.

B. F. Skinner's name is nearly synonymous with the methods of operant conditioning, which emphasize the theory that behavior is shaped not from within the organism but from without—by reinforcement. By rewarding parts of a desired behavioral sequence, Skinner conditioned pigeons and rats to perform extraordinary feats. From his work with animals, Skinner concluded that behavior could be explained in terms of the contingencies of reinforcement. Skinner's methods have had a strong influence on the study of behavior.

4. The cognitive approach stresses the importance of what intervenes between stimulus and response—the psychological experience. Behavior is viewed as the outward manifestation of internal psychological processes. The cognitive approach is particularly applicable to such functions as the learning process, perception, thinking, memory, and consciousness. Many cognitive theorists see the individual as a kind of computer, an information processor that receives inputs from stimuli, retrieves stored-up memories, makes comparisons and decisions to solve problems, and produces outputs in the form of behavioral responses.

Jean Piaget showed that the thought processes of children differ from those of adults. Using observational techniques, Piaget distilled a new theory of cognitive development, a universal and relatively stable schedule of four stages. Piaget demonstrated that practically all children will inevitably develop intellectually and learn.

5. The psychodynamic approach, based on the work of Sigmund Freud, sees human behavior as the result of a complex interplay of psychological processes, both conscious and unconscious. Emphasis on unconscious processes concerns many experimental psychologists because of the difficulties in scientifically observing and measuring them. Nonetheless, the psychodynamic approach remains a strong influence on research attempting to understand personality, sexual behavior, and emotional disturbance.

6. The humanistic approach opposes the reduction of behavior to mechanistic processes. The humanistic approach stresses subjective factors—the individual's own perception, interpretation of external events, and personal goals—and, in particular, the wholeness of human experience as keys to understanding the nature of human behavior. The methods of the humanistic approach are highly intuitive and have been criticized by some psychologists as unscientific.

Carl Rogers is a clinical psychologist whose humanistic theories have greatly influenced the study of personality and the treatment of emotional disturbances. Rogers' work with deprived and delinquent children during the 1930s led to his formulation of nondirective, or client-centered therapy. In client-centered therapy, no formal guidance is provided the client: the task of the therapist is to facilitate an inner force for growth—what Rogers calls the "self-directed process of becoming."

7. The biological approach focuses on the physiological and chemical bases of behavior, relating those behaviors to the workings of the brain and nervous system. In addition, the biological approach investigates the possible genetic bases of behavior—inborn predispositions toward a given level of intelligence, for example.

Roger Sperry has made many contributions to the biological approach. Two of his discoveries are especially important. First, he demonstrated that nerves are not functionally interchangeable as had been thought. His experiments with amphibians showed that the neural interconnections for vision are genetically preprogrammed. Sperry's second major contribution came from his split-brain studies, which showed that each of the hemispheres is highly specialized for the processing of information, can work independently, and has distinctly different consciousness and emotions associated with each.

8. Psychologists use two basic methods of formulating and testing hypotheses about behavior: correlational research and experiments. In both methods, researchers seek evidence of a relationship between two or more variables. When they are not able to control the independent variables under study, in-

vestigators use correlation to study how one variable changes as the other changes. Among the techniques used in correlational studies are observation, asking people (tests, interviews, questionnaires, and surveys), case histories, and archival studies.

9. In experimental research the variables can be systematically controlled in order to arrive at a conclusion of cause and effect. All variables, except the one being studied, are controlled, and the independent and dependent variables are precisely measured. The experimenter manipulates the independent variable while the dependent variable is affected by the changing independent variable.

10. Animals are widely used as subjects in psychologists' experiments. Some animal experimentation is done to study the evolution of behavior. Other researchers seek to translate their findings from animal research into application to human behavior. Animal research offers the advantages of studying behaviors that are less complex than those of humans and thus are easier to observe and measure; moreover, practical and ethical considerations dictate the use of animals in some experiments.

The experimental method offers researchers a number of safeguards for ensuring that all variables except those they want to manipulate are kept constant—control groups, random assignment, "blind" techniques, and most important, replication.

11. The experiment is the psychologist's most important tool in exploring behavior. Its great advantage is in the control that enables researchers to establish a reliable linkage between cause and effect. The correlational approach, by definition, allows the researcher only to find relationships between variables. Ideally, the two methods complement each other; the correlational method is a rich source of ideas that can be put to the test in more highly controlled experiments.

FOCUS: The goal of neuropsychology is to understand the functional relation of the brain and nervous system to psychological processes and behavior. One impressive line of research has involved the study of how the opiates, particularly morphine, affect neurotransmitter substances. Research done by Candace Pert and Solomon Snyder showing that the brain contains opiate receptors paved the way for the remarkable discovery that the brain manufactures and secretes its own opiate-like painkiller.

2

Perception
and
Consciousness

CHAPTER

2

The Nervous System

Paul Broca, a French surgeon, specialized in disorders of the nervous system.

Santiago Ramon y Cajal first demonstrated that the nervous system is a coherent network of neurons.

On April 11, 1861, a patient in a mental institution near Paris was taken to see Paul Broca, an eminent French surgeon who specialized in disorders of the nervous system. Although the patient's immediate problem was a severe infection in his right leg, Broca was more interested in a problem of longer standing. The patient could not or would not talk, but there was apparently nothing wrong with his vocal cords. Because the authorities reasoned that no sane man would consciously choose silence, the patient's failure to talk had kept him in the institution for 21 years. They called him "Tan"; except for an occasional swear word, that syllable was his only utterance.

Broca could not alleviate his patient's infection or speech problem, and six days later Tan died. At the autopsy, he examined Tan's brain. On its surface, in the front part of the left side near the temple, he found a lesion—that is, a mass of scar tissue—that apparently had resulted from disease or an old injury. Broca concluded that the site of the lesion was the area of the brain that controls speech.

About two decades later, in the early 1880s, a little-known Spanish anatomist named Santiago Ramon y Cajal began studying human behavior at a radically different level. Cajal had become obsessed with the new science of histology, the study of organic tissue under a microscope. Working with nerve tissue taken from the brain and spinal cord of birds and other small animals, Cajal (1909–1911) painstakingly pieced together the first coherent picture of the brain at its most basic structural level. The nervous system, he concluded, is a complex communications network of tiny self-contained cells, or neurons.

In Cajal's day very little was known about how nerve cells work, although it was already clear that the basic mechanism of a nerve cell's action is electrical. It is now clear that conduction in the nervous system is accomplished by electrical changes across the outer membrane of nerve cells. Cajal's most important contribution was to recognize that the nervous system, like the rest of the body, is made up of a complex set of individual cells. Successive nerve cells along a sensory pathway, for example, are not fused. In most cases, as we shall see, the actual transmission from one nerve cell to the next is brought about by the release of a tiny amount of a specific chemical substance.

The discoveries of these two men, the Frenchman Broca and the Spaniard Cajal, illustrate two of the foundations of physiological psychology. Drawing on knowledge from a variety of disciplines, including medicine, anatomy, histology, physiology, and chemistry, physiological psychologists seek the answers to fundamental questions about the relationship between the brain and behavior. Like Broca, they ask: Where are the control centers for behavior? Like Cajal they ask: How are the nerve circuits that control behavior organized at a microscopic level? A third, and related, question is: How is behavior related to the functioning of individual nerve cells?

Consider these questions as you read the words on this page. Even though you are sitting quietly, specific nerve cells in your head and body are bustling with electrical and chemical activity. Some guide your eyes along printed lines. Others register the shapes of the letters and, matching these forms against memory, render them into words. Still others monitor and regulate the actions of your heart and lungs, indicate the feel of your hands upon the book, and perhaps even order one hand to your mouth to stifle a yawn.

The most complex circuits of all make you conscious of the fact that you are reading about all of this unseen, unfelt activity in the nervous system. They enable you to ask mentally the questions that confront physiological psychologists and to understand, along with them, the basic what, where, and how of the nervous system.

CHAPTER 2 THE NERVOUS SYSTEM

Structures and Functions of the Nervous System

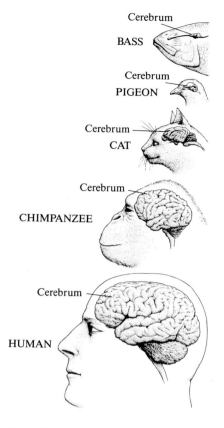

The **nervous system,** of which the brain is the principal part, refers to all of the nerve cells in the body and to all their supporting cells and is one of the body's main communications networks. The nervous system consists of two major subdivisions: the central nervous system and the peripheral nervous system. The central nervous system includes the nerve cells and fibers within the brain and spinal cord.

Organs and muscles in the periphery are connected to the central nervous system by the peripheral nervous system, which is made of groups of nerve cells called *ganglia* and fiber tracts that lie outside of the central nervous system. The peripheral nervous system carries information from the senses, muscles, and organs of the body to the central nervous system. Nerve fibers in both systems serve to conduct nerve impulses along great distances in the body, within the brain and spinal cord, and from the brain and spinal cord to and from sense organs and muscles in the body.

The central and peripheral nervous systems are, of course, interrelated. The so-called peripheral nerves, for example, are made up of large bundles of nerve fibers, many of which have cell bodies that are actually located in the spinal cord. The peripheral nerves connect the brain and spinal cord with **effectors,** or muscles and glands, and with **receptors,** in the skin and deep structures of the body. A similar set of motor and sensory nerves called **cranial nerves** serve the muscles and sense organs in the head.

The Central Nervous System

The **central nervous system** regulates and controls the activity of the entire body. In the very simplest animals there is either no nervous system, as in one-celled animals, or a very primitive nervous system, as in the starfish. But all vertebrate animals, and many of the higher invertebrates, have a well-developed collection of nerve cells and fibers, at the head end of the animal, which receive sensory impressions and regulate behavior. Figure 2.1 shows diagrams of the brains of different animals. The differences among the brains are apparent. It is clear that ''clever'' animals have bigger brains, but it is not true that intelligence within any species is correlated with brain size. For example, human geniuses have brains that are average in size.

In our own discussion of brain structure we will concentrate on the human brain. The brain and spinal cord, which together make up the central nervous system, are clearly the best protected parts of the body (see Figure 2.2). Both are encased in bone. But bone is only the beginning of the protection afforded the brain and spinal cord. Imagine the head from the outside inward. After removing layers of scalp, we come to the skull. If we continue our dissection with appropriate bone-cutting tools and cut through the skull, we come to three heavy, skinlike membranes, or **meninges.** The first membrane we encounter, which is heavy and leathery and surrounds the entire brain and spinal cord, is called the **dura mater,** or hard mother. It is the outermost of the three meninges that surround the central nervous system. The innermost is a delicate membrane called the **pia mater,** the tender mother. Between the pia, the innermost covering, and the dura, the outermost, is the third of the meninges, the **arachnoid.**

Figure 2.1

The size of the brain increases as we move "up" the vertebrate ladder, but it is not true that intelligence within any species is correlated with brain size.

Figure 2.2

Outer layers of brain and spinal cord.

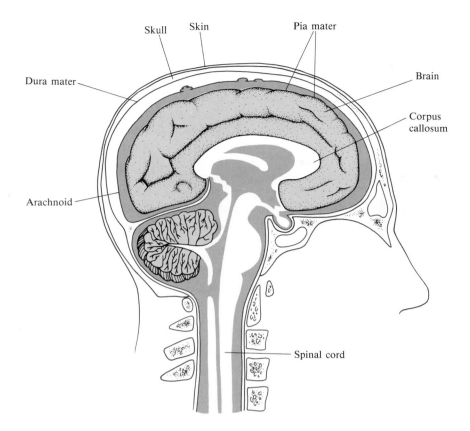

Figure 2.3

Cross section of spinal cord showing spinal tracts and afferent and efferent nerve fibers. The nerve fibers surrounding the butterfly-shaped mass make up the funiculi.

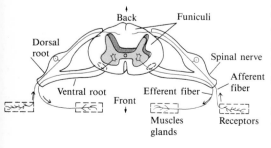

In the thin layer of space between the arachnoid and the pia mater is yet another protective element, **cerebrospinal fluid.** This fluid supplements the brain's arterial circulatory system by supplying nutrients and removing waste matter. It also serves as a buoyant shock absorber, not only further cushioning the brain from the impact of blows to the head but also protecting it from the pull of gravity. Brain tissue is so soft that, if the brain were placed unsupported on a hard surface such as a table, gravity alone would distort it.

Continuing our imaginary dissection, we remove the dura and the arachnoid from the surface of the brain. The pia, which clings to the brain tissue, would be harder to remove. But the pia is so thin that it presents no problem in allowing us to see the true shape of the brain and spinal cord. If the spinal cord were completely exposed, it would be seen as a long cylinder (in humans about as thick as a thumb and about 18 inches long) connecting directly to the brain.

Suppose we cut across the spinal cord at some level (see Figure 2.3). We would see a butterfly-shaped gray mass made up of nerve cell bodies surrounded by white nerve fibers which together are called the **funiculi.** Among these fibers are **afferent tracts** that carry sensations of warmth, cold, touch, pain, and body awareness from the receptors, or sense organs, to the spinal cord, and up to the brain. Others are **efferent tracts** that carry messages from the brain, down the spinal cord to the effectors, or muscles and glands. By severing the spinal cord we would cut off communication to and from the brain, thus depriving the brain of all information from the areas served by these sensory fibers and of all voluntary movement in the muscles served by these motor fibers. A few reflexes, or automatic movements, would remain. For example, a leg might still be withdrawn if a noxious stimulus were applied to the toe, but the person would not feel pain.

The **peripheral nervous system** transmits information back and forth between the various organs in the body and the central nervous system. It comprises the **somatic nervous system**—peripheral nerves that control movement and receive sensory information—and the **autonomic nervous system**—neural networks that control the functioning of the internal organs such as the arteries, heart, stomach, and sweat glands (**viscera**). The autonomic nervous system, in turn, has two parts: the **sympathetic nervous system** and the **parasympathetic nervous system** (see Color Plate 2.1, following p. 44). These two systems tend to have opposite effects on the organs that they control and from which they receive information. For example, the parasympathetic system decreases the rate of the heartbeat, while the sympathetic system speeds it up—a function that occurs during emotional arousal. Generally speaking, the sympathetic system mobilizes resources for emergencies; the parasympathetic system, by contrast, tends to conserve bodily resources.

Structures and Functions of the Brain

Everything we do—from kicking a ball to solving an equation, from flying a kite to composing a song, from firing a gun to picking up a wounded bird—is made possible and is controlled by the elegant and complex processes that take place in our brains. It would seem logical that the brain would have to be much larger than it is to encompass and perform all its myriad tasks. But the brain is a marvel of miniaturization.

All human brains look very much alike but show some variation in size. Popular lore would have it that the bigger the brain the more intelligent the creature. However, there appears to be no relationship between size and function in the human brain, except in extremely rare cases where the brain never attains full growth.

Without any appreciable advancements to the neural sciences, the brains of a number of notable historical figures—among them Lenin and Napoleon—

Everything we do is made possible by the complex processes that take place in our brains.

Early anatomists explored the brain with little clear knowledge of the functions of its structures. Typically they named the structures in terms of their appearance.

have been weighed and measured with great interest after their deaths. On the average, the human brain weighs about 1500 grams. The brain of the Russian novelist Ivan Turgenev weighed more than 2000 grams, but that of another gifted writer, the American poet Walt Whitman, weighed only 1282 grams. Such variations appear to be related in part to body weight. The average weight of a woman's brain, for example, is about 10 percent less than that of a man—approximately the same difference as in average body weight. The largest brain, in fact, belongs to the whale. Its brain weighs 6000 grams, four times the human average, but then whales often tip the scales at 50 tons.

Although brain size does not have important influence on our behavior, just where in the brain certain processes take place is quite important to our movements and thoughts and perceptions. Broca's discovery of the speech area furnished some of the first evidence for a theory of brain function that began to receive increasing support in the last part of the nineteenth century. This theory, known as **localization,** held that control of many aspects of behavior could be traced to specific regions of the brain.

Localization marked a great step forward in the orderly study of the biological basis of behavior. In ancient times most observers were unable even to link behavior to the brain and nervous system. The early Egyptians thought the heart and liver were the seats of human emotions. The Greek philosopher Aristotle was certain the brain could not be the source of feelings because he observed—correctly—that nerve tissue itself is insensitive to pain.

But in about 400 B.C. a fellow Greek, Hippocrates, the father of medicine, was able to draw the correct conclusions. After observing the behavior of patients who had suffered head injuries, Hippocrates, or one of his students, wrote: ''Men ought to know that from the brain and from the brain only arise our pleasures, joys, laughter, and just as well our sorrows, pains, griefs and tears.''

The functions of many parts of the brain have been learned by a variety of methods. One method, as we have seen in the work of Broca, is to observe behavioral symptoms in humans and then to examine their nervous systems at autopsy. Another method is to create lesions surgically in experimental animals and then observe the resulting behavior. Newer methods involve the stimulation of a test animal's brain by electrical or chemical means. Electrical activity from the individual nerve cells is recorded by means of ultrafine microelectrodes—very fine wires or fluid-filled glass tubes about one-thousandth of a millimeter at their tips that record the electrical activity of individual nerve cells.

As the early anatomists explored the brain and the rest of the nervous system, however, they had little clear knowledge of the functions of the various structures. Typically they named the structures in terms of their appearance. Hence, much of the terminology used today to describe parts of the nervous system derives from Greek and Latin roots and bears no relationship to function. One structure in the brain, for example, which we now know is related to emotional control, appeared to be shaped like an almond; thus, it was named amygdala—Greek for almond. Similarly, the hippocampus, a structure involved in learning and memory, got its name from the Latin for seahorse, which—at least in the anatomist's fancy—it resembled.

The Brain Stem

At the base of the skull, rising stalklike from the spinal cord into the skull, is the **brain stem** (see Figure 2.4). From an evolutionary standpoint it is the oldest part of the brain. The lowest part of the brain stem is the **medulla.** Just above the medulla at the base of the brain is an arching band of nerve fibers, which marks the region known as the **pons.** The pons and the medulla control

Figure 2.4

Basic structure of the human brain. In this drawing the brain has been split in two vertically, and the view is of the inner surface of one of the two halves, showing the positions of the spinal cord, brain stem, medulla, pons, midbrain, cerebellum, cerebral hemisphere, corpus callosum, thalamus and hypothalamus (see also Color Plate 2.2).

such largely automatic functions as heart rate and respiration. A broken neck may bring on death by suffocation if it severs nerve connections between the brain stem and the muscles that control chest expansion.

The Cerebellum

Attached to the rear of the brain at the level of the pons is the **cerebellum,** a large structure about the size of a peach (see Figure 2.4). The cerebellum is densely fissured and consists of two distinct hemispheres separated by a central, unpaired region, called the **vermis.** It is now known that the cerebellum helps to maintain the body's equilibrium and to coordinate muscles during fine movements such as threading a needle. There is recent evidence demonstrating that not only is the cerebellum involved in the control of movement, it may also be a major center for motor learning (Gellman & Miles, 1985). Its physical prominence made the cerebellum the subject of much erroneous speculation among early investigators, one of whom, noting that it was especially large in bulls and stallions, concluded that the cerebellum must be a sex center.

The Midbrain

The **midbrain,** which is joined to the pons (see Figure 2.4), contains a large number of nerve fibers that connect structures above and below it. Attached to the base of the brain just in front of the brain stem is a small gland called the **pituitary.** Attached to the top of the brain stem is another small gland called the **pineal.** Though not composed of nerve cells, both serve as regulators of body chemistry and thus influence behavior so markedly that they are considered to be functional parts of the brain. The pituitary secretes hormones that influence a wide range of functions, from body growth to human reproduction. The pineal gland was thought by the seventeenth-century philosopher René Descartes to be "the seat of the soul." In some amphibians, such as the frog, its light-sensitive cells function as a kind of third eye. In humans, recent research suggests, the pineal serves as a built-in timekeeper for the menstrual cycle and manufactures hormones involved in the development of sexual organs.

Septum region   Hypothalamus

Amygdala   Hippocampus

Figure 2.5

View of the interior of the brain through the right hemisphere showing the structures of the limbic system, including the amygdala, hippocampus, and septum (see also Color Plate 2.2).

The interior of the midbrain is made up of a structure called the **reticular formation,** which plays an important role in our state of arousal or awareness. If an animal's reticular formation is massively damaged, it will fall into a coma. The reticular formation also may influence our ability to focus attention by acting as a type of filter permitting some messages from the sense receptors to pass on to conscious awareness while blocking or toning down other messages.

The Cerebrum

The brain stem and its associated structures are practically hidden by the two massive connected bodies that arch above and around them, the **cerebral hemispheres** (see Figure 2.4). Taken together, these hemispheres form the **cerebrum,** which is the center of higher thought and perceptual processes. Several bands of nerve fibers, or **commissures,** join the two hemispheres of the cerebrum across the middle. The largest of these is the **corpus callosum** (Latin for hard body), which is about 3½-inches long and ¼-inch thick and contains an estimated 200 million nerve fibers. It is the relative size of the cerebrum—about four fifths of the brain's volume and weight—and especially its wrinkled gray surface, or cerebral cortex, that distinguishes the human brain most from that of other organisms.

Deep within the cerebrum, clustered around the top of the brain stem, are a number of complex structures: the **thalamus** (see Figure 2.4); which serves as a relay station through which nerve fibers carry all the sensory impressions except smell, which has its own private connection to the higher centers of the brain; the **hypothalamus** (see Figure 2.4); which governs the autonomic nervous system and the pituitary gland, and hence is involved in the regulation of body temperature, appetite, thirst, and sexual acitivites; and the **limbic system** (see Figure 2.5), a ringlike collection of centers including the almond-shaped **amygdala,** the seahorse-shaped **hippocampus,** and the **septum.** Together the hypothalamus and the limbic system are involved in intense emotions, such as anger, fear, and even pleasure. These structures and their apparent functions will be described in detail in chapter 10.

The Cerebral Cortex

The brain is very roughly spherical. Viewed from the top, it is pink and gray and wrinkled like a walnut. This wrinkled, or fissured, surface, which covers much of the brain's exterior, is the **cerebral cortex** (see Figure 2.6). Its grayish color has given rise to the popular expression for people of high intelligence—they have "lots of gray matter." In the brain and the rest of the nervous system, gray matter is made up of masses of nerve cells. The uniqueness of the human brain resides principally in the convoluted folds of the cerebral cortex. These folds or grooves are known as **fissures.** In this crumpled covering, the gray matter of nerve cells is about 2 to 3 millimeters deep and is arranged in a series of parallel layers, each of which tends to have nerve cells of different sizes and shapes. Fish and amphibians have no cortex, and in reptiles and birds it it less well developed than it is in mammals. All mammals have cortex; but in some, like the rat, it is relatively smooth. Human cortex, by contrast, folds in upon itself so much that it triples the surface area that can fit inside the skull. Stretched out flat, it would constitute a sheet of gray matter of about 2.5 square feet. As many as 100 million nerve cells may be packed into a single cubic inch of cortex.

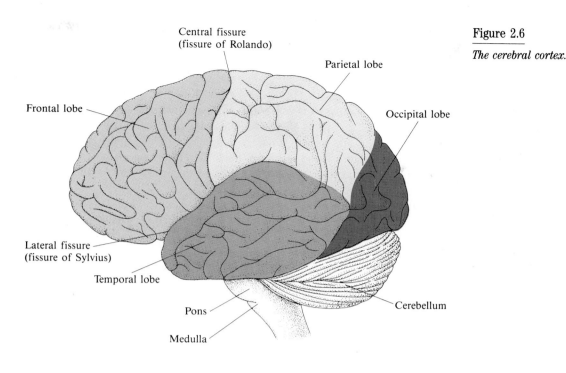

Figure 2.6

The cerebral cortex.

Central fissure
(fissure of Rolando)

Parietal lobe

Frontal lobe

Occipital lobe

Lateral fissure
(fissure of Sylvius)

Temporal lobe

Cerebellum

Pons

Medulla

The deep fissures between the folds create a series of landmarks that serve as convenient reference points on the cortical terrain. Two of them serve as major landmarks and appear on the surface of each half, or hemisphere, of the brain. Both are named for early anatomists: the **central fissure,** also called the **fissure of Rolando,** which cuts laterally across the surface, and the **lateral fissure** or **fissure of Sylvius,** which emerges from the bottom of the hemisphere and curves upward and back along the side. These fissures demarcate each hemisphere into distinct regions, or **lobes.** Each lobe has functions that will help us associate the name and region with particular phenomena of everyday behavior such as speech, movement, and sight. The lobes, which take their respective names from prominent nearby bones in the skull, and some of their functions are as follows:

Occipital lobe, at the back of the head, contains the visual cortex, which processes the sensations of light originating in the eyes.
Parietal lobe, at the top of the head, monitors such sensations as pressure on the skin, heat and cold, and awareness of the location of the body's limbs.
Temporal lobe, next to the temple, has areas concerned with hearing, visual recognition, and the understanding of language.
Frontal lobe, behind the forehead, contains the motor cortex, which helps control voluntary movements. Near the motor cortex is the area, discovered by Broca, which helps control speech.

Mapping the Cortex

The first major attempt at mapping or localizing precise functions in the cerebral cortex was carried out in about 1800 by a Viennese physician, Franz Joseph Gall (Gall & Spurzheim, 1810–1819). Gall was an early champion of localization but his methods and conclusions were all wrong.

Gall was intrigued by the bumps he observed on the heads of his patients and others. These bumps, he theorized, were caused by the mental exercise of certain centers in the cortex that Gall thought bulged like overused muscles. From his everyday observations he pinpointed 24 different areas and related

Figure 2.7

Chart used in the pseudoscience of phrenology, which expanded the concept of localization of mental activity.

them to behavioral traits. For example, he put the capacity for speech in the very front of the brain because he had observed that the eyes of prominent public speakers seemed to bulge there. He even claimed to have pinpointed a "destructiveness center" just behind the ear of a medical student who was "so fond of torturing animals," Gall observed, "that he late became a surgeon."

Gall and his followers expanded his erroneous version of localization into the pseudoscience known as **phrenology** (see Figure 2.7). Phrenology became a craze in both Europe and the United States, attracting thousands of adherents, including Karl Marx. These followers flocked to their nearest phrenologist to have their skull bumps read so they could better understand their own character and mental abilities.

Gall's notion, for all its wrongheadedness, helped further the theory of localization. As we have seen, Broca's discovery of Tan's speech area in 1861 gave the idea of localization a scientific foundation. Broca's method of mapping the cortex—postmortem examination coupled with observation of the patient's previous behavior—tended to be slow and cumbersome, however.

A much more direct method was inaugurated a few years later by two German physicians, Gustav Fritsch and Eduard Hitzig. Fritsch had served in the Prussian War and, while treating wounded soldiers, had noted that the muscles of the men sometimes twitched if he accidentally brushed against head injuries where the brain was laid bare. He had even experimented by applying a weak electric current to the exposed brain of several of his patients, a stimulation that produced movement. In 1870, back home in Berlin after the war, he and Hitzig contrived an epic experiment, which, because they lacked laboratory space, was carried out on Frau Hitzig's dressing table. They cut open the skull of a dog and placed the tips of electric wires on its brain. Current at one point of the cortex moved the dog's legs on the opposite side of its body. At another point, it twitched the muscles of the dog's head. Fritsch and Hitzig had found in the frontal lobe an area that controls voluntary movement, the motor cortex.

From this bizarre beginning on Frau Hitzig's dressing table, electrical stimulation became one of the prime tools for mapping the functions of the cortex. Since most nerve tissue is insensitive to pain, it is possible to stimulate the human brain during the course of brain surgery with the patient awake and alert. When the electrode is placed on the cortex of the occipital lobe at the back of the head, the patient reports seeing flashing lights and other visual phenomena. Stimulation in the sensory area of the parietal lobe brings reports of an odd prickly feeling in the skin. In the auditory area of the temporal lobe, it produces bursts of unintelligible sounds.

Among the most precise cortical maps are those describing the motor cortex, the region where Fritsch and Hitzig conducted the first experiment in electrical stimulation. Patients whose motor cortex is stimulated during surgery will move an arm or a hand or a leg without seeming to will the movement. They invariably report a feeling that the movement is completely automatic. For example, a patient does not choose to move an arm: it just moves.

The Motor Cortex

The organization of the **motor cortex** is of particular interest. Here, stretched around the curving surface of cortex, is in effect an upside-down map of the entire body's topography, from toes and ankle to tongue and throat. Neighboring points of cortex represent neighboring regions of the body so faithfully, in fact, that a *homunculus,* or little man, can be drawn. This homunculus illustrates the proportion of cortex devoted to control of the various muscles in the body.

As Figure 2.8 shows, the little man is amusingly distorted, revealing the disproportionate amounts of cortex necessary for control of different muscle groups. These distortions demonstrate two important traits that help distinguish

CHAPTER 2   THE NERVOUS SYSTEM

humans from their fellow animals. The little man has enormous hands, reflecting the large area of cortex necessary to control intricate manual tasks such as handwriting. And he has a large mouth, reflecting the extensive area necessary for controlling the tongue, throat, and lips in speech.

If we were to depict the organization of the motor cortex in other mammals, the resulting image similarly would reveal something of those animals' special behavioral traits. A drawing of a raccoon brain, for example, would show a large area of cortex devoted to its fingers, with which it carefully feels objects.

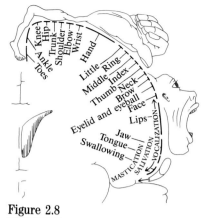

Figure 2.8

The motor homunculus, showing the proportion of cortex devoted to control of the body's various muscle groups.

The Silent (Association) Areas

The mapping of localized functions in the cerebral cortex is far from complete. There are less well-understood regions, which are sometimes called **silent areas** because electrical stimulation there fails to elicit either movement or sensation. They also are called **association areas** because they are presumed to integrate or associate information arriving at the precisely mapped cortical centers for sensation and movement. If so, centers for the so-called mental processes such as learning, memory, and thought presumably would be here. But large portions of association cortex can be lost to injury, disease, or the surgeon's scalpel without clearly defined effects on behavior. Much of the current research in the neurosciences is directed toward learning the functions of these uncharted areas.

The Connecting Pathways

Our discussion of structures and functions of the brain should not be taken to suggest that the nervous system consists of discrete and independent units. Rather, these anatomical parts are complexly interdependent, intricately linked by tracts or bundles of nerve fibers. Most voluntary movement, for example, depends upon the close coordination not only of the motor cortex but also of the cerebellum and other structures deep within the brain.

Nerve fibers and their connections are usually so intertwined that they can be sorted out and identified only with the aid of specialized staining methods and microscopic study. In some instances, however, large fiber tracts may stand out distinctly and can be followed by simple dissection for considerable distances. By tracing these connecting pathways with the naked eye, we can often deduce a great deal about the functions of a given part of the brain.

For example, we can see at the back of the eye a large fiber tract that proceeds toward the brain. After entering the brain, it is called the optic tract (see Figure 2.9). Physiological study shows that each of the fibers of the optic tract—about a million in monkeys and humans and 100,000 in cats—carries visual information. If we follow the course of the optic tract, we can see that it goes to, among other structures, a subdivision of the thalamus called the **lateral geniculate body.** All of the cells in the geniculate are involved in the transmission, or regulation of transmission, of visual information from the eye to the cerebral cortex.

Similar fiber systems originate in other sensory structures and project upward in the brain, connecting at one or more relay stations along the way. Most wind up in the cerebral cortex, where they end in separate and identifiable areas. Thus in the human visual system the fibers of cells in the lateral geniculate body project to a fissure in the occipital lobe at the back end of the cortex, the **calcarine fissure.**

Just as there are many sensory pathways from peripheral structures to the cortex, there are also motor pathways. These, however, originate in the brain and descend to connect to the nerve cells that control muscles. One of the major motor systems, the **pyramidal tract,** projects from the cerebral cortex

Figure 2.9

Visual pathways from the optic nerve that form the optic tract upon entering the brain, where it proceeds to the lateral geniculate body, fibers from which proceed to the calcarine fissure in the occipital lobe at the back of the cortex.

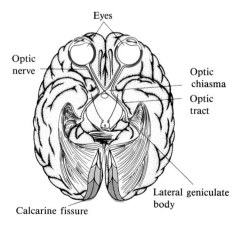

all the way down to the spinal cord. In humans and the higher primates some pyramidal tract fibers end directly on spinal motor nerve cells. These cells in turn send fibers via spinal nerves to connect directly to muscles.

Symmetry of the Brain

One of the most striking characteristics of brain anatomy has been only touched on so far in our discussion of structures. Like most parts of the body, these structures either come in pairs, or are arranged symmetrically. Just as we have two lungs, two arms, and two legs, we have two cerebral hemispheres, each the mirror image of the other. Even single structures, such as those in the brain stem, are divided in halves, and each half mirrors the other. This arrangement by which structures are paired or divided into similar halves is called **bilateral symmetry.**

Not only the brain but also most of the nervous system is bilaterally symmetrical. The brain and nervous system can be visualized as split vertically down the middle. Some nerve fiber tracts cross over to the opposite side within the spinal cord and some cross within the brain itself. The effect of this crossover is that each side of the brain presides principally over the opposite side of the body. Thus, movement of the right hand is controlled largely by the left side of the brain. Similarly, a pain in the left leg is represented principally in the right side of the brain.

A dramatic illustration of this crossover is found in the neurological disorder called **parietal lobe syndrome.** One area of the parietal lobe monitors skin sensations and body awareness. Parietal lobe syndrome affects half of this area. If it occurs in the right hemisphere, the patient loses awareness of the left side of the body and may completely neglect it. Often, the patient appears to be two people, with the right side of the body well-groomed, the left side unkempt.

Cerebral Dominance

Though the cerebral hemispheres appear to be anatomical twins, they are not identical in function. Each hemisphere has uniquely developed capabilities in carrying out certain tasks. The most evident instance of this specialization is the universal tendency of human beings to favor one hand over the other for tasks, such as writing or throwing a ball, that require finely tuned coordination. Most of us (an estimated 90 percent) are right-handed, meaning that highly developed control is exerted by the left hemisphere. For right-handedness, then, the left hemisphere is said to be dominant. The specialization of one or the other hemisphere is known as **cerebral dominance.**

A less obvious but even more pronounced instance of cerebral dominance is the fact that, in practically all human brains, the capacity for speech and language also resides on the surface of a single hemisphere. In 97 out of 100 persons, it is the left hemisphere. For this reason, a stroke that paralyzes the right side of the body (controlled by the left hemisphere) often also impairs the victim's language abilities.

During a stroke, blockage in the blood vessels serving the brain may cut off the oxygen supply to any of several language centers on the surface of the left hemisphere, killing millions of nerve cells. The result is **aphasia,** a term used for the impairment of the ability to speak, write, or understand language.

As a result of success in mapping much of the cortex, the symptoms of stroke-related language difficulty, or aphasia, often suggest the precise site of damage (see Figure 2.10). In one type of aphasia, for example, the patient speaks with great difficulty in an abbreviated style that omits the endings of verbs and nouns. These symptoms suggest that the damage is to Broca's area in the frontal lobe near the motor cortex. In a second type of aphasia, articulation seems normal, but the patient has poor comprehension of spoken language, and speech may be vague and roundabout—for example, "What you use to cut with" instead of "knife." These symptoms usually indicate damage to Wernicke's area. Inability to comprehend written language implicates an area farther back in the cortex, a region with direct connections to the visual cortex in the occipital lobe.

The dominant hemisphere also contains other regions, less precisely mapped, that appear to be involved in language. The simple act of handwriting, for example, may engage many portions of the cortical surface, including areas in the frontal lobe that, some researchers suggest, are essential to purposeful action. A woman with frontal-lobe damage wrote the following letter to a Russian neurosurgeon, repeating the same words page after page: "Dear Professor, I want to tell you that I want to tell you that I want to tell you. . . ."

In many cases of aphasia, the brain demonstrates a remarkable adaptability. If the damage to a relevant area is slight, the language capability may be restored after a short time. If the area is destroyed, however, it cannot recover, because, unlike other cells, nerve cells cannot replace themselves. But the brain possesses built-in backup mechanisms that often take over when things go wrong. This duplication of functions, or **redundancy,** is especially evident in young children. During the first years of life, both hemispheres apparently have an independent capacity for language. A young child can lose the entire left hemisphere and still regain speech through the right hemisphere.

However, the right hemisphere is unable to completely mediate all the language functions normally controlled by the left hemisphere. For example, patients with only a right hemisphere have problems understanding statements when they hear sentences containing a syntactic error (e.g., "Cash shouldn't send people through the mail since it might be stolen"). Thus, language development in the isolated right hemisphere remains incomplete (Dennis & Whitaker, 1976). By approximately age 10, the opposite hemisphere no longer seems able to assume control of language functions.

The localization of cerebral dominance for handedness and language predominantly in the left hemisphere raises obvious questions: what of the right hemisphere? Does it possess its own special behavioral capabilities? For many years these questions went unanswered, indeed largely unasked. Scientists labeled the left hemisphere the **major hemisphere** and relegated the right hemisphere to a limited role as the **minor hemisphere.**

Nonetheless, the early medical literature offered an occasional tantalizing hint of the right hemisphere's special abilities. One such ability appears to relate to music. In 1745 a physician wrote of a stroke victim whose symptoms, we now know, indicated damage to the language center of the left hemisphere (Bogen, 1969). The patient's spoken utterances were limited to the word "yes." However, the physician noted, "He can sing certain hymns, which he had learned before he became ill, as clearly and distinctly as any healthy person."

The Split Brain

These early hints about the right hemisphere went largely unexplored until the early 1950s when the American psychologist Roger Sperry (1961) and his associates began the remarkable series of experiments known as the "split-brain" studies. These studies, which would yield extraordinary new insights into the roles played by both hemispheres, began on a somewhat different track. Sperry wanted to investigate the route by which visual learning is transferred from one hemisphere to the other.

Sperry put the problem to one of his graduate students, Ronald Myers, suggesting he work with cats. Myers' first step was to eliminate one means by which visual information was known to reach both hemispheres. Recall that in mammals such as cats, visual information from each eye is normally transmit-

Figure 2.10

Approximate locations of the "speech" areas in the human brain. Damage to Broca's area causes prolonged aphasia, but recovery usually occurs, while damage to Wernicke's area causes devastating and permanent aphasia.

ted directly to both hemispheres via the optic nerve and optic tract. For his experiment, however, Myers (1955) changed this. He divided the **optic chiasma**—the optic nerve fibers that cross the brain's midline—leaving intact only those fibers that connected the right eye to the right side of the brain and the left eye to the left side of the brain. Thus, what the cat saw in its left eye would be transmitted only to the left hemisphere; what it saw in its right eye would be received only in the right hemisphere.

Myers then covered one of the cat's eyes with a leather mask and, using food as a reward, taught the animal a simple task in visual learning: to discriminate between a circle and a square. Next, Myers reversed the mask and covered the eye that had been trained. Because of Myers' surgical interruption of the optic chiasma, we might expect the untrained eye to show no recognition or memory of the circle-square task. But, in fact, the cat had no problem with it. Information from the trained eye had reached not only its corresponding cerebral hemisphere but also had somehow "leaked" to the other hemisphere as well. This transfer of information, Myers and Sperry suspected, might have occurred through the corpus callosum, the most prominent of the several commissures that connect the two hemispheres.

To test this possibility, Myers (1956) proceeded with new surgery on his experimental cats. He repeated his surgical procedure on the optic chiasma and also completely severed the corpus callosum between the two cerebral hemispheres. This time the results of the visual learning test were far different. When the untrained eye was exposed to the circle and square, the cat acted as if it had never seen the problem before. Indeed, it was as if the cat's two hemispheres were now two separate brains: one brain had learned the task; the other was completely ignorant of it. In subsequent experiments, split-brain cats were taught to make opposite choices with each eye—the square with one, the circle with the other. The cats learned to obey these conflicting instructions without the slightest evidence of confusion, confirming that their newly bisected hemispheres were functioning as independent units.

Though these experiments were fascinating, they had limited significance in terms of cerebral specialization. In cats and other mammals tested, both hemispheres are functionally equal; unlike human beings, these animals show no cerebral specialization. Humans, with their left hemispheric dominance for language and handedness, could be expected to exhibit far more interesting results if their brains could be safely split.

In fact, people did exist whose corpus callosum had been split in a surgical attempt to alleviate severe epilepsy. This neurological disorder is marked by seizures during which the victim suffers convulsions and sometimes falls on the ground. During a seizure, nerve signals in one cerebral hemisphere go awry in a way that is still not fully understood, often generating a mirror image of the aberrant nerve activity in the opposite hemisphere. Many cases of epilepsy can be controlled by drugs. However, some neurosurgeons tried the radical practice of cutting the corpus callosum in hopes that such surgery might prevent the spread of a seizure from one hemisphere to the other. In some cases the surgery was helpful; it almost totally eliminated the worst seizures and produced no noticeable changes in temperament, personality, or general behavior.

When Roger Sperry began studying patients whose brains had been split, he was struck by their apparent normality. One of the subjects he interviewed was a 48-year-old veteran of World War II whose seizures had begun after bomb fragments penetrated his brain. Sperry (1968) later wrote of this man whose cerebrum had been bisected: "In casual conversation over a cup of coffee and a cigaret, one would hardly suspect that there was anything at all unusual about him."

To examine more closely the behavioral effects of the split brain in these human subjects, Sperry and his graduate student Michael Gazzaniga (1967),

Figure 2.11

In split-brain experiments using touch, a subject could not identify an object hidden behind a screen by grasping it with the left hand because no information about the object reached the left hemisphere (after Gazzaniga, 1967).

had to devise a series of special tests. The aim of the tests was to restrict sensory information so that it would reach only one hemisphere or the other of the subject's bisected brain.

This could be done in the case of vision because of the way in which the eyes connect to the brain. If we stare straight ahead at an imaginary vertical line on the wall, everything to the right of that line is transmitted to the brain's left hemisphere; everything to the left goes to the right hemisphere. In one test, split-brain subjects had no trouble reporting a light's presence when it was flashed onto the right of a screen in front of them. Information about the light was transmitted to the left hemisphere, which contains the speech center. But when the light was flashed onto the left part of the screen, the subjects denied having seen it. The information had reached only the right hemisphere, which lacks speech, and the subjects had to remain mute. There was no question that the right hemisphere had perceived the light: when the subjects were asked to show where the image had been flashed on the screen, they quickly pointed with their right-hemisphere-controlled left hand, to the correct place.

In the case of touch, the problem of restricting information to one hemisphere was easily solved. For example, the subject would be told to grasp an object with the left hand. The object—for example, a pencil or spoon—was hidden from view behind a partition so that the only information about its nature reaching the brain came from the left hand (see Figure 2.11). This information was transmitted principally to the right hemisphere, because, as we noted earlier, the sensory nerves cross over to the opposite side en route to the brain. Because no information about the object had reached the left hemisphere, subjects could not name or describe the objects placed in their left hands. Instead, they would simply guess, calling a pencil, for example, a can opener. The "talking" left hemisphere—and the right hand—did not know what the left hand was doing.

Some results of these special tests are easily predictable based on our knowledge of the left hemisphere's dominance for language. However, tests demonstrated that the right hemisphere had unexpected abilities of its own. By manipulating objects with the left hand, it could add up to 10. And it even demonstrated an elementary capacity to reason. On one test, a picture of a spoon was flashed onto the left of the screen so it could be "seen" only by the right hemisphere. Subjects could not name the spoon, of course, because the image was not available to the left hemisphere. But they were orally instructed to select with their left hands the matching item from an assortment of hidden objects. The left hand—and right hemisphere—came up with the spoon (see Figure 2.12).

At certain tasks, the right hemisphere actually turned out to be superior to its counterpart on the left. It was better at recognizing faces and, through its control of the left hand, it was better at copying drawings and at arranging blocks to match a pictured design.

From the split-brain experiments a fascinating new picture of cerebral specialization has emerged, a picture later confirmed and extended by research using new techniques on normal subjects in which the corpus callosum is intact (Rizzollatti, Umilta, & Berlucchi, 1971). The left hemisphere appears to be verbal, analytic, and gifted in the step-by-step logic necessary for understanding science and mathematics. The right hemisphere appears to be intuitive, nonverbal, superior at spatial perception, and more attuned to art and music, where it seems able to perceive patterns as a whole.

The differences are so great that Sperry (1968) was led to hypothesize that all of us have, in effect, two brains, each with a will of its own. These two brains, connected by the corpus callosum, normally cooperate. But in the instance of the split-brain subjects, Sperry has observed, the two brains sometimes seemed to belong to "two different selves." The potential for conflict between the two hemispheres was dramatically illustrated in the behavior of one of the split-brain subjects (Gazzaniga, 1970). His two hands, directed by two separated hemispheres, had a tendency to be quarrelsome. He would sometimes attempt to pull his pants up with one hand while pulling them down with the other. In experiments involving the manipulation of blocks, his hands would similarly battle for control of the task. And on one occasion, he grabbed his wife with his left hand and shook her violently until his right hand came to her aid.

Such observations have spurred much speculation and sparked many new investigations into the relationship between cerebral specialization and the brain's highest function, consciousness itself. These issues will be described in chapter 5.

So far, we have considered the nervous system only in terms of the control centers of behavior. We have surveyed the where of the structures of the nervous system and attempted to localize the control of the various forms of behavior. Now we must look at how the nervous system works at the most basic level.

PARASYMPATHETIC

Constricts pupil

Inhibits tear glands

Increases salivation

Slows heart

Constricts bronchi

Increases digestive functions of stomach

Increases digestive functions of intestine

Contracts bladder

SYMPATHETIC

Dilates pupil

Stimulates tear glands

Inhibits salivation, increases sweating

Accelerates heart

Dilates bronchi

Decreases digestive functions of stomach

Secretes adrenalin

Decreases digestive functions of intestine

Inhibits bladder contraction

Chain of sympathetic ganglia

Spinal cord

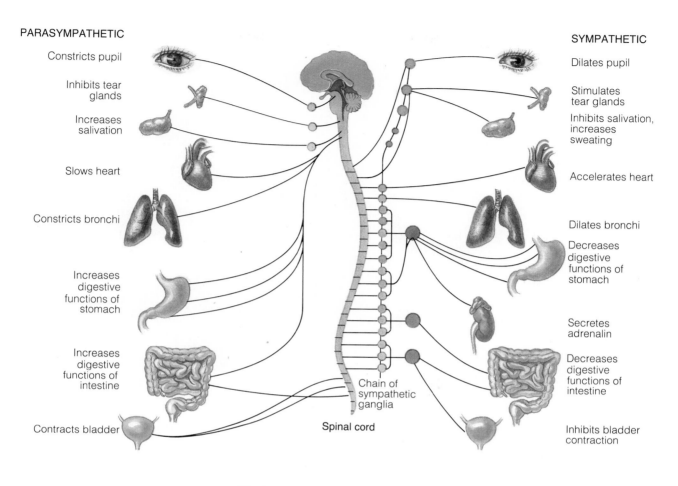

The Autonomic Nervous System

This schematic layout of the autonomic nervous system shows both the sympathetic and the parasympathetic systems, as well as their typically opposite effects on various bodily organs.

Color Plate 2.2

Perspectives of the Brain

On the cerebrum of the brain (far left, top), the lobes of the brain—occipital, parietal, temporal, and frontal—are identified, with the area of specialization for each noted in parentheses. In the drawing (far left, bottom), the cerebrum is shown as transparent, giving us a view of many of the basic structures of the human brain. Finally, cross-section views of the brain are shown on this page, revealing from a different perspective, the basic structures of the forebrain, midbrain, and hindbrain.

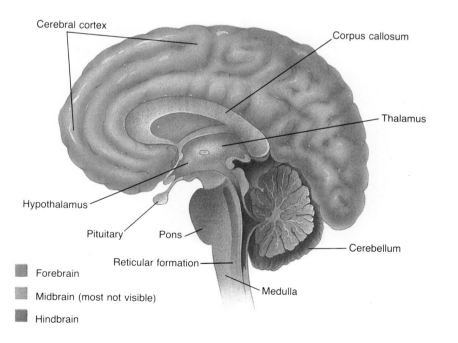

Cerebral cortex

Corpus callosum

Thalamus

Hypothalamus

Pituitary

Pons

Reticular formation

Medulla

Cerebellum

■ Forebrain

■ Midbrain (most not visible)

■ Hindbrain

Color Plate 2.3

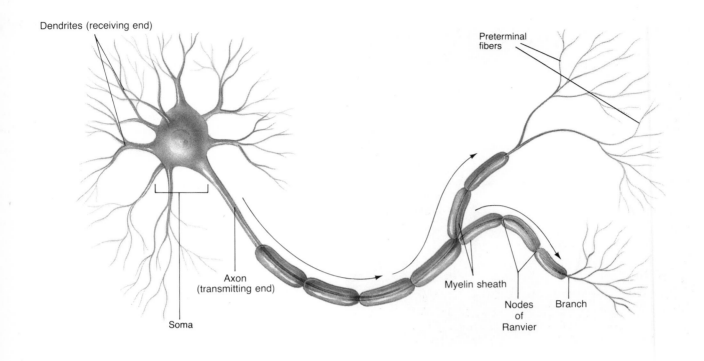

Dendrites (receiving end)

Preterminal fibers

Axon (transmitting end)

Soma

Myelin sheath

Nodes of Ranvier

Branch

The Neuron

Shown here above is a schematic drawing of a typical neuron, with cross-section photographs below of several different neurons found in the human brain. In each of the photos, note, where possible, the soma or cell body, axon, and dendrites.

Structures and Functions of the Neuron

The basic mechanisms of behavior can be viewed in three stages. First is the nerve cell, or neuron, the fundamental unit of all the structures of the nervous system. Second is the generation and propagation of electrical impulses within the individual neuron. Third is the transmission of those impulses between neurons. Considered together, these three stages will demonstrate the basic means by which all behavior—our every thought, feeling, sensation, action—is governed by the nervous system.

The Neuron

One of the fundamental insights in all biology was the recognition by the German scientist Theodor Schwann in 1838 that all living tissue is made up of cells. These are individual elements, typically microscopic in size, each of which usually contains its own nucleus and a surrounding membrane. The fundamental principle of neuroanatomy, called the **neuron doctrine,** which was first enunciated most clearly in its modern form by Cajal in the 1880s, is simply an extension of Schwann's insight. The neuron doctrine is the realization that the nervous system also is made up of cells called **neurons,** and that they interact with one another.

There are billions of neurons in the central nervous system of a human being, perhaps as many as 100 billion. Practically all of these neurons are present at birth and, unlike other cells, they do not multiply. Nor can a neuron be regenerated once it dies. Because of redundancy in the nervous system, a human may lose millions of neurons during his or her lifetime without apparent effects on behavior.

Neurons come in assorted sizes and shapes. Most of them are tiny—a cubic inch of brain matter contains up to 100 million neurons. They can resemble stars, pyramids, uprooted trees, or even strangely shaped balloons on a long string. But all neurons share certain essential properties. Hence, if we comprehend the structure of a single neuron, we will have a basis for understanding all nerve cells.

Let us look at a neuron under the light microscope. This neuron belongs to nerve tissue taken from the front portion of the spinal cord. The tissue was fixed with formalin or alcohol to preserve its structural features, then hardened by freezing or embedded in a solid material like wax. The tissue was then sliced into transparent sections with a guillotinelike instrument called a microtome. Finally, it was treated with one of a variety of stains, chemical agents that enable the viewer to distinguish particular features in the densely packed section of nerve cells. In this instance, the method was one favored by Cajal, the Golgi stain, a solution of silvery salts that affect only a few of the neurons, so that they stand out clearly under the microscope.

The view we see under the microscope shows the neuron's three essential parts: the cell body or **soma,** which uses oxygen and glucose and other material from the blood to manufacture protein and other materials necessary for the neuron's survival and functioning; a network of projections called **dendrites** that jut out from the cell body and receive messages from adjacent neurons; and from the other side of the body, a single long appendage known as the **axon,** which transmits messages to other neurons or to muscles and glands.

In appearance, the dendrites and axons differ in several important characteristics. Neurons typically have many dendrites but only one axon. Dendrites often branch and rebranch, forming an elegant treelike expansion. The pattern of dendritic branching varies widely among cell types and, indeed, it is usually either the pattern of dendritic branching or the shape of the cell body itself that gives classes of neurons their names. For example, two principal types of nerve

A stellate neuron with its axon, which can be seen running from the neuron to the bottom of the photograph.

Carolina Biological Supply

Figure 2.13

Drawing of a typical neuron of a vertebrate animal. The neuron can carry nerve impulses for a considerable distance. The nerve impulses originate near the cell body and are propagated along the axon, which is folded here for diagrammatic purposes but would be a centimeter long at actual size. The axon's preterminal fibers form synapses with as many as 1,000 other neurons through the dendrites.

Figure 2.14

Experimental arrangement for recording axon resting potential. One electrode is inserted through the neuron's axon, and the second electrode is placed in the salt solution surrounding the neuron. The voltmeter measures the resting potential.

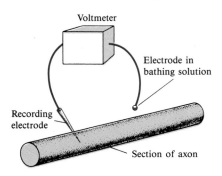

cells in the cerebral cortex are the **stellate cell,** so named because the radial pattern of its dendrite branches gives it a starlike appearance, and the **pyramidal cell,** which takes its name from the pyramidal shape of its cell body.

Another significant difference between dendrites and axons is their surface texture. Whereas axons are typically smooth, dendrites are often covered with spines or thorns. These dendritic spines serve as specialized receptor surfaces for receiving information from incoming axons.

Dendrites are short, extending at most a millimeter or two. The axon, by contrast, may extend for a relatively great distance. In a tall person, the axon extending from a spinal cord neuron that controls a muscle in the foot may be more than 3 feet in length. Many axons are grouped together in bundles called **nerves.** Nerves are often thick enough to be seen by the unaided eye.

The axon originates on the nerve cell body in a gentle swelling known as the **axon hillock.** Sometimes an axon extends to its target, such as a muscle or another neuron, and ends there without branching. More commonly, it branches near the end into a number of fine **preterminal fibers** before terminating at the target neuron or muscle. A single axon may make several contacts with another neuron via that neuron's cell body or one of its dendrites. (See Figure 2.13 and Color Plate 2.3 for a schematic diagram of a neuron.)

Electrical Activity in the Neuron

The portrait of the neuron painted above is essential to an understanding of the second element in our study of the basic mechanisms of behavior—electrical activity in the neuron.

The nervous system's basic means of communication is the **nerve impulse,** an electrically measured stimulus that travels down the axon of the neuron, usually in a direction away from the cell body. Though the nerve impulse is measured electrically, its nature differs markedly from a familiar example of electricity such as household current. It is slower, much less powerful, and depends on certain chemical characteristics of the neuron and the fluid that surrounds the neuron.

Much of what is known about the propagation of the nerve impulse along the axon derives from the research of two English neurophysiologists, Alan Hodgkin and Andrew Huxley (1952). Beginning in the late 1930s, Hodgkin and Huxley analyzed electrical activity in single axons taken from giant sea squids. These axons are sufficiently large so that electrodes can be inserted into them in order to study the nerve impulse. Indeed, a single squid axon is so thick that the scientist who discovered it at first mistook it for an artery.

In order to understand how the nerve impulse is transmitted down the axon, let us begin by imagining an experiment not unlike those conducted by Hodgkin and Huxley. Our hypothetical neuron, like all living cells, is surrounded by a thin membrane that encases the neuron's dendrites, cell body, and axon. There are charged molecules in fluid inside and surrounding the neuron.

Our testing apparatus consists of two fine-tipped electrodes connected to a voltmeter (see Figure 2.14). The device registers the voltage between two points. If we insert one electrode through the membrane of the neuron's axon and place the second electrode in the fluid that surrounds the neuron, a dramatic change will occur on the voltmeter. It will show an electric potential difference—or voltage—between the inside and outside of the axon. This difference is known as the **resting potential.** The inside and outside of the axon are electrically charged like the poles of a battery, with the inside of the cell negative and the outside positive. Hence, the axon is said to be polarized.

Polarization of the axon is caused by a slightly uneven distribution of electrically charged molecules, or **ions,** across the membrane. Ordinarily, ions

CHAPTER 2   THE NERVOUS SYSTEM

would migrate in or out until an even distribution change across the membrane was achieved. But when the neuron is at rest, the membrane does not permit all ions to pass through freely. For example, although the membrane does permit some sodium ions to leak into the axon from the outside, sodium is continuously pumped back out by the membrane. As a final result of the pumping of sodium ions, the inside of the axon acquires a negative charge (see Figure 2.15).

The resting potential can change quickly if the neuron is stimulated by an outside electrical force. Suddenly, the membrane becomes permeable to sodium ions, which pour into the axon, depolarizing it—changing the inside potential to positive, relative to the outside.

This sudden change can be recorded as a sudden change of voltage across the axon membrane called the **action potential** (see Figure 2.16). This occurs in a very short section of the membrane, perhaps only a few centimeters long, and it lasts a very short time—less than a millisecond (1/1,000 second). The action potential is so quick because the permeability of the axon membrane undergoes another sudden change: it stops letting in sodium ions and starts letting out potassium ions. The result is that the axon returns to its original state, that of polarization or the resting potential.

Nonetheless, the action potential has lasted long enough to affect the adjacent section of the axon membrane. It depolarizes that next patch of membrane, triggering the same sequence of changes in permeability to the sodium and potassium ions. Hence the inside of the membrane at that point also swings briefly from negative to positive. This process of repeated action potentials begins at the axon hillock and proceeds down the length of the axon in a manner analogous to the burning of a firecracker fuse: each patch sets off the patch next to it. Altogether, the nerve impulse at each point on the axon takes about a millisecond for completion. Then that portion of the axon is ready to begin the entire process again (see Figure 2.17).

We have not yet described how the electrical excitation of the axon actually begins in the neuron. This excitation is usually received at the neuron's dendrites. How does this excitation travel from the dendrite, through the cell body, to the beginning of the axon? The excitation depolarizes the dendrite membrane, but it usually does not spread by means of an action potential, as in the axon. Instead, it travels to the axon in a passive manner, like a ripple spreading in a pond.

It is important to note that the excitation reaching the axon hillock must be of sufficient intensity if the action potential is to be triggered there. If the excitation falls below the necessary **threshold,** no action potential will occur. By the same token, once the action potential is triggered, it does not vary much in intensity or speed along the axon, no matter how strong the original excitation. In other words, the neuron either fires or it does not. When it does fire, the action potential is always the same. This phenomenon is called the **all-or-none law** of nerve conduction. We will see the important implications of this law in chapter 3 when we consider the coding of sensory messages in the nervous system. The pressure of a finger on one's skin, for example, is coded by how many neurons fire and how fast they fire. It is not controlled by the intensity of the firing, which does not change.

The speed of the nerve impulse depends, in part, on the thickness of the axon; the thicker the axon, the faster the impulse. One probable function of the giant squid axons studied by Hodgkin and Huxley is to enable the creature to transmit fast nerve impulses. These impulses coordinate a system of jet propulsions used to escape predators. But such oversized axons cannot be accommodated in the anatomy of most creatures, including human beings. For example, human vision would require optic nerves more than an inch in diameter (and a much larger head) if axon diameter were the sole factor in the speed of the nerve impulse.

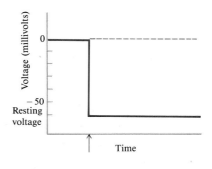

Figure 2.15

Resting potential across membrane of neuron. The electrode entered the axon at the time indicated by the arrow and recorded a negative charge.

Figure 2.16

An action potential. The stimulus was applied at the time indicated by the arrow and a positive charge or action potential was recorded.

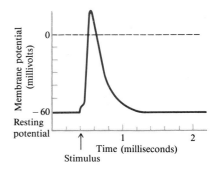

Most of the axons in the peripheral nervous system of vertebrates and many in the central nervous system have a special provision for greatly speeding up the nerve impulse. They are encased in a sheath of a fatty white substance, **myelin,** which serves to insulate the axon, preventing the free passage of sodium and potassium ions from taking place across each adjacent patch of membrane during an action potential.

How, then, can the action potential take place at all in a myelinated axon? If we look at the axon and its sheath under the light microscope, we can see that myelin is not continuous but is interrupted by gaps at intervals of about a millimeter or so. These gaps where the axon is left bare of myelin are the **nodes of Ranvier,** named after the nineteenth-century French anatomist, Louis Antoine Ranvier (1871), who first described them. In a myelinated axon, an action potential can occur only at these bare nodes. Consequently, the nerve impulse leaps from node to node instead of being slowed by the laborious process of repeating action potentials across each patch of membrane. Such transmission of the nerve impulse along myelinated axons is termed **saltatory conduction.**

Figure 2.17

Arrows indicate the direction in which the repeated action potentials are propagated along the length of the axon. At the front of the impulse, sodium ions rush into the axon making the inside briefly positive relative to the outside. Potassium ions then rush out of the axon, restoring the resting potential. At the site of the action potential the cell membrane is depolarized, which triggers the same sequence of changes in the flow of sodium and potassium ions (see also Color Plate 2.4).

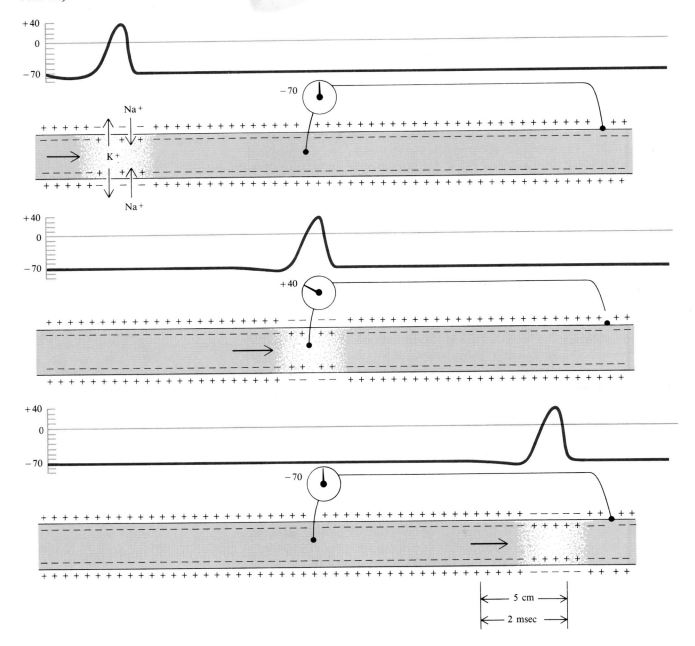

CHAPTER 2 THE NERVOUS SYSTEM

The speed of saltatory conduction in the fastest mammalian nerve fibers is about 225 miles per hour, approximately 20 times faster than the speed of the nerve impulse in an unmyelinated axon of the same diameter (see Figure 2.18). Thanks to saltatory conduction, for example, it takes only about 1/50th of a second for the nerve impulse to travel from toe to brain in the myelinated neuron that signals a touch on the big toe.

The importance of myelin to normal function becomes dramatically evident in the disease multiple sclerosis. The disease attacks the myelin sheath and replaces it with a hard fibrous tissue. As a consequence, timing of the nerve impulse is thrown off. Because motor pathways function poorly without precise timing, control of movement is impaired. If the disease affects nerve cells controlling respiration, it can lead to death by suffocation. Saltatory conduction probably also explains the delayed development of such motor skills as crawling and walking in human infants: the myelin sheath of many motor tracts is not fully developed until about a year after birth.

The production of myelin is one of the principal functions of a group of supportive cells found throughout the brain and nervous system. In the peripheral nervous system, they are known as **Schwann cells,** honoring Theodor Schwann (1839), the biologist who first described them. In the central nervous system, they are called **neuroglia,** or simply **glia,** from the Greek word for glue. There are so many glial cells in the brain (they outnumber neurons) that they appear to seal up the spaces between the neurons, literally sticking them together. Schwann cells and glia create the myelin sheath by fastening onto the bare axon and wrapping around it again and again (see Color Plate 2.4).

Other functions of the supportive cells are less well known. In the brain and spinal cord, the glial cells probably are important in nourishing the neurons and in directing their pattern of growth. One function, however, becomes graphically evident when an injury occurs in the brain. Glia proliferate rapidly in the affected region and serve as **phagocytes,** cells that eat up the debris left by the damage. Under the microscope, these cells can be seen engorged with bits of the ingested material.

Transmission of Impulses Between Neurons

Our picture of a single neuron in action has been relatively simple. A neuron becomes excited by an external stimulus, produces an action potential that is generated again and again as it passes down the axon as the nerve impulse. The voltage change of the nerve impulse is always the same in a given cell: only the frequency of firing changes. But changes in frequency are limited; during and just after each firing, the neuron is inexcitable. There is a small **refractory period** before it can fire again.

How, then, does the nervous system derive its unmatched complexity as a communications network? The answer lies in the remarkable manner in which nerve cells communicate with one another. Typically, communication occurs between the axon of one neuron and the cell body or dendrite of another neuron.

The Synapse

The minute space between the axon of one neuron and the cell body or dendrite of another neuron is called a **synapse.** The existence of the synapse and its nature have been the subject of two of the most fascinating and bitter controversies in the history of the neural sciences. To understand both the structure of the synapse and the debates that raged around it, let us consider the neural theory that prevailed until the late nineteenth century.

In those days most scientists believed that nerve cells were physically connected to one another. Under a light microscope, sections of nerve tissue

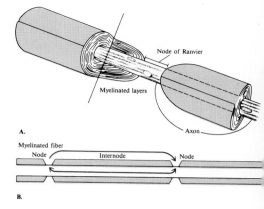

A. Myelinated fiber

B.

Figure 2.18

(a) View of myelin. The lengthwise view of a node of Ranvier shows the layers of myelin wound around the axon. (b) Saltatory conduction moves the nerve impulse very quickly along a myelinated fiber from one node of Ranvier to the next.

Italian physician and anatomist Camillo Golgi invented the staining method that bears his name.

looked like a trellis network, a net, or reticulum, of neurons in which axons were literally fused to dendrites or cell bodies in a continuous web. This point of view was known as the **reticular theory.** Its leading proponent was the Italian physician and anatomist Camillo Golgi (1883), who invented the staining method that bears his name.

Ironically, it was the Golgi stain that enabled Cajal to support a conflicting theory about the connections between nerve cells. Using the Golgi stain, Cajal (1909–1911) put forward evidence for the radical new theory, the neuron doctrine, that we described at the start of this chapter. The nervous system, he said, is composed of cells that make contact with one another but do not actually fuse. Cajal illustrated his theory with elegant drawings so accurate that they are still used in neuroanatomy textbooks today.

The debate between the old reticular theory and Cajal's neuron doctrine was a bitter one. Cajal could only infer the nature of the contacts between nerve cells, that is, the synapses: their structure was far too small to be seen under the light microscope. Since Cajal could not prove the existence of synapses, his old foe Golgi clung to the reticular theory. In 1906 the two men shared the Nobel Prize in medicine, but the bitterness did not abate. Cajal in his autobiography (1937) viewed Golgi's Nobel acceptance speech as an attempt to revive the reticular theory. It is said that, although they had nearby rooms in a Stockholm hotel, the two scientists passed without speaking.

Nearly half a century later, the powerful electron microscope vindicated Cajal's brilliant insight and revealed the true nature of the synapse. Under this new microscope, which can magnify up to 500,000 times, it is clear that nerve cells do not fuse; they are separated by a narrow cleft of about one millionth of an inch—a space 1000 times smaller than the finest hair. The synapse is actually a gap.

The second great debate about the synapse concerned the nature of the activity that occurs there. If the synapse is indeed a gap, scientists asked, how does the nerve impulse from the axon of one neuron cross it to excite the adjacent neuron? In their answers, scientists tended to divide into two opposing schools: the "spark" group versus the "soup" camp (Eccles, 1964). The "spark" theorists believed that synapses worked by direct electrical coupling across the synaptic cleft in the manner of a spark crossing the cap in a spark plug. The "soup" theorists believed that the transmission of the nerve impulse across the synaptic cleft was effected by means of a chemical. We know now that both schools were right, although the "soup" theorists were closer to the truth. The great majority of synapses in the vertebrate nervous system are chemical, but there are also demonstrable examples of electrical synapses. In these rare cases in which the presence of electrical synapses has been proven, the synaptic cleft between nerve cells is much narrower than in chemical synapses. Such electrical synapses are seen in certain giant neurons in the brain stem of a fish, for example.

With the insight provided by the electron microscope, let us construct a simplified picture of a typical chemical synapse (see Figure 2.19). We see an axon, which is called the **presynaptic element,** and a dendrite, or **postsynaptic element.** The membranes of these two elements are separated by the very thin **synaptic cleft.** On the presynaptic side, the tip of the axon is swollen into a knob. Inside this knob is an assemblage of tiny spheres called **synaptic vesicles.** These vesicles, each surrounded by a membrane, very likely contain an all-important chemical called a **neurotransmitter.**

Now, let us imagine the nerve impulse traveling down the length of the axon. When the nerve impulse reaches the tip of the axon, it triggers a series of events whereby the synaptic vesicles inside the axon become mobilized. They fuse with the axon's membrane and then release their tiny quantities of neurotransmitter into the synaptic cleft. Then, it is believed, the neurotransmit-

CHAPTER 2   THE NERVOUS SYSTEM

ter diffuses across the cleft. When the neurotransmitter reaches the other side of the cleft, the postsynaptic dendrite, it binds with special **receptor sites** on the dendrite membrane. The effect of this binding is to depolarize the membrane of the postsynaptic neurons. If the depolarization is great enough, it triggers a nerve impulse in the neuron's axon. Thus, by means of a neurotransmitter, electrical activity in one neuron is communicated to the next nerve cell in the pathway.

Neurotransmitters

The first direct evidence of neurotransmitters was discovered in the nervous system during a classic experiment carried out in 1921 by an Austrian physiologist named Otto Loewi. It has been said that the idea for the experiment came to Loewi one night during a dream. He woke up, scribbled notes for the experiment, and went back to sleep. The next morning Loewi could not decipher his own handwriting. That night, however, the same dream returned to Loewi and, when he woke up, he rushed to his basement to begin the experiment.

The experiment involved a simple preparation using the hearts from two frogs and a bundle of nerve fibers called the vagus nerve. The vagus nerve includes a group of long motor axons whose cell bodies are in the brain; these axons make contact with cells in the heart and other visceral organs. Interestingly, the heart does not require this neural connection to be intact in order to function: it has its own built-in conduction system that is capable of maintaining heartbeat without input from the brain. As Loewi knew, the vagus nerve is part of the parasympathetic nervous system, and one of its functions is to slow down heartbeat. The question Loewi asked was how it did this.

Loewi placed a frog heart and its attached vagus nerve in a saline solution to keep it beating. He then stimulated the vagus nerve electrically. As he expected, the heart rate slowed down. During stimulation, Loewi collected the saline solution surrounding the heart. He found that this fluid alone, when injected into the heart, had the same effect as stimulation: it slowed down the heart. By contrast, if the saline solution was collected when the nerve had not been stimulated, if failed to slow down the heart.

Obviously, stimulation of the vagus nerve had released a substance that, when injected back into the heart, could slow it down. Loewi correctly suspected this substance was a chemical called acetylcholine, but since he could not be certain, he gave it the neutral name Vagusstoff.

Later research in the 1930s by the English biologist Henry Dale (1938) confirmed that Vagusstoff was indeed acetylcholine. Dale's work focused on the synapselike cleft between axons and voluntary muscles in the tongue of a cat and in the legs of various animals. Dale proved that acetylcholine serves as the neurotransmitter in these nerves also. The difficulty of his search for the substance at the axon endings is illustrated by his finding that a single nerve impulse in a neuron triggers the release of a very small amount of acetylcholine—only 10^{-16} gram.

Loewi (1935) had also identified a second neurotransmitter. When he stimulated a frog's sympathetic nerves, which speed up heartbeat, tiny amounts of a different transmitter, later identified as noradrenalin, were released by axon endings. Chemically, noradrenalin is a close relative of the hormone adrenalin, which is secreted by the body's adrenal gland and also has the effect of speeding up heartbeat.

The existence of neurotransmitters helps explain the effects of many drugs on the nervous system. One example is the paralysis caused by curare, the poison once applied by South American Indians to their arrow tips. Curare, it is now clear, blocks the action of acetylcholine in the synapse and thus prevents

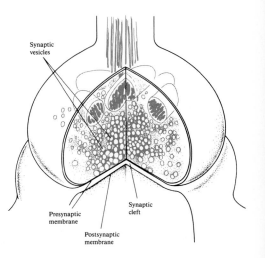

Synaptic
vesicles

Presynaptic
membrane

Synaptic
cleft

Postsynaptic
membrane

Figure 2.19

Simplified diagram of a synapse, the relay point where information is conveyed by chemical transmitters from neuron to neuron. A synapse consists of two parts: the knoblike tip of a presynaptic element (axon) and the receptor region of the postsynaptic element (dendrite). Chemical neurotransmitters, stored in the synaptic vesicles, are released into the synaptic cleft and depolarize the membrane of the postsynaptic neuron, which fires if the depolarization is great enough (see also Color Plate 2.4).

FOCUS

The Brain's Own Opiates

Perhaps the most remarkable discovery about the nervous system in the past decade is that it produces its own painkillers. These chemical substances are called **endorphins**—a contraction of two Greek words meaning "the morphine within"—because they appear to inhibit the perception of pain much in the same manner as morphine and other opiates.

The story behind this fascinating discovery begins with an understanding of how neurotransmitters function in the narrow synaptic cleft between nerve cells. When a neurotransmitter is released by the axon of one neuron, it crosses the synapse and then excites or inhibits the firing of the nerve impulse in the adjacent, or postsynaptic, neuron. The transmitter's effect on the postsynaptic neuron is assumed to occur at specific regions in the cell membrane known as receptor sites. These receptors appear to interact selectively with a given transmitter, binding with it chemically. Certain drugs can simulate the effect of a transmitter by similarly binding with its particular receptors.

As we saw in chapter 1, two neuropharmacologists at Johns Hopkins University set out to determine whether morphine worked in this way (Pert & Snyder, 1973). Morphine containing a radioactive substance was injected into experimental animals. If specific receptor sites existed for morphine and other opiates, they would thus become tagged with radioactive "labels." That is precisely what happened, and the researchers were able to map the location within the brain of the opiate receptors. The highest concentrations were in two different pathways of the central nervous system. One was deep in the brain in the limbic system, which is involved in the regulation of mood. The other ascends from the spinal cord along the midline of the brain, and is a pathway long believed to convey sensations of chronic pain. Localization of the opiate receptors in these two pathways coincides with the behavioral effects of morphine: the euphoric change in mood and the alleviation of severe pain.

These findings were fascinating, but the questions were even more intriguing. Why do opiate receptors exist in all vertebrates studied, including the hagfish, which evolved some 350 million years ago? Would evolution have provided us with special receptors that modify mood and alleviate pain just in case we might not discover the healing effects of the poppy's juice?

One obvious possibility was that the receptors existed to serve some morphinelike substance, probably a neurotransmitter, that occurred naturally in the brain. Soon afterward, a group of investigators in Scotland (Hughes et al., 1975), succeeded in isolating two morphinelike substances from the brain of the pig. It was found that these two substances bind selectively to the opiate receptor sites mapped at Johns Hopkins. Meanwhile, other morphinelike chemicals had been found in the pituitary

transmission of the nerve impulse. Nerve gases developed for warfare work in a different, but no less insidious, manner. Ordinarily, acetylcholine does not accumulate after crossing into the postsynaptic neuron: it is destroyed by chemical catalysts known as enzymes. In the case of acetylcholine the enzyme is called cholinesterase (Ach). But nerve gases interfere with Ach, and the resulting accumulation of neurotransmitter blocks the normal functioning of the victim's muscles, heart, and lungs. Similarly, as we will see in chapters 5 and 15, mood-altering drugs such as marijuana, LSD, antidepressants, and tranquilizers are capable of changing our behavior because they interfere with the synthesis, storage, release, or reuptake into the presynaptic membrane of the neurotransmitters.

Many serious disorders of the nervous system or motor system appear to be related to the presence of too much or too little of a particular neurotransmitter. The classic instance of a deficit in neurotransmitter production is the disorder known as Parkinson's disease, which is characterized by the progressive loss of control over simple movements. Even at rest, patients with this disease exhibit uncontrollable tremors and masklike facial expressions.

For years, physicians who examined the brains of Parkinson's victims during autopsies did not find definite focal damage that could account for the gland of various mammals, including camels (Li & Chung, 1976).

The biological function of these latter substances is still something of a mystery because hormones secreted

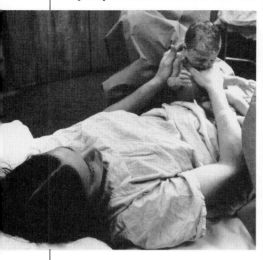

Endorphins might somehow account for how women react to pain during childbirth.

by the pituitary gland apparently do not function directly in the central nervous system. Nonetheless, all the endorphins seem closely related to opiates in a number of ways. They are similar in chemical structure, they bind to opiate receptor sites, they modify response to chronic pain, and they exert a pronounced effect on mood. Evidence suggests that the two endorphins found in the brain are neurotransmitters that serve to inhibit or excite transmission of the nerve impulse. For one thing, they are highly concentrated in nerve endings—the tip of the axon where neurotransmitters normally accumulate.

Discovery of the endorphins has stimulated a number of new suggestions about the physiological mechanisms of behavior (Wei & Loh, 1976). Some researchers now think that certain psychiatric disorders may result from an abnormality in the brain's level of endorphins. It also has been suggested that endorphins might somehow account for certain unusual reactions to pain that long have intrigued psychologists. Among these are the familiar instances of badly wounded soldiers who seem indifferent to pain during the heat of the battle and of religious holy men who walk on searing coals without complaint.

The endorphins also suggest a neurological basis for human addiction to opiates such as morphine and heroin. Perhaps the presence of morphine at the opiate receptors signals neurons to stop releasing their own "opiates," the endorphins. To make up for this lack, more and more of the morphine would have to be taken just to maintain a constant state at the opiate receptors. Then, if morphine is withdrawn, the receptors would lack both the drug and the endorphins and would signal the body to exhibit symptoms of drug withdrawal such as shaking and diarrhea.

Although the discovery of endorphins initially raised hopes for the synthesis of a chemically similar painkiller that would be nonaddictive, the history of analgesics is not encouraging. When heroin was first synthesized in the late nineteenth century, it was hailed as a nonaddictive substitute for morphine. And the results of early tests of various endorphins similarly give little cause for hope. Experimental rats were injected with repeated dosages of endorphins. After the injections were stopped, the rats suffered all the physical withdrawal symptoms of human drug addicts. ■

disease. Then, in 1959, an important clue to Parkinson's was discovered by a Swedish pharmacologist, Arvid Carlsson. He was testing the tranquilizer chlorpromazine on rats and noted that the drug produced tremors closely resembling those of Parkinson's. Since the drug was known to block the action of a neurotransmitter called dopamine, Carlsson's finding suggested that the tremors might be related to a lack of dopamine. This suggestion was substantiated by autopsies performed on human victims that showed virtually no dopamine.

All of this indicated that patients might be helped if normal dopamine levels in the brain could somehow be restored. Dopamine cannot be administered directly because it does not pass freely from blood vessels into the brain. However, a researcher at Long Island's Brookhaven National Laboratory, George C. Cotzias (Cotzias, Papasilou, and Gellene, 1969), found a way around the impasse. He gave patients a drug called L-Dopa, a chemical that the brain then converts into dopamine.

The dramatic success of this combination of basic research and clinical application has been a model for further research into the mechanisms of other diseases caused by irregularities in the production or use of neurotransmitters. In fact, the dopamine story has yielded tantalizing clues about the possible physiological basis of schizophrenia, which will be discussed in chapter 14.

In all, a dozen or more different neurotransmitters have been identified in the human nervous system. Not all of these serve to excite the postsynaptic neuron by triggering a nerve impulse. If they did, a kind of electrical storm, like a seizure of epilepsy, would constantly beset the nervous system. Some neurotransmitters serve to inhibit the firing of the nerve impulse: instead of depolarizing the membrane of the postsynaptic membrane, they hyperpolarize it, increasing the voltage outside the membrane. **Hyperpolarization** lessens the likelihood that a nerve impulse will be set off.

Several neurotransmitters are known to be both **excitatory** and **inhibitory.** Acetylcholine, for example, excites the voluntary muscles, but as we have seen in Loewi's experiment, it inhibits cells in the heart. This apparent contradiction probably results from subtle differences in the nature of the receptor sites, those areas on the postsynaptic neuron where the neurotransmitter chemically binds with the nerve cell's membrane. Receptor sites seem to recognize chemically their own particular neurotransmitter, although they can be fooled by certain drugs. In fact, recent investigations of morphine's relationship to receptor sites led to the discovery that the brain produces its own opiatelike painkillers, which apparently function as neurotransmitters (see Focus, p. 54).

The fact that the neurotransmitters may be excitatory or inhibitory complicates our picture of communication within the nervous system. So, indeed, does the fact that a given neuron may make synaptic contact with many other neurons. It is estimated, for example, that some neurons in the cerebral cortex have as many as 60,000 synapses. In such cells, several different neurotransmitters may be conveying conflicting information across the synapses. Some of these messages are excitatory; they say "fire." Others are inhibitory; they say "do not fire." The net sum of these messages determines whether or not the neuron will fire. If this sum equals or exceeds the neuron's threshold for depolarization, it will fire a nerve impulse.

A "Wiring Diagram"

We now have seen how the nervous system works at the most basic level. Individual neurons generate nerve impulses. Then, by making functional connections at the synapse through the release of neurotransmitters, they form pathways or circuits that transmit the nerve impulse. Such circuits of neurons comprise the various structures of the nervous system and also serve to connect the structures. The motor cortex, for example, is connected to the cerebellum and other nuclei deep in the brain and thence is linked to clusters of nerve cell bodies in the spinal cord, and finally to the muscles of the arm or leg. Thus even the simplest of these circuits, involving perhaps only a few neurons, intersect with many other circuits in complex grids that resemble the intricacy of a spider's web, multiplied a millionfold. The act of jumping out of the way of an oncoming car may require the action of numerous interconnecting grids that may involve millions of neurons—circuitry concerned with seeing, hearing, feeling, memory, and, of course, movement (see Research, p. 57).

The continuing challenge of the neurosciences is to map what might be called a "wiring diagram" of the nervous system, tracing the circuits neuron by neuron and relating them to behavior. This enormous task has been facilitated in recent years by the development of sensitive new laboratory techniques. One method, for example, enables scientists to record the firing of the nerve impulse in a single neuron in an animal's brain. Other methods involve the injection into live animals of radioactive substances that are taken up selectively by nerve cells. When these sections of nerve tissues are mounted on

RESEARCH

A fundamental aim of neurobiological research is to find precise relationships between human behavior and the activities that occur at the basic level of nerve cells. How do microscopic circuits of nerve cells, propagating minute bursts of electrical activity, enable us to walk, see, think, learn, and remember? Because simple ethics preclude tampering with the human nervous system, the search for answers typically focuses on the brains of other mammals. Cats, monkeys, and rats are among the favorite experimental animals in the research laboratories.

One problem with all of these animals is the enormous complexity of their nervous systems. Even a rat contains billions of nerve cells making trillions of connections with one another and tangled together in labyrinthine complexity. For this reason, many researchers concerned with the neural basis of behavior choose to study simple invertebrates. These creatures, such as the crayfish, insects, and snails, may have as few as 10,000 neurons. Their nerve cells are grouped in clusters called ganglia, consisting of about 500 to 2000 cells. The ganglia are capable of fairly complex behavioral responses, and the fact that there are relatively few nerve cells makes it possible to relate the function of individual neurons directly to a particular behavior.

For nearly two decades, Eric Kandel and his associates (1970, 1976, and 1979) have been investigating the neural mechanisms of aplysia, a giant marine snail that grows to about a foot in length. In particular, they have studied the neural activities underlying the creature's gill-withdrawal response. Touching the animal in a particular place causes its gill to withdraw into a cavity for self-protection, and much as the hu-

man hand pulls back reflexively from a potentially damaging stimulus such as a hot stove.

To study the neurons responsible for this reflex, Kandel made a small slit in the living animal and lifted out the abdominal ganglion, which consists of about 1800 nerve cells, some of them nearly a millimeter in diameter. By inserting microelectrodes into various cells and firing them one at a time, he was able to identify five motor neurons that produce movements of the withdrawal reflex.

Next, Kandel stimulated the surface of the animal's body with light brush strokes and recorded the resulting cellular electrical activity through microelectrodes. By this means, he was able to map the sensory neurons that activate the motor neurons and thus set in motion the gill-withdrawal response. All of these cells, Kandel found, are identifiable; that is, the same cells occur at the same place in every aplysia and make the same synaptic connections with one another. They also use the same neurotransmitters—chemicals that transmit the nerve impulse across the synaptic gap between neurons—as do cells in the human nervous system.

Now that he had a "wiring diagram" of the simple nerve circuits in-

volved, Kandel went on to study the neural mechanisms underlying the elementary form of learning known as habituation. Habituation is the gradual decrease in behavioral response to a repeated stimulus. In effect, it is learning to ignore stimuli that have lost their novelty. Habituation occurs in aplysia when the area near the gill is touched repeatedly; after awhile, the novelty ceases and the withdrawal reflex gradually diminishes.

Kandel found that the electrical activity of the neurons paralleled behavior. Repeated stimulation of the sensory neuron caused a reduction in the electrical activity of the motor neuron. This led him to focus on the synaptic connection between the two nerve cells. He found that repeated stimulation of the sensory neuron apparently resulted in a decrease in the amount of chemical neurotransmitter released by that nerve cell into the synaptic gap. Because the transmitter triggers the firing of the nerve impulse in the neighboring motor neuron, this reduction in the amount of the transmitter would explain the habituation of the gill-withdrawal response.

In short, this rudimentary form of learning appears to result from a change in the functional effectiveness of the synaptic connection. The leap from this finding to complex learning in the brain of a human being is obviously an enormous one. But Kandel has shown that elementary aspects of mental processes can be found in just a few neurons. This is an important beginning, a significant step forward in understanding the links between behavior and activity at the cellular level. ■

slides and coated with photographic emulsion, the radioactive substance exposes the emulsion, revealing the appropriate circuits of nerve cells.

Let us conclude our discussion of the what, where, and how of the nervous system by sketching a very rudimentary sort of wiring diagram and relating it to simple behavior. The simplest forms of behavior controlled by the nervous system are the automatic reflexes. These reflexes can occur automatically without intervention by the brain; in fact, when Charles Sherrington (1906) made his intensive study of reflexes in the early part of this century, he worked with animals that were decerebrate; that is, the cerebrum had been surgically removed. Among the reflexes studied by Sherrington was the flexion reflex, the neural action by which a hand automatically draws back from a hot stove. Sherrington even investigated the so-called scratch reflex by devising a kind of artificial flea. He inserted a pin into the skin of a dog; when a slight electric current passed through the pin, it stimulated the nerve endings so that the dog automatically lifted its leg and began to scratch.

The simplest of these automatic actions studied by Sherrington was the stretch reflex. Sherrington showed that when a muscle is stretched it will contract forcefully. A familiar example of the stretch reflex is the knee jerk, which physicians often test to determine whether there is damage to the spinal cord. The physician uses a rubber hammer to tap the knee just below the kneecap. Tapping the knee stretches the muscles of the upper thigh. The response in the healthy nervous system is powerful: the leg jerks up instantly, on its own. The stretch reflex enables muscles to adjust immediately to sudden changes in load. When an actor in a television Western leaps onto the back of a horse, it is the stretch reflex that keeps the poor animal from collapsing.

For our purposes here, the stretch reflex is significant because it reveals, in miniature, the fundamental mechanisms of the nervous system. In essence, the knee jerk can be understood in terms of only two nerve cells—a sensory neuron and a motor neuron—connected by a single synapse. These two neurons form the circuit. It is a simple loop beginning at the quadriceps muscle on the top of the thigh, traveling up to the base of the spinal cord, and then circling back to the original muscle.

Now, with this wiring diagram, we can follow the neural basis of the knee jerk (see Figure 2.20). The tap of the rubber hammer stretches the muscle slightly. This, in turn, stretches a fiber from the sensory neuron that is wrapped

The flexion reflex is the neural action by which a hand automatically draws back from a hot stove.

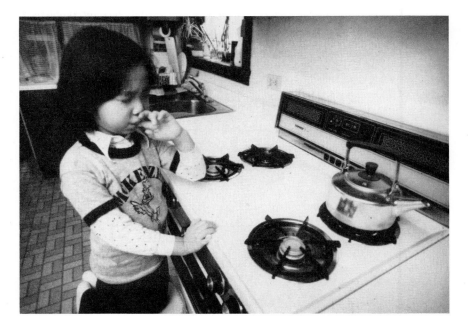

CHAPTER 2   THE NERVOUS SYSTEM

like a tentacle around a specialized muscle cell, called the **muscle spindle.** The stimulation excites the sensory neuron, setting off the interchange of sodium and potassium ions across the cell membrane and triggering the nerve impulse in the axon. The axon tip releases neurotransmitter into the synapse separating it from the dendrite of the motor neuron. The neurotransmitter sets off the nerve impulse in the motor neuron. The axon of the motor neuron releases its neurotransmitter, acetylcholine, into the gap between neuron and muscle. This same process, occurring simultaneously in perhaps hundreds of simple two-neuron loops, causes the muscle to contract and the leg to jerk up.

From this simple beginning, we will turn in later chapters to explorations of the circuitry that controls far more complex functions of the nervous system such as seeing, feeling, and remembering.

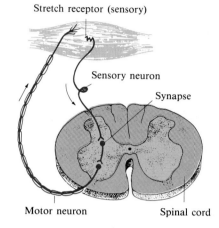

Summary

1. All vertebrates and many invertebrates have a nervous system that varies in size and complexity with the sensory, motor, and intellectual capacity of the animal. In man and other vertebrates, the nervous system consists of two major subdivisions: the central nervous system and the peripheral nervous system. The spinal cord and the brain make up the central nervous system, and the peripheral nervous system is made up of groups of nerve cells called ganglia and nerve fibers that lie outside the central nervous system. Nerve fibers in both systems are called axons—long processes of nerve cells that conduct nerve impulses. The central and peripheral nervous systems are complexly interrelated.

Figure 2.20

Wiring diagram of the stretch reflex. The tap of the hammer stretches the muscle, which, in turn, stretches the neuromuscular spindle. This stimulation excites the sensory neuron, which sets off a nerve impulse in the motor neuron causing the muscle to contract and the leg to jerk up.

2. The central nervous system regulates and controls the entire body. The brain and spinal cord are highly protected, by bone and by three membranes, or meninges: the dura mater, the arachnoid, and the pia mater. Among the fibers that make up the spinal cord are afferent nerves that carry sensations from the sense organs, or receptors, to the brain. Efferent nerves or effectors carry messages from the brain, down the spinal cord, to the muscles and glands.

3. The peripheral nervous system transmits information between the various body organs and the central nervous system and is made up of the somatic and autonomic nervous systems. The autonomic nervous system is made up of, in turn, the sympathetic and parasympathetic nervous systems.

4. The brain stem is composed of nerve cells and fibers. The lowest part of the brain stem is the medulla, and just above it is the pons. These centers control automatic functions such as heart rate and respiration. The midbrain is situated near the top of the brain stem. Just above the midbrain are the pineal and pituitary glands which, although not composed of nerve cells, regulate body chemistry, influence behavior, and are considered functional parts of the brain. Attached to the rear of the brain at the level of the pons is the cerebellum, which helps to maintain body equilibrium and to coordinate fine movements.

5. Two cerebral hemispheres form the cerebrum, whose wrinkled, gray surface, the cerebral cortex, and its associated fiber system, makes up about four-fifths of the brain's volume and weight. Within the cerebrum are the thalamus, a relay station for sensory impressions; the hypothalamus, governor of the autonomic nervous system and regulator of body temperature, appetite, thirst, and sexual activities; and the limbic system which, along with the hypothalamus, is involved in intense emotions such as anger, fear, and pleasure.

6. Each hemisphere of the cerebral cortex is demarcated by fissures into four distinct regions, or lobes: (1) the occipital lobe, which processes the sensation of vision, (2) the parietal lobe, which monitors skin sensations and lo-

cation of the body's limbs; (3) the temporal lobe, which is concerned with hearing and the understanding of language; and (4) the frontal lobe, which receives the sensations of smell and contains the motor cortex.

7. The motor cortex, stretched around the curving surface of the cerebral cortex, controls movements. The association areas make up the rest, and the bulk, of the cortex.

8. Not only the brain but also most of the nervous system is bilaterally symmetrical. Because of the crossover of nerve fiber tracts within the spinal cord and brain, each side of the brain controls the opposite side of the body: movement of the left hand is largely controlled by the right hemisphere of the brain. The specialization of one or the other hemisphere (as evidenced in handedness) is known as cerebral dominance. The left, or major, hemisphere appears to control verbal, analytic, and mathematical skills; the right, or minor, hemisphere, appears to control intuitive, nonverbal, and spatial perception skills. The two cerebral hemispheres are connected by a band of nerve fibers, the corpus callosum.

9. The principal functional units of the nervous system, numbering in billions, are neurons, and they interact by contacting one another. Most neurons have three essential parts: the cell body, or soma; a network of projections called dendrites; and the appendage known as the axon. Typically, the axon of one neuron makes contacts with another neuron via that neuron's cell body or one of its dendrites.

10. The nervous system's basic means of communication is the nerve impulse or action potential, an electrical wave that travels down the axon of the neuron away from the cell body. The action potential involves the successive passage of charged sodium and potassium ions through the axon's membrane. Insulation provided by the myelin sheath surrounding some axons speeds up the nerve impulse.

11. Neurons do not actually fuse. Neurotransmitters, chemical intermediaries, activate neurons across a very narrow gap, the synapse. The neurotransmitter diffuses across the synaptic cleft and binds with receptor sites on the dendrite membrane of the next neuron. This binding depolarizes the membrane and triggers a nerve impulse in the neuron's axon. Thus, by means of a neurotransmitter, electrical activity in one neuron is communicated to the next nerve cell in the pathway.

12. A dozen or more different neurotransmitters have been identified in the human nervous system. Some are excitatory, and trigger the nerve impulse; some are inhibitory, and retard the nerve impulse; several neurotransmitters are known to be both excitatory and inhibitory.

RESEARCH: The complexity of the mammalian nervous system has required that researchers interested in the neural basis of behavior study the nervous systems of simple invertebrates. These animals have fewer nerve cells than vertebrates, making it easier to relate the function of individual neurons to particular behavior. Eric Kandel has been able to map the sensory neurons that activate motor neurons involved in the control of the gill-withdrawal reflex in the giant sea squid *aplysia*. Kandel has shown that repeated stimulation of the sensory neurons decreases levels of neurotransmitter substance, thereby causing habituation of the reflex.

FOCUS: The discovery of opiate receptors in the brain together with the discovery of endorphins—the brain's own painkiller—has stimulated several new avenues of psychophysiological research. These include experiments exploring the link between psychiatric disorders and abnormal levels of endorphins and the development of a neurological model of opiate addiction. Rats injected repeatedly with endorphins experience withdrawal symptoms when endorphins are no longer administered.

Sensation

Johannes Müller's work on senses and sensation laid the groundwork for perception research.

The wages were good, and the work was easy. The student volunteers at McGill University had only to lie around for a few days in an isolation chamber (Bexton, Heron, & Scott, 1954). Lying on cots, the volunteers wore translucent goggles over their eyes to filter out most of the light. Fans and an air conditioner in the room emitted a steady, unvarying hum as the students lay with heavy gloves on their hands and cardboard mailing tubes on their arms. The experiment aimed to see what happens when we are largely deprived of sensations: the vision, hearing, and touch that ordinarily enrich our lives.

This sensory deprivation proved so difficult for some subjects that a few quit before the first day was over. The students who stayed on underwent stressful, even frightening, experiences. They had difficulty with motor coordination, could not solve simple problems, and found it almost impossible to concentrate.

Most of us have tried to imagine at one time or another what it would be like to be blind or deaf. But these volunteers learned what it is like to have their main windows to the world closed. Following these early reports, a number of studies were done on sensory deprivation in which the techniques were modified. In many of these the experience was not as disruptive as earlier reported (Suedfeld, 1975) and was even found to be useful in some cases of psychological therapy (Suedfeld & Kristeller, 1982).

In this chapter we will examine the sensory mechanisms through which we keep in touch with the world and our body's place in it. These mechanisms include seeing, hearing, the chemical senses (smell and taste), the skin senses (touch, temperature, and pain), and the sense of position and movement. For our purposes here, **sensation** is the process by which we receive and code a stimulus such as a spot of light or a musical tone. **Perception,** on the other hand, which will be discussed in chapter 4, is the process by which we recognize a pattern such as the familiar face of a friend.

Characteristics of the Senses

All of the senses, no matter how diverse, share certain characteristics. These characteristics hold true even for the senses peculiar to some animals, which receive information about their world in fascinating and sometimes bizarre ways (see Focus, p. 92).

All sensation can be described in three stages: stimulation, detection, and neural coding. To begin with, there must be some form of physical or chemical energy such as light or odor to stimulate the sensory mechanisms. Specialized organs such as the eye or nose receive or detect that energy. Finally, a means of converting the energy into a code understood by the central nervous system must exist.

Stimulation

ELECTRICITY: GREAT NON - AD. STIMULUS

The type of stimulus to which a sense organ normally responds is called the **adequate stimulus.** The adequate stimulus for the eye is the range of electromagnetic radiation that we call light. Why do we see light and not hear it? One of the fundamental principles of sensory coding was formulated by Johannes Müller during the nineteenth century (Müller, 1838/1948). His **law of specific nerve energies,** in its modern interpretation, simply states that only one kind of sensation is transmitted over a given nerve fiber. Axons in the optic nerve, for example, carry information to the visual centers of the brain, which, in turn, interpret the signals as visual. This is not to imply, however, that only light can serve as the stimulus for visual information. A punch in the eye will indeed make the victim "see stars." You can experience a less painful demonstration if you poke gently at your eyelid with a fingertip or the blunt end of a pencil. Two sensations occur. You feel the sense of touch as a result of the pressure on the skin around the eye. You may also perceive a hazy blob of light because the pressure also activates the visual mechanisms. The important point is that even though visual fibers may be activated by a stimulus other than light, the brain perceives that activation as caused by light. Müller's reasoning led to the assumption of a direct link between the peripheral sensory organs and specific cortical neurons.

Detection

The remarkable structures that detect the physical and chemical stimuli are called **receptors.** Receptors come in various forms. They are either modified nerve endings or specialized nonneural cells that contact a nerve ending. Good examples of the nonneural type are the light-sensitive receptors of the eye. Although not actually neurons, these photoreceptors have special properties that enable them to respond electrically to changes in light intensity. In other cases, just as the skin responds to touch, temperature, and pain, the receptors may be elaborate connective tissue structures that encase the endings of nerve fibers, or they may be the free endings of the nerve fibers themselves.

Neural Coding

In addition to detecting the stimulus, receptors have a second key function: they convert, or transduce, that physical energy into the nervous system's language—electrochemical signals or codes. This process resembles the generation of nerve impulses described in detail in chapter 2. To review, the stimulus causes a change in the ionic permeability of the receptor's membrane. In most cases the stimulus depolarizes the receptor. The depolarization in response to a stimulus is called a **generator potential.** The generator potential is usually continuously variable over a range of values: the more intense the stimulus, the bigger the generator potential. If the generator potential reaches and maintains a certain threshold of intensity, it in turn creates a series of nerve impulses, or action potentials, that travel down the fiber of the sensory neuron. At the junction between the sensory neuron and the next cell in the pathway, the nerve impulse causes the release of a chemical, the neurotransmitter. This action across the synapse serves either to excite or inhibit the next neuron.

By successive connections across one or more synapses, sensory information is brought from the periphery into the brain and within the brain to the cerebral cortex. In some cases the same cell does two jobs; it detects the sensory stimulus and codes it into a train of action potentials. In other cases the receptor cell does not fire action potentials but can produce them in subsequent cells to which it is connected. The rods and cones of the eye, for example, do not fire action potentials, nor do the next cells within the eye, the bipolar cells. But eventually all sensory information that reaches the brain must do so by a train of action potentials. In the eye it is the third cell in the pathway, the retinal ganglion cell, that fires action potentials. The axons of the retinal ganglion cells constitute the **optic nerve,** which connects the eye to the brain.

Receptors vary in their response to the sensory stimulus. Some will maintain their generator potential and keep firing impulses as long as the stimulus is present. They are known as **sustained receptors.** Others, known as **transient receptors,** fire when the stimulus is first applied but quickly return to their normal state, the resting potential, even if the stimulus is maintained.

How does the firing of the receptor code the intensity of the stimulus? How can this process convey the apparent loudness of a noise? As we saw in chapter 2, it cannot mirror the stimulus intensity by the size, or amplitude, of its action

Table 3.1	ABSOLUTE THRESHOLDS FOR SEVERAL DIFFERENT SENSES

Approximate Absolute Thresholds

Sensory modality	Threshold
Vision	A candle flame at 30 miles on a dark, clear night
Hearing	The tick of a watch at 20 feet in a quiet room
Taste	One ounce of quinine sulfate in 250 gallons of water
Smell	One drop of perfume diffused throughout a six-room house
Touch	Wing of a bee falling on the cheek from a distance of 1 centimeter

potential. Under the all-or-none law of nerve-impulse propagation, the voltage change of the action potential is always the same; only the frequency of the firing varies. Nerve cells in the sensory pathways thus usually represent the intensity of the stimulus only by firing more frequently. Alternatively, there might be specialized receptors whose thresholds differed. In such a case intensity could be signalled by *which* receptors were activated: a more intense stimulus would be needed to activate a high threshold receptor.

Psychophysics

The branch of psychology concerned with the measurement of relationships between the physical attributes of stimuli and the resulting sensations is called **psychophysics.** Psychophysicists are interested in studying how the physical characteristics of a stimulus, such as its intensity, affect a person's sensory impression, or judgment, of that aspect of the stimulus. For example, they would be interested in finding out how a person's impression of the brightness of a light would change when the physical intensity was doubled.

Sensory Thresholds

Sensory thresholds are the levels at which a stimulus or changes in a stimulus can be detected. They are a major concern of psychophysicists. How much sugar (amount of stimulus) must be put into a glass of water before we can first taste its sweetness? How much more intense must the second of two tones (change in stimulus) be before it sounds louder than the first?

Absolute Thresholds
The minimal level of intensity at which we can perceive a sensation is the **absolute threshold.** Suppose an experimenter sets the intensity of a tone well below the level at which you can hear it. The intensity is gradually raised until you say, "I hear it." The tone is then set well above that particular level and then decreased gradually until you say, "I don't hear it." In both cases, that point of transition between hearing and not hearing is your absolute threshold for sound intensity.

Table 3.1 shows approximate absolute thresholds for different senses. As you can see, the human senses are, appropriately enough, remarkably sensitive. For example, with normal vision on a dark clear night, you can probably spot a candle flame 30 miles away. It is important to note, however, that the figures listed are only approximate. Absolute thresholds may not be precisely the same from individual to individual and even may vary slightly for the same observer on different occasions. Obviously, the absolute threshold cannot be a discrete value. Psychologists usually define the absolute threshold as that value at which the stimulus can be detected 50 percent of the time.

Interestingly, at extremely low levels of intensity the stimulus itself may vary and such variability can affect threshold measurements. An example is the stimulus for vision—light. Light can be thought of as tiny particles of energy, called **quanta.** We might assume that the same light source, say a light bulb, would emit the same number of quanta per second whenever it is switched on. But there is an inherent variability in the number of quanta given off by a light source. Normally this variance is very small when compared to the total number of quanta. But at very low levels of light intensity, this variance in the number of quanta that are emitted in a given time adds variability to any measurement of the absolute threshold. The human eye is so sensitive that at the threshold for vision much of the apparent variability in threshold is really due to this inherent variability in the number of quanta emitted by the light.

CHAPTER 3   SENSATION

Although most psychophysical experiments are carried out with human subjects, the same sorts of procedures are applied to animals. For example, Donald Blough (1956) set out to determine the absolute threshold at which pigeons perceive light. He trained pigeons to peck a key for food reward in a box containing two keys. The animal was trained to peck at Key A when the light was on and Key B when the light was off. The electronic circuit was arranged so that Key A not only recorded the fact of pecking but also lowered the intensity of the light. Key B recorded the pecking and increased the illumination. Thus, the absolute threshold for light perception could be determined by measuring at what level of luminance the pigeons began frequent back and forth switching from Key A to Key B. The decreasing luminance necessary for this key-switching to take place, indicated by the descending curve after the "Break" in Figure 3.1, is a result of the pigeons' gradual adaptation over time to darkness. Note that after 60 minutes the key-switching has finally stablized at slightly above the 4.0 level of luminance. With a similar procedure, other researchers have measured the absolute thresholds for hearing, touch, and pain, as well as vision, in a large number of animals.

Difference Thresholds

The absolute threshold describes only the minimal level of intensity at which we can perceive a sensation. But we also have the ability to discriminate between two stimuli of different intensities. The smallest difference between two stimuli that can be discriminated reliably is the **difference threshold.** Like the absolute threshold, the difference threshold is defined by the amount of change that is necessary for a subject to detect a difference between two stimuli in 50 percent of the trials. The nineteenth-century German physiologist Ernst Weber (reprinted 1978) pioneered the scientific study of difference thresholds in experiments based on lifting small weights. If a subject could discriminate between a 51-ounce weight and a 50-ounce weight, the difference threshold was 1 ounce.

The 1 ounce was the **just noticeable difference,** or **jnd.** Weber found that over a surprisingly wide range, the difference threshold, or jnd, tended to be a constant ratio to the intensity of the stimulus. Thus, if the jnd between a 50-ounce weight and one that feels heavier is 1 ounce, the jnd for a 100-ounce weight and the next weight detected as heavier is 2 ounces. **Weber's law** can be expressed as a formula: $\Delta I / I = K$, where ΔI stands for the change in intensity, I is the intensity of the reference stimulus, and K is a constant. In the example given, if $I = 50$ ounces, $\Delta I = 1$ ounce; hence $\Delta I / I = 1/50$. The law says that this ratio will be constant no matter what value of I we choose. Weber's law works reasonably well for a number of senses and over a wide range of intensities, although it is usually inaccurate for stimuli with intensities that are either very small or very large.

Psychophysical Scales

Weber's work helped lead to a proposed solution to a problem that had troubled nineteenth-century researchers: how to measure precisely the relationship between the intensity of a stimulus and the intensity of the resulting sensation. This problem arose because it was clear there was not a one-to-one relationship between stimulus intensity and sensation magnitude. Doubling the physical intensity of a sound, for example, does not mean that we will perceive it as twice as loud.

Researchers needed a general principle for formulating scales that would relate stimulus intensity to its psychological magnitude, that is, how strongly we perceive the intensity of the stimulus. The clues for such a scale were found in Weber's law. Suppose that all difference thresholds, or jnds, were of roughly

Figure 3.1

Sample curve from one pigeon in a single hour obtained in a series of absolute threshold experiments. The curve can be separated into two continuous segments joined at a rather sharp "Break." The run began with the stimulus (light) at a superthreshold luminance (not shown). The responses in the first three minutes were all to Key A, which served only to reduce the luminance to threshold (Blough, 1956).

Physiologist Ernst Weber pioneered the scientific study of difference thresholds.

German physicist and philosopher Gustav Fechner derived a scale that would measure how we perceive the intensity of stimuli.

equal psychological magnitudes. For example, in the discrimination of weight differences, suppose that 1 ounce added an equal amount of "heaviness" to a 50-ounce weight as 2 ounces added to a 100-ounce weight. One added ounce would be equal in psychological magnitude to 2 added ounces, depending on how much we were adding it to. We could construct a scale in which equal increments of psychological magnitude were based on the jnd at each stimulus value. Reasoning this way from Weber's law, the German physicist and philosopher Gustav Fechner derived in 1860 just such a scale. His solution climaxed a decade of Herculean effort by Fechner who, by his own account, made no fewer than 24,576 separate judgments of difference thresholds using various small weights. Fechner also conducted numerous experiments investigating the just noticeable differences between varying stimulus intensities of both light and sound.

Although by today's standards Fechner's work may seem rather uninteresting, his insights into the quantitative relationship between mental sensation and physical stimulation constituted a monumental discovery relevant to the mind-body problem—an issue of considerable historical importance.

Fechner's law states that the relationship between stimulus intensity and the strength of sensation is a logarithmic one in which a constant ratio of stimulus change produces a constant difference in sensation. This logarithmic relationship between stimulus intensity and sensation is a logical consequence of treating just noticeable differences as psychological equivalent units.

Fechner's elegant formulations bridge the gap between mental and physical phenomena in a manner not previously thought possible. His experimental methods proved applicable to a broad range of psychological endeavors, and with slight modifications continue to be employed today. Fechner's empirical approach to the measurement of mental abilities challenged the long-held dictum of German philosopher Immanuel Kant that psychology was relagated to the status of a nonscience insomuch as it was not possible to quantify mental acts. While some of his findings have not withstood the tests of time, his various contributions when viewed in historical perspective remain profoundly important for the then newly emerging field of psychology. Indeed, without Fechner there would have been:

> "little of the breadth of science in the experimental body, for we hardly recognize a subject as scientific if measurement is not one of its tools. Fechner, because of what he did and the time at which he did it, set experimental quantitative psychology off upon the course which it has followed. One may call him the 'founder' of experimental psychology, or one may assign that title to Wundt. It does not matter. Fechner had a fertile idea which grew and brought forth fruit abundantly" (Boring, 1950, pp. 294–95).

By using more direct methods of estimating the relationship between stimulus intensity and the magnitude of sensation, S. S. Stevens has shown that Fechner's law is not as generally applicable as it once was thought to be. Stevens presented subjects with a series of stimuli to which they had to assign numbers proportional to the corresponding subjective impressions of sensations (Stevens, 1957). For example, he would present subjects with a stimulus of a certain light intensity and tell them it had a brightness of 10. Then he would present another light intensity and ask them to assign it a number indicating its brightness relative to the first light. If subjects believed the second light was twice as bright as the first, they would assign it the number 20; if they thought it was half as bright as the first, they would assign it the number 5. Using this method, Stevens found that increases in light intensity produce progressively smaller changes in perceived brightness—the same general conclusion that Fechner drew. However, he also found that this relationship is not true for all types of stimuli. Doubling of an electric shock, for example, results in consid-

CHAPTER 3   SENSATION

erably more than a mere doubling in the reported sensation. As a result of numerous studies with different senses, Stevens concluded that the relationship between stimulus intensity and magnitude of sensation differs for each sense but remains constant over a wide range of stimulus intensities for a single sensory system. He summarized his findings in what is known as **Stevens' Power Law,** which states that the magnitude of a sensation is equal to the physical magnitude of the stimulus producing the sensation raised to a certain power, which varies depending on the sensation that is being measured (Stevens, 1961).

Although some of his conclusions must be modified, Fechner's lasting contributions to psychophysics, a term that he coined, cannot be underestimated. He showed that psychological processes could be measured and, in doing so, gave the study of sensation its first tools. In addition, his law also indicated a compression in perceptual capabilities as stimulus intensity increases. This compression reflects the fact that the nervous system's ability to code and discriminate is less effective at the extremes of stimulus intensities.

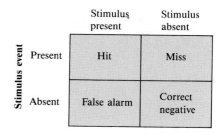

Figure 3.2

The four possible outcomes in a signal detection task.

Signal Detection Theory

The early psychophysicists were primarily concerned with the relationship between the characteristics of a physical stimulus and the sensory experience produced in the subject. As noted previously, however, absolute and difference thresholds depend not only on the stimulus itself, but on the observer's attitudes and beliefs at the time of the detection task. That is, an individual's sensitivity to a particular stimulus depends in large measure upon motivational factors that are independent of variations in the stimulus. The recognition that factors extraneous to changes in stimulus strength exert a powerful influence upon a subject's ability to detect a stimulus event underlies the modern approach known as **signal detection theory.** Signal detection theory is based upon the notion that the recognition of external stimuli is due to two factors: **sensitivity,** or simply how well an individual can actually detect a given stimulus, and **response bias,** or the readiness of a subject to report that a stimulus has occurred under conditions of uncertainty.

A typical procedure in a signal detection experiment dealing with absolute thresholds would be to make extensive use of **catch trials** when no stimulus is presented to the subject, thus providing an opportunity for the subject to report a stimulus presentation when in fact none has been given. If the subject commits such an error, it is termed a **false alarm.** Another type of error, called a **miss,** occurs when a subject fails to report that a stimulus was presented. Similarly, correct responses come in two forms: **hits,** when the subject reliably detects a true signal, and **correct negatives,** in which the person accurately states that no stimulus was given (see Figure 3.2).

A person's response bias will be a consequence of the payoffs and penalties associated with correct judgments and errors, respectively, with reference to the stimulus event. Put another way, a subject's degree of caution with reference to the reporting of a stimulus will be partially determined by the magnitude of the consequences that follow any given decision about whether a particular event has taken place. A host of real-life situations can be viewed from this perspective. For example, consider the case of a single woman living alone in a high-crime neighborhood whose "detection task" involves the identification of a burglar's efforts to unlock the front door against the background sounds (termed "noise" by signal detection theorists) of city traffic and howling cats. The consequences of a miss—failing to notice the burglar's illegal entry—might be fatal, forcing the woman to adopt lenient criteria which then lead her to detect many burglars when in fact none are present. It is reasonable to anticipate this sort of pattern when a stimulus is of relatively low intensity,

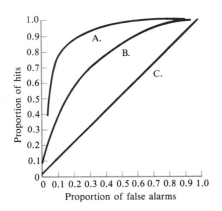

Figure 3.3

Signal detection theory is demonstrated in this ROC (receiver operating characteristic) curve. The number of "hits" and number of "false alarms" are recorded over numerous trials at different intensities.

and any failure to judge that a stimulus event has occurred results in dire consequences in comparison to the outcome of false alarms—in this case an unjustified, albeit understandable, call to the police department. Remember that either stimulus factors or the woman's expectancies will influence the proportion of hits and misses: a loud, clumsy burglar will almost certainly be noticed, while having recently viewed the horror film *Halloween* will probably promote the woman's bias toward false alarms.

Signal detection theory offers a method for separating the effects of response bias and stimulus sensitivity by systematically manipulating various aspects of the detection experiment. By changing the consequences of a subject's decision, such as making misses more costly by imposing a penalty of some sort, response bias can be manipulated while stimulus strength is held constant. The results of these experimental manipulations are consistent with the example presented previously: when subjects are induced to become more conservative in their judgments or relatively less prone to reporting stimulus occurrences, the proportion of both false alarms and hits decrease dramatically. Correspondingly, when the subject adopts a lenient strategy and is quick to report a stimulus, even if uncertain in his or her conviction, there is a marked increase in the percentage of hits and false alarms. These effects can be represented graphically by plotting the proportion of false alarms against the proportion of hits on the X- and Y-axes, respectively. The resulting plot is called a **Receiver Operating Characteristic Curve,** and is usually referred to simply as an **ROC** curve (Figure 3.3).

Signal detection theory rejects the notion of threshold in favor of analyzing detection tasks as decision-making situations in which a stimulus must be identified above background noise. The theory emphasizes that an individual's internal state of sensory readiness and cognitive preparedness play a crucial role with respect to any act of perceptual awareness, independent of the external stimulus itself.

Signal detection theory was developed by scientists studying detectability of signals on a radar screen, but has proved useful in many other contexts. It provides a handy way of analyzing the detectability of a sensory stimulus and the reliability of a human observer in a great number of detection tasks.

Whatever senses are measured and however they are measured, all follow a common path from stimulation to detection to neural coding. In the next section we shall examine in some detail just how the specific senses—sight, hearing, smell and taste, skin sensations, and movement and position—follow this three-stage pattern.

Vision

We begin our study of the specific senses with vision for two reasons. First, much of our knowledge about the world around us comes to the brain via the eyes. Second, researchers have devoted more effort to studying the mechanisms of vision than any other sensation. As a result, our understanding of how we see, although far from complete, exceeds our knowledge of any other sense.

Visual Stimulation: The Nature of Light

The stimulus for vision is light, a type of electromagnetic energy. Such energy can be thought of as traveling in waves. Wavelengths vary enormously, and the relative lengths of the waves determine the place in the spectrum of a given type of electromagnetic energy. At one end of the **electromagnetic spectrum** (the entire range of wavelengths or frequencies of electromagnetic radia-

The image we see is reversed on the retina.

tion) are radio waves that may be many miles in length. At the other end are the shortest cosmic rays (gamma rays), which measure about 10 trillionths of an inch. Neither are visible to the eye (see Color Plate 3.1, following p. 84).

Somewhere in between radio waves and cosmic rays is the narrow range of the electromagnetic spectrum that we can see: the **visible spectrum.** The wavelengths of light are measured in units called **nanometers.** A nanometer is one billionth (10^{-9}) of a meter. The visible spectrum ranges from wavelengths measuring about 400 nanometers to those of about 700 nanometers. In other words, that range of electromagnetic energy activates the light-sensitive receptors of the human eye (See Research: "How Much Light Do We Need for Seeing?").

Structure of the Eye

If an animal such as a white rat is killed and its eye removed, an interesting observation can be made. We can hold its eye up to a brightly lit scene and, at the back of the eye, a tiny image of the scene appears. The image is reversed: it is upside down and backwards. Precisely the same sort of reversed image is formed at the back of the human eye by our own vision. How is the image formed at the back of the eye? How is it converted into signals that can be interpreted by the nervous system? How are those signals conveyed to the brain and to what part?

To understand the answers to those questions, let us consider in detail the structure of the eye and how it responds to light. For simplicity's sake, we can liken the structure of the eye to the workings of an ordinary camera. As Figure 3.4 shows, light passes through the **cornea,** a transparent tissue, and through the hole formed by a structure called the **iris.** The iris changes shape to make the hole, called the **pupil,** larger and smaller. Like the aperture setting of a camera, the size of the pupil regulates the amount of light by constricting (getting smaller) and dilating (getting larger). The light entering the eye is focused by the cornea and the **lens**—suspended by ligaments within the eye—working together. Muscles within the eye can change the shape, or curvature, of the

Figure 3.4

The major structural features of the eye and its formation of an image. Similarities to a camera are illustrated in the lower drawing.

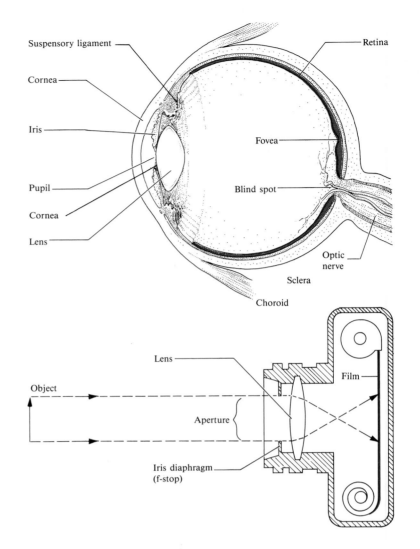

Figure 3.5

Two examples of optic arrays from objects, along with their retinal images. Only lines from the extremities of the objects are shown. In (A) the object is far away, so the visual angle is small and a correspondingly small image is projected on the retina. In (B) the object is closer, so there is a larger visual angle and a larger retinal image. To provide a sharp focus on the retina the lens has to change its curvature—a process called accommodation—so that it becomes thicker for close objects and thinner for distant ones.

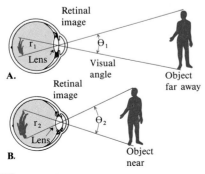

lens and hence the focus as objects approach or recede. This process is called **accommodation** (see Figure 3.5). As we view objects at close distances the lens becomes fatter; as we view distant objects it flattens. Finally, as in a camera, the light is focused onto a light-sensitive surface—the **retina.**

The eye does not really look like nor operate as simply as a camera, of course. As Figure 3.6 shows, it is basically a sphere that bulges a bit at the front. The bulge is filled with a watery fluid, **aqueous humor,** and most of the interior of the sphere is filled with a transparent jellylike substance, **vitreous humor.** These substances help maintain the shape of the eye, which is critical to precise vision. In fact, most defects in vision result from abnormalities in the shape of the eyeball. If the eye is too long, the cornea and lens focus images slightly in front of the retina and distant objects appear fuzzy. This is called nearsightedness, or myopia. If the eyeball is too short, images are focused behind the retina and nearby objects are blurred. This is called farsightedness, or hypermetropia.

The sphere is made up of three layers of tissue. The outermost layer, or white of the eye, is the **sclera**—from the Greek for "hard." The sclera is the major structural element of the eye, providing its firm outer framework. At the front, the sclera is modified to form the transparent cornea, through which we can see the colored iris with its pupil in the middle. The middle layer, the **choroid,** is a dark-pigmented lining, rich in blood vessels, that serves to keep out all light except for that which enters through the pupil. The innermost layer contains the retina—the structure where light is converted into electric signals and transmitted to the brain.

The Retina

The word *retina* derives from the Latin for "net" and, indeed, it is a net of millions of cells that, in connections and in function, resembles the neurons of the brain. The cells of the retina are clumped into three distinct layers (see Figure 3.7). One layer consists of the **rods** and **cones,** the light-sensitive receptor cells that receive and detect the electromagnetic energy, light, and convert it into neural signals. The second layer is the **inner nuclear layer,** consisting of **horizontal cells, bipolar cells,** and **amacrine cells.** These cells of the inner nuclear layer organize the information that comes from the rods and cones and transmit it to the third layer, the **ganglion cells.** Fibers projecting from the genglion cells bundle together to form the optic nerve, which carries the electrical signals to the brain.

As we look at a microscopic view of the retina, there appears to be a paradox in the arrangement of the three layers of cells. The rods and cones, which are the receptors, are farthest from the light, and their tips, which contain photosensitive chemicals, face away from the light. In order to reach them, the light has to penetrate a network of blood vessels, the ganglion cell layer, and the inner nuclear layer. This strange arrangement makes sense, however. All of the layers except for the blood vessels are transparent and hence present no obstacle to the passage of light. And, as we shall see later, the eye has an ingenious mechanism that renders the blood vessels invisible. Moreover, the positioning of the rods and cones permits their tips to come into intimate contact with the **pigment epithelium,** a single cell lining between the rods and cones and the choroid, the middle layer of structures surrounding the eyeball. The pigment epithelium has three important functions: it absorbs stray light, it serves as a metabolic channel for nourishment of the receptors and, as has recently been discovered, it plays a role in the continuous renewal of the light-sensitive outer segments of the rods.

Rods and Cones

Rods and cones are light receptors, but there are several important differences between them. The rods are slender and roughly cylindrical; each eye contains about 100 million rods. The cones vary in their width. Those in the periphery of the retina are plump and have a cone-shaped tip; those in the very center of the retina are as slender as rods. Each eye has some 6 million cones. Both rods and cones contain photosensitive chemicals, or pigments, that absorb light. When they absorb light, a chemical change occurs in the structure of the pigment molecule. This chemical change, in ways that are not yet completely understood, changes the voltage across the receptor membrane, and this generator potential is relayed to cells in the inner nuclear layer. Visual receptor cells of vertebrates are unlike most other sensory receptors in that they are hyperpolarized by light. Most of the receptor cells are depolarized by their adequate stimulus.

Rods and cones differ not only in shape and number but, most dramatically, in function. We can gain important clues to the differing functions of rods and cones in the human eye if we look first at the retina of two very different animals. For example, the retina of the hedgehog contains rods but very few cones. The hedgehog is a nocturnal animal, one that is active almost exclusively at night. By contrast, the retina of the tree shrew has only cone receptors. The tree shrew sleeps during the night and is active by day.

Similarly, in humans, the rods function principally in dim illumination such as at dusk and at night. With the rods, we see no true colors, only black, white, and shades of gray. With the cones, which function principally in bright illumination, we see black, white, and colors such as red, green, and blue. You can see for yourself the level of light at which the rods function best and at which the cones cease to operate. As the light fades at night, the world gradually loses its color: the rods have taken over. Indeed, it is sometimes said that humans really have two visual systems—a cone system and a rod system.

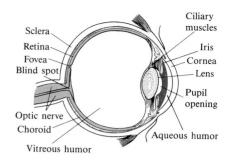

Figure 3.6

The eye is a complicated structure with many parts. Its purpose is to present an optical image of the world to the retina, where that image is transformed into nerve impulses.

Figure 3.7

Light entering the retina is processed by three layers of cells. It first activates the rods (R) and cones (C) where it is converted into neural signals. These neural signals then pass through the inner nuclear layer consisting of horizontal cells (H), bipolar cells (B), and amacrine cells (A), which organizes the information and transmits it to the third layer of ganglion cells (G). Fibers projecting from the ganglion cells bundle together to form the optic nerve, which carries the signals to the brain.

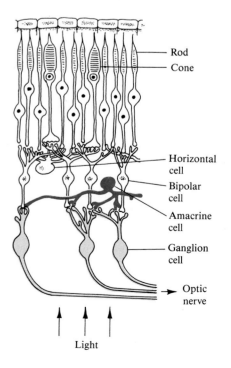

RESEARCH

Researchers who study sensation must necessarily bridge two quite different realms of science—psychology and physics. This was recognized by Gustav Theodor Fechner, the nineteenth-century German pioneer in the study of sensation, when he founded the branch of psychology that he called psychophysics. The central concern of psychophysics is the measurement of the relationships between the physical attributes of a stimulus such as light or sound and the sensations that it produces.

From the beginning, psychophysicists attempted to measure what they labeled the absolute threshold—the minimum amount of physical energy that can be detected by our sensory apparatus. The absolute threshold of vision was of particular interest: How much light is necessary before we can see? At least a dozen attempts were made to answer this question over a period of half a century. The failings in these studies typically were ones of methodology. It was not until the early 1940s that a team of investigators at Columbia University were able to answer the question, and then only by means of their painstaking approach to the problem (Hecht, Shlaer, & Pirenne, 1942).

Because this work by Selig Hecht and his colleagues is still considered a classic in psychophysical research, let us examine the highlights of their approach. The subject was placed in a dark room in a dark cabinet with his head immobilized. Through a complex optical arrangement, a light of brief duration was flashed onto one part of his eye. The subject controlled when the light was flashed, but the experimenters controlled the intensity of the light, systematically

How Much Light Do We Need for Seeing?

varying its amount, which is measured in quanta.

The conditions of the experiment were arranged so as to yield the maximum possible sensitivity of the subject's retina. For example, the part of the retina exposed to the light was in a portion of the retina where the relative concentration of light-sensitive receptors, the rods, is greatest. Moreover, the subject was required to sit in the dark for at least 30 minutes before testing because the process of dark adaptation heightens the sensitivity of the rods. In addition, the wavelength of light used in the experiment—510 nanometers—was selected because the rods are most sensitive to this particular wavelength.

Seven subjects were tested in the experiment, four of them at sessions extending over 18 months. Each of a series of light intensities was presented to each subject many times, and the frequency of the subject's report of seeing the light was determined for each intensity. The subject had to report seeing a given intensity of light at least 60 percent of the time in order for it to be considered as his absolute threshold. Hecht found that, among these subjects, the minimum amount of light necessary

for seeing ranged from 54 quanta to 148 quanta.

These results, however, were only the experiment's raw data, which had to be further processed. They represented the amount of light measured at the cornea. To calculate the light actually reaching the rods in the retina, Hecht had to make adjustments. He had to correct for the considerable amount of light that was lost in at least three ways: reflection from the cornea, absorption by other parts of the eye en route to the retina, and passage through the retina without actually affecting the light-sensitive chemicals in the rods.

After these corrections, Hecht found that a range of only 5 to 14 quanta was necessary to activate the visual systems of his subjects. Statistical probability dictated that none of the rods affected by the light absorbed more than 1 quantum of light. Therefore, for human beings to see, he concluded, it is necessary for only 1 quantum of light to be absorbed by 5 to 14 rods. Further statistical analysis reduced this minimum to 5 to 8 rods.

Hecht also studied the variability of each subject's performance—why an individual's absolute threshold might be 5 quanta on one occasion, for example, and 6 on another. It previously had been assumed that such fluctuations depended upon the subject's psychological or biological variability from test to test. Hecht was able to show that these fluctuations were actually related to the inherent nature of light itself. The amount of quanta emitted by any light source is never constant but varies slightly. ∎

This is known as the duplicity theory of vision.

The pigment that absorbs light in rods is called **rhodopsin** from two words meaning rose-colored and in the eye. One of the important components of rhodopsin is vitamin A. A deficiency of vitamin A can produce night blindness by not allowing the production of enough rhodopsin.

The rods are distributed relatively uniformly throughout the retina. The cones are thinly distributed in the periphery and become much more densely packed toward the center of the retina. In fact, in the very center of the retina, an area of less than one square millimeter called the **fovea,** there are only cones, no rods. Because of this tight packing of receptors, our daylight vision is most acute in the fovea. When we fix a small object with a direct gaze, an image of that object is formed on the fovea. In bright light the densely packed cones of the fovea function to provide maximal visual sharpness, or **acuity.** By the same token, as the light dims, the foveal cones decrease in efficiency to the level where we can no longer make out that object. Indeed, in very dim light and in darkness we are blind in the fovea. If you look at a dim star at night you can make it disappear by looking directly at it, thus calling the fovea into play. When you look away slightly it reappears; the image now is projected onto a region of the retina that contains rods. The rods and cones of the retina translate bright and dim stimuli into messages that are later carried by the ganglion cells to the brain.

✳ Dark and Light Adaptation

The dual workings of the rods and cones of the retina allow our eyes to adapt to changing conditions of light and dark. Some time is required for this adaptation to take place. When we enter a darkened theater, a short period of adaptation is required before we can find our way down an aisle and to a seat.

Adaptation to darkness occurs in two stages (see Figure 3.1). When we enter a dark room the cones adapt first, reaching a stable level of vision in less than 10 minutes. While increased sensitivity of the rods takes nearly half an hour or more for completion, when fully dark-adapted, the eyes are around 1000 times more sensitive then they were after the cone system adaptation.

The reverse process of adaptation to light—leaving a dark theater and entering a brightly lighted space, for example—is much faster. We may squint briefly, but the adaptation of cones and rods to light occurs quickly.

Dark adaptation within the rods is due in part to the resynthesis of rhodopsin. During normal daylight vision, rhodopsin in the rods is broken down into a protein (opsin) and a yellow pigment (retinene). In darkness the protein and pigment recombine into rhodopsin, which sensitizes the rods to low light.

Rods and cones are shown here synapsing with other cells in the retina. The rods are slender and roughly cylindrical; the cones vary in their width.

Color Vision

Seeing in color is so much a part of our visual world that we seldom give it any thought. Yet, in dim illumination, when the retinal cones are not operating, color is lost. At night, it is as if the television screen we have been watching all day in full color fades and becomes old-fashioned black and white.

The scientific understanding of color vision began in 1671 with a simple experiment by Isaac Newton, the great English physicist. Newton darkened his room by closing the shutters; he then cut a small hole in one of the shutters. A thin shaft of sunlight came through this small hole. Newton placed a prism in the path of the light. On the opposite wall the prism produced a long rectangular patch of light made up of a series of rainbowlike colors. On one side of this rectangle, the light was red; next to it was orange, then yellow, green, and blue, to violet at the opposite end of the rectangle (see Figure 3.8).

Thanks to the understanding pioneered by Newton, we know that light that appears white is made up of many **wavelengths;** a prism bends light rays in inverse proportion to their respective wavelengths—the shortest wavelength light is bent the most, the longest wavelength light is bent the least. Different wavelengths of light are seen as different colors. Once a particular wavelength is isolated from white light, it maintains its characteristic color over a certain

Figure 3.8

When white light is shone through a prism, it is split into rays of different wavelengths, visible as different colors.

Newton's sketch of a prism in the path of light.

range of intensities. Newton, further and correctly, interpreted the colors of natural objects, such as green grass, brown soil, and so on, on the basis of their ability to absorb some of the rays of light and reflect others. Green grass is green because it absorbs the short and long wavelength rays and reflects light in the middle portion of the spectrum that is seen as green.

How do we see the great number of colors that we can distinguish? One suggestion was that the eye might contain receptors that are selectively tuned to different wavelengths of light. The problem with this view was that the human eye makes subtle color distinctions: the average person probably can distinguish a thousand or more different colors. If every hue had its own special receptor, a thousand colors would require 1000 different receptors at each point on the retina.

Early in the nineteenth century, the English physicist Thomas Young (1802) suggested an ingenious solution to this problem. He speculated that there are only three types of broadly tuned receptors. Each of these, he suggested, is maximally sensitive to a different wavelength. These receptors would also respond, but less vigorously, to light whose wavelength was longer or shorter. Any color could be produced by mixing three wavelengths in correct proportion.

Color Mixing

Color mixing has proved to be an important source of data about the nature of human color vision. Color can be mixed in several ways. Imagine that you had two slide projectors, both projecting onto the same screen. Instead of the usual 35mm slides, you have a set of colored filters. You can mix the color on the screen as you choose. If you have three projectors, you can mix three colors. Another simple way to make a color mixture would be by spinning a disk with several colors on it. The disk is now spun fast enough so that the eye fuses the colors. Suppose you paste different colored triangles on a circle of cardboard. Like pie cuts, you make a wedge of yellow, a wedge of green, and a wedge of white. You could mix colors together by spinning the circle so fast that the eye cannot see the individual portions of the pie.

The spinning-disk method was adapted in the nineteenth century by James Clerk Maxwell (1855) for studying effects of mixtures of colors. Maxwell and others found that with appropriate mixtures of any three colors we can duplicate the appearance of any other color. Another giant of nineteenth-century science, Hermann von Helmholtz (1896), summarized his own view of the nature of color vision: "If we think of the colors as plotted on a color chart . . . , it is evident from the rules given for the construction that all colors that are to be

James Clerk Maxwell

made by mixing three colors must be contained within the triangle whose vertices are the places in the chart where the three fundamental colors are.'' Helmholtz then went on to show that a simple triangular representation of the colors was insufficient and finally concluded that, ''the boundary of the color chart must be a curved line [see Figure 3.9] which differs considerably from the perimeter of the triangle.'' Helmholtz's diagram allowed the color of any mixture of wavelengths to be predicted with reasonable accuracy.

Helmholtz clarified another problem that confused most people, even Newton: a mixture of yellow and blue lights does *not* produce green as we would think. Rather, it produces a pale gray. The confusion comes from the difference between a mixture of different lights and a mixture of different pigments. A mixture of light of different wavelengths is called an **additive mixture,** that is, mixing two or more wavelengths will add up to a new color. On the other hand, a mixture of pigments—paints, for example—produces what is called a **subtractive mixture.** Pigments absorb and reflect light selectively: in effect, pigments subtract, or take away. They do not reflect all wavelengths falling on them. A leaf is green because its pigments absorb other wavelengths and reflect green. Lights add their wavelength to a mixture; pigments absorb or subtract some wavelengths and reflect remaining wavelengths to produce a given hue (see Color Plate 3.2).

The early insights by Young, Maxwell, and Helmholtz proved remarkably accurate and useful for understanding color mixture. Although the three-color theory, or **trichromatic theory,** first proposed by Young remained highly controversial until recent years, we now know that the human eye does indeed have three different types of color-sensitive cones. Each of these three types of cones has a different pigment, just as the rods have their particular pigment, rhodopsin. One cone responds at peak sensitivity to the long wavelengths, another to the middle wavelengths, and a third to the short wavelengths.

Thanks to new developments in experimental techniques, it is now possible to measure the color sensitivity of cones very much as you might test a color filter. For example, by placing a color filter in a beam of light that is composed of a relatively equal mixture of all wavelengths, you can determine, using appropriate tests, how much of that light is absorbed at each wavelength. The same sort of test might be performed on a single human cone by employing a very narrow beam of light such as that provided by shining a light backwards through a microscope. How much light is absorbed by shining the light through the sensitive part of an individual cone would have to be tested first, and then measurements corrected for light absorption by other structures outside of the cone. Testing a large number of cones from the eye of a recently deceased person would reveal the results shown in Figure 3.10, which illustrates the spectral sensitivity for the three classes of color-catching cones.

As Young first suggested, the combinations in various degrees of the action of cones make up all of the color richness of our world. Precisely how these combinations are put together by the eye and brain is less clear. Some important clues have been discerned from a hypothesis set forth more than a century ago by Ewald Hering (1878), who disagreed with Young's trichromatic, or three-receptor, theory. Hering focused on the appearance of colors instead of the receptor mechanisms. He argued that there are four basic colors, not three. These colors include yellow as well as red, green, and blue. He noted that certain pairs of these colors (blue versus yellow, and red versus green) seem to be opposite in a psychological sense: when combined, they cancel out each other (so that they appear gray). These are called **opposing colors.**

Although Hering's notion about the initial reception of colors by the cones was imprecise, the **opponent process** mechanism is in fact at work in cells farther along in the retina and the visual pathways (Svaetichin & MacNichol, 1958; DeValois, Smith, Karoly, & Kitai, 1958). These cells appear to code opposing colors by increasing or decreasing their rate of firing. A cell might

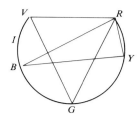

Figure 3.9

In Helmholtz's colored circle the positions of the colors are indicated by the initial letters of their names—that is, indigo blue (I), blue (B), yellow (Y), violet (V), red (R), and green (G). All the colors that can be made by mixing red, blue, and yellow are comprised within the triangle RBY. The triangle VRG includes the colors obtained by mixing violet, red, and green.

Hermann von Helmholtz

Figure 3.10

Idealized spectral sensitivities of the three classes of color-catching cones. Curve A illustrates cones most sensitive to red, curve B illustrates cones most sensitive to green, and curve C illustrates cones most sensitive to blue.

WAVE LENGTH
DET. HUE

AMPLITUDE
DET. LOUDNESS

be excited by long wavelengths of light in the red, for example, but inhibited by shorter wavelengths in the green. Another cell might show just the opposite responses. Recordings from microelectrodes have found an opponent process is already at work in the retinal ganglion cells where information is coded before transmission to the brain and in cells of the lateral geniculate body of the thalamus, the visual system's first way station in the brain itself (Wagner, Mac-Nichol, & Wolbarsht, 1960).

The occurrence of colored afterimages also supports the opponent process theory. If you stare at a red patch and then look at a neutral gray or white surface, you are likely to see a gray spot tinged with green. This is a **negative afterimage** because red is the complementary hue of green. The stimulus persists (briefly), but in a reversed state; chromatic and black-and-white effects are reversed. Less frequently encountered is a **positive afterimage** in which the perception of the stimulus persists in its original chromatic or black-and-white configuration. Positive afterimages occur most often after dark-adapted eyes have received a brief but intense stimulation (see Color Plate 3.4).

Recent findings would suggest that both the trichromatic theory and the opponent process may be partially correct in terms of explaining color vision. Although the retina contains three types of cone pigments which respond selectively to different wavelengths of light, this information is later encoded into two-color, opponent signals by cells in the lateral geniculate body further along the visual pathways. Current theories of color vision take into account this two-stage processing of visual information.

The further processing of color information in the brain is still something of a mystery. New discoveries suggest the existence of specific centers in the cortex, which receives its inputs from the visual cortex, whose cells are specially tuned to the analysis of color (Zeki, 1980).

The Psychological Nature of Color

Newton's experiment with the shaft of light and the prism indicated that the perception of color depends on the wavelength of light. In psychological terms colors have three subjective, but measurable, attributes: hue, brightness, and saturation.

Hue is what we normally refer to as color itself—red, green, blue, yellow (the psychologically pure colors), or mixtures of them; gray, black, and white have no hue at all. We perceive a new color with a different hue when lights of two or more wavelengths are combined. Most often, light reaching our eyes' cones is a mixture of wavelengths; the dominant wavelength determines the hue we experience. Wavelengths themselves are unaffected by mixture; the colors we experience are psychological products of the excitation of our receptors. **Brightness** is an aspect of the physical intensity of the color. **Saturation** refers to a hue's vividness, richness, and purity. Deep, ruby-red is a highly saturated color, whereas pale pink is a desaturated color; saturation is an indication of the physical purity of a hue's wavelength. If a mixture of other wavelengths is added to the psychologically pure hues, the color is desaturated and may be altered to a different hue.

The **color spindle,** or solid, visually represents the relationship among hue, brightness, and saturation. Hue is shown along the conical perimeter of the sphere. The vertical dimension depicts brightness; the horizontal axis represents saturation, from black at the base to white at the top (see Color Plate 3.3).

Remember that color is sensed, received, and coded, and then in turn perceived by the wavelength-sensitive cones of our eyes and by our brains. The wavelengths of mixed lights do not physically combine or change; the combinations take place in the retina of our eyes and in our brains. All of us, however, do not sense and perceive all colors.

CHAPTER 3   SENSATION

Color Blindness

Because normal color vision is trichromatic—that is, it requires three different types of color-sensitive cones—we now can better understand some of the common problems in seeing color. Roughly 6 to 8 percent of the men in the world, and less than 1 percent of the women, suffer from some form of a hereditary visual disability, commonly called **color blindness.** The vast majority are not truly color-blind; rather, they differ in various degrees from the normal in their mechanisms of color vision (see Color Plate 3.4).

In some instances of color blindness, the retina has only two types of cones instead of three. If the red-sensitive long-wavelength pigment is missing, the condition is called **protanopia.** If the green-catching middle-wavelength pigment is absent, the condition is called **deuteranopia.** (There is a condition, tritanopia, in which the short-wavelength, blue-sensitive pigment is missing, but that is very rare.) An even more common condition is one in which the pigment in the middle or long-wavelength cones is present but has a different maximal sensitivity from the pigment of the cones in the normal eye. People with this condition are called **anomalous trichomats** because they still require the three wavelengths to match the spectrum.

A few people called **monochromats** suffer from an extreme and rare form of true color blindness. One type of monochromat may have very few cones: such people have only about 5 percent or less of the normal number of cones. They tend to have very poor visual acuity and to be overly sensitive to even moderate levels of light, much as the person with normal vision finds daylight uncomfortable when emerging from a dark movie theater.

Neural Coding of Light

Let us now look at the retina as an extension of the central nervous system and consider how light is coded and what sorts of information are transmitted from the eye to the brain. To do this, we need to analyze individual cells within the retina. A concept crucial to such an exploration is that of a cell's **receptive field.** A receptive field is simply that region of the visual world that acts on a given cell. In the simplest case, light might increase the firing of a visual cell, but light can also inhibit the cell. For example, suppose that a cell were firing at some steady rate in the dark. Light imaged on a part of the retina might activate the cell, thus speeding it up or inhibiting it, thereby slowing its firing rate. The receptive field is the region of the visual field that can affect a given cell's response—either to excite or inhibit it.

Lateral Inhibition

Much of the research in the neural activity of vision stems from work that began during the early 1930s (Hartline and Graham, 1932). H. K. Hartline recorded nerve impulses in the eye of the horseshoe crab. This creature has a compound eye composed of many small units called ommatidia, or "little eyes." Each ommatidium contains a dozen cells, which are clustered in segments around a single nerve fiber that projects to the brain.

Hartline beamed a light at a single ommatidium and then recorded nerve impulses from the individual nerve fibers that came from that ommatidium. He found that, as might be expected, these fibers fired faster when the intensity of the light was increased. The relationship was a relatively simple one, in which the frequency of firing was roughly proportional to the logarithm of the magnitude of the stimulus.

Subsequent experiments on the horseshoe crab, however, brought a more surprising finding. When Hartline first illuminated one ommatidium and then a

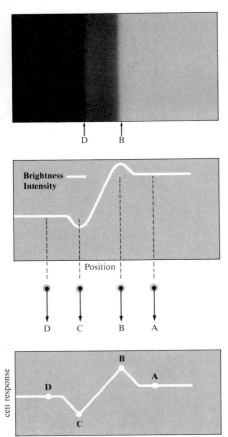

Figure 3.11

(a) Pattern of light which produces Mach bands is indicated at D and B. (b) Graph of the physical intensity (black line) and the brightness perceived across the pattern (white line). (c) Receptive fields of some selected ganglion cells which receive light at various points along the pattern. (d) Response or neural picture produced by the ganglion cells. (a and b from Visual Perception, *T. Cornsweet. Copyright 1970 by Academic Press. Reprinted by permission of Academic Press, Inc.)*

neighboring one, an interesting thing happened: the frequency of firing in the original receptor unit decreased. The firing of nerve impulses in the second receptor served as a brake, or inhibitor, on its neighboring receptor.

This phenomenon is known as **lateral inhibition.** Although the compound eye of the horseshoe crab differs markedly from the eye of the human, a similar sort of physiological mechanism seems to be peresent. The idea of lateral inhibition has important implications for the understanding of human vision. In the human retina a similar mechanism is produced by the cells of the inner nuclear layer, the structure containing the cells that connect the receptors, the rods and cones, with the ganglion cells. The net effect is to enhance the contrasts between different levels of illumination. In other words, lateral inhibition tends to emphasize contours or edges in what we see, and to ignore a steady level of illumination.

A process of this sort is at work, for example, in the so-called **Mach bands** shown in Figure 3.11. Notice that the perceived brightness is greatest at the contrast points across the pattern. Because of lateral inhibition, the contrast at the edges is enhanced, although the light intensity is unchanged. This illusion was observed some 100 years ago by the Austrian physicist Ernst Mach (Ratliff, 1965), who even then suspected that some sort of inhibitory effect in the retina might be responsible for it.

Stabilized Images

Lateral inhibition provides striking evidence of the retina's sensitivity to changes in the amount of light falling on different parts of it. Temporal changes also have profound implications for vision. In ordinary circumstances, images are never still on the retina. Even when we try to keep our eyes still by staring at a fixed point, they are making tiny spontaneous movements, like small pendulum swings, at the rate of up to 70 per second, as well as movements in slower drifts and flicks. These movements mean that light from the fixed scene keeps falling on different receptors in the retina (Ratliff & Riggs, 1950).

In the early 1950s Lorrin Riggs and his collaborators at Brown University (Riggs, Ratliff, Cornsweet, & Cornsweet, 1953) and Robert Ditchburn (1973) at Reading University in England discovered that if the eye did not move, the resulting stabilized image would quickly fade and disappear. This can be demonstrated in the laboratory using a special device that stabilizes an image on the retina (see Figure 3.12). A contact lens with a mirror on it is placed over the subject's eye. Targets can be reflected by the mirror onto a screen so that every time the eye makes one of its movements, the image on the screen moves with it. The image is thus stabilized on the retina of the eye wearing the contact lens.

When a stimulus is first turned on, the eye sees the image sharply and clearly. But within a few seconds, the image fades and soon disappears. This stabilized image falls constantly upon the same receptors. After a few seconds, information about that image no longer is transmitted to the brain.

The concept of **stabilized images** explains a visual phenomenon of which we are not ordinarily aware. Recall from our description of the retina's structure that light entering the eye has to pass through an intricate network of blood vessels before it reaches the rods and cones. Why don't we see the shadows of all those blood vessels? The answer is that they are stabilized on the retina. Because these shadows fall constantly on the same sets of rods and cones, we do not see them.

You can make the shadows appear, however, with a simple demonstration. Take a slender flashlight, a penlight, switch it on, and place it firmly on the corner of your eye. Then jiggle the penlight. The eccentric source of light and the jiggling motion move the shadows of the blood vessels sufficiently so that they now fall on a different from normal set of rods and cones. These new

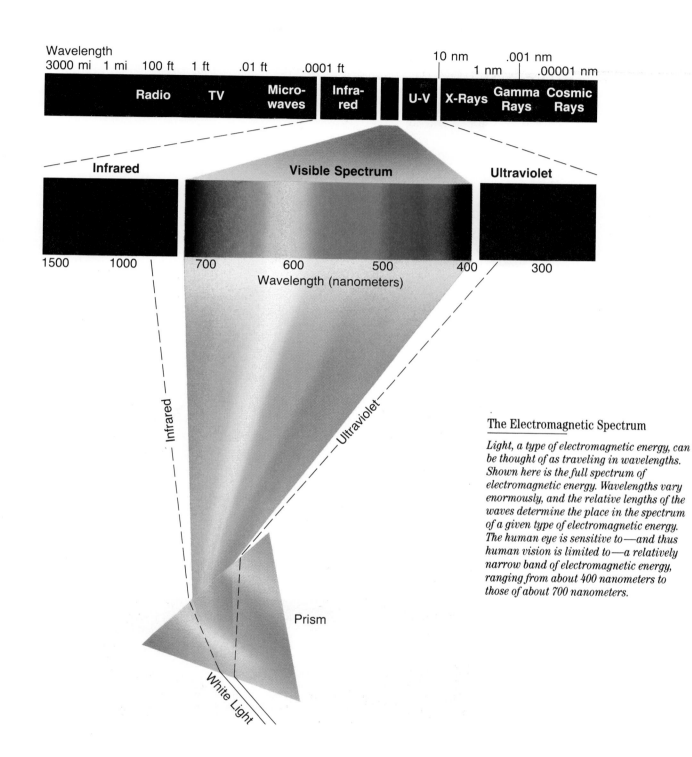

The Electromagnetic Spectrum

Light, a type of electromagnetic energy, can be thought of as traveling in wavelengths. Shown here is the full spectrum of electromagnetic energy. Wavelengths vary enormously, and the relative lengths of the waves determine the place in the spectrum of a given type of electromagnetic energy. The human eye is sensitive to—and thus human vision is limited to—a relatively narrow band of electromagnetic energy, ranging from about 400 nanometers to those of about 700 nanometers.

Color Plate 3.2

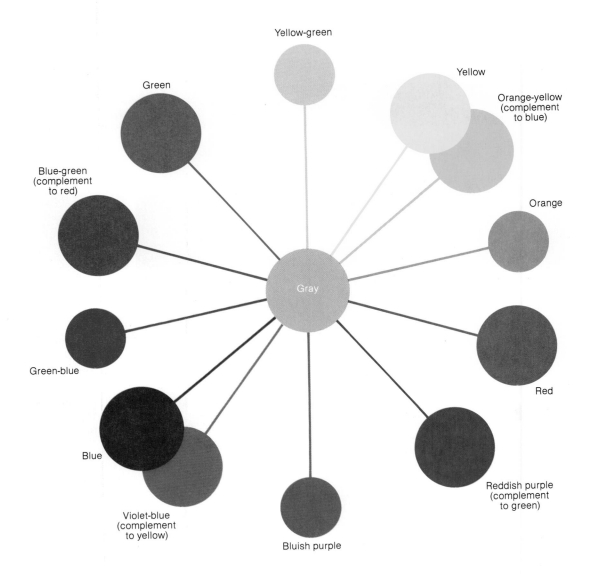

Additive Color Mixing

In light, red, blue, and green are considered primary colors because they are not a mixture of any other colors, but they can be mixed to produce other colors. Complementary colors are those opposite each other on the color wheel above (such as blue and orange-yellow); when mixed, complementary colors will result in gray. The mixing of any two wavelengths that are not opposite each other will result in an intermediate color. The actual effect of additive color mixing is demonstrated in the photo right, in which filters of red, green, and blue light from three slide projectors are mixed. In this case, mixing two colors produces a third color, and mixing all three colors produces white.

White

Brightness

Saturation

Hue

Black

The Color Spindle

The three dimensions of hue, saturation, and brightness form the color spindle (top left). The hues, at the rim of the circle, represent the same amount of brightness. The radius from the perimeter in toward the center represents decreasing amounts of saturation. The very center is that degree of grayness in which there is not even a hint of hue. The degree of brightness is represented by different color circles stacked on top of one another. A complete color spindle would contain 350,000 patches of discriminable colors. A detail of the color wheel is shown (lower right) highlighting one "patch," or hue—blue—and how it differs visually as brightness and saturation change; here the right edge of the triangle represents the vertical axis of the color spindle, which ranges from white to black.

A Demonstration of Colored Afterimages

Stare at the flag, fixating on the white dot in the center, for at least 30 seconds. Then look immediately at the black dot in the white box below. If you see the American flag in its familiar red, white, and blue, you have just experienced an afterimage.

Color-Blindness Tests

These two patterns are samples of those used to test people for color blindness. People with normal vision can see the number 26 in the pattern on the left and the number 12 in the pattern on the right. People with red-green color blindness will see something different—for example, they may see no numbers at all or only parts of the numbers. These reproductions of color recognition tests cannot be used for actual testing; they are only representative examples of the total of 15 charts necessary for a complete color recognition examination.

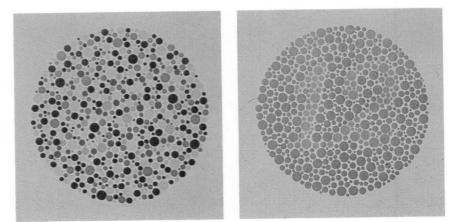

receptors respond to the shadow of the blood vessels and begin signaling information to the brain. You will see a beautiful pattern of treelike forms—the shadows of the blood vessels you had never seen before.

Center-Surround Organization of Visual Receptive Fields

So far, we have considered the neural responses that apparently occur in two layers of the retinal structure: the rods and cones and in the inner nuclear layer. The rods and cones make synaptic connections with the bipolar and horizontal cells of the inner nuclear layer. By way of bipolar and amacrine cells in the inner nuclear layer, information reaches the last way-station within the retina, that is, the ganglion cells. In humans the neural pathways converge like a funnel into the ganglion cells. Whereas there are something like 106 million receptor cells—rods and cones—in each eye, there are only about a million ganglion cells. One ganglion cell may have connections, via the inner nuclear layer, from over 100 rods. On the other hand, certain ganglion cells may have connections with only a small number of foveal cones where daylight vision is most acute.

Another way to examine the process of vision is to consider the sequence of cells, first in the retina and then in the brain, which respond to visual stimulation. A visual scene is imaged in the very first cells in the pathway, the rods and cones. For a well-focused image, each rod or cone "sees" only a tiny portion of the visual scene. Each ganglion cell sees a somewhat larger portion of the visual scene, though that portion is still very small when compared to the total scene. But the ganglion cell has already coded the visual information for further processing. The area of the retina associated with a given cell is called the cell's **receptive field.** The receptive field of a ganglion cell is much larger than that of a rod or cone. Typically, ganglion cells receive an input from several receptors by way of an intermediate set of cells in the inner nuclear layer of the retina. As a result of the processing within the inner nuclear layer, most ganglion cell receptive fields are organized in a concentric fashion called center-surround.

There are roughly equal numbers of "center on" and "center off" ganglion cells. "Center off" ganglion cells are activated when the center of the receptive field is darker than the surround. In a "center on" type ganglion cell, light shining in the center of the receptive field activates the cell (see Figure 3.13). There is a surround region in which light inhibits the cell or stops it from firing. Thus the ganglion cell responds to *differences* in illumination between a small region in the center of its receptive field and an area just outside that region. As a result, the ganglion cell is relatively insensitive to gross differences in the overall light on the retina. The center-surround organization of retinal ganglion cells is a useful first stage in neural processing of the visual image, providing mechanism whereby objects appear the same independent of the absolute amount of light falling on them.

The Brain and Vision

The ganglion cells send some one million nerve fibers from each eye directly to the brain. These fibers are bundled together in the two optic nerves, each of which exits from the eye about 15° from the fovea. Because there are no rods or cones at this point, a blind spot is created in the visual field of each eye. You can locate your own blind spot with a simple experiment. Close one eye, stare at the wall, and move a pencil slowly out of the field of vision. The pencil tip briefly disappears at the blind spot.

The bundled fibers of the two optic nerves, before reaching the brain, meet and partially cross over at the optic chiasma. Here roughly half of the fibers

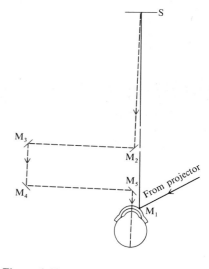

Figure 3.12

Apparatus for producing a stabilized retinal image. The image of a target is projected onto a contact lens with a mirror on it, which is placed over the subject's eye. The mirror reflects the image onto the screen S. The image from S reaches the subject's eye through the path indicated by the dotted line, reflected at points M_2, M_3, M_4, and M_5. Whenever the eye moves through a given angle, the mirror on the contact lens also moves, which in turn causes the image on the screen to move. Thus, the image that reaches the retina remains fixed in location despite normal eye movements.

Figure 3.13

Receptive fields of ganglion cells in the retinas of cats and monkeys are grouped into two main classes: "on" center and "off" center fields. "On" center cells respond best to a spot of light shone onto the central part of their receptive fields. Illumination (indicated by bar above records) of the surrounding area with a spot or a ring of light reduces or suppresses the discharges and causes responses when the light is turned off. Illumination of the entire receptive field elicits relatively weak discharges because center and surround oppose each other's effects. "Off" center cells slow down or stop signaling when the central area of their field is illuminated and accelerate when the light is turned off. Light shone onto the surround of an "off" center receptive field area excites (after Kuffler and Nicholls, 1976).

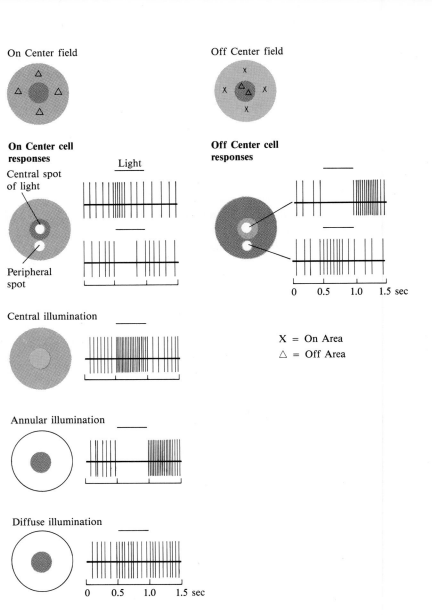

from each eye stay uncrossed, while half cross over and project to the opposite side of the brain (see Figure 3.14). The result of this arrangement is that each side of the brain receives information from both eyes: the retina on the right side of both eyes projects to the right half of the brain; the retina on the left side of both eyes projects to the left half of the brain. Because of the optical inversion by the eye, information from the left half of each visual field is thus sent to the right side of the brain and information from the right half of each visual field is sent to the left side of the brain.

The early anatomists could easily trace the path of the optic nerves by dissecting the brains of recently deceased humans and animals. They could see the optic fibers enter the brain at the thalamus. Only in the last century, however, did it become clear precisely where in the brain the visual fibers project after they emerge from the thalamus.

The actual site of the visual cortex was the subject of much controversy among neural scientists. In 1876, for example, the eminent English physician and scientist David Ferrier incorrectly identified the parietal lobe as the site of the visual cortex (Glickstein, 1985). Ferrier came to this erroneous conclusion through an interesting experiment. He removed the parietal lobe from both hemispheres of a monkey and observed that the animal no longer seemed to respond to visual stimulation. One of Ferrier's observations was that a monkey,

CHAPTER 3   SENSATION

who was very fond of tea, no longer reached out for the teacup when it was offered. When the cup was placed in its hands, however, the monkey would eagerly drink it. Thus, Ferrier argued that the monkey still liked tea but could no longer see the cup. What probably happened was that Ferrier destroyed those regions of the cerebral cortex that are a way-station between the visual and the motor cortex. The monkeys probably were not blind, but were unable to guide their movements under visual control.

In fact, it is in the occipital lobe that the visual cortex resides. This was established by the turn of the century on the basis of experiments with monkeys and later confirmed on the basis of reports of partial blindness—scotomas—in patients whose brains were damaged in the occipital lobe. Later, during the Russo-Japanese War and World War I, cases of combat gunshot wounds enabled researchers to map accurately the organization of visual fields in the cortex (Inouye, 1909). Dramatic confirmation came when the German brain surgeon, Ottfried Foerster (1929), was called on to treat a patient with recurrent epileptic fits stemming from a wartime brain injury. Foerster surgically removed the damaged area, which was under a local anesthetic. While the brain was still exposed, he electrically stimulated the region of the occipital lobe. (Remember that the brain itself is insensitive to pain because it lacks the nerve endings that signal this particular sensation.) When this region was stimulated electrically at various points, the patient reported seeing small spots of light. The location of these spots of light was consistent with the maps that had been constructed earlier on the basis of scotomas that followed gunshot wounds. Thus, the location of the visual cortex and the map of the visual fields was confirmed.

In recent years, researchers have begun recording electrical activity from single cells within the visual cortex of experimental animals, much as Kuffler did in the ganglion cells of the retina of cats. This work has yielded fascinating clues about how the brain recognizes the patterns of light that fall upon the retina. We will discuss these single-cell responses when we take up visual perception in the next chapter.

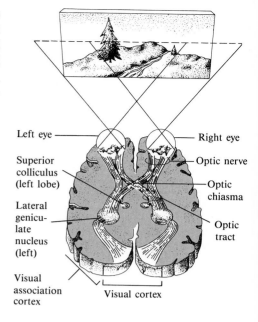

Figure 3.14

Each side of the brain receives information from both eyes. Light from the visual field projects onto the two retinas and neural messages are then sent to the two visual centers of each hemisphere (after Frisby, 1980).

Audition

Philosophers and physicists used to debate endlessly the answer to the old question: "If a tree falls in the forest and no one is around to hear it, will there be a sound?" The philosophers, insisting that sound is a sensory experience perceived by the listener, said no. The physicists, pointing out that sound is a movement of molecules caused by a vibrating body in a medium such as air or water, said yes.

The modern psychologist avoids the debate by saying that both the philosophers and the physicists were partially right. **Audition,** or the act of hearing, requires both rhythmical variations in the pressure of a medium near us *and* the reception of those variations by the ear, which in turn codes and transmits the information to the brain.

Auditory Stimulation: The Nature of Sound

Vision begins with light, a kind of electromagnetic energy. Sound begins with a mechanical disturbance; that is, vibrations create waves in a medium such as air or water. These waves resemble the ripples of water that radiate outward when you throw a stone into a pond. To understand this process more precisely, look at the musical tone represented in Figure 3.15. The dots are a highly schematic representation of the air molecules that transmit the tone. If air is pushed forward rapidly by a loudspeaker whose cone moves in the direc-

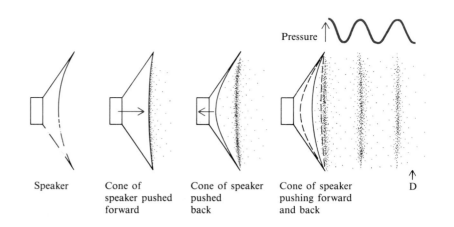

Figure 3.15

Representation of the concept of pressure and rarefaction in a loudspeaker. The dots represent the air molecules that transmit a tone. As the speaker moves forward, molecules are compressed, and as it returns to its original position the density of the molecules decreases. An observer at point D would experience a sequence of rarefaction and pressure that would result in sound.

Speaker

Cone of speaker pushed forward

Cone of speaker pushed back

Cone of speaker pushing forward and back

tion shown by the arrow, the air momentarily compresses just in front of the speaker (see Figure 3.15). If the speaker is returned to its original position with the same speed as it had moved earlier, it will leave a small region of rarefaction, or thinner air, adjacent to the loudspeaker. The molecules in this thinner air will be less densely distributed than is normal.

Suppose now that the loudspeaker cone moves back and forth continuously. The sequence of pressure and rarefaction will be transmitted through the air near the speaker. If the speaker continues to vibrate, there will be an orderly sequence of pressure and rarefaction in the surrounding air.

At room temperature sound waves travel in air at about 700 miles per hour, roughly 1100 feet per second. Note that individual molecules of air do not move at this speed; it is the sequence of pressure and rarefaction involving millions of molecules that is moving at 1100 feet per second.

Characteristics of Sound Waves

Sound waves have three important physical characteristics: frequency, amplitude, and phase (see Figure 3.16). **Frequency** is the measurement of how many waves occur each second. The musical note A above middle C—the standard to which American instruments are tuned—consists of a frequency of 440 waves per second. During 1 second, there would be 440 complete cycles of pressure and rarefaction in the air around the tuning fork or instrument sounding the note. Researchers honor the nineteenth-century German physicist Heinrich Hertz, who did the first definitive studies of energy waves, by utilizing the unit **hertz** (abbreviated Hz) to denote 1 cycle per second. Hence our musical note A above middle C would have a frequency of 440 Hz.

Whereas the frequency of a sound wave determines **pitch** (that is, apparent highness or lowness of a note), the intensity or loudness is determined by the **amplitude.** The higher the peak of the sound wave, the greater its amplitude, and the louder it usually sounds. Amplitude and frequency are not quite enough to characterize sound waves, however. A third important characteristic is **phase,** which relates to the precise timing of a sound wave. Consider the pairs of waves shown in Figure 3.16. In pair C the waves have the same amplitude and frequency, but they are out of step with each other. They have a different phase. The peak of one wave occurs before the peak of the other wave. If two sound waves are completely "out of phase," the instant of compression in one coincides precisely with the instant of rarefaction in the other. In such a case, they would tend to cancel each other and would be perceived by the ear as silence.

Pitch and loudness are psychological characteristics of sound that are related to the physical dimensions of frequency, amplitude, and phase. A third

Figure 3.16

Schematic diagram showing the differences between the amplitude, frequency, and phase of a sound wave. (A) Two waves with the same phase and frequency but different amplitudes. (B) Two waves with similar phase and amplitude but different frequencies. (C) Two waves with the same amplitude and frequency but different phases.

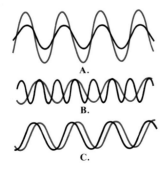

A.

B.

C.

CHAPTER 3   SENSATION

psychological quality of sound is **timbre,** which is a measure of a sound's purity. Most instruments produce sounds that are mixtures of frequencies. The complex mixture of sound waves produces an instrument's unique timbre.

Additional psychological characteristics of sound are **consonance** and **dissonance.** When two tones are sounded together, we usually sense and perceive consonant pairs as pleasant and dissonant pairs as unpleasant. Custom and culture play a role in our perception of combined tones as consonant or dissonant. During the first part of the twentieth century, the works of Igor Stravinsky were considered to be highly dissonant; today the composer's *Firebird Suite* is a popular staple of the orchestral repertoire. A physical explanation of consonance or dissonance lies in frequency difference. Dissonance occurs when two tones sounded together produce a third tone, based on the difference in their frequencies, that does not harmonize with the fundamental tones sounded and thus produces a "roughness" in the sound. When the frequencies of the two tones are sufficiently different to be heard as distinct sounds, the pair is perceived as consonant.

To measure the relative intensity of sound, scientists have worked out a unit called the **decibel**—*deci* from the Latin for one-tenth and *bel* after Alexander Graham Bell, the inventor of the telephone. Decibels refer to the ratios between the physical energy in a sound and a standard sound (see Figure 3.17). On the decibel scale, the usual zero is near the absolute threshold for hearing a tone of 1000 Hz—roughly the faintest sound audible to the average ear. Ordinary conversation usually measures between 60 and 80 decibels. Sounds about 140 decibels above threshold at 1000 Hz feel uncomfortable to the human ear, and more intense sounds produce structural damage. Note that the decibel scale is a logarithmic scale: 30 decibels has 10 times the physical intensity of 20 decibels.

In terms of frequency, the limits of human hearing range from about 20 Hz to 20,000 Hz. We do not hear equally well at each frequency, however. Humans hear best in a range of 1000 to 4000 Hz. The notes on a piano coincide roughly with this scale, ranging from 27 to 4200 Hz. Not surprisingly, human speech also falls within the optimal range of hearing.

Among different animals, there are great variations in auditory capacity. Cats, for example, can hear tones of 40,000 Hz—at least twice as high as the

Figure 3.17

The decibel (dB) scale indicates intensities of various common sounds.

Most instruments produce sounds that are mixtures of frequencies.

upper limit of human hearing. Dog-calling whistles emit frequencies up to 25,000 Hz, sufficiently above the human range so that we cannot hear them. One of the highest auditory capacity ranges belongs to some species of bats. These bats emit tones of up to 100,000 Hz or more and, by hearing and following the echoes of their own high-pitched squeaks, hunt prey, and navigate around objects in the dark. Like the bat, most animals do not make sounds that exceed their range of hearing frequencies. One exception is the grasshopper, which creates a ''song'' (by rubbing its legs against its own rough abdomen) of up to 100,000 Hz—too high to be picked up by the creature's primitive auditory system.

The auditory capacities of many different animals can be established easily in the laboratory. One very useful method has been developed by William Stebbins and his colleagues and used for assessment of damage to the ear (Stebbins, Miller, Johnsson, & Hawkins, 1969). For example, monkeys are trained to press a key, which turns on a loud tone. When the tone is on, the monkey is rewarded with a bit of food if it presses a second key. The monkey is taught that it can turn on a tone by pressing the first key. When the tone is on, and only when it is on, the monkey is rewarded with food for pressing the second key. Thus, switching to the second key tells the researcher that the monkey hears the tone. Since the monkey has auditory capacities similar to humans (although its upper range is about twice as high), such experiments can help analyze sounds that are potentially damaging to the human ear. For example, hearing thresholds can be measured before and after the animal is subjected to an intense sound.

Structure of the Ear

The function of the ear is to detect sound waves and transform them into neural impulses, the language of the nervous system. The manner in which the various parts of the ear achieve this is through a system of membranes, mechanical levers, and hydraulic fluids (see Figure 3.18).

Sound waves are funneled by the outer portion of the ear into its visible opening, the **auditory canal.** This hollow tube concentrates the sound waves and carries them to the **eardrum,** a taut membrane that vibrates rhythmically with the cyclical waves of pressure and rarefaction.

On the inner side of the eardrum is the **middle ear,** which contains three tiny bones, or **ossicles.** These ossicles are connected in sequential fashion to the eardrum: attached to the eardrum is the **malleus** or hammer, which it resembles; then comes the **incus** (anvil) and the **stapes** (stirrup). The stapes, the last bone in the ossicular chain, and about half the size of a grain of rice, couples directly with the **oval window,** a membrane that separates the middle ear from the **inner ear.**

The linkage of the three little bones of the middle ear acts as levers. It ''gears down'' the vibrations of the eardrum, multiplying their power severalfold. Moreover, the smallness of the oval window (about 1/25 the area of the eardrum) serves to further concentrate and thus amplify the forces reaching the inner ear. By the time a sound wave has set up vibrations in the oval window, the force may have been amplified up to 180 times that of the sound entering the outer ear.

The oval window is the gateway to the inner ear and to its principal structure, the **cochlea** (see Figure 3.18). No bigger than the tip of a little finger, the cochlea, as its Latin name suggests, looks like a snail shell. It is essentially a long, rolled-up bony tube filled with fluids. Inside the cochlea, running its coiled-up length, is the **cochlear partition.** On the bottom side of the cochlear

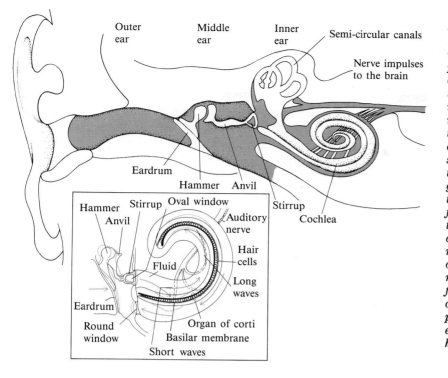

Figure 3.18

The structure of the human ear. Sound waves are funneled by the external portion of the ear through the auditory canal to the eardrum, which vibrates with the cyclical waves of pressure and rarefaction. The three little bones of the middle ear (hammer, anvil, and stirrup) together gear down the vibrations of the eardrum, multiplying their power severalfold. These vibrations are then transmitted through the oval window, the gateway to the inner ear, which opens to the cochlea, a long, rolled-up bony tube filled with fluids. On the bottom side of the cochlear partition, which divides the cochlea along its length, is the basilar membrane, to which is attached the organ of Corti that consists of thousands of receptor cells from which project hairlike fibers. Sound vibrations cause these hair cells to bend, thereby creating an electric potential. Through the auditory nerve the electrical impulses associated with hearing travel to the brain.

partition is the **basilar membrane.** Attached to the basilar membrane is the command post of hearing, the **organ of Corti.** This structure is a gelatinous mass about an inch and a half long, consisting of thousands of receptor cells from which project fine, hairlike fibers.

The mechanical vibrations of the oval window reach the hair cells of the organ of Corti by displacing the fluids adjacent to the cochlear partition, causing the basilar membrane to vibrate. The vibrations of the basilar membrane cause the hairs to bend. Finally, the bending of the hairs converts mechanical energy to electrical energy; that is, the bending motion creates a generator potential. If this potential is great enough, it triggers a nerve impulse in the connecting fibers of the auditory nerve in the inner ear. Via the auditory nerve, the electrical impulses concerned with hearing travel to the brain.

Neural Coding of Sound

Scientists generally assume that the amplitude of a sound wave is coded by the number of nerve fibers that are activated. There are about 30,000 such fibers projecting from the inner ear, a sufficient number to code the loudest of sounds. How the frequency of a sound wave is coded, however, was long the subject of dispute. Two theories of how the ear codes pitch were postulated.

The first of these, the **place theory,** was set forth in the nineteenth century by Hermann von Helmholtz (1875). Helmholtz suggested that the pitch we hear depends on the place on the basilar membrane that is stimulated by the sound waves.

Later, an alternative hypothesis of pitch discrimination, the **frequency theory,** was put forward. Known also as the telephone theory, it postulated that the coding process was much like that of a microphone. According to this theory, the pitch we hear is determined by the frequency of the firing of nerve impulses in the auditory nerve fibers. Each nerve impulse in one fiber was said to coincide with 1 Hz, or one complete cycle of pressure and rarefaction. Thus,

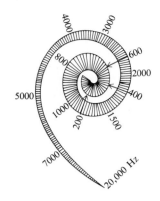

Figure 3.19

The location on the basilar membrane that receives the maximum stimulation depends on the frequency of the sound. Note that at high frequencies the vibration is greatest at the end of the basilar membrane closest to the oval window.

A direction finder for sound, the topophone, augmented a listener's powers of sound localization because its two ear trumpets are widely spaced and collected more sound than human ears. Patented in 1880, this device was designed for use by ship captains to determine with precision the direction of a whistle in the fog.

a tone of 500 Hz would cause a single nerve fiber to fire 500 times in a second. A major problem wtih the frequency theory was the built-in limitation on firing of a nerve fiber. A nerve fiber can fire only up to about 1000 times per second—not nearly enough to account for the human hearing range of up to 20,000 Hz (not to mention the bat's range of more than 100,000 Hz).

Much of the place versus frequency debate was resolved by the work of the Hungarian engineer and physiologist Georg von Békésy (1960), for which he was awarded the Nobel Prize in 1961. Using guinea pigs as his experimental animals, von Békésy watched through a microscope as the oval window was stimulated by tones of varying frequencies. He found that, in accordance with the place theory, as the frequency of sound varied, there was a different place in the basilar membrane that was maximally vibrated (see Figure 3.19). For high frequencies the vibration was greatest at the end of the basilar membrane nearest the oval window. But the fact that low tones activated the entire basilar membrane suggests that the frequency theory may also have some validity. For low frequencies the coding may indeed depend upon the number of firings by an individual nerve fiber.

In the brain itself there is also evidence that many of the cells in the successive relays in the brain that are concerned with hearing, from the medulla to the auditory cortex in the temporal lobe, respond selectively to various frequencies. Generally speaking, these auditory structures are organized **tonotopically;** that is, neighboring cells respond best to similar frequencies, and these frequencies change progressively from one place to another.

The Brain and Audition: Binaural Hearing

We are **binaural;** that is, we have two ears instead of one. The second ear might seem redundant because both ears send nerve connections to both the left and right sides of the brain. Loss of hearing in one ear does not substantially affect our ability to discriminate pitch and loudness. One reason for binaural hearing was offered more than 2000 years ago by the Greek philosopher Zeno. "Nature," he said, "has given man one tongue, but two ears, that we might hear twice as much as we speak."

Zeno's wishful thinking notwithstanding, our two-eared system functions mainly to locate the precise direction from which a sound originates. To test the effectiveness of binaural hearing as a sound locator, try this demonstration. Blindfold a friend. Then move quietly around that person, stop, and suddenly snap your fingers. The friend will be able to point quite precisely in the direction the sound came from.

How does the friend know where the sound came from? Two different cues are responsible for direction finding. One is the relative intensities of the sound wave as it successively reaches each of the two ears. This cue works better for higher-frequency sound waves. The wavelengths of higher-frequency sounds are shorter than the diameter of the head. The head acts as a barrier to such waves and thus casts a kind of sonic shadow on the side of the head farthest from the origin of the sound. As a result, tones are detectably louder on the near side of the head than on the far side. Difference in intensity works less efficiently for lower-frequency sounds, however, because lower-frequency sounds have longer wavelengths. These wavelengths can bend around the head, thus reducing detectable differences in intensity.

A second cue, namely, difference in phase or time of arrival, governs the location of lower-frequency sounds. As we noted earlier, sound travels rather slowly, about 1100 feet per second, or slightly more than 1 foot in a millisecond. If a person's ears are 6 inches apart, a sound originating at 90° from the right ear would arrive at the left ear about half a millisecond later than at the right ear. This means each ear would receive a different phase of the wavelength. The sounds in the ears, in other words, would be slightly out of phase with each other.

In your experiment on sound direction you might note that people sometimes make 180° errors in pointing to the source of a sound because both intensity and phase differences are lost when the sound source is directly in front of, or behind, the head.

How does the brain resolve small differences in time or intensity detected by the two ears? A structure in the brain stem probably serves as a major relay station for auditory signals en route to the cortex. Cells in this structure have dendrites projecting in two directions. On one side they receive connections from auditory fibers activated by the left ear; on the other side they receive connections from auditory fibers activated through the right ear. Thus these cells are in an excellent position to serve as a comparison mechanism for intensity and time differences in the two ears. Two other pieces of evidence support the belief that these cells play a crucial role in binaural sound location. Damage to these cells in experimental animals results in a loss of directional hearing without apparent harm to the ability to discriminate pitch or intensity. Moreover, these cells fire only when there are differences of time or intensity in the sounds reaching the two ears.

Interestingly, the basic scientific research that led to our understanding of binaural sound location has yielded an electronic bonus: stereophonic sound reproduction. Stereo recordings that are made with two microphones set some distance apart detect the same differences in sound as the ears, and, when played back over two speakers, simulate our normal hearing in depth.

Workers use ear protectors to prevent deafness caused by prolonged exposure to intensive noise.

Deafness

There are two major types of deafness, or hearing loss: conduction deafness and nerve deafness. Conduction deafness results from deficiencies in the conduction mechanism of the auditory system, particularly the ear canal, the tympanic membrane, or the ossicles. Nerve deafness results from deficiencies or damage to the auditory nerves, the basilar membrane, or other closely linked neural connections in the cochlea. Some malfunctions in parts of the conduction mechanism, such as impairment of the ability of the ossicles to conduct sound vibrations, can be alleviated by the use of a hearing aid, which amplifies the sound stimulus so that it will still travel through the normal channels. When the neural mechanisms of hearing are destroyed, a hearing aid will not help: no hearing aid can force a nonexistent nerve cell to fire.

The causes of deafness vary. It may result from chronic infection of the middle ear, the overall effect of aging, and prolonged exposure to intensive acoustic stimulation including excessive exposure to rock bands (Lipscomb, 1969).

The Chemical Senses

As we have seen, many of our important sensory organs respond to physical stimuli in the world around us: the eye responds to light; the ear responds to sound. Smell and taste, however, are chemical senses. Smell is a response to certain chemicals in the air we breathe; taste is a response to chemicals in the foods and liquids we ingest. The senses of taste and smell are quite interrelated in our sensing of food. Flavor is a combination, largely, of smell and taste. Aside from the sensations encountered in eating, the two chemical senses are usually quite different in humans. They are not as distinct in some animals,

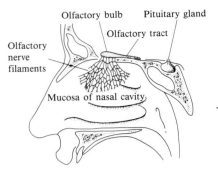

Figure 3.20

Olfactory structures in the nasal cavity. Receptors high in the nasal cavity carry the sensation of smell directly to the two olfactory bulbs, which are joined to the olfactory cortex of the brain.

Moonshine, a bloodhound, is used to trail an accused killer who escaped from jail in Troy, New York.

however. Certain species of fish, for example, possess tastelike chemical sensors on the surface of their bodies. These taste receptors serve a function similar to the mammalian sense of smell, detecting odorants that are dissolved in the water.

Smell

Our sense of smell literally helps make life more pungent, but it is not essential. People who are deprived of this sense can get along quite well in the world. A clue to its importance in evolution can be found, however, in the anatomy of neural connections for smell. Of all the senses, olfaction has the most direct route to the brain. Receptors high in each nasal cavity carrying this sensation travel directly to the two **olfactory bulbs,** which lie just below the frontal lobes of the brain. The olfactory bulbs are joined to the olfactory cortex of the brain. No other synaptic connections need be made along the path of smell (see Figure 3.20).

Smell plays surprisingly diverse roles in different animals. When a recently mated mouse, for example, smells the urine of a male mouse other than her mate, her pregnancy is usually blocked (Bruce, 1959; Whitten, Bronson, & Greenstein, 1968). In certain animals, olfaction also is involved in a form of chemical communication. One process by which this occurs involves certain chemical substances called **pheromones,** which are secreted by specialized glands of the skin or through the urine (see chapter 11).

Odor is detected through receptor cells embedded in a small mucus-covered surface on the roof of each of our two nasal passages. Although for humans each of these areas is only about the size of a postage stamp, together they contain about 5 million receptor cells. Some species of dogs have 200 million or more receptor cells and a proportionately larger area of the brain devoted to smell. Dogs are so sensitive to certain odors that United States Customs officials use them to sniff out contraband drugs such as marijuana.

From the receptor cells, hairlike filaments (cilia) project into the mucous area (see Figure 3.21). These filaments make contact with the molecules in odorants (the stimulants), and this process triggers a train of nerve impulses to the brain. Although the contact between odorant molecules and the nose's receptors is clearly chemical, the precise neural mechanism of it is still a puzzle. Some 2000 years ago, the poet Lucretius guessed that tiny odorant molecules somehow entered tiny pores in what he called the "palate." One modern theory of olfaction holds that Lucretius was essentially right. This theory suggests that the geometry of a particular odorant molecule fits into certain sites on the filaments extending from the receptor cell in a way analogous to a key fitting into a lock (Amoore, 1970). Recent findings, however, indicate that in certain molecules changes that do not alter size or shape appreciably have a profound impact on smell quality, which brings into question the accuracy of the lock-and-key theory (Schiffman, 1974).

How do we distinguish one odor from another? Many researchers assume that olfactory receptors respond selectively to certain classes of odors. A number of attempts have been made to classify odors in a system that might correspond to selectively sensitive receptors. One early attempt at a classification scheme was suggested by Hans Henning (1916). He postulated a smell prism consisting of six corners labeled putrid, ethereal, resinous, spicy, fragrant, and burnt. All smells, he suggested, are combinations of these six elementary odors, just as all colors result from mixtures of light of different wavelengths. More recently, researchers have attempted to classify odorous molecules on the basis of their chemical similarities. None of these classification schemes is universally accepted.

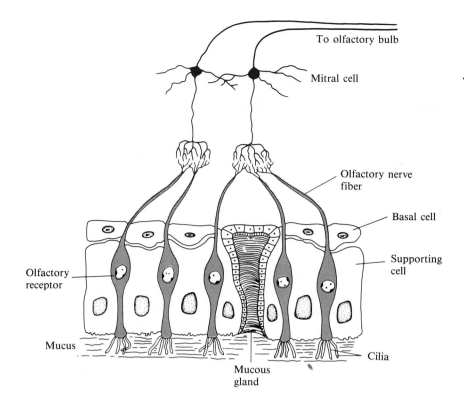

Figure 3.21

Schematic representation of olfactory receptor cells from which hairlike filaments (cilia) project into the mucous area. When these filaments make contact with the molecules in olfactory stimulants, a train of nerve impulses is triggered to the brain.

To olfactory bulb

Mitral cell

Olfactory nerve fiber

Basal cell

Supporting cell

Olfactory receptor

Mucus

Cilia

Mucous gland

One promising line of research seeks out human subjects who cannot smell certain substances (Amoore, 1971). For example, some people lack the ability to smell sweat. By analyzing the spectrum of smells that are not perceived or are perceived differently, it might be possible to characterize receptors that are sensitive to a particular class of odors.

Taste

The mechanisms of taste are somewhat better understood than those of smell. The primary sensory receptors that detect taste are contained in the taste buds, which are located on dark red spots known as **papillae.** There are an estimated 9000 taste buds in the human tongue and soft palate; limited quantities are also found on the hard palate, pharynx, larynx, and other parts of the oral cavity. Each taste bud contains a variable number of receptor cells. A bundle of nerve fibers from these cells connect each taste bud to the cortex via relay nuclei in the medulla and thalamus. The nature of the contact between the stimulants of flavor molecules and these receptor cells has not been clearly established, although, as in smell, it is believed that a lock-and-key mechanism may trigger the nerve impulse.

Researchers usually classify taste into four basic qualities: sweet, salty, sour, and bitter. Evidence for these four distinct taste qualities is suggested by the specific action of certain chemicals. For example, the leaf of the plant, *Gymnema sylvestre,* contains a substance that temporarily abolishes sweet taste. If you rinse your mouth in a weak solution made from this plant and then eat sugar, the sugar will be tasteless for about an hour. The other tastes—salty, bitter, and sour—are not affected.

Another plant, *synsepalum dulcificum,* has a totally different effect. Grown in Africa and known as "miracle fruit," it complicates taste in a remarkable way. After it is chewed, sour substances taste both sweet and sour. A lemon, for example, tastes like sweetened lemonade. "Miracle fruit" apparently alters

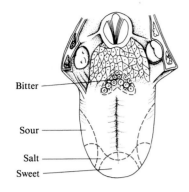

Figure 3.22

Location of four separate taste qualities on the tongue.

sweetness receptors in such a way that they can be temporarily activated by sour substances as well as remaining normally sensitive to sweet ones.

Additional evidence for the existence of four separate taste qualities comes from regional differences in the sensitivity of the tongue (see Figure 3.22). The back of the tongue is most sensitive to bitter substances. The tip of the tongue is most sensitive to sweet taste. Salty taste, however, seems uniformly distributed over the tongue.

Despite the apparent existence of these four distinct taste qualities, clear physiological evidence that the receptors are so neatly parceled out has yet to be established. Laboratory experiments in which neural activity is recorded from receptors have so far failed to show a precise relationship between a single receptor and a given taste.

Somesthesis

Sensations arising from the skin are known collectively as **somesthesis,** Greek for "body knowledge." Researchers have identified four distinct skin sensations: touch, warmth, cold, and pain. Other sensations, such as tickle or itch, represent variations on these basic types.

Areas of the skin that are stimulated by touch, temperature, and pain are distributed all over the surface of the body and have been mapped in minute detail in the laboratory. You can map "cold spots" on the back of your own hand with a simple experiment. Probe gently with the point of a pencil until you feel the sensation of cold. Although the receptors here ordinarily respond to cold temperatures, they can also be activated by touch.

The existence of such spots uniquely sensitive to the four basic sensations at first led researchers to a logical hypothesis: perhaps there are structurally distinct types of skin receptors that detect only a given sensation. Indeed, several kinds of receptors are found in the skin. Some are free nerve endings—the branching fibers of sensory neurons. Other receptors are specialized structures of various sizes and shapes that encapsulate the endings of nerve fibers.

In early attempts to correlate the types of receptors with specific skin sensations, researchers conducted heroic experiments whose subjects were usually the researchers themselves. The subjects were tested first for the distribution of sensation spots on a small section of skin. These spots were marked and then the patch of skin was removed surgically (Wollard, 1935). When sections of the skin were studied under the microscope, however, there was seldom a perfect correlation between specific touch spots and receptor type. Nevertheless, it is likely that nerves are specialized for one or another class of skin sensation. Certain free nerve endings in the skin are almost certainly associated with pain sensations. Other nerve fibers coil around the base of hair follicles and respond to the slight bending of the hairs and hence are sensitive signals that the region has touched something.

The neural mechanisms by which the central nervous system locates skin sensations on a particular part of the body are much better understood. Generally speaking, sensory fibers leading from the skin travel in bundles that may contain fibers that respond to one or more classes of sensation. The thickest nerve fibers arise from specialized receptors in the muscles and joints. A middle-thickness myelinated fiber carries touch sensation. The finest fibers, some of which are unmyelinated, carry only sensations of pain and temperature and travel at relatively slow speeds. Sensory cell bodies are situated just outside the spinal cord in a group of cells called the **dorsal root ganglia.** From here, the sensory pathways ascend by way of one or more relays to the thalamus deep in the brain and then to the cortex of the parietal lobe at the top. These pathways cross over en route to the brain or within it so that skin sensations from the right side of the body register in the left part of the parietal lobe and vice versa.

The portion of the parietal lobe devoted to skin sensations is sometimes called the **somatic sensory cortex.** Like the areas of cortex devoted to motor control (see chapter 2) it is mapped somatotopically. Adjacent points on the cortex represent neighboring points on the surface of the body in such a way that a homunculus, or "little man," can be drawn. As in the case of the motor cortex, this little man (see Figure 3.23) reflects the disproportionate distribution of skin sensitivity. The skin of the back, for example, while occupying a vast expanse is represented in a very modest region of the cortex. At the same time, large areas of cortex are devoted to inputs from our sensitive fingertips.

This disproportionate representation of sensation takes fascinating forms in various animal species. Whereas humans and monkeys have sensitive fingers, rats and mice possess enormously sensitive whiskers that are represented disproportionately in their cortexes. Thus equipped, the mouse can feel its way, literally whisker by whisker.

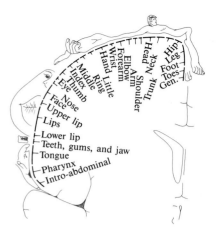

Figure 3.23

Homunculus, or "little man," depicting the disproportionate distribution of skin sensitivity in the somatic sensory cortex.

Senses of Position and Movement

The senses of position and movement are often regarded as the least important because we seldom are consciously aware that they even exist. Without these senses, however, each of us would be reduced to a helpless mass, unable to move and unable to stand upright against the force of gravity. Thanks to them, we constantly are aware of the position of our bodies in space, know when we move a limb, and know when we are standing up or lying down.

These least-appreciated of the senses can be classfied into two broad categories. One category involves the vestibular system, which deals with the movement and position of the head. The other is our sense of the body and its parts, which is detected principally through receptor cells in muscles, tendons, and joints. It is sometimes called **kinesthesis.**

Kinesthesis

To test the sense of position that we usually take for granted, try this experiment. Ask a friend to close her or his eyes and extend an arm to the side with the index finger pointing down. Next, lift the arm so that it points to a definite spot on the wall. Now ask the subject to drop the arm to the side and then try to reposition it precisely in the same place it was before. You will find that people can do this with a great deal of accuracy, often within an inch or two of the original target.

This accuracy is made possible by sensations from two different types of receptors. One type is found in the joints. Nerve impulses signaling the position of the limbs from these receptors are transmitted to the brain. The sensory role of a second type of receptor, **muscle spindles,** has been discovered more recently. Muscle spindles, which are specialized organs located within voluntary muscles, have sensory nerve endings that signal to the spinal cord and the brain when a muscle is stretched. As we saw in chapter 2, it long has been known that muscle spindles are involved in the regulation of the length of the muscle in stretch reflexes such as the knee jerk. Recent evidence indicates that muscle spindles also contribute to our sense of position and movement (Goodwin, McCloskey, & Mathews, 1972). During laboratory experiments, if a subject's limb is held in one position while muscle spindles are activated by vibrating the muscle, the subject experiences a feeling that the limb is actually being moved.

FOCUS

Senses We Do Not Have

Although evolution has endowed humans with an ingenious and highly useful array of sensory organs, the rest of the animal world has not been neglected. Most mammals, of course, are equipped with sight, hearing, and the other senses for perceiving the world. In other animals, however, special senses altogether lacking in humans have evolved that serve unique functions.

The Electric Sense
Certain species of fish, such as the electric eel, produce a discharge that stuns or kills their prey. But several other species possess a subtler form of electrical organ that helps guide their locomotion and detects objects in space. One such species, the elephant-nose fish of Africa, can be purchased in many pet stores.

Perhaps the most extensively studied species with the "electric sense" is the African knife fish. An organ in the tail of the knife fish generates a high-frequency alternating current. This current creates around the fish's body an electric field, which is distorted when objects enter it. These distortions are sensed by detectors lining the surface of the fish's body. Curiously, whereas human sensory organs send their information to the cerebral cortex of the brain, responses from the electric sense of the knife fish go to the cerebellum, a neural structure normally involved in movement.

Thermoreception
Boa constrictors and pit vipers such as the rattlesnake, though gifted with sight, also use a remarkable sensitivity to heat in detecting their prey. The sensory capability was discovered by Gaylord Noble and A. Schmidt (1937) in a fascinating series of experiments. They blindfolded snakes and presented them with a pair of light bulbs. Neither of the light bulbs was illuminated, but one had just been switched off and hence was slightly warmer than the other. The snakes struck repeatedly at the warm bulb. In boa constrictors the heat sensors, or thermoreceptors, are lined up in a row that runs roughly parallel to the animal's lips. In rattlesnakes the thermoreceptors can be found on each side of the head, between the eye and nostril, in the small pit that gives the family its name, pit viper.

In 1952, Theodore Bullock and R. B. Cowles recorded electrical activity in the nerve endings that connect to the rattlesnake's pit organ. They found that minute amounts of heat were enough to speed up markedly the firing of nerve impulses. The thermoreceptors are so sensitive that they can distinguish a human hand from its surroundings at a distance of more than a foot.

The Power of Smell
In some animals the olfactory sense,

Vestibular System

The inner ear contains, in addition to the organ for hearing, two sets of structures vital to our balance and posture (see Figure 3.24). One set, which helps control posture, consists of two saclike organs, the **utricle** and the **saccule.** Inside the utricle and the saccule are sensory hairs. Attached to these hairs, and embedded in a gelatinous mass, are crystals. If the head is tipped away from the upright position, these crystals serve as weights. They deflect the sensory hairs and trigger nerve impulses that signal the change in posture.

A second set of structures, the three **semicircular canals,** detect changes in the angular movement of the head. When the head moves, fluid in the canals is pressed against a series of hair cells. The bending of the hair sets off electrical impulses in nearby nerve fibers. Because the three canals are arranged at right angles to one another, they can detect movement in any direction.

As in the instance of the body's position detectors, we are unaware of the vestibular system until things go wrong. A disorder of the inner ear known as Ménière's syndrome affects the vestibular system and causes dizziness and feelings of disorientation. In extreme cases, the patient may not be able to remain upright.

A more familiar disruption of the vestibular system is motion sickness. The motion of a ship, for example, stimulates the vestibular system in a way

Figure 3.24

The vestibular system, located in the inner ear, is vital to balance and posture. The utricle and saccule help control posture. The three semicircular canals, which are arranged at right angles to each other, can detect movement in any direction and hence serve to control balance.

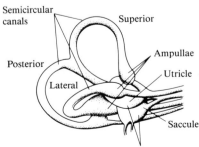

which is relatively unimportant in the human, serves as a powerful regulator of behavior. For example, in two widely disparate species, the salmon and the silkworm moth, smell plays a significant role in sexual reproduction. Salmon are born in freshwater rivers and streams and then migrate to the sea in the first year of life. But in the fourth year they return to spawn in the freshwater place where they were first hatched. The salmon's extraordinary homing ability stems from its olfactory organ. On the early outward journey, the salmon codes the turns and junctions of the water's branches and tributaries by recording their distinctive odors; returning to its birthplace, the salmon "reads" this well-remembered smell map to navigate its way home.

Among silkworm moths, smell is the cue for mating. The female releases a chemical odorant called a pheromone—the biologists's term for any chemical that triggers innate behavior patterns in a member of the same species. The male moth's olfactory organ, which is located in its antennae, can detect the pheromone from many miles away. Humans use the same chemical as the female odorant to attract males of certain insect species and then destroy them.

Echolocation

Bats are not blind. They see better than legend would have it, but vision provides the night-flying bat with only crude recognition of the terrain during flight. To hunt small flying insects at night, bats rely on a sensory system of echolocation, a kind of sonar. They give off very high-frequency sounds—much higher than the human threshold for hearing—and then locate insects and other objects by listening as the sounds bounce off them (Griffin, 1958). Interestingly, the bat's high-frequency cry can also be detected by one of its favorite prey, a night-flying moth. This moth has two simple and primitive ears on either side of the center portion of its body. Each ear has only two auditory fibers; these two fibers have different auditory thresholds. When the more sensitive of these two

In hunting small flying insects at night, bats rely on echolocation, a sensory system resembling sonar.

fibers detects bat cries at a distance, the moth responds by flying in the opposite direction. Higher intensity cries, indicating the bat is nearby, activate the other auditory nerve fiber. The moth thereupon takes dramatic evasive action, diving toward the ground or zooming away on a zigzag course. ∎

that is quite different from its normal functioning in head-rotation. It cannot simply be activation of the vestibular system that produces motion sickness, because it is constantly activated by normal head movement. Rather, it must be the particular pattern of activation produced by moderately high waves or by bends in the road.

The vestibular system also has reflexive nerve connections with the muscles of the eye. This is evident if you rock back and forth in a rocking chair. The angular movement of the head induces activity in the semicircular canals. This activity, in turn, signals the eyes to move in a direction opposite to the chair rotation. The net effect of this so-called **vestibuloocular reflex** is to hold the visual world steady even when the head is moving. Try reading this page while moving your head rapidly back and forth or from side to side. Because of the vestibuloocular reflex, you can still read the page. If you move the book at the same rate instead of your head, however, the text will blur.

Sometimes it may be useful to override this reflex. Say you want to read while being rocked back and forth in the rocking chair. The reflex, by pushing your eyes in the opposite direction of the chair's rotation, would make reading impossible. But if you consciously choose to hold your eyes still, you can overcome the reflex. This ability, it has recently been suggested, may stem from nerve connections through the cerebellum (see chapter 2), which plays an important role in voluntary movement.

Astronauts must adjust to the effect of zero gravity on their vestibular systems.

As we noted at the beginning of the chapter, all the senses go through a three-stage process in delivering their varying messages to the brain where necessary control, direction, and reaction take place. A stimulus (salt on the tongue or a sound wave entering the ear) must enter or touch the body; detectors (taste buds or eardrums) must sense and react to the stimulators; finally, those reactions of the receptors must be translated into nerve impulses that tell the brain what is happening. All those stimulant-receiving detectors and receptors and their corresponding neural networks are appendages and servants to the marvelous brain, which, finally, perceives all sensations, both physically and psychologically. That complex perception is the subject of the following chapter.

Summary

1. Sensation is the process by which we receive and code a stimulus such as a pattern of light or darkness, a sound wave, or a smell or taste. The sensory mechanisms include seeing, hearing, the chemical senses (taste and smell), the skin senses (touch, temperature, and pain), and the sense of position and movement. All human and animal senses can be described in three stages: (1) stimulation—some form of physical or chemical energy must stimulate the sensory mechanisms; (2) detection—receptors, either modified nerve endings or non-neural cells that contact a nerve ending, detect, or receive, stimuli; receptors function as converters, or transducers of physical and chemical energy; and (3) neural coding—the electrical change in the receptor is converted into the nervous system's language, a train of nerve impulses.

2. Psychophysics measures the relationships between the physical attributes of stimuli and resulting sensations. Sensory thresholds are the levels at which a stimulus or changes in a stimulus can be detected. The absolute threshold is the minimal level of intensity at which we can perceive a sensation. A difference threshold is the smallest difference between two stimuli that can be reliably discriminated. The just noticeable difference, or jnd, is that point at which discrimination is possible.

3. There is not a one-to-one relationship between the physical intensity of a stimulus and its sensation magnitude. In Fechner's law, sensation increases geometrically: the logarithm of the stimulus intensity, rather than its absolute value, determines it psychological magnitude.

4. Signal detection theory uses an orderly way of analyzing the detectability of stimuli. Stimulus detectability can be represented on graphs called ROC curves (receiver-operating characteristics).

5. Much of our knowledge about the world around us comes to the brain via the eyes, and a great deal of research has been devoted to the mechanisms of vision. The stimulus for vision is light, a kind of electromagnetic energy that travels in varying wavelengths. The wavelength of light is measured in nanometers (billionths of a meter); the visible spectrum for humans ranges from about 400 to 700 nanometers.

6. In the eye, light passes through the cornea, a transparent tissue, and then through the pupil. The light is focused by the cornea and the lens onto a light-sensitive surface, the retina. The retina is made up of millions of cells that, in connection and function, resemble the neurons of the brain. The cells of the retina are arranged in three distinct layers: (1) rods and cones, which receive and detect the electromagnetic energy of light; (2) the inner nuclear layer, which organizes the information from the rods and cones and transmits it to the ganglion; (3) fibers projecting from the ganglion cells bundle together to form the optic nerve, which carries the electric neural signals to the brain.

7. The human eye has about 100 million rods and 6 million cones. The rods function primarily in dim illumination; when the rods alone are working

we can see only black, white, and shades of gray. With the cones, which function primarily in bright light, we see chromatic colors such as red, green, and blue as well as shades of gray. Rods are distributed relatively uniformly throughout the retina; cones are thinly distributed in the periphery and are more densely packed in the center of the retina. In the center of the retina, in an area of about 1 square millimeter called the fovea, there are cones but no rods.

8. Our eyes adapt to darkness in two stages. The cones reach a stable level of vision in less than 10 minutes; full sensitivity of the rods requires around 30 minutes or more. Reverse adaptation to light occurs much more rapidly.

9. We see different wavelengths of light as different colors. The average person can distinguish a thousand or more different colors. The human eye has three types of color-sensitive cones, each with different pigments, just as rods have their own pigment, rhodopsin. The three types of cones respond at peak sensitivity to long, middle, and short wavelengths. The processing of color information in the brain is still something of a mystery, but recent research suggests the existence of centers in the cortex whose cells are specially tuned to the analysis of color.

10. Perception of color depends on the wavelength of light. In addition, the colors we perceive have three psychological attributes: hue, brightness, and saturation. When lights of two or more wavelengths are combined, we see a new color. A mixture of wavelengths is an additive mixture; conversely, a mixture of pigments is a subtractive mixture. Each hue has a complementary one that lies directly opposite it on the color circle.

11. A negative afterimage is the persistence of a stimulus in a reversed state of chromatic and black-and-white effects. Less frequently occurring is a positive afterimage in which the stimulus persists in its original chromatic state.

12. The usual so-called color blindness is not really a true blindness to colors. Such color blindness is caused in some cases by retinas that have only two types of cones instead of three. In other cases the pigment in the red and green cones is present but has a different maximal sensitivity from normal pigment. A few people, monochromats, have very few cones at all, and poor general vision as well as complete color blindness.

13. Each cell of the retina has a receptive field, which is the region of the visual field that affects a given cell's response to light—either to excite it or inhibit it. Lateral inhibition is a process whereby cells inhibit neighboring cells, thus enhancing the contrasts between different levels of illumination and emphasizing the contours or edges of what we see. The rods and cones make synaptic connections with cells in the inner nuclear layer and send information by way of these cells to the ganglion cells, which transmit visual information to the brain.

14. Ganglion cells send about a million nerve fibers from each eye directly to the brain. These fibers are bundled together into two optic nerves, which meet and partially cross over at the optic chiasma before reaching the brain. In this way, each of the brain's hemispheres receives information from each eye. The optic nerves enter the brain at the level of the thalamus and proceed to the visual cortex, which is located in the occipital lobe.

15. Audition, or the act of hearing requires both rhythmical variations in the pressure of a medium near us and the reception of those variations by the ear, which in turn codes and transmits information to the brain. Sound waves travel through air to our ears in a sequence of pressure and rarefaction.

16. Sound waves have three important characteristics: frequency, amplitude, and phase. Frequency is the measurement (in hertz units) of how many waves occur each second. It is frequency that principally determines the pitch of a sound; intensity, or loudness is largely determined by amplitude. The phase of a sound wave determines whether or not the wave is in synchronous frequency and amplitude with another wave.

17. The function of the ear is to detect sound waves and transform them into electrical impulses. Sound waves enter the ear through the auditory canal and travel to the eardrum, which is next to the middle ear. The ossicles (malleus, incus, and stapes) of the middle ear transmit the sound waves next to the oval window, which is the gateway to the inner ear and its principal structure, the cochlea. Inside the cochlea is the cochlear partition; on the bottom side of the cochlear partition is the basilar membrane. Located on the basilar membrane is the organ of Corti, which contains sensitive hair cells, the receptors of the inner ear. Vibrations of the basilar membrane cause the hairs to bend, converting mechanical energy to electrical energy, which triggers a nerve impulse to the auditory nerve; the electrical impulses concerned with hearing travel to the brain.

18. Smell and taste are chemical senses. Of all the senses, smell, or olfaction, has the most direct route to the brain. Receptors high in each nasal cavity carry smell directly to the two olfactory bulbs, which lie in the frontal lobes of the brain and are joined to the olfactory cortex.

19. The primary taste organs are the papillae, dark red spots on the tongue. There are some 9000 taste buds in the human tongue and each bud contains several receptor cells. The nature of the contact between these receptor cells and the stimulants of flavor molecules has not been clearly established. Taste has been classified into four basic qualities: sweet, sour, salty, and bitter.

20. Skin sensations—touch, warmth, cold, and pain—are known collectively as somesthesis. Some skin receptors are free nerve endings, the branching fibers of sensory neurons; others are specialized structures that encapsulate nerve fibers. Some large fibers are coated with myelin, which speeds up the transmission of the nerve impulse. Other, finer fibers, some unmyelinated, carry only sensations of pain or temperature. Sensory cell bodies lie in a small group of neurons just outside the spinal cord called the dorsal root ganglion. One branch of the sensory fibers ascends by relays to the thalamus deep in the brain and then to the cortex of the parietal lobe. Generally speaking, sensory fibers travel within the spinal cord in nerve tracts that are segregated for different sensations. The sensory pathways cross en route to the brain so that skin sensations from the right side of the body register in the left part of the parietal lobe, and vice versa.

21. The senses of position and movement are extremely important even though we are seldom conscious of them. One category of these senses is detected principally through receptor cells in muscles, tendons, and joints and is called kinesthesis. Kinesthesis encompasses the senses by which we discriminate body movement and position. The other category involves the vestibular system, which deals with the movement and position of the head and is important to equilibrium.

RESEARCH: The question of how much light is necessary for vision has long been studied by psychologists. In a carefully controlled experiment, Selig Hecht showed that 5–14 quanta of light were necessary to activate his subjects' visual receptors. Hecht also showed that fluctuations in the absolute threshold for light were not due to changes in the receptor, but were due to the fluctuation in the amount of quanta emitted by the light source.

FOCUS: In some species, specialized senses have evolved that are altogether lacking in humans. Certain species of fish produce electrical discharges that can be used to kill prey or to establish an electric field that permits the fish to detect objects that pass through it. Some snakes, such as those of the pit viper family, have thermoreceptors that are used to detect the presence of warm-blooded prey. Bats emit high-frequency sounds, similar to sonar waves, that are used to detect prey and other objects in their enivronment. Other animals have powerful senses of olfaction that allow them to detect pheromones or other minute odors essential for finding a potential mate or establishing a territory.

CHAPTER

4

Perception

The late American brain researcher Karl Lashley liked to tell his friends stories about his migraine headaches. These headaches often were preceded or accompanied by large **scotomas,** or blind spots, in his field of vision. On one occasion, Lashley recalled, the scotoma was so large that it momentarily beheaded a colleague who happened to be standing in front of him. But Lashley's perceptual mechanisms instantly filled in the gap with vertical stripes from the wallpaper in the background. Lashley also remembered vividly the time on a Florida road when a pursuing patrol car disappeared in his scotoma, which was then filled in by patterns from the surrounding landscape (Gore, 1971).

Lashley's experiences help us make a distinction between the operation of the sensory systems, which we discussed in the preceding chapter, and the process of perception. By receiving and coding stimuli around us, such as light and sound waves, the senses provide the raw materials for perception. **Perception** is the transformation of the evidence of our senses into mental representations. Perception implies that one *interprets* the information provided by the senses. Facts, or data, are fed into computers, but they mean nothing until the machine has processed the coded information and arranged it in a meaningful way. In a similar way our senses feed information to our brains. It is only after the brain has processed stimuli from the senses that we preceive. Through perception, a mosaic of light and darkness is transformed and interpreted as the beauty of an autumn sunset; pressure waves in the air become a Bach fugue; signals from touch receptors in our skin are felt as the caress of a lover.

In his book *Eye and Brain* (1977), the English psychologist Richard Gregory calls perception ''a dynamic searching for the best interpretation of the available data.'' Such interpretations are made in the light of expectations, existing or preconceived notions that may be quite independent of incoming sensory data. Such cues are dramatically illustrated in those fascinating puzzles known as visual illusions, which can mislead us to incorrect interpretations of the sensory data (see Figure 4.1). Other expectations depend on psychological concepts and processes discussed elsewhere in this text: learning and memory (we know it's a Bach fugue because we have heard it before); emotion and mood (which can determine whether stimulation of the pressure receptors in the skin is interpreted as a loving caress or an irritant). Even individual personality can influence perception: witness the varying ways in which people interpret the chaotic forms that comprise the Rorschach inkblot test (see Chapter 12).

In this chapter we will focus principally on visual perception, the dominant means by which we build up mental representations of the world. A majority of the external stimuli to which we respond is visual. Vision is the ''dominant'' sense: if we receive conflicting information from our visual apparatus and a different sensory modality—touch, for example—we will usually respond to the visual appearance.

We will begin with an introduction to visual perception, then go on to discuss the mechanisms of form vision and the perception of depth and motion.

Figure 4.1

Visual illusions. (A) The center circles in both patterns are equal in diameter but appear unequal. (B) The heavy form in the lefthand figure is a perfect circle and the heavy form in the righthand figure is a perfect square, although they appear to be distorted by the background pattern. (C) The three cylinders are the same size but appear to be different sizes. (D) The two lines are equal but appear unequal.

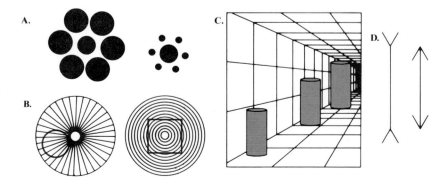

CHAPTER 4   PERCEPTION

Next, we will consider several issues relating to the roles of heredity and learning in the development of visual perception. Following that is a brief discussion of auditory perception, a subject no less fascinating than vision but one about which far less is known.

Visual Perception: An Introduction

From childhood, we have looked out at the world and recognized familiar objects and faces. Small children can go through a large and elaborate picture book and correctly identify all of the objects in it. We walk to school or work in the morning and guide our footsteps over the pavement without thinking about it. We watch a tennis ball coming across the net and organize all of our movements to meet it with the racket. Visual perception is so natural, so much a part of our everyday life, that it is difficult to think about it analytically. It seems evident to us that things look as they do because they are there.

Yet vision requires an enormous amount of active registration, analysis, sorting, filtering, and comparing by our perceptual mechanisms—first in the eye itself, but chiefly at centers within the brain. For example, although we are not aware of it, all of us have a blind spot in each eye, a smaller version of the scotoma that occurred in Karl Lashley's migraine attacks (see chapter 3). Ordinarily we are unaware of this small hole in our vision because the perceptual mechanisms of the brain fill it up with the surrounding patterns.

We will look first at three characteristics of visual perception that long have intrigued researchers—perceptual adaptation, visual capture, and perceptual constancy.

Small children can go through a large and elaborate picture book and correctly identify all of the objects in it.

Perceptual Adaptation

For more than a century, a favorite experimental tool of researchers who study visual perception has been goggles that distort what is seen. In his treatise on physiological optics, the nineteenth-century researcher Hermann von Helmholtz (1910) suggested the following experiment:

Take two glass prisms with refracting angles of about 16° or 18° and place them in a spectacle frame, with their edges both turned toward the left. As seen through these glasses, the objects in the field of view will all apparently be shifted to the left of their real position. At first, without bringing the hand into the field, look closely at some definite object within reach, and then close the eyes, and try to touch the object with the forefinger. The usual result will be to miss it by thrusting the hand too far to the left. But, after trying for some little while, or more quickly still, by inserting the hand in the field, and under the guidance of the eye, touching the objects with it for an instant, then on trying the above experiment again, we shall discover that now we do not miss the objects, but feel for them correctly. It is the same way when new objects are substituted for those with which we have become familiar. Having learned how to do this, suppose now we take off the prisms and remove the hand from the field of view, and then after gazing steadily at some object, close our eyes, and try to take hold of it. We find then that the hand will miss the object by being thrust too far to the right; until after several failures, our judgment of the direction of the eyes is rectified again

This simple effect of a prism on visual reaching is easy to replicate. When you first put a prism in front of your eye and reach for an object, you miss the object by about the same degree that the prism displaces the visual world. After a few tries with the prism in place, your reach becomes accurate again. When the prism is taken away, you misreach in the opposite direction.

The ability to compensate for an artificially displaced visual field is called **perceptual adaptation.** Perceptual adaptation is a form of learning or relearn-

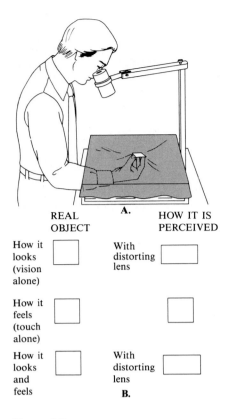

	REAL OBJECT	**A.**	HOW IT IS PERCEIVED
How it looks (vision alone)	☐	With distorting lens	☐
How it feels (touch alone)	☐		☐
How it looks and feels	☐	With distorting lens **B.**	☐

Figure 4.2

The experimental arrangement used to demonstrate visual capture includes a distorting lens and a cloth to cover the subject's hand to prevent him from detecting the distortion. The object being grasped is a small plastic square. As the schematic drawings of the results indicate, if the square is viewed through a distorting lens, it is perceived as a rectangle; if it is felt without being seen, it is perceived as a square; if it is viewed with a distorting lens and felt at the same time, it is perceived as a rectangle.

ing. In the first few days after beginning to wear eyeglasses, one's entire visual apparatus has to adjust to a changed sensing of stimuli. The perceptual apparatus is altered or adapted. We might assume that this perceptual adaptation takes place in the mechanisms that control visual direction. However, Charles Harris (1965) found that subjects who adapt to a prism and then are asked to point in the direction of a sound source do not point accurately. If perceptual adaptation involved only vision, such an error should not occur.

Moreover, when Harris's subjects were adapted to the prism with their right arm and could successfully point to the target, they showed no sign of such adaptation with the left arm. When they were asked to point at the target with the left arm while looking through the prism, they missed. This finding further supports the argument against a simple visual mechanism of prism adaptation. Harris concluded that the adaptation actually occurred because of a recalibration in the felt position of the arm—that is, the kinesthetic sense by which we determine position and movement in various parts of the body.

In summary, although perceptual adaptation may be induced visually, its principal effect may be on other senses.

Visual Capture

The findings on prism adaptation suggest another important characteristic of visual perception. When visual perception and another sense come into conflict, vision tends to win. In the Harris experiment, seeing was indeed believing. What the subjects saw was more convincing than what they felt in their arms. Vision, for humans, seems to be the dominant sense.

The tendency of vision to dominate the other senses has been called **visual capture.** Experiments have shown that if we view a square through a distorting lens that makes the square appear as a rectangle and feel the square object at the same time, we will still perceive the object as a rectangle. (Rock & Victor, 1964). Vision dominates touch in this example of visual capture (see Figure 4.2). Another instance of visual capture was dramatically demonstrated half a century ago by James J. Gibson (1933), who had his subject wear prism spectacles that created the illusion that everything was curved. Then he presented her with a rulerlike straightedge. As expected, the subject saw the straightedge as a curved rather than a straight object. When she ran her hand along the edge of the object while looking at it through the prism spectacles, an additional illusion was created. Not only did the straightedge look curved, it also felt curved. The subject's visual perception mechanisms had dominated her sense of touch; that is, her sense of touch had been visually captured.

What happens when hearing comes into conflict with vision? The illusion created by ventriloquists depends on visual capture. Ventriloquists do not actually throw their voices. They merely assume that our vision, fixed upon the moving lips of the dummy, will win out over our hearing, which if not for visual capture, would perceive that the sound was in fact coming from the ventriloquist. The discrepancy between visual and auditory information is thus resolved in favor of vision.

Perceptual Constancy

Another highly important characteristic of visual perception is the stability, or **perceptual constancy,** of the shape, size, lightness, and color of objects in our visual fields. We recognize the same objects at a variety of angles, at various distances, and even under sharply differing kinds of light. We perceive a piece of coal as black whether it is in shade or bright sunlight. We perceive

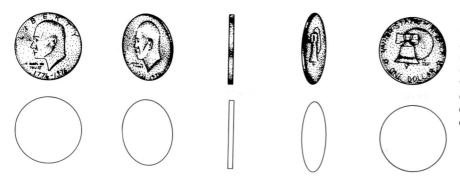

Figure 4.3

Demonstration of shape constancy. As a coin is rotated, its image becomes an ellipse that grows narrower and narrower until it becomes a thin rectangle, an ellipse again, and then a circle. At each orientation, however, it is still perceived as a circular coin.

people to be the same size whether they are 5 or 15 meters away. We perceive a door as a rectangle whether it is closed or half open. Although the sensory stimuli imaged on the retina change with shape, size, and lightness, we recognize the objects as stable, and our perception of them tends to remain the same. The mechanisms of constancy produce adaptive perception: we perceive objects as having relatively permanent physical properties in spite of variation in physical stimulus.

Shape

Probably the easiest kind of perceptual constancy to demonstrate is **shape constancy.** Hold up a coin in front of your eyes and rotate it. As you rotate the coin, the image of it on your retina becomes an ellipse that grows smaller and smaller, then it becomes a line, and finally an ellipse again (see Figure 4.3). Nonetheless, at each orientation it is still perceived as a circular coin. Similarly, a square rotated in front of your eyes becomes a distorted trapezoid on your retina; yet if you are aware that the figure is being rotated, you still perceive it as a square. A door or window casts a rectangular image only when viewed from a certain point; however, both appear rectangular from whatever point we view them. Thus, objects maintain their apparent constancy of shape despite rotation or differences in the point from which we view them.

Size

Look at someone standing near you and then compare that perception with your perception of someone standing across the street. They look about the same size to you even though the actual size of the respective images on your retina may differ by a factor of 10 to 1 or more. Perceived size does not regularly follow retinal size. As we will discuss in detail later, we interpret the size of objects in terms of their distance from us; we interpret relative size appropriate to the distance. This tendency for the perceptual apparatus to take into account the distance of an object in judging its size is called **size constancy.** It also further illustrates the adaptative nature of perceptual constancy.

The concept of size constancy provides a reasonable explanation for why we are fooled by certain visual illusions. In the **Ponzo illusion,** for example, two lines of equal length are drawn between two converging lines (see Figure 4.4). Although the drawing is two-dimensional, the converging lines appear to add the third dimension of depth or distance. As the converging lines come closer together like railroad tracks receding in the distance, we interpret them as parallel lines that are becoming more and more distant. Thus, the top horizontal line in the Ponzo illusion appears to be farther away. Because the top line appears to be more distant, the principle of size constancy is called into play; our expectation would be that the top line would appear shorter than the bottom line. Because it is the same length as the bottom line, however, the distance cue makes the top line actually appear to be longer.

Figure 4.4

The Ponzo illusion, demonstrated in a photograph and a sketch. The converging lines add a dimension of depth, and hence the distance cue makes the top (or "more distant") line appear larger than the bottom line even though they are actually the same length.

Figure 4.5

The apparent lightness or darkness of a gray disk is influenced by what surrounds the disk. If the disk is surrounded by a white band, it appears much darker than an identical disk surrounded by a black band.

Lightness

A lump of coal in sunlight reflects a larger amount of light than does a white paper in a dimly lit room. Yet the coal still looks black in the sunlight and the white paper still looks white in the dimly lit room. This tendency of our perception of an object's lightness to remain stable over a wide range of illumination is called **ligntness constancy.**

To understand lightness constancy, we need to review the process by which we perceive whether an object is white or black. We know that white surfaces reflect more light than do black surfaces. However, perception of lightness does not dpend on the absolute amount of light reflected from an object, but on the relative amount. T. K. Gelb (1929) demonstrated this principle in a classic experiment. Gelb positioned a spinning disk of black paper in a doorway so that when he projected a light on it, the illumination would fall only on the disk. The result was that the black disk actually looked white. However, when Gelb placed a bit of white paper in front of it, the disk appeared to turn black. In the absence of an external clue such as the bit of white paper, the brightly lit disk gave off more light than anything in its surroundings and hence was perceived as white. The presence of the white paper changed this perception because the white paper reflected much more light than the black disk. Thus, the relative amount of light—not the absolute amount—determines our perception of lightness (see chapter 3).

A phenomenon based on similar principles of lightness perception is shown in Figure 4.5. Suppose we draw a disk of neutral gray. The apparent lightness or darkness of the gray disk is influenced powerfully by what surrounds the disk. If we surround the disk with a black band, the gray of the central disk appears quite light. If we surround the disk with a white band, it appears much darker. Again our perception is influenced by the relative amount of light (Cornsweet, 1970).

Animal vision operates in a similar manner. In one of the best experiments in modern animal psychophysics, Donald Blough (1961) showed that pigeons are influenced powerfully by the lightness of the surround in their judgment of the lightness of a center target. Even pigeons take background illumination into account and thus show lightness constancy.

Color

We perceive the colors of an object as a constant if we are able to see the object's surroundings. The color of a lemon viewed through a tube so that only the lemon is visible may or may not be perceived as yellow, depending on the wavelength of the light rays striking it. If, however, we can see the lemon on a table or in a bowl of other fruit, we will see a yellow lemon because we have background clues as color referents. **Color constancy** is analogous to brightness constancy in that the light falling on an object and its surroundings determines the hue we perceive.

Perception of Shape and Form

When we look at the world around us, we organize it into meaningful units of shape and form without thinking. How do we perceive form? How are the stimuli of light imaged on the retina transformed into the pattern that we recognize as the familiar face of our grandmother? There are many ways to approach the study of form perception. We will consider first early psychological studies by the Gestalt theorists and then describe in detail the more recent attempts to understand the neural basis of form perception.

Figure-Ground Differentiation

The Danish psychologist, Edgar Rubin, in 1915 presented evidence that parts of any differentiated visual field will stand out from other parts. That part appearing as a distinct, delineated shape is the figure; the remainder is the ground. Shape and form tend to stand out against a background. This is called the **figure-ground relationship.** There are instances in which the relationship between figure and ground is ambiguous. For example, in the classic visual illusion shown in Figure 4.6, figure and ground keep changing; in panel B, the white vase against the dark background is clearly the figure until we perceive the two faces against the white background. Ambiguous relationships between figure and ground are frequently encountered in the natural world in the form of protective camouflage.

An early contribution to our thinking about form vision came from the group who called themselves *Gestalt* psychologists, from the German word for shape or form. This group, working mainly at the University of Berlin during the 1920s, studied several important phenomena in the organization of perception. Through a combination of description, intuition, and experimentation, the Gestalt psychologists attempted to formulate underlying principles by which we organize the visual field into figure and ground. These principles include the following:

Closure
The perceptual tendency to fill in gaps in an otherwise continuous pattern is known as **closure** (see Figure 4.7).

Continuity
A principle closely related to closure is **continuity.** We perceive elements that form a meaningful pattern as being grouped together (see Figure 4.8). When continuity prevails it is as though a pattern were generated that creates a sense of organized shape that takes precedence over any of the separate elements that make up the actual pattern.

Proximity
Elements that are physically close to one another look as if they go together. For example, when we see an array of dots like the following

```
. . . . . . . . . . . . . . . . . . . . . . . . . . . . . . . . . . . . . . . . . . . . . . . . . .
. . . . . . . . . . . . . . . . . . . . . . . . . . . . . . . . . . . . . . . . . . . . . . . .
. . . . . . . . . . . . . . . . . . . . . . . . . . . . . . . . . . . . . . . . . . . . . . . .
```

Figure 4.6

The Rubin vase is often used to illustrate the distinction between figure and ground. In (A) the figure-ground relationship is ambiguous. If the lines are perceived as marking the edges of the shaded space in the center, then the shaded space is the figure, the white space is the ground, and we see a vase; if the lines are perceived as marking the right and left edges of the white space, then the white space is the figure, the shaded space is the ground, and we see two facing profiles. In (B) the ambiguity is reduced to accent the vase, and in (C) the profiles are accented.

Figure 4.7

Because of closure, the tendency to fill in gaps, we perceive the sketch at the left as a circle and the sketch at the right as a horse and rider.

Figure 4.8

Because of continuity, the square element in this illustration is perceived as belonging to the wave-shaped pattern, while the dot to the right is perceptually isolated.

PERCEPTION OF SHAPE AND FORM

103

we see it as three horizontal rows of dots. But if we see

. . . .
. . . .
. . . .

we interpret it as eight short columns of dots. **Proximity** organizes the total pattern into meaningful subunits.

Similarity

We perceive similar elements (if proximity is equal) as being grouped together. **Similarity** organizes the elements as part of a meaningful pattern.

Some of the Gestalt principles are very similar to ideas suggested by contemporary scientists interested in the computer analysis of visual scenes. In this sense, Gestalt psychologists were pioneers in a new and important way of studying perception. But when the Gestalt theorists attempted to infer what might be happening in the brain itself during form perception, they did not have enough information. Gestalt theorists speculated that what we see is generated on the surface of the brain in electrical patterns that are the same as (or similar to) the shapes imaged on the retina. Such speculation occurred because at that time the major tool for the study of the physiological processes in form perception was not yet available. It is this tool—the recording of responses of individual cells in the visual pathways—that has given the first insights into how form is processed in the brain.

Feature Detectors

How is the stimulus of light processed and transformed by the nervous system into recognizable forms? Although the answer to that complex question is still far from clear, research over the past few decades has supplied some tantalizing clues. The aim of such research is to establish systematically the response properties of individual cells at the various way stations that comprise the visual pathways. To do this, a microelectrode is placed near a given cell in the eye or brain of a research animal; the electrical responses there are measured when various stimuli are presented to the eye.

As we saw in the preceding chapter, such experiments have shown that cells at the early stages in the visual pathways have relatively simple spatial response properties. For example, at the very first stage the rods and cones of the retina are activated in response to the absolute amount of light that falls upon them. Farther along in the retina, the ganglion cells respond to a very specific distribution of light and shade or to changes in illumination in their receptive field. The individual retina cells react only to tiny regions of light and dark; they are, in effect, indifferent to the overall shapes on the retina.

These discoveries, although important to our understanding of the physiological basis of vision, do not yet explain how the perception of form takes place at the cellular level. For clues to that process we must look farther back in the visual pathways, at the brain itself.

The work of David Hubel and Torsten Wiesel (1962) has made clear that the visual cortex contains nerve cells that respond to specific features of shape or orientation in their receptive fields. These cells have been called **feature detectors.** The features they appear to detect are linear in nature—for example, lines, bars, and edges at a particular orientation. Such feature detectors are doubtless one of the building blocks of perception.

Working first with cats and then with monkeys, Hubel and Wiesel placed microelectrodes near individual cells of the visual cortex and recorded the cel-

The work of David Hubel (top) and Torsten Wiesel (bottom) clarified that nerve cells in the visual cortex respond to specific features of shape or orientation. Such feature detectors are the building blocks of perception.

CHAPTER 4 PERCEPTION

lular activity that occurred when simple shapes were projected onto a screen in front of the animal. Hubel and Wiesel have described three different types of cells found in the visual cortex that are quite different in complexity in their response properties (see Figure 4.9).

Simple cells respond best to a linear shape or edge at a particular orientation and place in their receptive field—for example, a vertical line.

Complex cells resemble simple cells in their sensitivity to a line or edge at a given orientation, but unlike simple cells, certain complex cells also respond to an edge or line at any place in their receptive field.

Hypercomplex cells, as their name implies, have even more complex and selective response properties. One class of hypercomplex cell responds to a line anywhere in the visual field, but only if the edge has a specific length as well as orientation.

The relationships among these three classes of cells are still not entirely clear. Hubel and Weisel suggested a serieslike schema whereby complex cells receive their input from many simple cells, and hypercomplex cells in turn are activated by several complex cells. But the fact that complex cells may be activated at the same time or even before simple cells suggests that simple cells do not necessarily provide the functional inputs to complex cells.

Pattern Recognition

Feature detectors probably represent a relatively early step in recognizing patterns such as letters of the alphabet or specific shapes. Somehow and somewhere in the brain there must be a further synthesis of the simple information extracted by the feature detectors. Some neural mechanism for comparison that matches a given pattern with our stored memory of what it looks like must exist. Although feature detectors may prove to be the building blocks of perception, it is unlikely that the further processing necessary for pattern recognition actually takes place in the first way station for vision—the primary visual cortex. For one thing, the nerve cells there are highly localized in their responses; they fire only when an appropriate target is placed in just the right region of the visual field. Our perception of forms is inconsistent with such a strict organization of the visual fields. We can recognize things, no matter what their size, orientation, or position. It is pattern of activation to which we respond, not its precise position or size.

In humans and monkeys, the visual cortex makes connections with other cortical areas and with several targets deep in the brain. There is excellent evidence that a part of the temporal lobe is heavily involved in pattern recognition. During the 1950s, Kao Liang Chow (1951) and Mortimer Mishkin and Karl Pribram (1954) established that lesions in the inferior temporal cortex of monkeys greatly impair the animal's ability to learn form discrimination. The resulting deficit was even greater than that produced by lesions of an equal size in the visual cortex itself. When tested for visual acuity, the ability to resolve fine detail, the monkeys with temporal lobe lesions were entirely normal. Specifically, it was visual pattern recognition and visual learning that were disturbed.

Is There a Grandmother Cell?

A possible relationship between nerve cells and pattern recognition has led to speculation that in some cases the firing of a specific cell might be the neural equivalent of a specific perception. Brain scientists have given a colorful shorthand name to such a supposed processing mechanism: the **grandmother cell.** The idea is that either in the temporal cortex or somewhere else in the brain there might be a cell that is able to recognize all the features that add up to the

Figure 4.9

Cellular hypothesis on the synthesis of receptive fields, by simple, complex, and hypercomplex receptive fields. For each cell class, lower order neurons converge to form receptive fields of higher order neurons. (A) Fields of simple cells are created by the convergence of many geniculate neurons with concentric fields all arranged in a straight line on the retina corresponding to the axis of orientation of simple receptive fields. (B) The summation of simple cells responding best to a vertically oriented edge at slightly different positions is believed to account for the behavior of a complex cell, which responds well to a vertically oriented edge situated anywhere within its field. (C) In turn each of the two complex cells responds best to an obliquely oriented edge. But one cell is excitatory and the other is inhibitory to the hypercomplex cell so that an edge that covers both fields is ineffective, while a corner restricted to the left field excites (from Kuffler & Nicholls, 1976, after Hubel & Wiesel, 1965).

Figure 4.10

In this Florentine painting depicting the death of Savonarola, depth is achieved through use of the technique of linear perspective. The buildings on both sides of the canvas are drawn so that they appear as if they are on parallel lines that would converge at some distant point. Also, distant objects are drawn much smaller than nearby ones.

Figure 4.11

As you look at these rows of equally spaced telephone poles along the side of a road, the edges of the road appear to converge, the poles get progressively smaller, and the distance between poles seems to decrease.

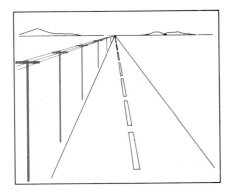

pattern that constitutes your grandmother. If you see someone who looks something like your grandmother, the cell will fire, but not at optimal frequency. It fires best only when it recognizes your grandmother.

The notion of a grandmother cell is only speculation, of course, and few neural scientists believe that the activity of any one cell is the key to understanding pattern recognition.

One obvious problem with the idea of a grandmother cell is that we would have to have a master cell for recognizing each of the people, objects, and patterns we know—a number so large that it might be difficult for the brain to accommodate them. But there is some evidence that a process like a grandmother cell may be involved in some instances of visual recognition. Charles Gross and his colleagues found cells in the inferotemporal cortex of a monkey with highly specific sensitivity to a most complex shape. One of these was activated briskly by the image of a monkey's hand (Gross, Rocha-Miranda, & Bender, 1972) or face (Bruce, Desimone, & Gross, 1981).

Ensemble Coding

An alternative view of pattern recognition is that it involves a group of nerve cells firing in some definite pattern. According to this view, each perception must be represented by some kind of **ensemble code**—that is, the firing of various combinations of the same set of nerve cells that should signify different perceptions.

How ensemble coding might work is harder to grasp intuitively than the grandmother cell concept. It may be useful to think of your memory cells as having a ''feature list.'' Such a list for your grandmother might include the angle of her eyebrows, the width of her nose and mouth, her browline, and so forth. When you see a woman of your grandmother's age and size (or anyone, for that matter), the feature detectors are activated and messages are sent to the memory cells. Your brain would compare the face you now see to the list associated in your memory cells with your grandmother. If the list matches, then it is, indeed, your grandmother.

Perception of Depth

One of the most prosaic and yet profound statements about visual perception is that we live in a three-dimensional world. Although the retina is essentially a flat, two-dimensional surface, we perceive depth and distance: our visual landscape unfolds in an orderly manner with some objects appearing to be near us and others farther in the distance.

What are the visual cues that enable us to perceive depth? Some of these cues require the use of only one eye and are thus **monocular.** Other cues are **binocular,** requiring the use of both eyes.

Monocular Cues

An interesting way to identify the monocular cues for perceiving depth is to consider the techniques painters use to portray the three-dimensional world on a two-dimensional canvas.

Perspective

Artists typically discuss the problem of representing three-dimensional space in terms of perspective—that is, cues that are important to our perception of depth. Although perspective is so widely used in painting that we take it for granted, the idea is a comparatively recent one. One technique for portraying depth on a canvas is **linear perspective.** Parallel lines are drawn so that they seem to converge on a distant spot known as the vanishing point. Distant objects are drawn much smaller than nearby objects (see Figure 4.10).

We experience linear perspective often in everyday perception. Imagine, for example, a row of equally spaced telephone poles along the roadside. As you look down the road, the edges of the road appear to converge, the telephone poles get progressively smaller, and the apparent distance between the equally spaced poles seems to lessen as the distance increases (see Figure 4.11 on the previous page).

Another instance of linear perspective, with its apparent convergence of parallel lines as they recede, can be experienced when we look up at a tall building. The two sides of the building seem to converge toward the top, giving the impression that the building is tapered (see Figure 4.12). To counteract this impression, some architects actually have designed buildings that are wider at the top than at the bottom. A notable example is the Bell Tower in the Cathedral of Florence (see Figure 4.13). The increase in width at the top helps compensate for the effects of linear perspective. As a result, the building looks more uniformly rectangular than would a building whose sides were truly parallel.

In addition to linear perspective, painters use **aerial perspective** as another cue to depth perception. Light reflected from a distant object is partially scattered or absorbed by small particles in the atmosphere before it reaches our eyes. The longer the distance, the more the light is affected by the atmosphere. Light reflected from distant mountains may travel many miles before reaching our eyes; hence, the outline of the mountains appears blurred and fuzzy and bluish in color. Painters use aerial perspective to achieve the impression of great distance (see Figure 4.14).

Overlap

Perhaps the simplest monocular cue is **overlap,** or **interposition.** If, in a painting or in our view of a scene, a park bench partially obscures the grass behind it, we know that the bench is nearer to us than is the grass. In a drawing of two circles, if one overlaps the other, the fully exposed one is perceived as nearer.

Figure 4.12

When we look up at a tall building that is actually rectangular, such as New York City's World Trade Center, the sides appear to converge at the top, and the building appears to be tapered.

Figure 4.13

The Bell Tower of the Cathedral of Florence was designed to be wider at the top than at the bottom to compensate for the tapering effect shown in Figure 4.12.

Figure 4.14

The use of aerial perspective permitted the artist to achieve the impression of great distance in this painting. The outline of the mountains is blurred to indicate what happens to light reflected from distant objects, which is partially scattered and absorbed before it reaches the viewer's eyes.

Actual walls

Illusory
walls

Opening for one eye

▲ Actual place and size of "smallest" man

▴ Illusory place and size of "smallest" man

△ Actual place and size of "medium" man

▵ Illusory place and size of "medium" man

□ "Largest" man

Figure 4.15

Top: A diagram of the Ames "distorted room," as seen from the top; Bottom: The Ames room as seen from the front. The man on the left is actually the same height as the other two men.

Relative Size

Another monocular cue to depth is the **relative size** of objects. If we look at a large crowd, the people closest to use look bigger than the ones farther away. Because we assume that people do not vary all that much in size, we interpret the smaller-appearing person as being more distant. The American psychologist Adelbert Ames, who was formerly a painter, has made clever use of this effect in several illusions (Ittelson, 1952). One of the most celebrated is the Ames Room (see Figure 4.15), which is viewed from an observation station in the front wall. The two adjacent walls are parallel, but the far wall is highly distorted. It angles away from the observer and, as this far wall recedes, the height increases. Yet, the room looks normal. However, when people of equal height are positioned along the far wall, the room still appears normal, but the people appear grotesquely different in size. Because we see the far wall as rectangular, the person whose head nearly reaches the ceiling looks huge compared to the person whose height appears to be half that of the ceiling. Relative size and distance are thus closely linked to each other. On normal viewing, distant people appear smaller and people that appear much smaller are seen as further away. The Ames room is so constructed that our usual distance cues are fooled.

Texture

The American psychologist James Gibson (1950) has called attention to the importance of another cue in determining depth—that of **texture.** Texture is a form of microstructure characteristic of most sufaces and is generally seen as a grain. If we look out at a textured surface such as a rock-strewn beach, the appearance of the texture varies with distance. As the distance increases, the texture, or grain, appears to change gradually from coarse to fine (see Figure 4.16).

Motion Parallax

A final monocular cue for depth perception, **motion parallax,** involves movement by the perceiver. Motion parallax is the difference in the apparent rate of movement of objects at different distances. For example, when you take a walk in the country, nearby objects such as fence posts and trees appear to change their position in step with your movements, while distant objects such as a mountain on the horizon seem to stay fixed in place. This difference in the apparent rate of movement helps us perceive relative depth. As you move, close elements (the fence posts) in the visual field appear to move faster than far objects (the mountains). The relative amount of apparent movement is less for far-away objects, and is therefore a cue to distance.

Binocular Cues

Although some monocular cues serve the painter and other perceivers quite well, even Leonardo da Vinci, who first formulated clearly the laws of linear perspective, recognized that a painting can never produce an impression of depth as compelling as that in the original scene. When we view a real scene, all of the objects in it are seen in slightly different positions relative to each other by the left and the right eye. This binocular disparity provides important cues for the perception of depth. A painting lacks the advantages inherent in binocular vision. We can see and perceive with each eye singly, but the images from each eye are also combined in the brain. We become aware of this mechanism of binocular fusion only when something goes wrong with it. If the coordination of the position of the two eyes does not work properly, we can have double vision or suppression of the image from one of the two eyes. When coordination works normally, the brain gives us single vision from each of two eyes and these two *different* images produce information for depth.

Convergence

One cue from binocular vision is the angle formed by the **convergence** of our two eyes as they pivot inward to focus on a single object. The function of convergence is to regulate the pattern of stimulation on each eye so as to avoid double images, which arise because the two eyes view the world from different positions on the head. Ordinarily, we are not consciously aware of these double images, but they can be illustrated by a simple demonstration (Woodworth, 1938). Hold a pencil vertically at a reading distance between your eyes, and fixate on a conspicuous and somewhat isolated object at the far end of the room. You will see a double image of the pencil. In order to yield a single image, the input from the two eyes must converge, which occurs when you look *at* the pencil.

Convergence occurs only when objects are nearby—that is, less than about 3 meters away (Gogel, 1977). At these nearby distances, the eyes can serve as a rangefinder, signaling distance to the brain by recording the angle of convergence, which then indicates the relative depth. Because single vision for objects at different distances requires different degrees of inward pivoting of the eyes, kinesthetic feedback from the extraocular muscles, which control the movement of the eyeballs, might also provide cues to the depth and distance of a nearby object. At greater distances the visual axes of the two eyes are parallel, and hence there is no convergence. A major limitation of convergence is that the depth of only a single object can be gauged at any one time. In addition, the role of convergence as a primary source of depth or distance information has been difficult to assess, and its importance as a spatial cue is not agreed on (Ogle, 1962; Gregory, 1973).

Stereoscopic Vision

The existence of two separate eyes provides an even more important cue for depth than convergence. Because our eyes are about 6.3 centimeters apart, each one has a slightly different point of view and thus records an image that is slightly different from that of the other eye. This slight disparity results in the perception of depth through **stereoscopic vision.**

The first clear account of the role of disparity was given in 1838 in a classic paper published by Charles Wheatstone, the English physicist. Wheatstone began to wonder whether a painting could ever represent a scene so perfectly that we could not tell it from reality. For the representation of distant scenes or objects his answer was affirmative: it should be possible for a painting to "render such perfect resemblances of the objects they are intended to represent, as to be mistaken for them." Then Wheatstone went on to point out how the accurate rendering of nearby scenes or objects was complicated by the problem of **disparity.** Each eye sees a subtly different aspect of the same nearby object. If, for example, you rapidly blink first the left and then the right eye, it is clear that each eye sees a somewhat different view.

To test the effects of disparity, Wheatstone constructed a simple device using a pair of right-angle mirrors that simulated the effects of binocular perception. He drew a picture of two flagpoles at different distances as seen by his left eye only; then he drew the same flagpoles as viewed by his right eye only. When Wheatstone viewed this pair of two-dimensional drawings on his new device, he saw in three dimensions. A powerful impression of depth was created—a stereoscopic view similar to that which occurs when the different views from each eye are fused in the brain.

Wheatstone had discovered stereoscopic vision and, in the process, had invented the stereoscope (see Figure 4.17). This instrument, perfected by Whatstone and others, became a popular form of home entertainment toward the end of the nineteenth century, making it possible for people to view scenic wonders, such as the Grand Canyon, in three dimensions. The photographs for the device were sold in stereo pairs—that is, two pictures made by a pair of cameras separated by the same distance that separates our two eyes.

Figure 4.16

Texture can be used as a cue for determining depth. As we look down a rock-strewn field, the texture of the rocks appears to vary with distance. As the distance increases, the texture gradually appears to change from coarse to fine.

Figure 4.17

The adjustable stereoscope provided an early method of looking at photographs in three dimensions through the use of two pictures separated by the same distance that separates our two eyes.

Figure 4.18

When the two random dot stereograms shown here are viewed one at a time, they are identical, except for the dots in an area in the center: in the one on the right, the dots are moved slightly to the right. However, if they are viewed together in a stereoscope, a center square is seen floating above the background in vivid depth (after Julesz, 1971).

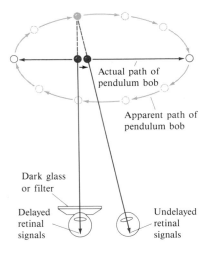

Figure 4.19

The Pulfrich pendulum effect occurs when a pendulum, swinging in a straight arc in a plane perpendicular to the line of sight and viewed with a filter over one eye, appears to swing in an ellipse. This is due to the fact that the signals from the eye covered by the filter are delayed, causing an apparent displacement of the pendulum bob away from the viewer when it moves from the filtered to the unfiltered side of the visual field and a displacement toward the viewer when the pendulum bob moves in the opposite direction.

A modern tool for the study of the mechanism of stereoscopic vision is a device called the **random dot stereogram,** invented by Bela Julesz (1971) of the Bell Telephone Laboratories. The stereogram consists of a pair of patterns of computer-generated randomly positioned dots (see Figure 4.18). The stereograms are identical except that, in one of them, one group of dots in the center has been moved slightly to one side or the other. The group that has been moved forms a recognizable shape such as a square. If these stereograms are viewed one at a time, the square shape is not apparent. But in the stereoscope, the pair of them create a powerful illusion of depth. The square seems to float in space above a background of random dots. The disparity between the two squares has been converted to a perception of depth.

Just where in the brain that fusing of stereoscopic images takes places is not entirely clear. Most likely, fusion occurs in the brain at a level beyond the primary visual cortex.

The Pulfrich Effect

The role of disparity as a cue for depth perception is illustrated in a curious illusion known as the **Pulfrich effect.** Though actually discovered earlier, it is named for Pulfrich, who studied the phenomenon even though he was blind in one eye. The effect cannot be seen without two functional eyes. To see the Pulfrich effect, try the following experiment:

Tie a weight onto a string and allow the weight to swing back and forth in front of you. The weight should move like a pendulum without coming toward or away from you. As you watch the weight swinging back and forth with both eyes, place a filter over one eye so that the amount of light reaching that eye is less than the amount reaching the other. A neutral gray filter, a photographic negative, one lens of a pair of sunglasses, or even a piece of colored cellophane will work. When you look at the weight moving back and forth with the filter in front of one eye, you will notice an interesting effect. The weight now appears to move in an elliptical orbit, coming closer at one end of its pendulum swing and then moving away from you on the other end. If you now shift the filter to the other eye, the direction of the ellipse is reversed (see Figure 4.19).

In order to understand the Pulfrich effect, we need to remember that a slight disparity in the position of an object on the two retinas can serve as a cue for depth. We also need to know that weak stimuli take a longer time to be processed by the eye and the brain than strong stimuli: the retina of the eye viewing such a scene would take a longer period of time to get its messages going to the brain than the retina of the eye viewing a more brightly illuminated scene (Enright, 1970; Gregory, 1973). If less light enters the right eye than the left, the image from the right eye is received by the brain a bit more slowly than the image from the left eye. Because the pendulum is moving, the right eye sees it slightly behind the place where the left eye sees it. A small disparity is thus created between the two eyes in your perception of the location of the pendulum. This disparity is interpreted by the brain as a depth cue. The weight appears to move first toward you and then away from you. You can produce this same effect on your own television screen. If you put a filter in front of one eye, the screen will appear to have depth when there is movement across the screen.

Perception of Motion

Our visual world is seldom still. We are moving most of the time, and many of the objects around us are in constant motion. How do we tell whether something is moving or standing still?

Real Motion

An object must reach a certain speed before we can detect that it is moving. This threshold for motion perception varies, however, with circumstances such as the background. Against a uniform background, a small spot will appear to be moving only if it moves at least a third of a degree per second. Put another way, you will be able to see the spot only it if takes six seconds or less to move across the width of your thumb held at arm's length. Most normal perception of movement demands a frame of reference in order to sense that movement is taking place. It is possible, however, to perceive motion without movement actually taking place. When this occurs we are no longer dealing with real motion.

Apparent Motion

Objects do not have to move at all and can still be perceived as moving.

The Phi Phenomenon

Consider the following motion experiment. A few feet in front of you are two lights, A and B, separated by a short distance. These lights are alternately illuminated, each for a brief time. What you perceive will depend upon the length of the interval between the illumination of the two lights. If the interval between the illumination of A and B is less than 1/50 second, both appear to light up at the same time. If the interval is longer than 1/5 second, you will perceive what has in fact happened, A lights, and then B lights. If the interval is about 1/20 second, however, an illusion of movement is created. The light appears to move across the space from A to B.

This illusion of apparent movement is known as the **phi phenomenon** (Wertheimer, 1912). It is the basis for one of the most instructive and entertaining illusions of our time: motion pictures. Movies are a series of still pictures that are projected at a speed (24 frames per second for commercial films) that approximates the 1/20-second interval in the phi phenomenon. Films give a total illusion of movement; whatever perceptual mechanism is responsible for the phi phenomenon neatly fills in the gaps between the frames. If you have ever made films with a home movie camera at very slow speeds—say about eight frames per second—you have noticed that the movement appears to be unnatural and jerky. This is because the film, at eight frames per second, is so slow that it is on the threshold of being perceived as a succession of still pictures rather than as motion pictures.

RESEARCH

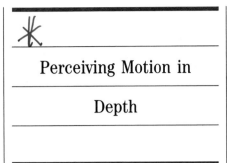

Perceiving Motion in

Depth

- The baseball zooms toward home plate at nearly 90 mph; the bat lashes out, catches the ball squarely and sends it over the left-field wall.
- The jet aircraft hurtled toward the ground; the pilot's precise touch on the controls eases the plane to a landing so gentle the passengers scarcely know they have touched ground.

Both of these highly skilled performances depend upon acute perception of the position and direction of the motion of objects in three-dimensional space. What is so remarkable is that such judgments are made by the brain on the basis of visual information that would seem to be woefully unsuited to the task: the flat two-dimensional images formed on the retina of each eye.

How can these two-dimensional retinal images provide the information necessary for the brain to make judgments about motion in three-dimensional space? Psychologists have identified several types of informational cues contained in the retinal images. They call these cues stimulus correlates of motion. The pilot, in order to achieve a safe landing, must make visual judgment of his own motion relative to a stationary world. A stimulus correlate in this instance is the flow pattern he sees as the plane

approaches the ground—the manner in which objects in his visual field appear to flow radially away from the landing point. The baseball batter, on the other hand, depends upon other stimulus correlates of motion, including the changing size of the ball, which appears to grow larger as it comes closer.

A group of researchers at Dalhousie University in Canada, David Regan, Kenneth Beverley, and Max Cynader (1979), have investigated the ways in which the stimulus correlates of motion are perceived and interpreted. Their theoretical approach derives from a widely held view that the information on the retinal image is broken down into a number of abstract features that are processed separately by different channels in the visual pathways of the brain. For example, color-processing channels detect wavelength differences in the retinal image. Other channels appear

to process form or shape. This view is based in part on direct physiological evidence showing that certain nerve cells respond selectively to various stimulus features.

Regan and his colleagues postulate the existence of two distinct channels that process information concerning motion in depth. One of these channels appears to be involved in two stimulus correlates, changing size and flow pattern, both of which are monocular—that is, available to one eye. The other channel is related to the processing of stereoscopic information requiring the use of both eyes.

Their channel hypothesis has been developed and tested using modern electronic equipment that can generate on the screen of a cathode ray tube various examples of stimulus correlates. For example, in one experiment, the researchers exposed human subjects to electronically simulated flow patterns like those seen by a pilot landing an airplane. They also exposed the subjects to a square pattern that appeared to change in size, giving the illusion of moving toward or away from this observer. Regan and his associates found the exposure to flow patterns for ten minutes made it more difficult for the subjects to see apparent changes in the size of the test square. This finding suggests that both of these stimulus correlates of motion—flow

The Autokinetic Effect

Another instance of apparent motion is the **autokinetic effect,** so named because it creates an illusion of spontaneous (auto) motion (kinetic). If you gaze at a small spot of light in a totally darkened room, the spot appears to move erratically, drifting back and forth or even swooping off in one direction. The autokinetic effect is so powerful that, in the earlier days of flying, navigational beacons and other steady light sources at night caused pilots considerable confusion.

What creates the autokinetic effect is not entirely clear. Our own eye movements probably provide at least part of the explanation (Matin & MacKinnon, 1964). But eye movements cannot be the entire explanation because the illusion abruptly disappears when the background is even faintly illuminated (Levy, 1972).

pattern and changing size—are processed by the same channel.

A separate channel investigated by Regan and his associates appears to respond only to binocular cues—information from both of the eyes. One possibility is that the brain uses the same stereoscopic mechanisms that enable us to perceive position in depth. If so, however, the brain of the baseball batter would have to create, in effect, a sequence of snapshots of the successive positions of the ball as it whizzed toward him. This would appear to be too sluggish a process to make possible the batter's split-second judgments of the ball's speed and direction of motion.

Regan and his associates postulate instead a stereoscopic channel responsive to the relative velocities of the left and right retinal images of the moving object. The accompanying figure illustrates how this might work. When the left and right retinal images of the object move in the same direction (A, B, H, I), the object being observed will pass wide of the observer's head. But when these images move in opposite directions at the same speed (E), the object will hit him directly between the eyes. Moreover, if the left eye's image moves more slowly than the right eye's image, the object will pass closer to the left eye than to the right eye, and vice versa.

The postulated channel for the de-

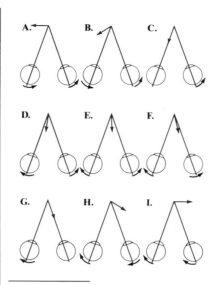

Relative velocities of the left and right retinal images of an object provide a cue to the object's direction of motion in depth. For example, if the left and right images of the object are moving in the same direction (A, B, H, I), the object will pass wide of the observer's hand, whereas if only one image is moving (C, G), the object will hit the observer directly in one eye. If the images are moving in opposite directions at the same speed (E), the object will hit the observer directly between the eyes. In addition, if the left image is moving slower than the right one (D), the object will pass closer to the left eye than to the right eye, and if the right image is moving more slowly (F), the object will pass closer to the right eye than to the left eye.

tection of the direction of motion in depth appears to be different from the mechanisms that detect the position of objects in depth. By recording

the electrical activity in single nerve cells in the visual cortex of cats, the researchers found cells that responded to the direction of motion in depth, but not to simple position in depth. Some neurons fired strongest in response to trajectories directed straight at the animal's head.

Which of the channels—changing size and flow pattern or stereoscopic motion—provides the more effective means of perceiving motion in depth? The researchers found that this depended in part on the object's velocity and the duration of the observer's sight of the object. The changing-size channel appeared to be more effective for a slowly moving object glimpsed for only 0.2 second. The stereoscopic motion channel was more effective for a rapidly moving object seen for about a second. In addition, the researchers found that relative effectiveness varied with the individual. In some people, for example, the stereoscopic channel appears to play little role in perception of motion in depth.

This finding may help explain the results of an experiment in which pilots landing jet aircraft were suddenly deprived of the vision of one eye. There was surprisingly little loss in landing performance, suggesting that these pilots may rely primarily on the monocular channel—changing size and flow pattern—rather than the stereoscopic mechanism. ■

Corollary Discharge

You can create the perception of apparent motion by placing your finger at the corner of your eye and then gently tapping it. As you can see, the world appears to jump back and forth. If you stop to think about it, this is remarkable: we are constantly moving our heads or eyes, but our movement does not make the scenes in front of us jump back and forth.

Researchers believe the reason for this lack of perceived motion lies in a hypothetical neural event they have labeled the **corollary discharge** (von Holst & Mittelstadt, 1950; von Holst, 1954). When the brain gives the command for the eyes to move, a second signal is also sent as a corollary of that command. The second signal, or corollary discharge, travels to some way station on the visual pathways within the brain and, in effect, tells the perceptual mechanisms to compensate for the fact that the image on the retina will be moving. Thus, when our eyes move we perceive no motion. By this reasoning we can understand why the world appears to jump back and forth when we jiggle the eye with a finger. There is no corollary discharge to register the intention to move the eye and prepare the brain to compensate; hence movement on the retina is perceived as real motion.

Let us imagine an interesting variation of this process involving the corollary discharge. Suppose you were to command your eyes to move but, for some reason, they failed to do so. The corollary discharge would be given in the brain, setting up the expectation of an eye movement, but there would be no motion across the retina. This very scenario was undertaken recently in an experiment carried out by a vision researcher who served as his own subject. (Stevens et al., 1976). To prevent his eyes from moving on command, he had himself paralyzed by an injection of a drug. (Because this drug also abolished normal respiratory movement of the chest, he had to be artificially respirated.) When the researcher attempted to move his eyes, they were paralyzed, and would not move. But in the process of his willing the eyes to move, the corollary discharge presumably was given in the brain.

In this experiment it was found that when the eyes were partially paralyzed, the visual world indeed appeared to jump if the subject attempted to move the eyes. But when the paralysis was complete, no apparent movement was seen. It seems possible that the jumping of the visual world when the eyes were partially paralyzed may have been an illusion caused by the corollary discharge.

Development of Visual Perception

Several central questions in the study of perception concern its development. How much of human perception is innate? How much must be learned? Are the mechanisms for such perceptions as form, depth, and motion present in infancy or are learning and experience necessary for their operation? There are no simple answers to these questions but, as we will see, evidence has been accumulated in support of both innate and learned factors: some mechanisms of perception appear to be innate, while early experience plays a critical role in the normal development of other functions.

We know, for example, that blind people whose vision has been restored have a great deal of trouble learning to interpret what they see. Cataracts are opacities in the lens, and they can black all patterned light to the retina, resulting in blindness. Now cataracts are routinely removed surgically, even in children. When cataract surgery was first introduced, adults who had been functionally blind all of their lives experienced normal retinal images for the first time. Some of these adults were never able to develop normal vision. For example, if they could discriminate a given triangle from a circle, they could not discriminate the two objects when the triangle was rotated several degrees. Such evidence suggests that there are periods early in life that are critical for learning various aspects of visual perception.

In an influential book, *The Organization of Behavior*, D. O. Hebb (1949) concluded as a result of experiments with the formerly blind that there are two categories of visual skills: **unity** and **identity.** Hebb used the term *unity* to describe the ability to detect the presence of an object—that is, to separate an object from its background. Identity goes further and requires the ability to distinguish classes of objects—for example, a triangle from a circle. Hebb concluded that unity is innate, while identity requires learning or experience. The acquisition of the perceptual skills of identity in infants may be similar to the process the resighted people went through. Let us look at some of the experiments that have helped us to understand the role of experience in vision.

Visual Perception in Infants

If newborn infants demonstrate the ability to perceive form, depth, and motion, then clearly these abilities are innate. But before perceptual ability in infants can be studied, a formidable hurdle must be overcome. The testing of visual functions in humans typically requires verbal responses, and infants cannot talk.

Robert Fantz (1961) invented a simple but highly effective method for determining what visual stimulus an infant prefers (see Figure 4.20). The baby is placed in a crib and then a pair of targets are placed on the ceiling above the baby—one to the left, the other to the right. The researcher watches from a chamber behind the targets to see if the baby turns its eyes or head to look at one of the two targets. As a safeguard against simple position preference on the part of the baby, the left-right position of the two targets is changed from time to time. The situation also is varied so that the researcher does not know which target is on the left and which is on the right; the researcher sees only the infant's face. Time spent staring at each stimulus is the measure for degree of preference.

Fantz's apparatus has given psychologists reliable methods for studying such aspects of visual learning as visual acuity and face preference.

Visual Acuity

The Fantz preferential looking method can be used to study several aspects of perception. For example, it can be employed to test a child's **visual acuity**—the ability to resolve fine detail. Through this method, it has been determined that young infants will look at a striped target in preference to a gray card. When the stripes are very narrow, however, they are beyond visual acuity of the infant; the child cannot distinguish them from a neutral gray. By presenting targets of varying stripe widths and noting the child's preference, researchers can calculate a rough measure of the child's visual acuity. With this method, several researchers, including Janette Atkinson and Oliver and Fleur Braddick (1974) and Davida Teller (Teller, Morse, Borton, & Regal, 1974), have found that newborn infants have only about one-tenth of the visual acuity of adults. Visual acuity improves gradually in the first few months of life and is essentially normal, at nearly adult level, by one year of age.

Face Preference

One of the most fascinating findings achieved through the Fantz method was that very young infants display a marked preference for the human face. Fantz presented the infants with a sketch of a face on one target and, as the other target, either a figure with facial features drawn in a scrambled pattern or two solid patches of color separated by a straight line (see Figure 4.21). Even infants as young as four days showed a preference for looking at the sketch of a real face. This tendency is probably based on a preference for certain visual components that comprise a human face such as curved rather than straight contours (Fantz, 1970). This finding suggests that there is an innate predisposition to look at facelike forms that requires no learning.

Directional Vision

One of the simplest of visual functions is **directional vision,** the ability to determine accurately the direction of a stimulus. If someone holds a light above or below your eyes or to the left or to the right, you can describe its location and point to it accurately. Is this ability innate or learned?

At the turn of the twentieth century, a German physician named Walter Schlodtmann set out to answer that question in a classically simple experiment

Figure 4.20

Visual preference in infants is demonstrated by the use of equipment originally designed by Robert Fantz.

Figure 4.21

Infants using Fantz's apparatus looked at the simple face longer than they looked at the design with scrambled facial features.

Figure 4.22

The "visual cliff," actually a solid glass surface, reveals a checked material that cascades to the floor. When infants of six months and older were placed on the center board, they seldom ventured onto the "cliff" side, even when coaxed.

(1902). Schlodtmann went to a home for blind children in Germany. He sought children who had been blind from birth and thus never had experienced normal patterned light but who had at least one eye with a retina that was functional. Cataracts or corneal irregularities allowed light to pass, but not patterned light. Schlodtmann found three such children, aged 11, 14, and 18, and tested them for directional vision. His three subjects were totally incapable of pointing to the direction of a window in daylight or a lamp in darkness; when a bright beam of light was shone at their faces, they were aware of the light but could not localize its position.

Then Schlodtmann made use of a simple technique that you can try on yourself. If you gently push at the outer corner of your eye with a pencil eraser, you will see a diffuse flash of grayish light. (Because the optics of the eye are inverted, pressure on the lower point of the eye produces light at the top of the visual field.) The flash of light is called a **phosphene,** and it occurs because the pressure activates cells in the retina.

Schlodtmann tested the three blind children for the presence of pressure phosphenes by gently pushing with a blunt probe on the corner of the eye. He asked each child to point to where the sensation of light seemed to come from. In all three cases, the children were able accurately to localize the phosphenes; they reported that the apparent light source was a direction opposite to that from which the retina had been stimulated. Thus, through this novel method, the children demonstrated evidence of directional vision.

Because these children had never experienced patterned light, Schlodtmann concluded that directional vision must be an innate capacity genetically wired into our perceptual apparatus.

Perception of Depth: The Visual Cliff

Among the most ingenious experiments in the study of perceptual development are those conducted by Eleanor J. Gibson and her collaborator Richard Walk (1960). The aim of these experiments was to study depth perception in infants. They grew out of some thoughts Gibson had one day while enjoying a picnic on the rim of the Grand Canyon. Peering over the rim, she wondered whether a young baby could perceive the perilous depths and avoid crawling off.

Back in the laboratory, she and Walk designed a kind of miniature Grand Canyon, which they called the **visual cliff** (see Figure 4.22). A board is placed in the middle of a large sheet of heavy transparent glass. At one side of the board is a covering of checkerboard material that is mounted practically flush with the underside of the glass. At the other side of the board the same material is placed at a depth of a foot or more below the glass. To an adult standing on the center board, this latter side has the appearance of a small cliff.

When infants of six months and older were placed on the center board, they rarely ventured onto the cliff side of the board, even when the mother coaxed them with rattles. It was not a question of leaving the board; three fourths of the children who were tested crawled off the board but nearly always toward the "shallow" side.

Which of the possible depth cues—monocular or binocular—enable young beings to perceive the visual cliff? In a number of visual cliff experiments in which binocular cues were eliminated and textural cues were neutralized, both human infants and animals, permanently and temporarily monocular, behaved as did binocular subjects even when using only one eye: they avoided the "deep" side of the cliff. From these experiments, Gibson and Walk concluded that motion parallax is an adequate cue for depth perception.

Because six-month-olds already have considerable visual experience, these experiments do not necessarily establish that depth perception is innate. However, experiments with very young animals—chicks, goats, and kittens—on the visual cliff substantially bolster the argument that these depth perception mech-

CHAPTER 4 PERCEPTION

anisms are inborn. For example, newly hatched chicks never hopped off the board onto the deep side of the cliff. A one-day-old goat, when placed on the deep side, extended its forelegs in a defensive posture and, when it saw the shallow side, leaped onto it. Young kittens avoided the cliff side even when they had been raised in the dark and thus lacked any visual experience. In short, several different animals, and probably people, appear to possess innate mechanisms that enable them to discriminate depth.

Learning and Visual Perception

The evidence presented thus far does little to support contentions that the perceptual world of the infant is, as William James described it nearly a century ago, "a booming, buzzing confusion." To the contrary, we have seen aspects of a remarkable orderliness in the development of perception. Directional vision and an apparent preference for the human face seem present from birth. Depth perception probably develops over the first ten months of life.

Feature Detectors

Another dramatic instance of the brain's **plasticity**—that is, its capacity for modification through experience—has been demonstrated in experiments showing changes in the response properties of cells in the visual cortex. These cells are the feature detectors, described earlier, that respond to small targets presented at various orientations in the visual field.

Helmut Hirsch and Nico Spinelli (1970) raised kittens with goggles that presented one eye with only vertical stripes and the other with only horizontal stripes. The kittens later were tested by placing microelectrodes near individual cells of the visual cortex. Cells activated from the eye that had been exposed to vertical stripes responded mostly or only to vertical bars; similarly those activated from the eye exposed to horizontal stripes responded mostly or only to horizontal bars.

These experiments suggested that the response properties of the feature detectors are shaped by interaction with the environment. Kittens, and presumably humans, deprived of the experience of vertical or horizontal stripes during a critical period (apparently the first four months of life in kittens) fail to develop fully normal perception of form.

Binocular Vision

There is also an early period that is critical for development of binocular vision. This has been established in recent animal experiments that permit normal vision experience for each eye but not for simultaneous use of the two eyes. Researchers have found that if one of the extraocular muscles of a kitten is cut so as to produce a misalignment of the eyes, subsequent testing shows a marked reduction in the number of cortical cells that can be activated from either eye (Hubel & Wiesel, 1965). Cells in the visual cortex of the brain can be activated by one eye or the other, but rarely by both.

A similar deficit has been demonstrated in animal experiments in which binocular fusion of the images from both eyes is prevented optically (Van Sluyters & Levitt, 1980). For example, a prism fixed over one eye prevents the placement of that eye in ways that normally would allow fusion of the images in the two eyes. Animals in these experiments are analogous to children who are born with an eye that deviates in direction, a condition called **strabismus** or "crossed eyes." Although surgery can correct the extraocular muscle imbalance, these children may fail to develop normal binocular vision. In order to perceive depth, they must depend solely upon monocular cues (such as motion parallax) available to each of the eyes.

The critical period for the development of binocular vision in cats seems to occur during the first few months of life. During that period normal binocular connections are made from eye to brain. In normal circumstances, when the eyes are correctly aligned, an orderly and roughly equal division of inputs from each eye make connection to the cortex. But without binocular experience, the fibers representing one eye or the other lose out. Normal binocular vision fails to develop.

Adaptability of Visual Perception

The role of learning in modifying the visual perception mechanisms is not limited to critical periods early in development. That plasticity is possible even in adults has been shown in experiments involving the vestibuloocular reflex. This reflex, as we saw in chapter 3, originates in the three semicircular canals of the inner ear, which are vital to our sense of position, and serves the important function of stabilizing our body and eyes in space.

The usefulness of the vestibuloocular reflex is illustrated in the following example. If you move this page of text back and forth rapidly while keeping your head still, you will not be able to read the words. If, however, you move your head back and forth rapidly instead of the book, you are able to read the text due to the vestibuloocular reflex. The semicircular canals in the inner ear register the position of your head as it moves and automatically signal the muscles controlling the position of your eyes. This signal causes the eyes to move an equivalent distance in the opposite direction. As a result, your eyes stay lined up on the text even though your head is moving.

Now let us suppose you are wearing an optical device that distorts the visual world—say, a pair of spectacles that shrinks the size of everything you see by half. Thus, if you were to move your eyes or head 6 degrees, the world would appear to move only 3 degrees. The vestibuloocular reflex would overcompensate. For a move of the head 6 degrees to the right, the reflex would move the eyes 6 degrees to the left—twice as much compensation as would be needed to stabilize the visual world, which has moved only 3 degrees. Hence, the eyes would overshoot the target.

What happens if you wear these spectacles for several days? Fred Miles and his collaborators found in monkeys that the strength of the vestibuloocular reflex decreased steadily from day to day until it nearly adjusted to the new magnification of the visual world. Similarly, when monkeys wore lenses that magnified the visual world, the reflex at first underestimated the amount of correction needed and then increased after a few days to almost adapt to the new magnification (Miles & Eighmy, 1980).

Studies with human subjects indicate that the vestibuloocular reflex can adapt to even more severe rearrangements of the visual world. G. Melvill Jones and his associates wore special prisms that reversed the world (Gonshor and Melvill Jones, 1976). They wore these for 2 to 27 days and tested the reflex periodically. As could be expected, at first the reflex went in a direction that was maladaptive for perception through reversing prisms. Because the prisms reversed the world, the subjects had to turn their heads to the right to look at things that were actually to their left. The vestibuloocular reflex, as usual, attempted to compensate for the rightward movement of the head by moving the eyes to the left. Ordinarily, this would stabilize the eyes in space. Because of the reversing prisms, however, the apparent movement of the world on the retina increased. Jones and his colleagues found that, over time, the vestibuloocular reflex and the disconcerting perception of motion slowly weakened. In fact, after a week or so, the direction of the reflex actually changed. Now a movement of the head to the right would cause a weak tendency for the eyes to move to the right. Because the visual world was reversed this is a proper adaptation.

Precisely how this remarkable adaptation takes place in the brain is not yet clear. But its occurrence in a system formerly thought to be "hard-wired"—that is, immutably fixed at birth—points to the possibility that other instances of perceptual plasticity may occur not only in infancy but also over the entire life span.

Auditory Perception

Much of what we know about perception is really about one type of perception—visual. Our perception of sound is less clearly understood. If you look at a picture on the wall, your perceptual mechanisms instantly provide a great deal of information without taking much time to analyze it. By contrast, even the simplest auditory perceptions—such as hearing a friend say your name or recognizing a short melody on the harmonica—require the analysis of sequential sensory information.

Neural Processing of Sound

As we saw in chapter 3, the auditory structures in the inner ear and the pathways leading into the brain are characterized by tonotopic organization. Neighboring cells of the cochlear nucleus are most sensitive to similar frequencies, and there is an orderly shift from low to high tones at different positions. This tonotopic organization appears to be preserved in the pathways leading to the auditory cortex of the brain. At these higher stations, however, the properties of auditory cells are far more complex and far more difficult to discern. Let us look at research concerning two different aspects of the neural processing of sound.

The Role of the Cortex

Although it is assumed that hearing depends on processing within the auditory cortex, there are surprisingly few data on the precise cortical functions. Cortical injuries often lead to profound disorders of language but seldom to deafness.

One likely role of the auditory cortex has been suggested by the experiment of Irving Diamond and William D. Neff (1957). Cats were trained to respond differently to tones of two different frequencies and to distinguish between two simple melodic sequences of three notes. Then the auditory cortex on both sides of each cat's brain was removed surgically. Diamond and Neff found that the cats were able to relearn the frequency discrimination task, but the ability to detect the sequence of notes was permanently lost. From this result it seems that the auditory cortex is critical for perceiving or learning sequences of tones, but that simple aspects of hearing can be handled by subcortical auditory structures.

Directional Hearing

We perceive not only the presence of a sound but also the direction from which it comes. This ability depends upon neural processing of differences in intensity, in time of arrival, or in phase of the sound that are registered at the two ears. At high frequencies the intensity of the sound at the two ears differs because the head acts as a kind of "sound shadow." At low frequencies, where the head shadows the sound much less, a cue for direction is the disparity in time of arrival of the sound at the two ears.

FOCUS

The Study of ESP

In the late 1920s, a young Duke University researcher, Joseph Banks Rhine, set out to study a phenomenon beside which even the mysteries of normal sensory perception seemed quite pale. Rhine wanted to investigate evidence of what he called extrasensory perception (ESP)—perception that is said to occur independently of the known senses. Reports of people capable of "mind reading" and possessing other paranormal abilities have persisted throughout history, but Rhine pioneered in the attempt to study such matters in the laboratory using the scientific method.

Rhine's basic method was simple. He recruited Duke students and faculty members as his subjects and asked them to guess the symbols contained in a special deck of cards. The deck consisted of 25 Zener cards, each imprinted with one of five symbols—square, wavy parallel lines, circle, star, and cross—as in the figure shown here. In the test for telepathy (mind-to-mind communication), the subject attempted to perceive the identity of the card, which was known only to the experimenter. In the test for clairvoyance (direct extrasensory perception of an object or event), the subject sought to identify the card, which was not known to the experimenter. And in the test for precognition (perception of the future), the subject tried to predict accurately the order the cards would take after they had been shuffled.

To these areas of ESP investigation, Rhine later added experiments for psychokinesis—that is, influence over external matter through the force of mind. In the psychokinesis experiments, subjects were asked to attempt mental influence over the outcome of rolling dice. ESP and psychokinesis, taken together, are now sometimes referred to as psi—from the twenty-third letter of the Greek alphabet. People who study psi and other paranormal phenomena such as psychic healing and out-of-body experiences are called parapsychologists—literally "beyond psychologists."

In assessing the results of their experiments, Rhine and other psi researchers relied on statistical measures widely used in psychology and other experimental sciences. Because the Zener deck contains 5 suits of 5 cards each, a subject can be expected by mere chance to score, on the average, 5 correct guesses in a run through the 25-card deck. The laws of probability indicate that results will occasionally exceed chance levels—for example, 9 hits in a 25-card run—which by itself does not indicate the presence of ESP, but merely a rare finding that can be expected to happen a few times over many experimental trials.

In 1935 Rhine published the results of his early experiments in clairvoyance and telepathy. He reported that a number of subjects had scored significantly above chance, including one who, in long-distance telepathy tests, had achieved odds against chance of an astronomical number consisting of 10 followed by 22 zeros against 1. Since that first monograph, positive results of thousands of experiments in ESP and psychokinesis have been published. The Zener cards and dice have been supplanted by automated equipment such as the random number generator, which presents experimental targets on the basis of the unpredictable decay of radioactive nuclei.

In addition to establishing to their own satisfaction that ESP and psychokinesis exist, parapsychologists have described a number of characteristics of the various psi phenomena. One is the decline effect (the tendency of subjects to score significantly higher early in the experiment), an effect attributed to fluctuations in mood and interest. Another is the sheep-goat effect—the tendency for subjects who believe in ESP to go along with the experiments like sheep and achieve higher scores than the goats, who are skeptical and balk at demonstrating ESP.

Recent work by Eric Knudsen and Masakazu Konishi (1978) suggests that some animals have a brain structure that is specially organized for representing directional sound. In the midbrain of the owl, Knudsen and Konishi found nerve cells that appear to form a kind of sound map of the auditory world with neighboring points in this structure responding to neighboring regions in the auditory space.

Two phenomena of auditory perception—auditory masking and selective attention—are of special interest. They help explain why we sometimes hear a pattern of sounds and at other times fail to do so.

Despite a large accumulation of experimental data in support of ESP and despite widespread popular interest, most psychologists and other scientists remain skeptical. (In a recent survey of scientists, only 9 percent accepted ESP as "established fact," although 45 percent described it as "a likely possibility.") Parapsychologists have largely been excluded from the mainstream of science, and their findings have been ignored by the leading journals. Not until 1969 was the Parapsychological Association accepted for membership by the prestigious American Association for the Advancement of Science. Only a handful of American universities have funded psi research or given faculty status to parapsychologists. Even Duke University, where ESP research began, withdrew its support after J. B. Rhine's retirement in 1965.

Why does science continue to shun the study of ESP? One reason is that mind reading and clairvoyance smack of the occult, of supernatural phenomena that science, by definition, seeks to reduce to the known, to natural laws; ESP, by definition, depends upon the unknown. In fact, ESP is assumed to have properties that are inconsistent with our knowledge of energy. For example, ESP researchers assert that it does not obey the inverse-square law: they say that ESP does not typically improve when a subject moves closer to a purported transmission source.

Another reason for skepticism fo-

The five symbols that appear on the Zener cards most commonly used in ESP research. Each card has a distinctive pattern.

cuses on methodology of ESP research. It is difficult to develop appropriate control groups for experiments because researchers do not know what to control. The case has been well summarized by a leading critic, the British psychologist C. E. M. Hansel, in his book *ESP and Parapsychology* (1979). Hansel suggests that because negative data from ESP experiments are seldom reported, overall statistical results are biased. He also suggests that slipshod experimental controls and sensory cues can account for many of the positive results: for example, the Zener cards used in Rhine's early work had a flaw that permitted them to be read from the back under certain kinds of illumination. When controls are tightened up, Hansel says, positive results typically decline.

Hansel also points to the difficulty in replicating ESP experiments. Disinterested researchers often have been unable to replicate the results of others and, indeed, even Rhine

and other ESP enthusiasts often could not replicate their own results. In experimental science, successful replication is essential in order to rule out the possibility of error or fraud. This latter possibility, fraud or its suspicion, long has haunted parapsychology. Although no branch of science is immune from unethical researchers who tamper with evidence or fabricate data, parapsychology is particularly vulnerable because of its admitted difficulty in reliably replicating experimental results. Although Rhine himself was virtually above suspicion, one of his trusted associates was caught tampering with the automated apparatus in order to produce positive results in a psychokinesis experiment. (Other parapsychologists brought the fraud to light.)

Beyond the issues of methodology and possible fraud, however, there remains a further barrier to acceptance of psi studies by the mainstream of science. Parapsychologists have failed to develop plausible theories to account for phenomena that seem so implausible and so incompatible with our current knowledge of both physics and perception. Without such theories, the study of ESP is likely to remain, as one critic has described its current status, "a no-man's-land between the lunatic fringe on the one hand and the academically unorthodox on the other." ■

Auditory Masking

If you are trying to listen to music and a fire engine happens to race by your window, you may fail to hear the music. This is an instance of **auditory masking.** Auditory masking is not simply a matter of one sound's drowning out another because of its intensity. It occurs most strongly for tones whose frequencies are close to the one you are attempting to listen to. Tones that are more distant in frequency fail to mask. For any given frequency, there appears to be a **critical band** of nearby frequencies capable of masking it.

It has been suggested that the concept of critical bands may help account for our perception of whether music sounds dissonant, where the notes when simultaneously played sound "wrong" together. For example, some musical intervals might sound dissonant because they lie within the critical band in which one tone masks the other; a major third may sound harmonious because it is outside the critical band for auditory masking.

Selective Attention

What we hear often depends upon what we pay attention to. Suppose, for example, you are at a party in a large crowded room, and a dozen or more people are talking. At first, all you hear is a low, buzzing noise. Now a friend with whom you want to talk begins to speak. Despite all of the other noises, you can hear and understand what your friend is saying. This ability to track someone's voice in a crowded, noisy room has been called the **cocktail party effect.**

Psychologists study selective attention in a laboratory situation that simulates the cocktail party setting. In a listening experiment, the subject wears earphones and is presented with two separate spoken tape-recorded messages, one to each ear. The subject is asked to attend to one of the messages. Typically, subjects have no difficulty following the attended message; they can even repeat the words as they listen despite the fact that a second message is droning on in the other ear. But subjects understand virtually nothing of the second message; they are typically unaware of it even if the voice suddenly switches from English to another language such as German.

This research suggests that people usually cannot listen to more than one conversation at once. It is as if somewhere in the central nervous system a selective filter tunes in the message we are paying attention to and tunes out all other auditory stimuli. Certain messages can break through this hypothetical filter, however, causing us to switch channels. Dichotic listening experiments have established what cocktail party guests long have known: a subject fully occupied listening to a message in one ear will suddenly hear what's happening in the other ear if the words carry an unusual significance (such as the subject's own name).

The term cocktail party effect *has been given to the ability to track individual voices in a crowded, noisy room.*

Summary

1. Our senses receive and code stimuli such as sound and light waves. Perception is the transformation of the evidence of our senses into mental representations. Perceptions are interpretations made in the light of existing or preconceived notions that may be independent of incoming sensory data. Vision requires an enormous amount of registration, analysis, sorting, filtering, and comparing by our perceptual mechanisms—first in the eye itself, but chiefly at centers within the brain.

2. A basic understanding of perceptual adaptation, visual capture, and perceptual constancy helps in understanding how we perceive ourselves and the world around us. Perceptual adaptation is the ability to compensate for an artificially displaced visual field. Visual capture refers to the tendency of vision to dominate input from the other senses. Perceptual constancy is the stability of the shape, size, brightness, and color of subjects in our visual fields; we recognize the same objects at a variety of angles, at various distances, and under different kinds of light.

3. Objects maintain their apparent constancy of shape despite differences in the point from which we view them. Size constancy is the tendency of the perceptual apparatus to take into account the distance of an object in judging

its size. Brightness constancy refers to the tendency of our perceptions of an object's brightness to remain stable over a wide range of illumination. Objects have color constancy if we are able to see the object's surroundings—that is, if we have references for perceiving an object's hue.

4. The shape and form of an object tend to stand out against a background. In a differentiated visual field, that part appearing as a distinct, delineated shape is the figure; the remainder is the ground. This is called the figure-ground differentiation. Among the perceptions by which we organize a visual field into figure and ground are closure, continuity, similarity, and proximity.

5. The stimulus of light is processed and transformed into recognizable forms by both the receptors in our eyes and by the nerve cells of the visual cortex. These latter cells have been called feature detectors. Feature detectors—simple, complex, and hypercomplex—appear to detect features that are linear in nature. It is postulated that some neural mechanism in the brain compares complex features with a stored memory of patterns. Visual synthesis likely takes place in a part of the temporal lobe.

6. We perceive depth through monocular cues that require the use of only one eye and through binocular cues that require the use of both eyes. Among the monocular cues for depth perception are perspective, overlap, relative size, texture, and motion parallax. Binocular cues include convergence and stereoscopic vision.

7. Perception of slow motion normally demands a frame of reference in order to sense that motion is taking place; however, it is possible to perceive motion without movement actually taking place. The phi phenomenon and autokinetic effect are examples of apparent motion.

8. Some mechanisms of perception appear to be innate, while early experience plays a critical role in the normal development of other functions. Visual acuity, a preference for faces, and directional vision all seem to be present at birth. It seems likely that some depth perception mechanisms are inborn.

9. Some aspects of perception do not seem to be innate; they develop only with learning and experience. The brain's plasticity—its capacity for modification through experience—has been demonstrated in experiments showing changes in the response properties of the feature detectors in the visual cortex. In cats, normal binocular vision seems to develop during the first few months of life. Experiments have shown that even adults can adapt seemingly hardwired mechanisms, such as the vestibuloocular relfex, which is vital to the sense of position and for stabilizing the body and the eyes. Other instances of perceptual plasticity may occur over the entire life span.

10. Auditory perception requires the analysis of sequential sensory information. Animal research indicates that neural processing in the auditory cortex is necessary for perceiving sequences of tones; however, simple aspects of hearing can be handled by subcortical auditory structures. Directional hearing depends upon neural processing of differences in intensity, in time of arrival, or in phase of sound that are registered at the two ears.

11. Auditory masking, the blocking of one of two sounds, occurs most frequently when the frequencies of the conflicting sounds are close. Auditory and visual perception are selective; we are able to choose between conflicting stimuli by a process of selective attention.

RESEARCH: Highly skilled behavior such as that involved in landing an aircraft depends upon the perception of position and direction of moving objects in three-dimensional space. David Regan and his colleagues have proposed the channel hypothesis to explain how two-dimensional retinal images provide the brain with the correct information needed to make decisions about movement in three-dimensional space. Regan proposed two different channels: one that processes monocular cues regarding changes in object size and flow pattern and the second that processes binocular information regarding stereoscopic cues. The stereoscopic channel appears to be sensitive to changes in the relative velocity of objects while the monocular channel appears to be sensitive to the distance between the observer and the target stimulus.

FOCUS: Despite Joseph Banks Rhine's attempt to establish ESP and other paranormal phenomena as legitimate topics for scientific inquiry, most psychologists do not take such research seriously. Problems with methodology and replication of experiment results, its association with the occult, and the fact that ESP is assumed to have properties inconsistent with natural law, represent some of the barriers to recognizing ESP and related phenomena as suitable topics for psychological inquiry.

CHAPTER

5

Consciousness

American psychologist William James

"Our normal waking consciousness, rational consciousness as we call it, is but one special type of consciousness, whilst all about it, parted from it by the filmiest of screens, there lie potential forms of consciousness entirely different. We may go through life without suspecting their existence; but apply the requisite stimulus, and at a touch they are there in all their completeness. . . . No account of the universe in its totality can be final which leaves these other forms of consciousness quite disregarded . . . they forbid a premature closing of our accounts with reality."

These words, which sound so contemporary, were written more than 80 years ago by the American psychologist William James and published in 1900 in his *The Varieties of Religious Experience*. James was describing his own introspective experiences after experimenting with nitrous oxide, the so-called laughing gas then used by dentists and surgeons as an anesthetic. In those days the study of consciousness was a principal focus of the new science of psychology. But the study of what goes on in people's minds soon proved to be too subjective for most practitioners of psychology; it was difficult to measure and verify. Psychology was a latecomer to the family of scientific disciplines and, after the turn of the century, psychologists increasingly sought to emulate the apparent methodological purity of physics and chemistry by emphasizing quantitative, objective measurements of behavior. Through much of this century, subjects such as sleep and dreams, hypnosis, meditations, and drug-induced states were relegated to abnormal psychology or simply regarded as irrelevant to science.

Only in recent years has the study of consciousness begun to reenter the mainstream of psychology and employ standard experimental procedures. The resurgence of interest stems partly from the growth of cognitive psychology, but it also results from the groundswell that has arisen in the general culture, beginning largely with the youth of the 1960s who turned inward in search of what James described as those "potential forms of consciousness entirely different."

Normal Versus Altered States of Consciousness

Some aspects of altered states are frequently present in normal waking consciousness.

Psychologists describe the Jamesian "forms of consciousness" as **states of consciousness.** These states may be seen as sets of structural conditions that are distinct from the actual content of consciousness. Structure denotes the major features that influence the ways in which we experience ourselves or the world; that is, different patterns of mental functioning that affect the way a person perceives, understands, or thinks about internal and external events. Content is the experience itself. For example, imagine that a soldier on night guard duty at the front line hears a rustle in the bushes outside the camp. His state of consciousness—in this case, his vigilance—determines the content of his consciousness; he responds very differently than he would on hearing the same sound while sunbathing at the same spot in peacetime. His state of consciousness greatly influences his consciousness in two different domains—the cognitive (how he solves problems) and the affective (how he responds emotionally).

Another common distinction differentiates normal states from **altered states of consciousness** (ASC). The soldier's high vigilance might be described as a **normal waking state of consciousness;** that is, maintaining maximum alertness to the external environment is necessary for survival. By contrast, altered states are variously typified by such characteristics as lack of self-awareness, hallucination, altered time perception, and loss of contact with present reality (Tart, 1975).

The distinction between normal and altered states of consciousness implies that altered states are abnormal. It suggests that the alert, rational mode of experiencing the world is normal while all other states of consciousness are abnormal. In fact, some aspects of altered states are frequently present in the normal waking consciousness of quite normal people. Ronald Shor (1960) found in a group of college students that hallucinations (perceptions of scenes that do not exist) and other phenomena similar to those thought to be characteristic of altered states of consciousness, were rather common in ordinary life. In a recent study, Kenneth Pope and Jerome Singer (1980) asked subjects to report ongoing mental experiences while the subjects were "sitting and doing nothing." The results contrasted sharply with the picture of purposeful mental activities such as reacting to the present environment, solving problems, making plans, and generally thinking rationally, all of which are typically associated with normal waking consciousness. Most of the content of consciousness, it was found, consisted of a kaleidoscope of chaotic imagery, including fantasy, the reliving of past experiences, and the like. Indeed, excerpts from the subjects' reports resembled fiction's stream-of-consciousness technique.

"Water and scotch," reported one subject, "scotch with water, with ice, with uh soda, with soda on the side, uh wine, beer, uh vomit, nausea, headaches, uhm aspirin. No-doz, Tums, uh Tums, little metal cases with railroad pictures on them and uh the trains into clouds of smoke and dust and the paintings in the Fogg museum and fog also, and uhm California and uhm California and uhm P. G. Wodehouse in Jeeves and Little Orphan Annie" (Pope & Singer, 1980).

The occurrence of such phenomena in normal people leading normal lives has led to the suggestion that the terminology be changed. It has been suggested that instead of referring to altered states and normal waking consciousness, we should use the term **alternate states** to cover all forms of consciousness. This change has not yet been generally adopted.

By any name, altered states are difficult to define, and there is, as yet, not general agreement on what constitutes an altered state. In this chapter we will consider two major and distinct altered states, sleeping and dreaming, which can be defined both in terms of subjective experience and physiological measurement, along with four other areas of vital interest to the study of consciousness: biofeedback, meditation, hypnosis, and drug-induced states. Finally, we shall see that human consciousness is enriched by a great variety of unusual, or anomalous phenomena that resemble certain aspects of altered states.

(A) French philosopher René Descartes; (B) A woodcut of Descartes's view of the mechanical nature of the nervous system. Light transmits images to the retinas of the eyes, stimulating animal spirit to activate the teardrop pineal gland. It then energizes nerves in the arm to produce movement.

Neural Approaches to Consciousness

The study of altered states of consciousness is of particular interest to neuroscientists. Altered states provide important models for investigating the complex and elusive relationships between mind and brain—the so-called mind-body problem, which has baffled philosophers and scientists for many centuries.

The Mind-Body Problem

The **mind-body problem** (or the mind-brain problem) is the difficult question of how the mind affects the behavior of the body and how the body affects the behavior of the mind. René Descartes, the French philosopher, believed that the mind and body are closely related and interact with each other (Descartes, 1862/1911). Three centuries later, Descartes' statement is just about as accurate a one as can be made.

Scientists prefer to study what can be measured, and the chemical and electrical workings of the brain can be, more and more, precisely observed. The workings of the mind—the individual consciousness and personality that we each possess—still cannot be tracked in as accurate a fashion as researchers would want.

In chapter 2 the findings of Paul Broca and of Gustav Fritsch and Eduard Hitzig were described. Broca located the speech center in the left half of a patient's brain. Fritsch and Hitzig made some of the first findings about the effect of electricity on brain functions. In the years that followed (roughly the end of the nineteenth century onward), scientists were torn between the view that either specific brain sites for each and every behavior existed or that the entire brain functioned in an equivalent and complex way to cause behavior. The truth lies somewhere between these two views.

Because it is not conceivable to most of us how mental events could be reduced to the physical-chemical processes with which scientists deal, science cannot lay claim to being able to "solve" the mind-body problem. What can be done is to look for correlations between subjective experience and physiological variables and then attempt, as far as possible, to unravel the tangled skein of cause and effect. In this pragmatic fashion we may learn to understand more and more of the ways in which mind and body influence each other, an attainable goal of immense practical importance in relation to psychosomatic (the combination of psychological and physical) health. It is generally accepted in this regard that emotional factors such as stress can exert a profound influence upon our physical condition and precipitate serious problems such as heart disease.

A key tenet of the neural sciences is that all conscious experiences depend upon activity in the brain, in particular, in the cerebral cortex. It is in the cortex, with its many folded convolutions multiplying the available surface area of the brain, that the human nervous system reaches its highest level of development. Here too, in the cortex, electrical stimulation of the temporal lobe can evoke conscious experiences. Wilder Penfield was able to stimulate long-forgotten memories in the exposed brains of neurosurgical patients who relived events out of the past while on the operating table (Penfield & Roberts, 1959).

Neurophysiology

For evidence of the biological events that underlie conscious experience, we must look to the two major scientific disciplines involved in the study of the brain, neurochemistry and neurophysiology. Later in this chapter, in the discussion of drug-induced states of consciousness, we will describe some of the most recent findings about the brain's chemistry. Here, however, let us focus on neurophysiology.

Localization

The methods of neurophysiology have demonstrated a great deal about the control of specific behavioral functions by specific areas of the brain. One area of the cortex, for example, controls voluntary movement; another mediates vision, and so on (see chapter 2). Such findings represent the localization of psychobiological functions in the cortex.

Localization is complicated, however, by the brain's *plasticity*—that is, its capacity to compensate for damage to a given neural area. How this occurs is not yet understood. Even speech, one of the earliest functions neurophysiologists were able to localize, does not always disappear permanently after a stroke or injury damages the relevant brain areas. President Eisenhower, for example, suffered a stroke while in office and showed considerable aphasia, or speech difficulty, but later recovered his powers of speech. Clearly this property of plasticity is a tremendous asset to the survival of a species. Though it

(A) Wilder Penfield was able to stimulate long-forgotten memories in the exposed brains of neurosurgical patients. He used this technique in assessing brain disorders; (B) The numbers shown on the brain above refer to where the brain was stimulated in an epileptic patient.

immensely complicates the job of the neurophysiologist, it illustrates the fact that the brain is not merely a machine akin to a computer.

Consciousness has not been localized in any specific area of the cerebral cortex. It seems likely that the neural basis of consciousness is widely distributed, perhaps involving virtually the entire brain. Indeed, regions of the brain far removed from the cortex, such as the reticular formation, play a vital role in consciousness. This neural system receives information from the various sensory modalities; through its activity noise or touch can waken a sleeper. Destruction of the reticular formation of a cat can result in permanent coma. But when this system is destroyed in multiple stages, with a few days intervening between each stage, an astonishing demonstration of plasticity occurs: the brain somehow reorganizes itself, takes over for the destroyed areas, and maintains the waking state. In the same way, the human brain, with its 10 billion neurons, appears capable of molding itself to the needs of human consciousness, overcoming trauma by recruiting other cells to take on new functions.

Electroencephalographs: Recording Brain Waves

An instrument that has been widely used in the study of consciousness is the **electroencephalograph,** or **EEG,** which records gross electrical activity in the brain. The EEG was invented by a German psychiatrist, Hans Berger, who had long been intrigued by the relationship between mental events and the electrical activity of the brain. Berger succeeded in obtaining his first electroencephalogram in 1929 by pasting metal disks on the scalp of his teenage son, Klaus, and connecting them to a simple recorder.

The wavy patterns, or **brain waves,** that Berger recorded represent fluctuations or oscillations in voltage, which in turn reflect the sum of many nerve cells firing in the cerebral cortex. Berger delineated two different EEG patterns. When his subject was awake but relaxed, with eyes closed or not attending to external stimuli, Berger recorded a relatively slow synchronous rhythm (neurons firing in an orderly pattern) with a frequency of about 10 waves per second. He called these **alpha waves.** When the subject was more alert, mentally active, and attending to external stimuli, Berger recorded more rapid waves of smaller amplitude (height) and less synchrony, which he called **beta waves.**

The modern EEG machine greatly amplifies the weak signals and graphs them on a strip of paper or on the display of a monitor (see Figure 5.1). In

Figure 5.1

The contrast between alpha waves (relaxed subject) and beta waves (mentally alert subject) can be seen on this typical EEG.

Excited – beta

Relaxed – alpha

50μv

1 sec.

addition to its use in the study of consciousness, the EEG has been used clinically in the diagnosis of epilepsy, brain tumors, and injuries to the brain.

In recent years, new high technology screening methods make it possible to obtain detailed images of the interior of human brains without damage to the tissues, thus providing a research tool of tremendous potential to the neurophysiologist. One of the most promising approaches is positron emission tomography (PET scanning), which allows the physician or scientist not only to ''see'' inside the brain but to find out which brain parts are actively functioning. Radioactive tracers administered to the subject are taken up by active brain cells and ''photographed'' by the positron emission camera. The information is then ''stacked up'' in the computer to provide a three-dimensional view of the levels of activity in the specific brain areas.

In the near future, brain scientists will likely be using PET scanning technology widely to identify the areas of the brain that are active during different states of consciousness. Presently, this technology is very expensive.

The Split Brain

Of all the findings in the recent mushrooming of neuroscientific research, the most influential in developing new concepts of consciousness derives from Roger Sperry's Nobel prizewinning research on the split brain (Sperry, 1974). This work is discussed in detail in chapter 2. Here it will suffice to recall that Sperry studied men and women whose corpus callosum (the principal connection between the two cerebral hemispheres) had been surgically cut to alleviate severe epilepsy. Before Sperry's work, the left hemisphere in most people was known to be dominant for language, but the right hemisphere was thought to have little importance. After Sperry's studies and the body of research inspired by his work, we now know that both hemispheres have vital functions but that they are specialized for different modes of information processing. The left hemisphere dominates in situations where linear, or sequential, processing of information is required (speech, for example); the right dominates in situations that require the simultaneous processing of information, as in problems involving the relationships between different elements (spatial perception, for example).

These findings are of enormous importance to the understanding of the brain, of course, and their implications for the study of consciousness are startling. They imply that each of us has two quite different minds coexisting in one body, each with its ''own private sensations . . . thoughts and ideas . . . memories and learning experiences'' (Sperry, 1974). Often during the Sperry experiments, two different hemispheres seemed to demonstrate different and even conflicting levels of consciousness. Consider the split-level responses of one of Sperry's female patients. She was seated at a special instrument on

CHAPTER 5 CONSCIOUSNESS

which a series of ordinary images could be flashed at random to parts of one eye or the other in such a way that the information about the image reached only the opposite hemisphere. When a picture of a nude was unexpectedly flashed onto the right part of a screen, she laughed and had no trouble identifying the image because it was available to her verbal left hemisphere. But when the same picture was shown to her left visual field, and thus was registered in her mute right hemisphere, she denied seeing anything. But the right hemisphere, although it could not verbalize the image, could respond to it emotionally because she could not help chuckling. When the subject was asked what was wrong, her left hemisphere could only convey a vague feeling of embarrassed amusement: "I don't know . . . nothing . . . oh—that funny machine." In fact, much split-brain research indicates that the two hemispheres may participate in different kinds of conscious experiences; this could be the basis for much of our ambivalence and the internal conflicts that often generate psychiatric problems (Galin, 1976).

But perhaps the most important effect of Sperry's work was the impact on the mind-body problem. Sperry (1982) himself believes that "The key development is a switch from prior noncausal, parallelist views to a new causal, or "interactionist" interpretation that ascribes to inner experience an integral causal control role in brain function and behavior. In effect, and without resorting to dualism, the mental forces of the conscious mind are restored to the brain of objective science from which they had long been excluded on materialist-behaviorist principles." Sperry believes that consciousness and mental functioning operate as causal factors in relation to cerebral activity and do not merely represent byproducts of the brain's physiological activity. Thus, conscious experience results from the complex interaction of mental (mind) and physical (brain) forces. "There is no implication that mind is separate from matter in the dualist sense" (Sperry, 1984, p. 672).

Since Sperry's split-brain experiments, a variety of methods have been developed to investigate hemispheric functions in normal subjects. One method used in neurosurgery is to inject an anesthetic into the main artery serving one hemisphere. In effect, this puts that hemisphere to sleep while leaving the other alert and awake. Another method is to record an EEG separately from the two sides of the head while the subject is engaged in different tasks. It has been found, for example, that there is a greater incidence of slow, synchronous alpha rhythm on the right side when the subject is reading or speaking. Because alpha is regarded as a manifestation of relaxation and less neural activity, this suggests the greater involvement of the left hemisphere in verbal tasks. By the same token, there is more alpha—and hence less neural—activity on the left side during spatial tasks such as pattern recognition by touching objects (Ornstein, 1972). It is of interest to note that, on the average, women are significantly more adept than men at verbal tasks, while men perform better on visuospatial ones.

Researchers have implicated the right hemisphere—the side of the brain once thought to be "silent"—in a remarkable array of functions. Among the functions that investigators suspect to be largely related to the right brain are musical and artistic appreciation, visual imagery, fantasy, and emotional experiences. There is also evidence that the right brain is highly involved with hypnotic and other altered states of consciousness and even with the unconscious mind in general.

Research on hemispheric specialization has generated a great deal of excitement among people far removed from the neurosciences—educators, philosophers, artists, and lay people. With this growing interest some tendencies to take preliminary research findings and even wild speculation for established fact have appeared. Individuals, professions, behaviors, and cognitions have been assigned as right or left brain in cavalier fashion. Among the really difficult questions raised by split-brain research are the following:

- How can two quite different brains (or minds) coexist in one person?
- How are the different, sometimes conflicting, messages from the two hemispheres integrated?
- How does one hemisphere dominate the other?
- In what ways are the six differences in the organization of right-left hemispheric functions related to behavioral differences between men and women?
- How and why did this strange dichotomy evolve in the human brain?

The possible evolutionary benefit and the cost of such an arrangement has been described by David Galin (1976): ''The evolutionary advantage of having two different minds is obvious; possession of two independent problem-solving organs increases mightily the likelihood of a creative solution to a novel problem. At the same time there is an enormous increase in the likelihood of internal conflict. And so we have man, the most innovative of species and at the same time the most at odds with himself.'' In considering the possibilities and problems of the split brain, however, it is important to emphasize that in normal circumstances and regardless of whether one hemisphere is more active at a given time, both function together in an integrated fashion. A growing body of research is providing evidence that the two hemispheres are more integrated (less asymmetric) in women than in men. This finding is likely related to that mentioned above in which women, on average, possessed greater verbal ability and lesser spatial ability than men.

State-Dependent Learning

An important question for neural scientists and other students of consciousness concerns the possible continuity of physiological and psychological functions in altered states. Are altered states episodic events that are separate and distinct from normal patterns of mental activity?

Evidence to the contrary comes from a phenomenon known as **state-dependent learning,** which has been demonstrated in experimental animals. One of the pioneers in this research, D. A. Overton (1974), taught rats to turn right in a T-maze while under the influence of a drug. Later, when the drug had worn off, the rats could not perform this task: it was as if they had never learned it. But when Overton administered the same drug again, the rats ''remembered'' their earlier lesson. What was learned in the drug state apparently was simply unavailable to the rats in their normal conditions: availability of the learning depended upon a return to the drug state; it was state-dependent learning.

There are several human parallels to state-dependent learning. One such parallel is evident in studies where subjects under hypnosis were able to recall, for the first time, experiences that had occurred while under anesthesia; they could remember, for example, hearing the doctors discussing their case (Levinson, 1967). Even closer parallels to state-dependent learning are the frequent reports of alcoholics who can recall events that occurred while they were intoxicated but only when they get drunk again. A classic example is depicted in Charlie Chaplin's film *City Lights:* the hero saves a drunk millionaire from attempting suicide. Each time the millionaire is drunk again and sees Charlie, he is lavish with his friendship, but the next morning when sober, he forgets the whole incident and has Charlie thrown out of his house.

A phenomenon similar to state-dependent learning also has been observed in studies of radical mood fluctuations. Herbert Weingartner and his associates

(Weingartner, Miller, & Murphy, 1979), studied manic depressives who swung rapidly between mania and depression. He found that they could recall information more easily during recurrence of the state during which they first acquired it—whether mania or depression. This finding has been reproduced in normal volunteers who underwent cyclical mood swings after being deprived of sleep (Reus, Weingartner, & Post, 1979).

These findings suggest that certain learned psychological reactions may be related to a given physiological state and that these reactions become available when the brain enters this state.

Sleep and Dreams

Among the general public, the very phrase "altered states of consciousness" often conjures up images of mystical trances or drug-induced euphoria. In fact, the most common and familiar of the altered states is experienced by all of us each day. Typically, we spend seven or eight hours a day in a state in which we are incapable of experiencing the environment or relating to people—sleep. And often during this period of sleep, perhaps four or five times a night, we experience yet another altered state—up to half an hour of fantasy and hallucination that seem achingly real and yet inexpressibly different from waking consciousness.

Because of its universality, sleep, with or without dreams, fascinates students of biology and psychology. Furthermore, it provides a rich model for investigating the interaction of body and mind. We will look first at the structure of sleep, a subject about which investigators have learned a great deal in the past two decades or so, and then we will examine the far more difficult questions of why we sleep and why we dream.

Our Biological Clock: The Circadian Rhythm

Our daily round of sleep and waking is governed by a biological cycle known as a **circadian rhythm**—from the Latin for "about one day." Internal timekeeping mechanisms, often called the **biological clock,** control the circadian rhythm, of which there are many examples in human and animal physiology. Human body temperature, for example, typically fluctuates in a daily cycle, peaking in the second half of the day (see Figure 5.2). Travelers become uncomfortably aware of the biological clock when they pass through different time zones and feel the internal effects of "jet lag," the discomfort resulting from having to reset daily rhythms.

The biological clock is set for roughly 24 hours. Ordinarily, the clock is reset by the environmental cues of light and dark. But the clock reverts to its built-in circadian rhythm when we are removed from the environmental cues. Volunteers who have lived experimentally in caves and mines typically maintain a circadian cycle of sleep and waking of between 23 and 25 hours.

Until 1972 the precise location of the internal timekeeper in humans had eluded neuroscientists. Then Irving Zucker and others pinpointed a specific area in the hypothalamus, the **suprachiasmatic nuclei,** located where the two optic nerves cross as they enter the brain. Experimental destruction of this area in rats and other animals wipes out the normal cycle of sleep and wakefulness along with other processes involving a circadian rhythm such as eating, drinking, and production of adrenal cortical hormones (Zucker, 1980).

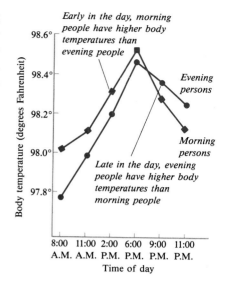

Figure 5.2

Individual differences in one circadian rhythm. As shown, morning people tend to have higher body temperatures early in the day than do evening people. After about 8 P.M., however, this difference is reversed.

Figure 5.3

(A) In the first of normal sleep's four stages, small, fast brain waves appear on EEG record (below sleeper); (B) In the second stage, brain waves show short bursts of activity (resembling spindles) as light sleep begins to deepen; (C) In the third stage, larger, slower brain waves appear as the half-hour descent to deep sleep continues; (D) In the fourth stage, the large delta waves of deep sleep increase in number.

A. **B.**

C. **D.**

The Structures of Sleep

The basic instrument for recording neural measurements during sleep is the electroencephalograph. For many years, sleep was assumed to be a single state. Investigators using the EEG were able to differentiate four sequential stages of this single state (see Figure 5.3):

1. The alpha waves that characterize the EEG as we close our eyes and relax show a decrease and slower **theta waves** of 4 to 6 cycles per second appear, along with slow rolling eye movements. This drowsy interval between waking and sleeping is known as the **hypnagogic state.** During this brief period short, hallucinatory, dreamlike experiences appear that resemble vivid still photographs. These experiences are often forgotten, but it has been hypothesized that the imagery in them in conducive to creativity, potentially leading to solutions to scientific or artistic problems.
2. **Sleep spindles,** short periods of rhythmical responses, with a frequency of 13 to 15 cycles per second, appear as light sleep begins to deepen.
3. Large slow **delta waves** of 1 to 4 cycles per second show up on the EEG as the descent into deep sleep continues.
4. The delta waves of deep sleep increase in number.

These four stages comprise the state sometimes called "quiet sleep," a not quite accurate description because snoring, sleep-talking, sleepwalking, and bed-wetting typically occur in Stage 4. It is quiet, however, when compared with another stage of sleep, a stage so different from quiet sleep that it constitutes a distinct state of consciousness. This separate state was discovered in 1953 by the University of Chicago sleep researcher Nathaniel Kleitman and one of his students, Eugene Aserinsky (Aserinsky & Kleitman, 1953). Like many important discoveries, it was triggered by a kind of "chance" observation. Aserinsky and Kleitman noticed that as infants went to sleep their eyes moved rapidly though the rest of the body was still. To study these eye movements in adults without disturbing the sleeper, the researchers attached electrodes to two places on the skin of the eyelid and wired the electrodes to their recording machine in the next room. When the sleeper's eyes moved, the machine recorded a potential difference that reflected a voltage developing between the cornea and retina.

These bouts of rapid eye movements began after their subjects had passed through the four stages of quiet sleep, about 70 or 80 minutes after the onset of slumber. When the sleepers were awakened during these rapid eye movements, they almost invariably reported they had been dreaming. This new state of sleep has come to be known as **rapid-eye-movement (REM) sleep.** It also has been termed paradoxical sleep, because, while the EEG shows that the brain is in a state of high "wakefulness" or activity, the subject is hardest to awaken during this stage (see Figure 5.4).

Interestingly, a quiet sound is more effective in arousing subjects during both REM and non-REM sleep if it has a personal significance, such as the sleeper's name. As Figure 5.5 shows, we typically go through several periods of REM sleep in a cycle. Toward the end of the cycle, the REM periods are separated by increasingly more wakeful states.

REM Sleep and Dreams

Researchers now assume that REM sleep in adults is virtually always accompanied by dreams. In recent studies, subjects reported dreams about 85 percent of the time when they were awakened during REM sleep; it is quite possible that the remaining 15 percent can be accounted for by simple failure to recall dreaming. Something like dreaming also occurs during non-REM sleep. Subjects awakened then frequently report mental activity (words and phrases, for example), but the activity is more thoughtlike—more conceptual and plausible and less visual—than actual dream content, which more closely resembles hallucinations.

Everyone dreams, it is now believed, whether or not the dreams are actually remembered. Dreaming follows a fairly regular cycle, beginning after completion of the four stages of non-REM sleep. A notable exception to this pattern occurs among people with **narcolepsy,** a disorder characterized by uncontrollable seizures of sleep during waking hours. Narcoleptics may fall asleep unpredictably—at the wheel of a car, during conversation, even while making love—and many of them bypass the other four stages of sleep and plunge directly into REM. Most people dream in cycles of about 90 minutes that recur about four to six times a night. Typically, the duration of REM periods increases through the night to a maximum of about an hour. Babies spend a higher percentage of their time in REM sleep, although there is no way of knowing when and what they dream.

In fact, all mammals that have been studied show REM sleep. Does this mean that these animals dream? Dog owners watching their pets twitch and paw during sleep have long suspected that their dogs do indeed dream. Because animals cannot tell us, there is no final answer to this old question. However, one piece of experimental evidence suggests that monkeys experience dreamlike visual images during REM sleep. C. J. Vaughan (1963) trained monkeys to press a lever every time pictures were flashed onto a screen. When the monkeys went to sleep and no pictures were being shown, they pressed the lever—but only during periods of REM.

Awake-like activation

Rapid eye movements

Muscle tone absent

Figure 5.4

In REM sleep, when dreams take place, a volunteer shows brain waves similar to waking state (top row), intense rapid eye movement (middle), and virtually no activity of chin muscles (bottom).

Figure 5.5

A young adult's typical night of sleep, showing wakeful (W), sleeping (S), and dreaming (D) states. The heavy lines indicate dreaming sleep accompanied by rapid eye movements.

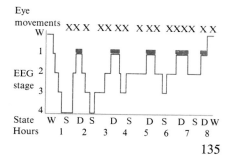

135

Dreaming and Waking

What does research in REM sleep tell us about relationships between the dream state and normal waking consciousness? Some findings support Sigmund Freud's contention that we integrate the residues of the activities of the previous day into the dream. However, they also contradict his assertion that it is always necessary to look beyond the manifest, or surface, content of dreams and focus on the latent, or hidden, meaning.

In fact, studies of children and adults, including cross-cultural investigations, show a very clear continuity between the manifest content of dreams and the concerns of an individual's waking life. We tend to take to bed with us our waking interests and worries. For example, a man with an unusually intense daytime preoccupation with the American sport of football reported that 36 percent of his remembered dreams were about football (Hall & Van de Castle, 1966).

Studies indicate that dreams even reflect the differences in social relations between men and women of different cultures. For example, a recent study of Americans has shown that women's dreams have more characters, friendly interactions, emotion, indoor settings, and themes of home and family than do men's dreams. Men's dreams, meanwhile, manifest more frequent aggression, striving for achievement, and overt hostility (Hall & Van de Castle, 1966). These elements of dream content seem to reflect traditional sex roles in our society. Future studies may reveal different dream contents for women and men as changing sex roles evolve.

Other links between the dreaming and waking states have been demonstrated (Dement & Wolpert, 1958). Investigators sprayed cold water on a sleeping subject shortly after REM sleep had begun. When they woke up the subject he reported the following dream: "I was walking behind a leading lady when she suddenly collapsed and water was dripping on her. I ran over to her and water was dripping on my back and head. The roof was leaking" (Dement, 1972). Thus, in addition to including residues from the previous day as Freud suggested, dreams can also incorporate events occurring in the environment at the time the dream is taking place.

The same experiment helped demonstrate another link to waking consciousness: dreams occur in real time—not, as it was once thought, compressed into a few moments. The subject was awakened a measured time after the water spray and, after reporting the dream, was asked to repeat it in pantomime. The amount of time it took for the water to awaken the subject in the pantomime was close to the actual time it took the water spray application to awaken the subject during the experiment.

A fascinating manifestation of the relationship between waking and dream consciousness is the phenomenon of the lucid dream—when the dreamer becomes aware he or she is dreaming and consequently can actually control the events in the dream from that perspective. In the work of Stephen LaBerge (1980) of Stanford, dreamers were able to communicate with sleep researchers while in a lucid dream by providing prearranged signals consisting of eye or hand movements. The investigators were able to verify that their subject was sleeping by following EEG and other physiological recordings indicative of the REM sleep stage.

A most dramatic illustration of a link between dreams and waking is that the two states actually appear to overlap. Researchers have reported a 90-minute cycle of minimal REMs during a 10-hour waking period, which appeared to coincide with daydreaming (Kripke & Sonnenschein, 1973). In a study of cognitive activity during relaxed wakefulness, subjects lay alone in a room and were periodically interrupted to be asked about their mental activity (Foulkes & Fleischer, 1975). About one fourth of the reports involved internal sensory imagery; of these reports, 44 percent were regarded by the subjects as either hallucinatory (had been accepted by the subjects as unreal during the experience) or considered bizarre or distorted.

Physiology of Dreaming

One important line of research growing out of the discovery of REM sleep is the attempt to relate physiological events to dreaming. Two classes of physiological events have been found during REM sleep.

Phasic (abrupt) **events** include the rapid eye movements and increases in various phenomena controlled by the autonomic nervous system such as pulse, respiration, and blood pressure.

Tonic (longer-lasting) **events** include penile erection in men and increased blood supply to the vagina in women and a decrease in muscle activity in both men and women.

How do these physiological events relate to the content of dreaming? It has been suggested that the rapid eye movements may represent a scanning of the dream image by the sleeper. William Dement (1972) reported an instance where side-to-side eye movement seemed to reflect a dream about watching a Ping-Pong game, but this rare observation does not exemplify any generally accepted principle. Similarly, penile erection might seem to suggest dream content of a sexual nature. However, studies indicate that only a small percentage (about 12 percent) of dreams manifest sexual content while male erection almost inevitably accompanies any REM sleep (Fisher, Gross, & Zuch, 1965). In fact, penile erections persist into non-REM sleep when laboratory subjects are deprived of REM sleep by awakening them whenever REM begins.

Investigators have attempted without success to link dream content to other signs of arousal during REM such as increases in heartbeat and respiration. These events, like penile erection, occur irrespective of the emotional content of the dream.

Peter Tripp, after 67 sleepless hours, with 133 hours still to go.

Why Sleep? Why Dream?

Why do we sleep and why do we dream? What is the biological value of sleep and dreams? We do know that sleep is necessary for survival. In the laboratory, sleep-deprived animals will eventually die; in medieval times, historians recorded instances where people were executed by being deprived of sleep. But why is sleep necessary?

Studies on experimental sleep deprivation have shown dramatic short-run effects but nothing lasting. In 1959 Peter Tripp, a New York disc jockey, stayed awake for 201 hours in a booth in Times Square to raise money for charity. Throughout his eight-day marathon he was studied by a highly qualified group of psychological and medical personnel. On his third day he began to see cobwebs in his shoes and rabbits in his booth and he began to suffer memory impairment. Halfway through his ordeal, he found it unbearable to attempt psychological tests requiring attention or even minimum mental agility. By 110 hours he showed signs of delirium and was still hallucinating. At 120 hours he showed signs of paranoia: he imagined that flames were spurting out of a drawer and that these had been set deliberately in order to test him. Yet at 150 hours (almost a week without sleep), although he was so disoriented that he was not sure where or who he was, he was able to summon up his energies for his evening broadcast from 5 to 8 P.M. He functioned as an effective disc jockey, but his brain waves showed deep sleep rhythms while he was in fact behaviorally awake.

On the last day of Tripp's marathon, a distinguished neurologist came to examine him. He was carrying an umbrella and wore rather old-fashioned clothes. Tripp imagined that he was an undertaker and jumped off the examining table in an attempt to escape from this apparent conspiracy of his doctors. Yet he managed to complete the day and get through his last broadcast. After a final hour of tests, he fell asleep for 13 hours, to awake totally restored except for a slight depression that bothered him somewhat for three months thereafter (Luce & Segal, 1966).

In addition to such naturalistic studies, there have been a number of laboratory experiments in which subjects were deprived of REM sleep only. This was accomplished by waking them every time the rapid eye movements began. Studies of both humans and animals show an apparent tendency for subjects to experience extra amounts of REM sleep after deprivation as if to catch up (Dement, 1960). However, in contrast to earlier data suggesting that REM deprivation produced impulsiveness and other temporary behavioral changes in humans, there is no acceptably clear-cut evidence of specific emotional or physiological effects.

A number of theories about why we need to sleep and dream have been advanced. Freud, for example, said dreams were the "guardian of sleep," giving vent to thoughts and images that otherwise would awaken the sleeper, but this notion has found little support in laboratory studies. Most current theories of sleep and dreams emphasize a restorative role for physiological or psychological functioning. Ernest Hartmann (1973) proposed that quiet sleep may enable the body to recuperate from physical fatigue caused by muscular exercise, and dreaming enables the brain to recuperate from mental fatigue caused by intellectual effort and stressful emotional experiences. Or, as Shakespeare put it more poetically long before the discovery of REM, sleep is "the chief nourisher of life's feast" and "knits up the ravelled sleave of care."

Uses of the Dream

Long before the discovery of REM sleep, of course, dreams were the subject of mystery, fascination, and speculation. In biblical days dreams were considered prophetic. In more recent times they have provided the inspiration for literature and even scientific discovery. The idea for Samuel Taylor Coleridge's poem "Kubla Khan" came to him in a dream. The German chemist Friedrich Kekulé deciphered the ringlike molecular structure of benzene after a dream in which a snake devoured its own tail. Even stranger perhaps, in view of the brain's role in REM sleep, the chemical nature of nerve impulses was demonstrated by Otto Loewi in an experiment that was dream-inspired.

Freud (1900) called dreams the "royal road to the unconscious." His formulation of psychoanalysis at the beginning of this century made use of dream content to reveal urges and problems of which the patient was not conscious (see chapters 12 and 15). To Freud dreams were often a form of wish fulfillment or manifestations of a primitive, irrational, childlike type of thinking that he called **primary process.** His disciple, Carl Jung, who later broke with Freud, also used dreams in his therapy, analytical psychology, but he took a more positive view. He believed dreams were symbolic messages from neglected parts of the dreamer's psyche that could help point the way to individual development. Moreover, to Jung dreams expressed not only unconscious themes of an individual's life but also the grand themes of human existence—ideas and images that were inherited by all mankind and resided in what Jung called the **collective unconscious** (1936).

The use of dreams in psychotherapy to fish material out of the unconscious mind, as it were, is now common in the Western world (see chapter 15). But they are or were nowhere more important to daily life than among the Senoi, an aboriginal tribe of Malaysia. An unusual anthropological study by the late Kilton Stewart described the ways in which the Senoi made use of dreams to solve everyday problems and improve human relations. Stewart reported that families would conduct regular "dream clinics" each morning. Parents would discuss the night's dreams with their children and, if an interpersonal problem manifested itself in a dream, efforts would be made during the day to placate any offended individuals by giving them presents. This therapeutic use of dreaming was believed to be an important factor in the life of the Senoi, contributing perhaps to a peaceful social order in which violent crime reportedly was extremely rare (Stewart, 1969).

Biofeedback

A potentially important area of research grew quite incidentally out of the pioneering sleep studies at the University of Chicago during the 1950s. Joseph Kamiya noted that volunteers in the sleep laboratory seemed able to guess when their brain waves, as recorded by the EEG, were registering the slow, relaxed alpha rhythm (Kamiya, 1969). He put subjects in a darkened, soundproof room, hooked them up to the EEG machine, which sounded a pleasant musical tone every time they produced alpha waves. With the tone providing the feedback, many volunteers soon learned to produce alpha waves at will, although they were never quite sure how they did it. Kamiya's work helped launch a new area of research and clinical application known as biological feedback, or **biofeedback.** In biofeedback training, the subject is given information, or feedback, on physiological processes that do not ordinarily reach awareness, such as brain waves and blood pressure, so that the subject can consciously attempt to control them.

Brain-Wave Control

The subjects in Kamiya's experiments reported that increasing the alpha rhythm seemed to be accompanied by a serene state of consciousness not unlike that reported in the literature on meditation. These reports caught the public fancy and alpha control was touted, and even commercially exploited, as a means of attaining higher or mystical consciousness. The public interest was spurred by ingenious stunts such as the demonstration of a young boy operating his toy electric train by amplifying his alpha rhythm. Electrodes on his scalp picked up the brain waves and activated an electronic switching mechanism; the more alpha, the faster the train went (Brown, 1974).

Although alpha control undoubtedly contributes to relaxation, subsequent research has failed to establish a significant correlation between the alpha rhythm and a specific state of consciousness. In fact, high alpha conditions can coexist with the conscious experience of anxiety. Studies indicate that simply sitting quietly and closing one's eyes matches biofeedback training in increasing the alpha rhythm. Opening the eyes suppresses alpha; suppression of eye movements increases it (Miller, 1978).

Visceral Control

Another form of biofeedback research and training aims at achieving conscious control over such visceral activities as heart rate, blood pressure, and even skin temperature. These functions are controlled by so-called smooth or involuntary muscles, which in turn are regulated by the autonomic nervous system. Until recently, control of the autonomic nervous system was thought to be automatic and not subject to the kind of conscious control that we have over our voluntary, or skeletal, muscles.

Although Eastern yogis were said to be able to perform such feats as slowing their metabolic rate and making their hearts slow down or stop, these claims were usually dismissed for various reasons including the presumption that skeletal muscles were responsible. In the so-called Valsalva maneuver, for example, Indian yogis can use their skeletal muscles to give the appearance that their heart has stopped. The yogis take a deep breath, hold it in, close their windpipe, lock their chin against their chest, and contract chest and abdominal muscles. This builds up pressure in the chest cavity, blocking blood return to the heart and preventing the heartbeat from being detected by a stethoscope, although the heart may actually be beating more rapidly.

During the 1960s Neal Miller tried to determine if it was possible to control autonomic activities consciously. One of the key experiments, conducted with his student Leo V. DiCara, tested whether rats could learn to change their heart rate and blood pressure through expanding and contracting their blood vessels (Miller, 1969). To rule out the possibility that the rats might "cheat" by using their skeletal muscles, they were given curare, a poison that paralyzes the skeletal muscles but not the nerves and smooth muscles of internal organs and blood vessels. (Surgeons learned this the hard way during the 1940s while experimenting with curare as an anesthetic: their patients had to suffer through the pain of the knife in silence because the skeletal muscles controlling speech were paralyzed.) Since chest muscles are necessary for breathing, the animals had to be artificially respirated. They were rewarded for achieving success in regulating their blood vessels or punished for not succeeding.

Miller and DiCara reported positive results: one rat, it was said, even learned to blush in one ear by dilating the blood vessels. Interestingly, Miller and others have had great difficulty in replicating the results of the experiments with curare, and their results are still the subject of debate. Nonetheless, the work gave a great impetus to biofeedback research. Later experiments appear to bear out Miller's hypothesis that conscious control of autonomic functions can be learned. Some humans have learned to control different responses simultaneously—for example, increasing blood pressure while decreasing heart rate, or vice versa—and this cannot be explained in terms of skeletal muscle effects. Recent work has shown that patients paralyzed by polio or muscular dystrophy can learn to increase their blood pressure.

While the mechanisms by which biofeedback works are still subject to dispute, there is little doubt that a primary role is played by cognitive factors. The first thing a subject does in trying to exercise control over visceral activities is to concentrate on the goal. One male subject raised his heart rate 30 beats a minute by imagining that he was running to catch a train.

Whatever the controversies surrounding brain wave control and visceral control, the techniques of biofeedback offer a great deal of promise for the treatment of psychosomatic disorders (psychologically induced diseases) by their focus on mind and body functioning together.

Biofeedback of skeletal muscle activity has been used to train patients with neuromuscular disorders to alleviate tension headaches. Biofeedback also has been successful in helping patients control various visceral functions in addition to heart rate and blood pressure—for example, by increasing blood flow to the hands instead of the head by warming them in order to relieve migraine headaches. Epileptics have reduced the frequency of their seizures by learning to increase certain brain waves that are associated with muscle inactivity. Since the conditions treated with biofeedback are generally stress-related, it is relevant that biofeedback training is usually very relaxing.

Meditation and Peak Experiences

Whereas biofeedback represents a recent method for developing conscious control over bodily functions, a means for achieving the same or similar goals has existed for many centuries in the practice of **meditation.** Most forms of meditation, of course, aim higher, seeking to alter consciousness and attain something like the state described by the nineteenth-century writer and social reformer Edward Carpenter:

> Of all the hard facts of science, I know of none more solid and fundamental than the fact that if you inhibit thought (and persevere) you come at length to a region of consciousness below or behind thought . . . and a realization of an altogether vaster self than that to which we are accustomed. . . . It is to die in the ordinary sense, but in another sense, it is to wake up and find that the ''I,'' one's real, most intimate self, pervades the universe and all other beings.

For many centuries, mystics in every major religion, particularly in the East, have reported such transcendental experiences. In recent years, however, meditation has become a subject of widespread secular interest in the West. To many people, it represents a way to transcend the self, a kind of spiritual ''high'' without drugs. To psychologists, it offers promise for the treatment of psychosomatic disorders and for a better understanding of the relationship between the mind and body.

Because of the plethora of meditational methods, effects, and goals, it is not easy to formulate a comprehensive definition of meditation; Deane Shapiro's working definition is as good as any: ''Meditation refers to a family of techniques which have in common a conscious attempt to focus attention in a nonanalytical way in an attempt not to dwell on discursive, ruminating thought.''

Types of Meditation

From the psychological point of view there are two principal types of meditative practice: concentrative and mindfulness (Goleman, 1977; Ornstein, 1972).

Concentrative Meditation

In **concentrative meditation,** such as that practiced in the Hindu tradition, alteration of consciousness is sought through detachment from both external environment and internal thought processes. To avoid distraction, the individual concentrates on a single thought, image, sound, or movement. For example, the meditator may use a mandala, a fixed visual image on which all attention is focused, or a mantra, a word repeated silently to oneself. Moslem Sufi, "whirling dervishes," sometimes concentrate on continuous and prolonged body movement or, more commonly, the rhythm of their own labored breathing while whirling. For the successful practitioner, this concetration can result in a state of consciousness that Daniel Goleman (1977) summarizes as "loss of sense awareness, one pointed attention to the exclusion of all other thoughts, and sublimely rapturous feelings. . . . The concentrative path leads the meditator to merge with his meditation subject . . . and then to transcend it."

A variant of the concentrative type known as **transcendental meditation (TM),** is the meditative practice most familiar in the Western world. Founded and led by Maharishi Mahesh Yogi, the TM organization is largely responsible for making the practice of meditation accessible to many Americans and others who know little of the mystical traditions of the East. TM is a simple technique, common to many schools of concentrative meditation. Novices are instructed to sit with their eyes closed, relaxed but with an upright spine, and to repeat silently a specially chosen mantra. Meditation takes place for about 20 minutes, twice a day, in a quiet environment. Meditators make no active attempt to control their mental experiences but try with a minimum of effort to keep their attention on the mantra, thereby indirectly resisting the intrusion of thoughts.

Devotees of TM have emphasized the physiological responses that occur in meditation, asserting that TM produces a unique psychophysiological state. This unique state, however, has not been scientifically described by practitioners. The TM organization has sponsored, directly and indirectly, programs of physiological research as well as work aimed at demonstrating the benefits of TM. These benefits, it is said, range from psychological well-being to changes in perception and diverse improvements in health (Davidson, 1976).

Mindfulness Meditation

In **mindfulness meditation,** such as that practiced in the Zen tradition of *shikan taza,* the process is quite different. Instead of ignoring internal and external stimuli, the meditator deliberately directs attention to all such distractions—the chirping of a bird, for example, or the tenderness in a leg that comes from prolonged sitting, or simply random thoughts that pass through the mind. The object is to observe these impressions and thoughts with detachment, to receive them while striving not to react to them. A Zen master has described this as "noticing every person one sees on the street but not looking back with emotional curiosity." Paradoxically, while the process demands increasingly intense immersion in the present, the ultimate goal is to achieve a state of nirvana, a state that is the negation of self-awareness, the total absence of ordinary experience.

In both basic types of meditation, the usual normal relationship between an individual and the internal and external environments seems to be eliminated so that stimuli from neither exert control over thought processes or behavior. The internal dialogue—the mind's ongoing stream of consciousness—disappears and, with it, planning, problem solving, imagining, remembering, and daydreaming.

Physiological Responses

What physiological changes actually occur during meditation? Widely publicized studies on TM practitioners have reported a number of physiological responses (Davidson, 1976). These are decreases in the heart and respiration rates and in the consumption of oxygen (see Figure 5.6). Electroencephalograph measurements show increases primarily in amount (and amplitude) of alpha waves, which are characteristic of relaxed wakefulness. Various changes in blood chemistry also are reported, including a decrease in blood lactate, a substance believed to be correlated with a high level of anxiety. Most of these responses are the opposite of those occurring during the stress that seems to be associated with many psychosomatic disorders such as high blood pressure (Benson, 1975).

The major question about these findings is whether the reported physiological responses are in any important way unique to meditation. It is possible, for example, that most of them simply denote a general state of relaxation, which can be induced by various nonmeditative techniques such as self-hypnosis or biofeedback training (Davidson, 1976). From a clinical point of view, meditation can be used successfully to treat psychosomatic stress-related and other psychological complaints, much in the way that relaxation therapies and other behavioral self-regulation methods are used (Shapiro, 1980).

Although physiological relaxation seems to be a characteristic of many forms of meditation, evidence of increased arousal has also been found. In studies of Zen adepts, yogis, and others, EEG responses that may be related to specific experiences in meditation have also been reported. These include increases in fast frequencies of the dominant beta rhythm (indicative of increased arousal) and also increased theta, both in connection with more profound meditative experiences (Corby, Roth, Zarcone, & Kopell, 1978; Kasematsu & Hirai, 1966).

Appropriately, the Corby study presented evidence that increased physiological arousal (EEG beta as well as increased heart and respiration rates) may be related to those meditative disciplines that stress a more active struggle toward the achievement of higher states, or peak experiences.

Peak Experiences

Meditation is a potential means for achieving those mysterious states of consciousness that have been called **peak experiences** by Abraham Maslow (1971), a founder of the modern tradition of humanistic psychology (see chapter 1). The practice of meditation, however, is not the only means, nor in itself necessarily sufficient, for producing peak experiences. Such states have been described by mystics and others in a vast literature deriving from all parts of the world and throughout recorded history. William James called them "mystical experiences"; Saint Paul spoke of "the peace that passeth understanding";

Figure 5.6

Physiological changes that occur during transcendental meditation are demonstrated by the dramatic drop in metabolic rate as reflected by the decrease in oxygen consumption.

Transcendental meditation is a simple technique in which one sits with eyes closed, in a relaxed position but with an upright spine, and repeats silently a specially chosen mantra.

In the late eighteenth century, Anton Mesmer first demonstrated hypnosis.

Quakers refer to the "inner light"; Zen Buddhists aspire to "satori" and yogis to "samadhi." These experiences have been induced not only by meditation but also by other conditions such as intense stress, creative efforts, or even (apparently) spontaneously.

What constitutes a peak experience is obviously highly subjective and may have nothing to do with intellectual profundity. Winston Churchill is said to have awakened once in the middle of the night with a sense of having discovered the secret of the universe. He wrote it down and then read his message the next morning in the hard light of normal waking consciousness: "The whole is pervaded by a strong smell of turpentine."

According to an extensive analysis of mystical literature, peak experiences share a number of characteristics (Stace, 1960). First and foremost is the experience of "unity" or "union," which can be expressed negatively as a loss of the sense of separateness of self from others and from the outside world. Six other characteristics were noted: a feeling of bliss; a sense of sacredness; ineffability or difficulty in describing the experience; enhanced sense of reality or meaning; transcendence of time and space; paradoxicality or reconciliation of propositions that seem contradictory in normal consciousness. For example, a mystic might claim to have died or to "have experienced an empty unity that at the same time contains all reality" (see Research, p. 145). Many of these categories were mentioned earlier by William James (1900).

Physiologically, little is known about peak experiences because they do not lend themselves to reproduction upon demand in the scientist's laboratory. As we will see later in this chapter, descriptions of mystical experiences often resemble the reports of subjects in drug-induced states. Arnold Mandell (1980) has proposed that the same series of complex chemicals interactions in the brain may underlie all peak experiences from the meditative "high" to the drug-induced state.

Hypnosis

One of the least understood phenomena of consciousness is the hypnotic state. **Hypnosis** was first demonstrated in the late eighteenth century by a Vienna physician named Anton Mesmer. Mesmer was fascinated, as were many scientists then, by naturally occurring electrical phenomena such as magnetism. He used hypnosis to treat his patients for a variety of physical and mental ailments but could explain it only in terms of an "animal magnetism" that flowed from him to his patients.

First known as mesmerism, hypnosis received its current name from the Greek for "sleep," because the hypnotic state was wrongly thought to represent a kind of psychological sleep. Freud was an early practitioner and experimented with hypnosis in treating patients with symptoms that lacked any physiological basis. The fact that some patients were able to recall long-forgotten childhood traumas under hypnosis helped lead Freud to hypothesize the existence of an unconscious, the bedrock on which he founded psychoanalysis.

Hypnotism is a relatively simple procedure, although folklore has endowed it with various properties of magical hocus-pocus. The hypnotist may use any number of methods, all aimed at relaxing the subject and narrowing normal consciousness. The subject may be instructed to focus attention on a shiny object while the hypnotist keeps repeating that the subject is getting relaxed and sleepy. Some subjects can even hypnotize themselves by listening to a tape recording of their own voice or the amplified sounds of their own breathing.

Characteristics of the Hypnotic State

Under hypnosis, people sometimes report regressing to early childhood and remembering events that they had forgotten. They lift weights and perform

RESEARCH

The publication in 1976 of the book *Life After Life* introduced a fascinating concept to the reading public, "the near-death experience." The author, Raymond Moody, Jr., who was trained in philosophy and medicine, reported on interviews he had conducted with a number of people who had experienced a close brush with death or who had been revived after apparent clinical death. These people told Moody that during this near-death state they had undergone an extraordinary series of phenomena, which he summed up in the following version of the "ideal" or "complete" experience:

A man is dying and, as he reaches the point of greatest physical distress, he hears himself pronounced dead by his doctor. He begins to hear an uncomfortable noise, a loud ringing or buzzing, and at the same time feels himself moving very rapidly through a long dark tunnel. After this, he suddenly finds himself outside of his own physical body . . . and he sees his own body from a distance, as though he is a spectator. . . . He glimpses the spirits of relatives and friends who have already died, and a loving, warm spirit of a kind he has never encountered before—a being of light—appears before him. This being asks him a question, nonverbally, to make him evaluate his life and helps him along by showing him a panoramic, instantaneous playback of the major events of his life. . . . He is overwhelmed by intense feelings of joy, love, and peace. Despite his attitude, though, he somehow reunites with his physical body and lives.

Although Moody's book understandably created a stir among the

The Near-Death Experience

general public, selling more than 3 million copies in the United States alone, it was at first generally disregarded by psychologists. Moody's report was anecdotal in nature; it had not been published in a scientific journal; his data were not quantified in a scientific manner. (For example, he did not spell out how many people he had interviewed or how many of them did not report the near-death experience.)

Recently, however, a number of psychologists and medical scholars have begun systematic research into the near-death experience. Of particular interest is the study conducted by Kenneth Ring (1980). Ring studied 102 persons who had been resuscitated after showing signs of clinical death. Of these subjects, 49 percent reported experiences almost identical in some major respects to those described by Moody.

Separating these near-death experiences into subcategories, Ring stated that 60 percent reported a sense of peace and well-being, 37 percent had the out-of-body feeling, 53 percent "entered the darkness," 33 percent "saw the light" and 20 percent entered it, 25 percent re-

viewed their lives, and 33 percent said they had chosen, bargained, or willed themselves to return to life. Ring also investigated the impact on the individual's subsequent life: 37 percent of those who had a near-death experience reported an increased appreciation of life; 29 percent of those who did not have a near-death experience reported an increased appreciation of life.

Since this report, Ring has interviewed more than 100 additional subjects. He has found that the earlier rate of about 50 percent reporting near-death experiences holds true for the new sample. His studies appear to have been conducted in such a manner as to exclude such easy explanations as lying by the subject or self-delusion by subjects who had read Moody's book. Although it is very difficult to obtain truly random samples of people who have been near death, there is no longer any doubt that substantial numbers have undergone the near-death experience.

Thus, for the first time, science has taken seriously a profound experience that surely must have existed since time immemorial but that, until Moody's book, had been noted only in fragmentary references in popular literature. The near-death experience must be regarded as occurring during an altered state of consciousness. How and why this particular state happens is far from clear, although its frequency suggests to many psychologists that the human species may have a genetic predisposition to the near-death experience. ■

other feats of strength that they are not apparently capable of under ordinary circumstances. They respond to things that do not exist in their present environment. They sometimes report themselves to be psychologically deaf or blind or insensitive to pain. Teeth have been pulled or even legs amputated without the patient's having an apparent conscious awareness of pain. It is a myth, however, that hypnotized subjects can be forced to do things they normally would adamantly refuse to do under ordinary circumstances.

A leading modern investigator of hypnosis, Ernest Hilgard has delineated a number of characteristics of the hypnotic state (Hilgard, 1977), including the following:

- High suggestibility (responsiveness to hypnotic suggestions), which is often regarded as the defining condition of hypnosis but actually is only one of many characteristics. Studies indicate an increase in suggestibility after hypnotic induction.
- Easy access to mental imagery and imagination—an ability that is also highly correlated with susceptibility to hypnosis. People with vivid imaginations are frequently good subjects for hypnosis.
- Decline of the conscious planning function. Subjects wait for the hypnotist to suggest actions.
- Reduction in reality testing; that is, subjects tend to see and hear things that are not there. Under deep hypnosis, a subject might "eat" an imaginary pear.

Subjects who are particularly susceptible can be placed in deep hypnosis. The method is to induce hypnosis and then suggest that subjects deepen this state by themselves. In deep hypnosis, subjects may no longer respond to the suggestions of the hypnotist but experience, on their own, ego loss (lack of self-consciousness or awareness of self), feelings of timelessness and bliss, and other feelings removed from normal consciousness.

Alterations in consciousness can endure beyond the hypnotic state. This is achieved through **posthypnotic suggestion.** While still hypnotized, subjects are told that they will forget everything that occurred during hypnosis (**posthypnotic amnesia**) and then remember it all at some prearranged signal. The hypnotist may also suggest that, after hypnosis, the subject will be capable of performing unusual skills: a common example is automatic writing, the act of writing understandably without awareness of what is being written.

Despite the fact that hypnotism has been well documented in the laboratory, so many enigmas remain that some investigators have suggested that it does not constitute an altered state of consciousness at all (Barber, 1970). For example, previous investigators have reported that great feats of memory are possible under hypnotic suggestion. However, more recent research suggests that hypnosis tends to make subjects more willing to report confabulations or "made up" information as a genuine memory than they otherwise would. The end result is that the hypnotized person produces some additional correct memories, and also more false reports. These findings cast doubt on the ability of hypnotized subjects to accurately report early childhood memories they had previously "forgotten."

Not everyone is equally susceptible to hypnotism, and although it is not clear what factors lead to susceptibility, children and imaginative people tend to be more susceptible. Hypnosis can take place during various kinds of physiologic states. Although the usual situation is extreme relaxation, subjects can be hypnotized during strenuous activities such as bicycling. A final enigma is that all attempts to find distinguishing physiological characteristics of the hypnotic state have met with failure. Unlike sleep and dreams, for example, which are characterized by distinct EEG patterns, the brain waves present in the hypnotic state do not appear to differ from the rhythms of normal waking consciousness. The clear distinction between hypnosis and the physiologically well-defined states of sleep contrasts sharply with the common instruction of hypnotists to their subjects that they are falling asleep.

However, failure to identify physiological correlates of hypnosis is likely due to the past inadequacy of rapidly developing methodologies for studying the waking human brain. Recently, EEG analyses of hemispheric assymetry have yielded evidence of right hemisphere dominance during hypnotic experience, at least in hypnotically susceptible subjects (Hilgard & Hilgard, 1983).

The "Hidden Observer"

A concept that can help explain the psychological processes occurring in hypnosis is **dissociation.** This concept describes a postulated process whereby certain mental processes split off from normal consciousness and function independently. It was first used in 1889 by the French psychologist and neurologist Pierre Janet, who employed hypnosis in treating mental disorders. An example of dissociation as described by Janet was the automatic writing performed by one of his patients, Lucie. Under posthypnotic suggestion, Lucie could write letters or solve mathematical problems on paper while chatting blithely along. She was unaware of what her hand was doing and she had no subsequency memory of the writing. The automatic writing was dissociated from her normal consciousness (Hilgard, 1977).

Hilgard (1977), using the dissociation concept, postulates a kind of divided awareness at work during hypnosis—two levels of consciousness each operating independently. One level is the consciousness that is apparent on the surface; the other is concealed and has been described by Hilgard as the "hidden observer."

The apparent presence of the **hidden observer** has been demonstrated in a number of Hilgard's experiments, especially those involving a painful stimulus during hypnosis. For example, subjects are told that they will feel no pain when they put their hand in a bucket of ice water. The subjects do as they are instructed and their surface consciousness reports no feeling of pain. If, however, the subjects are told to tell about their feelings through automatic writing, the hidden observer will report the pain.

Hypnosis in the Treatment of Pain

The clinical usefulness of hypnotic suggestion in reducing painful experience has been amply demonstrated. The practice is not limited to dentists' offices; it has been used successfully, for example, to suppress chronic pain suffered by cancer patients. Recent research has shown it to be more effective in this respect than biofeedback or acupuncture. In fact, the effectiveness of acupuncture and biofeedback may be related to suggestion, the essence of hypnosis (see Hilgard & Hilgard, 1983). The explanation that endogenous opiates are responsible for hypnotic analgesia has not been substantiated by research; naloxone, an effective antagonist of opiate action, did not prevent the beneficial effects of hypnosis.

A disquieting question is whether the presence of the "hidden observer" during hypnotic analgesia means that the pain is still being fully experienced, despite the apparent analgesia reported by the subject. The leading hypnosis researcher Ernest Hilgard has found, however, that the painful experience accessible through the hidden observer is only minimal. Physiological measurements show that this response is similar to the "mild excitement of knowing that a stressful stimulus is about to occur" (Hilgard & Hilgard, 1983).

Chemistry and Consciousness

With the exception of hypnosis, the alterations of consciousness we have discussed so far are for the most part self-induced. Sleep and dreams, for example, occur spontaneously; biofeedback and meditation are achieved basically through the individual's own efforts; and even hypnosis, as we have noted, can be self-induced. By contrast, the use of drugs represents a kind of external tinkering with the consciousness, a fact that may explain some of the controversy that surrounds the topic of drug use in our society.

The chemical approach to consciousness is both radically new and very old. It is new in the sense that the past three decades have witnessed a dramatic increase in **psychoactive drugs**—chemical substances that affect mood, thought, and behavior. As we will see more fully in chapters 14 and 15, the development of mood-influencing (psychoactive or psychotherapeutic) drugs for the treatment of schizophrenia, depression, and other disorders has exerted a powerful impact on our understanding of abnormal behavior. At the same time, the synthesis of psychedelic ("mind manifesting") drugs such as LSD and the widespread use of cannabis, or marijuana, have introduced millions of others to the effects of chemistry on consciousness. The latter group of drugs have been used primarily for recreational, rather than psychiatric, purposes.

From before the time of recorded history, people have experimented with drugs derived from herbal and other plants. The drug alcohol was used by the Egyptian and Indo-Aryan civilizations around 6400 B.C. and possibly as early as 9000 B.C. in the Indus Valley. Cannabis was also in use around 3000 B.C. in Indian and Chinese civilizations. It is believed that opium was used by Sumerians and Egyptians around 3500 to 4000 B.C. Records exist of the use by Indians of the New World of many plants containing psychedelic substances including mimosa, morning glory, *datura* (ginseng weed), peyote, various mushrooms including psilocybe, and coca (cocaine). In many tribal cultures, however, the use of psychoactive substances has seldom been accompanied by the problems of drug abuse that we associate with drug use in modern industrial societies. Later in this section we will examine some of the reasons.

Alcohol

Perhaps the most widely used, and abused, drug in modern Western societies is a depressant, alcohol. Alcohol, like other depressants, or downers, slows down neural activity as well as breathing and other physical activities. A small amount of alcohol acts as an intoxicant, presumably releasing "lower" brain mechanisms from inhibitory controls by the cortex. After a couple of drinks, however, most people become more lethargic, and deterioration in their locomotor skills and moods occurs.

A small amount of alcohol acts as an intoxicant, presumably releasing "lower" brain mechanisms from inhibitory controls by the cortex.

CHAPTER 5 CONSCIOUSNESS

Table 5.1   MAJOR CLASSES OF PSYCHOACTIVE DRUGS BASED ON GENERAL BIOLOGICAL OR BEHAVIORAL EFFECTS

Drug Class	Group	Trade or Common Name	Example	Evidence of Addiction?
Anesthetics and analgesics	General anesthetics	"laughing gas"	nitrous oxide	no
			diethyl ether	no
			chloroform	no
	Local anesthetics	coca	cocaine	yes
		Novocaine	procaine	no
	Narcotic analgesics	morphine, heroin	opium derivatives	yes
Sedative-hypnotics	General		alcohol	yes
	Barbiturates	Luminal	phenobarbital	yes
	Nonbarbiturates	Quaalude, Sopor	Methaqualone	yes
	Bromides		potassium bromide	no
Stimulants	Analeptics	Metrazol	pentylenetetrazol	no
	Nicotinics		nicotine	yes
	Sympathomimetics	Benzedrine, speed	amphetamine	yes
	Xanthines		caffeine	yes
Psychedelics	*Cannabis sativa*	hemp, hashish	marijuana	no
	Ergot derivative	LSD, "acid"	lysergic acid diethylamide	no
	Lophophora williamsii	peyote buttons	mescaline	no
	Psilocybe mexicana		psilocybin	no

Source: pages 170–171 in *Introduction to Physiological Psychology* by Richard F. Thompson. Copyright © 1975 by Richard F. Thompson. Reprinted by permission of Harper & Row, Publishers, Inc.

Alcohol is not even regarded as a drug by most people, but a drug it is. Excessive consumption of alcohol can result in addiction and in both psychological and physical impairment. Some researchers consider **alcoholism,** or alcohol addiction, to be a disease, meaning that it constitutes a pathological process within the organism. Others classify it as a behavioral disorder, or as a way of behaving in response to environmental contingencies. Some studies have even suggested the possibility of a genetic disposition to alcoholism (Cruz-Coke & Varela, 1966; McClearn & Rodgers, 1959).

The amount of alcohol consumed and its effects are measured in percentages of blood alcohol concentration—that is, the proportion of alcohol per unit of blood. After two cocktails on an empty stomach, an average-sized person will have a blood alcohol concentration of around 0.06 percent and feel "high" and mildly intoxicated. When blood alcohol concentrations reach the order of 0.1 percent, reflexive behaviors are seriously affected; the person is "drunk." When concentrations reach the order of 0.15 percent the individual will appear obviously to be drunk. However, given our current knowledge, it is impossible to specify with any precision the specific contribution of personal, social, and biological factors to the development of alcohol addiction. The ultimate answer will undoubtedly be complex, and may involve interactions between different sets of variables.

Classification of Psychoactive Drugs

Table 5.1 shows the main drug groups that affect consciousness, classified as to general effects and chemistry. It should be noted that a drug may have very different effects depending on the dose used. For this reason, and because drugs have multiple effects, their classification is somewhat arbitrary. The terms **stimulant** and **depressant** refer to stimulation or depression of the central nervous system in the present context. We will focus here on two categories: anesthetics and analgesics, and psychedelics.

Anesthetics and Analgesics

Anesthetics and **analgesics** are both drugs used to block pain. Anesthesia was introduced in the nineteenth century when Hollis Wells, a dentist in Hartford, Connecticut, began using nitrous oxide when pulling teeth. **General anesthesia,** or the loss of sensation with the loss of consciousness, was first used by William Morton who introduced ether for surgery. This was strongly opposed by the churches on the basis that people are meant to suffer. Apparently the most effective argument against this opposition was that God anesthetized Adam during the creation of Eve. General anesthetics may produce altered-state experiences during the induction of anesthesia and in awakening from it if the transitions to unconsciousness are not too rapid. Even **local anesthetics,** which produce **analgesia—**loss of pain without loss of consciousness when used at the site of the source of pain—may alter the conscious state when taken internally. The best-known example of this reaction comes from cocaine, also a stimulant, which produces a sense of well-being and is widely used today as a recreational drug. Freud was the first modern scholar to study cocaine's effectiveness as a local anesthetic and its behavioral effects. In the process he became an enthusiast and addict.

The **narcotic analgesics,** such as the opium derivatives morphine and heroin, ease pain while inducing significant elevation of mood. Opium is believed to have been used in ancient Greek rituals during the classical period as well as in ancient Egypt and Sumeria. Its derivatives are among the most addictive drugs. **Addiction** has two main aspects, the first of which is psychological dependence, wherein the addict develops a need for the drug in order to maintain feelings of well-being. The second is physical dependence, in which withdrawal of the drug from an addict results in severe illness and in some cases even death. A less extreme phenomenon common to many addictive and nonaddictive drugs is **tolerance** or the need to increase the dose, following repeated use of the drug, in order to achieve the same effect previously experienced from a smaller dose.

Many things are still not understood about anesthetics and consciousness; people sometimes remember at a later point statements made by the surgeon while they were deeply anesthetized, but the reasons for this are not clear. Such memories can be recovered under hypnosis, a fact that can be most embarrassing to the surgeon.

Sedatives and Hypnotics

Barbiturates and other sedative-hypnotic drugs in large doses induce general anesthesia. In smaller doses, they are considered **sedatives** (minor depressants). Unlike local anesthetics and analgesics, sedatives suppress the sensation of pain but impair consciousness in the process; subjects get sleepy as they lose sensation.

Stimulants

The most commonly used stimulants are amphetamines and related drugs, known popularly as speed. These drugs increase locomotor activity in animals at doses well below those that produce convulsions.

In humans, amphetamine and similar sympathomimetics also increase psychomotor activity. More relevant to the nonmedical user is the extreme euphoria experienced, particularly when the drug is injected intravenously. This state encompasses a great increase in perceived energy and self-confidence for social and other activities. Other common effects of acute intoxication with

Cocaine shares some of the characteristic behavioral effects of amphetamines, including the "rush" and "crash" sequence, and may produce other harmful effects with chronic use.

these drugs are less pleasant. Extreme aggressiveness with repeated or higher doses, as well as tremor, agitation, and even paranoid delusions can accompany the desired "rush," which is also soon followed by a highly unpleasant "crash." This stage can include a variety of dysphoric conditions from mild fatigue and anxiety to extreme depression. At this point the addict experiences intense need to take another dose.

The widespread use of amphetamines and similar psychostimulants for many years resulted from their commonly being prescribed for appetite control and as general stimulants. Not until the 1970s was it generally realized that the depression of appetite is effective only in the short run, for reasons not yet thoroughly understood but presumably related to the development of tolerance. In addition, amphetamines are no longer regarded as useful antidepressants. These agents are now officially prescribed in the U.S. only for treating hyperactive children and controlling narcolepsy. Cocaine, though classed as a local anesthetic, is also a brain stimulant showing somewhat similar effects on brain neurotransmitters as do amphetamines (cocaine inhibits reuptake of norepinephrine/dopamine and thereby increases the activity of neurons using these transmitters). Moreover, cocaine shares some of the characteristic behavioral effects of amphetamines, including the "rush" and "crash" sequence, and may produce other harmful effects with chronic use.

Psychedelics

The most interesting of the drugs from the standpoint of altered consciousness are the **psychedelics,** a term that means "mind manifesting." They are also sometimes referred to as **hallucinogens.** This is a misnomer because, contrary to popular belief, psychedelics do not generally induce true hallucinations, which are perceptions of scenes that do not exist. Rather, psychedelics typically modify the normal perceptual environment by greatly intensifying the sensory intensity of characteristics such as color and texture.

Several psychedelics occur naturally. The minor (less powerful) psychedelic, marijuana, derives from the hemp plant, *Cannabis sativa*. Mescaline is present in buttons of the peyote cactus and psilocybin is found in certain mush-

The psychological effects of marijuana include decreased performance on simple intellectual and psychomotor tests, including some impairment of driving ability, decreased activity levels, and distortions in the sense of time.

rooms. Other psychedelics are products of the laboratory. The most potent of the well-known psychedelics is LSD (lysergic acid diethylamide-25).

The known physiological effects of marijuana are not particularly dramatic: most characteristic are increased heart rate, increased pulse, and reddening of the eyes. The change in heart rate reaches its maximum about half an hour after ingestion of the drug, whose total time course is about three hours. This effect is the main basis for suggestions that the drug may be hazardous to people with heart problems. Other physiological effects are indicated by the fact that marijuana is finding medical applications in the treatment of glaucoma and the nausea induced by cancer chemotherapy.

The psychological effects of marijuana include decreased performance on simple intellectual and psychomotor tests, including some impairment of driving ability, decreased activity levels, and distortions in the sense of time. Generally these effects are less intense for experienced users (Grinspoon, 1977). However, marijuana in some cases shows what seems to be a reversed tolerance—with naive users needing to take more of the drug to get "high" (Weil, 1973). From the point of view of the user, of course, the important effects are the mood changes: feelings of well-being or euphoria and enhancement of sensory pleasure.

Although marijuana is physically nonaddictive, some users feel they need it regularly for the sense of well-being it provides. More research into the effects of marijuana is still needed. However, it is not nearly as potentially dangerous as the major psychedelics, one of which is LSD.

Just one tenth of a milligram of LSD can induce an immense transformation of the conscious state. LSD, a light chemical modification of compounds present in a certain fungus that attacks rye, is the product of both nature and the psychopharmacologist's laboratory. Its powerful effects on consciousness were discovered by the Swiss pharmacologist Albert Hofmann, who accidentally ingested a large dose of LSD in his laboratory one memorable May day in 1943. As Hofmann described it: "there surged upon me an uninterrupted stream of fantastic images of extraordinary plasticity and vividness and accompanied by an intense, kaleidoscope-like play of colors" (Sankar, 1975).

As shown in Figure 5.7, physiological effects of LSD include feelings of weakness, dizziness, and slight nausea early in the "trip" (Sankar, 1975). Pupillary dilation is an effect that is easily recognized (and therefore used by the police). A decreased threshold for arousal is usually seen along with increased sensory perception in all modalities. An increase in body temperature and blood sugar with a reduced urge for food intake is common. Thus the major observed physiological alterations reflect increased central sympathetic arousal, which clearly is insufficient to explain the profound psychological effects.

Psychological changes with LSD include alterations in body image, dreamy, detached feelings, time distortions, transformation of the visual environment often including apparent undulations, heightened suggestibility, and a variety of mood changes (Sankar, 1975). The effectiveness of the drug seems to depend upon personality; it is less effective in rigid, dogmatic, controlled people and more effective in esthetic, imaginative introverts.

Several explanations have been proposed for the psychological and physiological effects of LSD. For example, it has been speculated that time appears to pass more slowly because there is a higher density of intense conscious experiences. Some of the visual effects may be caused by pupil dilation, which increases the light reaching the retina. This results in decreased depth of focus, which maximizes spherical and chromatic aberrations and causes blurring and rainbow effects at the edges of the visual field (Barber, 1970).

It is interesting to note that among LSD, psilocybin, and mescaline there is **cross tolerance;** that is, development of tolerance to one of them by repeated use renders not only it, but also the others, less effective. However, there is no cross tolerance between these three drugs and marijuana. This indicates a

CHAPTER 5 CONSCIOUSNESS

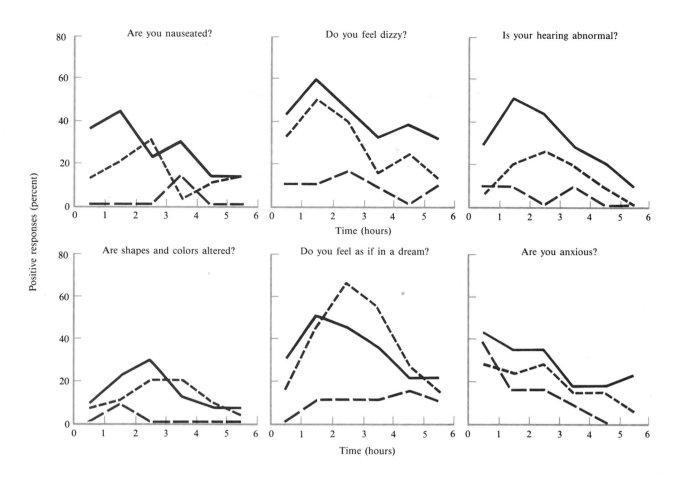

Figure 5.7

A subjective report on the physiological and perceptual effects of LSD was obtained by means of a questionnaire containing 47 items. Six of these are presented here. Volunteers were questioned at one-hour intervals beginning half an hour after they took the drug. The curves show the percentage of the group giving positive answers at each time. The long-broken curves are for those given an inactive substance, the short-broken curves for those given 25 to 75 micrograms of LSD, and the solid curves for those given 100 to 225 micrograms of LSD.

substantial difference between the action of marijuana and of the major psychedelics.

More than any other class of drugs, the psychedelics have inspired debate and controversy in our society, and their possession and sale is illegal in the United States except for carefully prescribed medicinal or experimental purposes. (Prohibition of drugs is nothing new, of course; a number of societies have banned tobacco; among them Russia in the seventeenth century where the use of snuff was thought to have such ill effects on the breath that one penalty authorized slitting the nose of the offender.)

In an attempt to clarify myths and misconceptions, let us consider two important questions in the debate over psychedelics.

Are Psychedelics Dangerous?

A variety of deleterious effects have been ascribed to marijuana. Early reports of brain damage and chromosome destruction have not survived the test of careful scientific research. In several studies, marijuana was shown to lower blood levels of the male sex hormone testosterone; it is not known if the change is sufficient to have ill effect (Kolodny, Masters, Kolodner, & Toro, 1974). A further danger of marijuana may be the "amotivational syndrome"—loss of motivation for work or studies. In fact, it is impossible so far to distinguish cause and effect; propensities to "amotivation" may themselves be the cause of heavy drug usage. For good or ill, marijuana is now being used by many millions of Americans. Further research on marijuana is needed; given the present state of knowledge, however, some investigators have concluded that, in normal usage, marijuana is a safer drug than either tobacco or alcohol, both of which are potentially lethal.

LSD, for all its potency and profundity of effect on consciousness, at present appears to be devoid of destructive effects on the body despite earlier unsubstantiated claims. The known dangers relate primarily to its psychological effects. Like marijuana, it is physically nonaddictive; unlike marijuana, it seldom seems to cause psychological dependence. Often a person will be deeply affected by an experience with LSD and yet never return to it.

The major known danger with LSD is the possibility of a "bad trip." Particularly when LSD is taken without appropriate supervision, the experience can be profoundly fearful with deleterious emotional effects outlasting the period of drug action. While there is no reliable evidence that LSD can induce a psychotic state in an individual with normal metal health, severely disturbed people should certainly avoid the drug, with the possible exception of its use in carefully supervised psychotherapy (Smart, 1967).

Any discussion of the possible dangers of psychedelic drugs must take into account the circumstances in which they are used. Many tribal groups have used psychedelic herbs for the purpose of seeking spiritual experiences, including the Native American Church, a North American Indian religion whose members are legally permitted to use peyote in their rituals. In such circumstances there seem to be no problems with abuse of the drugs. One reason, according to Andrew Weil (1973), who did the first modern laboratory research on the effects of marijuana, is that tribal societies use psychedelics in natural— and therefore less potent—form. Weil suggests that the variety of substances contained in the plants may somehow lessen overall deleterious effects.

Perhaps more important, the drugs are used in tribal societies in highly ritualized ways. Some are used only by medicine men or shamans for divination or diagnosing illness; others are used only in particular rites of passage when hallucinations are sought to arouse visions of the spirit realm. For instance, Zuni Indian rain priests take toloache (datura) before going out to commune with the bird kingdom to intercede for rain (Schultes, 1972). The rituals surrounding the preparation and ingestion of the herbs, along with the support of the group and the presence of religious leaders to provide guidance, appear to channel the effects of the drugs in desired directions. It is not merely coincidental that people in industrial societies whose use of alcohol is connected with ritual—drinking only with food, for example, or in the company of others—are much less likely to become abusers of this drug.

The ritual use of psychedelics exemplifies the well-documented fact that psychedelics do not necessarily impose specific experiences on the individual. Rather, the nature of the resulting alterations in the state of consciousness depends to a great degree on two psychological factors: **set** (the mental state of the individual before ingestion) and **setting** (external conditions). The importance of set and setting applies to the use of marijuana as well as to the more potent psychedelics such as LSD. Use of marijuana by an individual trying to counter depression often leads only to intensification of that depression. Finally it should be emphasized that research on marijuana and particularly on LSD has not been sufficient to regard them as "safe" drugs.

Do Psychedelics Produce Mystical Experiences?

This question is raised by the many similarities between psychedelic states and those states we have previously described as peak or mystical experiences. For one thing, it is often impossible to distinguish between first-person reports of the two experiences. Consider the following two accounts. The first is a first-person description of experiences under the influence of LSD:

Suddenly I burst into a vast, new, indescribably wonderful universe. Although I am writing this over a year later, the thrill of the surprise and amazement, the awesomeness of the revelation, the engulfment in an overwhelming feeling-wave of gratitude and blessed wonderment, are as fresh, and the memory of the experience is as vivid, as if it had happened five minutes ago. And yet to concoct anything by way of description that would even hint at the magnitude, the sense of ultimate reality . . . this seems such an impossible task. The knowledge which has infused and affected every aspect of my life came instantaneously and with such complete force of certainty that it was impossible, then or since, to doubt its validity.

The second passage is an account by R. M. Bucke of a spontaneous experience that he called "cosmic consciousness" and published in a book of that name in 1900:

> All at once, without warning of any kind, I found myself wrapped in a flame-colored cloud. For an instant I thought of fire . . . the next, I knew that the fire was within myself. Directly afterward there came upon me a sense of exultation, of immense joyousness accompanied or immediately followed by an intellectual illumination impossible to describe. Among other things, I did not merely come to believe, but I say that the universe is not composed of dead matter, but is, on the contrary, a living Presence; I became conscious in myself of eternal life. . . . I saw that all men are immortal: that the cosmic order is such that without any peradventure all things work together for the good of each and all; that the foundation principle of the world . . . is what we call love, and that the happiness of each and all is in the long run absolutely certain (Bucke, 1900).

Other apparent similarities can be found in the lasting beneficial effects on personality that have been reported in the aftermath of both states. These include enhancement of creativity (Harman, McKim, Mogar, Fadiman, & Stolaroff, 1966) and decreased anxiety, guilt, and repression; increased capacity to experience wide ranges of emotions; tolerance of ambiguity; and enhanced acceptance of self (Chwelos, Blewett, Smith, & Hoffer, 1959; Smart, 1967).

The writer Aldous Huxley believed that psychedelic and mystical experiences were essentially the same. His experiments with mescaline came against a background of scholarly involvement in Eastern religious thought. The issue was beclouded, however, by the antics of such drug prophets of the 1960s as Timothy Leary, the former psychologist who founded the League of Spiritual Discovery (LSD) and handed down the new commandments: "Tune in, turn on, and drop out." The publicity accorded Leary, along with the spread of irresponsible use of psychedelic drugs, helped create the climate in which psychedelics were essentially banned during the 1960s for scientific research on humans.

Table 5.2 SUMMARY OF PERCENTAGE SCORES AND SIGNIFICANCE LEVELS REACHED BY THE EXPERIMENTAL VERSUS THE CONTROL GROUP FOR CATEGORIES MEASURING THE TYPOLOGY OF MYSTICAL EXPERIENCE

Category	Percent of Maximum Possible Score Experimental	Control
I. *Unity*	62	7
A. Internal	70	8
B. External	38	2
II. *Transcendence of time and space*	84	6
III. *Deeply felt positive mood*	57	23
A. Joy, blessedness, and peace	51	13
B. Love	57	33
IV. *Sacredness*	53	28
V. *Objectivity and reality*	63	18
VI. *Paradoxicality*	61	13
VII. *Alleged ineffability*	66	18
VIII. *Transiency*	79	8
IX. *Persisting positive changes in attitude and behavior*	51	8
A. Toward self	57	3
B. Toward others	40	20
C. Toward life	54	6
D. Toward the experience	57	31

Source: W. Pahnke, "The Contribution of the Psychology of Religion to the Therapeutic Use of Psychedelic Substances." In H. Abramoon (ed.), *The Use of Psychotherapy and Alcoholism* (Indianapolis: Bobbs-Merrill, 1967), pp. 629–52.

Before the drugs became generally unavailable for human research, an experiment conducted by Walter Pahnke (Pahnke & Richards, 1966) produced evidence of parallels between psychedelic and religious-mystical experiences. The circumstances of the experiment, which has been dubbed "the miracle of Marsh Chapel," were carefully arranged to make maximum use of both mental set and environmental setting. On Good Friday, 20 Protestant theological students were assembled in a room adjacent to the chapel where services were being conducted. The students were given either psilocybin or a placebo under a double-blind procedure. For the next two and a half hours, the Good Friday service next door was piped into the room.

Later, the experience and its aftermath were assessed through questionnaires, written reports, and interviews. These assessments were aimed particularly at eliciting information relating to the categories of mystical experience, which we discussed in the section on meditation and peak experiences. The subjects who took psilocybin reported more lasting positive changes in attitude and/or behavior than did the subjects who took a placebo (see Table 5.2). Interestingly, one of the categories that showed the least difference between the psilocybin- and placebo-treated subjects was a sense of "sacredness." The control subjects had high scores on this item in part because they were affected by the carefully prepared religious environment. Although Pahnke did not assert that these subjects had true mystical experiences, the basic elements clearly were present.

One case against the equation of psychedelic states and mystical experiences presents some convincing arguments (Zaehner, 1972):

> Psychedelics heighten sensory experiences, whereas mystical experiences such as those induced by meditation are devoid of sensations.

- Psychedelic experiences are "involuntary" and dependent upon an outside stimulus, whereas individuals in the mystical state apparently can control their thoughts and feelings. R. H. Ward (1957) likens the psychedelic experience to "being on an express train at night, with no driver and no brakes."
- Psychedelic, as opposed to "true" mystical experiences, are devoid of the "Love of God."

One key point in the debate focuses on differences in personal effort. Drug taking is essentially a passive activity, whereas mystical experiences often come only after years of effort, study, and perhaps of suffering. This has been described as essentially the difference between climbing the Matterhorn and going up it in a cable car. The philosopher Huston Smith has pointed out that people sometimes report deep suffering in the psychedelic state. This suffering, he suggests, may be so intense that it telescopes into a few vivid hours of radically altered consciousness the troubles that are ordinarily experienced over many years.

Finally, it must be reemphasized that, regardless of any possible value of psychedelics, those contemplating their use cannot afford to disregard the potential health hazards of these very potent drugs, not to mention the legal consequences involved.

Drugs and the Brain

The study of how psychoactive drugs affect the brain is among the most intriguing and potentially rewarding areas in the neurosciences. This research focuses on neurotransmitters, the chemical substances that convey electric impulses across the synaptic gap between nerve cells in the brain (see chapter 2).

Drugs can influence the action of neurotransmitters in a number of ways. For example, they may increase or decrease the levels of certain neurotransmitters. Mood-affecting drugs such as antidepressants (used to treat severe psychological depression), and antipsychotics (used to treat the major psychoses) appear to work in this way. Antipsychotic drugs such as chlorpromazine have been used in the treatment of schizophrenia; antidepressants such as impramine are mood elevators. As we will see in chapter 15, the effects of such drugs have provided the basis for new theories about the neurochemical underpinnings of abnormal behavior. The opiate, morphine, seems to mimic the role of a neurotransmitter by occupying its receptor sites on the postsynaptic nerve cell. This discovery led to the startling finding that the neurotransmitter(s) that ordinarily use those sites are endogenous painkillers—in effect, the brain's own opiates (see chapter 2).

It is now clear that neurotransmitter action is a highly complex process and that psychoactive drugs can affect the process at practically any point (see chapter 2). Thus, a drug might alter the process anywhere from synthesis of the neurotransmitter in the nerve cell body through subsequent steps, including the breakdown of excess transmitter by enzymes, the action of the transmitter in binding to receptor sites on the postsynaptic cell, and the reuptake of excess transmitter by the presynaptic neuron (see Figure 5.8).

Various active drugs, including amphetamines and LSD, are known to interfere with the action of the neurotransmitter serotonin. Serotonin has a generally inhibitory effect on a variety of brain-behavioral functions, including sensory thresholds. The psychedelics (particularly LSD) are believed to decrease the level of serotonin, each drug achieving this in a different manner in the synaptic transmission process. In effect, they apparently inhibit the inhibitor, thereby likely removing the brake that serotonin ordinarily imposes on consciousness.

Figure 5.8

Diagrams showing how LSD serves as a neural blocking agent that prevents a nerve cell from firing.

What we call "normal" waking consciousness can be marked by an extraordinary range of irregularities, or anomalies, that in many respects resemble the altered states described in this chapter. A familiar instance of these anomalous experiences—as Graham Reed (1972) has labeled them—is the *déjà vu* (already seen), the overpowering feeling of having been in a place or situation before, though one has no conscious recollection of it. Less common is the converse, *jamais vu* (never seen), a sense that a scene, though consciously known to be familiar, suddenly seems completely strange.

Anomalous experiences often occur under conditions of high stimulation. Examples include the alterations of consciousness sometimes experienced during religious revival meetings, long-distance running, and orgasm. Other anomalous experiences involve extreme reduction of stimulation. Subjects deprived of most of their normal sensory input—by float-

Anomalous Experiences

ing in a dark water tank for a long time, for example—sometimes have hallucinations not unlike those that mark mental disorders (Lilly, 1977). Although these experiences are at least as intense as the altered states described in this chapter, they may occur in the context of a person's normal regular activities such as going to church, jogging, or having sex.

Something akin to a mystical experience has been reported by many people who suffered severe physical trauma or disease bringing them close to death. For example, people who have had an apparently fatal

heart attack or received seemingly mortal injuries in an auto accident and are clinically dead but "restored to life" by emergency medical care, have been able to describe afterward the sensation of having floated above the operating table, calmly observing doctors trying to resuscitate their body (Moody, 1976; Ring, 1980).

Even that familiar butt of campus jokes, the absentminded professor, can be considered guilty more of having an anomalous experience rather than a memory lapse. A passerby once encountered the mathematician Norbert Wiener in a corridor at M.I.T. After a brief conversation, Wiener asked the passerby in which direction he (Wiener) had been going when they met. The passerby told him, and Wiener smiled in relief. "Ah, good," he said, "That means I have already had my lunch." According to Reed (1972), absentmindedness stems not from a lack of attentiveness but, on the contrary, from an extreme degree of attentive-

The study of consciousness, of the workings of the mind, and of the effects of drugs on the brain is likely in its infancy. Further research into neurotransmitter action may reveal exciting possibilities for curing psychosomatic illnesses and neurological impairments. Social attitudes toward both medical and recreational use of drugs may change drastically.

Perhaps most important, research into the causes and workings of altered states may lead to a much greater understanding of human consciousness in its normal, or unaltered, states (see Focus; this page). A great deal of our discussion has centered on altered states of consciousness, but the majority of us live in unaltered states most of the time. The expectation of learning more about normal consciousness is an exciting prospect.

Summary

1. States of consciousness are sets of structural conditions that are distinct from the actual content of consciousness. Structure denotes the major features that influence the ways in which we experience ourselves or the world; content is the experience itself. The state of consciousness influences consciousness in two different domains: the cognitive (how we solve problems) and the affective (how we respond emotionally). Altered states of consciousness may be differentiated from normal states by such characteristics as lack of self-awareness, hallucination, altered time perception, and loss of contact with present reality.

ness to an internal conscious matter of more immediate concern than external things.

Here, as is usual in altered states of consciousness, ordinary self-awareness seems to disappear. This loss of self-awareness also appears to be important in the performance of highly skilled motor functions such as expert skiing or even of highly creative artistic endeavors such as music, painting, or writing. One is aware of the activity, superaware in fact, and yet unaware that one is aware. Self-consciousness is sacrificed or at least reduced; this seems to ensure a more intense involvement in the act—whether it be play, work, or creative thought.

This latter anomaly has been called the flow experience by psychologist Mihalyi Csikszentmihalyi (1975). In many ways, the flow experience resembles an altered state. Conscious thought disappears: "When I get hot in a game . . . like I said you don't think about it at all," said

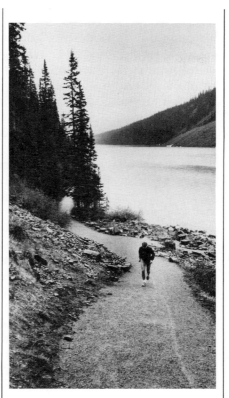

Anomalous experiences often occur under conditions of high stimulation, such as long-distance running.

a high school basketball player. Perception of time undergoes change: "Time passes a hundred times faster," said a chess player. "A whole story can unfold in seconds, it seems." And the sense or control that is present in normal consciousness seems to vanish: "You yourself are in an ecstatic state to such a point that you almost don't exist," said an eminent composer: "I have nothing to do with what is happening. I just sit there watching it in a state of awe and wonderment. And it just flows out by itself" (Csikszentmihalyi, 1975).

While arduous training is obviously essential to skilled activities and to creativity in science and the arts, it is becoming widely recognized that the flow experience may also be vital to success. Even athletic coaches are now experimenting with meditation and other relaxation techniques to help their teams "go with the flow." ■

Altered states are not necessarily abnormal; some aspects of altered states are frequently present in normal waking consciousness.

2. The study of altered states may eventually lead to some insights into the mind-body problem—whether the body causes the mind to think or whether the mind causes the body (the brain) to act (think). A key tenet of neural science is that all conscious experiences depend upon activity in the brain—in particular, in the cerebral cortex where the human nervous system reaches its highest level of development.

3. The three major research methods of neurophysiology are: (1) selective destruction of specific brain areas in animals and the study of brain damage in humans; (2) observation of the effects of electrical stimulation of the brain; and (3) recording the electrical activity of the brain. Localization of some specific psychobiological functions in the cortex is well established. Localization is complicated, however, by the brain's plasticity—that is, its capacity to compensate for damage to a given neural area of the cerebral cortex. It seems likely that the neural basis of consciousness is widely distributed, perhaps involving virtually the entire brain.

4. The electroencephalograph, or EEG, is an instrument that has been widely used in the study of consciousness and in clinical applications such as the diagnosis of epilepsy and brain tumors. The patterns produced by an EEG represent fluctuations, or oscillations, in voltage, which in turn represent the sum of many nerve cells firing in the cerebral cortex. Relatively slow, synchronous waves—alpha waves—generally indicate a subject who is relaxed, but

awake. Smaller waves of less amplitude and synchrony—beta waves—generally indicate a more alert and mentally active subject.

5. As a result of the research of Roger Sperry and others on the split brain, we now know that both hemispheres of the brain have vital functions but are specialized for different kinds of information processing. The left hemisphere dominates whenever linear, or sequential, information processing is required (speech, for example); the right dominates whenever simultaneous processing is required (spatial perception, for example). In normal circumstances, regardless of whether one hemisphere is more active than the other, both function together in an integrated fashion.

6. Research with both animals and humans indicates the existence of a phenomenon known as state-dependent learning: certain learned psychological reactions may be related to a given psychological state, and these reactions become available when the brain enters this state. Most research into state-dependent learning has been based on psychological reactions acquired in some kind of altered state of consciousness.

7. The most common forms of altered states are the sleeping and dreaming we all experience daily. Sleeping and waking alternate in a daily biological cycle known as a circadian rhythm. Internal timekeeping mechanisms, the biological clock, control this rhythm. Research has pinpointed a location of these internal mechanisms in a specific area of the hypothalamus, the superachiasmatic nuclei.

8. By use of the EEG, researchers have identified four stages of sequentially occurring sleep depth; later study has disclosed a fifth stage known as rapid-eye-movement (REM) sleep, during which dreams commonly occur. After passing through the four stages of "quiet" sleep, sleepers normally enter a period of REM sleep. When awakened from REM sleep, subjects in experiments have typically reported that they were dreaming. Researchers now assume that REM sleep is virtually always accompanied by dreams. Dreaming follows a fairly regular cycle, beginning after completion of the four stages of non-REM sleep. Most people dream in cycles of about 90 minutes that recur four to six times a night. An exception to this pattern occurs among people with narcolepsy, a disorder characterized by uncontrollable seizures of sleep during waking hours.

9. Investigations show a clear continuity between the manifest content of dreams and the concerns of waking life; that is, we take our interests and worries to bed. Experiments have also demonstrated that dreams occur in real time—not, as it was once thought, compressed into a few moments.

10. Two classes of physiological events have been found during REM sleep: (1) phasic (abrupt) events include the rapid eye movements and increases in various phenomena controlled by the autonomic nervous system such as pulse, respiration, and blood pressure, and (2) tonic (longer-lasting) events include penile erection in men, an increase in the blood supply to the vagina in women, and a decrease in muscle activity in both sexes.

11. Sleep is necessary for survival; however, studies on experimental sleep deprivation have shown dramatic short-term effects but no lasting ones. Most current theories of sleep and dreams emphasize a restorative role for physiological and psychological functioning.

12. Psychoanalysts from Freud and Jung onward have used the content of patients' dreams in their therapies. The use of dreams in psychotherapy, to draw material from the unconscious mind, is now common in the Western world.

13. In biofeedback training, subjects are given information, or feedback, on physiological processes that do not ordinarily reach awareness, such as brain waves, so that the subjects can attempt to control them consciously. The ability to produce alpha waves undoubtedly contributes to relaxation, but research has

failed to establish a significant correlation between the alpha rhythm and a specific state of consciousness. Biofeedback training has had some success in helping subjects achieve conscious control over such visceral activities as heart rate, blood pressure, and skin temperature (visceral control). The techniques of biofeedback training offer a great deal of promise for the treatment of psychosomatic disorders by their focus on mind and body functioning together.

14. While meditation to many people represents a way to transcend the self, to psychologists it offers promise for the treatment of psychosomatic disorders and for a better understanding of the relationships between mind and body. From the psychological point of view, there are two principal types of meditative practice. In concentrative meditation, alteration of consciousness is sought through detachment from both the external environment and internal thought processes: to avoid distraction, the individual concentrates on a single thought, image, sound, or movement. In mindfulness meditation, conversely, meditators deliberately direct attention to all distractions. The goal is to achieve nirvana, the state that is the negation of self-awareness, by receiving sense impressions while striving not to react to them. In transcendental meditation (TM), a form of concentrative meditation, meditators seek altered consciousness by repeating a mantra, an individually assigned Hindu word. Widely publicized studies on TM practitioners have reported a number of measurable physiological responses; however, these responses may not be unique to meditation. The responses may denote a general state of relaxation.

15. Mysterious states of consciousness that have been called peak experiences have been reported by mystics and others throughout recorded history. Little is known about the physiology of certain peak experiences, but descriptions of mystical experiences often resemble reports of subjects in certain drug-induced states.

16. Characteristics of the hypnotic state include high suggestibility, a decline of the conscious planning function, and a reduction in reality testing by those hypnotized. Alterations in consciousness can endure beyond the hypnotic state through posthypnotic suggestion. The hypnotic state is not characterized by any specific identified physiological responses.

17. The psychological processes occurring in hypnosis can be partially explained by a postulated process called dissociation, whereby certain mental processes split off from normal consciousness and function independently. Two levels of consciousness seem to be operating during hypnosis. One level is the consciousness that is apparent on the surface; the other is concealed and has been described as the hidden observer.

18. Altered states of consciousness may also be produced by drugs. The development of mood-influencing (psychoactive or psychotherapeutic) drugs has increased our understanding of abnormal behavior. Synthesis of psychedelic ("mind-manifesting") drugs, such as LSD, and the use of marijuana have introduced many people to the profound effects of chemistry on consciousness. The most widely used, and abused, mind-altering drug is alcohol.

19. Anesthetics produce a loss of sensation and, in large doses, a loss of consciousness; analgesics produce a loss of pain without loss of consciousness. Barbiturates in large doses induce general anesthesia; in smaller doses, they are considered sedatives (minor depressants). Sedatives suppress pain but impair consciousness. Narcotic analgesics, such as the opium derivatives morphine and heroin, ease pain while inducing significant elevation of mood. Addiction to these drugs produces both psychological and physical dependence.

20. Psychedelics, sometimes erroneously referred to as hallucinogens, modify normal perceptions by intensifying sensory reactions to color and texture. The most common psychedelics, LSD and marijuana, both produce a number of readily identifiable physiological and psychological effects. The use of psychedelics has been, and continues to be, widely debated.

21. A great deal of recent research has been devoted to the effect of psychoactive drugs on the action of the brain's neurotransmitters. The effects of drugs on neurotransmitters have provided the basis for new theories about the underpinnings of abnormal behavior.

RESEARCH: Near-death experience is a type of altered state of consciousness about which little systematic research has been conducted. One study (Ring), however, has reported that 49 percent of individuals who were revived after showing signs of clinical death report having a near-death experience. Explanations for this phenomenon are not yet clear, though some researchers suspect it may have a genetic basis.

FOCUS: Anomalous experiences are those that, similar to altered states, are not within the realm of "normal" waking consciousness. They typically occur during periods of either high or low stimulation and involve alterations and even loss of self-consciousness during the experience. In the latter case, the loss of self-consciousness or "flow experience" may create a more intense involvement in the act—be it play, work, or a creative task—which in turn may be a vital factor in its successful completion.

3

Growth, Learning, and Language

CHAPTER

6

Development

One of the most fascinating aspects of human behavior is its infinite variability: thought and action vary from individual to individual and from moment to moment even within the same individual. Perhaps most marked of all is the manner in which behavior changes over an individual's life span. Such changes, while most prominent in the first two decades of life, can be nevertheless quite remarkable in adulthood as well. As a rapidly maturing adult in your early twenties, you think and behave differently than you did as a child of eight or nine. And as an eight- or nine-year-old, you thought and behaved quite differently than you did as an infant.

In this chapter we examine **human development,** the branch of psychology concerned with the scientific study of changes that occur in individual growth, thinking, learning, personality, social, and emotional behavior over the life span. Within the broad field of psychology, developmental psychology operates as a growing subset of the discipline. How humans develop—from conception through old age—is a complex question and one that is frequently difficult to quantify. The study of development embraces all areas of human life and has profound implications for society. Its findings affect how parents raise their children, how schools educate the young, and how individuals of all ages can be helped to lead more fruitful lives. The amount of research generated by developmental psychologists in recent years is so enormous, in fact, that this chapter must necessarily be highly selective, covering just a few topics.

Other chapters will discuss in detail development as it pertains to a number of specific subject areas: for example, perception (chapter 4), language and cognition (chapter 9), sexual behavior (chapter 11), personality (chapter 12), and intelligence (chapter 13). In this chapter we will emphasize physical, cognitive, social, and moral development in turn. These divisions are arbitrary, though. It is important to remember that different types of development are actually intertwined and interactive. The way we look, for example, affects the way we think about ourselves, which in turn affects our social and emotional development and adaptation. As a foundation for understanding development, we will first examine the relationship between genetics and environmental influences on human behavior.

Determinants of Development

The debate over what determines development is one of the oldest controversies in recorded history. When the ancient Greeks speculated about this issue, the answer they arrived at was the same one confronting us today. Development is a function of both *heredity*—the genetic endowment of the individual—and *environment*—the broad array of experiences that the individual is exposed to from conception until death. Although the ancient Greeks did not conceptualize heredity and environment as scientists do today, nor understand the complex way in which these forces interact to influence development, they were aware that both factors contributed to the individual's behavior and development.

The Nature-Nurture Controversy

A major controversy that has dominated the field of developmental psychology in this century is over the relative contribution of heredity and environment to development. This controversy, known as the **nature-nurture controversy,** concerns which factor is more important for determining specific traits and behaviors in the individual, as well as the person's unique developmental path.

When we refer to a behavior as genetically determined, we generally mean that the behavior has somehow been preprogrammed in the structure of the nervous system of the organism at the time of conception. This implies that the behavior is independent of the previous experience of the individual. On the other hand, when we label a behavior as learned, we mean that the behavior is the result of some specific previous experience that resulted in the necessary learning. On the face of it, it seems that it should be possible to divide behavior into two categories—those that are genetically determined and independent of previous experience (nature), and those that are dependent on previous experience (nurture). Although this is a temptingly neat classification, it is not a particularly good one. Most researchers in human development now emphasize the *interaction* of genetic and environmental influences on behavior.

In describing the way in which heredity and environment interact, Anne Anastasi (1958) developed a model which she referred to as the **continuum of indirectness.** The model represents the varying degrees of influence of heredity on the developing organism. The most direct influence of heredity occurs in situations in which the individual inherits a characteristic that cannot be changed by the environment. A person's race, for example, is determined genetically at conception and will not change, regardless of the type of environment to which the person is exposed. Similarly, there are various forms of mental retardation that are the result of genetic defects and, so far, cannot be prevented or significantly altered by environmental intervention. A less direct influence of heredity on development can be seen in situations in which the person inherits characteristics whose impact can be altered by the environment. Take, for example, the case of inherited deafness. Without medical and educational intervention, such individuals are very likely to have serious intellectual and academic problems. With intervention, however, deaf individuals not only learn to communicate—either through speech, sign language, or both—but show normal levels of adjustment in intellectual and academic areas. Heredity plays an even more indirect role in development in situations in which the individual inherits the *potential* for a specific characteristic. For example, many people seem to be genetically susceptible to certain diseases. Whether the disease is manifested, however, is very much a function of the environment in which the person lives. Someone with inherited asthma is more likely to manifest the disease in humid or urban, industrialized areas such as New York

These children, in a multiracial kindergarten, are exposed to varying attitudes and behavior that may help them avoid social stereotyping.

Gregor Mendel, an Austrian monk who formulated the laws of heredity.

or Los Angeles than in desert climates such as Arizona. Finally, a still more indirect influence of heredity on development may occur as a result of social stereotypes. Sex and race, for example, are genetically determined physical characteristics that people often use as cues for determining how to respond to others. Although the specific attitudes and behavior that people display in stereotyping clearly are culturally determined, the cues that elicit such behavior (for example, the person's sex, skin color, facial structure, etc.) are often due to heredity.

The nature-nurture controversy no longer turns on the question of which determines development. Instead, researchers are more interested in *how* heredity and environment interact so as to influence the course of human development. For example, investigators are concerned with explaining the different ways in which people's intellectual potential (assumed to be partly genetic in origin) is manifested when they are raised in widely varying environments. In order to understand the interaction process, it is necessary to examine the basic principles of genetic transmission and, in particular, the way in which traditional models of genetics have been modified to take into account heredity-environment interaction.

Genetics

The classic laws of heredity were first proposed more than a century ago, by Gregor Mendel, an Austrian monk. Mendel's formulation of the laws of heredity stemmed from years of research in the monastery garden. He experimented with peas, crossbreeding different varieties. By breeding these plants selectively for characteristics such as height and color, he was able to work out mathematically the laws of probability under which these characteristics were passed on to the plants' progeny.

Since Mendel's pioneering work, genetic researchers have developed a much more precise model of the mechanisms of human heredity. Each of the reproductive cells—the male sperm and the female ovum, or egg—carries half of the genetic information normally present in a body cell. Each reproductive cell contains 23 **chromosomes,** microscopic rodlike units. There are thousands of **genes** contained inside each chromosome. The genes, in turn, contain the transmitter of the genetic code, the complex nucleic acid known as DNA, or deoxyribonucleic acid. At conception, the sperm and ovum merge, forming a single cell within which the chromosomes—half from each parent—form 23 pairs. This cell divides, and the subsequent process of cell division results in the embryo and, eventually, the human organism. Because of the astronomical number of possible gene combinations, practically every human being is genetically unique. The exceptions are identical twins, both of whom result from the same fertilized egg, or zygote (hence, they are monozygotic twins). Fraternal twins develop from two different zygotes (hence they are dizygotic twins) and are no more similar genetically than are ordinary siblings.

The sex of the progeny is determined in the 23rd pair of chromosomes in the fertilized egg. The cells of the female parent have a pair of X chromosomes (XX); those of the male parent have an X chromosome and a Y chromosome (XY). The female's contribution to the fertilized egg can be only an X chromosome, but the male's may be either an X or a Y. Thus, it is the father's sperm that determines the sex of the offspring (see Figure 6.1).

Like the chromosomes, the genes themselves are also paired together. Genes controlling physical characteristics are classified as either dominant or recessive. *Dominant* genes control the development of a characteristic, regardless of the nature of the genes with which they are paired. *Recessive* genes, by contrast, do not control development of a specific characteristic unless they are paired with similar recessive genes.

Figure 6.1

Sex is determined by the chromosomes in the fertilized egg. The cells of the female parent have a pair of X chromosomes (XX), whereas those of the male parent have an X and a Y (XY) chromosome. Because the female can contribute only an X, but the male can contribute either an X or a Y chromosome, it is the sperm of the father that determines the sex of the child.

CHAPTER 6 DEVELOPMENT

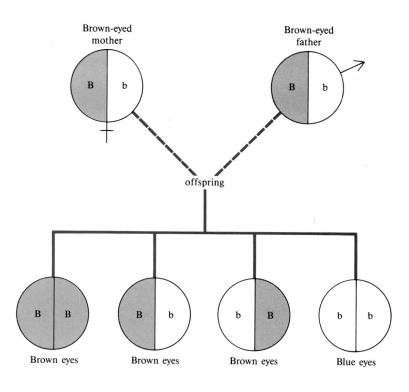

Figure 6.2

Because the gene for brown eyes (B) is dominant, whereas the gene for blue eyes (b) is recessive, the pairing of two brown-eyed parents who both carry the recessive blue-eyed gene will generally result in three-brown-eyed children for every blue-eyed child.

To see how this works in a simple case, take the example of eye color. Since the gene for brown eyes is dominant, an offspring whose pair of genes specify both brown and blue eyes will have brown eyes. The gene for blue eyes is recessive; thus a blue-eyed offspring can result only if the blue-eye gene is paired with another recessive blue-eye gene (see Figure 6.2). From these facts of comparative gene power, it is possible to compute the statistical probability of the offspring's eye color if the genetic makeup of the parents is known. If one parent has brown eyes that are determined by two brown-eye genes, then all offspring will have brown eyes. However, if the parent's brown eyes are due to a pairing of a dominant brown-eye gene and a recessive blue-eye gene and this parent pairs with a mate of similar genetic eye-color determination (dominant brown-eye gene and recessive blue-eye gene), there is a 25 percent chance that the offspring will have blue eyes.

This example raises an important distinction made by geneticists. **Genotype** refers to the genetic makeup of an individual; **phenotype** refers to the outward expression of that genetic makeup. Brown eyes are visibly the phenotype; the individual's genotype, on the other hand, might be composed of either of a pair of brown-eye genes or a pairing of a dominant brown-eye gene with a recessive blue-eye gene. Thus the phenotype brown eyes can be the result of either of two genotypes.

A New View of Genetics

The classical view of genetics is one of simple control of physical traits by individual genes or chromosomes. Modern approaches—especially that of **behavior genetics,** which studies the relative influences of heredity and environment—have developed several important concepts that modify the traditional view of heredity as it applies to human development (McClearn, 1970).

A trait such as eye color is a relatively simple one; the classic view that it is directly controlled by a given pair of genes makes sense. However, most developing systems are not nearly as simple as eye color. What we call intelligence, for example, is a complex concept covering a number of different functional systems. A single intelligence test, as will be seen in chapter 13, covers a number of different types of performance, including mathematical

Figure 6.3

The epigenetic landscape depicts development in terms of both biological and environmental constraints of varying degrees. The biological constraints are depicted as pathways that control the direction of a ball rolling down an incline. The environmental constraints are likened to forces that can jar the ball out of its pathway. The pathway followed by the ball in this illustration, begins with an alternative: the ball can go either right or left. Along the path to the right there is another alternative: the ball can either follow the main path to the left or branch off to the right. The pathway followed by the ball corresponds to the actual developmental history of the organism.

ability, knowledge of the world, vocabulary, spatial knowledge, and pattern discrimination. It is highly doubtful that a simple gene-trait model of the kind appropriate for eye color would apply to such complex systems as intelligence. Instead, the modern view regards the genetic contribution to complex systems as itself complex. Presumably, many different genes and gene combinations contribute to intelligence and other complex systems. Many important developing systems are thus thought to be **polygenetically determined**—related to the control of many genes rather than to the control of a single gene.

A second important modification of the classic view of heredity relates to the timing by which genetically determined features appear. Traits such as eye color are relatively well fixed early in development, but other systems take a much longer time to appear. Indeed, many developmental systems—motor coordination, for example, and language—are characterized by the gradual emergence of different behaviors at different ages. These behaviors seem to follow one another in a fixed sequence and occur at approximately the same ages for different individuals. To account for this fixedness of order and apparent universality of age of appearance, modern genetics assumes the existence of **pacing genes.** Such genes, in effect, set the pace for emerging systems of development.

Modern genetic theory has led to attempts to account for the relationship between genetically determined and paced factors and the interaction between the developing organism and its environment. One model for the relationship between genetics and environment is known as the **epigenetic landscape** (Waddington, 1957). The epigenetic landscape depicts the biological control of development in terms of constraints of varying strengths (see Figure 6.3). The biological constraints are likened to pathways that control the direction of a ball rolling down an incline. The environmental constraints are likened to forces that can jostle the incline and threaten to jar the ball out of its pathway depending on the pathway's characteristics. If the pathway is shallow and broad, the environment might succeed in deflecting the ball. If it is deep and narrow, the pathway would tightly constrain the path of the ball even in the face of a great deal of environmental jostling.

For example, characteristics such as eye color, hair color, and body hair distribution are under close genetic control. Regardless of the environment in which the child is raised, these physical attributes will follow the hereditary program passed along from parent to offspring. In terms of the epigenetic landscape model, we would say that these characteristics are following a steep and narrow pathway, one that is unlikely to allow for deflection except under the most extreme circumstances. Such characteristics are described as highly **canalized:** in the genetic-environment interaction, the genetic influence is very strong. Other characteristics, however, such as personality and interpersonal skills are under much less direct genetic control. The genotypes inherited by the child for these characteristics allow for a relatively wide range of developmental outcomes. In these cases, the nature of the socializing environment plays a major role in determining the specific form that these characteristics will take. In terms of the epigenetic landscape model, we would say that these characteristics are following a shallow and wide pathway, one that is very much open to the possibility of deflection. In contrast to eye color and hair color, characteristics such as personality and interpersonal skill are described as having a low level of canalization: in the genetic-environment interaction, the genetic influence is relatively weak.

A Model of Development

The discussion of the role of heredity and environment can be summed up by posing a basic model of development that is framed in terms of the interactions between biological constraints, on the one hand, and environmental influences on the other. In a developing organism, a number of systems come into play by virtue of maturational changes that are genetically paced. These maturational changes are the organism's biological contribution to interaction with a caregiving environment. The interaction between organism and environment allows for environmental modification and lays the foundation for the next developing system to come into place. Succeeding development will be jointly influenced by the history of interactions with the environment and by genetically paced biological factors. Thus, biology and experience are constantly interacting.

For example, the development of perceptual-motor accuracy depends upon both experiential and maturational factors. A child's motor control will improve with continued practice and feedback, although biological constraints will establish parameters that confine the rate and degree of improvement. All subsequent gains in psychomotor skill depend in effect upon the baseline established at the previous developmental level. In this way, all human abilities develop as a consequence of complex biological and environmental interactions so that the relative influence of either factor cannot be understood by a simple additive model. As noted earlier, however, highly canalized behaviors like walking occur on schedule primarily as a result of maturation and are relatively independent of experience.

It is important to keep in mind the relationship between genetically paced biological factors and the environment when considering the physical, cognitive, social, and moral development of human beings. Although everyone goes through developmental stages in the same sequence and the same general chronology, an individual does so at his or her own particular pace. Therefore, ages and stages are approximate and should be considered as such. This can be readily seen by focusing on any major developmental achievement. For example, although the average child says his or her first word around one year of age, some children begin to produce words at nine or ten months and others not until 15 to 16 months. Individual variability is a hallmark of human growth and development, not just in the early years of life, but across the entire life span.

Physical Development

The study of physical development is primarily a biological one. Physical development is defined as the changes in an individual's physiological functioning over the life span reflecting the process known as physical maturation. Physical development is reflected in growth, maturation, and eventual deterioration of specific organ systems (for example, the central nervous system), in the size and weight of the individual, and in the emergence and refinement of motor abilities. As a process, physical development is characterized by two patterns of growth: *cephalocaudal* (head to toe) and *proximodistal* (center to periphery). In other words, the upper parts of the body develop before the lower, and the central parts of the body, such as the heart and lungs, develop before the extremities.

Prenatal Period

Prenatal development—the time from conception until birth—lasts an average of 266 days. During this nine-month span remarkable changes take place in physical growth and maturation. There are three recognized stages of prenatal development. The first, which is called the **ovum stage,** begins at conception and ends approximately 10 to 14 days later when the fertilized egg (zygote) becomes implanted in the uterine wall. During this stage there is rapid growth in the number of cells, but as yet no differentiation of cells according

The sucking reflex, present in all newborn infants, is critical to survival.

to specific function; that is, the primitive organ systems of the body have not yet begun to form. The second stage of prenatal development, which lasts from approximately the fourteenth day to the end of the eighth week of pregnancy, is called the **embryo stage.** During this time the organism is not only growing larger, but, more importantly, the tissues and organs of the body, such as the skeletal system, nervous system, circulatory system, and so on, are beginning to emerge. The growth of the developing organism from approximately the eighth week of pregnancy until birth is called the **fetal stage.** Technically, though, the fetal stage begins when bone cells first emerge. This is a period of dramatic growth in size. It also is the time during which the organ systems mature to the point where they can sustain life outside the womb.

At one time it was thought that the prenatal organism was invulnerable or protected from the influence of extrauterine forces. We now know, however, that the developing organism is quite sensitive to the influence of certain drugs, chemicals, diseases, malnourishment, and, other factors, particularly during the first trimester of pregnancy—that is, during the first three months following conception. Such environmental agents—which are called **teratogens**—may produce abnormalities in the developing child.

Prenatal Environment Influences

The prenatal organism is protected from most diseases that the pregnant mother contracts, although there are important exceptions. For example, if a pregnant woman contracts rubella (German measles) in the first three months of pregnancy, she is likely to give birth to a child with a congenital abnormality such as cataracts, deafness, or mental retardation. Other illnesses that can cause problems for the unborn child are syphilis, diabetes, and maternal toxemia (a condition characterized by excessive weight gain, abnormal fluid retention, swelling of limbs, and high blood pressure). Maternal nutrition also is an important factor in the development of the prenatal organism. A pregnant woman whose diet is low in certain vitamins, minerals, and proteins is more likely to have a baby who suffers from anemia, bone malformation, and other growth problems. In particular, a study by Vore (1973) found that malnutrition in the prenatal period and infancy is related to deficits in the development of the central nervous system which can lead to learning problems and even mental retardation.

It is now well known that a variety of drugs and chemicals also produce abnormalities in the developing fetus. Women who are addicted to narcotics, such as heroin or morphine, are likely to give birth to addicted babies. Furthermore, these babies are more often characterized by abnormal reflex activity, sleep disturbances, excessive crying and irritability, attentional problems, and hyperactivity (Kolata, 1978). In extreme cases, they may die from complications associated with drug withdrawal. A more common drug that has been linked to fetal abnormalities is alcohol. Women who drink heavily while they are pregnant are significantly more likely to give birth to children suffering from **fetal alcohol syndrome,** a condition associated with prematurity, physical and motor deficiencies, and mental retardation. Other common drugs and chemicals linked to prenatal and birth complications include nicotine (from cigarette smoking), certain hormones (which are often used to sustain a pregnancy), and environmental contaminants such as mercury and lead. In addition to diseases, malnourishment, and chemical agents, prenatal development also is influenced by maternal stress, blood incompatibility between mother and offspring (so-called rh factor), and radiation.

Only a small percentage of unborn children are affected by teratogenic agents. Even if a child is born with some congenital problem caused by one of these agents, the child's later development will not necessarily be abnormal. Research suggests that the presence or absence of prenatal and reproductive complications is not a good predictor of later development. Rather, developmental outcome in later childhood and even adulthood is a function of the interaction of reproductive risk factors and the quality of the caretaking environment in which the child is raised (Sameroff & Chandler, 1975). Children who are born at risk for certain problems by virtue of their prenatal and reproductive history at times can overcome these problems if their caretaking environment is sufficiently nurturing and stimulating.

Infancy

The newborn, or **neonate,** usually cries and breathes immediately, then is weighed, measured, and examined for abnormalities. The head may appear abnormally elongated because the bones may have been squeezed together during birth. There is no lasting damage, however, because the skull bones do not fuse until several months after birth. Almost all hospitals now assess a neonate's physical condition at one and five minutes after birth by use of the Apgar scale. This scale, which measures the infant's physiological adaptation to the external world, includes observations of the baby's reflexes, color, muscle tone, breathing, and heart rate (Apgar, 1953).

Babies are born with dozens of reflexes—some indicative of brain maturity and some necessary for life itself. In the first category, normal, full-term neonates have the following five reflexes:

1. *Babinski reflex.* Toes fan upward when the feet are stroked.
2. *Stepping reflex.* Legs move as if to walk when the feet touch a flat surface.
3. *Swimming.* Arms and legs stretch out when the baby is held horizontally, stomach downward.
4. *Grasping reflex.* Hands grip tightly when anything touches the palms.
5. *Moro reflex.* Arms are flung outward and then brought together over the chest when someone bangs the table on which the neonate is lying.

These reflexes, which disappear in the first months of life, are signs that the baby's body and brain are functioning normally.

In the second category, three sets of reflexes are critical for survival and become stronger with maturity:

1. The first set helps the neonate maintain constant body temperature and includes crying, shivering, and tucking the legs close to the body.
2. The second set helps ensure adequate nourishment and includes the sucking, rooting, swallowing, and crying reflexes.
3. The third set maintains an adequate oxygen supply. The most obvious reflex in this set is breathing.

An infant's physical growth is astoundingly rapid. Between birth and age two, most children grow about 15 inches and gain about 20 pounds, nearly four times their birth weight. By age two, most males have reached half their adult height, and most females have passed the halfway mark by an inch or two.

Infants develop major motor skills at different rates. On average, infants can grab at 6 months, pick up objects with their thumb and forefinger between 9 and 14 months, and take their first steps soon after age 1.

Brain Growth

At birth, the brain already weighs about 25 percent of its adult weight. By age two, the brain is about 75 percent of its adult weight; the body weight at age two is only about 20 percent of its adult weight (Tanner, 1970). In the first months, those areas that control the senses and simple motor abilities—the primary motor areas of the cortex and the primary sensory areas of the cortex—

Table 6.1   TYPICAL MILESTONES OF INFANT MOTOR DEVELOPMENT

Motor Skill	Age (in months) when 25% of infants have mastered the skill	Age (in months) when 50% of infants have mastered the skill	Age (in months) when 90% of infants have mastered the skill
Lifts head 45° when lying on stomach	—	—	2.6
Lifts head 90° when lying on stomach	1.3	2.2	3.2
Sits propped up (head steady)	1.5	2.9	4.2
Rolls over	2.3	2.8	4.7
Bears some weight on legs	3.4	5.0	6.3
Sits without support	4.8	5.5	7.8
Stands holding on to something	5.0	5.8	10.0
Pulls self to standing position	6.0	7.6	10.0
Walks holding on to furniture	7.3	9.2	12.7
Stands momentarily	9.1	9.8	13.0
Stands alone well	9.8	11.5	13.9
Stoops and recovers	10.4	11.6	14.3
Walks well	11.3	12.1	14.3
Walks backwards	12.4	14.3	21.5
Walks up steps	14.0	17.0	22.0
Kicks ball forward	15.0	20.0	24.0

Source: from The Denver Developmental Screening Test by W. K. Frankenburg and J. B. Dodds, *Journal of Pediatrics*, 71, pp. 181–191, 1967. Reprinted by permission of The C. V. Mosby Company.

grow most rapidly. The brain develops faster than any other part of the human body. Not only does the size and number of nerve cells increase, but the "association" fibers connecting various parts of the brain also increase. These association fibers are the groundwork for the emergence of higher order thinking. By age five, a child's brain is at about 90 percent of its eventual weight, even though the average five-year-old's body weight is less than one-third of the average adult's (Tanner, 1970).

Development of Motor Abilities

Most babies first learn to move from place to place by crawling, lying on their stomachs, and pulling themselves ahead with their arms. Creeping, which involves coordination of arms and legs, begins anywhere from 5 to 12 months after birth. Most babies take their first steps soon after age one and walk and run well by age two. After they begin to walk, babies are called toddlers, although, technically, children are infants until they begin to talk (see Table 6.1).

By six months, most babies can reach, grab, and hang on to a dangling object, but they have trouble letting go of the object. Usually in a month's time they will have mastered this skill as well. As babies attempt to use their fingers to pick up objects, they progress through stages that end with the ability to use thumb and forefinger together between the ages of 9 and 14 months.

Infants develop major motor skills at different rates. Norms, or averages, vary from place to place and time to time. The average Swedish baby walks a month earlier than the average French baby (Hindley, Filliozat, Klakenberg, Nocolet-Meister, & Sand, 1966). The earliest walkers in the world seem to be from Central Uganda, where the average baby walks at ten months (Ainsworth, 1967). The interaction of inherited and environmental factors determines the age at which a particular child begins to evidence specific motor skills.

Childhood

Growth is less rapid during the childhood years. From ages two through six, children gain about 4½ pounds and grow almost 3 inches a year. During middle childhood, the youngster will gain an average of about 5 pounds and grow 2½ inches taller each year.

Gross motor skills, which involve large body movements such as running, improve dramatically between the ages of two and six. In fact, almost any gross motor skill that does not require much strength or judgment can be learned by most healthy five-year-olds.

Fine motor skills—painting a picture, for example—involve smaller body movements that are much harder for young children to master because they have not developed the muscular control or careful judgment needed to accompany delicate tasks. Their efforts are further complicated by their short, chubby fingers.

Children gain skill in controlling their bodies during middle childhood, in part because they grow more slowly. Children from 7 to 11 can perform almost any motor skill as long as it does not require much power or judgment. Males and females are about equal in physical abilities, except that males have greater forearm strength (Tanner, 1970), and girls have greater flexibility.

Growth Variation

The two most significant causes of height differences are ethnic origin and nutrition (Meredith, 1978). Partly because of better nourishment and health care, urban, upper-class, and firstborn children are generally taller than rural, lower-class, and later-born children. Children of mothers who did not smoke during pregnancy tend to be taller (about a half inch) at age five than children of mothers who smoked during pregnancy. Ethnic differences in the height of Americans are primarily genetic: Afro-American children are tallest, followed by Caucasian Americans, and then Asian-Americans (Meredith, 1978). In some regions of the world, variations in height are caused by malnutrition. In North America, heredity, rather than diet, causes most variation in size (Eveleth & Tanner, 1976).

Adolescence: Ages 12 to 18

Childhood comes to a close and adolescence begins with the advent of puberty. Technically speaking, **puberty** refers to the physical changes that result in the capacity of the person to reproduce sexually. Besides sexual maturity though, other important physical changes are taking place at this time. Dramatic increases in size and weight and changes in body proportions bring the young adolescent closer to the adult's physical form.

The development of sexual characteristics and the overall growth pattern of the adolescent are both regulated by the presence of hormones secreted by the endocrine system. Specifically, the pituitary gland (often called the master gland) located in the brain transmits chemical messages to the sex glands—the ovaries in the female and the testes in the male—which, in turn, produce specific sex hormones. In males, **androgens** are produced primarily; in females, **estrogens** and **progesterone** are the hormones secreted. It should be noted that the different types of sex hormones are found in both males and females; however, in males androgens predominate, and in females, estrogens and progesterone predominate. It is these sex hormones that regulate the physical and sexual changes typically observed in the maturing adolescent.

The Growth Spurt

Even before the young adolescent reaches sexual maturity, the presence of sex hormones has begun to act on the individual. Toward the end of middle childhood, young people begin to experience rapid physical growth—the **growth spurt.** In girls, the growth spurt usually begins around 10½ years, but may occur as early as 7½ years or as late as 11½ years. Young adolescent boys generally are two years behind girls in physical maturation. Typically, for boys, the growth spurt begins around 12½ years, but may occur as early as 10½ years or as late as 16 years (Tanner, 1971).

Painting a picture and tying shoes are both examples of fine motor skills that children learn to master.

During the growth spurt, rapid changes are taking place in height, weight, and body proportions. At the peak of this period, girls may gain as much as 20 pounds and grow 3½ inches taller in one year; in the same length of time, boys may gain up to 26 pounds and add 4 inches in height (Tanner, 1971). Physical growth does not occur in all parts of the body simultaneously, though (Katchadorian, 1977). Adolescents often find that their extremeties—hands and feet—are growing faster than their arms and legs, and certainly faster than their trunk, which is usually one of the last areas of the body to increase in size. This pattern of growth—distalproximo (periphery to center)—is opposite the pattern found in earlier periods of development. In addition, when adolescents look at themselves in the mirror, they often notice a certain unevenness to their facial features. This is because the two sides of the body do not always grow in a synchronous or even way. In response to all of these changes, adolescents frequently feel uncomfortable with the way their bodies look. Their large hands and feet and gangly arms and legs make them feel awkward. In a few years, however, the rest of the body catches up with the early growth changes and adolescents attain the shape and proportions of an adult.

Sex Characteristics

Primary sex characteristics, those related to the genitals and internal reproductive organs, are the most obvious indication of the onset of puberty. In girls, the uterus, fallopian tubes, and vagina grow rapidly in early adolescence. The first menstruation, or **menarche,** is usually taken to be the beginning of puberty or sexual maturity. Actually, though, young female adolescents may be very irregular and infertile for the first six months to one year or so following menarche. For boys, this period is characterized by enlargement of the testes and prostate gland and by growth in the length and width of the penis. Although there is no single event similar to menarche that marks the onset of puberty for boys, ejaculation of seminal fluid containing active sperm is usually taken as an indication that the boy is sexually mature.

In addition to changes in the reproductive organs, other parts of the body, so-called secondary sex characteristics, also are undergoing dramatic changes and are signaling the emergence of sexual maturation. For girls, there is first an enlargement of the breasts and the development of light-colored, soft pubic hair. Somewhat later, there is the development of axillary (armpit) hair, a wid-

CHAPTER 6   DEVELOPMENT

ening of the hips, and an increase in fat tissue in both the hip and breast regions. These fatty deposits create a more rounded appearance for the sexually mature, adolescent girl. Eventually, the light-colored pubic hair becomes coarser, darker, and more curly. Boys' secondary sex characteristics generally develop in the same sequence as girls'. Initially, there is the development of sparse patches of soft, light-colored pubic hair and minor changes in voice quality. Somewhat later, axillary hair appears, as well as a broadening of the shoulders and chest. Toward the middle of adolescence enough facial hair has developed so that boys need to begin shaving. Finally, there is a noticeable deepening of the voice and the development of coarse, dark, curly pubic hair.

Although the sequence of sexual maturation is similar for most individuals, the actual tempo or rate of development is highly variable from person to person. Individual differences in rate of sexual maturation are associated with a variety of factors, including heredity, nutrition, health, and, of course, the person's sex.

Psychological Consequences of Early Versus Late Maturation

Does it matter whether one matures early or late? And if so, are the consequences of the timing of sexual maturation the same for boys and girls? These questions have sparked a number of research studies. For example, research by Jones (1957, 1958) and Mussen and Jones (1957) suggested that early maturation was a distinct advantage for boys. Early maturing boys were better at sports, had a more positive self-image, were more popular with peers, were more composed and skilled in social situations, and were more interested in girls than their late maturing counterparts. For girls, however, the consequences of the timing of sexual maturation were less clear-cut. On the whole, these researchers found that early maturation was associated with less prestige in the elementary school years, but more prestige in the junior high school years. The problem for early maturing girls is that there is almost no one as well developed as they are. Thus, they often feel out of place and disconnected from their peers—at least until such time as their peers catch up to them in sexual maturation.

Early and Middle Adulthood: Ages 20 to 65

Females reach their full adult stature at an average age of 17.3 years; males do not reach full growth until an average of 21.2 years (Roche & Davila, 1972). Today's twenty-year-olds tend to be taller and to mature earlier than their parents because of improved standards of living and nutrition (Roche, 1979).

Muscular strength peaks for most people somewhere between 25 to 30 years of age (Bromley, 1979). A gradual loss of strength occurs between ages 30 to 60—about 10 percent. Most body functions begin to decline during early adulthood, but the changes are so imperceptible that little effect is actually felt until after age 40. Motor skills and dexterity peak between 19 and 26; agility begins to lessen in the midthirties (Troll, 1975). The brain continues to grow during young adulthood; brain size and weight diminish thereafter (Bischoff, 1976).

There is considerable individual variation in physical development and adaptation in adulthood. For the most part, however, how people have lived for the preceding years of their lives "comes home to roost" during middle adulthood. Smoking-related illnesses, such as emphysema and cancer of the mouth, throat, and lungs, manifest themselves at this time. Nonsmokers have only half the health problems of smokers (Turner & Helms, 1979). Obesity is another

People who exercise probably feel less the decline of motor skills and dexterity that begins in the midthirties.

critical health problem. The probability of dying in middle age increases by 40 percent for those who are 30 percent or more overweight (Turner & Helms, 1979).

Research also has shown that adults who have experienced a greater number of life event stressors, for example, death of a loved one, divorce, loss of a job, or physical illness, are more likely to have problems of adjustment at this time of life (Hultsch & Plemons, 1979), particularly when the stressors are experienced simultaneously, or one right after another (Palmore, Cleveland, Nowlin, Ramm, & Siegler, 1979). But clearly, not all individuals who experience life stress become ill or have serious problems of adaptation. What differentiates those individuals who succumb to the stresses of life from those who do not? Research by Kobasa and associates has indicated that people who take more active control over their lives, who feel a greater sense of purpose and meaningfulness in their activities, and who are challenged rather than burdened by life events are less vulnerable to the impact of traumatic life experiences (Kobasa, 1979; Kobasa, Maddi, & Kahn, 1982). Kobasa uses the term *hardy personality* to characterize individuals who are better able to withstand life stress.

The median age among females for the occurrence of menopause, the cessation of menstruation, is 49.5 years (Olds, 1970). Although much has been written about the emotional upheaval (irritability, depression) and unpleasant physical symptoms (hot flashes, headaches, insomnia, and weight gain) experienced by menopausal women, research suggests that for the majority of women such problems either are absent or are relatively minor in nature. Some evidence for male mid-life biological changes, the male climacteric, exists. These include a decreased rate of testosterone production, decreased fertility, decreased sexual desire and an increase in impotency (Beard, 1975).

Late Adulthood: After 65

The choice of age 65 for a dividing line between middle and old age is arbitrary. Some people refer to early old age—ages 65–74—and advanced old age—from 75 on—the point at which physiological changes occur to a marked degree (Butler, 1975).

Senescence, that period during which people grow old, begins at different ages for different people. Declines in body functioning begin late for some people but early for others. This physical aging is the critical point for the beginning of late adulthood. And yet, the way a person acts and feels is a more satisfactory index of aging than chronological years. Some people cope very well with the obvious physical signs of aging: wrinkling of skin, graying of hair, loss of muscular strength, and slowing of response time. Others, however, are devastated by those physical changes and never make an adequate adjustment to old age.

Several theories have been proposed to explain the aging process. Genetic programming may determine an outside limit for life's length. Within this genetic program, wear and tear takes place. As cells grow older, they are less able to repair or replace damaged components and so they die. As the parts of a machine wear out, so do the organs of the body. Internal and external stresses seem to aggravate this process of wear and tear. Researchers are investigating the roles of DNA and enzymes, various chemical changes, and the weakening of the body's immune system in efforts to understand aging better (Rockstein & Sussman, 1979).

From conception to death, physical development and aging are complex processes that are continuous throughout the life span. Cognitive and social development and aging are equally complex processes, but not as obviously continuous.

Cognitive Development

In the course of development, human beings acquire a variety of flexible strategies that allow them to adapt to the demands of the environment. Essential to this adaptation is the process of thinking, or cognition. The major theories about **cognitive development** attempt to explain the processes of intellectual growth and the stages at which they come into play.

Piaget: The Growth of Logic

The most comprehensive and influential theory of cognitive development was formulated by the eminent Swiss genetic epistemologist Jean Piaget, who died in 1980. Originally trained as a biologist, Piaget began his studies of child development in the 1920s. He worked first with his own son and two daughters, and later investigated cognitive development in thousands of children. From his studies came more than 150 articles and more than 30 books that attempt to formulate a coherent and detailed view of how cognition develops from infancy onward (Piaget, 1970).

Piaget's careful analysis showed that, contrary to previous assumptions, children do not think the same way as adults. Their thinking is qualitatively different, and this difference is reflected in the growth of logic. As children develop, their thoughts go beyond a merely accurate reflection of the objective properties of the world in which they live. By applying the rules of logic, developing children learn to ascertain realities that are not directly perceivable. That is, they learn to make generalizations about aspects of the world that they have not, and sometimes cannot, directly observe. For Piaget, this fact posed one of the fundamental questions concerning human thought: how do we get from the physically real world—that which impinges on our sensory systems—to a world whose reality is conceptual? In other words, how do we get from the actual to the theoretically possible?

Piaget attempted to account for the growth of logic in terms of a continual interplay between the individual's current understandings and the external reality that the individual encounters. Specifically, Piaget looked to the interaction of two cognitive processes that he called assimilation and accommodation. **As-**

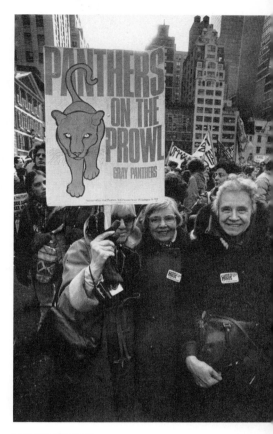

The way a person acts and feels is a more satisfactory index of aging than chronological years.

If food is not available, the infant may suck the next closest thing—a finger.

similation is the process through which individuals take in and incorporate their environment in terms of their current understandings of the world. **Accommodation** is the process through which these understandings of the world are modified by new information from the environment.

Underlying these two processes are several important themes. The child encountering the world has a number of hypothetical internal psychological structures or organizations that Piaget calls **schema.** In their interaction with the environment, children attempt to assimilate it into the internal schema that they currently have available to them. In other words, children's interpretation of reality is linked to the rules or principles that make up their internal schema. As they attempt to assimilate the world, children necessarily will encounter discrepancies between what a given scheme is prepared to deal with and the reality of the world. In the course of such discrepancies the assimilatory schema will undergo a slight modification, or accommodation, to deal with the objective properties of the world. Each modification of an assimilatory scheme that results from some accommodating encounter with the world serves to elaborate and differentiate the schema available for future encounters.

For example, a two-month-old infant's schema, or organized capacities for acting on the world, are limited to little more than a few reflexes. One of these reflexes is sucking, which involves opening the lips in a certain manner and then sucking whenever the surfaces around the mouth are stimulated. This reflex pattern typically has a very stereotyped form, so that the mouth opens in the shape of an ''O.'' The reflex is also rigidly organized so that opening the mouth is immediately followed by swallowing. Obviously, the reflex is very suitable for feeding, especially at the breast. But one of the first facts about babies—and about assimilation—is that infants continuously act on the world in any way they can. If they can only suck, they will attempt to suck everything in sight, such as a blanket or finger. But the sucking reflex that we have described will be less suitable for a blanket or a finger: the shape of the object is different, and it will not deliver milk. At first, infants will attempt to suck on these objects in the same way that they have nursed. Soon, however, accommodation will occur: the shape formed by the mouth will change as will the relationship between mouthing and swallowing. In the future, the infant will have more than one way of encountering the world: the choice to suck with the ''nipple mouth'' or with the ''blanket mouth'' must be made. This simple and yet subtle change is, in Piaget's view, the beginning of the growth of logic.

For Piaget, the balancing of assimilation (''what you already know how to do'') with accommodation (''how you have to change what you know to get something done here and now'') defines the child's adaptation to the world. Through successive encounters with the world, the range of internal assimilatory schemes gradually increases so that more and more the world is understood and hence acted on in an adaptive manner.

Besides assimilation and accommodation, Piaget also emphasized the process of **organization** as a mechanism of cognitive change. Organization refers to the tendency of the individual to coordinate and integrate information about the various objects that are encountered in the environment. As children develop, the process of organization results in a more coherent and unified system of knowledge. Although the tendency to organize information is inherent in the organism at birth, the differences between the very young child and the adult in the quality of their organizational capacity is quite dramatic. For example, young infants come to know the objects in their world through the separate schema they have available. A common object, such as a blanket, is known through the sucking scheme, looking scheme, grasping scheme, and so on. Unlike adults, who have an organized and unitary conception of the blanket as an object composed of various visual, tactile, olfactory (smell), and auditory qualities, young infants may well perceive the blanket as several distinct objects. In other words, the blanket that is mouthed is known to the sucking scheme and need not relate to the blanket as seen through the looking scheme.

Table 6.2 PIAGET'S STAGES OF COGNITIVE DEVELOPMENT

Piagetian Stage of Development	Approximate Age Range	Some Characteristics of this Stage
Sensorimotor Stage	Birth to about 18–24 months	Child knows world through motor activities and sensory impressions. Verbal symbols and even images not present. Child lacks understanding of *object permanence* (for instance, will not search for hidden objects).
Preoperational Stage	18–24 months to about 7 years	Child can use mental symbols (for instance, words) and shows some intuitive thought. However, both *serialization* (ability to order items along a dimension) and *conservation* are absent. Child is also *egocentric*—has difficulty in understanding that others may perceive the world differently.
Stage of Concrete Operations	7 years to about 11 or 12 years	Conservation and serialization are present. Child also understands *reversibility. Logical thought* appears, but only about objects that are present and observable.
Stage of Formal Operations	12 years and on	*Deductive reasoning* and *abstract thought* appear. Individual can take many different factors into account in making decisions, solving problems, and so on.

According to Piaget, cognitive development involves orderly movement through the stages described here. Please note that the age ranges shown are approximate. Many factors can influence the age at which a given child moves from one stage to another.

This phenomenon is rather like the story of the blind men and the elephant; each touches a different part of the elephant and fails to relate his perception to that experienced by the others. Thus, they each identify what they think the elephant is only in relation to the small section they have experienced. Because they fail to pool their knowledge, they are unable to identify the elephant as such. Only when children's various schema for knowing are organized can they achieve an integrated view that unites an object's various properties.

Thus, the world as adults know it is in fact *constructed* out of the integration of various cognitive schema. The knowledge of separate parts of the world are organized in respect to one another and from this process comes an organized view of the world.

Using the major themes of assimilation, accommodation, and the organization of knowing, Piaget traced the development of cognition through four major stages:

- Sensorimotor period—from birth through age 1
- Preoperational period—from age 2 through about age 6
- Period of concrete operations—from about age 7 through age 10
- Formal operational period—from age 11 through age 16

These stages are assumed to occur in a fixed sequence based on the interaction of biological maturation and experience and at approximately the same ages in all cultures (see Table 6.2).

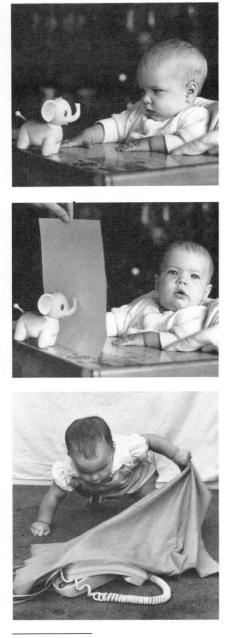

The concept of object permanence was first noted by Piaget. In the first few months of life an infant (above) attends only to objects that are physically present. If the object is obscured, it ceases to exist in the infant's mind. On the other hand, an older infant (below) will look for an object that has been covered or otherwise obscured.

During the first two years, children explore the relationship between sensory processes and their own bodily movements. This period is marked by a gradual shift from newborns' rudimentary reflexes, which are at first only minimally modified by contact with the environment, to the development of planned action that involves mental representation—that is, visual pictures of the results of actions.

To account for the many changes that occur during the first two years, the **sensorimotor stage** is subdivided into six separate substages.

Substage 1   In the first month, infants are largely a bundle of relatively isolated reflexes such as sucking. Although these reflexes are triggered by stimuli from the environment, such encounters cause little modification of the reflex. For instance, when an object is placed in an infant's hand, the infant will grasp it. The grasp may conform to the shape of the object, but on other occasions of grasping, there is no observed change—the initial grasp will be the same.

Substage 2   By about the second month, infants begin to show evidence of slight modification of reflex schema as a result of experience. As was discussed earlier, the shape of the open mouth may be altered during the sucking reflex to fit a blanket or a finger. Moreover, a highly significant pattern of activity now occurs that Piaget terms the **circular reaction.** Infants begin to repeat interesting activities. For example, infants whose sucking reflex has been modified to deal with a blanket instead of a breast will keep repeating this new scheme of action as if experimenting with it. For Piaget, the circular reaction is a general model of how new behaviors are acquired and perfected. Key to this concept is not just that children learn through repetition, but that children themselves generate the repetition as they attempt to explore their effective actions.

Piaget divides the circular reaction into three phases: primary, secondary, and tertiary. The primary circular reaction is characteristic of children in the second substage of sensorimotor development. In substage 2, the repetitions of behavior that define circular reactions are limited to the exercise of innate reflexes.

Substage 3   From the fourth to the eighth month, children become interested in the relationships between their own activities and the effects of those activities on the world. The repeated exploration of these relationships make up Piaget's secondary circular reaction. A characteristic secondary circular reaction has been termed "procedures to make interesting sights last." Suppose, for example, that an infant is lying in bed kicking its legs and looking at a mobile suspended above the bed. By chance, the infant's kicking causes the mobile to move. The infant, suddenly intrigued by the movement of the mobile, would engage in a circular reaction, kicking the legs and looking at the mobile for signs of movement. The infant might do this repeatedly, indicating its growing sense that its actions might somehow affect the world. Such "procedures to make interesting sights last" thus demonstrate a new orientation of the infant's activities—that is, an awareness of the relationship between action and result. But these procedures also show the limitations of infants' abilities because they still do not have a notion of precisely how action and result are related.

Substage 4   From the eighth to the twelfth month, infants begin to show evidence of a rudimentary understanding of cause and effect. In substage 3, infants' achievements are limited to attempting to reproduce accidental effects that their actions might be related to. In substage 4, infants' behaviors indicate that they are beginning to have some understanding of the relationship between means and ends. For example, they have discovered **object permanence**—that is, the fact that an object continues to exist even though it can no longer be seen. Thus they will remove a barrier to get at a ball or rattle that has been hidden behind the barrier. The independent schema of action for solving such practical problems may already have existed, but in isolation from one another. Now these independent schema become organized with respect to one another. The coordination of these schema produces the ability to solve a number of practical problems that require complex action sequences.

Substage 5   From approximately the twelfth to the eighteenth month, children display a new form of circular reaction that transcends the limitations of the previous stage. The tertiary circular reaction describes activities in which infants actively experiment with available action schema. They discover, for example, that there is more than one way to knock down a tower of blocks: the thrust of their legs will work as well as the sweep of their arms. During this stage, infants explore the equivalences that can be established among various ways of accomplishing the same end. In contrast to the secondary reaction, where they attempt to repeat the same environmental effect by repeating a single means to that end, they now experiment with various ways in which to alter the world. Children also are no longer limited to the action schema already in their repertoire; by experimenting with means, they discover in this substage new ways of acting on the environment.

Substage 6   From 18 months to 24 months, children show evidence of mental planning. In a given problem situation, for example, children no longer are limited to discovering solutions through trial and error manipulations. Instead, at this substage they are beginning to use mental representations of possible actions—that is, mental images of the different possibilities in a given situation. Using these representations, they can sort out the combinations of possible actions and select the action they will take. Now they are interested not only in the means but in the means to an end.

Thus cognitive development during the six substages of the sensorimotor stage takes children from a bundle of simple reflexes to individuals capable of imagining possible actions and of planning intelligently.

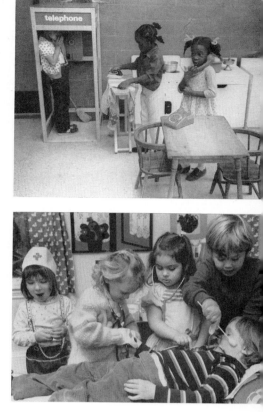

During the preoperational stage, children begin to imitate things they have observed in the past.

Childhood

At the end of the second year, children enter a long period of transition that extends to their sixth or seventh year. With the acquisition of language, they begin to extend their adaptations from a reality that can be acted on to a reality that can be talked and thought about.

The Preoperational Stage

During the **preoperational stage,** children begin to deal with the world symbolically: they begin to recognize that one thing can stand for another. This is evidenced in play, for example, where a cardboard box becomes a "house" and a group of dolls the "family" that lives there.

In addition to language and play, children's ability to deal with the world symbolically is seen in the development of representational drawing and their use of representational gestures. It is also seen in their capacity for **deferred imitation**—that is, their ability to imitate something such as a parent working that was observed some time in the past. Deferred imitation requires that the child form a mental image of the event he or she has observed which is then used at some later time to guide specific imitative actions.

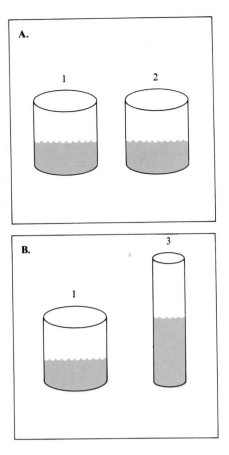

Figure 6.4

When a five-year-old child is shown two beakers of liquid, as shown in (A), and asked, "Which contains more, 1 or 2?" The child will say that they contain equal amounts. When the contents of 2 are poured into 3, a taller and thinner beaker as shown in (B), and the child is again asked, "Which contains more?" he or she will answer, "3." The child is said to be unable to conserve continuous quantities.

However, although preoperational children have become competent practical actors on their world, they have difficulty in organizing their thoughts about practical actions. They act on the world in a perfectly coherent way but are unable to present an equally coherent formulation of the action. For example, Piaget reported in *The Grasp of Consciousness* (1976) on studies in which children were asked to describe how they could crawl. Although the children could indeed crawl efficiently, their descriptions bore little relationship to what they actually did while crawling. Even while in the act of crawling, children would describe their actions in terms quite different from what they were doing with their arms and legs. Invariably, the children said crawling was accomplished by moving the left hand and left foot forward at the same time followed by the right hand and right foot. As anyone who has ever tried this can attest, it does not work: the hand and foot advanced at the same time have to be contralateral—that is, left hand, right leg.

In addition to such problems as describing simple actions with language, preoperational children also have difficulties with information that can be encoded only in language. A three-year-old boy might not understand, for example, that he is his brother's brother or that, if he has two brothers, his family contains three brothers.

The lack of logical organization that characterizes thinking during this stage can best be understood when contrasted with the next stage of cognitive development, the stage of concrete operational thought.

The Concrete Operational Stage

Between the ages of 7 and 11, children display a logical organization of thought that contrasts sharply with the previous period. Children in the **concrete operational stage** reason logically—that is, they perform mental operations or mental actions that previously had to be carried out in actuality—although largely in terms of concrete objects.

A dramatic example of the new logical organization of thought is the acquisition of the concept of conservation, which says, in essence, that the amount of a substance is not changed when its shape is altered. One of the many forms of conservation that Piaget studied was the conservation of continuous quantities. Piaget devised a simple test for children. The researcher takes two short stubby glasses of the same size and fills them equally with milk or lemonade (see Figure 6.4A). The child looks at the two glasses and agrees they contain the same amounts of liquid. Then the researcher transfers the liquid from one of the stubby glasses into a third glass that is taller and much thinner (Figure 6.4B). Then the child is asked whether the short glass and the tall thin glass contain the same amount of liquid. Younger children, still in the preoperational stage, typically will assert that the tall thin glass has more liquid because it is taller. By contrast, children in the concrete operational stage will correctly assert that both glasses contain the same amount. Nothing has been added and nothing has been taken away, they might point out.

More recent evidence suggests that even preoperational children possess the ability to conserve number (see Figure 6.4). In an important study, Gelman (1972) showed three-year-old children two platters, each containing a row of two or three toy mice. The platter with the larger number of mice, for example, three, was designated the "winner" without specifically implicating the number of mice as the critical attribute. The plate with fewer mice was designated as the "loser." Each plate was then covered with a large lid before being shuffled. Each child was provided with a prize for correctly choosing the three-mouse plate and calling it the winner. On several trials, Gelman lengthened or shortened the three-mouse row. Despite this spatial transformation, the children continued to correctly identify the three-mouse row as the winner.

Later, Gelman surreptitiously changed the three-mouse row by removing one of the toy mice and moving the remaining two toys in the row further apart or closer together. In marked contrast to the previous spatial change, almost all the children noticed the missing mouse and felt that such a modification disqualified it as a winner. Most thought it was now a loser. The children were acutely sensitive to the conservation of number and were not swayed by spatial-perceptual alterations as the traditional Piagetian approach might suggest. Unlike most Piagetian conservation tasks, Gelman's procedure avoided using the term ''more,'' which children use in a less restrictive manner than do adults. Thus, when children in previous experiments were observed to associate a longer row with its containing ''more'' items, an alternative explanation might be that the children are making use of the term ''more'' as analagous to taking up more space. This type of study illustrates how a child's level of language comprehension can exert a powerful influence on studies of cognitive development and result, as in this case, in a vast underestimation of a child's actual cognitive ability.

Note the crucial difference in the ways that preoperational and concrete operational children make their judgments of the amount of liquid in the glasses in Figure 6.4. Preoperational children base their judgments on appearances: the taller glass looks bigger. Concrete operational children base their judgments on the relationship between actions. This logical functioning reflects the developing organization of various schemes with respect to one another. Thought proceeds from what is known to what can be known by definite rules of implication. Using these rules of logic, concrete operational children override their perceptions of the appearances of things.

The development of logical thinking also can be seen in children's ability to classify or categorize objects in the world around them. Although preoperational children often are able to group things together on the basis of a single attribute (for example, they can put all the squares together in a pile), they do not recognize that objects can be members of more than one category simultaneously (a red square belongs to the class of ''red things'' and the class of ''square things''). By contrast, concrete operational children do appreciate the multiplicative nature of object classification. They also are knowledgeable about the relationship between subordinate and superordinate classes—known as **class inclusion.** For example, a child is shown ten wooden beads (eight red and two yellow) and is asked, ''Are there more wooden beads or more red beads?'' The concrete operational child would answer correctly that there are more wooden ones. The preoperational child, because of the overwhelming perceptual difference between the number of red and yellow beads, mistakenly would answer that there are more red ones.

The development of logical thought allows the child to organize the world in a very efficient manner. No longer is the child limited by the appearance of things; now reality can be inferred by the rules of logic. This achievement allows for a greater range of intellectual adaptation than was possible during the preoperational stage.

Adolescence

Beginning in about the twelfth year, children's formulations of the world in terms of logical principles take a highly significant turn. In the concrete operational period the ability to reason logically was limited to concrete situations. Now in the fourth and final stage of cognitive development, the **formal operational stage,** the ability to reason logically extends to more abstract matters. Children's intelligence is no longer limited to operating on things themselves but can reason in terms of hypotheses about reality. Hypothetical thinking—reasoning on the basis of a number of related ''if such is true, then so and so must also be true'' statements—is the hallmark of this stage of logical thinking; it also lies at the heart of scientific research and discovery. More

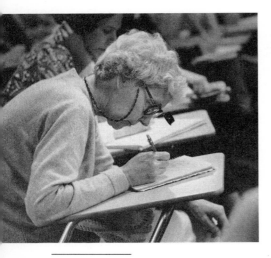

The broad-based loss of skills that we often imagine are by no means an inevitable part of aging. In fact, many elderly adults find that they can at last find the time to continue their education.

generally, it makes possible human formulations of moral, religious, and philosophical principles. Piaget's model goes only through adolescence in explaining intellectual development. Many other psychologists, however, have been interested in intellectual development beyond adolescence.

Early and Middle Adulthood

For many years, Piaget argued that formal operational thought was achieved by all individuals during adolescence. More recently, he acknowledged that this advanced level of reasoning may not be fully consolidated until young adulthood, and importantly, may not be expressed equally in all areas of a person's life (Piaget, 1972). For example, the scientist may manifest formal operations in devising experiments in his laboratory, but revert back to developmentally earlier forms of thinking in areas where he has less expertise, such as fixing his car's engine. Likewise, the artist may be capable of formal thought in analyzing modes of artistic expression, but have difficulty in applying similar rules of logic in solving an engineering problem. Thus, formal operations may be more narrowly expressed by people than previously was thought.

Another controversy in Piagetian theory has to do with the possibility of new forms of thinking beyond formal operations. According to Piaget, the final stage of thought is formal operations. Other researchers, however, believe that a more advanced level of thought exists that is displayed for the first time in adulthood. For example, Kramer (1983) has identified three characteristics that are mentioned frequently in conjunction with advanced adult thinking. First, adult thought is said to be *relativistic*. Unlike adolescents, who tend to think in absolutistic ways, adults are more likely to accept the idea that truth is relative—that it depends on one's point of view. A second feature of mature adult thought is the realization that *contradiction is an inherent aspect of reality*. Instead of always trying to resolve contradiction, adults often seek it out. Finally, adult thought, according to Kramer, also is characterized by its tendency to *organize contradictory knowledge into higher order systems*. Thus, whereas the adolescent is restricted to the development of a single abstract system of thought organized around formal operational principles, the adult thinker is said to view knowledge as the integration and coordination of multiple, potentially incompatible, systems of beliefs.

In the past, psychologists believed that general intellectual activity peaked in young adulthood and then declined. However, this theory was based on results of cross-sectional studies that compared test scores of different groups of people at different age levels and that did not control for group differences in such factors as education, experience, exposure to television, and so on. On the other hand, longitudinal studies, which test the same group of people periodically over years, show that a number of intellectual abilities appear to increase until at least the fifties (Owens, 1966).

There is no question that young adults do better on intelligence tests (particularly on tests that are timed or require speed) than middle-aged adults. Many of the factors that affect test performance—speed, motivation, health, sensory abilities, and so on—may be influenced by increasing age, resulting in lower test scores for older adults. Middle-aged adults, conversely, may bring wisdom and experience to problem solving that make them better able to cope than young adults. In fact, in certain areas such as vocabulary and social knowledge, middle-aged adults consistently outperform younger adults. Although sensory abilities do decline from young adulthood onward, there is virtually no evidence that any meaningful psychological changes that affect intellectual activity occur in the brain during middle adulthood (Welford & Birren, 1965).

CHAPTER 6 DEVELOPMENT

Age-related changes in creativity also have been observed in the adult years. In one classic study, Lehman (1953) reported that unique, high quality creative work among artists and scientists was more likely to be found in young adulthood than later in life. Albert Einstein, for example, made most of his important breakthroughs in the development of relativity theory when he was still in his early twenties. Other researchers have noted that productivity—the number of creative contributions a person makes—generally peaks in the middle adult years (Dennis, 1968). Productivity is quite variable, however, from profession to profession. Dennis observed that artists generally are more likely to reach their peak productivity earlier than scientists and scholars whose work may require extensive collection and evaluation of data.

It seems that although certain sensory processes and intellectual abilities begin to wane in middle adulthood, general experience, comprehension, and flexibility in thinking more than compensate for those minor reductions in cognitive efficiency (Baltes & Schaie, 1974).

Late Adulthood

It is commonly believed that people lose many of their mental abilities as they get older. The stereotype of the slow-to-respond, confused, and forgetful elderly adult is a reflection of this belief. And yet what seems clear from psychological research is that the broad-based loss of skills that we often imagine are by no means an inevitable part of aging.

Investigators have found that abilities and skills based primarily on education and cultural experience, such as general information, vocabulary, social knowledge, and mechanical knowledge, are maintained, or actually increase, during old age. These types of abilities are part of what is called **crystalized intelligence.** By contrast, **fluid intelligence,** which involves abilities related to perceiving relations, forming concepts, reasoning, and abstracting information, have been found to peak between the ages of twenty and thirty, and thereafter to decline, with a greater loss of ability occurring in old age (Cattell, 1963; Horn & Donaldson, 1980).

One area in which older individuals do seem to have trouble is when they must divide their attention between two or more input sources (trying to listen to more than one conversation at a time), or between information being held in memory and a particular response that is required (Craik, 1977). This suggests that there may be a decline in attentional capacity as people get older. If there is, however, it does not appear to have much effect on short-term memory. Research indicates that in most situations requiring short-term memory older adults are able to remember the same number of words, letters, or numbers as younger adults, although the older person may need more time to scan through short-term memory for the relevant information. By contrast, there is a growing body of evidence to indicate that older people do have significantly more difficulty than younger people in remembering information that is no longer being actively attended to or focused upon. This long-term memory deficit is related to problems in three areas: registration of information in memory, storage of information, and retrieval of information (Craik, 1977; Hartley, Harker, & Walsh, 1980).

Age-related changes in cognitive functioning are affected by many factors. One of the most important is health. Elderly adults in good health show little, if any, loss of mental abilities; older people who are fighting illness or approaching death show a marked decline in intellectual functioning (Riegel & Riegel, 1972). A decrease in blood supply to the brain or extensive hardening of the arteries may also cause changes in thinking.

Another factor influencing intellectual performance is the speed of response required on the task. Older people are unduly penalized in situations that demand "speeded" performance because there is a significant slowing of central nervous system activity with increasing age (Marsh & Thompson, 1977). The slower the central nervous system transmits information, the slower the response of the individual. But this does not mean that older people necessarily are incapable of solving these tasks. With a more liberal time requirement the elderly very often are successful in completing and solving tasks that they have failed under more stringent time constraints.

Research also suggests that "age is kinder to the initially more able"; that is, people with high ability tend to show less decline in intellectual functioning in old age than people with lower ability (Blum & Jarvik, 1975). This probably is because brighter individuals are better educated, more often seek intellectual challenge, and more frequently use their skills in their daily lives. As an example of this principle, consider the high level of achievement and productivity maintained into the seventies and eighties by such individuals as Albert Einstein, Sigmund Freud, Jean Piaget, Pablo Picasso, Bertrand Russell, George Bernard Shaw, Arthur Rubenstein, and Vladimir Horowitz.

The variability among people in intellectual functioning (and in other areas of life) is extremely broad in old age—possibly broader than at any other time in the life span. And yet, on the whole, the skills and knowledge of our senior citizens, a growing percentage of the population, are too often unrecognized and underutilized by society.

Information Processing Theory

Piaget's theory of cognitive development focuses on the *structure* of thought. The primary issue he has been concerned with is describing the developmental changes in the organizational schemes underlying specific forms of intellectual adaptation. Other researchers, however, have taken a different approach to understanding cognitive development. Rather than focusing on the structure of thought, these investigators have been concerned with the *process* of thought—that is, the way people attend to, transform, represent, organize, store, and retrieve information in problem-solving situations. **Information processing theory,** as this latter approach is called, is a relatively new way of looking at cognitive development. Its origins can be traced to scientific advances in communication theory, computer science, cognitive theory, linguistics, engineering, and information theory (Miller, 1983; Siegler, 1983). In reality it is not a single theory, but rather a framework characterizing a number of approaches to understanding cognitive processing. Common to all of these approaches is a concern for understanding how information flows through a cognitive system during problem solving. From a developmental perspective, the concern is with describing how the processing of information changes with age.

Information processing theory has likened the human mind to the workings of a computer. Both humans and computers are considered to be symbol manipulating devices. Each is assumed to have certain limited capacities for processing information. The limitations may be related to attentional capacity, the number of symbols that can be manipulated simultaneously, the speed with which information can be transmitted, the depth to which memory can be scanned, and so on. Understanding the nature and scope of these limitations and the means by which people of different ages attempt to overcome them is the central focus of this approach (Siegler, 1983).

From a developmental point of view, information processing theory has been particularly useful in providing researchers with insights into how people remember things. For example, Ann Brown (1975) distinguishes between involuntary and deliberate memory. Involuntary memory "just happens"; it involves simple recognition of objects or people that a person has encountered previously. This type of memory does not change very much across the life

CHAPTER 6   DEVELOPMENT

span—even young infants are capable of this sort of activity. By contrast, deliberate memory is a purposeful attempt to remember something; it involves strategies for organizing information, strategies for coding information, and strategies for effective retrieval of information. Deliberate memory improves significantly across the childhood years. Preschoolers, for example, seldom show spontaneous use of strategies that would aid them in remembering things. Most often they behave as if simply looking at something will be sufficient to remember it later on. As children enter the elementary school years, however, a number of specialized memory strategies emerge. One such strategy is **verbal rehearsal,** repeating over and over the things to be remembered. Another strategy is **clustering,** grouping together objects that are alike in some way and using a conceptual label (fruit) as a cue for remembering the individual items (pear, apple, orange, etc.).

Besides the development of specific memory strategies, children also show increases in their understanding of how memory works—what psychologists call **metamemory.** In other words, as children get older their knowledge about what is necessary for effective memory, and what factors might inhibit memory, improves dramatically. In one study, for example, Kreutzer, Leonard, and Flavell (1975) asked children in kindergarten and fifth grade whether it mattered if, after being told a phone number, they made the call immediately or got a drink of water. Only 40 percent of the kindergarten children, but over 75 percent of the fifth-graders, realized that postponing the phone call while getting a drink might result in the person forgetting the number.

Information processing theory is having a tremendous impact on current thinking about cognitive development, not just in the childhood years, but across the entire life span. Recently investigators have attempted to integrate the structural approach of Piaget with the process approach of information processing theory (Pascual-Leone, 1980; Siegler, 1981).

Erik Erikson distinguished eight different stages in a lifelong process of psychosocial development.

Social Development

Young human beings acquire the social skills and knowledge needed to function as members of their culture through the process of **socialization.** The emerging needs of the individual are expressed in interactions with a social environment—at first the parents, then an ever-widening context of people. The organization of the social environment may vary considerably from culture to culture, subculture to subculture. Some social organizations may allow for smooth transitions to occur from stage to stage; others might lead to an excessive crisis around a developing need.

Erikson's Theory of Psychosocial Development

Social development throughout life is a process of integration—of adapting inherited and learned traits to the social environment. A detailed view of social integration has been offered by Erik Erikson (1950) to account for social and emotional development over the entire life span. Erikson's view attempts to link in a closely knit fashion three key elements—highly canalized elements of biological development, child-rearing practices, and the social-cultural context within which the first two elements occur. It is derived from the analysis of case histories of abnormal development, not from experimental psychology.

Erikson distinguished eight different stages in a lifelong process of what he calls **psychosocial development.** Biological factors, social context, development over the life span, and the continuity of stages all interrelate in the eight stages proposed by Erikson. As illustrated in Table 6.3, these stages range from the first year of life, through adolescence, and into the aging years.

Each of these stages is characterized by new social situations and a central psychosocial crisis point that can have either a favorable or an unfavorable outcome. Successful resolution of each crisis depends essentially on the smoothness with which the developing individual satisfies needs particular to that stage and then is able to express that resolution in social life.

Infancy and Toddlerhood

According to Erikson, the first psychosocial crisis that confronts the person is learning to trust the world. This crisis takes place in the context of the first social relationships, which are with the principal caregivers—usually the mother and father. The special bond that forms between infant and caregiver is known as **attachment.** Much information about this relationship comes from research that has been done with monkeys. It is necessary to use caution in generalizing the results of animal studies to humans, but, for ethical or practical reasons, many important experiments can be carried out only with animals.

Table 6.3 ERIKSON'S STAGES OF PSYCHOSOCIAL DEVELOPMENT

Psychosocial Stage		Task or Crisis	Social Conditions	Psychosocial Outcome
Stage 1 (birth to 1 year)	Oral-sensory	Can I trust the world?	Support and provision of basic needs	Basic trust
			Lack of support and deprivation	Basic distrust
Stage 2 (2–3 years)	Muscular-anal	Can I control my own behavior?	Permissiveness and support	Autonomy
			Overprotection and lack of support	Shame and doubt
Stage 3 (4–5 years)	Locomotor-genital	Can I become independent of my parents by exploring my limits?	Encouragement to explore	Initiative
			Lack of opportunity to explore	Guilt
Stage 4 (6–11 years)	Latency	Can I master the necessary skills to adapt?	Adequate training and encouragement	Industry
			Poor training and lack of support	Inferiority
Stage 5 (12–18 years)	Puberty and adolescence	Who am I? What are my beliefs, feelings, and attitudes?	Internal stability and positive feedback	Personal identity
			Confusion of purpose and unclear feedback	Role confusion
Stage 6 (young adulthood)	Young adulthood	Can I give fully of myself to another?	Warmth and sharing	Intimacy
			Loneliness	Isolation
Stage 7 (adulthood)	Adulthood	What can I offer succeeding generations?	Purposefulness and productivity	Generativity
			Lack of growth and regression	Stagnation
Stage 8 (maturity)	Maturity	Have I found contentment and satisfaction through my life's work and play?	Unity and fulfillment	Integrity
			Disgust and dissatisfaction	Despair

Source: Adapted from E. H. Erikson, *Childhood and Society,* 2nd rev. ed. (New York: W. W. Norton & Company, Inc., 1963).

The classic, pioneering research on attachment in monkeys was done by Harry and Margaret Harlow (1965). Their observations demonstrate the importance and potency of mother-infant attachment in the species they have studied, the rhesus monkeys. Infant rhesus monkeys show the strength of their attachment to the mother in many ways.

A number of indirect measures are used to study the strength of an infant's response to its mother. One such measure is the frequency of proximity-seeking behaviors such as looking at the mother, attempting to touch the mother, or approaching the mother. Another measure is the degree of separation protest, such as crying or huddling in a corner, when the mother is not present. Infant rhesus monkeys show both of these types of behaviors: they spend a great deal of time in contact with their mothers and become very agitated when separated from them.

The dynamics of this attachment and its functional significance were demonstrated by experiments in which young monkeys were raised with artificial mothers, called surrogates. These surrogate mothers were made with soft cloth bodies, and the infants became quite attached to them (see Figure 6.5). During the developmental stage that the Harlows called the *comfort and attachment stage,* infants stay in very close proximity to their mothers. In the case of infants with cloth surrogates, the infants often spent 17 hours a day in contact with the surrogates, even though food was obtained away from the surrogate mothers. The Harlows believe that during this stage the infant establishes a bond of trust, which is later used as a base for the development of broader social contacts and behaviors.

In the next developmental stage, which the Harlows called the *stage of security,* the infants appear to gain a sense of self-confidence from the presence of the mother. For example, in one study infants were introduced into an open field, a room containing many new objects. Sometimes the surrogate mothers were present; sometimes they were not. When the surrogates were absent, the infants appeared very distressed—vocalizing, crouching, huddling, and rarely exploring the room. When the surrogates were introduced, the infants' behavior was much different. They rushed to the "mother" and clutched it intensely; then they relaxed, and all signs of apprehension disappeared. The surrogate mothers became a base for exploration of the room and manipulation of the objects in it. The presence of the "mothers" seemed to impart a sense of security to the infants.

These observations show how the attachment between infant and mother serves a critical function in promoting the interactions of the developing organism and its environment. With the mother present, the infant monkey interacts with, and presumably begins to learn how to manipulate, its environment. But the absence of the mother prevents such interaction. Infants raised without effective surrogate mothers failed to interact effectively with the environment. For example, infants raised with surrogate mothers made only of wire mesh failed to develop attachments to the surrogates, and when placed in the open field, these infants appeared terrorized whether or not the surrogate was present.

Human development studies show an overall pattern similar to that of rhesus monkeys—a system that is particularly tuned to the development of interaction with the environment. Proximity-seeking behaviors and separation protest associated with the process of attachment are manifested very early in human infancy. For example, very young infants seem to be more attracted to human beings than to objects. According to one study, infants discriminate between social objects: infants as young as two weeks tend to look longer at the mother than at a stranger (Carpenter, 1975). Another study indicates that four-week-old infants display a tendency to move toward people rather than objects (Brazelton, Koslowski, & Main, 1974).

Figure 6.5

The importance of infant-mother attachments was demonstrated in studies by Harry and Margaret Harlow. Surrogate mothers, made with soft cloth bodies, were used in experiments with infant rhesus monkeys. The infants developed quite an attachment to the surrogate mothers, which appear to provide a sense of security.

Figure 6.6

The results of the Shaffer and Emerson study suggest that attachment becomes specific as development proceeds.

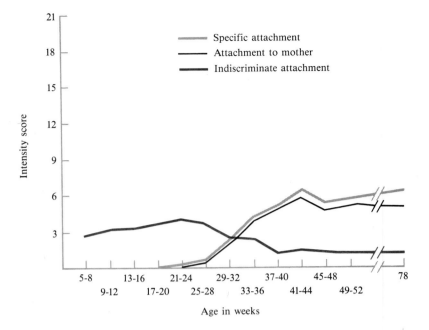

An ambitious field study of separation protest investigated the intensity and age of onset of separation protest in a sample of 60 Scottish infants (Schaffer & Emerson, 1964). Every four weeks for more than a year the researchers visited the infants' homes and asked their mothers to report the infants' behaviors in a variety of situations—for example, when the infant was left alone in a room with strangers or when left in a carriage outside a place of business. The results of this study are shown in Figure 6.6. The youngest infants—between 5 and 29 weeks—showed moderate amounts of separation protest when they were left alone not only by the mother but also by a large array of other individuals, even strangers. However, at about 29 weeks of age and beyond, indiscriminate protest declined and more intense protest to the departure of specific individuals—most often the mother—increased. These discriminate protests reached a peak at between 12 and 18 months of age. These results suggest that as development proceeds, attachment becomes specific—to mother, father, or other primary caregiver.

Studies suggest that adults may possess innate responses to several built-in signaling systems from infants. Physical features, such as the size and shape of the head, are recognized as "babyish" by adults who respond favorably to them (Alley, 1983). In addition to babyish features, infants display another characteristic that serves to strengthen the social bond with adults—smiling, which occurs so early in life and so universally that it is probably a highly canalized activity. Most newborn babies smile, sometimes even in the absence of any external stimulus; even blind babies smile. After the first month, smiling becomes more pronounced. It can clearly be elicited by anything that resembles a human face—even a schematic drawing or a cardboard mask. Thus, several months before attachment is well developed, smiling provides a mechanism for establishing social interaction with human caregivers.

Further evidence of such early social mechanisms comes from videotaped social interchanges of cooing and looking between mothers and infants as young as three months of age (Stern, 1974). These videotapes make clear that a "fine-tuned" relationship exists between mothers and young infants. Both mothers and infants adjust their behavior relative to one another, with mothers engaging in highly rhythmic interchanges with the infants. Infants, in turn, are able to reciprocate and often to pace the interaction.

Babyish features, smiling, "fine tuning"—all of these characteristics suggest that the infants are well equipped to attain and maintain social interactions with caregivers. Infants' physiognomy and behavior combine in a way that is satisfying to caregivers, who themselves seem specially attuned to infants' social signals.

Patterns of Attachment

Although infants and caregivers may, as evidence suggests, come pre-equipped to be mutually responsive, there is nonetheless considerable variation in their degree of social integration. Many intervening factors—biological or environmental—can disturb the mutually fine-tuned relationship between caregivers and infants. Some infants may be colicky or have irritable temperaments and thus display patterns of distress that caregivers find difficult to ameliorate. This can result in frustration that might disrupt the caregivers' responsiveness. Similarly, environmental stresses, such as economic problems or having no adult social outlet, can intervene to divert caregivers' abilities to respond to children's social signals.

Smiles are certainly an important part of the "fine-tuned" relationship that exists between mothers and infants.

Variations in infant-caregiver relationships have been investigated by Mary Ainsworth and her colleagues (Ainsworth, Bell, & Stayton, 1971). These researchers make an important distinction between two types of mother-child interaction patterns—sensitive and insensitive. In this distinction, sensitivity relates to the caregiver's ability to be aware of the presence of social signals from the infant and the ability to interpret correctly the meaning of these signals; insensitivity implies a lack of such awareness and a tendency to force compliance with commands without regard for the particular situation or the particular state of the child. Ainsworth and her colleagues have found that the relative sensitivity of the caregiver's responsiveness affects the quality of attachment shown by the infant. To assess quality of attachment these investigators devised a laboratory method called the *strange situation,* which involves a precise sequence of events. The mother and child first enter a room containing a number of toys scattered around on the floor. After several minutes an unfamiliar adult enters and takes a seat. Mother leaves the child in the room with the toys and stranger. She then returns to the room while the stranger leaves. The mother leaves again, leaving the child alone for a few minutes. The stranger returns and, shortly thereafter, so does the mother. During this sequence of two separations and two reunions, the child's behavior is observed and recorded on videotape.

Based upon these observations, Ainsworth and her colleagues have been able to identify three primary patterns of attachment:

- *Securely attached* (Group B): This group is active in seeking physical contact or interaction on reunion—contact that is effective in terminating distress and promoting a return to play activity.
- *Insecurely attached, avoidant* (Group A): This group avoids the mother upon reunion, especially in the instance of the second reunion when the child's distress at separation presumably has built up and is greater.
- *Insecurely attached, ambivalent* (Group C): This group has difficulty becoming settled on reunion, sometimes trying to get away from the mother; the child acts anxious even when mother returns and seems ambivalent about using mother as a secure base for promoting a return to play.

These findings were bolstered by a more recent study that looked at face-to-face interactions between mothers and infants aged 6 to 15 weeks—a stage at which attachment behaviors are not yet evident (Blehar, Lieberman, & Ainsworth, 1977). The results showed considerable differences among the mother-infant pairs in the degree of mutuality of interaction patterns. These variations, in turn, were related to the security of attachment later measured when the infants were 12 months old.

Secure attachment and a sense of trust allows for adaptive exploration of the environment.

Attachment and Autonomy

One important function of secure attachment is to provide the infant with protection and a sense of trust that allows for adaptive exploration of the environment. In Erikson's theory, trust and security set the stage for the emergence of autonomy.

Confirmation of the relationship between attachment and autonomy and exploration comes from the work of Ainsworth and her colleagues (Ainsworth, Bell, & Stayton, 1971). Their research demonstrated that the infant's exploratory activities depended on the strength of attachment, which in turn depended on the sensitivity of mutual interaction with the caregiver. Infants with secure attachments used the mother as a base from which to explore wider aspects of the environment; those with anxious attachments tended to orient toward the mother instead of the wider environment and were thus limited in their exploratory activities.

Successful adaptation to the environment, as shown by characteristics such as active exploration and the emergence of autonomy, is related to the smooth intercoordination of factors on both sides of the social equation—the meshing of the child's emerging needs and capacities with caregiving routines that are sensitive to the infant's own agenda. As the child's behaviors change with maturation, a number of crisis points crop up in the interactions between caregiver and child. The caregiver's recognition that the child is developing and changing, coupled with the infant's characteristics such as smiling that provide a reward for the caregiver, help to maintain a system that is both protective and liberating.

Continuity of Adaptation

Erikson has suggested that successful resolution of early psychosocial crises paves the way for more effective adaptation at later developmental levels. Conversely, difficulty in resolving these early crises can lead to certain psychosocial problems later on. With respect to the development of parent-child attachment, and the feelings of trust and security that follow from it, studies generally have supported Erikson's speculations. In one study, for example, Waters, Wippman, and Sroufe (1979) demonstrated that 18-month-old infants who were securely attached showed more effective social interactions with their mothers at 24 months than either insecurely avoidant or ambivalent groups of infants. Furthermore, these researchers also noted that quality of attachment at 15 months predicted levels of personal and interpersonal competence at 3 1/2 years. Specifically, preschoolers who were securely attached as infants received higher ratings in such areas as "peer leader," "sympathetic to peer distress," "other children seek his or her company," and "suggests activities." By contrast, preschoolers who were insecurely attached as infants received higher ratings for "hesitates to change," "basically withdrawn," and "spectator (versus participant) in social activities."

More recent research suggests that quality of mother-infant attachment may even serve to predict patterns of psychopathology in children (Lewis, Feiring, McGuffog, & Jaskir, 1984). One hundred and thirteen twelve-month-olds were first observed by the researchers in a modified version of the strange situation procedure. When these children were 6 years old, mothers were asked to complete the Child Behavior Profile, a paper-and-pencil measure of children's social competencies and behavior problems. The results of the study indicated that insecurely attached boys, but not girls, were more likely to be rated higher in behavior problems at age 6 than securely attached boys. Specifically, insecurely attached boys received higher ratings on schizoid behavior, depression, social withdrawal, uncommunicative behavior, and somatic complaints. Lewis and his colleagues noted, however, that only 40 percent of the males classified as insecurely attached at 12 months showed psychopathology at age 6 years.

Thus, other factors, besides quality of attachment, must be present before psychopathology will be manifested. The most important factors in this study discriminating between insecurely attached children with psychopathology and those without psychopathology were whether the pregnancy was planned, the number of life stress events the child had experienced (illness, divorce, accidents, economic hardships, etc.), birth order, and number of friends. Specifically, unplanned birth, greater life stress, second-born birth status, and fewer friends were more characteristic of those insecurely attached boys manifesting psychopathology.

It is clear that early socioemotional relationships between children and caregivers are extremely important for fostering effective adaptation, not only during infancy, but at later developmental levels as well. And yet it also is apparent that these attachment relationships are not the only factor determining quality of psychological adjustment. Parental attitudes and expectations, life events, and the child's social network, among other factors, also contribute to the adjustment of the child (see Focus, p. 196).

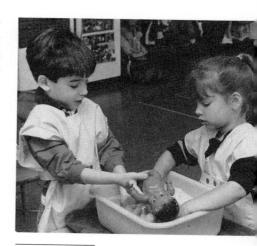

Children love to play and make-believe.

Childhood

In the preschool years children struggle with the psychosocial crisis of developing initiative versus guilt. This is a time when children are moving away from the dependency on parents and toward the ability to meet their own needs. If children are given support for their efforts and encouraged in them, then they will likely develop a sense of initiative. By contrast, when their efforts at independence are usually met with criticism, or even punishment, children are likely to believe that they have done something wrong, and thus feel guilty.

As children enter the elementary school years a new psychosocial crisis emerges—industry versus inferiority. This is a time when societal expectations take precedence over other needs and the ability to master certain cultural skills becomes paramount. Success in meeting these tasks leads the child to feel industrious, a feeling that is associated with a sense of pride or positive self-regard. On the other hand, children who are seldom given the opportunity to master their world and to test themselves, or whose accomplishments are often belittled, are very likely to develop feelings of inferiority that may persist into later developmental periods.

Childhood is a time of social expansion. At first these social interactions take place in the home with siblings; later on they extend beyond the family as the child begins to play with neighborhood children, preschool classmates, and so on. Young children love to play. They spend hours engaged in make-believe activities that not only provide intellectual stimulation, but also teach children social skills and help them work through emotional conflicts.

The peer group is important to young children in that it forces them to consider the thoughts, feelings, and needs of others.

Peer groups assume an even more influential role in middle childhood because children spend more and more time away from home and in the company of friends. The peer group plays a number of important roles in the life of the child. For one thing, peer interactions help to break down the natural egocentrism that characterizes young children; that is, they force children to consider the thoughts, feelings, and needs of others. Children also learn about the norms and values of society in the context of peer relations. Furthermore, feedback from peers is a major factor in the development of identity and self-esteem.

Being popular is an important goal for school age children. But what is it that makes a child popular? Hartup (1983) notes that popular children are friendlier and more outgoing, more attractive, brighter, and, for boys, more athletic. They also are more likely to be good listeners and to show enthusiasm and concern for others. Children often go to great lengths to achieve popularity.

FOCUS

Styles of Parenting

As children enter the toddler and preschool years, a parent's role shifts from primarily a caregiver to an agent of socialization. This role transition, which parallels the child's development of autonomy, involves the establishment of family rules and the development of parenting techniques to insure compliance with the rules. The dramatic nature of this transition is highlighted by research indicating that whereas very little discipline is used by parents in the first year of life (Tulkin & Kagan, 1972), nearly 60 percent of all parent-child interchanges at 27 months involve some type of discipline or control technique to shape the child's behavior (Minton, Kagan, & Levine, 1971).

Although all parents begin to actively discipline, and otherwise socialize, their children during the toddler and preschool period, there is great variability in the way they go about it. Research has shown that parents adopt different styles of parenting during the course of socialization, and that these styles differentially influence the child's behavior and development.

Diana Baumrind (1971, 1973) has been in the forefront in identifying different dimensions or styles of parenting. She has observed that many parents can be classified into one of three broad categories: authoritative, authoritarian, and laissez-faire (permissive).

Authoritative parents are those individuals who believe in the use of firm control, and consequently place a high value on rules. Administration of control, however, is carried out in a rational and fair manner, with extensive verbal give-and-take between parent and child. Furthermore, parent-child interactions are characterized by emotional warmth, acceptance, and mutual respect. Baumrind notes that children of authoritative parents generally are more friendly, cooperative, socially skillful, responsible, independent, and achievement-oriented than are other children. The second category, *authoritarian parents,* also involves the use of firm control. In this case, however, control is administered arbitrarily without consideration of the child's needs, point of view, or feelings. Furthermore, parents are restrictive of the child's activity and generally do not foster independent thinking and behavior. Overall, the family atmosphere is characterized by coolness rather than warmth and acceptance. In contrast to the authoritative style, this type of parenting is often linked to maladaptive social behavior in children, and to anxiety, distrust, and low self-image. The third category, *laissez-faire,* or *permissive parents,* contrasts with the other two in the degree to which parents use demands, limits, or other forms of control in interacting with their children. Permissive parents, as the name implies, place relatively little importance on controlling their children's behavior. Indeed, in the context of a warm and accepting environment, children are given considerable freedom to determine what it is they want to do and how they want to do it. Although parents will often give advice, if asked, they usually remain uninvolved in their children's decision making and activities. Research indicates that children of permissive parents, as opposed to other children, are socially immature,

In the process, however, they usually come to realize just how short-lived this status can be. The child who is the center of attention one week may be on the fringe of the group the next week. Fluctuations in popularity, which are common in middle childhood, often leave children feeling frustrated and confused.

Adolescence

Adolescence is a time of heightened self-awareness (Harter, 1983). Preoccupation with the self is related, in part, to the bodily changes associated with puberty and to newly emerging personal and social roles. It is also related to the development of abstract cognitive skills that allow adolescents to focus attention on themselves in ways that were beyond their capability just a few years earlier.

According to Erikson, the primary psychosocial crisis of adolescence is identity versus role confusion. Ideally, adolescents resolve this crisis by developing a sense of their own uniqueness and an understanding of their relation-

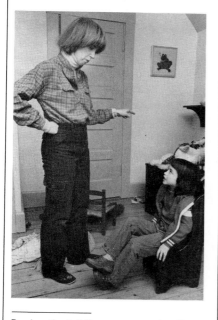

During the toddler years, nearly all parents use some sort of control technique to shape their child's behavior.

socialization history and personality characteristics of the parents themselves. Adults who were exposed to warmth and nurturance as children and whose own parents encouraged them to seek independence and take responsibility are likely to adopt similar styles of childrearing when they become parents. By contrast, adults who were treated harshly and arbitrarily as children and whose parents were unduly demanding and excessively controlling are more likely to adopt a harsh, restricting pattern themselves. In fact, the latter finding is dramatically illustrated in research on child abuse. Gelles and Straus (1979) reported that abusing parents were much more likely to have been abused as children than were nonabusing parents. In essence, family violence begets more violence.

Other important factors determining parenting style are the characteristics and behavior of the child. Richard Bell and his associates (Bell, 1979; Bell & Harper, 1977) have argued that children play a more active role in influencing the socialization process, and specifically parental behavior, than previous researchers had thought. For example, young children who are irritable, oppositional, or aggressive are more likely to elicit

limit-setting behavior by their parents than are friendly, respectful, and cooperative children.

Although research indicates that many adults have a predominant style of parenting, it should not be assumed that they respond to all childrearing situations in the same way. Grusec and Kuczynski (1980) found that when they asked mothers of four- to eight-year-old children how they would respond to various types of child misbehavior, the mothers' chosen discipline techniques were determined more by the specific situation than by some consistent childrearing approach on the mother's part. For example, mothers chose power-assertive techniques (threats of punishment) for dealing with most child misdeeds that did not involve harm to another. On the other hand, when the child's behavior did cause harm to another person, mothers were more likely to choose a reasoning and discussion approach to discipline. These results not only point out the variability in parenting style that can be found even within the same adult, but they also support Bell's contention that parenting strategies are often linked to the behavior and characteristics of the child. ∎

likely to regress behaviorally under stress, have difficulty with self-control, show lower levels of curiosity and exploratory behavior, and have difficulty in assuming a leadership role.

What determines the differences in the way parents raise their children? Undoubtedly, one factor is the

ship to the larger society, establishing a sexual, ethnic, political, moral, and vocational identity in the process (Erikson, 1968).

Adolescence has often been characterized as a period of storm and stress for the individual. Psychoanalytic theorists, in particular, have portrayed the adolescent years as a time of personal and interpersonal upheaval (Freud, 1958). Feelings of self-doubt, moodiness, anxiety, rebellion against parents and other authority figures are the most common behaviors associated with adolescent turmoil. But do all adolescents, in fact, experience this type of upheaval? Is adolescent rebellion an inevitable part of growing up? Research by Offer (1969) and Dusek and Flaherty (1981) suggests that there is considerable variability in adolescent development. Whereas some adolescents do show the type of rebellion and dramatic personality change described by psychoanalytic theorists, other adolescents pass through this period in a more gradual, consistent, and harmonious way.

There is no doubt that peers are an important influence on adolescents today. They are the main source of information about sex (Dickinson, 1978) and the chief encouragers of drug use (Kandel, 1974) and cigarette smoking

Though some adolescents experience turmoil and rebellion, others pass through this period in a more gradual, harmonious way.

(Krosnick & Judd, 1982). Adolescent subculture provides a buffer between the world of children and that of adults, allowing, for example, a social context for the development of mature friendships and sexual relationships. Sexual gratification is now aimed at developing satisfactory relationships with people outside the family and in finding a suitable partner.

Most adolescents identify strongly with their peer groups and their generation. In fact, teenagers identify with other teenagers more than with older people of their own race, religion, community, or sex (Sorenson, 1973). And they consider themselves more idealistic, less materialistic, healthier in their sexuality, and better able to understand friendship than members of the older generation (Sorenson, 1973).

Parents remain, however, vital influences on adolescents. Despite the need to be autonomous from their parents, most adolescents find that their basic values and sense of morality is not much different from that of their parents; nor do they differ that much in their standards of achievement and vocational preferences (Newman, 1982). Parental influence tends to be greatest when there is open communication and respect among family members. Adolescents whose parents are indifferent or overtly strict tend to identify more strongly with peers and to depend on them for social support (see Research, p. 202).

Early and Middle Adulthood

Young adulthood is a time when people make commitments in personal relationships and work. The roles of lover, spouse, parent, and worker are adopted and incorporated into the developing self-system. According to Erikson, the primary psychosocial crisis of this period is developing intimacy with another human being. This is the stage of life when true **mutuality** emerges— a feeling of concern for another that intertwines and complements the concern for self. Erikson (1968) theorizes that the ability to become intimate with another necessitates a satisfactory resolution of the identity crisis (see Research, p. 202). When people avoid intimate relationships out of fear of losing a sense of identity, feelings of isolation and self-absorption usually result.

In young adulthood people begin to think about settling down: finding someone with whom they are compatible and beginning a family. The choice of a marriage partner is influenced by many factors. According to Murstein (1970; 1982), physical appearance plays a major role in determining whether two people initially will be attracted to one another. Following this rather superficial start, the couple begin a process of discovering the similarities and differences in their values and attitudes toward life, male-female roles, sex, politics, religion, and the like. Should the couple determine that they share many similar qualities and ideas, they may then go on to explore the possibility of marriage and the role that each would play in the relationship. Murstein notes that although similarity between people usually benefits a marriage, this is not always the case. At times, two people with similar needs (for example, two high-strung, hot-tempered, self-centered individuals) may clash, resulting in marital discord. What is most important for marital success, Murstein observes, is that the needs of both partners be met at a reasonably satisfactory and equal level.

In starting a family, the roles of husband and wife are augmented by the additional roles of father and mother. For many people, becoming parents marks the final transition to adulthood—it is a process that often leads young people to feel grown-up and responsible.

As joyous and universally accepted as parenthood is, there a growing recognition among psychologists and family sociologists that the process of be-

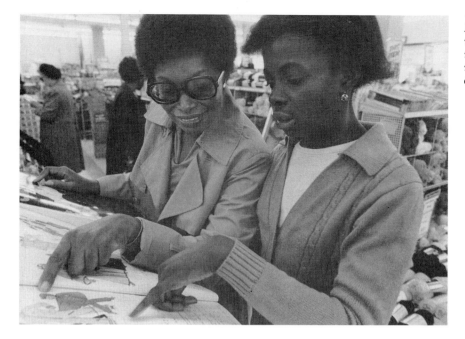

coming parents for the first time is associated with considerable stress for the couple. Sollie and Miller (1980) have noted four general classes of problems associated with the transition to parenthood. First, caring for a child is physically demanding. Parents, especially mothers, routinely report increased fatigue following the birth of a child. This problem is particularly evident when mothers are trying to juggle the roles of parent, spouse, homemaker, and employee. A second area in which problems arise is in the husband-wife relationship. In this case, the birth of a child usually is associated with reductions in time spent together as a couple, with disruption in the sexual relationship, and with lower levels of interpersonal intimacy in general. A third set of problems associated with the transition to parenthood relates to the emotional stresses experienced by parents. The feeling that one is totally responsible for the care and welfare of the young child and that the responsibility represents a long-term commitment often is experienced as emotionally draining. Parents may question whether they actually are competent to handle the vastness of these responsibilities. The fourth area in which problems arise involves the restrictions and lost opportunities associated with parenthood. Parents usually find that their social life is reduced considerably following the birth of the child. In addition, the loss of income (in conjunction with the added expense of a young child) and the restrictions on career development also are experienced as stressful by the couple. These problems, as well as others, help to explain the consistent research finding that marital satisfaction declines with the arrival of children and then increases again when children reach young adulthood and are "launched" into the world (Schram, 1979).

Couples vary considerably in the extent to which the transition to parenthood is experienced as stressful. One important factor affecting this transition process is the degree to which expectations of parents regarding parenthood have been confirmed or disconfirmed by actual experiences following the birth of the child. Jay Belsky and his colleagues, for example, had 61 middle-class couples who were having their first child complete a series of questionnaires and interviews during the last third of the pregnancy, and then again at three- and nine-months postpartum (Belsky, Ward, & Rovine, 1986). The questionnaire and interview measures focused on expectations about and actual effects

The process of becoming parents for the first time is associated with considerable joy and considerable stress.

of parenthood on marriage, social and family relationships, and shared caregiving. These investigators found that when parents' (especially mother's) initial expectations concerning the impact of parenthood on individual and family life were violated—that is, when the transition was more difficult than expected—there was a greater likelihood that parents would report dissatisfaction with the marital relationship.

Although the transition to parenthood inevitably involves stress for the couple, it would be a mistake to assume that there are few, if any, rewards associated with this experience. As noted previously, parenthood most often has a maturing effect on people. It usually enriches their emotional life, providing them with a greater sense of love and happiness than they ever have had before; it also fosters feelings of being competent, responsible, and generative or productive. Finally, as Belsky and Rovine (1984) have noted, parenthood generally strengthens relationships with extended family and helps to integrate the couple into the broader community.

Besides relationships with one's spouse and children, friendships also play an important role in the life of the young adult. People make friends as couples as well as individuals. Couple friendships allow the partners to be involved with others, avoid isolation, and find extra stimulation (Leefeldt & Callenbach, 1979). Many of the friendships people form are through the workplace. Most are with individuals of approximately the same age and background as the person, and are purely social. Others, however, involve **mentor-protégé relationships**—friendships with older and more experienced people—that are very influential in helping the young person move up the career ladder (Levinson, 1978).

Middle-aged people tend to invest less time in developing friendships, especially new ones, because their energies are devoted to family, work, and building up security for retirement. When new friendships do develop, they evolve from similarities in life stage, such as age of children, duration of marriage, or occupational status, rather than chronological age (Troll, 1975). Robert Peck (1968) identified four psychological developments critical to successful adjustment during middle age.

First, middle-aged adults must come to value wisdom over physical strength and attractiveness. They must learn to accept and adjust to the inevitable physical declines of this life period and to appreciate the role played by experience, knowledge, and mental processes in general adaptation and life satisfaction. Second, people must also change their perception of their relationships with others. Instead of sexualizing most human relationships, middle-aged adults must learn to appreciate people within a broader social context as individuals and companions. Third, during the middle years of life, people must be able to demonstrate what Peck calls *cathected flexibility*. That is, people must be able to shift their emotional investments to new people or activities as they confront an increasing number of losses in their lives—for example, death of parents, launching children into the world, a change in job or career, and so on. Finally, successful adjustment in middle age also requires that people remain mentally flexible and open to new experiences so that they do not become slaves to their past.

According to Erikson (1963), the central crisis for middle-aged adults is the resolution of generativity versus stagnation. Generativity involves the concern for establishing and guiding the next generation. For most people, generativity is expressed in the context of loving and nurturing children. It can also be expressed, however, in the context of work as one generates new ideas and products and guides the development of younger, less experienced workers. Erikson emphasizes that generativity is the person's link to the future—it is the means by which the person transcends his own mortality. In the absence of

CHAPTER 6 DEVELOPMENT

generativity, people are likely to feel stagnated, personally impoverished, and bored.

In middle adulthood, family life changes dramatically. Both parents and children are likely to vacillate between "holding on" and "letting go," as plans are made to launch the children into the world. At some point during this period, most couples find themselves alone again for the first time in twenty or so years. The children are now grown and living independent lives. Although this postchild period of family life requires considerable readjustment for the couple, research indicates that it is one of the most satisfying stages of marriage (Schram, 1979).

Even though middle-aged parents and their adult children are now living apart, they still maintain close ties. Troll, Miller, and Atchley (1979) note that young adults often rely on their parents for financial help, child care, and emotional support. In turn, middle-aged parents receive companionship, a sense of achievement, and emotional satisfaction from their children. Middle-aged adults also must adjust to the aging of their own parents. In many families, the middle-aged couple provides emotional and physical support and assumes some of the financial burden for their parents. Alpert and Richardson (1980) report that regular contact between adult children and their aged parents is extremely important for older people's psychological well-being.

Middle age is the time when most people first become grandparents. Troll (1983) notes that the typical age of attaining this status is around 49–51 for women and 51–53 for men. For some individuals, grandparenthood is a reminder of advancing age and hence is resented; most people, however, adjust quite well to their new family status and find it easier, and at times, preferable, to parenting. Research indicates that grandparents play an important role in family systems. In particular, they serve as resource persons for the younger generations, dispensing advice, emotional support, and child care as needed (Troll, 1983). Tinsley and Parke (1983) also note that grandparents, especially maternal grandmothers, are very important for promoting well-being in single parent childrearing units, particularly those involving teenage mothers.

Much has been written about the so-called "midlife crisis." Popular stereotypes suggest that many people undergo dramatic changes in personality and life adjustment at this time. Daniel Levinson (1978), in particular, has been an active proponent of the view that people undergo major reorientation during midlife. He suggests that sometime around the fourth decade of life people begin to reexamine their life goals in light of current and anticipated future achievements. Questions such as "Who am I?" and "Where am I going?" become important once again. Successful resolution of the midlife crisis, according to Levinson, involves working through discrepancies between one's ideal life goals and the realities one has experienced. In many cases, this involves readjusting lofty goals downward—settling for a managerial position within the company, for example, instead of the senior vice-presidency long sought after. Or, it may involve an actual career change in situations where there is the realization that personal and career satisfaction can be achieved only in a new field.

The concept of midlife crisis as a developmental syndrome has not gone unchallenged. A number of researchers have argued that personality development in middle age is largely an undramatic, non-crisis-oriented process. Costa and McCrae (1978, 1980), for example, have found little evidence that men in their forties report more symptoms of crisis than younger or older men. The fact that some people experience life crisis during middle age seems inevitable, "and must not be confused with the concept of midlife crisis as a universal, developmental stage that all persons experience." What should also be obvious, however, is that life adjustment during this period, like in all other

At some point during middle adulthood, most couples find themselves alone again for the first time in twenty or so years. This is, for many, a time of readjustment, but it can also be one of the most satisfying stages of marriage.

RESEARCH

From Identity to Intimacy

The passage from adolescence to adulthood is complex and involves many tasks. Perhaps most fundamental to this transition is the establishment of a unique identity and the gradual merging of the identity with another, as one develops intimate, mutually satisfying adult relationships.

Erikson (1963, 1968) has emphasized that adolescence is the time during which the identity crisis is most acute. Choice of an occupation, the development of religious principles, the clarification of a personal ideology or value system, the establishment of appropriate sex-role behavior, and the development of a satisfying sexual orientation are all part of the adolescent's self-exploration. Although all adolescents share these concerns, the actual resolution of the identity crisis in these areas varies considerably from one person to another. In an early extension of Erikson's theory, James Marcia (1966) interviewed 86 college age males regarding their degree of exploration of alternative solutions to identity is-

sues and the extent of commitment they had made to specific choices. Marcia focused primarily on the resolution of identity crisis in the areas of occupation, religion, and politics. He found that college age males could be classified into one of four identity statuses. *Identity achievers* were individuals who had struggled with crisis in one or more areas of life and had reached a personal decision or commitment that may or may not have corresponded with parental desires and beliefs. Other individuals, while also actively struggling with identity issues, showed no evidence, as yet, of firm commitment to any one particular set of values. These young people were classified as being in *moratorium*. A third group of college youth were characterized by

identity foreclosure. These individuals generally avoided identity crisis by giving in to parental desires and committing themselves to parental values and points of view. Marcia suggested that although these individuals showed strong ideological and career commitments, they actually lacked strong ego identity because they had avoided personal confrontation and crisis in their lives. The fourth group of college students were called *identity diffuse*. These individuals had never experienced true identity crisis and they had found no particular beliefs or set of values to which they could commit themselves.

Since Marcia's original study, numerous investigators have explored the psychological correlates of these identity statuses (Marcia, 1980; Waterman, 1982). Generally, research indicates that identity achievers are high in self-esteem, independence, and moral reasoning, and low in anxiety. Individuals in moratorium also share these attributes, except that they are characterized by high levels of anxiety. In contrast, the foreclosed

---

developmental periods, is highly variable from individual to individual. Whether a major life crisis occurs during middle adulthood is dependent on a variety of factors, including previous experience, personality style, degree of life stress, and availability of social support.

Late Adulthood

Erikson's model makes clear that development is an ongoing process, extending from birth to death. Each stage of the life cycle involves transitions and conflicts that need to be confronted and resolved. In old age, the individual experiences the psychosocial crisis of ego integrity versus despair (Erikson, 1963). This is a time during which the individual looks back over his or her life in an attempt to understand and give meaning to it. Ego integrity reflects an experience of emotional integration—a feeling of transcendence over the self and an acceptance of the one and only life that one has. Individuals who have had difficulty resolving earlier developmental crises are unlikely to achieve a high degree of ego integrity. Instead, for these individuals old age is accompanied by feelings of despair, bitterness, fear, and regret. In addition to the crisis of ego-integrity versus despair, Peck (1968) has identified three ad-identity pattern is associated with rigidity, submissiveness to authority, low levels of personal insight, and a more authoritarian personality style. Finally, identity diffuse individuals generally show low self-esteem and moral reasoning and high anxiety.

One of the more intriguing questions regarding ego identity is its relationship to interpersonal intimacy. Erikson (1963, 1968) argued that the development of adult intimacy relationships necessitated the resolution of the identity crisis. It is only after one has achieved a stable sense of self that it becomes safe to attempt merging it with that of another.

Research by Orlofsky, Marcia, and Lesser (1973), Marcia (1976), and Kacergius and Adams (1980) has generally confirmed the notion that active exploration and resolution of identity issues lead to greater degrees of interpersonal intimacy than does avoidance of personal confrontation and crisis. One interesting qualification of this pattern, however, has to do with potential differences between males and females in the na-

ture of the identity-intimacy relationship. Several researchers (Douvan & Adelson, 1966; LaVoie, 1976) have argued that because of traditional socialization practices, resolution of identity issues related to occupational and political areas are more important for males, and more predictive of their intimacy status, whereas for females, resolution of identity issues related to affiliative or dependency dimensions, such as in religion and interpersonal relations, are more predictive of intimacy. Fitch and Adams (1983) tested this hypothesis. A total of 78 college youth, 28 males and 50 females, were presented with Marcia's ego identity interview, as well as with a semistructured interview measuring intimacy status that was developed by Orlofsky et al. (1973). In line with their hypothesis, the results indicated that occupational identity was the best predictor of intimacy for males, whereas religious identity was the best predictor of intimacy for females. In other words, males with low occupational identity, and fe-

males with low religious identity, were also likely to show low levels of interpersonal intimacy.

These results, while generally supporting Erikson's notion that the development of adult intimacy is based upon a stable sense of self, also point out the complexity of this relationship. Identity is a multifaceted component of the self. Resolution of certain identity issues does not imply resolution of all identity issues. Furthermore, it is clear that certain aspects of the self are more central to the resolution of developmental issues than others. For males, who are socialized to be instrumental and achievement oriented, resolution of occupational identity paves the way for the establishment of adult intimacy. For females, on the other hand, who are socialized to be expressive and concerned with interpersonal issues, resolution of affiliative or social identity is more important for establishing true intimacy. ■

ditional developmental tasks that confront the aging adult. They include: adapting to physical decline, adjusting to occupational retirement, and confronting human mortality. As is true for each developmental period, there is wide variation in the way in which older people adapt to these specific tasks.

Variability among older people is also seen in the way in which they adapt socially during this period. Some researchers have argued that successful adaptation to aging typically involves a disengagement process—that is, a gradual detachment from societal concerns and a reduction in social and psychological commitment to others, especially those outside the family (Cumming & Henry, 1961). Other researchers, however, view successful aging as involving the continuation of relatively high levels of social activity into the elderly years. As Neugarten (1973) points out, however, personality type and long-standing life-styles are the primary factors predicting individual differences in social adaptation among the aged. Whereas some elderly adults seek a simpler, less hectic way of life in their later years, others desire constant social and intellectual stimulation. Both patterns can lead to successful aging as long as they meet the ongoing needs of the individual.

Change in family life is another factor influencing the adjustment of older people. Although the majority of elderly adults prefer to live independently of their middle-aged children (Yankelovich, Skelly, & White, 1977), they never-

Grandchildren can be a source of joy and friendship to the elderly adult.

theless become increasingly dependent on them during this period of life. This is particularly true in times of illness and when one's spouse dies. Widowhood represents a very serious psychological and social loss for the person, one that is related to increased physical and mental illness (Atchley, 1975). Part of the problem is that the remaining spouse sometimes is left alone with few family members or friends. When this happens loneliness sets in, which, in turn, can lead to depression, apathy, and generalized psychological and physical withdrawal. Fortunately, many people are able to overcome the grief of losing a spouse. With the help of siblings, children, and friends, the surviving adult can reorganize his or her life and plan constructively for the future—which may well include remarriage.

In late adulthood, many people experience a loss of control over their lives. Forced retirement, decreased income, declining health, and death of relatives and friends are factors that feed into this perception of reduced control and increased helplessness. These feelings, in turn, are important for determining the way in which older people adapt to the aging process. Ellen Langer and Judith Rodin (1976), for example, have shown that the ability of nursing home residents to control aspects of their lives not only influences their psychological well-being, but their mortality rate as well. These investigators, in cooperation with the nursing home staff, allowed one floor of elderly residents to take responsibility for selecting and caring for their own plants, and for choosing the movies they could watch. By contrast, another floor of elderly residents were exposed to the usual nursing home procedures which involved allowing the staff to make virtually all the decisions and to take all the responsibility for the older adults, including caring for the plants and choosing the movies. Langer and Rodin used several different measures to indicate what effect these changes might have on the patients' lives. One measure was activity level of the residents. On this measure the results of the experiment were quite striking. Residents on the choice-and-take-responsibility floor maintained a much higher activity level than those on the passively-cared-for floor. Even more remarkable, follow-up studies found that death rates on the two floors proved to be markedly different. Over a two-year period, there were far fewer deaths on the choice-and take-responsibility floor.

CHAPTER 6   DEVELOPMENT

The final task of life is, of course, death. Interestingly, research indicates that it is middle-aged adults, not the elderly, who are most preoccupied with death fears (Bengston, Cuellar, & Ragan, 1977). Thus, although older people anticipate and prepare for death, they usually are not overwhelmed by it.

The most well-known research on reactions to dying has been done by Elisabeth Kübler-Ross (1969). Her work indicates that people go through several distinct stages during the dying process. At first, there is shock and denial in response to the news that one is dying. However, denial is usually short-lived and is followed by a second stage, which involves feelings of anger and resentment. In essence the person is asking the question, "Why me?" The third stage of dying involves bargaining. Here the person has developed some hope that death somehow can be postponed or averted. In response to this feeling the person attempts to negotiate—with God, the doctor, etc.—for more time. However, the individual is forced to recognize that death is inevitable. This leads to the fourth stage, which involves depression. Kübler-Ross argues that this depression is part of a preparatory grief process; it is normal and should not be discouraged. Finally, if the person has progressed through the first four stages, and it should be noted that some adults do not, there is the possibility of achieving acceptance, the fifth stage of this process. Acceptance does not imply happiness, however. According to Kübler-Ross, it represents the final detachment from others as the individual prepares for the last journey of life.

A number of researchers and practitioners have been critical of Kübler-Ross's stage theory of dying (Shneidman, 1980; Schulz, 1978). They note that the stages themselves are highly subjective and difficult to identify in patients. More telling, however, is the criticism that people often show more variability in the process of dying than is suggested by Kübler-Ross's theory. Specifically, these investigators see the dying person as constantly alternating between feelings of anger, hope, despair, depression, yearning, bewilderment, and envy.

Regardless of how one conceptualizes the dying process—as a sequence of order stages or a continual intermingling of varied and, at times, opposing emotions and behaviors—there is general agreement that patients need to be told the truth about their condition so that they can be helped to face their impending death with a sense of dignity, warmth, and even hope.

Moral Development

An important aspect of growing up in any society is **moral development**—that is, the growth of the ability to distinguish between right and wrong. Life within social groups requires adherence to common sets of rules and principles that transcend the mutual attractions and attachments of familial relationships and friendships. How do we come to tell right from wrong? The answer to this question has been pursued in substantially different ways by two research traditions in psychology. One tradition, established by learning theorists, focuses on the effects of parental socialization and disciplinary practices. The other tradition, espoused by Piaget and other cognitive theorists, stresses developmental differences in the child's ability to reason about moral matters.

The Learning Approach

The learning approach has placed great importance on reward and punishment as teaching mechanisms of morality. Although the precise effectiveness of reward versus punishment depends on a number of conditions, reward gen-

Table 6.4 KOHLBERG'S STEPS OF MORAL DEVELOPMENT

Level	Stage
Level one Step 1	*Premoral* Punishment and obedience orientation. Obey rules to avoid punishment.
Step 2	Naive instrumental hedonism. Conform to obtain rewards, have favors returned.
Level two Step 3	*Conventional role conformity* Good boy/girl morality. Conform to avoid disapproval or dislike by others.
Step 4	Law and authority maintaining morality. Conform to avoid censure by authorities.
Level three Step 5	*Self-accepted moral principles* Morality of contract, individual rights, and democratically accepted law. Conform to maintain community welfare.
Step 6	Morality of individual principles of conscience. Conform to avoid self-condemnation.

erally emerges as a better teacher of moral behavior. A new learning model emphasizes the role of moral explanation in early disciplinary encounters between parent and child (Hoffman, 1983). According to this model, children's moral behavior is best enhanced when a moral explanation for the discipline is provided. For example, "Don't do that because it might hurt the other person" is more effective than a simple "don't do that."

Parents also influence the moral behavior of their children by serving as models. The tendency of children to imitate the behavior of others—expecially of their parents—is legendary, and this effect has been repeatedly demonstrated in the observational learning experiments conducted by Albert Bandura and his colleagues. Children also are likely to pay more attention to, and emulate, what parents actually do in practice rather than what they preach should be done (Hetherington & Morris, 1978).

The Cognitive Approach

The second major tradition in attempting to explain moral development, the cognitive approach, has been most vigorously espoused by Lawrence Kohlberg (1963). Kohlberg's model, like the theory of cognitive development constructed by Jean Piaget, distinguishes a series of sequential stages in the development of reasoning. Kohlberg began to think seriously about the problem of moral development after World War II when, as a seaman in the U.S. Merchant Marine, he helped Jewish immigrants break through the British blockade of Palestine. In that situation, Kohlberg was confronted by a moral dilemma: was he justified in breaking the law in order to attain what he considered a greater good?

Kohlberg's research method hinges upon the consideration of such moral dilemmas. He presented children with hypothetical dilemmas in which there is a clear conflict between obedience to social rules or laws and the needs of others. For example, if a man's wife is dying of cancer for want of an expensive drug that he cannot afford, would he be justified in stealing the drug? If a physician is confronted by a fatally ill patient who begs to be relieved of pain, should the physician consent to the patient's request to die?

Kohlberg asked such questions not only of American children but also of children in different countries. By analyzing their answers and, more importantly, the reasoning behind the answers, he delineated six stages in the development of moral reasoning. These six stages were grouped by Kohlberg on three major levels (see Table 6.4):

1. *Premoral level.* Children evaluate their behavior in terms of its consequences. Does a given action bring reward or punishment? In Step 1, the child justifies moral choice in the framework of avoiding punishment from powerful people. In Step 2, rewards or the return of favors dominate the child's reasoning about moral choices. This often takes the form of a "tit for tat" notion of social relationships—"I'll lend you my blocks if you let me play with your wagon."

2. *Conventional level.* At the conventional level of morality, the child's choices invoke the concept of social rules and obligations. In Step 3, the desire for approval from others, to be considered a "good boy" or "nice girl," is uppermost. In Step 4, the child's concepts of duty and of established law and authority play the major role in justification of moral choice.

3. *Postconventional level.* Self-accepted moral principles that are arrived at by increasingly abstract reasoning characterize Kohlberg's third level of development. Obedience to a rule no longer depends upon the mere existence of

the rule; the rule itself may be put into question and subjected to a developing self-standard of moral behavior. Thus, at this level, personal morality and conventional morality may come into conflict. In Step 5, the child tends to resolve conflicts between individual and social morality in favor of social. Unlike Step 4, in which the concepts of duty and law are predominant, the choice here is based on the principle of social contract; the child may decide that the rules are unfair, but since they have been agreed upon by the members of society and they are in the general interest of people, they should be obeyed—at least until the societal members choose to change the rules. Thus, rules are nothing more than social contracts between people. In Step 6, the child's inner compass rather than social rules dictates moral choice. The commandments of the individual conscience, based on universal principles such as the golden rule, take precedence. When there is conflict between one's own self-accepted principles and the rules established by society, the individual at this stage acts according to his own inner conscience—even though he recognizes that he may be punished by society for breaking its rule.

According to Kohlberg, the progression through three levels of moral development does not simply reflect social teachings but also intellectual changes. Kohlberg asserts that the six stages occur in an orderly progression. As in Piaget's theory of cognitive development, each stage builds upon previous stages and is determined by the increasing intellectual capacities of the child.

Evidence for the logical ordering of these stages comes from several studies. Kohlberg, himself, (1963) shows that children in the age range from 7 to 16 demonstrate decreasing amounts of premoral reasoning (Level 1), sharply increasing amounts of conventional morality (Level 2), and slightly increasing amounts of postconventional morality (Level 3). These changes are shown in Figure 6.7. In addition, instead of skipping stages, children tend to take moral reasoning a stage at a time (Turiel, 1966). When children were presented with models that reasoned either at one stage above, one stage below, or two stages above their own level, they showed maximum change to the model that reasoned one stage above their own level.

Although Kohlberg does not attempt to predict a direct relationship between age and moral maturity, some general conclusions can be drawn from his work. Premoral reasoning (Level 1) occurs in children age 7 and younger. Conventional morality applies predominantly from age 8 through adolescence, and in some cases into adulthood. In fact, many people never exceed this level. Postconventional morality seldom emerges before late adolescence or early adulthood. In Kohlberg's research, fewer than 10 percent of his subjects over 16 reached Step 6 in Table 6.4—the point at which individual conscience provides the guide for moral decisions.

The development of postconventional moral reasoning necessitates more than just the ability to think about moral issues in an abstract way. Kohlberg (1973) has argued that the higher levels of morality require certain personal experiences as well: in particular, ones that force the individual to confront conflicting values and varying notions of right and wrong. Leaving home and entering a college environment, for example, typically exposes young people to new ways of thinking, to new value systems, to emotional choices, and to new perceptions of self. These experiences, and others, foster a relativistic view of moral/ethical issues in the adult (Murphy & Gilligan, 1980)—that is, they help the person to recognize and accept multiple perspectives in moral situations. Thus, although people usually begin to think about moral issues in an abstract way in adolescence, consolidation of higher-order moral principles and a commitment to their ethical use generally does not develop until adulthood (Kohlberg, 1973).

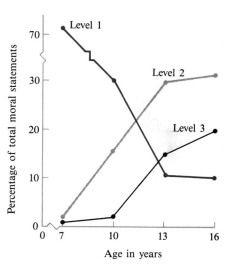

Figure 6.7

According to Kohlberg, children between 7 and 16 years old show decreasing amounts of premoral reasoning (Level 1), dramatically increasing amounts of conventional morality (Level 2), and slighty increasing amounts of postconventional morality (Level 3).

Summary

1. Developmental psychology is concerned with the scientific study of changes that occur in individuals over time. For simplicity's sake, development, which continues over the life span, is traced through its physical, cognitive, social, and moral aspects. However, these divisions are arbitrary: development in one sphere affects development in all the other spheres.

2. Although the controversy over causes of development—nature versus nurture or heredity versus environment—continues, most researchers emphasize the interaction between genetic and environmental influences. Heredity dictates normal individual characteristics such as eye color and bone structure through the genetic mechanisms of chromosomes and genes. Genotype refers to the genetic makeup of an individual; phenotype refers to the outward expression of that makeup. The modern view of genetics regards the development of complex systems, such as intelligence, as being polygenetically determined—related to the control of many genes. In addition, research with animals has modified the classic view of heredity regarding the timing in which genetically determined features appear. In physical maturation the process of change is apparently largely controlled by a special type of gene known as a pacing gene, which sets the pace for emerging systems of development. By virtue of maturational changes that are genetically paced, the organism interacts with its environment, laying the foundation for further interaction in the process of development.

3. The study of physical development focuses on the biological growth of the organism from conception to death. Heredity sets the boundaries for physical development, but an impoverished environment can have adverse influence. Developmental processes cannot be skipped, but wide variation exists in the age at which humans go through these processes. Normal physical development is orderly, sequential, and maturational; for example, all children crawl, stand, and walk in the same sequence and at roughly the same age.

4. The prenatal period—from conception to birth—is divided into three stages: ovum, embryo, and fetus. During the first three months or so of pregnancy, the developing organism is highly susceptible to the influence of environmental agents such as maternal diseases (German measles, syphilis), drugs and chemicals (narcotics, alcohol), nutritional deficiencies, maternal stress, X ray, and blood incompatibility between mother and offspring. The environmental agents, called teratogens, may produce abnormalities in the child.

5. Physical growth is fastest during the prenatal period, infancy, and early childhood, slows its pace during middle childhood, and speeds up again during adolescence. In adolescence, physical growth is accompanied by the emergence of sex characteristics. Most people reach peak physical development in their early twenties; thereafter, the physical development processes become those of aging.

6. Jean Piaget traced cognitive, or intellectual, growth through four major stages: (1) sensorimotor period—birth to age 2; (2) preoperational period—ages 2 to 6; (3) concrete operational period—ages 7 to 11; and (4) formal operational period—ages 11 to 16. Important events in these periods, respectively, are the discovery of object permanence, the use of symbols, the development of logical thought (conservation, classification) and the emergence of abstract thought, including systematic hypothesis testing.

7. Scores on IQ test typically peak in early adulthood, taper off gradually, and decline in old age. IQ tests are not reliable indicators of adult competencies and wisdom, however. Factors such as reaction speed, motivation, and health tend to penalize adults on IQ tests. Recent research indicates that peak intellectual achievement may come as late as age 50 for some people particularly in

areas tapping social knowledge, verbal-conceptual abilities, vocabulary, and arithmetic skills—that is, crystalized knowledge. Many people are mentally active and alert well into old age.

8. Piaget's view of cognitive development basically focuses on the structure of knowledge. An alternative view of knowledge development is provided by information processing theory, which focuses on the process of thought—that is, how people attend to, make sense of, and remember things. Information processing theory has been particularly useful in providing researchers with insights into how children and adults remember things. For example, clear developmental changes have been observed in children's use of memory strategies such as verbal rehearsal and clustering, and in their understanding of how memory works (metamemory).

9. Social development requires psychological adjustments throughout the life span. Erik Erikson proposed eight psychosocial crises that must be confronted by all people at various points in life. The crises range from trust versus mistrust in the first months of life to integrity versus despair as death approaches. The beginnings of social development can be observed in the very young through such processes as attachment, exploration, and autonomy.

Social interactions and peer groups are important throughout the life span. Interaction with siblings and other children begins in the preschool years and intensifies in middle childhood. Adolescents identify strongly with their peer groups, but parents remain strong influences on young people. In adulthood and in old age, social interaction is based strongly on similarity; friends are likely to be of the same sex, marital status, race, socioeconomic class, and about the same age.

10. Young adulthood is the time for starting a family. Many young couples find that the transition to parenthood brings not only considerable joy, but much additional stress to their lives as well. When, in middle adulthood, couples finally launch their children into the world, they often find a reduction in their stress level and, correspondingly, an increase in marital satisfaction.

11. Middle adulthood is the time when most people become grandparents. Although some people resent grandparenthood because it reminds them of their aging, most people adjust very well to their new status and find it easier than parenting. Although much has been written about the so-called midlife crisis, research suggests that it is by no means inevitable. Adjustment during middle adulthood is highly variable and dependent upon previous experience, personality style, degree of life stress, and social supports.

12. Contrary to popular stereotypes, it is not the older adult, but the middle-aged adult, who is more preoccupied with death and dying. Nevertheless, older people do experience considerable loss in their lives—declining physical health, retirement, loss of income, loss of prestige, and death of friends and spouse. Research indicates that adjustment to old age is highly dependent upon the availability of social supports and on the perception that one still has some control over one's life.

13. The final task of life is death. Research by Elisabeth Kübler-Ross suggests that people go through several distinct stages during the dying process: shock and denial, anger and resentment, bargaining, depression, and finally, acceptance. Other researchers believe that the dying person does not necessarily experience these emotional and behavioral reactions in the strict, sequential order outlined by Kübler-Ross. Rather, they suggest that the dying person may show alternating feelings, moving from shock to anger, denial, depression, and back to anger again.

14. The development of morality—the ability to distinguish between right and wrong—is an important aspect of growing up in any society. Learning theorists explain the growth of moral understanding by focusing on the effects

of parental socialization and disciplinary practices. Piaget and other cognitive theorists stress developmental differences in the child's ability to reason about moral questions.

Lawrence Kohlberg, using Piaget's work on moral reasoning as a base, proposed three levels (including six steps) of moral development. These range from obeying rules simply to avoid punishment to the morality of individual principles of conscience.

RESEARCH: According to Erickson, the transition from adolescence to adulthood is marked by the resolution of identity crisis and the establishment of one's unique identity; only then can this identity merge with another in the form of an intimate, mutually satisfying adult relationship. James Marcia identified four ways in which individuals approach identity crises, and each of these correlates with different personality characteristics. In addition, research suggests that some aspects of the identity crisis are more important than others, depending on one's sex: for men, the resolution of occupational identity is more important for establishing adult intimacy; for women, the resolution of affiliative or social identity is more important.

FOCUS: When it comes to childrearing and discipline, three broad categories of parenting styles have been identified. Authoritative parents believe in using firm, though fairly administered, control, and their children are typically friendly and independent; authoritarian parents administer control arbitrarily, and their children often are anxious and have a low self-image; laissez-faire, or permissive, parents exert little control, and their children are often socially immature and have difficulty with self-control. Factors that influence choice of parenting style are the socialization history and personality of the parents themselves and the child's personality; in addition, parenting style often varies depending on the specific childrearing situation.

CHAPTER

7

The Varieties of Learning

In learning to read and write, this child is learning ways to order information mentally.

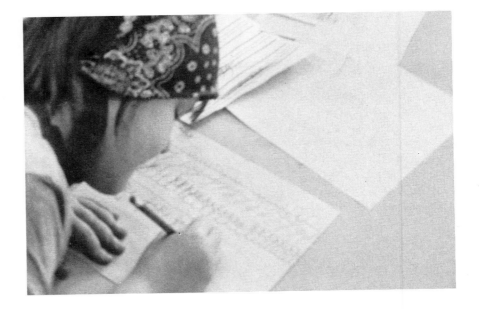

Because learning is such a vital aspect of both human and animal behavior, its underlying processes are of key importance in psychological thought. From birth until death there are continuous changes in behavior in most organisms from which learning can be observed or inferred. In humans, learning is most dramatic during the acquisition of basic skills in the preschool and school years. Children learn to read and to write; they acquire vast amounts of information; they learn ways of ordering that information mentally. Children begin amassing vocabularies that typically amount to more than 50,000 words over a lifetime. In addition to these cognitive skills, the continuous accumulation of social skills and attitudes characterizes interactions with others. Learning continues to be of central importance throughout our lives: adults must learn the skills required for a particular job, how to care for home and family, and how to adjust to their constantly changing world.

As an area of psychological study, learning can be broadly described as a relatively permanent change of behavior that results from prior experience. The use of the term **learning** is usually restricted not only to relatively permanent changes in behavior but also to continued demonstrations of knowledge and skill. A traditional part of most definitions of learning has been the role of experience. This is perfectly reasonable because much of what we learn requires considerable practice; that is, learning is often a gradual process. Changes in behavior that result from learning often would not occur without particular experiences, even though the specific contribution of experience may differ from one learning situation to another. In addition, changes in behavior such as those resulting from intoxication, illness, or fatigue are not considered to be learned because they are temporary and not relatively permanent and stable. For that matter, even permanent changes in behavior like those due to injury or long-term exposure to drugs such as LSD are not considered to be learned.

It is important to distinguish between learning and **performance.** Performance is the carrying out of an act; it is behavior. Learning involves coming to an understanding of the relationship between a given act and the circumstances under which it occurs. Learning, as opposed to performance, cannot be observed directly. As a result, learning is said to be inferred from performance.

The distinction between learning and performance can also be described in terms of capability and action: learning reflects what we are able to do, whereas performance pertains to what we actually do. The fact that a person is not dancing at a given moment does not imply that the person has not learned how to dance. An organism must be motivated before learning will be demonstrated by performance. If a dog is not motivated by hunger, it ignores the food dish even though it knows the location of the dish.

Because learning plays such a central role in most forms of behavior, its processes necessarily are discussed throughout this book. Memory, for example, is intimately related to learning and will be examined in chapter 8. Other varieties of learning, such as the acquisition of language and those relating to social and abnormal behavior, will also be discussed in separate chapters. In this chapter we will focus on several varieties of learning.

All varieties of learning—no matter how fundamental they may be—depend on complex interactions. These interactions involve a number of variables: the species of the learner, the particular setting or task, and what the organism brings to the situation in terms of prior experience and internal processes. Throughout this chapter we will see examples of species-specific learning, the influence of different tasks on learning, and the contribution of past experience to what is learned.

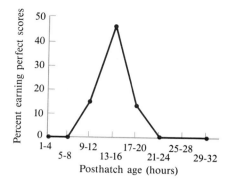

Figure 7.1

Imprinting as a function of age at exposure to imprinting stimulus. In studies by Eckhard Hess, maximum sensitivity for ducklings was found to be about 13 to 16 hours after hatching (after Hess, 1959).

Programmed Learning

In this section we will consider two examples of learning that clearly illustrate the complex interactions noted above. The first of these is song learning in birds. The main facets of song learning in birds can be shown by referring to Peter Marler's (1970) series of experiments done with white-crowned sparrows. This sparrow's song is typically learned between the birds' 10th and 50th day of life. If the male sparrow hears the song during this interval, he will develop a long and elaborate song. However, if he hears the song only outside this interval, the bird will sing a white-crowned sparrow song of minimal detail. Interestingly, if these sparrows are exposed to songs of other birds, even closely related species, this exposure has no effect on song development.

The process of song learning illustrates the way programmed learning works. The song is normally learned long before the birds begin to sing. As their vocal musculature develops the birds gradually begin to produce a song that matches the one they had previously learned. The songs produced by white-crowned sparrows have many features in common, although there is an effect of the environment in which the song was learned. In effect, the songs have local dialects analogous to the regional dialects manifest in the speech of human beings. Thus, these birds are programmed to learn the song of a specific species of bird within a specifiable period during their lives. However, they must be exposed to the song before true song learning takes place.

A second example of programmed learning comes from the study of imprinting. **Imprinting** is the process by which certain young animals learn to follow their mothers. Although it has been found in several species including dogs and sheep, imprinting is most pronounced in young birds—geese, for example—that are able to swim or walk immediately after birth. Imprinting typically occurs very soon after hatching, usually within a day or two, and it does not occur at all—or only very weakly—outside of this **critical period.** Eckhard Hess (1959) reports maximum sensitivity for ducklings within the first day and a peak at 13–16 hours of age (see Figure 7.1).

Ordinarily, the stimulus for imprinting is the movement of the young animal's mother. But the Austrian Konrad Lorenz (1937) and other **ethologists—** scientists who study animals in their natural environments—have shown that, in the absence of the mother, ducklings and chicks may imprint on other prominent moving objects such as a wooden decoy or even a flashing light. However, under conditions of a normal and natural environment, the mother is the only likely object for imprinting. Notice also that imprinting serves an impor-

Ethologist Konrad Lorenz, followed by some ducklings that imprinted upon him.

RESEARCH

A basic assumption of classical learning theory was that any stimulus can be attached to any response through repeated association. However, modern psychologists realize that some things are learned more easily than others. Examples of complex learning by animals provide some of the best opportunities to explore the reasons for both species differences and individual differences in learning.

The song of oscine songbirds (canaries, sparrows, and mockingbirds, to name a few) is one of the most complex behaviors known. Several types of early experiments have shown that the song of these birds is to a large extent learned. For example, young birds deafened in infancy or reared in isolation from the songs of their parents, produce abnormal songs as adults. Furthermore, as we saw earlier in this chapter, in some species exposure to certain songs during a sensitive period in infancy increases the likelihood that these songs will become part of the adult vocal repertoire. Such is the case with one species that has been studied extensively—the swamp sparrow.

For the swamp sparrow, exposure to songs of same-species birds during the sensitive period of infancy is necessary for normal vocal learning to occur. Male swamp sparrows will selectively learn songs of same-species birds even when they are presented with songs of birds of a different species. Of course, whether or not a particular song pattern has been learned can only be determined at a later time (almost a year) when the bird sings the song.

Robert Dooling and Margaret Searcy (1980) were interested in what accounts for this phenomenon of selected vocal learning in the swamp sparrow. They considered perceptual preferences and motor constraints as likely possibilities. That is, it may be that these young birds,

Song Learning in the Swamp Sparrow

without prior experience, already know what to listen for among the sounds in their environment. Later, they sing those songs that they prefer perceptually or that have "caught their attention."

Alternatively, it may be that the young songbird has no predisposition to learn certain songs. Instead, the young bird may simply learn every sound it hears, but be capable of producing only a narrow subset of these sounds. Perhaps the songbird syrinx (the sound-producing apparatus that is functionally equivalent to the larynx in humans) can produce only a restricted subset of the sounds to which the young bird was exposed. It is not possible to decide between these two alternatives by studying only what the adult bird sings.

Dooling and Searcy designed an experiment to evaluate whether or not young swamp sparrows reared in isolation from their normal acoustic environment still responded in any special way to their species-specific vocalizations. In other words, do swamp sparrows know what to listen for even before they have had exposure to the vocalizations they must learn?

Previous research with both humans and animals has shown that there are changes in heart rate associated with orientation or attention toward a pleasant or interesting stimulus. The technique of monitoring changes in heart rate was chosen by Dooling and Searcy because young

birds still in the nest offer few opportunities for other methods of perceptual testing.

Young swamp sparrows and young song sparrows were taken from the nest when they were only a few days old and reared by hand in the laboratory. Electrocardiographic (EKG) recordings were obtained from the young birds in a conventional way. Sensors were gently attached to the birds' skin to record electrical potentials generated by the heart. The young birds sat quietly in the dark in an artificial nest. Natural songs of both species of sparrows as well as canary songs were played to the young birds over a loudspeaker. Canary song was used as a control in this experiment because neither species of sparrow would be expected to have a biological preference for canary vocalizations. EKG potentials were monitored by computer and the time between each beat was stored in computer memory following each song presentation.

Analysis of the cardiac potentials to a number of different songs showed that swamp sparrows responded with greater heart rate deceleration to same-species song than to songs of other species. Song sparrows, on the other hand, showed no difference in cardiac response to vocalizations of the same species and those of other species. Interestingly enough, song-learning experiments also show that swamp sparrows are more selective than song sparrows in the sounds they will choose to imitate.

The results reported by Dooling and Searcy show that swamp sparrows may know what to listen for even before they have experience with songs of their own species. Young swamp sparrows, faced with the task of learning species-specific vocalizations, apparently bring to the task a perceptual predisposition that guides the song-learning process. ■

       CHAPTER 7   THE VARIETIES OF LEARNING

tant adaptive function by keeping the young chicks and geese close to their mothers.

Song learning and imprinting have a great deal in common as illustrations of programmed learning. The stimulus or cue for learning in both cases is species specific (the song or the mother). There is a definite period of time during which learning normally takes place in both song learning and imprinting and very little is learned outside of this critical period of time. Programmed learning is of particular importance because it illustrates the way in which species-specific biological factors interact with environmental experiences to determine what is learned. In chapter 9, we will see that at least certain aspects of language learning in humans bear a striking resemblance to this form of learning.

Classical Conditioning

Some people become frightened every time they see a snake or an insect. Others might giggle every time they recall a certain joke. Still others might become melancholy when they hear a song on the radio that they associate with a special event or time in their life.

How might these rather diverse behaviors be explained? Psychologists believe that they are the result of **classical conditioning,** one of the most extensively investigated varieties of learning.

Classical conditioning is based on an organism's learning that two stimuli go together. It primarily involves simple reflexive behavior. Reflexive behavior is usually produced involuntarily by a specific stimulus: for example, blinking when a strong puff of air hits your eye or salivating at the sight of food if you are hungry. These and other reflexive behaviors can be classically conditioned to some neutral stimulus.

One of the first students of classical conditioning was the eminent Russian physiologist Ivan Petrovich Pavlov, who performed what is probably the most famous series of experiments in the history of psychology. Pavlov's influence on the study of classical conditioning has been so great that many writers refer to this form of learning as **Pavlovian conditioning.**

Pavlov came upon classical conditioning by fortuitous accident just after the turn of the twentieth century. He was studying the digestive system in dogs and thereby successfully demonstrating the link between digestion and the nervous system, a research finding for which he won the Nobel Prize in 1904. It was a chance discovery, however, that led to his lasting fame.

Pavlov's dogs, like all hungry animals, salivated when food was placed in their mouths. This, Pavlov knew, was a *reflex;* it was built into the nervous system and required no prior learning. However, Pavlov noticed something he did not expect: the dogs would also salivate in response to stimuli merely associated with the food—the sight of the food dish, for example, or even the sound of the footsteps of the attendant who brought the food. This required learning.

Although Pavlov was irritated at first because the premature salivation interfered with his experiments on digestion, the phenomenon intrigued him nonetheless. He reasoned that, unlike an automatic reflex, it constituted a form of learning that might involve higher centers in the brain's two cerebral hemispheres. For this reason, Pavlov referred to the salivation as "psychic secretions." Pavlov knew that the cerebral hemispheres were of unquestioned importance in humans; he presumed that, in dogs also, they governed complex learning activities, such as guarding or hunting, that these animals had been taught for centuries. Thus, he began his epic experiments with dogs, hoping the study might lead to a means of measuring the brain's learning activity (Pavlov, 1927).

In contemporary applications, classical conditioning is often used to explain many physiological reactions, especially those related to emotional states. For example, irrational fears or phobias are thought to be the result of classical conditioning (Wolpe & Lazarus, 1969). Thus, fear of snakes may result not from any actual experience with snakes but from merely seeing a picture of a snake in some emotional context.

Acquisition: Stimulus and Response

The essence of Pavlov's classical conditioning experiments involves procedures that have since been repeated countless times in psychologists' laboratories. We will recreate Pavlov's experiments, beginning with the dog's natural response (salivation) to a particular stimulus (the presentation of food). Because the response is not learned, the salivation is termed the **unconditioned response (UR),** and the food is termed the **unconditioned stimulus (US).** We also need to select a neutral stimulus, such as a tone or bell, that does not ordinarily elicit the salivary response.

Now we are ready to replicate the experiment by surgically attaching a small capsule to an exposed part of the dog's salivary gland so that the amount of salivation can be measured. The hungry dog is then placed in a restraining harness in a soundproof laboratory where there will be no distractions (see Figure 7.2). The tone is sounded and, as might be predicted, the dog does not salivate. However, the dog does turn its head and shoulders toward the direction from which the tone is sounded, prick up its ears, and look attentive. This reaction to the tone is called an **orienting reflex,** which Pavlov sometimes called the "What-is-it? reflex."

A short time after the tone is sounded the food is presented, and the dog does salivate. If we repeat this sequence of events several times, with the tone always preceding the food presentation, the dog will begin to salivate in increasing amounts at the sound of the tone—even when the food is no longer presented. Learning has taken place, and we can describe the learning in the language used by investigators who employ classical conditioning techniques. The tone is now termed the **conditioned stimulus (CS),** and the salivary response to the tone alone is termed the **conditioned response (CR).** Usually the

Figure 7.2

Laboratory set-up for conducting Pavlovian or classical conditioning experiments. After several repetitions in which a tone is followed by the presentation of food—which causes a natural reflex, salivation—the dog will begin to salivate in increasing amounts at the sound of the tone even if food is no longer presented.

Tube for collecting saliva from subject's mouth

Harness (to restrict movement by subject)

Amount of saliva recorded here

CHAPTER 7   THE VARIETIES OF LEARNING

CR is very similar to the UR, but they are not identical. In salivary conditioning, for example, the UR is greater in volume and richer in digestive enzymes than the CR. What we have seen is the essence of classical conditioning: the dog has learned to associate a previously unrelated event, the sound of the tone, with salivation (see Figure 7.3).

Essential Features and Measurement

Pavlov's relatively pure form of classical conditioning is a rather passive process for the learner. It requires no active participation by the subject; the response to be conditioned is a reflex; presentation of the conditioned stimulus (tone) and unconditioned stimulus (food) are controlled by the experimenter. We can thus sum up the three essential features of classical conditioning:

1. A reflexive relationship exists between some stimulus (the US) and some response (the UR).
2. Prior to conditioning, there is some other stimulus, or potential conditioned stimulus (such as the tone), that does not elicit the unconditioned response but prepares the organism for the unconditioned stimulus to come.
3. Conditioning involves repeated pairings of the conditioned and unconditioned stimulus with the conditioned stimulus occurring a fixed interval before the unconditioned stimulus.

In classical conditioning there are two primary measures of the extent to which learning has occurred. One is the regularity with which the conditioned response occurs; the other is the intensity or magnitude of the conditioned response. These two variables are often plotted on a graph known as a learning curve, on which the vertical axis represents some measure of response strength and the horizontal axis represents learning trials (see left-hand graph in Figure 7.4). As you might expect, these measures often are closely related. As the salivary response occurred more regularly in Pavlov's dogs, for example, the number of drops of saliva also increased. An additional measure is the permanence of the conditioned response.

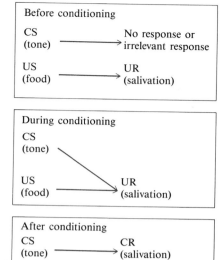

Figure 7.3

Diagram of classical conditioning. The association between the food— unconditioned stimulus (US)—and salivation—unconditioned reponse (UR)—exists at the start of the experiment and does not have to be learned. The association between the tone—conditioned stimulus (CS)—and salivation—conditioned response (CR)— is learned. It arises through a pairing of the CS and US followed by the UR.

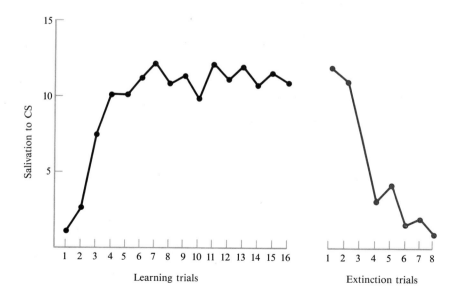

Learning trials

Extinction trials

Figure 7.4

The graph on the left depicts the acquisition phase of a classical conditioning experiment. Drops of salivation in response to the conditioned stimulus are plotted on the vertical axis, and number of trials on the horizontal axis. After 16 acquisition trials the experimenter starts extinction, the results of which are presented in the graph on the right. The conditioned response decreases the more trials the conditioned stimulus is presented alone (after Pavlov, 1927).

Figure 7.5

Time relationships define the types of classical conditioning. In simultaneous conditioning, the conditioned stimulus (CS) and the unconditioned stimulus (US) are presented together. In delayed conditioning, the conditioned stimulus (CS) precedes by at least several seconds the unconditioned stimulus (US), and then they continue to be present together. In trace conditioning, the conditioned stimulus (CS) is presented briefly and then removed, followed after a short interval by the unconditioned stimulus (US). Conditioning becomes progressively poorer in both delayed and trace conditioning as the CS-US interval increases.

Figure 7.6

Stimulus generalization refers to the fact that similar stimuli will produce a conditioned response. Note, however, that the generalization decreases as the stimuli become less similar to the original conditioned stimulus (in this case a tone of 1000 Hz).

Time Factors

One of the important factors in classical conditioning is the time interval between the two stimuli—the conditioned stimulus (tone) and the unconditioned stimulus (food). Time relationships define the types of classical conditioning. In **simultaneous conditioning,** the conditioned stimulus and the unconditioned stimulus are presented together at exactly the same time. This is not very effective. Conditioning is best when the conditioned stimulus precedes the unconditioned stimulus, although the time interval need not be large. In fact, an interval as short as 0.5 second, depending on the response being conditioned, often leads to very rapid conditioning. Classical conditioning also can be demonstrated with substantially longer intervals between the conditioned stimulus and the unconditioned stimulus. When the conditioned stimulus begins before the unconditioned stimulus and continues to the onset of the unconditioned stimulus, the resulting learning is termed **delayed conditioning.** This term is used because there is a delay between the onset of the conditioned stimulus and the onset of the unconditioned stimulus. The offset of the conditioned stimulus either coincides with or follows the onset of the unconditioned stimulus. In another type, **trace conditioning,** the conditioned stimulus is presented briefly and then removed; then, after an interval, the unconditioned stimulus is presented. Trace conditioning is so named because some residue or "trace" of the conditioned stimulus is presumed still to be present when the unconditioned stimulus occurs. Generally, the shorter the interval between the conditioned stimulus and the unconditioned stimulus, the more effective the association will be (see Figure 7.5).

Extinction and Spontaneous Recovery

Pavlov found that, once a conditioned response has been well established, it can be weakened by continuously presenting the conditioned stimulus (the tone) without the unconditioned stimulus (food). He called this **extinction,** or weakening of the response (see right-hand graph in Figure 7.4). Pavlov also found, however, that the conditioned response may not be completely extinguished even if it no longer occurs in one set of tests, or trials. If the animal is tested again a few days after extinction has been demonstrated, the conditioned stimulus again will often elicit the conditioned response although in weaker form. This phenomenon of partial recovery of the conditioned response following extinction has been called **spontaneous recovery.** The strength of a conditioned response is also demonstrated by the subject's response to similar, but not identical, stimuli.

Generalization and Discrimination

The following experiment demonstrates a striking characteristic of classical conditioning. First, a dog is conditioned so that salivation occurs whenever a tone of a particular frequency or pitch is sounded. Interestingly, if that tone is changed to differing frequencies the dog will also produce the conditioned response, salivation. This phenomenon, in which similar stimuli evoke the conditioned response, is called **stimulus generalization.** As might be expected, however, generalization decreases as the stimuli become less similar to the original conditioned stimulus. In this experiment, for example, salivation would decrease as the tone sounded less and less like the tone used to condition the dog (see Figure 7.6).

A classic but controversial study reported in 1920 by John B. Watson and Rosalie Rayner illustrates generalization of a conditioned response in humans. The chief investigator was Watson, and enthusiastic follower of Pavlov's work. Watson, who had hopes that Pavlovian conditioning techniques could be used to improve the quality of American education, was studying a particular conditioned response, fear or anxiety. In everyday life, certain irrational fears may be conditioned in humans—fear of snakes, for example. But Watson was the first to condition fear in a human in a laboratory.

His subject was Albert, an 11-month-old boy. Watson and his assistant, Rayner, placed Albert in a room with a gentle white rat. At first the boy petted the rat and showed no fear. Then, just as Albert was reaching for the animal, one of the experimenters stood behind the boy and made a loud noise by striking a steel bar with a hammer. Not surprisingly, the noise frightened Albert and he began to cry. The experimenters repeated this process several times, pairing the white rat and the loud noise, and Albert soon produced the conditioned response, fear, every time he saw the conditioned stimulus, the white rat (see Figure 7.7). Moreover, as we might expect from our experiment with the dog and tones of differing frequencies, Albert's fear of the white rat generalized to similar stimuli. When other white objects, such as a fur coat or a rabbit, were introduced into the room, they elicited the same fearful response. Albert's conditioned response seemed to generalize to any white soft and furry stimuli.

Figure 7.7

Depiction of John B. Watson's experiment in which he conditioned an infant, Albert, to fear a gentle white rat by striking a steel bar loudly each time the rat approached.

Other experiments have shown that stimulus generalization can occur to stimuli related on one or more physical dimensions such as color or tone frequency. We can demonstrate this with a typical classical conditioning procedure that is based on a measure of emotional reaction known as the galvanic skin response (GSR). The galvanic skin response is a measure of changes in electrical conductivity in the palm of the hands. These changes result from the increase in sweat gland activity that typically accompanies an emotional response. The galvanic skin response is used as part of lie detector tests on the grounds that sweaty palms—and hence an emotional reaction to a particular question—might suggest guilt. In the psychologist's laboratory the galvanic skin response can be easily elicited by administering a mild shock to a human subject's skin. The galvanic skin response can then be conditioned in the subject by pairing a flashing light with the shock. Let's say the light—the conditioned stimulus—is blue. After conditioning, a striking instance of generalization often occurs. The spoken word ''blue'' alone can cause the conditioned response, the galvanic skin response, to appear. This type of generalization, which is based on a meaningful relationship as opposed to a physical relationship between the conditioned stimulus (flashing blue light) and the test stimulus (spoken word ''blue''), is called **semantic generalization** (Kimble, 1961).

Generalization, Pavlov noted, has obvious biological significance for an animal's survival. Natural stimuli that have survival value for an organism—for example, the sound of a predator—are not constant. Thus, generalization of stimuli enables an animal to flee even though the predator's sound may vary widely in pitch or loudness.

At the same time, extreme generalization—fleeing from any sound—would have little survival value for the animal. The animal obviously must make appropriate and relatively precise choices, or **discriminations,** among stimuli. Pavlov (1927) tested several procedures in his studies of discrimination. The first method involved repeated presentation of a single conditioned stimulus (tone) with the unconditioned stimulus (food). The dog failed to learn to discriminate one particular conditioned stimulus tone from other tones differing in frequency, even after a thousand pairings. The second procedure proved more effective. During the conditioning sessions Pavlov presented several tones differing in frequency. Only one of these, however, was followed by the unconditioned stimulus, food. With this procedure, which Pavlov called the **method of contrast,** precise and rapid discrimination among tones was produced.

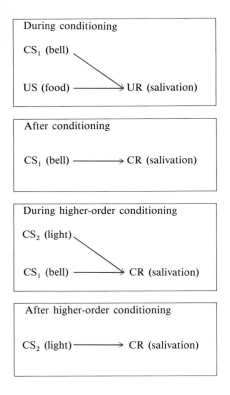

Figure 7.8

Diagram of higher-order conditioning of salivation from one conditioned stimulus to another. After traditional conditioning to a bell, another conditioned stimulus, a light, is introduced followed only by the bell (without the unconditioned stimulus of food). Eventually the light alone produces the conditioned response of salivation. The original conditioned stimulus (the bell) reinforced a new association in much the same way as the original unconditioned stimulus (food) had done.

Special Types of Conditioning

Classical conditioning can be investigated using variations on the basic stimulus-response pattern. Three such variations are higher-order conditioning, temporal conditioning, and taste aversion.

Higher-Order Conditioning

Once the relationship between the conditioned stimulus and the unconditioned stimulus is strongly established, the conditioned stimulus can serve to condition other stimuli. Pavlov demonstrated this phenomenon, known as **higher-order conditioning,** by first conditioning a dog to salivate at the sound of a bell and then training the dog to make a further association: the animal was presented with a light followed only by a bell (and not with the unconditioned stimulus of food). The animal began to salivate at the presence of the light alone (see Figure 7.8). The original conditioned stimulus (the bell) functioned as the unconditioned stimulus for a new association in much the same way as had the original unconditioned stimulus (food).

Higher-order conditioning, unlike stimulus generalization, involves a new association with a new stimulus that may be quite different from the original conditioned stimulus. Higher-order conditioning, however, is fairly weak because the new unconditioned stimulus—for example, the light in Pavlov's experiment—is never paired with the original unconditioned stimulus—food. The process of higher-order conditioning has been demonstrated only as far as third-order conditioning—using the light as the unconditioned stimulus for establishing yet another association. The process cannot go on indefinitely because the initial unconditioned stimulus on which the original association was based is no longer present, and the conditioned response to the earlier stimulus begins to extinguish. While the salivation response to the bell is established, salivation to the light extinguishes.

Temporal Conditioning

A remarkable range of stimuli can serve as the conditiond stimulus—even the mere passage of time itself. Observations of such **temporal conditioning** in the dog were reported by Pavlov (1927). A dog was given food every 30 minutes. Then, after this pattern was well established, a feeding was omitted. Nonetheless, the dog salivated: it was as if the lapse of 30 minutes had acquired the properties of a conditioned stimulus.

As most parents can attest, temporal conditioning seems to occur quite regularly in hungry infants. Experimental evidence of this is reported by Donald Marquis (1941). In this study, one group of newborn infants was fed on a three-hour schedule for eight days and then was shifted to a four-hour schedule on the ninth day. Predictably, between the third and fourth hour on the ninth day, the general activity level of these infants was substantially higher than that of infants fed on a four-hour schedule since birth. It should be noted, however, that the infants may have eaten only enough to tide them over for three hours and simply and naturally got hungry at the fourth hour. Caution is always necessary in interpreting the results of any experiment.

Taste Aversion

Innate factors work together with conditioning factors in producing behavior changes. Suppose a rat is permitted access to a novel, sweet-tasting solution. Shortly after drinking, the animal is given an injection that will make it violently ill. When the animal is fully recovered, it is again permitted access to the same solution; this time, however, the rat avoids drinking it. In just one trial, the rat apparently has been conditioned to avoid drinking the solution even though the interval between the taste and illness is relatively long. In fact, rats can learn to avoid a flavor when the interval between taste and illness is as long as 12 hours (Revusky & Garcia, 1970).

Rapid learning of taste aversion is of considerable survival value to any species; what serves as the effective conditioned stimulus, however, may vary from one species to another. For example, quail made ill after drinking blue-colored sour water subsequently show a much stronger aversion to blue water than to sour water. In contrast, rats tested under the same conditions avoid sour water more than blue water (Wilcoxin, Dragoin, & Kral, 1971).

One factor that is of considerable importance in the phenomenon of conditioned taste aversion is the novelty of the conditioned stimulus. If rats have experiences with a particular taste prior to the situation in which they are made ill, taste aversion does not occur. Apparently, these prior experiences or familiarity with the taste inoculate the animals from an aversion to that taste.

Taste aversion is also found in humans—as the following real-life story illustrates. The reader is cautioned not to repeat the procedure because it can be quite dangerous. The situation involved a teenage boy, call him Bill, who drank a fifth of Scotch whiskey in less than 30 minutes. Shortly thereafter, Bill passed out and remained unconscious for several hours. While unconscious he was violently ill and was still quite sick after regaining consciousness. For the next four to five years Bill experienced stomach contractions characteristic of retching whenever he smelled any kind of whiskey. However, this response did not generalize to beer and, perhaps unfortunately for Bill, the conditioned response to the smell of whiskey weakened in subsequent years and eventually disappeared.

Temporal conditioning is likely to play a role in an infant's feeding schedule.

Limitations of Classical Conditioning

Despite the widespread demonstrations of classical conditioning, it is important to keep in mind the limitations of this variety of learning. For the most part, the responses that have been classically conditioned are those largely controlled by the autonomic nervous system. In natural—as opposed to laboratory—settings, emotional reactions such as sweaty palms and increased heartbeat appear to be largely involuntary and hence can occur without conscious control.

Moreover, the conditioned response measured in most laboratory studies may be only one of several learned responses that occur. For example, responses characteristic of excitement, such as a speedup in heartbeat or respiration, may be elicited by the unconditioned stimulus—food—used to condition salivation. These responses may also be conditioned to appear at the presentation of a tone or other conditioned stimulus. A dramatic example of the multiple responses occurring in classical conditioning was reported from Pavlov's own laboratory. A dog, after it was released from the restraining harness, approached the harness, wagged its tail, and begged for food. This dog evidently had learned something during classical conditioning that was never part of the unconditioned response to food.

Although classical conditioning is a way of learning, it is a limited one. It is an unconscious, usually passive, process that does not involve an active acquisition of knowledge. For the kind of learning humans and animals need to cope with their environments, a different and more sophisticated process is needed. It can be called instrumental learning, operant conditioning, or, simply "trial and error."

Instrumental and Operant Conditioning

Instrumental or operant conditioning refers to a situation in which an organism learns to make a particular response in order to achieve a certain goal. The goal may be to obtain a desirable outcome such as satisfying a need or to

American psychologist E. L. Thorndike formulated the doctrine of trial and error learning, which is a cornerstone of what has become known as instrumental conditioning.

avoid some undesirable outcome such as receiving an electric shock. In either case the learned response is said to be instrumental in achieving the goal. It also typically involves operating on the environment in some way, by pressing a lever or pulling a string, for example.

Instrumental Conditioning

In the 1890s, even before Pavlov had begun his investigations of classical conditioning, the American psychologist Edward L. Thorndike was studying another variety of learning. Pavlov was able to work with his dogs in a laboratory, but Thorndike, who was still a graduate student at Columbia University, had to improvise. He collected scores of stray cats from the streets and alleys of New York and took them to his quarters in a rooming house. There, using packing boxes, he constructed cages that he called ''puzzle boxes.'' The puzzle confronting the cat was to find a way to open the box's latch. If the animal succeeded in pulling the string, it could escape and gain access to a bowl of food placed outside the box. Because the necessary response—pulling the string—was instrumental in obtaining the food, this variety of learning has been called **instrumental conditioning.**

Thorndike's vivid description of this form of learning was included in his doctoral dissertation:

> When put into the box the cat would show signs of discomfort and an impulse to escape from confinement (not a reaction to the sight of food, but only a blind attempt to escape). It tries to squeeze through any opening; it claws and bites at the bars and wire; it thrusts its paws out through any opening and claws at everything it reaches; it continues its efforts when it strikes anything loose and shaky; it may claw at things within the box. It does not pay very much attention to the food outside, but seems simply to strive instinctively to escape confinement. . . . Whether the impulse to struggle be due to an instinctive reaction to confinement or to an association, it is likely to succeed in letting the cat out of the box. The cat that is clawing all over the box in her impulsive struggle will probably claw the string or loop or button so as to open the door. (Thorndike, 1898)

In this quotation we see the basic elements of Thorndike's doctrine of **trial and error learning.** The cat did not appear to solve the problem of escape in an orderly manner; rather, it responded almost at random until the correct response was made by chance. Thorndike did not deny insightful learning, especially in humans, but it was not assigned any special role in the learning process.

On subsequent trials, however, the cat took less and less time to find the latchstring and to escape successfully. Thorndike plotted on a graph the times required for escape: the first trial-and-error attempt might take nearly four minutes, but by the seventh trial the cat might succeed in only about 30 seconds (see Figure 7.9). As Thorndike described the process, ''And gradually all the other nonsuccessful impulses will be stamped out and the particular impulse leading to the successful act will be stamped in by the resulting pleasure until, after many trials, the cat will, when put in the box, immediately claw the loop or button in a definite way.''

The basic principle of learning by trial and error, according to Thorndike, was the **law of effect.** Rewards strengthened, or ''stamped in,'' connections between stimuli and responses, whereas punishment ''stamped out'' such connections. Thorndike (1932) subsequently revised his position on punishment, concluding it had little or no effect on learning—an issue we will return to later in this chapter.

Figure 7.9

A plot of Edward L. Thorndike's experiment with a cat's attempt to escape from a puzzle box. The seventh trial shows a remarkable improvement in ability to solve the puzzle (after Thorndike, 1921).

CHAPTER 7   THE VARIETIES OF LEARNING

Operant Conditioning

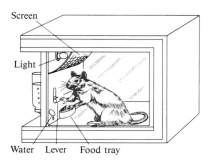

Figure 7.10

An experimental chamber, often called a "Skinner box," is used for many studies of operant conditioning. When the rat pushes the lever, a pellet of food automatically drops into the food tray.

During the late 1930s, research into instrumental conditioning took a new turn, and this form of learning took a new name. The Harvard psychologist B. F. Skinner (1938) called it **operant conditioning** because, in his pioneering experiments, the animal had to operate on the environment in order to produce a particular consequence such as obtaining food.

Skinner's early experiments in operant conditioning involved placing a rat in a chamber that has come to be known as a "Skinner box" (see Figure 7.10). The chamber was empty except for a food cup and small bar extending from one wall. The apparatus was designed so that the animal received a small pellet of food each time the bar was depressed. If the animal was deprived of food, it could be taught to press the bar to obtain the food pellets. When this happened, operant conditioning occurred. The learned behavior—bar pressing—was termed **operant behavior.**

Many investigators reserve the term *operant* for situations in which a subject is freely able to respond (Skinner's rat is free to press the bar at any time) and the term *instrumental* for situations in which the experimenter must initiate each trial that a subject experiences (Thorndike's cat could not start a new trial until it was again placed in the apparatus). Thus, Skinner's learning situation would be called operant learning and Thorndike's learning situation would be called instrumental learning.

One of the experimental advantages of Skinner's approach over Thorndike's is that the bar-pressing behavior can be brought under rather precise stimulus control. For example, a light can be placed above the bar and the animal rewarded for pressing the bar only when the light is turned on. Because the animal learns to discriminate by pressing only when the light is on, the light is called a **discriminative stimulus.** Discriminative stimuli set the occasion for responding.

Before beginning an operant conditioning experiment, the investigator must take into account the fact that the animal, say a rat, is apt to press the bar randomly even in the absence of reward. Therefore, it is necessary to establish an **operant baseline** for that response before the food is introduced. For example, the experimenter might count the number of times the rat presses the bar during a ten-minute interval in the absence of reinforcement. The operant level provides a standard against which the effects of subsequent conditioning can be compared.

The consequence produced by an operant response is known as reinforcement, which will be discussed in detail later in this chapter. Not surprisingly, the frequency of reinforcement—whether it occurs after every response, every other response, and so on—influences the rate of operant responding. The timing of the reinforcement is also important—at least in animals: the quicker the reinforcement, the faster learning occurs. The significance of immediate reinforcement to humans is more difficult to demonstrate. It no doubt plays a role in learning, but it is likely that knowing what one is being reinforced for is more important than the immediacy of the reinforcement. Of course, immediate reinforcement usually makes it clearer what the reinforcement is for.

Similarities Between Operant and Classical Conditioning

The procedures used to demonstrate these varieties of conditioning are quite different; nonetheless, many of the phenomena observed are the same. The learning curves of classical conditioning and operant conditioning are quite similar, as are the extinction curves. For example, an operant response can be

The stars serve as secondary reinforcers for this child's good behavior.

extinguished by withholding reinforcement; the animal's response rate may then return to its operant level. A classically conditioned response often returns to previous levels. In addition, when an animal exposed to extinction training is returned to the operant chamber it may well show spontaneous recovery of the response without additional reinforcement. Spontaneous recovery also occurs in classical conditioning situations. Reexposure to the conditioned stimulus will produce the conditioned response. Relearning after extinction in both conditioning processes can be accomplished much more rapidly than the original learning.

However, one main difference between the processes of classical conditioning and operant learning lies in the way that reinforcement is used and interpreted.

Reinforcement

The presentation of an unconditioned stimulus in contiguity (closeness) with the conditioned stimulus makes up the reinforcement aspect of classical conditioning. In operant conditioning, **reinforcement** is often defined as any stimulus that, when made contingent upon a response, increases the likelihood of that response occurring in the future. There are, as we shall see, multiple types of reinforcers.

To begin with, there are two broad categories of reinforcement—primary and secondary. **Primary reinforcers** have usually been defined as those stimuli that meet biological needs of the organism—food when we are hungry, water when we are thirsty, and so on. However, the reinforcers that affect human behavior are more likely to be ones we have learned to value rather than those that satisfy our biological needs. These are termed **secondary reinforcers.**

Among the most effective secondary reinforcers in humans are money and praise. We value a secondary reinforcer such as money for many reasons, but one reason is the obvious association with obtaining a primary reinforcer, food. This association is illustrated in laboratory experiments involving chimpanzees. In a now classic study, J. B. Wolfe (1936) taught chimpanzees the value of secondary reinforcers. Using a laboratory vending machine known as a Chimp-O-Mat, the chimps learned that by dropping tokens similar to poker chips into the machine, they would receive a food reward such as grapes (see Figure 7.11). Having learned this, the chimps could be conditioned to perform another task—pulling a lever—if they were given a secondary reinforcer—the tokens previously associated with getting food.

A similar phenomenon can be found in demonstrations of both classical and operant conditioning. Pavlov demonstrated that, once a dog had learned to salivate to a tone, the tone could then serve to condition salivation to a new conditioned stimulus such as a flashing light. In this instance of higher-order conditioning, the tone was associated with the relationship between the flashing light and salivation just as the food was associated with the original connection between tone and salivation.

Secondary reinforcement is readily demonstrated in operant conditioning. For example, suppose a rat learns to press a bar for food reward. Then suppose that, when the bar is depressed during training, the mechanism makes a noise when it releases the pellet of food. Because of the pairing of noise and food delivery, the noise itself will acquire the properties of a secondary reinforcer. That is, sounding the click following a response keeps the animal responding. This is easily shown during extinction by comparing resistance to extinction in animals that still hear the noise from the empty food mechanism with other animals who do not hear it because the mechanism has been disconnected.

Another distinction that is important to note here is the difference between negative reinforcement and punishment. This distinction often seems confusing because the same event—for example, use of electric shock—can constitute either negative reinforcement or punishment. **Punishment** is the correct term to use when the noxious event is used to suppress undesirable or unwanted behaviors. **Negative reinforcement** is used when the noxious event is present and it is removed when certain behaviors take place. For example, when we learn to perform certain actions in order to escape or avoid a noxious event, the noxious event is serving as a negative reinforcer: its removal increases the likelihood of our making the same escape or avoidance response in the future.

In contrast, punishment, seems far less effective in learning situations. As we noted previously, that early advocate of punishment, Edward L. Thorndike, changed his views. He revised his original law of effect so that it excluded punishment as an influence on connections between stimuli and responses. This view was supported in subsequent research (Estes, 1944; Skinner, 1938), which appeared to indicate that, although punishment temporarily suppresses responding, it does not have long-lasting effects. In addition, it is clear that punishment often has unintended aversive consequences—such as creating hostility toward whoever administers it. In view of these facts, psychologists have generally emphasized reinforcing desirable behavior rather than punishing undesirable behavior.

It is true, of course, that punishment is effective in certain situations. For example, if punishment is used to suppress undesirable behavior while alternative behaviors are being reinforced, the outcome may be quite positive. It is also true that guidelines intended to make punishment more effective can be garnered from studies in the laboratory. These include the following: it should be as intense as possible; the delay between response and punishment should be as short as possible; punishment should be administered consistently; the punished response should not be rewarded in any way. These guidelines, however, are much easier to apply in the laboratory than in the everyday world.

Some of the problems associated with punishment are quickly evident if we consider a fairly typical example of adolescent misbehavior. A teenage boy begins drinking beer and whiskey. His parents strongly oppose his drinking and punish him in various ways if he is caught at it. Our guidelines for effective punishment would prescribe intensity, immediacy, consistency, and a complete absence of reinforcement. However, will the parents employ severe punishment and possibly incur the hostility of their son? How soon after drinking and how regularly following drinking can punishment occur? Above all, how can the parents cope with the fact that the boy's drinking is reinforced by his peers, who consider it a sign of masculinity?

A major problem in assessing the effectiveness of both reinforcement and punishment is the difficulty in identifying, in advance, which is which. One person's punishment may be another's reinforcement. For example, punishing stimuli are aversive to most children, but to a child who feels neglected punishment by parents may seem welcome; their sudden attention serves as reinforcement rather than punishment and thus tends to make misbehavior more likely.

Figure 7.11

Like human beings, chimpanzees can be trained to work for money (secondary reinforcement) that can be exchanged for food (primary reinforcement). The chimp shown here is about to put its money (a poker chip) into a "Chimp-O-Mat," which will dispense bananas or grapes. Chimps can be trained to work all day for poker chips if they have first learned that the poker chips can be used to obtain food.

Schedules of Reinforcement

As we noted previously, much of the work in operant conditioning has focused on the control of behavior. An effective way to manipulate behavior is to manipulate the schedule under which reinforcement is provided. At first, because it produces rapid learning, an operant response is conditioned by reinforcing every occurrence of the response—a schedule known as **continuous reinforcement.** But after conditioning, the response can be maintained by a schedule of **partial reinforcement** under which the response is only occasionally reinforced. In this way the desired behavior becomes increasingly resistant to extinction.

In fact, very high rates of responding over long periods of extinction have been demonstrated under a variety of schedules of partial reinforcement. How-

Figure 7.12

Patterns of behavior that might typically occur under four simple schedules of reinforcement—fixed-ratio, fixed-interval, variable-ratio, and variable-interval. The steeper the lines, the higher the rate of responding.

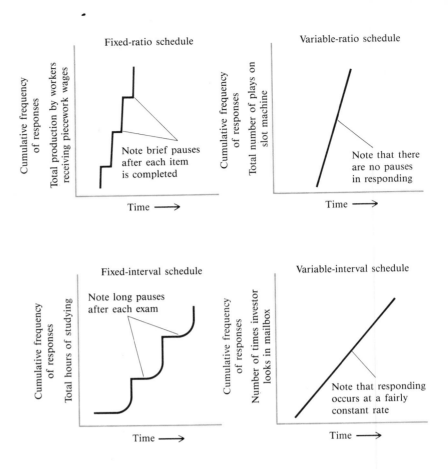

ever, the pattern of behavior that occurs as a result of partial reinforcement depends on the particular schedule that is employed. Of the various forms of partial reinforcement that have been studied extensively, only a few basic schedules need concern us here.

Fixed Schedules

Under a **fixed-ratio (FR) schedule** (see Figure 7.12), reinforcement is given only after a specific number of responses have been made. Fixed-ratio schedules produce very high and steady rates of responding. They resemble the piecework systems of payment used in some industries. Just as a rat may be rewarded only after 15 bar presses, a worker may get paid a certain amount for every 15 articles produced. However, if a rat experiences a long fixed ratio schedule, it takes a time out after each reinforcement—that is, it does not go back and press the bar immediately. But once the rat starts to press the bar again, it will do so at a high steady pace until the next reinforcement.

A different pattern of responding accompanies reinforcement schedules in which the reward depends on a lapse of time instead of the organism's behavior. In a **fixed-interval (FI) schedule,** (see Figure 7.12), reinforcement follows the first response that occurs after one minute has elapsed since the last reinforced response. In this situation, the response rate drops to near zero following a reinforced response and then accelerates as the end of the next interval approaches.

Variable Schedules

A **variable-ratio (VR) schedule** (see Figure 7.12) produces high and steady response rates. Although a variable-ratio schedule might require an overall average of 15 responses for reinforcement, the rate is varied so that, at one point, five unreinforced responses may precede a reinforced response while at another point 25 unreinforced responses may be required. Slot machines are an example of a device that operates on a variable-ratio schedule. If fixed-ratio and variable-ratio schedules of the same length are compared, the variable ratio schedule usually will produce higher and steadier (no pauses) rates of responding.

A **variable-interval (VI) schedule** (see Figure 7.12) is one in which the average interval might be one minute, although responses will be reinforced after time lapses of 5 seconds or 115 seconds. Interestingly, when a variable interval is employed, the response rate does not fluctuate as much as in the fixed-interval schedule because the organism cannot learn to anticipate when a particular interval will end. A variable-interval schedule produces the steadiest rate of responding of the four schedules discussed.

Constraints on Conditioning

Traditional theories of both classical and instrumental or operant conditioning held that all responses that an organism was capable of making could be conditioned with equal ease. However, in the following sections we will examine several constraints of a biological or a cognitive nature that clearly show this assumption to be incorrect. Each section will deal with a basic facet of conditioning and then the biological or cognitive limitations. Let us first examine some of the biological constraints on conditioning.

Trainers used behavior shaping to teach these animals to perform their tricks. The rabbit's natural tendency to pull and tug at twigs and roots transfers readily to the ability to pull the lever that fires the cannon. The raccoon's dextrous hands facilitate its learning to play basketball.

Behavior Shaping

The training of novel behavior or sequences of actions—ones obviously not normally performed by the organism—is called **behavior shaping.** Behavior shaping typically is accomplished by breaking up the desired sequence of action into small steps and then reinforcing the subject as it approaches closer and closer to the proper response in each step. This method of **successive approximations** is evident in training household pets to do tricks. For example, a dog can be taught to retrieve the newspaper by successively reinforcing the animal with food for coming closer and closer to the paper, withholding reinforcement until the dog picks up the paper with its mouth, and finally reinforcing it for returning with the paper. At any given point in the sequence, the desired next step is reinforced and all others become part of the chain of behavior leading to that response.

The simple procedures involved in behavior shaping have been applied to teaching elaborate tricks and complex action sequences to thousands of animals. Porpoises have been taught to jump through hoops and circus seals to play musical instruments. A pig has learned to clean house, turn on a television set, and eat breakfast at a table. In fact, psychologists Keller Breland and Marian Breland have turned behavior shaping into a large business, Animal Behavioral Enterprises, and have trained thousands of animals of many species for television shows and tourist attractions around the world.

Techniques of behavior shaping are also applied in the human world: teaching machines, computer-assisted instruction, and other types of programmed learning use the method of successive approximations. A learning problem is broken down into steps. At each stage the student who makes the appropriate response by providing the correct answer receives immediate reinforcement—perhaps praise from the teaching machine. In addition, behavior shaping has been used as a therapeutic technique. Obesity, stuttering, and a variety of other problems have been treated successfully with such methods. In one notable instance a schizophrenic who had not spoken for 19 years was taught to speak again. Using chewing gum as the reward, the therapist rein-

Computer-assisted instruction, a technique of behavior shaping, provides the learner with immediate reinforcement at each step.

forced a series of successive approximations by the patient—first, facing the therapist, then communicating through head gestures, and, finally speaking (Isaacs, Thomas, & Goldiamond, 1960).

Successful behavior shaping is contingent on the effectiveness of the reinforcement. Birdseed would be effective in training pigeons to play Ping-Pong; it would not be much help in training a dog to retrieve the newspaper. Even when the reinforcement is known to be effective for a particular organism, shaping may not be possible. Several interesting cases of conditioning failures are reported by the animal trainers Breland and Breland (1961). One example involved their frustrating attempts to teach a raccoon to deposit coins in a piggy bank. The raccoon seemed to be a good candidate for the task. It normally conditions readily, has a good appetite, and possesses paws quite similar to the hands of primates. Using food for reinforcement, the Brelands had no difficulty in teaching the raccoon the first step in the sequence—picking up a coin. Then the troubles began. Once the coin was picked up, the raccoon behaved in a most miserly fashion, clutching and rubbing the coin before finally placing it in a metal box. And when the Brelands indicated that the raccoon was to drop two coins in the box prior to reinforcement, it became totally uncooperative, spending several minutes rubbing the coins together and dipping them in and out of the container. Making the raccoon hungrier only increased the "misbehavior."

The Brelands concluded that the raccoon was engaged in a biologically natural response pattern known as "washing behavior," which is normally exhibited when the animal cleans shellfish for food. This instinctive behavior overrode the powerful inducement of food. Similarly, the inborn tendencies of pigs to root for food and of chickens to scratch for it sometimes foiled efforts to shape their behavior. When these reactions are activated in a given species, reinforcement no longer exerts its usual influence. The raccoon and other species cannot be trained to perform arbitrary actions when more basic instinctive reactions are aroused.

Superstitious Behavior

In conventional behavior shaping, as we have seen, delivery of the reinforcement is contingent on performance of the desired response. Another type of shaping has been identified in which a learned response results when there is no contingency between the response and reinforcement.

The setting for the experiment is one widely used in operant conditioning: a Skinner box with a food hopper and, on the wall, a small round disk that pigeons are taught to peck. Suppose a hungry but inexperienced pigeon is put in the box and provided with grain every 12 seconds no matter what the bird does. Under these conditions, Skinner (1948) reported that the pigeons tended to repeat whatever they happened to be doing when the reinforcement occurred—wing flapping, walking in circles, and so on. Because the responses were not instrumental in obtaining food but coincidental with it, he referred to them as "superstitions."

The resemblance to superstitious behavior among humans seemed obvious. Athletes, especially, act out little rituals of superstition that they associate with past success. Basketball players wear the same socks game after game; baseball players stepping into the batter's box tug their caps, dig holes with their spikes, and go through other such rituals. This behavior has been reinforced in the past by coincidental success just as Skinner presumed the antics of his pigeons were reinforced by the coincidental arrival of food.

Although it is true that superstitious behavior in humans may sometimes result from such coincidental rewards, subsequent research has cast doubt on Skinner's original interpretation of his pigeon's actions. Two other researchers, (Staddon & Simmelhag, 1971) repeated Skinner's experiment but ran their pigeons for many sessions. They noted that the birds eventually developed stereotyped responses after being fed; however, as the time for the next feeding approached, they were likely to engage in pecking responses directed at the food hopper. That is, as the time for feeding approached, the pigeons responded in a manner characteristic of the response of eating even though the pecking response had nothing to do with the birds being fed. The pecking response also occurred with increasing regularity as training progressed. Thus, the biologically natural response to food (pecking) was the last response made before food was presented and not some arbitrary form of behavior such as wing flapping that had been coincidentally reinforced. Notice also that the observations of J. E. R. Staddon and V. L. Simmelhag are strikingly similar to Pavlov's observation of temporal conditioning discussed earlier in this chapter. Just as Pavlov's dogs learned to salivate "on time," these pigeons learned to peck "on time."

Autoshaping

Now suppose the experiment described above is repeated, but this time the round disk is illuminated for a few seconds prior to the delivery of food. Under these conditions the pigeons rapidly learn to peck at the lighted disk. This phenomenon has been called **autoshaping** (automatic shaping). That is, the pecking response is automatically shaped by establishing a contingency between the lighted disk and reinforcement, even though the pecking response does not produce the reinforcement. In fact, simply pairing the illuminated disk with food delivery (the conditions for autoshaping) results in more rapid conditioning of the pecking response than is found with the more traditional method of behavior shaping through successive approximations.

What we see here as well as in the preceding section are examples of biologically prepared response patterns: that is, patterns of behavior that are natural responses when the reinforcement is food or escape from aversive stimuli. Anyone familiar with operant conditioning knows that it is easy to train pigeons to peck for food or rats to press levers for food. However, while possible, it is more difficult to train these same responses as ways of avoiding electric shock.

Other experimental findings support the interpretation that autoshaping involves a biologically prepared response rather than an arbitrary response that just happened to be reinforced. An autoshaped response of pecking at an illuminated disk is different in form depending on whether the bird is hungry and food is provided or the bird is thirsty and water is provided. When autoshaped pecks are based on water, the pigeon appears to be trying to drink the disk. Autoshaped pecks based on food appear to be eating motions. If access to a sexually receptive mate follows illumination of the disk, the pigeons will "court" the disk: they coo at it just as they would a prospective mate. In each of these cases the autoshaped response is not at all arbitrary: the response is intimately related to the reward, even though it does not produce the reinforcement. Finally, it should be noted that the contingency between the lighted disk and reinforcement is critical if autoshaping is to occur. Thus, if food is provided when the disk is not illuminated as well as when it is, autoshaped pecking will not occur (Jenkins, 1973). It appears that for autoshaping to occur, the lighted disk must serve to signal a forthcoming reinforcement. This observation suggests a cognitive constraint in conditioning that has been more closely examined in studies of escape and avoidance learning.

Escape and Avoidance Learning

Suppose a dog is placed in a shuttle box, a rectangular box with a low partition dividing the box into two sections. Let us further suppose that electric shock is delivered through the grid floor of the box and that the animal can escape shock by jumping over the partition to the other side of the box. Learning to jump the partition to escape shock is termed **escape learning.**

Now suppose a tone is sounded 10 seconds before each shock delivery so that the dog can avoid the shock by jumping the partition whenever the tone is heard. This type of learning is termed **avoidance learning,** and it involves a combination of classical and operant conditioning. Through classical conditioning the aversive properties of the shock become associated with the tone. In the presence of the tone, jumping has been negatively reinforced, since only by jumping can the dog avoid shock.

The Predictability Hypothesis

The procedures of avoidance learning have been used extensively in recent years to test an important new point of view about classical conditioning. This

A typical shuttle box, in this case for a rat.

idea, initially developed by Robert Rescorla and Richard Solomon (1967), posits a much more cognitive interpretation of classical conditioning. Organisms learn to predict the occurrence of the unconditioned stimulus on the basis of the occurrence of the conditioned stimulus (the tone). The dog, for example, learns to predict that the conditioned stimulus (tone) signals the imminent presentation of the unconditioned stimulus (shock). This idea does not deny conditioning of a response such as fear but rather shifts the emphasis to the more cognitive notion of predictability of events.

Tests of this idea involve training dogs in avoidance learning in the same manner that we described earlier. Then, after avoidance learning, the dogs are placed in situations where they receive unavoidable shocks. The shock always follows presentation of a high-frequency tone. Occasionally a lower-frequency tone is also presented, but it is never followed by shock. Now we return the dogs to the shuttle box. This time the two different tones are presented, but no shocks are administered.

What do you think the dogs would do under these conditions? In an experiment very similar to the one we have described, the animals jumped the shuttle box partition three times as often as their operant level, or baseline rate, when the high-frequency tone was presented. When the lower tone was presented, frequency of jumps dropped to near zero. When the tones were terminated, response rate gradually returned to the baseline level (Maier, Seligman, & Solomon, 1969).

These results support a highly cognitive interpretation of the predictive properties of the two stimuli. In effect, presentation of the high tone served as a "danger" signal; presentation of the lower tone served as a "safe" signal. The dogs apparently had learned that the lower tone was a reliable predictor of a time period safe from shocks.

Other experiments have tested an important implication of the **predictability hypothesis.** This implication is that classical conditioning will not occur unless the conditioned stimulus serves as a reliable basis for predicting the occurrence of the unconditioned stimulus. An appropriate test would be to train three groups of animals in avoidance learning and then expose them to unavoidable shock. For the first group the shock is reliably signaled by a tone. For the second group the shock is always preceded by a tone but sometimes the tone is sounded without the shock follow-up. For the third group, the shock is sometimes preceded by a tone, but there are tones not followed by shock and shocks not preceded by a tone.

In which groups would you predict that fear conditioning actually occurs? According to our hypothesis, it should occur in the first group because the tone is a reliable predictor of shock. It should also occur in the second group because the shock never comes without being preceded by the tone warning signal, although some tone presentations are not followed by shock. But in the third group, conditioning should not occur because the tone is an unreliable predictor of shock. These basic predictions have been confirmed in several experiments (Schwartz, 1984). Thus there is considerable support for the hypothesis that in classical conditioning the conditioned stimulus—in this case, the tone—must serve as a reliable basis for predicting the unconditioned stimulus—shock.

Learned Helplessness

Avoidance learning depends upon the ability of the organism to control its environment. The dog learns that its response—leaping over the partition in the shuttle box—will avoid electric shock. Suppose, however, that inexperienced dogs are placed in a situation over which they have no control: they are sub-

Figure 7.13

Results of an experiment in learned helplessness. The rapid rise in the solid line shows how quickly normal dogs learned how to cope with an electric shock delivered in a shuttle box, as explained in the text. The shaded line shows the very different behavior of animals that had acquired learned helplessness and, therefore, seemed incapable of learning how to do anything about the shock.

jected to a series of brief, intense shocks that cannot be avoided. This painful experience strongly affects their future capability for avoidance learning.

Investigators did, in fact, subject a group of dogs to unavoidable shock and then placed them in a shuttle box for avoidance training. The dogs now could avoid shock if they jumped over the partition within a specified period of time. Not many did. Only one third of the dogs showed avoidance learning. By contrast, among a control group of dogs not previously exposed to unavoidable shock, 94 percent successfully demonstrated avoidance learning (Seligman, Maier, & Solomon, 1971).

For the dogs who were unable to learn the avoidance response after being exposed to unavoidable shocks, it was as if they had concluded that "nothing they do matters." The investigators termed this phenomenon **learned helplessness** (see Figure 7.13). In other experiments, learned helplessness occurred even when the dogs were given warning. For example, during both the unavoidable shock and the avoidance-learning situations, a tone preceded the shock. Inasmuch as the tone reliably predicted the shock, it should have served as a warning signal to the dogs; nonetheless, they seemed helpless to escape. The experimenters found that learned helplessness could be overcome if they actually pulled the dogs back and forth over the partition. After being given that helping hand, the dogs were able to learn avoidance (Seligman, Maier, & Geer, 1968).

It is significant that when dogs are given avoidance training before being subjected to unavoidable shocks, learned helplessness does not occur. This is another illustration of the powerful influence exerted by prior experience in determining what is learned in a given situation.

Learned helplessness has been demonstrated in humans as well as in a variety of animals and may have important implications for understanding several aspects of human behavior (Seligman, 1975). It has been suggested, for example, that learned helplessness may account for some cases of chronic failure in school: students who have failed often in the past may come to feel that nothing they do in school will enable them to avoid further failures. Moreover, as we will see in chapter 14, the striking similarities between the behavior of the helpless dogs and that of some humans suggest new insights into one of the most common emotional disorders, depression. Depressed individuals often behave as if they think that "nothing they do matters."

Partial Reinforcement and Extinction

Acquisition training with partial reinforcement produces greater resistance to extinction than does continuous reinforcement. After training under partial reinforcement an animal will respond for a much longer period of time and respond more often in the absence of reinforcement than after training under only continuous reinforcement. This phenomenon has been termed the **partial-reinforcement effect.**

This effect is partially explained by the similarity between extinction sessions and training sessions on a partial-reinforcement schedule. In partial-reinforcement training, animals experience periods of no reinforcement that are comparable to the conditions during extinction sessions. While explanations of this sort have intuitive appeal, they are difficult to evaluate experimentally. For example, when animals are trained first on partial reinforcement and then on continuous reinforcement, they still show the partial-reinforcement effect during extinction when compared to animals trained only on continuous reinforcement (Jenkins, 1962; Theios, 1962). This effect holds even though the change in conditions between the end of training and extinction is the same for both groups of animals. The animals given initial training under partial reinforcement appeared to "remember" something about their initial experiences.

The possible importance of cognitive factors in explaining the partial-reinforcement effect is nicely illustrated in a study reported by Stewart Hulse (1973). Hulse used a modified Skinner box in which the bar was automatically withdrawn after each response. This allowed separate trials in which a response could be either reinforced or not. At first, the responses of his rats were reinforced on a random 50 percent of the trials. Then they were shifted to a schedule in which every other response was reinforced. Finally, training was concluded under continuous reinforcement. The surprising result was that the behavior of these animals extinguished even faster than animals trained only on continuous reinforcement. A possible explanation for this result is that the animals "noticed" that reinforcement was becoming increasingly predictable during training, changing from random, to single alternation, to continuous reinforcement. If this indeed was the case, the animals may have become increasingly attuned to the likelihood of reinforcement and more readily set to discriminate the beginning of extinction.

Reward or Punishment

As with many other aspects of our lives, learning through reinforcement involves a complex interaction between the learner, the task or situation, and what the learner brings to the situation both in terms of species-specific characteristics and past experiences. Behavior that might at first seem bizarre often becomes perfectly logical if we understand the prior experiences of a person or animal.

A graphic illustration of this can be found in a report by James Barrett (1978), who worked in the laboratory using squirrel monkeys. These monkeys, on a five-minute, fixed-interval schedule of reinforcement, showed the same pattern of bar pressing whether the last event in each interval was reinforcement (the presentation of food) or punishment (an intense electric shock). After each presentation of food or shock, the monkeys responded at a low rate that then increased steadily as the time for the next reinforcement approached (see Figure 7.14).

At first glance these response patterns seem incomprehensible; it is as if the monkeys could not tell reinforcement from punishment. But information about the monkeys' prior experiences makes their behavior more understandable. These animals had previously been trained to avoid shock by bar pressing. They had learned that pressing the bar would postpone the shock for 25 seconds and that not pressing the bar would lead to shocks every 5 seconds. Once we know this, the monkey's behavior on the fixed-interval schedule makes more sense. Having previously learned that bar pressing postpones shock, they continued to press the bar although this response no longer worked. Using human terms, we might say the monkeys concluded that even though shock was no longer totally avoidable by pressing the bar, at least the shock occurred only every so often. The monkeys could learn that bar pressing was no longer effective only if they were willing to endure the possibility of more frequent shocks.

Summary of Conditioning

As the preceding discussions indicate, the analysis of learning in terms of the phenomena of conditioning has been popular in psychology for a very long time. This analysis has proved to be quite successful in providing us with an

Figure 7.14

Performance of squirrel monkeys under five-minute, fixed-interval schedules of reinforcement. The first response after five minutes either produced a food pellet (top) or an electric shock (bottom). In both cases, patterns of responding were comparable regardless of the consequent event (Barrett, 1978).

Figure 7.15

One of Wolfgang Köhler's insight experiments, in which an ape stacked boxes on top of each other to reach food suspended from the ceiling.

Figure 7.16

Theoretical curves illustrating the relationship between speed of problem solving and degree of prior practice. According to trial-and-error theory, solution speed gradually increases with practice. According to insight theory, it increases on an all-or-none basis, independent of practice.

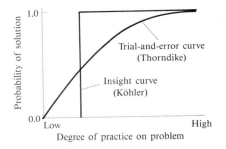

understanding of a variety of learned behaviors. It has also provided the basis for a number of practical applications. Conditioning principles form the basis of a popular type of psychotherapy known as behavior modification (see chapter 15). These same principles have provided a strong impetus for the development of systems for programmed instruction. As we have already seen, animal training techniques are almost exclusively based on principles established in the study of conditioning.

However, as we have also seen, there are important biological and cognitive constraints that influence behavior in conditioning situations. Biological characteristics often determine whether learning is easy or even possible in a given situation. Cognitive factors such as the predictability of success and the interpretation or meaning of particular experiences also play a role in conditioning situations. Thus, conditioning, like other varieties of learning, often depends on complex interactions between the species of the learner, the particular situation that is presented, and the learner's past experiences.

Cognition and Learning

In various conditioning phenomena we have seen a number of instances in which cognitive factors—perception and knowledge—influence conditioning. These cognitive influences are most likely to arise in conditioning situations when memory structures established through prior experience determine the way new experiences are interpreted. Instances of these influences include the partial-reinforcement effect, learned helplessness, and the importance of conditioned stimulus/unconditioned stimulus predictability in classical conditioning. As you might expect, cognitive factors play a major role in situations having little to do with conditioning. This fact has led many psychologists to abandon the study of strict conditioning paradigms in favor of procedures that are better suited to revealing the cognitive activities of the learner.

Insight Experiments

An early example of cognitive analysis can be seen in Wolfgang Köhler's work on **insight** in learning. Around 1913 he began a series of experiments with apes that demonstrated an important role for insight in problem-solving tasks. Köhler's basic argument with previous experiments such as Thorndike's was that they revealed only trial-and-error behavior because the tasks employed did not encourage insightful solutions. He argued that, with more appropriate tasks, insight in the form of novel (unpracticed) solutions would be quite common.

Köhler (1925) described the problem-solving behavior of apes in situations that were more or less natural for them. One famous example was that of the ape Sultan, who was unable to reach food with either of two short sticks but solved the problem by joining the sticks together. In another example the animal piled boxes on top of one another in order to reach food suspended from the ceiling (see Figure 7.15).

The ability of these apes to repeat these solutions without difficulty was taken as evidence that the original solution was not a random trial-and-error affair. This does not mean that such insightful solutions might not be facilitated by random behavior, but that the random behavior involves intelligent groping toward a solution and not a blind thrashing about, as Thorndike had implied (see Figure 7.16).

Insight during learning is a common phenomenon in humans, often associated with an "aha" experience. Such insightful solutions are not only readily repeated but also can be applied in new situations in which the solution is not specifically tied to the circumstances of initial learning. What is learned is a cognitive relationship between the responses and the goal and not just a conditioned response.

Learning Abstract Concepts

A **concept** refers to the properties or relationships common to a class of objects or ideas. Concepts vary widely in terms of both concreteness and complexity. A triangle is a concept, a quite simple one; abstract ideas such as freedom and justice are concepts as well. Much of what we learn consists of concepts. When you finish reading this book, we hope you will have learned a large number of concepts. **Concept learning** is a way of ordering our experience and our perceptions of the world around us. Concepts enable us to grasp the important similarities between things while ignoring the irrelevant details.

Concepts are learned in a variety of ways. Many of the concepts we learn are directly taught to us by parents, friends, and teachers. Concepts also are learned through reading or by exposure to radio and television. In fact, almost every activity we engage in provides opportunities to learn new concepts or to modify previously learned concepts.

In the following chapter we will examine in some detail the nature of the memory structures that result from learning concepts and the way these structures relate to one another. At this point in our discussion of cognitive aspects of learning, let us simply consider one experiment that deals with the learning of an abstract concept. There are two important things to note about this experiment. The first is that the concept that is learned is one the learners are never actually exposed to but one they learn nevertheless. The second is that the experiment is only one of many that show that such abstract concepts are learned, even though little is known as yet about the way they are learned.

The experiment to be considered did not involve the learning of a particular concept, such as a triangle or square, per se. Rather the experimenters, Jeffrey Franks and John Bransford (1971), presented a series of stimulus objects under the guise of an immediate memory experiment and subsequently used a recognition test as a basis for inferring what had been learned. Let us first consider the way in which stimulus materials were constructed.

The investigators began by selecting an arbitrary configuration consisting of four common shapes as a prototype. The prototype could be modified using a set of rules called transformation rules. One of the prototypes used, along with examples of the transformation rules, is shown in Figure 7.17. For example, applying the left-right reversal rule to the prototype results in the configuration shown just below the prototype.

The stimulus objects used in this experiment were configurations obtained by applying one or more transformations to the prototype. When two or more transformations were used, they were applied successively. For example, the prototype might first be modified using the left-right reversal rule. The resulting configuration could then be modified using the right-top-bottom reversal rule, and then the deletion rule could be applied. The resulting configuration, shown in Figure 7.17, is said to be three transformational steps away from the prototype. Configurations ranging from one to four transformations from the prototype were constructed for this experiment.

A subset of these configurations, but not including the prototype, was presented during the learning phase. Each stimulus object was presented for 5 seconds, followed by a short distractor task. The learners were then asked to

This child is learning but has not yet mastered the concept of the telephone and its use.

Figure 7.17

Sample of visual forms to demonstrate the learning of abstract concepts (Franks & Bransford, 1971).

(1) Prototype	■ ♥ ▲ ♦
(2) Left-right reversal	♥ ■ ♦ ▲
(3) Left figure ground reversal	▲ ♥ ■ ♦
(4) Right figure ground reversal	■ ♦ ▲ ♥
(5) Deletion	♥ ▲ ♦
(6) 2 + 4 + 5	♥ ▲ ♦

FOCUS

Observational Learning

The tendency of humans and many animals to learn by imitation is summed up by the adage, "Monkey see, monkey do." Particularly in the young, observational learning obviously is one of the most important varieties of learning. Children learn not only by imitating what they see but also by copying what they hear. The latter is evident whenever we listen with astonishment while a youngster, not old enough to understand the meaning, utters an explosive string of four-letter expletives.

Examples of observational learning among the young abound. By imitating the behavior of models (parents in particular), young children acquire much of their vocabulary, learn such motor tasks as tying their shoes, and attain many of the attitudes that characterize their social interactions with others. One explanation for the widespread importance of observational learning is its efficiency. Learners can often avoid the tedious trial-and-error procedures characteristic of instrumental conditioning: they can observe not only the behavior of the model but also whether or not the behavior is successful.

Perhaps the very fact that observational learning is so obvious helps explain why it has been relatively ne-

glected by psychologists until recent years. Recent interest has been given increased impetus by controversies surrounding possible effects of mass media—especially television—on behavior. The most prominent of these controversies is the issue of whether or not exposure to violence on television can increase violent behavior on the part of children. Although this issue is not likely to be settled for some time, indirect evidence concerning the issue is available.

This indirect evidence stems from the work of Albert Bandura, pioneer in the study of observational learning. In the basic Bandura experiment, groups of nursery school children were exposed to an adult model who behaved aggressively toward "Bobo," a 4-foot-high inflated plastic doll. In some experiments, the demonstration was live—that is, the model was present in the room with the children; in others, the demonstration was on film. After both live and filmed demonstrations the chil-

dren tended to imitate the models' aggressive behavior. They copied specific acts of aggression such as lifting, throwing, and kicking the plastic doll; they even reported some of the same hostile comments used by the model—"Pow!" and "Sock him in the nose!" (Bandura, 1974; Bandura, Ross, & Ross, 1963). Interestingly, the filmed demonstrations resulted in greater observational learning than did the live demonstrations.

Variations on these experiments suggest some of the factors that may influence observational learning. For example, the status of the model proved to be important, a finding echoed by the fact that people tend to imitate the behavior of celebrities. Rewards also had a significant impact; in experiments where the model was rewarded for aggressive behavior, the resulting imitation was greater than when the model was punished.

To many psychologists, the Bandura findings have a double significance. Violence on television may increase the tendency of viewers to behave aggressively; it may also teach them a repertoire of particular forms of violent behavior. Recall that the children in the experiments not only were more aggressive after viewing the film but also imitated specific acts of the model. There also has

reproduce the configuration they had just seen. This procedure was continued until each stimulus object had been presented twice.

In the recognition test a large number of configurations, including the prototype, were presented one at a time. The learners were asked to indicate whether or not each configuration had been presented during the learning phase and how confident they were of their answer. Other than the prototype, the configurations presented ranged from one to four transformations from the prototype. However, none of these configurations was actually presented during the learning phase.

The learners were most confident that they had seen the prototype before. Responses to the other configurations reflected the number of transformations applied to the prototype; that is, the configurations only one transformation

Illustration of Bandura's experiment on learning aggression by imitation involving use of "Bobo" clown doll. In the top row an adult model exhibits four different ways to hurt the doll. The next two rows show a boy and a girl duplicating the model's efforts.

been much speculation, though little data, that adults may learn new forms of violence by observing television and other media. In recent years, extensive media coverage of skyjackings, political assassinations, and other novel forms of violence has frequently been followed by waves of similar crimes.

Because the study of observational learning is still in its infancy, the limits on this variety of learning have not yet been fully established in the laboratory. Certainly one limit is the complexity of the behavior observed. We obviously do not learn to play the violin merely by watching and hearing a great violinist. ∎

away from the prototype were judged as next most likely to have been seen before. The further a configuration was from the prototype, the greater was the likelihood that it would be called a new one. However, the responses indicated that the learners thought that most of the configurations had been presented previously.

Franks and Bransford viewed their findings as indicating that what was learned was the prototype and the transformation rules rather than the specific configurations presented during the learning phase. Thus is appears that individuals are capable of abstracting a concept (the prototype) that was not presented as well as rules that were never presented formally. It should also be noted that these results cannot be explained on the basis of simple frequency with which the four shapes were presented.

A baseball pitcher relies on motor learning, which is an ongoing process involving verbal and cognitive aspects as well.

Another study (Spear, 1972) further suggests that learning specific configurations is not necessary for abstraction of the prototype and rules to occur. Using essentially the same task as Franks and Bransford, M. E. Spear compared a group of severely brain-damaged people with a normal group. The recognition results for both groups were comparable to those noted above. However, she also evaluated performance in reproducing the stimulus configurations as they were presented during the learning phase. As expected, the normals were essentially perfect, but the brain-damaged people did very poorly. Thus, learning the configurations presented does not seem to be necessary for the abstraction of concepts involving prototypes to take place.

Motor Learning

Cognitive approaches to learning often place considerable emphasis on the establishment of, or modification of, cognitive structures during learning. In the case of motor learning the important cognitive structures are those referred to as motor programs. The existence of such programs is inferred from the nature of motor performance; however, before we consider motor programs further, let us first examine motor learning in more detail.

Many of the varieties of learning previously discussed in this chapter involve the body's motor system. Obviously, behavior such as bar pressing, key pecking, and leaping to avoid electric shock would be impossible without muscles and motor nerves. As we will use the term here, however, **motor learning** refers to a distinct variety of learning. It involves the learning of a sequence of highly coordinated responses that are systematically related to one another: each response or component response is integrally related.

Investigations of motor learning can be traced back at least to studies of learning curves for apprentice telegraph operators developing their skill (Bryan & Harter, 1897). Such learning is often called motor-skill learning or sensorimotor learning. The latter term reflects the fact that sensory systems such as seeing and hearing play important roles both in directing the motor pattern and in providing feedback, including knowledge of results. It is clear also that there are verbal and other cognitive aspects of motor learning. For example, a baseball pitcher not only executes a predetermined movement sequence involving the entire body, but also must make decisions: the pitcher must decide where to pitch the ball—low and over the outside corner of home plate, for example. Similarly, the batter intentionally gets set for a particular type of pitch—say, a fast ball or curve—although the cognitive plan may or may not facilitate hitting the ball.

One important characteristic of motor learning is that it appears to be an ongoing process (Schmidt, 1975). This contrasts with other varieties of learning, such as conditioning and rote memorization, where the limitations on improvement are fairly restricted. In those varieties, performance usually reaches a peak level within relatively few trials.

Let us examine two examples of continuous improvement in motor learning. E. Crossman (1959) provides data in which factory workers, using a simple tool called a jig to make cigars, showed improvement over a period of seven years in the time required to make each cigar. Although the gains were greatest in the early days of this period, some improvements were still taking place seven years later, after the workers had produced 10 million cigars. The second illustration concerns the ability of a baseball outfielder to run after and catch a fly ball. This skill, which may seem routine to the uninitiated, is in fact an exceedingly complex sensorimotor skill that continues to improve over many years of practice. The expression "getting a good jump on the ball" lies at the heart of this skill. Although running speed obviously contributes to what the outfielder can accomplish, it is the skill in abstracting the trajectory that constitutes the ability of a good outfielder. The development of this skill begins in the young ballplayer and may not reach its upper limit even after several years of professional experience. It may well be that the main constraint on further improvement occurs when the process of aging limits what the body is physically capable of doing.

There are at least two ways to conceptualize the stages in motor learning. One way involves tasks or situations that consist of a series of levels. A particularly good example is the skill of typing. The first stage in acquiring this skill requires learning finger control and the location of the keys. This stage usually shows rapid improvement in terms of both speed and accuracy, although the beginning typist may feel that initial progress seems slow. The next stages involve moving from letter to word habits and from word to phrase habits. During each stage, initial improvement in performance tends to be followed by a plateau showing little improvement until the learner moves on to the next higher stage. Similar patterns of improvements followed by plateaus characterize learning to play musical instruments such as the piano.

A second way to analyze the stages of motor learning was provided by Paul Fitts and Michael Posner (1967). Their analysis is focused on the stages the learner passes through in terms of the way the learner performs.

In the first stage, termed the **cognitive stage**, the learner needs to know what the elements of the task are and what is expected in terms of performance. During this stage, learners draw upon reasoning abilities and past experiences to employ cognitive strategies that are subsequently modified as they gain experience with the task.

The **associative stage** enters in as the prior cognitive activities begin to drop out. Major errors are greatly reduced during this stage as the learner refines the responses to be made. Whereas the cognitive stage places initial emphasis on what responses to perform and in what order, the associative stage emphasizes how best to coordinate and intergrate those responses.

The third stage, or **autonomous stage**, of motor learning refers to extremely advanced levels of performance. Errors are greatly reduced, and the performer seems to become more automatic in performing the task. At this stage less attention is required to perform the task, and more attention can be devoted to other activities at the same time.

These stages are illustrated in the process of learning to drive a car. At first, a certain amount of instruction is usually required. Following this the learner begins to drive, but it is usually necessary to devote full attention to the various components of this sensorimotor task. These demands may be so great that directions being given by the driving instructor are not even heard. After considerable practice, however, simultaneous activities such as carrying on a conversation and driving can be accomplished quite easily. Nonetheless, when the driver is faced with a novel situation, such as negotiating an unfamiliar highway, more attention may be required for successful and safe driving.

The level to which a motor skill can become automatic is demonstrated by a story about the author of this chapter. He frequently was so deep in thought that he often arrived at his office without even recalling that he had driven from home. The route was five miles long and involved making a series of turns, monitoring stop lights, and crossing a major thoroughfare and a busy railroad track. Yet upon arrival at the office he had no awareness of having performed these functions. Obviously, such a high level of automaticity is impressive, although it is certainly not to be recommended behind the wheel.

Once a skill becomes automatic, we can say that a **motor program** has been acquired. The learner has established a sequence of highly coordinated movements that are integrated in time and characterized by a rhythmic structure of their own. There are several types of evidence that point to the existence of

This individual is combining two unusual and highly skilled motor programs.

motor programs. One consideration is the speed of certain highly skilled movements. For example, the fingers of one pianist were clocked at 16 movements per second (Lashley, 1951). Because this is apparently faster than the fingers could be controlled by sensory feedback, only a motor program could account for the speed.

The notion that highly integrated motor programs are acquired during advanced stages of motor learning is also supported by other observations. One is the ability to perform two tasks at the same time. Ulric Neisser (1976) cites cases of skilled pianists who can read prose while sight-reading music and professional typists who can type from copy while reciting nursery rhymes from memory. Perhaps the most persuasive evidence for motor programs derives from the extent to which well-learned skills can be performed despite years of nonuse. Examples we are all familiar with include bicycle riding, swimming, and even typing. To be sure, it may take some time and practice to regain the fine details of these skills, but—unlike other examples of human learning—motor skills are incredibly resistant to forgetting. It is as though the basic elements of these skills had become so highly integrated that they were retained as an intact unitary skill.

We have discussed a number of ways in which varieties of learning occur. All these varieties include relatively permanent behavior changes that result from prior experience. In the following chapter we will examine the vital role of memory and its structure in producing learning.

Summary

1. Learning can be broadly described as a relatively permanent change of behavior that results from prior experience. Learning is inferred from performance, but it is not the same thing. Motivation is usually necessary for learning to be manifest in performance. Also, certain changes in performance do not reflect learning because either they are temporary or they are due to innate factors. The difference between learning and performance can also be described in terms, respectively, of capability and action.

2. Imprinting is the process by which certain young animals learn to follow their mothers. Imprinting is most pronounced in young birds that are able to walk or swim immediately after birth. Ethologists, scientists who study animals in their natural environments, have found that, in the absence of the mother, ducklings and chicks will imprint on almost any prominent moving object. Imprinting points to the importance of innate factors in some forms of learning.

3. Pavlov's experiments in classical conditioning demonstrated the stimulus-response relationship in some basic forms of learning. Pavlov observed that dogs salivated (unconditioned response) at the presentation of food (unconditioned stimulus). The dogs then learned to salivate (conditioned response) in response to a previously neutral stimulus (conditioned stimulus), a bell.

4. Time relationships between the conditioned stimulus and unconditioned stimulus are important in classical conditioning. A short time between the conditioned stimulus and the unconditioned stimulus is often optimal for conditioning. Pavlov also demonstrated extinction, or weakening of a conditioned response, and the phenomena of stimulus generalization and discrimination.

5. E. L. Thorndike identified another variety of learning—learning by trial and error—that has become known as instrumental learning. B. F. Skinner developed procedures for studying operant conditioning, which involves controlling behavior by manipulating its consequences. Any stimulus event that, when made contingent upon a response, increases the future likelihood of that response, is called reinforcement.

6. Primary reinforcers are those that meet biological needs, such as food and water; secondary reinforcers, such as praise and money, are learned and are more likely to be effective in human learning.

7. An operant response is generally conditioned by reinforcing every occurrence of the response—a schedule known as continuous reinforcement. After conditioning, the response can be maintained by a schedule of partial reinforcement, under which it is only occasionally reinforced. Partial reinforcement schedules include fixed-interval, fixed-ratio, variable interval, and variable-ratio schedules. Partial reinforcement usually produces greater resistance to extinction than does continuous reinforcement.

8. The training of novel behavior or sequences of actions—ones not normally performed by the organism—is called behavior shaping. Behavior shaping is typically accomplished by breaking up the desired sequence of action into small steps with rewards in a method known as successive approximations. Successful behavior shaping is contingent upon the effectiveness of the reinforcement. In another type of shaping, autoshaping, a learned response results even when there is no contingency between the response and reinforcement.

9. Avoidance learning involves a combination of classical and instrumental conditioning: a classically conditioned fear response serves as the stimulus for an instrumental avoidance response. The predictability hypothesis states that in classical conditioning the conditioned stimulus must serve as a reliable basis for predicting the occurrence of the unconditioned stimulus.

10. Punishment is pain or annoyance administered in an attempt to eliminate a particular behavior; negative reinforcement, by contrast, results when a response leads to removal of a negative reinforcer, which serves the same purpose as would a positive reinforcer. Punishment seems less effective in learning situations than reinforcers that increase the probability of desired behavior.

11. Cognitive factors—perception and knowledge—influence various conditioning phenomena and are most likely to arise in conditioning situations when memory structures, established through prior experience, determine the way new experiences are interpreted. Insight experiments have demonstrated an important role for insight in problem-solving tasks: solutions achieved through insight can be applied to new problems.

12. A concept refers to the properties or relationships, both abstract and concrete, that are common to a class of objects or ideas. Concept learning, which orders our experience and perceptions, enables us to grasp the important similarities between things and to ignore irrelevant details. Concepts are learned in a variety of ways, not all of them yet understood.

13. Motor learning involves the learning of a sequence of highly coordinated responses that are systematically related to one another: Each response or component response is integrally related. Sensorimotor learning involves the sensory systems such as seeing and hearing both in directing the motor pattern and in providing feedback, including knowledge of results. Motor learning, in contrast to other varieties of learning such as conditioning and rote memorization, appears to be an ongoing process.

14. Once a skill, such as typing, becomes automatic, we can say that a motor program has been acquired. The learner has established a sequence of highly coordinated movements that are integrated in time and characterized by a rhythmic structure of their own.

RESEARCH: Robert Dooling and Margaret Searcy have demonstrated that selected vocal learning in the young swamp sparrow is facilitated by the birds' perceptual predisposition to attend to the song of the adult swamp sparrow. Swamp sparrows were raised in the laboratory and were not permitted to hear any bird songs until the time of testing. During testing, EKG readings were obtained from the young birds while they listened to different songs, including those from other types of sparrows. The young swamp sparrows responded with greater heart deceleration to songs of other swamp sparrows than to songs from other birds, indicating an innate recognition of their species' vocalizations.

FOCUS: Learning through imitation is called observational learning. Albert Bandura has demonstrated that children learn to behave more aggressively after watching a model perform aggressively, particularly if the model is a significant individual or is rewarded for aggressive behavior. Viewing violence on TV may increase the tendency of some persons to behave aggressively as well as suggest particular acts of violence. Observational learning is unlikely to account for the learning of highly complex skills such as playing a musical instrument.

CHAPTER

Memory and Cognition

Memory refers to the brain's ability to store and to recreate or reproduce past experiences and thoughts. The term *cognition* refers to a complex set of processes studied by psychologists that pertain to the acquisition and use of knowledge. In the preceding chapter we saw how several aspects of cognition relate to learning. Cognition is also very much involved in such diverse phenomena as attention, perception, problem solving, judgment, decision making, thinking, and memory. However, in a very fundamental sense, memory is the basic building block on which all of human cognition is based. Because of this relationship between memory and cognition, this chapter will emphasize only those aspects of cognition in which memory plays a primary role.

An intimate relationship exists between learning and memory. You will recall that learning is defined as a relatively permanent behavior change as a result of experience. It is the brain's memory capability that allows most learning to take place. Not only is learning inferred through performance measures based on memory of prior experiences, but, as we have also seen, what is learned in a particular situation (for example, learned helplessness) is often influenced by the presence or absence of memories of previous events. Similar relationships exist between memory and other cognitive processes. For example, when driving a car we must remember what to attend to and what can be ignored. When we see a friend approach, the act of perceiving that friend is intricately involved with memory. Many forms of cognition involve creative aspects, but all of our cognitive processes are closely tied to the contents of memory. In fact, the close interrelationships among our cognitive processes are such that it is impossible to discuss any one of them without at least implicit reference to other aspects of cognition.

Perhaps the most important reason for studying human memory is that memory is the repository of our knowledge of the world, including facts, beliefs, attitudes, and so on. It is for this reason that much of what you will encounter in other chapters involves human memory to a large degree.

Stages of Memory

In developing theoretical models of the stages and processes involved in memory, psychologists have found that many of the information-processing concepts formulated for communications, engineering, and computer science can be applied to human beings. The information-processing approach analyzes memory in stages and examines the processes that take place at each stage. In this vein, we shall look at three stages of memory: sensory memory, short-term memory, and long-term memory (see Figure 8.1). Although these stages of memory can be distinguished both in terms of the ways they are studied and the processes being examined, they need not be considered as separate isolated stages in any very fundamental sense. Rather, the distinction among these stages is offered for convenience in discussing various phenomena of memory.

The stage model represents a hypothetical construct that allows us to organize and better understand various memory phenomena. Although the idea of memory stages has important heuristic value, it may be somewhat artificial in the sense of fragmenting what is actually an integrated, coherent process.

Figure 8.1

Illustration of the three stages of memory: sensory, short-term, and long-term memory.

| External events | → | Sensory memory Visual Auditory | → | Short-term memory (STM) Limited capacity | ⇄ | Long-term memory (LTM) Unlimited capacity |

CHAPTER 8   MEMORY AND COGNITION

Sensory Memory

While the phenomenon of **sensory memory**—the momentary lingering of sensory information after a stimulus has been removed—was discovered in the last century, it is only since 1960 that any substantial amount of research dealing with the sensory effects of stimuli has been reported.

Visual Stimuli

A typical experiment on sensory visual memory might involve the simultaneous exposure of nine different letters of the alphabet arranged in three rows of three letters each (Sperling, 1960). The letters are exposed to observers for a very brief period of time, say 50 milliseconds. Because it requires approximately 200 milliseconds (1/5 of a second) to begin a directed eye movement, the observers do not have time to scan the array of letters, although they do see them all. Now the observers are asked to report all of the letters they have seen. Although the observers report having ''seen'' all of the letters, they can report only about four or five letters correctly. However, if the observers are asked to report only a single row of these letters, they can do so without error.

The row to be reported is indicated by the presentation of a cue following exposure to the letters. This is referred to as the partial-report technique. Because the observers have no way of knowing which row is to be reported until the letters disappear, this observation suggests that all, or at least most, of the letters were available for recall. Why then should the observers fail to report all letters correctly using the full-report procedure?

George Sperling and others have provided at least a tentative answer to this question (Sperling, 1960; Baddeley, 1976). When the cue, in this case a signal tone, used to indicate which row of letters to report occurs after only a brief delay following letter presentation, accuracy of reporting declines (see Figure 8.2). In fact, if the cue is presented as little as one second later, the observers' performance, in terms of percent correct, is no better than obtained in full report. Sperling attributes these findings to a visual memory trace, or the persisting aftereffects of stimuli, called the **icon,** or **iconic trace** (Sperling, 1960), which has a relatively large storage capacity but a duration of not more than one second. Thus, when using the full-report procedure, the trace or icon continues to decay while the observers are reporting the letters. By the time four or five letters have been reported, the icon is so faint that it is no longer possible to distinguish and report any more letters. However, the icon is present long enough to report all of the letters in any particular row.

Auditory Stimuli

Apart from the visual system, sensory memory has been clearly established only for audition. Ulric Neisser (1967) refers to this auditory trace as **echoic memory,** and it should be noted that its main characteristics are similar to those of iconic memory—that is, both refer to the persisting effects of sensory stimuli without regard to the nature of the observer's or listener's response. The capacity of the iconic trace is probably greater than that of the echoic trace because the spatial nature of the visual system permits simultaneous processing of several items at the same time. In contrast, the auditory system is designed to

Figure 8.2

Sperling's study of sensory memory, the number and percentage of correct letters recalled over a 1-second interval declined the longer the delay between the presentation of the letters and the cue (signal tone) indicating which row of letters was to be reported (Sperling, 1960).

process information serially, one item at a time. However, at least under some conditions, there is evidence to suggest that the duration of the echoic trace may be somewhat longer (up to 2 seconds) than is found for the visual trace (Darwin, Turvey, & Crowder, 1972).

As an example of echoic memory, recall the feeling that someone just said something to you and of going back to "listen" to it. Perhaps what was said was in the form of a question. You may even have responded with "What?" before going back to listen to what was said and stored in echoic memory. You may be able to process the question and answer it before the original speaker has repeated the question.

Short-Term Memory

Sensory memory, at best, plays only a small role in most everyday activities, simply because we are seldom exposed to events of such brief duration. In contrast, **short-term memory (STM)** is used by all of us constantly. A common illustration involves looking up a telephone number, holding it in short-term memory until the number has been dialed, and noting a few minutes later that we may have no recollection of the number we dialed. Several exposures to an arbitrary sequence of items such as telephone numbers are usually required before they become part of our relatively permanent long-term memory.

Short-term memory has been assigned numerous labels including primary memory, working memory, what we are currently "paying attention to," and even consciousness. These various labels have been introduced to emphasize theoretical distinctions, which will be considered shortly, and to focus on the way we use short-term memory as well as on the contents of short-term memory.

Capacity Limitations

One reason for our interest in short-term memory stems from the fact that human beings can deal with only a limited amount of information at any given moment. For example, when you go to a grocery store you cannot usually remember a long list of things to purchase unless you write it down.

In his classic studies of memory, Hermann Ebbinghaus (1885/1964) memorized hundreds of lists of nonsense syllables on which he later tested himself for retention. Nonsense syllables are three-letter sequences, usually containing a vowel between two consonants, which have no meaning or inherent associations. Ebbinghaus chose nonsense syllables because he thought meaningful words already contained too many associations and he wanted all the lists to be equally difficult to learn. He reported that the number of nonsense syllables he could recall following a single presentation was about seven. This observation suggested a fixed capacity for short-term memory or what has been called the *span of immediate memory*. Over half a century later, this notion was systematically developed in a paper by George A. Miller (1956). In reviewing the results of numerous studies, Miller proposed that the limit of the human short-term memory span was on the order of seven units plus or minus two units.

Studies of the memory span for arbitrarily related digits, for example, 2, 8, 5 . . .) show that most people have a capacity within this range. However, Miller's proposal went beyond single units such as digits or letters arranged in arbitrary sequences. Instead, Miller introduced the psychological concept of a **chunk of information.** Chunks refer to memory units that result from recoding units or integrating together more elementary units. For example, the digits 1, 4, 9, and 2 could be recoded as 1492, the date of Columbus's discovery of America. Words also constitute chunks in which several letters become integrated into a single meaningful unit. Thus, a sequence of seven arbitrarily re-

We typically rely on short-term memory when dialing a phone number.

Herman Ebbinghaus' research with nonsense syllables suggested a fixed capacity for short-term memory.

lated but familiar words would be almost as easy to recall as a string of seven consonants, even though the seven words taken together contain many more than seven letters. In this case, the letters within each word have become integrated into a single chunk.

In general, **chunking** refers to the organization of material in such a way as to include more items of information per chunk. The analogy here is to a memory span consisting of seven bins, each of which may contain several items as long as the items within each bin are coherently related. However, chunks are not defined by the materials themselves. Instead, chunks are imposed on the materials by the individual and will vary from one person to another. For someone unfamiliar with American history, the digits 1, 4, 9, and 2 may not form a chunk. Similarly, words that are unfamiliar to us do not form single chunks of information but remain as strings of arbitrarily arranged letters.

Attention

Psychologists have been well aware of capacity limits in short-term memory for many years, but the question we wish to address here is whether attentional processes place even further constraints on what can enter into our memory. The issue is not whether our attentional abilities are limited, because we all know they are. Rather, the issue is whether attentional limitations are any different from those that characterize short-term memory.

The study of attention has a long history is psychology but current interest in this topic was stimulated by the work of E. Colin Cherry (1953). The topic that interested Cherry has been described as the "cocktail party phenomenon," and it refers to our ability to attend selectively to one conversation while ignoring others (see chapter 4). The experimental task employed by Cherry is known as **shadowing:** two or more spoken messages are presented simultaneously to a listener whose task is to repeat one of the spoken messages aloud as it is heard, word for word. The repeated message is said to be shadowed, and the listener is instructed to stay as "close behind" the speaker's voice as possible. What is remembered of the message that is not shadowed is the main question of interest.

Cherry's findings indicate that subjects remember very little about the nonshadowed message. When speech is the nonshadowed message, the listeners always identify it as speech, but if the speech is changed from English to German or even to English speech played backwards, the listeners do not notice the change. They will notice a change in voice (a man's voice to a woman's voice) as well as a nonspeech signal such as a pure tone.

Although all of the words in the shadowed message are correctly repeated, the listeners remember very little of the content of that message. Apparently, the shadowing task of repeating the message is sufficiently demanding that little processing of meaning tasks place.

Findings such as Cherry's have led to considerable research and theorizing over the past two decades. One of the most important theoretical approaches to attention is the **filter theory** proposed by Donald E. Broadbent (1958). He proposed the existence of a series of sensory channels over which information can be transmitted in parallel—with information coming in over several channels at the same time. What counts as a channel has not been well defined, but channels usually refer to different physical or spatial characteristics. For instance, a physical characteristic might refer to the difference between a male and a female voice, while a spatial characteristic might refer to different locations from which auditory or visual messages might be transmitted.

While sensory information is transmitted in parallel, the basic element in Broadbent's theory is a selective filter that allows information only on a single channel to enter short-term memory while excluding or blocking out information on all other sensory channels. This means that some information never

If a student organizes lecture material into meaningful chunks, it is likely she will remember more of the lecture than those who make no attempt to structure the information.

Figure 8.3

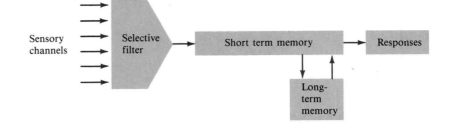

reaches short-term memory: it is not even perceived (see Figure 8.3). This theory helps account for results such as those reported by Cherry. The few characteristics of the nonshadowed message that are noticed by listeners can be explained on the basis of rapid filter switching to detect those physical characteristics such as voice quality that can be stored briefly in sensory, or echoic, memory. Note, however, that the physiological location of such a filter has not been identified, and therefore a physiological process description is lacking.

Since Broadbent's filter theory was introduced, the volume of research on attention has expanded enormously. The general pattern of this research has not been supportive of the operation of a selective filter. For instance, in a shadowing task, Neville Moray (1959) showed that information in the nonshadowed message was often noticed when it was preceded by the listener's own name. In another study, Anne Treisman (1964) had bilingual listeners shadow a message in English presented to one ear, while a foreign language translation of the message was presented to the other ear. About half of the listeners realized that the two messages had the same meaning. These results do not support the notion of a selective filter that allows information to be transmitted over a single channel while blocking out all information on other channels. Rather, if the content of the irrelevant message is salient enough, it will exceed the filter threshold and be processed. The problem for filter theory is that meaning is supposed to be processed only on the attended channel.

A number of questions remain about attention and short-term memory. Do we give any meaning to and perceive unattended information before rejecting it? Does material from secondary channels actually enter short-term memory, even briefly, before it is lost?

A series of studies quite convincingly indicated that selective attention to particular sensory channels takes place after initial registration (Shiffrin, Pisoni, & Castenada-Mendez, 1974). The stimuli presented to the listeners in these studies are often very simple—for example, single syllables. Listeners' prior knowledge of the channel on which a stimulus will appear (left or right ear) has no facilitory effect in terms of accuracy of response. The researchers interpreted these findings as an indication that the important capacity limitation is one involving short-term memory. They suggest that all incoming information is registered in short-term memory. However, because short-term memory has a fixed capacity, when the amount of information entering short-term memory exceeds this capacity, only some portion of the information can be processed further (rehearsed) and subsequently remembered. The remaining information is necessarily lost, even though it had been registered in short-term memory briefly.

In most shadowing experiments, the very act of shadowing occupies most of the capacity of short-term memory, and although information in the nonshadowed message may enter short-term memory and may be noticed at the time, it cannot be processed without interrupting the shadowing process. Therefore, it is not recalled when the retention test is administered. Support for this viewpoint was reported by Donald Norman (1969), who found that when listeners are interrupted during shadowing and asked to report on the nonshadowed message, they can report the last few items even though there is no evidence of any lasting memory for the nonshadowed message overall.

Advocates of selective attention or filter theory could argue that the findings reported by Norman simply reflect the recall of items that had not yet faded from sensory memory. However, a fairly commonplace experience tends to favor Shiffrin's interpretation. Suppose you look up an unfamiliar telephone number that you intend to dial. While you are walking over to the telephone, a friend, either intentionally or unintentionally, repeats aloud a series of numbers. You certainly perceive those numbers; they enter short-term memory. But if you are successful in maintaining the telephone number you looked up after dialing it, you will probably not remember the numbers your friend uttered. According to this view, attention does not restrict our ability to process and remember information in the sense of providing a capacity limitation. The capacity limitation is due to short-term memory, and attention refers to the act of processing information in short-term memory, which allows the information to be remembered subsequently.

As another illustration of this point imagine yourself in a situation in which you are very busy doing something, but you must be somewhere else soon. You hastily look at your watch but soon thereafter realize you do not know the time. You recall looking at your watch but the capacity of your short-term memory was sufficiently occupied that the time cannot be recalled. Illustrations such as these suggest that more information enters short-term memory than can subsequently be recalled and that Miller's magical number 7 plus or minus 2 refers to the number of chunks of information that can be attended to or processed sufficiently to be recalled.

Neisser (1976) proposed a similar view of attention, although it was stated in quite different terms. His view is that attention has no independent status apart from the perceptual process: attention is perception in that we choose what to look at, what to listen to, and so on. That is, we do not selectively block out inputs; rather, we simply do not pick them up.

Neisser offers several general criticisms of theories of selective attention based on either filtering or other capacity limitations. Among these is the failure to distinguish between the performance of skilled and unskilled observers on the secondary (nonattended) task. For example, he reports that after practicing for several hours on a number-detecting task while shadowing another message, performance on number detecting increased to 83 percent correct. In contrast, inexperienced listeners average only 4 percent correct in number detecting. The point here is that "dual attention" should be thought of as an acquired skill.

Neisser reports several other impressive demonstrations of such acquired skills including one mentioned in the previous chapter relating to skilled pianists who can shadow prose while while sight-reading music at the piano. An important point to be emphasized in this context is that apparent limitations in performance may not reflect absolute capacity limitations. They may simply reflect lack of interest, practice, or skill. As Neisser points out, most theories of attention do not as yet provide for distinctions between the performance of adults and children; that is, they do not explain developmental changes in capacity.

In spite of what some people may think, dual attention is an acquired skill.

Long-Term Memory

Long-term memory (LTM), because of its central role in all of our cognitive activities, is one of the most fascinating areas of psychological investigation. What is stored or represented in long-term memory quite obviously depends to a large extent on our previous experiences. At one level we can say that our experiences result in memory for a multitude of facts, concepts, skills, and beliefs (including attitudes, stereotypes and so on) as well as programs and rules for guiding mental operations. That is, long-term memory represents the organized store of general information or knowledge we have about the world we live in, whether or not our knowledge is correct, as well as programs and rules for carrying out overt behaviors and mental action sequences (reasoning, decision making, thinking, and so on). This vast store includes knowledge of our language (which will be discussed in the following chapter), and plans for dealing with everyday, and, in some cases, not so everyday experiences. Thus long-term memory is not only the repository of our prior experiences, but it also includes information and beliefs derived from these experiences as well as plans for guiding what we shall do in the future.

We know a great deal about what is represented in our own long-term memory, but we are consciously aware of the specific details only when this information is reinstated into short-term memory. First consider our example of looking up a telephone number, dialing it, and noting that when the conversation is over the number is totally forgotten. The experience of briefly holding information in consciousness, after which it is no longer consciously available, is characteristic of short-term memory. In this example the telephone number can be reinstated in short term memory only by looking it up again.

We do recall some well-known and frequently used telephone numbers. These telephone numbers are stored in long-term memory. However, soon after dialing one of these numbers, it is not consciously available either—unless we make the effort to reinstate it in short-term memory. We are aware of information present in short-term memory, and this does not depend on the information source. The information can enter from long-term memory or from an external source such as a telephone book. We consciously know what is currently in short-term memory and can report it immediately; in contrast, the contents of long-term memory are typically not available consciously, even though we do know quite a lot about what is stored in our long-term memory. For example, if asked whether or not you know the mailing address of a particular person, you might well answer affirmatively without recalling the address at all. You know that you know the address, but until the address is reinstated in short-term memory you may not be aware of it consciously or be able immediately to report it.

Another relationship between short-term memory and long-term memory derives from the study of patients suffering from bilateral damage to the tem-

CHAPTER 8   MEMORY AND COGNITION

poral lobes as well as to the hippocampus. These patients perform normally on short-term memory tasks such as immediate memory span for digits or for randomly presented words and show unimpaired general intelligence. However, they are grossly defective when it comes to transferring new material from short-term memory to long-term memory, irrespective of practice. Such patients have little difficulty recalling events prior to the brain damage. Thus both long-term memory and short-term memory appear unimpaired, and although material in long-term memory can be recalled and reinstated in short-term memory, new material in short-term memory is not stored in long-term memory. We might note that a similar pattern of memory performance is found in certain cases of senility.

A particularly striking example of this memory pattern is found in a patient called H.M., as described by Brenda Milner (1970). The patient's condition resulted from brain surgery performed because of severe epileptic seizures. Generally speaking, H.M. showed normal memory for things learned prior to surgery. He had command of language and could maintain new experiences in short-term memory for short periods of time by verbal rehearsal. His problem was that new material either was not stored in long-term memory or could not be retrieved from long-term memory. For example, H.M. had difficulty remembering the surroundings of the house where he had lived for six years and in recalling the names of regular visitors if he met them on the street. During the years since surgery there has been little or no improvement in this situation (see Figure 8.4).

What are we to conclude about memory from cases such as that of H.M.? At one time it was generally believed that such a problem was one of being unable to store information in long-term memory because of some disruption of the consolidation process. This interpretation was consistent with the view, based on the differences between short-term memory and long-term memory noted previously, that short-term memory and long-term memory were separate memory systems. However, both of these views have been challenged in more recent years. While it is still useful to talk about short-term memory and long-term memory separately in order to emphasize different aspects of memory, the existence of separate storage systems is questioned.

At this point a number of questions may occur to you. For example, how is information extracted from experience? How is this information subsequently represented in long-term memory? How can we best remember the information? These are important issues and we shall turn to them shortly. However, there are several rather abstract aspects of long-term memory that govern a substantial portion of our lives, and are often overlooked in such discussions. Therefore, let us begin with a general examination of the abstract contents of long-term memory before returning to the issues mentioned above.

Cognitive Maps

At least in terms of guiding our daily activities, **cognitive maps** constitute an important part of the human memory system. Cognitive maps, like other maps we are familiar with, have a distinctly spatial character. We all have cognitive maps of endless varieties, including those of the places where we live, work, and play. Once established, cognitive maps allow us to move about in the world in which we live without constant attention to everything around us. In fact, our cognitive maps are so efficient in guiding many daily activities that they are frequently taken for granted.

Cognitive maps are typically represented in terms of landmarks, routes or paths, and boundaries. When we talk of cognitive maps, we are often referring to representations of cities, buildings, or even the arrangement of furniture in a room. The degree of detail represented in our cognitive maps depends to a large extent on both the frequency with which we experience particular spatially arranged situations and our need to attend to the details that exist in those

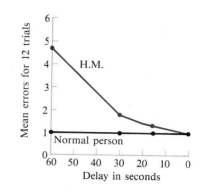

Figure 8.4

In comparison to normal subjects H. M.'s recall ability varied as a function of time. In each trial subjects were presented with successive stimuli and were to say whether a stimulus was the same as the preceding one. The time interval between presentation of each stimulus and its recall was increased from 0 to 60 seconds. Normal subjects averaged 1 error per 12 trials. With 0 seconds delay, H. M. made only 1 error; with 60 seconds delay, he averaged close to 5 errors (Milner, 1970).

A mail carrier's cognitive map of a neighborhood is probably much more detailed than that of many of its residents.

Students may misunderstand what they read in a text because they interpret it in terms of one of their old schemata.

situations. Our cognitive maps not only assist our own activities but also allow us to assist others by giving directions or telling someone where to find, for example, a particular book in a room. Of course, cognitive maps also allow us to plan in advance which routes we will take when going somewhere, whether or not we actually make the trip.

At least for adults, cognitive maps seem to be acquired without a great deal of effort. Perhaps this is because as adults we know a great deal about the world and about the kinds of elements that go into the spatial nature of such maps. In addition, the elements represented in cognitive maps are highly concrete and easily imaged. Imagery, as we shall see later in this chapter, plays an extremely important role in memory.

Some cognitive maps, such as those used in telling someone how to get to where you live, are gradually developed through daily experiences. When you move to a new place, you gradually build up and elaborate upon your cognitive map of that place. Other cognitive maps, such as one of the continental United States, are more likely to be acquired by repeated exposure to actual maps.

The spatial information represented in cognitive maps is relational and relative in character. That is, the landmarks and routes represented in cognitive maps are located in relation to each other, although absolute distance and location may not be well preserved. If you mentally scan a cognitive map, it will take longer to travel between places that are far apart—New York to Los Angeles—than between places that are close together—Chicago to St. Louis, (Kosslyn, Ball, & Reiser, 1978; Richman, Mitchell, & Reznick, 1979). This does not necessarily indicate that you are scanning a mental picture, but it does mean that the spatial organization represented in memory does include knowledge of at least relative distance.

Schemata

We can think of much of our general knowledge of the world as being represented in long-term memory in terms of **schemata.** A particular schema can be loosley thought of as an organized body of information. Much of what is stored in long-term memory, including beliefs, attitudes, and stereotypes, is organized in terms of schemata. Cognitive maps can be considered schemata in which the information represented in memory is highly spatial in character. An example of a schema for a particular activity would be going to a restaurant. Information organized in this schema would include knowledge of kinds of food served, procedures involved in ordering, and how to pay the bill, including how much of a tip should be included.

In the psychological literature, the notion of schemata is most closely linked to Sir Frederick Bartlett and his classic book *Remembering* (1932). Bartlett viewed schemata as the ways in which we organize our knowledge of the world based on our past experiences. These schemata are then used when we attempt to learn something new. Bartlett suggested that what is remembered about a new experience depends both on the character of the experience and our existing schemata at the time of the experience. He saw remembering as an active, constructive process that uses both what is retained from the new experience and our preexisting schemata. In this way existing schemata at any time may influence what we perceive, learn, and remember (Neisser, 1976).

Schemata play an important role in the educational process; for example, students may misunderstand what they read in a text because they interpret it in terms of one of their old schemata and not the schema that the author had in mind. Similar misunderstandings may occur in everyday interactions—even among friends.

Bartlett's work, as well as much subsequent research, focused on distortions or inaccuracies in remembering that result from conflicts between aspects of the to-be-remembered events and aspects of existing schemata. Numerous investigations have demonstrated that attitudes and prejudices can produce

The extent to which someone enjoys a sporting event depends on having a well-developed schema for that event.

CHAPTER 8   MEMORY AND COGNITION

marked distortions in what is remembered about a particular story or event. Can you remember a situation in which you or someone you know misrecalled or misperceived an event because his or her attitude or prejudice at the time of the event did not "fit" with what actually happened?

It is important to emphasize that existing schemata are modified by new experiences, with the result that distortions in remembering are minimized. Schemata are dynamic, not static, and new learning experiences provide opportunities to modify or elaborate existing schemata. As you read this text there will be numerous opportunities for you to modify or elaborate many of your existing schemata, including your conception of human memory.

Schemata are not only important in learning and memory, they also play a critical role in many other activities. We have schemata that guide our behavior in different social situations. The extent to which someone enjoys a sporting event or appreciates an outstanding performance by an individual player depends to a large degree on having a well-developed schema for that event. Well-developed schemata include general knowledge of the rules of the event as well as an appreciation of more subtle factors that allow you to evaluate both good and poor performances.

Schemata may influence memory performance in at least two ways: one way is when existing schemata are used to interpret experiences at the time of initial learning. That is, existing schemata are used to *construct* memories of current experiences or events. A second way schemata can influence memory performance is when schemata are used to *reconstruct* a memory of a prior experience. In this case schemata are used to reconstruct what "probably happened," but not necessarily what took place. However, when memory distortions are observed it is often difficult to determine whether they are due to constructive processes operating during learning or reconstructive processes operating during remembering, or to some combination of both sets of processes.

The influence of schemata on both constructive and reconstructive processes is well illustrated in comparisons of individuals who are high versus low in knowledge about activities such as playing chess, computer programming, or watching baseball. Consider the work by de Groot (1965, 1966) comparing memory performance of expert chess players with that of novices. The one major difference between these two groups was that expert or master chess players could reproduce a chessboard arrangement much better than novices could. That this difference was due to the experts' schemata and not simply to more exposure to chess boards was shown in a later study by Chase and Simon (1973). These investigators replicated de Groot's findings and went on to show that when chess pieces are placed on the board at random (positions that would not normally occur in chess), experts are no better at reproducing the arrangement than are novices. This indicates that the information contained in the experts' schemata is specific to how chess games flow and not to a superior memory for any location of chess pieces.

Inaccurate eyewitness testimony is an example of memory distortion that can have serious repercussions. On the basis of eyewitness testimony, the man on the top was imprisoned for 5 years for a crime committed by the man on the bottom.

Motor Programs

The acquisition of motor programs that guide many of our daily activities was discussed in chapter 7. In most instances overt instruction is not of much help in acquiring a motor program because these programs can be described only in very general terms. You can tell someone how to change a tire on a car and, assuming knowledge of the tools involved, he or she can change the tire. However, written or verbal instruction is not of much help in learning to run, speak, or swim.

Once established, motor programs allow us to carry out complex sequences of movements without requiring a great deal of attention to the movements themselves. This is not to imply that sensory information is not important to the effective execution of a motor program. Visual input is essential when driving a car; once a motor program for driving a car is well established, however, much of the visual information provided may not be consciously processed.

Reading is another skill that psychologists and educators have long tried to understand. Many components go into good reading, and one of them functions like a motor program. All of us have experienced this aspect of reading, which is mind wandering. That is, at some point while reading a book, we may become preoccupied with something else. When this happens we sometimes stop reading altogether; at other times, we continue the superficial act of reading in the sense of carrying out the appropriate motor program, until we realize that we do not know what we have just "read." This experience is not unlike Cherry's (1953) shadowing task mentioned earlier in this chapter. The text being read becomes the unshadowed message, and what we are thinking about becomes the shadowed message. The words in the text enter short-term memory, but because the capacity of short-term memory is largely devoted to other thoughts, there is not sufficient capacity remaining to process the sense or meaning of the text message.

The phenomenon illustrated here, which might be called "mindless reading," has some parallels to driving a car over a very familiar route without remembering or being aware of having done so: in both cases the individual is preoccupied with other thoughts. The driver of the car no doubt notices appropriate places to turn, stops for stop signs, and executes the motor program accordingly. Because the route is familiar, and in the absence of anything unusual, very little short-term memory capacity is required, and the driver can successfully reach the destination. Unfortunately, in mindless reading the same happy conclusion does not result. The reader may process the meaning of the familiar individual words at some level that is sufficient to allow the motor program to continue. However, the goal of understanding what has been read is not met.

Motor programs can also be characterized as being highly rhythmic in nature. That is, the particular elements or muscular movements are organized in time relative to one another—the timing of the elements in a sequence is relative and not absolute. We can run, swim, ride a bicycle, or speak at various speeds, and our motor programs are sufficiently flexible to guide the timing of each element relative to the other elements. It is tempting to speculate that this rhythmic character of motor programs plays a major role in their permanence in memory, even after many years of disuse.

Encoding, Storage, and Retrieval

Three basic questions arise in considering the way we store and use information in memory. First, what factors are involved in the way we extract information or encode information from our experiences? Second, how is the encoded information represented or stored in memory and how is it related to other information stored in memory? Finally, how do we successfully retrieve information from memory? Answers to these questions will be discussed in the following sections.

Encoding

In order to make use of any information, it must first get into memory. **Encoding** refers to the extraction of information from events we experience—under the conditions that the events are experienced. For instance, with the

Table 8.1 CONFUSION MATRIX FOR A SHORT-TERM MEMORY EXPERIMENT USING *AUDITORY* STIMULUS PRESENTATION. THE HIGHER THE NUMBER, THE MORE OFTEN THE TWO LETTERS COMING TOGETHER AT THAT POINT WERE CONFUSED.

		Stimulus Letter Presented									
		B	C	P	T	V	F	M	N	S	X
Stimulus Letter Recalled	B	–	171	75	84	168	2	11	10	2	2
	C	32	–	35	42	20	4	4	5	2	5
	P	162	350	–	505	91	11	31	23	5	5
	T	143	232	281	–	50	14	12	11	8	5
	V	122	61	34	22	–	1	8	11	1	0
	F	6	4	2	4	3	–	13	8	336	238
	M	10	14	2	3	4	22	–	334	21	9
	N	13	21	6	9	20	32	512	–	38	14
	S	2	18	2	7	3	488	23	11	–	391
	X	1	6	2	2	1	245	2	1	184	–

Source: R. Conrad, ''Acoustic Confusions in Immediate Memory,'' *British Journal of Psychology*, 1964, *55*, pp. 75–83. Reprinted by permission of British Journal of Psychology, Vol. 55.

very brief exposures provided in studies of sensory memory, what is initially encoded appears to be the physical characteristics or features of the events such as shape, size, location, and voice quality. The encoding of these features appears to be a relatively automatic process that is governed by the characteristics of our sensory systems (see chapter 3). As noted previously, these features are lost very rapidly, unless they are quickly encoded into short-term memory. In studies in which the event was exposure to an array of letters of the alphabet, encoding into short-term memory involved naming the letters (Sperling, 1960). Of course, the letter names themselves had to be retrieved from long-term memory before encoding into short-term memory could be accomplished. Thus, even in this rather simple experiment, we see some of the complexities that arise in attempting to distinguish among various stages of memory.

Studies of sensory memory indicate that with very brief exposures, more information is encoded into sensory memory that can be subsequently encoded into short-term memory. Of course, under most everyday situations such brief exposures are rare. However, these studies also suggest that the encoded information is different in kind. Encoding into sensory memory involves the extraction of physical characteristics or features of the event. Encoding into short-term memory involves a deeper level of processing, such as the name of a particular shape, and typically requires some interaction with long-term memory where shape names are stored.

Acoustic Encoding

A common process observed in encoding information into short-term memory is verbal rehearsal, or **naming.** This type of encoding is often observed even in situations where the events are presented visually. For example, R. Conrad (1964) presented both visual and auditory sequences of six consonant letters to observers and then asked for immediate recall. The patterns of errors found with both modes of presentation were quite similar, and they suggested that encoding was auditory or acoustic in nature—that is, letters with similar-sounding names, such as *B* and *V,* were often confused with each other whether the mode of presentation was auditory or visual. Neither of these letters, however, was likely to be confused with the letter *X* (see Tables 8.1 and 8.2).

Conrad's findings indicate that with visual presentation of consonant letters the observers encode the name of the letter rather than the visual form pre-

Table 8.2 CONFUSION MATRIX FOR A SHORT-TERM MEMORY EXPERIMENT USING *VISUAL* STIMULUS PRESENTATION. COMPARE THE SIMILARITY OF THE CONFUSIONS IN THIS CONDITION WITH THOSE OF THE AUDITORY CONDITION SHOWN IN TABLE 8.1.

		B	C	P	T	V	F	M	N	S	X
	B	–	18	62	5	83	12	9	3	2	0
	C	13	–	27	18	55	15	3	12	35	7
	P	102	18	–	24	40	15	8	8	7	7
	T	30	46	79	–	38	18	14	14	8	10
Stimulus Letter Recalled	V	56	32	30	14	–	21	15	11	11	5
	F	6	8	14	5	31	–	12	13	131	16
	M	12	6	8	5	20	16	–	146	15	5
	N	11	7	5	1	19	28	167	–	24	5
	S	7	21	11	2	9	37	4	12	–	16
	X	3	7	2	2	11	30	10	11	59	–

Stimulus Letter Presented (column header spanning B–X)

Source: R. Conrad, "Acoustic Confusions in Immediate Memory," *British Journal of Psychology*, 1964, *55*, pp. 75–83. Reprinted by permission of British Journal of Psychology, Vol. 55.

sented. Given the nature of the observers' task, the outcome seems quite reasonable. The observers were only required to report which consonants they saw or heard. They were not required to notice any other aspect of the consonants such as where they occurred in the alphabet. The names of the consonants are names for shapes and, in our daily experiences, shapes can vary considerably and still have the same name. Letter shapes can be in capitalized form or in lowercase. They can also vary in size and tilt. What is usually important is the identity of the letter and not the particular instance of the shape presented. Thus, unless there is some reason for doing otherwise, the most natural thing to do when presented with a sequence of shapes, be they letters or other shapes, is to encode them acoustically by naming them.

Given the capacity limitations of short-term memory, acoustic encoding is not only a natural process, but also a very efficient one. Encoding the names of five or six concepts allows us subsequently to retrieve more information about any one of them from long-term memory, if we need to do so. When we go to the grocery store to buy bread, butter, eggs, milk, and cheese, encoding these names allows us to retrieve more information later about each of them—what type of bread we want, what brand of butter, and so on. However, acoustic encoding is certainly not the only form of encoding observed in short-term memory. Other forms of encoding in short-term memory such as by visual form (imaging) or by meaning are used when the situation requires such encoding.

Recoding

As we saw earlier in this chapter, encoding into short-term memory often requires the **recoding** or chunking of information. This process involves an interaction between long-term memory and short-term memory. For example, consider the following string of digits: 149–217—761—812. This string of 12 digits is beyond the capacity of short-term memory. However, if we recode the string as 1492—1776—1812 we have three meaningful chunks of information that easily fall within the capacity of short-term memory. This example also indicates the importance of attentional processing in encoding. In this example we must actively search through the digit string to find units that constitute meaningful chunks. To someone never exposed to American history, these units would not constitute meaningful chunks of information and would exceed the capacity of short-term memory.

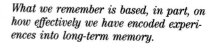

What we remember is based, in part, on how effectively we have encoded experiences into long-term memory.

Encoding Physical Sensible Factors

As in the case of short-term memory, encoding in long-term memory is inferred from observing what we remember and what we fail to remember in a variety of situations. However, encoding in long-term memory as opposed to short-term memory is both more complex and more permanent. Physically sensible aspects of our experiences are often attended to, and encoded in, long-term memory, which allows us subsequently to remember familiar people, objects, and places. These encodings also allow us to remember familiar songs and voices as well as the way things taste, smell, or feel. This is not to say that any physically sensible aspect of a particular experience will be automatically encoded. As noted previously, attentional processing is usually required for encoding to occur.

In addition to the directly sensory aspects of experiences, we also encode their meanings. When we learn concept names, whether names of digits, letters, words, places, or people, we encode how to pronounce those names and, most important, what the names mean.

Principle of Encoding Specificity

A particularly important aspect of encoding is what Endel Tulving and his associates have called the **principle of encoding specificity** (Tulving & Pearlstone, 1966; Tulving & Osler, 1968). The principle states that what is encoded about a particular event depends on the context in which the event occurs. Broadly speaking, this principle refers to the interactions between prior knowledge and the context of new experiences. We have referred to this interaction a number of times previously and will do so again. The principle of encoding specificity can be illustrated in a very simple task.

Suppose you are shown a list of words to be remembered. Each word to be remembered is typed in capital letters and is presented with another word typed in lowercase letters. You are told the word typed in lowercase is not important to remember but that looking at it might help recall the word to be remembered. Now suppose you see pairs of words like *ground/COLD, train/BLACK,* and so on. After the list of pairs is presented you are shown a list of words that includes all of the to-be-remembered words typed in capital letters. Your task is to indicate which words were presented previously. Following this recognition task a cued recall task is presented: the words previously appearing in lowercase letters (context words) are presented one at a time and you are asked to remember the words with which they were paired. The surprising finding here is that memory performance is better in the cued recall task with prior context words as cues than it is in the recognition task when the to-be-

Table 8.3 RECALL AS A FUNCTION OF ORIENTING TASKS

Orienting Tasks	Average Number of Words Recalled
Pleasantness rating	16.3
E-Checking	9.4
Intentional instructions	16.1

Source: Adapted from T. S. Hyde and J. J. Jenkins, "Differential Effects of Incidental Tasks on the Organization of Recall of a List of Highly Associated Words," *Journal of Experimental Psychology*, 82(1969):472–81.

Figure 8.5

In Craik and Tulving's recall studies, words that were followed by sentence questions were recalled better than words followed by rhyme questions or by case questions. With all methods the recall was better for words whose processing question was answered by "yes" rather than "no" (after Craik & Tulving, 1975).

remembered words are actually presented (Tulving & Thomson, 1973; Watkins & Tulving, 1975).

The operation of the encoding specificity principle as illustrated above suggests that what is encoded and hence stored in long-term memory depends on the context in which the encoding takes place. Retrieval is facilitated by reinstating this context. On the other hand, presenting a cue that might be effective in a different situation does not facilitate retrieval in this situation.

Depth of Encoding

Some psychologists have argued that the differences between short-term and long-term memory might be attributed to differences in the way information is processed rather than to separate memory systems. If information is processed shallowly, instatement into memory will be weak; if information is processed deeply, it is more likely to be remembered longer. This notion of **depth of encoding** implies a greater degree of semantic or cognitive analysis with a consequent improvement in memory. On several occasions we have mentioned the importance of attentional processing in encoding. A particularly good illustration comes from work on depth of encoding (Craik & Lockhart, 1972). For example, suppose a list of familiar words is read aloud to subjects in each of three conditions (see Table 8.3). One group, intentional learners, is simply asked to learn the words for subsequent recall. Two other groups, incidental learners, are asked either to rate each word on a scale ranging from pleasant to unpleasant or to indicate when each word is read aloud whether or not it contained the letter *E*. Notice that the incidental learners are not told that a recall test will follow. In a number of studies like this, incidental subjects who are required to attend to the meaning of each word as in pleasantness rating recall as many words as do the intentional learners. However, when subjects attend to superficial aspects of words as in *E*-checking, recall is much poorer (Jenkins, 1974; Hyde & Jenkins, 1969).

A series of studies reported by Fergus I.M. Craik and Tulving (1975) further supports the role of depth of encoding. In general these studies involved presenting words and asking various questions about the words. For instance, after presentation of a word, the subjects were asked if it appeared in uppercase or lowercase type, or they were asked if the word rhymes with another word, or if the word fit into a blank in a sentence (for example, "He met a _____ in the street"). As you might expect, both recall and recognition were shown to be an increasing function of depth, with best recall and recognition for words followed by sentence questions, next best for words followed by rhyme questions, and poorest for words followed by case questions (did it appear in uppercase or lowercase?) (see Figure 8.5).

It should be noted that there is a relationship between these depth-of-encoding studies and the principle of encoding specificity, which was discussed previously: the particular question asked about each word specifies the aspect or feature of the word that is attended to and encoded. This is illustrated in a study that compared the rhyme and sentence conditions employed by Craik and Tulving using recognition tests exclusively (Morris, Bransford, & Franks, 1977). Their results replicated those of Craik and Tulving. However, when a second group of subjects was given a new recognition list and was asked to indicate which words rhymed with the words presented initially, performance was better for words initially followed by rhyme questions. While depth of processing generally leads to better memory, a match between the context at the time of encoding and the context at the time of retrieval is also an important factor in memory.

Elaboration During Encoding

A concept that has been emphasized in recent years is that of elaboration during encoding. Elaboration refers to establishing a richer or more complete encoding without necessarily increasing the depth of encoding. A study by

Barry Stein and John Bransford (1979) nicely illustrates the influence of elaboration.

Stein and Bransford presented subjects with a series of adjectives to be recalled. However, the adjectives were presented in sentences such as "The fat man read the sign" that were elaborated as "The fat man read the sign that was two feet tall" or "The fat man read the sign warning of thin ice." Retention was tested by presenting the basic sentence minus the adjective (The _____ man read the sign). As you might expect, the elaboration concerning the thin ice led to superior memory performance. That is, simply elaborating the basic sentence does not improve retention unless the elaboration reflects the significance of what is to be remembered (the word *fat* in the example above).

Stein and Bransford also had subjects provide their own elaborations using prompt questions such as "What else might have happened here?" or "Why might this man be doing this?" In the case of the example about the fat man, the latter prompt, which focuses attention on the man, proved to be much more effective. This observation also suggests that the type of questions we ask ourselves during learning will influence our memory performance. Questions that are relevant to what we are trying to learn and remember will be the most effective.

Episodic memory involves storing aspects of experiences that are highly autobiographical. Being in a flood is an experience these people will never forget.

Storage

The preceding discussion clearly indicates that encoding and storage are intimately related. Our main emphasis in encoding was on either the processes of encoding—such as naming, imaging, and chunking—or the factors that influence encoding—such as the specific context or the depth of encoding. Note that in all of these instances, encoding was influenced by the existing contents of memory. In discussing **storage,** we will emphasize both the contents of long-term memory and the way these contents are represented and organized.

Episodic and Semantic Memory

In terms of what is stored in long-term memory, Tulving (1972) distinguishes between episodic and semantic memory. **Episodic memory** involves storing spatial and temporal aspects of experiences that are of a highly autobiographical nature. That is, the experiences or events stored in episodic memory are unique to a given person, and the time at which these experiences occurred may be just as important as the experiences themselves. Tulving suggests that most psychological studies of memory have a strongly episodic character to them.

Semantic memory, according to Tulving, refers to our organized store of general knowledge including our knowledge of the world, rules that guide our mental operations, the solution of problems, and so on. Semantic memory is necessary for storing information in episodic memory in many instances. Remembering one's own wedding would represent episodic memory; the knowledge of what a wedding is would be held in semantic memory. In another example, learning a list of familiar words in an experiment involves an interaction between episodic memory and semantic memory. Remembering the time and place that the experiment took place may help us remember the words in the list from episodic memory, but the words are also stored in semantic memory where the time and place of original learning is not important.

Tulving's distinction between episodic and semantic memory is quite important. The most obvious reason is the notion that contents of memory can be organized in different ways, one highly personal and the other much less so. Of course, because what we experience and learn is determined in part by what we know at the time, even semantic memory is personal in that sense. Both episodic and semantic memory are likely to be organized variously while retaining their distinctive functions.

RESEARCH

Posthypnotic Amnesia and the Episodic-Semantic Distinction

One of the more controversial issues in the study of human memory concerns the extent to which episodic and semantic memory constitute functionally distinct systems. A major problem here is that it is difficult to rule out a possible role for semantic memory in what appears to be an episodic task or a possible role for episodic memory in what appears to be a semantic task.

An investigation by John F. Kihlstrom (1980) appears to show a functional distinction between episodic and semantic memory under certain conditions. The subjects in this experiment were 40 Stanford University students who had been given a scale designed to measure hypnotic susceptibility. The subjects were classified into four groups ranging from low hypnotic susceptibility to very high hypnotic susceptibility. There were 10 subjects in each group. When recruited by telephone for the experiment, the subjects were told that they would learn a list of familiar words while hypnotized. They were reminded of this at the beginning of the experimental session.

A standard hypnotic procedure was employed with each subject; thereafter, all subjects were treated as though this procedure had been effective. Each subject learned a list of 15 words by the free recall method until a criterion of two successive errorless trials was reached. During learning, the words were presented at a rate of one word every 3 seconds. After presentation of the entire list the subjects were asked to recall, in any order, all of the words they could remember. Trials were repeated in this manner until the criterion was satisfied. Prior to being removed from the hypnotic state the subjects were told that they would not remember learning the list of words until the experimenter said, "Now you can remember everything."

Following awakening from hypnosis, each subject was asked what happened under hypnosis. If the subject did not mention learning the list of words, the experimenter specifically reminded him or her. The subjects were then asked to recall any words from the list they could remember (Test 1). This was seen as an episodic memory task.

Next, each subject was given a semantic memory task involving word associations. Subjects were given a list of stimulus words and asked to indicate the first three words that each stimulus word suggested to them. On the basis of word association norms it was known that half of the stimulus words had a high probability of eliciting words from the list previously learned under hypnosis, while the remaining stimulus words were not likely to elicit list members.

The results of the semantic memory task indicated a priming effect in semantic memory for members of the word list learned under hypnosis. That is, in the word association task the stimulus words could be divided into two sets, each of which was equally likely to elicit certain response words on the basis of word association norms. For example, the stimulus word *boy* elicits the re-

Support for the episodic and semantic memory distinction can be found in studies comparing the memory performance of amnesic patients and normal individuals. Subjects in both groups are presented a list of common words to study. Their memory for these words is then tested in two ways. One is a standard recognition memory test in which the previously presented words and an equal number of distractors are presented and the subject's task is to indicate which words were presented before. The other memory test is called **word fragment completion.** In this task some letters from a given word and appropriately spaced blanks are presented and the subject's task is to complete the word. For some of these stimuli the correct word was presented before and for others it was not. Better performance on words previously presented would indicate a memory effect for those words.

Typical findings in studies such as the one described above indicate that amnesics perform much poorer than normals on the recognition memory task, but do just as well as normals on word fragment completion (Warrington & Weiskrantz, 1974). The argument that is made concerning these findings is that sponse *girl* just as often as the stimulus word *lamp* elicits the response *light.* However, for half of the subjects *girl* was a member of the previously learned list and *light* was not. For the remaining subjects *light* was a list member and *girl* was not. It turned out in the word association task that list members were more often given as responses to the appropriate stimulus words than were words that did not appear on the previously learned list. This finding suggested that prior list learning had primed or increased the availability of these words in semantic memory. However, the priming effect was the same for all four levels of hypnotic suggestibility. In all four groups, eight to ten list words were recalled.

Following the word association task, each subject was again asked to recall as many words from the previously learned list as he or she could remember (Test 2). Then the experimenter said, "Now you can remember everything," and again asked the subjects to recall the list words (Test 3).

The results for the three episodic memory tests are shown in the adjacent figure. Although the performance of all four groups was graded as a function of hypnotic suggestibility, the most striking comparison was

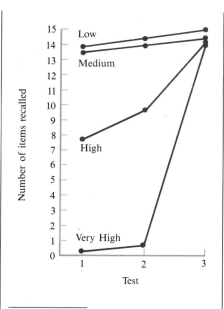

Number of items recalled on three tests of posthypnotic memory for a word list memorized during hypnosis (Experiment 1). Tests 1 and 2 occurred during suggested amnesia, before and after the word-association test, respectively; Test 3 occurred after administration of the reversibility cue (after Kihlstrom, 1980).

between the low and very high susceptibility conditions. Notice that the low susceptibility group performed very well on Test 1 and had little room for improvement on the subsequent tests. It seems likely that the subjects were not hypnotized. How-

ever, the subjects in the very high susceptibility group probably were hypnotized, and their performance on both Test 1 and Test 2 was very poor. Recall that the word association task occurred between these two episodic tests, and that even though these subjects reported a large number of list words in the word association task, they could not recall them as list members until after the posthypnotic suggestion had been removed (Test 3). On the final test these subjects performed comparably to those in the other three conditions.

The results of Kihlstrom's investigation appear to indicate that it is possible to separate the effects of episodic and semantic memory, at least under certain conditions. In his study the high susceptibility subjects showed just as strong a priming effect in semantic memory as the low susceptibility subjects, although they performed very poorly on the episodic task until the posthypnotic suggestion was removed. Furthermore, these findings suggest that at least with very high susceptibility subjects the posthypnotic suggestion did in fact remove any awareness of prior list learning or awareness of remembering in individuals with no brain damage or prior amnesia. ■

recognition memory is an episodic task and that amnesics are deficient in episodic memory. However, word fragment completion is seen as a semantic memory task and the priming of semantic memory from seeing the words during study is just as great for amnesics as it is for normals.

In a related study, Jacoby and Witherspoon (1982) asked amnesic and normal subjects a series of questions designed to bias a less frequent spelling of homophonic words (same sound, different spelling and meaning). For example, a question like "Can you name a musical instrument that employs a reed?" was intended to bias the spelling "reed" over "read." Following the questions the subjects were given an oral spelling test and a recognition memory test.

Again the amnesics were much poorer than the normal subjects in recognition memory, but they were comparable to the normals on the spelling test. These findings are also consistent with the episodic/semantic memory distinction, although Jacoby and Witherspoon raise an interesting point concerning these findings. They note that in both the spelling task and the word fragment completion task explicit awareness of remembering is not required. The subjects are simply asked to spell words or to complete word fragments. In contrast, recognition memory requires the subjects to indicate which words were presented previously and which were not. Perhaps both the amnesics and normals learned the words equally well but the amnesics have no memory of the learning experience. If this is the case, when asked to indicate which words were old and which were new in the recognition memory task, the amnesics would perform poorly because they have no awareness of having a prior learning experience.

Implicit in the issue of how knowledge and experience are represented in memory is the question of the organizational principles that characterize these representations. Organizational principles are typically inferred by studying retrieval from long-term memory. As you might expect, the task employed in a particular study has a major influence on the organization that is revealed. Nevertheless, studies indicate that human memory is highly complex and organized. The idea that different contents of long-term memory would be organized in different ways was implicit in our earlier discussion. Let us look next at some of those factors involved in the organization of memory.

Spatial Organization

Cognitive maps appear to be organized in a spatial manner that reflects the nature of the learning experience. Spatial representation is also characteristic of our mental picture of concrete objects, which preserve much the same type of relative information that characterize cognitive maps. For example, your mental picture of a basketball may not include its absolute size, but it probably includes the fact that a basketball is substantially larger than a baseball.

Mental representations of objects such as a basketball are highly particular, as are representations of particular objects such as your favorite chair. However, we also have representations of a more general nature. These representations (such as a table) are spatially organized too, but they are not representations of a particular instance of the category (all tables). Such representations include our knowledge about kinds of objects, and they enable us to imagine things we know do not exist (for example, a cat larger than the Empire State Building).

Serial Organization

Certain contents of memory are organized serially and in a specific sequential order. The best example of such serial organization is the letters of the alphabet. The English alphabet consists of 26 arbitrarily related symbols that have names. Because most of us learn those names only serially, beginning with A and ending with Z, our memory for them has that specific directional character. Any normal adult can rapidly recite the alphabet from A to Z and use that sequential information to perform a variety of tasks that involve ordering the names of things alphabetically. However, it is very difficult to recite the alphabet in reverse order unless you have practiced that task a large number of times. Try reciting the alphabet backward and notice what you do.

Another example of serial organization is the order of months in the year or days in the week. Again there is a directional component to the organization in memory, although most people can recite the days in the week or months in the year backward with much less difficulty than the alphabet.

When we memorize materials by rote learning, or mechanical repetition, the materials are usually organized serially with a strong directional component. This is the case when we memorize prose such as Lincoln's Gettysburg Address in order to reproduce it in the correct order. In the case of prose, however, it is the order of the lines or phrases that is most difficult to memorize, not the individual letters or words. Notice also that understanding the meaning of a prose passage such as the Gettysburg Address is not a prerequisite of memorizing it by rote learning.

The kinds of organizational principles we have been discussing so far are fairly easy for most people to understand. This is not only because they are part of our common experience but also because they are externally imposed on the memory system. If your cognitive map for going somewhere is not a good one, you are likely to get lost or at least waste considerable time getting there. Similarly, the letters of the alphabet are organized in an externally imposed manner, and if we do not learn that order well, we could not readily perform alphabetizing tasks. Notice also that these organizational principles are applied to closely prescribed materials. There are, however, some organizational principles that appear to be less externally imposed on memory.

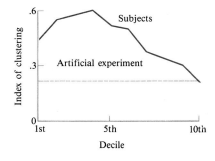

Figure 8.6

Index of clustering in successive tenths of total items recalled. The dashed line indicates expected clustering if the items were recalled at random (after Bousfield, 1953).

Associative Organization

Several aspects of what is stored about words are revealed in a study by Roger Brown and David McNeill (1966). These investigators presented their subjects with dictionary definitions (but not the words themselves) of relatively uncommon words—for example, *nepotism* or *sampan*—and asked them to give the words corresponding to the definitions. The words of particular interest were those that the subjects reported as being on the "tip of the tongue" but that could not be produced. We all have experienced this phenomenon of being on the verge of being able to recall something that just will not come. When this "state" was signified, the subjects were asked a number of questions about the word such as initial letter, number of letters or syllables, words similar in sound and meaning. The overall results indicated that the subjects could answer these questions with considerable accuracy, even though they could not recall the words themselves.

The Brown and McNeill study suggests several important characteristics of storage in long-term memory. The questions answered suggest aspects or dimensions of storage. These include initial letter, syllable structure, sound pattern, and general meaning; that is, words may be stored in memory as a bundle of features loosely tied together. Evidence from studies of word association, which date back to the work of Sir Francis Galton (1883), support a number of these features as aspects of organization in memory.

The word association technique involves presenting a list of words and asking someone to report, for each word, the first word that comes to mind. Under these conditions of free association, the responses given typically reflect the general and most common meanings of the words presented. For instance, the word *table* usually leads to *chair*, *hot* leads to *cold*, *mother* leads to *father*. In each of these examples it is easy to see the aspects of general meaning reflected in the responses given to each stimulus word.

The free recall task has often been employed to investigate organizational factors in memory. This task involves presentation of a list of words, one at a time, which the subjects are then asked to recall in any order they choose. When the words in a list are common free associates or instances of semantic categories (bird names, items of clothing, or names of four-legged animals), the related words are likely to be closely clustered in recall even though they were spaced far apart when the list was presented (Jenkins & Russel, 1952; Bousfield, 1953)—that is, the free associates are likely to be recalled together as are the members of a particular semantic category (see Figure 8.6).

The clustering of free associates suggests organization of general aspects of meaning, whereas clustering of category members involves more specific aspects of meaning. For example, free associates tend to come from the same grammatical class, although adults show this tendency much more than do young children. Nouns are names of things, and free associates to nouns are usually names of other things *(table-chair)*. Verbs are names of actions, whereas adjectives are names of properties of things, and they are usually responded to with the names of other actions or properties *(run-walk, hot-cold)*. In these cases rather general aspects of meaning are shared. In contrast, clus-

Figure 8.7

Mean number of words recalled out of 112 over several trials for subjects who studied organized versus random conceptual displays (after Bower, 1970).

tering of category members suggests organizational structures of things that share a number of more specific properties. Items of clothing share the characteristic of things we can wear.

Hierarchical Organization

In recent years psychologists have become quite interested in examining the way in which semantic categories themselves are represented and organized in memory—an extremely important issue because it deals with the representation of knowledge. Some aspects of our semantic knowledge involve particular concepts: a canary is a bird. Other semantic aspects appear to involve making inferences about concepts: even if you have never seen a canary, you would probably say that it can fly because you know a canary is a bird and you know birds can fly. But do all birds fly?

One approach to investigating the structure of semantic categories suggests that much of human conceptual knowledge could be represented in memory in terms of hierarchically organized structures. Investigators (Bower, Clark, Winzenz, & Lesgold, 1969) have shown that hierarchically organized materials are learned and remembered better than randomly organized materials (see Figure 8.7). In addition, as we shall see in the next chapter, hierarchical organizations are thought to play an important role in language.

A. M. Collins and M. R. Quillian (1969) provide an example of one such hierarchically organized structure (see Figure 8.8). Note that the classes at each level are characterized by sets of properties that define the members of each class. In this example, the animal level is superordinate to all other levels. Thus, the bird class and fish class are subordinate to the animal class but are coordinate with each other. Similarly, the bottom classes are subordinates of classes above them but are coordinate with each other. Collins and Quillian assumed that each class is represented as a set of properties or features. They also assumed a principle of **cognitive economy** in the representation of these properties. For example, because most birds can fly, the property of flying is represented at the bird level and not at the level designating a particular class of birds (for example, canaries). Only when a property of a superordinate does not apply to a subordinate is that represented in the memory structure. Thus, "can't fly" is a property of the ostrich class. An important assumption of cognitive economy is that particular properties are not represented more than is necessary. This, in turn, requires making inferences about relationships among concepts. The concept of bird contains the information that they can fly but not that they eat. To discover that birds eat requires further search up the semantic hierarchy to the animal level.

Before testing their hypothesis about hierarchical representations, Collins and Quillian had to make some additional assumptions. The most basic were that it takes time to retrieve properties from a class (retrieving "can sing" from the canary class) and to move from one level to another searching the hierarchical structure. For example, if you were asked to verify a statement such as "a canary can fly," it would require moving from the canary level to the bird level to retrieve the property "can fly."

The basic experiment involved presenting statements such as "a canary can sing," "a canary can fly," and so on. When each statement was presented, the subject pressed one of two buttons to indicate that the statement was true or false. The measure of interest was reaction time to true statements because reaction time to false statements should, in general, be long. The results of this experiment indicated that not all aspects of our knowledge are equally accessible. Thus, it takes longer to verify that "a canary is an animal" than "a canary is a bird," which in turn takes longer to verify than a "canary can sing." "A canary can sing" is verified most rapidly. The results also showed that inferences can be made even about things never actually experienced and that the time taken to make such inferences increases as the number of steps involved increases. Thus, it takes longer to verify that "a canary has skin" than it does to verify that "a canary can fly."

The classes or categories employed by Collins and Quillian were assumed to be organized according to a strictly logical hierarchy, with properties or features represented at the highest possible level in a particular hierarchy. There is reason, however, to question both of these assumptions. For example, if these assumptions were correct, it should take longer to verify the statement "a horse is an animal" than the statement "a horse is a mammal." As you might well expect, just the opposite outcome has been found (Rips, Shoben, & Smith, 1973). Observations such as this have led psychologists to question the strictly logical nature of hierarchies as well as the assumption that properties or features are stored only at the highest possible level in a given hierarchy.

Historically speaking, the treatment of conceptual knowledge in psychology has often involved the assumption that concepts are defined logically—that is, that concepts are clearly defined by a specific set of attributes or features and that all instances of a particular concept possess these defining features to an equal degree. Notice that in the Collins and Quillian model (see Figure 8.8) the properties represented at a particular level are considered to be equally representative of the concept.

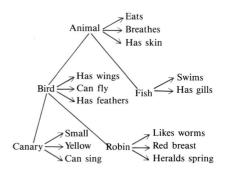

Figure 8.8

A simple hierarchy in semantic memory. The hierarchy consists of levels, properties of levels, and relationships among levels (after Collins & Quillian, 1969).

Alternative Structures of Organization

There is also evidence that organizations in memory may be quite flexible in that the same information may be organized in more than one way. For example, studies have shown that the same information is remembered equally well whether it is presented in a hierarchical organization or according to some other organizational principle (Broadbent, Cooper, & Broadbent, 1978). Thus, different people may organize the same information in different ways depending on their previous experiences. Because what we learn depends on complex interactions, it is not surprising that the way memory is structured or organized also reflects these interactions. The principle of encoding specificity also applies to organizational aspects of long-term memory; that is, organizations in long-term memory result from the interactions of prior knowledge and the context of new experience.

Alternative conceptions have been provided concerning the way concepts or categories might be organized without necessarily questioning the possibility of hierarchical relations among categories. Eleanor Rosch (1975) suggests that many natural categories or concepts are organized around prototypic features that are "most representative" of particular categories. For the category of "birds," her adult subjects rated robins and sparrows as being central to the concept and chickens and ducks less so because chickens and ducks were marginal to the prototype. They also verified statements such as "a robin is a bird" faster than statements such as "a turkey is a bird." Thus, Rosch sees category membership as being a matter of degree that depends on the features shared with the prototype. This requires that features or properties be represented at both the superordinate and subordinate levels. The importance of prototypes in Rosch's work is also supported by studies such as the Jeffrey Franks and John Bransford (1971) experiment we considered in the previous chapter. Recall that in their experiment subjects learned an abstract prototype that had never been presented to them.

Lance Rips, Edward Shoben, and Edward Smith (1973) also provide a model of conceptual knowledge that does not require strictly logical concepts. Their view is that concepts are represented in terms of both defining features and characteristic features. Defining features must be true of concepts. The concept "bird" might have defining features such as "has a head," "has wings," "has feathers," and so on. Characteristic features for "bird" might include "can sing" and "can fly," because they are not defining features of all birds.

According to Rips and his colleagues, verifying statements such as "a canary is a bird" first involves comparing all features, both defining and characteristic. If the degree of feature overlap is high, responding should be rapid. However, if the characteristic features are not shared, as in "an ostrich is a bird," then a second comparison is made on the basis of the defining features alone, which causes verifying such statements to be slower.

We have now examined a number of organizational principles that characterize storage in long-term memory. An important point to emphasize before concluding this section is that human memory is highly organized in one manner or another. It is also important to realize that the organizations described were presented in simple, single-word applications. Whole concepts are organized, drawn from, and shared among other items in memory just as single words are. All of memory is organized in some fashion, and these organizations are interrelated.

Retrieval

Much of what has already been discussed in this chapter deals with **retrieval** because what we know about human memory is often based on what we remember. In fact, some aspects of retrieval are at least implicit in the discussions of encoding and storage.

Organizational Structures

If someone asked you what letter of the alphabet followed the letter *B,* your answer would be prompt and correct. However, suppose you were asked what letter follows *J.* For most people this question is not as easy to answer and often requires retrieval of other information before the answer is given. You could begin by recalling that the alphabet begins with *A* and proceed through the alphabet until you arrive at the answer *K.* Most people do not have to start with *A,* however. They simply enter the serial organization at some well-known transition point, perhaps *G* followed by *H,* and proceed from there. The point of this example is that successful retrieval often requires recall of the organizational structure that is stored in memory before a specific piece of information can be provided. As more extreme examples of this point, what is the eleventh letter in the alphabet or what letter follows the letter *T?*

Retrieval of organization structures previously stored in long-term memory may allow us to provide information that has not been stored explicitly. For example, suppose you were asked how many windows there are in your home or in the place where you currently live. Most of us have not bothered to store that sort of fact in memory. Nevertheless, we can usually answer such questions by retrieving a mental image of the place in question and simply counting the number of windows. In this case, the relevant organizational structure is the mental image or cognitive map we have of where we live.

In the preceding discussion of storage in long-term memory, we noted that the same information may be organized in more than one way. It also turns out that certain aspects of retrieval depend on which organizational structure we are using. This is nicely illustrated by some work by Steven Kosslyn (1975, 1976) and his co-workers. They asked subjects to verify the truth of statements such as "cats have claws" and "cats have heads." When the subjects were responding on the basis of their semantic knowledge of cats, the statement "cats have claws" was verified faster. A model such as that of Collins and Quillian would explain this finding by noting that "having claws" is a property of cats, whereas "having heads" is a property of all animals. However, when the subjects of this experiment were asked to form a mental image of a cat before the statements were presented, the statement "cats have heads" was verified faster. Apparently, when we use the organizational structure provided by a mental image of a cat, the head is more prominent than the claws.

The preceding example illustrates some important aspects of retrieval from long-term memory. It shows that organizational structures not only influence what we retrieve but guide our search as well. Related aspects of memory and retrieval can be illustrated by considering the following questions:

What is the telephone number of the White House?
What is the telephone number of the king of France?
What is the telephone number of your closest friend?

Your answer to the question about the White House probably would be "I don't know." Notice that the answer did not follow a lengthy search of all telephone numbers that you know. You might have wondered why anyone would ask you such a question, and you would probably agree that such a number does exist. When we know some piece of information is not stored in memory, we do not bother to search for it.

Your answer to the question about the king of France illustrates another aspect of retrieval and its relation to other cognitive activities. Again, the answer is "I don't know." But in this case you probably retrieved the fact that you could not know this number because there is no king of France. You may also have retrieved other related information such as England has a queen, her name is Elizabeth, and she is the second queen of England to have that name. Retrieval of this last fact may even lead you to think about (retrieve?) at least some of what you know about the first Elizabeth.

The "Tip of the Tongue" Phenomenon

The preceding example shows that even when a piece of information is not stored in memory and hence cannot be retrieved, it may still lead to the retrieval of other, related information. The retrieval of related information is a common experience as is the experience of searchiing for something in memory that cannot be retrieved at the moment. We saw this in our previous discussion of the Brown and McNeill (1966) "tip of the tongue" study. Even when subjects could not recall the words being probed for, they could recall features of those words such as the initial letter, number of letters or syllables, or words similar in meaning.

Retrieval of related aspects of an experience or event often facilitates retrieval of the experience or event itself. Have you ever had the experience of trying to remember the name of someone you met at a party and not being able to do so? The experience is often quite frustrating. You may be able to recall the names of other people present at the party, what they were doing, and why the party was given. Still the elusive name will not come to mind. Nevertheless, if you can retrieve enough aspects of the party, the name you are searching for may eventually be retrieved. At least the mental search should help you recognize the name when you hear it.

Context

This example reinforces the importance of reinstating the context of encoding at the time of retrieval—what we referred to as the principle of encoding specificity. Recall that this principle states that what is encoded and subsequently stored in memory is to a large extent determined by the context at the time of encoding. Therefore, reinstating this context greatly facilitates retrieval, particularly in the case of our very personal episodic memories. This principle also helps us understand why cued recall and recognition are usually better than

Figure 8.9

Recall is often facilitated by cues. The first group does better on the second recall test because retrieval cues of category names have been presented. The second group does better than the first group on the first recall test because it benefits from the retrieval cues (after Baron, Byrne, & Kantowitz, 1980).

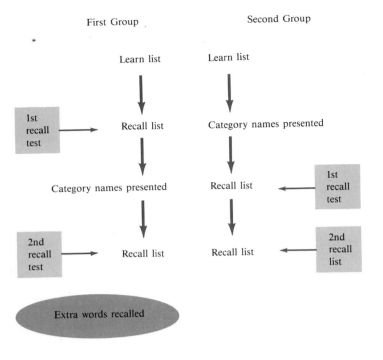

unaided recall (Tulving & Pearlstone, 1966; Tulving & Osler, 1968). In both of these cases more clues to the context of initial encoding are often provided (see Figure 8.9).

In some cases, cues presented at the time of retrieval often prove ineffective when we might think they should be effective. In one of our earlier examples, the world *cold* was presented in a list of words in the context of the word *ground*. *Ground* served as an effective cue for recalling that *cold* was a member of the list, while the semantically related word *hot* did not. Presentation of the cue word *hot* led to retrieval of the word *cold* but not to the fact that *cold* was a word in the list. This probably occurs because those features of the word *cold* having to do with *ground* were emphasized in episodic memory for the words on the list. Therefore, even though the cue word *hot* made the subjects think of the word *cold,* they did not recognize it as a list item. It is only when the same cues are presented during both learning and recall that they facililtate retrieval (Tulving & Thompson, 1973; Watkins & Tulving, 1975).

The importance of reinstating the encoding context at the time of retrieval appears to be quite general. Alan Baddeley (1976) discusses several studies pertaining to this issue. In one study, divers learned material either on land or under 10 feet of water, and retention was subsequently tested in one location or the other. Retention was much better when tested in the same environment in which original learning took place. If students are tested in the same room where they were taught, they will score higher than if they are tested in a different location. A related phenomenon, called **state-dependent memory** (Baddeley, 1976) occurs when material learned in an altered physiological state—usually drug-induced—is recalled in the same state (see chapter 5). For example, it has been shown that material learned under the influence of alcohol is best recalled under the influence of alcohol. There is clinical evidence of heavy drinkers who remember where they hid money while drunk only when they are again drunk (Goodwin, Powell, Bremer, Hoine, & Stern, 1969).

Although drug state-dependent memory is a well-established phenomenon, the effect is rather subtle. In an extensive review of the literature, Eich (1980) points out that drug state-dependency is not observed when explicit retrieval cues are provided. For example, the effect is not observed when the memory test is cued recall or recognition. It is when "implicit" retrieval cues due to reinstatement of the drug context are the only cues provided that drug state-dependent memory is observed.

Depth and Elaboration

Two concepts that were considered earlier were depth and elaboration of encoding. We noted that if subjects attend to relatively superficial aspects of words, such as the letters they contain or the way they sound, retrieval is quite poor. However, if they attend to aspects such as the meaning or pleasantness of words, retrieval is much better. In the case of elaboration at the time of encoding, what appears to be most important is that the elaboration be one that points up the significance of what we are trying to remember. Elaborations that do not accomplish this are ineffective at the time of retrieval.

Remembering and Forgetting

Now that we have reviewed the basic factors in encoding, storage, and retrieval, we might summarize in terms of some principles for better retrieval or good memory. In the case of short-term memory the major factor is attention. So long as we attend to information in short-term memory we can successfuly retireve it. Naturally, successful retrieval from long-term memory is more complex.

At the time of initial encoding, organize the material you want to remember and, if possible, relate this new material to your existing knowledge or schemata. Ask yourself questions that clarify the significance of what you want to remember. This procedure will lead to greater depth and elaboration during processing. Remember also that some kinds of information can be organized in different ways, and the more ways it is organized, the more accessible it may be across different retrieval contexts. In addition, multiple organizations result in deeper and more elaborate levels of processing. As an illustration of such multiple organization, recall that encoding specificity is a concept that is relevant not only to encoding but to storage and retrieval as well. While these principles for good memory were initially derived from studies using individual words or concepts, it is important to note that in recent years these principles have been extended to memory for materials such as sentences and stories (Horton & Mills, 1984). Several of these principles are clearly illustrated in the following section on mnemonics.

Mnemonics

The word **mnemonics** refers both to the centuries-old art of memory and to the devices, plans, or tricks that can be used as memory aids. Generally speaking, these aids are used to relate new material to some previously learned organizational scheme. As a result, the new material is both encoded and stored in an organized form and hence is easier to retrieve subsequently. Mnemonic aids can be useful in remembering many things. It is even helpful to invent a mnemonic for remembering how to spell the word *mnemonics*.

Almost any organizational scheme can be used as a basis for a mnemonic aid. However, the most commonly cited mnemonic aids involve the use of cognitive maps, images, or rhymes. Early Greek and Roman orators are reported to have used a combination of cognitive maps and images as mnemonic aids. To do this the Greeks created the **method of loci** (*loci* meaning "places"). For example, in preparing a speech the orators might mentally place the various topics at particular places along a well-known route or path. Topic *C* might be associated with the third house down the street. When it was time to give the speech, the orator would mentally travel along this route retrieving the topics to be talked about in the prescribed order. Because the places along the route were well known to the orator, retrieval of the order of topics would be facilitated. The tasks of encoding and storage of topics at particular places might have involved a great deal of effort, however.

In the discussion of motor programs we mentioned that the rhythmic nature of these programs could help explain why they are so resistant to forgetting. A similar reason could be given for the use of rhymes as mnemonic aids. Rhyme mnemonics can be quite effective if they are well constructed because mistakes in the order of recall destroy the rhyme.

A rhyme is commonly used to remember the number of days in each month of the year: "Thirty days hath September, April, June, and November, all the rest have thirty-one. . . ." The rhyme establishes an organization that, once learned, is easy to remember. Of course, recalling the number of days in a particular month, say July, may be difficult without recalling the entire rhyme.

A combination of a rhyme and images is employed in the frequently cited pegword system. This system is based on words that rhyme with a sequence of numbers. Once the rhyme is established, the material to be memorized must be attached to the rhyme words. For example, one is a bun, two is a shoe, three is a tree, four is a door, five is a hive, six are sticks, seven is heaven, eight is a gate, nine is a line, and ten is a hen. The main feature of a numeric pegword list is that the list must be learned only once. Each new list of material is associated with the old pegwords. Now, if a new list of items is to be remem-

Figure 8.10

A list of items can be remembered by forming an association between each item and a pegword (after Baron, Byrne, & Kantowitz, 1980).

bered, such as kite, duck, cow, elephant, giraffe, lamp, desk, watch, coat, and cone, it is necessary only to think of an association between the new items and the pegwords. For example, you might imagine a kite inside a huge bun, a duck putting on a shoe, a cow in a tree, an elephant squeezing through a narrow door, and so on (see Figure 8.10). In the pegword system the rhyme is fairly easily learned. The hard part comes in encoding the features of the words to be imaged and the construction of the image itself. The pegword system works best when a strong visual image can be formed (Bower, 1972).

Well-constructed mnemonic aids are effective for several reasons. First, the material to be memorized is integrated into a well-known organization scheme that can be retrieved readily. Second, the process of integrating new material into the existing scheme involves an encoding context (one-bun, two-shoe) that is easily reinstated at the time of recall. Third, the integration of the new material with the encoding context is likely to involve fairly deep levels of processing—for example, remembering things monkeys commonly do when constructing an image of a monkey swinging in a tree. However, despite the effectiveness of good mnemonic aids, it should be emphasized that they are not always easy to use: you have to work hard at them.

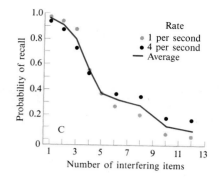

Figure 8.11

Probability of recall as a function of the number of digits following the digit to be recalled (after Waugh & Norman, 1965).

Forgetting

We seldom are concerned about why we remember (we just do), but we become very concerned about why we forget or fail to remember. And this concern becomes greater as we grow older. Although forgetting usually implies that something is lost from long-term memory, forgetting from short-term memory is relevant to the problem.

Forgetting from short-term memory is typically explained as being the result of displacement: new inputs displace old inputs in order to avoid capacity overload. This view of forgetting from short-term memory has been generally favored, at least since the work of Nancy Waugh and Donald Norman (1965). Prior to that time an alternative explanation held that forgetting from short-term memory would occur if material currently in short-term memory was not attended to, because the memory traces would decay over time.

To test these different explanations, Waugh and Norman devised an experiment using what is known as the probe technique. They presented subjects with several series of 16 digits. The last digit in each series was one that had appeared exactly once previously. This last digit is called the probe digit, and the subjects' task was to report the digit that followed the first appearance of the probe digit. Given a list such as 4, 9, 0, 4, 9, 8, 3, 5, 8, 2, 6, 3, 6, 2, 0, 5, the probe digit is 5, and the subject should recall the number 8.

The digits were presented verbally at either a fast (four per second) or slow (one per second) rate. For each list the probability of correct recall could be assessed as being due to either the number of digits or the amount of time occuring after the first presentation of the probe digit. Remember that the initial presentation of the probe digit had to be in short-term memory for the subjects to say what digit followed it. Thus, in the example above, eight digits follow the first presentation of the probe digit. With slow presentation eight seconds would elapse, and with fast presentation only two seconds would elapse. If the decay principle was correct, greater forgetting should be found with slow presentation than with fast presentation. However, if short-term memory operated according to displacement, presentation rate should make no difference. Of course, with displacement the number of digits following the first presentation of the probe digit should make a big difference.

The results of the Waugh and Norman experiment are summarized in Figure 8.11. The number of digits following initial presentation of the probe digit has a major effect. Presentation rate had no appreciable influence on recall. These findings strongly support the displacement principle as the major cause

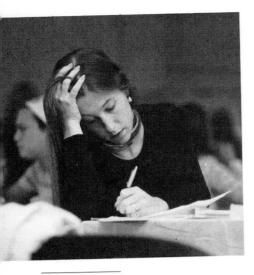

Too much anxiety when taking an exam can be a source of retrieval failure.

of forgetting from short-term memory. As the number of digits following the first presentation of the probe digit increases, the opportunity for displacement increases, and recall becomes increasingly poorer.

Before we discuss the reasons for forgetting from long-term memory, it is necessary to say something about the meaning of the word *forgetting*. When we forget something from short-term memory such as a recently looked-up telephone number, it is truly forgotten. If we need to dial the number again, we must look it up again. However, forgetting from long-term memory is much more complex. In fact, with long-term memory we can only be sure that we have failed to retrieve something; that is, we cannot be certain that a memory once in long-term memory has been truly forgotten, only that we cannot retrieve it. When we experience the "tip of the tongue" phenomenon in which some memory cannot be retrieved, we know it is still there. It is also fairly common to struggle to recall something, come to the conclusion that we must have forgotten it, and have the memory return at a later time.

We have considered several factors having to do with successful retrieval or good memory. Clearly the reverse of these factors will lead to memories that are easily forgotten or difficult to retrieve. Memory will be poor when materials to be learned are not well organized at the time of encoding and storage. Memory will also be poor when materials to be learned are not encoded at sufficiently deep levels or when the context at the time of encoding is quite different from that at the time of retrieval.

Proactive and retroactive interference are among the factors that make memories difficult to retrieve. **Proactive interference** arises when material learned previously interferes with retrieval of recently learned material. **Retroactive interference** is said to occur when the retrieval of previously learned material is interfered with by recently learned material. Notice that the terms *proaction* and *retroaction* refer to the temporal locus of interference. Thus, in proaction old memories operate foward in time to disrupt retrieval of newer memories, while in retroaction new memories operate backward in time to disrupt retrieval of older memories.

Either proactive or retroactive interference is particularly likely to occur when the same retrieval cue leads to different responses over time. Examples of such interference effects are commonly observed. A friend moves to a new home, and you have difficulty retrieving either the new address (proactive interference) or the old address (retroactive interference). A girlfriend you grew up with has been married for some time, and you have difficulty retrieving either her married name (proactive interference) or her maiden name (retroactive interference). In fact, proactive and retroactive interference effects are so common that the importance of these factors in explaining retrieval failures is often overlooked.

Another type of interference, which may be either proactive or retroactive in nature, is what is called mediated interference. **Mediated interference** is said to occur when some desired response is blocked by another response because both are linked to a common mediational concept. For example, suppose the office where you work has just purchased a photocopier; you know the name of the machine perfectly well, but you keep calling it a Xerox. In this case, the name Xerox is so strongly associated with the photocopying industry that you have difficulty retrieving the name of the copier used in your office. A person named Schick might occasionally be introduced to others, not without embarrassment, as Mr. or Ms. Gillette. You can, no doubt, supply many similar examples.

Finally, emotional states can cause retrieval failure or forgetting. As any student knows, either through personal experience or that of an acquaintance, anxiety at the time of an exam can be a major source of retrieval failure. It is not that anxiety is unusual when taking exams, but when the anxiety level gets too high it often is accompanied by extraneous thoughts or worries that interfere with retrieval of the relevant information (Holmes, 1974).

Perhaps the most frequently cited theory of emotional factors in retrieval failure is Freud's (1914/1938) theory of repression. Because this topic will be treated extensively in a later chapter (see chapter 12), it will only be outlined here. The basic theme of this theory is that certain childhood experiences as well as later experiences associated with them are so traumatic that the individual refuses to allow memories of them to enter consciousness. Repression is not a conscious process; it is unconscious, and the memories of these traumatic experiences are stored in the unconscious. Retrieval of such memories, according to Freud, occurs only when the emotion associated with them is reduced, usually through some form of therapy.

Memory and Thinking

At the beginning of this chapter we emphasized the extremely close relationship between memory and other cognitive activites. In the next chapter we will consider relationships among cognitive activities that are intimately related to language. Meanwhile, it is appropriate to conclude this chapter by illustrating some of the other relationships between memory and cognition.

The term **thinking** refers to a variety of cognitive activites including problem solving, planning, decision making, judgment—even remembering. In carrying out these activites we rely on the contents of long-term memory to a large degree. These contents include specific information, our knowledge of the world, and various organized schemata. Consider, for example, a fairly commonplace activity such as going out to dinner. Our schemata for this activity involves choosing a restaurant. Planning in turn involves making various decisions and judgments about what type of food we want to eat, how much we are willing to pay, what type of dress is appropriate, and so on. All of these decisions and judgments require remembering what we know about various restaurants, including where they are located and how best to get to them (cognitive maps). If we drive a car to the restaurant and have a flat tire along the way, problem solving may also be required, and our success at solving this problem will depend on our schemata for changing tires, including how to use the jack.

Retrieval of contents of long-term memory aids the cognitive activities involved in thinking, and they are constrained by failures of retrieval as well. Two examples illustrate these effects. First, suppose someone asked you where you were at 2 P.M. on the first Monday in March, two years ago. Unless that point in time was of particular significance for you, it would be difficult to answer the question. However, by drawing on episodic memory and semantic memory, you could probably come up with a reasonable answer that was fairly likely to be correct. For example, if you were a student two years ago, you would know that Mondays are usually school days. You would also know that there are no national holidays in early March in the United States, so school was probably in session. Now if you also can remember what class, if any, was meeting at 2 P.M., you would be able to reconstruct a reasonably good answer.

As a second illustration, imagine entering a room in which two strings are hanging from the ceiling. You are told that your task is to tie the two strings together. The problem is that the strings are too far apart to reach both at the same time. Scattered about the room are a variety of objects including a pair of pliers. This is a classic problem used in the study of problem solving that most people find difficult to solve without some sort of hint such as the experimenter brushing against one string to start it swinging. However, if you happen to retrieve the concept of a pendulum from long-term memory the problem is readily solved. You simply tie the pliers to one string and set it swinging toward the other string. Now you can grasp both strings at the same time and tie them together (see Figure 8.12).

Many adults can remember exactly what they were doing when President Kennedy was assassinated in 1963.

Figure 8.12

This is perhaps the most famous task used in laboratory studies of problem solving. The subject is required to figure out a way of tying two strings together, even though the two strings are too far apart to be held at the same time. A variety of objects are available for use in solving the problem, including a chair, tissue paper, a pair of pliers, and some paper clips. The solution involves tying the pliers to one of the strings and setting it in motion like a pendulum so that it can be reached while the subject is holding onto the other string (after McKenchie & Doyle, 1976).

FOCUS

In Search of the Engram

A fundamental assumption underlying memory research is that all learning somehow engraves a physical imprint on the nervous system. Karl Lashley, the distinguished pioneer in the investigation of learning's biological basis, labeled this presumed memory trace the *engram*—from the Greek for "that which is written in."

Lashley spent more than 30 years in search of the engram. His method was straightforward. He trained rats to negotiate a series of simple mazes, then surgically removed a portion of cerebral cortex from the brain of each animal. If the engram was stored in that particular portion of brain tissue, Lashley reasoned, then the rat would forget what it had learned about running the maze. The rat's loss of memory would be manifested in maze performance: it would be slower in running the maze and would make more errors.

Lashley conducted hundreds of such experiments, cutting lesions in many different parts of the cortex. To his surprise, Lashley found that the animal's performance in the maze was not affected specifically by damage to any single cortical area. Rather, the resulting deficits in maze performance seemed to be a function of the total amount of cortical tissue removed: the more tissue lost, the less the rat remembered. Near the end of this career, Lashley (1950) concluded with despair and irony: "I sometimes feel, in reviewing the evidence on the localization of the memory trace, that . . . learning is just not possible."

Lashley attempted to account for his frustrating results by proposing the principle of *mass action*. This principle suggested that the engram is actually everywhere, somehow distributed over the whole of the cortex rather than localized in a particular place. Critics, however, were quick to point to another possible explanation for Lashley's experimental findings. The rat's learning of the maze is contingent upon several different parts of the sensory apparatus. The rat learns by seeing the maze, of course; but it also learns by feeling with its whiskers. These different types of engrams would be stored in different parts of the brain; hence destruction of one memory trace would still leave intact the other engram.

Although Lashley failed to localize the engram, his pioneering ideas and experimental techniques paved the way for contemporary researchers. For example, it was a suggestion by Lashley that inspired the split-brain experiments of Roger Sperry (see chapter 2). One of the many interesting findings of the split-brain studies has permitted a reevaluation of the results of some of Lashley's experiments. Sperry's student, Ronald Myers (1961), provided evidence in cats that a visual memory may establish dual engrams—one in each hemisphere of the brain. It is now clear, from this and other findings, that Lashley's idea of mass action was probably in error and that the principle of *multiple storage* can account for his findings. A single memory may somehow engrave more than one engram, and these multiple traces are stored in different parts of the brain.

Other researchers, by probing structures deep in the brain below the cortex, have succeeded in localizing evidence of the engram. These

The difficulty of the two-string problem lies in the failure to retrieve the concept of a pendulum from long-term memory. This retrieval failure occurs because most people placed in this situation fixate on the most conventional uses of the objects in the room, including the pliers. This tendency is quite common in studies of problem solving and has been termed **functional fixedness.** However, functional fixedness is also an example of the principle of encoding specificity. The problem here is that an object, the pliers, is not a good retrieval cue for the concept of a pendulum.

Apart from retrieval failures, human memory also constrains the cognitive activities involved in thinking because of the limited capacity of short-term memory. Two illustrations of this constraint will illuminate the point. Suppose you are asked to place the months of the year in alphabetical order. You would have no difficulty recalling the names of the months, although for most of us the names are not stored in alphabetical order. You also know the alphabet quite well. With paper and pencil, the task is an easy one. However, try to perform this task without any external aids, and see how difficult it is to do.

experiments rely upon a modern technique not available in Lashley's time: microelectrodes that can monitor activity in a single nerve cell. Several such studies suggest that the structure known as the hippocampus, which is tucked up into the temporal lobe of the brain, may contain memory traces concerned with spatial representation of the visual world. In another part of the temporal lobe, Charles Gross and his colleagues discovered a nerve cell that fired when a monkey was presented with an image of the monkey's hand, a finding that implies the presence of the engram for a highly particular visual memory (Gross, Rocha-Miranda, & Bender, 1972).

The attempts to localize the engram seek to answer the question, *Where* is it?" A second question asks, "Precisely *what* is it?" The physical form in which a memory is embodied has been the subject of considerable speculation. Most theories focus on two different possible mechanisms. One idea is that learning causes some sort of structural change at the synaptic gap separating nerve cells; for example, new and very short nerve fibers may sprout here, strengthening neural connections that presumably constitute the engram. The other idea centers on chemical alterations within the nerve cells. This view has been given impetus by the recent advances in genetics showing the enormous amount of information that can be precisely coded by large nucleotide molecules such as deoxyribonucleic acid (DNA) and ribonucleic acid (RNA). Engrams, it is suggested, may similarly be stored in protein molecules within nerve cells. A number of interesting experiments have attempted to test this notion—researchers have even tried to show that engrams can be transferred from one worm to another through cannibalism—but the results have been widely criticized as inconsistent or inconclusive. All of the theories about the physical or chemical nature of the engram remain largely speculative.

Perhaps the most promising current investigation of memory's biological basis focuses on habituation, which is the gradual decrease in behavioral response to a repeated stimulus. People living near train tracks, for example, at first may be bothered by the noise of the trains passing during the night. After a period of time, however, they get used to the sound and sleep through the night. Eric Kandel (1976) has painstakingly investigated habituation in the sea slug, *aplysia* (see chapter 2 Research: "Studying Behavior at the Cellular Level"). Habituation occurs in *aplysia* when the gills are touched repeatedly. When first touched, the creature withdraws its gills vigorously, but repeated touching causes a gradual diminution of this reflex response. Kandel found that successive stimulation of the sensory neuron apparently caused a reduction in the amount of the chemical neurotransmitter released by that neuron into the synaptic gap. This reduction in transmitter provides biolgical explanation for the diminution, or habituation, of the gill-withdrawal response.

Kandel's work, together with other research, appears to have pinpointed the fundamental mechanism for habituation not only in *aplysia* but also in many vertebrates. Although this mechanism may be far more elementary than the engram that Lashley set out to find many years ago, its discovery marks a significant step forward. The brain sciences typically make their greatest progress by mastering the study of such simple systems. ∎

The difficulty is not due to any failure to retrieve information from long-term memory; rather, the capacity of short-term memory is overloaded by ''keeping track'' of the names while reordering them at the same time.

As a second illustration, try to multiply the number 23 by 67 in your head. Here again the problem is easy with paper and pencil, but doing it mentally, without external aids, is fairly difficult. The numbers 23 and 67 must be retained in short-term memory along with the numbers subsequently computed. Furthermore, short-term memory capacity is also taken up by applying the computational rules used to solve the problem. Both of the preceding examples illustrate the difficulty of thinking about anything that is complex in the sense of holding many components in short-term memory.

By no means is all thinking constrained by the limited capacity of short-term memory. Much of what is meant by thinking goes on beyond our conscious awareness, and only the products or results of those mental processes ever enter consciousness (Mandler, 1975). We referred to these mental processes as generative processes to reflect the inventive nature of their products.

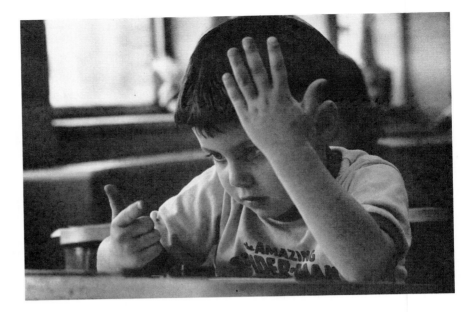

Young children often use their fingers as external aids to help them solve math problems.

That is, generative processes serve to lead to new ideas. Such processes are thought to play an important role in language, as we shall see in the next chapter.

The nature of generative processes and the role that they play in thinking are not well understood at present and probably will not be for some time to come. However, several different approaches to the study of such processes are currently being attempted. As noted, the study of language is closely related to the study of generative processes. Another approach is illustrated by attempts to characterize organizational principles in memory as, for example, in the work of Collins and Quillian. Here the attempt is to discover how information is represented and organized in memory so that we can make inferences about how that information might be used in thinking.

Still a third approach is computer simulation of mental operations. Computers are being programmed so that they perform tasks in ways similar to the ways humans perform those tasks. To the extent that the simulation is a good one, it may be possible to infer characteristics of human mental operations from the nature of the computer program. Alan Newell and Herbert Simon (1972) have developed a general-purpose program called the GENERAL PROBLEM SOLVER, which does a reasonably good job of solving certain mathematical problems and of playing chess. While this approach is interesting in a number of ways, it is questionable whether it will lead to any major clarifications of human mental operations.

Summary

1. Cognition is a complex set of processes that pertain to the acquisition of knowledge and its use. Memory is part of cognition and the basic building block upon which cognition is based. Learning and memory are closely interrelated.

2. For purposes of discussion, memory is classified into three types: sensory memory, short-term memory, and long-term memory. However, these varieties of memory are not necessarily separate and isolated stages. Sensory memory refers to the very brief span prior to perceptual processing. Visual memory trace, or iconic trace, has a relatively large storage capacity but a duration of not more than one second.

3. Short-term memory is longer in duration than sensory memory and has a limit of seven plus or minus two units of information, or chunks. Several

theories of attention have been proposed. It is likely that attention does not restrict our ability to process and remember information in the sense of providing a capacity limitation. Capacity limitation is due to short-term memory, and attention refers to the act of processing information in short-term memory. A similar view states that attention has no independent status apart from the perceptual process.

4. Long-term memory is not only the repository of our prior experiences but also includes information and beliefs derived from these experiences as well as plans for guiding what we shall do in the future. Several abstract contents of long-term memory govern a substantial portion of our lives: cognitive maps, schemata, motor-programs, and generative processes.

5. Encoding refers to the extraction of information from events we experience—under the conditions that the events are experienced. This information is transformed into codes that memory can accept and store. More information is encoded into sensory memory than can be subsequently encoded into short-term memory. Encoding into short-term memory involves a deeper level of processing and typically requires some interaction with long-term memory. Short-term memory is usually encoded acoustically, but can also be encoded by visual form or meaning. An important aspect of encoding is the principle of encoding specificity, which refers to the interactions between prior knowledge and the context of new experiences.

6. Storage refers both to the contents of long-term memory and the way these contents are represented and organized. Episodic memory involves storing spatial and temporal aspects of experiences that are of a highly autobiographical nature. Semantic memory refers to our organized store of general knowledge. Memory is variously and complexly organized, and different contents may be organized in different ways, including spatial organization, serial organization, associative organization, and most important, hierarchical organization.

7. Retrieval of information from memory often requires recall of the organizational structure that is stored in memory before a specific piece of information can be provided. Organizational structures not only influence what we retrieve, but they also guide our search of long-term memory.

8. It is not unusual to have a piece of information stored in long-term memory but not be able to recall it at a given moment. One example of this is known as the ''tip of the tongue'' phenomenon.

9. The principle of encoding specificity also applies to retrieval; that is, reinstating the encoding context greatly facilitates retrieval, particularly in the case of personal, episodic memories. If words or concepts have been encoded by meaning (depth of encoding), they will be more easily retrieved than if superficially encoded.

10. Mnemonics refers both to the art of memory and to the devices, plans, or tricks that can be used as memory aids. Generally speaking, mnemonic aids relate new material to some previously learned organizational scheme, such as a rhyme.

11. Forgetting from short-term memory is typically explained as a result of displacement; new inputs displace old inputs in order to avoid capacity overload. Forgetting from long-term memory is much more complex. In fact, we can only be sure that we have failed to retrieve something; we cannot be certain that a memory once in long-term memory has been truly forgotten. Among the factors that make memories difficult to retrieve are proactive and retroactive interference. Intense emotional states, such as anxiety, can also cause retrieval failure or forgetting.

12. Regardless of the source, long-term memory or an external source, information must enter short-term memory for it to be consciously available. The contents of long-term memory are typically not consciously available.

13. Thinking refers to a variety of cognitive activities including problem solving, planning, decision making, judgment, and even remembering. We rely

on the contents of long-term memory—specific information, our knowledge of the world, various organized schemata—to accomplish the acts of thinking. Constraints are placed on some forms of thinking by the limited capacity of short-term memory.

RESEARCH: An important issue in the study of human memory concerns the extent to which episodic and semantic memory constitute functionally different systems. John F. Kihlstrom has shown that under conditions of posthypnotic amnesia the effects of these two memory systems may be separated.

FOCUS: Lashley's view that the engram—the biological unit of learning—becomes distributed over the whole brain according to the principle of mass action has been displaced by the notion of multiple storage: that is, a single memory trace produces more than one engram. These multiple traces are then stored throughout the brain. Kandel's research with the gill-withdrawal reflex in *aplysia* points up the role of neurotransmitters in simple learning and thus substantiates the notion that learning does, indeed, have a biological basis.

CHAPTER

9

Language

Language is a complex vehicle for communication. It serves as the medium through which most knowledge is communicated.

Our language constitutes what is perhaps the most striking difference between humans and all other species. In no other species do we find such a complex vehicle for communication as the languages used by humans. As we shall see, this complexity is revealed in the way sounds make up words, in the way words make up phrases or sentences, and in the way sentences convey meaning.

The speed and ease with which human children acquire and learn language invites our curiosity and study. Language provides very good examples for examining the motor programs and generative processes that are found in human behavior. Once a natural language has been acquired, the motor programs for speech production rarely require any particular attention to the complex sequences of motor movements involved. When we have decided what to talk about, the muscle groups that control the shape of our mouth as well as movements of the lips and tongue seem to take over automatically to produce the desired sequence of speech sounds with little or no conscious effort on our part.

In addition, the generative processes involved in natural language are revealed by a very important facet of language—**creativity.** Setting aside clichés, direct quotations, and customary greetings, most utterances we produce or hear are novel—ones we have never produced or heard before. In addition, we can continue to produce and understand novel utterances without limit so long as the vocabulary contained in those utterances is known to us. The creativity found in natural language exemplifies the inventiveness of generative processes.

Another reason for treating language separately is its central importance in human cognitive activities. Language, spoken or written, serves as the medium through which most knowledge is communicated. We use language constantly in our daily activities for a variety of social, intellectual, and personal purposes. Thus, language serves as an important medium for observing the results of cognitive activities in human beings.

There are obvious parallels between spoken and written language. For example, when you read a sentence such as ''the car has a flat tire,'' the same meaning is conveyed to you as when you hear someone utter that sentence. Despite the parallels, however, the main emphasis in this chapter will be on spoken language. Spoken language is much older than written language, and it is the form of language that we all learn first because formal training is required to learn written language. In addition, there are good reasons for believing that the processes involved in writing and reading do not totally mirror those involved in speaking and listening. Written and spoken language clearly differ in terms of the sensory-perceptual systems involved (visual versus auditory) as well as in terms of the motor systems involved in production (fingers and hands versus mouth, tongue, and lips).

Spoken language is typically divided into three components. The first component is the sound patterns that are found in all natural languages. The study of these sound patterns is called **phonology.** The second component is the **syntax** of language. In English, as in any other natural language, it is this structure that determines whether or not a particular string of words ordered in a particular way constitutes an acceptable utterance. Most important, language is a vehicle for conveying the meaning of utterances, and the study of this component of language is called **semantics.**

Linguists study these components of language in order to determine the structure of language. Their goal is to specify rules of word formation, rules that indicate how words are combined to form sentences, and rules that indicate how meaning is determined. Psycholinguists also study these three components of language, but their focus is different from that of linguists. The primary concern of psycholinguists is with the way people produce and understand language, although the rules or structure specified by linguists often provide important insights concerning the way language is used. We shall see several

CHAPTER 9 LANGUAGE

examples of these insights in the following sections, but we shall also see instances where linguistic rules do not capture the way human beings use language. Thus, the rules, or structures, of language provided by linguists serve as an important reference point for psychologists who study language acquisition and use.

We will first explore phonology, syntax, and semantics and then see how each is used and acquired. Although these three components of language are clearly interrelated, it will be convenient in our discussion to treat them more or less separately.

Speech Production and Perception

Take an arbitrary English word such as the word *dog* and consider the relationship between its spoken and written forms. For present purposes we can ignore the meaning of the word because the relationship between the sound or spelling of a particular word and its meaning is essentially arbitrary. That is, the same class of objects is signified by different sounds and spellings in different languages. Now let us return to the English word *dog*. We know how to pronounce and spell it. However, if the spelling truly captured the pronunciation the word *dog* would be pronounced "dee–oh–gee." Suppose now that we try to pronounce the word by grouping the letters into adjacent pairs. Then we would have "do–og," which, if said rapidly, results in a better approximation to the word *dog*. Yet, it is only when we group all three letters into a single unit that the correct pronunciation is achieved. We shall return to this example later, but first let us consider certain aspects of speech sounds.

The Sounds of Speech

Phonologists have developed a complex system for describing the speech sounds that occur in language. These sounds are called **phonemes,** and they correspond roughly to the letters of the written alphabet. There are more phonemes in all languages combined than are found in any one particular language because some sounds that occur in one language do not occur in others. For example, in English there are different sounds for /r/ and /l/, but in Japanese this distinction does not exist. (It is conventional to put symbols for phonemes between slashes).

A phoneme is typically defined as the smallest unit of sound that makes a difference to the meaning of a larger sound unit such as a word. Consider the English word *tap,* for example. This word consists of three phonemes, and changing the middle one, the vowel, to /i/ changes the word to *tip*. Similarly, changing the initial consonant phoneme to /p/ gives us *pap,* whereas changing the final consonant to /b/ gives us *tab*.

The phonemes found in any particular natural language actually represent classes of speech sounds that are treated in the same way by native speakers of that language. The reason individual phonemes represent classes of speech sounds, rather than a single specific sound, is because the voices of speakers differ and because there are variations in the way a given speaker produces the same phoneme on different occasions. The way in which phonemes are identified and classified is not important for our discussion here, however,

For several decades it has been possible to represent the pattern of sound energy that occurs in speech in a visual form. An example of such a representation, called a **speech spectrogram,** is given in Figure 9.1. Three aspects of the speech signal are represented in a spectrogram. The vertical dimension represents the frequency of the sound in terms of cycles per second or hertz (Hz). Notice that the sound frequency is quite complex, with sound energy occurring

Figure 9.1

Typical speech spectrogram of the words "speech we may see."

at many different frequencies. The horizontal dimension represents elapsed time from the beginning to the end of an utterance in thousandths of a second, or milliseconds. The amplitude of the sound is represented by the degree of darkening, with the darkest parts of the spectrogram reflecting the greatest sound energy. Notice that the darkest aspects of the spectrogram occur at several different frequency levels and that in many cases a "dark bar" changes rapidly across several frequency levels.

These "dark bars" are called **formants** and they are differentiated in terms of the relative frequencies at which they occur. Thus, the lowest bar in a spectrogram is called the first formant, irrespective of its actual frequency. Similarly, the next lowest bar in terms of frequency is called the second formant, and so on until the main energy levels are all designated.

It is almost impossible to look at a particular spectrogram and determine which utterance might have produced it. There are striking contrasts between the visual representation of spoken language revealed in the spectrogram and the visual representation of the same message appearing in print. In the spectrogram there do not appear to be gaps between letters or words, as we see in the printed page of a book. It is even difficult to identify segments of the spectrogram that recur, although in terms of the phonemes involved in a particular message we know that some sounds must be recurring. Notice that the double "ee" in Figure 9.1 looks somewhat different in the word *speech* than it does in the word *see*.

Although spectrograms are difficult to read, they have made it possible for speech scientists to make important advances in the understanding of speech production and perception. These advances have been accomplished by creating imitation or synthetic spectrograms, developed partly through trial and error, that contain the essential elements required for particular patterns of speech sounds. These synthetic spectrograms can be converted into sound just as a phonograph needle can convert the grooves impressed on a record into sound. Sometimes very simple synthetic spectrograms are sufficient to generate an identifiable speech sound—one that would look very different and much more complex if you saw a spectrogram of the same sound produced by a human voice.

The simplicity of these synthetic spectrograms is possible because the human vocal apparatus produces a great deal of information that is not always required in order to identify a particular word or syllable. Much of the information produced by the human voice helps us determine such things as the age, sex, emotional state, and identity of the speaker. As a result, not all of the information represented in a spectrogram of natural speech is essential for identifying which words were said.

An illustration of the simplest elements that are sufficient to be heard as intelligible speech is shown in Fig. 9.2. The figure shows patterns that will produce the identifiable syllables *di*, *du*, *gi*, and *gu*. Notice that the lowest bar, or first formant, for each syllable shows a rapidly rising transition across frequencies before it levels off and remains in a steady state. However, the second formants all differ to a noticeable degree. What these differences among the patterns indicate is that what will be heard as a particular consonant-vowel combination depends both on the consonant and on the vowel. That is, the vowel provides the context for the consonant and the consonant provides the context for the vowel. The speech signal that leads to perception of particular syllables varies, depending on the contexts provided by the individual phonemes. Therefore speech is said to be characterized by **context-conditioned variation** (Liberman, Cooper, Shankweiler, & Studdert-Kennedy, 1967).

The importance of context-conditioned variation can be illustrated by comparing written and spoken language. In written language, as in this text, the symbols that represent letters of the alphabet are always the same. The symbols for the consonant letters just mentioned are d, D, g, G. Of course, different typefaces could be introduced, but there is little actual variation in the symbols used to represent a particular letter in written language. When spectrographs were first developed, researchers thought that the same would be true for speech elements or phonemes in spoken language. They thought that some fixed acoustic signal, some particular sound or sound pattern, would always represent a particular phoneme. However, as we have just seen, this is not the case. The sound pattern that represents a given phoneme in a word depends on the other phonemes present in that word.

An important consequence of context-conditioned variation is that you cannot pull the consonant and vowel apart and have two separate speech sounds remaining. For example, there is no way to modify the synthetic spectrograms shown in Figure 9.2 and hear only the consonant: information about both the consonant and the vowel is being transmitted at the same time. In other words, speech production involves **parallel transmission** of the phonemic elements, a factor not important in written language (Liberman, Cooper, Shankweiler, & Studdert-Kennedy, 1967). Try to produce a consonant sound such as b or d and notice what happens (bee or dee)!

Another illustration of parallel transmission is shown in Fig. 9.3. The synthetic spectrogram shown here, when converted to sound, would be heard as the single-syllable word *bag* (Liberman, 1970). The segments of the spectrogram associated with each phoneme indicate when information about that phoneme is being transmitted. Notice that vowel information is continuously present, whereas information about the consonants is present through approximately the first two thirds or last two thirds of the speech signal depending on the consonant. In other words, a change in the vowel *(bag to big)* would effect a change in the entire pattern, and changing a consonant *(bag to gag)* would effect a change in about two thirds of the pattern.

Now we are in a better position to understand our earlier example using the word *dog*. Only when the interrelated, context-dependent sound information is combined into a single package is the word *dog* properly produced and perceived. A simple illustration of this packaging during production can be achieved by pronouncing two similarly spelled words *sue* and *see* while paying close attention to what your mouth is doing. Notice that even as you begin the initial consonant your mouth is changing shape in anticipation of the following vowel. As another example, say the syllables *ba, da,* and *ga* and pay attention to the movements of your tongue. The complexity involved in the way speech sounds are produced and understood is particularly striking when we consider how easily very young children learn how to use these speech sounds.

Lateralization in Speech Perception

It was noted in chapter 2 that the human brain is highly specialized in the way it processes incoming signals. This specialization also holds for the perception of speech sounds, where the left hemisphere of the brain plays a dom-

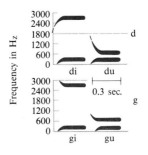

Figure 9.2

Spectrographic patterns that produce the syllables di, du, gi, *and* gu.

Figure 9.3

Parallel transmission of phonetic segments after encoding by the rules of speech to the level of sound. Here the single-syllable word bag *is represented.*

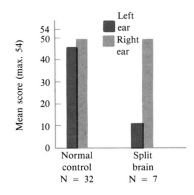

Figure 9.4

Listening performance of split-brain patients shows a marked left ear/right hemisphere disadvantage since no communication between brain hemispheres is possible in these patients.

inant role. This hemispheric dominance holds for right-handed individuals and for most who are left-handed as well. For example, suppose you were presented the speech sounds /da/ and /ka/, one to each ear at the same time, and you were asked to report both sounds. If you made an error in reporting one of these sounds it most likely would be the one presented to the left ear. This is because dominant projections in speech perception are those from the right ear to the left hemisphere. Interestingly enough, however, if the sounds presented were musical patterns, the left ear/right hemisphere connections would dominate.

As you would expect, the right ear/left hemisphere advantage in perceiving speech sounds is not great. We do not hear a telephone conversation better in the right ear than in the left ear. The advantage for right ear inputs occurs only when competing sounds are presented to the two ears. However, the advantage is greatly increased when the hemispheres cannot communicate with each other.

Brenda Milner, L. Taylor, and Roger Sperry (1968) report an investigation of speech perception in both normal and split-brain subjects. Recall from chapter 2 that in split-brain patients the two hemispheres cannot communicate with each other but the connection from each ear to both hemispheres is intact. In this study the subjects wore stereo headphones so that the sounds presented (spoken digits 1 through 9) could be presented to either ear separately or to both ears simultaneously. The results indicated no ear advantage for either group of subjects when the sounds were presented to only a single ear (either right or left). However, when competing sounds were presented to both ears, the right ear/left hemisphere advantage is revealed. As shown in Figure 9.4, the advantage for normal subjects is small but consistent. In the split-brain patients the advantage for right ear inputs is dramatic. This contrast between normal and split-brain subjects reveals the importance of the connections that go between the hemispheres in the perception of competing speech sounds.

The Speech Code

When we write or print in English we produce one letter at a time: we produce an alphabetic sequence consisting of individual letters. However, when we speak, information about more than one phoneme is usually conveyed at any given point. The parallel transmission of phonemes means that we can perceive speech at the rate of 15 or more phonemes per second. Such a rate would not be possible if each phoneme had to be perceived individually in an alphabeticlike order. Alphabetic sound sequences are thus much less efficient than human speech. This is well illustrated by studies of Morse code and by attempts to build reading machines for the blind. All of these systems are based on letter-by-letter transmission, and none of them is much better than one-tenth as efficient as human speech in terms of either sending or receiving (Liberman, Cooper, Shankweiler, & Studdert-Kennedy, 1967).

Because of the efficient packaging of speech sounds at the level of phonemes, speech has been characterized as a code rather than an alphabet. However, the efficient packaging is not the only reason that the term **speech code** has been used. Speech perception also does not seem to depend on any particular part of the frequency range. For example, filtering out all frequencies above 1900 Hz (about the middle of the frequency range for speech) does not impair the perception of speech. Filtering out the frequencies below 1900 Hz does not impair perception either. What does appear to be critical is the pattern of frequencies within whatever part of the frequency range that passes through the filter. Thus, to the extent that we can compare the phonemes of our spoken language to the letters of our written language, speech is best described as a code, and written language is best described as an alphabet.

CHAPTER 9 LANGUAGE

The differences between spoken and written language are of critical importance in understanding the complexity of natural language. Computers can be programmed to process printed materials, but computers have not yet been programmed to process any *substantial* amount of spoken language. The difficulty lies in the unending variation of sound patterns found in spoken language. Not only do the sound patterns that represent phonemes vary depending on context, but entire syllables may also change depending on the syllables near them. Humans have an impressive ability to produce and perceive such complex patterns of sound. Furthermore, humans perceive these patterns even though almost everyone's voice produces some difference in sound pattern.

Grammar and Syntax

While phonemes make up the sound elements of language, they alone do not convey meaning. They must be combined into meaningful utterances. The smallest combinations of speech sounds that have meaning in a given language are called **morphemes.** They include words that can stand alone, such as *big, small, car, odd;* prefixes, such as *un-, anti-, pre-;* and suffixes, such as *-ed, -er, -ly.* Many of the words in the English language are made up of combinations of morphemes. The word *unquestionable,* for example, is made up of the prefix *un-* meaning "not," the root word *question,* and the suffix *-able* meaning "capable of being."

Most authorities agree that to know a natural language, such as Enlgish, is to know a set of rules for generating and understanding the sentences of that language. These rules govern the grammatical structure or word-order relationships that characterize sentences of a natural language. For example, in English, "John hit the ball" is acceptable, whereas "hit John ball the" is not. All natural languages involve structure, even though the grammatical rules may differ from one language to another. These rules, called **syntactic rules,** serve as the means of translating morphemes into meaningful phrases and sentences.

The knowledge represented by syntactic rules constitutes implicit or tacit knowledge; for the most part, these rules were not explicitly taught to us, nor can we explicitly teach them to someone else. The notion that language use is governed by a tacit set of rules may seem strange, but this assumption appears to be required to account for the creativity that is characteristic of natural language. As we noted earlier, most utterances we produce and understand are ones we have never produced or heard before. Furthermore, we can continue to generate such novel utterances almost without limit.

A simple example serves to illustrate one aspect of the creativity that characterizes natural language. Suppose you said that your favorite number is the number seven. You could, of course, have picked any other number. Now, because there are an infinite number of numbers, there also are an infinite number of possible utterances concerning a favorite number. A sentence of potentially infinite length can be seen in the following example: "When she got up she put on her clothes, then she fed her cats, then she had breakfast, then she met her friends, then she went to school, then she came home, then she had lunch, then . . . ." The creativity found in natural languages is certainly not limited to these simple examples. However, these examples do serve as an illustration of the way our implicit knowledge of syntactic rules allows us both to produce and to understand an infinite number of utterances.

Despite the fairly obvious creativity revealed in natural language, the importance of this creativity was recognized in a scientific way only comparatively recently (Chomsky, 1957). In part, this was because many utterances do not contain new words, and we might conclude that the supply of sentences must also be limited. The creativity that characterizes natural language may also escape notice because it implies that we are capable, in principle, of doing things that in fact we cannot do. Because our life span is finite, we cannot generate an infinite number of sentences or a sentence of infinite length. Not many years ago the notion that human beings could have the knowledge or competence required for an act that could never be manifest in performance would have been quickly rejected by psychologists. The distinguished linguist Noam Chomsky (1957) has drawn the distinction between **linguistic competence** and **linguistic performance.**

We have already illustrated one facet of the competence-performance distinction that arises because of our finite life span. A second facet of this distinction has a close parallel in arithmetic. The rules of arithmetic, unlike the rules of language, are explicitly taught to us. And once those rules are learned, there is no limit to the number of problems that can be solved using those rules, beyond the limit imposed by our finite life span. There is, however, a restriction that influences arithmetic performance as opposed to arithmetic competence. Suppose you were asked to multiply two six-digit numbers. Without paper and pencil or a calculator you probably could not provide the solution, even though you clearly have the competence to do so. The constraint in this case is due to the limited capacity of our short-term memory, as we saw in chapter 8.

The limited capacity of short-term memory also influences language use. This sentence, ''The man the dog bit died,'' is an example of what linguists call an **embedded construction** because one sentence, ''The dog bit the man,'' is embedded within another sentence, ''The man died.'' This embedded construction is easily understood even though the related elements, *the man* and *died,* become separated as a result of the embedding. However, embedding cannot occur repeatedly and still result in a comprehensible sentence because of the load placed on short-term memory. For example, consider this sentence: ''The pen the author the editor liked used was new.'' Given paper and pencil and enough time, you would discover that ''the pen was new,'' ''the editor like the author,'' and the ''the author used the pen.'' The point is that because of short-term memory constraints, the competence we may have for understanding certain sentence constructions may not be realized in performance.

Grammars as Theories

The set of syntactic rules that describes any particular language constitutes the **grammar** of that language. Linguists attempt to write grammars for each natural language, although the set of rules that applies to English or any other natural language is far from being fully worked out. Some syntactic rules are unique to a particular language or set of related languages, while others may be common to most if not all languages. Rules common to all languages are called **linguistic universals.**

According to Chomsky (1957), the grammars that linguists write are best considered as **theories of linguistic competence;** that is, they are theories about the implicit knowledge that language users have. As such, these grammars must be capable of generating *all* and *only* the grammatical sentences found in a given language: they must account for the notion of infinitely many sentences and sentences of infinite length. As theories of competence as opposed to performance, they ignore human limitations such as finite life span and a limited capacity short-term memory. While grammars must be capable of generating infinitely many sentences, they must do so with a finite number of syntactic rules. And because languages are mastered over a relatively short period of time, there must be some limit on the number of rules contained in a grammar.

Primary sources of data used by linguists in writing grammars are the linguistic skills manifested by language users. Careful observation of linguistic

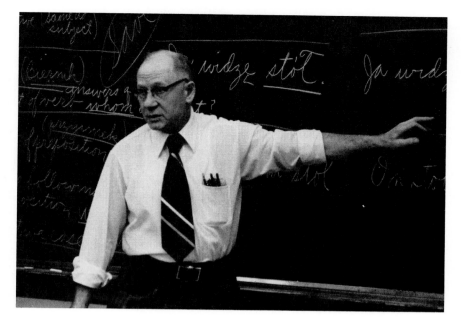

Each language has its own syntactic rules. Because languages are learned over a relatively short period of time, there must be some limit on the number of rules contained in a grammar.

performance thus aids the linguist in writing theories of linguistic competence. For example, one fairly common observation in linguistic performance is when the meaning a speaker intends to convey is not the same as the meaning actually conveyed to a listener. Unfortunately, this happens all too often in human communication, be it in the classroom, in the home, or elsewhere.

Consider the sentences given below, each of which is ambiguous in terms of its meaning:

(1) The sailors like the port.
(2) Flying planes can be dangerous.
(3) The shooting of the hunters was dreadful.

Sentence (1) illustrates **lexical ambiguity** because the word *port* can refer to either a type of wine or a harbor. Such ambiguities are not particular interesting because we are all aware that many English words have more than one meaning. However, the ambiguities revealed in sentences (2) and (3) are interesting. Sentence (2) can mean that either the act of flying planes is dangerous or the planes themselves are dangerous. Similarly, sentence (3) can refer to hunters being shot or to hunters being very poor at shooting. The fact that we can detect such ambiguities, not whether we usually notice them or not, is what is important here. This observation led linguists to distinguish between surface structure and deep structure. The **surface structure** refers to the form of the sentence we actually hear. The **deep structure** refers to the meaning of the sentence intended by the speaker. As sentences (2) and (3) illustrate, a single surface structure may have more than one deep structure, and it is the deep structure that determines the meaning of the sentence.

Just as one surface structure may result from more than one deep structure, the same deep structure can lead to more than one surface structure. Look at sentences (4) and (5) below. We all know that these two sentences mean exactly the same thing—that is, they have different surface structures based on the same deep structure:

(4) Mary sold the car.
(5) The car was sold by Mary.

Let us consider one more example of our linguistic skill before turning to a discussion of the form of syntactic rules. Sentences (6) and (7) below are

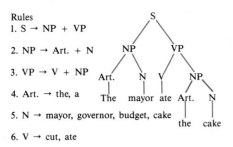

Rules
1. S → NP + VP

2. NP → Art. + N

3. VP → V + NP

4. Art. → the, a

5. N → mayor, governor, budget, cake

6. V → cut, ate

Figure 9.5

Tree diagram of phase structure rules and the way they are used to generate the sentence "The mayor ate the cake."

identical except for the words *eager* and *easy*. Yet speakers of English know that they are quite different in meaning.

(6) John is eager to please.
(7) John is easy to please.

Sentence (6), in which *John* is the logical subject, means that John is eager to please someone. However, sentence (7), where John is the logical object, means that it is easy for someone to please John. Observations such as these have led linguists to propose particular types of grammatical rules for natural language.

Phrase Structure and Transformational Rules

Contemporary approaches to the development of grammars usually begin with a **constituent analysis** of the sentence. The sentence serves as the basic unit of analysis and is broken down into its various components or constituents. The objective of constituent analysis is to identify the **phrase structure rules** that characterize a particular language.

An illustration of phrase structure rules and of the way they are used to generate a sentence is given in Figure 9.5. The diagram shown in the figure is called a tree diagram. The various levels shown in a tree diagram, going from top to bottom, represent the application of phrase structure rules in order to generate a particular sentence ("the mayor ate the cake"). The symbol (S), at the top, stands for sentence, and the arrow in Rule 1 means that whatever appears to the left is rewritten, or translated into whatever appears on the right—in this case noun phrase + verb phrase.

Notice that only a single element is rewritten at each step. By using Rule 1 we translate S into NP + VP, which is equivalent to subject plus predicate. Rule 2 translates the NP as Article (Art.) + Noun (N), and rule 3 rewrites VP into Verb (V) + NP. Applying the remaining rules gives us the surface structure of this sentence.

Quite obviously this illustration of using phrase structure rules is simplified: it does, however, show how a sentence can be generated according to these rules. In fact, even with the limited vocabulary provided in this illustration, several sentences can be generated. Thus, either the mayor or the governor or a mayor or a governor can "eat the cake" or "cut the budget." Clearly these rules are not sufficient by themselves because they also allow ungrammatical strings such as "The cake cut the budget."

Figures 9.6 and 9.7 illustrate the way constituent analysis can be applied to reveal the ambiguity of a sentence. In both cases the sentence (S) breaks down into a noun phrase (NP) and a verb phrase (VP), and the NP is translated into the pronoun *they*. However, in Figure 9.6 the main verb is *are*, which indicates that the pronoun refers to the planes. In Figure 9.7, *are* is an auxiliary verb, and the main verb is *flying*. Therefore, the pronoun refers to whomever is doing the flying.

Another type of phrase structure rule that is not shown in Figure 9.5 is of considerable importance. This rule is called a **recursive rule** because the symbol on the left also occurs on the right. For example, a rule such as S → NP + (S) + VP would allow embedding of one sentence within another, as we saw in "the man the dog bit died." Of course, additional rules would be needed to delete the duplicate reference to "the man" when "the dog bit the man" is embedded within "the man died." In this example the parentheses around the (S) on the right are used to indicate that the embedding is optional rather than required.

What are called **transformational rules** play an important role in theories of linguistic competence. Sentences (8) and (9) shown below have the same

Figure 9.6

Constituent analysis of the sentence "They are flying planes," in which the main verb is are.

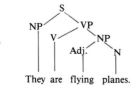

meaning, but it is both awkward and difficult to capture this fact with phrase structure rules alone.

(8) John kissed Mary.
(9) Mary was kissed by John.

To show that sentences (8) and (9) have the same meaning, linguists have turned to the use of transformational rules, which allow the deep structures generated by phrase structure rules to be modified before the surface structure form emerges. These transformational rules can be exceedingly complicated and are beyond the scope of our present coverage. However, they allow for various modifications in deep structure, such as rearrangement and addition of elements shown in going from sentence (8) to (9) as well as deletion of elements required when embedding the sentence ''the dog bit the man'' within the sentence ''the man died'' to produce ''the man the dog bit died.'' We do not say ''the man—the dog bit the man—died.''

With any reasonable vocabulary size, even a small number of these phrase structure and transformation rules will allow a large number of sentences to be generated. More important, when these rules are used in a theory of linguistic competence, they form the basis for explaining how words are grouped into phrases, how phrases are labeled in the surface structure (as NPs or VPs), and how meaningful relations may exist among words that do not occur together in the surface structure. In other words, these rules provide a way of understanding how the linguistic skills manifested by language users might come about. The use of these rules is not the only way to understand linguistic competence, however, as we shall see in subsequent sections.

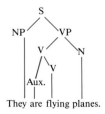

Figure 9.7

Constituent analysis of the sentence "They are flying planes," in which are *is an auxiliary verb, and* flying *is the main verb.*

Semantics and Syntax

When phrase structure and transformational rules were introduced, research suggested that these syntactic rules might play an important role in both sentence production and comprehension and even in memory for sentences as well. The basic idea was that a speaker would produce an utterance by unconsciously taking deep structures, which represent the meaning of a sentence, and applying the appropriate transformational rules to achieve the surface structure form. Of course, because the rules represent implicit knowledge, generation of a sentence would not involve a conscious application of the rules. The reverse of the production process would thus explain comprehension of a sentence by a listener. In other words, the surface structure form would be ''detransformed'' in order to recover the deep structure and, hence, the meaning of the utterance.

Although this theory is almost impossible to evaluate in the case of sentence production, a variety of experiments suggests that at least some aspects of the theory may characterize sentence comprehension. For example, it takes longer to comprehend the meaning of a sentence involving several transformational rules than one involving only one or two transformational rules (Miller, 1962). Thus, a simple declarative sentence such as ''the boy hit the girl'' should be understood more quickly than the passive question ''has the girl been hit by the boy?'' because the latter sentence involves both a passive transformational rule and a question transformational rule.

This theory can still be considered as providing a possible explanation for sentence production and initial comprehension of sentences. However, the explanation of what is subsequently stored in memory no longer holds. The notion was that if comprehension involved detransforming a surface structure to recover a deep structure, then sentence memory should involve recollection of both the deep structure and the transformational rules that were involved. However, research on comprehension and memory led to alternative conceptions of what is retained in memory.

In 1967, Jacqueline Sachs reported an important study that has a direct bearing on this issue. She had subjects listen to short stories and then tested their memory for a critical sentence. The story was constructed in such a way that the critical sentence could reasonably occur at several different places, thus providing several retention intervals. Depending on where the critical sentence occurred, the retention intervals were approximately 0 seconds, 27 seconds, or 46 seconds. Consider the three sentences below:

(10) He sent a letter about it to Galileo, the great Italian scientist.
(11) Galileo, the great Italian scientist, sent him a letter about it.
(12) A letter about it was sent to Galileo, the great Italian scientist.

Suppose sentence (10) actually appeared in the passage. Sentence (11) involves a change in meaning, while sentence (12) preserves the meaning but changes the syntactic form. After the entire story was heard, the subjects were shown sentences such as those given above and were asked whether or not they had heard the exact sentence.

When the test sentence immediately followed the critical sentence, the subjects were likely to detect a change. That is, with zero delay both semantic and syntactic changes were detected. However, at other delay intervals, detection of semantic changes was close to 90 percent, while detection of syntactic changes dropped to nearly chance levels. These findings led Sachs to propose a cognitive-processing model in which the original form of the sentence is retained only briefly. As soon as the meaning of the sentence has been captured, the syntactic form is forgotten. In other words, what is usually important in memory for language is the ''gist'' of what was said and not the particular syntactic form used. A recent study using deaf subjects and American Sign Language sentences also supports this conclusion (Hanson & Bellugi, 1982). In this study changes in semantic content of the sentences were more readily detected than were paraphrases that preserved sentence meaning.

John Bransford and Jeffrey Franks (1971) reported that memory for a particular sentence depends more on the meaning of the content than it does on the syntactic form. They took sentences composed of four basic elements for their experimental materials. For example, the sentence ''The rock rolled down the mountain and crushed the tiny hut at the edge of the woods'' contains the elements ''the rock rolled down the mountain,'' ''the rock crushed the hut,'' ''the hut was tiny,'' and ''the hut was at the edge of the woods.'' These four elements were presented to subjects either singly or in combinations such as ''tiny hut was at the edge of the woods.''

In the learning phase of the experiment, twenty-four sentences consisting of one, two, or three elements were presented to the subjects. Each sentence presented was derived in the manner just described from one of several four-element sentences. However, the four-element sentences were not presented. The memory test phase consisted of reading a number of sentences to the subjects and asking them to indicate which ones they had heard in the learning phase. The sentences presented in the memory test consisted of some of those previously presented (old) and some not presented previously (new). The new sentences included the four-element sentences from which both the old and new sentences were derived and some mixed sentences composed of elements taken from otherwise unrelated four-element sentences. For example, if one four-element sentence was about ''the rock rolling down the mountain'' and another was about ''ants eating jelly in the kitchen,'' a mixed sentence might be the one in (13).

(13) The rock rolled down the mountain and crushed the ants eating in the kitchen.

CHAPTER 9   LANGUAGE

The subjects were most likely to call a sentence "old" if it contained all four elements, even though no four-element sentences had been presented previously. In addition, three-element sentences, whether they were old or new, were more likely to be called old than two-element sentences. One-element sentences were least likely to be called old. The mixed sentences, however, were not confused with previously presented sentences: they were called new consistently.

The results (see Figure 9.8) of the Bransford and Franks study point strongly to contextual factors in abstracting the meaning of linguistic materials. The subjects were able to integrate the four basic elements from each four-element sentence into a single whole, despite the fact that sentences containing all four elements had not been presented. Once this mental integration had taken place, the subjects stored the entire four-element unit in memory and responded to each test sentence in terms of how closely it approximated the four-element unit.

Since the pioneering work reported by Sachs (1967) and Bransford and Franks (1971), evidence has accumulated supporting the importance of semantic as opposed to syntactic factors in the processing of linguistic materials. Much of this evidence relates to the role of context, and we shall examine some of it later in this chapter. For the moment, it is sufficient to point out that memory storage for linguistic material seems to rely on the type of semantic organization discussed in chapter 8, even though initial comprehension may also depend to an important degree on syntactic structures.

Figure 9.8

In a memory test, Bransford and Franks found that the degree of confidence that a sentence had been seen before depends on the number of familiar elements in that sentence. The greater the number of familiar elements the higher the rate of recall. Results of this kind support the importance of content as opposed to syntactic factors in memory (after Bransford & Franks, 1971).

Language Acquisition

Given the complexity that appears to characterize most aspects of natural language, it is rather remarkable that children learn language with such apparent ease. Indeed, available evidence suggests that children learn language with little or no systematic training.

Children acquire the sounds of speech quite readily. When these sounds are combined to produce words, children use these first words very efficiently. Children often use extra-linguistic context to expand the syntax of the message. In this way single words can be used in a variety of contexts to produce different messages.

Adult observers tend to interpret children's speech in terms of adult language. These twins were thought to be retarded because they spoke only "gibberish." However, when the gibberish was analyzed, it was found to have the components of language that allowed the twins to communicate effectively with each other.

Infants as young as one month of age can distinguish among some speech sounds before they can actually produce those sounds.

Gradually children add new rules, although the form of these rules is usually simpler than the adult form. Children also appear to develop strategies for encoding and decoding messages. These strategies grow in complexity as they develop. The content of what children talk about is directly related to their level of cognitive development. What is interesting about language development is that it appears to be unrelated to efforts to teach language. Even though adults adjust their language when talking to children, there is little evidence that children attempt to imitate others. Children as young as 4 years of age do, however, adjust their speech when talking to younger children. Children also appear to formulate broad rules and strategies for understanding and producing utterances. Despite the fact that individual children do vary, the formulation of these rules and strategies is quite regular both between children and across languages (Palermo, 1978).

Although the apparent ease with which children learn language is well known to all of us, the specific details of language development are not well established. Apart from the complexity of language, there are other reasons for this lack of knowledge. Most evidence concerning language development is necessarily observational or clinical in nature, particularly in the case of young children and infants. Such evidence is subject to misinterpretation by adult observers who tend to interpret children's speech in terms of adult language classifications. Adequate experimental evidence on language acquisition is difficult to get because young children and infants have severely limited attention spans.

Acquisition of Language Production

During babbling, speech sounds are produced according to a very definite pattern that seems to be comparable in most languages.

One general characteristic of language acquisition is that comprehension precedes production. This relationship between comprehension and production holds for all aspects of language including speech sounds, syntactic structures, and semantic interpretations or meaning. For example, infants as young as one month of age can distinguish between speech sounds such as /ba/ and /ga/ long before they can produce those sounds. Infants also can distinguish speech sounds from nonspeech sounds at very early ages (Molfese, 1972). The differential sensitivity of the left and right hemispheres of the brain to speech versus nonspeech sounds is present as early as the first week after birth (Palermo, 1978). Thus, it appears that the infant knows which sounds are speech sounds and which are not, essentially from birth.

On the production side, among the first characteristics of speech to be noted in the babbling of infants appears to be the intonation contour or rhythmic structure of utterances. Infants produce sound sequences that have recognizable intonation contours such as those characterizing questions or declarative statements (Lenneberg, 1967). It is likely that further development of the motor system is required before the fine movements needed for production of phonemes take place.

Once children do begin to produce phonemes with any appreciable frequency, vowel sounds occur most often. In fact, equality in the frequency of consonant and vowel sounds does not occur until around 30 months of age. After that, the relative frequency of consonant sounds increases dramatically as the children begin to produce words, phrases, and more complex utterances.

At one time it was thought that infants babbled all speech sounds but retained only those that occurred in their own language. However, that does not appear to be the case. During babbling, speech sounds are produced according to a very definite pattern that appears to be comparable across most, if not all, languages. Interestingly, the most common speech sounds produced in the first year of life, involving front vowels and back consonants, are among the last speech sounds to be included in word production. During the second year of life, when most children are producing recognizable speech, the most common speech sounds involve the consonants produced at the front of the mouth and the vowels produced in the back of the mouth. Thus, children speaking English say *tut* before *cut*, German children say *topf* before *kopf*, and Japanese-speaking children say *ta* before *ka* (Jakobson, 1968; McNeill, 1970).

The fact that comprehension precedes production, particularly between 1-1/2 and 3 years of age, suggests that language acquisition is not dependent on motor coordination. A young child who can't name the animals yet but can point to them if an adult names them is an example of the relative superiority of comprehensional skills. Of course there are maturational factors in phoneme and word production. Also, speech development is quite different from the development of other motor activities. Although speech develops with no particular training, most other motor skills, such as piano playing, require years of intensive training. In fact, speech (like walking) seems to have a basic maturational basis.

When children begin to utter meaningful speech, the majority of utterances consist of single words. This stage of development has been termed **holophrastic speech.** The utterances consist mainly of nouns and adjectives, with verbs appearing later in development. Students of language acquisition consider the holophrastic stage to be one in which single words are used to express relatively complex ideas. For example, the utterance "milk" may signify that the child "wants more milk" or that the child "sees a milk bottle" or even that "some milk has been spilled." In effect, an apparently simple word such as *milk* acts as a comment on some extralinguistic context that serves as the topic for that comment. However, quite different topics or situations may elicit the same comment with quite different messages intended by the infant.

Although it is interesting to speculate about the structures represented by holophrastic speech, it is only when words are combined that speech becomes noticeably grammatical. This period usually occurs around 18 months of age. Studying the acquisition of grammatical structures in young children is often a rather tedious task. Typical investigations involve recording utterances of children for several months and then attempting to determine the grammatical rules that characterize these utterances.

Acquisition of Grammatical Structure

When children first combine words, considerable evidence exists to indicate that they are using some kind of a system to construct utterances: even at this early stage, children do not combine words or order words at random. The task facing investigators of language acquisition is to unravel the system used to construct the utterances and to determine how that system is acquired.

Imitation and Grammatical Development

Before turning to imitation per se, we should consider what is available for children to imitate. That is, what language do they hear? Adults speak to children quite differently than they do to other adults. The sentences used by adults are well formed, but they are much shorter and simpler than those found in conversations between adults. With very young children, adults also slow their rate of speaking and use a great deal of repetition. In fact, adults seem to adjust the complexity of what they say to a child. As a child's mastery of language increases, the complexity of what an adult says increases. This appears to be the case irrespective of who the adults are (parents or others) or the language being spoken. Furthermore, there is not much difference between the speech of mother to child and the speech of one child to another child of the same age (Slobin, 1975).

Children demonstrate comprehensional skills by pointing to objects they cannot yet name.

ⓐ holophrastic
ⓐ jellographic

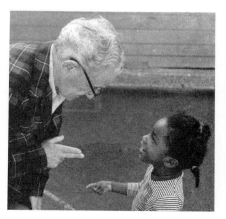

In conversations with young children, adults slow their rate of speaking and use repetition.

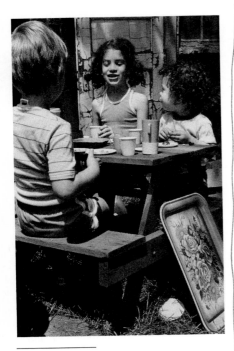

Children learn language through imitation; in playing together they often acquire the vocabulary of their playmates.

Although our knowledge of the way adults speak to children is quite extensive, we do not know a great deal about the way children use adult speech. The language environment that adults provide for children would seem ideal for learning language by imitation. However, the question of what is learned by imitation is difficult to answer.

There is little doubt that imitation plays a role in language acquisition. Children learn the language they are exposed to, and they acquire the vocabulary that they hear. However, children also produce utterances such as "all gone shoe" or "higher the swing" that they have never heard an adult say. Notice that the latter expression reflects the child's use of a rule. The reasoning process seems to go as follows: *high* means up, and *low* means down; therefore, if you can say "lower the swing," you should be able to say "higher the swing," as well.

Imitation and rule learning can both be seen even in the use of single words. When English-speaking children first use the past tense form of irregular verbs, they generally use them correctly and say "came," "went," "did," and so on. These verbs are common in adult speech, and it would not be surprising to find that children imitate them. However, regular verbs that use *-ed* to form the past tense are more numerous overall. Once children learn the rule for forming the past tense of these regular verbs, they generalize it to all verbs and say things like "comed," "goed, "or "doed" (Ervin-Tripp, 1964). In this case the child switches from a previously correct and supposedly reinforced form of the verb to an incorrect form that has never been heard in adult speech.

Beyond the level of single words, it is not clear what the child imitates. There is little evidence to indicate that the child imitates the syntactic form of adult speech, and adults do not seem to pay much attention to the syntactic form of child speech (Brown & Hanlon, 1970). For example, parents may accept utterances such as "he a girl" or "her curl my hair" but reject "the animal farmhouse" because the building that the child is talking about is a lighthouse. Apparently most corrections of children's speech by parents occur on nonsyntactic grounds.

Syntax

Early attempts to characterize the utterances of young children focused on the syntactic structure of these utterances; investigators attempted to specify classes of words used by children and then to develop rules to combine words (Braine, 1963; McNeill, 1970). The emphasis in this approach was on a set of rules for combining words and not on the meaning of the utterances. An example of this approach was David McNeill's (1970) effort to characterize the speech of a 28-month-old child, Adam.

McNeill was able to classify Adam's vocabulary into three categories: nouns (N), verbs (V), and pivots (P). The pivot class was heterogeneous in terms of classifications used for adult speech. McNeill then proposed three syntactic rules to describe Adam's utterances. The rules are given below and, as you will notice, they are similar to the phrase structure rules discussed previously. The use of parentheses indicates an optional element that may appear in an utterance but is not required:

S → NP and/or VP
NP → (P) N or NN
VP → (V) NP

Examples of utterances permitted by these rules include "ball," "that ball," "Adam ball," "Adam want ball," and "Adam mommy pencil." McNeill reports that these three rules described all of Adam's two- and three-word utterances. Even expressions such as "come eat pablum," which we might expect the child to imitate, do not appear in Adam's speech.

While McNeill's report is impressive, a major problem arises with all attempts to characterize these early utterances on the basis of syntactic rules alone. The problem arises from the fact that when a given expression is used by a child on more than one occasion it should always have the same meaning. However, as the following example shows, this is not always true of the utterances of young children. Lois Bloom (1970) reported that one child she studied used the expression "mommy sock" in two quite different contexts. In one case the expression was used when the child picked up her mother's sock; the other instance occurred when the mother was putting a sock on the child. Clearly the child was using the same words and word order to express quite different grammatical relationships. As with one-word utterances, it is necessary to consider the context of an utterance as well as the utterance itself in interpreting the child's speech.

Acquisition of Semantic Structure

Since Bloom's work, a number of investigations have dealt with the same issues. These studies indicate that early utterances of young children represent attempts to express grammatical relations that are quite different from those proposed by McNeill (1970) and others. These grammatical relations are called **case relations,** and they emphasize the semantic structure of the utterance, not just the syntactic form (Fillmore, 1968).

A sentence like "John hit the ball" illustrates both the agentive case and the objective case. The agentive case is expressed by indicating that a noun (John) is the agent or instigator of the action; the objective case is expressed when the role or state of a noun (the ball) depends on the meaning of the verb. In an utterance expressing the locative case, such as "the book was on the shelf," a noun (the shelf) indicates the location of a state or action. For a young child the expression "John ball" might reflect both the agentive and objective cases with the verb omitted.

Much of the early speech of young children can be characterized in terms of a relatively small number of case relations, perhaps six or eight (Bowerman, 1973). Even one-word utterances have been successfully analyzed in terms of case relations identified by context (Greenfield & Smith, 1976). In a cross-cultural study, Martin Braine (1976) looked at two-word combinations in the speech of English, Samoan, Finnish, Hebrew, and Swedish children. All the children expressed the three case relations illustrated above (agentive, objective, and locative), and while other case relations were observed, not all children used them all. As you might expect, different children tend to talk about different things. In one study, children tended to fall into one of two general categories: one group talked mainly about themselves and other people; the other group talked about objects around them (Nelson, 1973).

The emphasis on semantic considerations expressed in case relations is also congruent with the view that children use nonlinguistic information, such as prior knowledge of the world, in understanding language and in learning language (Macnamara, 1972). For instance, look at the four sentences below.

(14) Give the book to me.
(15) Give me the book.
(16) John hit Bill.
(17) Bill hit John.

✳ RESEARCH

An important part of the study of language acquisition in children is the nature of semantic development. Within this domain, an issue that is receiving increasing attention from researchers is that of underextension in children's use of concepts. For example, a child may readily apply the category label *bird* to a picture of a robin or sparrow but not to a chicken or duck. This failure to use the category label *bird* when referring to a chicken or a duck is an instance of underextension.

One common explanation for underextension is based on the prototypic feature theory (Rosch, 1975) which was discussed in chapter 8. According to this theory, natural concepts like *bird* are organized around prototypic features that are most representative of the concept or category. Instances of the category that share many features with the prototype are called typical instances of the category and are often assigned the category name, for example, *bird.* Instances that share only some features with the prototype are called atypical instances and are less likely to be assigned the category name. The issue that arises in studies of semantic development is why underex-

---

Underextension in Child

Language

---

tension occurs in children for atypical instances of a category but not for typical instances. Does underextension occur because atypical instances are perceptually less like the prototype than is the case for typical instances? Or, does underextension occur because adult naming practices are such that category labels like *bird* tend to be used with typical instances but not with atypical instances?

Thomas G. White (1982) has reported an investigation whose results relate to these questions. The first part of this investigation involved pictured instances from six common categories: animal, bird, food, clothing, plant, and furniture. The instances were either typical of the category or atypical. For the bird category, robin and bluejay were typical instances,

while turkey and chicken were atypical. Children ranging in age from 3 to 5 years were given two tasks. In one they were shown each pictured instance and asked if it came from the appropriately named category. There were also pictured objects that did not come from the category (noninstances) so that the children could not respond yes all the time. In the second task the children were shown pairs of items from the same category and were asked to indicate which member of the pair was most like the category label (for example, most like a bird).

The results of the second task clearly indicated that the children could distinguish between typical and atypical instances of all six categories. However, the results of the first task showed considerable underextension in the use of category labels as had been found previously. In the bird category underextension was not found at all for robin or bluejay but was common for turkey (70 percent) and for chicken (45 percent).

The second part of White's investigation examined naming practices of mothers in the presence of their children. The focus here was on the way pairs of instances from the same cat-

Notice that in (14) and (15) the order of the words "me" and "book" are reversed, but the sentences have the same meaning. However, in (16) and (17) the change in word order results in a semantic change as well. A child's ability to interpret correctly such changes is based on the knowledge that books can be given to people but people cannot be given to books. Thus, a child uses this nonlinguistic information to decide what semantic information was intended.

Semantic considerations in language acquisition raise an important issue concerning the relationship between language development and cognitive development. Although the evidence is somewhat sketchy, it appears that the earliest semantic relations expressed in children's speech have parallels in children's cognitive functioning as described by Jean Piaget (see chapter 6). During the sensorimotor period, for example, utterances about possession, location, recurrence, and other semantic relations are occurring (Brown, 1973). However, children do not use time-related linguistic structure (past, present, and future tense) before they have developed an adequate concept of time (Clark, 1971).

egory would be labeled when both instances were typical (robin, bluejay), atypical (turkey, chicken), or mixed (robin, turkey). In general, the results indicated that adult naming practices are quite systematic. The use of category labels was four times more likely to occur with typical than with atypical instances. Category labels are also more likely to be assigned to both members of a pair when both members are typical instances. In terms of specific examples, the following seem likely: turkey will be called a turkey, but a robin has a good chance of being called a bird; mothers are likely to call a tree a tree, but a fern may be called a plant; boots and mittens are usually called boots and mittens; and, while meat and peas are often called food, candy and ketchup are called candy and ketchup.

In the third part of this investigation White studied both degree of typicality of instances within a category and type of naming practice used. The category instances were pictures of fictitious animals made from Play-Doh. Two categories of animals were used: typical instances of each category had the same shape as one other typical instance and the same color as one other typical instance. Atypical instances had a unique shape and a unique color.

Kindergarten children were trained on the instances of one category and tested on instances from both categories. During training, pairs of instances were presented on each trial, and the naming practices emphasized either the use of category labels (superordinates) or the use of specific instance names.

As a test for underextension the children were shown each category instance and were asked if it was a member of the appropriately named category. If the answer was no the child was asked to name the instance. Following this test the children were shown pairs of instances with one being typical and the other atypical. They were then asked which instance was most like the appropriately named category (most typical).

The results of this study showed effects of both typicality and naming practices. When the children were trained using conventional naming practices in which pairs of typical items are usually assigned the category label and atypical items are assigned a specific name, underextension to atypical instances is quite common. That is, following conventional training, atypical instances usually are assigned a specific name rather than the category label and the typical instances are judged as best representing the category. However, following unconventional naming practices during training, very different results are found. When training emphasizes naming pairs of atypical instances with the category label and pairs of typical instances with the specific names, the children are more likely to reject typical instances as members of the category and accept atypical instances. Even when asked which of a typical and an atypical instance is most like the category labelled, they tend to favor the atypical member of the pair.

The results of these experiments when taken together clearly suggest an important role for adult naming practices in cases of underextension. The most important finding comes from the third experiment in which it was shown that unconventional naming practices could reverse the usual observation of underextension for atypical instances. In this case underextension was more common with typical instances that shared more features with the prototype. ■

Biological Basis for Language

In view of the enormous complexity of natural languages and the relative ease with which children learn these languages, it is not surprising to find that a number of writers (Lenneberg, 1967; Chomsky, 1965; McNeill, 1970) have suggested that there is an innate biological basis for language acquisition. Eric Lenneberg (1967) has also argued for a "critical period" in language acquisition similar to the critical period observed in behaviors such as song learning and imprinting (see chapter 7). The idea is that from sometime after birth (perhaps around age 2) until the time of puberty, when a number of biological changes occur, children are biologically prepared for language learning irrespective of the type of training they are given.

The biological basis of language learning is far from established, although there are a number of lines of supporting evidence. The observation that children show lateralization in the perception of speech sounds essentially from birth strongly suggests a biological or innate component of phonology, even though the motor development and coordination necessary for speech production take time to occur. Although languages differ remarkably in surface structure form, there are notable consistencies across languages. These language universals include syntactic rules relating deep structures to surface structures, the basic categories of subject and predicate of a sentence, and the consistent use across languages of subject-verb-object relationships.

Perhaps the most basic reason for believing that children are biologically prepared for language learning is that they learn languages of enormous complexity with such relative ease. Psychologists and linguists have been working for many years to determine the structures that characterize natural languages. Yet at least some of these structures seem to be apparent to children at a very early age, and others become apparent with little or no specific training.

Language Use in Adults

We do not give much conscious thought to the way we use language; we talk and we listen without being aware of the complex interrelated actions of our brains and speech programs. Further, we attend to content in speaking and hearing without much awareness of the form of our communication. Nevertheless, highly developed skills are at work in our use of language.

Subjective experience tells us that when we are speaking we are generally aware of the thoughts we are attempting to express but often are not aware of the particular grammatical constructions (sentence types) that we are using. Rarely do we attend to the particular lexical units we will utter more than two or three words in advance. In fact, James G. Martin (1971) has shown that during spontaneous speech, speakers pause more frequently before high information content words (nouns, verbs) than before low information function words (articles, prepositions, conjunctions). This observation suggests that, at least in some cases, word selection does not take place until the word needs to be produced by the speaker.

For a further example of automaticity in speech production, suppose you have memorized a prose passage or poem very thoroughly. Subsequent recitation of this passage requires very little thought or attention. In fact, you probably could recite the passage with little or no error while thinking at the same time about entirely unrelated ideas.

This observation should come as no surprise because the generative processes involved in sentence production are thought to be guided by tacit knowledge in the form of syntactic rules. Because this knowledge is implicit, and because the rules operate hierarchically, there is little reason to believe we should be consciously aware of their use in generating utterances. Much the same can be said about the phonological rules used to translate words and phrases into perceivable speech sounds during fluent speech. For the fluent speaker these production rules constitute a motor program that can run with little or no attentional control. For instance, it is quite common for parents to read stories to young children and have little recollection of what they have read.

The automaticity that characterizes so much of human speech does not imply that speech occurs without error. Sometimes errors are observed and corrected by the speaker; at other times they pass unnoticed. Speech errors are observed at many levels ranging from phonological to syntactic to semantic. At the phonological level, errors may involve interchange of syllables (butterpillar and catterfly) or interchange of individual phonemes (the nipper is zarrow). According to Merrill Garrett (1975), interchanges of this sort typically occur within a single phrase. For instance, Garrett reports the following error pattern:

"Children interfere with your nife lite" (night life). This example also illustrates a general characteristic of phonological errors, namely, that interchanges tend to occur among words that are similar in sound. An amusing illustration of such an interchange was observed when someone inquiring about a furnished apartment asked if it came with "rapes and drugs" instead of "drapes and rugs."

Speech errors of a syntactic or semantic nature are difficult, if not impossible, to disentangle. Purely syntactic errors presumably result from failure to apply syntactic rules correctly for translating mental representations into sentences. However, particular examples of such errors are often difficult to classify. An example cited by Donald Foss and David Hakes (1978) is: "Every time I put one of these buttons off, another one comes on." Here the interchange of the words *on* and *off* could result from either a syntactic or a semantic error.

Both syntactic and semantic errors occur when a speaker's attention is overloaded or distracted. For instance, when our thoughts "come too fast" the organized activity characteristic of fluent speech often fails. Similar disruptions of ongoing speech occur when our attention is diverted because of some distraction.

A particularly extreme illustration of failure of cognitive control can be found in schizophrenic speech. This form of speech, which is illustrated in chapter 14, has often been characterized as "word salad": individual words or, more commonly, phrases, are perfectly intact, but sequences of phrases do not form any coherent pattern. The schizophrenic speaker seems unable to control attention, and there is a fragmentation of experience, thought, and memories (Blumenthal, 1977).

Language Comprehension

As we have seen, the process of language comprehension involves those cognitive activities normally associated with thinking. The work of Sachs (1967), as well as Bransford and Franks (1971), indicates that language perceivers do more than store verbatim copies of the materials to which they are exposed. Both investigations suggest an active process of abstraction in which the essential meaning of an utterance, but not its formal syntactic structure, is represented in memory. A considerable body of evidence now exists to suggest that language comprehension involves fairly complex interactions among (1) various components of the materials presented, (2) the implications or possible implications of those materials, and (3) the relationship between the materials presented and an individual's general knowledge of the world. Among the factors that influence these interactions are inference, general knowledge and prior context, and schemata.

Inference

When we are exposed to language, written or spoken, we commonly draw conclusions about what we were exposed to that go beyond a literal interpretation. If you were presented with a sentence such as the one discussed earlier in this chapter and at a later time you were asked whether the man died because of the dog's bite, you might very well say yes.

(18) The man the dog bit died.

This is an example of drawing an inference from a sentence that goes beyond the literal meaning of that sentence. Sentence (18), you will recall, is constructed by embedding one sentence (The dog bit the man) within another sentence (The man died): there is no necessary implication that the dog's bite caused the man's death. The speaker could have uttered the sentence in that manner to simply identify which man was being discussed.

Bransford, Richard Barclay, and Franks (1972) studied inferences being drawn from sentences by presenting subjects with sentences like (19) and (20) below.

(19) Three turtles rested *on* a log and a fish swam under *it*.
(20) Three turtles rested *beside* a log and a fish swam under *it*.

After exposure to a number of sentences such as (19) or (20) the subjects were given a recognition test that included sentences they had seen previously as well as others they had not seen. Among the new sentences were ones like (21) and (22).

(21) Three turtles rested *on* a log and a fish swam under *them*.
(22) Three turtles rested *beside* a log and a fish swam under *them*.

Subjects presented with a sentence like (19) falsely concluded that they had also seen sentence (21), whereas subjects shown sentence (20) rarely made the mistake of thinking they had previously seen sentence (22) as well. What we see here is a situation in which individuals often cannot discriminate between a sentence they have seen before and a sentence that can be logically inferred from the previously seen sentence.

A related example of inference that does not depend on strict logic was reported by Walter Kintsch (1976). Kintsch and his associates had subjects read short paragraphs such as those shown in (23) and (24).

(23) A carelessly discarded burning cigarette started a fire. The fire destroyed many acres of virgin forest.
(24) A burning cigarette was carelessly discarded. The fire destroyed many acres of virgin forest.

On a subsequent retention test they were asked to indicate whether statements such as (25) were true or false.

(25) A discarded cigarette started a fire.

Notice that in (23) there is an explicit connection between the discarded cigarette and the fire. However, in (24) this relationship is only implicit. Nevertheless, subjects exposed to either (23) or (24) almost always indicated that (25) was true.

General Knowledge and Prior Context

The examples of inference mentioned above constitute a subclass of the effects of context on language comprehension. In those examples the context consists of the subjects' general knowledge about the concepts involved. For example, if the turtles rested *on* a log and a fish swam under it (the log), then the fish swam under them (the turtles) as well. The example of inference reported by Kintsch is less straightforward, but it depends on knowing that a fire was started, that a burning cigarette was discarded, and that something started the fire. From this the subjects inferred that the fire was started by the cigarette.

The following examples also illustrate the effects of knowledge and prior context. Read the short paragraph given in (26) below.

(26) With hocked gems financing him, our hero bravely defied all scornful laughter that tried to prevent his scheme. Your eyes deceive you, he had said, an egg not a table correctly typifies this unexplored planet. Now three sturdy sisters sought proof, forging along sometimes through calm vastness, yet more often over turbulent peaks and valleys. Days became weeks as many doubters spread fearful rumors about the edge. At last, from nowhere, welcome winged creatures appeared, signifying momentous success.

No doubt you had some difficulty making sense out of this passage. However, if you read the passage again and know that its title is "Christopher Columbus Discovering America," it will make a great deal of sense. The results of a study in which subjects were presented with just such passages, either with or without the title, indicated that subsequent recall of the passage was much better when the title had been presented (Dooling & Lachman, 1971).

This is an example of the role that memory or prior knowledge can play in language comprehension. The title activates the memories that allow the passage to be understood. While this illustration is quite extreme, it makes the point that language comprehension always involves some kind of interaction between the message being transmitted and what the listener already knows. Just as learning depends on contextual factors so does comprehension of language. As another illustration of the effects of context, read paragraph (27) below.

(27) If the balloons popped, the sound wouldn't be able to carry since everything would be too far away from the correct floor. A closed window would also prevent the sound from carrying, since most buildings tend to be well insulated. Since the whole operation depends on a steady flow of electricity, a break in the middle of the wire would also cause problems. Of course, the fellow could shout, but the human voice is not loud enough to carry that far. An additional problem is that a string could break on the instrument. Then there could be no accompaniment to the message. It is clear that the best situation would involve less distance. Then there would be fewer potential problems. With face-to-face contact, the least number of things could go wrong.

These co-workers share a general knowledge and understanding of the computer data they are discussing.

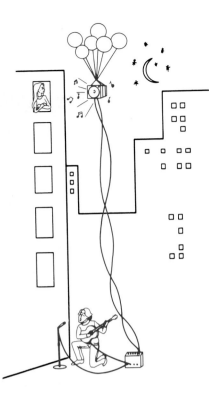

Figure 9.9

After you have studied this drawing of an "electronic serenade," go back and reread paragraph (27) and see whether the passage is easier to comprehend now that you have the relevant knowledge for understanding.

Again, you probably found this passage confusing. Now look at the picture in Figure 9.9, and then read the paragraph again. With the picture as context, the paragraph makes sense. Bransford and Marcia Johnson (1972) showed that with the appropriate context, subjects rated the paragraph as being more intelligible and recalled it better than without the picture context.

Both of the preceding examples illustrate important aspects of the use of language in communication. When attempting to communicate we all make assumptions about our audience: we assume certain general knowledge on the part of our audience; we make assumptions about the prior experiences of the person with whom we are communicating. The assumptions change as the audience changes. Different assumptions are made when talking to parents, friends, classmates, and teachers. Writers make assumptions about the background experiences of the readers of their books. If our assumptions about prior context are correct, we are much more likely to communicate what we intend than if our assumptions are incorrect.

Schemata and Comprehension

Among the assumptions we make about individuals with whom we are communicating are the presence and nature of certain schemata we expect our audience to possess. In chapter 8 schemata were loosely defined as organized bodies of information including beliefs and attitudes. The nature and organization of this information plays a major role in memory and in language comprehension as well. For example, if you tell someone about going to a certain restaurant and eating a good steak, you probably do not have to include any reference to ordering a steak. Unless the listeners lack a schema for "going to a restaurant," they will infer that you ordered the steak. However, this inference would not occur if your context was eating at a friend's home. The schema for "eating at a friend's home" does not usually include the notion of "ordering something."

In recent years psychologists have become quite interested in the role of very abstract schemata in processing language. Possible schemata that might be used in writing or comprehending stories are often called "story grammars." A schema might consist of a hierarchy of basic episodes for a story. At the top of the hierarchy the schema might include sections such as introduction, complication, and resolution. In the introduction the main characters are introduced. Various episodes in the introduction provide the setting for the main characters as well as background events relevant to the story. The basic ideas presented in the introduction are, therefore, organized under that part of our story schema. When we attempt to remember or paraphrase the story, these ideas or episodes are organized together.

The sections labeled "complication" and "resolution" contain those episodes describing the complications that occur in the life of the main character and, subsequently, the ways in which these complications are resolved. The basic assumption is that the reader will fill in the empty slots in the schema as the story unfolds. Our story schema is what allows us to comprehend and to organize a story we are reading; it also serves as a basis for deciding what counts as a good story. For instance, a story that does not develop in a way that is appropriate to our story schema is not likely to be appreciated by the reader or to be recalled very well (Rumelhart, 1975; Kintsch, 1977).

Different schema are required to comprehend different types of writing. Our story schema is fine for stories but not for reading scientific research reports. Schemata based on knowledge of the conventions of scientific writing will be necessary.

Abstract schemata are also subject to modification through experience—a child's story schema is likely to be quite different from that of an adult. Also, the nature of schemata is likely to be different in different cultures.

The Relationship Between Language and Thought

Human beings have demonstrably greater intellectual capacities than members of other species. To a large extent this superiority results from humans' capacity for thinking. Humans also have a unique system for communication—language—that serves as the primary vehicle for expressing thought. Therefore it is not surprising that psychologists are interested in the relationship between language and thought as well as the extent to which these aspects of cognition are uniquely human.

Various hypotheses concerning the relationship between language and thought have arisen in the history of psychology. One of the earliest views, proposed by John B. Watson (1913), was that language and thought were the same thing. According to Watson, thinking involved the same motor activities used in speaking: when we "think aloud," it is called speech; when we "speak covertly," it is called thinking. Too much contradictory evidence exists to take Watson's position seriously anymore. This evidence derives from the complex thought processes displayed by animals, nonspeaking humans, and humans who lose speech as a result of injury (Glucksberg & Danks, 1975). In addition, if thinking and speaking were the same activity, we would not correct ourselves while speaking by saying, "I didn't mean to say that."

The anthropologist-linguist Benjamin Lee Whorf (1956) proposed a sweeping, two-pronged hypothesis concerning language and thought. Whorf proposed first that all higher levels of thinking are dependent on language or that language determines thought (**linguistic determinism**). Because languages differ in many ways, Whorf also believed that speakers of different languages perceive and experience the world differently (**linguistic relativism**).

In short, his view was that the language we speak determines the way we perceive the world and hence the nature of thought. Whorf's views were based in part on a number of differences that he observed among languages used in various American Indian cultures. For instance, he noted that Eskimos have many words for *snow,* whereas most English speakers have only one. However, having only one name for snow does not mean that English speakers cannot perceive differences in varieties of snow. Any experienced skier, for example, is quite sensitive to a number of different types of snow.

In New Guinea there is a group of people called the Dani whose color names differ markedly from English. They use two names, *mili* (dark) and

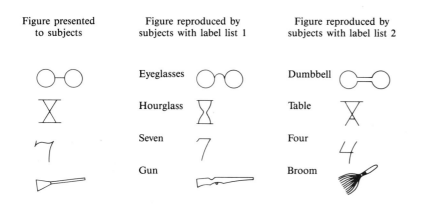

Figure presented to subjects	Figure reproduced by subjects with label list 1	Figure reproduced by subjects with label list 2
	Eyeglasses	Dumbbell
	Hourglass	Table
	Seven	Four
	Gun	Broom

Figure 9.10

Effects of verbal labels on memory for ambiguous figures. Subjects were presented with an ambiguous figure, as in column 1, along with a suggested label from either column 2 or column 3. In subsequent retention tests, descriptions of the figures were biased toward the description originally given.

THE RELATIONSHIP BETWEEN LANGUAGE AND THOUGHT

303

FOCUS

Language in Chimps

The use of natural language by human beings represents a unique system of communication. In no other species do we find a natural communication system that has the complexity and potential for creativity that characterizes human language. We have also seen that language plays a major role in human thinking and cognition. In fact, language plays such an important role for humans that it has often been argued that the cognitive processes required for language are uniquely human, that no other species is capable of mastering a skill as complex as human language. This claim is not without critics, and in recent years it has been challenged by several investigators working on communication systems with chimpanzees.

The earliest attempts to teach human language to chimps involved raising chimps in the homes of the investigators so as to increase the similarity to a human environment. Both of these efforts (Kellogg & Kellogg, 1933; Hayes & Hayes, 1951) were distinct failures. The chimp raised by the Kelloggs never produced any distinctly human speech sounds. The Hayeses were somewhat more successful. Their chimp, Viki, was finally able to produce the words, *papa, mama,* and *cup.* In addition she could understand other words to some degree. However, Viki's words were not clearly articulated and were often not understood by strangers.

These early failures to teach human language to chimps could have occurred for at least two reasons. The reason most often given is that the vocal apparatus of the chimp is not adequate for the production of human speech. The second reason given for failures to teach language to chimps is that they lack the necessary cognitive abilities.

Recently several attempts have been made to teach chimps communication systems that do not depend on the use of speech. The most widely publicized of these efforts is work with the chimp Washoe (Gardner & Gardner, 1971). The approach was to attempt to teach American Sign Language (ASL) to Washoe. The procedure involved the behavior shaping and instrumental conditioning techniques described in chapter 7. With these procedures, Washoe learned a fairly large vocabulary of signs and combinations of signs, and when she was 5 years old she could understand several hundred signs and could use more than 130 in various combinations.

David Premack (1971) reported that his chimp, Sarah, was taught to communicate using a variety of plastic forms that varied in size, shape, and color. The forms represented words that could be combined in various ways to produce sentences. Both Washoe and Sarah demonstrated an ability to produce simple sentences, many of which were novel. Sarah, for example, acquired a vocabulary of more than 60 nouns, 20 verbs, and 30 other words that could be combined to produce a variety of sentences. A chimp named Lana was taught to

---

mola (light), to refer to all the colors of the spectrum. Comparing Dani speakers with English speakers should provide strong support of Whorf's hypothesis. Yet the Dani were found to represent colors in memory in the same way as English speakers do (Heider & Oliver, 1972).

Although Whorf's linguistic relativity hypothesis was too sweeping, numerous situations exist in which language influences perception and memory as well as thought. For instance, subjects were presented with ambiguous figures, such as those shown in Figure 9.10, along with a suggested word label. The two circles connected by a straight line were said to resemble either eyeglasses or a dumbbell. In subsequent retention tests, drawings of the figures tended to be biased toward the particular verbal description that was provided at the time of original presentation (Carmichael, Hogan, & Walter, 1932).

A study that demonstrates a different way that language may influence thinking was reported by Elizabeth Loftus and John Palmer (1974). In this study subjects were shown a film of a traffic accident and then were questioned about the events they had seen. One question concerned the speed of the cars. Subjects who were asked how fast the cars were going before they ''hit each other'' judged the speed as slower than subjects asked how fast they were going communicate by typing on a keyboard console. The keys of the console represented about 100 words that Lana used to type messages (Rumbaugh, 1977). Finally, a gorilla named Koko was taught sign language (Patterson, 1978). Koko had a vocabulary of almost 400 signs and could combine them for longer utterances.

Although the accomplishments achieved by Washoe, Sarah, Lana, and Koko represent the most advanced communication systems taught to apes to date, there is still controversy over whether they can be said to use language in the human sense of the word. Some researchers believe that the achievements of these apes indicate that they do have some capacity for understanding syntax. Other researchers question whether the linguistic creativity of apes is limited to the ability to make word substitutions using restricted sentences—for example, "Sarah eat apple" to "Sarah wash apple" (Premack, 1976). It appears as though the level of syntactic and semantic complexity displayed by the animals is at best that displayed by a 2-year-old child and does not progress be-

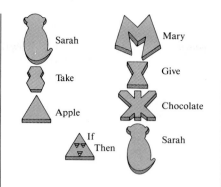

A few of Sarah's "words" as she arranged them to form a complex-sentence.

yond that. This is an impressive observation if true, but by age 3 the human child is displaying a considerably more complex language than the chimps have achieved.

Although it appears that nonhuman primates have the potential to create grammatical sentences, no satisfactory evidence exists that they can, in fact, acquire syntax. Terrace, Petitto, Sanders and Bever (1979) report an extensive study of a chimp called NIM which at first appeared to suggest that NIM could form grammatical combinations of signs. However, extensive videotape analyses

carried out by these investigators showed that most of NIM's utterances were, in fact, prompted by this teacher's prior utterance. There is no question that the linguistic abilities of nonhuman primates are probably greater than those of any other nonhuman animal, but whether there are limits to their ability to communicate symbolically, according to the rules of what we call language, remains to be seen.

Assuming chimps are not capable of acquiring a human-language-like communication system, what is suggested about the animals' cognitive capacities? It is tempting to think that chimps are lacking in certain cognitive characteristics, but it is virtually impossible to point out what these characteristics might be. Chimps demonstrate a wide range of cognitive structures in perceptual and motor tasks. Remember also that language acquisition in children bears little relationship to intelligence. As John Limber (1977) points out, it is no easier to identify the cognitive characteristics that are lacking in chimps than it is to identify those present in humans. ■

before they "smashed into each other." Just the difference between the words "hit" and "smashed" resulted in an appreciable difference in judged speed of the cars.

A week later the same subjects were again asked questions about the film. One question asked about the presence of broken glass—something not shown in the film. Nevertheless, subjects questioned the previous week with the word "smashed" reported having seen broken glass more often than those questioned with the word "hit." Here we see how subsequent linguistic experience can influence what we remember about a prior, nonlinguistic perception. We also see a demonstration of the way the wording of questions may influence eyewitness testimony.

A large amount of literature addresses the influence of language on perception, memory, and thought. We saw examples of this influence in our discussion of inference and the effects of context. Language is used to express concepts and relations as well as our thoughts about a variety of other things. However, language or speech, be it overt or covert, is but one way of thinking. In fact, most of the illustrations presented here concerning the influence of language on thought have also been demonstrated in nonlanguage situations.

Let us consider one illustration of thinking in a situation that does not require the use of language.

James J. Jenkins, Jerry Wald, and John Pittenger (1978) report an interesting demonstration of inference in a visual perception task. These investigators took a series of still pictures of a woman making tea. The scene involved activities such as heating water, making the tea, and pouring the tea. Subjects were shown some of the pictures and then, in a subsequent recognition task, they were shown a much larger set of pictures and were asked to indicate which ones they had seen before.

The pictures presented in the recognition test included some of those seen before as well as others from the scene that had not been shown before. These pictures had all been taken from the same camera location, and the subjects could not tell which ones had been seen previously. However, other pictures of the scene were also included from a different camera location. These pictures were the only ones that the subjects could discriminate as not having been presented earlier. The subjects seemed to have integrated the events pictured with their schemata for making tea and then could no longer discriminate what they had seen from what they had "filled in."

It should not surprise us to see that language and thought are closely related. In humans, language serves as the basic tool for communication. Therefore, when we label our experiences with words and phrases, our language will influence how we remember and think about those experiences. However, when we do not use language to label our experiences, the relationship between language and perception, memory, or thinking will be greatly reduced.

Summary

1. Natural language and the creativity of its generative processes constitute the most striking differences between humans and other species. Language is central to human cognition and to human communication. There are obvious parallels in spoken and written language, but they differ in terms of the sensory-perceptual systems involved (auditory versus visual) as well as in the motor systems involved in production (mouth, tongue, and lips versus fingers and hands).

2. For purposes of analysis and study, spoken language is broken down into three components: (1) phonology, the study of sound patterns, (2) syntax, the grammatical structure of language, and (3) semantics, the study of the meanings of utterances.

3. A phoneme is the smallest unit of sound that makes a difference to the meaning of a larger unit such as a word. Our perception of particular syllables varies depending on the contexts provided by individual phonemes of the syllables. Therefore, speech is said to be characterized by *context-conditioned variation*. Scientists study speech production and context-conditioned variations through the use of speech spectrographs.

4. Written language is an alphabetic sequence of individual letters; in spoken language, however, information about more than one phoneme is usually conveyed at any given point. Because of the efficient packaging of speech sounds at the level of phonemes, speech has been characterized as a code rather than as an alphabet.

5. Phonemes are combined to make up morphemes, which are the smallest groups of speech sounds that have meaning. Morphemes are then combined to produce words and sentences. To know a natural language is to know a set of rules for generating and understanding the sentences of that language. These syntactic rules govern the grammatical structure or word-order relationships of the sentences of that language. The knowledge represented by syntactic rules is implicit or tacit knowledge that cannot be explicitly taught.

6. The set of syntactic rules that describes any particular language constitutes the grammar of that language. Rules common to all languages are called linguistic universals. Grammars written by linguists are best considered as theories of linguistic competence about the implicit knowledge that language users have. They are theories of competence as opposed to performance because they ignore human limitations such as finite life span and a limited-capacity short-term memory.

7. The surface structure of a sentence refers to the form of the sentence we actually hear. The deep structure refers to the meaning of the sentence intended by the speaker.

8. Grammars are usually developed through a constituent analysis of the components of the sentence. Sentences can be generated through sets of phrase structure rules, including a recursive rule. Linguists have also developed transformational rules, which allow the deep structures generated by phrase structure rules to be modified before the surface structure form emerges.

9. As soon as we capture the meaning of a sentence, we seem to forget the syntactic form of that sentence. What is important for memory of language is the ''gist'' of what was said—that is, its semantic organization is retained.

10. Children learn language with ease and with little systematic training. Comprehension precedes production in language acquisition, a relationship that holds for speech sounds, syntactic structures, and semantic interpretations. Language acquisition does not appear to depend on motor coordination, although maturation is necessary for phoneme and word production. Most children begin meaningful speech by uttering single words, a developmental stage called holophrastic speech. Most children begin to combine words into identifiable grammatical structures at around 18 months of age.

11. The generative processes involved in sentence production are thought to be guided by tacit knowledge in the form of syntactic rules. Because this knowledge is implicit, and because the rules operate hierarchically, we are not consciously aware of their use in generating utterances.

12. Early utterances of young children represent attempts to express grammatical relations that are called case relations. Case relations emphasize the semantic structure of the utterance and not just the syntactic form. Children also use nonlinguistic information, such as prior knowledge of the world, in understanding and learning language. Although imitation certainly plays a role in language learning, beyond the level of single words it is not clear what children imitate.

13. Language comprehension involves those cognitive activities normally associated with thinking. Evidence suggests that language comprehension involves fairly complex interactions among (1) various components of the materials presented, (2) the implications or possible implications of those materials, and (3) the relationship between the materials presented and an individual's general knowledge of the world. Inference, general knowledge and prior context, and schemata are among the factors that affect these interactions.

14. Various hypotheses concerning the relationship between language and thought have been proposed. John B. Watson believed that thinking and speaking were the same thing. Benjamin Whorf held the view that the language we speak determines the way we perceive the world and hence the nature of thought. Whorf's hypothesis seems to have been too sweeping. Language or speech, overt or covert, is but one way of thinking.

FOCUS: Early attempts to study langauge in chimps failed for two reasons: first, chimps do not have the vocal apparatus necessary to speak words; second, chimps also may lack the cognitive ability necessary to comprehend and produce language. Linguistic research with chimpanzees has sought to teach them systems of symbolic communication such as American Sign Language. Several researchers have provided evidence that chimps can, in fact, learn symbolic communication, although apparently only to the level of children two years of age. Other researchers have shown that chimps' utterances are usually prompted by the teacher's own utterances and that chimps do not use symbolic communication spontaneously.

RESEARCH: Underextension occurs when a child applies the correct categorical labels to typical instances of that category but not to atypical instances. Thomas G. White's research has shown that: 1) children can readily distinguish between typical and atypical instances of a category; 2) when children are trained using conventional naming procedures underextension is quite common (to atypical instances); 3) unconventional naming practices can result in reversing underextension. In the latter case, underextension occurs to typical instances of categories.

PART

4

Motives and Emotions

10

Motivation and Emotion

Behavior is often organized so that specific goals can be obtained—food, water, a mate, good grades, a new car, and so on. In this chapter we will consider a number of the **needs**—physical states involving lacks or deficits—or **motives** that appear to impel certain goal-seeking behaviors. We will also consider the role of the emotions that are often closely associated with motivated behavior and the achievement of goals.

The concept of **motivation** has an interesting and rather tortuous history. For many years, psychologists attempted to explain motivation in terms of a single all-embracing theoretical construct. In the late nineteenth and early twentieth centuries, the pioneer psychologists William McDougall (1921) and William James (1890) ascribed motivation to **instincts**—innate patterns of behavior. They listed dozens of such instincts, ranging from hunting and fighting to acquisitiveness, curiosity, and jealousy. To James, instincts resembled reflexes in that they were called forth by specific sensory stimuli and elicited a specific type of behavior. However, unlike reflexes, which are localized to a specific organ or set of muscles, the instinct was presumed to direct all of the creature's behavior to a specific goal. A major problem with the instinctual view is that it lends itself to circular reasoning: people fight because they have fighting instincts. How do we know they have fighting instincts? Because they fight.

The instinctual view of motivation was largely superseded during the 1920s and 1930s by the concept of hypothetical states called **drives.** These hypothetical internal states are produced by a small number of primary biological needs such as water or food. If, for example, the organism is deprived of water, the need for water energizes an internal drive state that motivates and organizes behavior until that need is satisfied. For learning theorists such as Clark L. Hull (1943), the reduction of drive became a crucial concept. Motivated behavior was no longer considered to be reflexive, but was conditioned by the reinforcing property of drive reduction. According to this view, all drives and, therefore, all behavior, was motivated by eliminating or satisfying biological needs. The interpretation of all motivation in terms of a few primary biological needs now seems vastly oversimplified.

Today, neither instincts nor drives can be considered adequate as an all-embracing conceptual approach to the study of motivation. But there *is* a cer-

A part of the evolutionary process is natural selection. Animals that are best equipped to survive continue, and succeeding generations become more like the best-adapted animals of previous generations.

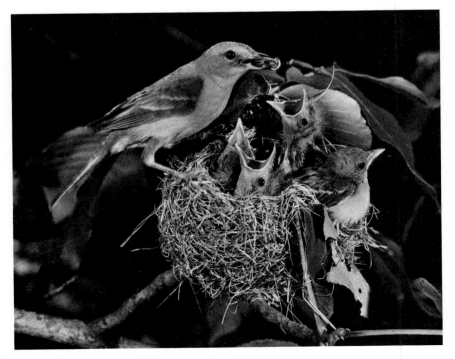

CHAPTER 10   MOTIVATION AND EMOTION

tain unity to the concept of motivation or motivated behavior. Motivated behavior is purposive, that is, goal-oriented. Purpose can be inferred from appetitive behavior, from the emotional responses that often accompany a motivated state, and from biological changes that produce the state. Although granting this sort of unity, in practice most modern researchers take a more restricted view of motivation, investigating the problems of motivation one at a time instead of attempting to answer all questions at once through the formulation of a single, all-encompassing theory. This has led to the development of several distinctly different approaches to the study of motivation. In the first part of this chapter we will discuss three of these approaches: the evolutionary approach, the physiological approach, and the social-learning approach. In the second part of the chapter we will look at emotions and their involvement in motivation. In the final part of the chapter we will see how all of these approaches can be put together in the case of one particularly important example of goal-directed behavior—aggression. In the next chapter we will continue our discussion of motivation and emotion by focusing on the biological and social aspects of sexual behavior.

Motivation and Evolution

When we study motivation we are often studying the ways in which animals behave to obtain the things they need to survive and reproduce. Motivated behavior plays a critical role in satisfying the needs of the organism. Therefore, we should expect the process of evolution to have affected motivated behavior, at least in the case of biological motives such as hunger, thirst, and sex.

There are two parts to the evolutionary process that interact with one another. The first is the **generation of variation** through a number of mechanisms among the members of a species. At least some of this variation will usually be the result of genetic differences among the animals. These differences will be carried in the genes, the basic units of heredity that transmit traits from one generation to the next. Genetically based characteristics produce the similarities in parents and offspring. For example, if the members of a species varied in size and this variation in size had a genetic basis, then the offspring of parents who were relatively large would themselves tend to be relatively large.

The second part of the evolutionary process is called **natural selection.** If the trait in which the animals vary is related to survival, some of the animals will be better equipped to survive than others, and these animals would leave more offspring. Such differential reproduction will lead to change in the population over time. As the animals that are best equipped continue generation after generation to be more successful, succeeding generations become more and more like the best-adapted animals of previous generations.

For example, suppose that a group of animals varied in their tendency to eat when they needed food and that these differences were genetic. Some of them ate too little, some about the right amount, and some ate more than they needed. Obviously, many of those who ate too little would starve or be too weak to escape from predators and would leave few offspring. The genes responsible for eating too little would sooner or later disappear as possessors of these genes became less and less numerous. It is equally true, though perhaps less obvious, that the animals that ate too much would also leave few offspring. Too much food might make the animals fat and slow them down so that they could not excape predators. After a period of such natural selection, all the animals should tend to eat about the optimal amount of food.

Several important implications can be drawn from this example. First, because the goals of motivated behavior are often biologically critical to the survival and/or reproduction of the organism, we should expect many motivational systems to be finely tuned to the needs of the organism. Second, evolution does not require the animal to "know" what it needs in any sort of subjective way. As long as an animal behaves appropriately, for whatever reason, it will leave offspring. Third, note that, strictly speaking, it is not survival that counts, but the leaving of offspring. An animal that engaged in no mate-seeking or sexual behavior, conserving time and energy for obtaining food and avoiding predators, might survive for a long time. But its genes would not be represented in the next generation.

Adaptive Behavior: Survival

This discussion of evolution and behavior clearly implies that behavior should often be adaptive, contributing directly to the number of offspring. How can the adaptive nature of that behavior be demonstrated? This question has been of special concern to ethologists, zoologists who study behavior—usually in the field under natural conditions. The ethologist most responsible for developing techniques for the study of the adaptive significance of behavior has been Niko Tinbergen, one of three ethologists to win the Nobel Prize in 1963.

Tinbergen and his students used experimental procedures in which variables hypothesized to influence animal behavior in the natural habitat were manipulated. For example, when young birds hatch they leave pieces of eggshell scattered in the area of the nest. This is particularly obvious in the case of ground-nesting birds such as the black-headed gull. The parents of black-headed gull chicks fastidiously clean up these eggshell pieces by eating them or, more often, carrying them away from the nest. Is there any adaptive significance to this behavior?

One possibility is that the eggshell removal reduces predation on the nest. The outside of the shells are covered with splotches of brown, green, and khaki: they are nicely camouflaged. But the insides of the shells are white, and eggshell pieces are very conspicuous. A simple experiment was performed (Tinbergen, 1963). Artificial nests, each with a single egg in it, were placed near a gull colony. Some of these nests had eggshell pieces nearby; some did not. Predation on the nests with eggshells was much higher than on the nests without eggshells. This directly demonstrated that eggshell removal reduces predation on the nest and therefore increases the number of young that survive.

Another approach to the problem of empirically demonstrating the adaptiveness of behavior is to measure selective pressure directly. If the behavior in question varies among the members of a species, it may be possible to measure directly the success of the animals in terms of numbers of young produced as a function of the behavior. For example, black-headed gulls, like many birds, nest in large colonies. They appear highly motivated to nest in the center of the colony and will struggle over these nest sites in the center, even though there are plenty of apparently satisfactory nest sites at the edges of the colony. There is some advantage to nesting in the center of the colony. It has been found that nests at the edge of the colony suffered much higher rates of predation than nests in the center of the colony (Patterson, 1965). Those gulls who more successfully compete to nest in the center will raise more young.

Optimization of Adaptive Behavior

Natural selection would serve to increase the proportion of animals whose goal-oriented behavior is optimized. Another approach to the study of the adapativeness of behavior, called **optimization theory,** has been developed during the past few years. The optimization approach is based on the assumption that the behavior of animals is organized to achieve some biologically significant goal. A mathematical or graphical model of the situation in which the behavior occurs is then constructed and used to figure out the best strategy

314

possible for obtaining the goal. Then experiments are conducted to see whether the behavior of the animal approaches the best—or optimal—solution.

Optimization theory represents a descriptive approach to assessing the efficacy of an organism's goal-directed actions under a given set of conditions. However, the theory does not further our understanding about which factors are initiating the behavior in question, nor does it explain why a less-than-optimal strategy was adopted.

Optimization theory has been applied to the study of foraging behavior. A foraging animal is an animal looking for food; the behavioral goal is unambiguous. Presumably, the behavior of the foraging animal should be organized for efficiency. This would minimize the amount of time required to obtain the needed food, leaving more time for other necessary activities such as finding a mate or caring for young. Therefore, optimal foraging models are constructed to discern the best possible strategy to follow when faced with a particular foraging problem. Experiments then determine the extent to which the behavior of the animals matches the results of the model building.

Optimal foraging models involve complex mathematical detail, but the basic logic can be seen through an example. A flycatcher is a bird that forages by sitting on a branch watching insects fly by and choosing certain insects to catch. Different types of insects fly by, some large and some small, some easy to catch and some hard to catch. Is there any rule the bird uses to determine which insects are worth chasing and which are not? The optimal foraging model developed originally by Robert MacArthur and Eric Pianka (1966) yields such a rule. They have shown mathematically that the bird should use a rule that depends on the abundance of the best types of insects. If the largest, easiest-to-capture insects are common, the bird should chase only these and ignore prey of less value. If the best types of prey are relatively rare, the bird should be less selective, taking all prey types.

Suppose there were only two types of insects, each requiring about 10 seconds to capture and eat, but the better type is twice as large, with double the dietary value of the lesser-valued type. If a small insect flies by the flycatcher, it will take 10 seconds to capture and eat, and the bird will miss any large insects that happen by. If the larger insects are very common, the flycatcher is better off ignoring small ones and waiting for the large ones. But if large ones are rare, then a large insect is unlikely to come around during the 10 seconds spent on a small insect, and the small insect is worth chasing. The flycatcher should be selective when large insects are plentiful but should go after all insects when the large ones are relatively rare. And it should make no difference how common the small insects are.

This model suggests what the behavior of the bird should be if the foraging behavior is organized to maximize efficiency in terms of the amount of food eaten per minute. Several experiments have observed foraging birds to behave as predicted by the model. For example, John Goss-Custard (1981) watched red shanks feeding on a mud flat in southern England. There were several different sizes of prey available to them. On days when large prey were abundant, the birds ate almost all large prey; when the large prey were less common, the red shanks broadened their diet to include smaller prey. Thus the optimization approach to foraging behavior seems to help us understand and predict what animals will do.

Physiological Bases of Motivated Behavior

As we saw in the previous section, motivated behavior is often organized in ways that ensure the survival and reproductive success of the organism. Some motives function to fulfill needs that are particularly necessary for survival. The needs that motivate such behaviors involve physiological and neural mechanisms within the organism.

Neural Control Mechanisms

Although many parts of the nervous system are involved in the control of motivated behavior, the hypothalamus is an important brain structure regulating motivated behavior, and the endocrine system is particularly important in its expression.

The Hypothalamus

The hypothalamus straddles the midline of the brain, extending from just below the thalamus to the base of the brain. Not much larger than the tip of a little finger and constituting less than 1 percent of the brain's entire weight, the hypothalamus is one of the principal brain structures involved in the regulation of hunger and thirst, body temperature, and sexual behavior. Through its connections to the autonomic nervous system, which controls glands and smooth muscles such as blood vessels and the heart, the hypothalamus also influences a great variety of emotional responses.

Many emotions, such as fear or anger, are accompanied by physiological arousal. Heart rate speeds up; blood is diverted from internal organs to the muscles carrying increased amounts of glucose or blood sugar. This process—the "fight or flight" response by which the body prepares for some kind of action—is regulated by the autonomic nervous system under the control of the hypothalamus.

The Endocrine System

A principal means of hypothalamic control of motivation is exerted through its connections to the body's endocrine system. The endocrine system, which works in parallel with the nervous system, consists of various ductless glands such as the adrenals and the pancreas that discharge vitally important substances called hormones directly into the bloodstream. (Other glands—for example, sweat glands—have ducts that carry their secretions to the body surface.) Several dozen hormones have been identified. The name **hormone** stems from the Greek meaning "to excite to action," and hormones excite an extraordinary variety of activity.

Originally hormones were thought to regulate purely peripheral physiological functions. For example, the first hormone to be identified, secretin, is secreted by the pancreas and helps regulate digestion. Thyroxin, which is secreted by the thyroid gland, controls the basic rate of metabolism. It became clear, however, that hormones are powerful regulators of and exert a direct influence upon behavior as well, and their secretion can be strongly influenced by environmental events. The adrenal glands just above the kidneys secrete two hormones, adrenalin and noradrenalin, that are associated with emotions such as fear and anger. They help increase blood pressure, heart rate, and respiration to arouse the body for action. This hormonal mechanism thus works in parallel with the autonomic nervous system during physiological arousal. As we will see in the next chapter, hormones released by the gonads—the testes in males, the ovaries in females—not only help control the development of sexual characteristics but also greatly influence sexual behavior.

The Guiding Principle: Homeostasis

A fundamental principle for understanding the neural control of motivation is the concept called **homeostasis.** The word (from the Greek for "maintaining stability") was coined early in this century by the American physiologist Walter B. Cannon (1929) to describe an organism's tendency to maintain its internal environment at a constant level.

Years before Cannon, French physiologist Claude Bernard (1865/1957) had correctly concluded that the principal regulator of this homeostatic har-

American physiologist Walter B. Cannon used the term homeostasis to describe an organism's tendency to maintain its internal environment at a constant level.

CHAPTER 10 MOTIVATION AND EMOTION

A number of automatic physiological mechanisms contribute to homeostatic control in humans. Shivering in a snow storm is actually a rapid alteration in the contraction of the muscles which creates heat.

mony is the nervous system. The brain—and, in large part, the hypothalamus—mediates the complex interplay of physiology and behavior in motivation. Part of the time the hypothalamus operates automatically in the regulation of homeostasis, but it also is subject to conscious control. This joint physiological and behavioral control of homeostasis is illustrated in the functioning of body temperature.

Humans and other mammals maintain a nearly constant body temperature. In humans the temperature is about 98.6 degrees Fahrenheit. A number of automatic physiological mechanisms contribute to this homeostatic control. When external heat threatens homeostasis, the peripheral blood vessels dilate and carry more blood to the surface of the body, cause the face to become flushed, and assist in cooling the body surface. The body's heat loss is speeded up by perspiration, which cools the skin as sweat evaporates. When cold threatens homeostasis, the peripheral blood vessels constrict, limiting the amount of heat loss; we also may begin to shiver—a rapid alteration in the contraction of the muscles that creates heat.

These physiological mechanisms are under the command of the preoptic area of the anterior hypothalamus, largely through its control of the autonomic nervous system. The hypothalamus senses temperature extremes through the neural pathways that arise from temperature-sensitive nerve endings in the skin. Another source of information is the hypothalamus's own thermostat—heat-sensitive cells that monitor the temperature of the blood circulating through it.

Obviously there is also behavioral control of temperature regulation. When it is cold, we wear coats or throw another log on the fire or turn up the furnace. Information about external temperature reaches the brain from the skin's nerve endings and motivates us to action. There is also evidence, however, that the hypothalamus itself can initiate behavioral responses. When a small heating probe is inserted into the hypothalamus of a rat, the animal will press a lever in order to receive a blast of cool air. This occurs even when the rat is in a cool environment (Corbit, 1970). But the hypothalamus cannot be the *only* place where behavioral temperature regulation is controlled. Although physiological temperature regulation is severely disrupted by hypothalamic lesions, *behavioral* temperature regulation is preserved (Carlisle, 1969). Rats will still press a lever to heat a cold chamber even after they sustain large hypothalamic lesions. Thus they can still maintain body temperature behaviorally. It appears as though the internal hypothalamic and voluntary behavioral systems of thermoregulation depend upon different central nervous system centers for their operation.

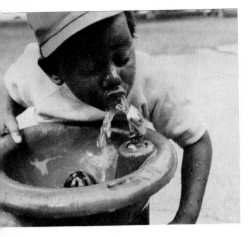

Thirst cannot be accounted for simply by dehydration in the mouth. There are precise mechanisms controlling thirst and water intake in homeostasis.

Thirst

The mechnisms that govern thirst and water intake provide a precise and classic model of the role of homeostasis in biological motivation. At one time it was believed that thirst could be accounted for simply by dehydration in the mouth—the familiar feeling of dryness that often precedes our desire to drink. But the dry-mouth theory failed on several counts. For example, even when sensory nerve connections arising from the lips, tongue, and mouth are severed, thirst and drinking are not significantly affected. In addition, merely moistening the mouth or throat has no lasting effect on thirst.

Modern research has demonstrated that two different systems control our intake of water. The osmotic and hypovolemic systems comprise intricate mechanisms that link the state of body fluids, nerve cells in the brain, and the secretion of hormones.

Osmotic Thirst

One system of thirst, **osmotic thirst,** depends upon the flow of fluids through the thin membrane that encloses each cell of the body. These fluids are of two basic types: the intracellular fluid contained within the cells and the extracellular fluid, which is made up of the liquid portion of the blood and of the interstitial fluid that surrounds and bathes body cells. The cell membrane is freely permeable to water but does not permit free passage to certain substances dissolved in the bloodstream and in the interstitial fluid, mainly sodium. As extracellular fluid is lost from the body in urine and sweat, the concentration of sodium outside the cells increases. Because of **osmosis**—the tendency of fluids to equalize concentrations of solutes on both sides of a semipermeable membrane—the water inside the cell passes out through the membrane. This osmotic process leaves the cell dehydrated and shrunken.

How could cellular dehydration tell us that we are thirsty? In its anterior portion the hypothalamus contains nerve cells that appear to be specialized to detect such cellular loss of water. Studies have shown that some cells in this region of the lateral preoptic area of the hypothalamus fire nerve impulses in response to changes in the osmotic pressure of blood (Cross & Green, 1959; Fitzsimons, 1971). These cells, called **osmoreceptors,** apparently are uniquely sensitive to the minute changes in volume that are associated with cellular dehydration.

The proof that the lateral preoptic area is crucial for osmotic thirst came from brain lesion experiments. Animals with large lesions of the preoptic area no longer drink in response to cellular dehydration (Peck & Novin, 1971; Blass & Epstein, 1971). Importantly, the other major mechanism producing thirst—decreases in blood volume—is still intact in animals with such lesions.

The osmoreceptors, through brain mechanisms that are not yet fully understood, tell us to drink fluids. At the same time, they set in motion another homeostatic means of regulating body fluids. They signal the pituitary gland to increase production of a chemical vitally important in the conservation of body fluids—the antidiuretic hormone vasopressin (see Figure 10.1). Vasopressin traveling through the bloodstream acts on the kidneys where urine is formed. Ordinarily, when plenty of water is available to the body, a large volume of urine is produced and excreted by the kidneys. But in times of water scarcity the presence of vasopressin causes the kidneys to reabsorb into the bloodstream much of the water that is ordinarily lost in urine.

One consequence of osmotic thirst is the high concentration of chemical waste products in the urine. For this reason, when we are thirsty or in the morning after a long period without drinking, our urine is a darker color than usual. Like the brain signals that tell us we are thirsty, this highly concentrated urine is a sign of the homeostatic process brought on by cellular dehydration or osmotic thirst.

Hypovolemic Thirst

Cellular dehydration produces thirst but is not necessary for it. There is a second system regulating water intake and recent evidence suggests that this system may be more important than osmotic thirst in regulating normal day to day drinking (Epstein, 1983). A hint of the nature of this mechanism long has been noted by surgeons who report that a sudden and dramatic loss of blood, such as might occur during hemorrhaging from a battlefield wound, produces immediate thirst. Laboratory experiments with animals have established that the loss of blood—and thus of extracellular fluid—results in low-volume or **hypovolemic thirst** (Russell, Abdelaal, & Morgenson, 1975).

Hypovolemic thirst constitutes a complex chain of events that is also not yet fully understood. When the volume of extracellular fluid is lowered, the kidneys release a chemical called renin, a substance long known to increase blood pressure. Renin acts as an enzyme to produce a blood hormone called angiotensin I, which in turn leads to the production of another hormone in the blood, angiotensin II. This latter hormone acts to conserve fluid by constricting the peripheral blood vessels, helping maintain normal blood pressure despite the loss of blood. In addition, angiotensin II affects certain nerve cells in the brain that signal thirst. When it is injected intravenously or directly into the brain of rats, it causes even a water-satiated animal to drink (Fitzsimons, 1972). Until recently the exact locus in the brain upon which angiotensin acts was not clearly known. It is now established that a small group of cells just next to the third ventricle, the subfornical organ, is the key structure that contains the receptors that are especially sensitive to angiotensin II and that plays a critical role in initiating hypovolemic drinking (Epstein, 1983).

In summary, there appear to be two different mechanisms of thirst—osmotic, which involves cellular dehydration, and hypovolemic, which depends upon a lowering of the volume of extracellular fluid.

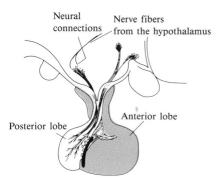

Figure 10.1

The pituitary gland, showing connective nerve fibers from the hypothalamus. One of the important pituitary hormones is vasopressin, which in times of water scarcity causes the kidneys to reabsorb into the bloodstream much of the water ordinarily lost in urine.

Hunger

To some extent the homeostatic mechanisms within our bodies compensate for lack of food. Sugar is stored in the liver and then released in times of deprivation. But when that supply is depleted, the motivation for food becomes so powerful that people will lie, connive, and even kill to get it. Hunger provides a good example of the control of motivated behavior by physiological factors and has been extensively investigated.

Feeding and Satiety Centers

An early suggestion about the sensation of hunger was that the familiar hunger pangs are simply contractions of the stomach. Cannon attempted to demonstrate the significance of stomach contractions when he had volunteer subjects swallow a recording balloon that was filled with air once in the stomach. Stomach contractions, as measured by increases in pressure in the balloon seemed to correlate with the subjects' reports of their hunger sensations (Cannon, 1911; Cannon & Washburn, 1912). However, other methods have shown that stomach contractions are not essential to experiencing the feeling of hunger. For example, people whose stomachs have been surgically removed still report feeling hungry.

In the 1940s researchers began to study the role of the brain in eating behavior. One group found that brain lesions in certain areas of the hypothalamus could produce dramatic changes in feeding (Hetherington & Ranson, 1942). Lesions in the ventromedial hypothalamus (VMH) spurred animals to overeat intensely—a state known as **hyperphagia** (see Figure 10.2). In some cases they actually burgeoned to three to four times their normal body weight. The initial interpretation of Ranson's work was that the VMH serves as a kind of **satiety center,** which, when functioning normally, tells us we have had enough to eat (see Figure 10.3).

This finding was paralleled by another related discovery: lesions placed in the lateral hypothalamus (LH) had the reverse effect (Epstein, 1971). Animals with such lesions were rendered unwilling or unable to eat—a state known as **aphagia.** These studies led to the theory that the LH is a **feeding center** that signals the need to eat.

A plausible and pleasantly simple picture of neural mechanisms involved in the control of feeding behavior thus arose. Eating was thought to be initiated and controlled by a set of neurons in the lateral hypothalamus, the feeding center. This feeding center was thought to be under inhibitory control from neurons in the ventromedial hypothalamus, the satiety center. As a consequence, lesions in the feeding center would be expected to impair normal eating in proportion to the severity of the damage; lesions in the satiety center would be expected to remove an inhibitory "brake" on the feedng center and produce overeating.

The Set-Point Theory

Another interpretation of these data was put forth by Richard Keesey and his colleagues. They argued that the hypothalamic centers play a different role in feeding: that they constitute the neural equivalent of a set point for body weight (Keesey & Powley, 1975). Like a thermostat in a home heating system, they sense body weight, turning on eating behavior when weight becomes too low and stopping it when weight is too high.

Keesey's **set-point theory** depends, in part, on the interpretation of experiments that preceded his own work. It was known, for example, that aphagic rats with lesions in the lateral hypothalamus feeding center would begin to feed again voluntarily if the animals were carefully nursed and force-fed following surgery (Teitelbaum & Epstein, 1962).

This was interpreted in terms of the feeding center perspective. Damage to the feeding center stopped the rats from eating; recovery of feeding behavior was thought to be a result of the remaining undamaged cells taking over control of eating.

Keesey had a different interpretation. He suggested that instead of disrupting the feeding center, the lesions actually had lowered the set point of the rats, thus turning off feeding. The rats eventually began eating again when their weight had dropped below the new set points. Feeding behavior turned on the way a furnace switches on when the thermostat senses that the temperature is too low.

In support of his idea, Keesey deprived rats of food for several days to drop their weight below the presumed post-lesion set point (Keesey & Powley, 1975). He then placed lesions in the lateral hypothalamus. According to feeding center perspective, these rats should have stopped eating after the surgery. In fact, they began eating normally after recovering from the anesthetic. Some of the rats—deprived of food longer than others—even began overeating. The lesioned rats kept eating until they reached their set point, at which time feeding behavior diminished. This set point appparently had been lowered by the lesions in the lateral hypothalamus. The weight of these rats leveled off at a point lower than that of a control group of rats, which had not received brain lesions.

Other observations suggest that a set point is normally operative for weight in other situations as well. If people of normal weight stop eating for any length of time, they lose weight, of course. But when they are allowed to eat freely, they rapidly return to precisely the same weight at which they started. The converse is also true. People who volunteered to eat an excessive amount of food—up to 8000 calories a day—predictably gained weight. But given free choice, they quickly lost it, returning to almost precisely their original level.

Some sort of set point is necessary to explain the remarkable constancy with which most people maintain their body weight over a long period of time. It has been estimated that merely an extra pat of butter each morning would increase one's weight by 10 pounds in one year and 100 pounds in 10 years. Experimental animals have been shown to eat the right amount of food to maintain constancy of body weight even when caloric content is greatly varied. For example, if the animal's food is adulterated with nonnutrients such as mineral oil or water, the animal adjusts the amount it eats so that the caloric intake is roughly constant over an extended period of time (Kennedy, 1950). Moreover, after they are force-fed a very rich diet by tube to make them grossly obese, rats consume far less food than control animals when they are allowed to eat freely. They continue to eat less until their weight roughly equals that of the control animals (Hoebel & Teitelbaum, 1966).

But the *nature* of the set point and the role of the hypothalamus in the control of eating are still controversial topics. For example, if the ventromedial hypothalamus (VMH) were, in fact, the "satiety center," then some of the factors that promptly stop feeding (for example, intravenous glucose injection or fillng the stomach) would be expected to exert their effects *via* the VMH. Thus, they should be ineffective after lesions of the VMH. But glucose injection and filling the stomach inhibit feeding even in VMH-lesioned animals. Since animals recover from either VMH or lateral hypothalamic lesions and eat meals that are essentially normal, neither the lateral hypothalamus nor the VMH is *necessary* for hunger or satiety. Hypothalamic lesions are known to produce endocrine abnormalities. Hence, it is possible that such abnormalities might indirectly produce the observed effects on feeding and weight.

There is difficulty in accounting for hunger and satiety in terms of a simple pair of activating and inhibitory centers. There is similar difficulty with the set-

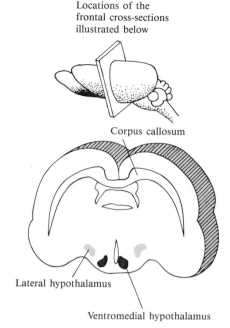

Locations of the frontal cross-sections illustrated below

Corpus callosum

Lateral hypothalamus

Ventromedial hypothalamus

Figure 10.2

The lateral and ventromedial hypothalamus in a rat's brain.

Figure 10.3

Rats with damage to the ventromedial hypothalamus often overeat and become greatly overweight. The rat shown below has suffered damage to this region.

Obesity is one of the most common health problems in the United States.

point idea. If animals recover normal feeding behavior when the lateral hypothalamus is destroyed, then the appetite-control mechanism—the comparator that *produces* hunger—must be elsewhere. We must conclude that the question of how and where in the brain hunger is regulated is still far from solved.

Partly in reaction to these difficulties, research in recent years has begun to reconsider more peripheral mechanisms in feeding control with considerable success (Smith, 1983). Rather than approach directly the question of how the *brain* controls feeding, this approach analyzes the role of peripheral structures in the mouth, the stomach, and the gut in the control of feeding. For example, experiments have shown that animals prepared so that the contents of their stomachs are immediately drained may nonetheless continue to eat for hours. Thus, neither the presence of food in the mouth nor the act of eating is enough to stop feeding. Some signal from the stomach or gut must be normally present after a meal.

Much contemporary research is directed at learning what the nature of that signal might be. Current research has suggested a plausible mechanism whereby the presence of food in the stomach or gut can stop feeding. In one ingenious experiment (Koopmans, 1981) an extra stomach was transplanted from one rat to another. The second stomach drained into the intestine but had no neural connection with the nervous system of the recipient rat. Yet food placed in the transplanted stomach and maintained there promptly caused the rat to stop feeding. This and other experiments point to a mechanism whereby a hormone is released from the stomach and/or the gut when food is present in it. This hormone acts on receptors elsewhere in the body or brain to terminate feeding. It seems likely that one important application of such studies will be a physiological approach to understanding and controlling obesity. Clearly, a deficit in production or response to such a "satiety" hormone might lead to obesity. If a normal "satiety" hormone could be delivered as a drug, it could be used to curb appetite without great risk and perhaps help obese people to regulate their weight.

Obesity

Obesity is one of the most common health problems in the United States. According to one study, 32 percent of males and 46 percent of females described themselves as being overweight; most of them had actively attempted at some point to lose weight.

In most cases of obesity, the excess weight is due to excess amounts of fat tissue. The human digestive system is remarkably efficient at extracting available energy from the food we eat, but if we consume more energy than we use, we store the excess as fat in special cells known as **adipocytes.** A logical question is whether obese people have more adipocytes or whether they simply store more fat in the same number of cells. Direct counts of the number of adipocytes in obese people and in people of normal weight indicate that most overweight people have more adipocytes (Knittle & Hirsch, 1968). Unfortunately, research suggests that the number of fat cells is fixed early in life, probably in the first two years (Lytle, 1977). According to one point of view, the number is partly determined through heredity and partly by eating habits in infancy (Knittle, 1975). Some researchers believe that adipocytes signal hunger when the cells are not full. This leads to a rather pessimistic view of the possibility of controlling obesity. Because obese people who reduce their weight still have the same number of fat cells, each adipocyte now contains less than the normal amount of fat. If these depleted cells signal hunger, then the obese person must either go chronically hungry or remain fat (Knittle, 1975). Unfilled adipocytes would be one possible intermediary in the biological basis of obesity. But any upward alteration of the set point for weight by any mechanism would produce obesity. Obese people would feel chronically hungry unless they reached their weight level (Nisbett, 1972).

Other researchers, while granting that such internal causes may mean that obesity is normal for some people, theorize that much overweight stems from a heightened responsiveness to cues in the external environment. Work with human subjects done by Stanley Schachter and Judith Rodin (1974) has shown that fat people tend to be more sensitive to environmental cues such as the time of day, social situation, and even the look and taste of food. For example, if obese subjects are erroneously informed that it is time for dinner, they eat more than subjects of normal weight do (Schachter & Gross, 1968). However, Herman and Polivy (in Stunkard, 1980) have found that nonobese subjects who were on restricted diets behaved similarly, suggesting that hunger and not obesity per se may underlie these behaviors. In addition, although obese subjects drink more of a good-tasting milk shake than do nonobese subjects, they drink less when the milk shake is laced with bitter-tasting quinine. This resembles the finickiness of rats with VMH lesions, who also overeat but reject food made bitter with quinine.

A Balanced Diet

Not only is it important to eat the right amount of food, it is also important that the food make up a balanced diet. Many organisms, including human children, will put together a proper diet from a menu that includes many foods, each containing one or a few necessary substances, without having received prior instruction about a proper diet (Davis, 1928). This ability is partially due to innate preferences, or **specific hungers** for some essential things such as salt (Stricker & Wilson, 1970). If rats are given two bottles to drink from, one containing pure water and the other containing salt water, the rats will prefer the saltwater solution as long as it is not too salty. If the need for salt is increased, the salt preference will become stronger. For instance, if a rat loses its adrenal glands, its need for salt is dramatically increased: without large amounts of salt, it will die. A rat without adrenals given access to strong salt solutions will drink them eagerly. Similarly, people with Addison's disease, which is due to a malfunction of the adrenal glands, will eat large amounts of salt.

The ability to select a balanced diet is also partially due to learning. Animals that have been fed on a deficient diet develop an aversion to that diet, so they will prefer any new diet when it is first introduced. If the new diet is a complete one, they will stay with it, ignoring the old diet and correcting the deficiency. This phenomenon has been investigated by Paul Rozin and his associates (Rodgers & Rozin, 1966). In this experiment, rats were first fed a diet that was deficient in thiamine. When a new diet was introduced and the rats had a choice between the two diets, all of the rats initially switched to the new diet. For some of the rats this new diet was complete, and they continued to eat it. For the rest of the rats the new diet was as deficient as the old one. After a few days these rats abandoned the new diet and returned to the old.

Another dramatic example of adaptive mechanisms in the control of feeding is the phenomenon of learned taste aversion (Garcia, Ervin, & Koelling, 1966). If rats are given a saccharin-flavored solution they will normally drink it. But if rats are given such a solution for the first time and later made ill, they will now no longer drink saccharin-flavored solutions. Rats learn to associate a distinctive new flavor with illness even though hours may elapse from the first taste of food to when they become ill. This mechanism is at the heart of "bait shyness." When faced with a new food, rats will nibble a small amount. If they become sick, they will then avoid that food.

So far, we have seen that the behavior of organisms is partially motivated by the evolutionary processes that produced them and that biological factors are vital in basic drives such as hunger and thirst. In addition, social motivations play important roles in the behavior of both animals and humans.

Social Bases of Motivated Behavior

Humans are social as well as biological beings. Hunger and thirst satisfy basic bodily needs, but other things move us. Many of these, like the need to affiliate with others or the need to achieve, are social in nature. These are called **social motives** because they are acquired or expressed largely through interactions with others.

A sharp distinction is sometimes drawn between biological and social motives. While the satisfaction of a biological motive is obviously and immediately necessary for survival, the satisfaction of a social motive appears less necessary. But this distinction may be misleading. The satisfaction of social motives may be critical not only for psychological well-being but also for biological success in evolutionary terms. The general goals of social motives include such things as recognition, affection, companionship, and power that may affect success in the long run. The study of the evolutionary significance of social behavior is the focus of a relatively new field, sociobiology.

The Adaptive Nature of Social Behavior: Sociobiology

Sociobiology attempts to study social behavior in terms of its adaptive value, with a particular emphasis on the optimization theory approach. As we saw earlier, models are constructed based on the assumption that animals maximize their foraging efficiency. Sociobiological models are constructed on the assumption that animals behave in ways to maximize their contribution to the next generation, measured in terms of the number of their genes represented in the next generation. This usually means maximizing the number of offspring successfully raised, but it can be more complicated when animals are related to each other.

Sociobiology is a relatively young discipline, dating from the 1970s. The sociobiological perspective appears to provide an extremely valuable way of looking at the social behavior of animals and will probably prove helpful, in the long run, in understanding human behavior (Wilson, 1975). We will look at two examples of sociobiological research with animals to get the general flavor of the approach and then discuss the applicability of sociobiology to our own species.

The Choice of a Mate

How animals select their mates is an issue of concern to sociobiologists. Mate choice can be a critical matter: the selection of an inappropriate mate may lead to relatively few healthy offspring. Furthermore, animal mating systems are enormously variable. For example, some birds are **monogamous** (one male paired with one female), some **polygamous** (one male paired with two or more females), and a rare few are **polyandrous** (more than one male paired with each female, see chapter 11). Can this variety in mating systems be interpreted in terms of maximizing the number of offspring?

One research effort that attempts to answer this question is an extensive field study of the lark bunting by Wanda Pleszczynska (1978). Lark buntings are fairly common birds in the midwestern United Sates during the spring and summer. They spend their winters in warmer climates, from Texas down into Mexico; in spring they migrate north to their breeding areas. The males arrive first on the breeding grounds—open grassland. They set up territories and begin to sing, advertising their presence both to other males and to females. The females begin to arrive about a week after the males do, and their arrival is staggered over a nine-day period. Some of the males obtain two females (polygamy) who both nest on his territory; others obtain only one female (monogamy); the rest are unable to obtain females. This pattern is due to systematic choices by the arriving females among the available males and territories.

The dynamics of this social system can be understood only after several facts are put together. First, the territories of the males vary widely in quality as nest sites. This is primarily determined by the amount of overhead cover present. Cover is important because it prevents the detection of the nest by predators and filters sunlight reaching the nest that can overheat the young birds. Second, during the nine-day interval in which females are arriving, there are three stages. During the early stage, arriving females pick males with the best territories. During the middle stage, some females choose unmated males with good territories, while other females choose already mated males with excellent territories. Finally, during the late stage, females choose among the remaining unmated males, selecting those with the best territories.

The critical stage is the middle one, wherein some females choose already mated males, while others choose unmated males. Essentially, females arriving during this period are faced with a choice. They can choose unmated males with good territories and be the primary mate, or they can choose an already mated male with an excellent territory and be a secondary mate (secondary mates receive less help from the male than do primary mates). If the differences in territory quality are large enough, a decision to be a secondary mate on an excellent territory may produce more surviving offspring than a decision to be a primary mate on a poorer territory.

These data support three ideas suggested by the sociobiological approach: (1) Females actively select mates (or at least territories) in which the number of young they can successfully raise is increased. Females arriving first select males who have the best territories in which the number of young successfully raised per nest is highest. (2) Monogamy or polygamy depends upon which strategy offers the best chance of having many surviving young. When faced with an unmated male with a relatively poor territory or a mated male with a good territory, the female attempts to maximize the number of young she will be able to raise successfully. (3) There is clear evolutionary pressure on the males to obtain the best possible territory; a male who obtains a poor territory is less likely to attract a mate. And without a mate, no offspring are produced.

Altruistic Behavior and Kin Selection

Other research also shows that animals tend to pick the best mates or best territories available. The sociobiological view suggests that the territorial, mating, and sexual behavior of many animals is organized around the adaptive goal of maximizing the number of offspring. But there are also examples of behavior that appear to violate this principle. The alarm sounding of many small, group-living animals when a predator approaches is one common, apparent exception.

Belding's ground squirrel is a small mammal that forms breeding colonies containing many burrows high in the Rocky Mountains. When a predator such as a hawk or a fox appears, the first squirrel to see it will sometimes give an alarm call. When they hear the call, the other squirrels in the vicinity usually stop what they are doing and either scan the environment for the predator or simply dive into their burrows. Because these animals do not always give the alarm call, it cannot be some simple innate response to the predators. But why give the alarm call at all? It would seem more adaptive for the animal just to dive for its burrow without calling attention to itself. This appears to be an example of **altruistic behavior**—behavior that helps others at some cost to the altruist. In sociobiological terms, altruistic behavior should not exist: animals that expose themselves to risk with no benefit to themselves should tend to leave few offspring.

However, sociobiology does offer some possible explanations for the evolution of altruistic behavior. Most important, close relatives have genes in com-

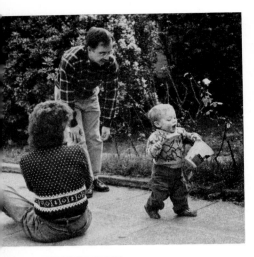

Humans have the longest period of need for protection, as evidenced by the prolonged dependency of children on their parents.

mon: full siblings share half their genes, aunts and nieces share one quarter, and cousins share one eighth. This is the basis for the concept of kin selection. If an animal acts in a manner that slightly reduces its own chances of surviving and reproducing but increases the prospects of some if its relatives, it could be increasing the number of its genes in the next generation because it shares genes with the children of its relatives.

The **kin selection hypothesis** predicts that helping behavior should be most common among closely related animals. Studies testing this idea are particularly difficult to carry out. Individual animals must be identifiable, either through natural markings or by marking of the animals by experimenters. In addition, studies must continue over several generations, so that kin relationships will be known. In spite of these difficulties, such experiments have been carried out, and the results of these studies are most often consistent with the kin selection hypothesis.

One of the best studies of the kin selection explanation for selective alarm calls is Paul Sherman's (1977) study of the Belding's ground squirrel. Individual squirrels were marked with blotches of colored dye so they could be recognized, and the group was observed over several generations. Within this colony, young males left the area before they were one year of age, and all of the adult males present had been born elsewhere. Thus, the adult males were not related to the females or young (except their own) in the area. Females, in contrast, tended to stay in the colony into which they were born, and many of them had relatives living in the immediate vicinity of their burrows. On the average, females are more related to animals in the area than are males. As one would expect from kin selection, females were more likely to give the alarm call after sighting a predator than were males. This could be a simple sex difference attributable to some factor other than relatedness. But Sherman also observed that some of the females had relatives living in the area (sisters, mothers, and descendants), whereas others did not. The females with relatives were much more likely to give alarm calls than were females without relatives.

Belding's ground squirrels take a risk by alarm calling—weasels and coyotes regularly stalked alarm callers and sometimes killed them. But this risk was probably offset by the gain to the relatives of the alarm callers. Other examples of cooperation among close kin exist in animals ranging from insects to birds to lions to primates. Kin relationships, with their genetic implications, appear to be basic to animal social behavior and organization.

Sociobiology, Motivation, and the Human Species

Can the sociobiological perspective be applied to human behavior? This problematic question has given rise to heated debate among psychologists, anthropologists, and zoologists. Sociobiological questions concerning various aspects of human behavior are easy to pose. Is nepotism (favoritism shown to a relative) due to kin selection? Does extended human courtship function to provide opportunities for the evaluation of prospective mates? In polygamous human societies, those men who have multiple wives were usually the richest. Is the parallel to the lark bunting more than coincidence?

In order to translate questions such as these into something more substantial, research is needed—research that will be difficult to carry out. A major factor limiting a sociobiological analysis of human behavior is cultural evolution, that is, the transmission of cultural mores, rules, maxims, etc., through language. Sociobiological researchers will have to develop methods to separate experimentally the effects of cultural evolution from those of biological evolution before adaptive behavior in humans can be said to have a biological basis.

Human Social Motives

Sociobiology suggests that the roots of human sociality are to be found in our biological heritage. But this does not mean that the social needs and behavior of humans are genetically predetermined in some narrow, inflexible way. Rather, human social needs are heavily influenced by experience; learning and social experience are crucial shapers of human social motivation. In this section we will look at two important human social motives: the need for affiliation and the need to achieve.

The Need for Affiliation

One of the most important of the social motives, **affiliation,** is summed up in the familiar statement—people need people. We need others for many reasons: to mediate rewards for us, to help us attain our goals, to help us learn things, to define social reality for us, to establish and validate our beliefs and values.

Our tendency to associate with others is so powerful that some psychologists have proposed that the need to affiliate is not only a social motive but also an innate biological need. As evidence they point to the prolonged dependency of human children on parents and other caregivers. Of all animals, humans have the longest period of need for protection and of learning to cope with the environment: a biological need for affiliation would thus have great survival value for individuals and for the human species.

Although the need for affiliation may indeed have a strong biological component, biology alone cannot explain our tendency to seek out others after we are adults and are able to survive physically quite well on our own. As our early needs are satisfied by others, social interaction becomes a learned source of reward and comfort. We learn that being with others is a necessary and enriching experience, and this social motive impels us throughout our lives.

In high-anxiety conditions, like those experienced by these people seeking refuge from World War II bombing, the need for affiliation appears to increase.

Anxiety and Affiliation

The factors that influence the need to affiliate have been studied extensively by Stanley Schachter. In *The Psychology of Affiliation* (1959), Schachter examined these factors and, in particular, the role of anxiety. Schachter's focus on anxiety stemmed in part from his study of case histories of individuals who had to endure long periods of time alone. For example, shipwrecked sailors and members of certain monastic religious orders often report experiencing bouts of severe anxiety during their loneliness.

Schachter reasoned that if being alone produced anxiety, anxiety might produce a desire to affiliate with others. To test this hypothesis, he conducted an experiment to measure the possible relation between anxiety and affiliation. To disguise the real purpose of the experiment, he told subjects that the aim was to test the effects of electric shock. Subjects were assigned to one of two conditions. In the high-anxiety condition, subjects were shown an ominous-looking complex of electrical gadgetry and were told that they would be given painful shocks. In the low-anxiety condition, the subjects were told the shocks would be extremely mild—scarcely more than a tickle. Then, in order to measure the effect of affiliation, the experimenter told the subjects that it would take a while to get the apparatus ready and that they could wait either in a room alone or in a room with others. Their decisions on how they would wait supported Schachter's hypothesis: 63 percent of the subjects in the high-anxiety condition chose to affiliate—wait in a room with others—but only 33 percent of the low-anxiety subjects made that choice.

Figure 10.4

A number of studies have shown the affiliation motive to be higher among first-born children than among their younger brothers and sisters, especially in the case of women.

In further research, Schachter tried to determine what sort of people anxious subjects would seek out. He varied the experiment so that there were two conditions of high anxiety. In one condition, anxious subjects were given the choice of waiting alone or waiting with others who were participating in the same shock experiment. In this condition, 60 percent of the subjects chose to wait with others. In the other condition, anxious subjects had the choice of waiting alone or of being with people who were ostensibly waiting in a room for a meeting with another professor. Interestingly, none of these subjects chose to wait with others. The anxiety-aroused desire to affiliate was directed only toward those who were presumably awaiting painful shocks and thus in the same boat. As Schachter put it, "Misery doesn't love just any kind of company; it loves only miserable company."

Schachter explained this phenomenon in terms of the **theory of social comparison,** which holds that, in ambiguous situations, we tend to look to other people for help in determining appropriate behavior. This theory will be discussed in greater detail in chapter 16. Although the subjects were undeniably anxious, the situation was so strange that they needed cues from others to help clarify their own feelings about it. Only those who were in the same state of anxiety—waiting to be shocked—would be useful in this process of social comparison.

The Effect of Birth Order

Having established a relation between anxiety and affiliation, Schachter wondered why there were individual differences in the need for others even among anxious people. One possibility quickly suggested itself: early experience. Perhaps people who had learned as children to rely heavily on others to allay their anxieties might develop the strongest need to affiliate when anxious. All children rely to some extent on others for relief from anxieties, of course, but Schachter reasoned that children without siblings are most likely to have their needs and anxieties taken care of by parents. Children without siblings would include those who were first in the order of birth and, hence, for a while were the only children in the family. Parents tend to be very solicitous with firstborn children. They respond to the slightest crying or hurt. By the time subsequent children arrive, however, they have come to realize that children are not all that fragile; they let children cry longer and do not fret over every fall or bruise. In any case, the proliferation of children means that parents simply do not have as much time to devote to any one child.

By this reasoning, firstborns ought to develop a stronger motive than later-borns to affiliate as a way of allaying anxiety. When Schachter reviewed his experimental data on anxiety and affiliation, he found support for this notion: only firstborns showed a great increase in the desire to be with others under high anxiety. In fact, he found that affiliative tendencies were precisely related to birth order. Firstborns showed greater affiliative tendencies when anxious than did second-borns, who in turn showed greater desire to affiliate than did third-borns, and so on (see Figure 10.4).

These findings imply that firstborns seek social means to cope with anxiety while later-borns are more likely to try avenues that are nonsocial. Such an implication, Schachter speculated, might apply in many real-life situations. People who are tense and anxious can attempt to cope with those emotions in many ways. One common way is through alcoholism—a distinctly nonsocial means. Another is through psychotherapy, which requires a form of dependency on another person. Schachter found support for these hypotheses. His analysis showed that later-borns were much more likely to become alcoholics than were firstborns. And firstborns were more likely to go into therapy and stick to it than were later-borns (although there was no difference in the extent to which the two groups suffered from psychological disturbance).

The Need for Achievement

Our society, and Americans in particular, put a high premium on **achievement.** From Little League baseball to Olympic competition, from third-grade spelling bees to the race for Nobel Prizes, doing well is highly valued by the participants and by those around them. Achievement often brings status and profit, of course, but even in the absence of external rewards, it makes us feel good.

David McClelland has found that individuals differ greatly in their need for achievement. An individual's level of need for achievement appears to be a stable and enduring characteristic that affects behavior in a variety of situations (McClelland, Atkinson, Clark, & Lowell, 1953). In addition, McClelland found that the need to achieve not only affects individual behavior, but also has a profound influence on economic and technological growth in a society (McClelland, 1961). Cultures and civilizations grow and prosper only when a significant number of people have a high level of achievement motivation; otherwise, the society will decline. To demonstrate this, McClelland analyzed the art, literature, and music of various cultures throughout history. These indicators showed high achievement themes, he found, just before a culture reached its zenith. But in the periods just prior to the decline of great civilizations, such as those of ancient Rome and Athens, the indicators showed a low need for achievement.

Measuring Achievement Need

McClelland's principal tool for measuring the need for achievement in individuals is the Thematic Apperception Test (TAT). The TAT, which is also used in measuring personality (see chapter 12), is called a projective test because subjects are presented with an ambiguous situation and then asked to tell a story about it, presumably projecting onto the situation their own inner feelings and needs. A typical TAT item for measuring achievement motivation might consist of a picture of a man sitting at a large desk and staring out the window. The subject is then asked to tell what led to this situation and what will happen in the future. In response to this picture, a person with a high need for achievement presumably will project that motive onto the situation. For example, the subject might suggest that the man is trying to get ahead on his job and has come to work on a Sunday morning; he is developing a new product for his company that will win him a promotion. On the other hand, the subject with a low need to achieve might conclude that it is Friday afternoon and the man is daydreaming about how relaxing the weekend will be; in fact, he will leave work early to be with his family.

High Need Versus Low Need

Through his work with the TAT and through experiments, McClelland has pinpointed a number of differences between high-need achievers and those with a low need to achieve. High-need achievers, for example, are motivated to succeed; low-need achievers are motivated to avoid failure. In choosing a task, a high-need achiever will typically pick one of intermediate difficulty—tough enough to create a challenge but not impossible. The low-need achiever typically picks either a task so easy that failure is impossible or a task so difficult that failure is to be expected and thus is unlikely to be condemned; in either case the possibility of true failure is avoided. This difference was demonstrated in a kindergarten class where children were asked to play a game in which they could choose the distance from which they attempted to throw rings over a stake. Children with a high need to achieve, as measured by the TAT, stood at medium distances—far enough to create a challenge but close enough to make success possible. The low-need achievers stood either right next to the stake or

Achievement often brings status and profit, and it makes us feel good.

McClelland used ambiguous pictures like this to analyze subjects' achievement motivation. Subjects are asked to tell what led to this situation and what will happen in the future.

so far away that they could not possibly succeed, but would not be condemned for their failure.

High- and low-need achievers differ in other important ways. High-need achievers don't like to gamble and far prefer skill to chance tasks. In addition, offers of money do not affect the performance of people with a high need for achievement. They do their best whether or not money is offered for good performance. Low-need achievers, on the other hand, try harder and perform better when rewards are at stake. Finally, the high-need achiever can easily delay gratification. He or she will choose to forgo a small reward now for a chance at a larger reward later. The low-need achiever prefers to take whatever reward is immediately available.

Response to Failure

High-need achievers become upset when they fail and are motivated to work even harder; low-need achievers expect to fail and tend to give up when it happens. Success has the opposite effect: high-need achievers expect success and ease up after they achieve it; low-need achievers are so excited by success because it is unexpected that they are spurred to greater effort (Weiner, 1970).

Parental Influences

Research indicates that parents who reward self-control and independence tend to have children with high achievement motivation (Teevan & McGhee, 1972). Such parents set high standards for their children but allow them to work at their own level and to make their own mistakes. By contrast, parents of low-need achievers typically set impossibly high goals for their children and make extreme demands. In addition, parents of high-need achievers encourage good performance but do not berate their children when they fail. If a child comes home from school with four As and one B on a report card, the parents focus on the As; parents of a potential low-need achiever tend to ask, "Why the B?" Parents of high-need achievers respond to mediocre grades with warmth and suggestions for reasonable goals and ways to reach them. Parents of low-need achievers might say, "You're dumb and lazy—you'll never amount to anything," and punish the child. When a child is having trouble with a math problem, the parent of a potential high-need achiever will suggest the general procedure and let the child work out the particular solution; a low-need achiever's parent will solve the problem and then hand the child the answer.

That needs for affiliation and achievement exist within all of us, to varying degrees, is undeniable. And although biological bases for at least the affiliation need have been proposed, a great deal more is known about the psychological bases of these needs and how they come about.

Closely related to motivation are emotions, which can activate and direct behavior in much the same way as physiological, social, and psychological motivations do. Emotions also accompany motivated behavior: love often goes with sex, anger with aggression, and so on. Although almost everyone feels emotions, they are difficult to define.

Emotions

Emotions such as rage, fear, love, hate, and joy are closely linked to motivation. Often they result from the fulfillment or frustration of biological or social motives. In addition, emotions themselves often serve as motivators of our behavior, moving us to actions that facts alone might never elicit.

What precisely constitutes an **emotion?** It usually consists of both a mental, or cognitive, component and a physiological response. Theories of emotions typically focus on the relation between these two components.

The James-Lange Theory

The earliest modern theory of emotions was proposed shortly before the beginning of the twentieth century by the American psychologist and philosopher William James (1890) and the Danish physiologist Karl Lange. Both researchers, though working independently, concentrated on physiological reactions—increased heartbeat, for example—that accompany strong emotions. Intuitively, most people believe that these physiological reactions are a response to the emotion. James and Lange said just the opposite: they argued that emotions are perceptions of physiological reactions that precede and cause the specific emotion. People realize they are afraid because their hearts pound rapidly. As James (1890) put it, "We are afraid because we run; we do not run because we are afraid."

The James-Lange theory suggests that each of our many emotions is produced by a distinct physiological state. This seems unlikely. In many cases the physiological differences that do exist between different emotional states are very subtle (Ax, 1953).

Cannon (1927) attacked the James-Lange theory on two grounds. First, the physiological changes associated with emotional states occur too slowly to produce an emotional reaction. If a gun is pointed at you, you feel fear immediately—too quickly to result from physiological reactions. Second, the physiological changes that accompany emotions come about in other situations in which they do not produce emotions. Heavy exercise often produces many of the same physiological changes that accompany fear—increased heart rate, breathing rate, blood pressure, and so on—without causing a fear reaction. Cannon argued that the thalamus plays a central role in emotion (Cannon, 1927). His idea was elaborated on by Philip Bard, and the theory, known as the **Cannon-Bard Theory** (Cannon, 1929), places the source of the emotions in the thalamus, which, he believed, sent impulses to the sympathetic nervous system (producing the physiological changes) and at the same time to the cerebral cortex (producing the feeling of emotion). Although the importance of the thalamus to emotion has not been substantiated, there can be no doubt that physiological factors play an important role in emotional experience.

Physiological Bases of Emotion

Physiological changes accompany most emotional experiences. Blood pressure, heart rate, and respiration may change; the pupils of the eyes may dilate; the body may break out in a sweat. These bodily reactions are controlled largely by the autonomic nervous system, which in turn controls the glands and smooth muscles of the heart, the blood vessels, and the gastrointestinal tract.

Other evidence for physiological bases of emotion has been provided by studies using electrical stimulation of the brain. Electrical stimulation of certain parts of the brain can produce what appear to be full-fledged fear or rage responses in rats and cats. A most intriguing discovery was made accidentally by James Olds and Peter Milner (1954). Olds was studying the effects of physiological arousal on learning. Other physiologists had recently found an area just behind the hypothalamus that is involved in maintaining wakefulness. Olds, attempting to insert an electrode in this area of a rat brain, missed his intended target and placed it in the hypothalamus. Unaware of the misplacement of the electrode, Olds began to give the rat brief bursts of electrical stimulation. The rat, with the electrode attached to wires strung from its head, was free to roam a tabletop enclosure. To the researcher's astonishment, the rat kept returning to the corner where the stimulation occurred. The rat, reported Olds, seemed to be "coming back for more."

Olds suspected that, for some reason, the rat liked the feeling elicited by the stimulation. To test this possibility, he arranged an experiment in which the

Figure 10.5

The presence of "pleasure centers" in the brain was discovered by James Olds. Using the apparatus shown, Olds studied the effects of electrical stimulation of the brain. Each time the rat pressed the lever, it received a weak pulse of electricity through a tiny electrode implanted in its brain.

animal could control the stimulation of its own brain. He put the rat in a Skinner box set up so that when the animal pushed a lever, it received a burst of electrical stimulation in the brain (see Figure 10.5).

The results of this and other experiments that followed were clear and dramatic. Rats would stage veritable orgies of self-stimulation. Certain centers in the hypothalamus proved to be the most powerful motivators. Rats would pump the lever up to 5000 times an hour. Some would press it as many as 2000 times an hour for 24 consecutive hours, collapse from exhaustion, and then return to the lever for still more self-stimulation. To reach the lever, rats would even cross an electrified grid, enduring painful shocks of strengths much higher than those that will stop a hungry animal from reaching a reward of food. Given a choice between pressing a lever to obtain food and pushing one for self-stimulation, some rats eventually gave up all interest in food and devoted full time to their electric reward; but for the intervention of the experimenter, they would have starved to death (Spies, 1965). These areas that elicited repeated self-stimulation were labeled **reward centers** by Olds, but they soon became popularly known as "pleasure centers."

At about the same time that Olds was carrying out his early experiments on the reward centers, a group of researchers at Yale University were experimentally stimulating neural centers in the nearby midbrain (Delgado, Roberts, & Miller, 1954). Under this stimulation, cats reacted as if in great pain. When they were presented with food and the current was switched on, they immediately stopped eating and would not return to the food. They would even perform difficult tasks in order to avoid stimulation in these so-called punishment or **aversive centers.**

How are these fascinating phenomena related to the emotions we experience upon satisfying a motive? The answer is not clear, although it must be assumed that these experiences are somehow represented in the brain. For example, the feeling of pleasure that comes from drinking a glass of cold water on a hot day must result from a change in the activity of nerve cells. It is also possible that electrical stimulation artificially activates the same circuits that are involved in normal mechanisms of pleasure or pain. The location of the reward center—near hypothalamic areas that help regulate eating, drinking, and sexual behavior—is suggestive. At the very least, these experiments show that events in the brain are related to feelings of pleasure and pain.

Cognitive Aspects of Emotion

Recent research and theory have placed considerable emphasis on the cognitive determinants of emotion.

Two-Factor Theory of Emotions

The clearest example of this approach is Schachter and Jerome Singer's (1962) **two-factor theory of emotions.** Schachter and Singer contend that the physiological arousal accompanying emotions is simply a general state. The exact nature of the emotion depends upon how the person interprets the cause and meaning of the physiological arousal. As we are aroused, we put a cognitive label on the arousal: we call it joy, rage, frustration, and so on—depending on how we interpret the feeling.

Schachter and Singer's two-factor theory indicates that an emotion consists of both arousal and cognition. If neither arousal nor the cognitive label is present, then there will be no emotion.

On what basis does a person determine the content of the cognitive label? The two-factor theory states that, in the absence of a ready explanation for arousal, we seek cues from the environment—signals from the situation itself or from other people in the situation to tell us what we are feeling. If we don't know whether to laugh or cry, we look to the situation—is it a party or a funeral?—and to the emotions others seem to be experiencing.

To test their theory, Schachter and Singer needed a basic experiment that would combine the two elements of arousal and environmental cues. They needed also to disguise the real purpose of the experiment. Their solution was a project ostensibly aimed at measuring the effects of injections of a vitamin supplement which they called "suproxin." In reality, suproxin was epinephrine, a drug that induces arousal by acting on the autonomic nervous system, much as the naturally occurring hormone adrenalin does.

Some subjects knew they would experience symptoms of arousal; they were told the suproxin would produce side effects such as increased heart rate, hand trembling, and flushed face—the normal effects of epinephrine. Thus informed, they presumably would not have to look to the environment to interpret their physiological state as a particular emotion. Other subjects were also injected with suproxin but were not told about any physiological symptoms. According to the Schachter-Singer theory, these subjects would look to situational cues in order to interpret their feelings of physiological arousal.

After the injection, the subjects were taken one at a time to a waiting room. There, each subject joined another "subject"—actually a confederate of the experimenters. The confederate then attempted to manipulate the unwitting subject's emotions by behaving in one of two ways: he acted either euphoric or angry. In the euphoric condition, the confederate began to act in a silly and bizarre manner: he played basketball by flipping wads of paper at a wastebasket, he folded paper airplanes and sent them flying around the room, he found a hula hoop behind a bookshelf and twirled it around his hips. In the anger condition, the confederate displayed annoyance and rage at a questionnaire that he and the subject were asked to fill out. Although it began innocently enough, the questionnaire gradually became very personal and insulting; the final item asked bluntly, "With how many men has your mother had extramarital relationships?" and then gave the respondent the choice of several numbers, none of which was zero. As the confederate proceeded through the questions, he displayed more and more annoyance, crossing out items and finally ripping up the entire questionnaire.

After all of this had taken place, the experimenters attempted to assess the mood of their subjects. They asked them to complete a questionnaire aimed at eliciting facts about mood. The results supported the two-factor theory. The subjects who had not been informed about the physiological symptoms reported more intense emotion than did the subjects who had been told that the suproxin would have side effects and thus had a ready explanation for their arousal. Moreover, in the anger condition, the uninformed subjects reported greater feelings of anger than did the informed subjects; in the euphoric condition they reported stronger feelings of happiness. In short, when subjects had no explanation for their feelings of arousal, they took their cues from the behavior of the confederate. If he seemed euphoric, they experienced the emotion of happiness; if he seemed angry, they were angry. The physiological state produced by the epinephrine injections produced increased happiness or increased anger, depending on the setting. This experiment demonstrates the influence of cognitive factors in the interpretation of our internal states (see Figure 10.6).

Transfer of Excitation

Imagine that you have just run a morning workout of three or four miles. Your heart is beating faster and you are feeling other signs of physiological arousal. Both factors in the Schachter-Singer theory of emotion are present: arousal, plus your cognition of the situation ("I've just finished a hard workout").

Let's further imagine that after you've stopped to catch your breath, you drive to the grocery store. On your way there, another car suddenly runs through a stop sign and cuts you off. Your reaction most likely would be anger at the other driver. But would the fact that you had just exercised a few minutes ago lead you to be even angrier than would be normal in this situation? Ac-

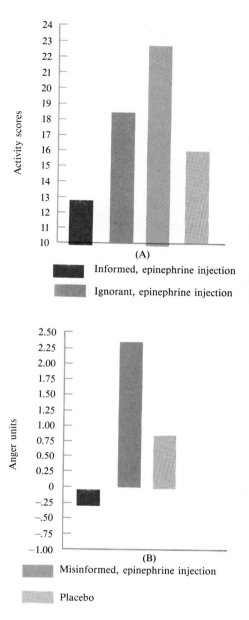

Figure 10.6

Bar diagrams of behavior in the euphoria (A) and anger conditions (B) of the Schachter and Singer experiment using "suproxin." The subjects who were not informed of the probable effects of suproxin as well as those who were misinformed were more active in the euphoria condition. The uninformed showed more anger in the anger condition (the misinformed were not tested in the anger condition). The subjects who were informed about the drug's effects were less active in the euphoria condition and showed no anger in the anger condition. The control subjects were more active than the informed subjects but less active than the uninformed or misinformed ones in the euphoria condition. In the anger condition they showed more anger than the informed subjects but much less than the uninformed subjects.

333

This baseball player's anger is evident in his tense body posture and facial expression. Physiological changes are also part of this emotional state.

cording to research by Dolf Zillmann, the answer is yes (Zillmann, 1971; Katcher, & Milavsky, 1972). Working from the two-factor theory of emotion, Zillmann has shown that arousal—whether caused by anger, physical exercise, or erotic stimulation—does not dissipate rapidly. Physiological excitation remains for a period of time even though we may not be aware of it. Zillmann calls this the phase of residual excitation.

The residual excitation from exercise, when added to the arousal of anger, leads to an especially high level of arousal. As you experience this high level of arousal, you attempt to interpret it in terms of immediate situational cues—your anger at the other driver. Thus, the effect is to transfer to the emotion of anger the residual excitation from physical exercise. According to Zillmann, this **transfer of excitation** will make you more angry, more willing to pick a fight with the other driver, than normally would be the case.

The enhancement of subsequent emotions by the transfer of residual excitation has been demonstrated by Zillmann and his colleagues in a number of experiments. One study, for example, created physiological arousal through physical exercise and then assessed whether this excitation was transferred to the level of sexual arousal. (Cantor, Zillmann, & Bryant, 1975). About five minutes after riding a stationary bicycle, and while they were in the phase of residual excitation, subjects were shown an erotic movie. Reports by these subjects of their feelings of sexual arousal were compared with those of subjects who either had not exercised first or who had watched the film immediately after or a long time after the exercise. The subjects in residual excitation reported being more sexually aroused by the film than did the other subjects.

The physiological and the cognitive aspects of emotions thus conjoin in varying ways, both to respond to, and to produce, the wide gamut of human feelings. One particular behavior that exemplifies this well is aggression: if the cognitive factor is anger or frustration, and it is accompanied by arousal, a strong emotion that might produce aggressive behavior is likely to result. Aggression has such powerful effects, in history and in the contemporary world, that it deserves a closer look.

Aggression

One of the most fascinating and important of all the behaviors that come under the scrutiny of psychologists who study motivation and emotion is aggression. Aggression is as commonplace as two neighbors quarreling and as immediate as daily newspaper headlines about assault, terrorism, and murder. In its most serious potential form, nuclear warfare, it threatens the very existence of humankind. In the course of this chapter, we have discussed several different approaches to motivation—sociobiological, physiological, and social. In this section, we will examine aggression in light of those three views.

The Sociobiological Approach

Konrad Lorenz, an ethologist who won a Nobel Prize in 1973, has proposed a theory of aggression that is based on studies of animal behavior. In his book *On Aggression* (1967), Lorenz argued that in many species fighting within the species is adaptive, fulfilling functions that enable the species as a whole to survive. For example, only the strongest win mates and reproduce, thus improving the species as a whole. In addition, because the losers may flee, Lorenz pointed out that the species will spread over a wider area, preventing overcrowding and insuring an adequate food supply.

Lorenz further postulated that because indiscriminate killing would not be adaptive, animals have evolved instinctive inhibitions against unrestrained aggression. These inhibitions are expressed in ritual behaviors that prevent fighting from resulting in death. For example, a defeated wolf turns and offers its throat to the victor, a gesture that ends their battle. The evolution of such inhibitors of aggression would be most developed in animals that have dangerous physical weapons like sharp teeth and claws. Lorenz suggested that over most of our evolutionary history, humans did not have such weapons. Therefore, humans did not evolve many effective inhibitors of aggression. When we began to manufacture weapons like knives, arrows, and rifles, the lack of such inhibitors became a lethal threat. We now had the weapons to kill with but not the ritualized gestures to stop the aggression. This argument makes some sense, but we probably do have inhibitors that are effective at close range, although not at a distance. It is easier to imagine killing someone with a rifle or a bomb than with a knife.

A critical and controversial part of Lorenz's arguments concerned the nature of an aggressive drive. Lorenz maintained that the aggressive drive was a **deprivation drive.** Deprivation drives are drives that, like hunger or thirst, get stronger and stronger as time passes without the satisfaction of the drive. Lorenz pointed out that as a drive gets stronger, less stimulation is needed to set off behavior associated with the drive. Thus, if aggression is based on a deprivation drive, aggressive behavior is virtually inevitable. However, there is no evidence, convincing or even semiconvincing, that aggression is based on a deprivation drive. Lorenz's assertion is rejected by most ethologists and psychologists.

In general terms, Lorenz viewed aggression as a relatively inflexible, innate mode of behavior. His theory thus has problems accounting for the wide variations in aggression that exist throughout human societies. Lorenz's views are often treated as though they were typical of the evolutionary approach to aggression. But this is not so. From the sociobiological point of view, Lorenz's position is flawed. Although Lorenz emphasized the value of aggressive behavior for the species as a whole, sociobiology emphasizes its for the individual's gene pool. From the sociobiological perspective, an animal should fight when the potential benefits of doing so outweigh the potential costs, and not otherwise. Benefits might include access to food, nesting sites, or potential mates. Costs might include the expenditure of time and energy and the risk of injury or death.

Informal observation supports the notion that costs and benefits determine aggression. Animals are most likely to fight over important resources when these are in short supply. For example, suppose you placed a bird feeder outside your kitchen window and kept it well stocked with birdseed all year round. During the winter, when other food is scarce, many birds would use the feeder, squabbling and fighting over the food. But during the summer, when other food is plentiful, birds coming to the feeder would not be very likely to fight.

This approach to aggression has been supported by several naturalistic studies. Frank Gill and Larry Wolf (1975) studied the territorial behavior of African sunbirds, which feed on the nectar of flowers. On some days these birds set up territories from which they aggressively chase other sunbirds. On other days, they do not set up such territories; instead they feed over a wide area without chasing other birds. Could this difference in behavior be due to the kind of cost-benefit relation suggested by sociobiology? To answer this question Gill and Wolf studied this behavior intensively. They found that whether or not the birds were territorial depended upon the number of flowers available each day. For instance, if there were very few flowers the birds were not aggressive. When there are only a few flowers, a territory has to be very large in order to contain enough food for the bird. But a large territory is very

Costs and benefits seem to determine aggression. Animals are most likely to fight over important resources such as food or nesting sites when these are in short supply.

Sniper, Charles Whitman prior to his killing spree on the University of Texas campus. Though an autopsy revealed a brain tumor, the relation between the tumor and the violence was not simple.

difficult to maintian. Thus the aggressive territorial behavior of the sunbirds was correlated with the relative costs and benefits of the behavior.

The sociobiological approach suggests that aggression is much more flexible than Lorenz's instinctive approach suggests. Aggression is simply another type of behavior that can serve an adaptive function under the right circumstances. Note that there is nothing in this view that says that aggression is either good or bad. It is just another behavioral alternative shown by animals under some conditions.

Physiological Mechanisms and Aggression

During the evening of July 31, 1966, Charles Whitman killed his wife and his mother. The next morning he carried a high-powered rifle to the top of the library on the University of Texas campus, barricaded himself in, and began to shoot at anything that moved. Before he was finally gunned down, Whitman shot 38 people, killing 14 of them. He left behind a note that said he had been experiencing overwhelming violent impulses, which he was afraid would overcome him. He asked that after his death an autopsy be carried out to see if there was any visible physical disorder. The autopsy revealed a tumor about the size of a walnut in the temporal lobe near the amygdala.

It is tempting to conclude that Whitman's tumor caused his aggressive behavior. But even if the tumor did contribute to what happened, and this seems likely, the relation between the tumor and the violence was not simple. For one thing, Whitman did not simply fly into a rage; he planned his attack over several days. And the murder of his wife was similarly premeditated. Before killing her he wrote, "It was after much thought that I decided to kill my wife Kathy. . . ." (Sweet, Ervin, & Mark, 1969).

Occurrences like the case of Charles Whitman suggest that violent behavior might be controllable through surgery. But in fact such attempts have rarely produced clear-cut effects. Often there are undesirable side effects or the desired effect is not obtained (Valenstein, 1973). These mixed results may reflect our ignorance of brain functioning. They likely reflect the complexity of the brain, where single centers of behavior are rarely physically separate.

But there is no question that neural mechanisms do play a crucial role in aggression. Much of the relevant evidence comes from animal studies: scientists have known for almost a century that damage to certain parts of the brain—the amygdala, hippocampus, and hypothalamus—affect aggressive behavior. In early studies on monkeys this damage was observed to decrease aggressiveness (Kluver & Bucy, 1937, 1938, 1939). More recent studies have found that damage to some parts of these structures may increase aggressiveness, whereas damage to other parts may decrease aggressiveness (Smith, King, & Hoebel, 1970).

The most impressive evidence for the role of neural mechanisms in aggression comes from studies using electrical stimulation of the brain. Electrical stimulation of various areas of the brain in many species elicits aggressive behavior, which often appears completely natural. In fact, these experiments have helped establish a distinction made on purely behavioral grounds: the distinction between predatory attack and within-species aggression. Aggression is usually defined as an attack on a member of one's own species. Predatory attacks on other species appear quite different from within-species aggression. A lion killing an antelope or a zebra shows little emotion. But when fighting with another lion, the animals display considerable emotion. Research using electrical stimulation of the brain shows that these two types of behavior have different neural substrates.

Many experiments have revealed that stimulation of different areas of the brain elicit two different kinds of attack behavior—affective attack and quiet-biting attack. John Flynn and his associates (Flynn, Vanegas, Foote, & Edwards, 1970) have done extensive research on the neural bases of rat killing by cats (it may seem strange, but laboratory cats do not spontaneously attack rats). When the medial hypothalamus is stimulated, affective attack is usually dramatically elicited: the cat behaves furiously; it arches its back; it erects the fur on its back and neck; it bares its teeth. The cat viciously attacks the rat with its claws, the attack often accompanied by growls or screams. Compared to this, the quiet-biting attack elicited by stimulation of the lateral hypothalamus is quite tame. When stimulated, the cat begins to search and when it sees the rat it pounces on it. In affective attack, the cat's behavior resembles that of a fight with another cat; quiet-biting attack, on the other hand, resembles normal hunting behavior.

The physiological approach to the study of aggression reveals several important facts. First, neural mechanisms are associated with aggressive behavior. In fact, the electrical stimulation research with animals suggests that aggressive behavior is integrated into the nervous system. Second, there are different types of aggressive behavior organized within the brain. Third, there is no single center for aggression within the brain: several different areas seem to be involved, including the hypothalamus, hippocampus, and amygdala. Finally, nothing in this information means that aggression, since it has neural bases, is inevitable. A normal cat, with the affective attack circuits in its brain, would never show such attack if it never encountered a situation that called for that behavior. Sociobiology and physiology cannot account for all aggression. Social and environmental factors are also important, and it is to these we now turn.

Verbalizing aggressive feelings allows us to "let off steam" and reduces the possibility of more violent aggression.

Psychosocial Approaches to Aggression

While the sociobiological and physiological approaches emphasize the adaptive and the neural aspects of aggression, psychological theories emphasize environmental and social influences. Psychologists seek to understand aggression by asking questions such as "How do people learn to be aggressive? What kinds of situations prompt us to be aggressive? What role does anger play?" In this section we will look at two influential psychological theories: one emphasizes emotional causes of aggression; the other examines the role of learning in aggression.

The Frustration-Aggression Hypothesis

In 1939, a team of five social scientists (Dollard, Doob, Miller, Mowrer, & Sears) theorized that frustration was the primary factor in aggression. "Aggression is always a consequence of frustration," they wrote, and "frustration always leads to some form of aggression."

Typically, frustration results when people are prevented from reaching goals or from engaging in desired activities. John Dollard and his associates reasoned that the frustrated person wants to aggress against the frustrating individual. Because this is not always possible, the frustrated person displaces aggression by directing it against another target. For example, the person's boss may refuse to give the employee a day off, but because the boss is not a suitable target, the person may aggress against less powerful targets—a family member or a fellow worker.

The **frustration-aggression hypothesis** has been criticized for a number of reasons but perhaps most logically for its unbending absolutism. People often are frustrated without subsequently engaging in aggression; aggression also occurs without the precedent of frustration. Insults, for example, often lead to aggression without necessarily causing frustration. Moreover, the hypothesis fails to take into account a major form of aggression, **instrumental aggression,** which is aimed at obtaining a reward—robbing a bank, for example—and may not stem directly from either frustration or anger.

How strange would appear to be this thing that men call pleasure! And how curiously it is related to what is thought to be its opposite, pain! The two will never be found *together* in a man, and yet if you seek the one and obtain it, you are almost bound always to get the other as well. . . . Wherever the one is found, the other follows up behind.

—Plato, *Phaedo*

The Costs of Pleasure, the Benefits of Pain

People as diverse as drug addicts and marathon runners would probably agree with Plato's ancient wisdom. The addict achieves the sudden rush of euphoria at the cost of the subsequent pain of withdrawal; the distance runner undergoes the pain of great physical exertion at the benefit of high exhilaration at the end of the race.

The reciprocal relations between pleasure and pain are the focus of an important new theory of motivation formulated by Richard Solomon of the University of Pennsylvania. Solomon (1980) calls his theory the opponent-process theory of acquired motivation. He believes that most acquired motives—such as love, social attach-ments, and even thrill seeking—as well as the needs for achievement, power, and affiliation, obey the same laws as various addictions. In his view, each of these motives is in fact a kind of addiction. Each addiction, whether to heroin, for example, or to social attachments, eventually produces a state opposite to that initially experienced: pleasure gives way to pain; pain turns to pleasure.

Solomon describes three phenomena that characterize the addictive type of acquired motive: (1) affective or emotional contrast, (2) habituation or tolerance, and (3) withdrawal or abstinence syndromes. These characteristics can be seen in the parallel emotional dynamics of two apparently contrasting types of acquired motivation—heroin addiction and thrill seeking. The first few doses of an opiate produce a state of euphoria. After the drug wears off, the user experiences the craving of withdrawal. If doses are repeated frequently, however, the tolerance to the drug builds up. The euphoria diminishes and gives way to the much more intense emotional and physiological pain of withdrawal. The positive reinforcement of pleasure loses power; the punishment of pain gains power.

By contrast, the acquisition of a thrill-seeking motive typically begins with negative or aversive stimulation. In a study of parachute jumping, Seymour Epstein (1967) found that novices experienced a great deal of terror during their first few jumps. A few minutes after landing safely, however, they became highly elated. Over many jumps, tolerance to the terror of free-fall built up. Epstein found that some experienced jumpers actually became severely distressed when bad weather grounded them. It was as if they were addicted to the sport and were experiencing withdrawal symptoms. Here, the thrill of the danger of jumping loses power,

Catharsis

An important corollary of the frustration-aggression hypothesis is **catharsis.** According to Dollard and his associates, realized aggression serves as a purgative: it reduces future tendencies to aggress and makes it relatively unlikely that the person will soon aggress again. This is reminiscent of Lorenz's idea of aggressive drive. The notion of catharsis is an ancient one, dating back at least as far as Aristotle, and over the centuries it has taken several forms. One long-standing theory holds that the mere act of fantasizing aggression or of watching another person aggress is cathartic. In this view, watching a boxing match or a football game has a cathartic value. It also has been suggested that verbalizing aggressive feelings enables us to "let off steam" and somehow reduces the possibility of more violent aggression. In fact, experimental evidence suggests that all of these notions about how to prevent aggression— fantasizing, watching, verbalizing aggression—are wrong. Indeed, these behaviors appear to increase the tendency to engage in aggression.

The cathartic effect has been established experimentally only when the frustrated or angered person is given an opportunity to harm the antagonist physically. In a study by Anthony Doob and Lorraine Wood (1972), subjects were angered by a confederate of the experimenters. In various conditions of and the positive reinforcement gains it. Although the heroin user begins with pleasure and the parachutist with terror, the result is the same—the craving that characterizes an acquired motive.

Solomon's theory assumes that the brain is somehow organized "to oppose and suppress many types of emotional arousals, whether they are pleasurable or aversive, whether they have been generated by positive or by negative reinforcers." He postulates two processes at work in acquired motivation. The primary process is set in motion by a positive or aversive stimulus such as heroin or parachute jumping. It eventually arouses an opponent process, which functions to oppose and suppress the emotional state generated by the primary process.

How can Solomon's fascinating theory be tested? One line of experiments deals with the growth of social attachment in young ducklings. Social attachment in young birds is acquired through the process of imprinting. As we saw in chapter 7, imprinting occurs when the newly hatched bird is first exposed to the movements of its mother or another object. If the imprinting stimulus is suddenly removed, however, the hatchling starts searching for the lost object and emits high-pitched cries, or distress calls. These distress calls are symptoms of withdrawal of the pleasurable stimulus and can be used as an index of the degree of social attachment, much in the way drug withdrawal symptoms can be used to measure dependence on heroin.

In an imprinting experiment, the opponent process, as indicated by the intensity of distress calling, increased as the number of trials, in which one-minute presentations were alternated with one-minute absences of the mother surrogate, increased.

Howard Hoffman and his colleagues (Hoffman, Eiserer, Ratner, & Pickering, 1974) exposed duck hatchlings to an imprinting stimulus for one-minute intervals that were alternated with one-minute periods in which the stimulus was removed. According to Solomon's theory, the opponent process—grief at the withdrawal of the mother surrogate—should be strengthened by use. As the figure indicates, that is precisely what happened in Hoffman's experiment. The opponent process, as measured by the intensity of distress calling, gradually increased.

Although Solomon's opponent-process theory still requires a great deal of testing before it can be widely accepted, the findings thus far may have important implications for the treatment of drug addiction. For example, the size and frequency of stimulus dosages appear to be crucial to the acquisition of an addictive type of motive. Solomon also suggests that there are implications for our understanding of psychosomatic disorders. He points out that we ordinarily think of physiological stress in terms of aversive events, but his theory "implies that often-repeated pleasures are just as fertile a source of physiological stress." ∎

the experiments, subjects were then either given opportunity to aggress against the confederate or not given opportunity to harm the confederate. Afterward, subjects were allowed to administer ostensibly painful shocks to the confederate. Shock intensity chosen by subjects served as the aggression measure. The least intense shock was administered by those subjects who had previously aggressed against the confederate. In this condition, presumably, the aggressive feelings of the subjects had been drained away through catharsis. On the other hand, the act of watching the confederate as he was harmed by the experimenter did not reduce later aggression: mere observation did not have cathartic value. Catharsis appears to occur only if one is frustrated and angered and then directly aggresses against the source of frustration.

Cues for Aggression

A modified version of the frustration-aggression hypothesis has been proposed by Leonard Berkowitz (1965). According to Berkowitz, frustration, insult, or attack produce anger or a readiness to aggress. Whether this anger actually prompts aggression depends upon the cues or stimuli present in the immediate situation.

FOCUS

Effects of TV Violence

For more than a decade, a highly significant focus of psychological research has been the effect of television violence on young children. Many American children spend more time watching TV than they spend in school, and what they see consists to a great extent of conflict, mayhem, and murder. According to George Gerbner (1972), 80 percent of TV dramas depict some form of violence. Other researchers have found that violence tends to be portrayed on TV as the most common way of achieving one's goals (Larsen, Gray, & Fortis, 1968). It has been estimated that, by age 16, the average TV-watching child will have witnessed no fewer than 13,000 murders (Waters & Malamud, 1975).

How does all this TV violence affect young children? One effect that has been convincingly documented in the laboratory is the physiological response of young TV viewers to real-life aggression. In one experiment (Thomas, Horton, Lippincott, & Drabman, 1977), researchers took physiological measures while young children watched either an aggressive TV show ("S.W.A.T.") or a championship volleyball game, which was equally exciting but nonaggressive. The physiological measures indicated both shows were roughly equal in the ex-

tent to which they aroused the viewers. Shortly after watching the TV show, and while they were still attached to the physiological monitoring apparatus, the children were exposed to a videotape of a real-life incident in which preschoolers engaged in a series of aggressive actions. (The children believed that they were viewing the preschool playground through a camera.) The children who had watched "S.W.A.T." were much less aroused by the preschoolers' fight than were the children who had seen the film of the volleyball game.

This apparent willingness to be more tolerant of real-life violence after watching the TV variety was also demonstrated by Ronald Drabman and Margaret Thomas (1974). In their experiments, children who had viewed a violent TV show were less likely to intervene in a fight between other children than were young subjects who had seen a nonviolent

show. Thus, faced by real-life aggression, children are less aroused and more willing to accept a fight than to break it up.

Does exposure to TV violence actually increase the likelihood that a child will engage in aggressive behavior? Two lines of psychological research discussed in our present chapter bear on this question; both suggest ways in which the tendency to aggress might be encouraged by watching TV violence. The social learning theory of Bandura, with its emphasis on observational learning, indicates that TV aggression provides a model for children to imitate. Such modeling has been demonstrated many times in the laboratory with children who view aggression either firsthand or in a filmed version. In addition, the research of Berkowitz on aggression cues as potential triggers of violence is similarly relevant. Through TV violence, many stimuli and cues can become associated with aggression and thus take on aggression-eliciting properties. Although the laboratory evidence strongly suggests the potential for engaging in aggression immediately after exposure to TV violence, psychologists are seeking answers to further questions. Does exposure to TV violence make it more likely that a child will be aggressive

Berkowitz placed a great deal of emphasis upon cues that have been associated with aggression in the past. An obvious example of such a cue is a gun. In one experiment, Berkowitz aroused his subjects with mild electric shocks. He then exposed half of his subjects to innocuous cues such as badminton rackets and shuttlecocks that were arrayed on a table. The other half were seated at a table containing cues that presumably would elicit aggression—a shotgun and a revolver. When all of the subjects were given the chance to retaliate against the experimenter by delivering electric shocks, those who had seen the guns demonstrated more aggression. Berkowitz concluded that the mere sight of a gun increases the tendency to commit aggression. "The finger pulls the trigger," Berkowitz wrote of guns, "but the trigger may also be pulling the finger."

Whereas Berkowitz's experiment has obvious implications for a society where guns are easily accessible, another experiment suggests that aggression-eliciting cues can be much more subtle than a shotgun or revolver. Berkowitz

340　　　CHAPTER 10　MOTIVATION AND EMOTION

later in life? Do all those TV-land murders lead a child to internalize and value aggression as a means of coping with life?

Probably the most impressive work addressing these questions was

boys who preferred TV violence also tended to be aggressive. This finding was not necessarily significant; it may be, for example, that boys who are aggressive happen to like TV violence.

turned out to be an accurate indicator of how aggressively he behaved at age 19. To rule out the possibility that aggressive boys prefer TV violence while young and simply continue to be aggressive later in life, Eron's group employed a variety of sophisticated statistical analyses. These analyses strongly implied that exposure to TV violence does increase aggressive behavior later in life.

a long-term study (Eron, Lefkowitz, Huesmann, & Walder, 1972) of a sample of several hundred boys living in a rural district of New York State. The researchers compiled data on a number of factors, including the boys' TV-watching habits and their tendency to be involved in real-life aggression. They found that those

What is important, however, is that Eron and his colleagues were able to study many of the boys again 10 years later when they were about 19. When the boys were again scored for aggressive behavior, a highly significant fact came to light: how much TV violence a boy had watched 10 years previously in the third grade

This research tentatively answered some questions but raised others. For example, Eron and his colleagues also studied a large sample of girls and found that preference for TV violence in the third grade did not relate to aggression 10 years later. One possibility for this negative finding is that at the time the girls were in the third grade only a few aggressive female characters were featured on TV. Now that TV gives greater prominence to violent women, a similar study might now find that girls too are adversely affected (Eron, 1980, 1982). Though further research is needed, the work to date does suggest that TV violence may be increasing our children's tolerance for aggression and enhancing the likelihood that they themselves will behave aggressively. ■

and Russell Green (1966) found that even a name can increase aggressive tendencies. Some subjects were shown a movie containing a great deal of violence. Afterward, they and other subjects were given the opportunity to shock an experimenter's confederate who had angered them. The most intense shocks were delivered by subjects who were led to believe that the confederate's first name was the same as that of an actor in the movie. Thus, according to Berkowitz, even an innocuous-sounding name, if previously associated with aggression, can elicit aggression from people who have been insulted, frustrated, or angered.

Lessons in Aggression

The social learning theory of Albert Bandura (1973) emphasizes the idea that aggression, like many other behaviors. is learned and that the learning occurs through two principal mechanisms. One mechanism is direct reinforcement. Children are often rewarded for acting aggressively, winning praise from peers and sometimes from parents. A second mechanism in the learning of aggression is modeling, or observation. By watching others who serve as models, children learn new ways of aggression and appropriate targets for that aggression. Observational learning is at issue in the continuing debate over the effects on children of the violence portrayed on television (see Focus on p. 340).

As we saw in chapter 7, Bandura's best-known work has focused on observational learning, most notably in the classic Bobo doll experiments. Although these experiments cast light on the vicarious acquisition of many behaviors, they are particularly relevant to the learning of aggression.

In these studies, children of nursery school age observed an adult model aggressing against a large inflatable clown called a Bobo doll (Bandura, Ross, & Ross, 1961). The model sat on the clown, punched it in the nose, hit it over the head with a toy mallet, kicked it around the room—all the while yelling "Sock him in the nose," "Sockeroo," "He sure is a tough fella." After observing this incident, the children were allowed to play freely in a room containing a number of toys including a "Bobo" doll. The children's behavior was carefully observed, and it was quite evident that the children were imitating the model's actions. The children's actions tended to match the aggressive behavior of the model, and the children also made some of the very same comments. Since the specific actions performed by the model were ones that were seldom performed by children in a control group who had not observed the model, the findings suggest that the children learned from the model. That is, they acquired new forms of physical and verbal aggressions.

In variations of his basic Bobo doll experiments, Bandura (1965) went on to investigate the effects of reward or punishment of the model. After the model had been aggressive, an adult walked into the room and said either of two things to the model. In the reward condition, the model was told that he had been a "strong champion" and that he deserved a treat, including a large glass of soda and an assortment of candies. In the punishment condition, the adult reprimanded the model—"Hey there, you big bully. You quit picking on that clown"—and threatened to give the model a "hard spanking." After observing either of these two scenes, the children were sent to the free-play room.

Interestingly, there was a vast difference between the behavior of those children who had seen the model rewarded and the behavior of those who had seen the model punished. The former group imitated the model's behavior; the latter did not. Despite this difference at the level of freely performed behavior, however, it was quite clear that all the children had learned the model's aggressive behavior. When the children were specifically asked to show the experimenter what the model had done and said, the children in the two conditions imitated the model's aggressive behavior equally well. Thus, all the children had acquired the behavior, but only those who saw the model rewarded chose to perform the behavior. Apparently, the children had learned not only how to aggress toward the Bobo doll but also, through observation of reward or punishment, whether it was appropriate to engage in aggression.

Summing Up Aggression

One of the reasons that psychology is a complex area of inquiry is that the phenomena that psychologists study need to be analyzed and understood at several different levels simultaneously. And it is often difficult to put multilevel analyses together into a single scheme. Such is the case with aggression. We have approached aggression from an evolutionary perspective, from a physiological point of view, and from a social point of view. What is the sum of those views?

We do not really know enough about aggression at present to put together a detailed picture, but an outline is beginning to emerge. As you recall, the epigenetic approach discussed in chapter 6 viewed the development of behavior as due to the interaction of genetic and environmental influences on the organism. The information we have reviewed on aggression shows that both factors almost certainly have a bearing on human aggression also. The biological bases of aggression are clear in both the sociobiological and physiological research we have reviewed. Aggression can be adaptive, at least under some circumstances, and therefore can be affected by natural selection. The neural basis of aggressive behavior demonstrates that aggressive behavior is wired into the brain, at least in lower animals and quite possibly in humans. On the other hand, the research of Bandura, Berkowitz, Doob, and others, shows that experience and the environment also affect aggressive behavior. Aggression in humans is probably a moderately canalized behavior, with some genetic basis. But how, when, and if a particular person will be aggressive at a given moment depends heavily on previous experience and the environmental situation. In terms of social policy, it may well be possible to control aggression because aggression is dependent on environmental factors. But this may not be easy, because aggression also apparently has biological roots.

Summary

1. Early psychologists ascribed motivation to instincts—innate patterns of behavior. The view was superseded by the concept of hypothetical states called drives—internal states that organisms sought to reduce. Today, instincts and drives do not seem adequate as all-embracing concepts for the investigation of motivation; instead, modern researchers investigate motives one at a time through various approaches. Among those approaches are the evolutionary approach, the physiological approach, and the social-learning approach.

2. The evolutionary emphasis holds that because the goals of motivated behavior are often biologically critical to survival and/or reproduction, evolution has finely tuned motivational systems to serve those goals. Strictly speaking, it is not survival that counts, but the leaving of offspring. Behavior is thus adaptive, contributing to the continuance of the species. Optimization theory assumes that animal behavior is organized to achieve biologically significant goals.

3. Physiological factors such as hunger and thirst are critical for survival, and neural mechanisms are involved in the regulation of these behaviors. The hypothalamus is an important regulator of hunger, thirst, body temperature, and sexual behavior, and a determiner of a variety of emotional responses. The endocrine system, which works in parallel with the nervous system, causes the secretion of hormones into the bloodstream; the hormonal mechanisms are also powerful regulators of behavior. An organism's tendency to maintain its internal environment at a constant level is called homeostasis. The hypothalamus operates automatically in the maintenance of homeostasis but is also subject to conscious control.

4. Two different systems control our thirst and intake of liquids. In the osmotic system, osmoreceptors sense cellular dehydration and prompt thirst. They also signal the pituitary gland to release an antidiuretic hormone (vasopressin) into the blood causing the kidneys to reabsorb water. The hypovolemic system senses lowered volumes of extracellular fluid and causes the kidneys to release renin, which acts as an enzyme to produce angiotensin I, which in turn leads to the production of angiotensin II. Angiotensin II affects certain nerve cells in the brain that then signal thirst. Research indicates that osmotic and hypovolemic thirst operate independently.

5. Homeostatic mechanisms in the brain help regulate hunger and food intake. One view was that the ventromedial hypothalamus is a satiety center that tells us when we have had enough to eat; the lateral hypothalamus is a feeding center that triggers hunger. Set-point theory holds that the hypothalamic centers play a different role, acting like thermostats to turn eating behavior on and off to maintain proper body weight. Obese people have a higher

than normal number of adipocytes, cells that store excess fat. Obese people also have heightened sensitivity to environmental cues about food. The ability to select a balanced diet is partially due to innate preferences for certain essential foods and partially due to learning.

6. Humans have social motives as well as biological needs. Sociobiology studies the interconnection of social and biological motivation. The sociobiological perspective has proved valuable in understanding the social behavior of animals and may prove equally illuminating in the long run in understanding human social behavior. Sociobiological research with human behavior is difficult to carry out and is still in its infancy.

7. Although human sociality may have some biological roots, learning and experience are crucial shapers of human social motivation. Among the strongest social motivators are our needs to affiliate and interact with others and our drives for achievement, which vary widely among individuals.

8. An emotion usually consists of both a mental, or cognitive, component and a physiological response. William James and Karl Lange believed that emotions are preceptions of physiological reactions that precede and cause the specific emotion. Although physiological factors play an important role in emotional experience, it is unlikely that each of our many emotions is produced by a distinct physiological state.

9. Physiological changes in functions such as heart rate and blood pressure accompany most strong emotional experiences. Experiments with animals suggest the existence of pain and pleasure centers in the brain. The two-factor theory of emotions contends that the physiological arousal accompanying emotions is a general state, and we must put a cognitive label on the arousal for it to be an emotion. We seek cues from the situation or the environment to tell us what we are feeling. Experiments with the drug epinephrine, which induces physiological arousal, have pointed up the influence of cognitive factors in the interpretation of our internal states.

10. Aggression is one of the strongest, most fascinating, and most potentially dangerous behaviors. Sociobiology suggests that aggressive behavior in animals should take place when its potential benefits—access to food, for example—outweigh its costs. Neural mechanisms involving the hypothalamus, the hippocampus, and the amygdala play a role in aggressive behavior, as animal research has shown. Psychosocial approaches to aggression emphasize emotional causes such as frustration, the need for catharsis, and the role of learning. Experiments have shown that children exposed to aggressive behavior will imitate it or condone it if the behavior is presented in a favorable light.

RESEARCH: Richard Solomon's opponent process theory of acquired motivation portrays acquired motives such as thrill seeking as being addictive. Addictive types of acquired motivation involve three components: (1) affective or emotional contrast; (2) habituation or tolerance to the danger and/or thrill involved; and (3) withdrawal or abstinence syndrome in which emotional upset is experienced when a person is not able to engage in that particular behavior.

FOCUS: Research examining the effects of television violence on the aggressive behavior of children has yielded two important findings, Viewing aggressive acts on television appears to: (1) increase children's tolerance for real-life aggression; and (2) increase the probability that a child will behave more aggressively when given the opportunity.

Sexual Behavior

When James Joyce's remarkable novel *Ulysses* was temporarily banned by the United States government half a century ago, it was not only the book's frank language that concerned the censors. They were also worried about the fact that Joyce's characters always seemed to be thinking about sex. His new stream-of-consciousness technique brimmed with erotic daydreams such as Molly Bloom's famous inner solilioquy that ends the novel: ". . . and then I asked him with my eyes to ask again yes and then he asked me would I yes to say yes my mountain flower and first I put my arms around him yes and drew him down to me so he could feel my breasts all perfume yes and his heart was going like mad and yes I said yes I will Yes." Even though the United States federal judge who handed down the landmark decision lifting the ban on *Ulysses* felt compelled to rationalize "the recurrent emergence of the theme of sex in the minds of his characters" by pointing out that Joyce's "locale was Celtic and his season Spring."

Today, as a result of the sexual revolution, most of us are willing to acknowledge that a mental preoccupation with sex is not the sole province of the Irish in the springtime. We spend a considerable amount of time thinking, daydreaming, and nightdreaming about sex—a subject that not long ago was generally taboo.

This should not surprise us, given the importance of sexual intercourse and related behaviors. To begin with, sexual behavior is obviously essential to the propagation of the species: any society that tried doing without it would not survive for long. Second, it is the source of much human pleasure and a medium for the expression of love and tenderness. Finally, as Sigmund Freud so forcefully suggested many years ago, sex sometimes plays an important role in seemingly unrelated areas of human behavior such as personality and even mental disorders.

For the student of psychology, sex is of additional interest. The study of sexual behavior offers a fascinating mode for the study of interactions between "mental" and "physical" mechanisms. In many ways, sexual behavior is a microcosm of human behavior in general, stemming from a complex interaction among biological, cognitive, experiential, and sociocultural determinants of how we think, feel, and act.

Although the importance of the evolutionary origins of human sexual behavior is conceded by most scientists, these factors are given the most emphasis by the new branch of science known as sociobiology (see chapter 10). The

Sociobiologists interpret sexual and other behaviors in terms of their evolutionary survival value.

CHAPTER 11   SEXUAL BEHAVIOR

sociobiologists tend to interpret sexual and other behaviors in terms of their evolutionary survival value (Daly & Wilson, 1978).

Sociobiology postulates, for example, that men want to have many sexual partners but women place greater emphasis on selectivity in the choice of mates. These and other apparent sex differences, say the sociobiologists, stem from differences in the parental investment of the two sexes. The male has large supplies of spermatozoa to expend and does not have to bear the child or, in many cases, help rear it. Thus he invests little in each offspring. The female has a much larger investment: pregnancy, lactation, and years of child care, along with the fact that she produces only one ovum per month. Sociobiologists conclude that much of sexual behavior is controlled by innate, genetically evolved mechanisms. Genes of males who inseminate many females and of females who select their mates carefully will be conserved by natural selection.

The evidence in support of sociobiology comes from the study of lower animal species. Its interpretations are highly speculative when applied to human beings. Such extreme claims about the genetic origins of human sexual behavior obviously must be measured against the tremendous importance of sociocultural factors.

Whether specific sexual behaviors spring from biological or environmental causes is a central issue in this chapter. We will thus focus frequently on the anatomy and physiology of sex. One section, for example, is devoted to the role of hormones in sexual behavior. The reasons for this emphasis are threefold. First, of all human behaviors, sex is the most subject to hormonal control. Second, a formidable body of experimental data exists, primarily animal research, that precisely shows the roles of the nervous and endocrine systems and that can be examined in human applications. Third, relatively little experimental research on the nonbiological aspects of sex has been performed, partly because of the taboos surrounding the subject until recent years and partly because of the obvious difficulties, even today, of studying human sex in the psychologist's laboratory.

Throughout the chapter, however, biological data will be evaluated in light of environmental factors that not only greatly influence sexual behavior but also appear to affect and modify our biology. At the end of the chapter, we will put the importance of both biological and the social determinants into perspective.

Pioneers in Human Sex Research

The scientific study of human sexuality is so new that its history covers less than a century. Four major figures dominate that short history—Sigmund Freud, Alfred Kinsey, and William Masters and Virginia Johnson. Each of these pioneers made a different kind of basic contribution to our present concepts of sexuality by using radically different methods of research.

Freud, a Viennese psychiatrist, depended upon the revelations of his patients as he explored the unconscious through his therapeutic system of psychoanalysis. Kinsey, a zoologist, used the survey-questionnaire method to collect data on people's sex lives. Masters and Johnson; a gynecologist and a psychologist, respectively, studied sexuality by a very direct means—observation of the sexual responses of volunteers in the St. Louis laboratory.

Freud: Psychosexual Development

Sexuality is central to Freud's formulation of psychoanalytic theory. Psychoanalytic theory, as we see elsewhere in the book, attempts to account for the development of normal personality (see chapter 12) and of psychopathol-

Reproduced by Special Permission of PLAYBOY Magazine;
Copyright© 1977 by PLAYBOY.

The suppression of childhood sexuality during the nineteenth century was symbolized by the war on masturbation.

ogy, or abnormal behavior (see chapter 14). Freud believed that inner conflicts could be traced to infancy and early childhood, to what he termed the **psychosexual stages** of development.

Freud's major treatise on sex, *Three Essays on the Theory of Sexuality,* was first published in 1905. The book was not much more than 100 pages long, only 1000 copies were printed, and it took more than four years to sell them. Nonetheless, this book, with its emphasis on infantile sexuality, had a profound impact.

To stunned Victorians, it appeared that Freud had "discovered" infantile sexuality. In fact, knowledge of childhood sexuality had been widespread until it began to be suppressed during the nineteenth century. The suppression of childhood sexuality was symbolized by the war on masturbation, which was alleged to cause insanity and various physical ailments. From 1856 to 1919, no fewer than 49 United States patents were granted for devices aimed at stopping masturbation. Some physicians advocated clitoridectomy, the removal of the clitoris, the most sensitive of the female genital structures. In Europe, physicians even recommended the use of a device to prevent little boys from having erections while sleeping: it consisted of a series of metal rings equipped with spikes that quickly awakened the culprit if his penis became erect.

Freud broadened the concept of sexuality by naming not only the genital region as an erogenous zone but also the mouth and anus. He then went on to describe the stages of psychosexual development in which the focus of sexual "energy," which he called **libido** (from the Latin meaning lust or desire) shifts successively in infancy and early childhood from **oral** (first year) to **anal** (second year) to **phallic.** A period of **latency** follows the phallic stage and is in turn followed in early adolescence by the **genital** stage, during which young people begin to direct their sexual interests toward others (see chapter 12).

Boys in the phallic stage (ages 3–5) focus on the penis and the fear of its removal. Freud misnamed this **castration anxiety** (castration means removal of the testes, not the penis). In girls, the phallic phase is characterized by attention to the clitoris and by anxiety at lacking a penis. Freud termed this **penis envy.** He contended that a healthy maturity depends on the successful resolution of the problems of the psychosexual stages, especially the phallic phase.

While Freud's influence upon the intellectual and cultural course of the twentieth century has been profound, the scientific validity of his specific concepts and conclusions has been seriously questioned. This is true not only of sexuality but also of his theories about personality and psychopathology. Freud's work is not generally amenable to experimental verification: concepts such as the castration complex and penis envy resist testing by the conventional methods of modern science. As a result, many of his concepts of psychosexuality have been either partially or totally rejected by most modern sex researchers.

As we shall see, modern researchers have taken a narrower, more manageable approach that is amenable to testing and verification. They owe, however, an immeasurable debt to Freud, who laid the intellectual foundation for subsequent study of human sexuality.

Kinsey: Asking About Sex

The second important pioneer in human sexual research was Alfred Kinsey. Until 1937, Kinsey, an Indiana University zoologist, had spent most of his career collecting and classifying gall wasps. When he was asked to teach a new course in sex and marriage, he went to the library to research the subject and concluded that science knew more about the sex lives of wasps than of humans.

Alfred Kinsey, an Indiana University zoologist, and his associates authored "The Kinsey Report," the most comprehensive study of sexual behavior ever undertaken.

Kinsey's approach to sex research differed markedly from that of Freud. Whereas Freud based his theories essentially on knowledge derived from a comparative handful of subjects—that is, his patients in psychoanalysis—Kinsey and his associates traveled the United States for 15 years, asking thousands of people to tell them about their sex lives. They asked, for example, how often respondents had intercourse and how often they masturbated. It is the most comprehensive study of sexual behavior ever undertaken: altogether, more than 5000 males and an equal number of females were interviewed.

The results were published in *Sexual Behavior in the Human Male* (Kinsey, Pomeroy, & Martin, 1948) and in *Sexual Behavior in the Human Female* (Kinsey, Pomeroy, Martin, & Gebhard, 1953). Both works were popularly known as "The Kinsey Report," and these accounts of how Americans actually behave both shocked and fascinated people. Despite the absence of photographs, they became best-sellers.

Kinsey's findings revealed the large disparity between what the public thought of as acceptable sexual conduct and actual sexual behavior. He noted high incidences of behavior generally regarded as unacceptable such as premarital and extramarital sexual intercourse, homosexuality, masturbation, and sexual fantasizing. For example, more than half of the married women interviewed reported that they had engaged in coitus (intercourse) before marriage: this compared shockingly with data from the nineteenth century (cited in Kinsey, Pomeroy, Martin, & Gebhard, 1953), which reported that only 14 percent of brides were not virgins.

Kinsey also was able to report fascinating variations in behavior among different groups. For example, male college graduates tended to engage increasingly in extramarital sex as they grew older, whereas such behavior tended to decrease with age among less-educated males. College-educated women masturbated more frequently than less-educated women, but had less premarital intercourse. Kinsey also found that masturbation was the most common means of experiencing orgasm for single women and the most reliable predictor of orgasm after they married. This finding was prophetic of current sex therapies that use masturbation in the treatment of **anorgasmia,** the inability to experience orgasm.

Scientists have criticized Kinsey's work because the sample of people interviewed was not representative of the United States population. The males were all white and did not represent an adequate geographical distribution. Nonetheless, his dryly fascinating statistics constituted a milestone in research. Indeed, more recent studies (Hun, 1974) have tended to support a great many of Kinsey's original findings. They provided a basis on which scientists and lay people alike could assess what was truly "normal" in American sexual behavior.

Masters and Johnson: Into the Laboratory

The first large-scale study of the physiological aspects of the human sexual response was begun in 1954 at Washington University in St. Louis by William Masters and his associate Virginia Johnson. Masters and Johnson brought human sex into the research laboratory. With instruments that monitored heart rate, blood pressure, and other physiological variables, they studied male and female orgasms resulting from masturbation or coitus.

It was not the first time scientists had attempted to measure the physiology of sex. One ill-fated study was carried out in the 1920s by the behavioral psychologist John B. Watson, whose early work in learning is discussed in chapter 7. Watson recorded his own responses and those of a female assistant until his wife, who had refused to join him in the experiment, found out about the assistant, sued for divorce, and confiscated his data. Watson's career at

William Masters and Virginia Johnson brought human sex into the research laboratory. In 1954 they began the first large-scale study of the physiological aspects of human sexual response.

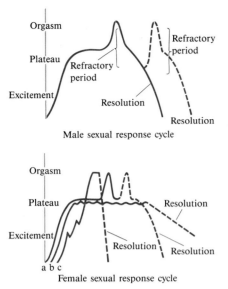

Figure 11.1

Diagrams of typical sexual response patterns in males and females. As the graphs show, sexual arousal in both increases until reaching a plateau phase. After this point, the male experiences orgasm as a brief, sudden surge of total arousal, followed by a refractory period during which he is incapable of further arousal; afterwards, he may experience either another orgasm or the onset of resolution. For the female, the cycle is more varied. She may experience orgasm twice or more before the onset of resolution (a); or she may never experience orgasm and then move slowly through resolution (b); or she may rapidly reach orgasm, stay in that phase for a time, and then move rapidly through resolution.

Johns Hopkins University was damaged, and he eventually married his assistant and went into advertising.

The Masters and Johnson project also ran into difficulties in the beginning. Their laboratory had to be moved off campus and was supported by funds from private foundations rather than the federal government. During the early days, many of the best-known medical journals refused to publish their findings.

Masters and Johnson first used prostitutes as experimental subjects. Later, members of the academic community were used as subjects. There were 694 volunteers, men and women aged 18 to 89. The majority of the volunteers were married couples. What the volunteers had in common was the ability to produce orgasms in the laboratory despite the presence of technicians, cameras, and elaborate monitoring equipment. In total they produced some 10,000 orgasms—2500 male and 7500 female. The orgasms were produced not only through coitus and self-stimulation but also through the use of an ingenious copulation machine. The machine consisted of a camera and a penislike probe, which was controlled by the female subject. The probe permitted the camera to record physiological events within the vagina.

In 1966 the results of the unprecedented investigation were published in the best-selling book *Human Sexual Response*. Most of the physiological events observed by Masters and Johnson fall under two principal headings: **vasocongestion**—increased blood flow to an area—and **myotonia**—increased muscle tone and contractions.

For both males and females, vasocongestion is seen primarily in the pelvic and genital areas but is also present in the abdomen, chest, neck, and face, where it causes the so-called sexual flush. Vasocongestion results in penile erections in the male and clitoral erections in the female and erections of nipples in both sexes, although in men there is no enlargement of the areola surrounding the nipple. Another consequence of vasocongestion is vaginal "lubrication," the appearance of a clear fluid that exudes from the walls of the vagina. Previously, it had been thought that the fluid was secreted by specific glands.

Like vasocongestion, myotonia also occurs in many areas of the body in both sexes. However, contractions of specific muscle groups are most dramatically pronounced during orgasm, when the muscles of the pelvic floor are affected. A series of rhythmic contractions in the muscles affecting the penis and the vagina occur during orgasm at about one-second intervals. Anal and other muscles in the region contract in synchrony with the genital muscles.

Masters and Johnson found that the physiology of human sexual response was basically the same for all subjects, both male and female, regardless of whether it was produced by coitus or masturbation. They somewhat arbitrarily subdivided the progression of events into four phases (see Figure 11.1):

1. *Excitement.* In the male, erection of the penis and perhaps of the nipples; in the female, erection of the nipples, swelling of the breasts, and lubrication of the vaginal lining.

2. *Plateau.* In the male, testes (reproductive glands located in the scrotum) swell to one and a half times normal; in the female, tissues around the outer third of the vaginal barrel swell and reduce the diameter of the vaginal opening (compared to the excitement phase), and the clitoris retracts under the hood that covers it.

3. *Orgasmic.* In the male, rhythmic contractions in the penis followed by ejaculation of the semen; in the female, rhythmic contractions of the outer third of the vagina and of the uterus; in both sexes, increase in respiration, heartbeat, and blood pressure.

4. *Resolution.* In both sexes, return of organs and tissues to normal conditions, which occurs more rapidly in the male than in the female. Men and women differ in their capacity to be rearoused after orgasm:

men generally experience an intervening period after orgasm during which they are not capable of sexual arousal. (see Focus on page 352).

The findings of Masters and Johnson contradicted some of the myth and folklore surrounding sexual response in women. For example, they showed that the size of the penis had little to do with female sexual pleasure. Also, they found no physiological difference between female orgasms resulting from direct clitoral stimulation and those resulting from vaginal stimulation (which causes indirect stimulation of the clitoris). Freud and others (mostly male) had contended that there are two types of orgasm—one produced by vaginal stimulation and the other by clitoral stimulation—and that vaginal orgasms were somehow superior.

Critics have faulted the Masters and Johnson study for widely varying reasons. Some observers charged that it constituted little more than a new kind of voyeurism under the veil of science; sex, they said, should be left to the bedroom. Others pointed out the volunteers were not representative of the general population because they were better educated and were selected for their ability to produce orgasm on demand. Still others charged that the laboratory approach, by reducing sex to its mechanics, depersonalized this most intimate of behaviors. The most important criticism was that Masters and Johnson had frequently violated common scientific procedure by failing to support their conclusions with sufficiently detailed information on experimental methods and results.

The major impact of the study was to usher in an era of concern and preoccupation with physiological responses in sex as opposed to the previous emphasis on psychological aspects that originated with Freud. Building on their laboratory research, Masters and Johnson went on to develop a novel approach to sexual therapy derived from the methods of both behavioral modification (see chapter 15) and conventional counseling. The new programs have helped men who suffer from premature ejaculation or impotence and women who are anorgasmic. Masters and Johnson's clinical observations were published in 1970 in *Human Sexual Inadequacy*.

Variations in Sexual Behavior

One of the most striking aspects of human sexual behavior is its wide variety. In recent decades the published work of Kinsey and other researchers has made evident what people had privately suspected for centuries: our sex lives differ in innumerable ways. These variations include who mates with whom, when, how, how frequently, and for how long.

In this section we will look at these differing patterns as they are manifested at four different levels: (1) among species, (2) among human cultures, (3) within a single culture, and (4) within the life cycle of the individual. This discussion begins with an examination of sexual behavior as a whole, in animals as well as in humans, then focuses on variations in smaller and more homogeneous groups, and ends with the individual.

Interspecies Variance

Animal behavior demonstrates that biology is an important determinant of different patterns of sexual behavior. Central to such a consideration is one overriding fact: although sexual behavior serves many purposes in humans and other higher species, it evolved principally to serve the aim of reproduction. In fact, we can understand much of the variety of sexual behavior evident in

FOCUS

The Nature of Orgasm

Only in recent years has science begun to explore one of the most intense, gratifying, and least-understood human experiences—orgasm. The word itself is derived from the Greek *orgasmos,* which means "to swell," "to be lustful." Physiologically, orgasm is typified by an explosive release of built-up neuromuscular tensions; psychologically, it can be characterized by a great variety of feelings, ranging from mild relief to something approaching a mystical experience.

Interestingly, there appears to be no direct evidence that the subjective experience of orgasm differs consistently between males and females. Ellen Vance and Nathaniel Wagner (1976) asked a group of men and women to submit written descriptions of their orgasms. These descriptions were given to a panel of qualified "judges" who lacked any overt clues as to the gender of each writer. The judges were unable to identify which descriptions came from men and which came from women.

Several important differences between the physiological responses of males and females during orgasm are apparent. The most obvious is that male orgasm typically is accompanied by ejaculation of seminal fluid. This must be preceded by emission of semen into the urethra from the testes and semen-producing glands by the contraction of involuntary muscles. Another difference is the occurrence of uterine contractions in the female, which has not yet been studied systematically. Masters and Johnson (1966) have established the capacity of the female, but not the male, to show multiple orgasms. Many females can go from one orgasm to another without pausing for the intervening refractory period characteristic of males and during which the male is not capable of sexual arousal.

This picture of apparent differences has been complicated by a report from California of men who seem capable of multiple orgasms, presumably after self-training (Robbins & Jensen, 1976). As in the female, the series of orgasms may continue to ten or more without a refractory period, which is characterized by loss of erection and sexual arousal. Each orgasm shows characteristic contractions of the pelvic floor muscles, including those of the penis. Women also show orgasmic contractions of the same muscles, which are found around the vagina, perineum, and anus. However, in men complete ejaculation of semen is found only during the final orgasm in the series. In other words, they can experience continued orgasms so long as seminal emission is prevented from occurring.

One explanation for multiple orgasms in men can be found in a new

different species of animals in terms of biological evolution. Each species has evolved a so-called **reproductive strategy** that meets the particular needs of the species in relation to its environment. These strategies, which differ from species to species, shape many aspects of behavior ranging from the duration of copulation to the extent of the father's participation in rearing the young.

In humans and some other animals, the reproductive strategy usually dictates sexual **monogamy**—that is, the practice of having only one mate at a time. The human young mature slowly and are defenseless during a prolonged period of development. Furthermore, at least in all primitive societies, the human mother is heavily involved in child care and needs the protection and assistance of the father in obtaining food. On the other hand, most small mammals, including rodents, which are used most often in experimental psychology, are promiscuous, as are some large mammals like the African buffalo. Songbirds are monogamous for a breeding season; geese and swans for a lifetime. In many species, **polygyny,** in which one male is bonded with a number of females, is the rule. **Polyandry,** in which one female is bonded with a number of males, rarely occurs. One well-studied instance of polyandry exists in a tropical bird, the American jacana. The female maintains a harem of two to four males and deposits a clutch of eggs with each. She trusts the males first to incubate and then to care for the newborn chicks. In humans, polygynous hypothesis proposed by Julian Davidson (1980). This theory, termed the *bipolar hypothesis,* suggests that male orgasm is linked to two different neural mechanisms. One neural mechanism fires "upward" to activate the altered state of consciousness that is the essence of the orgasmic experience. The other "pole" of this mechanism fires "downward" to produce the strong pelvic muscle contractions. The second neural mechanism Davidson hypothesizes also has two components: one is responsible for complete seminal emission via the smooth muscles controlled by the sympathetic nervous system, and the other causes the brain to activate the loss of sexual arousal after emission. Thus, according to this theory, it is the seminal emission that brings on the refractory period after a single male orgasm.

Davidson also has suggested that the bipolar hypothesis might be extended to female orgasm. He notes first that females lack seminal emission and have the greater capacity for multiple orgasm. Then he points out a direct analogy between seminal emission and uterine contractions. The contraction of the uterus is controlled by the same nerve that triggers seminal emission in the male. It is therefore possible that the nature of the uterine contractions may distinguish multiple and single orgasms (orgasms followed by a refractory period) in women.

If so, the bipolar hypothesis might also help clarify an issue first raised by Freud, who postulated two types of female orgasm, clitoral and vaginal. According to Freud (1905), vaginal orgasms were more satisfying and more "mature" than orgasms produced by stimulation of the clitoris, and this view became an important part of the psychoanalytic perspective on female sexuality. Kinsey (1953) questioned this. He asked five gynecologists to test the sensitivity to touch of various areas of the external and internal genitalia. Although all of the women responded with great sensitivity to touching the clitoris, the vaginal wall and cervix were largely insensitive to tactile stimulation. In fact, the vaginal wall and cervix have so few nerve endings that surgery is sometimes possible there without anesthesia.

Masters and Johnson (1966) could find no physiological difference between clitoral and vaginal orgasms. They pointed out that the thrusts of the penis during intercourse provide indirect stimulation to the clitoris by pulling on it; hence, perhaps all female orgasms are clitoral.

Nevertheless, many women seem to prefer one or the other mode of stimulation to orgasm. Davidson speculates that deep penile thrusting may induce uterine contractions, activating the same neural mechanism that causes seminal emission and loss of arousal in men. This could possibly result in a more satisfying orgasm that temporarily terminates arousal, in a way similar to the refractory period after male orgasm. ■

marriages have been permitted in a majority of societies, including the Mormons, but polyandry has scarcely ever been allowed.

A second aspect of reproductive strategy can be seen in the evolution of genital anatomy. For example, among animals that are heavily preyed upon, evolutionary survival suggests rapid mating and the anatomy to make it possible. In many male hoofed animals, a hard fibroelastic penis provides for a quick erection, with the organ shooting out like an arrow from a bow. The acme of such rapid performance occurs in the gerenuk antelope of eastern Africa, which can mate while literally on the run across the predator-infested plains. In contrast, mating tends to be a rather lengthy affair among carnivorous mammals, which have evolved a fleshy, slowly erecting penis. For example, in the dog, the penis swells within the female to form a kind of ball and socket joint that keeps the mating pair linked for a quarter or even a half hour of semen transfer.

Perhaps the most astonishing mating behavior, however, is that of the praying mantis. During copulation, the female has the unique habit of devouring her male partner's head. This cannibalism does have a salutory effect on reproduction of the species. Literally losing his head, the male also loses centers in his primitive brain that ordinarily inhibit sexual drive. Though headless, he lives for several hours and, with inhibitions gone, copulates much more

The role this father plays in rearing his child can be considered to be, in part, a product of human reproductive strategy.

vigorously, increasing the transfer of sperm. While this intriguing phenomenon is well known among animal behaviorists, it has recently been challenged. It may be that this cannibalistic behavior is largely due to the conditions imposed on the insects for optimal scientific observation.

Among our closest animal relatives—the three species of great apes—reproductive strategies differ markedly (Nadler, 1977). Orangutans tend to be antisocial, ranging alone over wide territories. Sexual behavior reflects this antisocial tendency. Because encounters between males and females are limited, it is important to maximize the opportunities for mating. Thus, sexual encounters often resemble a wrestling match, with the sexually dominant male forcing the female to the ground, if she is not "in heat" (hormonally prepared for mating).

Gorillas, on the other hand, are highly social animals, and mating is controlled by the female. Mating tends to be strictly limited to the period when the female is in heat or **estrus.** During this period of receptivity, the female may aggressively back her mate into a corner.

The third species of great ape, the chimpanzee, occupies a position somewhere between the gorilla and orangutan in terms of when mating occurs and which sex dominates the encounter. In each species, sexual behavior is adapted to conditions of social living.

By comparing the great apes and humans we can discern the parallels between the evolution of reproductive behavior and the evolution of reproductive anatomy (Short, 1978). For example, coitus occurs less frequently among humans than among chimpanzees. Likewise, the human testis is smaller, relative to body weight, than the chimpanzee testis. This correlation makes evolutionary sense because if men ejaculate more often than every two or three days, the volume of the semen and the density of the sperm decline, reducing the potential for reproduction.

Other evolutionary adaptations are consistent with the human maximization of sexual pleasure. The erect human penis is larger, relative to body weight, than that of any monkey or ape and is usually conspicuous when flaccid. Similarly, the human female breast is bigger and more prominent outside of pregnancy or lactation than that of any of the apes or primates. This plays a role in visual attraction between the sexes. Along with female orgasm, which does not occur in any subprimate species so far as is known, this attraction is believed to strengthen the development of a lasting **pair bond** between the two partners in a monogamous relationship. These pair bonds are important for the prolonged care of the slow-maturing human infant. However, the most important sexual factor cementing male-female bonding in humans is likely to be maintenance of sexual receptivity in women throughout the menstrual cycle, which is virtually unique to the human species (see Research, p. 356).

Intercultural Variance

The variations in patterns of sexual behavior found in different human societies are nearly as striking as those that occur among the different animal species. We are not always aware of these differences because our culture, like that of all societies, has its own value systems that label as deviant all behaviors that appear to fall outside of "normal" boundaries. Such behaviors are usually classified as pathological and then eliminated from consideration, except as they require suppression or "cure." Conversely, phenomena such as the incest taboo, common to so many profoundly different cultures, are more likely to be considered biological in origin. By turning to the data of anthropologists, however, we can see how differing value systems shape vastly different norms of sexual behavior.

The Trobrianders

The pioneer of modern anthropological studies of sex was Bronislaw Malinowski. For several years during World War I, Malinowski lived among the people of the Trobriand Islands in the South Pacific. His fascinating observations were published in 1929 in his classic study, *The Sexual Life of Savages in Northwestern Melanesia.*

The children of the Trobrianders were allowed a great deal of freedom. They roamed the village freely, forming what Malinowski called a "children's republic," in which they could engage in sexual games without parental restraints. This freedom of sexual play extended also to young unmarried adults, who were free to have premarital intercourse. Females were expected to experience orgasm and men encouraged to control ejaculation so as to maintain prolonged coitus.

RESEARCH

Female Sexuality and the

Menstrual Cycle

The importance of a scientist's methodology, which often seems less interesting than his or her results, is dramatically illustrated in the study of one highly significant aspect of sexual behavior: the suspected relationship between a woman's sexual desire and the phases of her menstrual cycle. In lower mammals, mating is limited to a brief period around the midpoint of the female's menstrual cycle, coinciding with ovulation, which is triggered by peak levels of the sex hormones. In humans, obviously, mating can occur at any time during the female cycle.

Nonetheless, important questions remain. Do changes in hormonal levels, as reflected in the various phases of the menstrual cycle, influence sexual responsiveness in the human female? Are women, as is widely believed, truly emancipated from hormonal control of their sexual behavior? These questions have more than academic interest, if only because of the widespread use of oral contraceptives, which profoundly influence hormonal levels. If cyclic hormonal changes do, in fact, affect female sexual behavior, then oral contraceptives can be expected to influence the responsiveness of women who use them.

Early attempts to answer these questions employed a simple methodology. Women were asked to describe their frequency of coitus in relationship to the phases of their menstrual cycles. Interestingly, most of these studies showed a peak in sexual activity not at midcycle but just before or just after menstruation. The problem with such studies was that the results did not necessarily reflect hormonal changes. For example, many women abstain from intercourse during menstruation. Thus, intercourse may well increase just before and after this period of abstention because of other factors such as the anticipation of abstention or the accumulation of desire after it.

Later studies produced opposite results, indicating a strong correlation between midcycle hormonal peaks and peaks in frequency of coitus or orgasm. But these studies, too, had methodological problems. Udry and Morris (1968) paid working-class women to report to the laboratory each day and record their sexual behavior for the past 24 hours. This was an improvement on unreliable retrospective methods in which women might be asked to record their sexual activities during previous weeks or months. But the study was severely criticized for failing to solve the problem of how to summate results from cycles of different lengths—and hence of how to estimate the time of ovulation. In fact, Udry and Morris (1977) later demonstrated that completely different conclusions could result from different methods of pooling and calculating data.

Regardless of results, all of the studies suffered from two critical shortcomings in methodology. One shortcoming was the implicit assumption that the frequency with which a woman participates in coitus depends upon her own feelings as opposed to the demands of her male partner. To remedy this problem, one study focused on female-initiated behavior, whether heterosexual or masturbatory (Adams, Gold, & Burt 1978). However, their findings—a midcycle peak of behavior coinciding with a midcycle peak of a particular sex hormone—illustrated the other shortcoming in such studies: they failed to measure the actual hormonal levels

of their subjects directly. Without these measurements, it is clearly impossible to reliably assess possible relationships between changes in sexual behavior throughout the menstrual cycle and the fluctuating hormone levels, which are postulated to cause these changes.

Since the 1970s, an accurate methodology for measuring hormonal levels by labeling the hormones with a radioactive substance has come into general use. This advance has made possible two new studies that confirm the early reports that sexual behavior reached a peak at times other than the midcycle surge of hormones. John Bancroft, a psychiatrist at the University of Edinburgh, and Diana Sanders found peaks of sexual interest just before menstruation and peaks of sexual activity just after the end of menstruation (Bancroft, 1981). An American investigator, Patricia Schreiner-Engel, and her colleagues have taken a different approach, using an instrument to record vaginal blood flow as a measure of sexual arousal, as well as measuring hormone levels in blood (Schreiner-Engel, Schiavi, Smith, & White, 1981). She found that maximal increases in sexual responsiveness and fantasizing when listening to an erotic tape recording occurred four to seven days before and just after menstruation. However, the changes in blood flow were small and two other studies (Hoon, Bruce, & Kinchloe, 1982; Morrell, Dixon, Carter-Porges, & Davidson, 1984) using video instead of audio tapes as erotic stimuli, failed to find any differences. The study last mentioned showed a small but significant decline in responsiveness at the time of menopause. Again, we do not know whether such small changes in vaginal vasocongestion have the significance to a woman's sexuality as analogous changes in erection would have to men. ∎

Some of the apparent permissiveness no doubt stemmed from the Trobrianders' ignorance about the relationship between sex and having babies. They believed that pregnancy occurred because the baby was placed on the hair of the prospective mother by a special spirit and then carried to the womb by the mother's blood. The belief that the blood helped nourish the baby explained to the Trobrianders why the pregnant women no longer menstruated.

For all of their apparent lack of constraints, the Trobrianders nonetheless put several important limits on sexual behavior. Incestuous relationships between brother and sister were so sternly forbidden that adult siblings were prohibited even from being together except in the presence of others. Adultery was also severely condemned, but as Malinowski observed, "The rules are as often and as easily broken, circumvented, and condoned as in our society."

Definite rules of propriety also governed the sexual techniques of the Trobrianders. They despised two important practices of Western society—namely, prolonged mouth-to-mouth kissing and the so-called missionary position (face-to-face copulation with the man prone over the woman). Trobrianders typically copulated with the woman on her back and the man squatting between her legs. Partners often scratched fiercely at each other and proudly wore the resulting scars as insignia of their pleasure.

The East Bay Society

A contrast to Trobriander sexual mores was found in the East Bay Society, a culture located on an island near the Trobriands. William Davenport (1965), who studied the East Bay Society, reported that the people had a positive attitude toward sex, but it differed from the Trobrianders in many respects, perhaps because, unlike the Trobrianders, they knew how babies are conceived. From the time boys and girls walked, they were separated socially, and any physical contact between them was a punishable offense after age five. Similarly, premarital sex between young men and women was forbidden, although masturbation was encouraged among both sexes and homosexuality among young men. Even after marriage, homosexual relationships between men and preadolescent boys were accepted.

Marital intercourse was reported to occur typically twice a day—in the morning, in the garden; in the evening, in the home. Unlike the Trobrianders, the East Bay people favored the missionary position. Following prolonged foreplay, the woman was expected to have an orgasm, although males were said to ejaculate in 30 seconds or less.

By comparing the studies from these two Melanesian peoples—the Trobriand Islanders and the East Bay Society—we can see readily how two cultures, which otherwise had much in common, differed radically in sexual behavior. These differences stemmed from differing social rules that governed not only the kinds of sexual acts that were permissible and with whom, but also at what age and even at what time of day.

A Tale of Two Tribes

The power of environmental circumstances to influence differing patterns of sexual behavior was shown in a recent study by Ernestine Friedl (1975). Friedl studied two neighboring tribes in New Guinea: one lived in the highlands, the other in nearby lowlands. The highland tribe had such negative attitudes toward sexual intercourse that it was not permitted in gardens for fear it would stunt plant growth. Coitus was believed to weaken men; contact with the menstrual blood of women was thought to be harmful. There was much general antagonism between men and women, who lived in segregated quarters.

The lowland tribe studied by Friedl regarded sexual intercourse as pleasurable and even a source of revitalization for men. In contrast to the highlanders,

Changes in our cultural norms regarding sex have been referred to as the sexual revolution.

these people wanted to perform coitus in gardens because it was thought beneficial to plant growth.

Friedl concluded that the striking differences in sexual attitudes between these neighboring societies probably resulted from a basic dichotomy in their immediate environments. The highland people lived in an area with scarce resources of land; they feared that any increase in their population would threaten food supplies. Conflict between the sexes and avoidance of intercourse were effective means of holding down the birthrate. The lowland people, by contrast, inhabited an uncrowded area that needed cultivation. A positive attitude toward relations between the sexes raised the birthrate and provided more farmers to cultivate the land.

Population control has also figured in the sexual norms of other societies. For example, on New Britain Island, men assiduously avoid sex to control population; they even worry about being raped by women (Reuben, 1971). Examples of sexual norms that increase birthrates can be found in organized religion. Roman Catholic prohibition of contraception (when effective) and the Orthodox Jewish avoidance of sexual relations during menstruation and the week after (and thus increased activity during the more fertile part of the menstrual cycle) both increase fertility rates among their adherents.

Cross-Cultural Variance and Similarities

The anthropological studies cited make abundantly clear how widely sexual behavior varies among cultures. This is not to suggest, however, that commonalities of sexual attitudes and practices do not exist that transcend cultural barriers. The best single source of such data is the classic cross-cultural review carried out by Clellan Ford, an anthropologist, and Frank Beach, a psychologist. Ford and Beach painstakingly reviewed data from 191 different human societies, many of them preliterate and with only one Western society included, the United States. Their findings were published in 1951 in *Patterns of Sexual Behavior*.

Although the data Ford and Beach reviewed are now quite old, and many of the societies have undergone profound changes, their findings help illuminate the question of which behaviors tend to be widespread. We will briefly describe two of their findings:

- Masturbation exists in almost all the human societies studied (and indeed, among nonhuman primates and other mammalian species). While techniques of self-stimulation vary little in different cultures, the range in attitudes toward masturbation is great—from encouragement as in the East Bay Society, to benign scorn as in the Trobriand Islands, to complete rejection as in the United States not long ago.
- Male homosexuality in some form was accepted or encouraged in 64 percent of the 76 societies on which Ford and Beach were able to obtain information. (Lesbianism was considerably less frequent or at least more carefully concealed.) Attitudes toward male homosexuality ranged from prohibition as in some Bedouin tribes where it was penalized by death, to total acceptance as in ancient Greek society where, during the Classical period, sexual relations between men and boys were regarded as a higher expression of love than heterosexual coitus.

Other findings included the following: face-to-face copulation is extremely widespread, as is stimulation of the female breast; frequency of coitus is higher in other societies than is the norm in the industrial West (up to 10 times a night among the Chagga tribesmen of Tanzania); manual stimulation of the partner's genitals is universal and considerably more common than oral-genital activity.

Intracultural Variance

Within a single culture, there are many variations from that society's general norms of sexual behavior. Variations such as homosexuality are discussed elsewhere in this chapter. A different sort of variance—namely, changes in overall sexual behavior in our own society over a period of time—is of great interest to psychologists.

During the past few decades, the changes in our cultural norms regarding sex have been so profound that we refer to them collectively as the sexual revolution. The most noticeable change has been the remarkable opening of channels of communication about explicit sexual matters. Books and movies that not long ago were prohibited by legal statutes are readily available and make James Joyce's *Ulysses* seem tame by comparison. Contraceptive devices that used to be kept under the druggist's counter are now displayed next to the colognes; *Consumer Reports* has devoted space to its ratings of the best condoms. People once modestly spoke of "limbs" instead of legs; now many people appear on television game shows and discuss the frequency of their sexual intercourse.

This change in attitudes about a subject that was once taboo has been accompanied by changes in actual behavior. Evidence points to real changes in the occurrence of certain sexual activities. Perhaps the most dramatic change is the incidence of premarital intercourse, especially among females (see Figure 11.2). About 40 years ago, Kinsey reported that among college-educated respondents 27 percent of females and 49 percent of males said they had engaged in premarital intercourse by the age of 21 (Kinsey, Pomeroy, Martin, & Gebhard, 1953; Kinsey, Pomeroy, & Martin, 1948). A comprehensive survey of American sexual behavior (Hunt, 1974) taken during the early 1970s showed a much higher incidence of premarital intercourse among the college students interviewed—depending on the group surveyed, 43 to 56 percent for females and 58 to 82 percent for males. It is interesting to note that this latter survey was sponsored by the Playboy Foundation, a benevolence of the magazine that both encouraged and symbolized the sexual revolution.

An even more dramatic increase in premarital intercourse, one that occurred over a single decade, from 1965 to 1975, is shown in Table 11.1. This study compares the incidence of such behavior among students at one American university located in the southeastern United States (King, Balswick, & Robinson, 1977). In ten years, the number of females reporting that they had engaged in coitus before marriage almost doubled.

Apart from the increased availability of effective birth control and abortion, the increased willingness of female college students to participate in coitus before marriage presumably reflects two interrelated phenomena. One is the decline of the old double standard of sexual morality that permitted certain behavior for men but not for women; the other is the rise of modern feminism. Significantly, surveys indicate that, in addition to premarital coitus, other forms of sexual behavior such as masturbation have also increased among women (King, Balswick, & Robinson, 1977).

Figure 11.2

Graph comparing the percentage of single females having had premarital intercourse in 1949, 1971, and 1977.

Table 11.1 INCIDENCE OF PREMARITAL INTERCOURSE IN COLLEGE STUDENTS AT A SOUTHERN UNIVERSITY (GROUPS OF 115–275 SUBJECTS EACH)

	Female	Male
1965	28.7%	65.1%
1970	37.3%	65.0%
1975	57.1%	73.9%

Source: K. King, J. O. Balswick, and I. E. Robinson, "The Continuing Premarital Revolution Among College Females," *Journal of Marriage and Family,* 39 (1977), 455.

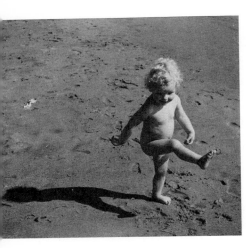

During the first year of life, spontaneous sexual arousal occurs frequently in both sexes.

Like the cross-cultural variations discussed previously, these examples of changes in a society's norms of sexual behavior over time reflect the importance of cultural attitudes. Next, we will narrow our focus to the cultural standards and the biological factors that influence individual, as opposed to societal, sexual behaviors.

Individual Variance: The Life Cycle

Our consideration of variance in sexual behavior has progressively narrowed to more homogeneous groups—from all beings including animals, to cross-cultural comparisons among humans, to a single culture. Now we will look at the individual human in order to identify varying sexual patterns as they are manifested over the entire life cycle.

Contrary to general belief, people seek sexual stimulation and gratification virtually from the cradle to the grave. Some of the quantitative and qualitative changes in the expression of sexual behavior during four broad phases of the life cycle—early childhood, prepuberty, puberty and beyond, and the declining years—concern us next.

Early Childhood

Episodes of spontaneous sexual arousal are found in both sexes during the first year of life. These endure from a few seconds to several minutes and may occur a number of times a day. As we saw earlier, Freud was castigated for calling attention to infant sexuality, but its existence has been long known to observant parents and more recently has been documented by scientific scrutiny.

Investigators believe that stimulation of the infant genitals takes place during periods of restless behavior involving stretching and bending of the legs. Boys show erections on these occasions, and it is thought that orgasm (although not ejaculation) sometimes follows. Moreover, pelvic thrusting motions are seen in infants from eight to ten months of age. During the first two years of life, there appears to be no difference between boys and girls in their sexual behavior. After that, however, boys are reported to masturbate more frequently than girls (Langfeldt, 1979).

Prepuberty

Despite Freud's suggestion that there is a period of sexual latency from about age 5 until puberty, youngsters continue to be sexually active during this period. Such activity was found by the anthropologist Malinowski (1929) in his study of the Trobriand Islanders and has been described much more recently by a number of observers. For example, one researcher noticed an increased frequency of male masturbation after age 7; in fact, the boys taught each other techniques of self-stimulation (Langfeldt, 1979). It is likely that Freud, in assuming a latency period, was misled by the effects of social sanctions in turn-of-the-century Vienna. Even in most modern societies, manifestations of sexuality in children are proscribed by the parents and consequently hidden by the child.

Puberty and Beyond

Puberty has traditionally been considered a period of great sexual awakening. Certainly, at this stage, which begins at about 14 years of age in the male and 12 in the female, profound sexual changes take place as both sexes become capable of reproduction. Amazing as it may seem, however, there is a lack of systematic data correlating sexual behavior with these physiological changes. Such data might help clarify the apparent contradiction between the concept of puberty as a time of sexual awakening and the evidence that there appears to be continuous sexual interest and activity from early childhood. For the moment, we must define behavioral puberty in terms of an increase in desire for sexual activity often accompanied by increased frequency of sexual outlet through masturbation and, most notably, through the development of a largely heterosexual social orientation. This is the time when the first manifestations of "falling in love" occur. This phenomenon, like other radically changed aspects of behavior during puberty, is often attributed by parents to "hormones." Later in this chapter we will take up the question of whether sexual behavioral changes can be reasonably related to changes in hormonal functioning. In any case, from early puberty, sexual capacity and activity generally are thought to build to a peak, which occurs at 15 to 18 years of age in the male but not until the late thirties or early forties in the female.

The Declining Years

After reaching a peak, sexual capacity and activity tend to decline. According to a longitudinal study of several hundred aging individuals started at Duke University in 1957 (Verwoerdt, Pfeiffer, & Wang, 1969), both men and women showed a pattern of declining sexual activity and interest with age, but about one half of the subjects surviving into their eighties and nineties reported "mild or moderate" sexual interest. The patterns differ between the sexes, however. In men there is a growing discrepancy between interest and capacity, with the former being maintained or even increased (25 percent of subjects) with age in the face of increasing **impotence**—the inability to perform coitus, generally because of failure of erection. In aging women, declining sexual activity in our society is often associated with lack of sexual opportunities due to lack of partners or of partners' interest or capacity to have intercourse.

Some of the effects of aging in men were observed by Masters and Johnson (1966) during the course of their laboratory studies. They found that male orgasm appears to be the aspect of sexual behavior most vulnerable to aging, possibly due to weakening of the penile muscles. In young men at their sexual peak, erection follows instantly upon stimulation, semen spurts from 12 to 24 centimeters during ejaculation, the penis takes about half an hour to return to its normal flaccid state, and sexual arousability is recovered soon (sometimes in less than a minute) after ejaculation. By contrast, men over 50 are slower to reach full erection, semen tends to seep out rather than spurt during ejaculation, the penis returns rapidly to its flaccid state, and the intervening refractory period before renewed sexual arousability may extend to 12 or even 24 hours.

It is also clear, however, that aging men can avoid absolute impotence through the maintenance of good health and the avoidance of serious psychological problems such as severe depression. As they grow older, men often insist that quantity of sexual experience is replaced by quality. Havelock Ellis, the English psychologist whose early writings on sex helped pave the way for Freud and the modern investigators of sex, became capable of sexual fulfillment through coitus only when he had reached his early fifties (Brecher, 1969).

The effect of aging on female sexuality is more complex and less well understood. Women may show increases, decreases, or lack of changes in their sexuality. What makes the difference is not precisely known. As we will see in the following section, **menopause,** the permanent cessation of menstruation that occurs during the late forties or early fifties as a result of fairly abrupt cessation of ovarian function, is marked by a sharp decrease in sex hormones. This deficiency can lead to dryness in the vagina and thinning of its walls, sometimes causing pain during coitus. But psychological factors also can play a role in changing sexuality. In some women mental stress and other problems can lead to a lack of interest in sex. In others, the end of childbearing years may bring liberation from sexual inhibitions related to the fear of conception. But even if women are interested, the lower survival rate of males and the societal constraints on having relations with younger men or on having extramarital relations may mean that older women will be sexually unfulfilled.

Behavioral puberty is defined in terms of an increase in desire for sexual activity. This is also often the time when we first "fall in love."

Both men and women show a pattern of declining sexual activity, but the patterns differ between the sexes.

The Role of Hormones in Sexual Behavior

The biological study of sexual behavior focuses principally upon the role of **hormones,** the chemical messengers that are manufactured by the various endocrine glands and released into the bloodstream. The brain is vital to hormonal functioning, and the study of relationships among hormones, brain, and behavior is known as psychoneuroendocrinology.

Each of us produces both male and female sex hormones that exert a profound influence on the anatomy and physiology of our sexual systems and largely govern the differentiation of male and female anatomy and physiology. At puberty, a large increase in the production of sex hormones is responsible for the sudden blooming of the physical and sexual characteristics. These include maturation of such primary characteristics as the male penis and testes and of the female clitoris and ovaries. They also include such secondary characteristics as the deepening of the male voice and the growth of facial hair and, in the female, enlargement of the breasts and broadening of the hips. Of great importance is the fact that beginning at puberty, hormones regulate the female reproductive cycle.

Beyond these well-established endocrine principles, the role of hormones in sexual behavior is less clear. Do so-called raging hormones cause premenstrual mood swings? Do male hormones cause an increase in aggressiveness and "machismo"? Does homosexuality result from hormonal action?

There is a reasonable possibility that the answer to the above questions is yes. A large percentage of the intelligent lay public and, indeed, of the medical profession shares such beliefs. The fact is, however, that none of the answers has been reliably established by experimental evidence. The answers are speculative or based on inadequate data, clinical impressions, or unverified extrapolation from animal research. Human sexual behavior is so profoundly affected by experience and sociocultural factors that it is often difficult to separate out the part played by hormones. In the following section we will evaluate the existing evidence and discuss the physiological and anatomical effects of hormones on sexual behavior.

Mechanisms of Hormonal Production

The production of hormones related to sex involves a complex interaction between brain and body. Hormonal production can be viewed as essentially a three-stage process:

1. The hypothalamus, a tiny structure at the base of the brain (see chapter 2), sends chemical signals via blood vessels that connect it to the so-called master gland, the pituitary.

2. The pituitary responds by manufacturing and releasing into the bloodstream two protein hormones, the **luteinizing hormone** (LH) and the **follicle-stimulating hormone** (FSH), both of which are essential for release of spermatozoa and eggs from the **gonads**—that is, the testes and ovaries. These hormones are called **gonadotropins.**

3. Gonadotropins, in turn, stimulate the production of sex hormones in the gonads. These gonadal hormones are called steroids, a class of hormones that also includes cortisone from the adrenal cortex. The main steroids produced by the male testes are **androgens,** the most important of which is **testosterone.** The primary steroids produced in the female's ovaries are estradiol (an **estrogen**) and **progesterone.**

Keep in mind that gonadotropin production is part of a process involving the brain and the pituitary gland. This process is a closed loop, and specialized cells in the brain and/or pituitary serve as a kind of thermostat. This "gonadostat" monitors the sex hormones circulating in the bloodstream; when they reach certain levels, it switches off production of the pituitary hormones, LH and FSH, that stimulate manufacture of the sex hormones. Contraceptive pills contain synthetic sexual steroids—artifical analogs of the natural female sex hormones, estrogen and progesterone. They prevent ovulation by signaling the pituitary to stop producing LH and FSH and have other antifertility effects such as preventing implantation of the fertilized egg in the womb.

Effects of Hormones in Females

The most pronounced effect of the steroid sex hormones in females is regulation of reproduction, including the production of eggs (ova), the menstrual cycle, and pregnancy. The length of the reproductive cycle varies widely among mammals—from 4 days in the rat to 36 days in the chimpanzee. This cycle is essentially a fluctuation from a state in which the female is physiologically prepared to receive sperm to a state in which she is prepared to receive the fertilized ovum. Thus, in the 28-day human cycle, it takes two weeks to make the egg available for fertilization, while during the next two weeks the reproductive tract is prepared for implantation and growth of the fertilized ovum. These effects are mediated by changes in the production of female steroid hormones, which are controlled in turn by the gonadotropins.

In most mammals the gonadal hormones exert a profound influence on mating behavior. Because they are produced in greatest amount around the time of ovulation, mating is generally limited to that short period around the time of ovulation, a limitation that increases the probability that copulation will result in conception.

One result of the action of sex hormones in animals is to make the female a receptive partner in mating. (Rape among animals is almost unknown.) In addition, the hormones may stimulate the female to initiate the sexual encounter by showing the male such stimuli as swollen or highly colored "sexual skin." This is known as **attractivity.** She also shows soliciting behavior or **proceptivity,** ranging from seductive hops, darts, and ear wiggles in the rat to the more brazen presentation of the rump in monkeys (Beach, 1976). If the source of these hormones—namely, the ovaries—is removed in a variety of subprimate species, all sexual behavior is suppressed. The behavior can be restored, however, with doses of estrogen and progesterone.

The principal mechanism by which hormones exert such a direct influence on sexual behavior in many female mammals was first proposed by Frank Beach in 1948. Beach suggested that hormones somehow affect nervous activity within the brain. Some years later two English investigators, Geoffrey Harris and Richard Michael, demonstrated this effect on a specific area of the brain. Harris and Michael (1964) worked with female cats whose ovaries had been removed, thus depriving them of sex hormones and, consequently, any interest in mating. They attached a small amount of estrogen to the end of a wire and inserted it into different parts of the cat's brain. When this hormonal implant was placed in certain areas of the hypothalamus, the cat soon became receptive to the male, and normal mating behavior occurred. More recently, other researchers (Barfield & Chen, 1978) have used smaller implants in rats to localize definitively hormone-responsive "sex centers."

Thus, in most mammals, there is an extraordinary coordination between the reproductive physiology and behavioral mechanisms. The brain signals the release of pituitary hormones, which control the ovarian production of sex hormones, which in turn act on the brain to influence behavior (as well as to "switch on" the pituitary to cause ovulation and to switch it off after fertilization to break the cycle).

In primates, however, this lock-step control of sexual behavior by ovarian hormones is not as strong as it is in other mammals. Although removal of the ovaries and treatment with sex hormones often have appeared to influence the behavior of female monkeys, the results may depend largely on a variety of social interactions that do not play important roles in subprimates. Not surprisingly, the male monkey's peak in sexual initiatives often coincides with ovulation in the female cycle. This suggests that the ovarian hormones of the female, peaking at ovulation, somehow produce maximal attractivity for the male. Another possibility is that the ovarian hormones stimulate subtle behavioral cues in the female that excite the male, although the female may be receptive to him even without midcycle hormones.

In humans the role of female hormones in sexual behavior becomes severely limited. Unlike any other species, the human female can continue an apparently normal sex life after surgical removal of her ovaries or the cessation of their function at menopause. It is true that a variety of studies have reported peaks of female sexual behavior occurring at various phases of the menstrual cycle. Because sex hormones also show considerable changes during these phases (see Figure 11.3), this suggests a hormonal role in women's sexuality. But such reports have also been explained in terms other than hormonal: for example, abstinence during menstruation or the conscious or subconscious desire to avoid or engage in coitus around the time of ovulation (Udry & Morris, 1977).

Similarly, there have been interesting observations about the possible link between female sex hormones and other behaviors. Many women report mood swings (the "premenstrual syndrome") during the final days before menstruation (Dalton, 1977). In addition, one correlational study of female convicts found they had a much greater likelihood of committing a violent crime during this period. Indeed, in France, women accused of crimes committed in the final days before menstruation are permitted a legal defense called "temporary impairment of sanity." Such observations have not been verified by experimental methods.

Figure 11.3

The menstrual cycle when fertilization does not occur. The events that take place within the pituitary, ovary, and uterus are precisely synchronized.

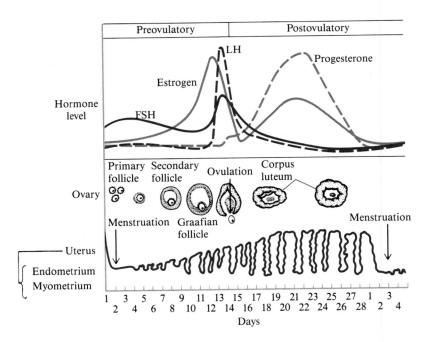

CHAPTER 11   SEXUAL BEHAVIOR

What is surprising, however, is that sexual behavior in women may be significantly influenced by androgens, the hormones that are vital to male sexuality. Androgens are produced both in the ovaries and in the adrenal glands. Clinicians have long believed that administering androgens to women can stimulate their sexual desire by affecting the brain or perhaps by increasing sensitivity and even growth in the clitoris. Moreover, it has been shown that blood levels of naturally occurring androgen often increase at the midpoint of the reproductive cycle (Judd & Yen, 1973). Whether androgens normally play a role in female sexual behavior or whether they have an effect only when large doses are administered awaits further research.

We have seen that hormones can affect female sexual behavior most dramatically in subprimate mammals. But such influence is not a one-way street. Data from animal experiments, and some from human research, indicate that behavior itself, along with environmental and social factors, affects production of sex hormones.

This evidence derives partly from observations of the apparent effects of emotional stress on menstrual cycles in human females. For example, gynecologists report that some college women experience irregular menstrual cycles under the stress of the school year but have regular cycles when they are relaxing at home during the summer (Matsumoto, Tamada, & Konuma, 1979). During World War II, many women in German concentration camps ceased menstruating altogether (Bass, 1947).

These apparent effects on hormonal functioning are still speculative, but the influence of social and environmental factors is well established in many animals. Cats and rabbits ovulate in response to copulation or even the mere presence of the male because sexual stimulation triggers release of LH. Female laboratory mice, when brought together in the same cage, cease their normal reproductive cycles. A newly pregnant female mouse will abort in the presence of a male other than the father. These effects on female reproductive function are caused by the presence of chemical substances or other excretions called **pheromones** in the urine of male and female mice. Such pheromones act chemically upon the glands of other mice to influence the production of their sex hormones.

A different kind of effect in animals is produced by the **signaling pheromones** (also known as sex attractants). These chemical messengers are excreted through the male's urine or through the female's vagina and activate sexual behaviors in the opposite sex, reaching the nervous system through the sense of smell. Signaling pheromones have been identified in many invertebrate animal species, particularly insects. One such pheromone, androstenone, is produced by boars and stimulates the mating stance in sows. This steroid is found in the sweat of men, and British psychologists have reported that its odor is attractive to women (Kirk-Smith & Booth, 1980).

Although pheromones have been chemically isolated in many animals, their possible existence in human females has been debated for many years. A study carried out by Martha McClintock (1971) provides evidence of the effect of social stimuli and perhaps of pheromones on menstrual cycles. She found that roommates or close friends living together in a college dormitory tended to have their menstrual periods at the same time. Moreover, shorter cycles were found among those women "who spent more time" with males. McLintock's hypothesis was that pheromones produced both by the females and the males were responsible for these apparent influences on hormonal functioning.

There is some evidence that women experience an increased acuity in the sense of smell at midcycle, the time of ovulation. For example, adult women can perceive a synthetic compound with a musklike odor that cannot usually be detected by males or by young girls before puberty (Le Magnen, 1952).

Figure 11.4

Effects of testosterone treatments on the sexual activity of men without functioning testes including mean frequencies of diurnal and nocturnal erections, coitus (including unsuccessful attempts), masturbation, and orgasms. All responses were normalized by expressing them as a percentage of the maximum weekly performance of that subject during the course of the cycle.

This perceptual ability reaches its peak at midcycle. Interestingly, musk, which is a common component of perfumes, is derived from a sex gland of the male Tibetan musk deer, where it is believed to perform a pheromonal function.

Effects of Hormones in Males

In contrast to females, where fluctuations in hormonal levels dictate the reproductive cycle, sex hormones in the male are produced at a fairly constant rate. Also in contrast to females, the key role of male sex hormones in mediating behavior is clearly established, from lower mammals to humans.

Classically, the first step in demonstrating the effects of a hormone is to remove the gland that produces the hormone and then observe the subsequent changes in behavior. The male sex hormones, androgens, including testosterone, are produced by the testes; removal of the testes—castration—has been a frequently used surgical technique throughout history.

Men were castrated to provide "safe" companions for ladies in ancient Rome and to furnish eunuchs for the harems of Arab sheiks. In fact, the very word *eunuch* comes from the Greek for "guardian of the bed." The medieval Roman Catholic church made use of a physiological fact that is now well known: castration before puberty eliminates the glandular source of testosterone that causes the adolescent voice to deepen. The "castrati" choirboys of Italy were men who kept their high-pitched voices because their testes had been excised before puberty. The Russian sect, Skoptsi, practiced castration to ensure male abstinence. Not surprisingly, this sect has died out.

Castration invariably produces a decrease and, frequently, a total disappearance of sexual behavior in males, although some of the effects may take several years to be manifested (Bermant & Davidson, 1974). After sexual behavior disappears, it can be restored by administering testosterone (Davidson, Camargo, & Smith, 1979). The rapid effects of administering testosterone to men without functioning testes can be seen in Figure 11.4. Recent studies have shown, however, that though testosterone-deprived men invariably lose libido (sexual drive, interest, pleasure) and spontaneous erections, they typically can experience erections in response to erotic films and presumably other strong sexual stimuli (Kwan, Greenleaf, Mann, Crapo & Davidson, 1982; Bancroft & Wu, 1983).

The importance of androgens to male sexual behavior is so obvious that the question arises: can differences in male sex drive and activity be related to differences in androgen levels? The answer was given in a recent study of 101 young adult men whose reported sexual activities were correlated with the level of testosterone in their blood (Brown, Monti, & Corriveau, 1978). No positive relationship was found between high sexual activity and high testosterone level. The probable explanation for this is that the normal range of testosterone levels exceeds that necessary to maintain sexual behavior. Nature apparently has provided a considerable excess of androgen (in rats, up to tenfold) over that necessary for normal sexual functioning. This is a kind of evolutionary safety factor to ensure survival of the species.

In late middle age, the decline in blood levels of testosterone is occasionally quite precipitous. In such cases, symptoms are similar to those found in female menopause, including hot flashes. Men with these symptoms are sometimes said to be undergoing the **male climacteric.** They show a rapid loss of sexual drive, indicating a clear relationship to the loss of male sex hormones. In contrast, as we previously noted, women often maintain or actually increase sexual behavior after menopause despite their sharp decline in female sex hormones.

Stressful events in a man's life can profoundly affect sex hormone level. Both physical trauma such as surgery and psychological stress have been shown to reduce the amount of testosterone in the blood (Davidson, Smith, & Levine, 1978). Although studies are lacking, it is a fair assumption that such environmental-biological interactions can result in impotence.

Effects of Hormones Within the Brain

The mechanisms by which male hormones affect sexual behavior have been the subject of much research in recent years. The prevailing hypothesis is that these hormones influence the action of nerve cells in the brain, especially in the hypothalamus, which, as we saw earlier, appears to be a site where female sex hormones affect behavior. Many investigators believe that hormones somehow influence the action of neurotransmitters—the chemical messengers between brain cells (see chapter 2). For instance, it has recently been shown that a single injection of yohimbine, a drug that stimulates the release of the brain neurotransmitter norepinephrine, immediately restores sexual behavior in castrated male rats (Clark, Smith, & Davidson, 1984). One widely held theory suggests that, at least in rats and some other animals, male hormones first must be converted in the brain to the female hormone estrogen before having an effect on male sexual behavior (Luttge, 1979).

The evidence that male hormones exert a direct influence on the brain comes principally from animal research. For example, a male rat that has become inactive following castration will resume the whole complex of mating behavior when solid testosterone is implanted in a specific area of the hypothalamus (Davidson, 1966). Sexual behavior can be eliminated in rats, mice, cats, dogs, and rhesus monkeys by destroying this same area in the hypothalamus. Injections of testosterone into these animals does not restore normal sexual behavior (Hart, 1985).

These experiments pinpoint at least one area of the brain as being specifically involved in controlling mating behavior in experimental animals. Other parts of the brain also have been implicated in sexual behavior. For example, when areas in the limbic system, which sends afferent nerves to the hypothalamus, are disrupted by a form of epilepsy in humans or by surgical lesions in experimental animals, increases or decreases in sexual behavior are reported. An example of "hypersexuality" in such an experiment involved a male cat with surgical lesions in the limbic system. The cat attempted to mate with a stuffed teddy bear and kept up his copulatory movements until he was put to sleep.

Increases in sexual behavior in female animals also have been observed from lesions in another area of the limbic system, the septum. One researcher, Robert Heath, has even implanted electrodes in the septa of a few human patients. Heath (1972) reported that electrical stimulation of the septum resulted in sexual arousal and generally pleasurable sensations. Questions have been raised, however, about both the results and the ethics of this research.

Sexual Differentiation

In recent years, the roles of the two sexes have begun to change radically in our society. These changes apply to practically all branches of human behavior, including sexual behavior.

At various places in this chapter we have described several differences between males and females in sexual behavior—for example, in the physiology of arousal and the incidence of premarital intercourse. To what extent are these factors determined by learning, culture, and other environmental factors? To what extent are they determined by the biological factors of anatomy and physiology?

The answers to these questions appear to be the easiest to obtain in the realm of animal research. Among subprimate species and among certain primates, biological determination predominates in sexual behavior and in many other sexually differentiated behaviors such as aggression, parenting, and emotions.

The "Reversed Adam" Principle

The Old Testament makes no bones about sexual differentiation: man came first, and from his rib was formed woman. In fact, however, the model of sexual differentiation provided by animal research is just the opposite. Anatomically and physiologically, the basic pattern is female. If the embryo is genetically destined to be a male, that is, if the father's fertilizing sperm carried a Y chromosome, masculinity is imposed by the presence of the male hormone androgen, which triggers development of internal and external male sexual structures. This androgen is provided at a critical stage in early development by the testes, which develop under the influence of the XY combination of sex chromosomes. Without androgen at the proper time, the developing animal remains female. (Androgen, in fact, takes its name from the Greek meaning "producer of males.") This principle of masculine superimposition on a basic female pattern is called the **reversed Adam principle.**

Animal Studies
Compelling and powerful in its simplicity and apparent universality, the reversed Adam principle derives from several decades of animal research. This research shows that the reversed Adam principle is responsible for sexual differentiation at the level of sexual anatomy, physiology, and behavior. Alfred Jost and associates (Jost, Jones, & Scott, 1969) established that androgen produced by the testes of the rabbit fetus was responsible for male anatomical differentiation, that is, development of the external genitalia and of the internal reproductive structures. Charles Barraclough (1966) demonstrated the drastic physiological effect of testosterone on newborn female rats: a single injection of the male hormone masculinized the physiology of their reproductive system so that they never cycled or ovulated in adulthood.

One of the key experiments in establishing the behavioral effects of the reversed Adam principle was carried out by Geofrey Harris and Seymour Levine (1965). Newborn male rats were castrated, depriving them of the male sex hormone produced by the testes, and an ovary was transplanted into the eye in front of the lens, where it could be observed. Although the external genitalia of these young rats were not feminized, they developed a female cycle of hormone production and ovulated. When males castrated at birth were given female sex hormones in adulthood, they displayed female patterns of sexual receptivity. These effects, it was found, could be prevented by a single injection of testosterone at the time of castration. Moreover, when newborn female rats were given testosterone, they grew up sterile and showed male mating and other behavior.

These findings were extended to monkeys by investigators Robert Goy and Charles Phoenix (Goy, 1970). Pregnant monkeys given testosterone produced female offspring with masculine genitalia: the clitoris, for example, grew to resemble a small penis. These females also displayed patterns of play typical of male monkeys: they were more assertive and engaged in rough games. They also displayed masculine sexual behavior such as the male pattern of mounting. Furthermore, there was a delay in the onset of puberty. Interestingly, however, when these females reached adolescence, there was little disruption of the typical female reproductive functions.

In summary, androgen is the key to sexual differentiation, especially in subprimate mammals. In its absence, the basic female pattern continues to develop. The female sex hormones produced by the ovaries have no known role in sexual differentiation. Research suggests that androgen brings about differentiation by laying down new patterns of neural activity in the hypothalamus, somehow changing the brain's future responsiveness to the gonadal hormones and to environmental stimuli. Actual changes in the growth pattern of certain neurons in the hypothalamic area, caused by sex hormone treatment at birth, have been demonstrated in rats (Harlan, Gordon, & Gorski, 1979). In fact, in the rat's spinal cord a whole nucleus that controls the muscles of the penis is formed due to the presence of male hormone and is virtually absent in females (Breedlove & Arnold, 1980).

Human Studies

Obviously, the findings about the reversed Adam principle cannot be extended to humans through direct experimentation. One possibility, however, is to study females who have been exposed in the womb to abnormal amounts of male hormones. For example, the genetic disorder known as **adrenogenital syndrome** produces a tumor or excessive growth in the adrenal glands that results in the production (commencing before birth) of large amounts of androgen. Other girls have had prenatal exposure to hormones with androgenic (masculinizing) actions that were given to their pregnant mothers to prevent spontaneous abortion. The degree of masculinization can vary from slight enlargement of the clitoris to its metamorphosis into a penis with fusion of the vagina and growth of a scrotum—albeit empty, because internal structures are feminine.

John Money and Anke Ehrhardt (1972) conducted long-term follow-up studies on such girls, most of whom had their anomalous genitals corrected by early surgery and lifelong hormone treatments. They found that prenatal exposure to male hormones resulted in unusually "tomboyish" behavior while growing up. This included a predilection for masculine dress and toys and a tendency, which had been observed previously in the female monkeys given testosterone before birth, to engage in masculine forms of rough-and-tumble play. There were, however, two important differences from the observations in most of the animal experiments described earlier: the reproductive cycles of the girls were not disrupted (in the monkeys, onset of menstruation was delayed), and they exhibited no deviance in later sexual behavior.

In humans, then, as well as in animals, the reversed Adam principle appears to be at work, although it is apparently less profound in its effects. Male hormones are secreted at critical periods in early development to bring about masculinization of reproductive anatomy and some aspects of behavior via action on the brain. In the human females studied, however, there was no clear change in sexual behavior nor in their feeling of gender identity: they regarded themselves as normal females.

The Influence of Learning in Sexual Differentiation

What explains the lesser effects of early androgen in humans? Money and Ehrhardt (1972) point to the importance of the social environment in establishing gender identity, sex roles, and behavior appropriate to the sex of the individual. That environment was shaped in such a way as to teach the androgen-exposed girls that they were indeed girls. They were given girls' names, usually treated early with plastic surgery and hormones to erase the masculinization of their genitals, and raised as girls.

Even more dramatic evidence of the vital role of social learning in sexual differentiation comes from work by these and other investigators. Money re-

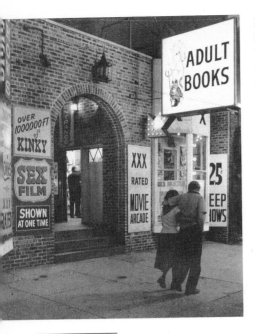

Kinsey found that women were less likely to be aroused by erotic material presented in visual form. However, more recent studies have found no significant differences between the sexes in response to erotic pictures.

ports, for example, on a pair of identical male twins. One of the twins had his penis removed shortly after birth because of damage during circumcision. He was reared as a girl and, at last report, had responded to this role by developing feminine play and dress behavior. The twin brother, meanwhile, was reared as a boy and shows normal male behavior (Money & Ehrhardt, 1972).

The most famous study of the effects of early social learning on sexual behavior was carried out by Harry Harlow (Harlow, 1965). Rhesus monkeys were raised in isolation without any contact with their mothers or peers during the first six months to one year of life. When they matured, these monkeys did not engage in normal sexual behavior. When placed with other monkeys, they were aggressive, showed symptoms typical of depression in humans such as withdrawal and inactivity, and failed to engage in appropriate mounting and copulatory activity.

Androgen and Environment

A fascinating recent observation apparently involved both hormonal and socio-environmental factors. In the early 1970s, endocrinologists (Imperato-McGinley, Peterson, Gautier, & Sturla, 1979) discovered a number of men in a village in the Dominican Republic with an enzyme defect that prevented utilization of testosterone by their tissues. Because of this defect, they were born with ambiguous or female-appearing genitalia and were raised as girls.

When these children reached puberty, however, their tissues began to respond to naturally occurring testosterone and they became masculine in anatomy, hence, the name by which they were known locally—*guevedoces,* or "penis at 12." Apparently, because of the accepting attitude of the community, they were able to make a satisfactory transition in gender from female to male. A few cases of this condition have now been discovered outside the Dominican Republic, including several individuals who made successful gender transitions at puberty. These late gender transitions contradict current psychiatric thinking (Hampson & Hampson, 1960), which insists that gender reassignment cannot be attempted after about two years of age without risking dire psychological consequences.

While social factors were clearly at work in the successful gender adaptations made by the boys both before and after puberty, biological factors were also important. Julienne Imperato-McGinley and her colleagues (1979) interpret it as strongly supporting the reversed Adam principle. They concluded that the boys were able to develop into normal adult males only because their brains were exposed to male sex hormones while they were still in the womb. That conclusion could be verified only by examining the susceptibility of the human brain to such hormonal influences, an examination that is not yet possible.

Sex Differences and Similarities in Humans

We have seen a sharp contrast in sexual differentiation between rats, for example, and human beings. In rats, the development of sexual behavior can be shifted between masculine and feminine simply by altering the level of male hormone at an early stage; in humans, some behaviors, but apparently not sexual behavior, are affected by such changes.

This contrast should not be surprising if we look closely at the apparent differences between males and females in sexual behavior. As science delves more deeply into male and female sexual behavior in humans, it becomes apparent that the similarities exceed the differences. This is evident if we reconsider, in the light of recent findings, two sex differences noted by Kinsey in his pioneering studies nearly three decades ago.

One difference noted by Kinsey was in masturbation. He reported that only 58 percent of female respondents engaged in self-stimulation while 92 percent of the male respondents did. This wide disparity has narrowed considerably in more recent surveys (Schmidt & Sigusch, 1973). Moreover, anthropological data suggest that such differences are likely to be culturally determined rather than dictated by biology.

A second difference reported by Kinsey was the apparent lower propensity of women to be aroused by erotic material presented in visual form—pictures of nudes, genitalia, or sexual behavior. This finding would seem to be borne out by everyday observation; the people who buy sexually explicit books and attend stag movies are predominantly male. However, recent studies have recorded physiological responses in young men and women to erotic pictures and have found no significant differences between the sexes (Schmidt & Sigusch, 1973). People either have changed in their responses to visual erotica or, more likely, Kinsey's data collection procedure was at fault in this case.

A third apparent sex difference—the differing nature of the orgasm—may also be less significant than formerly thought. For example, it has been suggested that men as well as women are capable of multiple orgasm (Robbins & Jensen, 1976); a new hypothesis raises the possibility that similar neural mechanisms may underlie orgasm in both sexes.

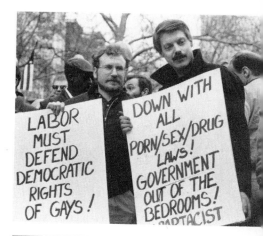

The factors that predispose some individuals to be homosexual are still not well understood.

Homosexuality

Differences in sexual behavior obviously also exist among the members of one sex. One dramatic example is homosexuality. The study of **homosexuality** is fraught with difficulties and ambiguities. Even the word *homosexual* is often used ambiguously. It usually is applied to men who prefer sex with other men, but it also applies to women who prefer sex with other women *(lesbians)*. Nor is it clear precisely what constitutes homosexuality. Kinsey (1948, 1953) found that one half of his male respondents and 28 percent of female respondents reported having had at least one homosexual experience (see Figure 11.5). Yet only 4 percent of males and 2 percent of females said they were exclusively homosexual. The classification of homosexual behavior as pathological is a cultural determination. The American Psychiatric Association no longer classifies it as a mental or emotional disorder, although many states still outlaw consensual sodomy. By contrast, in the East Bay Society studied by Davenport (1965), a male's refusal to engage in anal intercourse at a male friend's request was considered a serious breach of etiquette.

Figure 11.5

Alfred Kinsey's research established that homosexuality and heterosexuality are not mutually exclusive categories. Elements of both are found in most people in varying degrees. Kinsey's seven-point homosexual rating scale provides a way of measuring the balance in particular individuals. The scale runs from one extreme of exclusively heterosexual acts or feelings through the other extreme of exclusively homosexual acts or feelings.

Many studies have attempted to find a relationship between hormonal imbalance and homosexual behavior. Data collected in the United States, Britain, and Czechoslovakia, for example, show that about one third of the female homosexuals studied had higher than normal levels of the male hormone androgen. Studies of testosterone levels in male homosexuals have found differing levels of testosterone; some were above normal, some normal, and others below normal, indicating the lack of a relationship between testosterone levels and homosexuality in males. Administering hormones to hormone-deficient homosexuals may increase their sexual drive—as it does in heterosexuals—but does not alter their preferences for the same sex (Green, 1979).

In West Germany a few years ago, brain surgery was even carried out on criminal sex offenders who happened to be homosexual in an attempt to reduce homosexual behavior: lesions were placed in an area of the hypothalamus that controls sexual behavior in some animals (Roeder, 1966). Aside from the ethical considerations against this practice, there is no consistent evidence that homosexuality has a neuro-anatomical basis, let alone one that could be "cured" by brain surgery. Yet, it is possible, although not yet demonstrated scientifically, that hormonal factors acting upon the brain of the fetus may somehow predispose humans to homosexuality. If so, social factors might later elicit such predisposed behavior.

Psychological explanations for homosexuality focus on the role of early experience. The psychoanalytic view, first advanced by Freud, centers on certain unresolved conflicts in the young child. The child becomes sexually oriented to the parent of the same sex and for various reasons fails to outgrow this attachment. According to this view, male homosexuals harbor unconscious fears of women; female homosexuals have unconscious fears of men.

Increasingly, some researchers look to early learning experiences as the dominant factor in shaping homosexuality. Through the processes of conditioning and reinforcement that we described in chapter 7, children develop a preference for others of the same sex. Several longitudinal studies have investigated the relationship between early effeminate ("sissy") behavior in boys and adult sexual orientation. One study found that two thirds of male and female homosexuals described themselves as having experienced cross-gender ("sissy" or "tomboy") behavior as children (Saghir & Robins, 1973). More recently, Zuger (1984) followed 55 boys with early effeminate behavior and found that of those cases he was able to track into adulthood, 63 percent of the total were homosexual. Green (1979) has found similar results. The behavioral symptoms most frequently encountered in effeminate boys were an aversion to boys' games, an expressed desire to be born a girl and/or be dressed in girls' clothing, and feminine gesturing. In about one half of Zuger's cases, effeminate behavior was unmistakably present before 3 years of age, leading the author to conclude that the "basic organization" for effeminate behavior and a subsequent homosexual orientation is present at birth. However, this behavior pattern may be true of only a small proportion of all adult homosexuals.

The learning approach has gained credibility, in part, because of the recent success of conditioning techniques in changing sex preferences. In this therapy, individuals may be punished by mildly painful electric shocks when they become sexually aroused by visual images of homosexual behavior and rewarded for arousal in response to heterosexual images (Bancroft, 1974). It should be emphasized that most homosexuals are not candidates for this or any other "treatment" for their sex preferences, which need not be regarded as pathological.

Finally, whatever the clinical value of therapies derived from social learning theory may be, there is anthropological evidence showing that early homosexual experiences in boys do not necessarily determine future sexual orientation. In New Guinea tribes, notably the culture extensively described by the Stanford anthropologist Gilbert Herdt (1981), boys entering puberty regularly practice ritualized fellatio on the older postpubertal boys for a period of years, in order to ingest semen which helps them to become strong warriors. After puberty, the youths marry and homosexuality is prohibited.

Transsexualism

Transsexualism is commonly confused with homosexuality. Although transsexuals often are homosexual in sex preference, the chief distinguishing characteristic is a strong feeling of gender identity with the opposite sex. A male transsexual, for example, typically reports that he feels like "a woman in a man's body."

The attempts to explain transsexualism generally tend to coincide with the biological and psychological explanations of homosexuality. Gunter Dörner and his associates (Dörner, Rhode, Stahl, Krell, & Masius, 1975) have speculated that some instances of male-to-female transsexualism may result from androgen deficiency in the prenatal brain. Such an instance, it is postulated, might occur after the formation of the external genitals but before the brain has fully developed mechanisms that influence male and female behavior. Conversely, prenatal androgen excess could, in this view, account for female-to-male transsexualism.

Robert Stoller (1968) suggests that male transsexuals have mothers who are overprotective, confused, and unhappy about their own gender identity as females and maintain intimate physical closeness with the child for an unusually long period. Richard Green (1979) points out that many transsexual males were treated like girls by their mothers, who dressed them in feminine clothes; these males also preferred the company of girls as playmates during childhood. Green suggests that the causes of male transsexualism are probably complex, resulting from an interaction between prenatal androgen deficiency and an early socialization process in which feminine behavior is reinforced.

Several thousand transsexuals have undergone so-called sex-change surgery to make their outward appearance conform with their inward gender feelings. In males, hormone treatments (estrogen) help enlarge the breasts and reduce beard growth; in women, androgenic hormones can increase beard growth and muscle development and deepen the voice. Plastic surgery for males removes the testes and penis and creates an artificial vagina; for women, it reduces breast tissue, removes the ovaries and uterus, and creates an artificial penis.

Emotional adjustment after such surgery apparently varies widely. Many patients, such as Renee Richards, who became a woman tennis star after a sex-change operation, report successful adjustment. Recently, however, Johns Hopkins University, which pioneered in the surgery, announced it would no longer perform the operations, contending that surgery was no more successful than psychotherapy in helping transsexuals cope with their feelings. Most authorities dispute this view.

Transsexuals experience strong feelings of gender identity with the opposite sex. Debra Hardin, a transsexual who underwent sex-change surgery, is shown here holding an earlier photo of herself as a man.

Sex Differences and Sex Stereotypes

In previous sections of this chapter we have seen that males and females differ in some aspects of sexual behavior. For example, males are more likely to engage in premarital intercourse. The two sexes also differ in the age at which they experience a peak in sexual capacity. Furthermore, as men grow older changes in erection, ejaculation patterns, and refractory periods may occur; changes in female sexuality during the aging process are much less clear.

However, there are also many similarities between the sexes. For example, the subjective experience of orgasm is the same in males and females. Furthermore, research has shown that young women and men respond similarly to erotic pictures and that the sex difference in self-stimulation has decreased substantially in recent years. In addition, men seem to be capable of multiple orgasms, a capacity that was previously thought to be limited to women.

In this section, let us examine the issue of sex differences in other areas of human behavior. Once again, we will conclude that the similarities generally exceed the differences. We will also look at sex stereotypes, which are people's beliefs about men and women. We will see that people tend to respond differently to men and women, even though men and women actually behave quite similarly.

Sex Differences

The investigation of sex differences focuses attention on three areas that have attracted strong interest. These are cognitive performance, communication patterns, and social behavior.

Cognitive Performance

There are numerous areas in which men and women are similar in their cognitive abilities. For example, there are no substantial differences in general intelligence (Maccoby & Jacklin, 1974). Men and women are also equally competent when they form concepts, perform reasoning tasks, and solve problems. There are also no overall sex differences in creativity.

There are noteworthy sex differences in only three areas of cognitive performance: verbal, spatial, and mathematical abilities. However, even in these three areas, the differences are surprisingly small. For example, if we consider the variability of people's scores on any of these three kinds of cognitive ability, a *maximum* of only 5 percent of that variability can be attributed to sex (Hyde, 1981). This means that the average female's and the average male's scores on a particular test are not likely to be significantly different.

With respect to verbal ability, baby girls acquire language somewhat earlier than baby boys (Harris, 1977). Although sex differences in verbal ability in early childhood are typically small, young boys are more likely than young girls to be referred to reading clinics (Finucci & Childs, 1981). Beginning in high school, females are better at verbal tasks such as spelling, reading comprehension, speaking ability, and creative writing (Droege, 1967; Maccoby & Jacklin, 1974).

Spatial abilities involve shapes and figures, such as locating a particular object that is hidden in a larger design or determining what a shape would look like if it were rotated. Beginning in adolescence, males typically perform somewhat better than females on these tests (Peterson, 1980). However, these sex differences may disappear after a short practice session (Chance & Goldstein, 1971).

The sex difference in mathematics has attracted the most attention. For example, when gifted junior high school students took the mathematics portion of the Scholastic Aptitude Test, boys were more likely than girls to receive extremely high scores (Benbow & Stanley, 1983). However, other studies do not find significant sex differences in mathematical ability (Fennema & Sherman, 1977).

It must be emphasized that the differences in verbal and spatial abilities between the sexes are consistently quite small and are based on average differences between very large comparison groups. Individual cases may vary significantly. Interestingly, sex differences in cognitive ability seem to emerge in adolescence, and have been attributed to both differential patterns of socialization and biological changes concomitant with the onset of puberty. From a socialization standpoint, for example, adolescent boys may not be encouraged to pursue interests in poetry or literature and may come to view enhanced verbal skills as distinctly feminine in nature (Nash, 1979). Similarly, girls may experience a lack of support for their mathematical studies (Astin, 1974; Meece, Parsons, Kaczala, Goff, & Futterman, 1982). On the biological side, Waber (1977) has found that irrespective of sex, late-maturers outperform early-maturers on tests of visual-spatial ability, although no differences were evidenced on verbal measures. It has been hypothesized that these findings are a consequence of differences in the rate of maturation between the right and left cerebral hemispheres; the right hemisphere, which mediates spatial abilities, is presumed to mature more slowly than the left. Since females, on the average, mature earlier than males, the right hemisphere is provided with less time to consolidate its neurological integrity and thus its level of functioning, leaving females relatively weaker in spatial capacities in comparison to males. However, Kimball (1981) has argued that most biological explanations of cognitive differences between the sexes are inadequate.

Communication Patterns

Some of the greatest sex differences in human behavior seem to occur in the areas of verbal and nonverbal communication. Considering verbal communication, for example, men talk more than women when they are in mixed groups (Haas, 1979). Furthermore, men interrupt women more than women interrupt men. When Zimmerman and West (1977) recorded conversations in coffee shops and drug stores, they found that men interrupted more than 20 times as often as women. There also may be some differences in the content of verbal communication. In their conversations, women reveal somewhat more personal information about some aspects of their lives, in contrast to men; however, in other areas their self-disclosure patterns are similar (Derlega, Durham, Gockel, & Sholis, 1981).

One area of *nonverbal* communication in which sex differences are found is in the tendency to smile. Women are much more likely than men to smile when posing for yearbook pictures, for example (Ragan, 1982). Furthermore, women spend more time gazing at their conversational partners than men do (Frances, 1979). Women also stand and sit closer to each other than men do (Sussman & Rosenfeld, 1982). Finally, men touch women more often than women touch men (Henley, 1977).

Verbal and nonverbal communication is an area of great sexual difference. Studies show that men talk more than women in mixed groups, and men interrupt women more than women interrupt men.

Even though the sex differences in communication patterns are relatively marked, it is important to stress that there are also substantial individual differences. Undoubtedly, you know some men who look at you frequently when they are conversing and who smile readily. Similarly, you know some women who slap men heartily on the back and who interrupt constantly. Whenever we speak of sex differences, we must keep in mind that we are referring to general tendencies, rather than rules describing all men and all women.

Social Behavior

In their classic review of psychological sex differences, Maccoby and Jacklin (1974) concluded that aggression was the only area of social behavior in which sex differences are fairly well established. However, in a later analysis, Frodi, Macaulay, and Thome (1977) found that men were consistently more aggressive than women in less than half of the 72 studies they reviewed. Often, there are no sex differences. For example, when people are given a convincing justification for being aggressive, the sex differences in aggression evaporate. Also, men and women are equally likely to say that they approve of violence. In contrast, sex differences in aggression are exaggerated when people are asked to describe their own dreams, intentions, and customary behavior.

Clearly, whether sex differences in aggression are found is due in part to the type of aggressive behavior being sampled and the conditions specified for its expression. The manifestation of aggressive content in a dream represents something quite different from overt acts of hostility, although each might be operationalized as "aggression" for the purposes of a given study.

There is some speculation, incidentally, that sex differences in aggression may be biologically based. Some observational studies of child rearing practices by parents have indicated that children are not differentially reinforced for aggressive behavior as a function of sex (Birren et al., 1981). However, as Frodi and her coauthors conclude, "We would argue that behavior is largely shaped by social forces and that these may exaggerate or minimize whatever biological differences may exist" (p. 655).

Who are more helpful, men or women? According to Deaux (1976), the answer depends upon what we mean by "helpful." Men may be somewhat more likely than women to volunteer their assistance, particularly for jobs that require strength. When a person in need requests assistance, however, women and men are equally likely to help, and in some circumstances women may be somewhat more helpful (Pandey & Griffitt, 1974).

There may be some sex differences in the area of empathy. Women are significantly more accurate than men in decoding other people's facial expressions and judging the emotions underneath those expressions (Rosenthal & DePaulo, 1979). Women are also more likely than men to report feelings of concern for another person in distress (Eisenberg & Lennon, 1983). However, these sex differences in empathy disappear when empathy is assessed physiologically.

In general, then, women and men are similar in their social behavior. Sex differences in aggression, helpfulness, and empathy may exist in some circumstances, but—as we concluded about sexual behavior—the similarities generally exceed the differences.

Sex Stereotypes

We saw that sex differences in cognitive performance are generally minimal. Men and women differ in some areas of communication style, but these differences certainly do not apply to all men and all women. Furthermore, the similarities between the two sexes with respect to social behavior are more impressive than the differences. In other words, men and women actually behave rather similarly. Are these similarities reflected in people's ideas about men and women? Let us look at sex stereotypes.

Sex stereotypes are flourishing in our contemporary culture. For example, college students believe that women are more likely than men to be submissive, rattlebrained, fickle, complaining, affectionate, and talkative. They believe that men are more likely than women to be daring, adventurous, confident, rational, dominant, ambitious, and aggressive (Cowan & Stewart, 1977; Williams & Bennett, 1975).

One general tendency is for stereotypes to be more exaggerated than the sex differences that actually exist. For example, Kelley and his coauthors (1978) found that when dating couples were involved in conflict, females were somewhat likely to cry and males were somewhat likely to become angry. However, when people were asked to tell their ideas about what happens in conflicts, their stereotypes showed much greater sex differences than those that exist in reality.

Another characteristic of stereotypes is that men are often characterized in a more positive light than women. For example, Williams and Bennett (1975) found that adjectives used to describe women (submissive and rattlebrained) were usually negative, whereas the adjectives used to describe men (daring and adventurous) were usually positive. In other studies, college students read professional articles, half of the time labeled with a man's name, for example, John T. MacKay, and half of the time labeled with a woman's name, for example, Joan T. MacKay. People gave higher ratings to the article when they thought it had been written by a man (Goldberg, 1968; Paludi & Bauer, 1983).

A final characteristic of stereotypes is that they influence our perception and interpretation of behavior. For example, when adults saw a videotape of a crying baby whom they believed to be a boy, they concluded that the baby was angry. When other adults saw the same videotape, but believed the baby to be a girl, they concluded that she was afraid (Seavey, Katz, & Zalk, 1975). Summarizing the powerful influence of stereotypes, Hamilton (1981) remarked that people are essentially saying "I wouldn't have seen it if I hadn't believed it" (p. 137).

The Biosocial Complex

Sexual behavior is culturally determined; sexual behavior is biologically determined. Throughout this chapter we have seen examples of both kinds of effects. In experimental situations it is often possible to demonstrate specifically biological or specifically sociocultural causes for sexual phenomena. But in real-life situations the two types of determinants are typically so intertwined that it is often extremely difficult, and frequently impossible, to separate one from the other. It makes sense, then, to sum up the determinants of sexual behavior in terms of a **biosocial complex.**

This chapter has tended to emphasize the first part of that complex—the ''bio''—because of the wealth of carefully controlled experimental data available, especially from animal studies. At the same time, we should be on guard against hasty conclusions about biological determinants. Consider, for example, the clear-cut anatomical and physiological events of puberty. These occur earlier in the female than in the male, and yet the arousal of sexuality in the two sexes often follows a different pattern, which may be largely culturally determined. Sexual arousal in the young female may be inhibited by cultural factors—her anticipation of future domesticity and childbearing, for example, or by a double standard that encourages sexuality in young males but not in females. Here, biological processes, sociocultural expectations, and individual cognitive factors are involved in a mutually interactive system in which each component influences the other.

At the same time, the importance of biology should not be underestimated. This is particularly true when anatomical and/or hormonal differences seem to determine behavior (as in untreated androgenital syndrome or in males with inadequate testosterone production by their testes). Yet the cognitive evaluation of these differences may exert a crucial influence on sexual behavior rather than, or in addition to, the biology itself.

We can view biological factors less as determinants of sexual behavior than as constraints that often can be overcome if the environmental influence or the individual's will is strong enough. Thus, some people can fantasize to orgasm, and paraplegics often learn to enjoy sex despite the loss of genital sensation. Seldom must we regard biological factors as preordaining sexual behavior; they are always open to influence by cognitive, sociocultural, and learning factors.

Summary

1. Three major figures dominate the short history of research into human sexual behavior: Sigmund Freud, Alfred Kinsey, and William Masters. Freud based his theories on his observations of his patients in psychoanalysis. He formulated five stages of infantile psychosexual development in which the libido shifts successively from the oral, to the anal, and to the phallic stages. These stages are followed by a period of latency that is followed in early adolescence by the genital stage. Kinsey and his associates used the survey-questionnaire method to ask thousands of Americans about their sex lives. Masters and Johnson based their findings on laboratory observation of the physiology of sexual behavior.

2. One of the most striking aspects of sexual behavior, both human and animal, is its wide variety; however, most sexual behaviors evolved principally to serve the aim of reproduction of the species. Reproductive strategy in humans and many other animals usually dictates sexual monogamy, although the small mammals on which most research is done are generally promiscuous. In many animal species and human cultures, polygyny (one male mating with several females) is the rule; polyandry (one female mating with a number of males) occurs rarely. The evolution of genital anatomy seems also to have followed reproductive strategy. Humans exhibit evolutionary adaptations consistent with the maximization of sexual pleasure.

3. The value systems of different cultures shape vastly different norms of sexual behavior. The classic studies by Bronislaw Malinowski of the people of the Trobriand Islands and by William Davenport of the East Bay Society demonstrated striking differences in sexual norms between neighboring cultures, as did the studies by Friedl of neighboring tribes in New Guinea.

4. Within a single culture, many variations from a general norm of sexual behavior exist. Within our own society, the sexual revolution of the last few decades has produced profound changes in our cultural norms regarding sex: the increase in premarital intercourse, particularly among females, is the most dramatic of those changes.

5. People seek sexual stimulation from the cradle to the grave. Four broad phases of individual life cycles of sexual behavior have been described: early childhood, prepuberty, puberty and beyond, and the declining years. Episodes of spontaneous sexual arousal are found in both sexes during the first year of life; many older people are sexually active well into their eighties.

6. The biological study of sexual behavior focuses primarily on hormones, chemicals that are manufactured by the endocrine glands and released into the

bloodstream. The increase in the production of sex hormones at the onset of puberty is responsible for the emergence of primary and secondary sexual characteristics.

7. The production of sexual hormones is essentially a three-stage process: *1)* The hypothalamus sends chemical signals via blood vessels that connect it to the so-called master gland, the pituitary. *2)* The pituitary responds by manufacturing and releasing into the bloodstream two protein hormones, the luteinizing hormone (LH) and follicle-stimulating hormone (FSH), both of which are responsible for release of spermatozoa and eggs from the gonads (testes and ovaries). These two hormones are collectively called gonadotropins. *3)* Gonadotropins also stimulate the production of sex hormones in the gonads. These gonadal hormones are steroids, a class of hormones that also includes cortisone from the adrenal cortex. The main steroids produced by the male's testes are androgens, the most important of which is testosterone. The primary steroids produced in the female's ovaries are estrogens and progesterone. Small amounts of male sex hormones are produced in the female ovaries, and small amounts of female sex hormones are produced in the male testes.

8. The steroid sex hormones in females are produced in cyclically varying amounts and are responsible for regulation of many aspects of reproduction, including the production of eggs (ova), menstruation, and the fertility cycle. In most mammals the female gonadal (ovarian) hormones influence mating behavior by stimulating (and in some situations inhibiting) attractivity, receptivity, and proceptivity. In humans, however, the role of female hormones in sexual behavior seems to be minor, at least as indicated from the limited studies to date.

9. Sex hormones in the male are produced at a fairly constant rate, consistent with the noncyclic nature of male reproductive function, which they are instrumental in regulating. Their role in mediating sexual behavior is clearly established.

10. Current research suggests that male sex hormones influence the action of nerve cells in the brain, especially in the hypothalamus, which controls masculine sex behavior. This evidence comes principally from animal research.

11. The roles of the two sexes have begun to change radically in our society with profound implications for sexual behavior. Among subprimate species, and, to a lesser extent, among primates, biological determination predominates in sexual behavior. Learning and cultural-social factors seem to play a much larger role in determining human sexual behavior. Animal research has demonstrated what may be called the reversed Adam principle: the superimposition of masculine anatomy, physiology, and behavior on a basic female pattern. As science delves more deeply into male and female sexual behavior in humans, it becomes apparent that the similarities exceed the differences.

12. Homosexuals are men and women who prefer sexual partners of their own sex. At this point, research has not established a hormonal or genetic disposition toward homosexuality; psychological explanations for homosexuality focus on the role of early experience. In recent years a majority of psychiatrists have come to believe that homosexuality is not a pathological condition; rather, they view it as an alternate preference.

13. Transsexuals have strong feelings of gender identity with the opposite sex. A male transsexual, for example, typically reports that he feels like "a woman in a man's body." Current research does not show consistent biological explanations for transsexualism; psychologists focus on early learning as its basis.

14. Sexual behavior is both biologically and culturally determined. The two types of determinants are typically so intertwined that it is difficult, and sometimes impossible, to separate one from the other. The determinants of sexual behavior may be summed up as a biosocial complex.

FOCUS: Julian Davidson's bipolar theory of orgasm suggests that the male orgasm is linked to two distinct neurological processes: one that results in an altered state of consciousness and pelvic contractions and the other that results in the emission of seminal fluid and the onset of the refractory period after a single male orgasm. Davidson has also extended his theory to account for the female orgasm, suggesting that certain types of uterine contractions may result in the onset of the refractory period, thus explaining why some women have multiple orgasms and others do not.

RESEARCH: Early attempts to examine the effects of hormones on the levels of sexual desire and frequency of coitus in the human female were plagued with two major methodological flaws: 1) failure to measure levels of hormones directly and 2) failure to control the demands of the woman's sexual partner. Recent research has employed radioactive labels to determine the ebb and flow of hormones throughout the menstrual cycle and has shown that hormone level does not appear to be consistently linked to the level of sexual desire or the frequency of intercourse.

5

Personality and Intelligence

12

Personality and Its Assessment

None of us is what he or she appears to be at first sight. To accurately characterize people and predict their behavior is difficult.

Assume you have taken a test that purports to assess your personality. After a few days, the examiner sends you the following report: "You tend to be critical of yourself and have a strong need to have other people like you. Although you tend to be pretty well controlled on the outside, you frequently feel insecure inside. At times your sexual adjustment has been a problem for you. You like a certain amount of change in your life and become unhappy when you are hemmed in by restrictions and limitations. Sometimes you feel sociable and outgoing. At other times you tend to be very reserved and inward-looking."

If you feel this description sums up your personality, you are not alone. In experiments in which students were given an assessment report with statements like these, most of the students said the assessment fit them quite well—even though each student was given an identical report (Snyder & Larson, 1972).

This is an illustration of what psychologist Paul Meehl (1966) called the "Barnum effect" in personality description. The great circus showman, P. T. Barnum, believed that entrepreneurial success required the provision of a little something for everybody. The personality description has a little something for everyone because it is composed of statements that are true about almost everyone.

Astrologers, fortune-tellers, and others who purport to analyze personality and predict behavior have long known the power of the Barnum effect. They construct a series of general statements and make the client feel the description is prepared especially for him or her.

Any truly scientific theory of personality must avoid the easy temptations of the Barnum effect. A theory of personality must deal with both the ways individuals are unique and the ways individuals are similar. This is an enormous task, one that encompasses all branches of psychology. Consider the breadth of the definition of **personality:** the characteristic way in which a person thinks and behaves as he or she adapts to the environment. This includes visible behavior patterns as well as less apparent but relatively enduring characteristics such as values, motives, attitudes, abilities, and self-image.

Accurately characterizing people and predicting their behavior is difficult; even the origin of the word *personality* suggests its elusive quality. Its root is *persona,* from the Greek word meaning "mask." Greek actors wore stylized masks to represent the characters they were playing.

None of us is what he or she appears to be at first sight, and even our most intimate friends have great difficulty in discerning the whole of our personality. This is dramatically evident in the lives of many great women and men whose abilities were long hidden from their own families. Charles Darwin, who developed the theory of evolution by natural selection, is a classic example of a late bloomer. "You care for nothing but shooting, dogs, and rat-catching," his father once told him, "and you will be a disgrace to yourself and your family" (Good, 1974).

Although scientists have developed a number of theories of personality and many methods for assessing it, none is so all-encompassing that it can predict or explain the genius of a Darwin—or the uniqueness of any one of us. Nonetheless, personality theories have furthered our understanding of individual behavior and have had profound practical consequences, influencing how we raise children, why we are hired, and even how we use everyday language.

In this chapter we will examine the most influential theories of personality. These theories, in their assumptions about behavior and its development, fall into four general categories: psychodynamic, dispositional, phenomenological, and social learning theories. Each of the four perspectives we will consider reflects a distinguishably different way of viewing the complexity of personality. For each of these approaches we will describe the relevant theories and techniques for assessing personality. We will also consider in each category an example of research aimed at testing the theories and then discuss key issues.

Personality theorists are concerned with questions of consistency. They want to know why it is that a particular individual seems to behave in strikingly similar ways in a variety of different situations or on different occasions. In addition, personality theorists are interested in uniqueness. They want to know why it is that each individual's patterns of behavior and styles of interaction seem distinctive and singular. Why do two people in highly standardized situations behave in strikingly different ways? Much of what we will discuss in this chapter addresses the broad questions of how individual behavior is influenced by situational factors and by unique personality characteristics or past experiences. As we shall see, each of the approaches we discuss has different answers to these questions and frames them in different ways.

Psychodynamic Theories

One of the first comprehensive approaches to personality and its development was formulated by Sigmund Freud. His insistence that behavior is determined by the interplay of events and conflicts within the inner life of the individual is central to his approach and to that of other dynamic theories.

A crucial aspect of Freud's approach was his emphasis on psychological processes that are not ordinarily available to a person's consciousness. Freud saw evidence of such processes in his practice as a psychiatrist. Patients under hypnosis, for example, were able to recall traumatic events of childhood that normally eluded their conscious memories (Freud, 1916/1961, 1916/1963).

From these observations and from his later experiences with patients in psychoanalysis, Freud postulated three different provinces of mental activity (Freud, 1900/1953, 1933/1965):

Conscious mental activity includes all those thoughts and feelings that are being experienced at the moment. Although easily accessible, this activity represents only a small fraction of mental life.

Preconscious mental activity refers to all those thoughts and feelings that are outside immediate awareness but easily available—for example, a telephone number that can be summoned at will.

Unconscious mental activity is a vast reservoir of childhood and current memories, wishes and impulses, fears and hopes that lie beyond awareness. They are kept there, Freud believed, by a censoring process that protects the person from unacceptable wishes or threatening impulses. Although the unconscious could not be directly examined, its presence could be inferred from dreams, through hypnosis, and in the free association process of psychoanalysis. Of these three types of mental activity, Freud was convinced that the unconscious played the dominant role in shaping personality.

Central to Freudian theory is the concept of dynamic repression, the idea that there is an unconscious reservoir of wishes and ideas that are kept out of one's manifest mental activities. Repression refers to a mechanism of defense (chapter 14) in which unacceptable, anxiety-producing material is kept form being consciously expressed. According to traditional psychoanalytic theory, anxiety attaches itself to infantile memories, requiring that they be excluded from our awareness. Repressed wishes are thought to develop primarily as the young child begins to struggle with the constraints imposed by the environment to regulate his or her sexual and aggressive impulses. Freud believed that significant memories in one's life are never completely lost, but are relegated to the unconscious, where they defy our best conscious efforts to bring them forth.

Repressed wishes are relentless in their efforts to become manifest. As these impulses gain in strength, a counterforce is required to once again block the conflictual content from reaching preconscious levels. To the extent that

Table 12.1   STAGES OF PSYCHOSEXUAL ACTIVITY IN THE PSYCHOANALYTIC PERSPECTIVE

Stage of Psychosexual Development	Erogenous Zone	Prototypical Activity	Later Personality
Oral Stage (0–2 years)	Mouth	Sucking; incorporation; biting	Oral-incorporative; "sucker"; aggressive; oral sadistic
Anal Stage (2–3 years)	Anal sphincter	Urge for elimination; strict toilet training rewarded	Anal-retentive or expulsive; productive; creative
Phallic (4–5 years)	Genital organs	Masturbation; autoerotic activity; castration fear; penis envy	Oedipus complex; Electra complex; later relations with men *and* women
Genital (puberty–adulthood)	Genital organs	Sexual desire; sexual relations	Socialization; genuine friendships; stable, mature, long-term relationships; vocational choice

Source: Richard Price, *Abnormal Behavior,* 2d ed. (New York: Holt, Rinehart and Winston, 1978).

repression is incomplete, additional defense mechanisms are brought into play in order to regulate the amount of anxiety and keep it within tolerable limits and to control the extent to which the forbidden impulse is recognized. Thus, all behavior represents a compromise between the conscious and unconscious portions of the psyche. Freud theorized that when these compromise formations become grossly exaggerated and maladaptive in the individual's life, neurosis results. The Freudian model is based upon the belief that psychological tensions and the struggle to achieve some internal equilibrium is part of the human condition. It is a model of human behavior oriented in conflict between the rational and irrational elements of personality.

Moreover, Freud believed that slips of the tongue and the content of dreams provided evidence for the existence of these unobserved intrapsychic confrontations. For instance, the momentary inability to recall an acquaintance's name or to remember the location of an important object were phenomena understood as reflecting unconscious motives. From this viewpoint, lapses in memory are seen as motivated events, determined in large measure by dynamic forces operating beyond the horizon of the person's awareness. Freud thus rejected the notion of randomness in human activity and emphasized the coherence and interrelatedness of all behavior, "accidental" or otherwise.

Like Freudian slips of the tongue, dreams are recognized as expressions of wish-fulfillment or disguised representations of unconscious content. The latent dream thoughts or underlying content is unavailable to the dreamer by virtue of its association with anxiety. Instead, the dreamer is treated to a carefully laundered version that is remembered upon waking—the manifest content. Dreams, then, in a manner reminiscent of symptoms and indeed all behavior, constitute a compromise between the unrestricted realization of forbidden ideas and that which the person can reasonably tolerate and accept. The forbidden material is permitted only a partial, disguised expression, often in elaborately symbolic form unrecognizable to the dreamer.

Stages of Personality Development

Freud was one of the first investigators to insist that the early years were decisive in the formation of personality. Certain motives, aims, or drives may be arrested, or fixated, early in childhood because of overindulgence or deprivation, said Freud, and these **fixations** remain in the unconscious, shaping behavior throughout life.

Freud discerned four distinct stages of development: *oral, anal, phallic,* and *genital,* as shown in Table 12.1 (Freud, 1905/1962). As these names imply, Freud placed a great deal of emphasis on biological forces in the early shaping of personality. To Freud, not only the genitals but also the mouth and anus were erogenous (sensitive to sexual stimulation). The pleasure derived from each of the erogenous zones is related to one general source—the **libido** or energy of the sexual instincts. In each stage the libido focuses on the pleasure-giving zone that characterizes that stage. A person's experiences at each stage leave an imprint that influences future development.

Freud believed the primary erogenous zone is the mouth for children in the first year or two of life.

Oral Stage

During the first year or two of life, Freud argued, the primary erogenous zone is the mouth. Children gratify their hunger through sucking and then through biting. A child who becomes fixated at this stage—perhaps through early weaning—may later develop an **oral personality,** which may be characterized by oral aggression expressed through verbal hostility and feelings of deprivation or even gullibility.

Anal Stage

During the second and third years, the anus becomes a focus of discomfort or erotic pleasure. If the parents are strict and harsh in their methods of imposing toilet training, the child may hold back the feces. Fixation during this stage may later result in a **retentive personality,** which is characterized by overconcern with cleanliness or saving. On the other hand, a child praised for performance on the toilet may later become productive and creative in adult life, perhaps even as a writer or artist.

Phallic Stage

During the fourth and fifth years, the child's erotic interests shift to the genital organs. Sexual feelings are directed toward the parent of the opposite sex. The boy wishes to possess his mother and displace his father, a condition Freud called the **Oedipus complex,** after the legendary Greek king who murdered his father and married his mother. The boy associates sensations from his genital organs with his affection for his mother and fears his father will remove the offending organ. Freud called this fear **castration anxiety** and said it leads the boy to repress his lust for his mother and to identify with his father. According to Freud, the Oedipus complex takes a different form for girls—a form sometimes referred to as the **Electra complex,** after the princess in a Greek play who helped bring about the death of her mother. She blames her mother for the fact that she lacks a prominent exterior sex organ and desires her father because he has such an organ. Freud called these feelings **penis envy.** He said that problems arising during the phallic stage—for example, if the mother rejects her son's love, or the father disappoints his daughter by leaving home—can result in permanent damage to the child's sense of self and sexual identity.

In the phallic stage, during a child's fourth and fifth years, Freud maintained that a child directs sexual feelings toward the parent of the opposite sex.

Latency Stage

According to Freudian theory, the child enters a period of relative sexual inactivity following the resolution of Oedipal issues and identification with the same-sex parent that occurs during the phallic stage. During latency, interest in members of the opposite sex declines significantly. Freud thought that massive repressions keep the child's sexual impulses and Oedipal conflicts restrained until they are awakened once again by the onset of puberty. It was thought that in healthy people the Oedipal complex is negotiated satisfactorily so that the reemergence of such fears will not result in neurotic symptoms.

Genital Stage

After a period of five or six years of latency, the child enters a final active stage of psychosexual development. During adolescence, the self-oriented erotic concerns of the first three stages of development are directed outward onto other persons, usually of the opposite sex. The child becomes concerned with vocational choice, socialization, and peer relationships.

As we have seen, most stages of development carry potential crises for the child. Successful resolution of each crisis, Freud believed, was necessary for the child to arrive at a reasonably healthy personality in adulthood. Furthermore, how each stage is resolved was important for the shaping of the adult character or personality of the individual.

The Ego Psychologists

Many of the scientists who gravitated to Freud and his revolutionary view of personality later broke with him over theoretical issues. Usually, the differences revolved around Freud's belief that sex and other biological drives were the primary forces in shaping personality.

In the United States, influential theorists such as Karen Horney, Erich Fromm, and Erik Erikson were called **ego psychologists** because they felt the conscious ego was more important in shaping personality than were the instinctual drives of the id. Although the neo-Freudians retained many of the basic assumptions of Freud's dynamic theory, with its emphasis on unconscious processes and a fixed sequence of personality development, they were also greatly influence by the American social sciences. Cultural and social factors, they suggested, played a far greater role than had been granted by the biological determinism of Freud.

Fromm insisted that differences in the social environments markedly affect personality development. He suggested, for example, that a capitalistic society produces different personality types than would a "humanistic, communitarian socialism" (Fromm, 1947). Horney rejected much of Freud's thinking about women. Many years before the modern women's liberation movement, she detected male chauvinism in some of Freud's teachings. She pointed out, for example, that the idea of penis envy may not be built into women biologically but only reflects the favored position of men in most cultures (Horney, 1939).

CHAPTER 12   PERSONALITY AND ITS ASSESSMENT

Erikson, a Viennese who spent most of his life in the United States, proposed a life cycle of personality development comprising eight distinct sequential stages (see chapter 6) that differs substantially from the Freudian view. Unlike Freud's theory of psychosexual development, which focuses on early life events, Erikson's stages extend into adolescence, young adulthood, parenthood, and old age. In addition, each of the stages is characterized by personal or interpersonal crises that are more psychosocial than biological in nature (Erikson, 1963, 1968).

The most familiar of the developmental conflicts postulated by Erikson is the **identity crisis** of adolescence (Erikson, 1963). At puberty, the youth must face both the sudden bloom of sexuality and the need to adopt the roles to be played in adult society. Erikson summed up this identity crisis by citing the teenager Biff in Arthur Miller's play *Death of a Salesman:* ''I just can't take hold, Mom,'' says Biff. ''I can't take hold of some kind of a life.'' For all the emphasis on social processes, however, Erikson and the other ego psychologists still retain Freud's essential focus on the internal dynamics of personality development.

The most recent example of the focus on developmental conflicts has been research conducted by Levinson et al. (1978) in their book *The Seasons of a Man's Life*. Levinson and his colleagues studied 40 men in the 35–45 age group who were thought to be in especially critical transition years in their lives. They concluded that there are several age-linked periods in the development of every male adult, including an early adult transition from the ages of 17–22, and another as each man enters into mid-life around age 40. This is a time, they argued, when each person begins to realize that youthful dreams may not be fulfilled and that life is finite. Levinson et al. concluded that the structure of each person's life span can be viewed in terms of conscious choices and the outcomes of those choices. The choices are decisions about occupation, marriage and family, and friends, as well as long-range goals. Levinson's work can be seen as an extension of Erikson's ideas about adult development and personality change and reflects a growing interest in the understanding of adult personality development.

Carl Jung broke away from Freud's theory of personality and developed his own approach, analytical psychology.

Jung's Analytical Approach

Carl Jung, a Swiss psychiatrist, was one of Freud's earliest disciples, but Jung soon broke away to develop his own version of Freud's dynamic theory of personality (Jung 1916/1969, 1963). Jung called his new approach **analytical psychology.** It differed form the Freudian view on several important issues. Jung thought sexual forces and the Freudian concern with the early development of personality and the understanding of past childhood traumas were far less significant in shaping personality. Jung stressed the present conflicts and problems of his patients during therapy and believed that what he called **individuation**—psychological maturation—was a lifelong process (Jung, 1939/1969, 1916/1969).

Perhaps the most significant difference, however, was Jung's identification of an additional construct. He believed that all of us possess not only a **personal unconscious**—similar to the Freudian repository of forgotten or suppressed memories—but also share in the **collective unconscious.** He defined this as ''the all-controlling deposit of ancestral experience from untold millions of years, the echo of prehistoric world events in which each century adds an infinitesimally small amount of variation and differentiation.'' These ancient memories take the form of **archetypes,** master patterns of images that are transmitted from generation to generation. Examples of archetypes include such

The Problems with "Common Sense" in Assessing Personality

The interpretation of projective tests designed to measure personality is subject to a number of problems. Not the least of these is the preconceptions that the clinician may bring to the task of assessing test results. Loren J. and Jean Chapman (1967) have demonstrated how laypeople as well as experienced clinicians can fall into the trap of using "common sense" in the interpretation of projective test results. For example, in assessing the results of the Draw-a-Person test, clinicians and laypeople may believe that men who are concerned about their manliness will draw pictures of broad-shouldered, muscular physiques or they may believe that people who are particularly suspicious will emphasize the eyes in their drawings. The Chapmans found that these beliefs occurred even though such correlations did not actually exist in the clinical materials developed for their experiment.

This tendency of observers to find "illusory correlations" between preconceived projective-test indicators and personality traits was further investigated by the Chapmans (1969) in a series of studies based on interpretation of the widely used Rorschach Test. The personality trait chosen for the experiments was male homosexuality. Research has shown that, although clinicians commonly report a number of indicators of male homosexuality in their assessment of Rorschach results, only two indicators are valid signs of it. One sign is the client's description of a particular inkblot card as a "human or animal—contorted, monstrous, or threatening." The second sign is the description of another card as a "human or humanized animal."

In the first stage of these new experiments, the Chapmans sent questionnaires to a number of practicing clinicians asking them what signs of male homosexuality they had observed in their Rorschach results. Of the clinicians queried, 32 indicated they had seen the Rorschach results of a number of men with homosexual problems. Of these 32, only two listed either of the signs that research has shown to be valid. Most of the clinicians listed at least one of five signs, such as "human or animal anal content" or "feminine clothing," that research has found to be invalid.

These invalid signs are ones that appear to have a popular "common-sense" association with male homosexuality. That this is so was confirmed by the Chapmans when they asked a group of undergraduate students to rate these signs, along with

concepts as Mother, a Supreme Being, the Hero, and a sense of wholeness. Symbolic manifestations of these same archetypes, Jung said, can be found in all human cultures—in religion, in mythology, and even in a person's own dreams (Jung 1917/1966).

The interpretation of dreams was seen by both Jung and Freud as a source of data for understanding personality. But while Freud considered dreams a form of wish fulfillment, Jung perceived them as an unconscious effort to resolve personality problems. By bringing the forces of the personal unconscious and the collective unconscious into harmony with the conscious self, Jung believed, an individual can achieve psychological integration.

Psychodynamic Approaches to Assessment

Given their emphasis on the unconscious, dynamic theorists must necessarily penetrate that domain if they are to assess an individual's personality. One method used by Freud and his followers is **free association** (Freud, 1913/1958). In this process, which typically takes place during psychoanalysis, the person is instructed to give his or her thoughts complete freedom and to report all the daydreams, feelings, and images that flash through the mind no the two valid signs and a number of other filler items, for the strength of their associative connection to homosexuality.

The second phase of the Chapmans' experiments was designed to determine whether laypeople would make the same errors of diagnosis as those evidenced in the survey of clinicians. A total of 693 students in introductory psychology served as the subjects in three different experiments.

In one of these experiments, subjects were shown 30 Rorschach cards, each of which contained the purported response of a fictitious patient, along with two symptoms of this patient's emotional problems. The fictitious patient's responses were rigged so that they fell into five different categories: an invalid sign such as "feminine clothing," two valid signs of male homosexuality, and two filler categories—geographic features and food. The purported symptoms included two of the following: "He has sexual feelings toward other men." "He believes other people are plotting against him." "He feels sad and depressed much of the time." "He has strong feelings of inferiority." The responses and symptoms were deliberately paired in such a way that there was no valid relationship between them.

The subjects, after viewing each of the Rorschach cards for one minute, were given a questionnaire listing the four symptoms and asking if the subject had noticed "any general kind of thing that was seen most often by men with this problem." If so, they were to list that "kind of thing" and an example.

The results confirmed the prediction of the researchers: subjects reported that they had observed the five invalid signs as accompanying homosexual problems more than any other category of Rorschach response. By contrast, the valid signs of male homosexuality were not reported as correlates any more often than were the two filler categories. In short, these laypeople demonstrated the same errors of diagnosis as had the clinicians, even though the perceived relationships did not actually exist in the Rorschach materials. They were illusory correlates based on "commonsense" preconceptions.

Another experiment in the Chapmans' series is of particular interest. The researchers used essentially the same procedure that we have described but eliminated the five invalid signs of male homosexuality. In this instance, the subjects nearly doubled their accuracy in reporting valid correlates. The results of this experiment suggest to the Chapmans that preconceptions—the illusory correlates of male homosexuality—can "blind the observer to the presence of valid correlates of the symptom." This appears to be true whether the observer is a layperson or a highly experienced clinician. ∎

matter how incoherent or meaningless they might seem. These fragments are believed to provide a glimpse into the unconscious elements of personality.

A second major method espoused by Freud, Jung, and others is **dream interpretation.** Freud called dreams "the royal road to the unconscious" (1900/1953). He believed dreams had two primary psychological functions: they fulfilled wishes and they served as safety valves to release unconscious tensions. In both functions, he suggested, dreams give form to desires and impulses that would be unacceptable to the dreamer's conscious awareness.

Freud made a distinction between two different levels of dream content (1925/1961). He referred to the **manifest content,** which is what we remember about our dreams. **Latent content,** on the other hand, is the underlying psychic material that led to the manifest content. For example, a woman may dream of kissing her husband; this is the manifest content. However, the latent content may, in fact, involve the repressed desire to kiss her father.

Often the latent content of dreams is cloaked in symbols—objects or ideas that stand for something else. In dynamic theory, symbols usually substitute for unconscious desires that are threatening to the ego or superego. Thus, the appearance of children in a dream may be interpreted as symbols for the genital organs. Dream interpretation typically involves a description of the dream followed by the subject's free associations about the content.

Figure 12.1

The Rorschach test uses inkblots of the type illustrated for assessing personality. Typical responses might be to see animals or human beings in the pattern.

The assessment of personality through free association and dream interpretation is a lengthy process that depends largely on the intuition of the clinician.

Another major method of assessment used by dynamic theorists, **projective tests,** aims at preserving clinical judgments while providing a more standardized and objective means of glimpsing the unconscious. These tests require the person to respond to a series of deliberately ambiguous stimuli; they are called projective because it is assumed that in interpreting the stimuli, the person will project hidden aspects of personality onto them.

Projective tests of various kinds are widely used, according to self-reports by 500 clinicians surveyed by Wade and Baker (1977). Even clinicians who eschewed psychoanalytic theory found that projective techniques were often quite helpful in understanding the dynamics of personality.

The most familiar projective technique, the **Rorschach Test,** was developed in 1921 by the Swiss psychiatrist Hermann Rorschach. As a boy Rorschach dabbled so much in ink sketches that he was nicknamed Kleck—Swiss-German for inkblot. Appropriately, his test consists of a series of inkblots on ten separate cards (see Figure 12.1). Subjects look at the inkblots one at a time and tell the examiner what they see there—bugs, bats, humans, clouds, or whatever else. As in dream interpretation, the examiner looks for symbolic relationships to particular personality characteristics. If the subject sees masks among the inkblots, for example, this might be interpreted as revealing a preoccupation with the outward appearance of things. The examiner may also take into account other factors such as whether the subject responds to the entire inkblot or to only a part of it and whether the subject seems cooperative or defensive in response.

Evaluation of the Psychodynamic Approach

No approach to personality has so profoundly affected the modern view of human nature as Freud's dynamic perspective. His descriptions of unconscious motives and of early childhood development have penetrated every aspect of modern life from child-rearing practices to film and literature. Even the phrases associated with Freudian theory—unconscious, ego, Oedipus complex, Freudian slip, free association—are embedded in fabric of everyday conversation.

The undeniable impact notwithstanding, close evaluation of Freud's personality theory raises a number of perplexing issues. We will briefly examine one such issue—the status of the psychodynamic view as a scientific theory.

The dynamic view as a scientific theory has received criticism from contemporary theorists. One line of criticism focuses on the fact that the bulk of support for psychoanalytic theory derives from clinical evidence. Such evidence is subject to bias by the clinician. It does not tell us whether the childhood traumas reported by the patient actually occurred. It makes no provision for establishing that the reported childhood traumas actually led to the personality characteristics in question. And it makes no attempt to assess whether reported changes in the patient's behavior might not have occurred over time without psychoanalytic therapy.

Ernest Nagel (1959) has evaluated psychoanalysis as a scientific theory in terms of three criteria and found it lacking. He cites its inability to produce "if-then" statements that predict explicit consequences following from the theory, its failure to define clearly such concepts as the Oedipus complex, and its vague formulations that permit manipulation to fit the evidence at hand.

Another way of stating Nagel's criticism is that dynamic theory contains assertions that are true in every conceivable case—and hence by definition cannot be disproved or proved. Bert Kaplan (1964) singles out one such idea from

Freudian theory—the assertion that boys are sexually attracted to their mothers. If boys express this attraction, it fits the theory. "If, on the contrary," observes Kaplan, "they behave as though their mothers were detestable, this conduct only indicates a reaction against their own forbidden desires, and again the claims hold good; so it is true no matter what."

Phares (1984) has catalogued a number of theoretical and empirical problems with the psychoanalytic perspective on personality. These include the fact that many of the concepts are difficult to measure, that frequently the language is picturesque but difficult to use in a scientific context, that the approach is subject to excesses of interpretation, and that an overemphasis on childhood events may characterize the approach. Finally, there is a growing concern among feminists that the Freudian perspective often views women as vain, sensitive, and dependent on men. Phares (1984) notes that early in the development of psychoanalytic theory some analysts, including Karen Horney, also expressed their disagreement with Freud on these issues.

Many broad formulations of personality share this difficulty. Sweeping theories that attempt to capture universal truths about human personality are extremely difficult to test empirically, and the dynamic view is no exception. Despite the difficulty in conducting research on psychoanalytic concepts, however, literally thousands of studies have been conducted. Recently, a comprehensive review by Kline (1981) concluded that, while some of the results are equivocal, a great many studies support the value of psychoanalytic concepts, including research on defensiveness, anxiety, dreams, and psychosexual phenomena.

Dispositional Theories

A second major approach to understanding personality assumes that people have prevailing internal tendencies to behave in certain predictable ways. All of us, without quite realizing that we are dispositional theorists, tend to make that same assumption in our everyday judgments about people. We are constantly categorizing people in terms of a few characteristics that seem to typify them: "She has a pleasant disposition," or "He's the moody type." And hav-

Hippocrates proposed four basic human temperaments, illustrated in this medieval woodcut.

ing classified people, we tend to expect their future behavior to fit into that category.

Dispositional theories are of several kinds. One attempts to relate a person's physical or character type to his or her behavior. This view is familiar in the common assumption that a fat person, for example, is likely to be jolly. A second dispositional approach proposes to discover certain traits, such as aggressiveness, as the principal factors in personality. Finally, a third dispositional approach assumes that an understanding of individual needs, such as the need for love or respect, and their patterning will provide us with the clearest understanding of underlying personality dispositions.

Typological Theories

The possibility of a link between physical makeup and personality has long fascinated scientists. Nearly 2500 years ago, the Greek physician Hippocrates suggested that biochemistry shaped personality. He proposed four basic human temperaments corresponding to four body humours, or fluids: happy or sanguine (blood), hot tempered or choleric (yellow bile), sluggish or phlegmatic (phlegm) and sad or melancholic (black bile).

Much later, in the nineteenth century, scientists investigated associations between behavior and measurable physical characteristics. The founder of phrenology, Franz Josef Gall, thought bumps on an individual's skull were clues to personality (Gall and Spurzheim, 1810, 1819). It remained, however, for William Sheldon to undertake the first systematic study of personality and physical types.

Sheldon's Somatotypical Approach

In the 1940s, Sheldon conducted an extensive study in which 4000 male college students were photographed from the front, side, and rear (Sheldon, 1942, 1954). After examining the photographs, Sheldon concluded that there were three basic kinds of body structure and physique, which he called **somatotypes** (see Figure 12.2). His three somatotypes were **endomorph** (soft and round), **mesomorph** (sturdy and muscular), and **ectomorph** (thin and fragile).

Then, by studying other male subjects through interviews and observation, Sheldon developed his Scale of Temperament, which consisted of patterns of personality traits that seemed to characterize his subjects. Finally, in an attempt to find correlations between his somatotypes and temperament, he studied 200 male volunteers over a five-year period.

Sheldon reported striking correlations and, interestingly, they tended to confirm popular wisdom about such matters. The soft and round endomorphs were pleasure-loving, sociable, and relaxed (viscerotonic). Sturdy and muscular mesomorphs were outgoing, assertive, and dominating (somatotonic). Thin and fragile ectomorphs were inhibited, intense, and inward-looking (cerebrotonic).

Sheldon's somatotyping scheme did not purport to find pure endomorphs, mesomorphs, or ectomorphs. Instead, the person was somatotyped by assigning three numbers, each ranging from 1 to 7, that represented the relative strength of each basic type. A muscular person might be rated 1-7-1, thus nearing the somatotype of a pure mesomorph. A person of average physique could be somatotyped 4-4-4.

Although some correlational studies have found support for Sheldon's somatotypes (Brouwer, 1957; Hammond, 1957), others have not. For instance, Child (1950) reported only a moderate correlation between somatotype and temperament. The causes or mechanisms of the purported link between personality and physique have never clearly been established. Sheldon, who was the son of an animal breeder, believed the causes were genetic in origin. Indeed, he thought evidence of this genetic blueprint could be seen in the development of the human embryo and took his three somatotypes—endomorph, mesomorph, and ectomorph—from the names of three distinct layers of cells that develop respectively into the digestive system and internal organs (endomorph), bone and muscle (mesomorph), and the central nervous system (ectomorph). As these physical systems developed, Sheldon said, one became dominant, along with its associated personality type.

Obesity and Personality

Experimental evidence in support of the various typological theories is rare. In the case of Sheldon's somatotypes, for example, most of the follow-up studies have been correlational in nature. One notable example is the comparison of nearly 500 pairs of boys, one delinquent and the other nondelinquent, which indicated a clear relationship with somatotype differences (Glueck & Glueck, 1950, 1956). The findings from this study show a much higher percentage of muscular mesomorphs and much lower percentage of thin ectomorphs among the delinquents than chance would dictate. This does not mean that most mesomorphs become delinquent. The more plausible interpretation is that a muscular body lends itself to a physical orientation that might manifest itself in aggressive, even antisocial, behavior.

Such correlational studies, like Sheldon's original work with somatotypes, tell us little about the processes that might link physique and personality. However, one fascinating line of experimental research exists that suggests some possible clues. This research, initially concerned with patterns of eating, was done by Stanley Schachter.

Schachter had no particular interest in furthering Sheldon's theory, but he was intrigued by the relationship between physiological and psychological states in emotionality. This interest attracted him to the results of an experiment that suggested that fat people tended to report hunger even in the absence of a normal physiological indicator of hunger—stomach contraction (Stunkard & Koch, 1964). The obese subjects said they were hungry, as Schachter (1971) later described it, no matter what the state of their stomachs.

Intrigued by this evidence of a link between a person's physique and behavior, Schachter conducted his own experiment, carefully varying the body types of the subjects and their state of physiological hunger (Schachter, Goldman, & Gordon, 1968). Some of the subjects were first fed roast beef sandwiches; others were not. Then, under the guise of a taste preference experiment, all the subjects were encouraged to try five kinds of crackers. Schachter found that, as might be expected, persons of normal weight ate considerably more crackers when their stomachs were empty than when they were full. But among the obese subjects, having eaten roast beef sandwiches first did not seem to reduce the number of crackers consumed. In fact, the obese subjects actually ate slightly more crackers after their stomachs had already been filled.

From this and other experiments, Schachter concluded that external cues such as sight, smell, and taste of food, rather than the state of the gut, controlled the eating of fat people. He also began to suspect that fat people may also be more responsive to external stimuli in other kinds of behavior than are persons of normal weight.

To test this broader hypothesis, one of Schachter's students, Judith Rodin (1970), asked obese and normal subjects to perform a simple proofreading task. The environments varied according to the amount of distraction provided by tape recordings. As predicted by Schachter, the fat subjects were more prone to distraction and more responsive to external stimuli. However, in the absence of the distracting tapes, obese subjects were able to concentrate on their task even better than the normal subjects.

Predominant endomorph Predominant mesomorph Predominant ectomorph Average physique

Figure 12.2

Sheldon's three basic somatotypes include the entomorph (soft and round), the mesomorph (sturdy and muscular), and the ectomorph (thin and fragile). The average physique is also shown for purposes of comparison.

Figure 12.3

Eysenck's arrangement of the dimensions of personality is depicted by four quadrants that represent a combination of stability, instability, introversion, and extraversion.

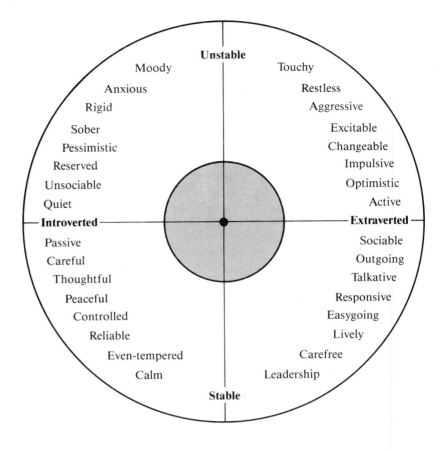

Whether such broad psychological dispositions can be linked to somatotype through further research remains to be seen. Of course, physical appearance can also affect the way in which others react to us and how we behave and feel about ourselves in social situations. Unraveling the relationship between physical type and personality will require disentangling a number of such factors.

Eysenck's Typological Approach to Personality

Another typological approach to personality is reflected in the extensive research and theory of H. J. Eysenck. Eysenck's approach is based on his belief, supported by elaborate research and sophisticated statistical methodology, that there is a small number, perhaps no more than two or three, of underlying personality dimensions along which all people differ.

For a number of years, Eysenck (1967, 1975) has argued that one of the most important of these dimensions is that of **introversion** and **extraversion.** As the name implies, extraverts are, on the average, more sociable, active, lively, and excitable than introverts, who tend to be quieter, more reserved, and less sociable.

A second major personality dimension suggested by Eysenck is stability and instability. In general, this dimension reflects the degree to which a person is calm and even-tempered as opposed to being moody and changeable. Figure 12.3 shows how Eysenck arranges these two dimensions to form four quadrants. These quadrants reflect a combination of introversion, extraversion, stability, and instability. Thus, in Eysenck's system, one may be a stable introvert or extravert or an unstable introvert or extravert.

In some of his research, Eysenck has suggested that a third factor, ''psychoticism'' may be an underlying third personality dimension reflecting insensitivity, oddness, hostility, and a lack of caring for others. Like many other dispositional theorists, Eysenck is concerned primarily with discovering a theoretical structure that provides for the arrangement of personality dimensions or traits so that any particular individual can be described using the terms of the system.

Trait Theories

As we suggested earlier, personality theorists are frequently concerned with developing theories of personality that help explain both the uniqueness of each individual and the fact that a person's behavior appears consistent across different occasions and situations. In some ways, this is the common-sense meaning of the term *personality*. In trying to understand and explain personal uniqueness and consistency, psychologists have used a variety of different theoretical strategies. One of the best-known strategies has been to argue that individuals have traits that help explain the uniqueness and consistency that we observe in behavior.

Gordon Allport describes a trait as a characteristic that summarizes a consistent pattern of behavior we can observe in an individual.

Allport: Traits as the Basic Units of Personality

One of the most influential trait psychologists is Gordon Allport, who developed and clarified a classical trait approach to describing and understanding personality (1937, 1961, 1966). Searching for distinctive styles of expressive behavior and personality traits, he has conducted intensive studies of single individuals and studies of groups of people.

Allport's concept of trait begins in much the same way as our everyday language usage of the term. For Allport, a trait is a characteristic that summarizes a consistent pattern of behavior that we can observe in an individual. Thus, we may say that a person is "aggressive" if we notice that in a variety of situations he or she behaves in forceful and brusque ways and if on the various occasions when we meet the person we notice that he or she leaves us with the same impression of aggressiveness.

However, Allport went further than simply arguing for the existence of traits. He suggested that we could differentiate between traits of different kinds and that it would be theoretically useful to do so. For example, he argued that traits may vary with respect to how generally they pervade the whole personality: **cardinal traits** should be extremely strong characteristics that shape the whole personality, whereas **central traits** would be important but not pervasive. Finally, **secondary traits** would reflect very narrow patterns of behavior or habits and be of less theoretical importance.

In addition to arguing that personality traits could vary in their generality, Allport also distinguished between what he called **adaptive traits,** which are necessary to carry out a particular task situation, and **expressive traits,** which are particular styles of behavior. In fact, Allport and Phillip Vernon conducted a study, which they summarized in a book entitled *Studies in Expressive Movement* (1933). The interesting thing about this study is that Allport believed that the uniqueness of individuals and their consistency over time could be captured only if many tests and measures were administered to large numbers of people on a number of different occasions. The unique expressive style of individuals would be reflected in the way in which these test results correlated with each other. In their study they used 300 different performance measures, including tasks of drawing and counting, rhythmic tapping, and physical strength. Allport and Vernon administered them to 25 men in a series of research sessions. Allport believed that if he was right about the unique expressive styles of individuals, then certain test results should correlate with each other reflecting distinctive personality traits such as speed or vigor.

While some tests revealed substantial correlations if repeated in the same session or if repeated for the same individual on two occasions, the correlations for different tests presumably measuring the same trait were not as high as Allport had hoped. Nevertheless, the study was intended to show that there were patterns of expressive styles reflected in the behavior of individuals and that these patterns could be observed over occasions.

Allport believed that personality traits vary according to whether they are common to most people or whether they are unique to a particular individual. He believed that some traits are common; that is, that they can be observed in most people to a greater or lesser degree. Thus, for example, one might discover that the trait of submissiveness would be relatively normally distributed in the population, with some people demonstrating a great deal of dominance and others considerably less so. Indeed, many psychologists have developed tests that they believe measure traits existing in varying quantities in the population. This approach, which involves studying many people with a relatively limited number of measures or tests to discover whether there is substantial individual variation in a characteristic, is called **nomothetic research.**

However, perhaps more than most personality theorists, Allport was fascinated by the unique characteristics of individuals. He believed that some personality traits are unique to particular individuals and can best be understood by studying a single individual intensively over a long period of time. This type of study, **idiographic research,** is illustrated by one of Allport's best-known studies summarized in his book *Letters from Jenny* (1965). This intensive case study was based on the letters written by Jenny Masterson between the ages of 58 and 70, which trace her personal relationships with her son and the rest of her family in great detail. Allport believed that much could be learned about her unique characteristics by studying these letters both in terms of their content and style. His strategy was to ask a large number of judges to read the letters and then to have the judges assign nearly 200 descriptive adjectives to Jenny based on their overall impressions of her personality. In addition, a content analysis of the frequency with which Jenny used various words was done to provide still another strategy for observing unique traits that Jenny might display. From these two research strategies of a variety of characteristics emerged that seemed important in describing Jenny's personality. They in-

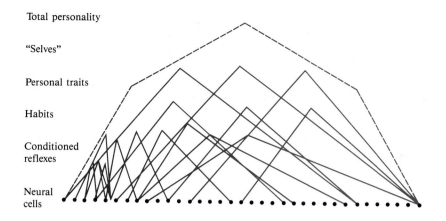

Total personality

"Selves"

Personal traits

Habits

Conditioned reflexes

Neural cells

Figure 12.4

Allport's concept of the structure of a total personality is based on a hierarchial structure. An individual's neural cells give rise to the formation of conditioned reflexes, which combine into habits. In turn, many habits combine to form personal traits. Combinations of traits make up the various "selves" we present to others. The entire integrated structure is known as the total personality.

cluded traits of aggressiveness, possessiveness, sentimentality, and a certain self-centered and self-pitying quality as well as strong indication of drama and intensity. Through careful study of the stylistic and personal documents of a single person's life, Allport attempted to understand the uniqueness of a single personality.

Although Allport was interested in studying the unique characteristics of particular individuals, he believed all personality traits existed in the context of a hierarchical structure. His concept of the structure of personality depended greatly on thinking of it as organized at the most basic level in terms of very small units of behavior along with physiological units such as "neural cells." Figure 12.4 shows how Allport believed these smaller units could then be combined into increasingly larger units, which he called conditioned reflexive habits; then at a somewhat broader level, personal traits; and finally overarching "selves." Selves were broad patterns of personal traits that emerged in different ways in different people in different situations. Thus, at a party we may show one "self," whereas at work we may show another. Nevertheless, all of these selves at the broader level are organized into the total personality of the individual shown at the top of the figure.

Allport was interested not only in dispositional traits, but also in the nature of human adjustment. He believed that psychological health reflected not just and absence of pathological traits, but instead an outgrowth of self-esteem and personal confidence. Hjelle and Ziegler (1981) have described a number of Allport's criteria for psychological maturity. They include a capacity to relate warmly to others, emotional security, realistic perception and skills, the capacity to see oneself objectively, and a unifying philosophy of life. Allport's dispositional theory of personality is particularly important to us because it is such a classic example of how the concept of trait has been used creatively to account for both the uniqueness and the consistency of personality.

Cattell: The Search for Source and Surface Traits

Another important trait theorist is Raymond Cattell (1950, 1952, 1957), who also believed that traits are the fundamental components of personality. Indeed, Cattell claimed that it is possible to understand the underlying structure of personality by discovering which traits are fundamental in behavior and which are less important. He believed that fundamental traits, which he called **source traits,** are the roots of overt behavior, and he identified 16 of them (see Figure 12.5). He described **surface traits** as clusters of overt behavior that seem to go together. Thus, nervous traits, such as trembling or stammering, may be surface traits that result from some more general source trait such as timidity or apprehensiveness.

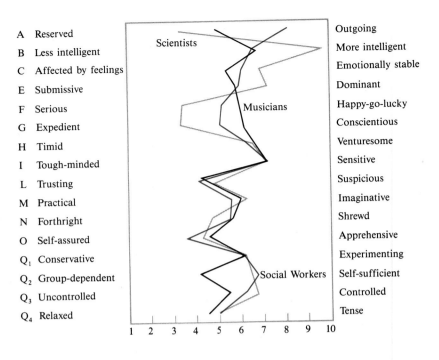

Figure 12.5

Cattell's personality traits are listed to the left and right of the graph. These traits, which are paired and describe the ends of the scale that make up the dimension, are personality factors obtained by factor analysis of many ratings. The profiles show the average scores on the 16 traits exhibited by groups of scientists, social workers, and musicians.

A	Reserved	Outgoing
B	Less intelligent	More intelligent
C	Affected by feelings	Emotionally stable
E	Submissive	Dominant
F	Serious	Happy-go-lucky
G	Expedient	Conscientious
H	Timid	Venturesome
I	Tough-minded	Sensitive
L	Trusting	Suspicious
M	Practical	Imaginative
N	Forthright	Shrewd
O	Self-assured	Apprehensive
Q_1	Conservative	Experimenting
Q_2	Group-dependent	Self-sufficient
Q_3	Uncontrolled	Controlled
Q_4	Relaxed	Tense

Unlike Allport, who relied heavily on his own theoretical intuition and observational skills in deciding which traits are central and which are less so, Cattell believed that the structure of personality can be discovered through the empirical means of **factor analysis**—a statistical strategy for extracting common factors or sources of variance that summarize test results from large numbers of people. Thus, a factor analyst may give 500 people a battery of tests with as many as 300 separate measures and then attempt to summarize either the characteristics of the people or the characteristics of the tests by correlating the results of each test to discover common sources of variance or "factors" in the test. Cattell believed that by conducting such studies repeatedly using different types of measures and different groups of people, common factors of personality ultimately would emerge.

On the face of it, this strategy seems to be logical. However, there are some real limitations on the use of factor analysis. One of them relates to deciding how many factors are to be used to summarize the data. In principle, as many factors as there are measures could be used, but by doing so the summarizing power of factor analysis would be lost, and the amount of variance accounted for by many of the factors would be extremely small. Similarly, many of the factors extracted may not reappear on subsequent tests using different measures and different individuals. This problem raises some questions about the degree to which some of the factors Cattell has described are replicable. Indeed, replicability is both a common demand of good scientific evidence and one that Cattell acknowledges is crucial in supporting his approach to describing the structure.

Is There a Biological Basis for Traits?
The Case of Aggression and Altruism

Dispositional approaches to personality frequently raise questions about the degree to which any particular trait reflects some underlying biological basis for personality. Two major traits, aggression and altruism, have received a great deal of attention. The Nobel Prize winner Konrad Lorenz (1974) has been an advocate of the idea that human aggression has instinctual origins. He argues that humans have difficulty controlling aggression because their ancestors never evolved an unwillingness to kill their own, as have other species. However, Wilson (1975) has suggested that other species such as hyenas do occasionally kill within their own species.

One recent series of studies linking genetic background to aggression involves the study of the XYY chromosome anomaly. Some evidence reported by Jarvik, Klodin, and Matsuyama (1973) suggested that an additional Y chromosome was overrepresented in prison populations and that it might provide a clue to the increased propensity for violence among some people. However, subsequent research by Kessler (1975) and Witkin and his colleagues (1976) suggests that this chromosomal anomaly is not necessarily associated with crimes of violence and that XYY males are not particularly prone to violence. Thus, this line of research attempting to link genetic factors to a personality disposition associated with aggression does not seem promising at this time.

Altruism seems, at first glance, to be a trait that is both uniquely human and likely to be learned in the context of family and community. But Wilson (1975) suggests that it is not the exclusive property of human beings. Sociobiology, a discipline that attempts to understand the biological basis of social behavior indicates that examples of altruism can be found throughout the animal kingdom. Frequently, animals will engage in behavior that either places them at risk or results in their death in order to preserve their infants or their biological community. Sociobiologists believe that altruism, particularly that which risks the individual, promotes what they call kin selection. By behaving altruistically, animals will increase the likelihood that closely related individuals will survive and reproduce. Since closely related individuals share genes with the altruistic animal, these genes are more likely to survive and thus promote the species. The altruistic behavior is "selfish" in the sense that it is designed to further the survival of one's genetic inheritance.

However, other evolutionary biologists such as Gould (1976) argue that many altruistic behaviors observed in human cultures can also be easily interpreted as learned behaviors transmitted from generation to generation through the traditions of the family. Thus, elderly Eskimos who commit suicide by abandoning their family when the group moves on to search for food could be .seen by sociobiologists as altruistic because they preserve the genetic group. But the same behavior could be interpreted culturally, since Eskimo children learn very early to celebrate the elderly as heroes who put the clan above their own individual lives (Phares, 1984).

Thus, the question of the degree to which traits such as aggression or altruism have a genetic basis remains. It serves both as a source of scientific debate and as a source of new hypotheses for understanding human traits and dispositions.

The question of the extent to which nature or nurture influences personality dispositions has been studied by Scarr and her colleagues (1981). These researchers studied adolescents who were adopted in infancy, as well as families with biologically related adolescents. A variety of personality measures were administered and similarities observed among the adopted relatives as well as the nonadopted biologically related individuals. They conclude from their research that neither environmental differences alone nor genetic differences alone account for the variance in personality measures. Instead, much of the variation observed actually suggested that individuals, even those who are biologically related in the same family, may proceed along quite different developmental lines. Scarr and her colleagues conclude that our models for understanding personality differences are still far too simple and that no theory yet exists to explain the individuality that they observed.

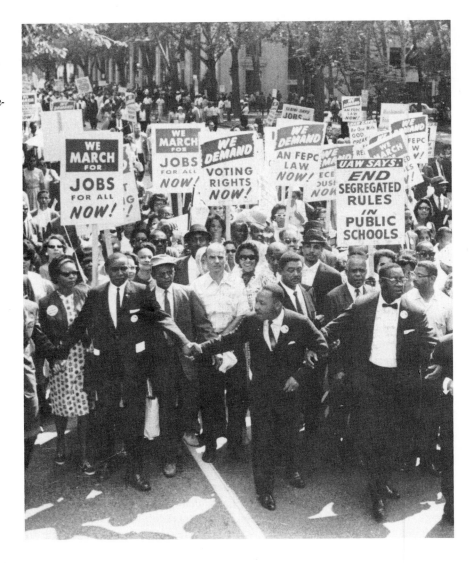

The situation we're in often defines or contributes to the needs we feel. The people who joined in the March on Washington showed a need for autonomy, which, according to Murray, means to resist influence or coercion and strive for independence.

Need Approaches

A third major approach to the understanding of personality through an examination of dispositions is one that emphasizes the concept of *need*. Unquestionably the major theorist in this area was Henry A. Murray. Murray inferred the existence of needs in people's behavior from the observation of various behavioral sequences (1938). For example, a sequence involving a person's being presented with a difficult problem, experiencing tension as a result, mastering the problem, and finally exhibiting pride may reveal a need for achievement (Bavelas, 1978). Repeated observation of such sequences, particularly when they involve a variety of different behaviors or circumstances, led Murray to suggest that distinctive needs exist for particular people. These needs include achievement, affiliation, aggression, autonomy, deference, nurturance, play, and understanding, among others.

Murray's approach to understanding personality in terms of needs requires some way for the researcher to take into account the social environment as well as the individual. Murray's approach, although oriented to the individual, relies heavily on the idea that needs are best understood in the context of the situations that may elicit them. As a consequence, Murray developed a second concept, which he called **press,** to describe the characteristics of situations that initiate or direct behavior. Thus, a situation may have a press of danger or achievement or affiliation or perhaps order.

Murray further distinguished between two kinds of press: **alpha press** and **beta press.** Alpha press reflects aspects of a situation that are objectively perceived, objectively exist, and are compelling to the individual, such as the objectively dangerous aspects posed by the situation of a car speeding directly toward you. Beta press characterizes those aspects of a situation that are perceived to be present by the individual and thus influence his or her behavior, such as seeing a classroom as a ''threatening'' place.

In developing his needs theory of personality, Murray (1938) was particularly interested in examining sequences or patterns of behavior that reflect the underlying needs that he assumed were so important to an understanding of the overall workings of the personality. Murray believed that in many cases it is possible to infer needs simply from examining overt behavior. By examining a pattern of behavior—such as the length of time that people engage in a task, their persistence in the face of difficult problems in accomplishing the task, and their apparent engagement in the task—a high need for achievement might be inferred. However, such a **manifest need**—a need observed in overt behavior—is not the only type that interested Murray. He also believed that each individual could be understood in terms of **latent needs**—needs reflected in fantasy, imagination, and thoughts and wishes about the world rather than in overt behavior.

As a strategy for measuring these latent needs, Murray developed the *Thematic Apperception Test (TAT),* which consists of a set of 20 pictures showing either one person or several people standing in relation to each other (Murray, 1951, 1962). An example of a TAT picture is shown in Figure 12.6. Murray and his colleagues assumed that when asked to tell a story about the TAT pictures, people would project their latent needs into the story as they do when they explain what they see in the inkblots of the Rorschach Test.

A subject tells a story about each of the 20 cards, and the stories are recorded. Then the stories are scored according to a standard for a variety of different needs, including achievement, recognition, order, dominance, autonomy, and affiliation. The themes that come out in these stories can also be scored to indicate what sorts of presses the pictures elicit from the subjects— that is, how he or she sees the press of each situation depicted in the pictures.

In recent years a number of Murray's colleagues and students have used the TAT in the context of studying a variety of different motives and needs (Atkinson, 1958; McClelland, Atkinson, Clark, & Lowell, 1953).

Figure 12.6

Typical example of a picture used in Murray's Thematic Apperception Test to measure latent needs. The subject is asked to tell a story about each of 20 such pictures. These stories are then scored against standards for a variety of different needs such as achievement, recognition, dominance, and affiliation.

Issues in the Dispositional Approach to Personality

Many psychologists feel that dispositional theories are no longer as important in the study of personality as they once were. Dispositional theories are better at describing personality than explaining the development of enduring behavior patterns. Type and trait theories capture something important about the ways in which people differ from one another.

For example, it is easy to find exceptions to Sheldon's somatotype scheme: one of the most renowned artists of our time, Pablo Picasso, was no frail ectomorph but a bull-necked mesomorph. On the other hand, it is equally easy to imagine how physique might influence temperament: it affects others' perceptions of us and hence our perceptions of ourselves.

The major drawback of the dispositional approach relates to its failure to take into account the role of the specific situation in behavior. The most influential attack on dispositional theories, mounted by Walter Mischel (1968), hinged on this failure.

Mischel focused on two important assumptions that underlie not only dispositional theories but also the dynamic approach of Freud and others. Both perspectives assume, in their theories and in their methods of assessment, that individual behavior is stable over time and general across situations. In other words, if a person is judged to be assertive, that person will be consistently assertive regardless of the particular circumstances.

In an extensive evaluation of evidence from assessment methods favored by both the dynamic and dispositional perspectives, Mischel found little support for either basic assumption, thus challenging a basic premise in most personality theories. When tests are repeated, he said, measures of traits tend to change, and the traits themselves fail to serve as reliable predictors of how a person will behave as situations change. Mischel (1977) has proposed that it is not possible to locate personality dispositions either in the actor or the person perceiving the actor. Instead, we must examine the continuous interaction between the observed and the observer to understand personality.

Mischel believes that we can take both dispositional (or personality) variables and situations into account by developing what he calls **cognitive learning person variables.** Such variables include the individual's competencies to construct or to generate a wide variety of behaviors under various conditions. Furthermore, such person variables include the individual's (1) ability to categorize and encode various social situations, (2) expectancies about the outcomes of those situations, and (3) self-regulatory systems and plans. Each of these major classes of variables, from Mischel's point of view, represents important person variables that are characteristics of the individual. Each will lead individuals to behave differently in different situations. Although Mischel has less to say about the characteristics of situations that bring out these differences among individuals, he does suggest that ambiguously structured situations are more likely to bring out individual differences than are highly structured situations (Price & Bouffard, 1974).

Learning Theories

While dispositional theories of personality focus on internal properties of the individual, learning theories focus outward on the environment. From the learning perspective, stable patterns of behavior are not evidence of traits or dispositions but are the consequence of repeated experiences with various stimulus situations. There are several learning approaches to the understanding of personality.

Skinner: Operant Approaches

One personality theory based on learning owes much to B. F. Skinner (1938, 1953, 1971, 1974). In effect, Skinner (1953) argues that there is no such thing as personality: there are only operant behaviors that are strengthened or weakened as a consequence of reinforcement. These behaviors are predictable and primarily controlled by measurable external stimuli. Behaviors that are positively reinforced tend to be repeated; those that are punished tend not to be repeated. Like many other learning theorists, Skinner says the key to understanding personality is to examine the stimulus conditions under which the behaviors have developed in the past and are maintained in the present.

Skinner's ideas about personality have been dramatized in a novel called *Walden Two* (1948), in which he creates a utopian community based on his principles of operant conditioning. The founder of this community argues that people's behavior can be predicted and controlled like chemical reactions in a test tube. The idea of an inner self, he asserts, is myth and superstition.

The operant learning emphasis on environmental and situational influences on personality inevitably requires different methods of assessment than those favored by other approaches. Because behavior is said to speak for itself, the aim is to observe behavior carefully in its natural setting and to describe accurately the situational factors that appear to influence it—an assessment called **functional analysis.** With this technique, psychologists not only observe and describe the conditions they suspect are shaping a particular behavior pattern, but they may also attempt to change the behavior. They may induce a modification of stimulus conditions and then observe whether or not this produces a predicted change in behavior. In this way, researchers can determine whether or not the stimuli that are apparently controlling the behavior are actually doing so.

A classic example of this method is the case of Ann (Allen, Hart, Buell, Harris, & Wolf, 1964). Ann was a bright four-year-old who came from an upper-middle-class home. After six weeks in nursery school, however, she seemed increasingly withdrawn and isolated from the other children, although she was clearly succeeding in winning the warm attention of teachers and other adults in the school.

Functional analysis of Ann's behavior began with a five-day observation period in the nursery school. Two observers each spent half of the morning recording at 10-second intervals what Ann was doing in relation to the other children and to the adults. The data collected during this five-day period showed that Ann spent about 50 percent of the time alone, 40 percent interacting with adults, and only about 10 percent interacting with the other children. The authors of the study concluded that Ann's isolate behavior was being maintained and probably strengthened inadvertently by adult social reinforcement.

It is interesting to note how this description of behavior differs from that of other personality theorists. Behavior that a trait theorist might describe as resulting from an internal disposition toward shyness with other children or that a dynamic theorist might interpret in terms of intrapsychic events is seen solely in terms of a particular stimulus condition—the situational presence of adult reinforcement. Note also the functions served by the five-day observation period. It establishes the solitary nature of Ann's behavior along with a hypothesis about the cause of that behavior. Moreover, it lays down a baseline of data against which to compare peer interaction after the investigators introduce a change in stimulus conditions. The change in stimulus conditions introduced was quite simple: the adults in the nursery school were instructed to stop giving Ann attention during her periods of withdrawal and during her attempts at interaction with them. They were told to give Ann attention only when she played with other children. Adult reinforcement in the form of attention thus became contingent on a change in her behavior—playing with her peers more often.

Now, whenever Ann started to interact with other children, even if that interaction was nothing more than standing or playing near another child, an adult quickly paid attention to her. For example, an adult would approach Ann and the others and say, "You three girls have a cozy house. Here are some more cups, Ann, for your tea party." And whenever Ann left the group, the adults immediatiely stopped paying attention to her.

Two observers continued to record Ann's social interaction every 10 seconds, and the change was immediately evident. On the very first day of the

Figure 12.7

This graphic presentation of the use of functional analysis in "case of Ann," shows that Ann's interaction with other children increased dramatically during periods when such behavior was reinforced by approval and attention from adults.

new arrangement, Ann spent nearly 60 percent of her time with other children—a sixfold increase over the five-day baseline. During one four-day period the researchers instructed the adults to revert to their former procedure—rewarding Ann with their attention for interacting with the adults but not the children—and Ann's interaction with children suddenly dropped dramatically. This drop helped confirm the researchers' hypothesis that the change in stimulus conditions was responsible for the change in Ann's behavior. Periodic checks after the 25-day study ended indicated that Ann's increased interaction with her peers remained fairly stable—presumably because the teachers continued to reinforce it. A graph displaying the entire analysis is shown in Figure 12.7.

This study lends some empirical support to the operant approach to understanding personality. Rather than interpreting Ann's behavior in terms of a trait, "shyness," the operant learning approach views the behavior as controlled, and controllable, by changing the reinforcement in the external stimulus environment.

Bandura: Social Learning Through Observation

Broader learning theories of personality than Skinner's have been offered by several investigators. The most prominent of these is the **social learning approach** developed by Albert Bandura. Although behaviorally oriented, Bandura (1971) rejects the concept of a one-way process involving the environment as the influencer of behavior and shaper of personality. Instead, his aim is to describe the two-way interaction between the individual and the environment:

"Behavior partly creates the environment, and the resultant environment in turn influences the behavior. In this two-way causal process the environment is just as influenceable as the behavior it controls" (Bandura, 1971).

Bandura's approach differs from the Skinnerian perspective in several important respects. It is based on human learning research rather than on animal conditioning. Furthermore, it stresses the importance of cognitive and social factors as opposed to simple classical or operant conditioning. As we saw in chapter 7, Bandura has shown that considerable learning takes place vicariously—through observational learning, or modeling. We watch the behavior of others—models—and take note of the consequences of their actions, observing whether they are reinforced or punished. These models may be parents, peers, or even performers on television.

In Bandura's social learning theory, the concept of reinforcement takes on a broader meaning. It may be direct—an external reinforcement experienced firsthand, or it may be vicarious—experienced through the observation of a model who is rewarded. In addition, reinforcement may be self-administered— the compliment, banana split, or other reward we give to ourselves for behaving in a certain way. "If actions were determined solely by external rewards and punishments," Bandura (1971) has written, "people would behave like weather vanes, constantly shifting in radically different directions to conform to the whims of others."

Thus, for Bandura, behavior depends on the special characteristics of the situation, the person's cognitive appraisal of the situation—the individual's awareness and expectations—and the history of reinforcements (direct, vicarious, or self-administered) in similar circumstances.

Unlike dynamic and dispositional theories, the social learning approach lends itself readily to testing by the experimental method. Because the primary emphasis is on external conditions rather than on internal structures or processes, the researcher can control and vary the stimuli that are said to shape behavior.

To test Bandura's social learning approach, Bandura and Mischel (1965) conducted an experiment that demonstrates the acquisition of behavioral characteristics through the observation of models. The characteristic in question involved self-control—in this instance, the willingness to delay gratification. Typically, the delay of gratification means postponing an immediate reward in favor of a potentially more valuable delayed reward. For example, a student decides to forgo dropping out of school to get a job in order to graduate and presumably to obtain a better job in the future.

To determine whether children can acquire this sort of self-control merely by observing, Bandura and Mischel worked with a group of fourth- and fifth-grade students. First, they classified the children according to whether they preferred high delay of reward or low delay of reward, by giving them a series of 14 choices between a small immediate reward (a small candy bar right away) and a larger postponed reward (a bigger candy bar a week later).

To test whether these initial preferences could be changed by observation of an appropriate adult model who made choices between immediate and postponed rewards, Bandura and Mischel exposed the children in the high-delay-of-reward group to a model who consistently opted for the immediate-reward choice and the children in the low-delay-of-reward group to a model who consistently selected the postponed reward. In some conditions the model was actually present, and in others written (symbolic) materials provided the modeling roles. The adult models, in making the choice, sometimes commented on the reasons for their choice. For example, in choosing a plastic chess set that was available immediately over a more expensive wooden set that would not be obtainable for two weeks, the model explained: "Chess figures are chess fig-

Albert Bandura developed the social learning approach emphasizing the two-way interaction between the individual and the environment.

Bandura has shown that considerable learning takes place through observation.

Figure 12.8

The results of Bandura and Mischel's social learning experiment indicate that children may acquire behavioral characteristics through the observation of models. The percentage of immediate-reward choices by children who initially preferred high-delay increased after exposure to immediate-reward models as did the percentage of delayed-reward choices by children who initially preferred low-delay after exposure to delay-reward models.

ures. I can get as much use out of the plastic ones right away'' (Bandura & Mischel, 1965).

The children were then given a delay-of-reward test. As predicted, the experiment produced marked changes in the children's willingness to delay gratification (see Figure 12.8). These changes remained moderately stable when the children were tested about a month later.

Self-efficacy

Recently, Bandura (1982) has begun to emphasize the role of self-efficacy in behavior. By self-efficacy, Bandura means the belief that one can successfully execute a given course of action or behavior. Our own capacity to estimate whether we can successfully carry out a course of action is of considerable importance because if our judgment is incorrect we may experience failure. Furthermore, our beliefs about how effective we will be in carrying out a given act also determines how carefully we prepare for that course of action and how we view ourselves. The idea of self-efficacy is an important extension of social learning theory and focuses on cognitions about the self. This recent development in social learning theory does much to bridge cognitive and phenomenological approaches with social learning theories of personality and represents an important new development in the social learning approach to personality.

Bandura and Schunk (1981) have conducted a number of studies to illustrate how immediacy of reward can affect one's sense of self-efficacy and how self-efficacy in turn can then motivate further performance. In their research, Bandura and his colleagues studied children who had a substantial lack of interest and skill in mathematical tasks. They offered them two self-directed programs of learning. One program used proximal goals the experimenter suggested—that the children complete material in small units of approximately six pages in each session. In a second group, only distal goals were given, suggesting that they complete the entire 42-page lesson by the end of the seventh session. With proximal goals the children progressed rapidly and developed a strong sense of self-efficacy. On the other hand, use of only long-term goals produced few effects, either in terms of performance or in terms of a sense of self-efficacy.

Perceived Control

An important line of research in the social learning tradition of personality has to do with our perceptions of whether we are in control of the outcomes of our efforts in life. Social learning theorists such as Phares (1976) and Rotter

(1954) have conducted an extended program of theory development and research attempting to understand both the antecedents and the consequences of perceived control over the outcomes in one's life.

A measurement instrument has been developed, the I.E. Scale, which measures a generalized expectancy about how best to construe the nature of reinforcement. People who score at the internal end of the scale construe a situation as one in which their efforts will make a difference in helping them resolve it. People who score at the external end of the scale, on the other hand, behave on the basis of their expectations that chance or other uncontrollable factors are the most critical. Internal and external orientations appear to be associated with an extremely wide variety of different behaviors. Internals are more likely than externals to seek information about their environment, show enhanced efforts to maximize their health and well-being, are more resistant to social influence, and tend to show higher levels of achievement.

Issues in the Learning Approach to Personality

After the elusive and sometimes metaphorical formulations of the dynamic and dispositional theories, the apparent straightforwardness of the learning approach to personality, has an immediate appeal. Unlike most other approaches to personality, the learning perspective purports to explain both the variation of personality over time and its consistency in given situations. In its methods of assessment and of experimental research, learning theory provides a sense of clear-cut cause and effect. If the stimulus condition that is believed to be determining a particular behavior is pinpointed and the stimulus is changed, then predictably the behavior will change.

This is an oversimplified view, of course. Implicit in the learning perspective are a number of issues. One is the widely held belief that Skinner's approach, in particular, reduces human beings to mere stimulus-response machines. Bandura's social learning approach is less susceptible to this criticism because it emphasizes internal processes, such as awareness and expectation, in individual responses to external stimuli.

On a more specific level, Janet Bavelas (1978) pointed out weaknesses in both Skinner's and Bandura's theories. Skinner, Bavelas points out, often confuses the concepts of the cause of behavior with those of behavioral control: "... it is wrong for any theory to conclude that whatever changes a behavior also illuminates the original cause of the behavior. For example, this author's vision is improved by wearing glasses. Does this mean that poor vision is caused by being born without eyeglasses? ... evidence that demonstrates that *operant* conditioning is *sufficient* to cause changes in behavior does not in addition demonstrate that operant conditioning is *necessary* to cause the behavior."

Evaluating Bandura's social learning theory and its emphasis on acquiring behavior through modeling, Bavelas identifies five shortcomings. First, as Bandura himself has acknowledged, mere exposure is not always sufficient to produce observational learning; in addition it is not yet possible to predict that, in a given situation, observational learning will actually occur. Second, the evidence is confusing as to how much children actually learn in modeling experiments. Third, there is also confusion as to what precisely constitutes a model in observational learning. Bandura has used verbal instructions—whether spoken by the model or simply in print—as a kind of model. Fourth, the Bandura theory fails to make clear what happens when there is a conflict between external reinforcement and self-reinforcement: which takes precedence, an individual's anticipation of good feelings or the promise of a concrete reward? The

A child's self-concept changes with experiences and the reactions of others.

research and theory development done recently on self-efficacy and perceived control begin to answer this question. It appears that these important developments in social learning theories of personality begin to bridge the gap between cognition and action, thought and behavior.

Phenomenological Theories

Phenomenological theories of personality take a very different view of the person: they focus on the conscious experience of the individual rather than on overt behavior, as in the behavioral approach, or on traits or types, as in the dispositional approach. Most other theories of personality view people from the outside, while phemenological theories attempt to enter into the person's own psychological experience in order to understand personality (Bavelas, 1978). Furthermore, like the later psychodynamic approaches to personality, the phenomenological approach is concerned primarily with conscious rather than unconscious experience.

Phenomenological theories are sometimes called "self theories" primarily because they are concerned with how one experiences one's own self. Carl Rogers is interested in the experience of the self and how this experience affects an individual's adjustment; Abraham Maslow, another theorist in this tradition, focuses primarily on how the self develops; George Kelly, although oriented to the individual phenomenology or experience of the self, is more concerned with how people develop categories for interpreting and evaluating their own experience.

Rogers: The Concept of Self-Actualization

Central to Rogers' view of personality, as to several of the humanistic theories, is the concept of **self-actualization.** This process has been described by Rogers (1961) as "the directional trend which is evident in all organic and human life—the urge to expand, extend, develop, mature—the tendency to express and actuate all the capacities of the organism."

Rogers (1959) believes the tendency toward self-actualization is innate as indicated by the goal-directed behaviors of infants—reaching, sucking, touching—which are their attempts to actualize themselves in terms of reality as each infant perceives it. As children engage in the actualizing process, they begin to symbolize—that is, to view their own behavior as a separate entity. Eventually their self-experience develops into a **self-concept,** the perceptual object that each child may experience as "me" or "I." This self-concept may change as a result of experiences with others and of reactions of others to the child. Thus, from the reality the child experiences evolves not only a sense of the outside world but also a sense of the self—the "I" or "me" of experience. The field of experience or **phenomenal field** contains a self as well as a view of others such as parents, teachers, and friends.

As the child's self-concept develops, the child also develops a need for positive regard on the part of others, a need Rogers considers so pervasive as to be universal. It is usually satisifed by children reciprocally: in satisfying other people's needs for positive regard, they also satisfy their own need. Sometimes this need becomes so compelling that children may seek the positive regard of others instead of seeking actualizing experiences. When this happens, Rogers suggests that **conditions of worth** develop. These conditions of worth are behaviors and experiences that a person perceives as being valued by others rather than as being valued intrinsically. For example, when a person strives for athletic achievement or excellence in school primarily because it will raise his or her value in the eyes of others rather than for the inherent pleasure that comes from mastering new skills, conditions of worth have been established as opposed to self-actualization.

When people begin to do things primarily because they are praised by others, the sense of self may become distorted and primarily shaped by others' approval. A gap can then develop between a person's actual experiences and his or her self-concept. Rogers calls this gap **incongruence.** He also says that incongruence can develop between an individual's self-concept and ideal self—the vision of what a person would like to be. In either case, the result of incongruence is likely to be anxiety and psychological maladjustment.

Rogers' view of personality primarily focuses on the individual's own experience, not on the person as seen by others or on the person as a bundle of traits, a set of behavior patterns, or a fixated developmental drive. In particular, how individuals view their own selves and their experiences is central to Rogers' theory of personality.

Most of the research on Rogers' theory has occurred in the course of psychotherapy, and effective therapy has been seen as a confirmation of Rogers' ideas. Among the attempts to verify aspects of the theory experimentally, the work most consistently cited by Rogers was the research carried out by B. Chodorkoff (1954). Chodorkoff sought to test different hypotheses derived from Rogers' self-theory, the most important of which states that if a person has a self-concept that agrees with other people's view of him or her, then there is congruency between self and experience and no need to distort perceptions or experiences.

In testing this, Chodorkoff sought to measure three characteristics of 30 male undergraduate students: (1) the degree to which their self-description is congruent with the description of them by others; (2) the degree to which threatening experiences are denied in awareness; and (3) the degree to which the individual is psychologically adjusted. Chodorkoff asked his subjects to attend three testing sessions. These sessions covered a variety of personality tests: a biographical inventory based on multiple-choice questions, the Rorschach inkblot test, a word association test, the Thematic Apperception Test, and finally a perceptual-defense test in which the subjects were confronted with words deemed to be most threatening and least threatening from the previous word association test. After these three sessions, the subjects were given a self-descriptive Q-sort test, which allowed them to identify adjectives that characterized their view of their ''real'' selves as they saw themselves and their ''ideal'' selves as they would like to be.

Chodorkoff and other judges scored each of the tests in terms of his three postulated characteristics—accuracy of self-description, perceptual defense, and psychological adjustment—and the results confirmed the hypothesis derived from Rogers' theory: students who were able to describe themselves accurately were also better adjusted and showed less perceptual defense. These findings have been criticized because of overlap (1) among the tests used to evaluate adjustment, and (2) the judges doing the ratings. However, more carefully designed studies of the type carried out by Chodorkoff could provide some evidence in support of Rogers' propositions.

A more recent experimental study of phenomenologically oriented concepts has been conducted by McFarlin and Blascovich (1981). These investigators attempted to manipulate the level of self-esteem reported by experimental subjects by giving them an anagram-solving task in which they received differing feedback about their success or failure. People with high, moderate, or low levels of self-esteem were told either that they did poorly, well, or were not told the results of their performance. Interestingly, none of the groups dramatically changed their reported level of self-esteem after receiving feedback about performance. This may suggest that self-esteem is a relatively enduring experience about the self.

Maslow: The Hierarchy of Needs

Abraham Maslow focused on the positive, growth-oriented aspects of personality.

Unlike Rogers, who derived his ideas about self-actualization from his practice of psychotherapy, Maslow (1962, 1963) studied friends as well as the lives of public figures whom he considered unusually creative—Abraham Lincoln and Albert Einstein, for example. From this study, Maslow compiled a list of characteristics of self-actualizers. Among these characteristics are an efficient perception of reality, autonomy, and an openness to mystical experiences.

Maslow also postulated a **hierarchy of needs** (see Figure 12.9). The basic physiological needs such as hunger and thirst are at the bottom of the hierarchy. Then come the needs for safety, and love and esteem. Self-actualization is the highest need of all. Maslow contended that the gratification of all the needs is necessary to psychological well-being, but that needs lower in the hierarchy must be satisfied before those above them can be satisfied.

One of Maslow's concepts that has entered into our general language is the **peak experience.** As defined by Maslow, the peak experience is a moment of self-actualization, a transcendent ecstasy in which perceptions are greatly sharpened. A peak experience resembles some of the altered states of consciousness discussed in chapter 5 and may occur in relation to music, religion, or other transcendent experiences.

Maslow was most interested in the positive, growth-oriented aspects of personality. Like other phenomenologically oriented theorists, he was concerned not so much with externally observed traits as with the experience of the fully functioning person.

Kelly: The Personal Construct Theory of Personality

Still another phenomenological approach to the understanding of personality has been developed by George Kelly (1955). While Rogers' approach to personality focuses on the person's self-concept, Kelly begins with the basic notion that the way the individual conceptually organizes his or her social world—the way the individual personally interprets and categorizes events and the behavior of others—is the essence of personality. The way people view other people and events is, according to Kelly, strikingly personal and individual. Kelly was always fascinated by the notion that people, no matter how much they seem to be living in the same public world, actually inhabit strikingly different personal worlds.

The key concept in Kelly's theory, that of **personal construct,** is essentially the idea that each of us has certain basic concepts or ideas that we use to understand the world. We see others as friendly or hostile; we describe situations as cooperative or competitive. It is these individual views that each of us holds that both help us understand and predict the behavior of others and affect the way we behave in interpersonal situations. In essence, Kelly believes that personality consists of the organized system of ideas and assumptions that each of us holds about other individuals in our world and the various roles that they may occupy.

Kelly's theory is essentially phenomenological in its orientation; it focuses on how each individual experiences the surrounding world. In particular, Kelly believed that the concepts or constructs that we use shape our experience of the world and our expectations about others in it. In addition, Kelly's theory relates to individual differences and the study of individuals' constructs rather than to developing generalizations about constructs or traits.

Kelly has developed a widely known personality test to identify and measure the personal constructs of each person as he defined them in his theory.

This **Role Construct Repertory Test** is designed to elicit from respondents their own constructs about other people and roles, particularly roles that are presumably very important to them, including the self, mother, spouse, pal, rejecting person, or attractive person (Kelly, 1955).

Kelly's strategy in eliciting the individual's personal constructs about each of these ideas is to ask respondents to think of at least three individuals or "figures" who occupy each of these roles. Then the respondent is asked to identify the ways in which two of these people are alike and are different from the third. The idea here is to identify the two ends of the personal constructs that best characterize a particular role. For example, a respondent might think of two fathers who are seen as "accepting" and different from a third father who is viewed as being "hostile." Thus, the two poles of the respondent's personal construct become "accepting" at the one end and "cold" at the other.

Once these personal constructs have been established, the respondent is asked to fill out a grid form by applying each of the constructs that have been elicited to each of the figures listed. This procedure should produce a grid in which important personal constructs in the respondent's life are used to rate important roles, resulting in a completely personalized perception of the respondent's own social role. Both the personal constructs obtained and the roles to which they are applied refer only to that particular respondent.

Results from the role repertory test have been used in a variety of ways. In particular they have been used as a basis for counselors and psychotherapists to understand the personal phenomenological worlds of their clients. A counselor may learn a great deal about the roles that are important to people, the ways in which they see their social worlds, their expectations about their relationships, and their own personal views of themselves.

Figure 12.9

Maslow's hierarchy of needs ranges from the basic physiological needs, including hunger and thirst, to self-actualization needs, the highest needs.

Issues in the Phenomenological Approach to Personality

Unquestionably, some of the strengths of the phenomenological approach are also its greatest weaknesses. This approach is distinctive in placing great importance on an appreciation of the subjective inner life of the person as a way of understanding personality. But, like any other perspective on the nature of human behavior, the emphasis on the phenomenological field of the individual neglects other important aspects of behavior. These theories have almost no behavioral content and are limited almost exclusively to subjective experience. Consequently, their ability to predict behavior or to link internal subjective phenomena to external behavior in the social world is severely limited.

Some of the phenomenological theories have been criticized as naively romantic (Liebert & Spiegler, 1974; Millon, 1967). This is truer of Maslow's perspective than it is of Kelly's.

As appealing as these theoretical approaches are in attempting to appreciate the inner psychological life of an individual, the research emerging from both Rogers' self-theory and Kelly's role-repertory orientation has been criticized because of its excessive reliance on self-report. In particular, Bavelas (1978) has noted that the reliability of individual role-constructs reported for the same people at different periods of time is relatively poor. Thus, the question of whether these personal constructs are indeed stable over time, as Kelly suggests they are, is not yet settled. Similarly, much of the research stimulated by Rogers' theory has relied on methods that have also been criticized because they depend so exclusively on the respondents' reports about their experiences and behaviors.

Reliance on self-report can also be problematic because these studies assume that respondents are aware of and able to report about significant aspects of their behaviors. It is just as plausible to assume that much of the important behavior that a personality theorist may wish to study is not directly accessible to a respondent's awareness but must either be observed by others or inferred from other aspects of overt behavior.

Phares (1984) has offered an insightful discussion of the dilemmas of doing research in the phenomenological tradition and points out a number of problems associated with measurement of the private world. He notes that for phenomenologists, assessing behavior by observing what people do is not particularly helpful because the meaning of that behavior may differ from person to person. However true this may be, the danger is that we are dealing with the observer's inferences about behavior: "The major problem with the phenomenological posture is determining the means whereby one person can become aware of another's experience and meaning. It is one thing to say, 'I understand where you are coming from,' and another to be sure that it is so, and this is no more true for the lay person than it is for the trained phenomenologist. In the latter case, the research literature is full of instances where phenomenological analyses have no supporting evidence of interjudge reliability. A great deal seems to be accepted on faith" (Phares, 1984, pp. 215–16).

Metatheories of Personality

The four perspectives we have discussed may appear to be so disparate as to make it very difficult to arrive at a coherent view of personality. These differences also concern many psychologists who are looking for ways to synthesize a single all-encompassing view of personality and behavior from the conflicting evidence.

Any attempt at synthesis must examine the theories for similarities as well as differences. If the root assumptions of the four personality perspectives are examined, two basic approaches or **metatheories**—theories behind the theories—emerge (Bavelas, 1978).

These two metatheories are essentially individual or social in their underlying assumptions. The individual metatheory, embracing the dynamic, dispositional, and phenomenological perspectives, views personality as a set of internal dispositions or intrapsychic mechanisms that differ from one person to another and help determine behavior. The social metatheory, including the various social learning theories, sees personality as a set of principles by which an individual interacts with the social environment. Bavelas (1978) has closely examined these two metatheories and described the five essential ways in which they actually differ and the ways in which they only appear to differ.

1. *Internal versus External Orientation.* Individual theories, while not denying that the environment plays a role in personality development, look for the basic determinants of personality—in the unconscious, in traits and types, or in the self-concept. Social theories emphasize conditions outside the individual—stimuli, reinforcers, models.

2. *Individual versus Situational Differences.* Individual theories suggest that individual differences arise out of early childhood experiences, while social theories assume that environmental forces continue to act on individuals throughout life so that people continue to change and to differentiate from one another as a result of situational differences.

3. *Stability versus Change.* Individual theories predict relative stability of personality once internal dynamics or structures have developed, while social theories assert that behavior will change as situations change.

4. *Cross-Situational Consistency versus Situational Specificity.* Individual theories see personality differences as not only stable but also general—that is, manifest in any relevant situation. By contrast, social theories look for situational changes that can evoke completely different behaviors—through the influence of modeling, for example.

FOCUS

Sex Stereotypes in Psychological Assessment

The various methods of personality assessment tend to assume that the assessor brings to the process an unbiased judgment, free of preconceptions about the individual in question. However, clinicians are confronted not with an abstract list of behaviors but with a living, breathing person who is the product of a lifetime of socialization in differing roles shaped by biological, ethnic, and cultural factors.

Given this human context, can the assessor truly be expected to bring a bias-free judgment to the assessment of personality? For example, might clinicians have preconceptions based solely on the gender of the subject? According to a study by Inge Broverman and her colleagues (Broverman, Broverman, & Clarkson, 1970), the answer may well be yes.

These investigators asked 79 clinically trained mental health workers to respond to a questionnaire. The task was to choose the adjectives that best characterized a male, a female, and a mature, healthy adult. The adjectives were bipolar choices such as "strong-weak."

Broverman and her colleagues found that there was a great deal of agreement about the attributes characterizing healthy men, healthy women, and healthy adults whose sex was unspecified. This is not surprising because most of us can readily call up images that conform to conventional sex role stereotypes in our society. For example, if a person were described as independent, objective, active, logical, worldly, direct, adventurous, and self-confident, a typical reaction would be to say the person was a male. Similarly, if the person were described as being emo-

tional, having sensitive feelings, disliking math and science, and being easily influenced, most people would likely say it was a female.

What was particularly interesting about the Broverman findings was that clinicians have different concepts of mental health for men and for women. These concepts parallel our sex role stereotypes. Their judgments about the mental health of a man vary with their perceptions of how closely he conforms to the male sex role stereotype. Women who conform to the female sex role stereotype also are judged to be healthier than women who do not.

The authors suggest that these findings show a powerful negative assessment of women. A healthy woman is defined by the clinicians as more submissive, more dependent, less adventurous, more easily influenced, and less objective than men. This constellation of characteristics, the authors note, is an unusual way to describe a mature healthy individual.

Moreover, Broverman and her co-workers also found that the mental health professionals' conception of an "adult healthy individual" more closely resembled the male stereotype than it did the female stereotype. This evident bias in favor of stereo-

typical male characteristics held regardless of the professional's own gender.

The authors feel that this bias reflects the general acceptance by mental health professionals of an "adjustment" notion of health. This notion assumes that people who conform to sex role stereotypes are better adjusted than people who do not conform to these roles.

Since this landmark study, a wide range of research has been done on the causes and consequences of sex role stereotyping (Unger, 1979). Recently, researchers have begun to explore the personality characteristic of androgyny, the idea that a person could exhibit both masculine and feminine behaviors and traits. Sandra Bem (1981) explored this idea and developed a scale to measure this sex role orientation. A number of studies have suggested that androgynous individuals have higher levels of psychosocial development, experience higher levels of psychological well-being, and are seen by others as well-adjusted. However, Taylor and Hall (1982) observe that androgyny should not be seen as an independent characteristic that certain people possess, but instead that it reflects the fact that masculinity and femininity are operating simultaneously to affect behavior in some people.

Previous researchers often conceptualized masculinity and femininity as opposite end points of a single dimension. Currently, most personality psychologists adhere to the view that masculinity and femininity are separate, independent dimensions. ■

---

5. *Correlational versus Experimental Research.* Individual theories must rely on correlational methods of research, which assess already existing differences in responses. Social theories frequently require the investigator to engage in experimental research, arranging different situations where responses can be measured.

Although these differences between the individual and social metatheories are compelling, Bavelas (1978) goes on to describe ways in which the two approaches often appear to differ but in fact do not. She calls these pseudo-differences.

One pseudo-difference is methodological rigor. Because the advocate of individual theories uses correlational methods, Bavelas points out, it does not necessarily follow that he or she is "more humanistic, more intuitive, or a more fuzzy or free-ranging thinker. Nor is the experimental psychologist (in this case the social personality theorist) automatically more precise, surer of cause-effect relations, less interested in individual human beings, or inclined to mistake rats and statistics for people."

A second pseudo-difference often attributed to the metatheories involves the importance of the individual. Individual theories are often said to respect human uniqueness, while social theories are said to favor an anonymous, deterministic version of human nature. In fact, with the notable exception of Skinner's learning theory, both approaches assume individual variations in behavior. The differences are a matter of emphasis.

"The error that leads to such propaganda on both sides," Bavelas (1978) concludes, "is in believing that one's theoretical position is a complete and final statement on human nature. None of the theories we have encountered encompasses all of human nature; all are tentative bets on where the major causal factors of some behaviors lie."

Summary

1. Personality is the characteristic way in which a person thinks and behaves as she or he adapts to the environment. Any theory of personality must explain why we behave in the ways we do and what makes each of us unique. Personality theories fall into four general categories: psychodynamic, dispositional, social learning, and phenomenological theories.

2. Freud's psychoanalytic theory insisted that behavior is determined by the interplay of events and psychological processes that are not normally available to a persons's consciousness. Freud placed a great deal of emphasis on sexual energy and motives in the early shaping of personality. He proposed four distinct stages of development: oral, anal, phallic, and genital. Each stage of development carries potential crises, and Freud believed that successful resolution of each crisis was necessary for a child to arrive at a healthy personality in childhood.

3. Neo-Freudians, the "ego psychologists," such as Karen Horney, Erich Fromm, and Erik Erikson, retained many of the basic assumptions of Freud's dynamic theory but felt that the conscious ego was more important in shaping personality than the instinctual drives of the unconscious. Carl Jung's analytical psychology proposed that the archetypes of the collective unconscious affect our personality development in a lifelong process of psychological maturation called *individuation*.

4. Dynamic theorists assess individual personality through the techniques of free association, dream interpretation, and projective tests in which subjects respond to deliberately ambiguous stimuli. Psychodynamic theories have been criticized for their inability to produce explicit "if-then" statements to predict consequences following from the theories, failure to define clearly such concepts as the Oedipus complex, and broad formulations that can be manipulated to fit the evidence at hand.

5. Dispositional theories assume that people have prevailing internal tendencies to behave in predictable ways. Dispositional theories may be broken

down into their emphases on types, on traits, and on individual needs. William Sheldon proposed personality patterns based on three basic body structure, or somatotypes: endomorph (soft and round), mesomorph (sturdy and muscular), and ectomorph (thin and fragile). Sheldon believed that as these physical systems developed, one became dominant, along with an associated personality type.

H. J. Eysenck proposed the existence of a small number of underlying dimensions of personality along which all people differ—introversion and extraversion, stability and instability, for example.

6. Gordon Allport proposed that individuals have traits that help explain the uniqueness and consistency that we observe in behavior. Allport argued that traits vary in their effect on the whole personality: cardinal traits are strong characteristics that shape the whole personality; central traits are important but not pervasive; secondary traits reflect very narrow patterns of behavior. Some traits can be observed in most people to a greater or lesser degree, whereas some traits are unique to particular individuals.

Raymond Cattell identified fundamental traits, which he called source traits, as underlying and fundamental roots of overt behavior. Surface traits were clusters of overt behavior that seemed to go together but have more than one source trait as their determinants. Cattell also believed that the structure of personality can be discovered through the empirical means of factor analysis.

Henry A. Murray proposed a theory of personality based on observable sequences of needs and the idea that individuals have distinctive needs. Murray also proposed a concept he called *press* to describe the characteristics of situations that initiate or direct behavior. Murray and his colleagues developed the Thematic Apperception Test (TAT), in which subjects are believed to project their needs onto stories they make up about pictures provided by the test.

7. Dispositional theories have been criticized because they are better at describing personality than in explaining the development of enduring behavior patterns. In addition, dispositional theories tend to slight the importance of the role of specific situations in accounting for behavior.

8. B. F. Skinner argues, in effect, that there is no such thing as personality: there are only operant behaviors that are strengthened or weakened as a consequence of reward and punishment. These behaviors are predictable and primarily controlled by measurable external influences, or stimulli. Operant learning emphasizes environmental and situational influences and must be assessed differently than other personality theories. Since behavior is said to speak for itself, it must be carefully observed in its natural setting, and the situational factors that appear to influence it must be accurately described—an assessment approach called functional analysis.

9. Albert Bandura's social learning approach to personality stresses the importance of cognitive and social factors and of observational learning, or modeling. In Bandura's theory, reinforcement may be experienced directly or vicariously, and it may be self-administered. For Bandura, behavior depends upon situational characteristics, a person's cognitive appraisal of the situation, and the history of reinforcement.

10. In its methods of assessment and experimental research, learning theory has a sense of clear-cut cause and effect. However, it is important to avoid confusing the concepts of the cause of behavior with those of behavioral control. Bandura's theory has been questioned because mere exposure is not always sufficient to produce observational learning, and it is not always possible to predict that, in a given situation, observational learning will actually occur.

11. Phenomenological approaches focus on the conscious experience of the individual and attempt to enter into the person's own psychological experience in order to understand personality.

Carl Rogers believes in an innate tendency toward self-actualization and that self-experience develops into a self-concept. How individuals experience and view themselves and their experiences is crucial to Rogers' theory.

Abraham Maslow postulated a hierarchy of needs with basic physiological needs at the bottom and self-actualization at the top. Maslow also proposed the peak experience, a transcendent moment of self-actualization in which perceptions are greatly sharpened.

George Kelly proposed that the way one conceptually organizes one's social world, and the way in which one personally interprets and categorizes events and the behavior of others, is the essence of one's personality. Kelly suggested that each of us develops a personal construct, a set of concepts and ideas that we use in order to understand ourselves and the world around us.

12. Phenomenological theories have little behavioral content. Consequently, their ability to predict behavior or to link internal subjective phenomena to external behavior in the social and interpersonal world is severely limited. These theories are also limited by their reliance on self-reports.

13. Bavelas has proposed that the four major approaches to personality fall into two overriding metatheories—social and individual. The social metatheory sees personality as a set of principles by which an individual interacts with the social environment. The individual metatheory embraces the dynamic, dispositional, and phenomenological views and sees personality as a set of internal dispositions or intrapsychic mechanisms that differ from one person to another and help determine behavior.

RESEARCH: In a series of similar studies, Loren J. and Jean Chapman demonstrated that both nonprofessionals (undergraduate students) and professionals often rely on common sense in interpreting the results of projective tests such as the Draw-a-Person and Rorschach tests. When asked to interpret the results of Rorschach tests from fictitious subjects, both students and experienced clinicians relied on the stereotypical correlates rather than known test correlates to assess the personality trait of homosexuality.

FOCUS: One assumption underlying personality assessment is that the assessor brings to the situation unbiased judgment, free of preconceptions about the individual in question. However, Broverman has shown that many clinicians have different conceptions of adjustment and mental health that depend on the sex of the person undergoing assessment. Clinicians judged men and women who conformed to their respective sex-role stereotype as being more mature and healthy than persons who did not. Broverman also found that clinicians' conception of the ''adult healthy individual'' typically possessed stereotypical male characteristics.

Intelligence

Consider these items from the news:

- A California businessman announced the creation of The Repository for Germinal Choice, a storage bank from which the sperm of Nobel Prize winners could be used for artificially inseminating women of exceptionally high IQs in order to produce offspring of unusual intelligence.
- Realizing the significance of mental ability for economic development in the industrialized world, the government of Venezuela has established a Ministry of Intelligence for the purpose of discovering how to raise the population's aptitude for education.
- In Virginia, it was revealed, more than 4000 men and women deemed mentally unfit had previously been legally sterilized by the state in order to prevent the birth of ''misfits'' and to raise ''the average intelligence of the people.''

As these news items suggest, in our culture intelligence is one of the most highly valued of human characteristics—and one of the most controversial. Few areas of psychological investigation have such volatile implications for society at large. Intelligence and the methods by which it is measured create social and political policy, shape our schools, and even influence some people's choice of mates.

What is intelligence? Most of us typically use the word in the dictionary sense of general knowledgeability or capacity for reasoning and understanding. Psychologists have learned a great deal about measuring intelligence but do not always agree about precisely what it is they are measuring. About 60 years ago several leading researchers were asked by the *Journal of Educational Psychology* to define the concept of intelligence. The ensuing disagreement prompted Edwin Boring, the eminent historian of psychology, to conclude wryly that intelligence is merely ''the capacity to do well in an intelligence test'' (Rice, 1979).

It would be a mistake, however, to treat intelligence and the efforts to measure it in a cavalier way. For both scientific and social reasons the study of intelligence and its measurement is central to psychology. We are just now beginning to understand the nature of intellectual abilities that produce effective problem solving. While individual differences in problem solving have been studied for years, it is only recently that scientists have taken this phenomenon into the laboratory in order to study some of the underlying components of intellectual ability and to answer additional questions about individual differences in intellectual ability.

Because intellectual ability is so highly valued in our culture, differences in intelligence as they are measured by various tests of intellectual promise form an important basis for social decisions regarding opportunities and responsibilities in our society. Because we live in a highly technological society that is growing more complex each year, intellectual ability may become an even more socially valued characteristic in the future. Because social opportunity, social environment, and genetic background play important roles in intelligence, environmental conditions that reduce the opportunity to develop intellectual ability are of great social concern. Thus, for both social and scientific reasons, the study of intelligence and its measurement have become important areas of study in modern psychology.

Theories of Intelligence

Psychologists who have developed theories about the nature of intelligence have taken one of two approaches. One approach, favored historically and underlying most forms of testing, was to view intelligence as a psychological structure, something that could be broken down into parts and then analyzed. The other approach, which has gained favor in recent years, looks at intelligence as a way of processing information.

Structural Theories

Theories of the structure of intelligence have been for the most part based on a technique called **factor analysis,** a statistical method that defines the common components or dimensions underlying multiple tests or measures. The aim is to find common factors that underlie performances on separate mental tests; for example, a vocabulary test and a reading comprehension examination may be analyzed for the intercorrelations among the test scores of a sample of respondents.

Spearman's "g" Factor

The pioneer in the application of factor analysis to intelligence was an English psychologist, Charles Spearman. His theory grew out of the simple observation that people who did well on one kind of mental test also did well on others; their scores tended to be positively correlated. In 1904 he posited the "universal Unity of the Intellect" and suggested that this unity was based on what he called general **mental facility** or simply *g factor.* In addition to this general factor, Spearman believed that performance on any particular intellectual task requires a **specific mental capability,** or the *s factor.* While excellence on a given test would depend on the operation of both *g* and *s,* overall excellence is based on the *g* factor, or general intelligence (Spearman, 1927).

Spearman's notion of the *g* factor fit well with the concept of standardized IQ tests, which came into widespread use in the 1920s and which purported to measure general intelligence. These tests greatly influenced education, particularly in England where the *g* factor became part of the underlying rationale for assigning British schoolchildren to separate schools at the early age of 11. Interestingly, no correlations at all have been found between an individual's scores on a number of the tests. This would suggest, contrary to Spearman's original theory of a unitary *g* factor, that intelligence does consist of many different components.

Thurstone's Primary Mental Abilities

During the 1930s, L. L. Thurstone developed a different theory of the structure of intelligence (Thurstone, 1938). Applying factor analysis to the same type of data used by Spearman, he concluded that intelligence was not a single entity but composed instead of seven components. He called these **primary mental abilities (PMAs)** and labeled them numerical ability, reasoning, verbal fluency, spatial relations, perception, memory, and verbal comprehension.

The operation of one or more of these PMAs, Thurstone said, could account for a subject's performance on a given test item. He believed that differ-

Figure 13.1

The sample items shown in this test correspond to Thurstone's primary mental abilities.

ent people display different patterns of mental ability, and he developed special tests to measure these different abilities (see Figure 13.1). On the basis of his factor analysis, he was able to prepare a profile of any test subject, showing the strength of each ability, from which reasonable predictions could be made about the subject's suitability for a given career.

Guilford's Theory of the Structure of the Intellect

The concept that intelligence comprises a number of different components was greatly expanded by J. P. Guilford, who postulated that no fewer than 120 separate factors, or mental abilities, exist. Guilford's interesting three-dimensional structure of intellect is depicted graphically in Figure 13.2 (Guilford, 1967). The three dimensions are contents (what the individual knows), operations (the processing of what is known), and products (the end results). Each dimension is subdivided into components, the interaction of which results in Guilford's 120 factors—4 content factors × 5 operation factors × 6 product factors equals 120.

Recently, Gardner (1983) argued in his book *Frames of Mind: The Theory of Multiple Intelligences* that our definition of intelligence has been too narrow.

His review of the evidence indicates that individuals have many potential domains of intellectual competence and that these various kinds of intelligence may operate independently of one another. Gardner suggests that there are at least six different types of intelligence, including language ability, logical reasoning ability, musical ability, spatial skills, bodily talents such as dance or athletic ability, and even the capacity to have access to one's own feelings.

An interesting aspect of Gardner's theory is that while these various forms of intellectual competence may work together at times, they also operate in isolation from each other. Thus, sometimes it is possible to discover people with extraordinarily developed abilities in one area but not in others. Later in this chapter we will examine some examples of such people, including ''idiot savants'' who may appear retarded except for their capacity to display one extraordinary ability or another.

Gardner's theory goes beyond simply arguing that there are many different kinds of intelligence. He suggests that each of these types of intelligence may have its own developmental sequence emerging at one point in life and fading at another. He cites as an example mathematicians whose contributions seem to occur relatively early in life. It may be that mathematical ability, at least a special talent in mathematics, seems to diminish by the time a mathematician is thirty years old or so. Drawing on a wide range of evidence in the field of clinical neurology, Gardner also argues that some of these intellectual abilities may be controlled by relatively discrete, small areas of the brain.

In general, society has valued only a few of these different abilities, such as the ability to reason and to use language; many other abilities such as access to one's own feelings have been largely ignored in our culture. If Gardner's theory is correct, there are clear implications for education. Teachers could match their curriculums and teaching strategies to each child's individual strengths and might be more alert to differences in abilities among children.

Gardner's theory is, in some ways, similar to Guilford's idea, since it suggests a number of different kinds of intellectual abilities. However, Gardner's suggestions that these abilities can operate relatively independent of each other and that they have specific locations in the brain goes well beyond earlier structural theories and brings together the study of intelligence with that of neurophysiology.

Information Processing Theory

In contrast to the structural theories of intelligence, the information processing approach, as the name suggests, views intelligence as a process. This theory attempts to break down the reasoning operation into distinct steps and then to explain how they are organized.

Robert J. Sternberg, a leading exponent of the information processing approach, has studied how people solve problems of the type found on IQ tests (Sternberg, 1977). Sternberg suggests that, during reasoning, information processing occurs on two different levels. One level consists of the sequential steps—components—that a person proceeds through in solving a complex mental problem. The other level consists of metacomponents—the processes that organize the components that a person goes through in deciding how to solve the problem.

As an illustration of this two-level process, Sternberg (1977) cites the following example:

Suppose that you want to convert Grecian drachmas to dollars, and you know that a drachma is worth about three cents. You need to know how many dollars you can get for 500 drachmas. Metacomponents are used to figure out how to solve the problem: The sum three cents has to be converted into its dollar equivalent, and then multiplied by 500. Components are used to actually obtain the solution: .03 × 500 equals $15.

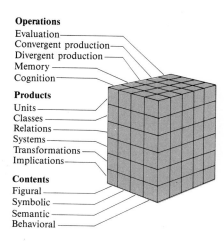

Operations
Evaluation
Convergent production
Divergent production
Memory
Cognition

Products
Units
Classes
Relations
Systems
Transformations
Implications

Contents
Figural
Symbolic
Semantic
Behavioral

Figure 13.2

According to Guilford's structure of the intellect, each cell of this three-dimensional block represents a unique intellectual ability.

Gardner suggests that each type of intelligence—for example, bodily talent—has its own developmental sequence emerging at one point in life and fading at another.

Components

Much of Sternberg's research focused on the processes involved in solving analogies, an ability considered highly indicative of general intelligence. In a typical experiment, the subject sits at a computer terminal, where the problem is presented in parts on the viewing screen, and responds one step at a time by pushing buttons.

Through such methods, Sternberg measured the speed of each step in the problem-solving process. Analogy solving, Sternberg believes, has six sequential components: encoding, inferring, mapping, applying, justifying, and responding.

Consider, for example, his componential analysis of an analogy typical of those found in IQ tests.

WASHINGTON is to ONE as LINCOLN is to: a. FIVE, b. TEN, c. FIFTEEN, d. FIFTY.

First, the person must encode the various terms of the analogy, identifying attributes that may be relevant to a solution. Both Washington and Lincoln were presidents of the United States, for example; both are portrayed on pieces of currency.

Next, the subject infers a relationship between the first two terms of the analogy, Washington and one; Washington's portrait appears on the $1 bill.

Then, the person maps this inference to the second half of the analogy, Lincoln and five. Lincoln also appears on currency.

The subject applies the relationship inferred to each of the possible answers and then attempts to justify an answer option as preferable to the others even if it does not seem ideal. Finally, the subject responds with the answer deemed best.

Metacomponents

Behind this analysis are the metacomponents, the higher-order decision processes. These processes help us decide what components to use in problem solving and what strategies to use to combine the components. Sternberg believes that metacomponents are more important to intelligence than are components. "IQ tests," he says, "may work as well as they do not only because they measure the speed and accuracy with which we solve various kinds of problems, but because they measure the speed and accuracy with which we go about deciding how to solve these problems" (Sternberg, 1977).

Surprisingly, Sternberg has found that people with high IQs may actually spend more time on a particular component than do people with low IQs (Sternberg & Dettermann, 1979). For example, in Sternberg's studies, higher-IQ people tend to take longer to encode the information presented by a problem. The time spent on this component, he suggests, pays off later in the problem-solving process, enabling them to carry out later steps more efficiently and more rapidly.

Sternberg's two-level theory may have important implications for improving individual reasoning ability. On the componential level, people can be helped to pinpoint the particular steps where they are having trouble solving problems. On the metacomponential level, people can be taught to think about how they are approaching the problem instead of the particular strategies for solving it.

Whether intelligence is a structure or a process, standards must exist for examining and judging it. Later in this chapter the methods of measurement designed by psychologists to tests intelligence will be explored.

Artificial Intelligence

In 1950 a somewhat eccentric English mathematician, Alan Turing, proposed a classic test of whether it would be possible to teach a machine to think and be intelligent. The test was, in effect, to place a human being and a machine behind a curtain and have each of them type answers to questions. If no difference could be detected between the two, then an intelligent machine would have been created.

Since Turing's original proposal for the creation of artificial intelligence, the fields of computer science and artificial intelligence in particular have grown rapidly. Most of us think of computer science as being primarily focused on questions having to do with the creation of increasingly complex computers. But the field of artificial intelligence is, its proponents claim, also of great relevance for our understanding of natural intelligence in human beings.

Two of the founders of the field of artificial intelligence, Allen Newell and Herbert A. Simon, a Nobel Prize-winning psychologist, suggest that the artificial intelligence is concerned with the question of whether it is possible to create a program that is sufficient to produce intelligence. This is, in effect, the Turing test.

Artificial intelligence also involves identifying tasks that require intelligent behavior and constructing programs for computers to accomplish those tasks. Indeed, artificial intelligence and cognitive psychology have begun to develop in parallel and to aid each other in developing new theory and research.

Newell and Simon (1981) suggest that the field of information processing theory has developed by conducting experiments and observations on human behavior and observing tasks that require memory, problem solving, concept attainment, symbol manipulation, and other psychological functions, and then attempting to program a symbol system that provides a model of the observed human behavior. From our point of view, the important question is whether the model so produced provides us with a new or more precise theory of human intelligence.

Is it possible that the creation of programs by computer scientists in the field of artificial intelligence can actually provide us with new and more searching theories of human intelligence? Pylyshyn (1979) proposes that artificial intelligence requires that we bring together the study of sensation, perception, learning, memory, and motivation in a single discipline to understand cognitive capacity or intelligence. Therefore, artificial intelligence requires that psychology redraw the boundaries of its field to bring together these various topics that have been studied separately in the past.

Imagine for a moment that we take the challenge of artificial intelligence seriously. Begin by considering the analogy between the human being and the computer. How do we think about this analogy, and what kinds of insights will provide about human intelligence? Pylyshyn (1979) suggests that three major problems are addressed when we consider this analogy.

The first of these is the problem of *organization.* How are the complex decisions and processing of information organized in both intelligent machines and in human beings? For Pylyshyn, the problem of organization is actually a problem in the allocation of complexity. In other words, how can we understand the relationship, for example, between a computer's software on the one hand and its hardware on the other? Are there analogies in human behavior? Is the brain programmed by experience? Are any of our perceptions already "wired in"? Will the human being/computer analogy actually sharpen our thinking about human intelligence?

Alan Turing, an English mathematician, proposed the idea of artificial intelligence in 1950.

An important concern in programming a computer to play chess is whether the program operates in the same way people do.

A second question addressed by Pylyshyn is the question of control, or the allocation of responsibility. What controls the artificial machine or computer? Computer scientists argue that *feedback* is critical in understanding the relationship of a machine to its environment. Similarly, in understanding human behavior, feedback produces a balance between the organism and the environment.

Finally, Pylyshyn asks whether analogies between computers and human intelligence are valid. Psychologists have frequently asked the question, "Maybe your program can perform the same tasks as people can, but how do you know whether it does it in the *same way* that people do?" Thus, for psychologists the crucial issue involving a program that can be taught to play chess is whether the program plays chess in the same way that people do. If not, then perhaps we do not have as much to learn about human intelligence from the creation of intelligent machines as we might hope.

Many researchers are skeptical about the value of the field of artificial intelligence in developing theories of human intelligence. Perhaps foremost among these is Ulric Neisser (1980), who argues that the Turing test of whether artificial intelligence has been achieved is a very poor test. He suggests that the Turing test puts its premium on deception and that you cannot say you have created artificial intelligence just because you can fool someone. Further, he argues, the test has nothing to do with whether a computer is like a person. Neisser observes that if you compare a human chess player with a computer program to play chess, each behaves in very different ways. The master chess player sees the whole board at a glance and observes patterns and configurations that suggest moves. The computer, because of its high speed and memory capacity, is able to explore a large number of possible moves and make a decision based on a list of possibilities, but it does not recognize patterns. Thus, there is no real analogy between the computer chess player and the human chess player. Nevertheless, research scientists in the field of artificial intelligence believe that their work will add insights into our understanding of the nature of human intelligence. The field will continue to grow rapidly and perhaps someday become a formal part of research on human intelligence.

Measurement of Intelligence

In recent decades practically every American schoolchild has been subjected to a test of intelligence. The social significance of intelligence tests is enormous. In the United States as well as in many other highly developed nations they lie at the heart of selection processes and are influential in determining the life course of many people. Typically, test scores determine who goes to college and who gets special education training; they often determine whether a child is placed in fast, average, or slow tracks in school (with all that implies in terms of teacher expectations and the child's own self-esteem); in the military they select who will serve in the front-line infantry and who will operate electronic equipment in the rear echelons.

The tests are also the subjects of several continuing controversies concerning their fairness to various cultural groups, what it is they actually predict, and to what uses they should be put. We will look first at the tests themselves and then present a framework for evaluating intelligence tests and the charges leveled against them.

The Binet Scales

The first practical measure of intelligence, and in its modern form still widely used, was developed by the French psychologist Alfred Binet. His study of children's mental abilities began when he noticed that his two daughters

Madeleine and Alice walked differently and wondered whether they might also think differently. He and his coworker, Theophile Simon, set about devising a way to test their intellectual performance (Binet & Simon, 1916). Binet's method was based on the simple observation that the intellectual performance of a child increases with age. By testing children of various ages, he could discover the intellectual milestones that marked each age.

In 1905, at the request of the Paris school authorities who wanted a means of identifying children who were slow learners, Binet prepared the forerunner of the modern intelligence test. Binet's test consisted of 30 questions corresponding in difficulty to the varying abilities of children between the ages of 3 and 13. The questions ranged from simple tasks, such as asking children to identify their eyes, nose, and mouth, to more complex activities, such as constructing a sentence around certain words. The questions were arranged so that a three-year-old would be expected to answer only the easiest ones correctly, while older children would be expected to answer progressively more difficult ones.

Binet was able to establish standards of performance by first giving the test to a sample composed of children of varying ages. He then carefully recorded their scores and specified norms—the distribution of scores obtained by children at different ages. Thus, a child's intelligence was operationalized as the number of items he or she was able to answer correctly. The level achieved indicated the child's mental age (MA). For example, if a child successfully completed all those items typically answered by the average five-year-old and none above that level, the child's MA was said to be five years.

French psychologist Alfred Binet believed that a child's intellectual performance increases with age.

The Stanford-Binet

Binet's test soon crossed the Atlantic and, in the hands of Lewis Terman of Stanford University, took a revised form. The revision, known as the **Stanford-Binet Test** and published in 1916, replaced Binet's test items with ones considered more suitable for American children and was standardized on a sample of 1400 children aged 3 to 16 (Terman, 1916). Terman's revision incorporated an idea suggested by William Stern (1914), a German psychologist, for representing the relationship between mental and chronological age. Mental age as shown on the Stanford-Binet was divided by chronological age (CA) and the resulting number multiplied by 100. The result was the child's **intelligence quotient** or **IQ.** Thus, if a child of six successfully completed all items expected of a nine-year-old, he or she was said to have a highly superior IQ of 150 (that is, 9/6 × 100).

The new test was enthusiastically welcomed in America, and while Binet's original intention was to use it to identify slow students who needed remedial instruction, the Stanford-Binet often became the primary means of selecting the intellectually superior. Despite Binet's warning against regarding the test results as fixed for life, it often was used to make long-term predictions about the intellectual abilities of young children.

Today the most popular of the IQ tests is the Stanford-Binet revision of 1960, which is considered appropriate for children from 3 to 18. The questions sample a wide variety of abilities, including memory, vocabulary, motor skills, comprehension, and reasoning. Typical test items for various levels are shown in Table 13.1.

The IQ determined by the modern Stanford-Binet no longer reflects the original formula of dividing mental age by chronological age and multiplying by 100. The problem with that simple formula was that the rate of growth in mental age typically slows down during the adolescent and adult years. But since chronological age continues to increase and thus exceed the mental age ceiling, the calculated IQ must decline. For instance, employing the original formula, a 35-year-old (CA) adult with an MA of 16 will obtain an IQ of 45

The Stanford-Binet revision of 1960 is the most popular IQ test for children from age 3 to 18.

Table 13.1 ITEMS OF THE TYPE INCLUDED IN THE 1960 EDITION OF THE STANFORD-BINET

Age 2:	Place geometric shapes into corresponding openings; identify body parts; stack blocks; identify common objects.
Age 4:	Name objects from memory; complete analogies (e.g., fire is hot; ice is _____); identify objects of similar shape; answer simple questions (e.g., "Why do we have schools?").
Age 6:	Define simple words; explain differences (e.g., between a fish and a horse); identify missing parts of a picture; count out objects.
Age 8:	Answer questions about a simple story; identify absurdities (e.g., in statements like "John had to walk on crutches because he hurt his arm"); explain similarities and differences among objects; tell how to handle certain situations (e.g., finding a stray puppy).
Age 10:	Define more difficult words; give explanations (e.g., about why people should be quiet in a library); list as many words as possible; repeat 6-digit numbers.
Age 12:	Identify more difficult verbal and pictured absurdities; repeat 5-digit numbers in reverse order; define abstract words (e.g., "sorrow"); fill in missing word in a sentence.
Age 14:	Solve reasoning problems; identify relationships among points of the compass; find similarities in apparently opposite concepts (e.g., "high" and "low"); predict the number of holes which will appear when folded paper is cut and then opened.
Superior Adult I:	Supply several missing words for incomplete sentences; repeat 6-digit numbers in reverse order; create a sentence using several unrelated words (e.g., "forest," "businesslike," and "dismayed"); describe similarities between concepts (e.g., "teaching" and "business").

Source: Douglas A. Bernstein and Michael T. Nietzel, *Introduction to Clinical Psychology* (New York: McGraw-Hill, 1980), p. 187.

$(16/35 \times 100 = 45)$. Such a score, if valid, would reflect severe mental retardation and obviously would not indicate the person's actual cognitive abilities. The old formula has been replaced by the **deviation IQ,** which reflects test performance relative to others of the same chronological age.

The Wechsler Scales

During the 1930s many clinicians criticized the Stanford-Binet because of its emphasis on verbal abilities and its built-in limitations for use on adults. One such clinician, David Wechsler, set about constructing an intelligence test aimed at overcoming both of these failings.

Wechsler's first test, the Wechsler Bellevue Intelligence Scale published in 1939, was intended for people 17 and older. Unlike the Stanford-Binet, it made no attempt to measure mental age; instead the Wechsler IQ reflected a comparison of points earned on the test with those achieved by test takers of the same age. Perhaps the most significant departure from the Stanford-Binet, however, was Wechsler's increased emphasis on nonverbal abilities. His test was subdivided into 11 groups, or subtests, each arranged in terms of increasing difficulty. There were six verbal subtests (information, comprehension, arithmetic, similarities, digit span, and vocabulary) along with five performance subtests (digit symbol, picture completion, block design, and picture arrangement and object assembly), examples of which are shown in Figure 13.3. This structure of subtests also was adapted for use in schools as the **Wechsler Intelligence Scale for Children (WISC),** which was substantially revised in 1974 and designated the WISC-R (Wechsler, 1974).

The Wechsler Bellevue Scale itself was revised in 1955 and renamed the **Wechsler Adult Intelligence Scale (WAIS),** and today it is the most popular means of measuring adult intelligence (Wechsler, 1955, 1958). In 1981 a revised version, WAIS-R, was made available (Wechsler, 1981). Typical items from the WAIS-R subtests are shown in Table 13.2. The popularity of the Wechsler scales stems from its subtests that enable clinicians to infer patterns of abilities; such inferences can be useful, for example, in assessing the possibility of localized brain damage.

Picture completion

What part is missing from this picture?

Picture arrangement

These pictures tell a story, but they are in the wrong order.
Put them in the right order so that they tell a story.

Block design

Put the blocks together to make this picture.

Object assembly

Put the pieces together as quickly as you can to make the picture on the right.

Evaluating the Tests

Recent controversies surrounding the measurement of intelligence have made it clear that not everyone agrees about the value of intelligence tests for making important social decisions. How do we judge, for example, whether tests measure what they claim to measure? Can we evaluate evidence and decide whether a test of intellectual ability actually predicts school performance? Should administrators use test scores to decide who should be admitted to universities? We will look at the principal criticisms of measures of intellectual ability in terms of three criteria for evaluating tests of all types: reliability, validity, and standardization.

Reliability

The **reliability** of a test can be shown if it measures the same thing consistently from occasion to occasion, if it is administered by different testers and gets the same results, or if two comparable forms of the test produce a similar result. In order to have confidence in a test score, we must be able to examine evidence of reliability and be convinced that the test produces consistent scores for the same person.

We can measure reliability in a number of different ways. The same person can be given the same test on two different occasions, and we can then assess

Figure 13.3

These items are similar to those appearing in the performance portion of the Wechsler Adult Intelligence Scale.

Table 13.2 ITEMS OF THE TYPE INCLUDED IN THE WESCHLER ADULT INTELLIGENCE SCALE (WAIS-R)

Information:	What is the shape of an orange? What does bread come from? What did Shakespeare do? What is the capital of France? What is the Malleus Malleficarum?
Comprehension	Why do we eat food? What should you do with a wallet found in the street? Why do foreign cars cost more than domestic cars? What does "the squeaky wheel gets the grease" mean?
Arithmetic:	If you have four apples and give two away, how many do you have left? How long will it take a person to walk 20 miles at 3 miles per hour? If four people can finish a job in 6 days, how many people would it take to do the job in 2 days?
Similarities:	Identify similar aspects of pairs like: hammer-screwdriver, portrait-short story, dog-flower.
Digit span:	Repeat in forward and reverse order: 2- to 9-digit numbers.
Vocabulary:	Define: chair, dime, lunch, paragraph, valley, asylum, modal, cutaneous.
Picture completion:	Find missing objects in increasingly complex pictures.
Block design:	Arrange blocks to match increasingly complex standard patterns.
Picture arrangement:	Place increasing number of pictures together to make increasingly complex stories.
Object assembly:	Arrange parts of puzzles to form recognizable objects (e.g., dog, flower, person).

Source: Douglas A. Bernstein and Michael T. Nietzel, *Introduction to Clinical Psychology* (New York: McGraw-Hill, 1980), p. 189.

how similar the scores are. This is assessing the test-retest reliability of the test. Another way to assess reliability is to divide the test into two equal parts and to assess whether or not the scores are similar on the two parts (split-half) for the same individual. Still another measure of reliability is to produce two tests that are parallel or comparable in form and examine the similarity of scores. Traditional tests such as the Stanford-Binet or the Wechsler scales have proved to be highly reliable. Test-retest or parallel forms of reliability correlations tend to be 0.9 or higher. Because correlations provide a measure of the degree to which the ranking of people on one measure is similar to their ranking on another basis, a correlation of 0.9 or higher suggests a high degree of consistency in measurement. It is important to note, however, that reliability reflects nothing about what the test measures; it only reflects the fact that whatever the test measures is being measured consistently.

Standardization

Test results usually refer to the distribution of scores among a group of respondents. In order to know whether a person's score is "high" or "low," psychologists compare it to the scores of others in the same age group who have taken the test. The meaning or usefulness of the test result, of course, depends on how similar the individual being tested is to the **standardization group** on which the test has been standardized. For example, if the test score of a person who is just learning English is compared with a standardization group of people who are all native English speakers, then the respondent's verbal ability may be underestimated because of the lack of comparability between the subject and the standardization.

When Lewis Terman adapted Binet's original scale for use in the United States, he standardized the test on a sample consisting only of native-born white Americans. Clearly many respondents from other groups may be disadvantaged by being compared only to this group. It wasn't until 1972 that the Stanford-Binet was standardized in order to reflect the diversity of the U.S. population. A 2100-child sample representing a broad range of socioeconomic, geographical, racial, and cultural groups was used in that standardization. Similarly, the Wechsler Adult Intelligence Scale was originally standardized on a white New York sample but now has been standardized on adequate comparison groups. Today most of the individually administered intelligence tests are regarded as being adequately standardized. If, however, the meaning of a score reflecting intellectual ability is being evaluated, it is important to know whether the respondent's score is being compared with a comparable standardization sample.

The most popular means of measuring adult intelligence is the Wechsler Adult Intelligence Scale or WAIS.

Validity

Another criterion that helps us to evaluate tests has to do with whether they measure what they are intended to measure. Researchers have several ways of determining the **validity** of a test. If, for example, a test had been designed to measure memory ability, the score that a subject obtains on the test can be compared with some other measure of memory, the **criterion measure.** If the relationship between the two measures is high, then a tester may conclude that the test is a reasonable measure of memory ability.

However, most tests of intellectual ability are designed for predictive purposes. That is, the intelligence test score is expected to predict outcomes such as later school achievements. This sort of validity is called **predictive validity** and is another important way in which to evaluate intelligence tests and other tests of intellectual ability. If a test is intended to predict school achievement, then it would be reasonable to examine the relationship between scores on the test and subsequent grades in school. If the relationship or correlation is high, then it is reasonable to conclude that the test is a valid predictor of scholastic achievement.

Generally, tests of intelligence have been quite effective in predicting how a child will fare in school. The correlation between IQ scores and academic grades is approximately 0.6 which, while far from perfect, is still relatively high. Of course, tests of intellectual ability designed to predict school achievement may do so relatively well without necessarily predicting other measures of achievement such as success in later life—a fact that suggests the limitations of the relationship between intelligence (or at least performances on tests) and worldly success.

Criticisms of Tests

The controversy over the value of intelligence tests has had some important ramifications in recent years. The National Education Association has formally called for the abolition of intelligence tests in the schools; in many school systems, such as New York City and Los Angeles, IQ tests actually have been abolished in the lower grades. Industry also has largely abandoned their use, in part because of a U.S. Supreme Court ruling in 1971—*Griggs* v. *The Duke Power Company*—in which the Court ruled that an electric utility worker in North Carolina had been deprived of his civil rights when he was denied promotion because of poor performance on an IQ test. Tests are proper to use, the Court said, only when they are used to predict specific job skills rather than overall intelligence.

Why is intelligence testing so controversial? We will examine three of the principal criticisms.

Achievement Versus Aptitude

It is important to distinguish between two types of tests: aptitude tests and achievement tests. The most important distinction has to do with the purposes to which they are put. In general, **aptitude tests** are designed to predict later performance, which as not yet been achieved. Thus, a test of aptitude for learning languages might be composed of various measures of abilities that are thought to be important in the learning of languages. Such a test might be composed of measures of memory ability, concentration, and verbal fluency. Intelligence tests have been historically thought of as general tests of aptitude, particularly scholastic ability.

Achievement tests, on the other hand, are tests designed to measure the degree to which a particular skill or body of knowledge has already been mastered. For example, written and performance tests of driving ability necessary to obtain a driver's license are achievement tests. Similarly, classroom tests, such as a final exam in introductory psychology, reflect the mastery and understanding of the material and are another specific type of achievement test.

A number of critics have argued that traditional intelligence tests reflect achievement as well as aptitude characteristics (Stalnaker, 1965). Most questions in intelligence tests require previous knowledge of language or the basics of arithmetic, for example. This criticism is true in the sense that intelligence test scores reflect what individuals have already learned as well as their aptitudes or learning potentials.

Cultural Bias

The issue of **cultural bias** represents a second major criticism of intelligence tests. Generations of blacks, Hispanics, and other minorities have been tested with questions that were standardized on a white, middle-class group.

Allegations of cultural bias focus on two aspects of discrimination. First, intelligence tests typically have required knowledge or perceptions that may be culture-specific: only a decade ago, for example, one test asked its subjects to fill in the word that best completed this sentence: "How the _____ roses flush up in the cheeks." The possible answers were red, pretty, yellow. The right answer was red, but, as *Testing Digest* pointed out recently, "only if the cheek in question is white" (*Time,* 1979).

The second form of discrimination is the language in which the test is written. Formal English puts at a disadvantage the sizable number of minority group members for whom English is a second language—Hispanics, for example, and even blacks who are exposed daily to black English.

Faced with such criticisms, test designers have attempted to eliminate the most obvious instances of cultural bias. In addition, there have been attempts to devise tests that are either culture-free or culture-specific—aimed at measuring special skills of minority groups. Culture-specific tests emphasize factors, such as minority languages, which may not play major roles in the larger culture.

Other approaches to the problem of cultural bias attempt to augment traditional tests with additional measures that take into account special traits or problems of minorities. Jane Mercer has developed an interlocking battery of measures for children from ages 5 to 11 called **System of Multicultural Pluralistic Assessment (SOMPA)** (Mercer & Lewis, 1977). The child is given the Wechsler scale but is also assessed for a number of other factors. For example, the examiner interviews the parent and prepares a sociocultural inventory of the family's background and an adaptive-behavior inventory of the child's performance in nonacademic activities. A thorough medical examination searches for problems, such as impairment of motor skills, that might affect the child's performance on the test and in school. The result is an **adjusted IQ** that is typically higher than the traditional IQ. In practical terms, this means children with a Wechsler IQ of 68, which would make them eligible for a class for the mentally retarded, might be shown to be capable of progressing in a regular class. SOMPA already has been adopted by the states of California and Louisiana for determining student placement in special-education programs.

The Pigeonhole Effect

A third major criticism of intelligence testing is that it fails to take into account varying rates of intellectual growth and risks locking young children into categories prematurely. This **pigeonhole effect** can stigmatize some youngsters unfairly by sidetracking them into classes for slow learners. It was concern over this issue that led the British to abandon their long-established "11-plus" system during the 1960s. Under this system an examination intended to measure intelligence and achievement was administered to all children around the eleventh birthday—hence the name 11 plus. The results determined whether children would be eligible for state grammar schools, which prepared them for university admission—and, therefore, the prospect of better jobs—or whether they would be sent instead to trade schools.

The possible effects of pigeonholing American children under fast or slow labels have been demonstrated in an experiment by Robert Rosenthal and Lenore Jacobson (1966). The experiment was conducted in an elementary school where children were tracked in classes according to the results of an IQ test taken at the beginning of the year. In 18 classes, teachers were given the names of children who purportedly had been identified by the IQ test as intellectual bloomers who would likely show marked improvement in their academic performance during the year. These children represented 25 percent of the pupils in the 18 classes. The story about their being specially marked for improvement was a ruse: they had not been chosen by the test at all but rather by random selection. By the end of the year, however, these randomly chosen "bloomers" had indeed bloomed. Their grades had improved and so had their IQs. Nearly half of the test population—47 percent—showed an increase of more than 20 points on the end-of-the-year IQ test; only 19 percent of the nonlabeled pupils showed similar improvement.

What can explain these startling results? One possibility is that the teachers expected more from the pupils labeled as bloomers and spent more time with them. Another possibility is that the teachers' expectations influenced their perception of the children's performance and thus the grades they awarded; the better grades, in turn, encouraged the children to work harder. A third possiblitiy is that the teachers' expectations were somehow communicated to the children who, believing themselves more capable than before, proceeded to be more capable.

Although some studies have qualified the original results obtained by Rosenthal and Jacobson, the effects of pigeonholing the children seem fairly clear: the intellectual performance of those students labeled as bloomers tended to improve more than the performance of those who were not so labeled.

While a number of researchers are working on devising accurate measures of intelligence, others are looking into the factors that determine the level of individual intelligence.

Determinants of Intelligence

Why is one person more intelligent than another? The answers proposed by psychologists are even more controversial than the various theories as to what intelligence is and the methods of measuring it. As in many of the other debates that arise from the study of human behavior, the controversy over the determinants of intelligence revolves around the two polarities of nature and nurture. Is intelligence essentially an inherited characteristic that is determined by our individual genetic makeup? Or is it largely the product of environmental influences such as education, child-rearing practices, social class, and culture?

Figure 13.4

Correlation coefficients for IQ test scores from 52 studies. Medians are shown by dots intersecting the horizontal lines, which represent the ranges. The relationship categories progress from totally unrelated persons reared apart to identical twins reared together.

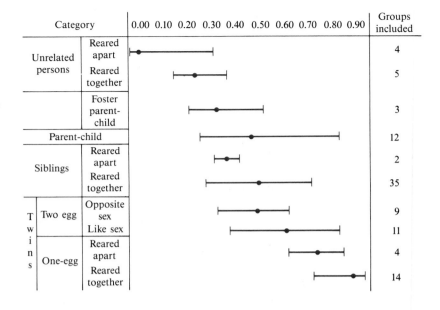

Category			Groups included
		0.00 0.10 0.20 0.30 0.40 0.50 0.60 0.70 0.80 0.90	
Unrelated persons	Reared apart		4
	Reared together		5
	Foster parent-child		3
Parent-child			12
Siblings	Reared apart		2
	Reared together		35
Twins — Two egg	Opposite sex		9
	Like sex		11
Twins — One-egg	Reared apart		4
	Reared together		14

Hereditary Influences on Intelligence

The case for inheritance of intelligence rests on evidence amassed from the pursuit of a simple proposition: if the primary influence on intelligence is genetic, then two individuals who have a close genetic relationship should have similar IQs. Such an approach depends on statistical correlations, because research in human genetics is not sufficiently advanced to explain the precise relationships between genetic endowment and complex behaviors or abilities such as intelligence.

Statistical correlations tend to bear out the proposed link between genetic relationship and IQ (Erlenmeyer-Kimling & Jarvik, 1963). Figure 13.4, which is based on data from 52 different studies, shows how correlations of IQ increase with increasingly closer genetic relationships. The categories of genetic relationship progess from one extreme, individuals who are totally unrelated, to the other extreme, identical twins, who are identical genetically. The systematic increase in correlation between IQs that is shown here strongly suggests a genetic influence on intelligence.

One problem with interpreting the possible cause of such correlations is obvious: closer genetic relationships also typically involve environmental similarities. Brothers, for example, not only draw from similar gene pools provided by their parents, but they also are exposed to similar environmental influences—class, culture, education, child-rearing practices.

The best method researchers can use to isolate the effects of heredity from those of environment is to study twins. Fraternal twins, who are said to be dizygotic because they originate in two separate eggs, are no more genetically alike than are other siblings. Thus, differences in intelligence between dizygotic twins are assumed to be determined by both genetic and environmental factors. Identical, or monozygotic, twins have identical genetic makeups because they originate in the same egg. As Figure 13.4 shows, the correlation of intelligence is usually much higher among monozygotic twins than among dizygotic twins.

Twin studies of unusual interest are those that compare identical twins who were raised together with twins who were separated soon after birth and raised apart. Studies of monozygotic twins raised apart tend to indicate such astonishing similarities and behaviors, despite differences in environment, that they buttress the argument for genetic influences. An important study by Thomas Bouchard (Holden, 1980) which is still in progess has provided preliminary but impressive evidence for such similarities (see Focus, p. 436). Bouchard and his colleagues are measuring a number of personality characteristics in addition to intelligence. In their studies to date, however, intelligence has shown the highest correlation of all the measurements—a tentative finding, but one that speaks powerfully for the heritability of intelligence.

At the same time, comparisons of monozygotic twins raised apart also provide evidence for the influence of environmental factors. Any differences between such twins are assumed to be environmentally based because the two individuals are genetically identical. Such differences are demonstrated by the higher correlation of intelligence for identical twins raised together, as shown in Figure 13.4.

The Evolution of Intelligence

Recently, sociobiologists have considered the evolution of a variety of social and behavioral characteristics and have proposed that many of the behaviors and traits that we have assumed were primarily a result of environmental influences can be explained equally well using evolutionary theory. The evolutionary record shows that primates have developed larger brains than would be predicted on the basis of their body size. This is particularly true of the genus *Homo*. The one intriguing exception in addition to the genus *Homo* is the bottle-nosed dolphin, who has a similarly large brain relative to its body size. From evidence of this sort, sociobiologists conclude that intelligent behavior can be seen as the product of evolution. One of the most outspoken critics of this view is Stephen J. Gould who, in his book *The Mismeasure of Man* (1981), argues that there is no evidence for biological change in brain size or structure since *Homo sapiens* appeared in the fossil record approximately 50 thousand years ago.

A critical distinction must be made here that helps to clear up the controversy. It may be that evolution of brain size has been important in the development of primates' intellectual capacities and, as Hunt (1983) suggests, it is almost certain that our larger brains allow us to process information more effectively than the tree shrew, for example. However, differences in intelligence among *Homo sapiens* do not appear to depend on differences in brain size. Thus, it may be that evolution contributes to the development of brain size and more intelligent behavior among primates compared to other species, but makes little difference among primates themselves.

One of the most interesting speculations about human intelligence from the evolutionary perspective has been offered by Jensen (1983). Jensen notes that the apparent inability of environmental factors to produce large changes in human intelligence can actually be thought of as a characteristic of evolutionary fitness. That is, Jensen suggests it could be that the biological basis of intelligence is like a gyroscope, a built-in stabilizing mechanism that safeguards the individual's intellectual capacity to cope with the demands of survival. Jensen suggests that, if this is the case, mental development would not be wholly at the mercy of environment events. If intelligence were malleable, it would provide little protection against the variables that exist in the environment. Thus,

The correlation of intelligence among identical twins is usually much higher than it is among fraternal twins.

FOCUS

Identical Twins as "Living Laboratories"

When identical twins James Arthur Springer and James Edward Lewis were reunited for the first time after being separated shortly after birth 39 years previously, they were astonished to discover a remarkable string of similarities and seeming coincidences. The apparent coincidences concerning names were the most obvious: each had been given the same first name by his adoptive parents, each had been married first to a woman named Linda and then to one named Betty, each had named a son either James Alan or James Allan, and each once had a dog named Toy. But Springer and Lewis also discovered other similarities: both liked to work with wood; both had served as auxiliary sheriff's deputies; both had vacationed at the same Florida resort, both smoked the same brand of cigarettes, drank the same beer, and drove the same model of automobile.

The reunion of the "Jim twins," as they came to be known, occurred in February 1979. About a month later, they became the first subjects in a new study by researchers at the University of Minnesota, of identical twins raised apart. Identical twins, because they develop from the division of a single fertilized egg, or monozygote, and thus have the same genes, have long been regarded as

"living laboratories" for the study of the effects of heritability and environment on intelligence, mental illness, and many other aspects of behavior (Chen, 1979). Identical twins are rare enough (they occur about 3.5 times in every 1000 live births), but ones who were separated early in life and reared apart are even rarer. The fact that they have been raised in differing environments can provide a measure of the importance of genetic factors in behavior.

The Minnesota project, headed by psychologist Thomas Bouchard, promises to be the most comprehensive study ever undertaken of twins raised apart (Holden, 1980). Subjects undergo an intensive six-day battery of tests, interviews, and examinations by psychologists, psychiatrists, and medical doctors. In addition to the Wechsler Adult Intelligence Scale, they are given tests for various mental abilities, such as memory and vocabulary, and no fewer than three different comprehensive psychological inventories. Thus far, more than a dozen sets of twins raised apart have been tested, and the publicity received by the project has helped generate leads to perhaps 20 other pairs.

Although Bouchard and his colleagues emphasize that their data have yet to be analyzed and that any conclusions are still highly tentative, even the raw data are fascinating. For example, many of the twins reported very similar medical histories. Springer and Lewis each described the onset at age 18 of a type of headache known as mixed headache syndrome—a tension headache that turns into a migraine—which had previously been thought to have no genetic basis. Electroencephalogram patterns for many of the twin pairs also tended to be similar. One pair of female twins shared the same phobias—fears of heights, bodies of water, and closed-in places.

Even more striking were the test results and researchers' observations on personality characteristics. In body language, their manner of speaking, the way they gesture, Springer and Lewis "were like bookends," Bouchard said. ". . . the genetic effect pervades the entire structure of personality" (Jackson, 1980).

mental development may have its own built-in timetable driven partly by evolutionary processes that protects it against being pushed too far in one direction or the other by environmental forces. Jensen's ideas suggest a sociobiological explanation for the relative stability of intelligence. In this view, intelligence stands as a relatively stable trait designed to protect the evolution of the species in the face of environmental change.

Environmental Influences on Intelligence

Studies of twins examine the relationship between intellectual variation and genetic variation. If there is a positive correlation between genetic similarity and similarity in intelligence test scores, we assume that intelligence and ge-

Although some similarities might conceivably be attributable to environment—the Jim twins were both raised in small-town Ohio working-class families—others had growing-up experiences radically different from those of their twin. For example, one set of twins were separated at age six months in Trinidad after their parents' divorce. One was raised there as a Jew by his Jewish father and later joined a kibbutz in Israel at age 17; the other was raised a Catholic by his grandmother in Germany and became involved in the Hitler Youth Movement. Although differences in attitude persist, they have a similar temperament and even similar idiosyncrasies—absentmindedness, the habit of storing rubber bands on their wrists, and a strange penchant for sneezing loudly in public to gain attention.

How might observable similarities in personality be explained in terms of genetic similarity? Bouchard speculates that the genetic background might create certain predispositions that are associated with certain patterns of behavior. Body language, for example, may be a function of predispositions in the anatomy and physiology of the muscles; color preferences may be more soothing to eyes with particular organic characteristics.

Identical twins James Arthur Springer and James Edward Lewis were reunited in 1979 after having been separated shortly after birth 39 years earlier. Although they were raised apart, there turned out to be a remarkable number of similarities between them.

On many of the psychological tests, the twin pairs scored so similarly to each other that they approximated the results obtained when one person takes the same test twice. Interestingly, the highest correlation was on the IQ test. In the few instances in which there was a marked difference in measured intelligence, the twin with the greater education had the higher score. These findings suggest that IQ has a high degree of heritability.

Bouchard suspects that identical twins reared apart may actually turn out to be more alike than those raised in the same environment. He speculates that in order to establish their own individuality, twins raised together sometimes exaggerate their differences. One twin, for example, might avoid pursuing an interest in music if the other twin is taking piano lessons. This interpretation is in marked contrast to the more usual speculation that identical twins may share more similarities in the family environment than fraternal twins because their similarity in appearance and manner elicits more similar responses from others.

It may be several years before the Minnesota project is completed and all of the data analyzed. Even then, it cannot be expected to furnish any definitive answers to the nature-nurture debate because the sample of subjects is so small. If the preliminary findings are any indication, however, it will provide further evidence for both perspectives: while the striking similarities in the behavior of identical twins raised apart may bolster the case for genetic determination, differences that are found will reflect and clarify the role of the environment. ■

netic background are related to one another. The impact of environmental factors on intelligence cannot be as easily compared as genetic makeup among individuals.

Scientists must either create or discover differences in the environments of individuals that may be related to differences in intellectual performance. If researchers can show that contrasting environments produce differences in intellectual attainment, then a case can be made for social, cultural, and environmental factors as well as genetic background in the development of intelligent behavior.

Family Environment: Birth Order and Intellectual Attainment
The impact of the family environment on intellectual behavior and on intelligence is unquestionably important. Language development, problem-solv-

Studies have shown a systematic relationship between birth order and intelligence.

Figure 13.5

Average transformed scores on the Raven test are shown as a function of birth order and family size (j indicates family size) with the score of the only child set at 100. The findings indicate that the larger the family, the lower the relative score. There also appears to be a systematic relationship between birth order and test scores.

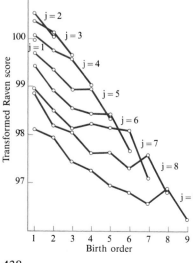

ing skills, and other critical intellectual abilities are first learned in the family context, not only from parents but also from siblings.

Lillian Belmont and Francis Marolla (1973) studied the results of intelligence tests given to nearly 400,000 19-year-old men in the Netherlands. This sample consisted of practically all males born in that country from 1944 to 1947. Belmont and Marolla found that firstborn males scored higher on the test than did later-borns within the same family. Moreover, IQ scores declined in relation to the ordinal position of birth within the family: second-borns scored higher than third-borns, who scored higher than fourth-borns, and so on. Similar conclusions have been drawn from a study of 800,000 U.S. students—both male and female—who applied for National Merit Scholarships.

This phenomenon is usually explained in terms of the amount of time and concern parents devote to their children. They are simply likely to lavish more attention on the firstborn. As the number of children increases, parents have less time and energy available to devote to any single offspring.

Another study of 400,000 19-year-olds reflects the impact of family environment on intelligence (Zajonc & Markus, 1975). Figure 13.5 shows the overall results of this study, which indicate several things. First, the IQs of children from larger families are somewhat lower than the IQs of children from smaller families. This difference is regular and systematic: the larger the family, the lower the relative IQ score. Second, there is a systematic relationship between birth order and intelligence, with individuals born earlier in the family showing some advantage in intellectual attainment over those born later.

In addition, the figures for the last child in the sequence show a decline in IQ level that is even larger than that for preceding children. It appears as if being a last child, particularly in larger families, produces a unique disadvantage of its own. Furthermore, the IQs for only children are systematically lower than for firstborn children with either one or two siblings. By way of explanation Robert Zajonc suggests that the family can be thought of as a group that provides intellectual resources to its members; this is the intellectual environment that affects intelligence. Zajonc concludes that increased family size is uniformly detrimental to intellectual development. He also believes that spacing between siblings is critical: larger spacing tends to benefit younger children, while it is detrimental to older siblings. Zajonc explains the comparatively lower IQs of last children and only children by the fact that neither has an opportunity to be a "teacher" to younger siblings. The opportunity to be a teacher to others tends to stimulate intellectual growth, whereas a lack of this opportunity will produce a somewhat lower level of intelligence.

All of the differences observed by Zajonc are small in the absolute sense, but are extremely regular. The fact that Zajonc and his colleagues were able to obtain birth order and intelligence test data on such a large sample means that even small differences associated with family size and birth order will be observable in the average values for various groups. On the other hand, numerous other factors also affect performance on intelligence tests, and family size and birth order are simply another set of contributors to performance. Thus, family size and birth order are part of a larger puzzle involved in understanding the role of environmental factors and genetic background in the development of intellectual ability.

Recently, Ernst and Angst (1983) have reviewed 35 years of research on birth order, including some 1500 studies. They conclude from their review that the effects of birth order on intelligence are smaller than previously thought. A critical issue, they argue, has to do with the fact that most research on birth order has ignored the fact that parents of large families tend, on the average, to have less money, less education, and lower IQs than parents of small families. Thus, the sample of firstborns is representative of all social classes, but a disproportionate number of fifth-borns tend to come from less-privileged homes. When such factors are taken into account, birth order effects on intelligence are minimal.

Moreover, recent evidence on the role prenatal and perinatal factors play with respect to postnatal behavioral capacities provides an alternative explanation to Zajonc's social model of birth order effects on intelligence. Maccoby et al. (1979) have discovered systematic relationships between hormonal levels in umbilical cord blood and the spacing of child births. Their findings suggest that there may be hormonal factors related to child birth spacing that might have similar effects upon various spheres of the infant's development, including intellectual ability.

Social Class and Ethnic Group Differences

In our society there are extremely large variations in the opportunities available to black versus white and wealthy versus less economically advantaged children. The degree to which ethnic or racial differences on the one hand and social class differences on the other affect intelligence or intellectual achievement is a subject of continuing debate. The issue is complex and researchers cannot easily disentangle the effects of class on IQ. For example, does restricted opportunity in lower socioeconomic groups produce lower levels of intellectual attainment or do individuals with lower levels of intellectual ability "drift" to the lower socioeconomic strata of society?

A recent study attempted to map some of the effects of race and social class on the intellectual and personality characteristics of young children (Yando, Seitz, & Zigler, 1979). The investigators studied 304 eight-year-old children from the Boston area. They carefully selected children representing higher and lower socioeconomic status as well as black and white children from both higher- and lower-status families. They were interested in what differences would remain after the variation in IQ was taken out of other measures. They studied a number of different characteristics including creativity, self-confidence, autonomy, curiosity, tolerance for frustration, dependency, and self-image. A number of fascinating results were obtained. For example, when social class effects were controlled in this study, few race differences were found. On the other hand, differences that appeared to be a consequence of social class were substantial. Less-advantaged children appeared to be creative problem solvers who were willing to take risks and persevere in the face of frustration.

Intellectual growth is often stimulated by the opportunity to be a teacher to others.

This picture of an allegedly "separate but equal" classroom in the early 1950s demonstrates sharply the extreme variation of opportunities available to black versus white children. Though educational reform has since taken place, the extremes of opportunities, in many cases, still exist.

Advantaged upper-class children, on the other hand, tended to be better at solving more conventional problems but also were overly concerned and anxious about failure.

One of the most important aspects of this study is the fact that the investigators designed it to allow assessment of differences that are a consequence of race and class where intelligence has been controlled. These differences, when they emerge, could be important factors that affect children's intellectual achievement as well as their achievement in other life domains.

A very different study illuminates the question of race differences and intelligence. This study capitalized on the "natural experiment" associated with adoption (Scarr & Weinberg, 1978). The researchers studied IQs of black children who had been adopted early in life by upper-middle-class white families with more than average educational attainment and income; they found that the average IQ of these adopted black children was 106, much higher than the national average of comparable children who had not been adopted. In addition, the investigators examined a number of different variables that presumably reflect differences in intellectual environment, and these variables also correlated with differences in IQ. Thus, the impact of environment differences on intellectual attainment of black children is considerable. It is worth noting from a methodological standpoint that the researchers had to assume low IQs in the biological parents of the black adoptee inasmuch as this information was not obtained. Still, this study throws doubt on the claim of Arthur Jensen (1969) who has argued that variation in IQ among blacks reflects genetic differences in intellectual potential.

The Heredity Versus Environment Controversy

Any attempt to sort out the evidence in the heredity versus environment debate over the determinants of intelligence faces a major hurdle. A great deal of educational and social policy—tracking of students, for example, and efforts to ameliorate poverty and upgrade slum schools—hinges on interpretation of the evidence, which often tends to be shaded by preexisting biases. These biases, in turn, sometimes lead to an exaggeration of the evidence and unwarranted conclusions. Several issues have clouded the debate in recent years.

CHAPTER 13   INTELLIGENCE

The Jensen Controversy

Too often the debate is obfuscated by the uses to which data and theories are put. A prime example is the work of Arthur Jensen, who in 1969 published a monograph alleging that about 80 percent of differences in IQ are attributable to differences in genetic background. This assertion was controversial, but Jensen went on to set off a much greater controversy. Jensen noted that the IQ scores of American blacks average more than 15 points below those of whites and that compensatory educational programs had done little to change that fact. In short, Jensen implied that the disparity between black and white IQs had relatively little to do with poverty, racial discrimination, inferior slum schools, or even cultural bias in testing.

Critics assailed Jensen on a number of counts:

- The IQ tests, on which Jensen built his theory, were culturally biased against blacks and hence invalid.

- The disparity in IQ scores between blacks and whites can be explained in terms of environmental factors such as nutrition, child-rearing practices, and poor schools (see Figure 13.6).

- Heritability of intelligence may account for differences in IQ within a group, but this does not justify the comparison across cultural or racial boundaries.

In order to understand this last criticism more clearly, it is necessary to consider the concept of heritability in more detail because this concept, often misunderstood, fuels the debate.

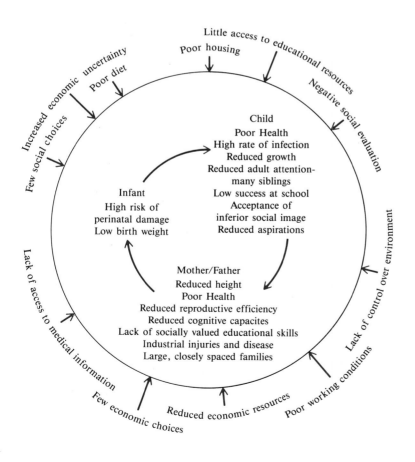

Figure 13.6

Multiple environmental factors can affect intellectual ability. Among populations in poverty, many of these factors may combine to produce a poor learning environment.

RESEARCH

A Classic Study of Environmental Influence

Researchers who want to investigate the effects of early childhood environment on human intelligence must overcome formidable obstacles. Because the presumed environmental effects occur over a long period of time, it obviously would be impractical to conduct experiments in the laboratory. Moreover, ethical considerations ordinarily constrain researchers from manipulating the real-life environment of a child.

In the classic study by Harold M. Skeels (1966), however, these obstacles were overcome because of the researcher's adroitness in seizing on a serendipitous "experiment in nature." Skeels' study began by chance during the 1930s when he was serving as a psychologist for the state of Iowa. Among his duties was the psychological testing of young children in an orphanage. One day he examined two baby girls who had been legally committed to the orphanage not long after birth because their feeble-minded mothers had neglected them. The girls were emaciated and pitifully inactive, spending their days in the orphanage rocking and whining. Skeels found that, although there was no evidence of physiological or organic defects, the girls showed developmental levels of children less than half their ages: the 16-month-old had

a level of seven months; the 13-month-old had a level of six months. In those days, intelligence was generally regarded by psychologists as a genetically determined characteristic that was relatively fixed at birth. The two little girls were given up as unadoptable and, two months later, they were transferred to the Glenwood State School, an institution for the mentally retarded.

Six months after the transfer, Skeels visited Glenwood. He scarcely recognized the two little girls. They were alert, smiling, and active. Skeels tested them again and found to his astonishment that they were now approaching normal mental development for their age. Subsequent tests when the girls were about three years of age confirmed their progress.

What could explain the remarkable changes in their behavior and

mental development? Skeels concluded that the change in environment had to be responsible. The orphanage where the girls spent their early months was understaffed and overcrowded. Much of the time, the young children were confined to large cribs with very little chance for human interaction. At Glenwood, by contrast, the two little girls had a homelike environment, rich in affection and interesting experiences. They lived in a ward with women ranging in age from 18 to 50 years (mental age from 5 to 9) who, in effect, "adopted" them. They also received a lot of affection and attention from attendants and nurses who bought them toys and picture books and took them out for auto rides and shopping excursions.

Skeels thereupon decided to undertake a bold experiment. He prevailed on the administrators of the orphanage to transfer 10 more children to the Glenwood State School, pointing out that the children all seemed destined for mental retardation in any case. His experimental group consisted of 13 children—the two little girls who had transferred earlier, a third girl who had been transferred at about the same time, and the ten new transfers. All were under three years of age, and all

The Concept of Heritability

The concept of **heritability** is a measure of relative variation. It indicates how much of the variation in a particular trait for a particular population is due to genetic as opposed to environmental factors. Thus, the first thing to recognize about the concept of heritability is that it depends on both environmental and genetic variation for a particular population. Measures of heritability in characteristics such as intelligence are applied to a specific group under a specific set of circumstances.

Herrnstein (1973) uses the example of skin color to illustrate the meaning of heritability. He points out that in the United States, which has a substantial mix of racial groups, the heritability of skin color is high. On the other hand, in a small, isolated Norwegian town, Scandinavians with generations of pale-skinned ancestors display little variation in skin color, and any variation observed is more likely to be due to environmental factors. Thus, in the Scandinavian town the heritability should be low—that is, any variation in skin color is likely to be caused by environmental factors such as exposure to the sun.

were certified as "seriously retarded by tests and observation before transfer was made." Their average age was 19.4 months; their IQ scores ranged from 35 to 89 with a mean of 64.3.

The progress of this experimental group at Glenwood was measured against that of a comparison group of 12 children who remained at the orphanage. The comparison group was slightly younger, with a mean age of 16.6 months, and considerably brighter, with a mean IQ of 86.7.

The contrasts between the two different environments—the drab, sterile orphanage and the lively, stimulating mental institution—became even more marked as the children grew older. At the orphanage, children over two years old lived in cottages where one matron, aided by three or four untrained girls, had charge of 30 to 35 boys and girls. The cottages were so crowded that the children had to be tightly regimented. At age six, the children attended the orphanage elementary school. Later, they were sent to public junior high school where there were few opportunities for individual attention and where the children quickly fell behind in their work.

Meanwhile, at Glenwood, the transfers from the orphanage were "adopted" by adults—attendants as well as the mentally retarded residents. Each child thus was afforded the opportunity for an intense one-to-one emotional relationship with an older person. The children could play outdoors often on tricycles, swings, and other equipment. And when they attended school at Glenwood, the matron in charge made it a regular practice to single out children in need of special attention, allowing them to spend stimulating time each day visiting her office.

After several months, Skeels tested the children in the experimental and comparison groups. The 13 children in the enriched environment at Glenwood showed an average gain in IQ of 27.5 points; 3 children gained over 45 points. In contrast, the 12 children in the deprived environment at the orphanage showed a decline in average IQ of 26.2 points.

Even more impressive were the results of the follow-up study conducted by Skeels 21 years later. All 13 children in the Glenwood experimental group—11 of whom had been placed for adoption—were self-supporting; in the comparison group, four were still wards of institutions and one had died in a state institution during adolescence. The median education level in the experimental group was the twelfth grade; in the comparison group less than the third grade. In the experimental group, subjects held jobs ranging from professional and business occupations to domestic service. Comparison group members who were not institutionalized tended to have low-level jobs.

Perhaps the most striking contrast occurred in the next generation. The experimental group had 28 offspring with IQs ranging from 86 to 125, with a mean of 104; in no instance was there any evidence of mental retardation. The comparison group had five children. Four, the offspring of one male subject, were of average intelligence. But the other second-generation child showed marked mental retardation with indications of probable brain damage.

Skeels' study had one methodological shortcoming: there was no way in which he could completely rule out possible innate differences in his subjects. Nonetheless, it provides extremely persuasive evidence—in the short run and over a period of more than two decades—for early environment as a powerful force in the shaping of intelligence. ■

When the race and IQ controversy stimulated by Jensen is considered, several factors must be carefully looked at. First, the estimates of heritability for intelligence are based on white populations; no adequate measures of heritability of intelligence for the black population is available. Furthermore, it is clear that the environmental circumstances for black people in the United States are dramatically different, on the average, than those for white people. Therefore, the heritability estimates for whites may tell us little or nothing about the heritability of IQ among blacks in the United States. Estimates of the heritability of intelligence are specific to particular populations under particular circumstances, and variations in environmental factors, such as blocked opportunity or deprived environment, may strongly affect heritability estimates.

However, there is an important corollary to this notion, as Herrnstein notes. If an environmental factor that would affect IQ were found—a diet or a particular type of educational program—and were provided to the American people, such an environmental factor would raise the average IQ of the American public and, at the same time, would actually increase the heritability of

IQ. Equalizing circumstances would mean that less and less variation in IQ would be due to environmental factors, and more and more would be due to genetic background. Thus, improving environmental circumstances may have the paradoxical effect of actually raising the degree to which intelligence runs in families.

Herrnstein offers the following syllogism, which draws out some of the social implications of these observations. He says "(1) if differences in mental abilities are inherited, and (2) if success requires those abilities, and (3) if earnings and prestige depend on success, (4) then social standing (which reflects earnings and prestige) will be based to some extent on inherited differences among people" (Herrnstein, 1973).

Herrnstein goes on to offer several corollaries of this syllogism. We have already discussed the first of these: the argument that as the environment becomes more favorable for intellectual development, the more certainly will differences in intelligence be inherited. In addition, as the social barriers to upward mobility are removed in our society, more and more of the barriers to upward mobility will be based on innate differences. He argues further that our society's technological advances will require intellectual ability to an increasing degree, and he suggests that "as technology advances, the tendency to be unemployed may run in the genes of a family about as certainly as bad teeth do now" (Herrnstein, 1973).

None of this should be seen as a justification for social discrimination based on group membership. Genetics may affect potential intellectual attainment of individuals, but environment, just as surely, determines the degree to which people fulfill their potential.

The Question of Modifiability

The evidence is substantial that genetic background helps determine intelligence, perhaps establishing upper and lower limits. At the same time, evidence is also substantial that life experiences help dictate where an individual's intelligence will fall within this assumed range laid down by nature. A recent comprehensive review of the research on the modifiability of intelligence (Detterman & Sternberg, 1982) suggests that it is indeed possible to modify a wide range of cognitive skills. However, it is unclear whether teaching these specific cognitive skills is the same thing as modifying general intellectual capacity.

It may be fruitful to look for those factors that may enable people to attain greater intellectual achievement as has been done with other conditions that clearly are genetic in origin and yet subject to environmental modification. One such condition is phenylketonuria (PKU), a disorder caused by the pairing of two defective recessive genes. Infants with PKU are unable to metabolize a certain amino acid. This deficiency interferes with the development of myelin, the white sheathing of nerve cells necessary for rapid transmission of electric impulses (see chapter 2), and can lead to irreversible brain damage and profound mental retardation. Many children with PKU never learn to walk or talk; more than half have IQs of less than 20. However, PKU can be detected in the postnatal blood test required by state laws. If the test is positive, a special diet low in the problem protein can allow normal brain development to occur. Thus, in the case of PKU, an environmental influence—a special diet—can modify or eliminate the behavioral effects of a genetically dictated condition.

The PKU example suggests one way of clarifying the debate over the determinants of intelligence. Even if intelligence has a genetic component, every effort should be made to provide the "special diet" of environmental influences that can help every individual attain full intellectual growth.

Changes in Intellectual Ability over the Life Span

We have already seen that the intelligence quotient is adjusted for an individual's chronological age. Thus, individuals actually are being compared to people of their own age when IQ is used as a measure of intellectual ability. A pertinent question is whether or not a person's IQ—that is, an individual's relative standing compared with people of a similar age—changes over time. In general, intelligence quotients remain relatively stable for most people, particularly after age seven.

Before age seven, tests of intelligence, particularly those given to infants, are not good predictors of future intellectual performance. One reason is that tests given to children early in life depend heavily on visual and motor ability, whereas tests given later in life depend much more heavily on verbal ability; results from one type of test of intellectual ability do not necessarily predict results in another domain. In addition, infant tests seem to be poor predictors of future performance because of the great plasticity of the behavior of infants.

Even though relative standing in IQ remains stable for most people over the life span, **intellectual ability**—that is, the ability to master a variety of tasks requiring memory, perception, reasoning, and other abilities—has a growth curve of its own. Figure 13.7 shows data that indicate that intellectual growth occurs very rapidly over the first 20 or so years of life and then levels out (Bayley, 1970).

Toward middle and old age, intellectual abilities begin to change again, but to say that intellectual ability simply declines in old age is much too simple. Some abilities remain relatively intact for most people even fairly late in life. Verbal ability, deductive reasoning ability, and general information retention remain constant well into later life (Blum, Jarvik, & Clark, 1970). Other abilities, however, do appear to decline in old age, particularly those requiring speed of response and short-term memory (Schaie & Strother, 1968; Craik, 1977). On standardized tests of intelligence such as the WAIS-R, psychomotor slowing contributes to the lower scores typically achieved by elderly individuals on timed measures of cognitive ability such as the Block Design, Object Assembly, and Digit Symbol subtests (Kramer & Jarvik, 1979). Again, there are wide individual differences in the size and rate of these changes: some people retain most of their intellectual vigor well into later life, whereas others lose it rather early. Changes in health and the degree to which an individual is intellectually challenged in daily life have a good deal to do with how rapidly intellectual abilities decline over time (De Carlo, 1971; Spirduso, 1973).

Figure 13.7

The scores in this theoretical growth curve of intelligence are based on age-appropriate tests, including Bayley infant scales, Stanford-Binet, and Wechsler Adult Scales. The curve shows rapid growth through childhood, with a leveling off at about age 20.

Extremes of Intelligence

In the wide spectrum of intelligence, the majority of us are clustered around the middle. For example, on the Stanford-Binet scale, the IQs of 46 percent of all Americans fall in the range between 90 and 109 (see Table 13.3). At either end of the spectrum are extremes that are of particular interest to the psychologist. About 3 percent of the population, approximately 7 million Americans, have IQs below 68 and are considered mentally retarded; about 1 percent of Americans have IQs above 140 and are considered mentally gifted.

Mental Retardation

"What is retardation? It's hard to say, I guess it's having problems thinking." This straightforward definition was offered by a 26-year-old man, who at the age of 15 had been placed in a state institution for the retarded. His case,

Table 13.3 PERCENTAGES OF POPULATION IN VARIOUS STANFORD-BINET IQ
RANGES

IQ	Percentage in Groups	Characterization
Above 139	1	Very superior
120–139	11	Superior
110–119	18	High average
90–109	46	Average
80–89	15	Low average
70–79	6	Borderline
Below 70	3	Mentally retarded
	100	

which was studied extensively, points up some of the difficulties in distinguishing between the intellectually normal and subnormal (Bogdan & Taylor, 1976).

Most formal definitions of mental retardation take into account not only subnormal IQ but also two other variables: the degree of social adaptation and the age at which intellectual problems are first manifested. The problems of retardation develop early in life, well before the eighteenth year. Thus the current manual of the American Association on Mental Deficiency (AAMD), an organization of professionals concerned with the problem, states that **mental retardation** "refers to significantly subaverage general intellectual functioning existing concurrently with deficits in adaptive behavior . . ." (Robinson & Robinson, 1976).

Levels of Retardation

The current AAMD manual recognizes four levels of mental deficiency. Significantly, the former category of borderline retardation has been dropped in response to criticism that people with IQs as high as 83 on the Stanford-Binet can adapt to conventional classrooms and should not be stigmatized. The following descriptions summarize key characteristics of each of the four levels of retardation recognized by the AAMD (Robinson & Robinson, 1976).

1. *Mild Retardation.* IQ 52 to 67 on the Stanford-Binet. This group comprises about 90 percent of the mentally retarded. Children in this group are eligible for classes for the educable mentally retarded and are expected to attain a sixth-grade level of academic performance. Adults usually can work in unskilled jobs.

2. *Moderate Retardation.* IQ 36 to 51. This group comprises about 6 percent of the mentally retarded. Children are eligible for classes for trainable retardates that emphasize self-care rather than academic skills. Few adults hold jobs but instead depend on their families or are institutionalized.

3. *Severe Retardation.* IQ 20 to 35. This group comprises about 3 percent of the retarded. Children require prolonged training just to learn to speak and take care of basic needs. Adults can usually communicate on a rudimentary level.

4. *Profound Retardation.* IQ below 20. This group comprises about 1 percent of the retarded. These individuals require total supervision, and it is assumed that they can learn little except possibly to walk, utter a few phrases, and feed themselves.

Not everyone of subnormal intelligence fits neatly into the four categories of mental retardation. A special and unusually interesting case in point is the **idiot savant,** a retardate who shows superior functioning in one narrow area of mental activity. Idiot savants have displayed extraordinary talents in music, mathematical calculation, and rote memory (Restak, 1982).

One of the best-documented case histories of an idiot savant is the study of L. (Scheerer, Rothman, & Goldstein, 1945). From his eleventh through sixteenth years, the investigators studied L., who had an IQ of 50 on the Stanford-Binet, which classified him as moderately retarded. Yet L. had several remarkable abilities. He could quickly spell forward or backward practically any word pronounced to him, although he did not necessarily know its meaning. He could play a number of melodies by ear on the piano but seemed to have no idea of what he was doing. He could add up to a dozen two-digit numbers as fast as they were recited to him but was unable to learn to add larger numbers. He could name the day of the week for any date between 1880 and 1950 but had no sense of chronology.

What explains such special talents in people who otherwise function on an intellectual level so far below normal? Bernard Rimland, a leading authority on savants and autism, believes that a defect exists within the brain that produces the savant's inability to associate incoming stimuli with already stored memories. This defect results in a reduction in the savant's ability to make generalizations or to think abstractly and may also account for the much greater apparent powers of concentration that savants display. This ''defective filter'' may lie within the brain's reticular activating system, an area associated with activation and alertness. However, if such a filtering mechanism exists, researchers have not yet been able to find it.

A child with Down's syndrome, which is the result of a chromosomal abnormality, usually displays moderate to severe retardation.

Determinants of Retardation

A number of factors are involved in the causes of mental retardation, depending in part on the severity of the deficiency. The more serious forms of retardation—moderate, severe, and profound—can typically be traced to organic factors such as chromosomal abnormalities or brain trauma. In mild retardation cultural-familial factors are believed to play the major role.

Organic causes of retardation can be grouped into three catagories—genetic, infectious, and traumatic. The most prevalent genetic cause is Down's syndrome (formerly known as mongolism), which accounts for at least 10 percent of the cases of moderate to severe retardation. In addition to low IQ—typically under 50—Down's syndrome victims have a number of physical abnormalities, including eyes that are slanted upward and outward, flat face and nose, and stunted growth. With proper encouragement and instruction, however, they can perform housework and simple carpentry and seem to thrive better in a loving home than in an institution. The cause of Down's syndrome is a chromosomal abnormality: victims have 47 chromosomes instead of 46, the extra one apparently resulting from a defective separation of pair 21 in the mother's egg cell before ovulation. For reasons that are still not clearly understood, about two thirds of all children with Down's syndrome are born to women over the age of 40.

Infectious diseases can cause retardation before or after birth. The fetus is particularly vulnerable during the first month of pregnancy, when its nervous system is developing at a rapid rate. If a mother is infected by rubella, or German measles, during this period, there is a 50 percent chance her child will suffer both mental and physical abnormalities. Young children born normal can suffer impairment of the brain, and hence mental retardation, if they are infected by encephalitis, an inflammation of the brain, or by meningitis, an inflammation of the brain's protective membranes.

Traumatic causes of retardation also can affect the brain before or after birth. These causes range from incompatibility between the blood of the mother and the fetus (leading to oxygen deprivation in the fetal brain), to excessive exposure to X rays in utero, to head injuries, and to ingestion by the child of poisonous metals such as lead (from automobile emissions or lead-based paints) and mercury (from industrial wastes consumed by fish).

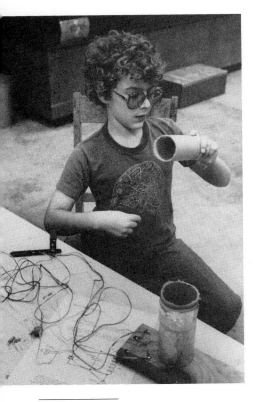

To prevent them from becoming bored, extremely bright children often need special education.

Another nonorganic factor believed to be widespread in the development of mental retardation is malnutrition. An estimated 300 million preschool children throughout the world have inadequate diets. Malnutrition is thought to be particularly harmful during the period of the brain's most rapid growth—in utero and in the first few months after birth. The evidence for the effects of malnutrition comes from a variety of sources. Much of it rests on animal studies demonstrating that the total number of neurons in the brain is permanently reduced if the creature suffers from malnutrition during periods of cell division (Davison & Dobbing, 1966). In addition, a study of human children at autopsy showed that children who had died from malnutrition had fewer than normal brain cells (Winick, Rosso, & Waterlow, 1970).

People whose retardation can be traced to organic causes are fairly evenly distributed throughout all socioeconomic, ethnic, and racial groups. Generally, those whose mental retardation is organic in origin fall into the categories below an IQ of 51—moderate, severe, and profound retardation. The greatest proportion of the mentally retarded, however, have an IQ above 51 and thus are considered only mildly retarded. Most of them show no indications of brain pathology, but typically are members of families in which the levels of intelligence and of socioeconomic status are low. These cultural-familial factors, many researchers believe, are responsible for mild retardation. Such home environments may not provide the early intellectual stimulation and encouragement thought necessary for normal mental growth. Children from such homes may also attend deficient schools.

The evidence for the cultural-familial view is correlational. Various studies have shown high correlations between mild retardation and homes of low socioeconomic levels where one or more parents or siblings have a subnormal IQ (Zigler, 1967). It may be that other environmental characteristics of poverty such as malnutrition—before and after birth—also contribute heavily to mild retardation. In any case, whether the causes are organic or cultural-familial or both, the majority of retarded children can achieve higher levels of intellectual functioning with appropriate training.

The Intellectually Gifted

The intellectually gifted sometimes face problems similar to those encountered by the mentally retarded. Like the mentally retarded, extremely bright children have been subject to popular bias and misunderstanding. Not too long ago, folk wisdom had it that "early ripe, early rot" and suggested that precocious children were prone to insanity and other severe problems. Such dire prophecies have not been borne out; nonetheless studies in recent years have shown that extremely bright children, like subnormal ones, may often need special education. They may become bored in conventional schools. Some studies indicate that gifted students account for up to 20 percent of all high-school dropouts (Hershey, 1976).

Concern about the gifted has resulted in several innovative educational programs. Several states now mandate special education programs for gifted students in public schools. These special programs usually consist of enrichment classes that meet once or twice a week, accelerated classes that cover traditional academic material faster than usual, or independent research projects or internships (Rice, 1980).

The task of identifying gifted students for special educational programs is not as simple as it seems. An exercise given to Arlington County teachers who are responsible for selecting gifted children demonstrates this difficulty. Teachers were asked to examine materials describing six prospects for programs for gifted students. The materials included teacher recommendations, IQ scores, family background, class performance, and descriptions of outside interests.

The teachers were allowed to choose only three cases for the gifted class. Actually, these materials were developed based on the backgrounds of extraordinary achievers. Typically, the teachers chose Isadore Duncan, Abraham Lincoln, and Senator Bill Bradley, a former Rhodes scholar and professional basketball player. But, at the same time, teachers typically rejected the materials describing Albert Einstein, who did not read until he was seven years old, and Thomas Edison, whose teachers thought he was not bright. Finally, Eleanor Roosevelt was frequently rejected because she was a withdrawn and troubled child.

Understanding of intellectually gifted children has benefited enormously from a long-term study launched in 1921 by Terman, who developed the Stanford-Binet IQ test. Terman and his coworkers selected 1528 California schoolchildren—857 boys and 671 girls—with IQs of 135 or higher for their study (Terman & Oden, 1947). Most of these subjects were between the ages of 8 and 12. For more than half a century since then, Terman and, after his death, other Stanford University researchers have kept track of this highly gifted group through periodic interviews and questionnaires—most recently in 1977 (Sears, 1977).

The data from the study have long since achieved Terman's original aim: to disprove the myth that exceptional intelligence is a handicap. For contemporary researchers, the results provide illumination, if not definitive answers, to a number of questions. What is the relationship between intelligence and later achievement? Does intelligence alone guarantee extraordinary accomplishment? Is there a correlation between IQ and creativity?

The group did extremely well in school, and the majority excelled in their careers. All but 11 finished high school, two thirds graduated from college, 97 received doctorates, 57 got medical degrees, and 92 earned law degrees. Careers ranged from letter carrier to brigadier general; there were a number of scientists and some corporation heads. Among the group was a leading writer of science fiction and an Academy Award-winning film director. In 1955, the group had an average income of $33,000, more than four times the national average of $8000.

At the same time, however, the group produced no towering geniuses, no Nobel Prize winners, "no Einsteins." Similarly, there is an absence of exceptional people in the creative arts—no poets, no great musicians, no painters. This suggests that although intelligence and creativity may overlap, they are not the same.

One important finding was that these bright people tended to produce bright offspring. The average IQ of their children was 133, although the range extended from a high of 200 to below 68, the upper limit of mental retardation. The high average cannot be attributed only to genetic factors, however, because the offspring typically were surrounded by environmental influences, such as the stimulation of high-IQ parents, that are known to be associated with above-normal intelligence.

Of particular interest in the Terman study is a comparison of career success among men within the group (Sears & Barbee, 1978). The criteria for job success included income, status as generally judged by society, and the respondent's self-assessment of whether he "had made use of his superior intelligence in his life work, both in his choice of vocation and in the attainment of a position of importance and responsibility in an area calling for a high degree of intellectual ability." By these criteria, the 100 most successful men were designated as the "A group," which included many university professors, lawyers, research scientists, physicians, and business executives. The 100 least successful men were designated as the "C group," which included only five professionals and mostly clerks, salesmen, and small businessmen.

The A group had originally scored only six points higher in IQ than had the C group, a difference so slight that it scarcely could account for the significant disparities in career success. An assessment of the backgrounds of the two groups, however, revealed several more important differences. For example, the As came from families in which the members were better educated and more stable. But the key difference appeared to lie in the need to achieve. Ratings by parents and teachers beginning when the subjects were still in elementary school showed that the one dimension that clearly distinguished As from Cs was "prudence and forethought, willpower, perseverance, and desire to excel." This theme was repeated in later ratings by parents, wives, and even the men themselves. As often singled out "persistence in working toward a goal" as the key factor in their success; Cs saw "lack of persistence" as responsible for their own lesser achievement.

Members of the A group also seemed happier than members of the C group. They were less concerned about making money (while making more). They were more likely to be satisfied with their careers and had more accurately predicted their vocation. They were less likely to report having personal problems such as overuse of alcohol. They were less likely to be divorced.

The Terman study thus appears to bear out other surveys suggesting that intelligence is only one factor in the achievement of a successful career. Other factors include family background, years of schooling completed, and early personality characteristics such as studiousness. But among those of virtually equal IQs, the most important factor seems to be a special need to achieve.

Intelligence in Perspective

Although intelligence is so highly valued in our society, its measurement so assiduously pursued, and its determinants so significant in the study of human behavior, it is important to keep intelligence and IQ scores in perspective for several reasons:

- Research increasingly suggests that intelligence is not a static, unalterable thing but a dynamic and still poorly understood process.
- While IQ scores are generally good at predicting academic performance, there appears to be less correlation with achievement in later life. It may be that motivation and interpersonal skills, such as sensitivity to others, which is sometimes called social intelligence, contribute more to successful performance in life than does a high IQ.
- No IQ test yet devised can measure all of the other dimensions, including common sense, intellectual independence, wit, and openness to experience, that are usually considered attributes of an intelligent person.
- Although intelligence and creativity obviously overlap, they are not the same; creative genius and even creativity in everyday life often require characteristics and processes that are seldom revealed in an IQ test.
- Finally, there is no evidence that a high IQ confers on its bearer two of the conditions that are prized even more than intelligence—wisdom and happiness.

Summary

1. The earliest theories of the nature of intelligence viewed it as a psychological structure that could be broken down into parts and analyzed. Charles Spearman proposed a "universal Unity of the intellect" which he labeled the "g" factor, or general mental facility. L. L. Thurstone divided intelligence into seven primary mental abilities: numerical ability, reasoning, verbal

fluency, spatial relations, perception, memory, and verbal comprehension. J. P. Guilford postulated a three-dimensional structure of intellect composed of contents, operations, and products. More recently, researchers have proposed an information processing view of intelligence. Robert J. Sternberg has proposed two levels in this approach: one level consists of the sequential steps— components—that a person proceeds through in solving a complex mental problem. The other level consists of metacomponents—the processes that organize the problem-solving components.

2. The first practical measure of intelligence was developed by the French psychologist, Alfred Binet. Binet established a level of performance for each age group; the results achieved by a child on the test constituted that child's mental age.

3. Lewis Terman of Stanford University revised the Binet test for American use. Mental age as shown on the Stanford-Binet was divided by chronological age and the resulting number was multiplied by 100, yielding an intelligence quotient, IQ. Modern versions of the Stanford-Binet test yield a deviation IQ, which reflects test performance relative to others of the same chronological age.

4. Two other intelligence tests in use today are the Wechsler Adult Intelligence Scale (WAIS) for people 17 and older and the Wechsler Intelligence Scale for Children (WISC). The Wechsler scales test nonverbal as well as verbal abilities.

5. All intelligence tests are judged by the criteria of reliability, validity, and standardization. If a test is reliable, test scores will be consistent over time; if it is valid, the test measures what it is intended to measure; if the test has been adequately standardized, one's scores are measured against those of a similar group of people.

6. Intelligence tests have historically been designed as aptitude tests, which predict later performance. Achievement tests, on the other hand, are designed to measure the degree to which a particular skill or body of knowledge has already been mastered.

7. Intelligence tests have been criticized because traditionally they have tested achievement as well as aptitude, because they have been culturally biased (improperly standardized), and because of the pigeonhole effect—that is, the failure to take varying rates of intellectual growth into account.

8. The controversy over the determinants of intelligence is linked to the nature-nurture debate; that is, whether intelligence is determined by our individual genetic makeups or whether it is the product of environmental influences such as education, family life, social class, and culture. Studies correlating the IQs of people with varying genetic relationships show a definite role for heredity in intelligence. The concept of heritability, however, is a measure of relative variation that attempts to tell us how much of the variation in a particular trait for a particular population is due to genetic factors or to environmental factors at any given time. Most likely, heredity is responsible for the possible range of a person's intelligence; environment determines how well the hereditary potential is realized.

9. Intelligence quotients for most people remain relatively stable, particularly after age 7; however, the ability to master a variety of intellectual tasks has a growth curve of its own, and peaks around age 40. The decline of intellectual abilities in later years varies widely among individuals.

10. In the wide spectrum of intelligence, most people fall around the middle of the scale. About 3 percent of the American population have IQs below 68 and are considered mentally retarded; about 1 percent have IQs above 140 and are considered mentally gifted.

11. Mental retardation has been classified as mild (IQ 52 to 67 on the Stanford-Binet); moderate (IQ 36 to 51); severe (IQ 20 to 35); and profound (IQ below 20). In mild retardation, cultural-familial factors are believed to play

the major role. The more serious forms of retardation—moderate, severe, and profound—are generally caused by organic factors such as chromosomal abnormalities or brain trauma. Organic causes of retardation are grouped into three categories—genetic, infectious, and traumatic. Malnutrition is also believed to play a role in retardation.

12. Data from research, such as the long-term Terman study, disprove the old myth that exceptional intelligence is a handicap. In general, people with superior intellects do well in school, excel in their careers, are happier than those with low IQs, and have bright offspring. There does not, interestingly enough, appear to be a high correlation between intelligence and creativity.

FOCUS: Identical twins reared apart are considered to be ideal subjects for psychological research investigating the separate contributions of nature and nurture to intelligence and other personality traits. One current project, headed by Thomas Bouchard, involves exposing identical twins to an intensive battery of psychological tests and interviews. So far, the research shows that many of the twins have similar medical and personal histories, suggesting that genetic factors contribute significantly to particular patterns of behavior and health. Differences in other aspects of life-style such as religious orientation are attributed to environmental factors.

RESEARCH: In the early part of this century intelligence was generally regarded as a genetically determined and immutable trait. This view was challenged by Skeels' (1966) longitudinal study in which children, originally diagnosed as being mentally retarded, showed considerable improvement in mental and emotional development after being transferred from an overcrowded and understaffed orphanage to a mental institution with a homelike environment. A comparable group of children who remained in the orphanage showed no such improvement. Today psychologists generally agree that early environmental influences play a crucial role in the shaping of intelligence.

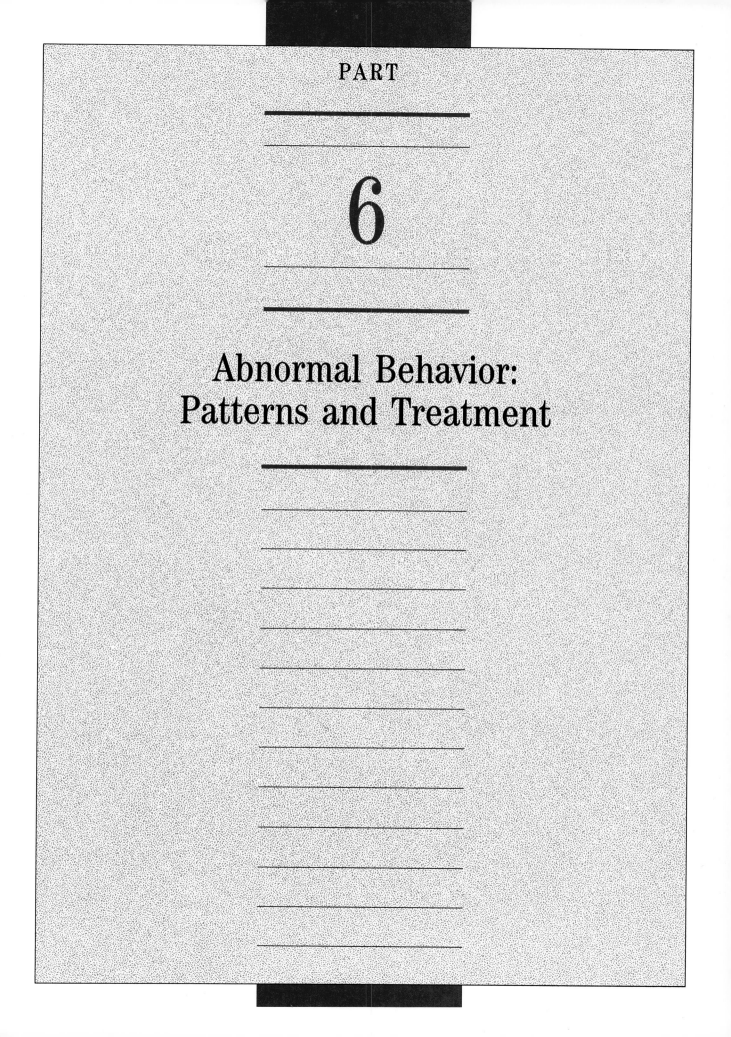

PART

6

Abnormal Behavior:
Patterns and Treatment

CHAPTER

14

Abnormal Behavior

- A middle-aged accountant finds it increasingly difficult to get to work on time because of the elaborate grooming he feels is necessary before he is ready for work. His preparations often start at three or four o'clock in the morning, with slow and meticulous washing, shaving, and dressing. Often he is unable to leave his apartment before four o'clock in the afternoon because he has not yet finished preparing himself for the day.
- William F., having just lost his job, decides to open a local automobile dealership. He has taken out loans from four different banks to do so, using his house as collateral in each case. Despite his recent job loss he seems full of enthusiasm and excitement. On his first day as an auto dealer he decides to open a nationwide network of car dealerships.
- Alice suffers from dramatic mood swings. At times she can barely contain her energy and enthusiasm. She needs little sleep and begins one new project after another. At other times she feels listless, loses her appetite, and bursts into tears at the smallest frustration. Her co-workers have begun to express concern for her and wonder what is wrong.

These examples of psychological distress reflect the range of human behavioral problems that are the subject of this chapter. Every year approximately 7 million Americans receive treatment for some form of psychological distress in public or private mental health facilities. The social and emotional costs of psychological disturbance are enormous, both in terms of personal distress and the loss of creativity and productivity to society at large.

There is no single definition of **abnormal behavior,** but most definitions fall into one or more categories. One definition of abnormal behavior focuses on *behavior that is disturbing to other people.* This definition suggests that an individual's behavior is literally "away from the norm" because it violates the values and expectations of others. It is important to note that this particular definition of abnormal behavior depends heavily on the cultural norms and rules of the local setting. What is seen as abnormal in central Africa may be highly appropriate in Wisconsin or Delaware.

A second definition of abnormal behavior suggests that **subjective distress** be the criterion because most forms of abnormal behavior involve at least some degree of subjective distress, including feelings of sadness, fear, or loss of control. As one of our examples above suggests, however, not all forms of abnormal behavior necessarily involve distress. Indeed, a person with some forms of mood disorder may feel temporarily elated.

A third definition emphasizes the *psychological handicaps* that interfere with or diminish an individual's ability to cope with the demands and stresses of life. Some severe forms of abnormal behavior—schizophrenia, for example—can be extremely disabling. However, other forms of abnormal behavior may exist in an individual's life with no serious debilitation.

As these three definitions of abnormal behavior indicate, it is very difficult to establish a sharp dividing line between what may be considered normal and abnormal behavior. Rather, behavior seems to range along a continuum, with most people clustering around the central point or average, and the rest spreading out toward the two extremes. From time to time, most people shift somewhat along the continuum. For example, some major change in a person's life, such as a divorce or a business failure, may temporarily result in severe depression or excessive drinking, until the person gets over the experience and begins to cope with the problem.

In fact, although patients in mental hospitals and clinics are often depicted as engaging in all types of unusual behavior—ranting and raving, crouching in corners, or posing as God—most hospitalized people are usually aware of what is going on around them, and only a small percentage continuously exhibit behavior that might be called bizarre.

The criteria for defining abnormal behavior help us to understand the multidimensional nature of behavior disorders, but they tell us little about the origin of abnormal behavior. Various investigators have offered theories to account for the causes of abnormality, and we shall examine several. One group of investigators searches for the causes of abnormal behavior in the social environment. A second group of investigators focuses on individual biology and searches for the causes of abnormal behavior in genetic, physiological, or biochemical makeup. Still other theoretical approaches concentrate on the psychological makeup of the person—human needs and conflicts and their ultimate translation into maladaptive behavior.

We will examine the historical evolution of these three approaches to understanding abnormal behavior and consider modern theories that have evolved from them. We will then examine different types of abnormal behavior, concentrating on psychological disorders associated with anxiety, with mood disorders, with major problems of perception and thought, such as schizophrenia, with personality disorders, and with substance abuse.

Theoretical Approaches to Abnormal Behavior

The study of abnormal behavior, perhaps more than any other area of psychology, requires an understanding of history. From the earliest times, humans have sought to explain and cure abnormal behavior. Three major ways of examining behavior have emerged in the modern era: the environmental, psychological, and biological viewpoints. Each must be viewed against the background of its origins.

Environmental Approaches to Abnormal Behavior

The first theoretical approach focuses on the social environment as the major cause—and potential cure—of abnormal behavior. The roots of this viewpoint can be traced to the emerging humanism of the Renaissance and the social and political awareness stimulated by the eighteenth-century French and American revolutions.

In Europe especially, the environmental approach took the form of revulsion against the harsh treatment of the mentally ill. Along with such "undesirables" as criminals and debtors, the insane were relegated to filthy and appalling prisons, as lepers had been in earlier centuries. Reformers in France and England, convinced that a more benign environment could alleviate madness, established mental hospitals where inmates could be treated with some kindness and concern.

In America, there was a widespread conviction that the rapid social change of the Jacksonian era was to blame for insanity and other deviant behavior. Social mobility, inflation, politics—all were seen as root causes. As a result, in 1829 reformers began placing severely disturbed people in asylums.

Scientists and physicians set out to create in the asylums an environment that would reduce tensions and stresses. David Rothman (1971) sums up the asylum solution in this way: "Create a different kind of environment, which methodically corrected the deficiencies of the community, and a cure for insanity was at hand."

The asylum program came to be known as a "moral treatment," and its heart was disciplined routine. To ensure the peace and serenity believed essential for curing the insane, asylums were placed in rural areas. The daily sched-

Reformers had hoped to cure the insane by placing them in asylums in which the environment was carefully ordered. However, achieving order among the inmates was not so readily obtained, as evidenced in this woodcut of Blackwell's Island, a nineteenth-century asylum in New York.

ule and the physical environment were both carefully arranged and ordered. Such institutions, it was believed, provided models of what society itself should be like.

Two perspectives on the nature and causes of abnormal behavior grew out of concerns with the social environment. The first, the **social perspective** argues that it is how others view deviant behavior and how they react to odd or puzzling behavior that is crucial. Thus, the social perspective is more concerned with perceptions of abnormal behavior than with the behavior itself.

The second view is the modern **learning perspective.** From the learning perspective, behavior—normal and abnormal—represents responses to stimuli and events in the environment. More specifically, the contingency between behavior and stimuli in the environment is critical. Both the social and learning perspectives bear closer examination.

The Social Perspective

Many advocates of the social perspective—for example Erving Goffman (1961) and Thomas Scheff (1966, 1984)—were trained in sociology. They emphasize that "abnormal" people are labeled as such because they violate certain norms, or socially agreed-upon rules of behavior. If no other likely explanation for puzzling behavior exists, it may be viewed as mental illness. Indeed, Thomas Szasz, a psychiatrist, has gone so far as to label mental illness a myth (1976) and has emphasized the disenfranchisement from society such a label produces. Furthermore, this label tends to alter the behavior of others toward the persons in question. They are cast in the role of "mental patients," and we tend to see their behaviors as consistent with that label. People so labeled, seeing changes in attitudes of others, may in turn act in even more puzzling ways. The social perspective sees this process of interactions as producing what they call a deviation amplifying system. This system finally leads to hospitalization. Once a person is hospitalized, deviation is further amplified.

This new role—that of "mental patient"—is illustrated in a study conducted by D. L. Rosenhan (1973). To find out whether the sane could be distinguished from the insane, Rosenhan contrived an elaborate hoax. He enlisted the aid of eight friends and collaborators—three psychologists, a pediatrician, a painter, and a homemaker—and asked them to become patients in mental hospitals.

These pseudopatients falsified their names and occupations and reported imaginary symptoms to the examining physician. Each was promptly admitted to the hospital. Moreover, all but one were diagnosed as suffering from schizophrenia.

This experiment confirmed Rosehan's suspicion that it may not always be possible to distinguish the sane from the insane. What happened to the pseudopatients after they were admitted to the hospital is also fascinating. When the pseudopatients exhibited perfectly normal behavior, such as asking the psychiatrists when they would be eligible for privileges, they were treated as disturbed people. "Good morning, Dave" was the nonreply of one doctor. "How are you today?" The doctor then moved away without waiting for a response. It is understandable how, in such circumstances, people labeled as mental patients eventually tend to accept their roles, question their own stability and, most significantly, behave in accord with the role.

The Learning Perspective

This recently developed approach to the study of abnormal behavior seeks to understand it through the principles of learning. According to this viewpoint, abnormal behavior is learned and maintained—and can be eliminated—largely through processes of conditioning.

Two of these processes, classical conditioning and instrumental (or operant) conditioning, were discussed at length in chapter 7. Recall that classical conditioning was first described by Ivan Pavlov. Using his methods, followers succeeded in classically conditioning laboratory animals to show that they exhibited various forms of abnormal behavior, which some scientists labeled "experimental neuroses." We also saw how the American psychologist John Watson conditioned abnormal behavior in a human being. By pairing a white rat with a frightening noise, Watson taught 11-month-old Albert to be afraid not only of white rats but also of other white furry objects (Watson & Rayner, 1920).

The second process used to explain how abnormal behavior is learned and maintained, instrumental conditioning, was developed by psychologists Edward Thorndike (1932) and B. F. Skinner (1938). Recall that, in this form of conditioning, positive or negative reinforcements greatly affect the likelihood that will occur again.

An example of the learning of abnormal behavior through instrumental conditioning has been provided by using the technique of behavior shaping, the contingent use of reinforcements to elicit gradually a particular pattern of behavior (Haughton & Ayllon, 1965). The subject of the study was a 54-year-old mental patient. The aim was to show that it was possible to shape her behavior so that she would do things that would appear senseless or peculiar—in this case to stand upright holding a broom.

The experiment began by depriving the woman of cigarettes. Next, whenever the patient was given a broom to hold, a staff member would approach, hand her a cigarette, and leave without explanation. As might be predicted, the woman began spending much of her time standing upright and holding the broom. Having succeeded in shaping this particular behavior, the investigators called in two psychiatrists. Without explaining how the patient had acquired the broom-holding behavior, they asked the psychiatrists to interpret her behavior. The psychiatrists saw it as a "magical act" in which the broom might represent either a "phallic symbol" or the "scepter of an omnipotent queen."

Clearly, this type of experiment raises fundamental ethical questions with regard to the conduct of mental health professionals in clinical settings and the adequacy of patient care. Ethical issues can never be artificially separated from the research enterprise and must remain paramount in the mind of the investigator. Nevertheless, from a learning perspective this experiment demonstrated that abnormal behavior could be produced in an unnatural setting by the rear-

Psychiatrist Thomas Szasz believes that labeling can alter the behavior of others toward the person in question.

rangement of external contingencies. The question was then raised about the extent to which similar learning mechanisms might be responsible for the development of abnormal behavior in natural settings.

The idea that the social environment is the source of stimuli and reinforcements for abnormal behavior—as well as normal behavior—is at the heart of the learning perspective. In considering various forms of abnormal behavior, we will encounter learning formulations that explain the development of psychological disorders.

Psychological Approaches to Abnormal Behavior

A second approach to the study of abnormal behavior—the psychological approach—emerged at the beginning of the twentieth century, but stemmed in part from the ideas of Anton Mesmer, a physician and mystic who worked in Austria more than 100 years earlier. As the word "mesmerize" suggests, Mesmer was the father of hypnosis. Mesmer believed that physical disease as well as some forms of irrational behavior resulted from an imbalance of magnetic fluids in the human body.

Although Mesmer was attacked as a fraud, he did manage to relieve a variety of disorders, albeit temporarily, including hysterical paralysis and psychosomatic ailments. His use of hypnotic suggestion helped to promote the psychological approach to human behavior. Mesmer's work fostered the idea that thinking could be both conscious and unconscious and suggested that one person could help another person remedy irrational behavior (Mesmer & Bloch, 1980).

The Dynamic Perspective

Others took up the use of hypnotic suggestion, but it was a young Viennese physician, Sigmund Freud, who formulated a uniquely psychological view of abnormal behavior. At first, Freud worked with another Viennese physician, Josef Breuer, who had developed a treatment that he called the "cathartic method," in which repressed emotional tension could be released (Freud, 1905/1953; Freud & Breuer, 1895/1966). Breuer hypnotized his patients, who were then encouraged to discuss their concerns while under hypnosis.

Freud was struck by the fact that much of what patients said under hypnosis was not ordinarily accessible to them. He called such thoughts "unconscious" and theorized that they were significant determinants of the patients' behavior, even though the patients were not ordinarily aware of them (Freud, 1905/1953; Freud & Breuer, 1895/1966).

Freud believed that irrational behavior resulted largely from internal conflicts between sexual or aggressive impulses and the demands of conscience and reality. It is important to grasp how Freud's point of view related to the nineteenth-century Victorian era in which it developed. The Victorian era emphasized tight control over personal impulses. Housewives went so far as to drape curtains over the legs of their pianos so as not to offend the moral sensibilities of guests! No wonder that Freud's patients revealed conflicts between natural sexual impulses and the prevailing prudish social standards.

Because it has been a major source of ideas in abnormal psychology, we will examine the dynamic perspective more closely, confining ourselves primarily to concepts intended to explain abnormal behavior. As we saw in chapter 12, much of the rest of the dynamic point of view focuses on personality development.

To Freud, behavior resulted from the dynamic interplay among three major mental structures, which he called the id, the ego, and the superego. Of course, these terms represented domains of thought and motivation rather than actual structures (Freud, 1933).

Color Plate 14.3

The Genain Quadruplets

The Genain quadruplets, born in the early 1930s, represented an important opportunity for researchers to study the role of genetic factors in schizophrenia. Genetically identical, each of the quadruplets became schizophrenic before the age of 25. Though genetic factors obviously played a major role in the development of the quadruplets' schizophrenia, the situation is not entirely cut-and-dried; it would appear that environmental factors played a role, too, in terms of the actual clinical picture and prognosis for each of the quads. Over the years, the Genains have been treated and studied, and their fascinating story is told in David Rosenthal's 1963 book entitled The Genain Quadruplets. *The Genains—Nora, Hester, Iris, and Myra—are shown here as infants and during a celebration of their 51st birthday. Also shown are PET scans of their brains.*

Nora

Iris

Hester

Myra

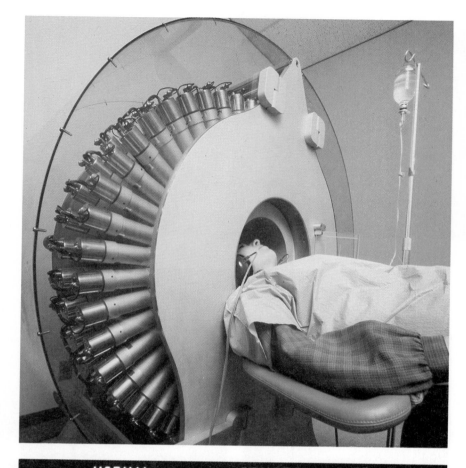

PET scans reveal metabolic activity in the brain by tracing the rate at which radioactive glucose, injected into the patient, is consumed in the brain. The rate of consumption is an indication of brain activity. Shown at left is a patient undergoing a PET scan, and below a sampling of PET scans of the brains of normal, schizophrenic, and depressed individuals. The red line through the outline of the head shows the actual section of the brain represented in the scans. Blue and green indicate low to moderate activity; yellow and red indicate moderate to high activity. It is important to note here that, fascinating as these scans of the brain may be, "researchers cannot yet make a causal connection between varying levels of brain activity and specific disorders" (Coleman, Butcher, & Carson, 1984).

Color Plate 14.2

Scanning the Brain

Two relatively new techniques for studying brain abnormalities are the CAT scan (computerized axial tomography) and the PET scan (positron emission tomography). Pictured at right is CAT scanning equipment (note the patient far left). During a CAT scan, a series of X-ray-like pictures are taken of the brain from a number of different angles; then a computer generates a composite picture of the brain structures. Lower left is a CAT scan of a normal brain and lower right, that of the brain of a person afflicted with senile dementia, a gradual deterioration of mental functioning. The dark blue areas of the afflicted brain indicate an enlargement of the ventricles (the large, hollow spaces in the brain) due to the degeneration of brain tissue.

The persistent actions of obsessive-compulsive behavior are illustrated in the paintings above. Both, done by a patient with obsessive-compulsive tendencies, are almost exactly the same in size, type of brush stroke used, and the seeming need to cover the entire surface. In an effort to break the patient from his rigid behavior, the therapist gave him a piece of paper twice as large as the ones on which he'd done the previous paintings. The patient, however, folded the paper to the same size as the previous paintings and proceeded to do the painting shown (unfolded) on the right—in the same size and style as his previous paintings.

The *id* represented the primitive biological drives of the organism. "A caldron of seething excitement," according to Freud (1933), the id had a single aim: to release its biological energy in either aggressive or erotic ways. Its self-seeking mechanisms are thus governed by the **pleasure principle.**

The *ego* was seen by Freud as a kind of executive judging the feasibility and appropriateness of our actions. While the id operates by the pleasure principle, the ego operates by the **reality principle.** It assesses the realism of engaging in aggressive or sexual acts demanded by the id.

The *superego* greatly resembles the familiar notion of "conscience." It controls and judges our actions as we plan or fantasize them and as we carry them out. The standards of the superego are laid down during the childhood socialization process of learning that certain acts and impulses are "good" and others "bad." The superego is also the home of the person's ideals and aspirations acquired from the parents.

It is inevitable that these three mental structures come into conflict. This conflict, said Freud, determines much of our behavior. A common example would be the conflict between the sexual demands of the id and the moral strictures of the superego. Such a conflict, if not readily resolved, produces tension and anxiety. To reduce the tension and anxiety, the ego brings into play a whole range of automatic and unconscious responses called **defense mechanisms.** The most important of these defense mechanisms is **repression.** In repression, unpleasant thoughts or dangerous impulses or wishes are barred from conscious awareness. For example, wishes arising from the id may signal to a married woman that another man is highly attractive. Since these reactions conflict with her superego—her moral notions about marital fidelity—she represses them into her unconscious. Freud found clues to repression in dreams and in memory lapses about certain names or events.

In addition to repression, Freud described a number of other defense mechanisms. They include:

- **Projection**—the attribution of personally unacceptable wishes to others. The married woman mentioned above might project her own sexual desires and impulses onto other women by accusing them of having "dirty thoughts."
- **Reaction formation**—the expression of conscious attitudes that are the opposite of an internal wish or impulse. It often takes the form of an intense and often exaggerated reaction to a seemingly commonplace circumstance. The woman's violent reaction to adulterous relationships, for example, might indicate a repressed attraction to men other than her husband.
- **Displacement**—the shifting of an impulse or wish directed at one person onto a substitute person or object deemed more acceptable. The woman directs her attentions to her brother, for example, instead of expressing her attraction to the other man.

Although defense mechanisms may seem irrational at first glance, they have an internal logic of their own. Defensive actions represent unconscious strategies whereby id impulses are permitted partial discharge or gratification at some expense to the actor's reality testing.

All of us have experienced them, but only when they begin to interfere with our functioning do they become a source of concern. In that event, understanding defense mechanisms may provide clues about the underlying conflict from which one suffers.

The idea that conflicting impulses can produce anxiety and that abnormal behavior may actually be a defense mechanism against that anxiety is at the center of the psychodynamic perspective on abnormal behavior. Later in the chapter the psychodynamic view will be discussed again in relationship to anxiety disorders.

Emil Kraepelin, through his classification efforts, helped turn the study of abnormal behavior into a medical discipline.

A third approach to studying abnormal behavior focuses on physiology. The nineteenth century ushered in a new age of technology and with it the conviction that science could solve problems of human behavior.

Medical scientists were beginning to understand the origins of many infectious diseases. Louis Pasteur had demonstratead that disease could be produced by bacteria, and there was a growing belief that microorganisms caused virtually everything that went wrong with people—even madness. This belief was strengthened by the observation that three of the most common diseases of the time—syphilis, tuberculosis, and typhus—sometimes produced irrational behavior in victims. The brain disease associated with syphilis is called general paresis, and the century-long chronicle of the discovery and successful treatment of this disease gave medical science enhanced credibility as an authority in the study of abnormal behavior.

At the same time, **neurology**—the study of the brain and nervous system—was becoming an important medical specialty. Physicians like Paul Broca (1861/1960), who discovered the speech area of the brain, were localizing specific behavioral functions in the brain.

Progress in neurology and in the general treatment of disease gave birth to a new specialized branch of medicine, **psychiatry.** Early psychiatry's approach to abnormal behavior was typified by the thinking of Emil Kraepelin. Kraepelin categorized and classified abnormal behavior in great detail so that it could be described in terms of diseases associated with symptoms (Kraepelin, 1896). Thus, he helped transform the study of abnormal behavior—once the province of witch doctors and magistrates—into a medical discipline.

A tradition of dealing with some forms of abnormal behavior as medical illnesses is reflected in our language, institutions, and ways of thinking. The disease model conceptualizes mental disorders as analogous to physical disease. Abnormal behavior is viewed as symptomatic of an underlying pathological condition, much as a germ causes a physical ailment. This perspective, if applied in its strictest sense, implies that all mental illness is a consequence of physical dysfunction. As noted above, this model has exercised a profound influence on the manner in which mental health professionals describe their activities; mental patients are *diagnosed,* given a *prognosis,* given various *treatments,* and expected to be *cured.* We must still explore the extent to which the origins of some types of abnormal behavior are in fact biological.

Evidence that some forms of abnormal behavior are at least partly organic in origin is accumulating rapidly. The **diathesis-stress model** (Zubin & Spring, 1977; Price & Lynn, 1981) seems to explain the origins of some mood disorders as well as some severe disorders of perception and thought. In general, this model suggests that some people may possess higher levels of vulnerability to stress and that this vulnerability is at least partly determined by genetic factors. Thus, when confronted by stressful events—the loss of a job or a loved one—people so predisposed are more likely to develop a behavior disorder than are people who are not so predisposed.

Scientists look for evidence to support this viewpoint in two areas. First, they may attempt to demonstrate that people who develop behavior disorders are more genetically similar to each other than to those who do not develop the disorders. If this can be demonstrated, then the case for genetic origins of behavior disorders is strengthened. Second, because any genetic disorder must express itself through biochemical pathways before manifesting itself as abnormal behavior, scientists may look for biochemical differences between normal and disturbed populations. Again, evidence that abnormal behavior is due to a disease process would be far from unequivocal, but it would strengthen the case.

Diagnosis and Classification of Abnormal Behavior

Classification has always been an important part of a developing science. The periodic table in chemistry, for example, is revised as new elements are discovered. Much of our understanding of evolutionary theory would not be possible without reliable classification of various species of animals and plants.

Psychologists studying abnormal behavior are still in the early stages of developing a classification system of mental disorders. The *Diagnostic and Statistical Manual of Mental Disorders* (DSM-III), published by the American Psychiatric Association, is in its third edition (1980). This latest version of the diagnostic system represents an attempt to provide reliable descriptions of patterns of abnormal behavior. In developing it, the framers attempted to include common disorders as well as the more unusual and severe forms of abnormal behavior (see Table 14.1).

Blashfield (1984) suggests that the DSM-III reflects four major innovations in developing a diagnostic classification system for abnormal behavior. First, in an attempt to increase comprehensiveness, the diagnostic categories have been greatly expanded. Critics of DSM-III have been concerned that this inclusive strategy increases the danger of labeling and stigmatizing people who have relatively mild difficulties as "abnormal." As we saw in discussing the social perspective on abnormal behavior, there is some evidence that such labeling can have negative effects for the individual.

Second, DSM-III urges clinicians not only to identify the major pattern of abnormal behaviors under consideration but also to classify individuals on other dimensions termed *axes*. Axis I is the primary mental disorder present. Axis II is reserved for personality disorders that may coexist along with an Axis I problem. Physical disorders and symptoms, the severity of psychosocial stressors, and the patient's highest level of adaptive functioning within the past year are coded on Axes III, IV, and V, respectively.

This second innovation, *multiaxial classification,* has the advantage of providing much more information about the individual, which can be useful in planning treatment. Furthermore, collecting information about personality characteristics and medical and psychosocial factors, as well as major psychological disorders, broadens the potential arena for research into the relationships among these domains. However, some of the axes, such as that estimating the severity of stressors, are poorly defined, and thus are likely to be of little value.

Third, DSM-III requires *specific diagnostic criteria* be met before a person can receive a diagnosis. For example, the criteria for diagnosis of a manic episode include the following: (1) distinct mood elevation; (2) duration of at least a week; and (3) at least three of the following symptoms: increases in activity, talkativeness, racing thoughts, inflated self-esteem, sleeplessness, inability to attend, and activities such as buying sprees, sexual indiscretions, or foolish business investments.

These specific criteria will greatly increase the chances of diagnostic agreement in a specific case. Thus, the reliability of the system is much improved. Unfortunately, however, the criteria were chosen intuitively by groups of expert clinicians rather than empirically on the basis of statistical analyses of symptoms associated with various diagnoses. Thus, the value of these criteria in discriminating among different diagnostic groups remains unclear (Blashfield, 1984).

Finally, the DSM-III contains a great deal of additional information about each disorder, including age of onset, course of the disorder, prevalence in the general population, sex ratio, and family patterns, if any. This provides a much fuller description of each diagnostic category, but the source of much of the information is not documented in DSM-III, leaving both the source and the validity uncertain.

The dangers of labeling are evident in the story of the man shown here. Born in a mental hospital to parents with mental problems, Jack Smith was assumed to be mentally retarded. It was not until 1976, when Mr. Smith was 54 years old, that a judge declared him not mentally ill or dangerous. Unfortunately, by that time, Mr Smith was considered "so impaired that it would be unwise to put him out on the streets" (New York Times, March 11, 1979, p. 26). He was placed in a nursing home.

Table 14.1 MAJOR DIAGNOSTIC CATEGORIES OF DSM-III

Disorders of Infancy, Childhood, and Adolescence
Includes mental retardation, problems of attention and conduct, anxiety disorders, eating disorders, and problems of language development.

Organic Disorders
Psychological or behavioral abnormalities associated with temporary or permanent dysfunction of the brain. May be due to diseases of aging, intoxication, or withdrawal from drugs or alcohol.

Substance Use Disorders
Behavioral changes associated with more or less regular use of substances that affect the central nervous system. Behavioral changes include impairment in social or occupational functioning, inability to stop taking the substance, or withdrawal symptoms.

Schizophrenic Disorders
Severe disorders involving delusions, hallucinations, incoherent speech, deterioration in role functioning, social withdrawal, and markedly peculiar behavior.

Affective Disorders
Disturbance of mood or emotion that generally involves depression or elation. May involve either bipolar disorders with shifting cycles of depression and elation, or episodes of major depression.

Anxiety Disorders
Anxiety is the predominant disturbance either when confronting a specific feared object or situation, or in a more generalized anxiety or panic disorder.

Somatoform Disorders
Physical symptoms such as pain, paralysis, or deafness that suggest a physical disorder, but for which there are no demonstrable organic findings. There is also strong evidence that psychological factors or conflicts are involved.

Dissociative Disorders
Sudden temporary alteration of consciousness, identity, or motor behavior. May involve amnesia, assumption of a new identity, or the existence of more than one personality within the individual.

Psychosexual Disorders
Includes gender identity disorders, sexual arousal by non-normative objects or situations, and sexual dysfunctions characterized by inhibitions in sexual desire or the sexual response cycle.

Factitious Disorders
Physical or psychological symptoms that are under the voluntary control of the individual, but with no obvious immediate goal.

Disorders of Impulse Control
Failure to resist an impulse that is harmful to oneself or others. Included are pathological gambling, stealing, fire setting, or explosive aggression.

Adjustment Disorders
Maladaptation to an indentifiable stressor such as business, school, or marital problems. The reaction to the stressor is in excess of what would be normally expected for that stressor.

Source: From American Psychiatric Association Diagnostic and Statistical Manual of Mental Disorders, Third Edition. Washington, DC, copyright APA 1980. Used with permission.

Schact and Nathan (1977) have also raised concerns about how well the system is able to assess people from a wide range of ethnic groups. Different ethnic groups may differ with respect to what they regard as the range of acceptable behavior under a given set of circumstances, and thus confound efforts to establish uniform standards of "normality" across various categories of individuals. In fact, all classification systems face this difficulty, but since the DSM-III has gained wide acceptance in the diagnosis of abnormal behavior, this concern becomes all the more compelling.

Perhaps the most critical issue is the question of how such a newly developed diagnostic and classification system will actually be used in practice. If it is used extensively to make decisions about the treatment of individuals before it has been rigorously tested, then abuses are possible. If, on the other hand, it is treated tentatively as a research instrument, potential benefits are great.

In our discussion of various forms of abnormal behavior we will present disorders on a rough continuum of severity (Menninger, Pruyser, & Mayman, 1963). We will begin by discussing reactions to environmental stressors, then move to more severe disorders such as anxiety and personality disorders. Next, we will consider very severe disorders such as effective disorders and schizophrenia. To conclude our discussion, we will examine substance use disorders, a source of increasing social concern and scientific interest.

Phobias

Ethel H., a married woman of 26, suffered her first acute anxiety attack two years before she began therapy. She was arriving alone by plane from England after visiting her parents there. As she entered the high-ceilinged terminal—no one met her—she felt suddenly terrified in the huge, empty space. She began ''shaking like a leaf''; she could not get her bags through customs without constant help; she had the impulse to tell everyone around who she was in case she went mad. A porter, sensing her anxiety, expressed open concern and this comforted her. She managed the rest of the trip by train without mishap, but reached home exhausted and unnerved, certain that something awful was happening to her (Cameron, 1963).

''Ethel H.'' suffers from a disorder known as **agoraphobia**—the irrational fear of wide-open places such as halls, fields, parks, and beaches. Phobias are among the most common of the anxiety disorders. The most familiar are **acrophobia** (fear of high places), **claustrophobia** (fear of enclosed places), and **zoophobia** (fear of certain animals such as dogs, horses, and snakes). But there have been notable instances of less familiar phobias. The composer Frederic Chopin had an intense fear of being buried alive, and the German philosopher Arthur Schopenhauer was so afraid of razors that he singed his beard with a flame rather than shave it (Kisker, 1964).

Phobias focus on a specific object or situation—one that presents no real danger to the individual. In the presence of that object or situation, the person may sweat profusely, shake, experience shortness of breath, or attempt to hide. By some estimates, perhaps 8 percent of the population suffers from phobias of varying types and intensity (Agras, Sylvestar, & Oliveau, 1969).

The fear of animals is often common among children between the ages of 2 and 4.

Phobias are even more prevalent in children than in adults. Between the ages of 2 and 4, for example, fear of animals is fairly common. Between 4 and 6, fears of the dark and of imaginary creatures are more prevalent (see Figure 14.1).

But these fears usually decline with the approach of adulthood. As Isaac Marks (1977) notes, "Fears and rituals appear in children for little or no apparent reason and disappear just as mysteriously." What then accounts for the persistence into adulthood of certain fears among people?

The psychodynamic view lists four basic stages in the development of phobias. First, the person experiences a threatening impulse, typically of an aggressive or sexual nature. Second, the person cannot repress these impulses—that is, he or she cannot keep them from intruding into conscious awareness. Third, intruding impulses crystallize in the shape of fearful fantasies. In the fourth and final stage of phobia development the fear is displaced onto another object that can be avoided.

Thus, according to the psychodynamic view, phobias result when forbidden impulses and the fear associated with them become transformed and externalized. Moreover, the feared object and the actual fear are frequently linked by a symbolic relationship. The fear of heights—acrophobia—may symbolize the fear of falling in the esteem of others. The fear of closed places—claustrophobia—may symbolize the fear of being left alone with one's own dangerous impulses and fantasies.

Learning theorists have questioned the interpretations of psychodynamic theorists. They argue that phobias can be accounted for by the mechanisms of classical conditioning. They do not regard phobias as being indicative of some type of underlying disorder but see them as resulting from a purely coincidental pairing of an intense emotional state with the phobic stimulus. In the view of learning theorists, "any neutral stimulus, simple or complex, that happens to make an impact on an individual at about the time that a fear reaction is evoked acquires the ability to evoke fear subsequently" (Wolpe & Rachman, 1960). This explanation of phobias is similar to that invoked in little Albert, whom we have discussed previously. Albert, you will recall, acquired a conditioned fear of white rats and other white furry things after he was frightened by a loud noise while playing with a white rat.

A third view of phobias does not rule out the learning perspective but suggests that certain fears may have a biological basis. This reasoning begins by looking at the objects or situations that are the foci of phobias. Phobias

Figure 14.1

Relative frequencies of various fear responses among children. It is clear that some childhood fears decline as children get older; while others dramatically increase.

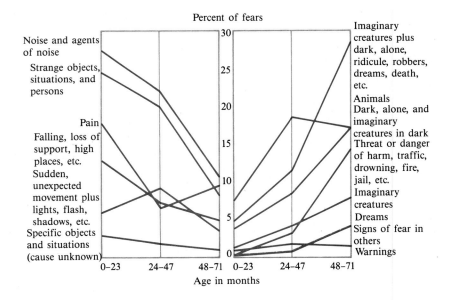

CHAPTER 14   ABNORMAL BEHAVIOR

involving naturally occurring pheonomena such as heights, snakes, or open spaces are relatively common; on the other hand, phobias involving manufactured objects, such as filing cabinets or plastic cups, are practically nonexistent. From the standpoint of evolution, fears of heights, snakes, or even open spaces make a great deal of sense—they have obvious survival value. Biological theorists describe them as **prepotent targets** for phobias.

Evidence in support of the idea of **biological preparedness** in the learning of phobias comes from a number of recent studies. For example, researchers found that skin-conductance measures of anxiety in response to pictures of snakes and spiders took longer to extinguish than did responses to pictures of nonprepotent targets such as houses (Ohman, Eriksson, Fredericksson, Hugdahl, & Oloffson, 1974).

In examining phobias we have considered three distinctively different views of the development of the disorder. The psychodynamic view sees phobias as fears associated with forbidden impulses; the learning perspective argues for a classical conditioning exploration; the biological preparedness approach suggests that the organism may be biologically predisposed to become fearful of some stimuli more easily than others.

It is unlikely that successful rock climbers experience acrophobia.

Obsessive-Compulsive Disorders

In DSM-III obsessive-compulsive disorders are classified as a form of anxiety state. The hallmark of obsessive-compulsive disorders is the experience of *persistent* thoughts, impulses, or actions. Often they are accompanied by a compulsion to actually engage in the behavior and a conflicting desire to resist it (Price & Lynn, 1981). These impulses or thoughts are usually frightening and seem irrational or senseless. Consider the following example:

"A housewife came for consultation because of sudden impulses to destroy objects which did not measure up to her perfectionistic standards. She tore up wallets and clothing which suddenly seemed to displease her because of some imperfection. If she did not give in to her impulses, she became nervous and jittery. It took her many hours to clean the three rooms of her apartment. Everything had to be in exactly the right place, and often she went to the extreme of measuring the distance between objects on the top of her dressing bureau to see that they were systematically arranged. Often, she had an impulse to soil objects after having cleaned them; for example, after having spent a great deal of time cleaning and polishing the surface of a mirror, she would feel compelled to spit on it and then clean it all over again" (Bucklew, 1960, p. 82).

As there are several other clinical phenomena that are easily confused with obsessive-compulsive disorders, some distinctions are needed.

Explanations for Obsessive-Compulsive Behavior

The psychodynamic interpretation of obsessive-compulsive disorders suggests that the symptomatic behavior is actually an attempt to control dangerous or unwanted impulses. In the following case, we see both id impulses and forces opposing them, called *countermeasures,* in open conflict with one another.

Frances T. was an unmarried typist, aged 24. She was trying to control erotic fantasies she could not repress. Her countermeasures put into practice, in a compulsive way, the advice often given to adolescents who are struggling with sex problems: "Think of something else!" Walking to work was an activity that permitted erotic fantasies to emerge easily. So each time Frances stepped on or off the curb at a corner, she made herself think of a different person. This kept her mind busy preparing for the next intersection. If she ran out of persons, she allowed herself to change streets and start the list over again (Cameron 1963, p. 383).

Some Vietnam veterans have experienced posttraumatic stress.

This case provides an excellent illustration of psychodynamic thinking about obsessive-compulsive disorders. Clearly, we can see the sexual fantasies as representations of id impulses in conflict with superego restrictions against acting out the impulses. Thus, from the psychodynamic viewpoint, Frances' symptoms—thinking of a new person in order to block out her sexual fantasies—are attempts to reduce anxiety. The anxiety, in turn, has been generated by the conflict between id and superego forces at war within her.

In attempting to understand how learning theorists might account for the development of compulsive behavior, a famous experiment by Skinner (1948) is of interest. Skinner placed hungry pigeons in an experimental cage in which food was automatically presented at regular five-second intervals. He observed the birds' behavior closely and discovered that in six out of eight cases the birds developed clearly defined ''ritualistic'' or ''superstitious'' behavior.

One bird, Skinner reported, began to turn counterclockwise in the cage, making two or three turns before receiving the food reinforcement. Another repeatedly thrust its head in one of the upper corners of the cage. These ritualistic responses seemed to develop because the bird happened to be executing a particular response as the food reward appeared. The response tended to be repeated and subsequently to be reinforced again. As Skinner notes, ''A few accidental connections between a ritual and a favorable consequence sufficed to set up and maintain the behavior, in spite of many unreinforced instances.''

Thus, the dynamic view of obsessive-compulsive behavior emphasizes the use of countermeasures to cope with forbidden id impulses, while the learning perspective sees the same behavior simply as the product of reinforcement (see Color Plate 14.1 following p. 460).

Adjustment Reactions: Responses to Traumatic Events

The disorders examined in this section frequently occur in response to a threatening or traumatic experience. The experience can be psychologically threatening, such as recent failure or rejection, or can be physically threatening, such as exposure to a natural disaster or combat. We will first consider the posttraumatic stress disorders, and then turn to the dissociative disorders.

Posttraumatic Stress Disorders

When people experience a psychologically traumatic event that is outside the range of usual human experience, such as natural disasters, war, or physical or sexual assault, they may develop a set of anxiety symptoms in response to the traumatic event. These could include reexperiencing the event, numbing of responsiveness, and withdrawal from the external world. The DSM-III lists these responses to traumatic events as **posttraumatic stress disorders.**

One famous case of posttraumatic stress disorder involved many inhabitants of Buffalo Creek, a community destroyed by flood. Erikson (1976) describes the terror the people experienced as the saw friends and relatives die. Even years later, many community members suffered residual effects of insomnia, night terrors, panic, and episodic depression that pervaded their lives and relationships.

Research on human responses to war and combat has provided some of the most detailed information about posttraumatic stress disorders. Williams (1983) has examined the research documenting posttraumatic stress responses among Vietnam combat veterans. She reports that a considerable body of research now indicates that some Vietnam veterans, particularly young men involved in heavy combat, are now experiencing delayed psychological difficulties. In a large-scale study, Egendorf (1981) surveyed Vietnam veterans and found that those who served in heavy combat continued to suffer from a variety of stress reaction symptoms, including memory trouble, loss of interest in the external world, thought confusion, nightmares, feelings of loss of control, and panic attacks.

One of the most striking characteristics of the posttraumatic stress disorder is the intrusive and recurrent recollection of the traumatic event, including flashbacks or involuntary reenactments of the event, night terrors and nightmares, and thoughts about the event that cannot be dispelled. At times, nightmares follow *environmental triggers* that remind the veterans of their war experience. Defazio et al. (1975) report that seeing a Vietnamese refugee on the street, or experiencing a sudden downpour of rain in the summer, or merely having that heat in one's home exceed 80 degrees can be sufficient triggers. Sometimes violent outbursts will follow these environmental stimuli. Williams (1983) describes one veteran who saw armed guards and thought he was back in Vietnam again. With no weapon to protect himself, he grabbed an innocent passerby for protection and forced the person into his home.

Another characteristic of posttraumatic stress disorder involves *intrusive memories* that cannot be dispelled. One veteran reports, ''Regardless of what I'd like to think about, it comes creeping back in. It's so hard to push back out again. It's old friends, their faces, the ambush, the screams, their faces . . .'' (Goodwin, 1980, p.2).

Dissociative Disorders

When a person encounters a severe stress or trauma, whether in the context of a natural disaster, combat, or individual trauma such as personal assault or child abuse, the development of a dissociative disorder is possible. According to DSM-III, the essential feature of **dissociative disorders** is a sudden and usually temporary change in the normal functions of consciousness, identity, or motor behavior (Price & Lynn, 1981). The person may develop a sudden inability to recall events or personal information, may engage in unexpected travel and assume a new identity, or may seem to develop two or more distinct personalities.

Amnesia
Joseph L. woke up one morning in what appeared to be a strange place. He had no memory of who he was or who was lying in the bed next to him. He appeared bewildered and confused. He was suffering from a dissociative disorder, *amnesia*.

A loss of memory with no organic involvement is one of the most common forms of dissociative disorder. Typically the person is unable to recall events or people associated with his or her own personal identity. Episodes of amnesia may last several hours or days, or, in some cases, weeks or months. When stopped by the police or interviewed by a mental health professional, the person may also appear to be dazed and mildly confused. Victims of dissociative reactions involving amnesia usually are experiencing intense emotional conflict or stress in their social, sexual, or economic life. They literally appear to be escaping from their distressing and conflict-ridden experience by forgetting who they are.

Fugue
Steve L. had just taken on a challenging new job in a law firm. It had not been going well. One day, he disappeared from his apartment and did not report to work. Two weeks later, his parents, having hired a private detective agency, located him working as a dishwasher in a restaurant in a nearby city. He had no recollection of his previous identity and had been drifting from job

William Mulligan, shown here while on trial for rape, was found by a psychiatrist to be an apparent sufferer of multiple personality.

to job. Steve L. was suffering from a dissociative disorder known as *fugue* (Price & Lynn, 1981).

In the case of fugue, which may be thought of as a special form of amnesia, victims not only forget their own identity and significant events in their lives, they actually flee their life circumstances. In many cases the person may move to another city some distance from home, and in some cases a secondary personality appears that has little or nothing to do with the person's previous life. The person may change his or her name and carry on an entirely new lifestyle for some period of time.

Multiple Personality

Christine is a loving three-year-old who likes to draw pictures of flowers and butterflies. David is a withdrawn little boy who bangs his head against the wall when upset. Adelena is a young lesbian. These distinct personalities, along with at least seven others, present a bizarre puzzle in a Columbus, Ohio, courtroom: they all exist within the same individual—William Milligan, 23, who was accused of rape. After a brief trial, the ten faces of Billy were found not guilty by reason of insanity (*Newsweek*, December 18, 1978, p. 106). William Milligan is an apparent sufferer of a dissociative disorder known as *multiple personality*.

Though rare, multiple personality is perhaps the best-known form of dissociative disorder. Multiple personality typically involves an alternation between two or more relatively well-defined personalities.

The most famous case of multiple personality was documented in Thigpen and Cleckley's book *The Three Faces of Eve* (1954). In this case, Thigpen and Cleckley reported different personalities associated with "Eve White," the original personality, "Eve Black," who typically was flamboyant and uninhibited, and a much more quiet, inhibited, and serious personality who appeared very different from the other two personalities.

Eve White began to suspect that something was going on when Eve Black would engage in carefree spending, promiscuity, and drinking, for which Eve White would later have to account. During her treatment, a third personality, "Jane," emerged. Jane was aware of the activities and personality of both Eve White and Eve Black. Finally, a fourth personality developed which seemed more stable than any of the three earlier versions.

More recently, the case of a twenty-two-year-old female given the pseudonym "Sybil" has been widely reported (Schreiber, 1975). During the course of her psychoanalytic treatment, a total of sixteen separate personalities were brought forth. These personalities differed significantly from each other in terms of talents, abilities, and interests, and ranged in age from infancy to middle age.

Affective Disorders: Depression and Mania

Clinical Descriptions

Imagine, for a moment that you are a clinical psychologist interviewing someone who has just come to you for help. The young man sitting across from you finds it hard to talk about what is bothering him. At first his conversation was animated, but now as he continues to talk his voice flattens into a monotone. His face loses its expression and becomes mask-like, suggesting the despair below the surface.

As the hour goes on, you begin to get a picture of his life. He maintains a pleasant, active facade only at great personal cost. Even the simplest activities, like dressing or driving to work, have become enormous acts of will. He reports difficulty sleeping, and, unaccountably, he wakes before dawn each day. Frequently at night this man withdraws into his apartment, refusing to answer the telephone. He lies listlessly for hours in front of the television set. Lately, he reports, he has begun to think about suicide.

As you listen to him you are struck by several things. His mood is obviously downcast and occasionally tears well up in his eyes. His thinking seems pessimistic and he frequently talks about himself in a disparaging way. The stains on his suit and his rumpled appearance suggest that he no longer cares as much as he once did about his appearance. The bagginess of his suit also suggests that he has lost a fair amount of weight recently. His world is gray and bleak, not very promising.

As you sit there, listening, you begin to notice your own mood. The world seems less exciting to you, too, now, and you feel somewhat depressed. As time goes on you begin to feel some mild irritation with this person. His apparent inability to "shake off" his feeling of sadness and his lack of response to your encouragements are frustrating and vaguely annoying.

You have just interviewed a person suffering from the typical symptoms of a moderately severe depression. Depression has been called the "common cold" of psychological disorders, and over a quarter of a million Americans are hospitalized for this disorder each year. Students, musicians, laborers, physicists, clerks, psychiatrists, and homemakers all are subject to depression. Lincoln and Hemingway, F. Scott Fitzgerald and Sylvia Plath all suffered from severe depression (Price & Lynn, 1981).

Major depression of the kind just described is a relatively common disorder with approximately 20 percent of all women and 10 percent of all men experiencing an episode at some time in their lives. According to DSM-III, major depressive episodes involve a sad and hopeless depressed mood and other symptoms, such as marked increases or decreases in appetite, sleep patterns, and level of activity, loss of interest in usual activities, fatigue, feelings of worthlessness, or recurrent thoughts of death or suicide.

However, affective disorders can also involve mood disturbances and may include intense episodes of elation called **manic episodes,** as well as alternating swings between elation and depression called **bipolar affective disorders.** Both are classified, by DSM-III as primary disturbances of mood. Of the two types of affective disorders, bipolar disorders are much rarer, with between one-half and one percent of the adult population having had a bipolar disorder (DSM-III).

Although it might seem that positive or elated moods would not be a problem to the person experiencing them, manic episodes can become extremely severe, as the following account by a forty-five-year-old homemaker suggests:

F. Scott Fitzgerald is known to have suffered from severe depression.

When I start going into a high, I no longer feel like an ordinary housewife. Instead I feel organized and accomplished and I begin to feel I am my most creative self. I can write poetry easily. I can compose melodies without effort. I can paint. My mind feels facile and absorbs everything. I have countless ideas about improving the conditions of mentally retarded children, of how a hospital for these children should be run, what they should have around them to keep them happy and calm and unafraid. I feel pleasure, a sense of euphoria or elation. I want it to last forever. I don't seem to need much sleep. I've lost weight and feel healthy and I like myself. I've just bought six new dresses, in fact, and they look quite good on me.

I feel sexy and men stare at me. Maybe I'll have an affair, or perhaps several. I feel capable of speaking and doing good in politics. I would like to help people with problems similar to mine so they won't feel hopeless.

It's wonderful when you feel like this. . . . The feeling of exhilaration—the high mood—makes me feel light and full of the joy of living. However, when I go beyond this stage, I become manic, and the creativeness becomes so magnified I begin to see things in my mind that aren't real.

I also experienced complete terror, as if it were actually happening, when I knew that an assassination scene was about to take place. I cowered under the covers and became a complete shaking wreck. As you know, I went into a manic psychosis at that point. My screams awakened my husband, who tried to reassure me that we were in our bedroom and everything was the same. There was nothing to be afraid of. Nevertheless, I was admitted to the hospital the next day (Fieve, 1975).

These examples illustrate some of the clinical characteristics of depression and elation. To get an even more detailed picture of the range of clinical behavior typically observed in mood disturbances see Table 14.2. The bipolar type of mood disorder is relatively rare, yet its dramatic mood swings make it the best-known type of mood disturbance. Joseph Mendels (1970) notes cases in which people have alternated between manic and depressive episodes every 24 hours for months. Such observations suggest that manic-depressive disorders may be affected by the body's biological rhythms.

Explanations for Affective Disorders

Because so many people suffer from depression at some time in their lives, research into its causes is an important area of study for psychologists. Although various explanations have been offered, no single one can account for this disorder.

Separation, Loss, and Change

Depression is often associated with stressful life events such as the death of a family member, the loss of a job, serious illness, or divorce. Not surprisingly, such stress often precipitates depression, which is separate and distinct from the normal sadness and grief that accompany these traumas. Depression apparently can occur in reaction to success as well as to trauma. The second man to walk on the moon, Colonel Edwin E. Aldrin, Jr., has written in his autobiography, *Return to Earth,* of the public adulation that attended his space flight—and of the progressive loss of his own confidence and self-esteem (Aldrin & Warga, 1973). Aldrin experienced crying spells after some speaking engagements and even developed physiological symptoms, including neck pains and numbed fingers. Aldrin recovered after undergoing psychotherapy and receiving antidepressant medication.

Both the dynamic and the learning perspectives emphasize the role of prior experiences in the development of depression. Research in this area has focused on the relationship between depression and losses (or other severe stresses) during early childhood. The psychodynamic hypothesis holds that losses or stresses might sensitize the person to depression in later life. For example, a child who lost a parent at an early age might find these early feelings of despair reactivated later when another relative dies.

There seems to be little question that separation from the mother can have an immediate and profound effect on offspring. Early emotional deprivation among humans has been studied most notably by Renee Spitz (1946, 1946), who observed the reactions of infants separated from their mothers between the ages of 6 and 12 months. These children typically displayed what has been called **anaclitic depression.** They cried continuously and showed apprehension, withdrawal, stupor, inability to sleep, weight loss, and retarded growth and development.

Table 14.2 MOOD SCALE USED TO MONITOR TREATMENT PROGRESS

(To be filled out in Metabolic Unit twice daily, before breakfast and before retiring, by both nurses [0–100] and patients [20–80]. Also adaptable to lithium clinic outpatients.)

100 Medical emergency. Wildly manic and psychotic; can't stop talking; incoherent, overactive, belligerent, c. elated. Not sleeping at all. At times delusional; hallucinating. May be either violent or paranoid.

90 Extreme elation so that patient can't rate self; in need of more medication and control. Completely uncooperative.

80 Severe elation. Should be admitted, or if in hospital usually wants to sign out of ward. Sleeping very little; hostile when crossed, loss of control. Needs medication.

70 Moderate elation. Overactivity and talkativeness; irritable and annoyed. Needs only four to six hours' sleep. Socially inappropriate; wants to control. Outpatient treatment has been advised by doctors.

60 Mildly elated mood and many ideas for new projects; occasionally mildly obtrusive. If creative, the energy is highly useful. Hyperperceptive. Feels wonderful, on top of the world. Increased sexual drive, wants to spend money and travel. Treatment may be contraindicated or not needed.

50 Mood is within normal range (45–55).

40 Mildly depressed mood, but noticeable lack of energy; chronic lack of optimism and pleasure. Feels slowed down. Treatment may not be desired, although it may be indicated. Decreased interest in sex. Decreased motivation.

30 Moderate depression. Loss of energy; disinterested in others; early weight, sleep, and appetite disturbance; able to function with effort but wants to stay in bed during day; doesn't want to go to work; feels life is not worthwhile. Little sexual interest. Outpatient treatment advised by doctors.

20 Severe depression. Takes care of daily routine but needs prodding and reminding; loss or gain of weight; sleep disorder is serious. Volunteers suicidal feelings; very withdrawn, may be paranoid.

10 Extreme depression. Actively suicidal, totally withdrawn or extremely agitated. Difficulty rating self on mood scale.

0 Medical emergency. Unable to eat or take medication; can't follow ward routine; delusional, suicidal. Stuporous. Stares into space, very little response on questioning. May require tube feeding.

Nurses' and psychiatrists' rating scale — covers 0–100.
Patient's self-rating scale — covers 20–80.

Source: "Manic-Depressive Mood Scale" from *Moodswing: The Third Revolution in Psychiatry* by Ronald R. Fieve, M.D. Text Copyright © 1975 by Ronald R. Fieve. Reprinted by permission of William Morrow & Company.

Perhaps the most famous research on separation, however, was that carried out by Harry and Margaret Harlow (1966) using rhesus monkeys. Working with monkeys instead of humans gave the researchers the opportunity to control closely a number of variables, including the length and type of separation and the age at which it occurred. The Harlows and their colleagues found that, once the mother-infant bond had been established, separation of the infants produced clinical effects in the infants very similar to the anaclitic depression reported by Spitz in human babies (Spitz, 1946, 1946). Moreover, separation of the young monkeys from peers of the same age also yielded reactions that resembled despair and depression (see Figure 14.2).

Research by the Harlow group suggests that separation not only causes immediate symptoms of depression in young rhesus monkeys but also seems to predispose them to later abnormal behavior (Harlow & Harlow, 1969). Monkeys separated from one another at three to four years of age show more abnormal behavior if they have been separated from their mothers during infancy. Separation thus seems to be important in depression both as a precipitating and as a predisposing factor.

Learned Helplessness

The learning perspective views depression as a state in which the person is not being rewarded for behaviors. Lacking reinforcement, the person shows fewer and fewer behaviors—or, in the terminology of learning, a low rate of response. For the causes of these symptoms, the learning theorists look to the individual's prior experiences.

In recent years, many such theorists have come to believe that depressed people suffer from a sense of helplessness that that they have learned. This hypothesis grows out of the experiments by Martin Seligman and his colleagues

Figure 14.2

Studies by the Harlows and their colleagues demonstrated that young monkeys reared alone exhibited reactions resembling despair and depression.

Table 14.3   PARALLELS BETWEEN LEARNED HELPLESSNESS AND DEPRESSION

	Learned Helplessness	Depression
Symptoms	Passivity Difficulty learning that responses produce relief Dissipates in time Lack of aggression Weight loss, appetite loss, social and sexual deficits Norepinephrine depletion and cholinergic activity Ulcers and stress	Passivity Negative cognitive set Time course Introjected hostility Weight loss, appetite loss, social and sexual deficits Norepinephrine depletion and cholinergic activity Ulcers (?) and stress Feelings of helplessness
Cause	Learning that responding and reinforcement are independent	Belief that responding is useless
Cure	Directive therapy: forced exposure to responses that produce reinforcement Electroconvulsive shock Time Anticholinergics; norepinephrine stimulants (?)	Recovery of belief that responding produces reinforcement Electroconvulsive shock Time Norepinephrine stimulants; anticholinergics (?)
Prevention	Immunization by mastery over reinforcement	(?)

Source: From Martin P. Seligman, *Helplessness: On Depression, Development and Death.* Copyright © 1975 W. H. Freeman and Company. Used by permission.

that were described in chapter 7 (Seligman, Maier, & Geer, 1968; Seligman, Maier, & Solomon, 1971; Seligman, 1975).

To Seligman and his colleagues there is a striking analogy between the apparent learned helplessness shown in animal experiments and the behavior of depressed humans. After closely examining the clinical literature on depression in light of his own research on animal helplessness, Seligman (1975) has described six types of parallel symptoms shown in Table 14.3. Seligman argues that the relationship between learned helplessness and clinical depression extends beyond these behavioral parallels. He believes that the feeling of helplessness is central to depression.

The original learned helplessness formulation of depression has been revised by researchers who believe that the critical aspects of depression are cognitive as well as emotional and behavioral. Abramson et al. (1978) have argued that the original learned helplessness model could not account for some important aspects of depression. For example, depressed people tend to blame themselves for failures even when self-blame is unwarranted. Furthermore, lowered self-esteem, another critical characteristic of depression, is not easy to account for using the learned helplessness model.

The reformulated model takes into account the attributions people make in attempting to explain and understand the world around them. According to the revised model, people prone to depression make internal attributions when they experience negative outcomes or failures and attribute success to events or forces outside themselves. Harvey and Weary (1984) have observed that this would help account for the fact that depressives also frequently show lower levels of motivation and performance.

Cognitive aspects of depression have also been emphasized by Beck and his co-workers (Beck, 1967; Beck, Rush, Shaw, & Emery, 1979). They believe that the most striking aspect of the depressive's behavior involves negative expectations and thoughts that are a continuous part of the depressed person's experience. These include negative conceptions of the self, negative interpretations of one's experiences, and negative expectations of the future. Beck believes that a habitual aspect of depressive thinking involves the use of cognitive schemata that shape the depressed person's experience and actually reinforce the negative experiences typically reported by depressives. For example, he observes that depressives often focus on small incidents in overgeneralizing about negative aspects of their own abilities.

Both the reformulated cognitive model of learned helplessness and Beck's cognitive view help account for features of depression that are not as well handled by dynamic or learning perspectives. Still other questions about depression are both raised and answered by recent biological research. It is to that research that we now turn.

Biological Determinants of Mood Disorders

Although the experiments conducted by Weiss and his colleagues are persuasive in reinterpreting the Seligman research with animals, they do not by themselves provide a broader base of evidence for assessing the degree to which genetic and physiological factors are important determinants of mood disorders.

Many scientists suspect that a family of neurotransmitters called catecholamines, including norepinephrine, dopamine, and epinephrine, play a key role in depression. It has been suggested that a depletion of norepinephrine in the brain results in depressed behavior (Shildkraut, 1978; Maas, 1978).

The evidence for this catecholamine hypothesis stems from several sources. One line of evidence indicated that drugs that increase the level of norepinephrine in the brain tend to produce overactivity in laboratory animals. Another line of evidence comes from the effects of drugs used in the treatment of depression. These drugs, called monoamine oxidase inhibitors (MAO inhibitors), are effective apparently because they maintain the level of norepinephrine in the brain. MAO inhibitors block the action of an enzyme, MAO, which breaks down neurotransmitters such as norepinephrine. Hence, scientists reason, depression may be associated with—and perhaps caused by—the lack of sufficient levels of norepinephrine or other catecholamines.

Evidence for genetic causes of some mood disorders have also been found. A study of bipolar effective disorders (violent mood alternation), found that when the disorder occurs in an individual with a twin sibling, both members of the pair are far more likely to be affected if they are monozygotic, rather than dizygotic, twins (Rosenthal, 1970). This finding suggests a genetic component in the disorder.

Another line of evidence involves the treatment of mood disorders. A new and effective pharmacological treatment, using lithium carbonate, indicates that the biochemistry of the brain is involved in some mood disorders (Tosteson, 1981). Lithium carbonate apparently reduces the brain's level of norepinephrine, the neurotransmitter that also has been implicated in depression. Interestingly, the element lithium is contained in mineral water, which probably explains why ancient Greek and Roman physicians prescribed mineral water for their manic-depressive patients, even though they could not have identified the chemical itself.

Thus mood disorders, like many other disorders, may be based in psychological trauma, may be learned, and may have biochemical or genetic origins. Strong evidence for organic causes of some mood disorders has emerged in recent years.

Schizophrenia: A Major Disorder of Perception and Thought

"Franz, 23, says he is a riddle of bones. He hears buzzing noises, penetrating squeals, and voices with messages he sometimes understands but cannot remember. He sees flashes of light and shadow in the middle of the room. Strangers, he says, can send their shadows to visit him in bed. He tastes soap in his mouth and absorbs poison from the bedpost. He chews his tie, hoards garbage, sits in a stupor for weeks, and hits his nurses. Occasionally he clowns and walks on his hands" (Rodgers, 1982, p. 85).

Sirhan Sirhan, the convicted assassin of Senator Robert F. Kennedy, was diagnosed as a chronic paranoid schizophrenic.

Schizophrenia is no respecter of race, religion, intelligence, economic status, or geographic boundaries. About 1 percent of the people in the United States will be diagnosed as schizophrenic at some point in their lives, but it is a worldwide disorder. A recent survey sponsored by the World Health Organization suggests a 1 percent incidence of schizophrenia in all of the countries studied: Nigeria, Colombia, Denmark, the Soviet Union, and India, as well as the United States (Tsuang. 1976).

Schizophrenics make up about half the patients in U.S. mental institutions; many more continue to live in society but must return to institutions periodically for treatment. Roughly one third of schizophrenics improve, about one third get worse, and the remaining third stay the same throughout their lives. Peak incidence occurs between the ages of 25 and 35 (Price & Lynn, 1981).

Despite thousands of scientific studies, schizophrenia remains one of the great puzzles confronting abnormal psychology. Perhaps more than any other area of abnormal psychology, schizophrenia is beset by questions and controversies, two of which are key to understanding the issues regarding it.

1. Is schizophrenia a single unitary disorder? Some scientists say yes. Others believe it is a group of similar-appearing disorders with different underlying causes. Still others argue that schizophrenia is merely a label for describing a range of behavior that we do not understand.
2. What are the causes of schizophrenia? Scientists are divided on this question and disagree markedly about the relative contributions of environmental and genetic factors causing the illness.

Clinical Descriptions

The word *schizophrenia* was coined by the Swiss psychiatrist Eugen Bleuler (1911/1950) from the Greek words *schizen* (''to split'') and *phren* (''mind''). Bleuler meant to emphasize the idea that the mind became ''split to chaos'' and the tissue of thoughts became loosened in schizophrenia. Unfortunately, this derivation of the term has led to widespread confusion between schizophrenia and multiple personality. Multiple personality is considered a kind of dissociative disorder that in actuality bears little resemblance to schizophrenia.

Bleuler suggested that following key characteristics of the disorder as a result of observing his schizophrenic patients:

- *Autism* is the tendency to withdraw from involvement in the external world and to become preoccupied with private fantasies. In autistic fantasies, perceptions frequently become distorted.
- *Associative disturbance* (also called ''loose associations'' or ''thought disorder'') often takes the form of language that wanders and skips from topic to topic in a vague, disjointed way. A graphic example of this can be seen in the reply of a man who was asked whether he felt that people imitated him.

  Yes . . . I don't quite gather. I know one right and one left use both hands, but I can't follow the system that's working. The idea is meant in a kind way, but it's not the way I understand life. It seems to be people taking sides, as I understand it. . . . To say things are all wrong means right in turn, but I don't appreciate it that way (Mayer-Gross, Slater, & Roth, 1969.)

- *Ambivalence* was Bleuler's way of describing the frequent juxtaposition of opposing emotions or impulses. For example, schizophrenics frequently report that they simultaneously experience love and hate for the same person.

- *Affective disturbance* refers to inappropriate emotional responses. Situations or stimuli that elicit joy or sadness in most of us may bring little response. Conversely, some schizophrenics may burst into laughter when told a friend or relative has died.
- *Delusions* are strongly held beliefs not shared by others in our culture.
- *Hallucinations* are sensations not experienced by others—seeing, hearing, or smelling things that do not actually exist but are perceived as being real (Feinberg, 1962).

Bleuler had a singular aptness for describing precisely the behavior he observed among his schizophrenic patients, and his descriptions remain useful when dealing with this disorder today.

Schizophrenics Describe Schizophrenia

Some valuable insights into schizophrenia also come from descriptions provided by James Chapman, who interviewed patients and asked them to describe their experiences as clearly as possible (Chapman, 1966). Based on these interviews, he reported that the first signs of an oncoming schizophrenic episode are often frightening changes in perception. "Last week I was with a girl," said one patient, "and she seemed to get bigger and bigger, like a monster coming nearer and nearer. The situations become threatening and I shrink back."

After such perceptual distortions, patients seem to have extreme difficulty in controlling their thoughts. "I can't keep thoughts out," says a patient. "It comes on automatically. It happens at most peculiar times—not just when I'm talking, but when I'm listening as well. I lose control at conversation, then I sweat and shake all over. . . . I can hear what they were saying all right, it's remembering what they have said the next second that is difficult. It just goes out of my mind. I'm concentrating so much on little things I have difficulty in finding an answer at the time." Such reports show that schizophrenics have trouble focusing their attention on external events.

Thus, clinical descriptions of schizophrenia clearly suggest that it involves severe disturbances of perception and thought. But what are the causes of the disorder?

Determinants of Schizophrenia

Most scientists would probably agree, in a general way, that both biology and experience play some role in the development of schizophrenia. But as one researcher notes, "After paying homage to the concept of genotype-environment interaction, most investigators, unwittingly or by choice, slip back into more comfortable modes of thought and place their etiological bets on one or the other side" (Kessler, 1969).

Consider the following evidence concerning the transmission of schizophrenia. It is well established that a child with one schizophrenic parent has a risk of developing the disorder that is 10 times greater than someone selected at random from the general population. Moreover, a child with two such parents has a risk 40 times greater.

Biologically oriented researchers view this as evidence of an inherited genetic defect. From the same set of facts, researchers whose perspective is social and environmental see schizophrenia as learned through constant exposure to the parent.

Biological Factors

The search for possible biological determinants of schizophrenia has proceeded simultaneously along two principal lines. Along one, researchers look for underlying genetic factors; along the other, scientists who for the most part

RESEARCH

Scientific experiments serve two important functions: to test existing theories and to provide the raw material for new ones. Sometimes, however, the findings of such experiments are subject to more than one interpretation. They may, for example, fit plausibly into two quite different theoretical approaches to human behavior.

A dramatic illustration of this occurred in the late 1960s when Martin Seligman and his colleagues observed the intriguing phenomenon that they labeled learned helplessness.

Seligman (1975) drew an analogy between the behavior of dogs subjected to inescapable shock in an experiment and that of depressed humans. "The depressed patient," he argued, "believes or has learned that he cannot control those elements of his life that relieve suffering, bring gratification, or provide nurture—in short, he believes that he is helpless."

Seligman's conclusions were of particular interest to another group of researchers. Like Seligman, Jay Weiss and his colleagues (Weiss, Glazer, & Pohorecky, 1976) were investigating the impact on behavior of stressful events such as unavoidable

shocks, but from a different theoretical perspective. The focus of their work was the biochemistry of the brain, particularly certain neurotransmitters thought to play an important role in human depression. Weiss did not question the results of the Seligman experiments, but he did question Seligman's explanation of those results as learned helplessness.

Weiss and his associates suspected that the behavior of the dogs, far from being attributable to learning could be explained in terms of biochemistry. They already had found in animal experiments that stress causes depletion of a particular neurotransmitter in the brain called norepinephrine. And as they studied the data from Seligman's work they were

struck by the fact that dogs tested 48 hours after being subjected to inescapable shock had no trouble jumping the shuttle-box partition. The helplessness thus appeared to be temporary—not characteristic of learned responses but just what they would expect if the norepinephrine had been depleted and then gradually returned to normal levels. Because norepinephrine was believed to be essential to active behavior, Weiss formulated an alternative hypothesis: unavoidable shock, instead of teaching the dogs they were helpless, simply lowered the levels of norepinephrine in the brain; this depletion, in turn, reduced the ability of the animals to produce the movements necessary to jump over the shuttle-box barrier.

Here then was a classic confrontation of two theoretical perspectives—learning versus biological—over how to interpret the uncontested results of an important experiment.

To test their alternative hypothesis, Weiss and his associates devised a series of experiments that have been praised for their logic and elegant simplicity. Let us look briefly at the major findings and how they were arrived at.

are already convinced of the importance of genetic factors seek specific solutions to schizophrenia in the biochemistry of the brain.

The strategy in genetic research is to study families where schizophrenia is prevalent. As we have already noted, however, the results of such family studies, which show much greater risk among children of schizophrenic parents, are subject to conflicting interpretations. Consequently, in an attempt to rule out the experience of living in a schizophrenic family as a possible cause, some genetic researchers have narrowed their focus by studying twins.

To understand the strategy behind these studies, remember that there are two genetic types of twins. Identical twins are monozygotic—they develop from the same egg and therefore are genetically identical. Fraternal twins, by contrast, are dizygotic—they develop from separate eggs and are no more genetically similar than other siblings. By comparing incidence of schizophrenia in identical and fraternal twins, researchers can help separate the possible effects of environment from those of heredity. If there is an important hereditary

1. Depletion of norepinephrine produces behaviors that look like learned helplessness. Weiss required laboratory rats to swim for 3½ minutes in cold water—an experience known to result in decreased norepinephrine. When these rats were later placed in a shuttle box, they showed behavior similar to the learned helplessness of Seligman's dogs; they were unable to jump the partition to avoid shock. To ensure that the cold water rather than the experience of swimming produced their behavior, Weiss exposed a control group to a similar swim in warm water. These rats had no trouble avoiding shock by jumping the partition in the shuttle box.

2. Norepinephrine depletion inhibits motor activity. To test his belief that norepinephrine depletion resulted in the lack of vigorous motor activity by Seligman's dogs, Weiss devised an experiment that would allow animals to avoid shock without having to leap a barrier. When his animals were exposed to inescapable shock and then given an opportunity to avoid shock by using a small movement, they were able to do so. Thus, they were not helpless when the motor activity required was small.

3. Animals recover from helplessness by adaptation. Weiss found that animals exposed to inescapable shock daily over a period of two weeks did not show helpless behavior in the shuttle-box situation. This conforms to the biochemist's expectation that the brain adapts to repeated experiences, showing norepinephrine depletion only at first. It also runs contrary to the learning theorist's expectation that repeated trials of inescapable shock would strengthen the helplessness rather than weaken it. Moreover, Weiss obtained direct measures of norepinephrine levels in his test animals. Although one session of inescapable shock produced depletion, repeated sessions did not. Adaptation apparently was occurring in the brain chemistry of the animals exposed to repeated sessions.

4. Pharmacological experiments support Weiss's interpretation. When drugs known to deplete levels of norepinephrine were injected into laboratory animals, the symptoms of learned helplessness resulted. By the same token, drugs that prevent depletion of norepinephrine levels served to prevent the animals from helplessness when they were exposed to inescapable shock; they could jump the barrier.

This chain of findings, each link fitting neatly into the next, provides persuasive evidence for Weiss's refutation of the learned helplessness interpretation. Weiss is careful to point out that the refutation applies only to the results of the original Seligman experiments. His findings do not necessarily rule out the existence of learned helplessness. It may indeed play a role, as Seligman suggests, in human depression, although apparently not in the behavior of the dogs in his original experiments.

The Weiss experiments also have illuminated the connection between psychosocial and biochemical factors in a particular instance of abnormal behavior. A stressful event—inescapable shock—leads to biochemical changes in the brain that, in turn, lead to a disturbance in behavior. This is a promising model for the understanding of disturbed behavior in general and may point the way to clarification of the precise determinants of human depression. ∎

factor in schizophrenia, it follows that both members of a pair of identical twins ought to be more likely to develop the disorder than would both members of a pair of fraternal twins.

Over the past half century, a number of such twin studies have been conducted. The results, with one or two exceptions, tend to buttress the arguments of the genetic perspective. Both members of identical twin pairs tend to develop schizophrenia more often than do fraternal twins. In summarizing the evidence from twin research, Kendler (1983) indicates that genetic factors are as important in schizophrenia as in such medical conditions as diabetes and hypertension (see Color Plate 14.3).

A convincing summary of the genetic research on schizophrenia is shown in Figure 14.3, which shows that the stronger the genetic relatedness between two individuals where one is already schizophrenic, the higher the risk of the other becoming schizophrenic as well (Gottesman & Shields, 1982; Nicol & Gottesman, 1983).

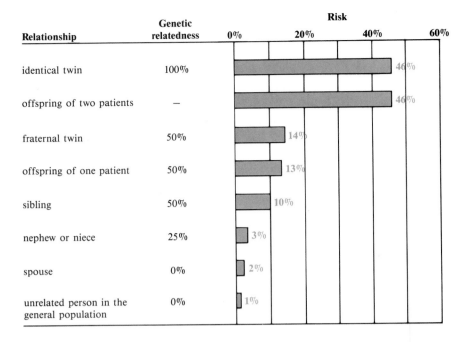

Figure 14.3

Lifetime risk of developing schizophrenia is strongly predicted by closeness of genetic relationship to a person who is already schizophrenic.

Even if there is a genetic component to schizophrenia, as evidence suggests, investigators are still interested in the form it might take in the physiological functioning of the person who develops the disorder. The search for answers has focused on two aspects of human biochemistry—the metabolism of the schizophrenic and the chemistry of the brain.

The history of the search for a metabolic mechanism has been discouraging. Researchers have so assiduously sought a biochemical "X-factor" unique to schizophrenics that there have been many premature reports of such a discovery (Kety, 1967). A dramatic instance of this was the report in the late 1950s of a "pink spot" in the blood and urine of schizophrenics (Hoffer, Osmond, & Smythies, 1954). This report, like many others, turned out to be a blind alley (see Focus, p. 483). Nonetheless, researchers continue to seek the elusive factor.

The newer—and more promising—biochemical approach, however, involves investigations into the chemistry of the brain. Instead of looking for some factor unique to schizophrenia, researchers try to understand the chemical functioning of the brain. They then build theories based on how chemical imbalances or malfunctions might lead to schizophrenic behavior.

The focus of their attention is the brain's neurotransmitters. As we saw earlier, several of these chemicals, which transmit electric impulses from one nerve cell to the next, have been implicated in the development of depression. About a dozen neurotransmitters have been positively identified and, as we pointed out in chapter 2, interference with their functioning by drugs or disease can dramatically affect behavior.

One particular neurotransmitter, dopamine, is the target of perhaps the most promising line of research into biochemical determinants of schizophrenia. Dopamine is known to be involved in the fine control of certain muscle movements; too little of it apparently leads to Parkinson's disease. Now, according to the so-called **dopamine hypothesis,** too much of it may cause symptoms of schizophrenia (see Figure 14.4).

The evidence for the dopamine hypothesis is indirect (Haracz, 1982). First, major tranquilizers such as the phenothiazines, which are used in the treatment of schizophrenia, have the effect of interfering with the action of dopamine: they inhibit the transmission of nerve impulses by blocking the nerve cell re-

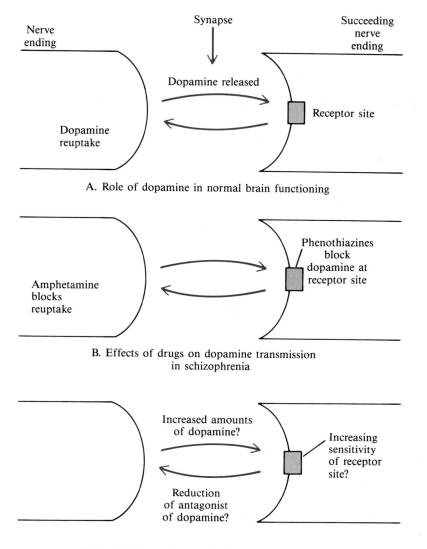

Figure 14.4

Representation of the hypothesis that the neurotransmitter dopamine is a biochemical determinant of schizophrenia.

Nerve ending

Synapse

Succeeding nerve ending

Dopamine released

Receptor site

Dopamine reuptake

A. Role of dopamine in normal brain functioning

Amphetamine blocks reuptake

Phenothiazines block dopamine at receptor site

B. Effects of drugs on dopamine transmission in schizophrenia

Increased amounts of dopamine?

Increasing sensitivity of receptor site?

Reduction of antagonist of dopamine?

C. Possible dopamine mechanisms in schizophrenia

ceptor sites where dopamine normally acts. Second, the amphetamines, which are known to stimulate the central nervous system, appear to "soup up" the transmission of nerve impulses by blocking the normal reuptake of dopamine. Because the dopamine is not taken up again in nerve endings, large amounts of it are left in the synaptic gaps between nerve cells, thus magnifying its effect. Moreover, amphetamines tend to worsen the symptoms of schizophrenia.

Thus, it appears that too much dopamine may somehow be responsible for the symptoms of schizophrenia. Several possibilities might account for the excess of dopamine (Nicol & Gottesman, 1983). The nerve endings could be producing too much for some reason, or some hypothetical chemical that normally reduces the amount of dopamine in the synaptic cleft might not be present in sufficient quantities. Whatever the mechanism, the question of how an excess of dopamine might produce schizophrenia still remains.

It is interesting to note that, even if the dopamine hypothesis is correct, it would not necessarily prove that schizophrenia is inherited. Some evidence suggests that the experience of learning may bring about biochemical changes in the brain (Rose, 1973). If so, a case could then plausibly be made that the imbalance of dopamine results from experience rather than genetics.

Still another important line of research has developed as a result of new methods of studying brain abnormalities and metabolism (Seidman, 1983). Techniques such as the PET scan (positron emission tomography) allow scientists to study radioactive traces of energy metabolism. The CAT scan, computerized axial tomography, provides a detailed computer image of the brain structures (see Color Plate 14.2).

Seidman (1983) reviews numerous studies that have shown physical abnormalities in the brain structure of between 20 and 30 percent of schizophrenics studied. Furthermore, studies of blood flow and energy metabolism in the brains of schizophrenics have shown that the frontal lobe blood flow of schizophrenics tends to "shut down" when confronted with complex cognitive tasks, while they tend to increase in normal individuals (Gur et al., 1983; Rodgers, 1982). It seems clear that not only brain chemistry, but actual structural abnormalities of the brain, may play an important role in at least some cases of schizophrenia.

Environmental Factors

The quest for environmental determinants of schizophrenia takes several forms. It looks at the role played by society at large, for example, but its most important focus is the family itself.

Support for the family approach can be found in at least three factors. First, to most psychologists, the family is seen as the focal point of learning. Second, the studies of twins discussed earlier, while suggesting a strong genetic component, cannot fully explain the incidence of schizophrenia. Third, it is a common observation among clinicians that the themes, preoccupations, fears, delusions, and hallucinations of their schizophrenic patients tend to center on the patient's family. In fact, the clinical literature persuades many psychologists that schizophrenic behavior can be understood only in the context of the family.

However, unusual behavior does not appear to be unique to families that produce schizophrenic children. A recent review could not find consistent evidence that conflict or either a positive or a negative emotion were uniquely characteristic of such families (Jacob, 1975).

Interestingly, however, the review did find evidence that there are more communication difficulties in schizophrenics' families (Jacob, 1975). Similarly, Lyman Wynne (1970) has found what he calls "communication deviancy" in the parents of schizophrenics, such as providing a child with conflicting messages simultaneously. Although Wynne emphasizes a family environmental interpretation of this phenomenon, it could also be explained in terms of genetics. The parents with this trait might be showing "communication deviancy" simply because they possess schizophrenic genes.

To avoid such ambiguous findings, researchers have attempted to examine the family over a long period of time. Ideally, a longitudinal study that looks at the same families over a period of time would have the advantage of examining the family environment before schizophrenic behavior appears in a child. This is usually impractical, however, because the researcher cannot know what families to study. One solution is the follow-up study, which examines clinical records of children made before they developed schizophrenia and then follows them up.

One follow-up study looked at children who had been seen early in life at a child guidance center and had later become schizophrenic (Waring & Ricks, 1965). The clinical records revealed some interesting information. For example, severely disturbed chronic schizophrenics were much more likely to have been raised in one of the following two kinds of family environments: (1) emotional divorce—an environment marked by much hostility and distrust between parents; or (2) symbolic union—an environment in which one spouse is dominating and overcontrolling, while the other is passive and accepting.

FOCUS

The Model Psychosis Hypothesis

For the past quarter century, scientists have been intrigued by certain apparent similarities between the subjective states induced by psychedelic drugs and those reported by schizophrenics. Those who experiment with drugs such as mescaline and LSD often report experiencing hallucinations and loss of self-identity resembling the symptoms of schizophrenia. In fact, another name for psychedelic drugs, psychotomimetic, literally means "capable of producing states that mimic psychotic states." Some investigators thus have hypothesized that drugs produce a kind of "model psychosis," which can help them better understand the nature of schizophrenia.

One research strategy suggested by this hypothesis is that the physiology of schizophrenics may produce some toxic substance resembling a psychedelic drug. For example, in 1962, two British scientists noted a chemical similarity between mescaline and adrenalin, the hormone that prepares the body for action during stress (Hoffer, Osmond, & Smythies, 1962). They speculated that perhaps adrenalin is metabolized by some people into a mescalinelike substance, which then produces schizophrenic behavior.

Soon afterward, Abram Hoffer reported a breakthrough that appeared to confirm the Osmond-Smythies speculation (Hoffer, Osmond, & Smythies, 1962). Hoffer said he had found a derivative of adrenalin called adrenochrome in samples of blood and urine taken from schizophrenics. This pink-colored chemical results when oxygen combines with adrenalin. Hoffer thus had reason to believe that the pink-spot substance,

which he thought was adrenochrome, might be the long-sought X-factor in schizophrenia—the biological cause. To test this possibility, he administered the substance to normal subjects. He reported that they experienced effects similar to those of people who took LSD.

Hoffer's report stirred great excitement. But when scientists all over the world attempted to repeat his experiments, they could not find adrenochrome in the blood of either schizophrenics or normal subjects. The general conclusion was that Hoffer's exciting results stemmed from poorly controlled laboratory procedures. The pink spots had appeared because the laboratory samples from schizophrenics had been allowed to remain in the open air for longer than those from nonschizophrenics. As for the reported psychedelic effects of the blood samples administered to normal subjects, it was quite likely the result of the placebo effect. Hoffer and his colleagues might have been so eager to demonstrate their theory that they unwittingly suggested the expected effects to their subjects, who obliged with reports of symptoms of disorientation that resembled those of schizophrenia.

A second research strategy for investigating the psychedelic experience as a "model psychosis" has focused on the apparent similarities of behavior between schizophrenics and people under the influence of psychedelic drugs. On closer examination, similarities as well as important differences emerge. For example, Leo Hollister (1962) conducted a simple but carefully controlled experiment. He asked a group of mental health professionals to listen to tape-recorded interviews. Some of the interviews were with normal subjects who were under the influence of LSD; the other interviews were with schizophrenics. The professionals had no difficulty distinguishing between the two groups. Hollister also reports a clear distinction in the disturbances experienced by the two groups. LSD seemed to affect perception primarily, whereas schizophrenia affected thought processes. Another investigator found differences in the types of hallucinations (Feinberg, 1962). Schizophrenic hallucinations tend to involve hearing voices, whereas psychedelic aberrations are primarily visual, involving alterations of color, size, shape, movement, and number.

Although these findings and the failure to pinpoint an X-factor in the metabolism of schizophrenics led many scientists to reject the model psychosis approach, others still feel it may yet shed light on schizophrenia. Researchers have found evidence of similarities to psychedelic breakdown (Bowers & Freedman, 1966). Another investigator suggests it is possbile that the prolonged experience of altered perceptions in schizophrenia may produce still other changes that mask essential similarities in the two states (Snyder, 1975). ■

In addition, in a third kind of environment, called *family sacrifice,* the child is openly rejected and frequently forced to leave the home. Children from this type of family fared better than those in the first two kinds of environment. This third group had the highest proportion of schizophrenics who were able to

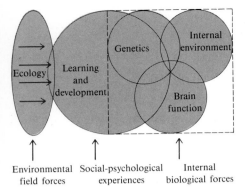

Environmental   Social-psychological   Internal
field forces   experiences   biological forces

Figure 14.5

The vulnerability model of causation in schizophrenia is based on the premise that the degree of vulnerability to schizophrenia in each of us is determined by some combination of biological and environmental factors.

be released from hospital settings after treatment and returned to the community. This study suggests that the severity of schizophrenic behavior may be significantly affected by the family environment.

The Vulnerability Model of Schizophrenia

There is little doubt that schizophrenia is at least partly hereditary. What is transmitted genetically is not yet clear, although the most promising new evidence suggests that the neurotransmitters of the brain—particularly dopamine—play an important role in the development of the disorder.

At the same time, it is clear that social and environmental factors, especially the family, are important. The social environment can affect the potential schizophrenic in two ways: it is the source of stresses, and it is the teacher of various abilities and skills that shape the way a person copes with those stresses.

Thus, there appear to be several determinants of schizophrenia, all of them intertwined in ways that are difficult to separate. Several models have been proposed in an attempt to incorporate all these factors in a coherent fashion. One such attempt is the **vulnerability model** (Zubin & Spring, 1977).

This model's basic premise is that each of us is endowed with some degree of vulnerability to schizophrenia (see Figure 14.5). The degree of vulnerability is determined by some combination of both biological and environmental factors. Whether this vulnerability will express itself in an episode of schizophrenia depends on the impact of any of a number of challenging life events. Among these events are bereavement, marriage, divorce, and unemployment. Moreover, the actual impact of a given event may differ depending on the person's vulnerability. For example, most of us are able to cope adequately with a death in the family, but for others who are more vulnerable, that loss may precipitate a schizophrenic episode. The model thus brings together genetic and environmental factors, including stress, and accounts for the episodic nature of schizophrenia.

Like all useful formulations, the vulnerability model raises as many questions as it answers. But it provides a model that can be applied not only to schizophrenia but also to other disorders, thus suggesting a way of incorporating evidence from conflicting perspectives into a more coherent picture of how severe disturbance in behavior may develop.

Personality Disorders

Many abnormal behaviors are characterized by sudden disruptions or changes in patterns. After the loss of a loved one a person may fall into a deep depression, or a traumatic event may trigger a phobic reaction. One set of disorders, however, does not happen suddenly; the patterns of behavior appear to be deeply ingrained and are manifested primarily as exaggerations. These are referred to as personality disorders. The DSM-III, as we indicated earlier, has a completely separate axis to describe the personality disorders, reflecting the view that these disorders are seen as distinct from other forms of psychological disorder.

Everyone has probably known people who act strangely but whose behavior hardly seems pathological. Everyone, too, has probably known people who are so neat and meticulous that, in this regard at least, they seem out of the ordinary. In the extreme, such patterns may make it difficult for people to cope effectively in the world because their behavior may negatively affect others and, therefore, disrupt personal relationships. Table 14.4 shows descriptions of **personality disorders** as they are listed in DSM-III.

Table 14.4 THE DSM-III CLASSIFICATION OF PERSONALITY DISORDERS

Eccentric Cluster	*Fearful Cluster*	*Erratic Cluster*
Paranoid personality: A pervasive and long-standing suspiciousness and mistrust of people in general. Individuals with this disorder are hypersensitive and easily slighted. They continually scan the environment for clues that validate their original prejudicial ideas, attitudes, or biases. Often their emotional experience is restricted. Introverted personality: A defect in the capacity to form social relationships; introversion and bland or constricted affect. Schizotypal personality: Various oddities of thinking, perception, communication, and behavior. Peculiarities in communication with concepts expressed unclearly or oddly.	Avoidant personality: Hypersensitivity to rejection, unwillingness to enter into relationships unless given an unusually strong guarantee of uncritical acceptance. Social withdrawal, yet a desire for affection and acceptance. Compulsive personality: Restricted ability to express warm and tender emotions, preoccupation with matters of rules, order, organization, efficiency, and detail. Excess devotion to work and productivity to the exclusion of pleasure. Compulsive personalities are often indecisive. Passive-aggressive personality: Resistance to demand for adequate activity or performance in both occupational and social areas of functioning. Resistance is not expressed directly. As a consequence, pervasive or long-standing social or occupational ineffectiveness often result.	Histrionic personality: Behavior that is overly reactive, intensely expressed, and perceived by others as shallow, superficial, or insincere. Often associated with disturbed interpersonal relationships. Narcissistic personality: Grandiose sense of self-importance or uniqueness, preoccupation with fantasies of unlimited success, exhibitionistic needs for constant attention and admiration. Antisocial personality: History of continuous and chronic antisocial behavior in which the rights of others are violated. Onset before age 15, failure to sustain good job performance, lying, stealing, fighting, truancy in childhood. Borderline personality: Instability in various areas of life including interpersonal relationships, behavior, mood, and self-image. Interpersonal relationships are often tense and unstable with marked shifts of attitude over time.

Source: From American Psychiatric Association Diagnostic and Statistical Manual of Mental Disorders, Third Edition. Washington, DC, copyright APA 1980. Used with permission.

It is important to note that these extreme patterns of personality disorders need not necessarily disrupt an individual's life adjustment. Indeed, for an accountant, extreme orderliness, as it is reflected in the compulsive personality, may be a distinct advantage. Similarly, a certain amount of suspiciousness in a police detective may be an asset rather than a liability.

Antisocial Personality

While little research has been done on most of the personality disorders, the antisocial personality, or sociopath, has received considerable attention. According to DSM-III, the primary characteristic of the antisocial personality is a history of continuous and chronic antisocial behavior. Violation of the rights of others and failure to sustain adequate job performance over an extended period of time are typical. Antisocial personalities are characterized by stealing, lying, fighting, and truancy in childhood. This disorder is observed much more commonly in males than females, and is estimated to occur in approximately 1 percent of the women and 3 percent of the men in the population.

This pattern of behavior is reflected in the following case history:

"A twenty-one-year-old male was interviewed by a psychiatrist while he was being detained in jail awaiting trial for attempted robbery. The patient had a history of multiple arrests for drug charges, robbery, and assault and battery. Past history revealed that he had been expelled from junior high school for truancy, fighting, and generally poor performance in school. Following a car theft when he was 14

Shoplifting can be a behavior characteristic of antisocial personality.

years old, he was placed in a juvenile detention center. Subsequently, he spent brief periods in a variety of institutions from which he usually ran away. At times, his parents attempted to let him live at home, but he was disruptive and threatened them with physical harm. . . . The patient has never formed close personal relationships with his parents, his two older brothers, or friends of either sex. He is a loner and a drifter, and has not worked for more than two months at any one job in his life. He was recently terminated, because of fighting and poor attendance, from a vocational training program in which he had been enrolled for about three weeks'' (Spitzer et al., 1981, p 34).

This example reflects some of the most important characteristics of the antisocial personality, a pattern of impulsivity and a disregard for social rules. The antisocial personality also seems unable to engage in close relationships with family and friends and is preoccupied with making sure that his or her own immediate needs are met. Typically, relationships with others are tolerated only so long as they continue to satisfy the person's needs (Price & Lynn, 1981).

In a famous book on antisocial personalities, Cleckley (1976) offers numerous case descriptions of the disorder. Many of Cleckley's cases include not just criminals but prominent businessmen, professionals, and others who fit the same pattern of behavior. Cleckley believes that these individuals are constitutionally unable to experience ''normal guilt'' in contemplating their own social behavior.

Research and Theory on the Antisocial Personality

Research from a dynamic, social learning, and biological perspective has been conducted in an attempt to understand the determinants of antisocial personality, and each of these perspectives has offered plausible, but far from definitive, explanations.

Psychodynamic theory has focused on the antisocial personalitys' limited ability to experience guilt or remorse. In normal development, the child internalizes the parents sense of morality, and by doing so is able to maintain parental approval and love. Thus, in normal development, according to the psychodynamic view, identification with the parent allows the child to internalize the traditional rules of society. However, if the child identifies with a parent who does not share society's values, he or she will not develop a strong superego, which prohibits antisocial behavior. Furthermore, the psychodynamic view suggests that a child who has experienced neglect or abuse will fail to develop a basic trust in others and that the child's distrust will become part of all future relationships. So, either through identification with a deviant caretaker or through failure in establishing basic trust, the antisocial personality is seen as the result of fundamental early processes in childhood socialization.

Researchers working from the learning perspective offer accounts that are in some ways similar, but that focus on the patterns of reinforcement that occur in the interaction between parent and child. For example, Maher (1966) suggests that when a parent reduces punishment or postpones it when a child repents and promises not to repeat the behavior, he or she is actually rewarding repentant behavior rather than suppressing disobedient behavior. The antisocial personality may then learn to be skillful at repenting but the disobedient behavior will continue, nevertheless. From a learning theorist's point of view, the consequence is that the child becomes adept at developing winning ways and devising elaborate patterns of repentance, but fails to develop appropriately socialized behavior.

Biological researchers have focused on constitutional characteristics of the antisocial personality, particularly those that may be associated with the development of anxiety and guilt. For example, Lykken, in a classic study (1957), observed that antisocial personalities may be deficient in their constitutional ability to develop conditioned anxiety responses. In a study comparing matched samples of antisocial personalities with other individuals who did not display the disorder, he observed that antisocial personalities were much less likely to develop a conditioned anxiety response, even when punished by a shock for errors in learning a standard laboratory task. Both groups, however, performed equally well when positively rewarded for correct responses in the task. Lykken concluded that antisocial personalities failed to avoid shock because of a constitutionally based inability to develop avoidance learning responses.

More recently, Hare and McPherson (1984) have found differences in the brain structures of antisocial personalities. Those studied appeared to have left hemispheres that are not as developed for language processing as they are in normal individuals. Hare and McPherson speculate that the antisocial personality's left hemisphere is not consistently dominant for language and that, as a result, language may not be as effective as a regulator of the antisocial personality's behavior. Clearly, some evidence is developing of a biological vulnerability to the development of antisocial behavior.

While psychodynamic, learning, and biological explanations for antisocial personalities remain plausible, it is important to recognize that this behavior pattern develops in the social context. The social norms for lying, truancy, and cheating can vary widely, and some individuals diagnosed as antisocial personalities may simply be responding appropriately to the social demands and norms of their environment. This may be particularly true in circumstances of poverty, where survival may demand duplicity and stealing, and where the rewards of staying in school or holding a steady job are nowhere in evidence.

Substance Abuse and Dependence

At the same time that some drugs are providing new insights into the causes and treatment of depression and schizophrenia, they are playing other quite different roles in our society. Increasingly, people are becoming dependent on both legal and illegal drugs in order to cope with stress, boredom, and fatigue. This coping pattern can have serious consequences and may evolve into chronic patterns of abuse and dependence.

The DSM-III distinguishes between substance abuse and substance dependence in abnormal patterns of substance use. **Substance abuse** involves a pathological pattern of use, such as inability to stop use or intoxication throughout the day, impairment in occupational or social functioning, and duration of at least a month. **Substance dependence** is a more severe form of disorder and involves increased tolerance to obtain a desired effect and the development of withdrawal symptoms if intake is reduced or stopped.

If we recall our definitions of abnormal behavior at the beginning of this chapter, substance abuse and dependence fit the definitions in several different ways. Abuse and dependence can be disturbing to other people because of the effects of drug use on social behavior. The recent movement of MADD—Mothers Against Drunk Drivers—is only one example. Both abuse and dependence can also produce subjective distress because of the development of psychological or physiological withdrawal symptoms. Finally, drug dependence and abuse can produce psychological handicaps in role functioning, either because of the drug effects or because of the more permanent physiological damage that may result. In our examination of substance abuse and dependence, we will begin by considering each of the five major classes of drug use and then focus on alcohol use in more detail.

Sedative drugs comprise the first class of drugs we will consider. This group includes alcohol, barbiturates, and mild tranquilizers. Alchohol and barbiturates are among the three most widely abused drugs in the United States. Tobacco is the third drug in the "top three." At relatively low levels of dosage, barbiturates have an anxiety-reducing effect, while at more moderate dosages they tend to induce sleep. They are readily available through prescription. The pattern of abuse may begin, however, when prescribed barbiturates are taken in order to relieve anxiety and induce sleep. As a tolerance for the drug increases, people tend to increase their dosages, frequently without notifying their physician. Abuse may not be recognized until the person's functioning is impaired, as reflected in slurred speech, acute intoxication, and even a staggering walk.

Sudden withdrawal from heavy barbiturate use can lead to convulsions, coma, and even death, making barbiturates one of the most dangerous drugs. In addition, while a person's need for increased dosages to produce a desired effect may grow, the lethal dose remains approximately the same. A person heavily dependent on barbiturates can thus approximate the lethal dose very rapidly as he or she increases the dosage to maintain a sedative effect.

Opiates and **narcotics** comprise a second major group of drugs that is frequently abused. By far the best known of these drugs is heroin, which can rapidly become addictive. A moderate daily dose of heroin over as little as a two-week period can produce physical dependence (Witters & Witters, 1975). Since the pleasurable effects of heroin are limited to only several hours, and withdrawal after abstinence occurs rapidly, another dose is needed to produce euphoria and to prevent withdrawal. Withdrawal can be quite painful, involving vomiting, abdominal cramps, sweating, and chills. Thus, heroin addicts frequently continue to use heroin as much to prevent withdrawal as for the pleasurable effect of the drug.

Some of the dangers of heroin dependence are associated with the way the drug is commonly taken. Because it is usually injected using unsterilized needles, infectious diseases including hepatitis, pneumonia, and Acquired Immune Deficiency Syndrome (AIDS), are sometimes transmitted. Higher death rates for heroin addicts are often associated with violent causes, such as murder, suicide, and accidents. In addition, accidental overdoses can be fatal and usually occur when the addict receives an unusually strong dose of the drug.

Stimulants comprise another class of drugs that is frequently abused. This group includes illegal drugs such as cocaine and amphetamines. Both of these drugs stimulate the central nervous system. Cocaine was hailed as a cure-all by doctors in the late 1800s, but in 1906 came under strict government control and is classified today as a narcotic drug. The use of cocaine is increasing rapidly in the United States. By the end of the 1970s it was estimated that over 8 million Americans had experimented with cocaine as a recreational drug (Ray, 1978). Cocaine is typically inhaled through the nose and absorbed through the nasal mucous membranes. Its effects last one-half hour or less and typically produce euphoria, increased feelings of confidence, and increased alertness. However, chronic use of cocaine frequently produces insomnia, weight loss, paranoid reactions, hallucinations, and digestive disorders.

Amphetamines are a second type of stimulant. Typically obtained as a prescription drug, amphetamines increase the rate of physiological processes through their action on the central nervous system. If intake of amphetamines increases gradually over time, the drug abuser may experience insomnia, which may in turn be countered through use of alcohol or sleeping pills. This can produce a cycle of stimulation and depression of the central nervous system that increases the likelihood of overdose. Severe patterns of amphetamine abuse may involve intravenous injection, in which the person may inject himself or herself repeatedly to prolong the feeling of euphoria. Hallucinations and delusions can develop in some cases with increasing use of amphetamines as the drug accumulates in the body. Furthermore, these symptoms may persist for extended periods of time after drug use has been discontinued.

Hallucinogens comprise the fifth and final major class of drugs we will consider. These drugs—including LSD, marijuana, mescaline, and peyote—produce profound changes in consciousness, and several patterns of experience have been identified. One pattern involves an experience that resembles psychosis, including paranoid delusions, panic attacks, depression, and severe bodily discomfort. A second pattern is primarily cognitive, in which the user experiences extremely lucid thoughts, novel perspectives on problems, and an increased appreciation for the complexity of ideas. Still other individuals experience an intensification of sensory experience, and may perceive great beauty in ordinary objects and the release of powerful emotions when listening to music.

Access and peer influence are two important factors in the initial use of an illegal substance like marijuana.

Researchers studying hallucinogens have concluded that the subjective effects are determined by a complex combination of several factors: the dosage of the drug, the personality of the user, the setting or psychological environment, and the user's expectations about the drug's effects. While hallucinogens do not produce physical dependence or withdrawal symptoms, psychotic reactions are occasionally reported that persist long after the end of the hallucinatory experience itself.

Explanations for Drug Dependence

No single explanation has yet emerged for drug abuse and dependence. One of the most important factors is the initial availability of the drug. When access is limited, the likelihood that people who are vulnerable to substance abuse will develop a problem is, of course, lower.

A variety of personal and social factors probably interact to increase the likelihood of substance abuse and dependence once a drug is available. Peer pressure, modeling of others' behavior, and a lack of alternative ways of coping with mood changes are among the likely explanations. However, once physical dependence on a drug has been created, both the subjective effect produced by the drug and the relief of withdrawal symptoms become powerful determinants of continued use. While social factors may be important in the initial pattern of drug use, physiological factors are likely to be strong determinants of the maintenance of a drug abuse problem. Let us now turn to alcohol, a major drug of abuse and dependence, for a more detailed examination.

Alcohol Abuse and Dependence

The recreational use of alcohol is now so commonplace that it is easy to forget that it is a potent and potentially dangerous psychoactive drug. For one person out of ten who drink, alcohol can be a serious personal problem and can create problems for families, friends, and employers (NIAAA Special Report, 1975).

There is a wide range of drinking patterns among those who drink excessively. However, the DSM-III classification identifies several specific criteria that distinguish the recreational use of alcohol from more destructive patterns of abuse. Alcohol abuse is diagnosed when (a) a continuous or episodic use of alcohol occurs for at least one month; (b) social complications arise, such as impairment in occupational or social functioning; and (c) the individual shows psychological dependence reflected in a compelling desire to use alcohol and an inability to cut down or stop drinking, or when binge patterns are observed. A person is diagnosed as dependent on alcohol when these criteria are fulfilled

Alcohol abuse is a common form of substance abuse.

and when a tolerance develops and symptoms of alcohol withdrawal occur, such as the "morning shakes" after a reduction or cessation of drinking.

The short-term effects of alcohol tend to be directly related to the amount of alcohol in the blood. Low doses produce talkativeness, euphoria, and reduced inhibitions. At higher doses, the sedating effects of alcohol become more obvious as the motor portions of the brain are affected, producing impaired muscular coordination and the inability to walk.

Typically, people who drink large amounts of alcohol regularly develop a tolerance to its effects. This often masks the problem, leaving family and friends unaware of heavy daily consumption. In contrast, other alcohol abusers may show dramatic changes in mood, as when, for example, a normally shy and retiring person becomes aggressive and assaultive. A relatively small proportion of the population will develop an idiosyncratic intoxication in those cases when the individual has virtually no tolerance of alcohol.

Psychologists have offered several alternative explanations for the development of alcohol abuse and dependence. Learning theorists have offered a tension reduction theory of alcoholism that suggests that alcohol serves to reduce tension and therefore reinforces drinking and increases probability of future drinking (Holroyd, 1978). However, other learning theorists (Marlatt, 1976) suggest that the explanation is more complicated and that drinking will be used to reduce stress only when the situation is perceived as stressful by the drinker and when the drinker believes that alcohol is an adequate response to the situation.

Psychodynamic theorists suggest that alcoholism is associated with unfilled needs and provides a way of the achieving gratification for needs that arise early in life. This account suggests that these needs develop early during the oral stage of development and that oral behaviors that provided security when a child was very young will be used to fulfill needs in ways that are no longer functional. This view suggests that alcohol may serve as a pacifier for easily frustrated, dependent, and demanding "oral characters" who have not matured beyond the oral stage of development. However, critics of this explanation have argued that these theories are difficult, if not impossible, to verify (Price & Lynn, 1981).

Cultural factors almost certainly play some role in the development of alcoholism, since Kinney and Leaton (1982) have identified very different cultural orientations to the use of alcohol. In societies where total abstinence is the norm, alcoholism exists only at low rates, while in societies where there are virtually no controls or sanctions against drinking the highest rates of alcoholism occur. Cultures where occasions for drinking are structured and somewhat ritualized may be best for preventing alcoholism. Of course, even within a particular culture there is a wide variation in individual problem drinking that cannot be accounted for entirely on cultural grounds. Even in societies with strong sanctions against alcohol use, a high rate of individual cases of alcoholism can be observed among those who do drink.

This wide individual variation within cultures has led researchers to search for biological and genetic bases for the development of alcoholism. For example, Goodwin (1979) has reviewed twin studies to identify possible genetic bases for alcoholism and has observed that identical twins tend to have higher concordance for rates of alcoholism than do fraternal twins.

Nevertheless, a large proportion of people who develop serious problems of alcohol abuse do not come from families in which one or both of the parents were alcoholics, thus leaving open the possibility that alcoholism may have multiple explanations rooted in cultural norms, different patterns of learning and reinforcement, and varying genetic predispositions to alcohol abuse and dependence.

Summary

1. Most definitions of abnormal psychology focus on (1) behavior that is disturbing to others, (2) subjective distress, or (3) psychological handicaps that prevent normal coping with the demands and stress of life. Theories to account for the causes of abnormal behavior fall into three general groups. Those concerned with the social environment focus on the social perspective, which considers abnormal behavior as a violation of social norms, and the learning perspective, which examines the contingency between behavior and stimuli in the environment. Biological theories search for behavior determinants in genetics, physiology, and biochemistry. Psychological theories, particularly those with a psychodynamic orientation, concentrate on inner conflicts that produce anxiety and, in turn, defense mechanisms.

2. The third and current edition of the *Diagnostic and Statistical Manual* of the American Psychiatric Association (DSM-III) represents an attempt to provide reliable descriptions of patterns of abnormal behavior. Among the important innovations reflected in the DSM-III are the use of specific criteria to identify various diagnostic categories and the capacity to offer diagnoses on several different dimensions including psychological and medical disorders, personality disorders, and environmental stressors.

3. Posttraumatic stress disorders are anxiety reactions to psychologically traumatic events outside the usual range of human experience. They may persist for long periods of time and may be accompanied by social withdrawal. Dissociative disorders involve a sudden change in the normal functions of consciousness or identity and may involve fugue, amnesia, or multiple personality.

4. Anxiety disorders take several different forms. Phobic reactions focus on specific objects or situations, but ones that present no actual danger to the individual. Obsessive-compulsive disorders involve persistent thoughts, impulses, or actions accompanied by conflicting desires to engage in or resist the impulse or action.

5. Personality disorders seem to be deeply ingrained and appear primarily as behavioral exaggerations. Some traits—compulsive neatness, for example—are not considered disorders until they become extreme, making it difficult for individuals concerned to cope effectively in their social worlds. One form of personality disorder, antisocial personality, has been studied more extensively than others. Antisocial personalities appear to have little regard for conventional social rules, seem unable to engage in close relationships, show a pattern of impulsive behavior, and appear unable to experience feelings of guilt. Dynamic learning and biological explanations all have been offered to explain the development of antisocial personality. Both learning and dynamic views focus on the process of socialization in childhood, while the biological views focus on constitutional inability to develop conditioned anxiety responses.

6. Disorders of mood and affect are among the most important forms of abnormal behavior. They include depression, manic episodes (intense periods of elation), and bipolar affective disorders (alternating states of elation and depression). Both the dynamic and learning perspectives emphasize the role of prior experiences as causes of these disorders. Biological research suggests some possible genetic and biochemical factors in such disorders as helplessness and bipolar affective disorders.

7. Schizophrenia is one of the major disorders of perception and thought. It is a functional psychosis with no known single cause; delusions and hallucinations are common symptoms. Most scientists agree that some combination of biological and environmental factors works to produce schizophrenia. Strong evidence exists for a genetic, inherited component; recent research suggests some biochemical basis; environmental theories focus on the role of the family.

The vulnerability model proposes that each of us has some vulnerability to schizophrenia. The degree of vulnerability is determined by some combination of biological and environmental factors.

8. Substance abuse and dependence can occur for a variety of drugs, both legal and illegal. Abuse is reflected in a pathological pattern of use, inability to stop use and impairment in role functioning. Substance dependence involves increased tolerance and development of withdrawal symptoms if use is interrupted or reduced. Major classes of drugs are sedative drugs, including alcohol and barbiturates, opiates and narcotics, including heroin and morphine, stimulants, including amphetamines and cocaine, and hallucinogens including mescaline, LSD, and marijuana. No single explanation exists for all forms of drug abuse, and availability, peer pressure, psychological or physiological dependence all may interact in the development of abnormal patterns of abuse and dependence.

RESEARCH: Animals exposed to inescapable electric shock fail to learn to avoid shock when later given the opportunity. Seligman's account of the phenomenon suggests that animals learn to be helpless since, in the past, they have been unable to control the occurrence of stressful events. An alternative account suggests that stressful events deplete the brain of norepinephrine, a neurotransmitter involved in the control of large-scale motor behavior. Thus, when norepinephrine is depleted the animal may not be able to execute the movements necessary to escape or avoid shock. To test this notion Weiss and his colleagues devised a series of ingenious experiments that pitted the biochemical account squarely against the learning account. The results supported the biochemical account.

FOCUS: Individuals who ingest psychedelic drugs may experience psychological states similar to those experienced by schizophrenics. This notion, known as the "model psychosis hypothesis," may lead to research that could help psychologists better understand the physiological dimensions of schizophrenia.

15

Behavior Change

In the early 1800s, a number of devices—including this "tranquilizing chair" designed by Benjamin Rush—were used to control unmanageable patients.

In this collage, Philippe Pinel—a driving force behind humanitarian reform of mental hospitals—is shown discovering the deplorable conditions of mental patients, urging reform, and, finally, freeing the patients from their shackles.

We all engage in attempts to change our own behavior and that of others every day. We may attempt to change our patterns of eating, to improve our own memory, or to persuade others to change their beliefs. Throughout this text, in fact, we have examined psychological principles that are often used for the purposes of changing behavior.

In chapter 14 we saw that most cultures have developed methods for offering help to people experiencing psychological disturbances and to change the behavior in question. More than most, our own society has invested resources in the development of effective methods of behavior change to help those who are experiencing intense personal distress or who are particularly disturbing to others.

Although psychological research in the area of behavior change is still in its early stages, knowledge is increasing rapidly. Techniques available for treatment of depression, schizophrenia, and other forms of psychopathology were sadly limited until this century. For many centuries people with behavioral disturbances were believed to be possessed by demons, and because treatment related to the presumed cause of the behavior, therapy consisted principally of trying to get rid of the demons. People were flogged, burned at the stake, and even had holes drilled in their skulls—a procedure called trephining—to let out the evil spirits. Even after the first mental asylum, Bethlehem Hospital, was founded in London in 1547, patients were chained and subjected to gawking tourists at a penny a look. Bethlehem was so noisy and chaotic, in fact, that *bedlam,* a word derived from the hospital's name, came into the language. As recently as the early 1800s in the United States, mental patients were sometimes treated by trying to break their will: one method was to place the patient in a coffinlike box with air holes and then submerge the box in water until the bubbles of air stopped rising, after which an attempt was made to revive the occupant.

We can identify a number of landmarks in the history of treatment of disordered behavior. One such noteworthy event occurred in 1792 when the reformer Philippe Pinel took over the Paris mental hospital Bicetre and unchained the patients, leading to an era of concern with humane treatment (Pinel, 1801/1962). A second landmark dates roughly from the turn of this century and Freud's formulation of mental illness as psychological in nature and psychoanalysis as a method of treatment. A third landmark came in the 1950s with the use of psychoactive drugs to treat certain disorders. A more recent landmark had its beginnings in the early 1960s and is known as the community mental health movement, which arose in part from opportunities and challenges provided by the introduction of the new drug therapies. These treatments, by allowing a large reduction in the population of mental institutions, brought into focus the role of the community in both the treatment and the prevention of mental illness.

Today, of course, behavior change methods are more benevolent and are provided in most cases by someone with professional training. The professionals who treat disordered behavior are classified principally according to their educational background:

- *Psychiatrists* are physicians who usually have spent a postgraduate residency training in psychotherapy and specialize in diagnosis and treatment of abnormal behavior.
- *Psychoanalysts* are practitioners, usually but not always physicians, who have received specialized training at a psychoanalytic institute in the methods of therapy first developed by Sigmund Freud.
- *Clinical psychologists* hold Ph.D.s in psychology and have completed a clinical internship training program. They have extensive training in research, psychological testing, and therapy techniques.

- *Counseling psychologists* have graduate training similar to that of clinical psychologists, but typically with less emphasis on research.
- *Psychiatric social workers* hold master's degrees in social work and have special training in treatment procedures, with emphasis on the home and community.

Mental health professionals administer two major categories of treatment—the psychotherapies and the biological therapies—which are sometimes used together.

Psychotherapies

Psychotherapy has been defined as "an interpersonal process designed to bring about modifications of feelings, cognitions, attitudes, and behavior which have proven troublesome to the person seeking help from a trained professional" (Strupp, 1978). There are many forms of psychotherapy. Freud, who started it all in Vienna nearly a century ago with his formulation of psychoanalysis, would surely be astonished at the remarkable range of therapies available today. Psychotherapists now treat children, entire families, drug addicts, alcoholics, prison inmates, the very old, and the terminally ill. They work with psychotics who were once thought to be unreachable and with clients who are simply seeking expanded personal awareness and more meaningful ways of living. Between these two extremes are those who seek help because of feelings of helplessness or social isolation, a sense of failure or lack of worth. Many feel excluded from the mainstream of life or blocked from living up to their potential.

There are four major classes of psychotherapy—psychodynamic, humanistic, behavioral, and group. In theory, these therapies differ markedly from one another; in practice, however, the theoretical lines between the types are blurred, and increasingly, psychotherapists describe themselves as eclectic. They select techniques from the various theoretical perspectives and tailor them to the problems of the particular patient. In fact, it is not uncommon for a psychotherapist to combine one of the psychologically oriented therapies with the use of drug treatment, one of the types of biological therapies.

Psychodynamic Therapy

Freud's original formulation of psychoanalysis (1904/1959) has been changed and adapted by later practitioners including Carl Jung, Karen Horney, and others. Whatever the dimensions of their dissent from Freudian doctrine, however, all of the psychodynamic schools have retained an emphasis on intrapsychic dynamics, or the conflicts that take place within a person's psyche.

Psychoanalysis

This approach to therapy begins with the first Freudian principle: the goal of **psychoanalysis** is to make conscious the images, fantasies, and wishes of the patient's unconscious (Freud, 1904/1959). This is achieved in large part through the development of a therapeutic relationship between patient and therapist and is aimed at providing insight into emotional problems.

Freud recognized that his technique would not work for everyone. He described the ideal patient in psychoanalysis as being younger than 50, fairly well educated, of good character, sufficiently motivated to seek therapy willingly, and neither psychotic, confused, nor deeply depressed. Freud also envisioned the ideal psychoanalyst—a person of irreproachable character who "must have overcome in his own mind that mixture of lewdness and prudery with which . . . many people consider sexual problems'' (Freud, 1904/1959). This latter requirement was important, of course, because Freud believed that repression of sexual impulses is basic to most emotional disturbances.

Techniques

Psychoanalytic treatment is a slow and gradual process; typically a patient will spend several hours a week for several years in psychoanalysis. Freud developed a set of procedures for psychoanalytic treatment that are basically still followed by modern psychodynamic therapists. Techniques may vary in nuance but seldom in essence.

Free Association Freud's fundamental rule of psychoanalysis is free association. In order to lower defenses the analyst instructs the patient to say freely whatever comes to mind and to avoid censoring the material no matter how silly, embarrassing, or illogical it may seem. To facilitate free association, the patient typically lies in a relaxed position on a couch. The analyst, to avoid distracting the patient, sits out of sight, maintaining an attitude of—as Freud put it—''evenly hovering attention'' (Freud, 1904/1959).

As the patient pours out whatever enters the mind, long-repressed wishes and impulses begin to well up. The analyst interprets the relationship between this formerly unconscious material and the patient's everyday problems as expressed during the therapy. From these data the analyst forms hypotheses regarding the origin and nature of the patient's difficulties. These hypotheses are articulated by the analyst and, eventually, the patient begins self-discovery of the implications of materials elicited during the free-association process.

Dream Analysis Closely related to free association and its interpretation is a second procedure—**dream analysis.** As we discussed in chapter 5, Freud viewed dreams as symbolic representations of hidden conflicts that were reawakened by the previous day's activities. The psychoanalyst looks at dream content on two levels: the *manifest* or surface, *content,* and the *latent,* or hidden, *content.* For example, an ogre in a dream would be the manifest content, but the analyst may interpret its latent, or true meaning, as representing the patient's secretly hated and feared father. According to Freudian theory, this process of **dream censorship**—the masking of real meaning—occurs because the meaning would be unacceptable to the patient's conscious standards of morality.

The analyst views the dream in the context of the particular patient's personality, relating it to the patient's conscious experiences and to the latent symbolic significance. Above all, the analyst will be guided by the patient's own comments about various aspects of the dream during free association. Freud maintained that, if clearly understood, dreams contain ''the psychology of the neurosis in a nutshell'' (Freud, 1897/1953).

Resistance Through free association and dream analysis patients become aware of previously unconscious aspects of their personalities. At this point, patients often show signs of **resistance:** they may miss therapy appointments, remain silent when asked to free-associate, or report that they have no dreams to relate.

According to psychoanalytic theory, resistance has the effect of protecting the patients' neurosis; unconsciously, they want to avoid the anxiety evoked by facing previously repressed impulses. To overcome resistance, the analyst attempts the following: (1) making patients aware that they are unconsciously resisting therapy, (2) pointing out to patients precisely how they are resisting the elimination of repressions, and (3) clarifying to patients just what it is they are avoiding (Reich, 1949).

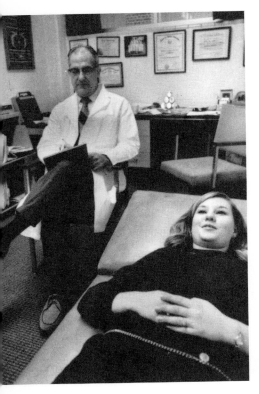

Many analysts use free association to interpret the relationship between unconscious material and everyday problems.

Interpretation   The process by which the analyst tries to overcome resistance is called **interpretation.** Typically, interpretation takes the form of a statement aimed at helping patients see the unconscious basis of a symptom that has been masked by resistance—for example: "Having these repeated accidents perhaps assured you of getting the attention you felt you could not get otherwise." Or interpretation may direct the patient's attention to a repressed impulse—for example: "Could it be that your present shyness is a defense against the aggressiveness your mother punished for when you were little?"

Analysts offer interpretation only when they have developed a reasonably clear picture of the dynamics of the patient's personality and the biographical roots of difficulties. Timing of interpretation is critical: if offered too soon, anxiety and resistance may be aroused; if timed correctly, a flow of new associations may be elicited leading to significant progress in the therapy.

Transference   As analysis progresses, patients may begin to express intense and unrealistic feelings and expectations toward the analyst. They may feel that the analyst is indifferent to them, for example, or that the analyst is attempting to manipulate them. If early ungratified strivings for love have been reactivated, they may begin to act seductively toward the analyst, bring presents, and spend hours rehearsing what they will say in the next therapy session. This process, through which the analyst becomes the focus of emotions once directed at parents or other significant people in the patients' childhoods, is called **transference.**

When transference occurs, the analyst points out to patients that their behavior is inappropriate and actually a form of resistance to getting better. This may trigger negative transference—focusing on the therapist feelings of frustration and violent anger that were once directed at disapproving parental figures. Ruth Munroe (1955), cites the case of a patient who actually pulled a gun on his analyst: "I admire the *sang-froid* of the analyst who looked in a gun . . . and said calmly, 'This is what I meant about your murderous feelings toward your father (laugh). Do you see it now?' According to the analyst, the patient laughed also, albeit a bit hysterically, and lay down on the couch—in such a position that the analyst could now unobtrusively wipe the sweat off his brow."

Munroe's dramatic example illustrates how the analyst's skillful use of interpretation can transform transference into a therapeutic instrument. By emotionally reliving painful aspects of childhood, patients in transference give the analyst a clear view of the unconscious determinants of their behaviors. And with the help of the analyst's interpretation, patients come to understand better the irrational expectations and demands that they bring not only to the analyst but also to people in everyday life.

On the other hand, transference can fail if analysts themselves have not resolved the conflicts in their own unconscious. When analysts respond to the hostile or seductive transference of patients with unconscious emotional reactions of their own, **countertransference** is said to occur. To prevent countertransference, analysts themselves must undergo thorough analysis before they attempt to treat patients.

Working Through   Difficulties often occur even when analysis appears to be on the way to successful completion. New experiences in a patient's life may threaten the recent and fragile adjustment, and neurotic responses may reappear. In the continuing therapy, resistance may once again become a factor, and, as Karl Menninger (1958) put it, "It often appears as if the patient had never heard the analyst's previous interpretation." Interpretations must be repeated and related again to the patient's past and present. In successful therapy, however, the healthy part of a patient's personality has been activated and ultimately works to integrate the insights so painfully achieved.

Psychoanalysis was not only Freud's method of treatment but also his primary mode of research. He developed the methods of interpretation and the

The Rogerian approach to therapy emphasizes the relationship between therapist and client.

analysis of transference, which are used in treatment, as ways of gaining insight into psychological conflict. The fact that treatment and research are so tightly intertwined makes psychoanalysis extremely difficult to evaluate.

Humanistic Therapy

Humanistic therapy developed in part as a reaction against the psychoanalytic view. Whereas psychoanalysis emphasizes the primitive sexual and aggressive impulses of the id and their management by the ego, humanism takes an optimistic view that stresses the human potential for growth. Clients, or patients, are regarded as having the freedom and capacity to choose their own goals in life. They are seen as integrated wholes rather than as conflict-ridden combinations of id, ego, and superego impulses.

Client-Centered Therapy

The most prominent example of the humanistic approach is the **client-centered therapy** of Carl Rogers (1957, 1959). Rogers believes that all humans have an innate tendency toward self-actualization (chapter 12) and, given the opportunity, will find their own paths toward self-development. Patients themselves set the goals of therapy, and the therapist refrains from giving advice 'or specific prescriptions for change, unlike the directive interpretation offered in psychoanalysis. With nondirective therapy the therapist neither defines patients' problems nor tells patients how to solve them.

The Rogerian approach emphasizes the critical importance of the relationship between therapist and client. Rogers' vision of the ideal therapist is expressed in the form of ten difficult questions therapists must ask themselves (Rogers, 1961).

1. Can I *be* in some way which will be perceived by the other person as trustworthy, as dependable or consistent in some deep sense . . . ?
2. Can I be expressive enough as a person that what I am will be communicated unambiguously . . . ?
3. Can I let myself experience positive attitudes towards this other person—attitudes of warmth, caring, liking, interest, respect . . . ?
4. Can I be strong enough as a person to be separate from the other . . . ?
5. Am I secure enough within myself to permit him his separateness . . . ?
6. Can I let myself enter fully into the world of his feelings and personal meanings and see these as he does . . . ?
7. Can I be acceptant of each facet of this other person which he presents to me? Can I perceive him as he is? Can I communicate this attitude? Or can I only receive him conditionally, acceptant of some aspects of his feelings and silently or openly disapproving of other aspects?
8. Can I act with sufficient sensitivity in the relationship that my behavior will not be perceived as a threat . . . ?
9. Can I free him from the threat of external evaluation . . . ?
10. Can I meet this other individual as a person who is in the process of *becoming* or will I be bound by his past and by my past . . . ?

Rogers also has cited six conditions that the therapist-client relationship must fulfill in order to be successful (Rogers, 1957):

1. Client and therapist must be fully aware of each other.
2. The client must be in a state of incongruence—that is, not freely and genuinely himself or herself—and thus feeling vulnerable or anxious.
3. The therapist must be congruent—an authentic person who wears no mask and plays no role.
4. The therapist must express unconditional positive regard, listening with a nonjudgmental attitude that permits clients to be themselves without threat of sanctions.

5. The therapist must relate to clients with complete empathy, sensing "the client's world as if it were your own, but without ever losing the 'as if' quality."
6. The client must feel, at least to some degree, the therapist's acceptance and understanding.

Techniques

Unlike psychoanalysts, Rogerian therapists make no attempt to trace the early roots of difficulties. The focus is on the client's present functioning, and therapy is concluded in a relatively brief period. Rogers (1957) defines therapy as the "releasing of an already existent capacity in a potentially competent individual, not the expert manipulation of a more or less passive personality." To this end, he advocates three principal techniques of therapeutic procedure:

- *Reflection of feelings.* The therapist accepts the client's feelings and communicates understanding by restating them in words that mirror their essence. For example:
  CLIENT: I was small and envied people who were large. I was—well, I took beatings by boys and I couldn't strike back.
  THERAPIST: You've had plenty of experience in being the underdog.
- *Clarification of feelings.* When the client becomes confused in trying to express feelings, it is up to the therapist to help clarify them so that the client can express them clearly. For example:
  THERAPIST: And so, little by little, you have come to hold back things that previously you would have communicated to your wife? Is that it?
- *Expression of therapist's feelings.* Rogers has recently concluded that, in order truly to be genuine, therapists should reveal their own reactions when it seems appropriate (Meador & Rogers, 1979).
  CLIENT: I think I'm beyond help.
  THERAPIST: Huh? Feel as though you're beyond help? I know. You feel just completely hopeless about yourself. I can understand that. I don't feel hopeless, but I realize you do.

Through these techniques, the therapist helps clients to see inconsistencies between their self-concepts and their behaviors and to accept feelings that previously had been denied. These insights facilitate a reorganization of the self on a more realistic level. With this restructuring comes behavior that is more adaptive, less anxious, and more effective (Rogers, 1961).

Rogers has increasingly acknowledged the difficulties inherent in attempting to carry out a truly nondirective treatment. Rogers' later writings emphasize the necessity for the therapist to become geniunely involved in the therapeutic process as an empathic, sensitive individual. Specific intervention procedures and techniques are considered secondary to the therapist's capacity to accept the client unconditionally and communicate his or her understanding of that person's experience.

Behavior Therapy

Psychodynamic and humanistic therapies are both based on the assumption that disordered behavior can be changed through insight into its internal causes. **Behavior therapy,** as its name suggests, focuses on the behavior itself rather than on subjective determinants. What a psychoanalyst would call the symptom of an underlying problem is, in the eyes of a behavior therapist, actually the problem. Behavior therapists assume that emotional disturbances are learned reactions to coping with various stresses. In therapy, they put into practice the principles of learning—and unlearning—developed in the laboratory by experimental psychologists.

Another notable departure in behavior therapy relates to the role of the therapist. Unlike psychoanalysts and humanistic therapists, many practitioners

Mary Cover Jones demonstrated that counterconditioning is possible by substituting a new response to a stimulus.

of behavior therapy minimize the importance of the relationship between therapist and patient and emphasize instead impersonal techniques of treatment (Parloff, Waskow, & Wolper, 1978). In fact, some therapists take the extreme position that the therapist is essentially a "social reinforcement machine" (Krasner, 1962).

There are five major behavioral approaches to treatment. Two of them—counterconditioning and operant techniques—are derived respectively from the principles of classical and operant conditioning. The third, modeling, originated in Albert Bandura's theory of observational learning. The fourth, cognitive restructuring, reflects the increasing interest of behaviorists in the processes of cognition. And finally, self-control procedures require individuals themselves to rearrange environmental contingencies in order to reduce undesirable behaviors and increase or strengthen desirable behaviors.

Counterconditioning

The aim of **counterconditioning** is to break the connection between a given stimulus and response that has been classically conditioned. Remember, for example, the story of Little Albert who was conditioned, through the use of a frightening noise, to fear white rats. A connection was established between the conditioned stimulus (white rat) and Little Albert's response (fear). A few years after this experiment, Mary Cover Jones (1925) demonstrated that such fears could be counterconditioned by substituting a new response to the stimulus. In this instance, the old response was a little boy's fear of rabbits. She eliminated this by feeding the boy in the presence of a rabbit, gradually moving him closer to the animal on successive occasions. The new response—positive feelings associated with eating—"crowded out" the old response—fear.

Three basic techniques are employed in counterconditioning—systematic desensitization, implosive therapy, and aversion therapy. Each uses entirely different methods.

Systematic Desensitization   The counterconditioning technique developed by Joseph Wolpe (1958), **systematic desensitization,** is based on the medical procedure of giving increasing doses of allergens to hay fever sufferers. In systematic desensitization, patients are taught a new response, deep muscle relaxation, and then gradually conditioned to substitute the new response for fear as they mentally visualize increasing "doses" of anxiety-provoking situations.

Suppose, for example, you have a terrible fear of flying. After you have learned a series of exercises that help you relax the entire body, the therapist asks you to draw up a list of all the situations that trigger your fear of flying—for example, the decision to buy a plane ticket, the drive to the airport, boarding the plane, the takeoff. You and the therapist rank these situations in an **anxiety hierarchy,** from the least to the most fear-evoking. The therapist then tells you to relax in a reclining chair and imagine the least fearful situation. When you are able to do this without muscular tension, you then contemplate the next situation in the hierarchy. This process may continue for ten separate sessions or more, until you can imagine the entire hierarchy of anxieties without feeling fear. In addition, the therapist may assign "homework" between sessions—actually placing yourself in the progressively frightening situations.

Does the effect of learning to relax while merely imagining the stressful situations carry over into real life? Studies have shown that it generally does, resulting in reduction of anxiety in situations imagined during therapy (Wolpe, 1958; Goldfried and Davison, 1976). Success has been reported with a wide range of complaints, including phobias, psychosomatic disorders, and depression brought on by external stresses (Phillips & Bierman, 1981).

Implosive Therapy   A second type of counterconditioning, **implosive therapy,** differs radically from systematic desensitization. Instead of fighting fear by gradually increasing the patient's tolerance for anxiety as in desensitization, implosive therapy fights fear by attempting to create a massive dose of it. At the outset, patients are instructed to visualize themselves in the most frightening circumstances imaginable—for example, trapped on a tiny island, with no means of escape, surrounded by hideous beasts. The aim is to create an inward explosion, or implosion, of anxiety. By repeatedly confronting this implosive panic the patient gradually becomes accustomed to it, and eventually anxiety is extinguished (Stampfl & Levis, 1967).

Implosive therapy is controversial and has been attacked as cruel and inhumane. The technique offends behaviorists because its theoretical underpinnings encompass not only classical conditioning but also certain tenets of psychoanalytic theory. The conditioned stimuli for fears, implosive therapists assert, originate in infantile aggression and sexuality, and these fears must be confronted.

Support for implosive therapy comes from both clinical experience and laboratory research with animals. An animal's fear of a stimulus that has previously been paired with shock can sometimes be rapidly extinguished if the animal is prevented from escaping shock. Clinical data indicate that implosion is about as effective as desensitization in reducing a variety of phobias (Gelder et al., 1973). Implosion using vivid or horrifying images is used a good deal less frequently today since researchers have found that prolonged exposure to a feared stimulus under more benign conditions is a more comfortable and more effective treatment.

Aversion Therapy   Another controversial technique of counterconditioning is **aversion therapy.** In desensitization the goal is to substitute a positive response, relaxation, for anxiety; in the aversion approach, by contrast, the aim is to substitute negative feelings for positive ones by conditioning aversion to stimuli that are considered inappropriately attractive. To reduce the attraction of cigarette smoking, for example, the therapist might give the client repeated electric shocks whenever pictures of cigarettes are presented. Thus, an anxiety response would be substituted for the good feelings a heavy smoker might ordinarily associate with cigarettes.

A second kind of aversion therapy, called **covert sensitization,** relies on the power of the imagination (Lazarus, 1958). Clients are asked to imagine the aversive effects of an undesirable behavior such as heavy drinking. A treatment

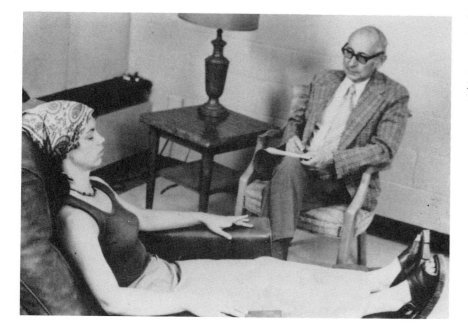

Psychiatrist Joseph Wolpe (pictured here) uses systematic desensitization to teach people to control fears and anxieties by visualizing anxiety-provoking situations while deeply relaxed.

Aversion therapy is often used to treat alcoholism.

program for alcoholics has been developed using covert sensitization (Cautela, 1966). It includes the following instructions from the therapist:

> As you are approaching the bar you have a funny feeling in the pit of your stomach. Your stomach feels all queasy and nauseous. Some liquid comes up your throat and it is very sour. You try to swallow it back down, but as you do this, food particles start coming up your throat to your mouth. . . . As the bartender is pouring the beer, puke comes up into your mouth.

Although aversive therapy has helped clients control such habits as overeating, heavy drinking, and cigarette smoking, it has been criticized for both ethical and scientific reasons. Critics question the wisdom of inflicting pain and discomfort on people; they also question how long people will react anxiously to a stimulus such as cigarettes once they are no longer being shocked.

The most controversial use of aversion therapy has been an attempt to change the sexual orientation of male homosexuals (Feldman & MacCulloch, 1971). Clients were presented with pictures of males and given electric shocks while they viewed the picture; then a picture of an attractive female was presented without the electric shock. Using this procedure, the researchers reported that more than half of 43 male homosexual patients were judged to have become significantly more oriented toward heterosexual activities. It should be noted, however, that homosexual feelings and behavior were not completely eliminated. Also, those who sought treatment did not accept their homosexuality and were desirous of change. The procedure has been strongly criticized by gay liberation organizations who contend that it contributes to the general impression of homosexuality as a form of aberrant behavior. Indeed, many researchers are now questioning the appropriateness of programs to reorient homosexual males and lesbians, and instead have recommended research on gay life styles and a recognition of the wide range of adjustments possible within homosexual populations (Davison, 1978).

Operant Techniques

The second major theoretical approach to behavior therapy stems largely from the research in operant conditioning by B. F. Skinner. **Operant techniques** are based on the use of positive and negative reinforcement to shape, or modify, the behavior of patients. For example, the process of shaping—rewarding each stage in a series of gradual approximations—has been employed to change the behavior of psychotics.

The most notable successes of operant therapy have been attained with children. By working with parents and teachers, operant therapists have been able to change reinforcement practices and eliminate a wide range of childhood problems, including aggression, bed-wetting, and asthmatic attacks. For example, in the instance of an overdemanding child, the operant therapist might make a **functional analysis** in the home, carefully noting the correlation between the child's demands and the parents' unwitting reinforcement policies. Then a strategy would be developed in which the parents would reinforce, through their attention and other rewards, the child's nondemanding actions.

Detailed operant techniques have been developed to teach normal speech to severely disturbed children (Lovass, 1977). Many of the children did not speak at all or were able to vocalize only simple vowels. The program begins by teaching the child a few recognizable words. Then it proceeds to teaching the child to label events and objects, then to verbalize relationships between events, and, finally, to develop spontaneous conversation skills. Reinforcement is used throughout the process. The following example shows how a child in the third month of language training begins to develop discriminations in the context of a conversation (Lovass, 1977). During the conversation the child received an M&M candy after each correct response.

E:	Ricky, what's your name?
RICKY:	Ricky.
E:	That's right.
RICKY:	How are you feeling?
E:	No. Ask me what I asked you. Ricky! Say what's your name?
RICKY:	Ricky.
E:	No. Say, what's . . .
RICKY:	What's (pauses) . . .
E:	Your . . .
RICKY:	Your (pauses) . . .
E:	Say, name.
RICKY:	Name.
E:	Now, say it all together.
RICKY:	What's your name?
E:	Joan. Good boy, Ricky. That's good. That's good. Come here, Ricky. Stand up, Ricky. Ricky, how are you feeling?
RICKY:	I am feeling fine.
E:	That's good. Ricky, come here. Ricky, come. Now you ask me.
RICKY:	How are you feeling?
E:	I am feeling fine. That's good. That's good.
RICKY:	Lie down, please. Lie down. (Preceding this hour Ricky had been taught how to order E to stand up, lie down, smile, etc.)
E:	Ricky, how old are you?
RICKY:	I'm 7 years old.
E:	That's right. Ask me, Ricky.
RICKY:	Ask me.
E:	No. That's not what I asked you. Ask me how old I am. Say, how . . .
RICKY:	Are you feeling?
E:	No. That's not what I asked you either. I asked you how old you are. Now, you ask me. Say, how . . .
RICKY:	Old . . .
E:	Say, are you.
RICKY:	Are you.
E:	That's right. Now say it all together. Say, how old are you?
RICKY:	I am 7 years old. How old are you?
E:	I am 21 years old. That's very good. That's good.

Operant techniques are also widely used in the so-called **token economy—** a system for changing behavior in an institutionalized setting. Ted Ayllon and Nathan Azrin (1968) set aside an entire ward of a mental hospital and instituted

Bandura has demonstrated the use of modeling therapy with clients who have an intense fear of snakes. By imitating models who handle snakes in a calm and confident manner, clients can learn to overcome their fear of these reptiles.

what they called a token economy. As reinforcement for activities such as making beds, brushing teeth, and combing hair, severely disturbed patients were given plastic tokens that could be exchanged for special privileges, including a private room or extra visits to the canteen. The token economy succeeded in bringing about a number of changes in overt behavior and has since been introduced at mental hospitals, prisons, and other institutions throughout the United States.

An example of a residential token economy is Achievement Place, a home-style facility for 12- to 16-year-old boys who have been referred to the courts for getting into trouble with the law (Fixsen, Phillips, & Wolf, 1972). The program is aimed at reducing antisocial behavior and increasing interpersonal skills as well as improving self-care and academic achievement. Target behaviors are identified, and a token system is developed in which the boys in the Achievement Place home receive points every time they complete the task or behave appropriately. They then can exchange their points for privileges or things they desire such as use of the telephone, tools, radios, record players, snacks, visits home, or allowances. Each resident of Achievement Place records the points he has earned on an index card, and at the end of the day the points can be exchanged for privileges to be used on the following day, if a stipulated number of points has been accumulated. Thus far, Achievement Place has been quite successful; for example, its graduates have had fewer contacts with the police and committed fewer acts that resulted in contact with the courts than children who received more traditional institutional treatment or had been placed on probation.

Token economy techniques also have been applied to the education of retarded children with encouraging results. In a six-week program at a school for retarded children, specially designed teaching materials were used, and performance was rewarded with tokens that could be exchanged for soft drinks, extra time watching television, and other privileges (Ayllon and Kelly, 1972). At the end of the program, tests showed that the IQ of the subjects had increased by an average of almost four points. Meanwhile, the average IQ of children in the control group not participating in the program had actually declined nearly three points.

A problem of operant therapy used in institutional settings is that of generalizing to real-life situations (Kazdin, 1979). If it is the reinforcement contingencies of real-life environments that are assumed to have produced the problems in the first place—as many behavior therapists assume—what happens when the client returns there? To make new behavior patterns more persistent, operant therapists have tried several approaches. One is to move patients away from a continuous schedule of reinforcement to an intermittent schedule so that reinforcement occurs regularly but infrequently. Another strategy is to encourage clients to reinforce themselves for the desired behavior. The staff of Achievement Place, for example, has dealt with the problem by phasing out the point system as quickly as possible and shifting to a merit system so that the boys do not come to rely on the token economy program.

Modeling

The third major theoretical approach to behavior therapy employs the concept of **modeling,** or observational learning, formulated by Albert Bandura. In treatment through modeling, the patient unlearns anxiety about a given stimulus by watching the therapist perform a behavior and then imitating that behavior (Bandura, 1971).

Bandura's most celebrated demonstration of modeling therapy was an experiment with people who had an intense fear of snakes (Bandura, 1971). Although, strictly speaking, these people were not patients (they were subjects who had answered a newspaper ad seeking individuals with a fear of snakes), their fear amounted to a phobia. Some of them so dreaded the possibility of encountering snakes that they had to forgo pleasures such as hiking and gardening. Bandura first tested their fear by confronting his subjects with a four-foot king snake. Then he divided the subjects into four groups and compared three different methods of treatment. One group underwent systematic desensitization, substituting a relaxed response while progressively imagining increasingly anxiety-provoking situations involving snakes. The second group, after learning muscle relaxation procedures, watched a movie on snake handling. The third group watched a live model, the therapist, play with a large king snake; then, in a series of stages, the members of this group were encouraged to approach the snake and imitate all the maneuvers the therapist had performed with the snake. The fourth group was the control group; members received no treatment at all.

The test to determine the effectiveness of the various treatments was dramatically direct: subjects had to sit in a chair for 30 seconds while a snake crawled over their bodies. Although only a few members of the other treatment groups passed the test, everyone in the modeling therapy group succeeded. Later, Bandura used modeling therapy to reduce snake phobia in members of the other groups.

Modeling also has been successful with childhood phobias such as fear of dogs or fear of dentists. In addition, something very much like modeling is evident in the procedure called *behavioral rehearsal* in which the therapist demonstrates how to handle an interpersonal problem in a better way and the patient then imitates the therapist, continually rehearsing this new behavior (Lazarus, 1971). Modeling also has been combined with other behavioral therapies, including operant approaches, in the effective treatment of schizophrenic patients (Bellack, Hersen, & Turner, 1976).

Albert Ellis' rational-emotive therapy is a method of cognitive restructuring.

Cognitive Restructuring

Another general approach in behavior therapy, **cognitive restructuring,** differs from the other methods in its emphasis on manipulation, or restructuring, of the cognitive processes. Until recent years, as we have seen previously, the behavioral perspective in psychology had focused on overt behavior, which could be measured objectively, and largely neglected the subjective processes of reasoning and thinking.

One important method of cognitive restructuring is the **rational-emotive therapy** of Albert Ellis (1976, 1977), which was long ignored by most behavior theoreticians. Ellis traced many emotional problems to internal sentences that people repeat to themselves. For example, depressed people may say to themselves, ''What a worthless person I am.'' Or anxious people may create internal problems by adopting unrealistic expectations such as those embodied in the internal sentence, ''I must win the love of everyone.'' External events are then interpreted in terms of these assumptions.

Recently, Beck argued that the cognitions of depressed persons play an important role both in causing and maintaining depression. He suggests that automatic, rigid cognitive schemata or ideas, when they are activated by stress, produce distorted perceptions and interpretations in depressed people. These automatic schemata tend to perpetuate people's unrealistic pessimism about themselves, the future, and their world. Beck and his colleagues (1979) have developed a method for helping depressed persons to restructure their rigid cognitions, and early results of comparative research by Rush et al. (1977) suggest that cognitive therapy is as effective or more effective than antidepressant medication in reducing symptoms and in maintaining improvement over the course of as much as an entire year.

Although cognitive behavior therapists may differ in the details of the specific procedures they employ, they agree that changing maladaptive thought patterns is central to the therapeutic effort (Price & Lynn, 1981). Cognitive behavioral methods have been used with success in treating test anxiety, lack of dating skills, chronic anger, and schizophrenia. Meichenbaum and his colleagues (1983) have also shown that cognitive restructuring techniques can be effective in preventing psychological problems that may emerge for individuals experiencing stressful situations.

Cognitive behavior therapists believe that it is unnecessary to assume that hidden motivations or unconscious processes are modifying behavior. The cognitive behavior therapist's direct focus on conscious thought patterns and their modification is what most distinguishes cognitive restructuring from other techniques of behavior modification and psychotherapy.

Self-control Procedures

One of the more recent developments in behavior therapy is the use of **self-control procedures.** With the therapist operating as a consultant, clients set up their own goals—for example, losing weight or stopping smoking—and provide their own reinforcements.

Clients use operant-oriented steps in their programs: (1) Desirable behavior is positively reinforced; negative behavior is not reinforced. (2) Reinforcement is contingent—that is, it is gained only if the desired behavior takes place. (3) Environments are controlled by the clients themselves to increase the possibilities of performing the targeted behaviors (Watson & Tharp, 1972).

Weight-control through behavior change is perhaps the most prevalent goal of self-control programs. By rearranging environmental cues that stimulate eating, clients attempt to increase the chances for performing the desired behavior of moderate eating. After a certain number of days of eating controlled-amount meals slowly, consciously, and in a particular setting, they reward themselves for changes in behavior with some type of reinforcement such as buying a new article of clothing.

In some ways, the techniques of self-control procedures resemble those of token economies, but they are not institutionalized programs, and clients administer their own reinforcements. Therapists serve as advisers and intervene only when needed.

Group Therapy

The therapies discussed so far typically occur on a one-to-one basis between therapist and patient or client. There are several potential advantages, however, if a therapist can treat more than one patient at a time. In recent

A popular form of therapy is group therapy, involving a therapist and up to a dozen patients.

CHAPTER 15 BEHAVIOR CHANGE

years, **group therapy** consisting of a therapist and up to a dozen patients has become highly popular in the United States. The following advantages are cited by proponents of group therapy:

- Therapists can use time more efficiently, see more patients, and presumably charge lower fees.
- Patients who have difficulty relating to other people can experience effective interaction firsthand.
- Patients are subjected to social pressures from others to change.
- Patients may be comforted by the knowledge that others have similar problems.
- Patients can learn vicariously—by watching the behavior of others—to solve their own problems.

Practically every theoretical approach or method of therapy used with individuals has also been applied in group settings. Behavioral methods are used in groups essentially as a time-saving device; these groups usually retain much of the therapist-to-patient relationship found in individual therapy. By contrast, the four types of group therapy we will examine—psychodrama, sensitivity training, encounter groups, and family therapy—all emphasize interaction among group members.

In T-groups, people are taught to be more sensitive in their relationships with others.

Psychodrama

One of the pioneers of group therapy was J. L. Moreno, who had an abiding interest in the theater and in 1921 founded a drama company. Out of this experience grew Moreno's inspiration for a type of group therapy that he called **psychodrama** (Moreno & Kipper, 1965).

In psychodrama the members of a therapeutic group act out their feelings as if they were actors in a play, improvising their lines. Often the psychodrama centers on the problems of one patient, with the others playing the roles of principal figures in the patient's life. Moreno believed that such role playing revealed the patients' deepest emotions and enabled them to change more effectively than by merely attempting to verbalize their feelings. In a special method of role playing, the **mirroring technique,** one member of the group portrays another member, giving that individual the opportunity to see himself or herself as others do. The director of the psychodrama is the therapist. Often the drama actually takes place on a stage in front of an audience. Moreno believed that members of the audience might be helped with their own problems if they saw them portrayed on the stage.

Sensitivity Training

The **sensitivity training group**—often called the **T-group** (*T* for training)—originated in 1947 at the National Training Laboratories in Bethel, Maine (Buchanan, 1964). It began as a method to make business executives more sensitive in their relationships with others, but has since burgeoned into an educational movement aimed at helping people who, although functioning well, want to improve interpersonal interactions.

Members of a T-group are encouraged to drop their guard, to speak frankly, and to listen attentively. The emphasis is on the process of interaction among the participants and the problems that arise during it. As the interaction develops, participants are encouraged to examine their reactions to the others and to analyze their own true feelings and perceptions.

The role of the leader, or trainer, differs from that of a one-to-one therapist: the trainer is a full member of the group (Aronson, 1972). Other members are free to comment on the trainer's feelings and reactions. Trainers are not supposed to impose their will or ideas on the other participants, although they sometimes intervene if one of the members is being subjected to undue coercion by the rest of the group.

Encounter Groups

While the **encounter group** movement developed from separate origins—Rogers (1970) traces it to his program of training counselors at the University of Chicago after World War II—its techniques are often difficult to distinguish from those used in T-groups. Rogers' groups tend to follow the tenets of his client-centered therapy, with the group leader, or facilitator, working to clarify the feelings of group members.

Encounter groups are widely employed in public institutions, especially juvenile correctional centers. They are best known, however, from their association with centers of the human potential movement such as Esalen. One form of encounter group is the *marathon,* a weekend-long session in which participants seldom sleep—the supposition being that fatigue will help participants drop their social masks and become more open with one another.

Critics of both T-groups and encounter groups contend that the group experience teaches members only how to participate in such groups. They assert that the insights and skills learned in these groups are difficult to transfer to real life, where complete openness and candor are seldom considered virtues (Houts & Serber, 1972). Some research suggests that participants view themselves more favorably after a group experience but, surprisingly, are not necessarily less prejudiced or more open-minded (Lieberman, Yalom, & Miles, 1973). There is also the danger that, if an individual's faults are pointed out but not fully dealt with by the group, problems may be aggravated rather than solved. A participant may leave feeling worse than before taking part in the therapy (Lieberman, Yalom, & Miles, 1973). For these reasons T-groups and encounter groups are not recommended for those with moderate to severe emotional problems.

Family Therapy

Many investigators believe that the family is instrumental in producing and maintaining disordered behavior, especially in children. Underlying this belief is the view, known as a *systems approach,* that the dynamics of family interaction may be responsible for the symptoms of the individual; the individual, in other words, is part of a larger, disordered system. Therefore, some therapists involve several members of the family in the treatment process.

Family therapy involves the discussion of problems with all the members of a family in an effort to uncover and modify aspects of family interaction that may be contributing to problems.

CHAPTER 15   BEHAVIOR CHANGE

Family therapists, by talking with all the members of the family, attempt to pinpoint disordered interactions. For example, take the case of Laura, a fourteen-year-old girl who refused to eat and had to be hospitalized because of excessive weight loss (Aponte & Hoffman, 1973). In the following excerpt from the first therapy session, the therapist asks Laura what happens when she refuses to eat:

THERAPIST: (To Laura.) When you get annoyed, how do you express your annoyance? What do you say to Dad? Say it now, the way you said it then.

LAURA: (To father.) No, I don't want any food. (Pause.)

THERAPIST: What do you do then? (Pause.) Dad, what do you do then, when she says that?

FATHER: I naturally insist.

THERAPIST: You insist. Insist now. I want to know how it works.

FATHER: (Overlapping.) Well, this is more present than recent. This is not . . .

THERAPIST: OK, yeah, OK. Make believe that it's happening.

FATHER: OK (To Laura.) I'm going downstairs, Laura. Do you want something?

LAURA: No.

FATHER: Nothing at all, no snitch, something, a piece of fruit?

LAURA: Nothing. I don't want anything.

FATHER: A little ice cream?

LAURA: No.

FATHER: OK.

THERAPIST: (To Laura.) Do the same thing with Mom. How does it go? (To Mother.) It goes also with you similar?

LAURA: Uh . . .

THERAPIST: (Indicating that Laura should continue.) OK.

FATHER: (To Laura.) Try it at the dinner table with Connie. I think that might be better because (to Mother) you don't go down as often as I do. (Laughter.)

Thus, the therapist focuses on Laura's problem as a struggle with her parents rather than as a symbol of an inner conflict, as in the psychodynamic approach. The therapist calls the attention of the family to such disordered interactions and suggests ways that such interactions can be modified. Family members are helped to express their desires and feelings directly and clearly to one another. The therapist may even have them rehearse such interactions. Often, family therapy sessions are videotaped and then rerun so that parents and children can see for themselves the nuances of their behavior toward one another.

Evaluating Psychotherapy

The effectiveness of psychotherapy is extremely difficult to measure because it is subject to so many variables—patient, therapist, and the nature of the disorder. Subjective reports by therapists or patients may be valuable but scarcely qualify as dispassionate evidence of effectiveness. Therapists have vested interests in proving the value of their efforts. The patients' own assessments may be influenced by what has been called the hello-goodbye effect: when they say "hello" to the therapist, there is a tendency to exaggerate their problems to make clear they really need help; when they say "goodbye" at the end of therapy, there is a tendency to exaggerate how much better they feel in order to show appreciation to the therapist and to convince themselves that the time and money were well spent.

RESEARCH

A Way to Find Out

Whether Psychotherapy

Works

One of the major problems in evaluating the effectiveness of psychotherapy is that the research in this field is extremely fragmented. It consists of large numbers of relatively small studies dealing with diverse treatment methods and employing different measures of effectiveness. All of these data, observe Mary L. Smith and Gene V. Glass, are "atomized and sprayed across a vast landscape of journals, books, and reports." The impressive achievement of Smith and Glass (1977) has been to search out all of these fragments of data, subject them to complex statistical analysis, and then provide tentative answers to two vital questions: Does psychotherapy work? Which type of therapy works best?

In their "meta-analysis," Smith and Glass carried out an exhaustive search of the literature that turned up no less than 1000 different evaluations of psychotherapy. Of these, 375 studies were selected for complete statistical analysis. One criterion for inclusion in the analysis was that a study had to compare at least one therapy treatment group to an untreated group or to a different therapy group. The following definition of

psychotherapy was used in the selection process:

> Psychotherapy is taken to mean the informed and planful application of techniques derived from established psychological principles, by persons qualified through training and experience to understand these principles and to apply these techniques with the intention of assisting individuals to modify such personal characteristics as feelings, values, attitudes, and behaviors which are judged by the therapist to be maladaptive or maladjustive (Meltzoff & Kornreich, 1970).

By this definition, the following were excluded from the analysis: drug

therapies, hypnotherapy, bibliotherapy, occupational therapy, milieu therapy, peer counseling, sensitivity training, marathon encounter groups, consciousness-raising groups, and psychodrama.

After selecting the studies, Smith and Glass classified the different types of outcomes assessed in the studies. There were ten categories, including such measures as fear and anxiety reduction, self-esteem, and achievement in school or on the job. Altogether, the 375 studies yielded 833 outcomes. (Some studies had more than one outcome because they measured the effect of therapy at more than one time or on more than one type of effect.) All of these outcomes measures were more or less related to "well-being" and thus are generally comparable.

Through statistical measurement, Smith and Glass then determined the magnitude of effect for each therapy outcome. (Magnitude of effect, or effect size, was the mean difference between the treated and control subjects divided by the standard deviation of the control group.)

The 833 effect-size measures represented about 25,000 subjects in the

---

Nonetheless, a number of attempts have been made to evaluate psychotherapy. Such studies typically ask two questions:

1. Does psychotherapy work?
2. Which method among the many approaches to psychotherapy works best?

Does Psychotherapy Work?

Given the enormous amounts of money, energy, and hope expended each year on psychotherapy, the question may seem superfluous. In fact, however, psychotherapy as a means of behavior change has long been subject to scientific skepticism.

The most forceful attack on the effectiveness of psychotherapy was mounted in 1952 by the British psychologist Hans J. Eysenck (Eysenck, 1952, 1965). Eysenck surveyed studied of several thousand people who either underwent psychotherapy or were not treated; psychoanalytic techniques were used on the majority of those who had been treated. As a result of this survey, Eysenck concluded that about 75 percent of neutorics got better within two treatment groups and a similar number in the control groups. On the average, the therapy clients were 22 years of age, and received an average of 17 hours of therapy from therapists with an average of about 3-1/2 years of experience. The effects of their treatment were measured on an average of a little less than four months after therapy.

How effective was their treatment? According to Smith and Glass, the average client receiving therapy was better off than 75 percent of the untreated members of the control groups. That finding was arrived at by lumping all of the 833 effect sizes together (see figure).

In order to compare the effectiveness of the general types of treatment, Smith and Glass asked 25 clinicians and counselors to classify the ten methods of therapy evaluated in the various studies. Two "superclasses" of therapy were perceived: behavioral therapies, including implosion, systematic desensitization, and behavior modification, and nonbehavioral therapies, including psychoanalytic therapy, Rogerian therapy, and eclectic therapy, among others.

Smith and Glass then selected 120

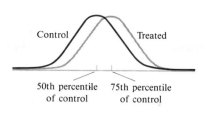

The results of the Smith and Glass study of the effectiveness of psychotherapy indicated that the average person receiving therapy was better off than 75 percent of the control group.

effect-size measures in which a behavioral therapy and a nonbehavioral therapy had been compared simultaneously with an untreated control group. Thus, for these studies, the two superclasses were equated for such important variables as nature of the clients' problems, duration of therapy, and experience of the therapists. In this analysis, Smith and Glass found that the behavioral and nonbehavioral therapies were about equally effective.

In further analyses, the researchers were able to manipulate statistically several of the variables. Consider, for example, a prototypical

subject of high intelligence, 20 years of age, being treated for a simple phobia by a therapist with two years' experience, and being evaluated immediately after therapy. Smith and Glass found that two behavioral therapies—systematic desensitization and behavioral modification—showed effects superior to psychodynamic therapy. This finding suggests that some therapies may be more effective than others for a particular type of person with a particular disorder. Overall, however, Smith and Glass reported that they could find only negligible differences in the effects produced by different therapy types.

In view of the continuing controversy over the effectiveness of psychotherapy and of competing types of therapy, the Smith and Glass meta-analysis is a highly significant contribution. It demonstrates a new strategy for summarizing research in a way that allows psychologists and mental health policymakers alike to draw overall conclusions. ■

years whether or not they received therapy. Eysenck's conclusions were disputed on several grounds: he focused on changes in behavior and ignored personality changes, and he also ignored the fact that many in the nontreated category actually were receiving help from their physicians. In attacking Eysenck's findings, one investigator used newer studies to conclude that although about 30 percent of neurotics improve spontaneously without treatment, about 65 percent improve in therapy (Bergin, 1971).

Which Psychotherapy Method Works Best?

Proponents of the various therapies have long debated the purported advantages of their own method and the shortcomings of other techniques. The psychodynamic approach is often challenged as too costly and too intellectual. Behavior therapies are accused of being mechanistic and of dealing with symptoms rather than root causes.

For the most convincing study of which therapy works best, we must look again to the ambitious analysis by Smith and Glass. In addition to their assessment of the effectiveness of psychotherapy in general, these investigators compared a number of individual therapeutic techniques. They then conducted a series of careful analyses. Their conclusions, while not likely to stop the debate over which therapy works best, is enlightening: there appears to be little or no difference in effectiveness among therapies.

As Smith and Glass put it: "Despite volumes devoted to the theoretical differences among different schools of psychotherapy, the results of research demonstrate negligible differences in the effects produced by different therapy types. Unconditional judgments of superiority of one or another type of psychotherapy and all that these claims imply about treatment and training policy are unjustified. Scholars and clinicians are in the rather embarrassing position of knowing less than has been proven, because knowledge atomized and sprayed across a vast landscape of journals, books, and reports has not been accessible" (Smith & Glass, 1977).

After a survey of patients, another group of researchers concluded that the relationship between patient and therapist plays a major role in the success of any type of therapy: "Psychotherapy was seen by our respondents as an intensely personal experience. Most important, the therapist's warmth, his respect and interest, and his perceived competence and activity emerged as important ingredients in the amount of change reported by the patients" (Strupp, Fox, & Lessler, 1969).

Although there is no convincing evidence that a particular type of therapy is clearly superior in all cases, researchers have suggested that there are certain common factors that provide the vehicles for effective change in psychotherapy (Murray & Jacobson, 1978):

1. Clients expect to be helped. Clients' expectations that they will be able to perform new behaviors successfully may be a powerful ingredient for change in both the insight- and behavior-oriented psychotherapies.

2. Changing maladaptive beliefs about the world may facilitate behavior change. The psychodynamic therapist's permissive attitude may encourage the client to rethink views about sexual behavior, for example. The rational emotive therapist's focus on "irrational thinking" may not only lead to changes in beliefs but also to behavioral change. Behavioral techniques, such as systematic desensitization, may change the client's beliefs about the phobic object or situation, and modeling and operant procedures may inform the client about real-world reinforcement contingencies.

3. Clients may come to alter their beliefs about themselves as a consequence of acceptance by the therapist. In the case of behavior therapy, the expectation on the part of therapists that they can positively change socially undesirable behavior often has a positive effect on clients' attitudes.

4. Clients develop skills in social living. In the case of many of the insight and behavior therapies, the therapist may provide an effective model for skillful social interaction. In the case of other therapies, such as client-centered therapy, feedback on the appropriateness or acceptability of certain feelings and thoughts may also promote the development of social competencies.

Thus it may be that the psychological methods of behavior change that we have reviewed share more in common than is at first evident. Even though hundreds of studies of the effectiveness of psychotherapy are now available, large-scale efforts to examine systematically the relative effectiveness of different therapeutic approaches for different types of problems, using commonly agreed-upon standards for success, are only now beginning. Studies of the kind conducted by Smith and Glass—as valuable as they are—only highlight the need for large-scale research to determine more definitively the relative effectiveness of different therapeutic approaches.

Biological Therapies

The psychotherapies attempt to bring about changes in behavior through manipulation of psychological processes such as learning and insight; the biological therapies seek the same goal through manipulation of the brain's physiological and chemical processes. The primary biological therapies consist of two highly controversial approaches to behavior change—electroconvulsive therapy and psychosurgery—as well as psychoactive drug treatment, a method that has proved to be dramatically effective in helping alleviate the symptoms of many people with emotional disturbances.

It is interesting to note that whereas psychotherapies tend to derive from theoretical formulations about behavior, biological therapies were discovered largely by happenstance. However, the effectiveness of drug therapy has led to promising new theories about the chemical mechanisms by which the brain mediates behavior.

Electroconvulsive Therapy

During the 1930s several European investigators began the experimental treatment of schizophrenia by inducing convulsions through the injection of various chemicals. They believed, erroneously, that schizophrenia and epilepsy were mutually exclusive disorders and that by inducing convulsions the schizophrenic could be cured. In 1939, the Italian psychiatrist Ugo Cerletti, who was interested in epilepsy, stumbled on a more effective way of inducing seizures. On a visit to a slaughterhouse he saw animals being rendered unconscious by electric shocks to the head. Soon afterward, Cerletti tried the technique on a schizophrenic patient—and **electroconvulsive therapy,** or **shock treatment,** was born.

Today shock treatment is used principally in cases of severe depression that fail to respond to other therapies. After being injected with an anesthetic, the patient is given a muscle relaxant and strapped down onto a bed to prevent bone fractures and bruises during the convulsions. Electrodes are placed on each side of the patient's forehead and, for about two seconds, a current is sent

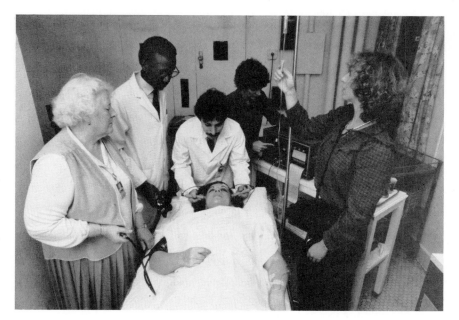

Electroconvulsive therapy is sometimes used to relieve symptoms of severely depressed individuals.

through the brain to produce a convulsion much like that of a *grand mal* epileptic seizure. Typically, the patient receives ten treatments over a period of about three weeks.

After a shock treatment, the patient often is confused and cannot remember the shock itself or events that occurred just before and after the convulsion. Impairment of long-term memory also has been reported in some cases. Ernest Hemingway, who underwent shock treatment for severe depression, asserted that it had ruined his writing career by erasing his store of long-term memories (*Time,* 1979). A new method of treatment, which causes convulsions only in one side of the brain (usually the nondominant hemisphere), apparently produces less confusion and memory loss.

A number of researchers (Greenblatt, Grosser, & Wechsler, 1964) have confirmed the effectiveness of shock treatment in relieving the symptoms of many, but not all, severely depressed patients, but no one knows how or why it works. The brain researcher Steven Rose (1975) has likened shock treatment to "attempting to mend a faulty radio by kicking it." More than 50 different explanations for its effectiveness have been offered, ranging from a modification of brain chemical levels to the old notion that shock punishes the unconscious, enabling patients to expiate the guilt said to be at the core of depression. The prospect of shock treatment terrifies many patients, a view held by the public at large and reinforced by the brutal shock scenes in the movie *One Flew over the Cuckoo's Nest.*

Psychosurgery

Like shock treatment, surgery performed to alter mental or emotional functioning and behavior—**psychosurgery**—is highly controversial, although apparently much less effective. History records a number of early instances of surgery aimed at controlling behavior, including the practice of castration, which eliminates the source of male sex hormones. Modern psychosurgery was launched in 1935 by Antonio de Egas Moniz, a Portuguese diplomat and psychiatrist. Moniz was impressed by a report by Carlyle Jacobsen, a Yale researcher who had removed a portion of the prefrontal lobe region from the brains of two chimpanzees, Becky and Lucy. The surgery eliminated the quarrelsome tendencies of the chimps who now "acted as though they had joined the happiness cult . . . and placed their burdens on the Lord" (Bailey, 1975).

Despite the fact that little was then known—or is now known—about the functions of this part of the brain, Moniz persuaded a colleague to perform a **prefrontal lobotomy** on a psychotic patient. The patient was calmer after the surgery, and soon lobotomies were being performed in the United States and elsewhere for all types of emotional disturbances. For his work, Moniz shared a Nobel Prize in 1949, although by then he was retired and partially paralyzed—the result of a bullet in the spine, which was fired by one of his lobotomized patients.

During the 1950s it became clear that the reports of dramatic improvements in lobotomized patients were premature, and the procedure fell out of favor. Although the surgery had a calming effect, it also often brought unintended side results, including stupor, impaired intellect, and epileptic seizures. Newer techniques have made lobotomies more precise, destroying much less brain tissue and resulting in fewer undesirable side effects. Nonetheless, this surgery is generally considered a last resort, suitable only for patients with long-term severe disturbances, such as obssessive-compulsive disorders, that do not respond to other therapies.

An even more controversial type of psychosurgery, **amygdalectomy,** involves destruction of centers deep in the brain that some researchers believe are responsible for violence and aggression. It has been suggested, for example, that malfunctions in the amygdala, a structure of the brain's limbic system, may trigger violent behavior (Mark & Ervin, 1970). Researchers implanted electrodes in the amygdala and then switched on an electric current in an attempt to locate the "aggression centers." If the patient reported a feeling of rage, these centers were then destroyed with a larger burst of current (Mark, Sweet, & Ervin, 1972).

Elliot S. Valenstein (1973), in an extensive critique of psychosurgery, has evaluated the cases of ten patients who underwent amygdalectomies. He found little evidence for optimism. Patients' violent episodes were not eliminated in all cases, and there were indications of undesirable side effects—including an instance of voracious appetite—presumably caused by damage to neighboring neural tissue. Aside from the ethical questions raised by psychosurgery, this latter consideration—damage to other neural tissue—is a decisive one for many investigators. So closely entwined are the myriad circuits of the brain that, given the present inadequacy of knowledge, it seems impossible to tamper with certain neural centers without affecting others.

Drug Treatment

Freud, who recognized that his talking cure was of limited effectiveness in helping severely disturbed patients, predicted: "The future may teach us how to exercise a direct influence by particular chemical substances" (Clark, 1979).

Beginning in the 1950s, this prediction came true with the development of psychoactive drugs. These drugs, while falling far short of providing permanent cures for disordered behavior, have had an extraordinarily dramatic impact on some types of mental illness. By relieving many of the worst symptoms of schizophrenia and depression, they have helped make possible a reduction in the population of mental hospitals, enabling patients to return to the community.

The psychoactive drugs used in treatment are classified into four categories—minor tranquilizers for anxiety, major tranquilizers for psychotic symptoms, stimulants, and antidepressants (see Table 15.1). None of these drugs is a panacea: practically all of them can produce undesirable side effects, and

Table 15.1 PSYCHOACTIVE DRUGS CATEGORIZED BY THEIR EFFECTS ON BEHAVIOR

Effect Group	*Chemical Group*	*Generic Name*	*Trade Name*
Minor tranquilizers	propanediols	meprobamate	Miltown, Equanil
	benzodiazepines	chlordiazepoxide diazepam	Librium Valium
Major tranquilizers (antipsychotics)	phenothiazines	chlorpromazine trifluoperazine thioridazine	Thorazine Stelazine Mellaril
	butyrophenones	haloperidol	Haldol
	thioxanthenes	chlorprothixene	Taractan
Stimulants	amphetamines	dextroamphetamine	Dexedrine
	piperidyls	methylphenidate	Ritalin
Antidepressants	tricyclics	imipramine amitriptyline doxepin	Tofranil Elavil Sinequan
	monoamine oxidase inhibitors	phenelzine tranylcypromine	Nardil Parnate

some are physically addictive. In addition, psychoactive drugs are typically used in conjunction with other therapies. When a patient stops taking the medication, symptoms usually return. Nonetheless, they have helped millions of people to overcome personal crises or simply to function in everyday life. They also have made it possible for many who previously could not be reached by psychotherapy to benefit from psychological as well as biological treatment.

Major Tranquilizers

The **major tranquilizers** are used to alleviate extreme symptoms of agitation and hyperactivity (Davis, 1975). For many centuries, people of Africa and India relied on a botanical remedy, the snakeroot plant, or *Rauwolfia sepentina,* for a variety of ailments including hysteria. This use of the drug was not known in the West until 1952, when Swiss chemists, who had experimented with *Rauwolfia* in treating high blood pressure, discovered the plant had a calming effect and extracted from it the first major tranquilizer, reserpine.

At about the same time, another series of events led to the synthesis of chlorpromazine, an even more effective tranquilizer. Chlorpromazine belongs to a remarkably useful class of compounds called the phenothiazines. The nucleus of these compounds was first synthesized in 1880 as a treatment for parasitic worm infections in animals. It was later used in the antihistamines, which were prescribed for a variety of conditions, including the common cold, allergies, and lowered blood pressure. The use of antihistamines during surgery to reduce shock led to the discovery of the chemical's calming effect. Soon after, chlorpromazine was synthesized, and it quickly became the treatment of choice for schizophrenia: in the decade after its introduction, it was given to an estimated 50 million patients around the world (May, 1968).

The effectiveness of chlorpromazine and the other phenothiazines in reducing the incidence of hallucinations and delusions and in enabling schizophrenics to leave mental hospitals has been established in a number of studies (May, 1968; MacDonald & Tobias, 1976).

The phenothiazines do, however, have some serious shortcomings. Not all schizophrenics are helped by the drugs. Moreover, often those who are helped are released from mental hospitals only to be readmitted later. This revolving-door pattern of admission, discharge, and readmission stems in part from disagreeable side effects, such as blurred vision, that lead patients to stop taking the medication when they are on their own. More serious side effects involve the motor systems. Patients may display symptoms such as rigidity of the facial muscles similar to that experienced in Parkinson's disease (Parkes, 1976). From 10 to 15 percent of patients treated with phenothiazines for a long period of time develop a neurological disorder called tardive dyskinesia (Jus et al., 1976), which is characterized by lip-smacking and chin-wagging motions. Tardive dyskinesia causes some patients such acute embarrassment that they avoid all contact with people (Widroe & Heisler, 1976).

A recent study by Estroff (1981) of mental patients in the community suggests that these secondary effects of the phenothiazines may place psychiatric patients in a dilemma. If they continue to take their medication, psychotic symptoms are reduced but the secondary motor symptoms of tardive dyskinesia are a signal to others in their social world that they are indeed psychiatric patients. If they cease their medication, their psychotic symptoms reemerge. Thus, drug treatment can have paradoxical effects on the well-being of the patient.

These effects on the motor systems were among the first clues to the neural chemistry now believed to underlie the action of the drugs. The major tranquilizers interfere with the workings of dopamine, one of the neurotransmitters that carries electric impulses between nerve cells. Dopamine is known to be active in neural systems mediating both emotions and voluntary movement. By mixing radioactively labeled drugs with brain tissue, Solomon Synder (1975) has shown that the drugs attach to nerve cell receptor sites normally occupied by dopamine. When the major tranquilizers attach to the dopamine receptors, they apparently block the action of dopamine, thereby blocking transmission of nerve impulses in these pathways. Snyder's research and the work of others strongly implies that the hallucinations and delusions of schizophrenia are linked to an excess of dopamine.

Minor Tranquilizers

The **minor tranquilizers** are antianxiety drugs that reduce excitability and cause drowsiness and are usually prescribed for patients who suffer anxiety or psychophysiological disorders. The first of the minor tranquilizers, Miltown, a propanediol, was introduced in the early 1950s, about the same time that the major tranquilizers came on the market. Later came the benzodiazepines (Librium, Valium), which are now among the most widely prescribed drugs in the world (Ray, 1978).

Recent brain research suggests that, like the major tranquilizers, Valium and the other minor tranquilizers exert their effects by occupying neural receptor sites in the brain (Schmeck, 1979). An earlier discovery by Candace Pert and Solomon Synder (1973)—of receptors to which opiates, such as morphine, would bind—led to the successful isolation of endogenous painkillers in the brain (see chapter 2). With this in mind, researchers now believe that the receptors to which Valium attaches are normally occupied by some naturally occurring chemical. This postulated chemical might be an endogenous tranquilizer, the brain's own means of controlling anxiety.

Like the other psychoactive drugs, the minor tranquilizers are a mixed blessing. Some of them can be addictive if taken regularly for a long period. A further danger is that many people resort to these pills instead of attempting to deal with everyday stress on their own.

Antidepressants

Whereas tranquilizers serve to calm arousal, **antidepressants** act to elevate mood and hence are sometimes called energizers. The first antidepressant, iproniazid, which belongs to a class of drugs called monoamine oxidase (MAO) inhibitors, originally was synthesized for treatment of tuberculosis patients. When researchers noticed in the late 1950s that iproniazid lifted the spirits of TB patients, it was given to people suffering from depression. The MAO inhibitors are highly toxic and cause harm to the liver, brain, and cardiovascular system. They also interact dangerously—sometimes lethally—with other chemicals and with foods and beverages containing tyramine (beer, certain cheeses, pickled herring). The MAO inhibitors generally have been supplanted by another class of antidepressants, the tricyclics, which were first tried as a treatment for schizophrenia because they have a molecular structure similar to that of the phenothiazine tranquilizers.

Like other psychoactive drugs, the antidepressants are thought to act on the brain by interfering with the neurotransmitters. The tricyclics, it is believed, increase the level of the transmitter norepinephrine by preventing the reuptake of that transmitter by the nerve cell after the firing of electric impulses (Baldessarini, 1977).

Another drug, lithium carbonate, has been reported effective in managing the wide mood swings of manic-depressives by reducing the frequency of both manic and depressive episodes. How lithium accomplishes these two contrary actions—elevating mood and reducing arousal—has not been established. Lithium is highly toxic and can be fatal if its level in the bloodstream becomes too high (Branchey, Charles, & Simpson, 1976).

Stimulants

The most familiar of the **stimulants** used in treatment are the amphetamines, which were developed in the early 1930s as medication for asthma. Soldiers during World War II took Dexedrine and other amphetamines to fight fatigue. Frequently called "pep pills" or "uppers," they have been widely abused for their euphoric effects. The amphetamines stimulate the central nervous system, increasing the available supply of the neurotransmitter dopamine; in excessive doses they produce symptoms resembling those of schizophrenia. This observation by Snyder (1975) provided further evidence for the hypothesis that schizophrenia is related to an excess of dopamine.

In recent years, the amphetamines and a piperidyl derivative, Ritalin, have been prescribed for hyperactive children. Although this use has been criticized, it has proved to be effective in managing hyperactivity (Gittelman-Klein, Klein, Katz, Saraf & Pollack, 1976). This may seem strange because a stimulant would be expected to stimulate, not calm, but these drugs have a pronounced effect on the attention of hyperactive children, making them less subject to distraction and thus exerting a calming influence (Conners, 1972).

Community Mental Health

The passage of the Community Mental Health Center Act of 1963 resulted in the creation of community mental health centers to provide care for the large numbers of patients being released from institutions and to bring low-cost psychological help to the general public, especially the poor. The centers typically provide short-term hospitalization, outpatient treatment, 24-hour emergency service, and community programs aimed at the prevention of psychological distress.

The community mental health movement primarily focuses on five new perspectives in helping: the trend toward community living, the emphasis on crisis intervention, the investigation of new methods of prevention, the increasing concern about legal and ethical issues, and the new role of the nonprofessional.

Community Living

The national trend toward deinstitutionalization has shifted much of the burden of looking after the mentally ill from hospitals to the community, a change that has brought about some problems (Price & Smith, 1983). The community is seldom ready to receive mental patients; the patients themselves, although their symptoms are temporarily under control, are seldom prepared to function on their own after spending many years in a hospital. Too often, there is a lack of follow-up therapy. Many former hospital patients live alone, often in slum conditions, and roam the streets aimlessly. Nearly 40,000 poor, chronic mental patients have been "dumped" in New York City alone—many in cheap residential hotels where they receive little or no care, subsist on public assistance, and rarely see a social worker (Koenig, 1978). One result of this situation is the previously mentioned revolving-door phenomenon, where as many as one half of all patients released from mental hospitals return within a year. Some critics argue that "decarceration" actually is not a reform but simply a less expensive way than mental hospitals of handling the mentally ill (Scull, 1977).

Price and Smith (1983) have traced the history of the deinstitutionalization movement over the last 20 years and suggest that the enthusiasm for cost reduction in the care of the mentally ill has not been matched by the provision for alternative forms of treatment. Also, future projections for the chronic mentally ill indicate that the burden of care will dramatically increase.

If there is a dark side to community living for the mentally ill, there also is a bright side. In many communities, there are halfway houses and other means of easing the transition from hospital living. Two demonstration projects exemplify how formerly hospitalized patients can be supported effectively in the community.

One highly persuasive project was carried out by George Fairweather and his colleagues (Fairweather, 1964; Fairweather, Sanders, Cressler, & Maynard, 1969). Fairweather began by teaching hospitalized patients skills in group decision making and problem solving. He moved his experimental group from the hospital to a house in the community that Fairweather later labeled a "lodge." The patients received training as gardeners and janitors, were placed in jobs and encouraged to become self-sufficient and self-governing at the lodge. The results were dramatic. Over a 40-month period the members of the lodge spent more than 80 percent of their time in the community and only 20 percent back at the hospital. Meanwhile, a control group, consisting of patients given similar hospital treatment but discharged individually into the community without benefit of the lodge, spent only 20 percent of the time in the community and 80 percent in the hospital.

Another kind of support system was provided by Training in Community Living, a program conducted by the Mendota Mental Health Institute in Madison, Wisconsin (Marx, Test, & Stein, 1973; Fields, 1978). Patients moving from the hospital into the community were helped by a staff that included a psychiatrist, a psychologist, nurses, an occupational therapist, and a number of aides and trainees. Before the patients left the hospital, staff members trained them in job and social skills. The staff also found them places to live and jobs and generally paved the way for the transition by talking with the police and other agencies in the community. Staff members went grocery shopping with patients and taught them how to cook and to do laundry. It was the staff's responsibility to keep tabs on each patient's progress and problems, and the members met regularly to discuss each patient.

The results of the first Training in Community Living project illustrate both the potential benefits and the perils of deinstitutionalization. After five months, the supported patients proved to be far more successful in the community than a comparable control group that did not receive special help. However, once the support program was withdrawn, many patients returned to the hospital. Without support, they could not cope in the community. A second study provided support for 14 months. On practically all measures, these patients fared better than did the unsupported control groups. They spent little time in institutions, were better adjusted to their homes, and experienced greater satisfaction in their jobs and social relationships. Interestingly, the cost was about the same for supported community living as for hospitalization of the patients.

Such projects demonstrate the potential of community living. They suggest what could be achieved on a much larger scale if sufficient resources and commitment were mobilized.

These former institutionalized patients now live in a halfway house and lead a productive life as a home-renovation team.

Crisis Intervention

More than 40 years ago a fire broke out in a Boston restaurant and hundreds of people were killed or injured. A young psychiatrist, Erich Lindemann, rallied his colleagues to see if they could help the bereaved parents and spouses of those who had died. Over a hundred people were interviewed by mental health professionals, and from this tragic beginning a realization of the process of grief and mourning in the face of the loss of a loved one began to develop (Lindemann, 1944). These researchers formed an understanding of the relationship between life crisis and psychological adjustment as well as a strategy for helping people cope with life emergencies. This short-term psychological strategy came to be called crisis intervention.

An important aim of community mental health programs is to provide a variety of immediate services for people caught up in emotional crises (Jacobson, 1980). Such crises may include threats of suicide, severe drug reactions, serious family conflicts, and other behavioral emergencies. *Crisis intervention* in these situations seeks to alleviate the precipitating stress and to mobilize the person's own capabilities for coping—without requiring expensive hospitalization.

Special facilities for crisis intervention take several forms. Walk-in clinics, usually part of a community mental health center and staffed by professionals, offer round-the-clock service without an appointment. A person may receive brief psychotherapy, consisting of several sessions over a short period of time, and may also receive medication such as tranquilizers or antidepressants. A variant of the walk-in clinic is the so-called free clinic, the first of which was established during the early 1960s in the Haight-Ashbury district of San Francisco to provide medical, psychological, and social services to the young people who had congregated there. Free clinics are usually staffed by volunteers, including trained professionals. However, it is typically the presence of knowledgeable and sympathetic nonprofessionals, such as former drug addicts with a great deal of experience on the street, that makes the free clinic appealing to many clients who might be wary of more traditional treatment facilities.

Hotlines are telephone emergency service centers that enable people with personal problems to talk to a trained and sympathetic listener. Although many hotlines offer conversation, advice, and referral for a variety of problems, others specialize in a particular problem such as drugs, rape, or suicide. A notable example is the suicide prevention movement launched around the turn of the century by the National Save-A-Life League, which established a 24-hour telephone answering service for suicidal people in New York City. Volunteers are trained to evaluate the caller's potential for suicide, convey a sense of empathy, give reassurance, and get the caller's name and phone number so the case can be followed up.

Family-crisis help is provided in several United States cities by police who have been specially trained to intervene in domestic emergencies. Such pro-

Crisis intervention centers provide "hotlines" to trained personnel who can offer conversation, advice, and referral services for a wide variety of problems.

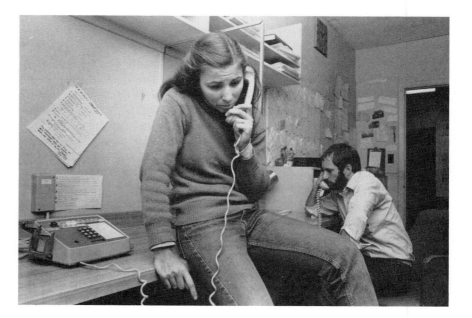

CHAPTER 15 BEHAVIOR CHANGE

grams were originated in New York City by researchers who noted that half of the calls for assistance to an urban police department may involve family crises or other complaints of a personal or interpersonal nature (Bard & Berkowitz, 1967; Bard, 1970). These crises range from juvenile delinquency to intrafamily violence. In a precinct on the upper west side of Manhattan, 18 police volunteers were selected and given an intensive 160-hour training program in crisis intervention. Then, for two years, these men served, one pair to a shift, as the Family Crisis Intervention Unit. Among the positive findings reported were a decrease in the number of assaults within families and the fact that none of the specially trained police sustained injuries in handling family disturbances (Bard, 1970).

Prevention

Another key characteristic of the community mental health movement is the focus on preventing disordered behavior before it occurs. Price and his colleagues have examined the variety of programs and approaches aimed at this goal (Price et al., 1980). The hope is to extend public health research, which has scored its greatest triumphs over disease and suffering through programs of prevention—vaccination programs, for example, and water purification.

Three basic strategies for the prevention of mental illness have been identified (Bloom, 1977):

1. Community-wide efforts include those programs, such as newspaper or television campaigns, that educate people in more effective parenting skills or that alert the public about child abuse. An analogy to public health would be community-wide programs to purify water and prevent typhoid fever.

2. Milestone programs expose people to help at specified intervals in their lives, much as couples are given a blood test before marriage or preschool children are immunized against certain diseases. At milestones such as the first year of marriage, the birth of the first child, and enrollment in school, people could be given training to help reduce the stresses of these critical life stages.

3. High-risk programs focus on those people who are deemed particularly vulnerable to specific disorders because of genetic makeup (children of schizophrenics), unusual personal experiences (a child whose parent dies), or extreme environmental stresses (survivors of disasters such as earthquakes or plane crashes).

Although widespread prevention of mental illness remains a goal rather than a reality, the results of several studies demonstrate great potential. Research has shown that the emotional hazards associated with medical treatment in young children can be prevented (Cassell, 1965). Working with children between the ages of 3 and 11 who were about to undergo cardiac catheterization—a diagnostic procedure in which a tube is first inserted into a vein and then fed through into the heart—the researcher rehearsed everything that would happen in the operating room with each child, using a puppet as the stand-in for the young patient. Then the child was asked to play the role of the doctor while the therapist acted out the role of the frightened child, asking for reassurance from the "doctor." Later, in the operating room, the children who underwent this anticipatory coping showed much less emotional upset than did a control group who did not receive such guidance.

George Spivack and Myrna Shure (1974) reasoned that training in solving social and cognitive problems would help children cope with interpersonal problems and reduce their vulnerability to stress. They provided four-year-olds

In an effort to minimize the trauma of surgery, this volunteer uses puppets to prepare a child for treatment.

with an intensive ten-week training program, teaching the abilities to sense problems, identify feelings, and look for alternative solutions. When these children were followed up a year later, they had retained their coping skills.

In recent years, there has been a substantial increase in research on preventive strategies in mental health. Preventive programs are being tested in schools, in hospitals, with the elderly, with children of divorcing parents, and in a wide variety of other settings and populations. Preventive psychology is now moving rapidly toward its goal (Cowen, 1982; Felner et al., 1983).

The Rights of Patients

Increased community responsibility for the treatment of mental patients has generated a new concern for the constitutional rights of mental patients. This reflects both the changing attitudes of the public at large toward the mentally ill and recent court decisions to safeguard the rights of patients.

Until about two decades ago the courts largely deferred to the expertise of mental health professionals in deciding what was best for hospitalized patients. Since then, however, the courts have taken a more direct hand, intervening on behalf of constitutional rights. The most notable decision, handed down by the United States Supreme Court in 1979, relates to the involuntary commitment of patients to mental institutions. The court ruled that patients who do not represent a danger to society must either be treated by the institution or released. This decision was aimed at eliminating the so-called warehousing of the mentally ill—locking up patients while failing to treat them. Other decisions have safeguarded the right of institutionalized patients to refuse treatment, requiring carefully defined procedures for obtaining the patient's informed consent before certain therapeutic techniques can be used. Among these techniques are psychosurgery, shock treatment, and aversion therapy. The courts also have limited effectively the types of reinforcers that can be used in behavioral techniques employing the token economy. For example, neither privacy nor meals can be offered as reinforcers because the patient has a legal right to these amenities without having to earn them. The result of such decisions is that the professional's judgment of what is best for the patient must now be weighed against the court's interpretation of the patient's rights.

The patient's right to refuse treatment can create a number of ethical dilemmas with which the mental health professional must cope (Price & Lynn,

1981). For example, consider the case of an extremely disturbed schizophrenic patient who reports hearing voices that are commanding suicide. Should this patient be given antipsychotic drug treatments, even if the patient refuses them because he or she believes that they will be harmful? The dilemma is a real one.

Because such dilemmas are encountered almost daily by many mental health professionals, particularly those dealing with people experiencing severe disturbances in behavior, a number of legal and ethical guidelines have been established to help mental health professionals decide when they can or should provide treatment over a patient's objections. One important guideline is whether the patients are judged by mental health professionals to be dangerous to themselves or others.

However, careful research on the capacity of mental health professionals to actually predict who will be violent and who will not indicates that mental health professionals tend to be poor at making this prediction and, in many cases, may overpredict violence, thus potentially depriving nonviolent persons of their rights and freedom (Monahan, 1981).

Guidelines are also being developed to establish procedures for informing patients about the kind of treatment they will receive and the likely outcome of the treatment. Before patients are asked whether they will accept treatment, psychiatrists are required to give patients information about the benefits and risks of the proposed treatments, alternative treatments, and the likely outcomes if the treatments are refused. Furthermore, if patients are unable to understand the information, psychiatrists are required to inform a responsible guardian or relative.

Programs like college peer counseling involve trained laypeople who give social support in a number of situations.

The Role of the Nonprofessional

The community mental health movement, by decentralizing treatment and attempting to reach out to a broader segment of the general public, requires large numbers of workers. This demand not only far outstrips the number of mental health professionals now available, it also exceeds the foreseeable prospects for training psychiatrists, clinical psychologists, and social workers. To meet the demand, professionals increasingly are turning to nonprofessionals.

The potential role of the nonprofessional in community mental health was first heralded in an important book titled *Americans View Their Mental Health* (Gurin, Veroff, & Feld, 1960). The authors pointed out that largely untapped human resources for helping already were available in the community. Through sympathetic day-to-day contacts with friends and neighbors, hundreds of thousands of Americans provide a kind of psychotherapy for those who lack the inclination or financial wherewithal to seek out professional help. These home-grown therapists—without psychiatric training or degrees but capable of warmth and caring—include religious leaders, homemakers, college students, bartenders, hairdressers, and others.

Major research interest has emerged in the important role of *social support* in protecting individuals from the negative effects of stressful life events. Gottlieb (1983) has surveyed the literature on social support and suggests that these informal helping relationships can be beneficial for a wide variety of individuals throughout the life span, including mothers during childbirth, persons who have recently been unemployed, and elderly people facing retirement.

In recent years, many such people have been enlisted by the community mental health movement, enabling the professionals who train them to multiply many times over the impact of their own knowledge and skills. These laypeople have been put to work as volunteers or paid staff in myriad programs, ranging from college peer counseling to crisis intervention services. After a comparatively brief training period, they qualify as paraprofessionals who can take their

FOCUS

All of the methods of treatment described in this chapter are rooted in the assumptions of Western culture. For example, biological therapies, such as drug treatments, reflect the direct cause-and-effect tenets of scientific materialism. Psychoanalysis, with its emphasis on intellect and verbal expression, still reflects the upper-middle-class values of Freud's turn-of-the-century Vienna.

Other societies have developed different means of treatment that are rooted in their own cultural assumptions. Western psychologists refer to these therapies as folk healing. In recent years, with the rise of the community mental health movement and the expanding importance of the non-professional, psychologists have taken a new interest in folk healing. Interestingly, researchers have noted several parallels between various forms of folk healing and the psychodynamic therapies of Freud and others (Fields, 1976). Here we will look briefly at two varieties of folk healing practiced by subcultures in the United States—Puerto Rican *espiritismo* and the treatment procedures of Navajo medicine men.

Espiritismo, or spiritism, flourishes in Puerto Rican communities in

Therapy Through Folk Healing

urban areas of the United States, such as New York City's South Bronx. It is based on the belief that everyone is imbued with benevolent and malevolent spirits. The healer, or *espiritista,* is thought to have the ability to get rid of evil spirits that inflict suffering and psychological disturbances and to get in touch with the good spirits. Although such beliefs may sound alien to Western science, Vivian Garrison, an anthropologist who has studied *espiritismo,* points out that healers often interpret the spirits symbolically, rather than literally, as "representatives of current or recurrent problems." In this sense, says Garrison, spiritism is not so far removed from Western psychodynamic theory. "Just as there is no empirical reality which corresponds

to the concept of an id, an ego, or a superego, the spirits are concepts which can be understood as behavioral manifestations" (Fields, 1976).

A wide variety of problems are treated in storefront *centros,* or healing centers, including nervous disorders and marriage and family crises. When a person first comes to the *centro* for help, the *espiritista* often conducts a kind of initial psychiatric interview, spending considerable time learning the background and problems of the person. From this consultation, the healer attempts to identify the particular *causas,* or spirits, responsible for the person's suffering. The *causas* are then treated at seances attended by the patient and a number of others, including several healers and perhaps members of the family. All who are present are encouraged to use their spiritual faculties and to communicate their visions about the patient. The seance resembles psychodrama, complete with an eerie candlelit setting and elaborate ritualistic props and with the healers entering trancelike states and acting out the roles of the malevolent spirits.

Garrison and other anthropologists who have studied the *espiritis-*

---

places alongside the fully trained professionals. In addition to recruiting lay helpers into the mainstream of mental health care, professionals have taken a new interest in the unconventional therapies practiced by indigenous folk healers (see Focus, this page).

Despite the widespread use of paraprofessionals in community mental health, there persists (at least among professionals) the assumption that professional clinicians are more effective psychotherapists than those without extensive training. This assumption has been called sharply into question in a study by Joseph A. Durlak (1979). Durlak examined 42 studies that compared the effectiveness of professionals and paraprofessionals in treating a number of different types of clients. Paraprofessionals were defined as mental health workers who had received no formal postgraduate clinical training in professional programs of psychiatry, social work, and psychiatric nursing. Durlak found that "paraprofessionals achieve clinical outcomes equal to or significantly better than those obtained by professionals." In addition, Durlak classified the studies under review by the particular purpose or method of therapy:

tas suggest that they are at least as effective as—and in some cases more effective than—traditional mental health services in helping members of the Puerto Rican community.

Like the *espiritistas,* the Navajo medicine men—sometimes known as singers—draw on the folkways of their own people. Traditional Navajo philosophy emphasizes the unity of all experience. Sickness—of body or mind—is considered a state of fragmentation. Healing involves becoming whole again and in harmony with friends, family, and nature. The Navajo makes no distinction between healing and worship, and the ceremonies conducted by medicine men involve both. Robert Fulton, a Navajo healer, has said: "Each man must have a prayer; he must dream of something and believe in something which is more than himself" (Fields, 1976).

Like psychotherapists, medicine men train for many years. In recognition of this, the National Institute of Mental Health has funded a training program that combines apprenticeship to established medicine men with teaching in Western principles of medicine. Apprentices must learn the songs, prayers, and stories of the ancient healing ceremonies by heart

A Navajo medicine man uses feathers to perform his ancient rites for therapeutic purposes.

because, by Navajo tradition, they cannot be written down.

Healing rituals typically are elaborate and lengthy, sometimes lasting for a week or more. Planning them requires a number of meetings between the medicine man and the patient's family—consultations that, in themselves, represent a kind of family group therapy. The healing ceremonies bring together family and friends in a *hogan,* the simple Navajo eight-sided earthen dwelling. A number of different ceremonies can be conducted depending on the symptoms of the patient. They usually involve ritual objects from the natural

world such as juniper branches, bird feathers, and dyes from berries and barks. These objects are used in reenactment of old Navajo religious stories that describe a problem similar to that afflicting the patient. Through the old songs and chants the medicine man takes on the role of the supernatural being who cured the patient in the ancient story. The emphasis on ancient myths is reminiscent of the teachings of Freud's former disciple Carl Jung, who postulated that archetypal symbols, revealed in dreams, art, and literature, were a vital part of the therapeutic process (Jung, 1964).

Navajo healing rituals often are effective in relieving depression, grief, and anxiety. This should not be surprising in light of the fact that such ceremonies have the effect of bringing patients closer to their families and their society. As Fields (1976) has observed, "The Navajos have been pulled between two cultures . . . often with tragic results. The medicine man, as he offers tales of noble adventures, sparks a renewed pride in Indian tradition. The ceremonies provide a structure to develop, support, and affirm this cultural pride and identity." ■

individual or group psychotherapy or counseling; academic counseling; crisis intervention; specific target programs for problems such as sleep difficulties, stuttering, overweight, and smoking; and other more general interventions. In general, paraprofessionals were even more effective relative to professionals when they were working with highly specific target problems such as sleep difficulties and stuttering.

How can we explain such surprising findings? One possibility is that the general enthusiasm of paraprofessionals and the basis for their selection made them more effective helpers. A second possibility is that the paraprofessionals were shown to be effective for the particular target problem and the techniques used before they were employed. If so, the superiority of paraprofessionals may be true only for well-defined problems where highly specific treatment methods are applicable.

In any case, Durlak's findings have forced professionals to reexamine the question of how much training is actually needed for various helping roles. If his findings are verified by additional careful research, it may be that the pool

This self-help group of parents of the mentally ill meets to share problems and help each other cope.

of helpers can be greatly increased at relatively little cost, expanding the available services and further accelerating the diffusion of responsibility for mental health from the professional to the community itself.

Mutual Support Groups

In surveying social and community interventions, Iscoe and Harris (1984) point to self-help groups as a major resource in the community, providing help for an extremely wide range of individuals. Katz (1981) estimates that there are at least 500,000 self-help groups in the United States comprising a total membership of about 23 million individuals. Gartner and Riessman (1980; 1982) have surveyed these groups. They include people experiencing similar circumstances or misfortunes such as single parent groups, parents without partners, Alcoholics Anonymous, and organizations such as Mothers Against Drunk Driving (MADD) aimed at dealing with a national problem at a local level. Typically, self-help groups do not see existing social institutions or agencies as able to meet their needs. They usually organize themselves around a shared belief system and the idea that they can help each other lead more satisfactory lives.

As the costs of professional services increase, as they surely will in the future, we can expect even more self-help groups to emerge in the United States. Some will work in collaboration with mental health or health professionals and others will work independently toward their own goals for well-being.

Summary

1. The professionals who treat disordered behavior are classified principally according to their educational backgrounds. Psychiatrists are physicians who have spent a postgraduate residency training in psychotherapy. Psychoanalysts, usually physicians, have received specialized training at a psychoanalytic institute. Clinical psychologists hold Ph.D.s in psychology, and have had extensive training in research, psychological testing, and therapeutic techniques. Counseling psychologists have graduate training similar to that of clinical psychologists, but typically with less emphasis on research. Psychiatric social workers hold master's degrees in social work and have special training in treatment procedures that emphasize the home and community.

2. The treatment of mental disorders through psychological means is a simplified definition of psychotherapy. A number of offshoots have arisen from Freud's original formulation of psychoanalysis, but all of the psychodynamic schools retain an emphasis on intrapsychic dynamics. The processes of classical psychotherapy include free association, by which repressed thoughts and feelings are brought to awareness. Analysts interpret these associations to help patients understand the roots of some of their problems. As they face previously unconscious aspects of their personalities, patients may begin to resist self-confrontation. They may also transfer to the analyst feelings about other important people in their lives; when transference occurs, the analyst points out to the patient that the behavior is inappropriate and actually a form of resistance to getting better. Successful analysis is often a lengthy and intense process, requiring working through neurotic responses and fragile adjustments several times over.

3. Humanistic therapies take an optimistic view of the human potential for growth. In Carl Rogers' client-centered approach, the clients themselves set the goals of the therapy and the topics to be discussed. The humanistic therapist takes a positive attitude toward clients and believes that they have an innate tendency toward self-actualization.

4 Behavior therapy focuses on behavior itself rather than on subjective determinants. Among the major behavioral approaches to treatment are counterconditioning and operant techniques—derived respectively from the principles of classical and operant conditioning; modeling of appropriate behaviors stems from Bandura's theory of observational learning; cognitive restructuring is based on altering maladaptive thought patterns; and self-control techniques are based on control of environmental techniques by the patients themselves.

5 Practically every approach and method of treatment used with individuals has also been applied to group therapy. Four types of group therapy that emphasize interaction among group members—as opposed to the therapist-client relationship—are psychodrama, sensitivity training, encounter groups, and family therapy.

6. Measuring the effectiveness and "success" of psychotherapy is difficult because of the many variables involved—patient, therapist, setting, goals, spontaneous remission, and so on. Research—most notably a major review by Smith and Glass (1971)—indicates that psychotherapy does help most patients and that different approaches to therapy do not differ greatly in effectiveness.

7. Biological therapies include electroconvulsive therapy (electroshock), psychosurgery, and drug treatment. Of these, drug therapy has been the most effective. The psychoactive drugs used in treatment are classified as major and minor tranquilizers, antidepressants, and stimulants. Tranquilizers such as chlorpromazine have been effective in the treatment of schizophrenia; antidepressants such as the tricyclics have served as successful mood elevators for depressed patients.

8. The role of the community in treating and preventing mental illness has grown enormously in the past 20 years as a result of the patients released from hospitals after drug therapy and by the enactment of the Community Mental Health Centers Act of 1963. Among the successful efforts have been community living programs for former mental patients, various forms of crisis intervention, and prevention programs. In recent years, the courts have moved to safeguard the rights of the mentally ill. Finally, the emergence of paraprofessionals in the community health movement has enabled highly trained practitioners to stretch their training in new and effective ways.

RESEARCH: With the aid of a complex statistical analysis, Smith and Glass were able to successfully address the difficult task of ascertaining the effectiveness of psychotherapy. In general, these researchers found that the average person undergoing therapy was better off than the majority of other persons who experience similar psychological problems but who do not undergo therapy. Although in a few instances (e.g., the treatment of phobias) behavioral therapies were found to be superior to psychodynamic therapies in terms of outcome effectiveness, only negligible differences were found between different types of therapies overall.

FOCUS: Various societies have developed different forms of therapy for abnormal behavior based on certain cultural assumptions. Two such therapies are *espiritismo*, practiced by Puerto Rican folk healers, and the healing rituals performed by Navajo medicine men. Both of these therapies are similar to Western psychodynamic approaches in that they focus on the symbolism and unity of life experiences as well as provide support systems for the afflicted person.

7

Social Influence and Interaction

CHAPTER

16

Social Influence

Social Psychology Focuses on People

Behavior and Stimuli

Arousal: The Mere Presence of Others
Social Reinforcement
Social Punishment
Information: Social Comparison

Conformity

Public Compliance Versus Private Acceptance
Information Versus Reinforcement: Two Different Processes
Factors Affecting Conformity

Learning About Ourselves

How Others Treat Us
Self-Perception

Intentional Social Influence

Obedience to Authority
Persuasion: Changing Attitudes by Changing Perceptions
Dissonance: Changing Attitudes by Changing Behavior
Brainwashing: Extreme Social Influence

Summary

Research: Dissonance and the $2 Bettor

Focus: The Process of Religious Conversion

While we may not hesitate to kick a machine when it frustrates us, we may think twice before kicking a person who might kick back.

By proposing a simple experiment we can illustrate, quite simply, social influence. Suppose that the students in your psychology class are asked to play a trick on the instructor, who for some reason tends to lecture primarily from the right side of the room. The students respond to the lecture with interested looks, well-timed nods, and smiles whenever the lecturer speaks from the left side of the room. When the instructor goes back to the right, they feign boredom and give little response. The hypothesis of our experiment is that the instructor will be visibly influenced by the contrasting behaviors of the class. In a class where this experiment was tried (Whaley & Malott, 1969), the instructor was so affected that he spent much more time lecturing from the left side of the room—the side on which his words had been rewarded.

In this chapter we will discuss such instances of **social influence**—the ways in which an individual's actions affect the behavior, attitudes, or judgments of another. As in the experiment above, the effects of social influence usually reflect simple one-way processes; the social world is not, however, always one way. The instructor's response to the looks of the students, for example, might in turn further affect the level of student interest and of class attendance. In turn, this would then affect the instructor's behavior. Thus, the effects of the instructor on students and vice versa are mutual and reciprocal. This two-way process is known as **social interaction** and will be discussed in the next chapter.

Social Psychology Focuses on People

The study of both social influence and social interaction is the province of social psychology. Social psychology examines how people, as opposed to impersonal stimuli such as word lists or drug levels, affect other people. It thus differs from other branches of psychology in a number of ways:

- People are clearly our most important stimuli. We are basically social animals, and people can arouse us, anger us, or delight or depress us more than anything else.

- People often change as we perceive or judge them: nonsocial objects, on the other hand, maintain a certain degree of object constancy. We can judge the length of a line, kiss a silver dollar, or kick a football without changing these objects. Judging a student's performance, kissing a date, or kicking a potential mugger are obviously different matters. People change in significant ways as we do things to them.

- Unlike objects, people typically react to our actions. Rather than passively accepting our behavior, people respond to us. We may not hesitate to kick a broken candy machine when it frustrates us, but we are likely to stop short of aggression if a person frustrates us because we know the person might kick back.

- Social judgments frequently have less basis in reality than our judgments of nonsocial objects do. We can measure the accuracy of our judgments about the length of a line (2 inches) or the weight of a rock (3 pounds). But how can we check the accuracy of our judgments about, for example, the honesty and aims of other people?

- Social psychologists focus on how people in general respond to given situations. Other branches of psychology, such as personality and development, focus primarily on how an individual or a type of individual behaves in different situations.

- Social psychology emphasizes the world as it is perceived. Whether we interpret another's remark as witty, mean, thoughtless, sarcastic, or friendly, influences our subsequent behavior toward that person. Such perceptions are often biased and distorted to fit our needs and wishes as was shown in a study by Albert Hastorf and Hadley Cantril (1954). Dartmouth and Princeton students were asked to watch a film showing an especially rough and dirty football game between the two schools and to state their perceptions of the game. Not surprisingly, the perceptions of the two groups differed sharply. Each group noted many more infractions by the other team and typically interpreted questionable calls by referees in their own team's favor. Obviously, such differing perceptions affect behavior both during and after a football game.

Performance and behavior may be affected when an audience is present.

To recap, the most important stimuli in our environments are people—who change as we perceive them. Our behavior is affected by the reactions of others to our actions. Our social judgments are not readily quantifiable. Social psychology focuses on how people, in general, perceive and respond to situations. We shall next examine the various stimuli that can affect those perceptions and responses.

Behavior and Stimuli

Stimuli affect our behavior in three basic ways:

1. *Arousal.* When our arousal level is affected by a loud clap of thunder, a day without food, or an injection of adrenalin, our behavior is influenced.
2. *Reinforcement.* Whether a flower smells good and "rewards" us or causes a skin rash and "punishes" us will affect our behavior toward that type of flower in the future.
3. *Information.* A red light tells us to step on the brakes: control of behavior is exerted by the stimulus of the signal—a source of information.

Other people are social stimuli, and they affect our behavior through these processes of arousal, reward and punishment, and information. A closer look at these three types of influence will help us to understand a wide variety of social behavior.

Arousal: The Mere Presence of Others

The behavior of others can arouse us in many ways. As we saw in chapter 10, people can anger us and cause us to behave aggressively. Members of the opposite sex can arouse us by the manner in which they dress. But can the mere presence of others increase our arousal level and thus affect our behavior?

Much anecdotal evidence from everyday life suggests that it can. A well-rehearsed speech suddenly falls apart when the speaker faces an audience and experiences stage fright. Tired joggers quickly perk up when they happen upon a group of other joggers. In these simple social situations, the other people are not offering rewards or conveying information: they are merely present.

Scientific investigation of the effects of an audience dates back over a century. In 1904, a German researcher conducted experiments concerned with muscular effort and fatigue (Meumann). He noted that his subjects were able to exert far more muscle effort on the days when he watched as compared to the days on which no one watched.

More recently, Bruce Bergum and Donald Lehr (1963) reported increases in performance on a quite different task when others watched. Subjects were

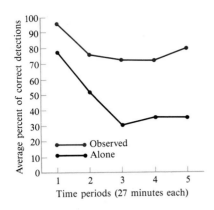

Figure 16.1

Accuracy on a monitoring task performed alone and under supervision. It can be seen that the scores were consistently higher when the task was performed in the presence of an observer.

placed in a booth where they observed a circle of red lamps lighting rapidly in sequence. They were asked to press a button whenever a light failed to blink on in proper sequence. Half of the subjects performed the task while alone in the booth; the other half had an observer with them. Subjects performed the task for 2 hours and 15 minutes. Figure 16.1 divides this period into five 27-minute segments and shows the average percentage of correct detections for each interval for both accompanied and solitary students. As the figure shows, the performance of both groups diminished over time because of boredom and fatigue. More important, the accuracy of subjects with a passive audience—albeit an audience of one—was consistently better than those who were alone. Behavior is thus affected by even a passive audience.

Behavior is also affected when one performs a task in the presence of others who are also engaged in a similar task—a situation called **coaction.** Many years ago, Floyd Allport (1920) administered various tests to subjects. On some occasions they worked alone in cubicles. At other times they worked while seated around a table (a coaction condition). Performance rates for simple tasks such as vowel cancellation and multiplication were much higher in the coaction situation.

Researchers have also observed increases in performance in coaction situations in several different species of animals. Chickens deprived of food and then allowed to eat until full will still eat half as much again when placed in the presence of another chicken that is eating (Bayer, 1929). Ants digging nests in groups of two or three dig more quickly and move more sand per ant than ants working alone (Chen, 1937).

Such results led psychologists to assume that the presence of others always increased or facilitated performance, a phenomenon known as **social facilitation.** This assumption, however, was contradicted by the results of several experiments. For example, human subjects who were instructed to learn lists of nonsense syllables performed better when alone (Pessin, 1933). Similarly, research shows that both humans (Husband, 1931) and cockroaches (Gates and Allee, 1933) learn complex mazes more quickly when alone than when fellow creatures are present. In other words, an audience sometimes facilitates performance; at other times the presence of others impairs performance.

Zajonc's Arousal Theory

This apparent contradiction has been explained by Robert Zajonc (1965) in terms of arousal. The presence of others energizes us and increases our drive level. An increase in drive strengthens the dominant response of the organism—that is, the response most likely to occur. At the same time, an increase in drive weakens responses that already are weak. In a simple or well-learned task, familiarity with what is required exists, or the task has been practiced several times. Thus the strongest and most likely response is the one that is appropriate and correct. In a complex and difficult task, on the other hand, the strongest response is likely to be the wrong one. Consider the task of backing a car into a tight parking space. For an experienced driver this is a well-learned behavior, and the "most natural" and most probable responses will get the car into the space. However, for a novice driver, the most likely responses are incorrect, and parking will be difficult. Because a passive or coacting audience strengthens the most likely response, an audience will improve the parking performance of the experienced driver but interfere with the performance of the novice driver. In the same way, an audience will improve performance on simple and well-learned tasks, such as weight pulling or eating, but impair performance on difficult tasks, such as list learning or negotiation of complex mazes. In Allport's coaction study, performance of tasks such as solving logic problems was worse with an audience, while simple tasks such as vowel cancellation improved in a coaction situation.

Zajonc's arousal theory has been supported by subsequent research. For example, although humans and cockroaches do worse on complex mazes in the presence of an audience, the presence of others facilitates performance when the maze is simple (Zajonc, Heingartner, & Herman, 1969). Recent studies have also reported that the presence of others enhances the dominant response and thus affects performance of relevant behaviors such as laughter in children (Chapman, 1973), game-playing behavior (Grush, 1978), and competitive swimming (Sorrentino & Sheppard, 1978).

If the presence of others acts as a source of arousal, we might expect that other, nonsocial factors that increase drive should have similar effects. That is, any source of arousal should enhance the dominant response and lead to better performance on simple tasks but result in diminished performance on complex tasks. This has been confirmed by other studies. Kenneth Spence, Janet Taylor, and Ronnie Ketchel (1956) found that high-anxiety people perform better on easy tasks and worse on complex tasks than low-anxiety people. In addition, George Mandler and Seymour Sarason (1952) reported that students suffering from test anxiety showed improved performance on easy tests but impaired performance on hard tests. Further, in a task where subjects had to recognize sets of words flashed on a screen, those who had been motivated by the offer of money more often guessed words that were strongest in their response hierarchy than did subjects not offered money. The offer of money enhanced the dominant response (Zajonc & Nieuwenhuyse, 1964). Interestingly, a similar experiment showed that the presence of others had similar effects (Zajonc & Sales, 1966). Subjects who guessed in the presence of others had their dominant responses strengthened when compared with subjects who guessed while alone.

Praise on the job is a type of social reinforcement.

Cottrell's Theory

One modification of Zajonc's original theory was made by Nickolas Cottrell (1968). **Cottrell's theory** suggested that it was not just the presence of an audience that aroused a person and enhanced the dominant response, but the presence of an audience capable of evaluating and rating the subject. In his own work (Cottrell, Wack, Sekerak, and Rittle, 1968) he found that, in word recognition tasks, blindfolding an audience did not lead to an increase in subjects' guessing the dominant response. Likewise, other investigators reported enhanced choice of dominant response words only when an expert audience was used (Henchy & Glass, 1968).

Arousal, then, does strengthen the dominant response—the one most likely to occur—but weakens responses that are already weak. The presence of others will most likely increase the dominant response if the audience, or observer, is capable of evaluating the subject's performance. Arousal seems to be a product of our concern over the impression we will make on others.

Social Reinforcement

Arousal through their presence is only one of the ways in which others influence our behavior. An even more prevalent means of social influence is **reinforcement.** People serve as real or potential sources of both reward and punishment. Others dramatically affect us through bribes, kisses and hugs, cash bonuses, good grades, praise, and other rewards. They also control our behavior through the use of threats, spanking, guilt, social rejection, and other punishments.

People may provide **primary reinforcers** that satisfy such basic physiological needs as food, water, or shelter; more important, however, they administer **secondary reinforcers** that are not inherently rewarding but that an individual

Parents often use verbal reinforcement as they socialize with their children.

has learned to associate with positive outcomes. Money, for example, serves no direct biological need, but it is associated with primary reinforcers that do satisfy primary needs since it can buy food, drink, and comfort. Some secondary reinforcers such as approval, love, and attention are by their very nature social: they cannot be obtained from the nonsocial environment.

Verbal Reinforcement

One of the most effective social rewards is praise. One experiment indicated that even a simple statement such as "good" or "mm hmm" could affect verbal behavior (Greenspoon, 1955). He asked subjects to utter words at random (as they thought of them) for 50 minutes. Some subjects were reinforced by an "mm hmm" or a "good" for every singular noun they generated, while others were rewarded only for plural nouns. For both groups, the **verbal reinforcement** significantly increased the generation rate for the type of word that was reinforced. Richard Centers (1963) studied the control of everyday conversation through the use of simple social reinforcers. While supposedly waiting for an experiment, subjects sat in the lobby of a psychology laboratory. A confederate of the experimenter (who acted like a subject) joined the real subjects and initiated conversation. Through the use of head nods, "mm hmms," and smiles, the confederate was able to influence the total verbalization of subjects, the number of statements they made conveying information, and the number of statements of opinion.

Can such verbal reinforcement also affect underlying attitudes and beliefs? Chester Insko (1965) sought to answer that question in an experiment involving students in an introductory psychology course at the University of Hawaii. Students were interviewed by telephone about their feelings toward a proposed springtime festival. Half of the students were rewarded with a "good" or "mm hmm" whenever they expressed feelings of support for the festival. The other half were verbally rewarded for statements opposing the festival. One week later during their psychology class, all subjects were given a general opinion survey. One item in the survey concerned opinions about a springtime festival. The answers of those who previously had been verbally rewarded for profestival statements showed more favorable attitudes toward the festival than did the answers of those who had not received the reinforcements. The verbal reinforcement during the telephone interview had evidently affected their opinions.

Verbal reinforcers often are used by parents as they socialize with their children. Parents, however, typically give so much attention and affection to their children that these reinforcers may lose their effectiveness. Indeed, a few kind words from a stranger may prove far more effective. Researchers observed preschool children playing a game that involved dropping marbles into various holes and found that verbal reinforcers from adult strangers ("that's good" or "you're terrific at this game") had a far greater influence on the children's responses than did similar reinforcers from parents (Stevenson, Keen, & Knights, 1963).

As the above findings suggest, the effect of verbal reinforcers is often dependent upon the particular situation. Jacob Gewirtz and Donald Baer (1958) reasoned that, just as an organism responds more powerfully to food reinforcement when it is hungry, people who recently have been deprived of social approval and attention will be far more responsive to verbal reinforcement. In their experiment, nursery school children dropped marbles into a box through two holes. Each child played the game twice, once after social interaction with others and again after spending 20 minutes alone with no social contact. The experimenter used the verbal reinforcers "good" and "mm hmm" in an attempt to influence which hole the children dropped the marbles through. As predicted, the children were far more responsive to the verbal reinforcement after the social deprivation period. Interestingly, this effect was even more pronounced in children whom their teacher previously had rated as high in seeking approval.

Social reinforcement takes forms other than verbal reinforcement, of course. Approval can be expressed subtly without a word being spoken—through a smile, nod of the head, or even increased eye contact. The unconscious use of social reinforcers may shape many significant behaviors. Since we are most likely to reinforce in subtle ways behaviors in others that we expect and desire, we are likely to bring about those behaviors. Clinical psychologists who expect their clients to improve may subtly reinforce their healthy-sounding verbalizations without really improving their mental health. One area where subtle social reinforcement is likely to have a significant effect is political polling. There are often differences noted in polls taken by the two major political parties in the United States. Democrats typically report that their polls indicate strong support for Democratic candidates, while Republican polls show just the opposite. Even if the same questions are used in different polls, we might conjecture as to why the results of the polls would differ. It is likely that the Democratic and Republican interviewers subtly reinforce their respondents—through a smile or nod of the head—for answers that support their own party. This subtle reinforcement may not only affect the expressed opinion of the respondents but also influence their subsequent behavior in the election booth.

Interpersonal Attraction

Psychologists are concerned with the various factors that determine why people like certain other people and show definite preferences in their choices of others as friends, roommates, or lovers. The area of study concerned with the question of why people like or dislike others is called **interpersonal attraction.** Both the actual and potential rewards that others might supply underlie most theories of interpersonal attraction.

1. *Propinquity.* One of the simplest facts about interpersonal attraction is that people generally come to like those who happen to live or work physically close to them—**propinquity.** Friendships typically develop between people who live in adjacent apartments or who are assigned seats that are close to each other in a classroom. Obviously it is difficult for friendships to develop between people who rarely see each other. On the other hand, neighbors are likely to engage in friendly hellos, to seek help from each other, and to borrow needed items from each other. It is through these kinds of interactions that friendships develop.

Friendships usually develop among people who live or work in close proximity to each other, like these college students.

537

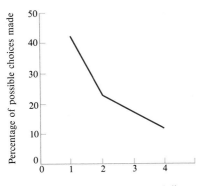

Figure 16.2

The relation between proximity and liking. "Units of approximate distance" represent how many doors apart people live. It can be seen that the closer together people live, the more likely it is that they will become friends.

People who share the same attitudes, views, and interests tend to be attracted to one another.

Leon Festinger, Stanley Schachter, and Kurt Back (1950) studied friendship patterns among residents of a housing complex. The closer the residents lived to each other in terms of sheer physical distance, the more likely they were to be close friends (see Figure 16.2). In addition, residents who lived in strategic locations that would put them in contact with many residents (at the bottom of a stairway or in the middle of an inner court) were most popular.

Theodore Newcomb (1961) acquired use of an entire dormitory at the University of Michigan and recruited students to live there free if they filled out questionnaires at various times throughout the year. A major determinant of liking in this study was how close the students lived to one another. Students who happened to be assigned as roommates became friends—even if their initial attitudes were incompatible. Other research confirms the effects of physical closeness on attraction. People who are physically close to each other during work are likely to become friends (Kipnis, 1957), and marriages are more likely among people who happen to live near each other (Bossard, 1932).

2. Familiarity. One reason why propinquity might lead to attraction is that we tend to see frequently and to become familiar with those who live nearby. Zajonc (1968) has proposed that the frequency with which we are exposed to people or objects is a major determinant of our liking. Mere continued exposure to a person's face (even in the absence of interaction) is sufficient condition for liking that person. In one study demonstrating this effect, subjects went from room to room in the laboratory to taste either pleasant or noxious drinks. As they went from room to room, they found themselves in the company of other subjects. According to plan, some of these subjects were encountered frequently during the experiment, whereas others were encountered infrequently. At the end of the experiment, subjects were asked how much they liked each of the other subjects. Those who had been encountered more frequently were liked better—even if the encounters took place while tasting noxious drinks (Saegert, Swap, and Zajonc, 1973)! More will be said about the relation between frequency of exposure and attraction later in the chapter, when theories of attitude change are discussed.

3. Similarity-attraction. Perhaps the most frequently cited theory of interpersonal attraction is the **similarity-attraction theory** offered by Donn Byrne (1969). In essence, Byrne's theory recalls the adage, "Birds of a feather flock together." People seem to like others of the same "feather." Attraction by similarity seems to apply on almost any dimension, ranging from personality traits, attitudes, and political views, to less important aspects such as city of birth, physical characteristics, and athletic ability. Examples of attraction by similarity abound in everyday life: computer dating services depend upon it by matching people in terms of their similar attitudes and characteristics.

To investigate the role of similarity in interpersonal attraction, Byrne has carried out an extensive research program. In his standard experiment (Byrne, 1961), subjects first fill out a questionnaire in which they describe many of their attitudes toward current issues. Later, they are shown answers purportedly given by other people to the same questionnaire and asked to judge the likability of those people. The other people do not exist, of course. Their answers are fabricated by the experimenter, who can manipulate them to be either very similar to those of the subject or very different. The more similar the attitudes expressed by the subject and the bogus "other person," the greater the liking expressed by the subject. Other work (Byrne, Ervin, & Lamberth, 1970) found that couples who were matched on similarity before a computer date liked each other more than couples who were not so matched. They even stood closer during a postdate interview with the experimenter.

Interpersonal attraction has been shown to reflect similarities not only in attitudes but also in abilities such as intelligence and athletic prowess and even physical similarity. For example, married couples are more similar in height (Berscheid and Walster, 1969) and attractiveness (Murstein, 1972) than would be expected by chance. A study of the 1971 New York mayoral election found that people who preferred the taller candidate were significantly taller than those who preferred the shorter candidate (Berkowitz, Nebel, & Reitman, 1971).

Among the most impressive studies of similarity in interpersonal attraction was the previously mentioned large-scale naturalistic study carried out by Newcomb (1961) in the dormitories of the University of Michigan. Recall that Newcomb discovered that physical closeness was a major determinant of attraction. In addition, he measured the initial attitudes of all residents and found that initial similarity of attitudes was also an important determinant of whether or not students liked each other later in the semester.

Why does similarity lead to attraction? The most likely reason is that people who are similar to us are rewarding in several different ways. Interaction with someone who shares similar interests and attitudes is likely to be smooth, effortless, and interesting to both persons. Similar people find it easier to share pleasant experiences and to find conversational topics of mutual interest. Beyond such obvious rewards, similarity of beliefs and attitudes offers another kind of reinforcement. Similar others help us confirm our own beliefs, reduce uncertainty, and validate our own way of viewing reality.

4. *Complementarity*. Despite the evidence given above, similarity can interfere with liking in some situations. The adage "opposites attract" has some support from psychological research. Two people who talk a lot may find each other irritating—a dominating woman and a dominating man cannot both control the relationship. On the other hand, a good talker and a good listener are likely to get along well; a dominating wife and a submissive husband (or vice versa) may have a smooth relationship. The meshing of people's different needs in such a way that each is satisfied is called *complementarity*. Television's "Odd Couple" was a dramatic demonstration of complementarity. Oscar Madison could be as sloppy as he liked, while Felix Unger could express his obsession with neatness by cleaning up after his roommate. In a complementary relationship, each person rewards the other by allowing and encouraging expression of important needs and desires. Some research supports the role of complementarity in attraction. James Palmer and Byrne (1970) reported that submissive subjects preferred dominant others, and Clyde Hendrick and Steven Brown (1971) found that introverted subjects preferred extraverts.

5. *Balance*. Fritz Heider (1958), in formulating his *balance theory* of interpersonal attraction, pointed out the tendency of people to seek consistency among their *own* thoughts, feelings, and actions. When inconsistency arises, people try to reduce the conflict by changing their attitudes and beliefs and thus restore the more rewarding state of affairs—consistency or balance. According to Heider, a relationship is balanced if two people either like or dislike each other. If one person likes the other but is disliked in return, the relationship is imbalanced. Thus, balance theory proposes that **reciprocity** is an important factor in interpersonal attraction. We will come to like those who like us and dislike those who dislike us. Zajonc and Eugene Burnstein (1965) showed that reciprocity is an important bias in interpersonal relationships. In three-person relationships, there is balance if the people who like each other share their likes and dislikes of other people.

For example, Romeo and Lord Montague (his father) love each other and share their dislike for Tybalt (a Capulet and Juliet's cousin). Figure 16.3A demonstrates this balanced and comfortable set of relationships. Imbalanced (or tension arousing) relationships exist when people who like each other disagree about their feelings for another person. Figure 16.3B illustrates such an imbalanced set of relationships. Romeo and Juliet love each other, but Juliet likes her cousin Tybalt while Romeo does not. Such relationships can become quite uncomfortable because of the conflict experienced by disagreement. For example, should Romeo and Juliet invite Tybalt to a party?

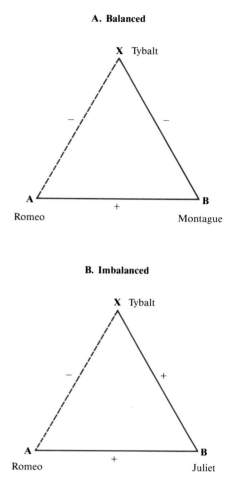

Figure 16.3

Demonstration of Zajonc and Burnstein's balance theory of relationships as represented in the characters of Shakespeare's Romeo and Juliet.

Balanced relationships, said Heider, make people feel comfortable. But imbalanced relationships feel wrong and will motivate people to restore balance by changing their pattern of likes and dislikes. For example, if you learn that someone you dislike is a good friend of your best friend, you can resolve the inconsistency and restore balance in two different ways. You can start liking the person you disliked, or you can stop liking—or at least think less of—your best friend.

6. *Gain-loss*. Suppose someone who previously disliked you starts to like you? How will you react to that person? Sometimes the approval of someone who in the past has disliked you is even more rewarding than the approval of an old friend. Eliot Aronson and Darwyn Linder (1965) have called this the **gain-loss theory** of interpersonal attraction. This theory says that we like someone better if the other person first dislikes us and then likes us than if the person had liked us all along. To test their theory, Aronson and Linder staged an experiment in which subjects interacted with an accomplice, or confederate, of the researchers in several meetings. After each meeting, the subjects heard the confederate's opinion of them. The subjects were grouped in four experimental conditions. In the consistent positive condition, all evaluations by the confederate were positive. In the consistent negative, all evaluations were negative. In the gain condition, the confederate began by giving negative evaluations but then became positive. In the loss condition, evaluations started as positive but then became negative.

As predicted by gain-loss theory, subjects in the gain condition liked the confederate most; subjects in the loss condition liked the confederate least. The gain of approval from someone who previously disliked you is somehow more rewarding than constant approval. Perhaps the initial dislike upsets you, and you feel a rewarding relief when the dislike changes. In addition, you are likely to view the person who changes from disliking to liking you as a more discerning and credible source—one who does not like just anyone but who is highly selective.

7. *Just-world*. It is reasonable to assume that we might feel sorry for, or even like, victims of accidents or bad fortune. But the set of beliefs and feelings that Melvin Lerner has called the **just-world hypothesis** suggests just the

In keeping with the just-world hypothesis of interpersonal attraction, 60% of those polled about the Kent State killings felt that the victims "got what was coming to them."

CHAPTER 16   SOCIAL INFLUENCE

opposite. This hypothesis refers to our tendency to believe that the world is fair, orderly, and just: people get the rewards and punishments they deserve and deserve what they get. When bad things happen to good people, it surprises and upsets us. Hence we rationalize that victims must deserve their fate.

An experiment demonstrates the just-world hypothesis at work (Lerner and Simmons, 1966). Subjects watched participants in a memory task learn series of words. These participants were actually confederates of the experimenters, and they intentionally made a number of errors. The experiment was rigged so that it appeared to the subjects that some of the participants received electric shocks for each error while other participants received no shock. Afterward, the subjects were asked to evaluate the participants. The subjects showed more dislike for those who had appeared to receive shocks. They apparently decided that, in a just world, innocent victims would not receive such punishment. Hence there must have been something wrong with the victims.

Similar dislike or derogation of victims often has been evidenced in the real world. In 1970, after four students were shot to death by the National Guard during an antiwar protest at Kent State University in Ohio, there was a tendency among Americans to suggest that the victims "got what was coming to them." In one public opinion poll, 60 percent of those questioned blamed the victims themselves, even though two of them were bystanders not even involved in the demonstration.

Social Punishment

Just as other people can influence our behavior by serving as sources of reward, they also can influence us by serving as sources of punishment. We often go along with other people simply to avoid punishment—social rejection or banishment to positions of low status, for example. We do not want to be thought of as different or deviant from group norms.

Deviance

Deviance describes behavior that departs in a marked and noticeable way from accepted group norms. The consequences of being considered deviant were powerfully demonstrated in a classic experiment carried out by Schachter (1951). The subjects of the experiment were organized into a series of "discussion clubs." Concealed in each group were three of Schachter's confederates, who pretended to be subjects. As the group began to discuss the prescribed topic, one of the confederates took a position similar to that of the group. A second confederate took a position deviant from the group and remained steadfast in this dissenting opinion. The third confederate began by taking a deviant position but eventually came to side with the group, pretending to be convinced by the group's arguments.

At the end of the discussion, when it came time to assign jobs, the groups punished the deviant by assigning him the jobs that no one wanted. Furthermore, on a measure that asked the subjects to consider how much they liked each of the others, the deviant was clearly disliked. Interestingly, the confederate who began as deviant but eventually agreed with the group was not punished. This person was liked just as much as the confederates who had agreed with the group right from the beginning.

The Schachter study demonstrates the harsh manner in which people are often treated for differing with the opinions of others. But deviance is not simply a matter of failing to listen to the wisdom of the group. The mere appearance of being different can lead to group rejection, even if the apparent deviance is meaningless. Jonathan Freedman and Anthony Doob (1968) asked groups of five or six subjects to take a written personality test. Then each subject was shown score sheets that purportedly contained the distribution of

When the fear of punishment is temporarily absent, a situation can often result in mob behavior. This may have been a factor when a riot broke out at the European Cup soccer championship at Brussels stadium, in which more than 250 people were injured.

When made to feel anonymous, the subjects shown here were more willing to engage in antisocial behavior (Zimbardo, 1969).

test results for all members of the group. In fact, these results had been fabricated by the experimenters and so rigged that one person was shown to have scored differently from all the others. This person was the deviant, although it was never made clear precisely how the score differed from the other scores in the group, not even whether it was more favorable or less favorable than the other scores. This manipulation was successful; the deviants felt different, and the rest of the group considered them so. The group was then asked to select a member for a learning experiment that would purportedly require the subject to receive occasional electric shocks. Not surprisingly, the groups selected the deviants. In an interesting variation of this experiment, Freedman and Doob arranged the situation so that the "learner" was to receive money rather than shocks; in this condition the group avoided selecting the deviant for the experiment.

The punishment of deviance and our fear of such rejection help explain much of our general social behavior. We are constantly in situations where we must comply with certain group or societal norms. We comply in part because we tend to believe in the norms and see their value. But we also comply because we fear that we might be punished by others if we do not.

Deindividuation

The crucial role of punishment in influencing our behavior, which we have seen in our consideration of deviance, also is dramatically evident when the fear of punishment is temporarily absent. Such a situation can result in mob behavior. During power blackouts, it is not uncommon to find roving gangs of residents looting local stores. In the old South, lynchings of blacks by white mobs occurred with sickening frequency. Victory celebrations after football games sometimes erupt into vandalism.

Common to all these instances of mob behavior is what researchers call a state of **deindividuation**—the submerging of the individual into the group. When individuals perform criminal acts alone, they can normally expect to be punished for their behavior. However, when they are part of a group in which all or most of the members are acting in the same way, individuals are relatively free of such concerns. Because the group provides a protective cloak of anonymity, individuals feel less responsible for their actions and hence less accountable to others.

Although the mere fact of membership in a mob tends to make people feel faceless, deindividuation is greatly enhanced when distinctive personal characteristics such as name or face are literally obscured. In typical laboratory investigations of deindividuation, subjects are made to feel identifiable by wearing name tags and by frequent use of their names or to feel anonymous by being required to wear lab coats or even hoods and by never having their names mentioned (Zimbardo, 1969; Singer, Brush, & Lublin, 1965). The subjects who are made to feel anonymous are much more willing to engage in antisocial behavior; for example, they might use much more obscenity during a group discussion or deliver higher levels of what they thought were electric shocks to another person.

Examples of deindividuation can be found in daily newspaper headlines. Members of terrorist groups such as the Ku Klux Klan wear hoods not only to hide their identity from the police but also to submerge their identity into the group. According to some reports, the murderers of three civil rights workers in Mississippi in 1964 passed the gun from hand to hand so that each would feel equally responsible and none would feel individually guilty.

But we need look no further for the experience of deindividuation than our own feelings of anonymity when as children we dressed up for Halloween. Behind our costumes and masks we felt unidentifiable and thus more likely to engage in mildly antisocial behavior such as soaping windows. A clever study of children's behavior was carried out during this naturally occurring state of deindividuation at Halloween (Diener, Fraser, Beaman, & Kelem, 1976). The researchers arranged to observe trick-or-treaters at a number of different homes. As the Halloweener approached the home, a hidden observer recorded one important variable—that is, whether the child was alone or in a group. At the door, the children were greeted by an experimenter who made appropriate approving comments about the costumes and set up a second variable of the study: half of the time, the children were asked their names and addresses; the other half of the time the children were allowed to remain anonymous. The experimenter next pointed to a table, told each trick-or-treater to take one piece of candy from the bowl, and then left the room. The children were being watched, however, by a hidden observer, who noted whether the children helped themselves to an extra piece of candy or to money from a bowl of pennies and nickels on the table.

Both anonymity and group membership affected the behavior of the children. The children were more likely to steal if their anonymity had been protected or if they had arrived in a group. As can be seen in the accompanying table, stealing was most prevalent among those children who were most deindividuated—anonymous and in a group. More than half of these children helped themselves to an extra piece of candy or to money from the bowl of coins.

	Percentage of Children in Each Condition Who Stole	
Anonymity	*Alone*	*Group*
Nonanonymous	7.5%	20.8%
Anonymous	21.4%	57.2%

Social reinforcement and social punishment do have an amply documented effect on many of our behaviors. Rewards and punishments, in addition to arousal, are stimuli that affect the way we act. In the next section we shall examine the ways in which other people serve as stimuli to our behavior by acting as sources of information.

In addition to serving as sources of arousal and of reinforcement, other people influence our behavior in a third major way—by serving as useful sources of information. We observe the behavior of other people in a given situation, and their behavior gives us information about how to act in that situation. Much of a child's learning is acquired through the observation of others. This same process influences adults, especially in ambiguous circumstances where what constitutes appropriate behavior may not be clear.

People are constantly making **social comparisons,** looking to others as a guide for their own interpretations of what is appropriate in a given situation. Cigarette smokers will frequently look around the room to see if anyone else is smoking before they decide to light up. Similarly, when we want to applaud a speaker or a musical performance, we turn to others to see if they are ready to applaud: they serve as models.

A theory of social comparison relevant to such situations was proposed in 1954 by Festinger. The basic tenet of the theory is that whenever we are uncertain about the validity of our own opinions or judgments, we turn to others for information. Their responses serve as guides for us in determining what our own interpretation or response ought to be.

Here is a typical example of the social comparison process at work on campus. In an exam where grades are assigned on a curve, you learn that your score was 42 out of a possible 65 points. How well did you do? You do not know how to interpret this score. It could be that everyone in the class did poorly and your score is actually in the top quarter of the class distribution— or it could be that everyone did well and your score is actually one of the lowest in the class. Typically, you will want to know immediately what other people's scores were. By comparing your score to theirs, you arrive at an interpretation of how well you did on the test.

Affiliation

One of the first experimental investigations of social comparison was conducted by Schachter (1959). Because people must at least get together in order to engage in the social comparison process, Schachter focused on **affiliation**— that is, the desire to associate and interact with others (see chapter 10 for an extended discussion of the need for affiliation). He hypothesized that fear would lead to affiliation, inasmuch as fearful individuals want to affiliate so that others can give them information that will help them evaluate how appropriate their feelings of fear are.

To test this hypothesis, Schachter ran an experiment in which subjects were told they would receive electric shocks. Half of the subjects were told the shocks would be very severe. The experimenter, an ominous-looking man dressed in a lab coat and supposedly named "Dr. Gregor Zilstein," warned them: "Now I feel I must be completely honest with you and tell you exactly what you are in for. These shocks will hurt. They will be painful . . . but, of course, they will do no permanent damage." For the other half of the subjects, the experimenter described the shocks quite differently: "Do not let the word 'shock' trouble you; I am sure that you will enjoy the experiment . . . I assure you that what you will feel will not in any way be painful. It will resemble more a tickle or a tingle than anything unpleasant." After hearing one of these two descriptions, subjects were given a choice of how they could spend their time while the shock apparatus was supposedly being put in order: they could wait with other people or wait alone. The subjects in the high-fear condition— those who were anticipating severe shocks—showed a stronger desire to wait with others than did those in the low-fear condition. In other words, high fear led to a desire for affiliation.

CHAPTER 16 SOCIAL INFLUENCE

Further research by Schachter (1959) suggests that in high-fear situations people do not want to affiliate with simply anyone. They prefer to affiliate with other subjects who are participating in the experiment and expecting to be shocked—that is, people with information about the situation at hand. This affiliation enables them to undergo the social comparison process, obtaining information from others around them about how to interpret the severity of the shock situation and their emotional state. Additional research (Gerard, 1963; Wrightsman, 1960) indicates that affiliation in the fear situation is due to a desire for social comparison along with a desire for reassurance and the reduction of fear.

Other work by Schachter (Schachter & Singer, 1962) has shown that during a state of physiological arousal subjects tend to interpret their own emotions in terms of social comparison. They variously report feelings of happiness or anger, for example, depending upon information cues supplied by others. See chapter 10 for a detailed description of the procedures and results of this experiment.

How a given situation is defined and what informational cues one takes from others may determine whether one offers assistance or not.

Bystander Intervention

One of the most dramatic situations where the behavior of other people serves as an important source of information is the apparent emergency. You are walking down the street and see an old woman sprawled on a patch of ice. Has she fallen and hurt herself? Is she merely drunk? Perhaps she is only shaken up and will easily get back on her feet unaided. Or she may have broken a bone and is in a true emergency situation. Are others standing by? What are they doing? The situation is obviously ambiguous. How you define it, what informational cues you take from other people, may be the determining factors in whether you intervene and offer help.

The factors that determine whether or not bystanders intervene in such situations have been investigated by Bibb Latané and John Darley. Their original interest was prompted by an extraordinary and tragic instance of nonintervention by bystanders that occurred in 1964 in New York City. Shortly after 3 A.M. a young woman named Kitty Genovese, who was returning from work, was attacked by a man in front of her apartment building. The man stabbed her, but she struggled free, crying out in terror and screaming for help. Then the man attacked her again and stabbed her to death. Kitty Genovese's death struggle lasted more than 30 minutes. During this period, reporters from the *New York Times* later learned, at least 38 residents of the building heard her scream and came to the windows. Yet not one of those people came to her aid or telephoned the police.

The incident received a great deal of publicity. It was interpreted in the press in terms of apathy and indifference, of people having "lost concern for our fellow man." Such explanations focused on the personalities of the bystanders who had failed to help: something was lacking in their character. However, Latané and Darley (1970) sought a different explanation. They attempted to determine precisely what situational variables and social psychological processes lead people in general to respond—or not—to an emergency.

Latané and Darley began by proposing a "decision tree" analysis showing that responding to an emergency requires more than personal altruism: it involves a sequence of appropriate decisions. First and most obvious, an individual must notice the incident. Second, that individual must resolve any apparent ambiguity and interpret the event as an emergency. Third, that person must assume some responsibility, must "make it his or her business" to intervene. Finally, the individual must know the appropriate form of assistance and then render it. Only if the bystander makes the appropriate decision at each point in the sequence will he or she intervene, and these decisions typically must be made in a matter of seconds.

In their experiments on **bystander intervention,** Latané and Darley isolated particular decision points and then examined the variables affecting that decision and the subject's response. In one experiment (Darley and Latané, 1968), the emergency was so obvious that it had to be noticed and interpreted as an emergency; thus the subject was at the third point on the decision tree—deciding whether to assume responsibility. Ostensibly, the experiment involved a discussion about adjustment to college life, with the subjects placed in individual booths connected by an intercom system. In fact, only one subject participated at a time; the other subjects were actually tape recordings prepared by the experimenters. During the discussion, one of the voices loudly announced the onset of an epileptic seizure: "I er um I think I need help er if if could er er somebody er er er er er give me a little er give me a little help . . . I'm gonna die er er I'm gonna die er help er help er er seizure er." The voice choked, then lapsed into silence.

How did the subjects respond to this obvious emergency? It all depended on how many people the subject thought were tuned in to the emergency on the intercom. The experimeters, by use of the appropriate number of tape recorders, manipulated this variable. Some subjects thought that the group consisted of only two people (subject and victim); others thought it consisted of three people (subject, victim, and one additional discussant) or six people (four additional discussants). The measure of helping was whether the subject stepped out of the booth and sought some help for the victim. Helping, as it turned out, was a direct function of the size of the group. The greater the number of other people the subject thought had heard the victim's plea for help, the less likely the subject was to respond. Eighty-five percent of the subjects who thought they were alone with the victim responded before the victim's taped voice ran out. Of those who believed that the group consisted of three, 62 percent responded. And of those who believed the group consisted of six, only 31 percent offered help.

Latané and Darley concluded that a **diffusion of responsibility** had occurred in the larger groups: knowing that others were present meant that the subject was not solely responsible for the victim's welfare. Thus, one variable that determines whether a bystander will intervene is the number of bystanders believed to be present. The larger the number of others present, the less responsibility the individual is likely to assume. (Bystanders in the Kitty Genovese case lived in a large apartment building. Listening from behind their windows, they must have assumed there were many others present.)

Another experiment by Latané and Darley (1968) focused on an earlier point in their decision-tree analysis—defining the event as an emergency. They created an ambiguous event and then examined variables that influenced how the event was defined. The setting for the experiment was a small waiting room where subjects sat filling out a questionnaire. Suddenly, a stream of smoke poured into the room through a wall vent. Some subjects were alone when this happened: 75 percent of these subjects stepped out of the room and reported the emergency. Other subjects were with two other people, actually accomplices of the experimenters who had been instructed to react passively and display no emotional reaction to the smoke. Of these subjects, only 10 percent reported the smoke. Faced with the apparent ambiguity of the situation, they went through the social comparison process to reduce their own uncertainties: they observed the passivity of the two others in the waiting room and defined the event as a nonemergency.

In a final condition of the experiment, three subjects were in the waiting room. All of them were naive; that is, none was a confederate of the experimeter. Reporting of the emergency was also relatively low in this condition. In only 38 percent of these groups did even one person report the smoke. Latané and Darley concluded that in the groups of three a state of **pluralistic ignorance** apparently had developed. They pointed out that, since our culture does not encourage display of emotions, each of the three subjects was probably attempting to appear calm. When these subjects made social comparisons, they saw everyone else acting undisturbed by the smoke. Hence they defined the event as a nonemergency. Later interviews with the subjects who had not responded to the emergency elicited an astonishing variety of interpretations of what the smoke was. These interpretations ranged from air-conditioning vapors to smog (introduced, it was thought, to simulate an urban environment) to a "truth gas" designed to make the subject reply honestly to the questionnaire.

Further research on the state of pluralistic ignorance that can develop among bystanders in an emergency has been conducted. In one such experiment, subjects working on a task overheard a loud crash from an adjoining room and subsequently heard a workman crying out in distress (Darley, Teger, & Lewis, 1973). As had been found in past research, subjects who were alone were more likely to help than were subjects who were paired with another subject. However, this state of pluralistic ignorance among subjects participating in pairs was much more likely to occur when the two subjects were seated back-to-back rather than face-to-face. Many fewer subjects in the nonfacing condition intervened than in the facing condition. In this latter condition, it was very easy for subjects to notice each other's startled response at the sound of the crash. Thus, despite subjects' desires to appear calm, they did emit cues that were noticeable to a facing partner and that enabled each person to decide that an emergency was indeed in progress. These cues were far less noticeable when subjects were seated back-to-back, thus leading subjects to interpret each other's presumed lack of a reaction as an indication that the event was not a serious cry for help.

Conformity

The underlying features of social comparison and affiliation as well as diffusion of responsibility are the comforts the individual has in knowing that others all essentially believe the same thing. The perception that others share our qualities and beliefs is rewarding because it confirms the idea that our beliefs and attributes are appropriate, valued, and correct. Might it be, then, that we bias our perception of the beliefs of other people and see them as being more like us than they really are? Lee Ross and his colleagues (Ross, Greene, & House, 1977) investigated the estimates that people made of the frequency of various traits and beliefs in the population (e.g., what percentage of people do you think have blue eyes? believe in capital punishment?). The main finding was that people perceived their own characteristics and beliefs as being relatively common. That is, blue-eyed people judged that there were more blue-eyed people than did people whose eyes were a different color. Believers in capital punishment estimated that more Americans believed in capital punishment than did those who opposed capital punishment. Ross et al. referred to this phenomenon as the **false consensus effect** to get across the idea that people mistakenly believe that many others feel and act the way they themselves do.

Not only do people believe that others share their own qualities, people are also willing to change their judgments and behavior to fit the ideas and judgments of other group members when it is obvious that the group does not share the individual's belief. In other words, the individual conforms.

Public Compliance Versus Private Acceptance

Sometimes **conformity** consists solely of a kind of public compliance. Other times it goes far deeper and results in private acceptance. The distinction between two of the types of social influence—reinforcement and information—

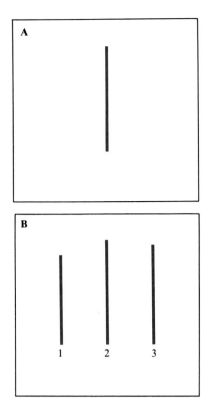

Figure 16.4

Cards used in Asch's conformity experiments. After viewing card A, *the subject is asked to pick the line from card* B *that matches card* A.

helps to differentiate between public compliance and private acceptance. The two processes operate in very different ways and with differing effects. The most important distinction is that the threat of social punishment brings about public compliance but not private acceptance. There is no change in private internalized beliefs. Once the person who has offered rewards or threatened punishment is no longer watching, behavior reverts to what it was prior to the attempt at social control. By contrast, social control achieved through the use of others as sources of information leads not only to public compliance but also to changes of internalized attitudes and beliefs. These changes persist even after the source of information is no longer present and watching.

Sherif: The Autokinetic Effect

The first systematic work in the study of conformity was carried out by Muzafer Sherif (1937). To demonstrate conformity, Sherif took advantage of a well-known optical illusion, the **autokinetic effect.** If an indivudal is placed in a totally dark room with no frame of reference and then a single point of light is introduced, the light appears to move erratically. This effect is caused by random movements of the person's own eyes (see chapter 3). (During World War II, two versions of this effect proved so distracting to American pilots flying in formation at night that blinking lights were introduced to eliminate the problem.)

Sherif asked his subjects to make judgments as to how far the light seemed to be moving. Different subjects tended to develop different, though stable, ranges for their estimates. Some estimates were in the 1/4-inch to 2-inch range, for example, while others ranged from 5 to 7 inches. However, when several people with differing individual ranges were brought together, the group quickly established its own range, which was an average of the individual ranges. After only a few trials, Sherif found that he could easily get subjects to change their estimates by placing accomplices in the room with the subjects. This proved true even when the purported judgments of the accomplices varied widely from the subjects' individual range. Sherif thus demonstrated a clear instance of conformity: subjects' judgments changed when faced with the differing judgments of one or more others.

Asch: The Length of Lines

Solomon Asch (1951) approached conformity in a different way. He felt that Sherif's research had misrepresented people as blind conformists. He believed that the subjects had conformed only because of the built-in ambiguity of the autokinetic effect. He reasoned that with a clear object of perception, subjects in groups would show much less conformity in judgment.

To test his ideas, Asch devised a set of simple and elegant experiments. His subjects were shown a pair of white cards (see Figure 16.4). On one card was a single black vertical line. On the other card were three vertical lines of

The only true subject (#6) in Solomon Asch's experiment looked bewildered and concerned when confronted by an obviously incorrect unanimous majority.

differing lengths. The subject's task was to judge which of those three lines exactly matched the standard line on the other card. It was an easy task because two of the lines were appreciably longer or shorter than the standard line. When subjects made their judgments alone, without group pressure, they almost never made an error.

In a group judgment situation, the subject's estimates were made after each of five other group members gave their judgments. The elegant twist in Asch's setup was that all of the members of the group, except for one real subject, were his accomplices. On the first couple of trials, the confederates behaved normally. Like the subject, they gave the correct answer when shown each pair of cards. Beginning with the third trial and on several later trials, however, the confederates all gave a prearranged incorrect answer, selecting lines that were obviously much too long or much too short. What would happen when the subject's senses indicated one thing and the group indicated something else? Would the subject stick to the perceptual evidence or conform to group opinion, no matter how obviously wrong?

Asch reported that subjects conformed to the group's incorrect judgment on more than one third of the trials. Indeed, more than 80 percent of all subjects conformed on at least one trial (see Figure 16.5). Thus, Asch had proved himself wrong: indeed, subjects did conform even when there was virtually unmistakable perceptual evidence upon which to base their judgments.

Figure 16.5

Asch's experiments clearly demonstrate conformity to group judgment. When the group told the truth (correct identification), the subject also answered correctly, as shown by the "No opposition" curve. However, when the group deliberately gave incorrect answers, the subject often conformed to the group's incorrect judgment, as shown in the "Alone against majority" curve.

Information Versus Reinforcement: Two Different Processes

Subjects in both the Sherif and Asch experiments conformed—but for different reasons. In the Sherif procedure the autokinetic situation was so ambiguous that subjects were impelled to look to the judgments of others. The others served as useful sources of information: the subjects were under informational social influence.

On the other hand, the subjects in the Asch experiments needed no informational cues. The relative lengths of the lines were not ambiguous and were easily judged when the subjects were alone. The subjects were under a different social influence, that of reinforcement. They conformed because of the rewards and punishments that could be administered by others. Conforming gave them the rewarding feeling of going along with the group, of acceptance by others. By conforming they avoided the possibility of rejection by group members. Remember from our earlier discussion of the deviance experiments how harshly groups treat deviance. Under reinforcement influence, people tend to conform to the standards of their group whether it be a fraternity, football team, or a board of directors, even when they feel the group might be wrong.

As we noted at the beginning of this section, reinforcement influence leads to public compliance but not internal change. This was clear when Asch's subjects were removed from the group situation and asked to make individual judgments. They immediately reverted to their earlier, correct judgements: their conformity to the group had involved public compliance, not internal change. On the other hand, for the Sherif subjects, the informational impact of the group judgments left a mark. They continued to conform to the group judgments even in the absence of the others: there had been internalized change.

The difference in process between the two conformity experiments is also demonstrated by the differing effects of anonymity. Asch's subjects made their judgments in a face-to-face setting. On the other hand, if subjects in this situation make their judgments anonymously (that is, when they are placed in private rooms where they can hear the judgments of others but no one is seen or identified by name), conformity drops off dramatically (Deutsch & Gerard, 1955). No such effect would be expected in the Sherif procedure. In fact, his subjects did make their judgments anonymously: subjects were in a dark room and could not identify each other. When we accept information from others as evidence of reality, we use the information regardless of whether we are in public or alone.

Factors Affecting Conformity

In addition to anonymity, several other factors can affect conformity as it develops through informational and reinforcement social influence.

Ambiguity

When the subject is under informational influence, uncertainty about the correct judgment leads the individual to look to others for information. Ambiguity thus has a major effect on conformity. Any increase in ambiguity should increase conformity, whereas decreases in ambiguity decrease conformity. Asch (1951), in a variation on his initial experiment, demonstrated this effect quite clearly. He found that as the lengths of the three test lines were made more similar, increasing the difficulty or ambiguity of the task, conformity also increased markedly.

Self-confidence

Another factor affecting conformity through informational influence is the confidence of subjects in their own ability to make accurate judgments. Conformity decreases in the group situation when subjects are first told they are very accurate in individual judgments. Conversely, conformity increases when subjects are told they are terrible at the task (Samelson, 1957). Varying the perceived competence of the confederates in the group also affects the confidence and the resulting conformity of the subject (Mausner, 1954). If, for example, the confederate in the Sherif procedure were introduced as a graduate student in visual perception, conformity would increase. It would decrease if the confederate were presented as a high school student with bad eyes.

Self-confidence also relates to the issue of sex differences in conformity. Generally speaking, one sex does not appear to conform any more than the other sex. Instead, research has indicated that the degree of conformity depends upon which sex feels less expert at the task in question (Sistrunk & McDavid, 1971). Females conform more than males when the task is one for which males feel more expert. However, when the task is one for which females feel more expert, males display more conformity than females.

Group Goals

One factor affecting conformity through the power of the group to reward or punish is the salience of the group's goals. For example, using the Asch procedure, Morton Deutsch and Harold Gerard (1955) introduced an attractive group goal. Subjects were told that each member of the five groups making the fewest total errors would receive a pair of tickets to a play. This goal induced a mutual dependence among the group members. The fact that each member cared more about the performance of others led to a large increase in conformity.

Allies

A second factor affecting the reinforcing power of the group—and hence conformity—is the presence of allies. When Asch (1951) provided the subject with a confederate who always gave the right answer no matter what the other accomplices did, conformity was drastically reduced. Two possibilities account for this effect: (1) having at least one ally reduces the likelihood of rejection by the group, and (2) if rejection does occur, one can at least share the deviant state with a friend and partner. Interestingly, additional research indicates that

CHAPTER 16 SOCIAL INFLUENCE

a very close bond develops between the subject and the ally (Darley, Moriarty, Darley, & Berscheid, 1974). In a later situation, the subject is very likely to conform to the judgments of the ally.

Cohesiveness

Finally, the cohesiveness of the group—that is, the attraction that members have for the group and for each other—influences conformity through reinforcement. Leonard Berkowitz (1954) established groups that were either high or low in cohesiveness. He did this by telling the groups that they had been preselected and had been put together because of their congeniality and the scientific prediction that they would like each other (high cohesiveness) or that it had been impossible to arrange a congenial group (low cohesiveness). The task of each group was to produce checkerboards made of cardboard. Although subjects worked alone in separate rooms, they could communicate with other members of their group by writing notes. The experimenter manipulated the conditions by intercepting the notes written by the subjects and substituting his own. In one condition, the notes requested the subjects to work hard and raise productivity. In the other condition, subjects were urged to slow down and not work so hard. Which groups conformed more significantly to the apparent wishes of other members? Relative to those in the low-cohesiveness groups, subjects in high-cohesiveness groups greatly increased productivity when asked to do so and greatly decreased productivity when asked to do that. The greater the cohesiveness of a group, the greater the tendency was for individual members to accept influence from others in the group.

Degree of conformity is influenced by many different factors. Reward and punishment bring about public compliance but not private acceptance, and information brings about both public compliance and changes in internalized attitudes and beliefs. Anonymity, ambiguity, self-confidence, the importance of group goals, the presence of allies, and the cohesiveness of the group all have important effects on conformity.

In addition to affecting how we define events, other people are also instrumental in helping us to define ourselves.

Learning About Ourselves

We already have discussed several examples of social influence in which others help us to define events. In bystander intervention, for example, the behavior of others helps us to decide whether an emergency is actually in progress. In conformity, the social comparison process provides information that influences our judgments about exterior phenomena. Social psychology also studies how others help us learn about ourselves and, indeed, help us define ourselves.

Clearly, social comparison is one way we define our own opinions, abilities, judgments, and emotions. Take a simple example of athletic ability. If you want to know how good you are at tennis, you compare your performance on the court with the performance of others. Let us consider several other ways in which others help define us.

How Others Treat Us

We can learn about ourselves by looking at how others treat us (Mead, 1934). Their treatment presumably reflects their evaluation of us, which in turn shapes our evaluations of ourselves.

This process is demonstrated clearly in an experiment by Robert Kraut (1973). The experimenter, posing as a door-to-door canvasser, approached residents of a middle-class neighborhood and asked them to donate money to a charitable agency. Half of those who donated money received an explicit label from the experimenter: "You are a generous person. I wish more of the people I met were as charitable as you." The other half who donated money were not labeled in any way. Similarly, half of those who did not donate received no label and the other half were directly labeled as uncharitable: "Let me give you one of our health leaflets anyway. We've been giving them to everyone, even people like you who are uncharitable and don't normally give to these causes."

Thus, half of the donors and half of the nondonors received explicit information about the canvasser's evaluation of them. How did these evaluations affect the subjects? A week to two weeks later, the same subjects were approached by a second experimenter, who was posing as a canvasser for another charitable agency. Those donors who previously had been labeled as charitable gave more money to this campaign than did donors who had not been labeled. Similarly, those who had not donated the first time, and who had been labeled as uncharitable, gave less than did the nondonors who had not been labeled. In sum, the evaluation by the first canvasser had apparently affected the subject's own self-image and hence the likelihood that the person would or would not donate to other agencies.

Self-Perception

Another way in which we can learn about ourselves is by observing our own behavior. For example, you walk home from a party, glance at your watch and, amazed at how late it is, remark to yourself, "Gee, I must have had a good time. Look how late I stayed." Or you eat a surprisingly large amount of food at dinner and exclaim, "I must have been hungrier than I thought."

Daryl Bem (1972) proposed a **theory of self-perception** to account for such phenomena: "Individuals come to know their own attitudes, emotions and other internal states partially by inferring them from observations of their own overt behavior and/or the circumstances in which this behavior occurs."

Observing One's Own Behavior

Self-perception processes have been demonstrated in another door-to-door canvassing experiment (Freedman & Fraser, 1966). The experimenter, posing as a canvasser, approached a number of homeowners and asked them to sign a petition promoting safe driving. It was a small request, and almost everyone who was asked complied. Later, these same subjects were approached by a second canvasser who asked them to comply with a more demanding request: they were asked to place on their front lawns a large, unattractive sign that said, "Drive Carefully." To provide a control group, the experimenter made the same request of some homeowners who had not been approached with the small initial request. Those people who had complied with the first request were more likely to agree to the larger request than were the control group subjects. In the process of complying with the first request, the subjects observed themselves as being "concerned citizens." This self-perception made them more willing to go along with the more demanding request.

This phenomenon has links to the conventional wisdom of door-to-door sales people who claim that if they can merely "get their foot in the door" (that is, get the homeowner to comply with the small request of letting them in house), they can subsequently make their sale.

How the self-perception process can lead to inferences about one's internal state is shown in a fascinating study by Stuart Valins (1966). Here, male subjects observed what they believed to be their own physiological reactions to external stimuli. They were rigged up with electrodes that supposedly measured heart rate. Then they were shown several centerfold photographs of nudes from *Playboy* magazine. As they viewed the pictures, the subjects were permitted to listen to what was purported to be their "amplified heartbeat." Actually, the sound was simulated by the experimenter and arranged so that the "heartbeat" increased when the subject was viewing certain of the nudes. Later, the subjects were asked to rate the attractiveness of each nude and asked which of the photos they would like to take home as a reward for participating in the experiment. The subjects liked best the photos that supposedly had stimulated increases in their heart rate. By observing their own physiological behavior, albeit bogus, they inferred how they must have felt toward each photo.

Overjustification: Too Much Reward

In self-perception we learn something about ourselves because of behavior that we attribute to internal forces. We also can learn about ourselves when we attribute the behavior to some strong external force. Suppose someone asks you to read ten books and promises you a reward for doing so. If you agree to the request, chances are that you will attribute your compliance to the promise of reward. But what if you would have read those books anyway without the offer of reward? Research indicates that you would still attribute your compliance to the reward and, as a result, grow to like the activity less. If it took a reward to get you to perform the activity, then you must not like it.

This phenomenon is called **overjustification** because the reward provides too large an external justification for performing a behavior. Overjustification was convincingly demonstrated in an experiment by Mark Lepper, David Greene, and Richard Nisbett (1973). The experimenter observed children in a nursery school and selected as subjects those who played with felt pens a great deal during free-play period. Thus, all the subjects already had an intrinsic interest in playing with felt pens. Each of the children was asked to draw a picture with some felt pens. There were three different conditions. In the "Expected Reward" condition, the children were told that as a reward for drawing the picture, they would be given a "Good Player Award," an attractive certificate with colored ribbons. In the "No Reward" condition, the children heard nothing of a reward. In the "Unexpected Reward" condition, the children were given a "Good Player Award" after drawing the picture, but the reward was unexpected: it had not been mentioned beforehand.

Several days later the experimenter observed these same children in the nursery school and recorded the amount of time each spent with the felt pens during the free-play period. The children in the "Expected Reward" condition played with the felt pens significantly less than did the children who had heard nothing of a reward or received the reward unexpectedly. The researchers concluded that agreeing to draw the picutre in order to earn a reward undermined the child's intrinsic interest in working with the felt markers. In effect, these children, by attributing their behavior to the external reward, learned that they were not really all that interested in the activity itself.

The experimental findings are an example of how rewards can sometimes produce atypical effects. To understand the negative effects of reward, it is necessary to understand the difference between extrinsic rewards and intrinsic rewards. Extrinsic rewards, such as trophies, prize money, applause of an audience, and praise, are those received as a result of performing an action. Intrinsic rewards, on the other hand, derive from the process of carrying out an action. For example, children are intrinsically motivated to learn; they find learning and discovery rewarding in their own right (Deci, 1975). However, it is possible in light of the results reported above that giving children gold stars for getting the right answers or offering them highly prized rewards for bringing home good report cards could undermine this interest in learning.

We saw earlier that rewards usually increase the likelihood of one's performing the rewarded behavior. But here, at least in the condition where the

The top photo shows the fake shock-generating machine used in Stanley Milgram's experiment. Second, the "learner" is strapped to the chair and wired with electrodes. Next, the subject receives a sample shock. Later (bottom photo), the subject gets up and refuses to administer any more shocks to the "learner."

reward was expected and the activity served as a means of obtaining the reward, just the opposite occurred. Apparently, if one is already intrinsically interested in the activity, the perception that one is performing the activity in order to obtain a reward can undermine that intrinsic interest. We can even sometimes learn about what it is that we do not like by observing that it seems to take a strong external force to get us to perform the behavior.

Intentional Social Influence

Most of the examples of social influence we have discussed thus far represent **unintentional social influence.** They are instances where others arouse us, reinforce us, or serve as sources of information inadvertently. But other people often clearly intend to influence us. Police give orders they clearly expect us to obey. Advertisers try to persuade us to buy their products. Politicians attempt to talk us into voting for them. We will examine next some instances of such **intentional social influence.**

Obedience to Authority

The most obvious and perhaps the most effective form of intentional social influence is a directive issued by an authority figure. Millions of people have died in wars because of the willingness to obey orders blindly and to kill others. This process of blind obedience to authority has been explored by Stanley Milgram (1963) in a research program widely publicized because of its relevance to events in Nazi Germany. For example, Adolph Eichmann, a Nazi official during World War II, justified his role in the deaths of hundreds of thousands of Jews by saying he was simply obeying orders.

Working at Yale University in the early 1960s, Milgram created an ingenious experimental design to measure obedience. He used the cover story that the purpose of the experiment was to investigate "the effects of punishment on learning." Subjects were told that they would serve as the teachers. They asked the learner—ostensibly another subject—a series of questions involving word pairs and then punished any mistakes with an electric shock. The shock apparatus contained a number of levers with the voltage level indicated above each lever. The voltages ranged in 15-volt increments from 15 volts to 450 volts, with the lower range labeled "Slight Shock" and the upper range labeled "Danger: Severe Shock." The highest level bore the label *XXX*. Subjects were told that each time the learner erred or failed to respond they should increase the shock level by 15 volts.

The learner was strapped into a chair in the next room with electrodes connected to the wrists. The learner was a fake, of course, an accomplice of the experimenter, and received no electric shocks. It had been prearranged for the learner to make many errors and to respond to the supposed escalation of shocks in a predescribed manner. At 90 volts, the learner began to cry out in pain; at 150 volts, the learner asked to be let out of the experiment. At 180 volts, the learner banged on the wall, and at 285 volts, the learner screamed in agony. At 330 volts and thereafter, through the 450-volt limit, there was only ominous silence.

The authority in this setting was the researcher, who sat next to the subject. In a white lab coat, the experimenter, in effect, personified the authority of "science." Subjects were not physically coerced into administering shocks. If the subjects hesitated in raising the shock level, the experimenter prodded them to proceed with instructions such as, "The experiment requires that you continue."

How would you respond in this situation? Before he conducted the experiments, Milgram suspected that only a few of his subjects would be willing to obey all the way to the 450-volt limit. As it turned out, nearly two thirds of Milgram's subjects—teachers, salespeople, laborers, clerks—obeyed the experimenter all the way and delivered the maximum shock of 450 volts. To Milgram, the lesson of the study was that "ordinary people, simply doing their jobs, and without any particular hostility on their parts, can become agents in a terrible destructive process" (Milgram, 1974).

In further research, Milgram (1974) attempted to examine what variables affect the level of obedience to an authority figure. One variable was the "psychological distance" between subject and learner. The closer the subject was to the learner, the lower the obedience level. Subjects obeyed most when they could neither see nor hear the learner's reactions to the shocks; they obeyed least when the subject was required actually to hold the learner's hand on a shock plate in order to deliver the punishment.

A second variable was the "psychological distance" between the subject and the authority figure. The greater the distance from the experimenter, the less the obedience level. Obedience was least when the experimenter delivered instructions to the subject via a tape recorder and was never actually seen by the subject. Interestingly, in the absence of the experimenter, several subjects disobeyed orders by using only the lowest level of shock: they were willing to undermine the experiment but not create an open break with authority.

Many critics in and out of the scientific community have raised questions about the ethics of Milgram's experiment. In fact, when Milgram's book, *Obedience to Authority,* was published in 1974, the *New York Times* Sunday reviewer was so incensed at the method used in the research that he virtually ignored the findings. The principal criticism was that the subjects were led under false pretenses into behavior likely to burden them with guilt. In reply, Milgram has pointed out that immediately after the experiment each subject was informed of the true purpose and given emotional support, whether the subject had obeyed or disobeyed. A follow-up questionnaire administered some time later found that only 1.3 percent of the subjects expressed regret at having participated in the experiment, whereas 83.7 percent were glad to have participated. Furthermore, a university psychiatrist interviewed 40 of the subjects and reported no evidence of emotional harm. In fact, many of these subjects said their participation in the experiment had been an enriching and instructive experience.

Persuasion: Changing Attitudes by Changing Perceptions

Another major form of intentional social influence is **persuasion.** Unlike orders from an authority figure, which aim directly at our behavior, persuasion aims only indirectly at changing our behavior. Persuasion aims first at changing our attitudes; attitude change, it is hoped, will lead to behavior change. Advertisers trust that, by persuading us of the worth of their products and thus changing our attitudes, we will be led to purchase those wares.

An **attitude** represents a categorization of an object along an evaluative dimension. The object can be an actual physical object, another person, or some issue, and the attitude represents one's degree of favorability. Social psychologists typically measure attitudes by having subjects judge objects on scales that range from "good" to "bad" or "agree" to "disagree."

It is obvious that we all have attitudes. Just think about how often you have been asked questions of this sort: "How was the movie?" "Do you like Joe?" "Do you want to see marijuana legalized?" An important issue that arises is why we form attitudes and what use they are to us. The most common answer is one that centers upon the "knowledge function" that attitudes serve (Katz, 1960; Smith, Bruner, & White, 1956). Attitudes help us to categorize the complex social environments in which we live. They are functional in the sense that they serve to simplify our environment. "Objects" are classified as

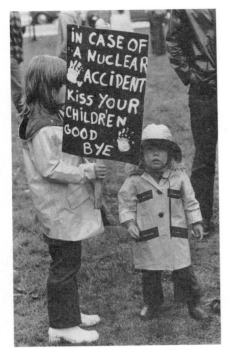

Socialization by parents exerts an important influence on a child's attitude formation.

"good" or "bad," and hence the behavior of these "objects" and additional qualities that they might possess are more easily predicted.

How are attitudes formed? They can be formed in any number of different ways, some of which we have already discussed. Attitudes can be formed through social comparison processes, through the informational social influence that all groups of which we are members can have upon us, and through self-perception processes. Socialization, in particular socialization by parents, undoubtedly exerts an influence upon attitude formation. For example, children tend to adopt the same political party affiliation selected by their parents.

Attitudes also form through classical conditioning processes (see chapter 7). Objects continuously associated with bad events take on negative value; those associated with positive events become valued positively. For example, Mark Zanna, Charles Kiesler, and Paul Pilkonis (1970) demonstrated that words that signaled shock onset for a subject came to be viewed more negatively than words that signaled shock offset. Such a process is clearly not unfamiliar to commercial advertisers, who frequently attempt to associate a catchy jingle or a pleasant muscial score with their product.

Attitudes are also made more positive by the individual's familiarity with the object. As we saw in the section on familiarity and attraction, Zajonc (1968) has demonstrated that frequency of exposure encourages positive attitudes toward the object. He found, for example, that students subsequently liked other students depicted in yearbook photographs to which they had been exposed frequently more than they liked those whose photographs they had seen less frequently. This hypothesis that familiarity, or frequency of exposure, shapes attitudes was given a clever test by Theodore Mita, Marshall Dermer, and Jeffrey Knight (1977). The experiment hinged on the fact that individuals typically see the mirror image of their faces while friends see the true image. Photographs of the subjects were reproduced in two ways: one showed the subject's true image and the other the subject's mirror image. Given a choice, the subjects preferred the mirror-image photo—the only image to which they had been exposed previously. However, friends of the subjects tended to select the true-image photo—the image to which they had been exposed previously.

The principle by which frequency of exposure, and thus familiarity, produces favorable attitudes is often used by commercial advertisers. Advertisers introducing a new product are likely to blitz television and various print media with their name and visual image in hopes that familiarity will breed increased sales.

There are thus rather simple methods for changing attitudes toward objects. These involve pairing an object with other objects in a classical conditioning procedure or merely increasing the frequency of exposure to the object. However, many attempts at attitude change involve quite a different procedure, the presentation of a persuasive message. Attitude change through persuasive messages depends on three kinds of factors: who presents the message (communicator factors), what the message is like (communication factors), and at whom the message is aimed (receiver factors). What characteristics of the communicator, communication, and receiver tend to promote attitude change and make a persuasive message effective?

Credibility of the Communicator

To test the effectiveness of credibility, researchers exposed two groups of subjects to the same persuasive message concerning the practicality of building nuclear submarines (Hovland & Weiss, 1952). In one condition, the message was attributed to the eminent physicist, J. Robert Oppenheimer. In the other condition, it was attributed to the official Russian Communist party newspaper *Pravda.* The source perceived as more credible, Oppenheimer, produced more attitude change. Communicator credibility, additional research has shown, consists of two important components: expertise and trustworthiness. Oppenheimer, the physicist, was regarded as more expert in the field of atomic energy than was *Pravda*. He also was perceived as more trustworthy—that is, less likely to be making statements for purposes of propaganda than would *Pravda*.

The use of experts as communicators is common in television commercials. Who can better extol the virtues of a particular tennis racquet than a professional tennis player, for example? Trustworthiness is a more subtle component of credibility. Is the communicator sincere? Does she or he have ulterior motives? Another study demonstrated how the perceived trustworthiness of an individual varies depending upon his or her message (Walters, Aronson, & Abrahams, 1966). A fictitious Mafia extortionist, Joe "The Shoulder" Napolitano, said to be currently in prison, argued that courts were too strict in sentencing criminals. Joe's trustworthiness was clearly in doubt: he obviously had an ulterior motive in advocating less stringent sentencing procedures. In this condition, Joe produced no attitude change. The result was different, however, when Joe argued that the courts were too lenient with criminals. He was taking a position in opposition to his own self-interest and the subjects perceived him as being sincere and trustworthy. In this case he produced a great deal of attitude change.

Television advertising often manipulates the perceived trustworthiness of the communicators to enhance their persuasiveness. For example, commercials sometimes make use of a hidden-camera ploy to create the impression that the communicator has nothing to gain by endorsing the product. Similarly, in political advertising, the camera eavesdrops upon candidates in situations where they appear to be talking privately, and hence candidly, to a friend.

Many sports personalities have a high degree of communicator credibility.

Attractiveness of the Communicator

Attractiveness is a second important characteristic of effective communicators. A number of experiments have demonstrated that the more attractive the communicator, the greater the change in attitudes. Television advertising's most frequently used ploy is probably the attractive and sexy celebrity who endorses a given product.

There is an important difference between attractiveness and the other communicator characteristic we have discussed—credibility. Changing attitudes through credibility is the more rational process in which the expertise and trustworthiness of the communicator are judged. Attitude change through attractiveness stems from a desire to be similar to those we admire.

The distinction between credibility and attractiveness is nicely illustrated in a recent experiment by Ross Norman (1976). The subjects, all females, read a message that advocated sleeping less than the typical eight hours a night. For half of the subjects, this assertion was supported by some plausible arguments; for the other half, there were no arguments in support of the message. In addition, half of the subjects were led to believe that the author of the message was highly credible—a forty-three-year-old professor of physiological psychology who had recently coauthored a book on sleep. These subjects were shown a picture of an unattractive, middle-aged man. The other subjects were led to believe that the author was not an expert but a highly attractive 20-year-old male undergraduate who was athletic and musical and recently was elected to the student government council. These subjects were shown a picture of a smiling, physically attractive young man.

Which characteristic proved to be more important, credibility or attractiveness? The attractive communicator produced attitude change in favor of less sleep regardless of whether or not he presented arguments to support his assertion. The other communicator was effective in producing attitude change only when he presented arguments to support his assertion.

Message and Audience Characteristics

In addition to characteristics of the source, factors concerning the audience and the message itself affect the extent to which persuasion is effective. Though many such factors have been investigated (see Petty & Cacioppo,

1981, for an excellent review of the many relevant variables), we shall focus on only one message characteristic and one audience characteristic. Which medium—oral or written—is the better vehicle for presentation of a message? How does the intelligence level of the audience relate to persuasion? There is no simple answer to either of these questions. One medium is not always more effective than another. And people of relatively low intelligence are not always more persuaded by a message than people of relatively high intelligence.

In order to address the questions of appropriate medium and audience intelligence level, it is useful to consider the process by which persuasion occurs. McGuire (1968) has proposed that attitude change in response to a persuasive communication involves two necessary steps, reception and yielding. The audience must receive, that is, attend to and comprehend, the message. Then the audience must yield to the message. In other words, the audience must find the arguments convincing. Messages differ in the degree to which they promote reception or yielding. A simple message is one that is very easy to understand, but is probably not very convincing. A complex message, on the other hand, may be much more difficult to understand because it likely includes a description of supporting research and data. Yet, these very features that make a complex message more difficult to receive also make it more convincing.

Which message medium is more effective has been found to depend upon the complexity of the message (Chaiken & Eagly, 1976). For a complex message, a written communication is more effective than an audible message. With a written message, the individual can reread parts that he or she did not immediately understand. As a result, it is far easier to receive the complex message when it is presented in a written format. Because it is more likely to have been received, it produces more attitude change than the same message presented orally. On the other hand, simple messages are easy to receive regardless of how they are presented. They are more effective, however, when presented orally, as a radio or television message, when the focus is on how convincing the speaker is.

In a similar manner, the intelligence of the audience relates to the effectiveness of simple versus complex messages (Eagly & Warren, 1976). With highly intelligent people comprising the audience, the source of the message does not need to be so concerned with reception, the audience's ability to comprehend the message. A highly intelligent audience could probably understand virtually any message. What the source does have to worry about is the yielding step. Highly intelligent people will notice logical flaws in the source's arguments and will be capable of counterarguing. So, the message must adequately convince an audience including highly intelligent individuals, suggesting that a complex message would produce more attitude change than would a simple message for such an audience.

For an audience of lower intelligence, the reasoning is reversed. Here, reception is the key concern. The source must ensure that the audience receives the message, suggesting that a simple message would be more effective than a complex message because an audience of relatively low intelligence might not be able to follow a complex message. Thus, for such individuals of lower intelligence a simple message produces more attitude change than does a complex message.

Dissonance: Changing Attitudes by Changing Behavior

Intentional social influence can take yet another form. As we have seen, persuasion aims at changing a person's behavior by first changing attitudes. But it is also possible for a person to change your attitude by first getting you to perform a behavior that is inconsistent with that attitude.

RESEARCH

Dissonance and the $2 Bettor

When we commit ourselves to a decision such as buying a car, choosing a college, or even making a small wager on a horse, we sometimes experience initial second thoughts about the decision. By choosing Alternative *X*, we have given up all the positive qualities of the other alternative—the sleek lines of Car *Y*, for example. In addition, we call to mind some of the negative aspects of the chosen Alternative *X*. Because these misgivings are inconsistent with our behavior of selecting a particular option, we experience cognitive dissonance, an unpleasant state of tension.

According to Festinger's theory of cognitive dissonance, one way in which we reduce this postdecisional conflict is by changing our thinking so as to increase the attractiveness of the choice to which we are already committed. A number of investigations of this theoretical proposition have been conducted in the laboratory, but Robert Knox and James Inkster (1968) wanted to test postdecisional dissonance as it occurs in real-life behavior in a natural setting. The setting they selected was the racetrack; the behavior was that of $2 bettors.

Knox and Inkster reasoned that $2 bettors have to make decisions about which horse they think will win the race, then commit themselves to that choice by going to the parimutuel window and placing their bets. If Festinger's theory is correct, once a person has placed a bet, postdecisional dissonance should arise and attempts should be made to reduce this dissonance by increasing the attractiveness of the chosen horse. In short, the bettor ought to feel more confident that the chosen horse will win after placing the bet than before placing it.

To test this experimental hypothesis, the two researchers interviewed

141 bettors at the Exhibition Park racetrack in Vancouver, British Columbia. Of these subjects, 69 were interviewed less than 30 seconds *before* making a $2 bet to win; 72 were interviewed a few seconds *after* making a $2 bet to win. In the interview, each subject was asked to rate on a 7-point scale his or her horse's chances of winning the race. "Never mind now what the tote board or professional handicappers say," each subject was instructed. "What chance do *you* think your horse has?" The rating scale shown to the subject ranged from 1 (slight chance to win) through 7 (excellent chance to win).

The results of these interviews appeared to confirm the researchers' hypothesis. The median rating given by the subjects in the prebet group was 3.48—only a little above a "fair" chance of winning. In the postbet group, by contrast, the subjects gave a median rating of 4.81; they rated the chances of their horse winning as close to "good." The table below shows the number of subjects in each group who believed that their chances of winning were above or below the overall median.

Though the results accorded with their predictions from dissonance

	Prebet Group	Postbet Group
Above the median	25	45
Below the median	44	27

theory, Knox and Inkster realized that the results might conceivably have been attributable to another factor. A substantial number of their postbet subjects might simply have made last-minute switches from relative long shots to favorites. If so, this could account for the greater confidence expressed by the postbet group. However, the researchers talked with a number of bettors on other days at the racetrack and found virtually no evidence to support this "switch-to-favorites" explanation. Moreover, in a second experiment at another racetrack, in which Knox and Inkster were able to replicate their general findings from the first experiment, none of the postbet subjects indicated that he or she had switched to the favorite just before placing the bet in question.

Thus the results of experiments at two different racetracks provided support for Festinger's notion of postdecisional reduction of dissonance. Bettors tended to feel more confident about their horse after committing their money than before. And this reduction in dissonance occurred very rapidly, no more than 30 seconds after the bet.

The authors summed up the overall effect observed in their research by citing the reaction of one subject in their first experiment. This subject had been interviewed by one researcher before he placed his bet. After making his bet, he approached the other experimenter and said: "Are you working with that other fellow there? Well, I just told him that my horse had a fair chance of winning. Will you have him change that to a good chance? No, by God, make that an excellent chance." The belief that his horse had an excellent chance to win obviously made the bettor feel better. "In the human race," the authors concluded, "dissonance had won again." ∎

This phenomenon is explained by Festinger's **theory of cognitive disso-nance** (1957). Like balance theory, Festinger's theory assumes that people pre-fer consistency. Dissonance theory and research emphasize consistency be-tween people's attitudes and their behavior. The theory proposes that when individuals behave in a manner inconsistent with their attitudes they experience **dissonance,** an unpleasant state of tension. Individuals can reduce the state of dissonance in either of two ways. One is to change one of the inconsistent cognitions—for example, by changing the relevant attitude. The other is to find justification for the inconsistent behavior—for example, by concluding that they were "forced" to perform the behavior or by perceiving the benefits to be derived from the behavior.

In one of the earliest experimental tests of the theory of cognitive disso-nance, Festinger and J. Merrill Carlsmith (1959) had subjects perform a very dull and boring task: the subjects had to place a large number of spools on pegs on a board, turn each spool a quarter turn, take the spools off the pegs, and then put them back on. As you can imagine, subjects' attitudes toward this task were highly negative. The subjects were then induced to tell a female "sub-ject," who was actually an accomplice of the experimenter, that this boring task she would be performing was really interesting and enjoyable. Some of the subjects were offered $20 to tell this falsehood; others were offered only $1. Almost all of the subjects agreed to walk into the waiting room and per-suade the subject-accomplice that the boring experiment would be fun.

Obviously, there is a discrepancy here between attitudes and behavior. Although the task was boring, subjects tried to convince another person it was fun. Why? To the subjects who received $20, the reason was clear: they wanted the money. The larger payment provided an important external justification consistent with the counterattitudinal behavior. There was no dissonance, and the subjects experienced no need to change their attitudes. But for the subjects who received only $1, there was much less external justification and more dissonance. How could subjects reduce the dissonance? They could do so by changing their attitude toward the task. This is exactly what happened. When the subjects were asked to evaluate the experiment, the subjects who were paid only $1 rated the tedious task as more fun and enjoyable than did either the subjects who were paid $20 to lie or the subjects in a control group who were not required to lie about the task. Since the external justification—the $1 pay-ment—was too low to justify the counterattitudinal behavior, the subjects sim-ply changed their attitudes to make them consistent with behavior.

Cognitive dissonance theory also suggests another way in which behavior influences attitudes. This is the notion of **effort justification;** that is, people like what they have chosen to suffer for. This notion was demonstrated in an interesting experiment by Aronson and Judson Mills (1959). College women were invited to join a group that supposedly was discussing various aspects of sex. Before the students could join, however, they had to undergo a screening process. For some of the subjects, this screening involved nothing more than reading aloud a number of ordinary but sexually related words. In the severe initiation condition, however, the subjects had to read aloud some rather em-barrassing material: a list of obscene words and two very explicit descriptions of sexual activity. Dissonance is created in this condition. The cognitions—that one does not like to be embarrassed but nonetheless has engaged in embarrass-ing behavior—are discrepant. A third group did not have to undergo any screening process. Then all the subjects in all three conditions listened to what was ostensibly a discussion by the group they were joining. Actually what they heard was a tape-recorded discussion of "secondary sex behavior in lower an-imals" that was intended to be very dull. Afterward, the subjects were asked to rate the club and the discussion. Those who underwent little or no effort to get into the group rated the discussion as it actually was—dull and boring. But the subjects who underwent the severe initiation procedure rated the discussion

CHAPTER 16 SOCIAL INFLUENCE

and the club quite high. In short, the greater the effort expended in order to join the group, the more attractive the group seemed. By convincing themselves that the club was worthwhile, subjects justified the effort and reduced dissonance: they came to like what they had "suffered" for.

This effort justification principle has important implications. One such implication concerns the marketing of new products. Dissonance theory suggests that, whenever we purchase a product, we feel a need to justify our expenditure of effort, that is, our expenditure of money. The more we pay for the product, the more we should come to like it. New products, however, are often introduced at a low price or with a coupon-discount offer. Purchases are then likely to be justified by the low price rather than the attractiveness of the product.

A study of the relation between dissonance theory and the actual marketing of new products was conducted by Doob and his colleagues (Doob, Carlsmith, Freedman, Landauer, & Toms, 1969). They arranged for the introduction of a number of products such as mouthwash and toothpaste at a number of different stores. In half the stores, the product was introduced at its regular price; in others, it was sold at a discount. Predictably, more sales occurred at the "discount stores" than at the "regular-price stores." After awhile, however, the discount offer was ended and all stores began to sell the product at the standard price. Now the sales trend was reversed. Over the next 20 weeks, the stores where the product had not been discounted in the beginning sold more of the product than the stores that had initially offered the discount (see Figure 16.6). Thus, in the long run, introducing the product at its regular price produced more sales than introducing the product at a discount. According to dissonance theory, the greater "effort" expenditure involved in paying more for the product led those people who initially purchased the product at the regular price to persuade themselves of the product's value, and, hence, to purchase the product on a regular, long-term basis. Their behavior—buying at the regular price—had affected their attitudes toward the product, and this new attitude in turn had influenced later behavior.

Another implication of the effort justification principle concerns therapy situations. Typically, an individual in therapy chooses to undergo considerable effort in order to produce some self-improvement. Money, time, the experiencing of some unpleasant thoughts and feelings all are expended in the hopes of improvement. A dissonance analysis of this situation would suggest that the individual would wish to justify this effort expenditure. He or she can do so by evaluating the desired goal state as very desirable. For example, a snake phobic who chose to undergo therapy may come to see snakes as more positive than previously and see the ability to approach snakes as more important than previously. Joel Cooper (1980) conducted an experiment to test this reasoning. He found that snake phobics who chose to participate in an effortful procedure later were able to approach a 6-foot boa constrictor more closely than could control subjects. Thus, therapies may be able to improve their effectiveness by judicious use of the effort justification principle. Indeed, other research (Cooper & Axsom, 1982) indicates that both assertiveness and weight reduction can be enhanced by increasing individuals' perceptions of the extent to which they have chosen to engage in considerable effort for the express purpose of improving their assertiveness or losing weight.

Brainwashing: Extreme Social Influence

An extreme form of intentional social influence is the process widely known as **brainwashing.** The term first was used during the late 1940s to describe the attempts of Chinese Communists to change the political thinking of the Nationalist Chinese and during the Korean War, of American and other Western prisoners of war. More recently, it has been applied to the political

Figure 16.6

Demonstration of dissonance theory. Introducing a product (in this case, mouthwash) at its regular price and maintaining that price, as shown by the red line, is more effective in the long run than introducing it at a discount price and then raising it to the regular price, as shown by the black line.

Nearly two months after her kidnapping, Patricia Hearst, a likely victim of brainwashing, proclaimed that she had chosen to join the SLA.

conversion of the young heiress, Patricia Hearst, after she was kidnapped by the Symbionese Liberation Army (SLA) in 1974. The young revolutionaries of the SLA considered her "a prisoner of war." During her captivity, Patty Hearst underwent marked changes; she renounced her former life and identity and announced that she had changed her name to Tania and joined her captors. She took part in a bank robbery, helped other SLA members escape from another robbery, and eluded arrest for nearly two years. When finally captured, she listed her occupation as "urban guerrilla." Then, over the next year, another transformation occurred, and Patty seemed to revert to her prekidnapping identity as an unaffected young woman.

How can we account for the dramatic changes in attitudes and behavior Patty Hearst underwent during captivity? As was true in the case of the Communist Chinese prisoner-of-war camps, our first impulse is to assume that brainwashing consists of coercive techniques of mind control and body abuse such as drug use, hypnosis, torture, and sexual abuse. However, several analyses (Szasz, 1976; Schein, Schneier, & Barker, 1961) have questioned whether the techniques involved in brainwashing are actually so radical or extreme. In fact, other commentators (Zimbardo, Ebbesen, & Maslach, 1977; Lifton, 1963) view brainwashing in terms of traditional methods of intentional social influence such as simple persuasion. (Many of these same methods are involved in the process of religious conversion; see Focus, p. 563.) They suggest several factors that determine the effectiveness of brainwashing, including victim vulnerability, milieu control, the cohesiveness and attractiveness of the captors, and the ability to come to a confession.

- *Victim Vulnerability.* Patty Hearst lacked a strongly held and well-thought-out set of political beliefs and was thus vulnerable to the dogmatic ideology of her captors. In addition, her wealth made her susceptible to guilt about the poor and oppressed people whom the SLA professed to speak for.

- *Milieu Control.* Like most effective agents of brainwashing, the SLA had total control over the victim's environment. They controlled all sources of information and all reward and punishment. Patty Hearst was exposed daily to the SLA philosophy and rhetoric, but she had no contact with past friends or family and little access to outside information sources such as newspapers and television. The SLA bombarded her with brief, oversimplified catch phrases that, through their ritual repetition, became familiar to the young woman and hence easy to accept.

- *The Captors.* The members of an effective brainwashing group must be cohesive, committed, and attractive. SLA members appeared strong and attractive and brooked no signs of disbelief or dissension. Thus they quickly became important sources of approval and identification for Patty Hearst.

- *Confession.* An important aspect of brainwashing involves confession of wrongdoing and renunciation of the past. This is all the more effective if the victim retains the illusion of free choice. Patty Hearst believed that her decision to remain with the SLA was made of her own free will. This is consistent with the theory of cognitive dissonance. Joining the SLA obviously created dissonance—in effect, "SLA is a bad organization; I'm not bad." Dissonance could be reduced in either of two ways: if she had been forced to join by threat of severe punishment or if she changed her attitude toward the SLA. In the absence of severe threat, she changed her attitude. This provided internal justification for her behavior and made her such a committed convert that she was willing to become a bank robber.

FOCUS

The Process of Religious Conversion

One of the most fascinating social phenomena of the past decade has been the conversion of large numbers of Americans, especially young people, to fringe religious cults. For example, during this period about 10,000 young Americans have abandoned their past social ties and identities to become followers of the Unification Church of the Reverend Sun Myung Moon.

The most dramatic instance of religious conversion involved the members of the People's Temple, a California cult that emigrated to the jungles of Guyana. There, in November 1978, members of the cult dutifully lined up and, upon the orders of their leader, Jim Jones, took cups of a soft drink spiked with cyanide poison. Parents squirted the poison into the mouths of infants and children, then drank some themselves. Nearly 800 people, including 200 children, died in this bizarre and shocking mass suicide.

The tragic drama at Jonestown suggests that some occult trauma must be at work in converting people into true believers willing to give up their money, their past identities, and even their lives. We can easily conjure up visions of converts to the People's Temple or to the Unification Church, being kidnapped, drugged, and tortured. But, in fact, evidence suggests otherwise. People become true believers through many of the same processes of social influence that affect the behavior of us all. For example, conversion to the Unification Church usually begins with a low-key exercise in friendly persuasion—an invitation to dinner. This pleasant meal is followed by a further invitation to spend a weekend on a quiet and lovely farm.

The potential convert is confronted with a cohesive group of happy, attractive, young people who appear to be supportive, open, and friendly. This is especially persuasive to potential converts who are uncertain about their own identities and are experiencing anxiety. (Recruiters often station themselves in campus libraries during exam time, a period of great student stress.) If the person has been religious in the past, the cult will likely be particularly attractive.

Another key factor is the isolation of the potential convert so that all other sources of social influence are removed. The weekend on the Moonie farm ensures there will be no social contact with noncultists. Similarly, the People's Temple moved from San Francisco to remote Guyana to isolate members. The absence of radio, television, and newspapers contributes to a situation in which

The members of the People's Temple followed the orders of their leader, Jim Jones, and committed mass suicide by ingesting a drink laced with cyanide (shown in the foreground).

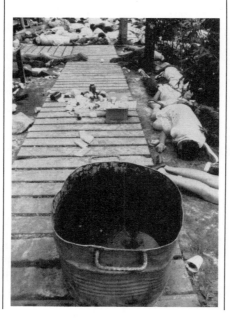

the only sources of social influence, and hence of information and reinforcement, are the cult members. Moreover, the cults tend to emphasize the here and now, dismissing concerns with the past or the future, and thus further strengthening isolation.

Attachment to the group is another important aspect of the conversion process. Passivity and dependency are encouraged, providing a psychological readiness for obedience to the dictates of the group. Cult members are the principal sources of social reinforcement. They freely offer smiles, compliments, and hugs. They profess sadness (though not anger) at the potential convert's "misdirected" thoughts, producing guilt and shame. As the individual identity is submerged into the group, a state of deindividuation develops. The "I" is lost in the "we." Cultists are referred to as "brother" or "sister" rather than by name, increasing the loss of personal identity.

Finally, the success of a cult, and of concomitant conversion, depends on the influence of a powerful and charismatic leader. The members of the cult and the potential convert come to believe that this leader is all-knowing and capable of solving the problems of the members and, indeed, of society. Typically, leaders such as Jim Jones and Sun Myung Moon are flamboyant in their behavior and spellbinding as speakers, filling their oratory with allegory and mysticism.

Once a person actually converts to membership in a cult, commitment gradually intensifies. Members come to perceive the world through the filter of the cult's language and ideas and to view everything in terms of what it means to the cult. Most of the sense of individual identity is lost. Now, any suggestion or perception by the cult leader is accepted without question. Violence and even mass suicide thus can become acceptable behaviors. ■

Although most of the social influences we encounter are considered unintentional, there are some instances when intentional social influence is brought to bear, including obedience to directives issued by people in authority and persuasion aimed at changing attitudes. The success of persuasion is influenced by the credibility of the communication and attractiveness of the communicator. Attitudes can also be changed by creating dissonance—a state of tension resulting from a situation in which people behave in a manner that does not coincide with their attitudes. People in this state often change the relevant attitudes in order to create consistency again. Taken to its extreme, intentional social influence becomes brainwashing. Though very few people ever experience brainwashing, almost everyone falls prey to some of the less extreme forms of intentional social influence on a daily basis.

Summary

1. Social influence is usually a simple, one-way process in which an individual's actions affect the behavior and attitudes of another. Mutual and reciprocal actions and reactions constitute social interaction.

2. Social psychology examines the most important stimuli in our environments—people, who change as we perceive them. Our behavior is affected by the reactions of others to our actions. Social psychology studies general, as opposed to individual, responses and perceptions. Social perceptions and judgments are not readily quantified.

3. Our behavior is affected by social stimuli through the process of arousal, reward and punishment, and information. The presence of others energizes us and increases our drive level: it arouses us. An increase in drive strengthens the dominant response (the one most likely to occur) of the organism; an increase in drive weakens responses that are already weak. By increasing the dominant response, arousal leads us to better performance on simple and well-learned tasks, but results in diminished performance on hard and complex tasks. The presence of others will most likely increase the dominant response if the audience, or observer, is capable of rating the subject's performance.

4. People serve as real or potential sources of reinforcement. People may provide primary reinforcers that satisfy basic physiological needs, or they may serve as secondary reinforcers, providing stimuli that are not inherently rewarding but that we have learned to associate with positive outcomes. Reinforcement from others can be verbal and nonverbal.

5. The following factors have been found to determine why we like some people and dislike others:

- Propinquity. Physical closeness increases interpersonal attraction.
- Familiarity. Frequency of exposure increases interpersonal attraction.
- Similarity-attraction. Interpersonal attraction reflects similarities in attitudes, abilities, and in physical likeness.
- Complementarity. In a complementary relationship, each person rewards the other by allowing and encouraging expression of important needs and desires.
- Balance. Balance theory proposes that reciprocity is an important factor in interpersonal attraction; we will come to like those who like us and dislike those who dislike us.
- Gain-loss. This theory says that we like someone better if the other person first disliked us and then likes us, than if the person had liked us all along. Gain of approval is more rewarding than constant approval.

Just-world. We tend to believe that the world is fair; people get the rewards and punishments they deserve. When bad things happen to good people, it surprises and upsets us. Hence we rationalize that victims must deserve their fate.

6. People influence our behavior not only by serving as sources of reward but also by acting as sources of punishment. Deviance, behavior that departs from accepted group norms, is often "punished" by others through rejection and relegation to undesirable social position. Our behavior is also dramatically affected when the fear of punishment is temporarily absent in a state of deindividuation. Individuals will perform, as members of groups, acts that they will not perform alone because the fear of punishment is removed or lessened.

7. Other people also influence our behavior by serving as useful sources of information: we observe their behavior in a given situation, and their behavior gives us clues as to how we should act in that situtation. By observing others we are engaging in social comparison. People are subject to affiliation, the desire to associate and interact with others so that they may engage in the social comparison process. Studies in bystander intervention, how we act to help others in emergencies, have provided striking evidence of our dependency on clues from the behavior of others.

8. Individuals change their behavior and judgments as a result of exposure to the ideas and judgments of a group. In other words, individuals conform. Conformity may result solely in public compliance; other times it goes far deeper and results in private acceptance. Reinforcement in the form of punishment usually results in public compliance but not private acceptance. Social control achieved through the use of others as sources of information, by contrast, leads not only to public compliance but also to changes of internalized attitudes and beliefs. Conformity drops when people have anonymity. In addition to anonymity, conformity is affected by the ambiguity of situations, by self-confidence, by group goals, by the presence of allies, and by group cohesiveness.

9. Other people help us to learn about ourselves and to define ourselves; we can learn about ourselves by analyzing how others treat us. The process of self-perception—observing our own behavior—is another avenue of self-knowledge.

10. Social influence can be unintentional and inadvertent, or it can be intentional. The most obvious forms of intentional social influence are directives issued by authority figures whom we obey. Another form of intentional social influence is persuasion, which aims first at changing our attitudes; attitude change will normally lead to behavior change. Attitude change through persuasion depends to a great extent on the credibility of the communicator, the source of the persuasive message, and on the attractiveness of the communicator.

11. Another form of intentional social influence is explained by Leon Festinger's theory of cognitive dissonance, which proposes that when individuals behave in a manner inconsistent with their attitudes, they experience dissonance, an unpleasant state of tension. The state of dissonance can be reduced by reducing the number of inconsistent cognitions, which can be accomplished by changing the relevant attitudes. Dissonance can also be reduced by increasing the number of consistent cognitions, by concluding that behavior has been forced.

12. The most extreme form of intentional social influence is the process known as brainwashing. The effectiveness of brainwashing is determined by victim vulnerability, milieu control, the cohesiveness and attractiveness of the captors, and the subject's ability to come to a confession.

RESEARCH: According to Festinger's theory of cognitive dissonance, post-decisional conflict is reduced by making thinking more consistent with behavior, thereby increasing the subjective attractiveness of decisions recently made. To test this notion, Knox and Inkster interviewed persons just before and just after they had placed bets at the parimutuel window of a horsetrack. Consistent with cognitive dissonance theory, the majority of bettors tended to feel more confident about their horse after placing their bets than before.

FOCUS: Religious conversion to cult ideology is an intensive process based on isolated and selected social support, obedience to the cult consciousness, and deindividuation of the convert. Cults are generally headed by a powerful and charismatic leader who potential converts and cult members believe to be an omnipotent and divine authority.

CHAPTER

17

Social Interaction

All of us who survive the often difficult relationships between parent and child, wife and husband, employer and employee, friend and friend, understand intuitively the distinction between social influence and social interaction. Social influence, as we saw in the previous chapter, is essentially a one-way process. For example, the socialization of children for many years was treated as an instance of social influence. These early conceptions emphasized the effects that parental attitudes and behavior had on the development of children. Among the main issues were the age of weaning, severity of toilet training, and the types of punishment administered.

It is clear now, of course, that this approach ignored the many effects that children, in turn, exert on their parents. Parents who must awaken for the 3 A.M. feeding or spend time driving children to Little League practice, ballet class, and swimming lessons are fully aware of how their behavior is shaped by children. Children can influence the intellectual and cultural tastes of their parents—the books they read, the music they like, the movies they see.

Child socialization is a prime example of the two-way process called **social interaction.** In this chapter we will be concerned with the mutual and reciprocal effects that people have on each other as they interact. This field of investigation covers an enormous range, from the study of two-person, or **dyadic,** relationships such as socialization and friendship, to the consideration of cooperation and conflict between groups and even nations. We will look first at a general theory of social interaction. Next, we will discuss the critical importance of social perception, that is, how we view other people and interpret their behavior. Then we will consider group interactions from two points of view—behavior within the group and behavior between two groups. Finally, we will focus on a different kind of social interaction—namely, the environmental effects people exert on one another through noise and crowding.

Social Relationships: Thibaut and Kelley's Theory of Social Interaction

The basic form of social interaction involves a relationship between two people. No matter what the nature of the relationship—husband and wife, teacher and student, boss and employee, storekeeper and customer—each person exerts influence on the other. Of course, the amount of influence differs in different types of relationships: husband and wife influence each other more than do storekeeper and customer. And although the traffic of influence may be two-way, it may flow more heavily in one direction; the boss, for example, typically has a greater effect on the employee than does the employee on the boss.

In order to understand how two people affect each other in this basic form of social interaction, let us consider a general theory that attempts to account for the formation, maintenance, and breakup of relationships. The theory was first developed in the field of economics and later applied to social relationships by John Thibaut and Harold Kelley (1959).

Rewards and Costs

The **Thibaut and Kelley theory of social interaction** postulates that relationships depend largely upon each participant's analysis of the rewards and costs of their behavior. This analysis occurs (usually unconsciously) whenever two people interact, and it shapes the responses of each person. Even in the simplest social situation, many responses are available. A person alone on an elevator with another person, for example, may intentionally look away or may make eye contact to get the other's attention and start to discuss the weather, the world situation, or the slowness of the elevator. The other person may respond in turn by ignoring the eye contact or by mumbling a brief reply or by joining or expanding the conversation.

According to Thibaut and Kelley, the choice of each response depends on an analysis of the potential costs (for example, embarrassment, boredom, or loss of esteem) and rewards (for example, pleasure, money, or affection) of that response. Each person tries to adopt the response and induce in the other the response that will yield the best outcome—that is, the greatest rewards at the least cost. In this view then, as people interact they are constantly computing the reward-cost ratio in order to determine the overall satisfaction of the relationship. Unless both participants compute the profit as greater than the costs, the interaction is likely to stop. The two people in the elevator might smile, nod their heads, and go their separate ways, moving on to relationships with greater potential for profit.

According to Thibaut and Kelley, people constantly compute the reward-cost ratio of a relationship.

The Comparison Level

Suppose that the two people on the elevator do begin a social relationship. What determines their feelings of satisfaction in the relationship? According to Thibaut and Kelley, satisfaction depends in part on one's expectations, or **comparison level** (CL). The comparison level for any interaction is the level of outcome you expect or feel you deserve. It depends on past experiences, what you have seen others get out of relationships, and your general level of optimism. Some people have high expectations in relationships, feeling they deserve more rewards than costs. They will not be happy on a date unless it is a special evening. Others are more pessimistic and expect costs to be relatively high: on a date they are satisfied with a moderately pleasant evening.

Thus happiness in a relationship is not determined by the absolute level of outcome but by the outcome relative to comparison level. Whenever the outcome is above a person's comparison level, that person will be satisfied and happy in the relationship. But when outcomes fall below the comparison level, unhappiness and dissatisfaction result.

Considering the Alternatives

Whereas the comparison level helps determine the general level of satisfaction, the make-or-break factor depends on the alternative relationships available. The outcome level from such alternatives—that is, what people feel they could get in another relationship—is called the **comparison level for alternatives** (CL$_{ALT}$). According to Thibaut and Kelley, any time the outcome of the present relationship falls below the comparison level for alternatives, the person will break up the relationship (see Figure 17.1).

The comparison level for alternatives is clearly an extremely important aspect of any two-person relationship because it determines one's level of power and dependency. The availability of an alternative almost as good as the present relationship reduces dependency and increases power. On the other hand, if the potential rewards from the next best available alternative are low, dependency on the present relationship is increased. Consider, for example, a marriage where the wife likes the relationship but has alternatives with very good reward potential—a new career she has thought about pursuing or other men who are interested in her. Let us assume that the husband, by contrast, has no possible alternatives that even come near the rewards he gets from the marriage. In such a relationship, the wife holds the power and the husband is very dependent. She can hurt him, and he will stay on. But anything he does to make her slightly unhappy might force the rewards of the relationship below those of her alternatives and cause her to break up the relationship.

Figure 17.1

Variations in a wife's comparison level (CL) and comparison level for alternatives (CL$_{ALT}$), and the outcomes (O) in four marriage situations. (A) Initial situation. The outcomes experienced in the relationship with her husband are above the CL and the CL$_{ALT}$ and provide the wife with a moderate amount of satisfaction. (B) When the wife hears about the divorce of friends, her CL is lowered, and the amount of satisfaction she has with her own marriage is increased. (C) Meeting an old boyfriend raises the CL$_{ALT}$ but the outcomes she experiences in her own marriage are still above the CL and the CL$_{ALT}$. If these outcomes should decrease, they could easily fall below the raised CL$_{ALT}$, and the wife would then end her marriage. (D) The husband has changed his behavior, and the wife's outcomes fall below the CL, but they are still above the CL$_{ALT}$. The wife will be dissatisfied but will stay in the relationship. Should the outcomes fall below the CL$_{ALT}$ the wife will leave her husband. These are only sample situations. The CL, the CL$_{ALT}$, and the outcomes can all vary in relation to one another. Both the amount of satisfaction or dissatisfaction and the maintenance of the marriage will depend on the relative positions of these variables.

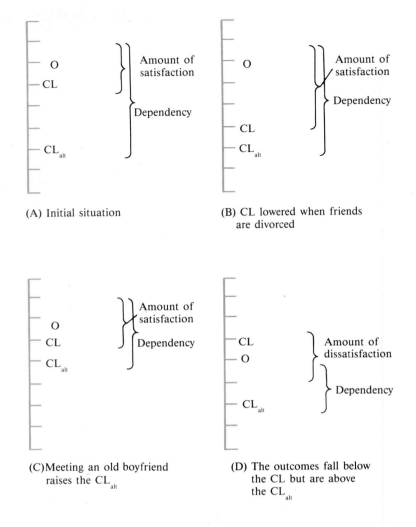

(A) Initial situation

(B) CL lowered when friends are divorced

(C) Meeting an old boyfriend raises the CL$_{alt}$

(D) The outcomes fall below the CL but are above the CL$_{alt}$

Limitations of the Theory

This view of people as constant calculators of rewards and costs presents a highly selfish model of human nature. As such, the Thibaut and Kelley theory is hard put to explain behavior such as pure altruism (helping others in need), which seems to occur without any explicit rewards. Another limitation of the theory is its inability to specify all the responses available in a social interaction and the rewards and costs associated with them. It is seldom easy to predict what might be rewarding or costly for each person. Not only is one person's reward another person's cost, a given individual's perception of what is rewarding often changes relative to situation and mood. A closer examination of these all-important perceptions is in order.

Social Perception

How we interact with other people depends to a great extent upon how we perceive them and how we interpret their behavior. These perceptions of people—what we *think* they are like—will influence how we respond to them. If you think the woman next door is hostile, you are unlikely to want to interact with her. In terms of interaction then, the true nature of that neighbor is less

CHAPTER 17   SOCIAL INTERACTION

important than your **social perception** of her. In this section we will take up two different processes that are important in social perception: (1) how we arrive at an overall impression of another person, and (2) how we interpret the causes of another person's behavior.

Impression Formation

Suppose you learn the following facts about your psychology instructor: she once went out of her way to help a lost little boy find his way home; she was a Phi Beta Kappa in college, is a fan of the Boston Celtics basketball team, and dislikes fast-food restaurants; she once fasted for three days just to see whether she could do it. As you learn these individual facts, you organize the information, integrate it, and arrive at your own general summary picture of what she is like—bright and helpful, but nutty. This is the essence of **impression formation**—the process by which we form global impressions of people based on specific facts we have learned. We can identify three important general features of impression formation: impressions are usually thought to be structured, stable, and constructive.

Structure: Categorizing People and Groups

We have convenient categories for classifying things: animals, vegetables, and minerals; furniture, appliances, and artwork. Having categories for non-human things with shared, identifiable attributes helps us to simplify a complex world. In this same way we create structure in the process of perceiving people, categorizing what they are like. One familiar set of categories, originally described by the Swiss psychologist Carl Jung (1939), consists of introverts and extraverts (see chapter 12). Introverts are passive, withdrawn, cautious, and reflective; extraverts are outgoing, sociable, active, impulsive, and fond of parties (Eysenck & Eysenck, 1967).

Although few people fit neatly into the introvert versus extravert dichotomy, this kind of general categorizing provides an important framework in impression formation. In fact, Nancy Cantor and Walter Mischel (1977) have shown that people learn and remember information about others more proficiently if they can code particular facts about them into trait categories such as introvert and extravert. In their study they presented subjects with selected adjectives to describe four characters: an extravert, an introvert, and two characters that fit no particular personality type. Tests showed that subjects could recognize more facts and recall more characteristics and behaviors of characters who fit the pure introvert or extravert personality types. Thus, personality traits serve as categories around which we organize information about people. Of course, as chapter 8 shows, organized information is more easily recalled than unorganized information.

Trait categories enable us not only to organize information about others but also to suggest other traits the people might possess. We have implicit theories about what trait categories are associated with what other traits; generous people, for example, are assumed also to be intelligent, honest, and considerate. Researchers have tried to develop a picture of what traits go with what other traits according to our implicit theory (Rosenberg, Nelson, & Vivekananthan, 1968). They asked subjects to describe people they knew by selecting personality traits from a list. By seeing which traits often occurred together in descriptions of people and which did not, they were able to identify the important dimensions in personality impressions and the traits that clustered together. Figure 17.2 shows that the two important dimensions in personality impression are social (from good to bad) and intellectual (from good to bad). That is, we tend to think of people mainly in terms of their social and intellectual qualities.

Introverts are typically passive, withdrawn, cautious, and reflective.

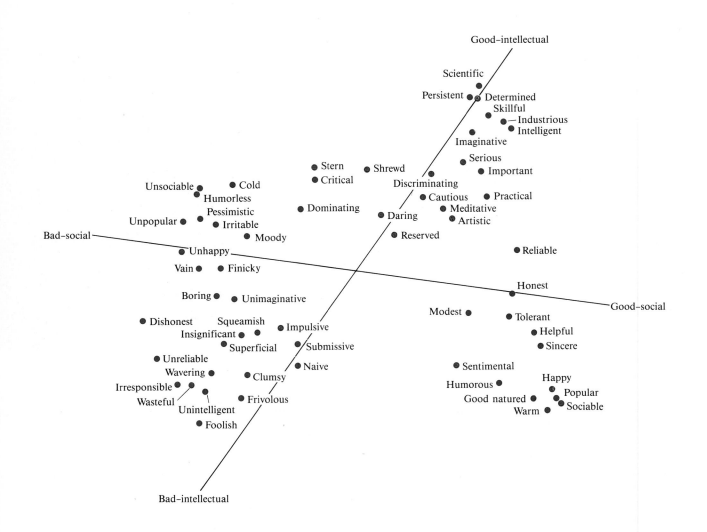

Figure 17.2

Two-dimensional configuration of 60 traits showing best-fitting axes of properties of social desirability and intellectual desirability. The farther apart two traits are in the diagram, the less likely they are to be perceived as occurring in a person's character.

The position of each trait in the figure shows the dimension to which it is relevant. For example, "scientific" and "determined" cluster together as "good-intellectual" traits. "Unsociable" and "humorless" are "bad-social" traits. The further apart two traits are in the picture, the less likely they are to be perceived as occurring together in a person's character. Thus, "happy" and "popular" are very likely to be judged as occurring together in a person's character; "irresponsible" and "imaginative" are very unlikely to be judged as occurring together.

Just as we make assumptions about what traits go together, we also have implicit theories about what kinds of traits are associated with various groups of people. We simplify and structure the complex world of other people by seeing them as members of groups and perceiving each group as having special and identifiable characteristics. These general pictures of large groups of people are called **group stereotypes.**

We can all call to mind such general pictures, or stereotypes, of a great variety of groups—races, nationalities, the sexes, occupational groups such as police, politicians, and college professors, even students grouped by college. Studies have shown that college students are consistent in their group stereotypes of students from other colleges (Fink & Cantril, 1939). Undergraduates of Yale, Princeton, Dartmouth, and Harvard were presented with 50 adjectives (for instance, brilliant, athletic, studious) and were asked to pick the five that best described a Harvard student, a Yale student, and so on. There was considerable agreement as to the nature of the students at each college. For example, in their choices of 5 adjectives from the list of 50 to describe a Harvard student, all subjects from Dartmouth used a total of only 10 different adjectives. Different sets of adjectives were consistently used to describe students from Yale or Princeton.

Agreement about ethnic stereotypes has also been demonstrated in both early and recent studies. The first empirical study of ethnic stereotypes was conducted in 1933 (Katz & Braly). One hundred Princeton students were asked to list the traits that they considered most characteristic of 10 groups: Negroes, Jews, Irish, Turks, Germans, Italians, Americans, Chinese, Japanese, and English. Subjects showed very high agreement on the assignment of traits. For example, Negroes were characterized as "superstitious" by 84 percent of the sample and as "lazy" by 75 percent; Germans were seen as "scientifically minded" by 78 percent. Most agreement was seen in the stereotypes of Negroes, and least stereotyping was done in the ratings of Turks. It is interesting that these were the two most disliked groups. Thus, degree of stereotyping seems to bear no relation to prejudice toward a group. Nearly 40 years later, a similar study at Princeton replicated the early results in showing consistent stereotyping of the various ethnic groups (Darley, Lewis, & Glucksberg, 1972).

Among the most widely held group stereotypes are those associated with the sexes. In our society, women are generally perceived as less creative, logical, aggressive, and proficient at quantitative tasks than men, and as more timid, dependent, and submissive than men. Most of these characteristics are merely stereotypes and have no basis in actual sex differences (see chapter 11).

Another common stereotype relates to physical appearance. Although most of us would say it is illogical to evaluate another person solely on the basis of physical appearance, we tend to do exactly that. Karen Dion, Ellen Berscheid, and Elaine Walster (1972) demonstrated that attractive people are perceived quite differently from unattractive people. They showed subjects a series of photographs of people and asked the subjects for their impressions. Some of the people in the photographs were very attractive; others were unattractive. The subjects, with no information other than the photographs, tended to judge the people in terms of the "beautiful is good" stereotype: they rated the attractive people as brighter, kinder, happier, and as having rosier futures—with more money and better marriages.

Later in this chapter we will consider the effects of such stereotyping on social interaction. For now, keep in mind the existence of group stereotypes and their role in structuring our impressions of other people.

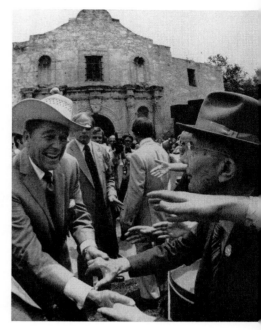

Stereotypes are often ascribed to people in public service—in this case, the "hand-shaking politician."

Stability: Sticking with Our Impressions

A second general feature of impression formation, in addition to structure, is that impressions tend to be stable. Early in a relationship, we try to discover permanent qualities in others. Once we find them, we are hesitant to change our perceptions. These impressions endure even though we may learn facts that seem to contradict them.

What explains the enduring quality of impressions? Once we have structured a meaningful picture of another person or group of people, we normally interpret any new information in the light of this impression. Thus if someone we perceive as considerate and friendly aims a negative remark at us, we interpret it as a joke. But the same remark by someone perceived as inconsiderate and unfriendly is seen as hostile. Remember from the previous chapter the study of spectator perception of a Dartmouth-Princeton football game (Hastorf & Cantril, 1954). Students from each college interpreted the many infractions committed on the playing field in the light of their existing impressions: players from their own college were rule-abiding athletes, and those from the rival college were not.

One way to maintain a stable stereotype of any group is to interpret the behavior of any group member as fitting that stereotype. This often occurs when racial stereotypes are involved. In one study (Duncan, 1976), white sub-

This female drill sergeant may not fit the stereotype many people have of women or of drill sergeants.

jects viewed a group situation in which an ambiguous shove was given by one actor to another. This act was perceived as far more violent when performed by a black actor than by a white actor. Such interpretations allow subjects to maintain stable stereotypes of blacks as an aggressive group.

Constructiveness: Inferring Other Qualities

In addition to structure and stability, there is a third general feature of impression formation: the process is constructive. Once we have categorized a person, we build on this general picture. We believe that all kinds of characteristics that seem to be consistent with our general picture are true. If we perceive a politician as a "liberal," we infer a host of characteristics consistent with this category: for example, most liberals have ordinarily been in favor of national health insurance and more funding for welfare programs. Any particular liberal may or may not really hold these positions: what is fascinating is how we make the assumptions even in the absence of relevant information.

This tendency to build on our existing impression was demonstrated in the laboratory study by Cantor and Mischel (1977) that was described earlier. They presented subjects with characteristics of a hypothetical person that were consistent with those of an extravert. When the subjects tried to identify elements in the specific information they had been given, they mistakenly chose many characteristics that, though consistent with extraversion, they had not been given. Significantly, they did not mistakenly choose characteristics associated with introversion. They simply built on general impressions of an extravert. Opposite effects were seen when subjects were presented with a typical introverted character. Then, they mistakenly recognized traits consistent with the introverted personality type. Thus, once we can categorize or "pigeonhole" a person, we tend to believe they have all the qualities and characteristics consistent with that category.

Major Determinants in Impression Formation

The process of impression formation naturally relies on information about the other person, but some facts are perceived as more important than others. We give special importance to when information is received, emphasize certain facts and disregard others, and interpret the facts in terms of their context. These three determinants in impression formation have been labeled **primacy-recency**, **central traits**, and **context.**

Primacy-Recency

When you get to know another student, you are apt to learn a number of facts about the person—their college major, hometown, ambitions for the future, food preferences. Which information has a greater effect on your overall impression? The earliest information you get—college major (primacy)—or the more recent information—food preferences (recency)?

Research indicates that the old advice "make a good first impression" is sound counsel. Abraham Luchins (1957) presented subjects with descriptions of people that contained the same facts but varied the order in which the information was presented. In one case, the first half of the description portrayed the target person as friendly, while the last half pictured an unfriendly character. In the other test condition, the order of presentation was reversed. In the friendly-unfriendly order, 78 percent of the subjects rated the target person as friendly. When the order was unfriendly-friendly, 87 percent rated the imaginary person as unfriendly. Thus, even when the total information presented was exactly the same, the first impression almost always won out.

The primacy effect also has been established for impressions of a person's ability. Edward Jones and his associates (Jones, Rock, Shaver, Goethals, &

Ward, 1968) had subjects watch a student attempting to solve a number of difficult problems. The "student," actually a confederate of the experimenter, solved 15 of the 30 problems correctly. In one case, the 15 correct answers were given very early in the series. In the other condition, the successes came mainly toward the end. Subjects were asked to indicate how intelligent they felt this student was. The "student" who solved more problems early in the test was seen as smarter than the "student" who solved the same number of problems but had arrived at correct answers later in the test.

Why should there be a primacy effect in the way we perceive others? To begin with, there is a greater need for information when we first meet someone. We want to form a stable picture quickly, and thus we pay more attention to early information. Another reason for the primacy effect is related to the general proposal made earlier, that impressions have stability. Once we form an initial impression based on early information, later facts, even if contradictory to the initial impression, tend to be interpreted in light of the first impression. They might be seen as circumstantial deviations from the person's true characteristics or even be ignored. In the Jones experiment the first impression of the "student" who quickly solved 15 problems was one of intelligence. Subsequent failure to solve problems was attributed to the difficulty of the problems or to the student's being bored and not trying hard.

Studies have shown that first impressions tend to have the most lasting effect on how a person is perceived.

Central Traits

Aside from the primacy effect, certain facts carry a special weight in the overall impression. Solomon Asch (1946) demonstrated this by focusing on the possibility that certain central traits might play a key role. Subjects were asked to form an impression of a person described as intelligent, skillfull, industrious, warm, determined, practical, and cautious. Almost all subjects felt that such a person was generous, happy, and good-natured. Then Asch changed one word in the list of traits: he left out *warm* and substituted *cold*. Now the impressions were quite different: only a small percentage perceived this person as generous, happy, or good-natured, although they did see the person as more important. When Asch tried alternating other traits such as polite versus blunt, there was little difference in overall impressions. Asch concluded that the warm-cold dimension was a central one around which general impressions of people were formed.

Context

We learn facts about people in the context of other information; this context has an effect on how we interpret the traits in question. Say, for example, we learn that a person is highly charitable but is also very wealthy. This context shades our interpretation of the person's charitable impulses and thus affects our overall impression.

Context is particularly important in interpreting the meaning of a trait such as aggressiveness. In the context of traits like intelligence and kindness, aggressiveness might imply that the person is a hard worker or a go-getter. In the context of dumbness and meanness, it might imply hostility.

Asch (1948) demonstrated just how markedly context can change the meaning of information. He had his subjects read the following statement: "I hold it that a little rebellion, now and then, is a good thing and necessary in the political world as storms are in the physical." When subjects were told that the author of the statement was Thomas Jefferson, they perceived the word *rebellion* in the context of known Jeffersonian traits and interpreted it as meaning agitation and civil disobedience. But when the statement was attributed to Lenin, subjects interpreted rebellion in terms of their perception of Lenin as a revolutionary communist and saw it as meaning full-scale revolution. Thus, the context of the information we receive about a person is an important determinant of our overall impression.

As we have seen, impression formation is an important part of social perception. A second significant process, closely linked to impression formation, is attribution—that is, the inferences we make about the *causes* of other people's behavior. How we perceive *why* people behave the way they do will greatly affect our interaction with them. **Attribution theory** deals with the underlying principles by which we decide the causes of another person's actions.

Attribution theory has implications for many areas of social policy. In education, for example, urban ghetto schools are a pressing issue. Why do children in such schools often fail? Is it because of the lack of individual ability or motivation? Is it because of racial discrimination, difficulties at home, or inadequate teaching? How society attributes the causes of failure will obviously determine its approaches to changing this behavior.

Dispositional Versus Situational Attribution

The perceived causes of other people's behavior can be classified into two general categories. If we think that a person acts in a certain way because of something internal in that person—for example, attitudes, personality traits, and mood—we attribute the behavior to **dispositional reasons.** If, on the other hand, the particular behavior seems to stem from external causes such as an offer of money or a threatened punishment, we attribute it to **situational reasons.**

Our perceptions of what a person is really like usually depend upon dispositional attributions. For example, if a person who has been offered $1000 to sign a petition in favor of saving the world's whales signs the petition, it tells us nothing about the person's attitude toward whales. The reasons for signing are obviously situational; we assume that practically anyone would sign such a petition in return for $1000. On the other hand, if a person freely chooses to sign the petition in the absence of external influences, we attribute the behavior to dispositional causes. We infer that the person actually wants the whales to be saved. In the absence of obvious rewards or punishments, behavior is assumed to reflect dispositional factors such as attitudes and traits. This fact helps explain the presumed effectiveness of "hidden-camera" commercials on television. If we are led to believe that a person has endorsed a product without being paid for it—indeed, without even knowing the camera is recording the endorsement—we are more likely to believe that the person really likes the product.

Key Factors in Attribution

Kelley (1967) has proposed that people attribute the causes of behavior by using three key factors—*distinctiveness, consensus,* and *consistency*—as well as by some additional basic principles. Kelley points out that we all behave much like scientists in seeking these three factors and in collecting evidence and arriving at logical conclusions.

1. *Distinctiveness.* Suppose we see Harvey crying at the movie and try to figure out why. Are the reasons dispositional: is he softhearted, emotional, easily moved to tears? Or are they situational: is the movie a real tearjerker or does Harvey have something in his eye? As we consider this question, a first useful piece of information is whether or not Harvey typically cries at movies. Here we are assessing the distinctiveness of Harvey's behavior. If he almost never cries at movies, his behavior is distinctive; thus we are likely to attribute the cause to situational reasons—the movie itself. But if the crying is nondis-

tinctive (he cries even during cartoons), we would conclude that the cause was dispositional and had something to do with Harvey's personality.

2. *Consensus.* A second factor in attributing Harvey's behavior would be information about how other people reacted to the same movie. If practically everyone came out of the movie with handkerchief in hand, there was obviously a high consensus that the movie was a tearjerker; thus Harvey's crying could reasonably be attributed to the situation. By the same token, if no one else cried, indicating low consensus, we would learn something about Harvey.

When people act much like everyone else, we learn little about them. Jones, Davis, and Gergen (1961) had subjects listen to tape recordings of people applying for a job as an astronaut. The experimenters described this job as requiring someone very introverted. Some subjects heard a job applicant behave in the expected introverted way—the right way to get the job. Others heard an applicant behave in a very extraverted manner. Subjects were then asked to give their impressions of what the applicant was really like. Those who had heard the introverted applicant were not confident in their attributions: the applicant had acted like anyone looking for the job would act. Consensus was high. The behavior was due to situational forces; hence little could be learned about the person. Those who heard the applicant behave in an extraverted way assumed that few others would have acted in this way (perceived low consensus). These subjects thus believed that the behavior reflected the dispositions of the actor and were confident that the applicant was outgoing and extraverted.

3. *Consistency.* A final factor in determining the cause of Harvey's crying is the consistency of his behavior when he sees this particular movie. If this is the only time Harvey cried at this movie, that is, if there is low consistency, we assume that the cause is situationally specific to this occasion (Harvey was in a very sad mood or had something in his eye). If Harvey always cries at this movie, that is, if there is high consistency, the reason he is crying could be either dispositional (something general about Harvey's personality), or situational (the movie is a real tearjerker).

4. *Principles in attribution.* In addition to these three factors, Kelley (1972) also has identified interesting principles that people use in attributing causality to behavior. One is the **discounting principle,** that is, we discount dispositional factors when situational causes are evident. Assume you are watching a child playing with a new puzzle. In the absence of plausible external causes, you will attribute the child's behavior to a dispositional reason: she likes to play with this puzzle. But if there is a plausible external reason—for example, the child's mother has told her if she does not play with the puzzle she will have to help with the dishes—you are likely to discount the dispositional possibility. Thus, when several possible causes for a behavior exist simultaneously, the perceived role of any one of them is discounted. Behavior is discounted as an indicator of dispositions when plausible external reasons exist.

The **augmentation principle,** by contrast, points to instances where the role of the dispositional cause is augmented, or increased. For example, if the child played with the new puzzle even though her mother had threatened her with a spanking for this behavior, we would infer intense dispositional causality: the child must really like the puzzle. The findings of the study cited earlier by Jones, Davis, and Gergen (1961) support the role of the augmentation principle. When subjects listened to job applicants who had pressing external reasons for acting introverted (it was a condition for getting the job), but who nonetheless behaved like extraverts, the subjects decided the applicants must really be extraverts. The perceived role of this disposition was augmented since the behavior emerged in the face of an external barrier. In a similar way, we tend to give a high credibility rating to politicians who take a position in the face of opposition from their audience. We judge them as really believing what they say (Mills & Jellison, 1967).

Salespeople probably rely on implicit rules—some that may be biased—to infer the attitudes and traits of their customers.

Biases in the Attribution Process

As we have described it thus far, attribution appears to be a relatively rational and logical process of assessing the causes of behavior. By attending to implicit rules and principles, we are able to infer the attitudes and traits of another person. In fact, however, we are not always as rational as attribution theory implies. In practice, certain biases creep into the process.

Foremost among these biases is the tendency to overattribute the behavior of another person to dispositional reasons. We assume people act in a certain way because they *are* that way. This tendency is nicely illustrated in the results of an experiment conducted by Jones and Victor Harris (1967). The task of the college student subjects was to read a speech about Fidel Castro and then to assess the attitude of the speechwriter, who was ostensibly a member of the university debate team. Half of the subjects read a speech that was favorable to Castro; the other half read a speech that was highly critical of the Cuban leader. Moreover, half of the subjects who read the pro-Castro speech and half who read the anti-Castro version were informed that the debater had freely chosen that position. The other half in each condition were told that the debater had no choice in the matter; the position for or against Castro had been assigned by the debate coach.

The logic of the attribution process ought to enable us to predict the results easily. But such predictions would be only half right. In the conditions in which the debater ostensibly had freely chosen the position taken in the speech, the subjects were quite logical. They saw the speech as reflecting the debater's true attitude toward Castro. They attributed strong pro-Castro attitudes to the author of the speech that was favorable to Castro, and anti-Castro attitudes to the author of the speech critical of him.

However, logic went awry in the conditions where the debater supposedly was assigned the position, pro or anti, and thus had no choice. Although the behavior logically should have been attributed to situational causes (the debater had no choice), the subjects attributed it to dispositional reasons. They judged the debater who was assigned the pro-Castro speech to be more favorable to Castro than was the debater who was assigned the anti-Castro speech.

Ross, Amabile, and Steinmetz (1977) presented another interesting demonstration of the tendency to ignore the situational causes of another's behavior and to misattribute it to dispositional reasons. In their experiment, subjects came to a laboratory three at a time and were randomly assigned a role as quizmaster or contestant or observer. The quizmaster was instructed to compose 10 challenging but not impossible questions. The contestant's job was to answer these 10 questions. Because everyone has specialized and idiosyncratic knowledge, it was not difficult for quizmasters to stump the contestants on many items. An observer (the third subject) watched the proceedings. The observer's job was to rate the intelligence and general knowledge of the quizmaster and contestant. Logically, an observer should realize that the contestant was at a disadvantage; had the roles of quizmaster and contestant been reversed, the quizmaster would have been stumped. But observers failed to take into account the situational causes of the contestant being stumped and saw the behavior as reflecting dispositions. Quizmasters were judged as far more intelligent and knowledgeable than contestants.

Thus, when we observe someone else's behavior, we tend to overemphasize the power of dispositional forces. But what happens when we are actors rather than observers? If you were the purported debater in the Jones and Harris experiment, would writing a pro-Castro speech that you had been assigned make you decide that you were in favor of Castro? Probably not. Chances are, you would perceive your own behavior—writing the speech—as a response to situational pressures, namely that you were assigned the task. As Jones and Richard Nisbett (1971) have pointed out, there tends to be an important difference between actors and observers in the attribution of causality. As actors we see our own behavior largely in terms of situational forces; as observers we perceive the behavior of others as stemming largely from their own dispositions.

This **actor-observer difference** has been documented in a number of studies, including a simple writing exercise conducted by Nisbett and his associates (Nisbett, Caputo, Legant, & Maracek, 1973). Male college students were asked to write paragraphs on several topics: why they liked their girlfriends and why they had selected their college majors; why their best male friend liked his girlfriend and why he had chosen his college major. The subjects, in explaining their own behavior, emphasized external reasons: the girl was attractive and had a nice sense of humor, their college major offered inviting career opportunities, and so on. But in explaining the behavior of their best friends, the subjects cited dispositional reasons that emphasized the friend's own personal qualities: he likes a certain kind of girl, and he is very logical and hence suited for a major and a career in computer programming.

In an even more direct test of the actor-observer difference, the same researchers presented subjects with a list of pairs of opposite traits such as quiet-talkative and cautious-bold. The subjects were asked to rate themselves or an acquaintance on each trait pair. They were also given the option of noting that a given trait "depends on the situation." The results showed that subjects selected this situational option much more frequently when rating themselves than when judging acquaintances. In the picture that emerged, their acquaintances possessed definite personality traits, but the subjects themselves merely responded to the demands of the situation.

Our tendency to attribute dispositional causes to other people's behavior may seem illogical, but it serves a function. Assigning personality traits and other characteristics to another person leads us to believe that we "know" the person. Such knowledge, whether objectively warranted or not, enables us to make predictions about how that person will behave (especially toward us) in the future. This feeling that we can predict what will happen gives us a sense of control over our interaction with the person.

This desire for control is not unlike that found in another kind of interaction, gambling. In gambling we attempt to control chance. People pursue all sorts of strategies aimed at controlling the outcome: at the craps table, for example, they talk to the dice, blow on them, roll them softly for low numbers or hard for high numbers, and even try intensely to visualize the desired out-

The illusion of control is a common phenomenon held by those who gamble.

come. All of these rituals are perceived by gamblers as ways of changing the odds in their favor, or of transforming what is clearly a chance event into a controllable one.

The **illusion of control** in gambling has been studied by Ellen Langer (1975), who found that people tend to infer a power over chance outcomes that in fact does not exist. Langer concluded that when people believed they had some control over a chance outcome they felt relatively likely to win. For example, subjects who were given the opportunity to select a lottery ticket felt more confident they would win than did those who were simply handed one by the ticket vendor.

In light of this powerful tendency to infer the ability to control what are obviously chance events, it is no wonder that we assume we "know" others and thus can predict their behaviors. Attributing dispositional traits gives us at least the illusion of control in social interaction. As we will see later in this chapter, this same desire for control tends to influence our perception of people who are members of groups that we have stereotyped, leading us to feel that we already "know" a lot about such people.

Links Between Social Perception and Social Interaction

The two processes of social perception—impression formation and attribution of traits—serve as guides in our behavior toward others. By acting in terms of our perceptions of another person, we forge another link in the complex chain connecting social perception and social interaction. Suppose that you have formed the impression that someone is hostile and attribute their hostility to dispositional traits. This perception is apt to affect your behavior toward that person; you are likely to behave coldly, if not with outright hostility. Social perception can influence social interaction even when the perception is false.

The Self-Fulfilling Prophecy

Let us assume that your perception of another as hostile is erroneous. You attributed the hostility to dispositional reasons when in fact it had a situational cause; for example, you observed that a male acquaintance ignored your greeting. In truth, the reason for this is that he had just flunked an exam and was angry and distracted. You, however, see it as an indication of unfriendliness. Thus, the next time you see him you act on your perception and behave in a cool and aloof manner. How will the other person react to this behavior? She or he is likely to respond in kind—with coldness and hostility. In short, your original perception, though erroneous, has become true.

Such an instance, in which the perceiver causes another person to behave in a manner that confirms the perceiver's expectations, is called a **self-fulfilling prophecy.**

Sociologist Robert Merton (1957), who first proposed this concept, has characterized the self-fulfilling prophecy in the following way: " . . . definitions of a situation (prophecies or predictions) become an integral part of the situation and thus affect subsequent developments. . . . The self-fulfilling prophecy is, in the beginning, a *false* definition of the situation evoking a new behavior which makes the originally false conception come *true*. The specious validity of the self-fulfilling prophecy perpetuates a reign of error. For the prophet will cite the actual course of the events as proof that he was right from the beginning."

The self-fulfilling prophecy, by perpetuating "a reign of error," has obvious implications for the study of stereotypes. The stereotypes we hold about various groups can bias the social interaction process in such a way that members of those groups will often conform to the expected stereotypical behavior. Thus false stereotypes are confirmed and the reign of error perpetuated.

A recent experiment (Snyder, Tanke, & Berscheid, 1977) convincingly demonstrated the self-perpetuating, self-fulfilling nature of false stereotypes. The aim was to test the effects of the physical attractiveness stereotype described earlier in this chapter—the assumption that says, in effect, "beautiful is good."

The subjects were male and female college students. A male and female were taken into separate laboratories without meeting each other and told that they would engage in a "get-acquainted" telephone conversation. The male was then given a photograph, which was purportedly a just-snapped Polaroid of the woman with whom he was to talk. The photograph, in fact, was a phony, the manipulation prearranged by the researchers. It showed either a beautiful woman or an unattractive one and was thus intended to generate the stereotypes associated with physical attractiveness.

After the males were shown the photo, they filled out a questionnaire that asked how they thought their telephone partner would behave. Males shown the attractive photo indicated that they expected her to be more sociable, poised, and humorous than did the males who were shown the unattractive picture. These expectations affected the behavior of the men once they got on the telephone. Judges listened to the males during the phone conversation and rated their behavior. The judges were unaware of the nature of the photograph the male subject had seen, and thus their ratings were unbiased by any knowledge of "whom" the male was talking to. (This procedure is referred to as keeping the judge "blind to experimental conditions.") The judges' ratings displayed an interesting effect. Those males who thought they were talking with an attractive woman were judged more sociable, interesting, outgoing, humorous, and animated than the males who thought they were talking with an unattractive woman.

These results should not surprise us in view of our earlier discussion on how stereotypes influence social perception and behavior. What is more striking is the behavior of the women during the phone conversation. They responded in the same way that they were treated by the males. According to the judges who listened to the females during the phone conversation, those speaking with males who thought they were attractive were more animated and sociable than the women talking with males who thought them unattractive.

Lest we forget, the males' impressions had been based upon bogus photographs; the females in the two experimental conditions were actually about equal in physical attractiveness. Even though the males' expectations about the warmth and sociability of their partner had no basis in reality whatsoever, those expectations had a pronounced effect on social interaction. They affected how the males behaved on the telephone; this in turn affected how the females behaved. The false male stereotypes of physical attractiveness started a chain of events culminating in the self-fulfilling prophecy: the females who were expected to be sociable became sociable.

The self-fulfilling prophecy is responsible for the maintenance of many of our false stereotypes, including those that relate to race and sex roles. For example, the stereotype that blacks are not competent for certain occupations may lead a white interviewer to behave in such a way that any job applicant—black or white—would become nervous and botch the interview. Because the applicant performs poorly during the interview, the person is judged unfit for the job, and the interviewer's false stereotype is confirmed (Word, Zanna, & Cooper, 1974). Similarly, stereotypes about female behavior can become reality through biased social interaction (Zanna & Pack, 1975). For example, imagine a male employer who never challenges a female employee with difficult assignments. As a result, the woman does not receive the kind of training and experience she needs. If and when she is finally asked to work on a difficult task, she is likely to fail because of lack of training. Such failure confirms original beliefs about her lack of ''male-type'' competence.

Biased Perceptions

Stereotypes also can be maintained through a second process. In the self-fulfilling prophecy, the behavior of the other person actually conforms to the perceiver's expectations. It is also possible for the perceiver only to *think* that the expected behavior is confirmed. In such instances, the perceiver's expectations are, in effect, self-confirming.

What explains **biased perceptions?** We saw earlier that our impression formation tends to be constructive and stable; that is, we build upon and embellish the impression that we have already. Two perceivers may interpret another person's behavior differently because they are building on differing impressions.

An experiment by Kelley (1950) makes essentially this point. A guest instructor was introduced to classes of students. Half the students received a biographical note describing the instructor as ''a rather cold person, industrious, critical, practical, and determined.'' The other students received a description that differed from this only in that it substituted the word *warm* for the word *cold*. After the guest instructor had finished leading the day's discussion, the students were asked to complete an evaluation form. Those students who had been informed that the instructor was warm consistently gave a higher rating than those who had been told that the instructor was a cold person. The students interpreted the teacher's behavior in such a way that their expectations, whether of warmth or coldness, were confirmed.

Similarly, our stereotypes may guide our perceptions so as to make it likely that we perceive just what we expected. Consider the following imaginary but highly plausible dialogue presented by Gordon Allport in his book *The Nature of Prejudice:*

Mr. X: The trouble with the Jews is that they only take care of their own group.

Mr. Y: But the record of the Community Chest campaign shows that they give more generously, in proportion to their numbers, to the general charities of the community, than do non-Jews.

Mr. X: That shows they are always trying to buy favor and intrude into Christian affairs. They think of nothing but money; that is why there are so many Jewish bankers.

Mr. Y: But a recent study shows that the percentage of Jews in the banking busines negligible, far smaller than the percentage of non-Jews.

Mr. X: That's just it; they don't go in for respectable business; they are only in the movie business or run night clubs. (Allport, 1954)

In this dialogue we see how contrary evidence can be misconstrued to appear to be consistent with the original negative stereotype. Each apparently favorable trait is twisted so as to confirm Mr. X's expectations. Other false stereotypes are maintained by similar biases in perception. Blacks thought to be "lazy" are said by racists to be "uppity" when they behave aggressively. Women said to be "passive" are then often viewed by male chauvinists as "pushy" when they perform competently in a professional occupation. No matter the nature of the behavior, it is construed so as to confirm expectations.

What is interesting in such examples from real life is that the same behavior can be interpreted in diametrically opposite ways depending upon our stereotypes. In the laboratory such bias was clearly demonstrated by Dion (1972), who presented adults with a description of misbehavior on the part of a seven-year-old child said to have thrown stones at a dog. The adults were also provided with a photo purportedly showing the child. Half were shown a photo of a physically attractive child; half saw a picture of a physically unattractive child. Although all of the adults were given precisely the same description of the child's misbehavior, they interpreted it according to the stereotypes of physical attractiveness ("beautiful is good"). Those who thought the child was attractive perceived the wrongdoing to be less severe and less likely to occur in the future than did those who saw the unattractive picture.

At one time or another we all can fall into the twin traps of perceiving others in a biased manner and behaving in ways that will create self-fulfilling prophecies. Such outcomes of social interaction can occur not only in one-to-one relationships but also in group interactions.

A physically attractive child who misbehaves is more likely to be perceived as less disruptive than a child who is physically unattractive.

Group Interactions

Much of our social interaction occurs in groups. We all belong to many groups—ranging from large aggregations such as political parties or college student bodies, to smaller, more intimate groups, such as families or circles of friends. In the following discussion, we will look first at interaction within groups, and then turn to relations between groups.

Intragroup Behavior

When we are in groups, we often behave differently than when we act alone or as individuals. In the preceding chapter we saw several examples of the profound effect of groups on individual behavior: the mere presence of others affects our performance on tasks; the operations of norms in a group can lead to conformity by its members and, through a process of deindividuation, members sometimes abandon their own personal sense of identity to that of the group. In addition, there are two other important ways in which behavior within the group can differ from that of the individual acting alone.

The Risky Shift

One fascinating line of research in group behavior has focused on the kinds of decisions that are made by groups as opposed to those made by individuals.

RESEARCH

Women behave differently from men. As we saw in chapter 11 in our discussion of sex-role development, many studies have found a number of apparent differences in the behavior of the two sexes. For example, women appear to conform to social norms more than do men and to perform less well on certain intellectual tasks such as a mathematical aptitude test.

There is disagreement as to the reasons for these apparent sex differences. One school of thought asserts that they stem from basic biological differences such as hormonal functioning. Others postulate personality differences that develop because of the differing ways in which socialization affects the two sexes.

In recent years, however, many social psychologists have focused on the role of interpersonal dynamics and, in particular, the effects of sex-role stereotypes. Stereotypes create expectations about how people will behave, and it may be that men and women behave differently because of society's expectations. A particular behavioral difference thus might be the result not of biological or personality differences, but of the self-fulfilling prophecy: a woman performs less proficiently on a mathematical aptitude test, for example, because

The Effects of Sex-Role Stereotypes

she is living up (or down) to society's expectations. Sex-role stereotypes may be particularly forceful when they are held by someone of the opposite sex who is attractive to the person.

An experiment designed to test this notion was conducted by Mark Zanna and Susan Pack (1975) at Princeton University. Their subjects were 80 female Princeton undergraduates. Their aim was to affect the attitudes and behavior of these women by manipulating two factors: the sex-role stereotypes held by hypothetical male partners and the desirability or attractiveness of those partners.

Before the experiment, each subject was asked to complete a battery of questionnaires about herself. The intent was to obtain initial data about how the subject viewed herself on 11 items related to sex-role stereotypes (for example, aggressiveness,

tenderness, and concern about personal appearance). Each item required responses on a six-point rating scale in such a manner that a higher number indicated agreement with a traditional female stereotypic trait.

About three weeks later, each subject returned to the laboratory for an experiment ostensibly concerned with the process by which people form impressions of one another. Each subject was given a set of questionnaires and told that they had been filled out by a young man whom she would get to meet later in the experiment. The male didn't exist, of course. Information about each hypothetical male partner had been manipulated by the researchers so that he seemed either highly desirable (tall, unattached, Princeton senior, has car, enjoys sports) or not very desirable (short, has a girlfriend, freshman at another university, does not particularly enjoy sports). Next, the subject was shown a questionnaire purporting to indicate her male partner's image of the ideal woman. This information indicated that the partner held either the traditional stereotype (for example, "the ideal woman would be very emotional," "very passive") or an untraditional, more liberated stereotype (exact opposite of the above).

Among the questions investigators have explored is whether groups tend to make decisions that are more conservative or riskier than those made by individuals.

Let us examine this question by considering a dilemma often used in the study of individual and group decision making. Mr. F needs help in making an important decision:

> Mr. F is currently a college senior eager to pursue graduate study in chemistry leading to the doctor of philosophy degree. He has been accepted by both University X and University Y. University X has a worldwide reputation for excellence in chemistry. While a degree for University X would signify outstanding training in this field, the standards are so very rigorous that only a fraction of the degree candidates actually receive the degree. University Y, on the other hand, has a less notable reputation in chemistry but almost everyone admitted is awarded the doctor of philosophy degree. As a result, the degree from University Y is much less prestigious than the corresponding degree from University X.

Each subject then completed a set of questionnaires on her own background and attitudes. Although these questionnaires were supposedly to be shown to the male partner, they actually were intended to elicit a self-description on the same 11 items concerning sex-role traits and behavior that had been contained in the questionnaires administered three weeks previously. The researchers wanted to measure how much a subject's answers had changed in response to the sex-role attitudes and attractiveness of her male partner.

Finally, the researchers administered an anagrams test—four-letter groupings that had to be transposed into words. Unlike the previous tests, this task was designed to provide a measure of actual behavior as opposed to attitudes.

The results of the experiment supported the notion that sex-role behavior is often shaped by the expectations of attractive others. Subjects who expected to meet a highly desirable male tended to live up to his expectations in her portrayal of her own attitudes. When the desirable male favored untraditional women, subjects described themselves as more untraditional; when he favored traditional qualities, subjects endorsed traditional traits. No such effects were observed when the male was undesirable. The table below shows the mean changes in subjects' self-descriptions in terms of the sex-role stereotypic traits.

In addition, on the anagrams test, subjects anticipating a meeting with a desirable male holding untraditional expectations of women outperformed subjects who anticipated a meeting with a desirable male holding the traditional stereotype. Poor performance, of course, fulfills the traditional sex-role stereotype. Again, there were no such differences when the partner was unattractive. This result is particularly important because it indicates an actual change in behavior as opposed to attitudes. The mean scores in the anagram test are shown in the table below.

Although this experiment dealt with the effects of stereotypes on female behavior, Zanna and Pack believe that men who are highly motivated to impress a woman will also behave in ways that live up to her expectations. The authors conclude that "Some apparent sex differences in behavior may be just that: only apparent and easily changeable; but only if traditional stereotypes are induced to change." ■

Partner's Desirability	Partner's Stereotypic View of Women	
	Untraditional	Traditional
High desirability	5.05	−2.35
Low desirability	.60	.60

NOTE: N equals 20 per condition. Positive scores indicate changes in self-presentation in the untraditional direction: negative scores, in the traditional direction.

Partner's Desirability	Partner's Stereotypic View of Women	
	Untraditional	Traditional
High desirability	44.25	37.40
Low desirability	41.50	40.35

NOTE: N equals 20 per condition. Scores range from a possible low of zero to a possible high of 50.

Suppose that you are asked to advise Mr. F in this matter. It is your job to determine the lowest possible chance of success at University X—the more difficult but potentially more rewarding course of action—that you would be willing to accept before advising him to go there. The risk of the decision about which university to attend hinges upon the level of the odds you are willing to accept; the lower the chance, the riskier the decision.

At the same time you are making your recommendation, five other people are individually going through the same decision-making process. You all arrive at individual decisions. Then the six of you are brought together and asked to discuss the dilemma and arrive at a unanimous decision. In which direction of risk do you think the group will go? Compared with the average individual decision, will the group's advice be riskier, more conservative, or about the same?

Common sense would seem to dictate that groups would be more conservative than individuals. Psychologists long assumed that groups were cautious and moderate, anathema to the extreme risk taker who would quickly be pulled into line. Research shows otherwise. Group decisions on problems like the one facing Mr. F turn out to be far riskier than the average individual decision. This tendency of the group to shift the direction of risk has been called the **risky shift.** It has been demonstrated in a variety of situations involving decisions of many types (Wallach & Kogan, 1965; Stoner, 1961).

In one such study, Michael Wallach, Walter Kogan, and Daryl Bem (1964) asked subjects individually to choose among a set of problems to try to solve in order to earn money. They could choose easier problems where correct solutions paid a minimum, or difficult problems where there was low probability of success but high payoffs. The harder the problems chosen the more risk, since there is a good chance of failing but some chance of earning a lot. After individuals made decisions, they were put into groups to come to a unanimous decision about the level of problems that each would then solve. Group decisions were significantly riskier. That is, groups were more likely to decide that members should attempt difficult, high-payoff problems.

Such findings of riskier decisions by groups have important implications in a world where increasingly crucial political, economic, and military decisions are made by groups rather than by individuals.

Why do groups make riskier decisions than do individuals? There are at least two reasons: *diffusion of responsibility* and *cultural values.*

1. *Diffusion of responsibility.* Acting as a member of a group lessens one's own feeling of responsibility about the outcome by diffusing it among the other members. As an individual decision maker, you might feel full of responsibility if Mr. F enrolled at University *X* on your personal recommendation and then flunked out; hence you would tend toward conservatism in your advice. Group decision makers, by contrast, can always point their fingers at one another and assert, quite rightly, that the decision was not theirs alone.

2. *Cultural values.* A second factor that helps account for the risky shift is that risk itself tends to be a general cultural value in our society, where ''nothing ventured, nothing gained'' is a popular maxim. The cultural value explanation implies that individuals making decisions alone try to take risks; however, a person acting alone may not realize just how far others are willing to go in level of risk (Brown, 1965). Once in a group a member can see that his or her own decision was really not that risky, and, in an attempt to achieve the cultural value of risk, that person is willing to go along with the other riskier members. Moreover, since risk is valued in the culture, most of the arguments brought up during group discussion will favor the risky alternative, pushing participants to become more daring in their decisions (Vinokur, Trope, & Burnstein, 1975).

If the cultural value explanation has validity, it also ought to apply in special situations where risk is not valued by the society. Where conservatism is valued (for example, making a decision about whether or not to perform life-threatening surgery) we would logically expect the group to make choices that are more conservative than those made by individuals acting alone. In fact, studies (Stoner, 1968; Rabow, Fowler, Bradford, Hofeller, & Shibuya, 1966) show that such group-induced conservative shifts do occur. Questions involving a dangerous operation, a potentially serious illness, or family savings all led to conservative shifts during group decision making. Thus, although both individuals and groups try to make decisions in keeping with cultural values, group decisions typically shift further in the direction of those values than do individual choices.

The Roles People Play

Another factor that helps differentiate behavior within the group is the existence of various roles that members are expected to play. All groups—families, fraternities, or professional football teams—have a number of different positions. The pro football team, for example, has an owner, a coach, an equipment manager, a number of cheerleaders, and, of course, a number of playing positions such as tight end. Each position has a set of prescribed and expected behaviors; these behaviors are what psychologists call **roles.** The role of tight end is essentially the same on any pro team. He is expected to learn the plays, listen to the quarterback in the huddle, block for the running backs, and catch passes. He is not expected to know how to fix a broken shoulder pad or to call the plays. The tight end who departs from his role during duty hours, say, by playing practical jokes on the halfbacks instead of practicing pass patterns, will not last long in his particular group, the pro football team. Groups expect all members to fulfill their particular roles. Whatever one's behavior outside the group, continued membership in the group usually hinges upon meeting the expectations associated with the role. It may be all right for our tight end to play jokes all he wants at home or in the off-season; when he is a member of the team, however, he had better behave like a tight end.

The powerful behavioral effects of playing a role have been demonstrated both in field studies and in elaborate laboratory experiments. In a field study the impact of various job roles on the attitudes of workers employed by a home appliance manufacturer was examined (Lieberman, 1950). All 2354 workers filled out an initial questionnaire designed to reveal various personal attitudes including how they felt about management and about their labor union. Nine months later, they filled out a similar questionnaire. During the intervening period, 23 workers had been promoted to foremen and 35 had been elected union stewards. The new questionnaire showed that these workers took on new attitudes to fit the expectations of their new roles. Those promoted to foremen became much more favorable to management; those elected stewards became more pro-union. A short time later, economic recession caused a cutback in the work force, resulting in the demotion of eight of the recently promoted foremen, who returned to their old roles as workers. In addition, several of the new union stewards did not seek reelection and they, too, returned to the worker role. As these foremen and stewards reverted to the worker role, their attitudes also reverted to those typical of the factory worker.

Laboratory explorations of role expectations have sometimes produced startling changes in behavior. We saw in the previous chapter how the subjects in the Stanley Milgram (1963) obedience experiments—normal, ordinary people—were willing to administer what they thought were dangerously high levels of electric shocks to another person even when that person was apparently screaming in pain. The discrepancy between their normal behavior and how they acted in the experiment can be understood in terms of roles. As subjects in an experiment, they had temporarily joined a group—"science"—and their

In Zimbardo's prison experiment, those assigned to the role of guards became actively cruel and hostile, while the "prisoners" were passive and obedient.

role was to follow the instructions of the researcher (whose own role was clearly defined by the white lab coat that was worn).

Whereas the Milgram study necessarily involved deceiving subjects about the real purpose of the experiment, an equally dramatic demonstration of role expectations required no such subterfuge. Philip Zimbardo (1975) set up an experimental mock prison in a basement at Stanford University. The subjects, 18 young male volunteers recruited through a newspaper ad, were told quite truthfully that the purpose of the experiment was to study the effects of imprisonment. They were paid $15 per day and randomly assigned to play roles as prisoners or guards. To simulate real conditions, the prisoners were picked up at their homes in a police car, fingerprinted, deloused, and locked in a cell. They wore smocks with stenciled numbers and, to simulate prison haircuts, pulled nylon stockings over their heads. The guards wore uniforms of khaki shirts and pants and, to prevent eye contact with the prisoners, silver sunglasses that were opaque from the outside. They were given billy clubs and told to maintain order but not to resort to physical violence.

Both prisoners and guards played their roles so convincingly that soon it was impossible for observers to distinguish acting from reality. The guards became authoritarian, tough, even brutal. They harassed prisoners by denying them toilet privileges and by calling them out of their cells in the middle of the night to do push-ups; when prisoners tried to rebel, the guards sprayed them with streams of foam from fire extinguishers. After their brief attempt at rebellion, the prisoners became servile and passive; in the first few days five prisoners developed symptoms of emotional disturbance, including depression, uncontrollable crying, and fits of rage, and had to be dismissed. So powerful were the effects of role playing that the experiment, which was scheduled to run two weeks, had to be terminated after six days.

Group interaction thus has strong effects on our behavior. The cultural values of groups and the roles molded into us by groups influence our decision making (rightly or not) and our general behavior.

Intergroup Relations

Just as individuals can interact, so too can groups that range in size from a family or teenage gang to nations. Interactions between groups parallel, in many ways, the processes in interpersonal relations that we discussed earlier in this chapter. Like two individuals, two groups can enjoy a relationship that leads to their mutual satisfaction; one group can be more powerful than the other or can be dependent on the other; two groups can be in a state of conflict with each other. Similarly, as in interpersonal interaction, the ways in which one group perceives the other group influences relationships between them. Groups, too, are prone to self-fulfilling prophecy, creating through their treatment of other groups the very characteristics they had mistakenly perceived in the first place. And, once a group forms an impression of another group, that impression tends to persist even in the face of contrary evidence, biasing perceptions of the other group's subsequent behavior.

At the same time, two important differences between interpersonal and intergroup interactions have particular impact on intergroup conflict, tending to render it unusually severe and persistent. First, no individual is absolutely essential to the group. The group and its conflict with another group can survive the loss of individuals; family feuds, for example, have been known to persist through several generations. Second, intergroup conflict increases group cohesiveness against the common enemy, reinforcing biased perceptions and increasing the likelihood of continuing hostility.

The Dynamics of Conflict

Perhaps the most ambitious study of intergroup dynamics ever undertaken was the classic research program carried out by Muzafer Sherif and his associates (Sherif & Sherif, 1953). Beginning in 1949, Sherif set up a series of summer camps for eleven- and twelve-year old boys. Because it was then widely believed that conflict between groups stemmed largely from racial or religious differences, Sherif purposely selected the boys for the homogeneity of their background; all were from stable, white, middle-class, Protestant homes. The boys were unaware that they were the subjects in an experiment because the behavioral manipulations were carried out under the guise of everyday camp activity. The camp staff consisted of Sherif's accomplices; Sherif himself watched the proceedings in the persona of "Mr. Mussee," the camp caretaker. Sherif set out to create groups, to generate hostility among them, and finally to reduce group conflict.

Sherif's most detailed study was conducted in the summer of 1954 and is known as the "Robbers Cave" experiment because of the camp's location near a landmark of that name in rural Oklahoma (Sherif, Harvey, White, Hood, & Sherif, 1961). In the first phase of the experiment, the researchers set about aligning the boys, who were previously unacquainted, into two distinct and cohesive groups. They segregated the boys into two separate residential groups in areas sufficiently far apart to eliminate most incidental contact between the two. Then they began to build cohesion within each subcamp by staging activities such as cookouts and overnight hikes that required the boys to cooperate closely with one another. Soon friendship patterns developed. The groups became such closely knit units that they even coined group names. One group was the "Rattlers"; the other was the "Eagles."

In the second phase of the experiment, Sherif and his associates deliberately attempted to create conflict between the Rattlers and the Eagles. Their method was to pit the two groups against each other in highly competitive tournaments. The two groups competed for attractive prizes in touch football, tug-of-war, and a number of other games. Since only one of two groups could win any given game, the atmosphere of highly charged competition soon gave way to intergroup hostility. The groups traded insults and engaged in food fights. They staged raids on the enemy cabins, vandalizing the possessions of the other group. They even began stockpiling apples to use as ammunition.

Biased perceptions of the opposing group were obviously quite prevalent during this stage of the research. Members overestimated the quality of their own group performance and underestimated the quality of the opposing group. For example, Sherif had the two groups of boys compete in a bean collection contest. Later, the beans collected by each boy were displayed, and campers were asked to estimate the number of beans that each boy had gathered. These estimates were strongly biased. The boys judged the collections of other members of their own group to be larger than the collections of members of the other group. Similar findings have resulted from other group evaluations of performance by opposing groups. (Hinkle & Schopler, 1979). Thus, as often occurs in interpersonal perception, evaluations of the behavior of the opposing group were distorted to be consistent with the hostility toward that group.

In the final phase of the experiment, the researchers sought to diminish the hostility and end the conflict. Several methods were tried without success. Camp counselors lectured on the necessity for friendly camp relations; pleasant social contacts such as mingling at movies were encouraged, but these contacts only heightened tensions. Interestingly, Sherif and his associates had succeeded in reducing tension between two groups at a previous summer camp, but only by employing a strategem often used by shaky national governments—the threat of a common enemy. When competitions were arranged with a team from a neighboring town, the two camp groups formed an all-star team and

From Sherif's study, the Eagles and the Rattlers are shown here, first in a fierce tug-of-war and later striving to achieve the superordinate goals of pulling the stalled food truck and fixing the water supply.

worked together. Such solutions are only temporary, however, and threaten an escalation of hostilities—the entire camp against an outside enemy.

For the Robbers Cave experiment, the researchers introduced a new approach. They had the two groups work together toward **superordinate goals,** tasks that appeal to both groups but lie beyond the resources of a single group. The reasoning behind this approach was described by Sherif: ". . . just as competition generates friction, working in a common endeavor should promote harmony."

In real life, superordinate goals often grow out of the necessities of a compelling emergency that calls for unusual human cooperation—for example, a flood, a catastrophic fire, or an earthquake. The Robbers Cave researchers created their own emergencies. When the camp's water supply was disrupted, the two groups worked together to find the cause—faucets the researchers had plugged up and a valve they had turned off. When a food truck "mysteriously" stalled, both groups literally pulled together—on the same rope they had used before in a fierce tug-of-war competition—to get the truck into the camp. The latter was a particularly clear example of a superordinate task because neither group could have pulled the truck without help from the other. Slowly, as the two groups had to cooperate on these and other staff-arranged tasks, the bickering and hostility decreased. Friendships formed against group boundaries. The two groups began cooperating even in the absence of superordinate goals, and the tendency to perceive the other group in a biased and unfavorable manner virtually disappeared. Indeed, at the conclusion of the camp, all the boys voted to go home on the same bus; en route home the Rattlers bought refreshments for all with the money they had won in one of the competitions with their former foes, the Eagles.

The Importance of Success

In the Robbers Cave experiment the researchers were careful to arrange tasks so that the groups would be successful in attaining their superordinate goals. Success in such cooperative ventures is essential if intergroup hostility

Figure 17.3

One technique for studying the effects of extreme crowding. In John Calhoun's "rat city," the conical objects are food hoppers and the winding staircases lead to burrows (the burrow in pen 1 is shown with its top removed). Originally there were 32 rats, but the population was allowed to expand rapidly. Although there was always ample food and water available, overcrowded conditions resulted in hostility, high infant mortality rate, aberrant sexual behavior, and even cannibalism.

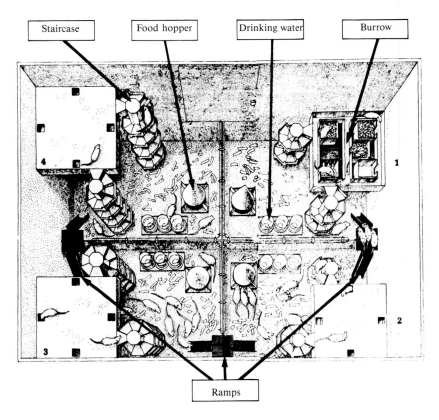

is to be reduced. This was illustrated in recent laboratory research by Stephen Worchel, Virginia Andreoli, and Robert Folger (1977). In a number of sessions, they created two competitive groups of college students and then had the groups cooperate on a series of superordinate tasks. In half of the sessions the two groups were told that their joint venture had been successful enough to win the monetary reward that had been offered. In the other half of the sessions the groups were told that their cooperative efforts had been unsuccessful, and therefore they would not receive the reward.

The results of a subsequent questionnaire administered to the subjects illuminate the importance of success in reducing intergroup conflict. Conflict fostered by competition was reduced only when working together led to success. When the joint efforts failed, there was no reduction in hostility; in fact, there was a slight increase in hostility. Worchel and his associates point out that when a cooperative endeavor between two conflicting groups fails, each group uses the other as a scapegoat, blaming the other for not pulling its own weight.

As we have seen, individuals, members of groups, and groups themselves, interact, perceive, and influence each other in many ways—positively and negatively, logically and illogically, safely and dangerously. Individuals and groups are subject to yet another force. Much of that force is created by people, but it is distinct from them individually: it is the environment.

Interaction with the Environment

A further kind of social interaction, namely, the interaction between the individual and the social and physical aspects of the environment, is the province of a relatively new branch of social psychology known as environmental psychology. Interaction with the environment is social because it typically entails mutual and reciprocal effects caused by people. For example, the two areas of investigation that we will discuss—crowding and noise—are created by people, and these environmental influences, in turn, exert psychological effects on individuals.

Crowding

Concern about the psychological effects of crowding stems from two closely entwined facts about world population. First, the earth's population is growing so rapidly that it is expected to double within the next 35 years. Second, world population is becoming increasingly urbanized, with more and more people being packed into less and less space; in urban areas such as New York's Manhattan Island, population density has now reached levels of up to 70,000 people per square mile.

Animals: A "Behavioral Sink"

One approach to the study of high population density has been to pack laboratory animals together in small spaces and to investigate the effects on their behavior. The best-known study of animal crowding was conducted by John Calhoun (1962), who formed a colony of 32 rats in a limited space and allowed the population to expand rapidly (see Figure 17.3). Although Calhoun ensured that ample food and water were available to serve the growing population, the rats' behavior became alarmingly pathological as density increased. Females were often unable to carry pregnancy to full term or to survive the delivery of their litters. The females who survived made poor mothers; at one point the infant mortality rate reached 96 percent. Sexual behavior changed; young rats of either sex were mounted by male rats. Aggression was common, and there were even instances of cannibalism. Some rats were hyperactive,

Riding on a bus full of people probably causes most people to feel crowded.

constantly dashing about their cages; others isolated themselves in their nests and emerged only to eat when the other rats slept. So staggering were the effects of the increased population density that Calhoun coined the term **behavioral sink** to refer to the negative behavior displayed.

Humans: Density Versus Crowding

The dramatic findings in animal experiments have fueled interest in, and helped lead to, a number of studies on human crowding. Typically, the early research involved examining the correlation between population density in an urban area and various indices of social pathology such as mental illness and crime. The studies have been conducted in a number of cities, including Chicago (Galle, Gove, & McPherson, 1972; Winsborough, 1965) and New York (Freedman, Heshka, & Levy, 1975). Usually, the city is divided into districts by the researchers, who then examine the potential relationship between density and, for example, crime rates in a given district.

Do those districts high in population density also have high crime rates? The answer is yes, but . . . . The important *but* is that the districts with the highest density and highest crime also are the poorest areas of the city. Thus it is quite possible that poverty may be the cause of both the high density and the high crime. In fact, when income is taken into account, there appears to be no correlation at all between density and crime; high-density, high-income areas did not have higher crime rates than low-density, high-income areas.

This sort of evidence has caused researchers to reconsider the issue of human crowding and to draw some important distinctions. Instead of looking for a strict cause-and-effect relation between density and negative social behavior, they have begun to investigate the particular conditions under which density and negative behavior might be linked. They also now draw a distinction between density and crowding. **Density** denotes the actual state of physical conditions—that is, how many people per square foot occupy a room or a square mile in a city. **Crowding** refers to a psychological state—that is, the discomfort associated with having more people around than one would prefer.

Viewed in these terms, density affects our behavior only as it produces the psychological state of crowding. It is clear that density alone does not always produce crowding. People often pack into a football stadium or rock concert arena without feeling crowded. In fact, football games and rock concerts are probably less exciting and less enjoyable when the house is only half full.

Excessive Stimulation

What are the conditions under which density produces the state of crowding? J. A. Desor (1972) has suggested that density is associated with crowding only to the extent that the situation results in **excessive stimulation**—the "overloading" of our cognitive capacities. At a football game, for example, density may be extremely high, but we are not paying attention to everyone in the stadium; we are not overstimulated by the people around us. Hence we do not feel crowded.

In order to test her excessive stimulation hypothesis, Desor staged a series of clever experiments. She built dollhouse-like rooms to scale and then had subjects place stick figures that represented people in the rooms. Subjects were instructed to put "as many people as you can without overcrowding them" into a room. In one experiment, Desor set up two rooms that were exactly alike in shape but different in size: one room had twice as much square footage as the other. In the smaller room, subjects placed an average of 18.9 "people." But in the larger room they placed only 34.1—less than twice the number placed in the smaller room. This result supports the earlier point that density alone does not determine crowding. If it did, the subjects would have put in the larger room precisely twice the number of people as in the smaller room.

In further experiments, Desor examined more directly the relation between excessive stimulation and the feeling of crowding. One method was to manipulate various architectural features that influence the level of stimulation. For example, when she divided a room with a partition, subjects placed many more people in this room than they did in an identical room without the partition. A partition has the effect of reducing stimulation from people on the other side of the room; thus it takes more people to make you feel crowded. Another architectural feature, the number of doors, also proved to be a factor. The more doors leading into a room, the fewer stick people the subjects placed in the room. Open doors open up the possibility of more stimulation and, with it, an increase in the feeling of being crowded.

Recent work by other researchers has tended to confirm Desor's proposition that stimulation is critical to the perception of crowding. For example, Jack Heller, Bradford Groff, and Sheldon Solomon (1977) created four different experimental conditions in terms of density and stimulation. To vary density they placed groups of six to eight subjects in either a small room or a large room. To vary stimulation, they had some of the subjects perform a task at a private little table so that the subjects could effectively ignore the other people in the room (low stimulation); other subjects had to walk around the room to collect materials necessary to perform the task, forcing them to pay a great deal of attention to the other people and thus to become highly stimulated.

The results highlighted the role of stimulation. In the low-stimulation condition, the density of the room had no effect upon performance. In the high-stimulation condition, density became important; many more performance errors occurred in the high-density condition than in the low-density condition. In short, it appears that high density produces a feeling of crowding and the ill effects from it only when there is also excessive stimulation.

One of the consequences of excessive stimulation is the feeling that one no longer has control over the situation. There are simply too many stimuli for one to control and manage the environment effectively. The relevance of feelings of control to perceptions of crowding is well illustrated by a recent experiment concerning crowding in elevators (Rodin, Solomon, & Metcalf, 1978). A team of confederates waited until they saw a person alone approaching an elevator at a library. When the elevator arrived they all entered, along with the subject. However, the confederates maneuvered in such a way as to force the subject to take a particular position in the elevator. Half the subjects were positioned in front of the elevator control panel. The other subjects were forced to a position away from the control panel. When the elevator stopped on the subject's floor, one of the confederates, posing as an architecture student, asked the subject to complete a questionnaire concerning the elevator. Subjects who had stood by the control panel reported feeling less crowded in the elevator and estimated the elevator to be larger in size than did subjects who were

Table 17.1 NUMBER OF SUBJECTS ASSUMING EACH SEAT POSITION

Expected Group Size	Seat Position		
	Corner	Wall	Middle
4 persons	5	11	23
10 persons	31	8	1

Source: A. Baum and C. I. Greenberg, "Waiting for a Crowd: The Behavioral and Perceptual Effects of Anticipated Crowding," *Journal of Personality and Social Psychology* 32 (1975): 671–79.

Figure 17.4

Classification of seat position of experimental room. When people expected the arrival of a small group, they tended to place themselves near the center of the room. However, when they were told a large group was expected, the corners and walls were overwhelmingly chosen.

distant from the control panel. Thus, the simple feeling that one is in control does affect the perception of crowding.

One way to avoid crowding in high-density situations is to assert control by attempting to reduce the stimulation that impinges on us. This stratagem was demonstrated by Andrew Baum and Carl Greenberg (1975) in an experiment that varied the expectations of subjects about the number of people who were to arrive in a room. Some of the subjects thought there eventually would be four people in the room; this was the low-density condition. Other subjects thought there would eventually be ten people; this was the high-density condition. The subjects who expected ten people reacted very differently from those who expected four. For example, as shown in Table 17.1, these subjects tended to avoid the middle of the room and sit in a corner of the room or against the wall—positions from which they could better control the amount of stimulation received. (The division of the room into its various components is displayed in Figure 17.4). Furthermore, they spent less time gazing at the face of the next person to walk into the room than did those who were expecting only four people.

Although such stratagems apparently enable people to cope with high density by reducing stimulation, there may be costs involved in such adaptations. We will return to this issue following our discussion of the environmental effects of noise.

Noise

An important environmental characteristic of urban areas usually associated with population density is the noise level. City dwellers tend to get used to it, but anyone who goes from the country into a densely packed urban area like San Francisco is immediately struck not only by the presence of all those people, but also by the presence of all that noise. The staccato thump of jackhammers, the banging of garbage cans against sanitation trucks, the roar of airplanes overhead and subways below, the blare of taxi horns, and the shouts of people all contribute to the disconcerting din.

Short-Term Effects

The classic studies of the effects of exposure to high levels of noise were carried out by David Glass and Jerome Singer (1972). Glass and Singer exposed subjects to 23 minutes of very loud bursts of noise over headphone sets and tested them during this exposure. Almost as soon as the noise began, there were immediate and marked effects on both the physiology and behavior of subjects. Physiological changes included increased heart rate and other signs of heightened arousal. Behavioral change was measured by testing the subjects' performance on various arithmetic and word problems. Those exposed to noise tended to make more errors than did those in the control group, who were not exposed to noise.

These particular effects proved to be short-lived, however. As the exposure to noise continued, subjects quickly adapted to it. Within a few minutes after the noise began, heart rate and other physiological measures returned to normal; performance on the arithmetic and word tasks equalled that of the no-noise control group.

Although this finding is a powerful demonstration of the ability of the human organism to adapt to stress, it does not tell the whole story. Glass and Singer also tested for aftereffects of adaptation to noise. After the noise was turned off, subjects had to perform a variety of cognitive tasks. One of these tasks was proofreading a typed manuscript to identify and correct errors. Those subjects who had earlier been exposed to noise did rather poorly, missing more of the typographical errors than did the subjects who had not been exposed to noise.

Even these findings, however, were subject to subtle variations. Glass and Singer showed, for example, that these aftereffects occurred only when the noise had been unpredictable in nature. Bursts of noise that occurred predictably—say, at regularly spaced intervals—produced little or no aftereffect. Predictability apparently enables individuals to prepare themselves for each burst of noise. This, in turn, may give them a feeling of some control over the noise and hence lessen the aftereffect.

The feeling of control also appeared to be at work in other experiments by Glass and Singer. Subjects were exposed to unpredictable noise but given control over the noise—a button that would stop it. After the researchers terminated the noise, subjects who had the control button available showed no aftereffect when tested at proofreading and other tasks. Interestingly, the subjects did not actually press the button: just the feeling that they had control over the noise was enough.

These findings again illustrate the importance of perceptions of control. Recall the earlier discussion of the illusion of control and the role that it plays in social perception and interaction. The desire for control appears to act as a basic human motive that underlies many social psychological processes, including person perception, attitude formation, gambling fallacies, and, as we have just seen, the effects of noise upon performance.

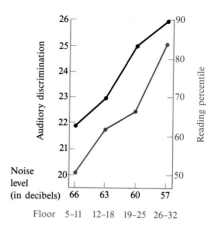

Figure 17.5

Reading and auditory skills of children are shown as a function of noise levels in their apartment building. Children living on the lower noisier floors scored significantly lower on auditory discrimination and reading tests than did children living on higher floors.

Long-Term Effects

The Glass and Singer experiments had built-in limitations because they were able to measure only short-term effects during and after short-term exposure. What about long-term effects of exposure to noise over long periods of time? A group of researchers hypothesized that prolonged exposure to noise may produce in people a "filtering mechanism" that makes them less attentive to sounds (Cohen, Glass, & Singer, 1973). An ideal natural laboratory for testing this hypothesis was found in a 32-story apartment building that was literally built over a heavily traveled expressway in New York City. Noise levels were particularly high on the lower floors of this building because they were closer to the highway. Measurements showed, for example, that the noise level on the eighth floor was twice as high as that on the thirty-second floor.

The subjects in this investigation were elementary school children who had lived in the building for at least four years. One important test was the measurement of their auditory discrimination. Each child was presented with two spoken words that sounded similar—gear-beer, for example, or coke-cope—and then asked whether they detected a difference between the two words. Children who lived on the lower, noisier floors were much poorer at this task than those who lived on the upper floors. Because auditory discrimination is related to reading ability, the investigators also gave each child a standardized reading test. Again, children from the noisier floors scored significantly lower than the children from the quieter floors—the lower the floor the lower the score (see Figure 17.5).

Prolonged exposure to noise thus appeared to adversely affect such important skills as hearing and reading. The children on the lower floors of the building apparently adapted to the highway noise, the authors suggest, by developing a filtering mechanism. But this ability to filter out sounds made them less sensitive to auditory cues and thus impaired their reading ability. In short, they adapted but had to pay a price.

Aftereffects of Crowding

The findings about the aftereffects of noise—decreased performance after adaptation—have inspired parallel research in crowding. As we saw in the earlier discussion of crowding, people sometimes adapt to high-density situations by controlling the amount of stimulation they receive—for example, by sitting

FOCUS

Proxemics: The Space We Call Our Own

A concept closely related to both interpersonal interaction and crowding is personal space—the physical distance that we maintain during interaction with others. The study of personal space is known as *proxemics,* a word coined by the anthropologist Edward T. Hall (1966). Hall and others have suggested that personal space constitutes a kind of portable psychological bubble that envelops us. Whenever personal space is intruded upon, we become uncomfortable or even angry.

Some of the aspects of personal space have been demonstrated in a series of field studies by Robert Sommer (1969). In one study, Sommer had a female confederate approach female students who were seated alone at tables in the library. When the confederate sat down at the table several chairs away from the subject, there was an apparent invasion of personal space. Subjects would variously turn away, draw in their arm or head, mark off personal boundaries on the table with a book or purse, or even get up and walk away.

Most of the time we avoid infringing upon the personal space of others. A clear instance of this was shown by Eric Knowles and his associates (Knowles, Kreuser, Hyde, & Schuchart, 1976) in a clever field study. Knowles set up his study in a 10-foot-wide corridor in which there was a shallow alcove containing a bench. He had confederates sit on the bench and then observed the behavior of passersby. Even though the bench did not protrude into the corridor, people passing made a slight detour in order to give the bench sitters a wide berth. Interestingly, when there were two bench sitters, passersby made a wider detour than when only one person occupied the bench.

The physical dimensions of personal space vary widely, depending upon a number of factors. Among these factors are the relationship between two persons, the setting, personal characteristics, and even ethnic and nationality differences. Lovers, for example, obviously stand closer together than do strangers; coworkers are likely to huddle at a cocktail party although they are at arm's length in the office. Hall has classified distances maintained during interpersonal encounters into four zones, the boundaries of which depend upon the nature of the interaction:

- The intimate zone ranges from touching to about 18 inches. This distance is used by mothers and children, by lovers, and by—quite literally—close friends.
- The personal zone extends from 18 inches to 4 feet. This zone is

against the wall or by paying less attention to the people in the room. Does such adaptation result in the kinds of negative aftereffects observed when people cope with exposure to noise?

To find out, Drury Sherrod (1974) adopted several of the techniques used in the Glass and Singer noise experiments. He placed groups of eight subjects in either a large room (150 square feet) or a small one (37 square feet). While in these rooms, the subjects were asked to perform various irrelevant tasks. Then, much as Glass and Singer turned off the noise in their experiments, Sherrod "turned off" the crowding by escorting the subjects into a much more spacious room. There, the subjects performed a task designed to measure their tolerance to frustration; they worked on a series of difficult paper-and-pencil puzzles, some of which were not solvable. The measure of frustration tolerance was the length of time in which subjects persisted in trying to find a solution to the unsolvable puzzles. Subjects who earlier had been in the smaller, more densely packed room displayed less tolerance to frustration than did those who had been in the larger, less densely packed room.

In addition to these two conditions of the experiment (large room and small room), Sherrod set up a third condition that gave subjects control over their ordinarily used for conversation by casual friends and acquaintances.

- The social zone is from 4 to 12 feet. Most formal and business contacts take place in this zone; it is close enough for clear seeing and hearing but sufficiently distant to preclude truly personal interaction.
- The public zone ranges beyond 12 feet and typically describes the space between listeners and a teacher or public speaker.

The actual dimensions of these zones tend to change with ethnic and cultural differences. For example, Hall and others have noted that Europeans typically carry on conversations at a closer range than do North Americans or the English and that Arabs and South Americans tend to converse almost toe to toe. These differences in the dimensions of our personal bubble of space can lead to misunderstandings and awkward social scenes. Jonathan Freedman, in his book *Crowding and Behavior*

Edward T. Hall and others have suggested that personal space represents a "psychological bubble" with which we surround ourselves. The dimensions of these zones tend to change with ethnic and cultural differences.

(1975), has vividly described the kind of minuet that can result when unspoken cultural concepts of personal space come into conflict:

When someone from England meets someone from Mexico, for example, they might execute a complex little dance. The Mexican stands a little closer than the Englishman would like, while the Englishman stands a little farther away than the Mexican considers appropriate. Naturally they cannot both have their way, so they shift back and forth. The Englishman backs up slightly to adjust the distance, the Mexican moves forward to readjust it, the Englishman moves some more, and so on. Eventually, the Englishman may find himself backed into a corner while the Mexican finds that he has been chasing the other all around the room. They both feel misused. The Englishman thinks the Mexican is pushy, aggressive, overly enthusiastic, and familiar. The Mexican thinks the Englishman is cold, distant, unfriendly, and defensive. Yet all that has happened is that they were both trying to stand a comfortable and appropriate (for them) distance apart. ■

situation. Subjects in this condition were placed in a dense environment, the small room, but given the freedom to leave it if they became uncomfortable. This condition paralleled that used in the Glass and Singer experiments where subjects were given a button to press if they wanted to turn off the noise. Interestingly, the results were also similar. Although subjects in this condition did not actually leave the small room, the mere availability of the option increased their sense of control over the situation. And the feelings of control, in turn, led to a decrease in the negative aftereffects on the frustration tolerance test. The frustration tolerance of these subjects ranked in the middle in the results of the three conditions; they were more tolerant to frustration than those subjects who had been in the small room without the option to leave, but less tolerant than those who had been in the large room.

The results of Sherrod's research, the Glass and Singer work on noise, and many other experiments make clear the remarkable adaptability of people in their interactions with the urban environment. But they also suggest that in the long run such adaptation is purchased at a price. These costs include decreased performance at certain tasks and even the tendency to become more easily frustrated (Sherrod & Downs, 1974).

Summary

1. Social interactions are mutual, reciprocal, two-way processes, be they two-person (or dyadic) relationships or interactions within or between groups. Another kind of social interaction can be found in the environmental effects people exert on one another through factors like noise and crowding. Social interactions are often affected by our physical environments.

2. Thibaut and Kelley's theory of social interaction proposes that relationships depend largely upon each participant's analysis of the rewards and costs: each person tries to adopt the response that will yield the greatest rewards at the least cost. Satisfaction in a relationship depends in part on one's expectations, or comparison level. The comparison level for any interaction is the level of outcome you expect or feel you deserve. Thus, satisfaction in a relationship is not determined by the absolute level of outcome, but by the outcome relative to the comparison level. The comparison level for alternatives is the expected outcome from alternate relationships. According to Thibaut and Kelley, any time the outcome of the present relationship falls below the comparison level of alternatives, the person will break up the relationship. This theory of social interaction presents a highly selfish model of human nature and does not explain behavior such as pure altruism.

3. How we interact with people depends to a great extent upon how we perceive them and how we interpret their behavior. Impression formation is the process by which we form global impressions of people based on specific facts we have learned. Impressions are usually structured, stable, and constructive. We create structure in the process of perceiving people by categorizing what they are like. A tool of categorization is the attribution of traits, which we assign, rightly or wrongly, to individuals and to groups. Our impressions of others tend to be stable and to endure, even though we may learn facts that contradict them. In addition to structure and stability, the process of impression formation is constructive: once we have categorized a person or group, we build on the general picture.

4. There are three determinants in impression formation: primacy-recency, central traits, and context. Primary-recency refers to the old saying that first impressions are lasting; we tend to rely more on our first impressions about others than on our latest information. Certain facts (is a person "warm" or "cold"?) are considered central traits, and we base a large part of our overall impression of others on these traits. We also learn facts about people in the context of other information; this context has an effect on how we interpret the traits in question.

5. Closely linked to impression formation is attribution, the inferences we make about the causes of other people's behavior. The perceived cause of other people's behavior can be classified into two general categories. If we think that a person acts in a certain way because of something internal in that person, we attribute the behavior to disposition. If we believe that a behavior stems from external causes, we attribute it to situation. Our perceptions of others usually depend upon dispositional attributions. We normally look for three key factors in attributing the causes of behavior: distinctiveness, consensus, and consistency. When situational causes are evident, we will frequently discount disposition (the discounting principle); conversely, there are instances when the dispositional cause is augmented, or increased (the augmentation principle), as we attribute causality to behavior.

6. In practice, certain biases creep into the attribution process. Foremost among these biases is our tendency to attribute the behaviors of others to disposition: we assume that people act in certain ways because they are that way. Another bias comes into play when we are actors rather than observers. As actors we tend to see our own behavior as situationally motivated; as observers we perceive the behavior of others as stemming largely from their own dispositions. In addition, we tend to attribute the behavior of others to dispositional

causes because that leads us to believe that we "know" those people, can predict their behaviors, and thus have a sense of control over our interaction with them.

7. The two processes of social perception—impression formation and attribution of traits—serve as guides in our behavior toward others. But social perception can influence social interaction even when the perception is false. In the self-fulfilling prophecy the perceiver causes another person to behave in a manner that confirms the perceiver's expectations. In addition, when we have biased perceptions it is possible for us only to *think* that expected behaviors have been confirmed.

8. While a number of the principles of social interaction apply both to individuals and groups, there are some notable differences in collective behaviors. One example is the risky shift, wherein research has shown that groups faced with difficult or controversial questions are more likely to decide upon or recommend more daring courses of action than would members of the group acting alone. This can be explained by the following: (1) a diffusion of responsibility—responsibility for outcomes is diffused among group members—and (2) cultural value—risk itself has a general cultural value in our society, and groups seem to be more affected by this value than are individuals acting alone. Group behavior is also differentiated from individual behavior by the fact that all groups have behavioral expectations of members that must be met for continued group membership; that is, groups assign us roles to play.

9. Interactions between groups parallel in many ways the processes in interpersonal relations. At the same time, two important differences between interpersonal and intergroup interactions have particular impact on intergroup conflict: (1) no individual is absolutely essential to the group, and (2) intergroup conflict increases group cohesiveness, often reinforcing biased perceptions.

10. In a classic study (the "Robbers Cave" experiment), Muzafer Sherif and his associates explored the dynamics of group conflict by creating two groups, generating hostility between them, and attempting to reduce the resulting conflict. Two factors were important in reducing conflict between the groups: (1) the introduction of superordinate goals, tasks that appealed to both groups but lay beyond the resources of a single group, and (2) ensuring success in the cooperative ventures.

11. A further kind of social interaction, that between the individual and the social and physical aspects of the environment is the province of a relatively new branch of social psychology known as environmental psychology. Interaction with the environment is social because it typically entails mutual and reciprocal effects caused by people. Two major areas of investigation for environmental psychology are crowding and noise.

12. Early research into the problems of densely populated urban areas showed a high correlation between population density and high crime rates; however, because districts with the highest density and the highest crime are also the poorest areas of the cities, it is quite possible that poverty may be the cause of both the density and the crime. Thus, instead of looking for a strict cause-and-effect relationship between density and negative social behavior, researchers have begun to investigate the particular conditions under which density and negative behavior might be linked. These researchers also now draw a distinction between density and crowding. Density denotes the actual state of physical conditions, that is, how many people per square foot occupy a room or square mile in a city; crowding refers to a psychological state: the discomfort associated with having more people around than one would prefer. Density produces crowding only to the extent that the situation results in excessive stimulation—the "overloading" of our cognitive capacities.

13. Another important environmental characteristic of urban areas is noise level. Studies have shown short-term negative effects of noise on human task ability; the same studies have also demonstrated a high degree of adaptability

to noise by the same subjects. Long-term effects of noise may adversely affect important skills such as hearing and reading ability. Studies have also shown that our adaptability to noise and crowding may be purchased at the price of decreased performance at certain tasks and the tendency to become more easily frustrated.

RESEARCH: Sex-role stereotypes may be particularly powerful in affecting an individual's attitudes and behavior when they are held by someone of the opposite sex to whom that individual is attracted. To test this notion, 80 women were given information regarding the sex-role stereotypes and the attractiveness of hypothetical male partners (Zanna & Pack, 1975). Women who expected to meet a desirable male partner tended to live up to his expectations regardless of whether the stereotype was traditional or untraditional. However, women led to believe that their partner was unattractive did not tend to live up to his expectations. These findings suggest that sex-role behavior is shaped by the expectation of attractive others.

FOCUS: The study of personal space is called proxemics. The physical dimensions of personal space appear to vary depending upon context, personality characteristics of the persons involved, and ethnic and nationality differences. The intimate zone ranges from touching to 18 inches and is common among parents and children, lovers, and good friends. The personal zone extends from 18 inches to 4 feet and is typical among casual friends. The social and public zones extend from 4–12 feet and 12 and beyond, respectively. These zones are found in formal business meetings and teaching settings.

APPENDIX

Statistical Methods

Statistical methods are essential to psychological researchers in the communication and interpretation of research findings. An understanding of basic statistics is also important to users of research findings for the proper analysis and evaluation of those findings. Statistical methods are used to describe and summarize the results of research **(descriptive statistics),** as well as to make inferences about the meaning of research findings **(inferential statistics).**

For example, if 100 students in basic psychology take a midterm examination consisting of 100 questions and the average score is 70, that average score is a descriptive statistic—a fact. If the professor hypothesizes that the average score for all students in the college would also be 70, that would be drawing an inference—and a highly suspect inference at that.

Some Uses of Numbers

Statistical methods are applied to numbers that refer to various characteristics of individuals, events, objects, and processes; however, not all of the ways numbers are used have the same meaning. For example, a particular basketball player has a uniform with a number on it. This basketball player's height is represented by a number as is his or her body temperature. Even preference for a food, such as hot dogs, can be assigned a number. Yet, from a mathematical point of view, each of these numbers has a different meaning. Let us briefly consider how these uses of numbers differ.

When numbers are used to identify members of a basketball team, for example, the numbers are usually assigned to each player in an arbitrary fashion. The only restriction is that each player has a different number; thus the numbers assigned have no mathematical meaning. The numbers assigned do not represent a player's skill or any other characteristic of the player. When numbers are assigned merely as labels for purposes of identification, we refer to this as the **nominal use of numbers.**

A more mathematically meaningful assignment of numbers is found in the **ordinal use of numbers.** Such a use of numbers might arise in a rank order of color preferences. The color most preferred would be assigned the rank of 1, the next the rank of 2, and so on. Unlike the nominal use of numbers, the ordinal use implies an underlying scale or dimension. In this example, the underlying dimension is color preference; the numbers assigned to various colors indicate locations along this dimension. However, the assigned numbers are only meaningful relative to each other. For example, the ranks 1, 2, and 3 might be assigned to three colors that were quite close together in terms of preference, or to three colors that differed greatly in terms of preference. The assigned ranks tell us the order of these colors and that they were the three most preferred of those ranked. But they do not provide any information about the degree of preference in absolute terms. If your favorite color was not among those being ranked, some other color would be assigned a rank of 1.

The number assigned to a person's body temperature, or more generally any use of either the Fahrenheit or Celsius scales of temperature, involves the **interval use of numbers;** the unit distance between all adjacent pairs of numbers is the same. For example, the change in body temperature from 98° to 99° is the same as the change from 100° to 101°. Similarly, in measuring air temperature in Fahrenheit, the difference in heat going from 50° to 60° is the same as the difference from 80° to 90°. The interval use of numbers allows us to locate points along a dimension and to determine how far apart they are in terms of scale units. However, the interval use of numbers gives us only relative information about any two numbers because the zero point does not indicate a total absence of what is being measured. As a consequence, an air temperature of 20° Fahrenheit cannot be said to be twice as warm as one of 10°. Such a comparison is meaningful mathematically only when the zero point is absolute, rather than being arbitrarily placed as it is in the Fahrenheit and Celsius scales.

When numbers are assigned in such a way that the scale units are equal and the zero point is absolute (indicating a total absence of what is being measured), we have an example of the **ratio use of numbers.** Examples of the ratio use of numbers include height, weight, and elapsed time. In each of these instances every assigned number is located along a dimension in an absolute sense. Therefore, it is possible to say that one person took twice as long as another to solve a problem, or that a growing child's weight had doubled in the past five years. In other words the ratio use of numbers allows us to perform all arithmetic operations (addition, subtraction, multiplication, and division) in a mathematically meaningful fashion.

Measurement Categories

Numbers are assigned and used to measure and categorize. Behavioral scientists employ three types of categorization and measurement: (1) unordered categorization, (2) ordered categorization, and (3) ordered categorization based on the natural number system. All categorization refers in some way to measurement, and these measurements are referred to as measurement scales.

- A **nominal scale** of measurement represents unordered classification. Classifying people as Texans, New Yorkers, and Alaskans is an example of a nominal scale: no meaningful descriptions are used or judgments made.
- An **ordinal scale** names the order or the rank in which the subject at hand falls. Ranking members of the basketball team by the number of quarters played in a season would represent an ordinal scale: Smith (1)—32 quarters; Jones (2)—29 quarters, and so on.
- The Fahrenheit and Celsius scales represent **interval scales.** They differ from ordinal scales in that difference in adjacent categories is the same in the number scale. The difference between 5°C and 6°C is the same as the difference between other adjacent categories—10°C and 11°C.
- A **ratio scale** differs from an interval scale in that the zero point is absolute. A weight system—ounces and pounds, for example—has an absolute zero point at which there is no weight.

Descriptive Statistics

Data, the plural of datum, refer to uncategorized and uncompared information: a group of test scores, for example, are data that have not been meaningfully processed. When researchers deal with large numbers of individuals, there is a need for making great amounts of data usable.

The main purpose of descriptive statistics is to answer the need for condensing and summarizing data. For example, suppose you wanted to describe the academic ability of the freshman class at a particular college as indicated by its performance on a scholastic aptitude test (SAT). The data, consisting of SAT scores for every student, might involve several hundred or several thousand scores. Out of this massive collection of scores, you will want to make some summary statements about the academic ability of the freshman class—for example, which score is most representative of the class as a whole. Statistics that provide such summary statements are called measures of central tendency. That is, these statistics provide ways of best representing the scores for an entire group of individuals.

Table A.1   SCORES ON A BIOLOGY EXAM FOR TWO GROUPS OF 10 STUDENTS

Section 1		Section 2	
41		90	
35		76	
34		34	
32		32	
32		32	
	Median 31.5		Median 31.5
31		31	
30		30	
29		29	
28		28	
28		28	

The mean ($\overline{X}$) is the sum of the scores (ΣX) divided by the number of scores (N).

Section 1

$$\overline{X} = \frac{\Sigma X}{N}$$

$$32 = \frac{320}{10}$$

Mean = 32.0

Section 2

$$\overline{X} = \frac{\Sigma X}{N}$$

$$41 = \frac{410}{10}$$

Mean = 41.0

Measures of Central Tendency

Central tendency is measured by the *mode* (the score that occurs most frequently), the *median* (the middle score in a distribution), and the *mean* (the arithmetic average).

The most widely used measure of central tendency is the **arithmetic mean,** or **average.** The mean of a set of scores is the number obtained by adding up all of the scores and dividing by the number of scores. Table A.1 provides an illustration of this procedure for two groups of students. It is typical to use the letter X to stand for any score for an individual. Then the symbol ΣX (the Greek letter sigma, "Σ," stands for "the sum of") indicates the result of adding up all of the individual scores. The letter N designates the number of scores added up. $\overline{X}$ is the symbol for the mean or average score. The bar over the X is thus used to indicate that it is the mean and not the score of an individual.

Although the arithmetic mean is the most widely used measure of central tendency, it is not always the value that is most characteristic of the scores as a whole. Because the computation of the mean takes into account the actual magnitude of each score, the mean is influenced considerably by extreme or atypical scores. When this is the case, the **median** is often used as the measure of central tendency. The median is the middlemost value in a distribution of scores. Determination of the median considers only whether a score is in the upper half or the lower half and not its absolute magnitude. To obtain the value for the median the scores are arranged in order of magnitude, as shown in Table A.1. The median is the value that divides the distribution of scores in half. If the total number of scores is even, as in Table A.1, the median is the value halfway between the two middle scores. When the number of scores is odd, the median value is the same as the middlemost score. For example, if a score of 27 was added to the scores for either Section 1 or Section 2 in Table A.1, the median value would then be 31. In all instances the number of scores above the median value must be the same as the number of scores below the median value.

The data shown in Table A.1 indicate that the means for the two sections differ substantially, although the medians are the same. This arises because the

Table A.2   FREQUENCY TABLE FOR INTRODUCTORY PSYCHOLOGY EXAM SCORES OF 118 STUDENTS (55 POSSIBLE POINTS)

Score (X)	Frequency of Each Score (F)
49	1
48	2
47	5
46	8
45	13
44	18
43	24
42	18
41	13
40	8
39	5
38	2
37	1

APPENDIX   STATISTICAL METHODS

two highest scores in Section 2 are extreme or atypical scores. In the case of Table A.1 the median is the better measure of central tendency because it is closer to the majority of the scores of the entire group than is the mean. Notice, for example, that the mean for Section 2 (41 as opposed to the median of 31.5) is larger than eight of the ten scores.

A third measure of central tendency is the **mode.** The mode is a relatively crude index, easy to calculate, and its value is equal to the score that occurs most often. To determine the mode you arrange the scores into a **frequency distribution,** such as Table A.2, and examine the column of frequencies to see which score occurred most often. The value of that score (43) is the mode.

Frequency Distributions and Central Tendency

A frequency distribution is a technique for showing the way in which the frequency of actually obtained scores is distributed over the range of possible score values. A frequency distribution may appear either in tabular form, as shown in Table A.2, or in graphic form, as shown in Figure A.1. In both cases the number of times each score occurred can be determined. A frequency distribution table is more convenient for computational purposes, such as determining a measure of central tendency, whereas a graphic presentation is superior for communicating the shape of a distribution.

Frequency distributions may take on any shape imaginable. For practical purposes, however, most frequency distributions that psychologists deal with are found within the range of shapes shown in Figure A.2. Notice that the top panel shows a **symmetrical distribution,** in which the value of the mean and median are the same. The distribution is symmetrical because the upper and lower halves (above and below 50) are mirror images of each other.

The distributions shown in the lower two panels of Figure A.2 are called **skewed** or **asymmetrical.** All skewed distributions have a longer "tail" on one end than on the other end. When the tail extends to the higher-score values, the distribution is said to be **positively skewed;** when the tail extends to the lower score values, the distribution is said to be **negatively skewed.** Notice also that in both of these distributions there is a particular relationship between the measures of central tendency. By definition, the mode is always the score occurring most often, or the score corresponding to the peak of the distribution. By comparison, the mean and median are toward the tail of the distribution, with the mean being furthest from the mode. Thus, in a positively skewed distribution the mean will be a larger score value than the median; in a negatively skewed distribution, the median will be a larger score value than the mean. This relationship exists because, as we noted previously, the extreme scores in the tail have more influence on the value of the mean than they do on the value of the median.

Measures of Variability

The most basic reason for using statistical methods is the existence of variation or individual differences. People differ from one another in height, weight, intelligence, attitudes, and most things of interest to psychologists. A crude but easily calculated measure of variability is the **range.** The range is obtained from a frequency distribution by subtracting the lowest obtained score from the highest obtained score. For example, the range of scores on the biology exam represented in the first section of Table A.1 is 13 (41 − 28 = 13); the range in Section 2 is 62 (90 − 28). The range of Section 2 is exaggerated by the two abnormally high scores. Because the range is based on only the two extreme scores, it tells us little about where each score lies. In addition, if

Figure A.1

Frequency polygon for the data presented in Table A.2.

Figure A.2

One symmetrical and two skewed distributions showing the relative locations of measures of central tendency.

ILLUSTRATION OF THE CALCULATION OF THE VARIANCE AND
STANDARD DEVIATION FOR TWO DISTRIBUTIONS OF SCORES

Distribution A			Distribution B		
X	$X - \overline{X}$	$(X - \overline{X})^2$	X	$X - \overline{X}$	$(X - \overline{X})^2$
42	+2	4	56	+16	256
42	+2	4	52	+12	144
41	+1	1	48	+8	64
41	+1	1	44	+4	16
40	0	0	40	0	0
40	0	0	40	0	0
39	−1	1	36	−4	16
39	−1	1	32	−8	64
38	−2	4	28	−12	144
38	−2	4	24	−16	256

$\Sigma X = 400$ $\Sigma(X - \overline{X})^2 = 20$
$N = 10$ $N = 10$
$\overline{X} = 40$ $\sigma^2 = 2.0$
$\sigma = 1.414$

$\Sigma X = 400$ $\Sigma(X - \overline{X})^2 = 960$
$N = 10$ $N = 10$
$\overline{X} = 40$ $\sigma^2 = 96.0$
$\sigma = 9.798$

either the highest or lowest obtained score is very extreme (as in Section 2), the range provides an exaggerated impression of the extent of individual differences.

The most commonly used measures of variability are the **variance** and **standard deviation.** The calculation of the variance and standard deviation is illustrated in Table A.3. Notice that the first step is to compute the mean for each distribution. In this example the means are the same (40) for the two distributions.

The next step is to calculate a **deviation score** $(X - \overline{X})$ corresponding to each obtained score. The deviation scores indicate how far from the mean of a particular distribution each obtained score is located. In Distribution A of Table A.3, the highest and lowest scores (42 and 38), deviate from the mean (40) by only 2 points each. For any given distribution the sum of the deviation scores will always be zero. This is because the mean is calculated to be the arithmetic balancing point of the distribution.

The next step is to square each deviation score in order to generate a variability measure that increases as the spread of a distribution increases. Then we add up these squared deviation scores and divide by the number of squared deviation scores (N). This calculation gives us the variance (σ^2), which can be defined in words as the average squared deviation score or the mean of the squared deviation scores.

$$\text{Variance} = \sigma^2 = \frac{\Sigma(X - \overline{X})^2}{N}$$

The standard deviation is simply the square root of the variance. In other words, it is defined as the square root of the mean squared deviation score. Thus,

$$\text{Standard deviation} = \sigma = \sqrt{\frac{\Sigma(X - \overline{X})^2}{N}}.$$

The symbol used to represent the variance and the standard deviation is the lowercase Greek letter sigma *(σ)*. Either the variance or standard deviation can be used to indicate variability. In either case, the larger the value the greater the variability because in wider distributions the scores are farther away on the average from the mean. Thus, the average squared distance is greater. For example, in Table A.3, greater variability is found for Distribution B than Distribution A with either measure. The variance and standard deviation could not be represented by a value below zero, and a value of zero would arise only when there was no variability among individuals.

Variability and the Normal Distribution

The **normal distribution** is one of many possible distributions that are symmetrical in shape. The normal distribution is particularly useful to students of statistical methods. A representation of a normal distribution is shown in Figure A.3. As a symmetrical distribution, the two halves are mirror images of each another—that is, if you folded the distribution at the mean, the shape of both halves would be the same. The normal distribution is bell-shaped, with most scores occurring near the mean value. As you move away from the mean in either direction, the frequency of occurrence of the score values decreases. How are the properties of the normal distribution of use to us?

Suppose a student took a psychology exam consisting of 100 multiple-choice questions. Further suppose that the scores obtained on the exam were normally distributed and that our hypothetical student received a score of 80 correct answers. Is 80 a good score? This question cannot be answered on the basis of the information given.

Next, suppose that the mean score on the exam was 75. Now you would know that the student scored in the upper half of the class because 80 is above the mean. Remember that the mean and median values are the same in a normal distribution. Because half of the scores are found below the median, a score of 80 is in the upper half of the class; however, we still do not know how good a score of 80 is. Unless we know the standard deviation of the scores, we do not know how far a score of 80 is above the mean. Given this additional information we can compute the student's **standard score.** For example, given that the standard deviation is 5, we can see that a score of 80 is 5 points above the mean score of 75 or one standard deviation above the mean. This calculation is shown below, where the standard score is obtained by dividing the student's deviation score by the standard deviation of the distribution.

$$\text{Standard score} = \frac{X - \overline{X}}{\sigma} = \frac{80 - 75}{5} = \frac{+5}{5} = +1.0$$

Standard scores, or z scores, can be computed for distributions of any shape, but in the normal distribution there is a particular relationship between standard scores and areas of the distributions. This relationship is illustrated in Figure A.4. (Note that standard scores are often called ζ scores when the distribution is normal in shape.)

Figure A.4 shows the percentage of obtained scores occurring between the various z score values. In the normal distribution almost all scores fall within six standard deviation units. Approximately 34 percent of the scores are found between the mean (z score = 0) and one standard deviation above the mean (z score = +1). Since the distribution is symmetrical, the same percentage of scores are found between the z scores of 0 and −1. If you add up the percentages shown in Figure A.4, you will see that more than 99 percent of the scores fall within three standard deviation units above and below the mean. This will always be the case whenever a distribution is normal in shape.

Now we can precisely evaluate the score of 80. We know that half, or 50 percent, of the scores are located below the mean, and that 34 percent are located between the mean and a z score of +1. Therefore, 84 percent of the

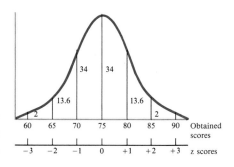

Figure A.3

Graphic illustration of the shape of the normal distribution.

Figure A.4

Illustration of the relationship between the normal distribution and z scores.

scores are below an obtained score of 80. In other words, this student's percentile rank is 84. Like a z score, a percentile score is a transformed score: it is the percentage of raw scores that are less than or equal to that particular raw score. Only 16 percent of the scores were better than or equal to our student's score.

The advantage of using standard scores when the distribution of scores is normal is that once we know the mean and standard deviation we can answer a variety of questions about the distribution. For example, IQ as measured by intelligence tests is normally distributed with a mean of 100 and a standard deviation of 15. Given this information we can draw a graph like that shown in Figure A.4 in order to answer such questions as the following:

1. How many people have IQs between 85 and 115?
   Answer: Approximately 68 percent.
2. How many people have IQs over 115?
   Answer: 16 percent.
3. How many people are below average in IQ?
   Answer: 50 percent.

These and other questions can be answered about any set of scores that are distributed normally once the mean and standard deviation are known.

Correlation and Regression

Correlation is one of the most useful statistical methods used by psychologists. It describes the relationship between two sets of score values, which can be related in a variety of ways. The numerical index of the degree of relationship between two sets of scores is called the **coefficient of correlation.** The value of the correlation coefficient may range from -1.00 to $+1.00$.

It is important to realize that the sign (plus or minus) refers only to the direction of the relationship and not to the degree of relationship. For example, if high scores from one set tend to go with high scores from the other set while the low scores similarly go together, the relationship is said to be a **positive** ($+$) or **direct correlation.** If you correlated height and weight for a group of people, the resulting correlation would be a positive value: people with large scores on height tend to have large scores on weight, and vice versa. On the other hand, a **negative** ($-$) or **inverse correlation** exists when high scores from one set go with low scores from the other set, and vice versa. For example, as elementary school children grow older—say age 7 to age 12—they make fewer spelling errors on standardized achievement tests. There is an inverse relationship between age and the number of errors.

The relationships described by the correlation coefficient can be illustrated graphically by means of the "scatter plot" as shown in Figure A.5. Notice in the figure that the score sets are labeled X and Y. Dots are placed in the scatter plot to represent each subject's X and Y scores. It is conventional to use the letter X to designate scores on the abscissa or X axis (the horizontal axis) of the scatter plot, and Y to designate scores on the ordinate or Y axis (the vertical axis).

Panel A illustrates a perfect positive correlation. Each dot in the plot represents two scores, one on X and one on Y, for the same individual. Panel A thus indicates for any two individuals that the one with the higher score on X also has the higher score on Y. The relationship between the two sets of scores is linear because all of the dots, or data points, fall on a straight line going from lower left to upper right. Now look at Panel D, where a perfect negative correlation is shown. Everything said about Panel A applies to Panel D except

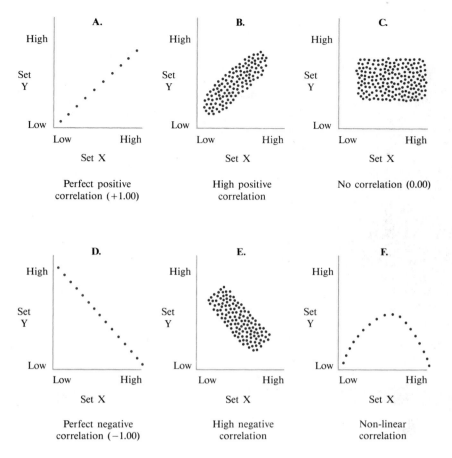

Figure A.5

Scatter plots illustrating several degrees of correlation between two sets of scores.

that the data points go from upper left to lower right. In both panels the degree of relationship is the same (1.00); only the sign indicating direction of relationship differs. Positive relationships are also referred to as direct relationships; negative relationships are also referred to as inverse relationships.

Panels B and E also indicate equally strong correlations, with B showing a positive relationship and E showing a negative relationship. However, the correlation is no longer perfect. In panel B, for example, you can readily find a pair of dots indicating that one individual has a higher score on X but a lower score on Y. Yet from the scatter plot you can also see a distinct trend for high scores on X to go with high scores on Y and for low scores on X and Y to go together; similarly in Panel E, there is a distinctly negative or inverse relationship between X and Y, although the trend is not perfect.

Panel C illustrates an absence of relationship between X and Y. Notice that the range of Y values for low scores on X is the same as the range of Y values that go with high scores on X. In other words, knowing the way an individual scores on X does not tell us anything about the way that individual would score on Y. We shall return to this aspect of correlation shortly. Panel F is included in Figure A.5 to illustrate a strong, in fact perfect, relationship between X and Y, but one that is not linear.

The coefficient of correlation is used to describe the relationship between two sets of scores. However, to understand better the meaning of a correlation coefficient it is necessary to show how it can be used to make predictions. This is illustrated in the hypothetical and partial scatter plot shown in Figure A.6. Suppose you wanted to predict a certain person's score on Y. If all you knew were the values on Y that were obtained, all you could say is that the score would be somewhere between 30 and 90, the most extreme scores on Y. However, if you also knew this person's score on X was, say 60, then you could narrow your prediction about the Y score to a value between 50 and 70, the

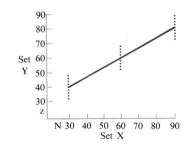

Figure A.6

Illustration of the use of a regression line in predicting scores on Y from scores on X.

Table A.4 ILLUSTRATION OF THE RELATION BETWEEN r (THE CORRELATION COEFFICIENT) AND r^2 (THE PROPORTION OF Y VARIATION ACCOUNTED FOR BY X)

r	r^2
1.00	1.00
.90	.81
.80	.64
.70	.49
.60	.36
.50	.25
.40	.16
.30	.09
.20	.04
.10	.01
.00	.00

range of Y scores that go with X equal to 60. A similar narrowing of the range of Y scores also occurs for X scores equal to either 30 or 90.

The most commonly used correlation method is the **Pearson product-moment correlation,** which is based on the index designated r. As we have already seen, r increases from 0.00 to plus or minus 1.00 as the degree of relationship between the two sets of scores increases. However, the important point to note here is that r^2 and not r itself is the appropriate index of the degree of relationship that exists between the sets of scores. What r^2 measures is the proportion of Y variation that is accounted for by X variation. Let us now return to Figure A.6 to get an idea of what this statement means.

In using correlational methods for predicting performance we begin by considering the extent of variation or individual differences in one set of scores, say, in the absence of any other information. In Figure A.6 the range of Y scores is from 30 to 90. However, suppose the relationship between X and Y is that shown in the figure. The straight line running from lower left to upper right is the line that best "fits" the data points, and it is called the **regression line.** In our illustration the regression line connects the average or mean Y score for each separate value of X. Thus, the average Y score is 40 for an X of 30. For X equal to 60, the average Y is 60, and for X equal to 90, the average Y is 80.

Now, if you knew that a particular person's X score is 60, your best prediction on Y would be the average Y score of 60. That is, the predicted Y score is the average Y score obtained by everyone having an X score of 60. Notice that errors in prediction will still occur, but the magnitude of the errors will be considerably reduced compared to a situation in which no knowledge of the relationship between X and Y is provided. If you know that X is 60, you no longer will be concerned about Y values below 50 or above 70 in making predictions. If you know that X is 90, the variations in Y below 70 will not be of concern. In other words, for any value of X, two thirds of the total range of Y scores will be eliminated from concern in making predictions about Y scores. Thus, in making any single prediction about a Y score on the basis of a given value of X, we can say that two thirds of the variations in Y have been accounted for by knowledge of X. For X and Y in general, we can say that two thirds of the individual differences in Y scores are accounted for by knowledge of the individual differences in X scores. Since this proportion (two thirds, or 0.67) equals r^2, we know that r equals 0.82. Table A.4 shows the relationship between r and r^2 for several values of r.

Notice that a correlation of 1.00 means that all of the Y variation is explained by knowledge of X. Look back at Panels A and D of Figure A.5 for an illustration. In both panels if you knew a person's score on X, you would also know the corresponding Y score. However, below values of 1.00 the relationship between r and the degree of actual relationship between scores on X and Y is not very similar. For example, an r value of 0.50 indicates that only one fourth, or 25 percent, of the variation in Y scores is accounted for by X. Thus, it is the square of the correlation coefficient that is the best indicator of the degree of relationship described.

Two additional points need to be made before we conclude our discussion of correlation. One is that in order to correlate two sets of scores meaningfully, each pair of scores must come from the same source. You can correlate individual characteristics of people (height, weight, IQ, and so on) with one another because everyone can be described in terms of these characteristics. But you could not meaningfully correlate the heights of one group of people with the weights of another group because the pairing of a given height and a given weight would be arbitrary.

Although the correlation coefficient is an index of relationship between two sets of scores, it is not an index of a causal relationship. That is, the fact of correlation does not mean that the two sets of scores are causally related. For example, suppose you identify a group of children between the ages of 4 and 12 and correlate their mental ages with the length of their big toes. You would find the correlation to be quite high, perhaps +0.80. Recall that the notion of mental age is such that at age 4 a child with an IQ of 100 would have a mental age of 4, and that the mental age would increase one year for every year of chronological age. Thus the high correlation does not indicate a causal relationship or indicate that the brain is in the big toe. Instead it describes the fact that between the ages of 4 and 12 big toes increase in length and intellectual functioning improves.

Inferential Statistics

The methods of inferential statistics are of considerable importance in psychology but are properly reserved for more advanced textbooks. However, on the basis of our rather brief treatment of descriptive statistics it is possible to introduce some of the questions that inferential statistics are designed to answer. We can also introduce a few concepts that are basic to the use of inferential statistics.

Few factual claims made by psychologists are based on studies of everyone belonging to a defined population. Most such claims are based on studies of a subset or sample of the population. The mean of the sample and the variation or individual differences observed in the sample provide a basis for making estimates about the population as a whole. Populations can be defined in a number of ways. For instance, if you wanted to know the average IQ of plumbers, then the population would consist of all plumbers.

The concepts of a sample and a population are vital to inferential statistics. A **population** might be all eighteen-year-old female college students in the United States. If you wanted to know how many of those young women had used marijuana, you would find it impossible to interview all of them. You could, instead, interview a sample of eighteen-year-old female college students, say 2000 of them. You would infer from your findings that the experience of the women in your sample would be similar to the experience of the population as a whole.

However a population is defined, it is important that a sample chosen for the purpose of estimation of characteristics of the population be representative of the population. This is typically done by taking a **random sample** of the population. Sampling randomly means that every member of the defined population has an equal chance of being included in the sample. Sampling randomly does not ensure correct estimation, but it does avoid any obvious sample bias. If you wanted to estimate the intelligence (IQ) of all Americans, you would not sample only from people living in Chicago. You would need samples from other urban areas, smaller towns, and rural areas.

All the descriptive statistics discussed previously, including the measures of central tendency and variability as well as the correlation coefficient, can be used for purposes of estimation. Other questions that arise in the case of estimation include those concerning the accuracy of estimates and the degree to which estimates for one population differ from estimates for another population. The following hypothetical example that arises in inferential statistics can be used to illustrate these issues.

Suppose you were wondering whether the students enrolled in College A were more intelligent than those enrolled in College B. To answer this question you select a random sample of the students at the two schools and give each sample an intelligence test. You find that the mean IQ for students from College A was 120, and from College B it was 115. Would you be justified in concluding that College A students were more intelligent? Let us consider some factors that might influence your answer.

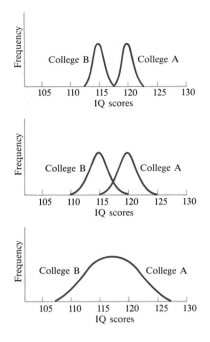

Figure A.7

Illustration of possible relationship between IQs of students at two colleges (populations).

Figure A.7 shows three pairs of population distributions that could give rise to the results given above. The top panel illustrates two nonoverlapping populations of IQ. The middle and bottom panels show two levels of overlap for the populations. In the middle panel the populations overlap somewhat, and in the bottom panel the overlap is complete. Even restricting ourselves to just these three possibilities, the question of interest is which pair of population distributions gave rise to our sample results.

Let us first consider the sample means of 120 for College A and 115 for College B. These sample means can be considered as estimates of the corresponding populations, although it should be clear that sample means can and do differ from the means of populations from which the samples are drawn. Notice, however, that the sample means in this case do not help us in answering our basic question. As you can see in Figure A.7, the respective population means are 115 for College B and 120 for College A in both the top and middle panels. In the bottom panel, where the distributions totally overlap, the mean between 115 and 120 could easily result from small errors in estimation due to unintentional sample bias. How then would we decide whether or not the students at College A were more intelligent?

Look again at Figure A.7, but this time consider the extent of individual differences in the three pairs of population distributions. In the top panel the range of IQs in both populations is about 5 points, in the middle panel it is about 10 points, and in the bottom panel it is about 20 points for both populations. Now, if the extent of individual differences in our sample, as indexed by the variance and standard deviation, was quite small, we would conclude that the top panel probably best represents the true populations. This conclusion would be particulary well justified if all IQs in the sample for College B were between 112 and 117, and all those in the College A sample were between 117 and 122. On the other hand, if the variances and standard deviations were large, with both samples including some IQ values such as 110 and 125, we would conclude that the lower panel best represents the true populations.

It should be apparent that the conclusions discussed above could be reached only if the samples for College A and B truly represented their respective populations. Obviously, it would be possible in the case of the bottom panel to select samples with small variances and standard deviations. For instance, the College B sample could contain IQs mainly clustered around 115, while the College A sample IQs were clustered around 120. If that were to happen we might easily make an incorrect inference concerning the true populations. However, incorrect inferences would be more likely to arise if the middle panel represented the true populations, because even fairly small errors in sample representativeness could result in incorrectly choosing the populations in the top and bottom panels. Notice that sample bias in samples selected from the populations shown in the middle panel of Figure A.7 need not be terribly large for those samples to look like samples chosen from the poulations shown in the top or bottom panels. In contrast, the sample bias in samples chosen from the bottom panel would have to be considerable before those samples would lead us incorrectly to infer that the top panel best represented the true populations.

Notice that in reaching any of the conclusions just mentioned, the major factors were the amount of variation, or individual differences, in the populations and the representativeness of the samples. As the variation increased, the overlap among the populations increased and the opportunity for error in estimating the population means increased. That is, the more variation that exists in a population, the greater the opportunity for a sample drawn from that population to provide a poor estimate of the population mean. Thus, in applying the techniques of inferential statistics there is always some risk of making incorrect inferences.

GLOSSARY

Designations in parentheses following definitions indicate the primary chapter(s) in which the term is discussed.

A

abnormal behavior Abnormal behavior is commonly defined in one of three ways: (1) as behavior that is disturbing to others, (2) as behavior that is characterized by subjective distress, or (3) as behavior characterized by impairing psychological handicaps. *(14)*

absolute threshold Minimum level of intensity at which we can perceive a sensation. *(3)*

accommodation Process in which muscles within the eye change the shape, or curvature, of the lens and hence the focus as objects approach or recede. *(3)*

achievement Social motive that causes us to strive for bigger and better accomplishments. *(10)*

achievement tests Tests designed to measure the degree to which a particular skill or body of knowledge has already been mastered. *(13)*

acrophobia Fear of high places. *(14)*

action potential In reference to electrical activity in the neuron, a sudden change of voltage across the axon membrane. *(2)*

actor-observer difference As actors we see our own behavior largely in terms of situational forces; as observers we perceive the behavior of others as stemming largely from their own dispositions. *(17)*

acuity Maximal visual sharpness. *(3)*

adaptive traits According to Allport, personality traits that are necessary in order to carry out a particular task situation; see also *expressive traits*. *(12)*

adequate stimulus The stimulus to which a sense organ normally responds; adequate stimulus for the eye is the range of electromagnetic radiation called light. *(3)*

addiction Drug dependence that may be psychological, physiological, or both. *(5)*

additive mixture A mixture of wave lengths of light; mixing two or more wave lengths will add up to a new color; see also *subtractive mixture*. *(3)*

adipocytes Special cells in which the body stores fat. *(10)*

adjusted IQ A measure that results from the System of Multicultural Pluralistic Assessment; typically yields a higher IQ than traditional measures. *(13)*

aerial perspective One of the monocular cues for perceiving depth in which outlines of distant objects appear blurred and fuzzy. *(4)*

affective disturbance Inappropriate emotional responses; a symptom of schizophrenia. *(14)*

afferent nerves Fibers that carry sensations of warmth, cold, touch, pain, and body awareness from the receptors, or sense organs, to the spinal cord and then to the brain. *(2)*

affiliation Social motive that impels us to associate with others; some psychologists believe affiliation need has some biological as well as social basis. *(10)*

alcoholism Addiction to the depressant drug alcohol. *(5)*

alloplastic view Literally, "change outside of self"; this approach to development stresses the ability of the organism to alter nature and thus affect canalization. *(6)*

all-or-none law In reference to nerve conduction, describes the fact that once a neuron fires, increases in the stimulus do not increase the action potential. *(2)*

alpha press According to Murray, those aspects of a situation that are objectively perceived, objectively exist, and are compelling to the individual; see also *beta press* and *press*. *(12)*

alpha waves EEG pattern produced by a subject who is awake but relaxed; characterized by relatively slow synchronous rhythms (neurons firing in an orderly pattern) with a frequency of about 10 waves per second. *(5)*

altered states of consciousness States of consciousness variously typified by such characteristics as lack of self-awareness, hallucination, altered time perception, and loss of contact with present reality. *(5)*

alternate states Term designating all forms of consciousness; implies that normal waking consciousness and altered states cannot be clearly differentiated. *(5)*

altruistic behavior Behavior that helps others at some cost to the individual. *(10)*

amacrine cells Unipolar nerve cells that are without axons; found in the inner nuclear layer of the retina and in other organs; see also *bipolar cells* and *horizontal cells*. *(3)*

ambivalence Behavior characterized by the frequent juxtaposition of opposing emotions or impulses; a symptom of schizophrenia. *(14)*

amplitude One of the physical properties of sound that measures intensity or loudness of a sound wave; see also *frequency* and *phase*. *(3)*

amygdala Almond-shaped structure of the limbic system that functions in the arousal and control of emotional and motivational behavior and apparently as a receptive center for reinforcing stimuli such as pain, food, and so on. *(2)*

amygdalectomy Through electrodes planted in the amygdala, the destruction of certain "aggression centers"; there is little evidence of success in those amygdalectomies that have been performed. *(15)*

anaclitic depression Reaction of some infants when separated from their mothers; characterized by continuous crying, apprehension, withdrawal, weight loss, and retarded growth and development. *(14)*

analgesia Loss of pain without loss of consciousness. *(5)*

analgesics Pain-blocking drugs that do not produce a loss of consciousness when used at the site of the source of pain. *(5)*

anal stage According to Freud, the second stage of psychosexual development during which sexual energy of the libido is anally directed; see also *genital stage, oral stage,* and *phallic stage*. *(11, 12)*

analytical psychology   The theories of Jung; characterized by less emphasis on early psychosexual development than Freud; focus on present conflicts and problems and on the concepts of the collective unconscious and archetypes. *(12)*

andrenogenital syndrome   Genetic disorder of the female that produces a tumor or excessive growth in the adrenal glands resulting in the production (commencing before birth) of large amounts of androgen (a male sex hormone). *(11)*

androgens   Main steroids (gonadal hormones) produced by the male testes. *(11)*

anesthetics   Agents that produce insensitivity to pain. *(5)*

anomalous trichomats   People with a type of color blindness caused by a condition in which the pigment in the middle- or long-wavelength cones is present but has a different maximal sensitivity than the pigment in the cones of the normal eye. *(3)*

anorgasmia   Inability to experience orgasm. *(11)*

antidepressants   Drugs that act to elevate mood. *(18)*

anxiety   State of uneasiness or apprehension, which is related to fear but less object-specific than fear. *(14)*

anxiety hierarchy   A list of situations to which a person responds with anxiety ranked in order from the least to the most fear evoking; used by behavior therapists in systematic desensitization. *(15)*

aphagia   State of being unwilling or unable to eat; lesions in the lateral hypothalamus have produced aphagia in laboratory animals. *(10)*

aphasia   Loss or impairment of the ability to use language, usually resulting from brain damage. *(5)*

aptitude tests   In general, tests that are designed to predict later performance that has not yet been achieved. *(13)*

aqueous humor   Watery fluid that fills the bulge at the front of the eyes. *(3)*

arachnoid   The middle layer between the dura and the pia mater, of the three meninges surrounding the central nervous system. *(2)*

archetypes   According to Jung, the master patterns of images that are transmitted from generation to generation; examples include such concepts as Mother, a Supreme Being, the Hero, and a sense of wholeness; see also *personal unconscious*. *(12)*

archival study   Study that attempts to find historical data that sheds light on a particular kind of behavior. *(1)*

arithmetic mean   The most widely used measure of central tendency that is obtained by adding up all of the scores and dividing by the number of scores; see also *median* and *mode*. *(App.)*

assimilation   Process through which individuals take in and incorporate information from their environment in light of their current understandings of the world. *(6)*

association areas   Regions of the cerebral cortex whose functions are not completely understood but that are presumed to integrate or associate information arriving at the precisely mapped cortical centers for sensation and movement; also called silent areas. *(2)*

associative disturbance   Behavior that takes the form of vague and disjointed language; a symptom of schizophrenia; also called loose associations or thought disorder. *(14)*

associative stage   The second stage in motor learning in which cognitive activities begin to drop out and coordination and integration of responses is learned; see also *autonomous stage, cognitive stage,* and *motor learning.* *(7)*

asymmetrical distribution   See *skewed distribution. (App.)*

attachment   Special bond formed between infant and caregiver. *(6)*

attitude   Disposition that makes a person categorize objects, people, or issues along an evaluative dimension. *(16)*

attractivity   Initiation of the sexual encounter by the female of the species by showing the male such stimuli as swollen or highly colored "sexual skin." *(11)*

attribution theory   Deals with the underlying principles by which we decide the causes of another person's actions; attribution refers to the inferences we make about the causes of other people's behavior. *(17)*

audition   The act of hearing; requires both rhythmical variations in the pressure of a medium near us and the reception of these variations by the ear. *(3)*

auditory canal   The visible opening of the ear; a hollow tube that concentrates sound waves. *(3)*

auditory masking   Drowning out of one sound by another not simply because of tone intensity but because of similarities in frequency of the two tones. *(4)*

augmentation principle   The practice of increasing or adding to dispositional causes in attributing causality to behavior; see also *discounting principle.* *(17)*

autism   The tendency to withdraw from involvement in the external world and to become preoccupied with private fantasies; a symptom of schizophrenia. *(14)*

autokinetic effect   If an individual is placed in a totally dark room with no frame of reference and then a single, stable point of light is introduced, the light appears to move erratically. *(16)*

automatic writing   Act of writing understandably without awareness of what is being written; a result of posthypnotic suggestion. *(5)*

autonomic nervous system   One of the two parts of the peripheral nervous system that controls the functioning of the internal organs such as arteries, heart, stomach, and sweat glands; see also *somatic nervous system.* *(2)*

autonomous stage   Third stage of motor learning in which the performer seems to become more automatic in performing the task; see also *associative stage, cognitive stage,* and *motor learning.* *(7)*

autoshaping   Development of a learned response under circumstances in which there is no contingency between the response and the delivery of reinforcement. *(7)*

average   See *arithmetic mean. (App.)*

aversive centers   Areas in the midbrain near the hypothalamus that seem to produce pain or discomfort in laboratory animals when those areas are electrically stimulated. *(10)*

aversion therapy   Type of counterconditioning, behavior therapy that aims at substituting negative feelings for positive ones by conditioning aversion to stimuli that are considered inappropriately attractive; see also *implosive therapy* and *systematic desensitization.* *(15)*

avoidance learning   Conditioning to a cue so that in anticipation of punishment the animal learns to avoid the punishing stimulus. *(7)*

axon   One of a neuron's three essential parts—a single long appendage jutting out from the soma on the side opposite the dendrites; see also *dendrite* and *soma.* *(2)*

axon hillock   A gentle swelling at the point on the nerve cell body from which the axon originates. *(2)*

B

balance theory   Theory of interpersonal attraction based on the tendency of people to seek consistency among their own thoughts, feelings, and actions. (*16*)

barbiturate   Sedative-hypnotic drug that induces general anesthesia when used in large doses. (*5*)

basilar membrane   A delicate fibrous membrane located within the coils at the base of the cochlea of the inner ear. (*3*)

behavioral rehearsal   A procedure similar to modeling in which the therapist demonstrates how to handle an interpersonal problem in a better way, and the patient then imitates the therapist, continually rehearsing the new behavior. (*15*)

behavioral sink   Term coined by Calhoun to refer to the negative behavior displayed by laboratory animals in an overcrowded situation. (*17*)

behaviorism   School that views psychology as the study of behavior that is observable and measurable and the ways in which stimulus-response relationships are formed. (*1*)

behavior shaping   The training of novel behavior or sequences of actions by breaking up the desired action into small steps and then reinforcing the proper response to each step until the desired behavior is learned. See also *successive approximation.* (*7*)

behavior therapy   Therapy that focuses on behavior itself rather than on subjective determinants; see also *cognitive restructuring, counterconditioning, modeling, operant techniques,* and *self-control procedures.* (*15*)

beta press   According to Murray, those aspects of a situation that are perceived to be present by the individual and thus influence his or her behavior; see also *alpha press* and *press.* (*12*)

beta waves   EEG patterns produced by subjects who are alert, mentally active, and attending to external stimuli; characterized by more rapid waves of smaller amplitude (height) and less synchrony than alpha waves. (*5*)

biased perception   A situation in which the perceiver of another person's behavior only thinks that expected behavior is confirmed, even when the other person's behavior does not actually conform to the perceiver's expectations. (*17*)

bilateral symmetry   Arrangement by which structures of the body and brain are paired or divided into similar halves. (*2*)

binaural   Refers to our two-eared system of audition. (*3*)

binocular cues   Cues for visual depth perception that require the use of both eyes. (*4*)

biofeedback   Process by which subjects can observe their own physiological processes that do not ordinarily reach awareness such as brain waves and blood pressure, so that they can attempt consciously to control them. (*5*)

biological clock   Internal time-keeping mechanisms that control an individual's circadian rhythm, or daily round of sleep and waking; see also *circadian rhythm.* (*5*)

biological preparedness   Theory suggesting that an organism may be biologically predisposed to become fearful of certain stimuli more easily than others. (*14*)

biosocial complex   The sum of the cultural and biological determinants of sexual behavior. (*11*)

bipolar affective disorders   Part of a cluster of disorders of mood and affect characterized by alternating swings between elation and depression. (*14*)

bipolar cells   Cells of the inner nuclear layer of the retina that organize information coming from the rods and cones and transmit it to the ganglion cells; see also *horizontal cells* and *amacrine cells.* (*3*)

brain stem   Stalklike portion of the brain rising from the spinal cord into the skull. (*2*)

brainwashing   Extreme form of intentional social influence. (*16*)

brain waves   Wavy patterns shown by an electroencephalograph that represent fluctuations or oscillations in voltage, which in turn reflect the sum of many nerve cells firing in the cerebral cortex. (*5*)

brightness   The psychological aspect of color that refers to the physical intensity of color; see also *hue* and *saturation.* (*3*)

bystander intervention   Refers to the decisions people must make about whether to step in and help in an emergency. (*16*)

C

calcarine fissure   Fissure in the occipital lobe at the back end of the cortex; involved in the human visual system. (*2*)

canalization   Development of systems in which genetic influence is relatively strong and environmental influence is relatively weak. (*6*)

Cannon-Bard theory   Theory that physiological arousal alone does not cause emotion but is produced simultaneously with the subjective experience of emotion. (*10*)

cardinal traits   According to Allport, extremely strong characteristics that shape the total personality; see also *central traits* and *secondary traits.* (*12*)

case history   Technique used in clinical psychology; a compilation of a kind of psychological biography of the client. (*1*)

case relations   Grammatical relations that emphasize the semantic structure of utterances, not just the syntactic form. (*9*)

castration anxiety   Freud's term for the fear of removal of the penis experienced by males during the phallic stage. (*11*)

catharsis   Relief of emotional tension by reestablishing the association between the present emotion and the past causal event. (*10*)

cell body   See *soma.* (*2*)

center-off   The process in which certain of the eye's ganglion cells decrease their firing rate when light falls in the peripheral area surrounding the center of the receptive field; see also *center-on.* (*3*)

center-on   The process by which certain of the eye's ganglion cells decrease their firing rate when light falls in the peripheral area surrounding the center of the receptive field; see also *center-off.* (*3*)

center-surround   The concentric organization of the receptive field of the eye's ganglion cells. (*3*)

central fissure   Major fissure of the cerebral cortex cutting laterally across the surface separating the frontal lobe from the parietal lobe; also called the fissure of Rolando. (*2*)

central nervous system   Made up of the brain and spinal cord that together regulate and control the activity of the entire body; see also *peripheral nervous system.* (*2*)

central traits   According to Allport, characteristics that are important but not pervasive in shaping personality; see also *cardinal traits* and *secondary traits.* Facts or perceptions that carry special weight in impression formation. (*17*)

cerebellum   Large structure attached to the rear of the brain at the level of the pons; helps maintain the body's equilibrium and coordinate muscles during fine movements. (2)

cerebral cortex   Fissured, grayish surface that covers much of the brain's exterior; controls the more complex functions of the organism. (2)

cerebral dominance   Specialization of one or the other of the brain's hemispheres for certain tasks or abilities. (2)

cerebral hemispheres   The two large connected bodies that make up the cerebrum; see also *cerebrum*. (2)

cerebrospinal fluid   Fluid in the thin layer of space between the arachnoid and the pia mater of the brain; supplements the brain's arterial circulatory system by supplying nutrients and removing waste matter; also serves as a buoyant shock absorber. (2)

cerebrum   The two massive connected bodies that arch above and around the brain stem and its connected structures; see also *cerebral hemispheres*. (2)

choroid   The dark-pigmented lining, rich in blood vessels, that forms the middle layer of the eye and serves to keep out all light except for that which enters through the pupil. (3)

chromosomes   Microscopic, rodlike units of the male sperm and the female ovum that contain the genes. (6)

chunking   Organization of material in such a way as to include more items of information per unit; see also *chunks of information*. (8)

chunks of information   Memory units that result from recoding or integrating more elementary units. (8)

circadian rhythm   Biological cycle that governs an individual's daily round of sleep and waking; see also *biological clock*. (5)

classical conditioning   A form of conditioning attributed to Pavlov in which a neutral stimulus, the conditioned stimulus (CS), is paired with an unconditioned stimulus (US), to produce a conditioned response (CR) similar to the unconditioned response (UR); primarily restricted to the acquisition of involuntary associations. (7)

claustrophobia   Fear of enclosed places. (14)

client-centered therapy   Humanistic therapy developed by Rogers, in which patients themselves set the goals, and therapists refrain from giving advice. (15)

clinical psychologist   A practitioner who holds a PhD in psychology and has had extensive training in research, psychological testing, and therapy techniques. (15)

closure   Perceptual tendency to fill in the gaps in an otherwise continuous pattern. (4)

cochlea   Principal structure of the inner ear; essentially a long, rolled-up bony tube filled with fluids that contains the basilar membrane, which stimulates the auditory receptors. (3)

coaction   Situation in which a person performs a task in the presence of others who are also engaged in a similar task. (16)

cochlear partition   Structure running the coiled-up length of the cochlea of the inner ear; on its bottom side is the basilar membrane. (3)

cocktail party effect   The ability to track a specific person's voice in a crowded, noisy room. (4)

coefficient of correlation   Numerical index of the degree of relationship between two sets of scores; value of the correlation coefficient may range from −1.00 to +1.00. (App.)

cognitive development   Processes of intellectual growth and the stages at which they come into play. (6)

cognitive economy   Principle at work in hierarchically orga-

nized memory structures; only when a property of a superordinate does not apply to a subordinate is that represented in the memory structure. (8)

cognitive learning person variables   Variables that include the individual's competencies to construct or to generate a wide variety of behaviors under various conditions. (12)

cognitive map   Representation in memory of what is where in terms of landmarks, routes or paths, and boundaries. (8)

cognitive restructuring   Approach in behavior therapy that emphasizes manipulation, or restructuring, of cognitive processes. (15)

cognitive stage   The first stage of motor learning in which learners draw on reasoning abilities and past experiences in order to learn the elements and skills of a new task; see also *associative stage, autonomous stage,* and *motor learning*. (7)

collective unconscious   What Jung defined as ''the all-controlling deposit of ancestral experience from untold millions of years, the echo of prehistoric world events in which each century adds an infinitesimally small amount of variation and differentiation''; these ancient memories take the form of archetypes. (12)

color blindness   A hereditary visual disability generally characterized by some abnormality of the cones of the retina or their pigmentation. (3)

color constancy   Tendency to perceive the colors of an object as constant whether in bright or dim light; see also *brightness constancy, perceptual constancy, shape constancy,* and *size constancy*. (4)

color spindle   A mechanism that visually represents the relationship among hue, brightness, and saturation of color. (3)

commissures   Several bands of nerve fibers that connect the cerebral hemispheres. (2)

comparison level   Level of outcome you expect or feel you deserve in any interaction; determines the degree of satisfaction attained in a relationship; see also *comparison level for alternatives*. (17)

comparison level for alternatives   The make-or-break-factor in a relationship that depends on the alternative relationships available; if the comparison level of the present relationship falls below the comparison level for the alternatives, the relationship will break up; see also *comparison level*. (17)

complementarity   Meshing of people's different needs in such a way that each is satisfied. (16)

complex cells   One of three types of feature detector cells in the visual cortex that are sensitive to a line or edge at a given orientation but also respond to an edge or line at any place in their receptive field; see also *feature detectors, hypercomplex cells,* and *simple cells*. (4)

concentrative meditation   Meditation in which alteration of consciousness is sought through detachment from both the external environment and internal thought processes. (5)

concept   Properties or relationships common to a class of objects or ideas. (7)

concept learning   A way of ordering experience and perceptions of the world in order to grasp the important similarities between things while ignoring the irrelevant details. (7)

concrete operational period   In Piaget's theory, the period from about age 7 to age 11 during which children display a logical organization of thought and can perform mental operations of actions that previously had to be carried out in actuality. (6)

conditioned response (CR) In classical conditioning, a response elicited by some initially neutral stimulus, the conditioned stimulus (CS), as a result of pairing between that conditioned stimulus and an unconditioned stimulus (US); similar but usually not identical to the original unconditioned response; see also *classical conditioning*. (7)

conditioned stimulus (CS) In classical conditioning, the neutral stimulus that comes to elicit the desired response through pairing with the unconditioned stimulus; see also *classical conditioning*. (7)

conditions of worth According to Rogers, behaviors and experiences that a person perceives others as valuing rather than as being intrinsically valued. (12)

cones Light-sensitive receptor cells of the retina that convert light into neural signals; they function principally in bright illumination and detect true colors as well as black and white; see also *rods*. (3)

conformity Situation in which an individual changes judgments or behavior as a result of exposure to the ideas and judgments of a group. (16)

conscious mental activity Freud's term for all those thoughts and feelings that are being experienced at the moment, which represent only a small fraction of mental life; see also *preconscious mental activity* and *unconscious mental activity*. (12)

consonance Occurs when the frequencies of two tones are sufficiently different to be heard as distinct sounds; see also *dissonance*. (3)

constituent analysis Breaking a sentence down into its various components in order to identify the phrase structure rules that characterize a particular language. (9)

context A determinant in impression formation; we learn facts about people in the context, or light, of other information. (17)

context-conditioned variation The characteristic of the speech signal that causes perception of particular syllables to vary, depending on the contexts provided by the individual phonemes. (9)

continuity Perceptual tendency to see elements in interesting patterns as being grouped together. (4)

continuous reinforcement In operant conditioning, the schedule of reinforcement in which an operant response is reinforced at every occurrence of the response. (7)

control group In experiments, a group of subjects that do not receive the conditions being studied; group used as a source of comparison to be certain the experimental group is being affected by the independent variable and not other factors. (1)

convergence A cue for binocular vision that results from the angle formed by the convergence of the two eyes as they pivot inward to focus on a single object. (4)

cornea Transparent, tissuelike coating of the front of the eye. (3)

corollary discharge In vision, an hypothetical neural event in which perceptual mechanisms somehow compensate for the movement of our own eyes. (4)

corpus callosum Largest of the bands of nerve fibers that join the cerebral hemispheres. (2)

correlation Describes the relationship between two sets of score values; see also *negative correlation* and *positive correlation*. (App.)

correlational research Methods for analyzing relationships between variables through observation, queries, or data gathering. (1)

Cottrell's theory Modification of Zajonc's theory to suggest that it is not just the presence of an audience that arouses a person and enhances the dominant response but the presence of an audience capable of evaluating and rating the subject. (16)

counseling psychologist A practitioner who has graduate training similar to that of a clinical psychologist but typically with less emphasis on research. (15)

counterconditioning Approach in behavior therapy that aims to break the connection between a given stimulus and a classically conditioned response; see also *aversion therapy, implosive therapy,* and *systematic desensitization*. (15)

countertransference In a therapy situation, the condition that occurs when analysts respond to the hostile or seductive transference of patients with unconscious emotional reactions of their own. (15)

covert sensitization A technique in aversion therapy in which clients are asked to imagine the aversive effects of an undesirable behavior, such as heavy drinking, in order to stop the behavior. (15)

cranial nerves A set of motor and sensory nerves (effectors and receptors) serving the muscles and sense organs of the head. (2)

creativity In natural language, the ability exemplified by the inventiveness of generative processes. (9)

crisis intervention A service of community mental health programs that provides immediate help to people who are experiencing serious emotional crises by attempting to alleviate the precipitating stress and to mobilize the person's own capabilities for coping. (15)

criterion measure In test validation, the measure to which subject's score on a test can be compared. (17)

critical period Period of maximum sensitivity for learning or acquiring certain skills or behaviors. (6, 7)

cross tolerance In drug use, the situation that occurs when tolerance to one drug renders other drugs less effective; see also *tolerance*. (5)

crowding The psychological state characterized by discomfort associated with having more people around than one would prefer; see also *density*. (17)

cultural bias Issue raised as a criticism of intelligence tests for being culture-specific and favoring native speakers of the testing language. (13)

D

data Uncategorized and uncompared information; the plural of datum. (App.)

decibel Unit for measuring the relative intensity of sound. (3)

deep hypnosis State in which subjects may no longer respond to the suggestions of the hypnotist but experience, on their own, ego loss, a sense of timelessness and bliss, and other feelings removed from normal consciousness. (5)

deep structure The meaning of a sentence intended by the speaker; see also *surface structure*. (9)

defense mechanisms A range of automatic and unconscious responses brought into play by the ego in order to reduce the tension and anxiety brought on by the conflict between the id and the superego. (14)

deindividuation   Submerging of the individual into the group; common to mob behavior. (*16*)

delayed conditioning   Learning that takes place when the conditioned stimulus begins several seconds before the unconditioned stimulus and continues to the onset of the unconditioned stimulus. (*7*)

delta waves   EEG patterns that appear as the descent into deep sleep progresses. (*5*)

delusions   Strongly held beliefs not shared by others in a culture; a symptom of schizophrenia. (*14*)

dendrite   One of a neuron's three essential parts—a projection that receives impulses from other neurons and conducts them to the cell body and axon; see also *axon* and *soma*. (*2*)

density   The actual state of crowded physical conditions; see also *crowding*. (*17*)

dependent variable   In psychological research, the response being measured; under the hypothesis being tested, it is presumed to be dependent on the independent variable. (*1*)

depressant   Any drug that has a depressing effect on central nervous system activity. (*5*)

depression   Part of a cluster of disorders of mood and affect; characterized by feelings of dejection and melancholy. (*14*)

deprivation drive   Theory proposed by Lorenz, that the drive toward aggression is a deprivation drive, that is, an unsatisfied drive. (*10*)

depth of encoding   Theory that the differences between short-term and long-term memory are due to how shallowly or how deeply information is processed. (*8*)

descriptive statistics   Use of statistical methods to describe and summarize the results of research. (*App.*)

determinants of intelligence   The combination of hereditary and environmental factors that determine intelligence. (*13*)

deuteranopia   A type of color blindness caused by an absence of green-catching middle-wavelength cones. (*3*)

development   Branch of psychology concerned with the scientific study of changes that occur in individual growth, thinking and learning, and social behavior over time. (*6*)

deviance   Behavior that departs in a marked and noticeable way from accepted group norms. (*16*)

deviation IQ   The IQ determined by the 1960 Stanford-Binet test, which reflects performance relative to others of the same chronological age. (*13*)

deviation score   A number that indicates how far from the mean of a particular distribution each obtained score is located. (*App.*)

diasthesis stress model   An explanation for the origins of some forms of abnormal behavior, which suggests that some people may possess higher levels of vulnerability to stress and that this vulnerability is at least partly determined by genetic factors. (*14*)

difference threshold   The smallest difference between two stimuli that can be reliably perceived. (*3*)

direct correlation   See *positive correlation*. (*App.*)

direct reinforcement   In Bandura's social learning theory, an external reward experienced at firsthand; see also *vicarious reinforcement*. (*12*)

directional vision   The visual ability to determine accurately the direction of a stimulus. (*4*)

discounting principle   The practice of discounting disposi-

tional factors when situational causes are evident in attributing causality to behavior; see also *augmentation principle*. (*17*)

discrimination   The process of learning to respond to certain stimuli and not to others. (*7*)

discriminative stimulus   In operant conditioning, a specific stimulus that comes to control a response. (*7*)

disparity   In visual depth perception, the subtle difference resulting from the slightly different point of view of each eye. (*4*)

displacement   A defense mechanism—the shifting of an impulse directed at one person onto a substitute person or object deemed more acceptable. (*14*)

dispositional reasons   One of the categories in the attribution process by which people make judgments about the causes of other people's behavior based on the belief that something internal in the other person is responsible for the behavior; see also *situational reasons*. (*17*)

disregulation theory   Theory proposed to explain psychophysiological disorders, based on disruption of the internal regulatory system. (*14*)

dissociation   Postulated process whereby certain mental processes split off from normal consciousness and function independently, which helps explain what occurs during hypnosis; see also *hidden observer*. (*5*)

dissonance   Occurs when two tones sounded together produce a third tone, based on the difference in their frequencies, that does not harmonize with the fundamental tones sounded thus producing a "rough" or "harsh" sound; see also *consonance*. (*3*)

dopamine hypothesis   Theory that dopamine, a neurotransmitter known to be involved in the fine control of certain muscle movements, may, when present in excess, cause symptoms of schizophrenia. (*14*)

dorsal root ganglia   A group of cells containing sensory cell bodies situated just outside the spinal cord. (*3*)

double-blind technique   Safeguard in drug experiments when neither the experimenter nor the subject knows which group is getting the drug and which is getting the inert substance or placebo. (*1*)

dream analysis   See *dream interpretation*. (*15*)

dream censorship   According to Freudian theory, a masking of the real meaning of dreams (latent content) because the meaning would be unacceptable to the patient's conscious standards of morality. (*15*)

dream interpretation   Method employed by Freud, Jung, and others to explore the unconscious; closely related to free association; patients report their dreams, which are analyzed by the psychoanalyst for manifest and latent content; see also *manifest content* and *latent content*. (*12*)

drive-reduction theory   A theory, that claims that all behavior is motivated by the need to eliminate or satisfy a biological drive. (*10*)

drives   Hypothetical internal states produced by a small number of primary biological needs such as water or food. (*10*)

dura mater   Heavy and leathery membrane that forms the outermost layer of the three meninges surrounding the central nervous system. (*2*)

dyad   A two-person relationship—the smallest social unit. (*17*)

E

eardrum   A taut membrane in the ear that vibrates rhythmically with the cycle of pressure and rarefaction from sound waves. (*3*)

echoic memory   An auditory memory trace, or the persisting aftereffects of stimuli, of very short duration similar to the visual, or iconic trace. (*8*)

ectomorph   One of Sheldon's somatotypes—describes those whose physiques are thin and fragile; see also *endomorph* and *mesomorph*. (*12*)

EEG   Acronym for electroencephalograph. (*5*)

effectors   Muscles and glands. (*2*)

efferent nerves   Nerve fibers that carry messages from the brain, down the spinal cord, to the effectors, or muscles and glands. (*2*)

effort justification   Notion that people like what they have chosen to suffer for. (*16*)

ego psychologists   Psychologists, including Horney, Fromm, and Erikson, who followed Freud but departed from strict psychoanalytical thought in believing that the conscious ego was more important in shaping personality than the instinctual drives of the id. (*12*)

eidetic imagery   A relatively rare form of memory characterized by extreme vividness of detail in recall; commonly referred to as photographic memory. (*8*)

Electra complex   According to Freud, a conflict that arises among females during the phallic stage when they blame the mother for their own lack of a prominant exterior sex organ; see also *Oedipus complex*. (*12*)

electroconvulsive therapy   A form of biological treatment principally used in cases of severe depression in which a brief electric current is sent through the brain to produce a convulsive seizure; also called shock treatment. (*15*)

electroencephalograph (EEG)   Instrument that records gross electrical activity in the brain. (*5*)

electromagnetic spectrum   Entire range of wavelengths or frequencies of electromagnetic radiation. (*3*)

embedded construction   A sentence within which another sentence is enclosed or "embedded". (*9*)

emotion   Any strong feeling consisting of both a mental, or cognitive, and a physiological component. (*10*)

empiricism   A philosophy, proposed by John Locke, that stresses experience of the world as the source of all knowledge. (*1*)

encoding   Extraction of information from events we experience under the conditions that the events are experienced. (*8*)

encounter group   A form of group therapy, group members are encouraged to relate intimately with one another and to express themselves more fully than in ordinary interpersonal interactions. (*15*)

endomorph   One of Sheldon's somatotypes—describes those whose physiques tend to softness and roundness; see also *ectomorph* and *mesomorph*. (*12*)

ensemble code   A theory of visual perception that proposes that the firing of various combinations of the same set of nerve cells should signify different perceptions. (*4*)

epigenetic landscape   One model for portraying the relationship between genetically determined and paced factors and the interaction between the developing organism and its environment; depicts the biological control of development in terms of constraints of varying strengths. (*6*)

episodic memory   Memory of spatial and temporal aspects of experiences that are of a highly autobiographical nature; see also *semantic memory*. (*8*)

escape learning   Form of learning in which an acquired response removes an organism from a painful stimulus; reinforcement consists of the reduction or cessation of an aversive stimulus. (*7*)

estrogen   One of the primary steroids (gonadal hormones) produced in the female's ovaries. (*11*)

estrus   In mammalian mammals, period in which the female of the species is sexually receptive (in heat). (*11*)

ethologists   Scientists who study animals in their natural environments. (*7*)

evoked potential   The brain's responses to sudden changes in stimuli, as measured by an electroencephalograph, that have been found to correlate with IQ scores from traditional tests; a technique used in neurometrics; see also *neurometrics*. (*13*)

excessive stimulation   The "overloading" of our cognitive capacities. (*17*)

excitatory neurotransmitter   Neurotransmitter serves to encourage the firing of a nerve impulse; see also *inhibitory neurotransmitter* and *neurotransmitter*. (*2*)

expressive traits   Particular styles of behavior as defined by Allport in his trait theory of personality; see also *adaptive traits*. (*12*)

extinction   Weakening of a conditioned response by continuous presentation of the conditioned stimulus without the unconditioned stimulus. (*7*)

extraversion   One of the major dimensions of personality proposed by Eysenck; extraverts are more sociable, lively, and excitable than introverts; see also *introversion*. (*12*)

F

factor analysis   Statistical method that defines the common components or dimensions underlying various tests or measures. In order to find commonalities that run through all or some of the tests. (*13*)

familiarity   Factor in interpersonal attraction—we tend to see frequently and become familiar with people who live nearby; see also *propinquity*. (*16*)

family therapy   Form of therapy that involves several members of the family in the treatment process; based on the belief that the dynamics of family interaction may be responsible for the symptoms of an individual; see also *group therapy*. (*15*)

feature detectors   Nerve cells of the visual cortex that respond to specific linear features of shape or orientation in their receptive fields; see also *complex cells; hypercomplex cells,* and *simple cells.* (*4*)

Fechner's law   The assertion that the relationship between stimulus intensity and the strength of sensation is a logarithmic one in which a constant ratio of stimulus produces a constant difference in sensation. (*3*)

feeding center   Term used to describe the role of the lateral

hypothalamus as an appetite activator that signals the need to eat; see also *satiety center*. (*10*)

figure-ground relationship   The differentiation of the visual field into a part (the figure) that stands out from the remainder (the ground). (*4*)

fine motor skills   Small body movements, such as drawing, that are difficult for very young children to master; see also *gross motor skills*. (*6*)

fissure of Rolando   See *central fissure*. (*2*)

fissure of Sylvius   See *laternal fissure*. (*2*)

fissures   Folds and grooves in the gray matter of nerve cells that make up the brain's cerebral cortex. (*2*)

fixations   According to Freud, those motives, aims, or drives that may be frozen, or fixated, early in childhood, remaining in the unconscious and shaping behavior throughout life. (*12*)

fixed-interval (FI) schedule   Schedule of reinforcement in which reinforcement depends on a lapse of a specified amount of time instead of the organism's behavior; see also *fixed-ratio schedule, variable-interval schedule,* and *variable-ratio schedule*. (*7*)

fixed-ratio (FR) schedule   Schedule of reinforcement in which reinforcement is given only after a specific number of responses have been made; see also *fixed-interval schedule, variable-interval schedule,* and *variable-ratio schedule*. (*7*)

follicle-stimulating hormone (FSH)   One of the two protein hormones, called gonadotropins, that is manufactured and released into the bloodstream by the pituitary gland and that is essential for release of spermatozoa from the testes and eggs from the ovaries; see also *luteinizing hormone*. (*11*)

formal operational period   In Piaget's theory, the fourth and final stage of cognitive development during which young people extend the ability to reason logically to abstract matters. (*6*)

fovea   Area in the center of the retina containing cones and no rods; daylight vision is most acute in the fovea. (*3*)

free association   A method for delving into the unconscious used in psychoanalysis in which clients are instructed to give their thoughts complete freedom and to report all the daydreams, feelings, and images that flash through their minds no matter how incoherent or meaningless they might seem. (*12*)

frequency   One of the physical properties of sound that measures the number of sound waves per second noted in units called hertzes (Hz); see also *amplitude* and *phase*. (*3*)

frequency distribution   A technique for showing, either in tabular or in graphic form, the way in which the frequency of actually obtained scores is distributed over the range of possible score values. (*App.*)

frequency theory   Theory of how the ear codes pitch, which proposes that the pitch we hear is determined by the frequency of the firing of nerve impulses in the auditory nerve fibers; see also *place theory*. (*3*)

frontal lobe   A lobe in each cerebral hemisphere of the brain that contains the motor cortex, which helps control voluntary movements. (*2*)

frustration-aggression hypothesis   Theory that aggression is always a consequence of frustration which results from people being prevented from reaching goals or engaging in desired activities. (*10*)

functional analysis   One of the techniques used in operant therapy with children in which the therapist visits the home to observe the child's behavior and the parents' unwitting reinforcement policies, notes correlations, and then devises a strategy to help parents reinforce desired behaviors. (*15*)

functional fixedness   The inability to recognize the various possible uses of an object beyond its conventional uses. (*8*)

functionalism   Early school of psychological thought that was concerned with the use of the mind rather than its contents. (*1*)

functional psychoses   Psychoses, such as schizophrenia, for which there is no known single cause and which are not the consequence of disease or brain damage; see also *organic psychoses*. (*14*)

funiculi   A butterfly-shaped gray mass in the spinal cord made up of nerve cell bodies surrounded by white nerve fibers of afferent and efferent nerves. (*2*)

G

g factor   See *mental facility*. (*13*)

gain-loss theory   Theory of interpersonal attraction that holds that we like someone better if the other person first dislikes us and then likes us, than if the person had liked us all along. (*16*)

ganglia   Groups of nerve cells that, along with fiber tracts lying outside of the central nervous system, make up the peripheral nervous system. (*2*)

ganglion cells   Third layer of the retina; fibers of which bundle together to form the optic nerve. (*3*)

general anesthesia   Loss of sensation accompanied by loss of consciousness. (*5*)

generation of variation   A part of the evolutionary process that ascribes variations among members of a species to a number of mechanisms, one of which is genetic differences; see also *natural selection*. (*10*)

generative processes   Mental programs for cognitive activities, such as thinking, reasoning, or remembering, that are similar to motor programs. (*8*)

generator potential   Depolarization of a receptor cell in response to a stimulus. (*3*)

genes   The basic units of hereditary transmission that contain the complex mucleic acid known as DNA, which provides the primary hereditary information and controls. (*6*)

genital stage   According to Freud, the period of early adolescence, in which the self-oriented erotic concerns of the first three stages of development are directed outward onto other persons, usually of the opposite sex; see also *anal stage, oral stage,* and *phallic stage*. (*11, 12*)

genotype   Characteristics that an individual has inherited and will transmit to his or her descendants whether or not the individual manifests those characteristics; see also *phenotype*. (*6*)

Gestalt psychology   German school of psychology that emphasizes the wholeness and organization of mental experience. (*1*)

glia   See *neuroglia*. (*2*)

gonadotropins   Two types of protein hormones—the luteinizing hormone and the follicle-stimulating hormone—both of which are essential for release of spermatozoa and eggs from the gonads and are manufactured and released by the pituitary gland. (*11*)

gonads   Reproductive organs—the ovaries of the female and the testes of the male. (*11*)

grammar The set of syntactic rules that describes any particular language. *(9)*

grandmother cell A hypothetical visual processing mechanism that postulates the existence of specific cells that are the neural equivalents of specific perceptions and that would be able to recognize all the features that add up to a particular pattern, such as your grandmother and only fires at optimal frequency when it recognizes that specific pattern. *(4)*

gross motor skills Large body movements, such as running and jumping, that improve dramatically between the ages of two and six; see also *fine motor skills*. *(6)*

group stereotypes The categorizing of other people by seeing them as members of groups and perceiving each group as having special and identifying characteristics. *(17)*

group therapy A form of therapy, using many techniques including psychodrama, sensitivity training groups, encounter groups, and family therapy, in which a therapist works with a group of up to a dozen patients at one time to help them work together in solving problems; see also *encounter groups, family therapy, psychodrama,* and *sensitivity training groups*. *(15)*

growth spurt A rapid period of physical growth that is the first readily observable sign of the onset of puberty. *(6)*

H

hallucinations Sensations not experienced by others—seeing, hearing, or smelling things that do not actually exist but are perceived as being real; a symptom of schizophrenia. *(14)*

hallucinogens Agents or substances that induce hallucinations or dreams. *(5)*

heritability A concept that relates to the measurement of the degree to which the variation in a particular trait for a particular population is due to genetic factors as opposed to other factors, presumably environmental; measures of heritability in characteristics such as intelligence are applied to specific groups under specific sets of circumstances. *(13)*

hertz (Hz) Unit employed to measure the frequency of sound waves; one hertz denotes one cycle per second. *(3)*

hidden observer Term used by Hilgard to describe the concealed level of awareness operating during hypnosis; see also *dissociation*. *(5)*

hierarchy of needs A concept, postulated by Maslow to explain personality development as occurring in a positive growth-oriented experience that proceeds in a progression in which the lower needs in the hierarchy must be satisfied before those above can be satisfied. *(12)*

higher-order conditioning Type of classical conditioning in which a new stimulus comes to elicit the conditioned response as a result of being paired with an effective conditioned stimulus, which serves as the unconditioned stimulus in the new conditioning situation. *(7)*

hippocampus Seahorse-shaped structure in the limbic system that is involved in learning, memory, and motivation. *(2)*

holophrastic speech Children's first meaningful utterances, which consist of single words—mainly nouns and adjectives. *(9)*

homeostasis Term describing an organism's tendency to maintain its internal environment at a constant level. *(12)*

homosexuality Sexual preference for members of the same sex. *(11)*

homunculus The little man that can be drawn by mapping the organization of the motor cortex, the neighboring points of which faithfully represent neighboring regions of the body. *(2)*

horizontal cells Cells of the inner nuclear layer of the retina that organize information coming from the rods and cones and transmit it to the ganglion cells; see also *bipolar cells* and *amacrine cells*. *(3)*

hormones Chemicals manufactured by the various endocrine glands and released into the bloodstream that play a major role in bodily function and behavior particularly sexual behavior. *(11)*

hue The psychological attribute of color that is usually referred to as color itself; see also *brightness* and *saturation*. *(3)*

humanistic therapy A form of therapy that is based on treating patients as integrated wholes rather than as conflict-ridden combinations of id, ego, and superego impulses and that takes an optimistic view of the human potential for growth. *(15)*

hypercomplex cells One of the three types of feature detector cells in the visual cortex, one class of which responds to a line anywhere in the visual field but only if the edge has a specific length as well as orientation; see also *complex cells, feature detectors,* and *simple cells*.

hyperphagia A disorder characterized by excessive appetite, seemingly without satiation. *(10)*

hyperpolarization Increase in the voltage outside of a nerve membrane caused by some neurotransmitters and resulting in a lessening of the likelihood that a nerve impulse will be set off. *(2)*

hypnagogic state Drowsy interval between waking and sleeping, characterized by an EEG pattern of theta waves and by brief, hallucinatory, dreamlike experiences that resemble vivid still photographs. *(5)*

hypnosis A temporary trancelike state of consciousness characterized by high suggestibility, easy access to mental imagery and imagination, decline of the conscious planning function, and reduction in reality testing. *(5)*

hypothalamus A small structure located at the top of the brain stem that governs the autonomic nervous system and the pituitary gland, and hence is involved in the regulation of body temperature, appetite, thirst, and sexual activities. *(2)*

hypothesis Tentative theory or supposition adopted provisionally to account for certain facts and to guide in the investigation of other facts. *(1)*

hypovolemic thirst One of two systems of thirst that results from loss of blood and thus of extracellular fluid; see also *osmotic thirst*. *(10)*

I

icon A visual memory trace, or the persisting aftereffects of stimuli, that has a relatively large storage capacity but a duration of not more than one second; also called iconic trace. *(8)*

iconic trace See *icon*. *(8)*

identity One of two categories of visual skills characterized by the ability to distinguish classes of objects, for example, a triangle from a circle; see also *unity*. *(4)*

identity crisis The conflict facing adolescents as they attempt to assimilate their own blooming sexuality and adopt the roles they will play in adult society. *(12)*

idiographic research   The long-term study of personality traits unique to a single individual. *(12)*

idiot savant   A retardate who shows superior functioning in one narrow area of mental activity. *(13)*

illusion of control   The sense of control over interactions with other people that results from attributing dispositional causes to other people's behavior, which enables us to feel that we know them and thus can predict their actions in the future. *(17)*

implosive therapy   Type of counterconditioning, a form of behavior therapy that creates a massive dose of fear in order to cause an inward explosion or implosion of anxiety and eventually to extinguish that anxiety; see also *aversion therapy* and *systematic desensitization*. *(15)*

impotence   Inability to perform coitus, generally because of failure of erection. *(11)*

impression formation   Process by which we form global impressions of people based on specific facts we have learned. *(17)*

imprinting   Process by which organisms acquire a learned attachment at a particular period in life. *(7)*

incongruence   Gap between one's actual experiences and one's self-concept that occurs when people begin to do things primarily to obtain praise from others, and the sense of self, especially one's ideal sense of self, becomes distorted and primarily shaped by others' approval. *(12)*

incus   Tiny bone of the middle ear that connects the malleus and the stapes. *(3)*

independent variable   In an experimental situation, the condition manipulated by the researcher. *(1)*

individuation   Jung's term for the lifelong process of psychological maturation. *(12)*

inferential statistics   Use of statistical methods to make inferences about the meaning of research findings. *(App.)*

inhibitory neurotransmitter   Neurotransmitter that serves to retard or discourage the firing of a nerve impulse; see also *excitatory neurotransmitter* and *neurotransmitter*. *(2)*

inner ear   That portion of the ear immediately past the oval window in which the mechanical energy of sound waves is converted into electrical energy; see also *middle ear* and *outer ear*. *(3)*

inner nuclear layer   Second layer of the retina that is made up of horizontal, bipolar, and amacrine cells. *(3)*

insight   A novel (unpracticed) solution to a task or problem that appears suddenly. *(7)*

instincts   Innate patterns of behavior. *(10)*

instrumental aggression   Aggression that is aimed at obtaining a reward—robbing a bank, for example. *(10)*

instrumental conditioning   Type of learning that uses reinforcers to change the frequency of a behavior; usually applied to situations in which the experimenter must initiate each trial that a subject experiences; see also *operant conditioning*. *(7)*

intellectual ability   Ability to master a variety of tasks requiring memory, reasoning, perception, and other abilities. *(13)*

intelligence quotient (IQ)   Measure of intelligence obtained by dividing the mental age as shown on the 1916 Stanford-Binet test by chronological age and multiplying the resulting number by 100. *(13)*

intentional social influence   Instances in which others purposefully arouse us, reinforce us, or serve as sources of information. *(16)*

interpersonal attraction   Area of study concerned with the question of why people like or dislike others. *(16)*

interposition   See *overlap*. *(4)*

interpretation   In psychodynamic therapy, the process by which the analyst tries to overcome resistance, usually by making a statement aimed at helping patients see the unconscious basis of a symptom that has been masked by resistance; see also *resistance*. *(15)*

interval scale   Type of measurement scale in which the difference in adjacent categories is the same in the number scale, examples include Farenheit and Celsius scales; see also *nominal scale, ordinal scale,* and *ratio scale*. *(App.)*

interval use of numbers   The assignment of numbers in which the unit distance between all adjacent pairs of numbers is the same; used to locate points along a dimension and to determine how far apart they are in terms of scale units; see also *nominal use of numbers, ordinal use of numbers,* and *ratio use of numbers*. *(App.)*

introversion   One of the major dimensions of personality proposed by Eysenck; introverts are quieter, more reserved, and less sociable than extraverts; see also *extraversion*. *(12)*

inverse correlation   See *negative correlation*. *(App.)*

ions   Electrically charged molecules that, in the transmission of nerve impulses, move across the membrane of an axon. *(2)*

IQ   See *intelligence quotient*. *(13)*

iris   Part of the eye surrounding the pupil that gives the eye color and serves as a diaphragm for regulating the size of the pupil and thereby the amount of light entering the eye. *(3)*

J

just noticeable difference (jnd)   A quantitative method of determining the smallest perceptible difference between stimuli. *(3)*

just-world hypothesis   Refers to the tendency to believe that the world is orderly, fair, and just and that people get the rewards and punishments they deserve. *(16)*

K

kappa-effect   Phenomenon in which the perception of experienced time and space is influenced by the manipulation of distance; see also *tau-effect*. *(4)*

kinesthesis   A general term for sensory information generated by receptor cells in the muscles, tendons, and joints that informs us of our skeletal movement. *(3)*

kin selection hypothesis   Predicts that helping behavior should be most common among closely related animals. *(10)*

L

latency period   According to Freud, the period that follows the phallic stage of psychosexual development. *(11)*

latent content   The underlying psychic material of dreams that leads to the manifest content, or specifics, of dreams; see also *manifest content*. *(12)*

latent learning   Learning that occurs without any apparent reinforcement and that is not manifest in behavior until reinforcement is introduced. (7)

latent needs   According to Murray, the needs of individuals that are reflected in fantasy, imagination, and thoughts and wishes about the world rather than in overt behavior; see also *manifest needs*. (12)

lateral fissure   Major fissure of the cerebral cortex that demarcates each hemisphere into lobes; also called the fissure of Sylvius. (2)

lateral geniculate body   Subdivision of the thalamus, the cells of which are involved in the transmission, or regulation of transmission, of visual information from the eye to the cerebral cortex. (2)

lateral inhibition   The tendency of adjacent neural elements in the visual system to inhibit each other that results in emphasizing contours or edges in what we see and in enhancing contrasts between different levels of illumination. (3)

law of effect   Thorndike's theory that in trial and error learning, the connections between a stimulus and a response are strengthened if reinforcement follows the response and weakened if the response is not followed by reinforcement. (7)

law of specific nerve energies   The principle that only one kind of sensation is transmitted over a given nerve fiber. (3)

learned helplessness   A condition created by exposure to inescapable aversive stimuli that retards or prevents learning in new situations in which escape or avoidance is possible. (7)

learning   A relatively permanent change of behavior that results from prior experience. (7)

learning perspective   Idea that conditioning is responsible for behavior—that normal and abnormal behavior represent responses to stimuli and events in the environment; see also *social perspective*. (14)

Learning Potential Assessment Device   A test-teach-test technique for measuring a child's learning potential. (13)

learning potential tests   Tests that measure the gap between children's present capabilities and their future potential; see also *zone of proximal development*. (13)

lens   Transparent structure in the eye that changes shape to focus the optic array on the retina at the back of the eye. (3)

lexical ambiguity   The characteristic of language that allows the assignment of different meanings to the same word. (9)

libido   According to Freud, the general source of sexual instincts, residing in the id. (12)

lightness constancy   Tendency to perceive an object's brightness as stable over a wide range of illumination; see also *color constancy, perceptual constancy, shape constancy,* and *size constancy*. (4)

limbic system   Ringlike structure located at the top of the brain stem that includes the *amygdala, the hippocampus,* and the *septal region* and is involved, along with the hypothalamus, in intense emotions such as anger, fear, and pleasure. (2)

linear perspective   One of the monocular cues for perceiving depth in which parallel lines seem to converge at a distant spot known as the vanishing point. (4)

linguistic competence   Implicit knowledge that language uses have of the syntactic rules that allow them both to produce and to understand an infinite number of utterances; see also *linguistic performance*. (9)

linguistic determinism   Theory that all higher levels of thinking are dependent on language or that language determines thought; see also *linguistic relativism*. (9)

linguistic performance   Constraints on language users, including a finite life span and the limits of short-term memory, that limit the capacity for generating an infinite number of utterances; see also *linguistic competence*. (9)

linguistic relativism   Theory that speakers of different languages perceive and experience the world differently; see also *linguistic determinism*. (9)

linguistic universals   Syntactic rules common to all languages. (9)

lobes   Distinct regions in each hemisphere of the cerebral cortex. (2)

local anesthetics   Pain-blocking drugs used at the site of the source of pain to produce analgesia. (5)

localization   Theory that many aspects of behavior can be traced to specific regions of the brain. (2)

longitudinal studies   Research in which the behavior of the same subjects is investigated over a long period of time. (1)

long-term memory (LTM)   Organized store of general information of knowledge about the world as well as programs and rules for carrying out overt behaviors and mental action sequences; see also *sensory memory* and *short-term memory*. (8)

luteinizing hormone (LH)   One of two protein hormones called gonadotropins, that is manufactured and released into the bloodstream by the pituitary gland and that is essential for release of spermatozoa and eggs from the gonads—the testes and ovaries; these hormones are called gonadotropins; see also *follicle-stimulating hormone*. (11)

M

Mach bands   A device used to demonstrate the phenomenon of lateral inhibition in which an observer perceives a narrow bright band on the lighter side of the boundary between two areas of markedly different light intensities and a narrow darker band on the other side even though the light intensity is unchanged. (3)

major hemisphere   Obsolete label applied to the brain's left hemisphere at a time when the right hemisphere was thought to have only a limited role in brain functioning; see also *minor hemisphere*. (2)

major tranquilizers   Drugs, such as chlorpromazine and the other phenothiazines, used to alleviate extreme symptoms of agitation and hyperactivity; see also *minor tranquilizers*. (15)

male climacteric   Term used to describe symptoms experienced by men in late middle age that are similar to those found in female menopause and that are related to loss of testosterone. (11)

malleus   Tiny bone of the middle ear that is attached to the eardrum at one end and the incus at the other. (3)

manic episodes   One of the disorders of mood and affect characterized by intense episodes of elation. (14)

manifest content   Remembered content of a dream, including the characters and their actions; see also *latent content*. (12)

manifest needs   According to Murray, the needs of individuals that may be observed in overt behavior; see also *latent needs*. (12)

mean   See *arithmetic mean*. (App.)

meninges   Membranes lying directly under the skull, surrounding the central nervous system; see also *arachnoid, dura mater,* and *pia mater.* (2)

median   The measure of central tendency that represents the middlemost value in a distribution of scores; see also *mean* and *mode.* (*App.*)

mediated interference   One of the factors that makes memories difficult to retrieve, which occurs when some desired response from memory is blocked by another response because both responses are linked to a common mediational concept. (8)

medulla   The lowest part of the brain stem that contains all ascending and descending tracts interconnecting the brain and the spinal cord. (2)

memory   The brain's ability to recreate or reproduce past experience and thoughts. (8)

menopause   The permanent cessation of menstruation that occurs in women during their late forties or early fifties and is marked by a sharp decrease in sex hormones. (*11*)

mental facility   Term used by Spearman to refer to the unity of the intellect or general intelligence; also called the *g* factor; see also *specific mental capability.* (13)

mental retardation   According to the current manual of the American Association on Mental Deficiency (AAMD), "significantly subaverage general intellectual functioning existing concurrently with deficits in adaptive behavior." (13)

mesomorph   One of Sheldon's somatotypes—describes those whose physiques are primarily sturdy and muscular; see also *ectomorph* and *endomorph.* (12)

method of contrast   Procedure in classical conditioning used to produce discrimination among similar stimuli by continuously presenting the unconditioned stimulus only after a particular conditioned stimulus and not after other, similar stimuli. (7)

midbrain   The part of the brain that contains a large number of nerve fibers, which connect structures above and below it. (2)

middle ear   That portion of the ear that contains three tiny bones called ossicles, which amplify the vibrations of the eardrum and pass them along to the inner ear; see also *inner ear* and *outer ear.* (3)

mild retardation   One of the levels of retardation characterized by IQ scores of 52 to 67 on the Stanford-Binet—children are eligible for classes for the educable mentally retarded, and adults can usually work in unskilled jobs; see also *moderate retardation, profound retardation,* and *severe retardation.* (13)

mind-body problem   Complex issue relating to how the mind affects the behavior of the body and how the body affects the behavior of the mind. (5)

mindfulness meditation   Form of meditation in which the meditator focuses on both internal and external stimuli in order to observe thoughts and impressions with complete detachment. (5)

minor hemisphere   Obsolete label applied to the brain's right hemisphere at a time when the left hemisphere was thought to have a major role in brain functioning; see also *major hemisphere.* (2)

minor tranquilizers   Drugs, such as the benzodiazepines (Librium, Valium), that are usually prescribed for patients who suffer anxiety or psychosomatic disorders; see also *major tranquilizers.* (15)

mirroring technique   One form of psychodrama in which one member of the group plays another member, giving that individual the opportunity to see himself or herself as others do; see also *psychodrama.* (15)

mnemonics   Devices, plans, and tricks that facilitate memory. (8)

mode   The measure of central tendency that represents the score that occurs most often in a distribution of scores; see also *mean* and *median.* (*App.*)

modeling   Approach in behavior therapy formulated by Bandura in which the patient unlearns anxiety about a given stimulus by watching the therapist perform a behavior and then imitating it. (15)

moderate retardation   One of the levels of retardation characterized by IQ scores of 36 to 51 on the Stanford-Binet—children are eligible for classes for trainable retardates that emphasize self-care, and few adults hold jobs; see also *mild retardation, profound retardation,* and *severe retardation.* (13)

monochromats   People who suffer from an extreme and rare form of color blindness, characterized by very poor visual acuity and extreme sensitivity to even moderate levels of light. (3)

monocular cues   Cues for visual depth perception that require the use of only one eye. (4)

monogamy   The practice of having only one mate at a time, which is common among human beings and many other animals. (*11*)

moral development   Growth of the ability to distinguish between right and wrong. (6)

morpheme   The smallest combination of speech sounds that have meaning. (9)

motion parallax   One of the monocular cues for perceiving depth, which relates to the difference in the apparent rate of movement of objects at different distances and depends on the observer's position (when the head moves, close objects appear to move faster than far objects). (4)

motivation   Those forces or influences that provide incentives for behavior. (10)

motive   An inferred process (desire, need, drive, or emotion) within people that consciously or unconsciously propels them toward specific goals. (10)

motor cortex   The part of the cerebral cortex that controls body movements. (2)

motor learning   Distinct variety of learning that involves the learning of a sequence of highly coordinated responses that are systematically related to one another and integrally related. (7)

motor program   The result of motor learning that occurs once a skill becomes automatic, and the learner has established a sequence of highly coordinated movements that are integrated in time and characterized by a rhythmic structure of their own. (7)

muscle spindles   Specialized receptors located within voluntary muscles that contain sensory nerve endings, which signal to the spinal cord and the brain when a muscle is stretched. (3)

myelin   Sheath of fatty white substance that insulates the axons of many neurons and prevents the free passage of sodium and potassium ions across each adjacent patch of membrane during an action potential. (2)

myotonia   Increased muscle tone and contractions that are part of the physiology of human sexual responses; see also *vasocongestion*. (*11*)

N

naming   Verbal rehearsal process used in encoding information into short-term memory. (*8*)

nanometer   Unit measurement of the wavelengths of light, equivalent to one billionth of a meter. (*3*)

narcolepsy   Disorder characterized by uncontrollable seizures of sleep during waking hours. (*5*)

narcotic analgesics   Drugs, such as the opium derivatives morphine and heroin, that ease pain while inducing significant elevation of mood. (*5*)

natural selection   A part of the evolutionary process in which animals that are better equipped to survive leave more offspring; see also *generation of variation*. (*10*)

nature-nurture controversy   Debate over which factor is more influential in development, nature—factors based on the genetic endowment of the organism—or nurture—factors based on the previous experience of the organism. (*6*)

needs   Physical states involving lacks or deficits such as hunger and thirst. (*10*)

negative afterimage   Phenomenon in which a visual stimulus persists (briefly), but in a reversed state; chromatic and black-and-white effects are reversed; see also *positive afterimage*. (*3*)

negative correlation   Relationship between two variables in which a high rank on one goes with a low rank on the other; see also *positive correlation*. (*App.*)

negative reinforcement   Results when a response leads to removal of an aversive stimulus or negative reinforcer and, therefore, increases the probability that the desired behavior will be performed. (*7*)

negatively skewed distribution   Distribution of scores in which extreme scores appear at the lower end; see also *positively skewed distribution*. (*App.*)

neonate   A newborn infant. (*6*)

nerve impulse   An electrically measured stimulus that travels down the axon of the neuron usually in a direction away from the cell body and is the nervous system's basic means of communication. (*2*)

nerves   Bundles of axons from separate cell bodies traveling together. (*2*)

nervous system   All of the nerve cells in the body and all of their supporting cells. (*2*)

neuroglia   Myelin-producing cells of the central nervous system; also called the glia; see also *phagocytes Schwann cells*. (*2*)

neurology   The study of the brain and the nervous system. (*14*)

neurometrics   New branch of intelligence testing that focuses on reactions within the brain and the body rather than on such responses as verbal answers. (*13*)

neuron doctrine   Fundamental principle of neuroanatomy, which states that the nervous system is made up of cells called neurons, and they interact by making contact with one another. (*2*)

neurons   Cells that make up the nervous system. (*2*)

neurotransmitter   Chemical released by the synaptic vesicles of a neuron through which electrical activity in one neuron is communicated to the next nerve cell in the pathway; see also *excitatory neurotransmitter* and *inhibitory neurotransmitter*. (*2*)

nodes of Ranvier   Gaps, or nodes, at which the axon of a myelinated neuron is bare of protective myelin; the only places in a myelinated axon at which an action potential can occur. (*2*)

nominal scale   A measurement scale representing unordered classification of information; see also *interval scale, ordinal scale,* and *ratio scale*. (*App.*)

nominal use of numbers   The assignment of numbers merely as labels for purposes of identification; see also *interval use of numbers, ordinal use of numbers,* and *ratio use of numbers*. (*App.*)

nomothetic research   Testing of many people with a limited battery of measures to discover whether there is substantial individual variation in a characteristic. (*12*)

normal distribution   Bell-shaped distribution of scores with most scores occurring near the mean value and with both halves having the same shape. (*App.*)

normal waking consciousness   State of consciousness in which an individual maintains maximum alertness to the external environment. (*5*)

O

obesity   Condition of being overweight. (*10, 12*)

object permanence   Term used by Piaget to refer to a child's realization that an object continues to exist even if it is hidden from view. (*6*)

observational method   Research technique in which psychologists observe the behavior of subjects in a systematic, objective, and precise manner. (*1*)

occipital lobe   Lobe in each cerebral hemisphere of the brain that contains the visual cortex, which processes the sensations of light. (*2*)

Oedipus complex   According to Freud, a conflict that arises among males during the phallic stage when they wish to possess the mother and displace the father; see also *Electra complex*. (*12*)

olfactory bulbs   Structures vital to the sense of smell that receive sensory information from receptors in the nasal cavity and are connected to the olfactory cortex of the brain. (*3*)

operant behavior   Any behavior that operates on or has an effect on the environment. (*7*)

operant conditioning   Type of learning in which the subject has to operate on the environment in order to produce a particular consequence such as obtaining food; usually applied to situations in which a subject is freely able to respond; see also *instrumental conditioning*. (*7*)

operant level   Frequency of an operant response, such as bar pressing, prior to conditioning or any reinforcement training. (*7*)

operant techniques   Approach in behavior therapy that uses positive and negative reinforcement to shape, or modify, behavior. (*15*)

operational definition   A definition that explains something in such a way that it can be measured and tested by others. (*1*)

opponent process theory   Mechanism in the retina and visual pathways through which cells appear to code opposing colors by increasing or decreasing their rate of firing. (*3*)

opposing colors   Certain pairs of colors (blue and yellow and red and green) that when combined cancel each other out and appear gray. *(3)*

optic chiasma   Point behind the eyes where the bundled fibers of the two optic nerves meet and cross over before reaching the brain. *(3)*

optic nerve   The axons of the retinal ganglion cells; connects the eye to the brain. *(3)*

optimization theory   An approach to the study of the adaptiveness of behavior, which proposes that the behavior of animals is organized to achieve some biologically significant goal. *(10)*

oral personality   According to Freud's psychodynamic theory of personality development, the type of personality that results when a child becomes fixated in the oral stage; often characterized by oral aggression expressed through verbal hostility and feelings of deprivation or even gullibility; see also *retentive personality. (12)*

oral stage   According to Freud, the first stage of psychosexual development during which sexual energy of the libido is orally focused; see also *anal stage, genital stage,* and *phallic stage. (11, 12)*

ordinal scale   A measurement scale that orders or ranks information; see also *interval scale, nominal scale,* and *ratio scale. (App.)*

ordinal use of numbers   Assignment of numbers on the basis of a rank order or preference; see also *interval use of numbers, nominal use of numbers,* and *ratio use of numbers. (App.)*

organic psychoses   Psychoses that occur as the consequence of a specific disease, such as syphilis, or from brain damage and that are characterized by definable changes in the central nervous system; see also *functional psychoses. (14)*

organ of Corti   The actual receptor for hearing, located in the inner ear attached to the basilar membrane and consisting of thousands of receptor cells with project fine, hairlike fibers, the bending of which converts the mechanical energy of sound waves into electrical energy. *(3)*

orienting reflex   In classical conditioning, an initial response including turning and looking attentive, to a new stimulus. *(7)*

osmoreceptors   Cells in the anterior portion of the hypothalamus that are apparently uniquely sensitive to the minute changes in volume that are associated with cellular dehydration and that stimulate drinking as well as signal the pituitary gland to increase production of antidiuretic hormone. *(10)*

osmosis   Tendency of fluids to equalize concentrations of solutes on both sides of a semipermeable membrane. *(10)*

osmotic thirst   One of two systems of thirst that results from cell dehydration due to osmosis; see also *hypovolemic thirst. (10)*

oval window   Membrane that transmits vibrations from the middle ear to the inner ear. *(3)*

overjustification   Phenomenon in which a reward provides too large an external justification for performing a behavior. *(16)*

overlap   One of the monocular cues for perceiving depth, also called interposition, in which things appear nearer that partially obscure other things behind them. *(4)*

P

pacing genes   Genes that set the pace for emerging systems of development, such as motor coordination, that are characterized by the gradual appearance of different behaviors at different ages. *(6)*

pair bond   Joining of two partners in a monogamous relationship. *(11)*

papillae   Dark red spots on the tongue that contain the primary sensory organs for detecting taste. *(3)*

parallel transmission   An aspect of speech; information about the consonant and the vowel is transmitted at the same time. *(9)*

parasympathetic nervous system   One of two parts of the autonomic nervous system, which tends to conserve bodily resources; see also *sympathetic nervous system. (2)*

parietal lobe   Lobe in each cerebral hemisphere of the brain that monitors such sensations as pressure on the skin, heat and cold, and awareness of the location of the body's limbs. *(2)*

parietal lobe syndrome   Neurological disorder that affects half of the parietal lobe and, depending on which half, causes lack of awareness of the opposite side of the body. *(2)*

partial reinforcement   Maintenance of a conditioned operant response by a schedule of occasional as opposed to continuous reinforcement; see also *partial reinforcement effect. (7)*

partial reinforcement effect   The result of any form of partial reinforcement, which produces greater resistance to extinction and which produces the response for a longer period of time and more often without reward than continuous reinforcement; see also *partial reinforcement. (7)*

Pavlovian conditioning   Another term for classical conditioning, after the first student of the topic, Ivan Petrovich Pavlov. *(7)*

peak experiences   Term used by Abraham Maslow to describe various mysterious states of consciousness generally characterized by a sense of unity with others and the outside world, a feeling of bliss, a sense of sacredness, difficulty in describing the experience, an enhanced sense of reality, transcendence of time and space, and reconciliation of contradictory propositions. *(5)*

Pearson product-moment correlation   The most commonly used correlation method based on the index designated *r. (App.)*

penis envy   Freud's term for the anxiety at lacking a penis experienced by females during the phallic stage. *(11)*

perception   Transformation of the evidence of the senses into mental representations; see also *sensation. (4)*

perceptual adaptation   Ability to compensate for an artificially displaced visual field. *(4)*

perceptual constancy   The tendency to perceive objects as having certain stable properties, such as shape, size, brightness, and color, despite variations in physical stimuli; see also *brightness constancy, color constancy, shape constancy,* and *size constancy. (4)*

performance   Observable responses or behavior in a given task; learning is inferred from performance, but it is not the same as performance. *(7)*

peripheral nervous system   Transmits information back and forth between the various organs of the body and the central nervous system; see also *central nervous system.* (2)

personality The characteristic way in which a person thinks and behaves as he or she adapts to the environment, including visible behavior patterns as well as such less apparent characteristics as values, motives, attitudes, abilities, and self-image. (*12*)

personality disorders Patterns of behavior that appear to be deeply ingrained and are manifested primarily as exaggerations—for example, excessive neatness. (*14*)

personal unconscious According to Jung, a repository of forgotten or suppressed memories that every person has, which take the form of archetypes. (*12*)

persuasion Form of intentional social influence that aims only indirectly at changing behavior. (*16*)

phagocytes Glial cells that eat up the debris left by an injury to the brain; see also *neuroglia.* (2)

phallic stage According to Freud, the third stage of psychosexual development during which the child's erotic interests shift to the genital organs, and sexual feelings are directed toward the parent of the opposite sex; see also *anal stage, genital stage,* and *oral stage.* (*12*)

phase Relates to the precise timing of a sound wave. (*3*)

phasic events One of two classes of physiological events that occur during REM sleep, characterized by rapid eye movements and increases in various phenomena controlled by the autonomic nervous system such as pulse, respiration and blood pressure; see also *tonic events.* (*5*)

phenomenal field One of the steps in the process Rogers calls self-actualization when the child's field of experience contains a self as well as a view of others such as parents, teachers, and friends. (*12*)

phenomenological theories Theories of personality that focus on the conscious experience of the individual rather than on overt behavior or on traits or types. (*12*)

phenotype Characteristics that are exhibited by the individual organism, such as eye color, that express the individual's genetic makeup; see also *genotype.* (6)

pheromones Chemical substances secreted by many animals that influence the production of sex hormones in other members of the same species. (*11*)

phi phenomenon An illusion of apparent movement that results when two stationary light sources are alternately illuminated about 1/20 of a second apart, and the light appears to move across the space from one to the other; the basis for motion pictures. (*4*)

phobias Intense, neurotic, and irrational fears of certain objects or situations; among the most common of the anxiety disorders. (*14*)

phonemes The smallest units of sound that make a difference to the meaning of a larger sound unit such as a word. (*9*)

phonology Study of the sound patterns found in all natural languages. (*9*)

phosphene A flash of light that occurs when pressure on the eye activates cells in the retina. (*4*)

phrase structure rules The rules by which sentences are generated and structured in a particular language. (*9*)

phrenology Pseudoscience based on reading the bumps of the skull in order to understand character and mental ability. (2)

physical development Changes in an individual's physiological functioning over time reflecting the process of physical maturation. (6)

pia mater Innermost of the three meninges surrounding the central nervous system. (2)

pigment epithelium A single cell lining between the rods and cones of the retina and the choroid that absorbs stray light, serves as a metabolic channel for nourishment of the receptors, and plays a role in the continuous renewal of the light-sensitive outer segments of the rods. (*3*)

pigeonhole effect The premature categorizing of young children that may result from intelligence testing that fails to take into account varying rates of intellectual growth. (*13*)

pineal Small gland attached to the top of the brain stem, which although not composed of nerve cells, serves as a regulator of body chemistry and thus influences behavior. (2)

pitch The apparent highness or lowness of a note, determined by the frequency of a sound wave. (*3*)

pituitary Small gland attached to the base of the brain just in front of the brain stem, which secretes hormones that influence a wide range of functions, from body growth to human reproduction. (2)

place theory Theory of how the ear codes pitch, which suggests that the pitch we hear depends on the place on the basilar membrane that is stimulated by the sound waves; see also *frequency theory.* (*3*)

plasticity The brain's capacity for modification through experience. (*4*)

pleasure principle According to Freud, the governing mechanism of the id, which seeks to release its biological energy in either aggressive or erotic ways; see also *reality principle.* (*4*)

pluralistic ignorance A situation that occurs when individuals in a group do not know that there are others in the group who share their feelings. (*16*)

polarization The slightly uneven distribution of electrically charged ions across the membrane of a nerve cell axon that causes the inside of the cell to be negative and the outside of the cell to be positive. (2)

polyandry Mating system of one female paired with more than one male. (*10, 11*)

polygamy Mating system of one male paired with two or more females. (*10*)

polygyny Practice found in a number of species in which one male is bonded with a number of females at the same time. (*11*)

polygentic determinism Refers to developing systems that are under the control of a number of genes. (6)

pons Arching band of nerve fibers just above the medulla at the base of the brain that controls such largely automatic functions as heart rate and respiration. (2)

Ponzo illusion The illusion of depth or distance created in two-dimensional drawing when what the viewer interprets as being parallel lines are drawn as converging lines. (*4*)

population Any group of individuals (persons, other organisms, objects, or items of data) making up the total of all possible cases from which samples may be taken for measurement. (*App.*)

positive afterimage   Phenomenon in which the perception of a visual stimulus persists in its original chromatic or black-and-white configuration; see also *negative afterimage*. (*3*)

positive correlation   Relationship between two variables in which a high rank on one goes with a high rank on the other or in which a low rank on one goes with a low rank on the other; see also *negative correlation*. (*App.*)

positively skewed distribution   Distribution of scores in which extreme scores appear at the higher end; see also *negatively skewed distribution*. (*App.*)

posthypnotic amnesia   A condition, achieved through posthypnotic suggestion, in which subjects under hypnosis forget everything that happened during hypnosis until they are signaled to remember. (*5*)

posthypnotic suggestion   A suggestion made to a person under hypnosis that he or she will feel or act in a prescribed way when no longer hypnotized. (*5*)

postsynaptic element   The dendrite of a neuron. (*2*)

preconscious mental activity   Freud's term for all those thoughts and feelings that are outside immediate awareness but easily available; see also *conscious mental activity* and *unconscious mental activity*. (*12*)

predictability hypothesis   Hypothesis that classical conditioning will not occur unless the conditioned stimulus serves as a reliable basis for predicting the occurrence of the unconditioned stimulus. (*7*)

predictive validity   Measure of a test's validity based on the correlation between test scores and some criteria of behavior the test predicted such as between scores on a scholastic aptitude test and subsequent grades in school. (*13*)

prefrontal lobotomy   A form of psychosurgery, in which a portion of the prefrontal lobe region of the brain is removed, that is used only as a last resort. (*15*)

preoperational period   In Piaget's theory, the period from about age two to age seven during which children begin to deal with the world symbolically, such as recognizing that one thing can stand for another. (*6*)

prepotent targets   Certain objects, organisms, and situations that hold some possible and actual threat to people and, therefore, from a biological viewpoint, are likely to become the foci of phobias. (*14*)

press   According to Murray, the characteristics of situations that initiate or direct behavior; see also *alpha press* and *beta press*. (*12*)

presynaptic element   The axon of a neuron. (*2*)

preterminal fibers   Fine branches at the end of the axons of some nerve cells. (*2*)

primacy-recency   A determinant in impression formation, which holds that first impressions tend to outweigh more recent ones even if the latter seem to contradict the former. (*17*)

primary mental abilities (PMAs)   Seven components of intelligence proposed by Thurstone: numerical ability, reasoning, verbal fluency, spatial relations, perception, memory, and verbal comprehension. (*13*)

primary process   According to Freud, a primitive, irrational, childlike type of thinking that is often manifested in dreams. (*5*)

primary reinforces   Those stimuli that satisfy basic physiological needs such as food, water, or shelter; see also *secondary reinforcers*. (*7, 16*)

principle of encoding specificity   A factor in memory that relates to the interactions between prior knowledge and the context of new experiences and suggests that what is encoded and stored in long-term memory depends on the context in which the encoding takes place and that retrieval is facilitated by reinstating the same context. (*8*)

proactive interference   One factor that makes memories difficult to retrieve, which occurs when material learned previously interferes with retrieval of recently learned material; see also *retroactive interference*. (*8*)

proceptivity   Sexually soliciting behavior by the female of the species. (*11*)

profound retardation   One of the levels of retardation, characterized by IQ scores of below 20 on the Stanford-Binet—individuals require total supervision and it is assumed that they can learn little except possibly to walk, utter a few phrases, and feed themselves; see also *mild retardation, moderate retardation,* and *severe retardation*. (*13*)

progesterone   One of the primary steroids (gonadal hormones) produced in the female's ovaries. (*11*)

projection   A defense mechanism—the attribution of personally unacceptable impulses to others. (*14*)

projective tests   Personality tests in which subjects reveal or ''project'' themselves through imaginative association with a stimulus; see also *Rorschach Test, Thematic Apperception Test*. (*12*)

propinquity   Factor in interpersonal attraction—we generally come to like people who happen to live or work close to us; see also *familiarity*. (*16*)

protanopia   A type of color blindness caused by the absence of red-sensitive long-wavelength cones. (*3*)

protensity   Perceived passage of time as contrasted with the duration of time. (*4*)

proximity   Perceptual tendency to see elements that are physically close to one another as belonging together. (*4*)

pyramidal tract   One of the major motor pathways in the nervous systems that projects from the cerebral cortex to the spinal cord. (*2*)

psychedelics   Drugs that typically modify the normal perceptual environment by greatly intensifying the sensory intensity of characteristics such as color and texture. (*5*)

psychoactive drugs   Chemical substances that affect mood, thought, and behavior. (*5*)

psychiatric social worker   A practitioner who holds a master's degree in social work and who has special training in treatment procedures with emphasis on the home and community. (*15*)

psychiatry   The branch of medicine concerned with mental health and mental illness. (*14*)

psychiatrist   A physician who usually has spent a post graduate residency training in psychotherapy and specializes in diagnosis and treatment of abnormal behavior. (*15*)

psychoanalysis   A form of psychotherapy, based on Freud's principle of making conscious the images, fantasies, and wishes of the patient's unconscious. (*15*)

psychoanalyst   A practitioner, usually but not always a physician, who has received specialized training at a psychoanalytic institute in the methods of therapy first developed by Sigmund Freud. (*15*)

psychodrama   A form of group therapy in which members act out their feelings as if they were performers in a play, improvising their lines; see also *mirroring technique*. (*15*)

psychodynamic approach   School of psychology based on the work of Sigmund Freud that looks beyond conscious awareness to unconscious desires and impulses. (1)

psychology The study of mind and behavior. (1)

psychometrics Branch of psychology concerned with testing of abilities, interests, traits, attitudes, and behavioral tendencies. (1)

psychophysics Branch of psychology concerned with the measurement of relationships between the physical attributes of stimuli and the resulting sensations. (3)

psychophysiological disorders A variety of body reactions that are assumed to be closely related to psychological phenomena—for example, stress. (14)

psychosexual stages According to Freud, the stages of development, each of which centers on a specific pleasurable area of the body and presents the opportunity for fixation, that all human beings pass through in early life. (11)

psychosocial development A lifelong process of social development that Erikson divided into eight different stages that all interrelate. (6)

psychosurgery A form of biological treatment that uses surgery to alter mental or emotional functioning and behavior; see also *prefrontal lobotomy*. (15)

psychotherapy An interpersonal process designed to bring about modifications of feelings, cognitions, attitudes, and behavior that are troublesome to the person seeking help from a trained professional. (15)

puberty Period of physical growth that ends childhood and brings the young person to adult size, shape, and sexual potential. (6)

Pulfrich effect An illusion, which illustrates the role of disparity as a cue for depth perception, that is caused by placing a filter over one eye to alter slightly the brain's processing of the speed of a moving stimulus. (4)

punishment Pain or annoyance administered in an attempt to eliminate a particular behavior. (7)

pupil Structure that regulates the amount of light entering the eye by constriction and dilation. (3)

pyramidal cell One of the two principal types of nerve cells of the cerebral cortex, so named because of the pyramidal shape of its cell body; see also *stellate cell*. (2)

Q

quanta Tiny particles of energy that make up light. (3)

R

random assignment Assigning of subjects to various experimental conditions by methods of chance, in order to neutralize the variables that are not being manipulated in the experiment. (1)

random dot stereogram A tool for the study of the mechanism of stereoscopic vision, which consists of a pair of patterns of computer-generated randomly positioned dots. (4)

random sample Unbiased sample of a population that is taken to be representative of the population as a whole. (1)

range A measure of variability, calculated from a frequency distribution by subtracting the lowest obtained score from the highest obtained score. (App.)

rapid-eye-movement (REM) sleep Stage of sleep characterized by eye muscle activity, a high state of brain activity similar to waking, and, frequently, dreaming. (5)

rational-emotive therapy A method of cognitive restructuring developed by Ellis that traces emotional problems to the sentences people repeat to themselves and attempts to get people to change these maladaptive thought patterns. (15)

ratio scale Measurement scale in which the zero point is absolute such as for weight; see also *interval scale, nominal scale,* and *ordinal scale*. (App.)

ratio use of numbers The assignment of numbers in such a way that the scale units are equal and the zero point is an absolute; see also *interval use of numbers, nominal use of numbers,* and *ordinal use of numbers*. (App.)

reaction formation A defense mechanism—the expression of conscious attitudes that the opposite of an internal wish or impulse. (14)

reality principle According to Freud, the governing mechanism of the ego, which assesses the realism of engaging in aggressive or sexual acts prompted by the id; see also *pleasure principle*. (14)

receiver operating characteristic (ROC) curve A graph of the results of a signal detection test that indicates a subject's percentage of correct versus incorrect responses in identifying the presence of a given stimulus, which is used by psychophysicists to obtain a clear picture of how well a given stimulus can be detected; see also *signal detection theory*. (3)

receptive field The region of the visual field that can affect the response of a given cell in the retina—either to excite or inhibit it. (3)

receptors Peripheral endings of sensory neurons that receive stimuli. (2)

receptor sites Sites on the postsynaptic dendrite membrane of a neuron to which neurotransmitters bind. (2)

reciprocity Factor in interpersonal attraction—we will come to like those who like us and dislike those who dislike us. (16)

recoding Process of encoding information into short-term memory by reorganizing it into more meaningful units; see also *chunking*. (9)

recursive rule A phrase structure rule in which an element on the left of a diagram also occurs on the right. (9)

redundancy A duplication of functions by built-in backup mechanisms of the brain. (2)

regression line In statistics, a procedure for prediciting a person's score on one variable when the person's score on another variable is not known but when the relationship between the two variables is provided. (App.)

refractory period A resting period during which a neuron is inexcitable and cannot fire. (2)

reinforcement The use of stimuli to increase the likelihood of responses occurring before their presentation. (7, 16)

relative size A monocular cue to visual depth perception—we assume that smaller-appearing objects are more distant. (4)

reliability One criterion for evaluating psychological tests—can be shown if a test measures the same thing consistently from occasion to occasion, when administered by different testers, or when two comparable forms of the test produce similar results; see also *standardization* and *validity*. (13)

repression The most important of the defense mechanisms—unpleasant thoughts or dangerous impulses are barred from conscious awareness. (14)

replication The ability of other researchers to perform an experiment in the same manner and obtain the same results as the initial researcher. *(1)*

resistance   The reaction of many patients in analysis when they become aware of previously unconscious aspects of their personalities, characterized by missing therapy appointments, refusing to free associate, and reporting they have no dreams to relate. *(15)*

resting potential   An electric potential difference—or voltage—between the inside and outside of the axon of a neuron. *(2)*

retentive personality   According to Freud, a personality type that results from being fixated in the anal stage and is characterized by over-concern with cleanliness or saving. *(12)*

reticular formation   Interior of the midbrain extending from the brain stem upward to higher portions of the brain that plays an important role in arousal and awareness. *(2)*

reticular theory   Nineteenth-century theory that the nerve cells were physically connected to one another. *(2)*

retina   Photosensitive surface at the back of the eye that contains the visual receptor cells. *(3)*

retrieval   Process of recalling information from memory, which often requires recall of an organizational structure before a specific piece of information can be provided. *(8)*

retroactive interference   One factor that makes memories difficult to retrieve, which occurs when material learned recently interferes with the retrieval of previously learned material; see also *proactive interference. (8)*

reward centers   Areas in the hypothalamus that seem to induce pleasure in laboratory animals when those areas are electrically stimulated. *(10)*

reproductive strategy   Strategy evolved by each species that meets the particular reproductive needs of the species in relation to its environment. *(11)*

reversed Adam principle   Model of sexual differentiation based on the principle of masculine superimposition on a basic female pattern. *(11)*

rhodopsin   Pigment that absorbs light in the rods of the retina. *(3)*

risky shift   The tendency of group decisions to shift in the direction of risk, away from more cautious individual decisions. *(17)*

ROC curve   see *receiver operating characteristic curve. (3)*

rods   Light-sensitive receptor cells of the retina that convert light into neural signals and that function principally in dim illumination and detect no true colors—only black white, and shades of gray; see also *cones. (3)*

Role Construct Repertory Test   Test designed by Kelly to elicit from respondents their own constructs about other people and roles such as self, mother, spouse, pal, rejecting person, or attractive person. *(12)*

roles   The set of prescribed and expected behaviors attached to each position in a group. *(17)*

Roschach test   Projective technique for personality assessment in which subjects look at a series of inkblots on separate cards and tell the examiner what they see; see also *projective tests. (12)*

S

s factor   See *specific mental capability. (13)*

saccule   One of two saclike organs of the inner ear that help control posture; see also *utricle. (3)*

satiety center   Term used to describe the role of the ventromedial hypothalamus as an appetite control that signals that we have had enough to eat; see also *feeding center. (10)*

saltatory conduction   Transmission of a nerve impulse along myelinated axons. *(2)*

saturation   The psychological aspect of color that refers to a hue's vividness, richness, and purity; see also *brightness* and *hue. (3)*

schemes   Intellectual structures or organizations proposed by Piaget that underlie the processes of assimilation and accommodation in cognitive development. *(6)*

schemata   In long-term memory, organized bodies of information representing our general knowledge of the world. *(8)*

schizophrenia   A functional psychotic disorder, characterized by a split between aspects of personality functioning, especially between emotion and behavior. *(14)*

Schwann cells   A group of supportive, myelin-producing cells found throughout the brain and nervous system; see also *phagocyte* and *Schwann cells. (2)*

sclera   The outermost layer, or white, of the eye, that is the major structural element of the eye, providing its firm outer framework. *(3)*

scotomas   Blind spots in the visual field of each eye, caused by the lack of rods and cones where the optic nerves exit from the eye near the fovea. *(3)*

secondary reinforcers   Those stimuli that an individual has learned to associate with positive outcomes such as approval, love, attention, and money; see also *primary reinforcers. (7, 16)*

secondary traits   According to Allport, characteristics that reflect very narrow patterns of behavior or habits and are of less importance in shaping personality than cardinal traits and central traits; see also *cardinal traits* and *central traits. (12)*

sedatives   Barbiturates taken in small doses that impair consciousness in the process of suppressing pain. *(5)*

self-actualization   According to Rogers, the central concept of personality development, based on the idea that all organisms tend to strive toward expressing all their capacities. *(12)*

self-administered reinforcement   In Bandura's social learning theory, the reinforcements we give to ourselves for behaving in certain ways. *(12)*

self-concept   According to Rogers, the perceptual object, developed through self-experience, that each child may experience as "me" or "I." *(12)*

self-control procedures   Approach in behavior therapy in which clients set up their own goals and provide their own reinforcements with the therapist operating as a consultant. *(15)*

self-fulfilling prophecy   An instance in which the perceiver causes another person to behave in a manner that confirms the perceiver's expectations. *(17)*

semantic generalization   The type of generalization that is based on a meaningful relationship as opposed to a physical relationship between a conditioned stimulus (flashing blue light) and a test stimulus (spoken word "blue"). *(7)*

semantic memory   Organized store of general knowledge, including knowledge of the world, rules that guide mental operations, the solution of problems, and so on; see also *episodic memory. (8)*

semantics   Study of the meaning of utterances. *(9)*

semicircular canals   A set of structures in the inner ear that serve to detect changes in the angular movement of the head. (*3*)

senescence   Period during which people grow old, that begins at different ages for different people. (*6*)

sensation   The process by which we receive and code stimuli such as a spot of light or a musical tone; see also *perception*. (*3*)

sensitivity training group   A form of group therapy aimed at helping people who, though functioning well, want to improve interpersonal interactions, which is often called a *T group* (*T* for training). (*15*)

sensorimotor period   In Piaget's theory, the first two years of life during which children explore the relationship between sensory processes and their own bodily movements. (*6*)

sensory memory   Momentary lingering of sensory information after a stimulus has been removed; see also *long-term memory* and *short-term memory*. (*8*)

sensory thresholds   Levels at which a stimulus or changes in a stimulus can be detected. (*3*)

septum   Wall-like region in the limbic system of the brain, located between the amygdala and the hypothalamus, that when operated on produces aggressive behavior in animals and when electrically stimulated seems to produce a pleasurable emotion in rats. (*2*)

set   In reference to the use of psychedelics, one of the two psychological factors that affect the nature of the resulting alterations of consciousness—the mental condition of the individual before ingestion; see also *setting*. (*5*)

set-point theory   In terms of hunger, theory that the hypothalamic centers act like a thermostat by sensing body weight and turning on eating behavior when weight goes too low and turning off eating behavior when weight goes too high. (*10*)

setting   In reference to the use of psychedelics, one of the two psychological factors that affect the nature of the resulting alterations of consciousness—describes the external conditions around the individual taking the drug; see also *set*. (*5*)

severe retardation   One of the levels of retardation, characterized by IQ scores between 20 and 35 on the Stanford-Binet—children require prolonged training just to learn to speak and take care of basic needs, and adults can usually communicate on a rudimentary level; see also *mild retardation, moderate retardation,* and *profound retardation.* (*13*)

shadowing   In the study of attention, occurs when two or more messages are presented at the same time to a listener, whose task is to repeat one of the spoken messages aloud word for word as it is heard. (*8*)

shape constancy   Tendency to perceive the shape of objects as constant despite rotation or differences in the point from which we view them; see also *brightness constancy, color constancy, perceptual constancy,* and *size constancy.* (*4*)

shock treatment   See *electroconvulsive therapy.* (*15*)

short-term memory (STM)   Memory of brief duration—example, remembering a telephone number only until it is dialed—also called primary memory, working memory, what we are currently "paying attention to," and even consciousness; see also *long-term memory* and *sensory memory.* (*8*)

signal detection theory   Method of determining how well a given stimulus can be detected, by presenting a stimulus at different intensities over a large number of trials and plotting the number of correct responses versus incorrect responses; see also *receiver operating characteristic.* (*3*)

signaling pheromones   Chemicals, also called sex attractants, excreted through urine or through the vagina that activate sexual behaviors in male animals, reaching the nervous system through the sense of smell. (*11*)

silent areas   See *association areas.* (*2*)

similarity   Perceptual tendency to see similar elements (proximity being equal) as being grouped together. (*4*)

similarity-attraction theory   Theory of interpersonal attraction that holds that people tend to like others who are similar to themselves on almost any dimension. (*16*)

simple cells   One of three types of feature detection cells in the visual cortex that respond best to a linear shape or edge at a particular orientation and place in their receptive field; see also *complex cells, feature detectors,* and *hypercomplex cells.* (*4*)

simultaneous conditioning   In classical conditioning, when the conditioned stimulus is presented at exactly the same time as the unconditioned stimulus. (*7*)

situational reasons   One of the categories in the attribution process by which people make judgments about the causes of other people's behavior based on the belief that something external to the other person is responsible for the behavior; see also *dispositional reasons.* (*17*)

size constancy   Tendency to perceive the size of objects as constant despite its distance from the viewer; see also *brightness constancy, color constancy, perceptual constancy,* and *shape constancy.* (*4*)

skewed distribution   Distribution, also called asymmetrical distribution, in which there are more values on one end than on the other end; see also *symmetrical distribution.* (*App.*)

sleep spindles   Short periods of rhythmical responses, with an EEG frequency of 13 to 15 cycles per second, that appear as light sleep begins to deepen. (*5*)

social comparison   Looking to others as a guide for an individual's own interpretation of what is appropriate behavior in a given situation. (*16*)

social facilitation   Phenomenon in which the presence of others increases or facilitates an individual's performance of a task. (*16*)

social influence   Ways in which an individual's actions affect the behavior, attitudes, or judgments of another. (*16*)

social interaction   Mutual reciprocal effects that people have on each other as they interact. (*16, 17*)

socialization   Process of social interaction through which the young acquire the social skills and knowledge needed to function as a member of the culture. (*6*)

social learning approach   Learning theory of personality developed by Bandura that aims at describing the two-way interaction between the individual and the environment. (*12*)

social motives   Needs that are acquired or expressed largely through interactions with others. (*10*)

social perception   The ways in which we perceive others and interpret their behavior. (*17*)

social perspective   Idea that it is how others view deviant behavior and how they react to odd or puzzling behavior that defines that behavior's abnormality; see also *learning perspective.* (*14*)

sociobiology   The study of social behavior in terms of its adaptive value, with a particular emphasis on the optimization theory approach. (*10*)

soma   One of a neuron's three essential parts—the cell body that uses oxygen and glucose and other material from the blood to manufacture protein and other materials necessary for the neuron's survival and functioning; see also *axon* and *dendrite*. (2)

somatic nervous system   One of the two parts of the peripheral nervous system that controls movement and receives sensory information; see also *autonomic nervous system*. (2)

somatic sensory cortex   Portion of the parietal lobe devoted to skin sensations. (3)

somatotypes   Three basic types of body structure and physique identified by Sheldon; see also *ectomorph, endomorph,* and *mesomorph*. (12)

somesthesis   Sensations arising from the skin—touch, warmth, cold, and pain. (3)

SOMPA   See *System of Multicultural Pluralistic Assessment*. (13)

source traits   According to Cattell, fundamental traits that are the roots of overt behavior; see also *surface traits*. (12)

specific mental capability   Term used by Spearman to refer to performance of any specific intellectual task; also called the *s* factor; see also *mental facility*. (13)

speech code   A term applied to speech because of the efficient packaging of speech sounds at the level of phonemes and the lack of dependency on any particular frequency for speech perception. (9)

speech spectrogram   Visual representation of the patterns of sound energy, including frequency, time, and amplitude. (9)

spontaneous recovery   Partial recovery of a conditioned response following extinction. (7)

stabilized image   Phenomenon in which a stimulus image fades and disappears if the image falls constantly on the same receptors. (3)

standard deviation   A measure of the variability or scatter of a frequency distribution that is obtained by calculating the square root of the variance; see also *variance*. (*App.*)

standardization   One criterion for evaluating psychological tests—developing a set of scores for a particular test, which reflect the diversity of the overall population who will take the test, against which any individual's score can be evaluated; see also *reliability* and *validity*. (17)

standardization-group   Group on which a test has been standardized, which should be representative of the overall population who will take the test. (13)

standard score   A score for each value in any distribution that expresses the deviation from the mean in standard deviation units. (*App.*)

Stanford-Binet Test   Revision of Binet's original intelligence test for use with American children, which was first published in 1916 and revised in 1960. (13)

stapes   The third and last bone in the ossicular chain of the middle ear that couples directly with the oval window. (3)

state-dependent learning   Learning that is profoundly affected by the learner's internal physiological state, which must be replicated for recall to occur. (5)

state-dependent memory   Phenomenon in which material learned in an altered physiological state (usually drug-induced) can only be recalled when the person is in the same state. (8)

states of consciousness   Sets of structural conditions that are distinct from the actual content of consciousness—the major

features that influence the ways in which we experience ourselves or the world as opposed to the experience itself. (5)

stellate cell   One of two principal types of nerve cells of the cerebral cortex, so named because the radial pattern of its dendrite branches gives it a starlike appearance; see also *pyramidal cell*. (2)

stereoscopic vision   The slight disparity between the images recorded by each eye that results in the perception of depth. (4)

stereotypes   Existing mental sets people may have about the traits or physical characteristics of an entire group of people. (8)

Stevens' Power Law   Law formulated by Stevens that the magnitude of a sensation is equal to the physical magnitude of the stimulus producing the sensation raised to a certain power, which varies depending on the sensation that is being measured. (3)

stimulants   Amphetamines and other drugs that stimulate the central nervous system increasing the available supply of the neurotransmitter dopamine. (15)

stimulus generalization   Phenomenon in which a conditioned response can be evoked by stimuli that are similar to but not the same as the original conditioned stimulus. (7)

storage   Refers both to the contents of long-term memory and the way in which these contents are represented and organized. (8)

strabismus   Condition commonly referred to as "crossed eyes," which is caused by an extraocular muscle imbalance. (4)

stress   State of psychological and physiological tension that is caused by threatening demands from the environment. (14)

structuralism   Early school of psychological thought that sought to understand the structure of the mind through analysis of the basic elements of mental experience: sensations, images, and feelings. (1)

subjective distress   Feelings of sadness, fear, or loss of control that accompanies most forms of abnormal behavior. (14)

subtractive mixture   A mixture of pigments, which absorb or subtract some wavelengths and reflect remaining wavelengths to produce a unique hue; see also *additive mixture*. (3)

successive approximations   Behavior shaping accomplished by breaking down the desired sequence of actions into small steps and then reinforcing the organism as it approaches closer and closer to the desired response at each step. (7)

superordinate goals   Tasks that appeal to more than one group but lie beyond the resources of any single group and, therefore, require that the groups work together toward accomplishing them. (17)

surface structure   The form of the sentence we actually hear; see also *deep structure*. (9)

surface traits   According to Cattell clusters of overt behavior that seem to go together; see also *source traits*. (12)

survey   Research technique in which the opinions, attitudes, and experiences of large numbers of people can be assessed through the use of written questionnaires or interviews. (1)

sustained receptors   Receptors that will maintain their generator potential and keep firing impulses as long as the stimulus is present; see also *transient receptors*. (3)

symmetrical distribution   Distribution in which the value of the mean and median are the same and both halves are mirror images; see also *skewed distribution*. (*App.*)

sympathetic nervous system   One of two parts of the autonomic nervous system, that tends to mobilize resources of the body for emergencies; see also *parasympathetic nervous system*. (*2*)

synapse   The contact between the axon of one neuron and the cell body or dendrite of another neuron. (*2*)

synaptic cleft   Very thin gap between the membranes of the presynaptic element (the axon) and the postsynaptic element (the dendrite). (*2*)

syntactic rules   The means of translating the sounds of speech into meaningful phrases and sentences. (*9*)

synaptic vesicles   Assemblage of tiny spheres in a knob on the tip of the axon, each of which is surrounded by a membrane and very likely contains a neurotransmitter. (*2*)

syntax   The grammatical structure of language. (*9*)

systematic desensitization   Type of counterconditioning behavior therapy in which patients are taught a new response, muscle relaxation, and then gradually conditioned to substitute the new response for fear as they visualize increasing "doses" of anxiety-provoking situations; see also *aversion therapy* and *implosive therapy*. (*15*)

System of Multicultural Pluralistic Assessment (SOMPA)   Battery of intelligence measures for children from 5 to 11 that produces an adjusted IQ that is typically higher than the traditional IQ. (*13*)

T

TAT   See *Thematic Apperception Test*. (*12*)

tau-effect   Phenomenon in which the perception of space is influenced by time; see also *kappa-effect*. (*4*)

temporal conditioning   Type of classical conditioning in which the subject is conditioned to give the conditioned response at certain time intervals, and time itself becomes the conditioned stimulus. (*7*)

temporal lobe   Lobe in each cerebral hemisphere of the brain that contains areas concerned with hearing, visual recognition, and the understanding of language. (*2*)

testosterone   Most important of the androgens (steroids, or gonadal hormones) produced in the male testes. (*13*)

texture   One of the monocular cues for perceiving depth, in which the grain of most surfaces appears to change gradually from coarse to fine as distance increases. (*4*)

T-group   See *sensitivity training group*. (*15*)

thalamus   Complex structure located at the top of the brain stem through which nerve fibers carry all sensory impressions except smell. (*2*)

Thematic Apperception Test (TAT)   Projective test for personality assessment that consists of a set of 20 pictures showing either one person or several people standing in relation to each other, about which subjects tell stories. (*12*)

theories of linguistic competence   According to Chomsky, the grammars that linguists write, which must be capable of generating all and only the grammatical sentences found in a given language. (*9*)

theory   A systematic explanation that consists of a group of unified hypotheses. (*1*)

theory of cognitive dissonance   Festinger's theory that proposes that when individuals behave in a manner inconsistent with their attitudes they experience dissonance, an unpleasant state of tension, which can be relieved either by reducing the number of inconsistent cognitions or by increasing the number of consistent cognitions. (*16*)

theory of self-perception   Bem's theory that people learn about themselves by observing their own behavior. (*16*)

theory of social comparison   Theory which holds that, in ambiguous situations, we tend to look to other people for help in determining appropriate behavior. (*10*)

theta waves   EEG patterns of from 4 to 6 cycles per second produced during the drowsy interval between waking and sleeping known as the hypnagogic state. (*5*)

Thibaut and Kelley theory   Postulates that relationships depend largely on each participant's analysis of the rewards and costs, which occurs (usually unconsciously) whenever two people interact and shapes the responses of each person. (*17*)

thinking   A variety of cognitive activities including problem solving, planning, decision making, judgment, and even remembering. (*8*)

threshold   The level of excitation necessary to trigger an action potential in a neuron. (*2*)

timbre   A measure of a sound's purity. (*3*)

token economy   An operant technique used for changing behavior in institutionalized settings in which severely disturbed patients are given plastic tokens as reinforcement for activities such as making beds and combing hair that can be exchanged for special privileges. (*15*)

tolerance   Level at which users need to increase the dose of a drug in order to achieve the same effect previously experienced from a smaller dose. (*5*)

tonic events   One of two classes of physiological events that occur during REM sleep, characterized by penile erection in men and probably increased blood supply to the vagina in women and a decrease in muscle activity in both men and women; see also *phasic events*. (*5*)

tonotopical organzation   Organization of the brain's auditory structures, in which neighboring cells respond best to similar frequencies, and these frequencies change progressively from one place to another. (*3*)

trace conditioning   Learning that takes place when the conditioned stimulus is presented briefly, then removed, followed after a relatively brief interval, by the presentation of the unconditioned stimulus. (*7*)

transcendental meditation   Variant of concentrative meditation in which the meditator makes no active attempt to control mental experiences but focuses on a mantra, thereby resisting indirectly the intrusion of thoughts. (*5*)

transfer of excitation   The transfer of residual excitation from one state or activity (such as physical exercise) to another state (the emotion of anger). (*10*)

transference   A frequent occurrence in analysis in which the analyst becomes the focus of emotions once directed at parents or other significant people in the patient's childhood. (*15*)

transformational rules   Rules that allow the deep structures generated by phrase structure rules to be modified before the surface structure form emerges. (*9*)

transient receptors   Receptors that fire when a stimulus is first applied but quickly return to their normal state, the resting potential, even if the stimulus is maintained; see also *sustained receptors*. *(3)*

transsexualism   Strong feelings of gender identity with the opposite sex. *(11)*

trial-and-error learning   Type of learning in which the subject begins a task with activity that is apparently random until the correct response is made by chance and reinforced. *(7)*

trichromatic theory   Theory that there are only three types of color receptors for visions. *(3)*

two-factor theory of emotions   Theory that emotions consist of both arousal and cognition and if neither exists there will be no emotions. *(10)*

U

unconditioned response (UR)   Response that automatically occurs, without training, whenever the unconditioned stimulus is presented; see also *classical conditioning*. *(7)*

unconditioned stimulus (US)   Stimulus that automatically elicits, without any training, the desired response; see *classical conditioning*. *(7)*

unconscious mental activity   Freud's term for the reservoir of childhood and current memories, wishes, impulses, fears, and hopes that lie beyond awareness, which he believed play the dominant role in shaping personality; see also *conscious mental activity* and *preconscious mental activity*. *(12)*

unintentional social influence   Instances where others inadvertently arouse us, reinforce us, or serve as sources of information. (16)

unity   One of two categories of visual skills characterized by the ability to detect the presence of an object, that is, to separate an object from its background; see also *identity*. *(4)*

utricle   One of two saclike organs of the inner ear that help control posture; see also *saccule*. *(3)*

V

validity   One criterion for evaluating psychological tests—can be shown if a test measures what it was intended to measure; see also *reliability* and *standardization*. *(13)*

variable-interval (VI) schedule   Schedule of reinforcement in which reinforcement is given after variable time intervals; see also *fixed-interval schedule, fixed-ratio schedule,* and *variable-ratio schedule*. *(7)*

variable-ratio (VR) schedule   Schedule of reinforcement in which reinforcement is given after a varying number of responses; see also *fixed-interval schedule, fixed-ratio schedule,* and *variable-interval schedule*. *(7)*

variance   The average squared deviation score or the mean of the squared deviation scores; see also *deviation score*. *(App.)*

vasocongestion   Increased blood flow to an area of the body, which results in penile erections in the male and clitoral erections in the female; see also *myotonia*. *(11)*

verbal reinforcement   Form of social reinforcement in which words or sounds are employed to indicate approval or disapproval of an action or response. *(16)*

vermis   Central, unpaired region that separates the two hemispheres of the cerebellum. *(2)*

vestibulo-ocular reflex   Reflex originating in the three semicircular canals of the inner ear that serves the function of stabilizing the body and eyes in space. *(4)*

vicarious learning   In Bandura's social learning theory, learning by observing others, or modeling. *(12)*

vicarious reinforcement   In Bandura's social learning theory, reinforcement that is experienced through observation of a model who is rewarded; see also *direct reinforcement*. *(12)*

visible spectrum   Narrow range of the electromagnetic spectrum that the human eye can see. *(3)*

visual acuity   The visual ability to resolve fine detail. *(4)*

visual capture   Tendency of vision to dominate the other senses. *(4)*

visual cliff   A laboratory apparatus designed for testing depth perception in infants. *(4)*

vitreous humor   Transparent jellylike substance that fills most of the interior of the eye. *(3)*

vulnerability model   Model of the determinants of schizophrenia based on the premise that everyone is endowed with some degree of vulnerability to schizophrenia, which is determined by some combination of biological and environmental factors. *(14)*

W

WAIS   See *Wechsler Adult Intelligence Scale*. *(13)*

wavelength   The difference between the crest of one light wave and the crest of the next light wave—determines color. *(3)*

Weber's law   The principle that the size of the difference threshold is proportional to the intensity of a standard stimulus. *(3)*

Wechsler Adult Intelligence Scale (WAIS)   The most popular means of measuring adult intelligence through a series of subtests designed to measure verbal and performance abilities. *(13)*

Wechsler Intelligence Scale for Children (WISC)   Adaptation of the Wechsler Adult Intelligence Scale for use in schools. *(13)*

WISC   See *Wechsler Intelligence Scale for Children*. *(13)*

working through   In psychoanalysis, the process of reeducation by having patients face the same conflicts repeatedly until they can face life independently and master the conflicts of everyday life. *(15)*

Z

Zajonc's arousal theory   Theory that the arousal produced by the presence of others strengthens the dominant response of the organism, which is, a simple or well-learned task is likely to be appropriate or correct, whereas in a complex and difficult task, it is likely to be wrong. *(16)*

zone of proximal development   The gap between childrens' present capabilities and their future potential. *(13)*

zoophobia   Fear of certain animals. *(14)*

REFERENCES

Abramson, L. Y., Seligman, M. E. P., & Teasdale, J. D. (1978). Learned helplessness in humans: Critique and reformulation. *Journal of Abnormal Psychology, 87,* 49–74.

Adams, D. B., Gold, A. B., & Burt, A. D. (1978). Rise in female-initiated sexual activity at ovulation and its suppression by oral contraceptives. *New England Journal of Medicine, 299,* 1145–1150.

Adams, G. R., & Fitch, S. A. (1982). Ego stage and identity status development: A cross-sequential analysis. *Journal of Personality and Social Psychology, 43,* 574–583.

Adrin, E., & Warga, W. (1973). *Return to earth.* New York: Random House.

Agras, S., Sylvester, D., & Aoliveau, D. (1969). *The epidemiology of common fears and phobias.* Unpublished manuscript.

Ainsworth, M. D. S. (1967). *Infancy in Uganda.* Baltimore, MD: Johns Hopkins Press.

Ainsworth, M. D. S., Bell, S. M., & Stayton, D. J. (1971). Individual differences in strange situation behavior of one-year-olds. In H. R. Schaffer (Ed.), *The origins of human social relations.* London: Academic Press.

Alcock, J. (1972). The evolution of the use of tools by feeding animals. *Evolution, 26,* 464–474.

Allen, K. E., Hart, B., Buell, J. S., Harris, F. R., & Wolf, M. M. (1964). Effects of social reinforcement on isolate behavior of a nursery school child. *Child Development, 35,* 511–518.

Alley, T. R. (1983). Growth-produced changes in body shape and size determinants of perceived age and adult caregiving. *Child Development, 54,* 241–248.

Allport, F. H. (1920). The influence of the group upon association and thought. *Journal of Experimental Psychology, 3,* 159–182.

Allport, G. W. (1937). *Personality: A psychological interpretation.* New York: Holt.

Allport, G. W. (1954). *The nature of prejudice.* Reading, MA: Addison-Wesley.

Allport, G. W. (1961). *Pattern and growth in personality.* New York: Holt, Rinehart and Winston.

Allport, G. W. (1965). *Letters from Jenny.* New York: Harcourt.

Allport, G. W. (1966). Traits revisited. *American Psychologist, 21,* 1–10.

Allport, G. W., & Vernon, P. E. (1933). *Studies in expressive movement.* New York: Macmillan.

Alpert, J. L., & Richardson, M. S. (1980). Parenting. In L. Poon (Ed.), *Aging in the 1980s: Psychological issues.* Washington, DC: American Psychological Association.

American Psychiatric Association. (1980). *Diagnostic and statistical manual of mental disorders* (DSM-III) (3rd ed.). Washington, DC: American Psychiatric Association.

Amoore, J. E. (1971). Olfaction. In L. Beidler (Ed.), *Handbook of sensory physiology: Vol. 4. Chemical senses: Pt. 1.* Berlin, Heidelberg, and New York: Springer.

Anastasi, A. (1958). Heredity, environment, and the question "how." *Psychological Review, 65,* 197–208.

Apgar, V. (1953). A proposal for a new method evaluation in the newborn infant. *Current Research in Anesthesia and Analgesia, 32,* 260.

Aponte, H., & Hoffman, L. (1973). The open door: A structural approach to a family with an anorectic child. *Family Process, 12,* 1–44.

Arieti, S. (1959). Manic-depressive psychosis. In S. Arieti (Ed.). *American handbook of psychiatry.* New York: Basic Books.

Aronson, E. (1972). *The social animal.* San Francisco: Freeman.

Aronson, E., & Linder, D. (1965). Gain and loss of esteem as determinants of interpersonal attractiveness. *Journal of Experimental Social Psychology, 1,* 156–172.

Aronson, E., & Mills, J. (1959). The effect of severity of initiation on liking for a group. *Journal of Abnormal and Social Psychology. 59,* 177–181.

Asch, S. E. (1946). Forming impressions of personalities. *Journal of Abnormal and Social Psychology, 41* 258–290.

Asch, S. E. (1948). The doctrine of suggestion, prestige, and imitation in social psychology. *Psychological Review, 55,* 250–276.

Asch, S. E. (1951). Effects of group pressure upon the modification and distortion of judgment. In H. Guptzkow (Ed.), *Groups, leadership and men.* Pittsburgh, PA: Carnegie.

Aserinsky, E., & Kleitman, N. (1953). Regularly occurring periods of eye motility and concomitant phenomena during sleep. *Science, 118* 273–274.

Astin, H. S. (1974). Sex differences in mathematical and scientific precocity. In J. C. Stanley, D. P. Keating, & L. Fox (eds.), *Mathematical talent: Discovery, description and development.* Baltimore, MD: Johns Hopkins University Press.

Atchley, R. C. (1975). Dimensions of widowhood in later life. *Gerontologist, 11,* 176–178.

Atkinson, J., Braddick, O., & Braddick F. (1974). Acuity and contrast sensitivity of infant vision. *Nature, 247,* 403–404.

Atkinson, J. W. (Ed.). (1958). *Motives in fantasy, action, and society.* Princeton, NJ: Van Nostrand.

Atkinson, R. C., & Raugh, M. R. (1975). An application of the mnenomic keyboard method to the acquisition of a Russian vocabulatory. *Journal of Experimental Psychology: Human Learning and Memory, 104,* 126–133.

Ax, A. F. (1953). The physiological differentiation between fear and anger in humans. *Psychosomatic Medicine, 14,* 433–442.

Ayllon, T., & Azrin, N. H. (1968). *The token economy: A motivational system for therapy and rehabilitation.* New York: Appleton-Century-Crofts.

Ayllon, T., & Kelly, K. (1972). Effects of reinforcement on standardized test performance. *Journal of Applied Behavior Analysis, 4,* 477–484.

Baddeley, A. D. (1966). Time-estimation at reduced body temperature. *American Journal of Psychology, 79,* 475–479.

Baddley, A. D. (1976). *The psychology of memory.* New York: Basic Books.

Bailey, R. H. (1975). *The role of the brain.* New York: Time-Life Books.

Bakal, D. (1975). Headache: A biopsychological perspective. *Psychological Bulletin, 82,* 369–382.

Baldessarini, R. J. (1977). *Chemotherapy in psychiatry.* Cambridge, MA: Harvard University Press.

Baltes, P. B., & Schaie, K. W. (1974, March). Aging and the IQ: The myth of the twilight years. *Psychology Today, 7* 35–40.

Bancroft, J. (1974). *Deviant sexual behavior: Modification and assessment.* Oxford: Clarendon Press.

Bancroft, J. (1981). Hormones and human sexual behavior. *British Medical Bulletin, 37,* 153–158.

Bancroft, J., & Wu, F. C. W. (1983). Changes in erectile responsiveness during androgen replacement therapy. *Archives of Sexual Behavior, 12,* 59.

Bandura, A. (1965). Influence of models' reinforcement contingencies on the acquisition of imitative responses. *Journal of Personality and Social Psychology, 1,* 589–595.

Bandura, A. (1971). Psychotherapy based on modeling principles. In A. E. Bergin & S. L. Garfield (Eds.), *Handbook of psychotherapy and behavior change.* New York: Wiley.

Bandura, A. (1971). *Social learning theory.* Morristown, NJ: General Learning Press.

Bandura, A. (1976). Social learning analysis of aggression. In E. Ribes-Inesta (Ed.), *Analysis of delinquency and aggression* . Hillsdale, NJ: Erlbaum.

Bandura, A. (1982). Self-efficacy mechanism in human agency. *American Psychologist, 37,* 122–147.

Bandura, A., Blanchard, E. B., & Ritter, B. (1963). The relative efficacy of desensitization and modeling approaches for inducing behavioral, affective, and attitudinal changes. *Journal of Personality and Social Psychology, 13,* 173–199.

Bandura, A., & Mischel, W. (1965). Modification of self-imposed delay on reward through exposure to live and symbolic models. *Journal of Personality and Social Psychology, 2,* 698–705.

Bandura, A., Ross, D., & Ross, S. A. (1961). Transmission of aggression through imitation of aggressive models. *Journal of Abnormal and Social Psychology, 63,* 575–582.

Bandura, A., Ross, D., & Ross, S. A. (1963). Imitation of film-mediated aggressive models. *Journal of Abnormal and Social Psychology, 66,* 3–11.

Bandura, A., & Schunk, D. H. (1981). Cultivating confidence, self-efficacy, and intrinsic interest through proximal motivation. *Journal of Personality and Social Psychology, 1,* 589–595.

Barber, T. X. (1970). *LSD, marijuana, yoga and hypnosis.* Chicago: Aldine.

Bard, M. (1970). *Training police as specialists in family crisis intervention.* Washington, DC: U.S. Government Printing Office.

Bard, M., & Berkowitz, B. (1967). Training police as specialists in family crisis intervention: A community psychology action program. *Community Mental Health Journal, 3,* 315–317.

Barfield, R. J., & Chen, J. (1978). Activation of estrous behavior in ovariectomized rats by intracerebral implants of estradiol benzoate. *Endocrinology, 101,* 1716–1725.

Baron, R. A., Byrne, D., & Kantowitz, B. H. (1980). *Psychology: Understanding behavior* (2nd ed.). New York: Holt.

Barraclough, C. A. (1966). Hormones and development: Modifications in the CNS regulation of reproduction after exposure of prepuberal rats to steroid. *Recent Progress in Hormone Research, 22,* 503–509.

Barrett, J. E. (1978). Operant paradigm. In G. U. Balis, L. Wurmser, E. McDaniel, & R. G. Grenell, (Eds.). *The behavioral and social sciences and the practice of medicine; the psychiatric foundation of medicine* (Vol. 2). Boston: Butterworth Publishers.

Bartlett, F. C. (1932). *Remembering.* Cambridge, England: Cambridge University Press.

Bass, F. (1947). *L'amènorrhée au camp de concentration de Térézin. Gynécologia 123,* 211.

Bateson, G., Jackson, D. C., Haley, J., & Weakland, J. (1956). Toward a theory of schizophrenia. *Behavioral Science, 1,* 251–264.

Baum, A., & Greenberg, C. I. (1975). Waiting for a crowd: The behavioral and perceptual effects of anticipated crowding. *Journal of personality and Social Psychology, 32,* 671–679.

Baumrind, D. (1971). Current patterns of parental authority. *Developmental Psychology Monographs, 4,* (1, Pt. 2).

Baumrind, D. (1973). The development of instrumental competence through socialization. In A. Pick (Ed.), *Minnesota symposium on child psychology* (Vol. 7). Minneapolis: University of Minnesota Press.

Bavelas, J. B. (1978). *Personality: Current theory and research.* Monterey, CA: Brooks/Cole.

Bayer, E. (1929). Beiträge zur Zweikomponenthentheorie des Hungers. *Zeitschrift für Psychologie, 112,* 1–54

Bayley, N. (1970). Development of mental abilities. In Mussen, P. (Ed.). *Carmichael's manual of child psychology.* New York: Wiley.

Beach, F. A. (1948). *Hormones and behavior.* New York: Hoeber.

Beach, F. A. (1976). Sexual attractivity, proceptivity, and receptivity in female mammals. *Hormones and Behavior, 7,* 105–138.

Beard, R. J. (1975). The menopause. *British Journal of Hospital Medicine, 12,* 631–637.

Beck, A. T. (1967). *Depression: Clinical, experimental, and theoretical aspects.* New York: Hoeber (Harper & Row).

Beck, A. T., Rush, A. J., Shaw, B. F., & Emery, G. (1979). *Cognitive therapy of depression.* New York: Guilford Press.

Békéy, G. von. (1960). *Experiments in hearing.* New York: McGraw-Hill.

Bell, R. Q. (1979). Parent, child, and reciprocal influences. *American Psychologist, 34,* 821–826.

Bell, R. Q., & Harper, L. V. (1977). *The effects of children on parents.* Hillsdale, NJ: Erlbaum.

Bellack, A. S., Hersen, M., & Turner, S. M. (1976). Generalization effects of social skills training in chronic schizophrenics: An Experimental analysis. *Behaviour Research and Therapy, 14,* 391–398.

Belmont, L., & Marolla, F. A. (1973). Birth order, family size, and intelligence. *Science, 182,* 1096–1101.

Belsky, J., & Rovine, M. (1984). Social network contact, family support, and the transition to parenthood. *Journal of Marriage and the Family.*

Belsky, J., Ward, M. J., & Rovine, M. (1986). Prenatal expectations, postnatal experiences, and the transition to parenthood. In R. D. Ashmore & D. M. Brodzinsky (Eds.), *Thinking about the family: Perspectives of parents and children.* Hillsdale, NJ: Erlbaum.

Bem, D. J. (1972). Self-perception theory. In L. Berkowitz (Ed.), *Advances in experimental social psychology* (Vol. 6). New York: Academic Press.

Bem, S. L. (1981). Gender schema theory: A cognitive account of sex typing. *Psychological Review, 88,* 354–364.

Benbow, C. P., & Stanley, J. C. (1983). Sex differences in mathematical reasoning: More facts. *Science , 222,* 1029–1031.

Bengston, V. L., Cuellar, J. B., & Ragan, P. K. (1977). Stratum contrasts and similarities in attitudes toward death. *Journal of Gerontology, 32,* 76–88.

Benson, H. (1975). *The relaxation response.* New York: Morrow.

Berger, H. (1929. *über das elektroenkephalogramm des menschen. Archiv Für Psychiatrie und Nervenkrankheiten, 87,* 527–570.

Bergin, A. E. (1971). The evaluation of the therapeutic outcomes. In A. E. Bergin & S. L. Garfield (Eds.), *Handbook of psychotherapy and behavior change: An empirical analysis.* New York: Wiley.

Bergum, B. O., & Lehr, D. J. (1963). Effects of authoritarianism on vigilance performance. *Journal of Applied Psychology, 47,* 75–77.

Berkowitz, L., & Geen, R. G. (1966). Film violence and the cue properties of available targets. *Journal of Personality and Social Psychology, 3,* 525–530.

Berkowitz, L. (1954). Group standards, cohesiveness, and productivity. *Human Relations, 7,* 509–519.

Berkowitz, L. (1965). The concept of aggressive drive: Some additional considerations. In L. Berkowitz (Ed.), *Advances in experimental social psychology* (Vol. 2). New York: Academic Press.

Berkowitz, W. R., Nebel, J. C., & Reitman, J. W. (1971). Height and interpersonal attraction: The 1969 mayoral election in New York City. *Proceedings of the 79th Annual Convention of the American Psychological Association. 6,* 281–282.

Bermant, G., & Davidson, J. M. (1974). *Biological bases of sexual behavior.* New York: Harper & Row.

Bernard, C. (1957). *An introduction to the study of experimental medicine* (H. C. Greene, Trans.). New York: Dover. (Originally published, 1865).

Berscheid, E., & Walster, E. H. (1969). *Interpersonal attraction.* Reading, MA: Addison Wesley.

Bexton, W. H., Heron, W., & Scott, T. H. (1954). Effects of decreased variation in the sensory environment. *Canadian Journal of Psychology, 8,* 70–76.

Binet, A., & Simon, T. (1916). *The development of intelligence in children.* (E. S. Kite Trans.). Baltimore. MD: Williams & Wilkins.

Birren, J. E. et al. (1981). *Developmental psychology: A life-span approach* Boston: Houghton-Mifflin.

Bischof, L. J. (1976). *Adult psychology* (2nd ed.). New York: Harper & Row.

Blashfield, R. K. (1980). *The classification of psychopathology: Neo-Kraepelinian and quantitative approaches.* New York: Plenum Press.

Blashfield, R. K., & Draguns, J. G. (1976). Evaluative criteria for psychiatric classification. *Journal of Abnormal Psychology, 85,* 140–150.

Blass, E. L., & Epstein, A. N. (1971). A lateral preoptic osmosensitive zone for thirst in the rat. *Journal of Comparative and Physiological Psychology, 76,* 378–394.

Blehar, M. C., Lieberman, A. F., & Ainsworth, M. D. S. (1977). Early face-to-face interaction and its relation to later infant-mother attachment. *Child Development, 48,* 182–184.

Bleuler, E. (1950). *Domentia praecox, or the group of schizophrenias* (J. Zinkin, Trans.). New York: International Universities Press. (Originally published, 1911).

Bloom, B. (1977). *Community mental health.* Monterey, CA: Brooks-Cole.

Bloom, L. (1970). *Language development: Form and function in emerging grammars.* Cambridge, MA: MIT Press.

Blough, D. (1956). Dark adaptation in the pigeon. *Journal of Comparative and Physiological Psychology, 49,* 425–430.

Blough, D. S. (1961). Experiments in animal psychophysics. *Scientific American, 205,* 113–122.

Blum, J. E., Jarvik, L. F., & Clark, E. T. (1970). Rate of change on selective tests of intelligence: A twenty-year longitudinal study. *Journal of Gerontology, 25,* 171–176.

Blum, J. E., & Jarvik, L. F. (1975). Intellectual performance of octogenerians and initial ability. *Human Development, 18,* 364–375.

Blumenthal, A. L. (1977). *The process of cognition.* Englewood Cliffs, NJ: Prentice-Hall.

Bogdan, R., & Taylor, S. (1976). The judged, not the judges: An insider's view of mental retardation. *American Psychologist, 31,* 47–52.

Bogen, J. E. (1969). The other side of the brain: An appositional mind. *Bulletin of The Los Angeles Neurological Societies, 34,* 135–162.

Boring, E. G. (1950). *A history of experimental psychology* (2nd ed.). New York: Appleton-Century-Crofts.

Boring, E. G. (1953). A history of introspection. *Psychological Bulletin, 50,* 169–189.

Bossard, J. H. S. (1932). Residential propinquity as a factor in mate selection. *American Journal of Sociology, 38,* 219–224.

Botwinick, J. (1967). *Cognitive processes in maturity and old age.* New York: Springer.

Bousfield, W. A. (1953). The occurrence of clustering in the recall of randomly arranged associates. *Journal of General Psychology, 49,* 229–240.

Bower, G. H., Clark, M., Winzenz, D., & Lesgold, A. (1969). Hierarchical retrieval schemes in recall of categorized word lists. *Journal of Verbal Learning and Verbal Behavior, 8,* 323–343.

Bower, G. H. (1972). Mental imagery and associative learning. In L. Gregg (Ed.), *Cognition in learning and memory.* New York: Wiley.

Bowerman, M. (1973). Structual relationships in children's utterances: Syntactic or semantic? In T. E. Moore (Ed.), *Cognitive development and the acquisition of language.* New York: Academic Press.

Bowers, M. B., Jr., & Freedman, D. X. (1966). Psychedelic experiences in acute psychosis. *Archives of General Psychiatry, 15,* 240–248.

Bowlby, J. (1960). Separation anxiety. *International Journal of Psychoanalysis, 4,* 89–113.

Bowlby, J. (1969). Attachment. In *Attachment and loss* (Vol. 1). New York: Basic Books.

Braine, M. D. S. (1963). On learning the grammatical order of words. *Psychological Review, 70,* 323–348.

Braine, M. D. S. (1976). Children's first word combinations. *Monographs of the Society for Research in Child Development, 41* (Serial No. 164).

Branchey, M. H., Charles J., & Simpson, G. M. (1976). Extrapyramidal side effects in lithium maintenance therapy. *American Journal of Psychiatry, 133,* 444–445.

Bransford, J. D., Barclay, J. B., & Franks, J. J. (1972). Sentence memory: A constructive versus interpretive approach. *Cognitive Psychology, 3,* 193–209.

Bransford, J. D., & Franks, J. J. (1971). The abstraction of linguistic ideas. *Cognitive Psychology, 2,* 331–350.

Bransford, J. D., & Johnson, M. K. (1972). Contextual prerequisites for understanding: Some investigations of comprehension and recall. *Journal of Verbal Learning and Verbal Behavior, 11,* 717–726.

Brazelton, T. B., Koslowski, B., & Main, M. (1974). The origins of reciprocity: The early mother-infant interaction. In M. Lewis & L. A. Rosenbaum (Eds.), *The effect of the infant on its caregiver.* New York: Wiley.

Brazelton, T. B. (1974). *Neonatal behavioral assessment scale.* Philadelphia, PA: International Ideas.

Brecher, E. M. (1969). *The sex researchers.* Boston: Little, Brown.

Breedlove, S. M., & Arnold, A. P. (1980). Hormone accumulation in a sexually dimorphic nucleus in the rat spinal cord. *Science, 211,* 1285.

Breland, K., & Breland, M. (1961). The misbehavior of organisms. *American Psychologist, 16,* 681–684.

Breland, K., & Breland, M. (1966). *Animal behavior.* New York: Macmillan.

Broadbent, D. E. (1958). *Perception and communication.* London: Pergamon Press.

Broadbent, D. E., Cooper, P. J., & Broadbent, M. H. P. (1978). A comparison of hierarchical and matrix retrieval schemes in recall. *Journal of Experimental Psychology: Human Learning and Memory, 4,* 476–497.

Broca, P. (1960). Remarques dur la siége de la faculté du langage articulé; suivies d'une observation d'aphémie (perte de lar parole). In G. von Bonin (Trans.), *Some papers on the cerebral cortex.* Springfield, IL: Charles C Thomas (Originally published, 1861).

Bromely, D. B. (1979). *The psychology of human aging* (2nd ed.). Baltimore, MD: Penguin Books.

Bronson, W. C. (1959). Dimension of ego and infantile identification. *Journal of Personality, 27,* 532–545.

Brouwer, D. (1957). Somatotypes and psychosomatic diseases. *Journal of Psychosomatic Research, 2,* 23–24.

Broverman, I. K., Broverman, D. M., & Clarkson, F. E. (1970). Sex role stereotypes and clinical judgments of mental health. *Journal of Consulting and Clinical Psychology, 34,* 1–7.

Brown, A. L. (1975). The development of memory: Knowing, knowing about knowing, and knowing how to know. In H. W.

Reese (Ed.), *Advances in child development and behavior* (Vol. 10). New York: Academic Press.

Brown, B. (1974). *New mind, new body*. New York: Harper & Row.

Brown, R. (1965). *Social psychology*. New York: Free Press.

Brown, R., & Hanlon, C. (1970). Derivational complexity and order of acquisition in child speech. In J. R. Hayes (Ed.), *Cognition and the development of language*. New York: Wiley.

Brown, R. W. (1973). Development of the first language in the human species. *American Psychologist, 28*, 97–106.

Brown, R. W., & McNeill, D. (1966). The "tip of the tongue" phenomenon. *Journal of Verbal Learning and Verbal Behavior, 5*, 325–337.

Brown, W. A., Monti, P. M., & Corriveau, D. P. (1978). Serum testosterone and sexual activity and interest in men. *Archives of Sexual Behavior, 7*, 97–103.

Bruce, C., Desimone, R., & Gross, C. (1981). Visual properties of neurons in a polysensory area in the superior temporal sulcus of the macaque. *Journal of Neurophysiology, 46*, 369–384.

Bruce, H. M. (1959). An exteroreceptive block to pregnancy in the mouse. *Nature, 184*, 105.

Bruner, J. S., Olver, R. R., & Greenfield, P. M. (1966). *Studies in cognitive growth*. New York: Wiley.

Bruner, J. S. (1966). On cognitive growth: II. In J. S. Bruner, R. R. Olver, & P. M. Greenfield, *Studies in cognitive growth*, New York: Wiley.

Bryan, W. L., & Harter, N. (1897). Studies in the physiology and psychology of telegraphic language. *Psychological Review, 4*, 27–53.

Buchanan, P. C. (1964). Innovative organizations: A study in organizational development. In *Applying behavioral science research in industry*. New York: Industrial Relations Counselor.

Bucke, R. M. (1900). *Cosmic consciousness*. New York: Causeway Books.

Bucklew, J. (1960). *Paradigms for psychopathology: A contribution to case history analysis*. Philadelphia: J. B. Lippincott.

Bullock, T. H., & Cowles, R. B. (1952). Physiology of an infrared receptor—the facial pit of pit vipers. *Science, 115*, 541–543.

Butler, R. N. (1975). *Why survive? Being old in America*. New York: Harper & Row.

Byrne, D. (1969). Attitudes and attraction. In L. Berkowitz (Ed.), *Advances in experimental social psychology* (Vol. 4). New York: Academic Press.

Byrne, D., Ervin. C. R., & Lamberth, J. (1970). Continuity between the experimental study of attraction and real-life computer dating. *Journal of Personality and Social Psychology, 16*, 157–165.

Calhoun, J. B. (1962). Population density and social pathology. *Scientific American, 206*, 139–148.

Cameron, N. (1963). *Personality development and psychopathology: A dynamic approach*. Boston: Houghton Mifflin.

Cann, M. A. (1953). *An investigation of a component of parental behavior in humans*. Unpublished master's thesis, University of Chicago

Cannon, W. B. (1911). *The mechanical factors of digestion*. London: Arnold.

Cannon, W. B. (1927). The James-Lange theory of emotions: A critical examination and an alternative theory. *American Journal of Psychology, 39*, 106–124.

Cannon, W. B. (1929). *Bodily changes in pain, hunger, fear, and rage* (2nd ed.). New York: Appleton-Century-Crofts.

Cannon, W. B., & Washburn, A. L. (1912). An explanation of hunger. *American Journal of Physiology, 29*, 441–454.

Cantor, J. R., Zillmann, D., & Bryant, J. (1975). Enhancement of experienced sexual arousal in response to erotic stimuli through misattribution of unrelated residual excitation. *Journal of Personality and Social Psychology. 32*, 69–75.

Cantor, N., & Mischel, W. (1977). Traits as protypes: Effects on recognition memory. *Journal of Personality and Social Psychology, 35*, 38–48.

Carlisle, H. J. (1969). The effects of preoptic and anterior hypothalamic lesions on behavioral thermoregulation in the cold. *Journal of Comparative and Physiological Psychology, 69*, 391–402.

Carlsson, A. (1959). The occurrence, distribution and physiological role of catecholamines in the nervous system. *Pharmacology Review, 11*, 490.

Carmichael, L. (1970). The onset and early development of behavior. In P. H. Mussen (Ed.), *Carmichael's manual of child psychology* (3rd ed.) (Vol. 1). New York: Wiley.

Carmichael, L., Hogan, H. P., & Walter, A. A. (1932). An experimental study of the effect of language on the reproduction of visually perceived forms. *Journal of Experimental Psychology, 15*, 73–86.

Carpenter, G. (1975). Mother's face and the newborn. In R. Lewin (Ed.), *Child alive*. London: Temple Smith.

Cassell, S. (1965). Effect of brief puppet therapy upon the emotional responses of children undergoing cardiac catheterization. *Journal of Consulting Psychology, 29*, 1–8.

Cattell, R. B. (1950). *Personality: A systematic, theoretical, and factual study*. New York: McGraw-Hill.

Cattell, R. B. (1952). *Factor analysis: An introduction and manual for psychologist and social scientist*. New York: Harper.

Cattell, R. B. (1957). *Personality and motivation: Structure and measurement*. New York: World Book.

Cattell, R. G. (1963). Theory of fluid and crystallized intelligence: The critical experiment. *Journal of Educational Psychology, 36*, 1–22.

Cautela, J. R. (1966). Treatment of compulsive behavior by covert sensitization. *Psychological Record, 16*, 33–41.

Centers, R. A. (1963). Laboratory adaptation of the controversial procedure for the conditioning of verbal operants. *Journal of Abnormal and Social Psychology, 67*, 334–379.

Chaiken, S., & Eagley, A. H. (1976). Communication modality as a determinant of message persuasiveness and message comprehensibility. *Journal of Personality and Social Psychology, 34*, 605–614.

Change, J. E., & Goldstein, A. G. (1971). Internal-external control of reinforcement and embedded-figures performance. *Perception & Psychophysics, 9*, 33–34.

Chapman, A. J. (1973). Social facilitation of laughter in children. *Journal of Experimental Social Psychology, 9*, 529–541.

Chapman, J. (1966). The early symptoms of schizophrenia. *British Journal of Psychiatry, 112*, 225–251.

Chapman, L. J., & Chapman, J. P. (1967). Genesis of popular but erroneous psychodiagnostic observations. *Journal of Abnormal Psychology. 72*, 193–204.

Chapman, L. J., & Chapman, J. P. (1969). Illusory correlation as an obstacle to the use of valid psychodiagnostic signs. *Journal of Abnormal Psychology 74*, 271–280.

Chase, W. G., & Simon, H. A. (1973). Perception in chess. *Cognitive Psychology, 4*, 55–81.

Chen, E. (1979, December 9). Twins reared apart: A Living lab. *The New York Times Magazine*, 112–126.

Chen, S. C. (1937). Social molification of the activity of ants in nest-building. *Physiological Zoology, 10*, 420–436.

Cherry, E. C. (1953). Some experiments on the recognition of speech with one and two ears. *Journal of the Acoustical Society of America, 25*, 975–979.

Chodorkoff, B. (1954). Self-perception, perceptual defense, and adjustment. *Journal of Abnormal and Social Psychology, 49*, 508–512.

Chomsky, N. (1957). *Syntactic structures*. The Hague: Mouton.

Chow, K. L. (1951). Effects of partial extirpations of the posterior association cortex on visually mediated behavior in monkeys. *Comparative Psychological Monographs*, 20, 187–217.

Chwelos, N., Blewett, D. B., Smith, C. M., & Hoffer, A. (1959). Use of d-LSD in the treatment of alcoholism. *Quarterly Journal of Studies on Alcohol*, 20, 577–590.

Clark, E. V. (1971). On the acquisition of the meaning of before and after. *Journal of Verbal Learning and Verbal Behavior*, 10, 266–275.

Clark, J. T., Smith, E. R., & Davidson, J. M. (1984). Enhancement of sexual motivation in male rats by yohimbine. *Science*, 225, 847–849.

Clark, J. T., Smith, E. R., & Davidson, J. M. (in press). Yohimbine stimulates mounting in castrate male and intact nonreceptive female rats.

Clark, M. (1979, November 12). Drugs and psychiatry: A new era. *Newsweek*, 98.

Cleckley, H. (1976). *The mask of sanity* (5th edition). St. Louis: C. V. Mosby.

Coburn, R. S. (1983, September). Schooling the precocious. *Science*, 68–83.

Cohen, J., Hansel, C. E. M., & Sylvester, J. D. (1954). Interdependence of temporal and auditory judgments. *Nature*, 174, 642.

Cohen, S., Glass, D. C., & Singer, J. E. (1973). Apartment noise, auditory discrimination and reading ability in children. *Journal of Experimental Social Psychology*, 9, 407–422.

Coleman, J. C., Butcher, J. N., & Carson, R. C. (1984). *Abnormal psychology and modern life* (7th ed.). Glenview, IL: Scott, Foresman.

Collins, A. M., & Quillian, M. R. (1969). Retrieval time from semantic memory. *Journal of Verbal Learning and Verbal Behavior*, 8, 240–247.

Collins, B., Henker, B., & Whalen, C. (1980). Ecological and pharmacological influences on behaviors in the hyperkinetic behavioral syndrome. In S. Salzinger, J. Antrobus, E. J. Glicks (Eds.), *The ecosystem of the 'sick' kid.*. New York: Academic Press.

Comeback for shock therapy? (1979, November 19). *Time*, 76.

Conners, C. K. (1972). Pharmacotherapy of psychopathology in children. In H. C. Quay & J. S. Werry (Eds.), *Psychopathological disorders of childhood*. New York: Wiley.

Conrad, R. (1964). Acoustic confusions in immediate memory. *British Journal of Psychology*, 55, 75–83.

Cooper, J., & Axsom, D. (1982). Effort justification in psychotherapy. In G. Weary & H. Mirels (Eds.), *Integrations of clinical and social psychology*. London: Oxford University Press.

Cooper, J. (1980). Reducing fears and increasing assertiveness: The role of dissonance reduction. *Journal of Experimental Social Psychology*, 16, 199–213.

Corbit, J. D. (1968). Cellular dehydration and hypovolaemia are additive in producing thirst. *Nature*, 218, 886–887.

Corbit, J. D. (1970). Behavioral regulation of body temperature. In J. D. Hardy, A. P. Gagge & J. A. Stolwijk (Eds.)., *Physiological and behavioral Temperature regulation*. Springfield, IL: Charles C Thomas.

Corby, J. C., Roth, W. T., Zarcone, V. P., Jr., & Kopell, B. S. (1978). Psychophysiological correlates of the practice of tantric yoga meditation. *Archives of General Psychiatry*, 35, 571–577.

Cornsweet, T. N. (1970). *Visual perception*. New York: Academic Press.

Costa, P. T., & McCrae, R. R. (1978). Objective personality assessment. In M. Storandt, I. C. Siegler & M. F. Elias (Eds.), *The clinical psychology of aging*. New York: Plenum Press.

Costa, P. T., & McCrae, R. R. (1980). Still stable after all these years: Personality as a key to some issues in aging. In P. B. Bolles & O. G. Brim (Eds.), *Life-span development and behavior* (Vol. 3). New York: Academic Press.

Cottrell, N. B. (1968). Performance in the presence of other human beings: Mere presence, audience, and affiliation effects. In E. C. Simmel, R. A. Hoppe, & G. A. Milton (Eds.), *Social facilitation and imitative behavior*. Boston: Allyn and Bacon.

Cottrell, N. B., Wack, D. L., Sekerak, G. J., & Rittle, R. H. (1968). The social facilitation of dominant responses by the presence of an audience and the mere presence of others. *Journal of Personality and Social Psychology*, 9, 251–256.

Cotzias, G. C., Papasilou, P. S., & Gellene, R. (1969). Modification of parkinsonism-chronic treatment with L-Dopa. *New England Journal of Medicine*, 280, 337.

Cowan, M. L., & Stewart, B. J. (1977). A methodological study of sex stereotypes. *Sex Roles*, 3, 205–216.

Cowen, E. (1982). The special number: A complete roadmap. *American Journal of Community Psychology*, 10, 239–250.

Craik, F. I. M. (1977). Age differences in human memory. In J. E. Birren & K. W. Schaie (Eds.), *Handbook of the psychology of aging*. New York: Van Nostrand.

Craik, F. I. M., & Lockhart, R. S. (1972). Levels of processing: A framework for memory research. *Journal of Verbal Learning and Verbal Behavior*, 11, 671–684.

Craik, F. I. M., & Tulving, E. (1975). Depth of processing and the retention of words of episodic memory. *Journal of Experimental Psychology*, 104, 268–294.

Cross, B. A., & Green, J. D. (1959). Activity of single neurons in the hypothalamus: Effect of osmotic and other stimuli. *Journal of Physiology*, 17, 347–392.

Crossman, E. R. f. W. (1959). A theory of the acquisition of speed-skill. *Ergonomics*, 2, 153–166.

Cruz-Coke, R., & Varela, A. (1966). Inheritance of alcoholism: Its association with color-blindness. *Lancet*, 2, 1282–1284.

Csikszentmihalyi, M. (1975). Play and intrinsic rewards. *Journal of Humanistic Psychology*, 15, 41.

Cumming, E., & Henry, W. (1961). *Growing old: A process of disengagement*. New York: Basic Books.

Dale, H. H. (1938). Acetylcoline as a chemical transmitter of the effects of nerve impulses. *Journal of Mt. Sinai Hospital*, 4, 401–415.

Dalton, K. (1977). *The premenstrual syndrome and progesterone therapy*. London: Heinemann.

Daly, M., & Wilson, M. (1978). *Sex, evolution and behavior*. North Scituate, MA: Duxbury Press.

D'Andrade, R. (1966). Cross-cultural studies of sex differences in behavior. In E. E. Maccoby (Ed.), *The development of sex differences*. Stanford, CA: Stanford University Press.

Darley, J. M., & Latané, B. (1968). Bystander intervention in emergencies: Diffusion of responsibility. *Journal of Personality and Social Psychology*, 8, 377–383.

Darley, J. M., Lewis, L. D., & Glucksberg, S. (1972). *Stereotype persistance and change among college students: One more time*. Unpublished manuscript. Princeton University.

Darley, J. M., Moriarty, T., Darley, S., & Berscheid, E. (1974). Increased conformity to a fellow deviant as a function of prior deviation. *Journal of Experimental Social Psychology*, 10, 211–223.

Darley, J. M., Teger, A. I., & Lewis, L. D. (1973). Do groups always inhibit individuals' responses to potential emergencies? *Journal of Personality and Social Psychology*, 26, 395–399.

Darwin, C. J., Turvey, M. T., & Crowder, R. G. (1973). An auditory analogue of the Sperling partial report procedure: Evidence for brief auditory storage. *Cognitive Psychology*, 3, 255–267.

Davenport, W. (1965). Sexual patterns and their regulation in a society of the Southwest Pacific. In F. A. Beach (Ed.), *Sex and behavior*. New York: Wiley.

Davidson, J. M. (1966). Activation of the male rat's sexual behavior by intracerebral implantation of androgen. *Endocrinology*, 79, 783–794.

Davidson, J. M. (1976). The physiology of meditation and mystical states of consciousness. *Perspectives in Biology and Medicine, 19,* 345–379.

Davidson, J. M. (1980). The psychobiology of sexual experience. In J. M. Davidson & R. J. Davidson (Eds.), *The psychobiology of consciousness.* New York: Plenum Press.

Davidson, J. M., Camargo, C. A., & Smith, E. R. (1979). Effects of androgen on sexual behavior in hypogonadal men. *Journal of Clinical Endocrinology and Metabolism, 48,* 955–958.

Davidson, J. M., Smith, E. R., & Levine, S. (In Press). Testosterone. In H. Ursin, E. Baade, & S. Levine (Eds.), *Psychobiology of stresses: A study of coping men.* New York: Academic Press (Article originally published, 1978).

Davis, C. M. (1928). Self-selection of diet by newly weaned infants. *American Journal of Disease Children, 36,* 651–679.

Davis, J. M. (1975). Overview: Maintenance therapy in psychiatry: 1. Schizophrenia. *American Journal of Psychiatry, 132,* 1237–1245.

Davison, A. N., & Dobbing J. (1966). Myelination as a vulnerable period in brain development. *British Medical Bulletin, 22,* 40–44.

Davison, G. C. (1978). Not can, but ought: The treatment of homosexuality. *Journal of Consulting and Clinical Psychology, 46,* 170–172.

Deaux, K. (1976). *The behavior of women and men.* Monterey, CA: Brooks/Cole.

De Carlo, T. J. (1971). *Recreational participation patterns and successful aging: A Twin study.* Unpublished doctoral dissertation. Columbia University.

Deci, E. L. (1975). *Intrinsic motivation.* New York: Plenum Press.

Defazio, V., Rustin, S., & Diamond, A. (1975). Symptom development in Viet Nam era veterans. *American Journal of Orthopsychiatry, 45,* 158–163.

DeGroot, A. D. (1965). *Thought and choice in chess.* The Hague: Mouton.

DeGroot, A. D. (1966). Perception and memory versus thought. In B. Kleinmuntz (ed.), *Problem solving.* New York: Wiley.

Delgado, J., Roberts, W., & Miller, N. (1954). Learning motivated by electrical stimulation of the brain. *American Journal of Physiology, 179,* 587–593.

Dement, W. C. (1960). The effect of dream deprivation. *Science, 131,* 1705–1707.

Dement, W. C. (1972). *Some must watch while some must sleep.* Stanford, CA: Stanford University Press.

Dement, W. C., & Wolpert, E. (1958). The relation of eye movements, bodily motility, and external stimuli to dream content. *Journal of Experimental Psychology, 53,* 543–553.

Dennis, M., & Whitaker, H. (1976). Language acquisition following hemidecortication: Linguistic superiority of the left over the right hemisphere. *Brain and Language, 3,* 404–433.

Dennis, W. (1968). Creative productivity between the ages of twenty and eighty years. In B. Neugarten (Ed.), *Middle Age and Aging.* Chicago: University of Chicago Press.

Derlaga, V. J., Durham, B., Gockel, B., & Sholis, D. (1981). Sex differences in self-disclosure: Effects of topic content, friendship, and partner's sex. *Sex Roles, 7,* 433–447.

Descartes, R. (1662). *Traité do l'homme.* (E. S. Haldane & G. R. T. Ross, Trans.). Cambridge, England: Cambridge University Press, 1911.

Desor, J. A. (1972). Toward a psychological theory of crowding. *Journal of Personality and Social Psychology, 21,* 79–83.

Detterman, D. K., & Sternberg, R. J. (Eds.). (1982). *How and how much can intelligence be increased?* Norwood, NJ: Ablex.

Deutsch, M., & Gerard, H. B. (1955). A study of normative and informational social influences upon individual judgment. *Journal of Abnormal and Social Psychiatry, 51,* 629–631.

DeValois, R. L., Smith, C. J., Karoly, A. J., & Kitai, S. T. (1958). Electrical responses of primate visual system: I Different layers of macaque laterial geniculate nucleus. *Journal of Comparative and Physiological Psychology, 51,* 662–668.

Diamond, I., & Neff, W. D. (1957). Ablation of temporal cortex and discrimination of auditory patterns. *Journal of Neurophysiology, 20,* 300–315.

Dickinson, G. E. (1978). Adolescent sex information sources: 1964–1974. *Adolescence, 13,* 653–658.

Diener, E., Fraser, S. C., Beaman, A. L., & Kelem, R. T. (1976). Effects of deindividuation variable on stealing among halloween trick-or-treaters. *Journal of Personality and Social Psychology, 33,* 178–183.

Dion, K. K. (1972). Physical attractiveness and evaluation of children's transgressions. *Journal of Personality and Social Psychology, 24,* 207–213.

Dion, K. K., Berscheid, E., & Walster, E. (1972). What is beautiful is good. *Journal of Personality and Social Psychology, 24,* 285–290.

Ditchburn, R. W. (1973). *Eye movements and visual perception* Oxford: Clarendon Press.

Dollard, J., Doob, L., Miller, N., Mowrer, O., & Sears, R. (1939). *Frustration and aggression.* New Haven: Yale University Press.

Doob, A. N., Carlsmith, J. M., Freedman, J. L., Landauer, T. K., & Toms, S. (1969). Effect of initial selling price on subsequent sales. *Journal of Personality and Social Psychology, 11,* 345–350.

Doob, A. N., & Wood, L. E. (1972). Catharsis and aggression: Effects of annoyance and retaliation on aggressive behavior. *Journal of Personality and Social Psychology, 22,* 156–162.

Dooling, D. J., & Lachman, R. (1971). Effects of comprehension on retention of prose. *Journal of Experimental Psychology, 88,* 216–222.

Dooling, R., & Searcy, M. (1980). Early perceptual selectivity in the swan sparrow. *Developmental Psychobiology, 13,* 499–506.

Dörner, G. E., Rhode, W., Stahl, F., Krell, L. & Masius, W. (1975). A neuroendocrine predisposition for homosexuality in men. *Archives of Sexual Behavior, 4,* 1–8.

Douvan, E., & Adelson, J. (1966). *The adolescent experience.* New York: Wiley.

Drabman, R. S., & Thomas, M. H. (1974). Does media violence increase children's tolerance to real-life aggression? *Developmental Psychology, 10,* 418–421.

Droege, R. C. (1967). Sex differences in aptitude maturation during high school. *Journal of Counseling Psychology, 14,* 407–411.

Duncan, B. L. (1976). Differential social perception and attribution of intergroup violence: Testing the lower limits of stereotyping of blacks. *Journal of Personality and Social Psychology, 34,* 590–598.

Durlak, J. A. (1979). Comparative effectiveness of paraprofessional and professional helpers. *Psychological Bulletin, 56,* 80–92.

Dusek, J. B., & Flaherty, J. F. (1981). The development of the self-concept during the adolescent years. *Monographs of the Society for Research in Child Development, 46,* (4, Serial No. 191).

Dweck, C. S., & Goetz, F. E. (1977). Attributions and learned helplessness. In J. H. Harvey, W. Ickes, & R. F. Kidd (Eds.), *New directions in attribution research* (Vol. 2). Hillsdale, NJ: Erlbaum.

Eagly, A. H., & Warren, R. (1976). Intelligence, comprehension, and opinion change. *Journal of Personality, 44,* 226–242.

Ebbinghaus, H. (1964). *Memory* (H. A. Ruger & C. E. Bussenius, Trans.). New York: Dover. (Originally published, 1885.)

Eccles, J. C. (1964). *The physiology of synapses.* Berlin: Springer.

Edson, L. (1975). *How we learn.* New York: Time-Life Books.

Egendorf, A., Remez, A., & Farley, J. (1981). Dealing with the war: A view based on the individual lives of Viet Nam Veterans. In A. Egendorf et al. (Eds.), *Legacies of Viet Nam: Com-*

parative adjustment of veterans and their peers (Vol. 5). Washington, DC: U.S. Government Printing Office.

Eich, J. E. (1980). The cue-dependent nature of state-dependent retrieval. *Memory and Cognition, 8*, 157–173.

Eisenberg, N., & Lennon, R. (1983). Sex differences in empathy and related capacities. *Psychological Bulletin, 94*, 100–131.

Ellis, A. (1976). Rational emotive therapy. In V. Binder, A. Binder & B. Rimland (Eds.), *Modern therapies*. Englewood Cliffs, NJ: Prentice-Hall.

Ellis, A. (1977). The basic clinical theory of rational-emotive therapy. In A. Ellis & R. Grieger (Eds.), *Handbook of rational-emotive therapy*. New York: Springer.

Emmerich, W. (1959). Parental identification in young children. *Genetic Psychology Monographs, 60*, 257–308.

Enright, J. T. (1970). Stereopsis, visual latency, and three-dimensional moving pictures. *American Scientist, 58*, 536–545.

Epstein, A. N. (1983). Neuropsychology of drinking behavior. In E. Satinoff & P. Teitelbaum (Eds.), *Handbook of behavioral neurobiology*. New York: Plenum Press.

Epstein, A. N. (1971). The lateral hypothalamic syndrome and its implication for the physiological psychology of hunger and thirst. In E. Stellar & J. M. Sprague (Eds.), *Progress in physiological psychology* (Vol. 4). New York: Academic Press.

Epstein, S. M. (1967). Toward a unified theory of anxiety. In B. A. Maher (Ed.), *Progress in experimental personality research* (Vol. 4). New York: Academic Press.

Erikson, E. H. (1950). *Childhood and society*. New York: Norton.

Erikson, E. H. (1963). *Childhood and society* (2nd rev. ed). New York: Norton.

Erikson, E. H. (1968). *Identity, youth and crisis*. New York: Norton.

Erikson, E. H. (1969). *Ghandi's truth*. New York: Norton.

Erikson, E. H. (1975). *Life history and the historical moment*. New York: Norton.

Erikson, K. T. (1976). *Everything in its path: Destruction of community in the Buffalo Creek flood*. New York: Simon & Schuster.

Erlenmeyer-Kimling, L., & Jarvik, L. F. (1963). Genetics and intelligence: A review. *Science, 142*, 1477–1479.

Ernst, C., & Angst, J. (1983). *Birth order*. New York: Springer-Verlag.

Eron, L. D. (1980). Prescription for reduction of aggression. *American Psychologist, 35*, 244–252.

Eron, L. D. (1982). Parent-child interaction, television violence, and aggression of children. *American Psychologist, 37*, 197–211.

Eron, L. D., Lefkowitz, M. M., Huesmann, L. R., & Walder, L. Q.. (1972). Does television violence cause aggression? *American Psychologist, 27*, 253–263.

Ervin-Tripp, S. (1964). Limitation and structural change in children's language. In E. H. Lenneberg (Ed.), *New directions in the study of language*. Cambridge, MA: MIT Press.

Estes, W. K. (1944). An experimental study of punishment. *Psychological Monographs, 57*, (Whole No. 263).

Estroff, S. E. (1981). *Making it crazy: An ethnography of psychiatric clients in an American community*. Berkeley: University of California Press.

Estroff, S. E. (1981). *Making it crazy: An ethnography of psychiatric clients in an American community*. Berkeley: University of California Press.

Eveleth, P. B., & Tanner, J. M. (1976). *Worldwide variation in human growth*. Cambridge, England: Cambridge University Press.

Eysenck, H. J. (1952). The effects of psychotherapy: An evaluation. *Journal of Consulting Psychology, 16*, 319–324.

Eysenck, H. J. (1965). *Fact and fiction in psychology*. Baltimore: Penguin.

Eysenck, H. J. (1967). *The biological basis of personality*. Springfield, IL: Charles C Thomas.

Eysenck, H. J. (1975). *The inequality of man*. San Diego: Edits Publishers.

Eysenck, H. J., & Eysenck, S. B. G. (1967). *Personality structure and measurement*. London: Routledge & Kegan-Paul.

Fagot, B. I. (1977). Consequences of moderate cross-gender behavior in pre-school children. *Child Development 48*, 902–907.

Fagot, B. I., & Patterson, C. R. (1969). An in vivo analysis of reinforcing contingencies for sex role behaviors in the preschool child. *Development Psychology, 1*, 563–568.

Fairweather, G. W., Sanders, D. H., Cressler, D. L., & Maynard, H. (1969). *Community life for the mentally ill: An alternative to institutional care*. Chicago: Aldine.

Fairweather, G. W. (Ed.). (1964). *Social psychology in treating mental illness: An experimental approach*. New York: Wiley.

Falk, J. L. (1971). Theoretical review: The nature and determinants of adjunctive behavior. *Physiology and Behavior, 6*, 577–588.

Fantz, R. L. (1961). The origin of form perception. *Scientific-American, 204*, 66–72.

Fantz, R. L. (1970). Visual perception and experience in infancy: Issues and approaches. In *Early experience and visual information processing in perceptual and reading disorders*. New York: National Academy of Science.

Fechner, G. T. (1966) *Elements of psychophysics* (H. E. Adler, Trans.). New York: Holt, Rinehart and Winston. (Originally published, 1860.)

Feder, H. H. (1984). Hormones and sexual behavior. *Annotated Review of Psychology, 35*, 170.

Feinberg, I. (1962). A comparison of the visual hallucinations in schizophrenia and those induced by mescaline and LSD-25. In L. J. West (ed.), *Hallucinations*. New York: Grune & Stratton.

Feldman, M. P., & MacCulloch, M. J. (1971). *Homosexual behavior: Therapy and assessment*. Oxford, England: Pergamon Press.

Felner, R. D., Jason, L. A., Moritsugu, J. N., & Farber, S. S. (1983). *Preventive psychology: Theory, research and practice*. New York: Pergamon Press.

Farber, S. S. (1983). *Preventive psychology: Theory, research and practice*. New York: Pergamon Press.

Fennema, E., & Sherman, J. (1977). Sex-related differences in mathematics achievement, spatial visualization and affective factors. *American Educational Research Journal, 14*, 51–71.

Ferrier, D. (1876). *Functions of the brain*. London: Smith, Elder & Co.

Festinger, L. (1954). A theory of social comparison processes. *Human Relations, 7*, 117–140.

Festinger, L. (1957). *A theory of cognitive dissonance*. Stanford, CA: Stanford University Press.

Festinger, L., & Carlsmith, J. M. (1959). Cognitive consequences of forced compliance. *Journal of Abnormal and Social Psychology, 58*, 202–210.

Festinger, L., Schachter, S., & Back, K. (1950). *Social pressures in informal groups*. New York: Harper.

Feuerstein, R. (1980). *Instrumental enrichment: An intervention program for cognitive modifiability*. Baltimore, MD: University Park Press.

Fields, S. (1976). Folk healing for the wounded spirit. *Innovations, 3*, 3–18.

Fields, S. (1978). Support and succor for the "walking wounded." *Innovations, 5*(1), 2–15.

Fieve, R. R. (1975). *Moodswing: The third revolution in psychiatry*. New York: Bantam.

Fillmore, C. J. (1968). The case for case. In E. Bach & R. T. Harms (Eds.). *Universals in linguistic theory*. New York: Holt, Rinehart & Winston.

Fink, K., & Cantril, H. (1939). The collegiate stereotype as frame of reference. *Journal of Abnormal and Social Psychology, 32*, 352–356.

Finucci, J. M., & Childs, B. (1981). Are there really more dyslexic boys than girls? In A. Ansara, N. Geschwind, A. Galaburda, M. Albert, & N. Gartrell (Eds.), *Sex differences in dyslexia.* Townson, MD: Orton Dyslexia Society.

Fisher, C., Gross, J., & Zuch, J. (1965). Cycle of penile erection synchronous with dreaming. *Archives of General Psychiatry, 12,* 29–45.

Fisher, R. (1967). The biological fabric of time. *Interdisciplinary Perspectives of Time: Annals of the New York Academy of Science, 138,* 451–465.

Fitch, S. A., & Adams, G. R. (1983). Ego identity and intimacy status: Replication and extension. *Developmental Psychology, 19,* 839–845.

Fitts, P. M., & Posner, M. I. (1967). *Human performance.* Belmont, CA: Brooks-Cole.

Fitzsimons, J. T. (1971). The physiology of thirst: A review of the extraneaural aspects of the mechanisms of drinking. In E. Stellar & J. M. Sprague (Eds.), *Progress in psychological psychology.* New York: Academic Press.

Fitzsimons, J. T. (1972). Thirst. *Physiological Reviews, 52,* 468–561.

Fixsen, D. L., Phillips, E. L., Phillips, E. A., & Wolf, M. M. (1972). *The teaching-family model of group home treatment.* Paper presented at the meeting of the American Psychological Association, Honolulu, Hawaii.

Flavell, J. H. (1978). Metacognitive development. In J. M. Scandura & C. J. Brainerd (Eds.), *Structural-process theories of complex human behavior.* Leyden: S. J. Thoff.

Flynn, J., Vanegas, H., Foote, W., & Edwards, S. (1970) Neural mechanisms involved in a cat's attack on a rat. In R. F. Whalen, M. Thompson, M. Verzeano, & N. Weinberger (Eds.), *The neural control of behavior.* New York: Academic Press.

Foa, E. B., Blau, J. S., Prout, M., & Latimer, P. (1977). Is horror a necessary component of flooding (imposion)? *Behavior Research and Therapy, 15,* 397–402.

Ford, C. S., & Beach, F. A. (1951). *Patterns of sexual behavior.* New York: Harper.

Forerster, O. (1929). Beiträge zur Pathophysiologie der Sehsphauare. *Journal für Psychologie und Neurologie, 39,* 463–485.

Foss, D. J., & Hakes, D. T. (1978). *Psycholinguistics.* Englewood Cliffs, NJ: Prentice-Hall.

Foulkes, D., & Fleischer, S. (1975). Mental activity in relaxed wakefulness. *Journal of Abnormal Psychology, 84,* 66.

Fraisse, P. (1963). *The psychology of time.* New York: Harper & Row.

Frances, S. J. (1979). Sex differences in nonverbal behavior. *Sex Roles, 5,* 519–535.

Frankenberg, W. K., & Dodds, J. B. (1967). The Denver Developmental Screening Test. *Journal of Pediatrics, 71,* 181–191.

Franks, J. J., & Bransford, J. D. (1971). Abstraction of visual patterns. *Journal of Experimental Psychology, 90,* 65–74.

Freedman, J. L., & Doob, A. N. (1968). *Deviancy: The psychology of being different.* New York: Academic Press.

Freedman, J. L., & Fraser, S. C. (1966). Compliance without pressure: The foot-in-the-door technique. *Journal of Personality and Social Psychology, 4,* 195–202.

Freedman, J. L., Henshka, S., & Levy, A. (1975). Population density and pathology: Is there a relationship? *Journal of Experimental Social Psychology, 11,* 539–552.

Freedman, J. L. (1975). *Crowding and behavior.* New York: Viking Press.

Freud, A. (1958). Adolescence. *Psychoanalytic Study of the Child, 13,* 255–278.

Freud, S., & Breuer, J. (1966). *Studies on hysteria* (J. Strachey, Trans.). New York: Avon Books. (Originally published, 1895.)

Freud, S. (1905). *Three essays on the theory of sexuality.* London: Hogarth Press.

Freud, S. (1914/1938). Psychopathology of everyday life. In A. A. Birell (Ed.), *The writings of Sigmund Freud.* New York: Modern Library.

Freud, S. (1953). A letter to Fleiss, 1897. In E. Jones (Ed.), *The life and works of Sigmund Freud* (Vol. 1). New York: Basic Books.

Freud, S. (1953). Fragment of an analysis of a case of hysteria. In J. Strachey (Ed. & trans.), *The standard edition of the complete psychological works of Sigmund Freud* (Vol. 7). London: Hogarth Press. (Originally published, 1905.)

Freud, S. (1953). The interpretation of dreams. In J. Strachey (Ed. and trans.), *The standard edition of the complete psychological works of Sigmund Freud* (Vols. 4 & 5). London: Hogarth Press. (Originally published, 1900.)

Freud, S. (1956). Analysis of a phobia in a five-year-old boy, 1909. In *Collected works of Sigmund Freud* (Vol. 10). London: Hogarth Press.

Freud, S. (1958). On beginning the treatment. In J. Strachey (Trans.), *The standard edition of the complete psychological works of Sigmund Freud* (Vol. 12). London: Hogarth Press. (Originally published, 1913.)

Freud, S. (1959). On psychotherapy. In E. Jones (Ed.), *Sigmund Freud collected papers* (Vol. 1). New York: Basic Books. (Originally published, 1904.)

Freud, S. (1961). Some additional notes on dream-interpretation as a whole. In J. Strachey (Trans.), *The standard edition of the complete psychological works of Sigmund Freud* (Vol. 19). London: Hogarth Press. (Originally published, 1925.)

Freud, S. (1961) Introductory lectures on psychoanalysis. In J. Strachey (Trans.), *The standard edition of the complete psychological works of Sigmund Freud* (Vol. 15). London: Hogarth Press. (Originally published, 1916.)

Freud, S. (1962). The interpretation of dreams. In J. Strachey (Ed. and trans.), *The standard edition of the complete psychological works of Sigmund Freud* (Vols. 4 & 5). London: Hogarth Press, 1962. (Originally published, 1900.)

Freud, S. (1962). *Three essays on the theory of sexuality* (J. Strachey, Trans.). New York: Avon Books. (Originally published, 1905.)

Freud, S. (1963). Introductory lectures on psychoanalysis. In J. Strachey (Trans.), *The standard edition of the complete psychological works of Sigmund Freud* (Vol. 16). London: Hogarth Press. (Originally published, 1916.)

Freud, S. (1965). *New introductory lectures on psychoanalysis* (J. Strachey, Trans.). New York: Norton. (Originally published, 1933.)

Friedl, E. (1975). *Women and Men.* New York: Holt, Rinehart & Winston.

Frisby, J. P. (1980). *Seeing.* Oxford: Oxford University Press.

Fritsch, G. T., & Hitzig, E. (1960). *über die elektrische Erregbarkeit des Grosshirns.* In G. Von. Bonin (Trans.), *Some papers on the cerebral cortex.* Springfield, IL: Charles C Thomas. (Originally published, 1870.)

Frodi, A., Macaulay, J., & Thome, P. R. (1977). Are women always less aggressive than men? A review of the experimental literature. *Psychological Bulletin, 84,* 634–660.

Fromkin, V., Krashen, S., Curtiss, S., Rigler, S., & Rigler, M. (1972/1973). The development of language in Genie: A case of language acquisition beyond the "critical period." *Brain & Language, 1,* 81–107.

Fromm, E. (1947). *Man for himself: An inquiry into the psychology of ethics.* New York: Rinehart.

Galin, D. (1976). The two modes of consciousness and the two halves of the brain. In P. Lee, R. E. Ornstein, C. T. Tart, A. Deikman, & D. Galin (Eds.), *Symposium on Consciousness.* New York: Viking Press.

Gall, F. J., & Spurzheim, J. C. (1810–1819). *Anatomie et phy-*

siologie du systéme nerveux en général et du cerveau en particulier (4 vols. & atlas). Paris: Schoell.

Galle, O. R., Gove, W. R., & McPherson, J. M. (1972). Population density and pathology: What are the relations for man? *Science, 176,* 23–30.

Galton, F. (1883). *Inquiries into human faculty and its development.* London: Macmillan.

Garcia, J., Ervin, F. R., & Koelling, R. A. (1966). Learning with prolonged delay of reinforcement. *Psychonomic Science, 5,* 121–122.

Gardner, B. T., & Gartner, R. A. (1971). Two-way communication with an infant chimpanzee. In A. M. Schrier & F. Stollnitz (Eds.), *Behavior of nonhuman primates* (Vol. 4). New York: Academic Press.

Gardner, H. (1983). *Frames of mind: The theory of multiple intelligences.* New York: Basic Books.

Garrett, M. F. (1975). The analysis of sentence production. In G. H. Bower (ed.), *The psychology of learning and motivation* (Vol. 9). New York: Academic Press.

Gartner, A., & Riesman, F. (1982). Self-help and mental health. *Hospital and Community Psychology, 33, 631–635.*

Gartner, A., & Riessman, F. (1980). *Help: A working guide to self-help groups.* New York: Franklin Watts.

Gartner, A., & Riessman, F. (1980). *Help: A working guide to self-help groups.* New York: Viewpoint, Franklin Watts.

Gartner, A., & Riessman, F. (1982) Self-help and mental health. *Hospital and Community Psychology, 33, 631–635.*

Gates, M. F., & Allen, W. C. (1933). Conditioned behavior of isolated and grouped cockroaches on a simple maze. *Journal of Comparative Psychology, 15,* 331–358.

Gazzangia, M. S. (1970). *The bisected brain.* New York: Appleton-Century-Crofts.

Gazzaniga, M. S. (1967). The split brain in man. *Scientific American, 217* 24–29.

Gelb, T. K. (1929). Die ''Farbenkonstauz'' der Schdinge. *Handbuch der Hormalen und Pathologischen Psysiologie, 12,* 594–678.

Gelder, M. G., Bancroft, J. H. J., Gath, D. H., Johnston, D. W., Mathews, A. M., & Shaw, P. M. (1973). Specific and nonspecific factors in behavior therapy. *British Journal of Psychiatry, 123,* 445–462.

Gelles, R. J., & Strauss, M. A. Violence in the American family. *Journal of Social Issues, 35,* 14–38.

Gellman, R., & Miles, F. (1985). A new role for the cerebellum in conditioning. *Trends in Neuroscience, 8,* 181–182.

Gelman, R. (1972). Logical capacity of very young children: Number invariance rules. *Child Development, 43,* 75–90.

Gerard, H. B. (1963). Emotional uncertainty and social comparison. *Journal of Abnormal and Social Psychology, 66,* 568–573.

Gerbner, G. (1972). Violence in television drama: Trends and symbolic functions. In G. Comstock, A Rubenstein, & J. Murray, (Eds.). *Television and social behavior* (Vol. 1). Washington, D.C.: U.S. Government Printing Office.

Gerwirtz, J. L., & Baer, D. M. (1958). The effect of brief social deprivation on behavior for a social reinforcer. *Journal of Abnormal and Social Psychology, 56,* 49–56.

Gibson, E. J., & Walk, R. D. (1960). The ''visual cliff.'' *Scientific American, 202,* 64–71.

Gibson, J. J. (1933). Adaptation, after-effect, and contrast in the perception of curved lines. *Journal of Experimental Psychology, 16,* 1–31.

Gibson, J. J. (1950). *The perception of the visual world.* Boston: Houghton Mifflin.

Gill, F. B., & Wolf, L. L. (1975). Economics of feeding territoriality in the golden-winged sunbird. *Ecology, 56,* 333–345.

Gilman, S., Bloedel, J. R., & Lechtenberg, R. (1981). *Disorders of the cerebellum.* Philadelphia: Davis.

Gittelman-Klein, R., Klein, D. F., Katz, S., Saraf, K., & Pollack, E. (1976). Comparative effects of methylphenidate and thiordazine in hyperkinetic children. *Archives of General Psychiatry, 33,* 1217–1231.

Glass, D. C., & Singer, J. E. (1972). *Urban stress: Experiments on noise and social stressors.* New York: Academic Press.

Glickstein, M. (1985). Ferrier's mistake. *Trends in Neuroscience, 8,* 341–344.

Glucksberg, S., & Danks, J. H. (1975). *Experimental psycholinguistics.* Hillsdale, NJ: Erlbaum.

Glueck, S., & Glueck, E. (1950). *Unraveling juvenile delinquency.* New York: Commonwealth Fund.

Glueck, S., & Glueck, E. (1956). *Physique and delinquency.* New York: Harper.

Goffman, E. (1961). *Asylums: Essays on the social situation of mental patients and other inmates.* Garden City, NJ: Anchor.

Gogel, W. C. (1977). The metric of visual space. In W. Epstein (Ed.), *Stability and constancy in visual perception.* New York: Wiley.

Goldberg, P. A. (1968). Are women prejudiced against women? *Transaction, 5,* 28–30.

Goldfried, M. R., & Davidson, G. C. (1976). *Criminal behavior therapy.* New York: Holt, Rinehart and Winston.

Goleman, D. (1883). Recherches sur l'histologie des centres nerveux. *Archives Italiennes de Biologie, 3,* 285–317.

Gonshor, A., & Melvill, Jones, G. (1976). Extreme vestibulo-ocular adaptation induced by prolonged optical reversal in vision. *Journal of Physiology, 256,* 381–414.

Good, P. (1974). *The individual.* New York: Time-Life Books.

Goodwin, D. W., Powell, B., Bremer, D., Hoine, H., & Stern, J. (1969). Alcohol and recall: State dependent effects in man. *Science, 163,* 1358.

Goodwin, D. W. (1979). Alcoholism and heredity. *Archives of General Psychiatry, 36,* 57–64.

Goodwin, G. M., McCloskey, D. I., & Mathews, P. B. C. (1972). The contribution to muscle afferents to kinesthesia shown by vibration induced illusions of movement and by the effects of paralysing joint afferents. *Brain, 95,* 705–748.

Goodwin, J. (1980). The etiology of combat-related post-traumatic stress disorders. In T. Williams (Ed.), *Post-traumatic stress disorders of the Viet Nam veteran.* Cincinnati, OH: Disabled American Veterans National Headquarters.

Gore, R. (1971, October 22). In search of the mind's eye. *Life.*

Goss-Custard, J. D. (1981). Feeding behavior of redshank, *Tringa totanus,* and optimal forging theory. In A. C. Kamil & T. D. Sargent (Eds.), *Foraging behavior: Ecological eathological and psychological approaches.* New York: Garland.

Gottesman, I. I., & Shields, J. (1982). *Schizophrenia: The epigenetic puzzle.* Cambridge University Press.

Gottlieb, B. H. (1983). *Social support strategies: Guidelines for mental health practice.* Beverly Hills, CA: Sage Publications.

Gottlieb, B. H. (1983). *Support support strategies: Guidelines for mental health practice.* Beverly Hills, CA: Sage Publications.

Gould, S. J. (1976). Biological potential vs. biological determinism. *Natural History, 85,* 12–22.

Gould, S. J. (1981). *The mismeasure of man.* New York: Norton.

Goy, R. W. (1970) Experimental control of psychosexuality. *Philosophical Transactions of the Royal Society, (B), 259, 149–162.*

Green, D. M., & Swets, J. A. (1966). *Signal detection theory and psychophysics.* New York: Wiley.

Green, R. (1979). Biological influences on sexual identity. In A. Katchadourian (Ed.), *Human sexuality—a comparative and developmental perspective.* Berkeley: University of California Press.

Greenblatt, M., Grosser, G. H., & Wechsler, H. (1964). Differential responses of hospitalized depressed patients to somatic therapy. *American Journal of Psychiatry, 120,* 935–943.

Greenfield, P. M., & Smith, J. H. (1976). *The structure of com-*

munication in early language development. New York: Academic Press.

Greenfield, P. M. (1966). On culture and conservation. In J. S. Bruner, R. R. Olver, & P. M. Greenfield, *Studies in cognitive growth*. New York: Wiley.

Greenspoon, J. (1955). The reinforcing effects of two spoken sounds on the frequency of two responses. *American Journal of Psychology, 68*, 409–416.

Gregory, R. L. (1973). *Eye and brain* (2nd ed.). New York: World University Library.

Griffin, D. R. (1958). *Listening in the dark*. New Haven: Yale University Press.

Grinspoon, L. (1977). *Marijuana reconsidered*. Cambridge, MA: Harvard University Press.

Gross, C., Rocha-Miranda, C. E., & Bender, D. B. (1972). Visual properties of neurons in inferotemporal cortex of the macaque. *Journal of Neurophysiology, 35*, 96–111.

Grusec, J. E., & Kuczynski, L. (1980). Direction of effect in socialization: A comparison of the parents' versus the child's behavior as determinants of disciplinary techniques. *Development psychology, 16*, 1–9.

Grush, J. E. (1978). Audiences can inhibitor facilitate competitive behavior. *Personality and Social Psychology Bulletin, 4*, 119–122.

Guilford, J. P. (1967). *The nature of human intelligence*. New York: McGraw-Hill.

Gur, R. E., Skolnick, B. E., Gur, R. C., Caroff, S., Rieger, W., Obrist, W. D., Younkin, D., & Reivich, M. (1983). Brain function in psychiatric disorders: Regional cerebral blood flow in medicated schizophrenics. *Archives of General Psychiatry, 40*, 1250–1254.

Gurin, G., Veroff, J., & Feld, S. (1960). *Americans view their mental health*. New York: Basic Books.

Haas, A. (1979). Male and female spoken language differences: Stereotypes and evidence. *Psychological Bulletin, 86*, 616–626.

Hall, C., & Van de Castle, R. L. (1966). *The content analysis of dreams*. New York: Appleton-Century-Crofts.

Hall, E. T. (1966). *The hidden dimension*. Garden City, NY: Doubleday.

Hamilton, D. L. (1981). Illusory correlation as a basis for stereotyping. In D. L. Hamilton (Ed.), *Cognitive processes in stereotyping and intergroup behavior*. Hillsdale, NJ: Erlbaum.

Hammond, W. H. (1957). The constancy of physical types as determined by factorial analysis. *Human Biology, 29*, 40–61.

Hampson, J. L., & Hampson, J. G. (1960). The ontogenesis of sexual behavior in man. In W. C. Young (Ed.), *Sex and internal secretions* (3rd ed.) (Vol. 2). Baltimore: Williams & Wilkins.

Hansel, C. E. M. (1979). *ESP and parapsychology: A critical evaluation*. Buffalo, NY: Prometheus Books.

Hanson, V. L., & Bellugi, U. (1982). On the role of sign order and morphological structure in memory for American sign language sentences. *Journal of Verbal Learning and Verbal Behavior, 21*, 621–633.

Haracz, J. L. (1982). The dopamine hypothesis: An overview of studies with schizophrenic patients. *Schizophrenia Bulletin 8*(3), 438–469.

Hardt, G. (1981). *The guardians of the flutes*. New York: McGraw-Hill.

Hare, R. D., & McPherson, L. M. (1984). Psychopathy and perceptual asymmetry during verbal dichotic listening. *Journal of Abnormal Psychology, 93*, 141–149.

Harlan, R. E., Gordon, J. H., & Gorski, R. A. (1979). *Sexual differentiation of the brain: Implications for neuroscience*. In D. M. Schneider (Ed.), *Reviews of neuroscience* (Vol. 4). New York: Raven Press.

Harlow, H. F. (1965). Sexual behavior in the rhesus monkey. In F. A. Beach (Ed.), *Sex and behavior*. New York: Wiley.

Harlow, H. F., & Harlow, M. K. (1965) The affectional systems. In A. M. Schrier, H. F. Harlow, & F. Stollnitz (Eds.), *Behavior of nonhuman primates* (Vol. 2). New York: Academic Press.

Harlow, H. F., & Harlow, M. K. (1966). Learning to love. *American Scientist, 54*, 244–272.

Harlow, H. F., & Harlow, M. K. (1969). *Effects of various mother-infant relationships on rhesus monkey behaviors:IV*. London: Methuen.

Harman, W., McKim, R., Mogar, R., Fadiman, J., & Stolaroff, M. (1966). Psychedelic agents in creative problem-solving: A pilot study. *Psychological Reports, 19*, 211–227.

Harris, C. S. (1965). Perceptual adaption to inverted, reversed, and displaced vision. *Psychology Review, 72*, 419–444.

Harris, G. W., & Levine S. (1965). Sexual differentiation of the brain and its experimental control. *Journal of Physiology, 181*, 379–400.

Harris, G. W., & Michael, R. P. (1964). The activation of sexual behavior by hypothalamic implants of estrogen. *Journal of Physiology, 171*, 275–301.

Harris, L. J. (1977). Sex differences in the growth and use of language. In E. Donelson, & J. Gullahorn (Eds.), *Women: A psychological perspective*. New York: Wiley.

Hart, B. L., & Leedy, M. G. (1985). Neurological basis of male sexual behavior: A comparative analysis. In N. Adler, D. Pfaff, & R. Goy (Eds.), *Handbook of behavioral neurobiology reproduction*. New York: Plenum Press.

Harter, S. (1983). Developmental perspectives on the self-system. In E. M. Hetherington (ed.), *Handbook of child psychology. Vol. IV: Socialization, personality, and social development*. New York: Wiley.

Hartley, J. T., Harker, J. O., & Walsh, D. A. (1980). Contemporary issues and new directions in adult development of learning and memory. In L. Poon (Ed.), *Aging in the 1980s: Psychological issues*. Washington, DC: American Psychological Association.

Hartline, H. K., & Graham, C. H. (1932). Nerve impulses from single receptors in the eye. *Journal of Cellular and Comparative Physiology, 1*, 277–295.

Hartmann, E. L. (1973). *Functions of sleep*. New Haven, CT: Yale University Press.

Hartorf, A., Cantril, H. (1954). They saw a game: A case study. *Journal of Abnormal and Social Psychology, 49*, 129–134.

Hartup, W. W. (1983). Peer relations. In E. M. Hetherington, (Ed.), *Handbook of child psychology, and social development*. New York: Wiley.

Harvey, J. H., & Weary, G. (1984). Current issues in attribution theory and research. *Annual Review of Psychology*.

Haughton, E., & Ayylon, T. (1965). Production and elimination of symptomatic behavior. In L. Ullmann & L. Krasner (Eds.), *Case studies in behavior modification*. New York: Holt, Rinehart & Winston.

Hayes, K. J., & Hayes, C. (1951). Intellectual development of a home-raised chimpanzee. *Proceedings of the American Philosophical Society, 95*, 105–109.

Heath, R. G. (1972). Pleasure and brain activity in man. *Journal of Nervous and Mental Disease, 154*, 3–18.

Hebb, D. O. (1949. *The organization of behavior*. New York: Wiley.

Hecht, S., Shalaer, S., & Pirenne, M. H. (1942). Energy, quanta, and vision. *Journal of General Physiology, 25*, 819–840.

Heider, E. R., & Oliver, D. (1972). The structure of the color space in naming and memory for two languages. *Cognitive Psychology, 3*, 337–354.

Heider, F. (1958). *The psychology of interpersonal relations*. New York: Wiley.

Heller, J. F., Groff, B. D., & Solomon, S. H. (1977). Toward an understanding of crowding. The role of physical interaction. *Journal of Personality and Social Psychology, 35,* 183–190.

Helmholtz, H. L. F. von. (1875). *On the sensations of tone* (A. J. Ellis, Trans.). Londond: Longmans, Green.

Helmholtz, H. L. F. von. (1924). *Helmholtz' treatise on physiological optics* (Vol. 2), (J. P. C. Southall, Trans.) Rochester, NY: Optical Society of America. (Originally published, 1896.)

Helmholtz, H. L. F. von. (1962). *Helmholtz' treatise on psychological optics* (J.P.C. Southall, Ed. and trans.). New York: Dover. (Originally published, 1910.)

Helson H., & King, S. M. (1931) The tau-effect: An example of psychological relativity. *Journal of Experimental Psychology, 14,* 202–218.

Henchy, J., & Glass, D. C. (1968). Evaluation apprehension and the social facilitation of dominant and subordinate responses. *Journal of Personality and Social Psychology, 10,* 446–454.

Hendrick, C., & Brown, S. R. (1971). Introversion, extraversion, and interpersonal attraction. *Journal of Personality and Social Psychology, 20,* 31–36.

Henning, H. (1916). *Das Geruch.* Leipzig: Barth.

Hering, E. (1878). *Zur Lehre vom Lichtsinne.* Gerhold's Sohn.

Herman, C. P., & Polivy, J. *(1980). Restrained eating. In* A. J. Stunkard (Ed.), *Obesity.* Philadelphia: Saunders.

Hernstein, R., & Boring, E. (1966). *A source book in the history of psychology.* Cambridge, MA: Harvard University Press.

Hernstein, R. J. (1973). *I.Q. in the meritocracy.* Boston: Atlantic-Little, Brown.

Hershey, M. (1976). *Characteristics of gifted children.* Kansas City, MO: Gifted Association Conference.

Hess, E. H., & Polt, J. M. (1960). Pupil size as related to interest value of visual stimuli. *Science, 132,* 349–350.

Hess, E. H. (1959). The conditions limiting critical age of imprinting. *Journal of Comparative and Physiological Psychology, 52,* 515–518.

Hetherington, A. W., & Ranson, S. W. (1942). The sponstaneous activity and food intake of rats with hypothalamic lesions. *American Journal of Physiology, 136,* 609–617.

Hetherington, E. M. (1966). Effects of paternal absence on sex-typed behaviors in Negro and White pre-adolescent males. *Journal of Personality and Social Psychology, 2,* 188–194.

Hetherington, E. M. (1967). The effects of familial variables on sex-typing, on parent-child similarity and on imitation in children. In J. P. Hill (Ed.), *Minnesota Symposium on Child Psychology* (Vol. 1). Minnesota: University of Minnesota Press.

Hetherington, E. M., & Morris, W. N. (1978). The family and primary groups. In W. H. Holtzman (Ed.), *Introductory psychology in depth: Developmental topics.* New York: Harper & Row.

Hetherington, E. M., & Parke, R. D. (1979). *Child Psychology: A Contemporary Viewpoint* (2nd ed.). New York: McGraw-Hill.

Hilgard, E. (1977). *Divided consciousness.* New York: Wiley.

Hilgard, E. R., & Hilgard, J. R. (1983). *Hypnosis in the relief of pain.* Los Altos, CA: Wm. Kauffman.

Hindley, C. B., Filliozat, A. M., Klakenberg, G., Nocolet-Meister, D., & Sand, E. A. (1966). Differences in agcof of walking in five European longitudinal samples. *Human Biology, 38,* 364–379.

Hinkle, S., & Schopler, J. (1979). Ethnocentrism in the evaluation of group products. In W. G. Austin & S. Worchel (Eds.), *The social psychology of intergroup relations.* Monterey, CA: Brooks/Cole.

Hirsch, H., & Spinelli, N. (1970). Visual experience modifies distribution of horizontally and vertically oriented receptive fields in cats. *Science, 168,* 869–871.

Hjelle, L. A., & Ziegler, D. J. (1981). *Personality theories: Basic assumptions, research, and applications* (2nd ed.). New York: McGraw-Hill.

Hjelle, L. A., & Ziegler, D. J. (1981). *Personality theories: Basic assumptions, research, and applications* (2nd ed.). New York: McGraw-Hill.

Hoagland, H. (1933). The physiological control of judgments of duration: Evidence for a chemical clock. *Journal of General Psychology, 9,* 267–287.

Hoagland, H. (1935). *Pacemakers in relation to aspects of behavior.* New York: Macmillan.

Hodgaes, A. (1983). *Alan Turing: The enigma.* New York: Simon & Schuster.

Hodgkin, A. L., & Huxley, A. F. (1952). A quantitative description of membrane current and its application to conduction and excitation in nerve. *Journal of Physiology, 117,* 500–544.

Hoebel, B. C., & Teitelbaum, P. (1966). Weight regulation in normal and hypothalamic rats. *Journal of Comparative and Physiological Psychology, 61,* 189–193.

Hoffer, A., Osmond, H., & Smythies, J. R. (1954). Schizophrenia: A new approach. *Journal of Mental Science, 100,* 29–45.

Hoffman, H. S., Eiserer, L. A., Ratner, A. M., & Pickering, V. L. (1974). Development of distress vocalization during withdrawal of an imprinting stimulus. *Journal of Comparative and Physiological Pathology, 86,* 563–568.

Hoffman, M. L. (in press). Parental discipline and moral internalization: An information processing analysis. In E. T. Higgins, D. Ruble, & W. Hastings. *New directions in social-cognitive development.* New York: Cambridge University Press.

Holden, C. (1980). Identical twins reared apart. *Science, 207,* 1323–1328.

Hollister, L. E. (1962). Drug induced psychoses and schizophrenic reaction: A critical comparison. *Annals of the New York Academy of Sciences, 96,* 80–88.

Holmes, D. S. (1974). Investigations of repression: Differential recall of material experimentally or naturally associated with ego threat. *Psychological Bulletin, 81,* 632–653.

Holroyd, K. A. (1978). Effects of social anxiety and social evaluation on beer consumption and social interaction. *Journal of Studies on Alcohol, 37,* 737–744.

Hoon, P. W., Bruce, K., & Kinchloe, B. (1982). Does the menstrual cycle play a role in sexual arousal? *Psychophysiology, 19,* 21.

Horn, J. L., & Donaldson, G. (1980). Cognitive development in adulthood. In O. Brim and J. Kagan (Eds.), *Constancy and change in human development.* Cambridge, MA: Harvard University Press.

Horney, K. (1939). *New ways in psycholanalysis.* New York: Norton.

Horton, D. L., & Mills, C. B. (1984). Human learning and memory. *Annual Review of Psychology, 35,* 361–397.

Houts, P. S., & Serber, M. (Eds.) (1972). *After the turn-on, what? Learning perspectives on humanistic groups.* Champaign, IL: Research Press.

Hovland, C. I., & Sears, R. R. (1940). Minor studies in aggression: VI. Correlation of lynchings with economic indices. *Journal of Personality, 19,* 301–310.

Hovland, C. I., & Sears, R. R. (1952). The influence of source credibility on communication effectiveness. *Public Opinion Quarterly, 15,* 635–650.

Hubel, D. H., & Wiesel, T. N. (1962). Receptive fields, binocular interaction and functional architecture in the cat's visual cortex. *Journal of Neurophysiology, 160,* 106–154.

Hubel, D. H., & Wiesel, T. N. (1965). Binocular interaction in striate cortex of kittens reared with artifical squint. *Journal of Neurophysiology, 28,* 1041–1059.

Hughes, J., Smith, T. W., Kosterlitz, H. W., Fothergill, L. A., Morgan, B. A., & Morris, H. R. (1975). Identification of two related pentapeptides from the brain with potent opiate agonist activity. *Nature, 258,* 577–579.

Hull, C. (1951). *Principles of behavior.* New Haven, CT: Yale University Press.

Hull, C. (1952). *A behavior system: An introduction to behavior theory concerning the individual organism.* New Haven, CT: Yale University Press.

Hulse, S. H. (1973). Patterned reinforcement. In G. H. Bower (Ed.), *The psychology of learning and motivation* (Vol. 7). New York: Academic Press.

Hultsch, D. F., & Plemons, J. K. (1979). Life events and life span development. In P. B. Baltes & O. G. Brim, Jr. (Eds.), *Lifespan development and behavior.* (Vol. 2). New York: Academic Press.

Hunt, E. (1983). Intelligence on intelligence. *Contemporary Psychology, 28*(12), 901–903.

Hunt, M. (1974). *Sexual behavior in the 1970's.* Chicago: Playboy Press.

Husband, R. W. (1931). Analysis of methods in human male learning. *Journal of Genetic Psychology, 39,* 258–277.

Hyde, J. S. (1981). How large are cognitive gender differences? A meta-analysis using w_2 and d. *American Psychologist, 36,* 892–901.

Hyde, T. S., & Jenkins, J. J. (1969). Differential effects of incidental tasks on the organization of recall of highly associated works. *Journal of Experimental Psychology, 82,* 472–481.

Imperato-McGinley, J., Peterson, R. E., Gautier, T., & Sturla, E. (1979). Androgens and the evolution of male gender identity in male pseudohermaphrodites with 5(alpha) reduce deficiency. *New England Journal of Medicine, 300,* 1233.

Inouye, T. (1909). *Die sehstöorungen bei schussverletzungen der kortikalen sehsphäre.* Leipzig: Engelmann.

Insko, C. (1965). Verbal reinforcement of attitude. *Journal of Personality and Social Psychology, 2,* 261–263.

Isaacs, W., Thomas, J., & Goldiamond, I. (1960). Application of operant conditioning to reinstate verbal behavior in psychotics. *Journal of Speech and Hearing Disorders, 25,* 8–12.

Iscoe, I., & Harris, L. C. (1984). Social and community intervention. *Annual Review of Psychology, 35,* 333–360.

Iscoe, I., & Harris, L. C. (1984). Social and community intervention. *Annual Review of Psychology, 35,* 333–360.

Itard, J. (1932). *The wild boy of Aveyron.* (G. Humphrey & M. Humphrey, Trans.). New York: Appleton-Century-Crofts.

Ittelson, W. H. (1952). *The Ames demonstrations in perception.* Princeton, NJ: Princeton University Press.

Jackson, D. D. (1980, October). Reunion of identical twins named Jim, raised apart for 39 years, reveals astonishing similarities. *Smithsonian,* pp. 48–56.

Jacob, T. (1975). Family interaction in disturbed and normal families: A methodological and substantive review. *Psychological Bulletin, 82,* 33–65.

Jacobson, G. F. (1980). *Crisis intervention in the 80's: New directions for mental health services.* San Francisco: Jossey-Bass.

Jacoby, L. L., & Witherspoon, D. (1982). Remembering without awareness. *Canadian Journal of Psychology, 36,* 300–324.

Jakobson, R. (1968). *Child language, aphasis, and general sound laws* (A. Keiler, Trans.). The Hague: Mouton.

James, W. (1890). *Principles of psychology* (Vols. 1 & 2). New York: Holt.

James, W. (1900). *The varieties of religious experience.* New York: Modern Library.

Jarvik, L. F., Klodin, V., & Matsuyama, S. S. (1973). Human aggression and the extra Y chromosome: Fact or fantasy? *American Psychologist, 28,* 674–682.

Jenkins, H. M. (1962). Resistance to extinction when partial reinforcement is followed by regular enforcement. *Journal of Experimental Psychology, 64,* 441–450.

Jenkins, H. M. (1973). Effects of the stimulus reinforcer relation on selected and unselected responses. In R. A. Hinde & J. Stevenson-Hinde (Eds.), *Constraints on learning: Limitations and predistions.* London: Academic Press.

Jenkins, J. J., & Russell, W. A. (1952). Associative clustering during recall. *Journal of Abnormal and Social Psychology, 47,* 818–821.

Jenkins, J. J., Wald, J., & Pittenger, J. B. (1978). Apprehending pictorial events: An instance of psychological cohesion. In C. W. Savage (Ed.), *Perception and cognition: Issues in the foundations of psychology.* Minneapolis: University of Minnesota Press.

Jenkins, J. J. (1974). Remember that old theory of memory? Well, forget it! *American Psychologist, 29,* 785–795.

Jensen, A. R. (1969). How much can we boost I.Q. and scholastic achievement? *Harvard Educational Review, 39, 1–123.*

Jensen, A. R. (1983). Again: How much can we boost IQ? *Contemporary Psychology, 28*(10), 756–758.

Jones, E. E., Davis, K. E., & Gergen, K. J. (1961). Role playing variations and their informational value for person perception. *Journal of Abnormal and Social Psychology, 63,* 302–310.

Jones, E. E., & Harris, V. A. (1967). The attribution of attitudes. *Journal of Experimental Social Psychology, 3, 1–24.*

Jones, E. E., & Nisbett, R. E. (1971). *The actor and the observer: Divergent perceptions of the causes of behavior.* Morristown, NJ: General Learning Press.

Jones, E. E., Rock, L., Shaver, K. G., Goethals, C. R., & Ward, L. M. (1968). Pattern of performance and ability attribution: An unexpected primary effect. *Journal of Personality and Social Psychology, 9,* 317–340.

Jones, M. C. (1957). The later careers of boys who are early- or late-maturing. *Child Development, 27,* 115–128.

Jones, M. C. (1925). A laboratory study of fear: The case of Peter. *Pedagogical Seminary, 31,* 308–315.

Jones, M. C. (1958). The study of socialization patterns at the high-school level. *Journal of Genetic Psychology, 93,* 87–111.

Jost, A., Jones, H. W., & Scott, W. W. (Eds.). (1969). *Hermaphroditism, genital anomalies and related endocrine disorders* (2nd ed.). Baltimore: MD: Williams & Wilkins.

Judd, H. L., & Yen, S. S. C. (1973). Serum androstenedione and testosterone levels during the menstrual cycle. *Journal of Clinical Endocrinology and Metabolism, 36,* 475–481.

Julesz, B. (1971). *Foundations of cyclopean perception.* Chicago: University of Chicago Press.

Jung, C. G. (1936). The concept of the collective unconscious. In H. Read, M. Fordham, & G. Adler (Eds.), *Collected works of C. G. Jung* (Vol. 9), (Pt. 1). Boston: Routledge & Kegan-Paul.

Jung, C. G. (1939). *The integration of the personality.* New York: Farrar and Rinehart.

Jung, C. G. (1954–1979). *The collected works of Carl G. Jung* (20 vols.) (G. Adler, M. Fordham, & H. Read, Eds; and, R. F. C. Hull, Trans.). Princeton, NJ: Princeton University Press.

Jung, C. G. (1963). *Memories, dreams, reflections.* New York: Pantheon.

Jung, C. G. (1964). Approaching the unconscious. In C. G. Jung (Ed.), *Man and his symbols.* London: Aldus Books.

Jung, C. G. (1966). Two essays on analytical psychological. In *The collected works of C. G. Jung* (Vol. 7). Princeton, NJ: Princeton University Press.

Jung, C. G. (1969). Conscious, unconsious and individuation. In *The collected works of C. G. Jung* (Vol. 9). Princeton, NJ: Princeton University Press.

Jung, C. G. (1969). General aspects of dream psychology. In *The collected works of C. G. Jung* (Vol. 8). Princeton, NJ: Princeton University Press.

Jus, A., Pineau, R., Lachance, R., Pelchat, G., Jus, K., Pires, P., & Villeneuve, R. (1976). Epidemiology of tardive dyskinesia, Part I, *Diseases of the Nervous System, 37,* 210–214.

Kacergius, M. A., & Adams, G. R. (1980). Erikson stage resolution: The relationship between identity and intimacy. *Journal of youth and adolescence, 9*, 117–126.

Kagan, J. (1958). The concept of identification. *Psychological Review, 65*, 296–305.

Kamiya, J. (1969). Operant control of EEG alpha rhythm and some of its reported effects on consciousness. In C. Tart (Ed.), *Altered states of consciousness.* New York: Wiley.

Kandel, D. (1974). Inter and intragenerational influences on adolescent marijuana use. *Journal of Social Issues, 30(2)*, 107–135.

Kandel, E. (1970). Nerve cells and behavior. *Scientific American, 223*, 107–135.

Kandel, E. (1976). *Cellular basis of behavior.* San Francisco: Freeman.

Kandel, E. (1979). Small systems of neurons. *Scientific American, 24*, 66–76.

Kaplan, B. (1964). *The conduct of inquiry: Methodology for behavioral science.* San Francisco: Chandler.

Kart, C. S. (1976). Some biological aspects of aging. In C. S. Kart & B. B. Manard (Eds.), *Aging in America: Readings in social gerontology.* New York: Alfred Publishing.

Kasematsu, A., & Hirai, T. (1966). An electroencephalographic study on the zen meditation. *Folia Psychiatrica et Neurologica, 20*, 315–336.

Katchedourian, H. (1977). *The biology of adolescence.* San Francisco: W. H. Freeman.

Katz, A. H. (1981). Self-help and mutual aid: An emerging social movement. *Annual Review of Sociology, 7*, 129–155.

Katz, D. (1960). The functional approach to the study of attitudes. *Public Opinion Quarterly, 24*, 163–204.

Kazdin, A. E. (1979). Fictions, factions, and functions of behavior therapy. *Behavior Therapy, 10*, 629–654.

Keesey, R. E., & Powerly, T. L. (1975). Hypothalamic regulation of body weight. *American Scientist, 63*, 558–565.

Keith, S. J., Gunderson, J. G., Reifman, A., Buchsbaum, S., & Mosher, L. R. (1976). Special report: Schizophrenia. *Schizophrenia Bulletin, 2*, 510–565.

Kelley, H. H., Cunningham, J. D., Grisham, J. A., Lefebvre, L. M., Sink, C. R., & Yablon, G. (1978). Sex differences in comments made during conflict within close heterosexual pairs. *Sex Roles, 4*, 473–492.

Kelley, H. H. (1950). The warm-cold variable in first impressions of persons. *Journal of Personality, 18*, 431–439.

Kelley, H. H. (1967). Attribution theory in social psychology. In D. Levine (Ed.), *Nebraska Symposium on Motivation* (Vol. 15). Lincoln: University of Nebraska Press.

Kelley, H. H. (1972). Attribution in social interaction. In E. E. Jones, D. E. Kanouse, H. H. Kelley, R. E. Nisbett, S. Valins, & B. Weiner (Eds.), *Attribution: Perceiving the causes of behavior.* Morristown, NJ: General Learning Press.

Kellogg, W. N., & Kellogg, L. A. (1933). *The ape and the child.* New York: McGraw-Hill.

Kelly, G. A. (1955). *The psychology of personal constructs* (Vols. 1 & 2). New York: Norton.

Kendler, K. S. (1983, November). Overview: A current perspective on twin studies of schizophrenia. *American Journal of Psychiatry, 140(11)*, 1413–1425.

Kennedy, G. C. (1950). The hypothalamic control of food intake in rats. *Proceedings of the Royal Society of London: B, 137*, 535–548.

Kessler, S. (1969), September 26). The ethiological questions in mental illness. *Science*, 1341–1342.

Kessler, S. (1975). Extra chromosomes and criminality. In R. R. Fieve, D. Rosenthal, & H. Brill (Eds.), *Genetic research in psychiatry.* Baltimore: MD: Johns Hopkins University Press.

Kety, S. S. (1967). Current biochemical approaches to schizophrenia. *New England Journal of Medicine, 276*, 325–331.

Kiester, E., Jr., & Gudhea, D. (1974, September). Albert Bandura: A very modern model. *Human Behavior*, p. 31.

Kihlstrom, J. F. (1980). Posthypnotic amnesia for recently learned material: Interactions with "episodic" and "semantic" memory. *Cognitive Psychology, 12*, 227–251.

Kimball, M. M. (1981). Women and science: A critique of biological theories. *International Journal of Women's Studies, 4*, 318–338.

Kimble, G. A. (Ed.). (1961). *Hilgard and Marguis' conditioning and learning* (2nd ed.). Englewood Cliffs, NJ: Prentice-Hall.

King, K., Balswick, J. O., & Robinson, I. E. (1977). The continuing premartial revolution among college females. *Journal of Marriage and Family, 39*, 455.

Kinney, J., & Leaton, G. (1982). *Loosening the grip: A handbook of alcohol information* (3rd ed.). St. Louis, MO: Mosby.

Kinsey, A. C., Pomeroy, W. B., & Martin, C. E. (1948). *Sexual behavior in the human male.* Philadelphia: Saunders.

Kinsey, A. C., Pomeroy, W. B., Martin, C. E., & Gebhard, P. H. (1953). *Sexual behavior in the human female.* Philadelphia: Saunders.

Kintsch, W. (1976). Memory for prose. In C. N. Cofer (Ed.), *The structure of human memory.* San Francisco: Freeman.

Kipnis, P. S. (1957). Interaction between members of a bomber crew as a determinant of sociometric choice. *Human Relations, 10*, 253–270.

Kirk-Smith, M. D., & Booth, D. A. (1980). Effect of androstenone on choice of location in others' presence. *Olfaction and Taste, 7*, 397.

Kisker, G. W. (1964). *The disorganized personality.* New York: McGraw-Hill.

Kline, P. (1981). *Fact and fantasy in Freudian theory* (2nd ed.). London: Methuen.

Kluver, H., & Bucy, P. C. (1937). "Psychic blindness" and other symptoms following bilateral temporal lobectomy in rhesus monkeys. *American Journal of Physiology, 119*, 352–353.

Kluver, H., & Bucy, P. C. (1938). An analysis of certain effects of bilateral temporary lobectomy in the rhesus monkey, with special reference to "physic blindness." *Journal of Psychology, 5*, 33–54.

Kluver, H., & Bucy, P. C. (1939). Preliminary analysis of functions of the temporal lobes in monkeys. *Archives of Neurology and Psychiatry, 42*, 979–1000.

Knittle, J. L. (1975). Early influences on development of adipose tissues. In G. A. Bray (Ed.), *Obesity in perspective.* Washington, D.C.: U.S. Government Printing Office.

Knittle, J. L. & Hirsch, J. (1968). Effect of early nutrition on the development of rat epididymal fat pads: Cellularity and metabolism. *Journal of Clinical Investigation, 47*, 2091.

Knowles, E. S., Kreuser, S. H., Hyde, M., & Schuchart, G. E. (1976). Group size and the extension of social space boundaries. *Journal of Personality and Social Psychology, 33*, 647–654.

Knox, R. E., & Inkster, J. A. (1968). Postdecision dissonance at post time. *Journal of Personality and Social Psychology, 8*, 319–323.

Knudsen, E. L., & Konishi, M. (1978). Space and frequency are represented separately in auditory midbrain of the owl. *Journal of Neurophysiology, 41*, 810–884.

Kobasa, S. C. (1979). Stressful life events, personality, and health: An inquiry into hardiness. *Journal of Personality and Social Psychology, 37*, 1–11.

Kobasa, S. C., Maddi, S. R., & Kahn, S. (1983). Hardness and health: A prospective study. *Journal of Personality and Social Psychology, 42*, 168–177.

Koenig, P. (1978, May 21). The problem that can't be tranquilized. *New York Times Magazine*, 14–16.

Kohlberg, L. (1963). The development of children's orientations toward a moral order: I. Sequence in the development of moral thought. *Vita Humana*, *6*, 11–33.

Kohlberg, L. (1973). Continuities in child and adult moral development revisited. In P. B. Batles & K. W. Schaie (Eds.), *Lifespan developmental psychology: Personality and socialization*. New York: Academic Press.

Kohlberg, L. A. (1966). A cognitive-developmental analysis of children's sex-role concepts and attitudes. In E. E. Maccoby (Ed.), *The development of sex differences*. Stanford, CA: Stanford University Press.

Köhler, W.. (1925). *The mentality of apes* (E. Winter, Trans.). New York: Harcourt, Brace and World.

Kolata, G. B. (1978). Behavioral teratology: Birth defects of the mind. *Science*, *202*, 732–734.

Kolodny, R. C., Masters, W. H., Kolodner, R. M., & Toro, G. (1974). Depression of plasma testosterone levels after chronic intensive marijuana use. *New England Journal of Medicine*, *290*, 872.

Koopmans, H. S. (1981). The role of the gastrointestinal tract in the satiation of hunger. In L. A. Cioffi, W. P. T. James & T. B. Van Italie (Eds.), *The body weight regulatory system: Normal and disturbed mechanisms*. New York: Raven Press.

Kosslyn, S. M. (1975). Information representation in visual images. *Cognitive Psychology*, *7* 341–370.

Kosslyn, S. M. (1976). Can imagery be distinguished from other forms of internal representation? Evidence from studies of information retrieval time. *Memory and Cognition*, *4*, 291–297.

Kosslyn, S. M., Ball, T. M., & Reiser, B. J. (1978). Visual images perserve metric spatial information: Evidence from studies of image scanning. *Journal of Experimental Psychology: Human Perception and Performance*, *4*, 47–60.

Kraepelin, E. (1896). *Lehrbuch der psychiatrie* (5th ed.). Leipzig: Barth.

Kramer, D. A. (1983). Post-formal operations? A need for further conceptualization. *Human Development*, *26*, 91–105.

Kramer, N. A., & Jarvik, L. (1979). Assessment of intellectual changes in the elderly. In A. Raskin & L. Jarvik (Eds.), *Psychiatric symptoms and cognitive loss in the elderly*. Washington, DC: Hemisphere.

Krasner, L. (1962). The therapist as a social reinforcement machine. In H. H. Strupp & L. Luborsky (Eds.), *Research in psychotherapy* (Vol. 2). Washington, DC: American Psychological Association.

Kraut, R. E. (1973). Effects of social labeling on giving to charity. *Journal of Experimental Social Psychology*, *9*, 551–562.

Kreutzer, M. A., Leonard, C., & Flavell, J. H. (1975). An interview study of children's knowledge about memory. *Monographs of the Society for Research in Child Development*, *40* (1, Serial No. 159).

Kripke, D. F., & Sonnenschein, D. (1973). *A 90 minute daydream cycle*. Paper presented at the meeting of the Association for the Psychophysiologic Study of Sleep, San Diego.

Krosnick, J. A., & Judd, C. M. (1982). Transitions in social influence at adolescence: Who induces cigarette smoking? *Developmental Psychology 18*, 359–368.

Kubler-Ross, E. (1969). *On death and dying.*. New York: Macmillan.

Kuffler, S. W., & Nicholls, J. G. (1976). *From neuron to brain*. Sunderland, MA: Sinauer Associates, Inc.

Kuffler, S. W. (1953). Discharge patterns and functional organization of mammalian retina. *Journal of Neurophysiology*, *16*, 37–68.

Kwan, M., Greenleaf, W. J., Mann, J., Crapo, L. & Davidson, J. M. (1983). The nature of androgen action on male sexuality: A combined laboratory—self-report study on hypogonadal men. *Journal of Clin. Endo. Metab.*, *57*, 557.

La Barre, W. (1954). *The human animal*. Chicago: University of Chicago Press.

LaBerge, S. P. (1980). Lucid dreaming as a learnable skill. *Perceptual and Motor Skills*, *51*, 1039–1042.

LaBerge, S. P., Nagel, L. E., Dement, W. C., & Zarcone, W. C. (1980). Lucid dreaming verified by volitional communication during REM sleep. *Perceptual and motor skills*, *52*, 727–732.

Laing, R. D., & Esterson, A. (1971). *Sanity, madness, and the family*. New York: Basic Books.

Langer, E. J. (1975). The illusion of control. *Journal of Personality and Social Psychology*, *32*, 311–328.

Langer, E. J., & Rodin, J. (1976). The effects of choice and enhanced personal responsibility for the aged: A field experiment in an institutional setting. *Journal of Personality and Social Psychology*, *34*, 191–198.

Langer, E. J., & Roth, J. (1975). Heads I win, tails, it's chance: The illusion of control as a function of the sequence of outcomes in a purely chance task. *Journal of Personality and Social Psychology*, *32*, 951–955.

Langfeldt, T. (1979). Child sexuality and problems. In J. M. Sampson (Ed.), *Childhood sexuality*. Montreal: Etudes Bivantes.

Larsen, O. N., Gray, L. N., & Fortis, J. G. (1968). Achieving goals through violence on television. In O. N. Larsen (Ed.), *Violence and the mass media*. New York: Harper & Row.

Lashley, K. S. (1950). Physiological mechanisms and animal behavior. In *Symposium of the Society for Experimental Biology* (Vol. IV). New York: Academic Press.

Lashley, K. S. (1951). The problem of serial order in behavior. In L. A. Jefress (Ed.), *Cerebral mechanisms in behavior*. New York: Wiley.

Latané, B., & Darley, J. M. (1968). Group inhibition of bystander interventions in emergencies. *Journal of Personality and Social Psychology*, *10*, 215–221.

Latané, B., & Darley, J. M. (1970). *The unresponsive bystander: Why doesn't he help?* New York: Appleton-Century-Crofts.

LaVoie, J. (1976). Ego identity formation in middle adolescence. *Journal of Youth and Adolescence*, *5*, 371–385.

Lazarus, A. A. (1958). New methods of psychotherapy: A case study. *South African Medical Journal*, *33*, 660.

Lazarus, A. A. (1971). *Behavior therapy and beyond*. New York: McGraw-Hill.

Leefeldt, C., & Callenbach, E. (1979). *The art of friendship*. New York: Pantheon.

Lehman, H. C. (1953). *Age and achievement*. Princeton, NJ: Princeton University Press.

LeMagnen, J. (1952). Les phenomenes olfactosexuals chez le rat blanc. *Archives Scientifiques Physiologiques*, *6*, 295–332.

Lenneberg, E. H. (1967). *Biological foundations of language*. New York: Wiley.

Lepper, M. R., Greene, D., & Nisbett, R. E. (1973). Undermining children's intrinsic interest with extrinsic reward: A test of "overjustification" hypothesis. *Journal of Personality and Social Psychology*, *5*, 189–202.

Lerner, M. J., & Simmons, C. (1966). Observer's reaction to the innocent victim: Compassion or rejection. *Journal of Personality and Social Psychology*, *4*, 203–210.

Levinson, B. W. (1967). States of awareness during general anesthesia. In J. Lassner (Ed.), *Hypnosis and psychosomatic medicine*. New York: Springer.

Levinson, D., Darrow, C., Klein, M., Levinson, M., & McKee, B. (1978). *The seasons of a man's life*. New York: Knopf.

Levy, J. (1972). Autokinetic illusion: A systematic review of theories, measures, and independent variables. *Psychological Bulletin*, *78*, 457–474.

Lewis, M., Feiring, C., McGuffog, C., & Jaskir, J. (1984). Predicting psychopathology in six-year-olds from early social relations. *Child Development, 55,* 123–136.

Li, C. H., & Chung, D. (1976). Isolation and structure of an untriakontapeptide with opiate activity from camel pituitary. *Proceedings of the National Academy of Science, U.S.A., 73,* 1145–1148.

Liberman, A. M. (1970). The grammars of speech and language. *Cognitive Psychology, 1,* 301–323.

Lidz, T., Fleck, S., & Cornelison, A. (1965). *Schizophrenia and the family.* New York: International Universities Press.

Lieberman, A. (1977). Preschoolers' competence with a peer: Relations with attachment and peer experience. *Child Development, 48,* 1277–1287.

Lieberman, A. M., Cooper, F. S., Shankweiler, D., & Studdert-Kennedy, M. (1967). Perception of the speech code. *Psychological Review, 74,* 431–461.

Lieberman, M. A., Yalom, I. D., & Miles, M. B. (1973). *Encounter groups: First facts.* New York: Basic Books.

Lieberman, S. (1950). The effects of changes in roles on the attitudes of role occupants. *Human Relations, 9,* 385–403.

Liebert, R. M., & Spiegler, M. D. (1974). *Personality: Strategies for the study of man* (Rev. ed.). Homewood, IL: Dorsey Press.

Lifton, R. J. (1963). *Thought reform and the psychology of totalism: A study of brainwashing.* Homewood, IL: Dorsey Press.

Lilly, J. C. (1977). *The deep self.* New York: Lippincott.

Limber, J. (1977). Language in child and chimp? *American Psychologist, 32,* 280–295.

Lindemann, E. (1944). Symptomatology and management of acute grief. *American Journal of Psychiatry, 101,* 141–148.

Lindsay, P. H., & Norman, D. A. (1977). *Human information processing* (2nd ed.). New York: Academic Press.

Link, R. (1980, February-March). The literary digest poll: Appearances can be deceiving. *Public Opinion,* p. 55.

Lipscomb, D. M. (1969). Ear damage from exposure to rock and roll music. *Archives of Otolaryngology, 90,* 543–555.

Loewi, O. (1921). über humorale übertragbarkeit der Herznervenwirkung. *Pflügers Archiv für die Gesamte Physiologie des Menschen und der Tiere, 189,* 239–242.

Loewi, O. (1935). The Ferrier lecture: On problems connected with the principle of humoral transmission of nerve impulses. *Proceedings of the Royal Society of London: Series B, Biological Sciences, 118B,* 299–316.

Loftus, E. F., & Palmer, J. C. (1974). Reconstruction of automobile destribution: An example of the interaction between language and memory. *Journal of Verbal Learning and Verbal Behavior, 13,* 585–589.

Lorenz, K. (1967). *On aggression.* New York: Bantam.

Lorenz, K. (1974). *The eight deadly sins of civilized man.* New York: Harcourt Brace Jovanovich.

Lorenz, K. Z. (1937). The companion in the bird's world. *Auk, 54,* 245–273.

Lorenz, K. Z., & Tinbergen, N. (1957). Taxis and Instinkthandlung in der Eirollbewegung der Graugans. In C. H. Schiller (Ed.), *Instinctive behavior.* New York: International Universities Press. (Originally published, 1938).

Lovass, I. O. (1977). *The autistic child.* New York: Irvington Publishers.

Luce, G. G., & Segal, J. (1966). *Sleep.* New York: Coward, McCann & Geoghegan.

Luchins, A. (1957). Primacy-recency in impression formation. In C. I. Hovland (Ed.), *The order of presentation in persuasion.* New Haven, CT: Yale University Press.

Ludolph, P. (1982). *A reanalysis of the literature on multiple personality. Paper presented at the American Psychological Association.*

Luttge, W. G. (1979). Endocrine control of mammalian sexual behavior: An analysis of the potential role of testosterone metabolites. In C. Beyer (Ed.), *Endocrine control of sexual behavior.* New York: Raven Press.

Lykken, D. T. (1957). A study of anxiety in the sociopathic personality. *Journal of Abnormal and Social Psychology, 55,* 6–10.

Lytle, L. (1977). Control of eating behavior. In R. J. Wurtman & J. J. Wurtman (Eds.), *Nutrition and the brain.* New York: Raven Press.

Maas, J. W. (1978). Clinical and biochemical hertergeneity of depressive disorders. *Ann. Int. Med., 88,* 556.

MacArthur, R. H., & Pianka, E. R. (1966). On optimal use of patchy environment. *American Naturalist, 100,* 603–609.

Maccoby, E., Doering, C., Jacklin C., & Kraemer, H. (1981). Concentrations of sex hormones in umbilical-cord blood: Their relation to sex and birth order of infants. In E. Hetherington and R. Parke (Eds.), *Contemporary readings in child psychology* (2nd ed.). New York: McGraw-Hill.

Maccoby, E. E., & Jacklin, C. N. (1974). *The psychology of sex differences.* Stanford, CA: Stanford University Press.

MacDonald, M. L., & Tobias, L. L. (1976). Withdrawal causes relapse? Our response. *Psychological Bulletin, 83,* 448–451.

Macnamara, J. (1972). Cognitive basis of language in infants. *Psychological Review, 79,* 1–13.

Maddi, S. R., Kobasa, S. C., & Hoover, M. (1979). *The alienation test. Journal of Humanistic Psychology, 19,* 72–76.

Maher, B. A. (1966). *Principles of psychopathology.* New York: McGraw-Hill.

Maier, S. F., Seligman, M. E. P., & Solomon, R. L. (1969). Pavlovian fear conditioning and learned helplessness: Effects on escape and avoidance behavior of (a) the CS-US contingency and (b) the independence of the US and voluntary responding. In B. A. Campbell & R. M. Church (Eds.), *Punishment and aversive behavior.* New York: Appleton-Century-Crofts.

Malinowski, B. (1929). *Sexual life of savages in Northwestern Melanesia.* New York: Harcourt.

Mandell, A. J. (1980). Towards a psychobiology of transcendence. In J. M. Davidson & R. J. Davidson (Eds.), *Psychobiology of Consciousness.* New York: Plenum Press.

Mandler, G., & Sarason, S. B. (1952). A study of anxiety and learning. *Journal of Abnormal and Social Psychology, 47,* 166–173.

Mandler, G. (1975). *Mind and emotion.* New York: Wiley.

Marcia, J. E. (1966). Development and validation of ego identity status. *Journal of Personality and Social Psychology, 3,* 551–558.

Marcia, J. E. (1976). Identity six years later: A follow-up study. *Journal of Youth and Adolescence, 5,* 145–160.

Marcia, J. E. (1980). Identity in adolescence. In J. Adelson (Ed.), *Handbook of adolescent psychology.* New York: Wiley.

Mark, V. H., & Ervin, F. R. (1970). *Violence and the brain.* New York: Harper & Row.

Mark, V. H., Sweet, W. H., & Ervin, F. R. (1972). The effect of amygdalectomy on violent behavior patients with temporal lobe epilepsy. In E. Hitchcock, L. Laitinen, & K. Vaernet (Eds.), *Psychosurgery.* Springfield, IL: Charles C Thomas.

Marks, I. M. (1977). Phobias and obsessions. In J. Maser, & M. Seligman (Eds.), *Experimental psychopathology.* New York: Wiley.

Marlatt, G. A. (1976). Alcohol, stress, and cognitive control. In C. D. Spielberger & G. Sarason (Eds.), *Stress and anxiety* (Vol. 3). Washington, DC: Hemisphere.

Marler, P. (1970). A comparative approach to vocal learning: Song development in white-crowned sparrows. *Journal of Comparative and Physiological Psychology, 71,* 1–25.

Marlow, A. H. (1971). *Farther reaches of human nature.* New York: Viking Press.

Marquis, D. P. (1941). Learning in the neonate: The modification of behavior under three feeding schedules. *Journal of Experimental Psychology, 29,* 263–282.

Marsh, G. R. & Thompson, L. W. (1977). Psychophysiology of aging. In J. E. Birren & K. W. Schaie (Eds.), *Handbook of the psychology of aging.* New York: Van Nostrand Reinhold.

Martin, J. G. (1971). Some accoustic and grammatical features of spontaneous speech. In D. L. Horton & J. J. Jenkins (Eds), *The perception of language.* Columbus, Ohio: Merrill.

Marx, A. J., Test, M. A., & Stein, L. I. (1973). Extrahospital management of severe mental illness. *Archives of General Psychiatry, 29,* 505–511.

Maslow, A. H. (1962). *Toward a psychology of being.* Princeton, NJ: Van Nostrand.

Maslow, A. H. (1963). Self-actualizing people. In G. B. Levitas (Ed.), *The world of psychology* (Vol. 2). New York: Braziller.

Masters, W. H., & Johnson, V. E. (1966). *The human sexual response.* Boston: Little, Brown.

Masters, W. H., & Johnson, V. E. (1970). *Human sexual inadequacy.* Boston: Little, Brown.

Matas, L., Arend, R. A., Sroufe, L. A. (1978). Continuity of adaptation in the second year: The relationship between quality of attachment and later competencies. *Child Development, 49,* 547–556.

Matin, L., & MacKinnon, G. E. (1964). Autokinetic movement: Selective manipulation of directional components by image stabilization. *Science, 143,* 147–148.

Matsumoto, S., Tamada, T., & Konuma, S. (1979). Endocrinological analysis of environmental menstrual disorders. *International Journal of Fertility, 24,* 233–239.

Mausner, B. (1954). Prestige and social interaction: The effect of one's partner's success in a relevant task on the interaction of observed pairs. *Journal of Abnormal and Social Psychology, 49,* 557–560.

Maxwell, J. C. (1855). Experiments on colour as perceived by the eye, with remarks on colour blindness. *Transactions of the Royal Society of Edinburgh, 21,* 275–298.

May, P. R. A. (1968). *Treatment of schizophrenia: A comparative study of five treatment methods.* New York: Science House.

Mayer-Gross, W., Slater, E., & Roth, M. (1969). *Clinical psychiatry.* Baltimore, MD: Williams & Wilkins.

McClearn, G., & Rodgers, D. (1959). Differences in alcohol preference among inbred strains of mice. *Quarterly Journal on the Study of Alcohol, 20,* 691–695.

McClearn, G. (1970). Genetic influences on behavior and development. In P. Mussen (eds), *Carmichael's manual of child psychology.* New York: Wiley.

McClelland, D. C., Atkinson, J. W., Clark, R. A., & Lowell, E. L. (1953). *The achievement motive.* New York: Appleton-Century-Crofts.

McClelland, D. C. (1961). *The achieving society.* New York: Van Nostrand.

McClintock, M. K. (1971). Menstrual synchrony and suppression. *Nature, 229,* 244–245.

McDougall, W. (1921). *An introduction to social psychology* (14th ed.). Boston: J. W. Luce.

McFarlin, D. B., & Blascovich, J. (1981). Effects of self-esteem and performance feedback on future affective preferences and cognitive expectations. *Journal of Personality and Social Psychology, 40,* 521–531.

McGuire, W. J. (1968). Personality and susceptibility to social influence. In E. F. Borgatta & W. W. Lambert (Eds.), *Handbook of Personality theory and research.* Chicago: Rand McNally.

McNeill, D. (1970). *The acquisition of language: The study of developmental psycholinguistics.* New York: Harper & Row.

Mead, G. H. (1934). *Mind, self, and society.* Chicago: University of Chicago Press.

Meador, B. D., & Rogers, C. R. (1979). Person centered therapy. In J. R. Corsini (Ed.), *Current psychotherapies.* Itasca, IL: Peacock.

Medawar, P. (1979). *Advice to a young scientist.* New York: Harper & Row.

Meece, J. L., Parsons, J. E., Kaczala, C. M., Goff, S. B., & Futterman, R. (1982). Sex differences in math achievement: Toward a model of academic choice. *Psychological Bulletin, 91,* 324–348.

Meehl, P. E. (1966). Some ruminations on the validation of clinical procedures. In E. Megargee (Ed.), *Research in clinical assessment.* New York: Harper & Row.

Meichenbaum, D., & Jaremco, M. E. (Eds.) (1983). *Stress reduction and prevention.* New York: Plenum Press.

Meletzky, B. M., & Klotter, J. (1974). Smoking and alcoholism. *American Journal of Psychiatry, 131,* 445–447.

Meltzoff, J., & Kornreich, M. (1970). *Research in psychotherapy.* New York: Atherton.

Mendels, J. (1970). *Concepts of depression.* New York: Wiley.

Menninger, K., Mayman M., & Pruyser, P. (1963). *The vital balance.* New York: Viking.

Menninger, K. (1958). *Theory of psychoanalytic technique.* New York: Basic Books.

Mercer, J. R., & Lewis, J. (1977). *System of multicultural pluralistic assessment.* New York: Psychological Corporation.

Meredith, H. V. (1978). Research between 1960 and 1970 on the standing height of young children in different parts of the world. In H. W. Rease & L. P. Lipsitt (Eds.), *Advances in child development and behavior* (Vol. 12). New York: Academic Press.

Merton, R. K. (1957). *Social theory and social structure.* New York: Free Press.

Meumann, E. (1904). Haus-und Schularbeit: Experimente an Kindern der Volkschule. *Dir Deutsche Schule, 8,* 278–303, 337–359, 416–431.

Michenbaum, D., & Jaremco, M. E. (Eds.). (1983). *Stress reduction and prevention.* New York: Plenum.

Miles, F., Eighmy, B. (1980). Long-term adaptive changes in primate vestibulo-ocular reflex: I. Behavioral observation. *Journal of Neurophysiology, 43* 1406–1425.

Milgram, S. (1963). Behavioral study of obedience. *Journal of Abnormal and Social Psychology, 67,* 371–378.

Milgram, S. (1974). *Obedience to authority.* New York: Harper & Row.

Miller, G. A. (1956). The magical number seven, plus or minus two: Some limits on our capacity for processing information. *Psychological Review, 63,* 81–97.

Miller, G. A. (1962). Some psychological studies of grammar. *American Psychologist, 17,* 748–762.

Miller, I. W. & Norman, W. H. (1979). Learned helplessness in humans: A review and attribution theory model. *Psychology Bulletin, 86,* 93–118.

Miller, N. E. (1969). Learning of visceral and grandular responses. *Science, 163,* 434–435.

Miller, N. E. (1978). Biofeedback and visceral learning. *Annual Review of Psychology, 29,* 375–404.

Miller, N. E., Bailey, C. J., & Stevenson, J. A. F. (1950). "Decreased hunger" but increased food intake resulting from hypothalamic lesions. *Science, 112,* 256–259.

Miller, P. H. (1983). *Theories of developmental psychology.* San Francisco: Freeman & Co.

Millon, T. (Ed.) (1967). *Theories of psychopathology.* Philadelphia: Saunders.

Mills, J., & Jellison, J. M. (1967). Effect on opinion change of how desirable the communication is to the audience the communicator addressed. *Journal of Personality and Social Psychology, 6,* 98–101.

Milner, B. (1970). Memory and the medial temporal regions of the brain. In K. H. Pribram & D. E. Broadbent (Eds.), *Biology of memory*. New York: Academic Press.

Milner, B., Taylor, L., Sperry, R. W. (1968). Lateralized suppression of dichotically presented digits after commissural section in man. *Science, 161*, 184–185.

Minton, C., Kagan, J., & Levine, J. A. (1971). Maternal control and obedience in the two-year-old. *Child Development, 42*, 1873–1894.

Mischel, W. (1968). *Personality and assessment*. New York: Wiley.

Mischel, W. (1977). The interaction of person and situation. In D. Magnusson & N. S. Endler (Eds.), *Personality at the crossroads: Current issues in interactional psychology*. Hillsdale, NJ: Erlbaum.

Mishkin, M., & Pribram, K. H. (1954). Visual discrimination performance following partial ablations of the temporal lobe: I. Ventral vs. lateral. *Journal of Comparative and Physiological Psychology, 47*, 14–20.

Mita, T. H., Dermer, M., & Knight, J. (1977). Reversed facial images and the mere exposure hypothesis. *Journal of Personality and Social Psychology, 35*, 597–601.

Molfese, D. L. (1972). *Cerebral asymmetry in infants, children and adults: Auditory evoked responses to speech and noise stimuli.* Unpublished doctoral dissertation, Pennsylvania State University.

Monahan, J. (1981). *The clinical prediction of violent behavior*. Rockville, MD: National Institute of Mental Health.

Money, J., & Ehrhardt, A. A. (1972). *Man and woman, boy and girl*. Baltimore: Johns Hopkins University Press.

Moody, R. (1976). *Life after life*. New York: Mockingbird Books.

Moore, R. (1977). Dependence on alcohol. In S. N. Pradhan & S. N. Dutta (Eds.), *Drug abuse: Clinical and basic aspects*. St. Louis, MO: Mosby.

Moray, N. (1959). Attention in dichotic listening: Affective cues and the influence of instructions. *Quarterly Journal of Experimental Psychology, 11*, 56–60.

Moreno, J. L., & Kipper, D. A. (1968). Group psychodrama and community-centered counseling. In G. M. Gazda (Eds), *Basic approaches to group psychotherapy and group counseling*. Springfield, IL: Charles C Thomas.

Morrell, M. J., Dixen, J. M., Carter, S., & Davidson, J. M. (1984). The influence of age and cycling status on sexual arousability in women. *American Journal of Obstetrics and Gynecology, 148*, 66.

Morris, C. D., Bransford, J. D., & Franks, J. J. (1977). Levels of processing versus transfer appropriate processing. *Journal of Verbal Learning and Verbal Behavior, 16*, 519–533.

Müller, J. (1838). *Handbuch der Physiologie des Menschen Coblentz, Holsher I*. (W. Baly, Trans.). London: Taylor & Walton. (Orignally published, 1833).

Müller, J. (1940). *Handbuck der Physiologie des Menschen Goblentz, Holsher II* (W. Baly, Trans.). London: Taylor & Walton. (Originally published, 1842).

Müller, J. (1948). The specific energies of nerves. In W. Dennis (Ed.), *Readings in the history of psychology*. New York: Appleton-Century-Crofts. (Article orignally published, 1838).

Munroe, R. (1955). *Schools of psychoanalytic thought*. New York: Dryden.

Murphy, J. M. & Gilligan, C. (1980). Moral development in late adolescence and adulthood: A critique and reconstruction of Kohlberg's theory. *Human Development, 23*, 77–104.

Murray, E. J., & Jacobson, L. I. (1978). Cognition and learning in traditional and behavioral therapy. In S. L. Garfield & A. E. Bergin (Eds.), *Handbook of psychotherapy and behavior change*, (2nd ed.). New York: Wiley.

Murray, H. A. (1938). *Explorations in personality: A clinical and experimental study of fifty men of college age*. New York: Oxford University Press.

Murray, H. A. (1951). Uses of the Thematic Apperception Test. *American Journal of Psychiatry, 107*, 577–581.

Murray, H. A. (1962). *Explorations in personality*. New York: Science Editions.

Murstein, B. I. (1970). Stimulus-value-role: A theory of marital choice. *Journal of Marriage and the Family. 32*, 465–481.

Murstein, B. I. (1972). Physical attractiveness and marital choice. *Journal of Social Psychology 22*, 8–12.

Murstein, B. I. (1982). Marital choice. In B. Wolman (ed.), *Handbook of developmental psychology*. Englewood Cliffs, NJ: Prentice-Hall.

Mussen, P. M., & Jones, M. C. (1957). Self-conception, motivations, and interpersonal attitudes of early- and late-maturing boys. *Child Development, 28*, 243–256.

Myers, R. E. (1955). Interocular transfer of pattern discrimination in cats following section of crossed optic fibers. *Journal of Comparative and Physiological Psychology, 48*, 470–473.

Myers, R. E. (1961). *Brain mechanisms and learning*. Springfield, IL: Charles C Thomas.

Myers, R. E. (1961). Function of corpus callosum in interocular transfer. *Brain, 79*, 358–363.

Nadler, R. (1977). Sexual behavior of the chimpanzee in relation to the gorilla and orangutan. In G. H. Bourne (Eds), *Progress in ape research*. New York: Academic Press.

Nagel, E. (1959). Methodological issues in psychoanalytic theory. In S. Hook (Ed.), *Psychoanalysis, scientific method, and philosophy*. New York: Viking Press.

Nash, S. C. (1979). Sex role as a mediator of intellectual functioning. In M. A. Wittig, & A. C. Petersen (Eds.), *Sex-related differences in cognitive functioning*. New York: Academic Press.

National Institute on Alcohol Abuse and Alcoholism (NIAA). (1975). *Alcohol and health: Second special report to the U.S. Congress, new knowledge*. U.S. Department of Health, Education and Welfare, DHEW Publication Number (ADM) 75–212. Washington, DC: U.S. Government Printing Office.

Neisser, U. (1967). *Cognitive psychology*. New York: Appleton-Century-Crofts.

Neisser, U. (1976). *Cognition and reality*. San Francisco: W. H. Freeman.

Neisser, U. (1980, January). Computers can't think. *Creative computing*.

Nelson, K. (1973). Structure and strategy in learning to talk. *Monographs of the Society for Research in Child Development, 38* (Nos. 1–2).

Neugarten, B. (1975, January 18). The rise of the young old. *New York Times*.

Neugarten, B. L. (1973). Personality change in late life: A developmental perspective. In C. Eisdorfer & M. P. Lawton (Eds.), *Psychology of adult development and aging*. Washington, DC: American Psychological Association.

Newcomb, T. M. (1961). *The acquintance process*. New York: Holt, Rinehart and Winston.

Newell, A., & Simon, H. A. (1972). *Human problem solving*. Englewood Cliffs, NJ: Prentice-Hall.

Newell, A., & Simon, H. A. (1981). Computer science as empirical inquiry: Symbols and search. In J. Haugeland (Ed.), *Mind design: Philosophy, psychology, artificial intelligence*. Cambridge, MA: MIT Press.

Newman, P. R. (1982). The Peer group. In B. Wolman (Ed.), *Handbook of developmental psychology*. Englewood Cliffs, NJ: Prentice-Hall.

Newsweek, December 18, p. 106.

Newton, I. (1704). *Opticks*. London: William Innys.

Nicol, S. E., & Gottesman, I. I. (1983). Clues to the genetics and neurobiology of schizophrenia. *American Scientist, 71*, 398–404.

Nisbett, R. E. (1972). Hunger, obesity, and the ventromedial hypothalamus. *Psychological Review, 79*, 433–453.

Nisbett, R. E., Caputo, C., Legant, P., Marecek, J. (1973). Behavior as seen by the actor and as seen by the observer. *Journal of Personality and Social Psychology, 27*, 154–164.

Noble, G. K., & Schmidt, A. (1937). Structure and function of the facial and labial pits of snakes. *Proceedings of the American Philosophical Society, 77*, 263–288.

Norman, D. A. (1969). Memory while shadowing. *Quarterly Journal of Experimental Psychology, 21*, 85–93.

Norman, R. (1976). When what is said is important: A comparison of expert and attractive sources. *Journal of Experimental Social Psychology, 12*, 294–300.

Nyrne, D. (1961). Interpersonal attraction and attitude similarity. *Journal of Abnormal and Social Psychology, 62*, 713–715.

Offer, D. (1969). *The psychological world of the teenager.* New York: Basic Books.

Ogle, K. N. (1962). The optical space sense. In H. Davson (Ed.), *The eye.* New York: Academic Press.

Ohman, A., Eriksson, A., Fredriksson, N., Hugdahl, K., & Oloffson, C. (1974). Habituation of the electrodermal at orienting reaction to potentially phobic and supposedly neutral stimuli in normal human subjects. *Biological Psychology, 2*, 85–92.

Olds, J., & Milnear, P. (1954). Positive reinforcement produced by electrical stimulation of the septal area and other regions of the rat brain. *Journal of Comparative and Physiological Psychology, 47*, 419–427.

Olds, S. W. (1970, May). Menopause: Something to look forward to? *Today's Health,* p. 48.

Orlofsky, J. L., Marcia, J. E., & Lesser, I. (1973). Ego identity status and the intimacy versus isolation crisis of young adulthood. *Journal of Personality and Social Psychology, 27*, 211–219.

Ornstein, R. (1972). *The psychology of consciousness.* San Francisco: W. H. Freeman.

Ornstein, R. E. (1969). *On the experience of time.* Baltimore, MD: Penguin Books.

Overton, D. A. (1974). Experimental methods for the study of state-dependent learning. *Federation Proceedings, 33*, 1800–1813.

Owens, W. A. (1966). Age and mental abilities: A second adult follow-up. *Journal of Educational Psychology, 57*(6), 311–325.

Pahnke, W. M., & Richards, W. A. (1966). Implication of LSD and experimental mysticism. *Journal of Religion and Health, 5*, 175–208.

Palermo, D. S. (1978). *Psychology of language.* Glenview, IL: Scott, Foresman.

Palmer, J., & Byrne, D. (1970). Attraction toward dominant and submissive strangers: Similarity versus complementarity. *Journal of Experimental Research in Psychology, 4*, 108–115.

Palmore, E., Cleveland, W. P., Nowlin, J. G., Ramm, D., & Siegler, I. C. (1979). Stress and adaptation in late life. *Journal of Gerontology, 34*, 841–851.

Paludi, M. A., & Bauer, W. D. (1983) Goldberg revisited: What's in an author's name. *Sex Roles, 9*, 387–390.

Parkes, J. D. (1976). Clinical aspects of tardive dyskinesia. In H. F. Bradford and C. D. Marsden (Eds.), *Biochemistry and neurology.* New York: Academic Press.

Parloff, M. B., Waskow, E., & Wolper, B. E. (1978). Research on therapist variables in relation to process and outcome. In S. Garfield & A. Bergin (Eds.), *Handbook of psychotherapy and behavior change.* New York: Wiley.

Pascual-Leone, J. (1980). Constructive problems for constructive theories: The current relevance of Piaget's work and critique of information processing simulation psychology. In H. Speda & P. Kluwe (Eds.), *Psychological models of thinking.* New York: Academic Press.

Patterson, F. G. (1978). The gestures of a gorilla: Language acquisition in another pongid. *Brain and Language. 5*, 72–97.

Patterson, I. J. (1965). Timing and spacing of broods in the black-headed gull *Larus ridibundis. Ibis, 107*, 433–459.

Pavlov, I. P. (1927). *Conditioned reflexes* (G. V. Anrep, Trans.). New York: Oxford University Press.

Peck, J. W., & Novin, D. (1971). Evidence that osmoreceptors mediating drinking in rabbits are in the lateral preoptic area. *Journal of Comparative and Physiological Psychology, 74*, 134–147.

Peck, R. C. (1968). Psychological developments in the second half of life. In B. L. Neugarten (Ed.), *Middle age and the aging.* Chicago: University of Chicago Press.

Pelletier, K. R. (1977). *Mind as healer, mind as slayer.* New York: Dell.

Penfield, W., & Roberts, L. (1959). *Speech and brain mechanisms.* Princeton, NJ: Princeton University Press.

Pert, C. B., & Snyder, S. H. (1973). Opiate receptor: Demonstration in nervous tissue. *Science, 179*, 1011–1014.

Pessin, J. (1933). The comparative effects of social and mechanical stimulation of memorizing. *American Journal of Psychology, 45*, 263–270.

Petersen, A. C. (1980). Biopsychosocial processes in the development of sex-related differences and sex roles. In J. E. Parsons (Ed.), *The psychobiology of sex differences and sex roles.* Washington, DC: Hemisphere.

Petty, R. E., & Cacioppo, J. T. (1981). *Attitudes and persuasion: Classic and contemporary approaches.* Dubuque, Iowa: Wm. C. Brown.

Phares, E. J. (1976). *Locus of control in personality.* Morristown, NJ: General Learning Press.

Phares, E. J. (1984). *Introduction to personality.* Columbus, OH: Merrill.

Phillips, J. S., & Bierman, K. L. (1981). Clinical psychology: Individual methods. *Annual Review of Psychology, 32*, 405–438.

Piaget, J. (1959). *The language and thought of the child.* New York: Harcourt, Brace. (Originally published, 1926).

Piaget, J. (1962). The stages of the intellectual development of the child. *Bulletin of the Menninger Clinic, 26*, 120–145.

Piaget, J. (1970). Piaget's theory. In P. Mussen (Ed.), *Carmichael's manual of child psychology.* New York: Wiley.

Piaget, J. (1972). Intellectual evolution from adolescence to adulthood. *Human Development, 15*, 1–12.

Piaget, J. (1974). *The origins of intelligence in children.* New York: Norton. (Originally published, 1963).

Piaget, J. (1976). *The grasp of consciousness.* Cambridge, MA: Harvard University Press.

Pinel, P. (1962). *A treatise on insanity,* (D. D. Davis, Trans.). New York: Hafner. (Originally published in 1801).

Plesczynska, W. (1978). Microgeographic prediction of polygyny in lark bunting. *Science, 201*, 935–937.

Pope, K. S. (1978). The flow of consciousness. In K. S. Pope & J. L. Singer (Eds.), *The stream of consciousness.* New York: Plenum Press.

Premack, D. (1971). On the assessment of language competence in the chimpanzee. In A. M. Schrier & F. Stollnitz (Eds.), *Behavior of nonhuman primates* (Vol. 4). New York: Academic Press.

Premack, D. (1976). Language and intelligence in ape and man. *American Scientist, 64*, 674–683.

Price, R. H., Ketterer, R. F., Bader, B. C., & Monahan, J. (Eds.). (1980). *Prevention in mental health: Research, policy and practice.* Beverly Hills: Sage.

Price, R. H., & Lynn, S. J. (1981). *Abnormal psychology in the human context.* Homewood, IL: Dorsey Press.

Price, R. H., & Smith, S.S. (1983). Two decades of reform in the mental health system. In E. Seidman (Ed.), *Handbook of social and community intervention.* Beverly Hills, CA: Sage.

Price, R. H. & Bouffard, D. L. (1974). Behavioral appropriateness and situational constraint as dimensions of social behavior. *Journal of Personality and Social Psychology, 30,* 579–586.

Price, R. N., & Lynn, S. J. (1981). *Abnormal behavior in the human context.* Homewood, IL: Dorsey Press.

Pylyshyn, Z. W. (1979). Complexity and the study of artificial and human intelligence. In M. Ringle (Ed.), *Philosophical perspectives.*

Rabow, J., Fowler, F. J., Bradford, D. L., Hofeller, M. A., & Shibuya, Y. (1966). The role of social norms and leadership in risk taking. *Sociometry, 26,* 16–27.

Rachman, S. J., & Hodgson, R. J. (1980). *Obsessions and compulsions.* Englewood Cliffs, NJ: Prentice-Hall.

Ragan, J. M. (1982). Gender displays in portrait photographs. *Sex Roles, 8,* 33–43.

Ramon y Cajal, S. (1909–1911). *Histologie du systéme nerveux de l'homme et des vértebrès* (2 vols.), (L. Azoulay, Trans.). Paris: Maloine.

Ramon y Cajal, S. (1937). *Recollections of my life.* (E. H. Craigie & J. Cano, Trans.). Philadelphia: American Philosophical Society.

Ranvier, L. A. (1871). Contributions a l'histologie et é la physiologie des nerfs periphériques. *Comptes Rendus Hebdomaoaires des Seances de L'Academie des Sciences, Paris, 73,* 1168–1171.

Ratliff, F., & Riggs, L. A. (1950). Involuntary motions of the eye during monocular fixation. *Journal of Experimental Psychology, 40,* 687–701.

Ratliff, F. (1965). *Mach bands: Quantitative studies on neural networks in the retina.* San Francisco: Holden-Day.

Raven, J. C. (1941). Standardization of progressive matrices. *British Journal of Medical Psychology, 19,* 137–150.

Ray, O. (1978). *Drugs, society, and human behavior* (2nd ed.). St. Louis: Mosby.

Ray, O. S. (1978). *Drugs, society, and human behavior* (2nd ed.). St. Louis, MO: Mosby.

Reed, D., Bevereley, K., & Cynader, H. (1979). The visual perception of motion in depth. *Scientific American, 24,* 136–151.

Reich, W. (1949). *Character analysis.* New York: Orgone Institute Press.

Rescoria, R. A., & Solomon, R. L. (1967). Two-process learning theory: Relations between Pavlovian conditioning and instrumental learning.

Restak, R. M. (1982, May). Islands of genius. *Science, 82,* 62–67.

Reuben, D. (1971). *Everything you always wanted to know about sex, but were afraid to ask.* New York: Bantam.

Reus, V. I., Weingartner, H., Post, R. M. (1979). Clinical implications of state-dependent learning. *American Journal of Psychiatry, 136,* 927–931.

Revusky, S. H., & Garcia, J. (1970). Learned associations over long delays. In G. H. Bower & J. T. Spence (Eds.), *The psychology of learning and motivation: IV.* New York: Academic Press.

Rheingold, H. L., & Eckerman, C.O. (1973). The fear of strangers hypothesis: A critical review. In H. Reese (Ed.), *Advances in child development and behavior* (Vol. 8). New York: Academic Press.

Rhine, J. B. (1935). *Extra-sensory perception.* Boston: Bruce Humphries.

Rice, B. (1979, September). Brave new world of intelligence testing. *Psychology Today,* p. 27.

Rice, B. (1980). Going for the gifted gold. *Psychology Today, 13,* 55.

Richman, C. L., Mitchell, D. B., & Reznick, J. S. (1979). Mental travel: Some reservations. *Journal of Experimental Psychology: Human Perception, 5,* 13–18.

Riegel, K. F., & Riegel, R. M. (1972). Development, drop, and death. *Developmental Psychology, 6*(2), 306–319.

Riegel, K. F. & Riegel, R. M. (1972). Development, drop and death. *Developmental Psychology, 6,* 306–319.

Riggs, L. A., Ratliff, F., Cornsweet, J. C., & Cornsweet, T. (1953). The disappearance of visual test objects. *Journal of the Optical Society of America, 43,* 495–501.

Ring, K. (1980). *Life at death.* New York: Coward, McCann & Geoghegan.

Rips, L. J., Shoben, E. J., & Smith, E. E. (1973). Semantic distance and the verification of semantic relations. *Journal of Verbal Learning and Verbal Behavior, 12,* 1–20.

Rizzollatti, G., Umilta, C., & Berlucchi, G. (1971). Opposite superiorities of the right and left hemispheres in discriminative reaction time to physiognomical and alphabetical material. *Brain, 94,* 431–442.

Robbins, M. B., & Jensen, J. D. (1976). Multiple orgasms in males. In R. Gemme & C. C. Wheeler (Eds.), *Progress in sexology.* New York: Plenum Press.

Robinson, N. M., & Robinson, H. B. (1976). *The mentally retarded child* (2nd ed.). New York: McGraw-Hill.

Roche, A. D. (Ed.). (1979). Secular trends in human growth, maturation, and development. *Monographs of the Society for Research in Child Development, 44* (Serial No. 179).

Roche, A. F., Davila, g. H. (1972). Late adolescent growth in stature. *Pediatrics, 50*(6), 874–880.

Rock, I., & Victor, J. (1964). Vision and touch: An experimentally created conflict between the two senses. *Science, 143,* 594–596.

Rockstein, M., & Sussman, M. (1979). *Biology of aging.* Belmont, CA: Wadsworth.

Rodgers, J. E. (1982, July-August). Roots of madness: The schizophrenic's reality is not ours. *Science, 82,* 85–89.

Rodgers, W., & Rozin, P. (1966). Novel food preferences in thiamine-deficient rats. *Journal of Comparative and Psychological Psychology, 61,* 1–4.

Rodin, J. (1970). *Effects of distraction on the performance of obese and normal subjects.* Unpublished doctoral dissertation. Columbia University.

Rodin, J., Solomon, S., & Metcalf, J. (1978). Role of control in mediating perceptions of density. *Journal of Personality and Social Psychology, 36,* 988–999.

Roeder, F. D. (1966). Stereotaxic lesion of the tuber cinereum in sexual deviation. *Confinia Neurologica, 27,* 162–163.

Rogers, C. R. (1942). *Counseling and psychotherapy.* Boston: Houghton Mifflin.

Rogers, C. R. (1957). The necessary and sufficient conditions of therapeutic personality change. *Journal of counseling Psychology, 21,* 95–103.

Rogers, C. R. (1959). A theory of therapy, personality, and interpersonal relationships as developed in client-centered framework. In S. Koch (Ed.), *Psychology: A study of a Science (Vol. III). Formulation of the person in the social context.* New York: McGraw-Hill.

Rogers, C. R. (1961). *On becoming a person.* Boston: Houghton Mifflin.

Rogers, C. R. (1970). *On encounter groups.* New York: Harper & Row.

Rosch, E. H. (1975). Cognitive representations of semantic categories. *Journal of Experimental Psychology, 104,* 192–233.

Rose, S. (1973). *The conscious brain.* New York: Knopf.

Rosenberg, S., Nelson, C., & Vivekananthan, P. S. (1968). A multidimensional approach to the structure of personality impression. *Journal of Personality and Social Psychology, 9,* 283–294.

Rosenhan, D. L. (1973). On being sane in insane places. *Science, 179,* 250–258.

Rosenthal, D. (1970). *Genetic theory and abnormal behavior*. New York: McGraw-Hill.

Rosenthal, R., DePaulo, B. M. (1979). Sex differences in eavesdropping on nonverbal cues. *Journal of Personality and Social Psychology, 37*, 273–285.

Rosenthal, R., & Jacobson, L. (1966). Teachers expectancies: Determinants of pupils I.Q. gain. *Psychological Reports, 19*, 115–118.

Ross, L., Amabile, T. M., & Steinmetz, J. L. (1977). Social roles, social control, and bias in social-perception processes. *Journal of Personality and Social Psychology, 35*, 485–494.

Ross, L., Greene, D., & House, P. (1977). The "False Consensus Effect": An egocentric bias in social perception and attribution processes. *Journal of Experimental Social Psychology, 13*, 279–301.

Rothman, D. (1971). *The discovery of the asylum*. New York: Little, Brown.

Rotter, J. B. (1954). *Social learning and clinical psychology*. Englewood Cliffs, NJ: Prentice-Hall.

Rotter, J. B. (1982). *The development and application of social learning theory: Selected papers*. New York: Praeger.

Rubin, E. (1958). Figure and ground. In D. C. Beardslee & M. Wertheimer (Eds.), *Readings in perception*. New York: D Von Nostrand. (Article originally published, 1915).

Rumbaugh, D. M. (Ed.). (1977). *Language learning by a chimpanzee: The Lana project*. New York: Academic Press.

Rumelhart, D. E. (1975). Notes on a schema for stories: In D. G. Bobrow & A. M. Collins (Eds.), *Representations and understanding: Studies in cognitive science*. New York: Academic Press.

Rush, A. J., Beck, A. T., Kovacs, M., & Hollon, S. I. (1977). Comparative efficacy of cognitive therapy and pharmacotherapy in the treatment of depressed outpatients. *Cognitive Therapy Research, 1*, 17–37.

Russell, P. J., Adbelaal, A. E., & Mogenson, G. J. (1975). Graded levels of hemorrhage, thirst, and Angiotensin II in the rat. *Physiology and Behavior, 15*, 117–119.

Sabom, M. B. (1982). *Recollections of death*. New York: Harper & Row.

Sachs, J. S. (1967). Recognition memory for syntactic and semantic aspects of connected discourse. *Perception and Psychophysics. 2*, 437–442.

Sackett, G. P. (1966). Monkeys reared in isolation with pictures as visual input: Evidence for an innate releasing mechanism. *Science, 154*, 1468–1473.

Saegert, S., Swap, W., & Zajonc, R. B. (1973). Exposure, context, and interpersonal attraction. *Journal of Personality and Social Psychology, 25*, 234–252.

Sagan, C. (1977). *The dragons of Eden*. New York: Random House.

Saghir, M. T., Robins, E. (1973). *Male and female homosexuality*. Baltimore: Williams & Wilkins.

Samelson, F. (1957). Conforming behavior under two conditions of conflict in the cognitive field. *Journal of Abnormal and Social Psychology, 55*, 181–187.

Sameroff, A. J. & Chandler, N. J. (1975). Reproductive risk and the continuum of caretaking casualty. In F. Horowitz (Ed.), *Review of child development research* (Vol. 4). Chicago: University of Chicago Press.

Sankar, D. V. S. (1975). *LSD—a total study*. Westbury, NY: PJD Publications.

Scarr, S., Webber, P. L., Weinberg, R. A., & Wittig, M. A. (1981). Personality resemblance among adolescents and their parents in biologically related and adoptive families. *Journal of Personality and Social Psychology, 40*, 885–898.

Scarr, S., & Weinberg, R. A. (1978). The influence of "family background" on intellectual attainment. *American Sociological Review, 43*, 674–692.

Schachter, S. (1951). Deviation, rejection and communication. *Journal of Abnormal and Social Psychology, 46*, 190–207.

Schachter, S. (1959). *The psychology of affiliation*. Stanford, CA: Stanford University Press.

Schachter, S. (1971). Some extraordinary facts about obese humans and rats. *American Psychologist, 26*, 129–144.

Schachter, S., Goldman, R., & Gordon, A. (1968). Effects of fear, food deprivation, and obesity on eating. *Journal of Personality and Social Psychology, 10*, 91–97.

Schachter, S., & Gross, L. P. (1968). Manipulated time and eating behavior. *Journal of Personality and Social Psychology, 10*, 98–106.

Schachter, S., & Rodin, J. *Obese humans and rats*. Washington, DC: Erlbaum/Halsted.

Schachter, S., & Singer, J. E. (1962). Cognitive, social, and physiological determinants of emotional state. *Psychological Review, 69*, 379–399.

Schact, T., & Nathan, P. E. (1977). But is it good for psychologists? Appraisal and status of DSM III. *American Psychologist, 32*, 1017–1025.

Schaffer, H. R., & Emerson, P. E. (1964). The development of social attachments in infancy. Monographs of the Society for Research in Child development of social attachments in infancy. *Monographs of the Society for Research in Child Development, 29*(3).

Schaie, K., & Strother, C. (1968). A cross-sequential study of age changes in cognitive behavior. *Psychological Bulletin, 70*, 671–680.

Scheerer, M., Rothman, E., Goldstein, K. (1945). A case of "idiot savant": An experimental study of personality organization. *Psychological Monographs, 58*, (whole No. 269).

Scheff, T. J. (1966). *Being mentally ill: A sociological theory*. Chicago: Aldine.

Schein, E. H., Schneier, I., & Baker, C. H. (1961). *Coercive persuasion*. New York: Norton.

Schiffman, H. R. (1976). *Sensation and perception: An integrated approach*. New York: Wiley.

Schiffman, S. S. (1974). Physiochemical correlates of olfactory quality. *Science, 185*, 112–117.

Schildkraut, J. J., et. al. (1978). Toward a biochemical classification of depressive disorders. *Archives of General Psychiatry, 35*, 1427.

Schildkraut, J. J., & Kety, S. S. (1967). Biogenic amines and emotion. *Science, 156*, 21–30.

Schlodtmann, W. (1902). Ein Beitrag zur Lehre von der Optischen Localisation bei Blindgeboren. *Archiv für Opthalmologie, 54*, 256–267.

Schmeck, H. M., Jr. (1976, June 10). Trend in growth of children lags. *New York Times*, p. 13.

Schmeck, H. M., Jr. (1979, April 10). Researcher's tracking brain's own tranquilizers. *New York Times*, Cl.

Schmidt, G., & Sigusch, V. (1973) Woman's sexual arousal. In J. Zubin and J. Money (Eds.), *Contemporary sexual behavior: Critical issues in the 1970's*. Baltimore: Johns Hopkins University Press.

Schmidt, R. A. (1975). A schema theory of discrete motor skill learning. *Psychological Review, 82*, 225–260.

Schram, R. (1979). Marital satisfaction over the family life-cycle: A critique and proposal. *Journal of Marriage and the Family, 41*, 7–40.

Schreiber, F. R. (1973). *Sybil* Chicago: Regnery.

Schreiner-Engel, P., Schiavi, R. C., Smith, H., & White, D. (1981). Sexual arousability and the menstrual cycle. *Psychosomatic Medicine, 43*, 199–214.

Schull, A. T. (1977). Community treatment and the deviant: A radical view. In *Decarceration*. Englewood Cliffs, NJ: Prentice-Hall.

Schultes, R. E. (1972). The utilization of hallucinogens in primitive societies: Use, misuse or abuse? In W. Keup (Ed.), *Drug abuse: Current concepts and research*. Springfield, IL: Charles C Thomas.

Schulz, R. (1978). *The psychology of death, dying and bereavement*. Reading, MA: Addison-Wesley.

Schwann, T. (1939). *Mikroskopische Untersuchungen über die üUbereinstimmung in der Struktur und dem Wachstum der Thiere und Pflanzen*. Berlin: Reimer.

Schwartz, B. (1984). *Psychology of learning and behavior* (2nd ed.). New York: Norton.

Schwartz, G. E. (1977). Psychosomatic disorders and biofeedback: A psychobiological model of disregulation. In J. D. Maser & M. E. P. Seligman (Eds.), *Psychopathology: Experimental models*, San Francisco: Freeman.

Sears, P. S., & Barbee, N. H. (1978). Career and life satisfaction among Terman's gifted women. In *The gifted and the creative: 50-year perspective*. Baltimore: Johns Hopkins University Press.

Sears, R. R. (1977). Sources of life satisfaction of the Terman-gifted men. *American Psychologist, 32*, 119–128.

Seavey, G. A., Katz, P. A., & Zalk, B. R. (1975). Baby X: The effect of gender labels on adult responses to infants. *Sex Roles, 1*, 103–110.

Seidman, L. J. (1983). Schizophrenia and brain Dysfunction: An integration of recent neuro-diagnostic findings. *Psychological Bulletin, 94*(2), 195–238.

Seligman, M. E. P. (1975). *Helplessness: On depression, development and death*. San Francisco: Freeman.

Seligman, M. E. P., Maier, S. F., & Geer, J. (1968). The alleviation of learned helplessness in the dog. *Journal of Abnormal and Social Psychology, 73*, 256–262.

Seligman, M. E. P., Maier, S. F., & Solomon, R. L. (1971). Unpredictable and uncontrollable aversive events. In R. F. Brusch (Ed.), *Aversive conditioning and learning*. New York: Academic Press.

Shapiro, D. (1980). *Meditation: Self-regulation strategies and altered states of consciousness*. New York: Aldine.

Shattuck, R. (1980). *The forbidden experiment*. New York: Farrar Straus Giroux.

Sheldon, W. H. (1942). *The varieties of temperament: A psychology of constitutional differences*. New York: Harper.

Sheldon, W. H. (1954). *Atlas of men: A guide for somatotyping the adult male at all ages*. New York: Harper.

Sherif, M., Harvey, O., White, B., Hood, W., & Sherif, C. (1961). *Intergroup conflict and cooperation: The robbers' cave experiment*. Norman, OK: University Book Exchange.

Sherif, M., & Sherif, C. *Groups in harmony and tension*. New York: Harper & Row.

Sherif, M. (1937). An experimental approach to the study of attitudes. *Sociometry, 1*, 90–98.

Sherman, P. W. (1977). Nepotism and the evolution of alarm calls. *Science, 197*, 1246–1253.

Sherrington, C. (1906). *The integrative action of the nervous system*. New Haven, CT: Yale University Press.

Sherrod, D. R. (1974). Crowding, perceived control, and behavior aftereffects. *Journal of Applied Social Psychology. 14*, 171–186.

Sherrod, D. R., & Downs, R. (1974). Environmental determinants of altruism: The effects of stimulus overload and perceived control on helping. *Journal of Experimental Social Psychology, 10*, 468–479.

Shiffrin, R. M., Pisoni, D. B., & Castenada-Mendez, K. (1974). Is attention shared between the ears? *Cognitive Psychology, 6*, 190–215.

Shneidman, E. (1980). *Death: Current perspectives* (2nd ed.). Palo Alto, CA: Mayfield.

Shor, R. E. (1960). The frequency of naturally occurring "hypnotic like" experiences in normal college population. *International Journal of Clinical and Experimental Hypnosis, 8*, 151–163.

Short, R. V. (1978). Sexual-selection and its component parts, somatic and genital selection, as illustrated by man and the great apes. *Advances in the Study of Behavior, 9*, 131.

Siegler, R. S: (1981). Developmental sequences within and between concepts. *Monographs of the Society for Research in Child Development, 46*, (2, Serial No. 189).

Siegler, R. S. (1983). Information processing approaches to development. In W. Kessen (Ed.), *Handbook of child psychology, Vol 1: History, theory and methods*. New York: Wiley.

Singer, J. E., Brush, C., & Lublin, S. D. (1965). Some aspects of deindividuation: Identification and conformity. *Journal of Experimental Social Psychology, 1*, 356–378. .

Sistrunk, F., & McDavid, J. W. (1971). Sex variables in conforming behavior. *Journal of Personality and Social Psychology, 17*, 200–207.

Skeels, H. M. (1966). Adult status of children with contrasting early life experiences. *Monographs of the Society for Research and Child Development* (Vol. 31).

Skinner, B. F. (1938). *The behavior of organisms*. New York: Appleton-Century-Crofts.

Skinner, B. F. (1948). Superstition in the pigeon. *Journal of Experimental Psychology. 38*, 168–172.

Skinner, B. F. (1948). *Walden two*. New York: Macmillan.

Skinner, B. F. (1953). *Science and human behavior*. New York: Macmillan.

Skinner, B. F. (1956). A case history in scientific method. *American Psychologist, 11*, 221–233.

Skinner, B. F. (1974). *About behaviorism*. New York: Knopf.

Skinner, B. F. *Beyond freedom and dignity*. New York: Knopf.

Slobin, D. I. (1975). On the nature of talk to children. In E. H. Lenneberg & E. Lenneberg (Eds.), *Foundations of language development: A multidisciplinary approach* (Vol. 1). New York: Academic Press.

Smart, R. G. (1967). *LSD in treatment of alcoholism*. Toronto: University of Toronto Press.

Smith, D. E., King, M. B., & Hoebel, B. C. (1970). Lateral hypothalamic control of killing: Evidence for a cholinoceptive mechanism. *Science, 167*, 900–901.

Smith, G. P. (1983, July 9). The peripheral control of appetite. *The Lancet*, 88–89.

Smith, M. B., Bruner, J. S., White, R. W. (1956). *Opinions and personality*. New York: Wiley.

Smith, M. L., Glass, G. V., & Miller, T. I. (1980). *The benefits of psychotherapy*. Baltimore, MD: Johns Hopkins University Press.

Smith, M. L., Glass, G. V. (1977). Meta-analysis of psychotherapy outcome studies. *American Psychologist, 132*, 752–760.

Snyder, C. R., & Larson, G. R. (1972). A further look at student acceptance of general personality interpretations. *Journal of Consulting and Clinical Psychology, 38*, 384–388.

Snyder, M., Tanke, E. D., & Berscheid, E. (1977). *Social perception and interpersonal behavior: On the self-fulfilling nature of social psychology, 35*, 656–666.

Snyder, S. (1977, March). Opiate receptors and internal opiates. *Scientific American*, 44–56.

Snyder, S. H. (1975). *Madness and the brain*. New York: McGraw-Hill.

Snyder, S. H. (1976). The dopamine hypothesis of schizophrenia. *American Journal of Psychiatry, 133*, 197–202.

Snyderman, M., & Herrnstein, R. J. (1983, September). Intelligence tests and the Immigration Act of 1924. *American Psychologist*, 986–995.

Sollie, D. & Miller, B. (1980). The transition to parenthood as a critical time for building family strengths. In N. Stinnett & P. Knaub (Eds.), *Family strengths: Positive models of family life*. Lincoln, NE: University of Nebraska Press.

Solomon, R. I. (1980). The opponent-process theory of acquired motivation. *American Psychologist, 691*, 691–712.

Sommer, R. (1969). *Personal space*. Englewood Cliffs, NJ: Prentice-Hall.

Sorenson, C. (1973). *Adolescent sexuality in contemporary America*. New York: World Publishing.

Sorrentino, R. M., & Sheppard, B. H. (1978). Effects of affiliation-related motives on swimmers in individual versus group competition: A field experiment. *Journal of Personality and Social Psychology, 36*, 704–714.

Spear, M. E. (1972). *Organizational aspects of memory in temporal lobatomy patients*. Unpublished doctoral dissertation, University of Maryland.

Spearman, C. (1927). *The abilities of man*. London: Macmillan.

Spence, K. W., Taylor, J., Ketchel, R. (1956). Anxiety (drive) level and degree of competition in paired associates learning. *Journal of Experimental Psychology, 53*, 306–310.

Sperling, G. A. (1960). The information available in brief visual presentations. *Psychological Monographs, 74* (Whole No. 498).

Sperry, R. (1984). Consciousness, personal identity, and the divided brain. *Neuropsychologia, 22*, 661–673.

Sperry, R. W. (1956). Neuronal basis of the spontaneous optic nerve responses produced by visual inversion. *Journal of Comparative Physiological Psychology, 43*, 482–489.

Sperry, R. W. (1961). Cerebral organization and behavior. *Science, 133*, 1749.

Sperry, R. W. (1964). The great cerebral commissure. *Scientific American, 210*, 42–52.

Sperry, R. W. (1968). In G. E. W. Wolstenholme & M. O'Conner (Eds.), *Growth of the nervous system*. London: Churchill.

Sperry, R. W. (1974). Lateral specialization in the surgically disconnected hemispheres. In F. O. Schmitt & F. G. Worden (Eds.), *The neurosciences third study program*. Cambridge, MA: MIT Press.

Sperry, R. W. (1982). Some effects of disconnecting the cerebral hemispheres. *Science, 217*, 1223–1226.

Spies, G. (1965). Food versus intracranial self-stimulation reinforcement in food deprived rats. *Journal of Comparative and Physiological Psychology, 60*, 153–157.

Spirduso, W. W. (1973). Reaction and movement time as a function of age and physical activity level. *Journal of Gerontology, 30*, 435–440.

Spitz, R. A. (1946). Anaclitic depression. *Psychoanalytic Studies of the Child, 2*, 313–342.

Spitz, R. A. (1946). Hospitalism: A follow-up report. *Psychoanalytic Studies of the Child, 2*, 113–117.

Spitzer, R. L., Skodol, A. E., Gibbon, M., & Williams, J. B. W. (1981). *DSM-III case book: A learning companion to the diagnostic and statistical manual of mental disorders* (3rd ed.). Washington, DC: American Psychiatric Association.

Spivack, G., & Shure, M. B. (1974). *Social adjustment of young children: A cognitive approach to solving real life problems*. San Francisco: Jossey-Bass.

Sroufe, L. A., & Waters, E. (1977). Attachment as an organizational construct. *Child Development, 48*, 1184–1199.

Stace, W. T. (1960). *Philosophy of mysticism*. New York: Macmillan.

Staddon, J. E. R., & Simmelhag, V. L. (1971). The "superstition" experiment: A reexamination of its implications for the principles of adaptive behavior. *Psychological Review, 78*, 3–43.

Stalnaker, J. M. (1965). Psychological tests and public responsibility. *American Psychologist, 20*, 131–135.

Stampfl, T. C., & Levis, D. J. (1967). Essentials of implosive therapy: A learning-therapy-based psychodynamic behavior therapy. *Journal of Abnormal Psychology, 72*, 496–503.

Stebbins, W. C., Miller, J. M., Johnsson, L. G., & Hawkins, J. E., Jr. (1969). Ototoxic hearing loss and cochlear pathology in the monkey. *Annals of Otology, Rhinology, and Laryngology, 78*, 598–602.

Stern, D. N. (1974). Mother and infant at play: The dyadic interaction involving facial, vocal and gaze behaviors. In M. Lewis & L. A. Rosenblum (Eds.), *The effect of the infant on its caretaker*. New York: Wiley.

Stern, W. (1914). *The psychological methods of testing intelligence*. (G. W. Whipple, Trans.). Baltimore, MD: Warwick & York.

Sternberg, R. J., & Dettermanm, D. K. (Eds.). (1979). *Human intelligence: Perspective on its theory and measures*. Norwood, NJ: Ablex.

Sternberg, R. J. (1979). *Intelligence, information processing and analogical reasoning: Componential analysis of human abilities*. Hillsdale, NJ: Erlbaum.

Stevens, J. K., Emerson, R. C., Gerstein, G. L., Kallos, T., Neufeld, G., Nichols, C., & Rosenquist, A. C. (1976). Paralysis of the awake human: Visual perceptions. *Vision Research, 16*, 93–98.

Stevens, S. S. (1957). On the psychophysical law. *Psychological Review, 64*, 153–181.

Stevens, S. S. (1961). To honor Fechner and repeal his law. *Science, 133*, 80–86.

Stevenson, H. W., Keen, R., & Knights, R. M. (1963). Parents and strangers as reinforcing agents for children's performance. *Journal of Abnormal and Social Psychology, 67*, 183–186.

Stewart, K. (1969). Dream theory in Malaya. In C. Tart (Ed.), *Altered states of consciousness*. New York: Wiley.

Stoller, R. (1968). *Sex and gender*. New York: Science House.

Stoner, J. A. F. (1961). *A comparison of individual and group decisions involving risk*. Unpublished master's thesis. MIT.

Stoner, J. A. F. (1968). Risky and cautious shifts in group decisions: The influence of widely held values. *Journal of Experimental Social Psychology, 4*, 442–459.

Stricker, E. M., & Wilson, N. E. (1970). Salt-seeking behavior in rats following acute sodium deficiency. *Journal of Comparative Physiology, 72*, 416–420.

Strupp, H. H., Fox, R. E., & Lessler, K. (1969). *Patients view their therapy*. Baltimore, MD: Johns Hopkins University Press.

Strupp, H. H. (1978). Psychotherapy research and practice. In S. Garfield & A. Bergin (Eds.), *Handbook of psychotherapy and behavior change*. New York: Wiley.

Stunkard, A., & Koch, C. (1964). The interpretation of gastric motility. I. Apparent bias in the reports of hunger by obese persons. *Archives of General Psychiatry, 11*, 74–82.

Stunkard, A. (1980). *Obesity*. Philadelphia: Saunders.

Suedfeld, P. (1975). The benefits of boredom: Sensory deprivation reconsidered. *American Scientist, 63*, 60–69.

Suedfeld, P., & Kristeller, J. L. (1982). Stimulus reduction as a technique in health psychology. *Health psychology, 1*, 337–357.

Sussman, N. M., & Rosenfeld, H. M. (1982). Influence of culture, language, and sex on conversational distance. *Journal of Personality and Social Psychology, 42*, 66–74.

Svaetichin, G., & MacNichol, E. F., Jr. (1958). Retinal mechanisms for chromatic and achromatic vision. *Annals of the New York Academy of Science, 74*, 385–404.

Sweet, W. H., Ervin, F., & Mark, V. H. (1969). The relationship of violent behavior to focal cerebral disease. In S. Garattini & S. Eigg (Eds.), *Aggressive behavior*. New York: Wiley.

Szasz, T. (1976). Patty Hearst's conversion: Some call it brain-washing. *The New Republic, 174*, 10–12.

Tanner, J. M. (1970). Physical growth. In P. H. Mussen (ed.), *Carmichael's manual of child psychology* (Vol. 1) (3rd ed.). New York: Wiley.

Tanner, J. M. (1971). Sequence, tempo, and individual variation in the growth and development of boys and girls aged twelve to sixteen. *Daedalus, 100*, 907–930.

Tart, C. T. (Ed.). (1975). *States of consciousness*. New York: Dutton.

Taylor, M. C., & Hall, J. A. (1982). Psychological androgyny: Theories, methods and conclusions. *Psychological Bulletin, 92*, 347–366.

Teevan, R. C., & McGhee, P. E. (1972). Childhood development of fear of failure motivation. *Journal of Personality and Social Psychology, 21*, 345–348.

Teitelbaum, P., & Epstein, A. (1962). Recovery of feeding and drinking after lateral hypothalamic lesions. *Psychological Review, 69*, 74–90.

Teller, D. Y., Morse, R., Borton, R., & Regal, D. (1974). Visual acuity for vertical and diagonal gratings in human infants. *Vision Research, 14*, 1433–1439.

Terman, L. M., & Oden, N. H. (1947). *The gifted child grows up*. Stanford, CA: Stanford University Press.

Terman, L. M. (1916). *The measurement of intelligence*. Boston: Houghton Mifflin.

Terrace, H. S., Petitto, L. A., Sanders, R. J., & Bever, T. G. (1979). Can an ape create a sentence? *Science, 206*, 891–902.

Theios, J. (1962). The partial reinforcement effect sustained through blocks of continuous reinforcement. *Journal of Experimental Psychology, 64*, 1–6.

Thibaut, J. W., & Kelley, H. H. (1959). *The social psychology of groups*. New York: Wiley.

Thigpen, Z. H., & Cleckley, H. (1954) *The three faces of Eve*. Kingsport, TN: Kingsport Press.

Thomas, M. H., Horton, R. W., Lippincott, E. C., & D., Drabman, R. S. (1977). Desensitization to portrayals of real-life aggression as a function of exposure to television violence. *Journal of Personality and Social Psychology, 35*, 450–458.

Thorndike, E. L. (1898). Animal intelligence: An experimental study of the associative processes in animals. *Psychological Review Monograph, 2* (Whole No–8).

Thorndike, E. L. (1932). *The psychology of learning*. New York: Teachers College.

Thurstone, L. L. (1938). Primary mental abilities. *Psychometric Monographs. 1*, 1–121.

Time. (1979, November, 26). A rebellion gathers steam.

Time (1971, September 20). Skinner's utopia: Panacea, or path to hell? 47–53.

Tinbergen, N. (1963). The shell menace. *Natural History, 72*, 28–35.

Tinsley, B. R. & Parke, R. D. (1983). Grandparents as support and socialization agents. In M. Lewis (Ed.), *Beyond the dyad*. New York: Plenum Press.

Tolman, E. C. (1932). *Purposive behavior in animals and men*. New York: Century Co.

Tolman, E. C. (1938). Determinants of behavior at a choice point. *Psychological Review. 45*, 1–41.

Tolman, E. C. (1948). Cognitive maps in rats and men. *Psychological Review. 556*, 189–208.

Tosteson, D. C. (1981, April). Lithium and maina. *Scientific American, 244*, 164.

Treisman, A. M. (1964). Monitoring and storage of irrelevant messages in selective attention. *Journal of Verbal Learning and Verbal Behavior, 3*, 449–459.

Troll, L. E., Miller, S. J., & Atchley, R. C. (1979). *Families in later life*. Belmont, CA: Wadsworth.

Troll, L. E. (1975). *Early and middle adulthood*. Monterey, CA: Brooks/Cole Publishing.

Troll, L. E. (1983). Grandparents: The family watchdogs. In T. Brubaker (Ed.), *Family relationships in later life*. Beverly Hills, CA:, Sage.

Tsuang, M. (1976). Schizophrenia around the world. *Comparative Psychiatry, 17*, 477–481.

Tulkin, S. R. & Kagan, J. (1972). Mother-child interaction in the first year of life. *Child Development, 43*, 31–42.

Tulving, E. (1972). Episodic and semantic memory. In E. Tulving & W. Donaldson (Eds.), *Organization of memory*. New York: Academic Press.

Tulving, E., & Osler, S. (1968). Effectiveness of retrieval cues in memory for words. *Journal of Experimental Psychology, 77*, 593–601.

Tulving, E., & Pearlstone, Z. (1966). Availability versus accessibility of information in memory for words. *Journal of Verbal Learning and Verbal Behavior, 5*, 381–391.

Tulving, E., & Thomson, D. M. (1973). Encoding specificity and retrieval processes in episodic memory. *Psychological Review, 80*, 352–373.

Turiel, E. (1966). An experimental test of the sequentiality of developmental stages in the child's moral judgments. *Journal of Personality and Social Psychology, 3*, 611–618.

Turner, J. S., & Helms, D. B. *Life span development*. Philadelphia: W. B. Saunders.

Udry, J. R., & Morris, N. M. (1968). Distribution of coitus in the menstual cycle. *Nature, 220*, 593–595.

Udry, J. R., & Morris, N. M. (1977). The distribution of events in the human menstrual cycle. *Journal of Reproduction and Fertility,, 51*, 419–425.

Ullmann, L. P., & Krasner, L. (1975). *A psychological approach to abnormal behavior* (2nd ed.). Englewood Cliffs, NJ: Prentice-Hall.

Unger, R. K. (1979). *Female and male: Psychological perspectives*. New York: Harper & Row.

Unger, R. K. (1979). *Psychological perspectives*. New York: Harper & Row.

Valenstein, E. S. (1973). *Brain control*. New York: Wiley.

Valins, S. (1966). Cognitive effects of false heartrate feedback. *Journal of Personality and Social Psychology, 14*, 400–408.

Vance, E. B., & Wagner, N. N. (1976). Written descriptions of orgasms: A study of sex differences. *Archives of Sexual Behavior, 5*, 87–98.

Vance Sluyters, R., & Levitt, F. (1980). Experimental strabismus in the kitten. *Journal of Neurophysiology, 43*, 686–699.

Vaughan, C. J. (1963). *The development and use of an operant technique to provide evidence for visual imagery in the rhesus monkey under ''sensory deprivation''*. Unpublished doctoral dissertation. University of Pittsburgh.

Verwoerdt, A., Pfeiffer, E., & Wang, H. S. (1969). Sexual behavior in senescence. *Geriatrics, 24*, 137–154.

Vinokur, A., Trope, Y., & Burstein, E. (1975). A decision-making analysis of persuasive argumentation and the choice-shift. *Journal of Experimental Social Psychology, 11*, 127–148.

von Holst, E., & Mittelstadt, H. (1950). Das reafferenz-princip. *Die Naturwissensdraften, 20*, 464–467.

von Holst, E. (1954). Relations between the central nervous system and the peripheral organs. *British Journal of Animal Behavior, 2*, 89–94.

Vonnegut, M. (1975). *The Eden express*. New York: Praeger.

Vore, D. A. (1973). Prenatal nutrition and postnatal intellectual development. *Merrill-Palmer Quarterly, 119*, 253–260.

Vygotsky, L. S. (1978). *Mind in society*. Cambridge, MA: Harvard University Press.

Waber, D. P. (1977). Sex differences in mental abilities, hemispheric lateralization, and rate of physical growth at adolescence. *Developmental Psychology, 90*, 29–38.

Waddington, C. H. (1957). *The strategy of the genes*. New York: Macmillan.

Wade, T. C., & Baker, T. B. (1977). Opinions and use of psychological tests: A survey of clinical psychologists. *American Psychologist, 32*, 872–882.

Wagner, H. G., MacNichol, E. F., Jr., Wolbarsht, M. L. (1960).

The response properties of single ganglion cells in the goldfish retina. *Journal of General Physiology, 43*, 45–62.

Wallach, M. A., Kogan, N., & Bem, D. J. (1964). Diffusion of responsibility and level of risk taking in groups. *Journal of Abnormal and Social Psychology, 68*, 263–274.

Wallach, M. A., Kogan, N. (1965). The rules of information, discussion, and consensus in group risk taking. *Journal of Experimental Social Psychology, 1*, 1–19.

Walters, E., Aronson, E., & Abrahams, D. (1966). On increasing the persuasiveness of a low prestige communicator. *Journal of Experimental Social Psychology, 2*, 325–342.

Walters, E., Wippman, J., & Sroufe, L. A. (1979). Attachment, positive affect, and competence in the peer group: Two studies in construct validation. *Child Development, 50*, 821–829.

Waring, M., & Ricks, D. (1965). Family patterns of children who become adult schizophrenics. *Journal of Nervous and Mental Disease. 140*, 351–364.

Warrington, E. K., & Weiskrantz, L. (1974). The effect of prior learning on subsequent retention in amnesic patients. *Neuropsychologia, 12*, 419–428.

Waterman, A. S. (1982). Identity development from adolescence to adulthood: An extension of theory and a review of research. *Developmental, 18*, 341–358.

Waters, E., Wippman, J., & Sroufe, L. A. (1979). Attachment, positive affect, and competence in the peer group: Two studies in construct validation. *Child Development, 50*, 821–829.

Waters, H. F., & Malamud, P. (1975, March 10). Drop that gun, Captain Video. *Newsweek, 85*(10), 81–82.

Watkins, M. J., & Tulving, E. (1975). Episodic memory: When recognition fails. *Journal of Experimental Psychology, 104*, 5–36.

Watson, D. L., & Tharp, R. G. (1972). *Self-directed behavior: Self-modification for personal adjustment.* Monterey, CA: Brooks/Cole.

Watson, J. B., & Rayner, R. (1920). Conditioned emotional reactions. *Journal of Experimental Psychology, 3*, 1–14.

Watson, J. B. (1925). *Behaviorism.* New York: Norton.

Waugh, N. C., & Norman, D. A. (1965). Primary memory. *Psychological Review, 72*, 89–104.

Weber, E. H. (1978). *The sense of touch.* New York: Academic Press.

Wechsler, D. (1949). *The Wechsler intelligence scale for children.* New York: Psychological Corporation.

Wechsler, D. (1955). *Wechsler adult intelligence scale manual.* New York: Psychological Corporation.

Wechsler, D. (1958). *The measurement and appraisal of adult intelligence.* Baltimore, MD: Williams & Wilkins.

Wei, E., & Loh, H. (1976). Physical dependence on opiate-like peptides. *Science, 193*, 1262.

Weil, A. (1973). *The natural mind.* Boston: Houghton Mifflin.

Weiner, B. (1970). New conceptions in the study of achievement motivation. In B. A. Maher (Ed.), *Progress in experimental personality research* (Vol. 5). New York: Academic Press.

Weingartner, H., Miller, H. A., & Murphy, D. L. (1979). Mood state-dependent retrieval of verbal associations. *Journal of Abnormal Psychology, 86*, 276–284.

Weiss, J. M., Glazer, H. I., & Pohorecky, L. A. (1976). Coping behavior and neurochemical changes: An alternative explanation for the original "learned helplessness" experiments. In G. Serban & A. Kling (Eds.). *Relevance of the animal model to the human.* New York: Plenum Press.

Welford, A. T., & Birren, J. E. (Eds.). (1965). *Behavior, aging, and the nervous system.* Springfield, IL: Charles C Thomas.

Wender, P. H., Rosenthal, D., Kety, S. S., Schulsinger, F., & Weiner, J. (1974). Crossfostering: A research strategy for clarifying the role of genetic and experiential factors in the etiology of schizophrenia. *Archives of General Psychiatry, 30*, 121–128.

Wender, P. H., Rosenthal, D., Kety, S. S., Schulsinger, F., &

Weiner, J. (1973). Social class and psychopathology in adoptees: A natural experimental method for separating the roles of genetic and experiental factors. *Archives of General Psychiatry, 28*, 318–325.

Wertheimer, M. (1912). Experimentelle studien über das schen von Vervegung. *Zeitschrift für Psychologie, 61*, 161–265.

Whaley, D. L., & Malott, R. W. (1969). *Elementary principles of behavior.* Kalamazoo, MI: Behaviordelia.

Wheatstone, C. (1838). On some remarkable and hitherto unobserved phenomena of binocular vision. *London Royal Society: Philosophical Transactions of the Royal Society*, 371–394.

White, T. G. (1982). Naming practices, typicality, and underextension in child language. *Journal of Experimental Child Psychology, 33*, 324–346.

Whitten, W. K., Bronson, F. H., & Greenstein, J. A. (1968). Estrus-inducing pheromone of male mice: Transport by movement of air. *Science, 161*, 584–585.

Whorf, B. L. (1956). *Language, thought and reality: Selected writings of Benjamin Lee Whorf* (J. B. Carroll, Ed.). New York: Wiley.

Widoe, H. J., & Heisler, S. (1976). Treatment of tardive dyskinesia. *Diseases of the Nervous System, 37*, 162–164.

Wilcoxin, H. C., Dragoin, W. B., & Kral, P. A. (1971). Illness-induced aversions in rat and quail: Relative saliences of visual and gustatory cues. *Science, 71*, 826–828.

Will, O. A. (1970). Analytic etiology: A primer. In J. O. Cole & L. E. Hollister (Eds.), *Scnizophrenia.* New York: MEDCOM.

Williams, C. C. (1983). The mental foxhole: The Viet Nam Veterans' search for meaning. *American Journal of Orthopsychiatry, 53*(1), 4–17.

Williams, J. E., & Bennett, S. M. (1975). The definition of sex stereotypes via the adjective check list. *Sex Roles, 1* 327–337.

Wilson, E. D. (1975). *Sociobiology: The new synthesis.* Cambridge, MA: Harvard University Press.

Wilson, E. O. (1975). *Sociobiology: The new Press.*

Winick, N., Rosso, P., & Waterlow, J. (1970). Cellular growth of cerebrum, cerebelium, and brain stem in normal and marasmic children *Experimental Neurology, 26*, 393–400.

Winsborough, H. H. (1965). The social consequences of high population density. *Law and Contemporary Problems, 30*, 120–126.

Witlin, H. A., Mednick, S. A., Schulsinger, F., Bakkestrom, E., Christiansen, K. O., Goodenough, D. R., & Stocking, M. (1976). Criminality in XYY and XXY men. *Science, 193*, 547–555.

Witters, W. L., & Jones-Witters, P. (1975). *Drugs and Sex.* New York: Macmillan.

Wolfe, J. B. (1936). Effectiveness of token-rewards for chimpanzees. *Comparative Psychology Monographs, 12* (Whole no. 60).

Wollard, H. H. (1935). Observations on terminations of lutaneous nerves. *Brain, 58*, 352.

Wolpe, J., & Lazarus, A. A. (1969). *The practice of behavior therapy.* New York: Pergamon.

Wolpe, J., & Rachman, S. J. (1960). Psychoanalytic "evidence": A critique based on Freud's case of Little Hans. *Journal of Nervous and Mental Diseases, 130*, 135–148.

Wolpe, J. (1958). *Psychotherapy by reciprocal inhibition.* Stanford, CA: Stanford University Press.

Woodrow, H. (1951). Time perception. In S. S. Stevens (Ed.), *Handbook of experimental psychology.* New York: Wiley.

Woods, S. C., & Porto, D. (1976). Insulin and the set-point regulation of body weight. In D. Novin, W. Wyrwicka, & G. Bray (Eds.), *Hunger: Basic mechanisms and clinical implications.* New York: Raven Press.

Woodworth, R. S. (1938). *Experimental psychology.* New York: Holt.

Worchel, S., Andreoli, V. A., & Folger, R. (1977). Intergroup cooperation and intergroup attraction: The effect of previous interaction and outcome of combined effort. *Journal of Experimental Social Psychology, 13*, 131–140.

Word, C. O., Zanna, M. P., & Cooper, J. (1974). The nonverbal mediation of self-fulfilling prophecies in interracial interaction. *Journal of Experimental Social Psychology, 10*, 109–120.

Wrightsman, L. S. (1960). Effects of waiting with others on changes in level of felt anxiety. *Journal of Abnormal and Social Psychology, 61*, 216–222.

Wynne, L. C. (1970). Communication disorders and the quest for relatedness in families of schizophrenics. *American Journal of Psychoanalysis, 30*, 100–114.

Yando, R., Seitz, V., & Zigler, E. (1979). *Intellectual and personality characteristics of children: Social class and ethnic group differences.* Hillsdale, NJ: Erlbaum.

Yankelovich, Skelly, & White, Inc. (1977). *Raising children in a changing society: The General Mills American Family Report, 1976–1977.* Minneapolis, MN: General Mills, Inc.

Young, T. (1802). On the theory of light and colours. *Philosophical Transactions of the Royal Society of London, 92*, 20.

Zaehner, R. C. (1972). *Zen, drugs, and mysticism.* New York: Random House.

Zajonc, R. B. (1965). Social facilitation. *Science, 149*, 269–274.

Zajonc, R. B. (1968). Attitudinal effects of mere exposure. *Journal of Personality and Social Psychology Monograph Supplement, 9*, 1–27.

Zajonc, R. B., & Burnstein, E. (1965). Structural balance, reciprocity, and positivity as sources of cognitive bias. *Journal of Personality, 33*, 570–583.

Zajonc, R. B., Heingartner, A., & Herman, E. M. (1969). Social enhancement and impairment of performance in the cockroach. *Journal of Personality and Social Psychology, 13*, 83–92.

Zajonc, R. B., & Markus, G. B. (1975). Birth order and intellectual development. *Psychological Review, 82*, 74–88.

Zajonc, R. B., & Nieuwenhuyse, B. (1964). Relationship between work frequency and recognition: Perceptual process or response bias. *Journal of Experimental Psychology, 67*, 276–285.

Zajonc, R. B., & Sales, S. M. (1966). Social facilitation of dominant and subordinate responses. *Journal of Experimental Social Psychology, 2*, 160–168.

Zanna, M. P., Kiesler, C. A., & Pilkonis, P. A. (1970). Positive and negative attitudinal affect established by classical conditioning. *Journal of Personality and Social Psychology, 14*, 321–328.

Zanna, M. P., & Pack, S. J. (1975). On the self-fulfilling nature of apparent sex differences in behavior. *Journal of Experimental Social Psychology, 11*, 583–591.

Zeki, S. (1980). The representation of colours in the cerebral cortex. *Nature, 284*, 412–418.

Zigler, E. (1967). Familial mental retardation: A continuing dilemma. *Science, 155*, 292–298.

Zillmann, D., Katcher, A. H., & Milavsky, B. (1972). Excitation transfer from physical exercise to subsequent aggressive behavior. *Journal of Experimental Social Psychology, 8*, 247–259.

Zillmann, D. (1971). Excitation transfer in communication-mediated aggressive behavior. *Journal of Experimental Social Psychology, 7*, 419–434.

Zimbardo, P. G. (1969). The human choice: Individuation, reason, and order versus deindividuation, impulse, and chaos. In W. J. Arnold & K. Levine (Eds.), *Nebraska Symposium on Motivation* (Vol. 17). Lincoln: University of Nebraska Press.

Zimbardo, P. G. (1975). On transforming experimental research into advocacy for social change. In M. Deutsch & H. Hornstein (Eds.), *Applying social psychology: Implications for research, practice, and training.* Hillsdale, NJ: Erlbaum.

Zimbardo, P. G., Ebbesen, E. G., & Maslach, C. (1977). *Influencing attitudes and changing behavior* (2nd ed.). Reading, MA: Addison-Wesley.

Zimmerman, D. H., & West, C. (1975). Sex roles, interruptions and silences in conversation. In B. Thorne, & N. Henley (Eds.), *Language and sex: Difference and dominance.* Rowley, MA: Newbury House.

Zubin, J., & Spring, B. (1977). Vulnerability: A new view of schizophrenia. *Journal of Abnormal Psychology, 103*–126.

Zucker, I. (1980). Behavior, and biologic rhythms. In D. Krieger, (Ed.), *Neuroendocrinology.* Sunderland, MA: Sinauer.

Zuger, B. (1984). Early effeminate behavior in boys, outcome and significance for homosexuality. *Journal of Nervous and Mental Diseases, 172*, 90–97.

CREDITS

Positions of photographs are shown in abbreviated form as follows: top (t), bottom (b), center (c), left (l), right (r). All photographs not credited are the property of Scott, Foresman, The first set of entries in a chapter refers to photos and the second set of entries refers to figure art.

Chapter 1

p. 5 (t) Library of Congress (b) The Bettman Archive
p. 6 UPI/Bettmann Newsphotos
p. 7 Ken Heyman
p. 8 Pfizer Inc.
p. 9 Richard Younker
p. 10 (t) Yves De Braine/Black Star (b) Phiz Mesey/Taurus
p. 11 UPI/Bettmann Newsphotos
p. 12 (t) The Bettmann Archive (b) Courtesy of Dr. Rollo May
p. 13 The Bettmann Archive
p. 14 James Holland/Stock, Boston
p. 15 (t) Courtesy of California Institute of Technology (b) Jean-Claude Lejeune
p. 18 Cary Wolinsky/Stock, Boston
p. 20 Courtesy of Chris Costner Sizemore, author of *I'm Eve,* Doubleday, 1977
p. 22 Ken Robert Buck/Stock, Boston
p. 26 Jean-Claude Lejeune

Chapter 2

p. 32 (t) The Granger Collection (b) The Bettmann Archive
p. 35 Michael D. Burkey/Gallery of Images
p. 36 From *De humani corpus fabrica* by Andreas Vesalius, 1543
p. 40 Figure 2.7. The Bettmann Archive
p. 52 The Bettmann Archive
p. 55 Sam Sweezy/Stock, Boston

Fig. 2.1, p. 33, from "The Brain" by David H. Hubel. Copyright © 1979 by Scientific American, Inc. All rights reserved. Reprinted by permission.

Fig. 2.3, p. 34, adapted from H. D. Patton, J. W. Sundsten, W. E. Crill and P. W. Swanson, *Introduction to Basic Neurology.* Philadelphia: W. B. Saunders Co., 1976, p. 35. Reprinted by permission.

Fig. 2.8, p. 41, Reprinted with permission of Macmillan Publishing Company from *The Cerebral Cortex of Man* by Wilder Penfield and Theodore Rasmussen. Copyright 1950 by Macmillan Publishing Company, renewed 1978 by Theordore Rasmussen.

Fig. 2.9, p. 41, adapted from C. B. Noback and R. J. Demerest, *The Human Nervous System.* New York: McGraw-Hill, 1975.

Fig. 2.10, p. 43, redrawn from Fig. X-4 from Wilder Penfield and Lamar Roberts, *Speech and Brain Mechanisms.* Copyright © 1959 by Princeton University Press, p. 201.

Figs. 2.11 and 2.12, pp. 45 and 46, Michael S. Gazzaniga, "The Split Brain in Man." Copyright © 1967 by Scientific American, Inc. All rights reserved. Reprinted by permission.

Photo, p, 48, D. A. Sholl, *The Organization of the Cerebral Cortex.* New York: Wiley, 1956, p. 13. Reprinted by permission of Menthuen & Co., Ltd.

Fig. 2.13, p. 48, after C. F. Stevens, "The Neuron." *Scientific American,* September 1979, p. 56. Reprinted by permission.

Fig. 2.14, p. 48, C. F. Stevens, *Neurophysiology: A Primer.* New York: Wiley, 1966. Reprinted by permission.

Figs. 2.15 and 2.16, page 49, C. F. Stevens, *Neurophysiology: A Primer.* New York: Wiley, 1966. Reprinted by permission.

Fig. 2.17, p. 50, C. B. Noback and R. J. Demerest, *The Human Nervous System.* New York: McGraw-Hill, 1975. Used by permission of the publisher.

Fig. 2.18, p. 51, A. M. Schneider and B. Tarshis, *An Introduction to Physiological Psychology.* New York: Random House, 1975.

Fig. 2.19, p. 53, after C. F. Stevens, "The Neuron." *Scientific American,* September 1979, p. 57. Reprinted by permission.

Chapter 3

p. 62 Culver Pictures
p. 65 The Granger Collection
p. 66 The Granger Collection
p. 69 Lennart Nilsson, *Behold Man.* Little, Brown & Co., Boston, 1974
p. 73 D. Bownds and S. Carlson, University of Wisconsin
p. 74 (t) Bodleian Library, Oxford, MS New College 361/2, fol. 45v (b) National Portrait Gallery, London
p. 75 The Bettmann Archive
p. 83 Courtesy of Chicago Symphony Orchestra
p. 86 Culver Pictures
p. 87 Robert George Gaylord
p. 88 Luanne M. Ferris/*The Sunday Record,* Troy, New York
p. 93 Stephen Dalton/The National Audubon Society Collection/Photo Researchers
p. 94 NASA

Fig. 3.1, p. 65, D. Blough, "Dark Adaptation in the Pigeon." *Journal of Comparative Physiological Psychology,* Vol. 49, 1956, p. 425. Copyright © 1956 by the American Psychological Association. Reprinted by permission of the publisher and author.

Fig. 3.4, p. 70, after George Wald, "Eye and Camera." *Scientific American,* August 1950. Reprinted by permission.

Fig. 3.7, p. 71, from *An Introduction to Physiological Psychology* by Allen M. Schneider and Barry Tarshis. Copyright © 1975, 1980, 1986 by Random House, Inc. Reprinted by permission of the publisher.

Fig. 3.8, p. 73, after F. W. Billmeyer and M. Saltzman, *Principles of Color Technology.* New York: Wiley, 1966.

Fig. 3.10, p. 76, G. Wald, "The Receptors of Human Color Vision." *Science,* Vol. 145, September 1964, pp. 1007–1016. Copyright © 1964 by the American Association for the Advancement of Science. Reprinted by permission.

Fig. 3.12, p. 79, after L. A. Riggs, F. Ratliff, J. C. Cornsweet and T. N. Cornsweet, "The Disappearance of Visual Test Objects." *Journal of the Optical Society of America,* Vol. 43, 1953, pp. 495–501.

Fig. 3.17, p. 83, adapted from A. Chapanis, *Man-Machine Engineering.* Belmont, Calif.: Wadsworth, 1965 and A. Chapanis, W. R. Garner, and C. T. Morgan, *Applied Experimental Psychology—Human Factors in Engineering Design.* New York: Wiley, 1949.

Fig. 3.19, p. 86, adapted from O. Stuhlman, Jr., *An Introduction to Biophysics.* New York: Wiley, 1943, Reprinted by permission of Mrs. William T. Couch.

Fig. 3.20, p. 88, adapted from E. Gardner, *Fundamentals of Neurology.* Philadelphia: Saunders, 1975.

Fig. 3.21, p. 89, adapted from E. Gardner, *Fundamentals of Neurology.* Philadelphia: Saunders, 1975.

Fig. 3.23, p. 91, Reprinted with permission of Macmillan Publishing Company from *The Cerebral Cortex of Man* by Wilder Penfield and Theodore Rasmussen. Copyright 1950 by Macmillan Publishing Company, renewed 1978 by Theordore Rasmussen.

Fig. 3.24, p. 92, redrawn from A. M. Schneider and B. Tarshis, *An*

Introduction to Physiological Psychology. New York: Random House, 1975.

Chapter 4
p. 99 Alan Carey/The Image Works
p. 104 (both) Courtesy of Harvard University News Office
p. 106 Figure 4.10. Alinari/Art Resource
p. 107 Figure 4.12. Erich Hartmann/Magnum Figure 4.13. Alinari/Art Resource Figure 4.14. George Inness: *The Lackawana Valley.* National Gallery of Art, Washington, Gift of Mrs. Huttleston Rogers, 1945
p. 108 Figure 4.15B. William Vandivert
p. 109 Figure 4.16. Jean-Claude Lejeune
p. 110 Figure 4.18. B. Julesz, *Foundations of Cyclopean Perception.* The University of Chicago Press, 1971. Reprinted by permission of The University of Chicago Press
p. 115 Figure 4.20. David Linton
p. 116 Figure 4.22. William Vandivert
p. 122 Alan Carey/the Image Works

Fig. 4.1, p. 98, from James J. Gibson: *The Perception of the Visual World.* Copyright © 1950, renewed 1978 by Houghton Mifflin Company. Adapted by permission.
Fig. 4.2, p. 100, I. Rock and C. S. Harris, "Vision and Touch." Copyright ©. 1967 by Scientific American, Inc. All rights reserved.
Fig. 4.18, p. 110, B. Julesz, *Foundations of Cyclopean Perception.* The University of Chicago Press, 1971. Reprinted by permission of The University of Chicago Press.
Fig. 4.19, p. 110, from *Eye and Brain* by R. L. Gregory. Copyright © 1973 by World University Library. Used with the permission of McGraw-Hill Book Company.
RESEARCH, p. 113, David Regan, Kennerth Beverley and Max Cynader, "The Visual Perception of Motion in Depth." Copyright ©. 1979 by Scientific American, Inc. All rights reserved. Reprinted by permission.

Chapter 5
p. 126 (t) The Bettmann Archive (b) Barbara Alper/Stock, Boston
p. 127 (t) Giraudon/Art Resource (b) The Bettmann Archive
p. 128 (t) Courtesy of Montreal Neurological Institute (b) Wilder Penfield, *The Excitable Cortex in Conscious Man.* Liverpool University Press, 1958. Second impression 1967
p. 129 Dan McCoy/Rainbow
p. 134 Figure 5.3. Sleep Photos—Ted Spagna, all rights reserved. From DREAMSTAGE Catalog © 1977 J. A. Hobson and Hoffmann-La Roche Inc.
p. 135 Figure 5.4. Sleep Photos—Ted Spagna, all rights reserved. From DREAMSTAGE Catalog © 1977 J. A. Hobson and Hoffmann-La Roche Inc.
p. 137 Ted Russell, LIFE Magazine © 1959 Time Inc.
p. 140 REPRINTED FROM PSYCHOLOGY TODAY MAGAZINE copyright © 1985 American Psychological Association
p. 143 Laimute Druskis/Taurus
p. 144 The Bettmann Archive
p. 148 Alan Carey/The Image Works
p. 151 Margaret Thompson/The Picture Cube
p. 152 Paul Conklin/Monkmeyer
p. 155 (all) Courtesy of Dr. Albert Hofmann
p. 159 Jean-Claude Lejeune

Fig. 5.1, p. 130, after R. A. Levitt, *Physiological Psychology.* Copyright © 1981 by Holt, Rinehart and Winston. Reprinted by permission of Holt, Rinehart and Winston.
Fig. 5.2, p. 133, from *Psychology: Understanding Behavior,* second edition, by Robert A. Baron, Donn Byrne, and Barry H. Kantowitz. Copyright © 1977 by W. B. Saunders Co. Copyright © 1980 by Holt, Rinehart and Winston. Reprinted by permission of Holt, Rinehart and Winston.
Fig. 5.4, p. 135, from E. Hartman, *The Biology of Dreaming.*

Charles C Thomas. Courtesy of Charles C Thomas, Publisher, Springfield, Illinois.
Fig. 5.6, p. 143, J. Allison, "Respiratory Changes During the Practice of the Technique of Transcendental Meditation." *Lancet,* No. 7651 (London, England, 1970) pp. 833–834.
Fig. 5.7, p. 153, Frank Barron, Murray E. Jarvik and Sterling Bunnell, Jr., "The Hallucinogenic Drugs." Copyright © 1964 by Scientific American, Inc. All rights reserved. Photo, p. 156, George E. Jones III, Photo Researchers. Reprinted by permission.
Fig. 5.8, p. 157, James V. McConnell, *Understanding Human Behavior.* Copyright © 1980 by Holt, Rinehart and Winston. Used by permission of Holt, Rinehart and Winston.

Chapter 6
p. 168 Österreichische Nationalbibliothek, Vienna
p. 172 Margaret Thompson/the Picture Cube
p. 173 (t, c) Elizabeth Crews (b) Robert V. Eckert, Jr./The Picture Cube
p. 175 (t) Elizabeth Crews (b) Shirley Zeiberg/Taurus
p. 176 Robert Drea
p. 178 Jerry Berndt/Stock, Boston
p. 179 Jim Anderson/Stock, Boston
p. 180 Elizabeth Crews
p. 182 (t, c) George Zimbel/Monkmeyer (b) Hazel Hankin/Stock, Boston
p. 183 (t) Elizabeth Crews (b) Carol Palmer/the Picture Cube
p. 186 Laimute Druskis/Taurus
p. 189 Jon Erikson
p. 191 Figure 6.5. Harlow Primate Lab, University of Wisconsin
p. 193 Elizabeth Crews
p. 194 Eric Kroll/Taurus
p. 195 (t) Shirley Zeiberg/Taurus (b) Jean-Claude Lejeune
p. 197 Paul Fortin/Stock, Boston
p. 198 Collins/Monkmeyer
p. 199 Michael Weisbrot and Family
p. 200 (t) Ulrike Welsch/Stock, Boston (b) Elizabeth Crews
p. 201 Miro Vintoniv/Stock, Boston
p. 204 Elizabeth Crews

Fig. 6.3, p. 168, C. H. Waddington, *The Strategy of the Genes: A Discussion of Some Aspects of Theoretical Biology.* London: George Allen & Unwin, 1957, pp. 29, 36.
Fig. 6.6, p. 192, H. R. Schaeffer and P. E. Emerson, "The Development of Social Attachments in Infancy." *Monographs of the Society for Research in Child Development,* 1964, 29 (3). Copyright © 1964 by The Society for Research in Child Development, Inc. Reprinted by permission.
Fig. 6.7, p. 207, from "Development of Moral Character and Moral Ideology" by Lawrence Kohlberg in *Review of Child Development Research Volume I* by Martin L. Hoffman and Lois Wladis Hoffman. Copyright © 1964 by Russell Sage Foundation. Reprinted by permission of Basic Books, Inc. Publishers.

Chapter 7
p. 213 Thomas McAvoy, LIFE Magazine © 1955 Time Inc.
p. 221 Elizabeth Crews
p. 222 The Granger Collection
p. 224 Michael Weisbrot and Family
p. 225 Figure 7.11. Yerkes Primate Research Center, Emory University
p. 227 (both) Animal Behavior Enterprises, Inc.
p. 228 Elizabeth Crews
p. 230 Courtesy of Dr. Philip G. Zimbardo
p. 234 Figure 7.15. Wolfgang Köhler, *The Mentality of Apes.* Routledge & Kegan Paul PLC, London, 1927. Reprinted 1948, 1973
p. 235 Elizabeth Crews
p. 237 Courtesy of Dr. Albert Bandura
p. 238 Wide World
p. 239 Michael McGovern/The Picture Cube

Fig. 7.1, p. 213, E. H. Hess, "Imprinting." *Science,* Vol. 130, 1959, pp. 133–141. Copyright © 1959 by the American Association for the Advancement of Science. Reprinted by permission.

Fig. 7.4, p. 218, after I. V. Pavlov, *Conditioned Reflex.* Oxford, 1927.

Fig. 7.9, p. 222, after E. L. Thorndike, *The Psychology of Learning.* New York: Columbia University Press, 1921.

Fig. 7.13, p. 232, adapted from I. V. Pavlov, *Conditioned Reflexes.* Oxford, 1927.

Chapter 8

p. 246 (t) Frank Siteman/Taurus (b) The Bettman Archive
p. 247 Rogers/Monkmeyer
p. 249 Elizabeth Crews
p. 250 Nancy Bates/The Picture Cube
p. 252 (t) Rogers/Monkmeyer (b) Jean-Claude Lejeune
p. 253 (both) Wide World
p. 257 Frank Siteman/The Picture Cube
p. 259 Wide World
p. 272 Laimute Druskis/Taurus
p. 276 Jean-Claude Lejeune

Fig. 8.2, p. 245, after G. Sperling, "The Information Available in Brief Visual Presentations." *Psychological Monographs,* 74, Whole No. 498, 1960. Copyright © by the American Psychological Association. Reprinted by permission of the publisher and author.

Fig. 8.3, p. 248, reprinted with permission from Perception and Communication by D. Broadbent. Copyright © 1958, Pergamon Books Ltd.

Fig. 8.4, p. 251, B. Milner, "Amnesia Following Operation of Temporal Lobes." In C. W. N. Whitty and O. L. Zangwill, eds., *Amnesia.* London: Butterworth, 1966.

Fig. 8.5, p. 258, adapted by permission of F. I. M. Craik and E. Tulving, "Depth of Processing and the Retention of Words in Episodic Memory." *Journal of Experimental Psychology,* Vol. 104, 1975, pp. 268–294. Copyright © 1975 by the American Psychological Association. Reprinted by permission of the publisher and authors.

Fig. 8.6, p. 263, after W. A. Bousfield, "The Occurrence of Clustering in the Free Recall of Randomly Arranged Associates." *Journal of General Psychology,* Vol. 49, 1953, pp. 229–240. Reprinted by permission of The Journal Press and the author.

Fig. 8.7, p. 264, G. H. Bower, "Organizational Factors in Memory." *Cognitive Psychology,* Vol. 1, 1970.

Fig. 8.8, p. 265, adapted from A. M. Collins and M. R. Quillian, "Retrieval Time From Semantic Memory." *Journal of Verbal Learning and Verbal Behavior,* Vol. 8, 1969, pp. 240–247.

Fig. 8.9, p. 268, adapted from E. Tulving and Z. Pearlstone, "Availability Versus Accessibility of Information in Memory for Words." *Journal of Verbal Learning and Verbal Behavior,* Vol. 5, 1965, pp. 381–391. Reprinted by permission.

Fig. 8.10, p. 270, from *Psychology: Understanding Behavior,* second edition, by Robert A. Baron, Donn Byrne, and Barry H. Kantowitz. Copyright © 1980 by Holt, Rinehart and Winston. Copyright © 1977 by W. B. Saunders Co. Reprinted by permission of Holt, Rinehart and Winston

Fig. 8.11, p. 271, after N. C. Waugh and D. A. Norman, "Primary Memory." *Psychological Review,* Vol. 72, 1965, pp. 89–104. Copyright © 1965 by the American Psychological Association. Reprinted by permission of the publisher and the authors.

Fig. 8.12, p. 273, after W. J. McKeachie and C. L. Doyle, *Psychology.* Reading, Mass.: Addison-Wesley, 1976. Reprinted with permission.

Chapter 9

p. 280 Strickler/Monkmeyer
p. 287 J. Berndt/Stock, Boston
p. 291 Wide World
p. 292 (t) Elizabeth Crews (b) Alan Carey/The Image Works

p. 293 (both) Elizabeth Crews
p. 294 Jean-Claude Lejeune
p. 301 Robert George Gaylord

Fig. 9.1, p. 282, R. K. Potter, G. A. Kopp, and H. C. Green, *Visible Speech.* Litton Educational Publishing, Inc., 1947. Copyright © 1947 by Bell Telephone Laboratories. Reprinted with permission.

Fig. 9.3, p. 283, A. M. Liberman, "The Grammars of Speech and Language." *Cognitive Psychology,* Vol. 1, 1970, pp. 301–323.

Fig. 9.4, p. 284, B. Milner, L. Taylor, and R. W. Sperry, "Lateralized Suppression of Dichotically Presented Digits After Commissural Section in Man." *Science,* July 12, 1968, pp. 184–186. Copyright © 1968 by the American Association for the Advancement of Science. Reprinted by permission.

Fig. 9.8, p. 291, adapted from J. D. Bransford and J. J. Franks, "The Abstraction of Linguistic Ideas." *Cognitive Psychology,* Vol. 2. 1971. Reprinted by permission.

Fig. 9.9, p. 302, J. D. Bransford and M. K. Johnson, "Considerations of Some Problems of Comprehension." In W. G. Chase, ed., *Visual Information Processing.* New York: Academic Press, 1973. Used with permission of the publisher and authors.

Fig. 9.10, p. 303, adapted from Carmichael, Hogan and Walter, 1932. Focus, p. 305, after A. J. Premack and D. Premack, "Teaching Language to an Ape." *Scientific American,* October 1972, p. 97. Reprinted by permission.

Chapter 10

p. 312 John H. Gerard
p. 316 The Bettmann Archive
p. 317 UPI/Bettmann Newsphotos
p. 320 John Sanderson
p. 321 Figure 10.3. Courtesy of Dr. Neal Miller
p. 322 Barbara Alper/Stock, Boston
p. 326 Elizabeth Crews
p. 327 Imperial War Museum, London
p. 329 Focus on Sports
p. 330 Courtesy of Dr. David C. McClelland
p. 332 Figure 10.5. Dr. James Olds
p. 334 UPI/Bettmann Newsphotos
p. 335 Wolfgang Bayer
p. 336 UPI/Bettmann Newsphotos
p. 337 Jim Harrison/Stock, Boston
p. 341 Reprinted by permission: Tribune Media Services

Fig. 10.1, p. 319, from *Psychology: Its Principles and Meanings,* third edition, by Lyle E. Bourne, Jr., and Bruce R. Ekstrand. Copyright © 1973 by the Dryden Press. Copyright © 1976, 1979 by Holt, Rinehart and Winston. Reprinted by permission of Holt, Rinehart and Winston.

Fig. 10.2, p. 321, from *Physiological Psychology* by Mark Rosenzweig and Arnold Leiman. Copyright © 1982 by D. C. Heath and Company. Reprinted by permission.

Fig. 10.4, p. 328, after W. N. Dember, "Birth Order and Need for Affiliation." *Journal of Abnormal and Social Psychology,* Vol. 68, 1964. Copyright 1964 by the American Psychological Association. Adapted by permission of the publisher and author.

Fig. 10.6, p. 333, from S. Schachter and J. Singer, "Cognitive Social and Physiological Determinants of Emotional State." *Psychological Review,* Vol. 69, 1962. Copyright 1962 by the American Psychological Association. Adapted by permission of the publisher and authors.

Research, p. 339, after H. S. Hoffman, L. A. Eiserer, A. M. Ratner and V. L. Pickering, "Development of Distress Vocalization During Withdrawal of an Imprinting Stimulus." *Journal of Comparative and Physiological Psychology,* Vol. 86, 1974. Copyright 1974 by the American Psychological Association. Reprinted by permission of the publisher and authors.

Chapter 11

p. 346 UPI/Bettmann Newsphotos
p. 348 (b) Photo by Dellenback. Reproduced by permission of the Kinsey Institute for Research in Sex, Gender, and Reproduction, Inc.
p. 349 Robert Levin/Black Star
p. 354 Mark Antman/The Image Works
p. 355 Victor Englebert
p. 358 Rhoda Sidney/Monkmeyer
p. 360 Jean-Claude Lejeune
p. 361 (t) Bob Kalman/The Image Works (b) Alan Carey/The Image Works
p. 370 Richard Stromberg
p. 371 Laimute Druskis/Taurus
p. 373 Eric Kroll/Taurus
p. 375 Eric Kroll/Taurus
Fig. 11.1, p. 350, William H. Masters and Virginia F. Johnson, *Human Sexual Response*. Boston: Little, Brown and Company, 1966.
Fig. 11.2, p. 359, adapted from M. Zelnik and J. F. Kantner, ''Sexual and Contraceptive Practices Experience of Young Unmarried Women in the United States, 1976 and 1971.'' *Family Planning Perspectives*, Vol. 9, 1977, pp. 55–71. A. C. Kinsey, W. B. Pomeroy, C. E. Martin and P. H. Gebhard, *Sexual Behavior in the Human Female*. Philadelphia: Saunders, 1953. Reprinted by permission of the Institute for Sex Research.
Fig. 11.4, p. 366, J. M. Davidson, C. A. Camargo, E. R. Smith, ''Effects of Androgen on Sexual Behavior in Hypogonodal Men.'' *Journal of Clinical Endocrinology and Metabolism*, Vol. 48, 1979, pp. 955–958. Reprinted with permission of The Endocrine Society.
Fig. 11.5, p. 371, after A. C. Kinsey, W. B. Pomeroy, C. E. Martin, *Sexual Behavior in the Human Male*. Philadelphia: Saunders, 1948. Reprinted by permission of the Institute for Sex Research.

Chapter 12

p. 384 Peter Southwick/Stock, Boston
p. 387 (t) Shirley Zeiberg/Taurus (b) Jim Whitmer
p. 388 Richard Younker
p. 389 The Bettmann Archive
p. 393 Michael Weisbrot and Family
p. 394 (both) Zentralbibliothek Zürich, Ms. C 101, fol. 25–26
p. 397 Courtesy of Harvard University News Office
p. 398 Richard Younker
p. 402 UPI/Bettmann Newsphotos
p. 403 Figure 12.6. Reprinted by permission of the publishers from Henry A. Murray, *Thematic Apperception Test*. Cambridge, Massachusetts: Harvard University Press, Copyright 1943 by the President and Fellows of Harvard College; © 1971 by Henry A. Murray
p. 407 (t) Courtesy of Dr. Albert Bandura (b) Jean-Claude Lejeune
p. 410 Alan Carey/The Image Works
p. 412 The Bettmann Archive

Fig. 12.2, p. 395, After Sheldon, 1942.
Fig. 12.3, p. 396, after H. J. Eysenck, ''Principles and Methods of Personality: Description, Classification and Diagnosis.'' *British Journal of Psychology*, Vol. 55, 1964, pp. 284-294.
Fig. 12.4, p. 399, after G. W. Allport, *Personality: A Psychological Interpretation*. Copyright © 1961 by Holt, Rinehart and Winston. Reprinted by permission of Holt, Rinehart and Winston.
Fig. 12.5, p. 400, taken from the Handbook for the 16 PF © 1970, by the Institute for Personality and Ability Testing, Inc. Reproduced by permission.
Fig. 12.7, p. 406, K. E. Allen, et. al., ''Effects of Social Reinforcement on Isolate Behavior of a Nursery School Child.'' *Child Development*, Vol. 35, 1964, pp. 511-518. Copyright © 1964 by The Society For Research in Child Development, Inc. Reprinted by permission.
Fig. 12.8, p. 408, A. Bandura and W. Mischel, ''Modification of Self-imposed Delay of Reward Through Exposure to Live and Symbolic Models.'' *Journal of Personality and Social Psychology*, Vol.

2, 1965, pp. 698-705. Reprinted by permission of the publisher and authors.

Chapter 13

p. 423 Shirley Zeiberg/Taurus
p. 425 Bassano & Vandyk Studios incorporating Elliott & Fry
p. 426 Steve Baratz/The Picture Cube
p. 427 (t) The Bettmann Archive
p. 431 Reproduced by permission from the WECHSLER ADULT INTELLIGENCE SCALE - REVISED. Copyright © 1955, 1980 by the Psychological Corporation. All rights reserved
p. 435 Elizabeth Crews
p. 437 *Minneapolis Tribune*
p. 438 Jean-Claude Lejeune
p. 439 Michael Weisbrot and Family
p. 440 Ed Clark, LIFE Magazine © 1949 Time Inc.
p. 448 Elizabeth Crews

Fig. 13.1, p. 422, from *Primary Mental Abilities* for Grades 9-12 by Thelma Gwinn Thurstone. Copyright © 1962, 1953, 1964, by Thelma Gwinn Thurstone. Reprinted by permission of the publisher, Science Research Associates, Inc.
Fig. 13.2, p. 423, J. P. Guilford, *The Nature of Human Intelligence*. New York: McGraw-Hill, 1967, p. 63.
Fig. 13.3, p. 429, from *Psychology: Understanding Behavior*, second edition, by Robert A. Baron, Donn Byrne, and Barry H. Kantowitz. Copyright © 1980 by Holt, Rinehart and Winston. Copyright © 1977 by W. B. Saunders Co. Reprinted by permission of Holt, Rinehart and Winston.
Fig. 13.4, p. 434, L. Erlenmeyer-Kimling and L. F. Jarvik, ''Genetics and Intelligence: A Review.'' *Science*, December 13, 1963. Copyright © 1963 by American Association for the Advancement of Science. Reprinted by permission.
Fig. 13.5, p. 438, R. B. Zajonc and G. B. Markus, ''Birth Order and Intellectual Development.'' *Psychological Review*, Vol. 82, 1975, pp. 74-88. Copyright © 1975 by the American Psychological Association. Reprinted by permission of publisher and authors.
Fig. 13.6, p. 441, K. Richardson and D. Spears, *Race and Intelligence*. New York: Penguin Books, 1972, p. 187.
Fig. 13.7, p. 445, N. Bayley, ''Development of Mental Abilities.'' In P. Mussen, ed., *Carmichael's Manual of Child Psychology*. New York: Wiley, 1970. Reprinted by permission.

Chapter 14

p. 458 The Bettmann Archive
p. 459 UPI/Bettmann Newsphotos
p. 462 Historical Pictures Service, Chicago
p. 463 Tom Damman/NYT Pictures
p. 465 Michael Weisbrot and Family
p. 466 Anna Kaufman Moon/Stock, Boston
p. 467 Stanley Rowin/The Picture Cube
p. 468 Larry Burrows, LIFE Magazine © 1965 Time Inc.
p. 470 Wide World
p. 471 E. Hazebroucq
p. 476 Wide World
p. 489 Joseph Szabo/Photo Researchers
p. 490 Courtesy National Council on Alcoholism Inc.

Fig. 14.1, p. 466, Reprinted by permission of the publisher from Arthur T. Jersild and Frances G. Holmes, *Children's Fears*. New York: Teacher's College Press. Copyright © 1935. All rights reserved.
Fig. 14.3, p. 480, from ''Clues to the genetics and neurobiology of schizophrenia'' by S. E. Nicol and I. I. Gottesman, *American Scientist*, 1983, July-August, 71, 398-404. Reprinted by permission.
Fig. 14.4, p. 481, Price and Lynn, *Abnormal Behavior in the Human Context*. Homewood, Ill.: The Dorsey Press, 1981, p. 300. Reprinted by permission of the publisher.
Fig. 14.5, p. 484, J. Zubin and B. Spring, ''Vulnerability: A New

View of Schizophrenia." *Journal of Abnormal Psychology,* Vol. 86, 1977. Copyright © 1977 by the American Psychological Association. Reprinted by permission.

Chapter 15
p. 494 (t) National Library of Medicine (b) Culver Pictures
p. 496 Van Bucher/Photo Researchers
p. 498 Eric A. Roth/The Picture Cube
p. 500 G. Paul Bishop
p. 501 Courtesy of Dr. Joseph Wolpe
p. 502 Curt Gunther/Camera 5
p. 503 Allan Grant
p. 504 (both) Courtesy of Dr. Albert Bandura
p. 505 UPI/Bettmann Newsphotos
p. 506 Bohdan Hrynewych/Stock, Boston
p. 507 Ian Berry/Magnum
p. 513 © Andy Freeberg
p. 519 Lionel J. M. Delevigne/Stock, Boston
p. 520 Paul Fortin/Stock, Boston
p. 522 Jean-Claude Lejeune
p. 523 Sandra Johnson/The Picture Cube
p. 525 The Bettmann Archive
p. 526 Ken Heinen/NYT Pictures

RESEARCH, p. 511, after M. L. Smith and G. V. Glass, "Meta-analysis of Psychotherapy Outcome Studies." *American Psychologist,* Vol. 33, 1977, pp. 752-760. Copyright © 1977 by the American Psychological Association. Reprinted by permission.

Chapter 16
p. 532 Charles Biasiny-Rivera
p. 533 Margaret Thompson/The Picture Cube
p. 536 Michael Weisbrot and Family
p. 537 Hugh Rogers/Monkmeyer
p. 538 Peter Menzel/Stock, Boston
p. 540 © *Valley Daily News,* Tarentum, PA. Photo: John P. Filo
p. 542 (t) Wide World (b) Courtesy of Dr. Philip G. Zimbardo
p. 543 Wide World
p. 545 Martin A. Levick/Black Star
p. 548 William Vandivert
p. 554 (all) Copyright 1965 by Stanley Milgram. From the film OBEDIENCE, distributed by the New York University Film Division and the Pennsylvania State University, PCR
p. 556 Eric A. Roth/The Picture Cube
p. 562 UPI/Bettmann Newsphotos
p. 563 Frank Johnston/*The Washington Post*/Woodfin Camp

Fig. 16.1, p. 534, after R. B. Zajonc, *Social Psychology: An Experimental Approach.* Wadsworth, 1966, p. 12. Copyright © 1967 by Wadsworth Publishing Co., Inc. Adapted by permission of the publisher, Brooks/Cole Publishing Co., Monterey, Calif.
Fig. 16.2, p. 538, adapted from *Social Pressures in Informal Groups* by Leon Festinger, Stanley Schachter, and Kurt Back with the permission of the publisher, Stanford University Press. Copyright © 1950 by Leon Festinger, Stanley Schachter, and Kurt Back. Copyright renewed 1978.
Fig. 16.3, p. 539, adapted from S. Worchel and J. Cooper, *Under-*

standing Social Psychology. Homewood, Ill.: The Dorsey Press, 1976.
Fig. 16.4, p. 548, adapted from S. Asch, "Opinions and Social Pressure." *Scientific American,* 1955. Reprinted by permission.
Fig. 16.5, p. 549, adapted from S. Asch, "Opinions and Social Pressures." *Scientific American,* 1955. Reprinted by permission.
Fig. 16.6, p. 561, A. N. Doob, J. M. Carlsmith, J. L. Freedman, T. K. Landauer, and S. Toms, "Effect of Initial Selling Price on Subsequent Sales." *Journal of Personality and Social Psychology,* Vol. 11, 1969, pp. 345-350. Copyright 1969 by the American Psychological Association. Reprinted by permission of the publisher and authors.

Chapter 17
p. 569 Michael Weisbrot and Family
p. 571 Jean Shapiro
p. 573 (t) UPI/Bettmann Newsphotos (b) David Kennedy/TexaStock
p. 575 Dave Schaefer/The Picture Cube
p. 578 Richard Younker
p. 580 Dan Brinzac/Peter Arnold
p. 581 Bob Kalman/The Image Works
p. 583 David S. Strickler/The Picture Cube
p. 586 Owen Franken/Stock, Boston
p. 588 Courtesy of Dr. Philip G. Zimbardo
p. 589 Courtesy of Dr. Muzafer Sherif, from Sherif, M. and Sherif, C., *An Outline of Social Psychology* (Rev. ed.). New York: Harper & Row, 1956
p. 592 Donald C. Dietz/Stock, Boston
p. 597 Hazel Hankin/Stock, Boston

Fig. 17.1, p. 570, J. W. Thibaut and H. H. Kelley, *The Social Psychology of Groups.* New York: Wiley, 1959.
Fig. 17.2, p. 572, S. Rosenberg, C. Nelson, P. S. Vivekananthan, "A Multidimensional Approach to the Structure of Personality Impression." *Journal of Personality and Social Psychology,* Vol. 9, 1968, pp. 283-294. Copyright 1968 by the American Psychological Association. Reprinted by permission of the publisher and authors.
Fig. 17.3, p. 590, after J. B. Calhoun, "Population Density and Social Pathology." *Scientific American,* Vol. 206, 1962, pp. 139-148. Reprinted by permission.
Fig. 17.4, p. 594, after Baum and Greenberg, 1975.
Fig. 17.5, p. 595, S. Cohen, D. C. Glass and J. E. Singer, "Apartment Noise, Auditory Discrimination and Reading Ability in Children." *Journal of Experimental Social Psychology,* Vol. 9, 1973, pp. 407-422. Reprinted by permission.

Color Inserts
Color Plate 2.2 (tr) Manfred Kage/Peter Arnold
Color Plate 2.3 (bl, bc) Manfred Kage/Peter Arnold (br) Ed Reschke/Peter Arnold
Color Plate 3.3 (tl) Courtesy of Munsell Color, Baltimore, Maryland
Color Plate 3.4 (bl, br) MacMillan Science Co., Inc.
Color Plate 14.1 (all) Al Vercoutere, Malibu, CA
Color Plate 14.2 (tl, tr, bl, bc) Dan McCoy/Rainbow (br) Brookhaven National Laboratory and New York University Medical Center
Color Plate 14.3 (all) NIMH

NAME INDEX

NAME INDEX

SUBJECT INDEX

and reinforcement, 537
Frontal lobe, 39, 40, 42, 43, 60, 96, 482
Frustration
    and aggression, 21, 337–338, 344
    from crowding, 595–599
Frustration-aggression hypothesis, 337, 339
Fugue, 469–470, 491
Functional analysis, 405, 417, 502
Functional fixedness, 274
Functionalism, 5, 8, 26
Funiculi, 34

G factor, 421, 450
Gain-loss theory, 540, 564
Galvanic skin response (GSR), 219
Gambling, 579–580
Gandhi's Truth, 11
Ganglia, 33, 57, 59
Ganglion cells, 71, 73, 76, 78, 79, 80, 94, 95, 104
Gender identity, 369, 373, 379
Gender reassignment, 370
General anesthesia, 149, 150
General knowledge, 299, 300–302, 307
General mental facility, 421, 450
GENERAL PROBLEM SOLVER, 276
Generalization, 218–219
Generation of variation, 313
Generative processes
    and language, 280, 298, 306, 307
    and thinking, 275–276, 277
Generativity vs. stagnation crisis, 190, 200–201
Generator potential, 63
Genes, 168–170, 208, 313, 314, 324, 325–326, 343
Genetics and heredity
    and abnormal behavior, 462, 475, 477–482, 491
    and behavior, 14, 27
    and color blindness, 77
    and development, 166–171, 175, 177, 208
    vs. environment, 166–171, 208, 440–444, 451
    and intelligence, 434–437, 440–444, 447, 451
    laws of, 168
    and motivation, 177
    and personality, 400–401, 436–437
    and schizophrenia, 477–482
    and sexual behavior, 347
Genital stage, 348, 378, 386, 387–388, 416
Genotype, 169, 170, 208
Gestalt psychology, 5, 8, 12, 26, 103–104
Glia, 51
Goals
    of group, 550, 590
    personal, 12, 27, 389
    superordinate, 590, 599
    in therapy, 506
    unrealistic, 330
Gonadotropins, 362, 363, 379
Gonads, 316, 362, 379
Grammar, 286–289, 293–294, 298, 307
Grandmother cell, 105–106

The Grasp of Consciousness, 184
Grasping reflex, 173
Grief, 204, 205, 519–520
Griggs vs. The Duke Power Company, 431
Gross motor skills, 175
Group
    anonymity of, 542–543, 565
    and attraction, 537–541, 564–565
    and conformity, 547–551, 565
    and decision making, 583–587
    and environment, 591–597, 599–600
    goals of, 550, 565
    and intervention, 545–546
Group interactions, 583–591
Group norms, 541, 542, 583
Group stereotypes, 572–574, 580, 581
Group therapy, 506–509
Growth spurt, 175–176
Growth variations, 175
Guilt, 190, 195, 486, 487, 491, 555

Habituation, 57, 60, 275, 338, 344
Hair cells of ear, 85, 96
Hallucinations
    and altered states of consciousness, 133, 134, 137, 151, 154, 158
    and schizophrenia, 477, 483, 492, 516
Hallucinogens, 151–157, 161, 489, 492
Hammer of ear, 84, 85
Handedness, and the brain, 42, 43, 44, 60
Happiness, 333, 450
Hardy personality, 178
Health
    and aging, 203–204, 209, 445
    and cognition, 187, 445
    and life style, 177–178
    of mother, 172, 208
Hearing
    and the brain, 39, 60
    effect of noise on, 595
    and thresholds, 64
    See also Audition
Heart rate, 152, 350, 594
    controlling, 139–140, 141, 161
    and emotion, 316, 331, 344
Hello-goodbye effect, 509
Helplessness, learned or biochemical, 473–475, 478–479, 491, 492
Hemispheres of brain, 15, 27, 38, 39, 42–46, 59, 60, 274
    and antisocial personality, 487
    and cognitive skills, 375
    and consciousness, 130–132, 160
    and sensation, 79–80, 95
    and speech perception, 283–284, 292
Heredity, *See* Genetics
Heritability, 442–444, 451
Heroin, 55, 149, 150, 161, 172, 338, 488, 492
Hertz, 82, 95
Hidden observer, 147, 161
Hierarchical organization, 264–265, 277
Hierarchy of needs, 412, 418
Higher-order conditioning, 220, 224
Hippocampus, 36, 38, 251, 275, 336, 344
Histrionic personality, 485
Hits, in signal detection, 67, 68
Holophrasic speech, 293, 307

Homeostasis, 316–317, 318–319, 343
Homosexuality, 349, 357, 358, 359, 362, 371–373, 379, 390–391, 418, 502
Homunculus
    motor, 41
    of skin sensitivity, 91
Horizontal cells, 71
Hormones, 55, 175, 439
    and motivation, 316, 343, 344, 362–369
    and sexual behavior, 347, 356, 361, 362–369, 372, 378–379, 380
Hospitalization, 458, 516, 518–519
Hostility, 589–590, 599
Hotlines, 520
Hue, 76, 95, 102, 123
Human potential, 12–13, 498
Human Sexual Inadequacy, 351
Humanistic approach, 12–13, 27
Humanistic therapy, 498–499, 527
Hunger, 319–322, 343, 395
Hyperactivity, 151, 516, 518
Hypercomplex cells, 105, 123
Hypermetropia, 70
Hyperphagia, 320
Hyperpolarization, 56
Hypnagogic state, 134
Hypnosis, 11–12, 132, 144–147, 150, 161, 385, 460
Hypnotic suggestion. *See* Post-hypnotic suggestion
Hypnotic susceptibility, 146, 147, 260–261
Hypothalamus, 37, 38, 59, 133, 160
    and motivation, 316, 317, 318, 320, 321, 331–332, 336, 337, 343, 344
    and sexual behavior, 362–363, 367, 369, 372, 379
Hypothesis, 16, 20, 21
Hypovolemic thirst, 319, 343

I. E. Scale, 409
Icon, 245, 276
Iconic trace, 245–246, 276
Id, 388, 460, 461, 468, 498
Identical twins, 168
    and abnormal behavior, 475, 478–479, 480, 490
    and intelligence, 434–435, 436–437, 452
Identity
    and group, 542–543, 563, 583
    vs. role confusion, 190, 195, 196–197, 198, 202–203, 210
    as a visual skill, 114
Identity achievers, 202
Identity crisis, 196–197, 202–203, 389
Identity diffuse, 202, 203
Identity foreclosure, 202–203
Idiographic research, 398
Idiot savants, 423, 446–447
Illusion of control, 580, 595
Illusions, 98, 101, 108, 112, 114, 548
Illusory correlates, 390–391
Imagery, and memory, 252, 256, 259, 270–271
Imitation
    aggression, 236
    and grammatical development, 293–294, 307
Implosive therapy, 500–501, 511

Nature vs. nurture, 166–171, 174, 208, 401, 440–444, 451
Navajo medicine men, 524–525, 528
Near-death experience, 145, 158, 162
Needs, 312–344
    for achievement, 329–330, 338, 344
    for affiliation, 327–328, 330, 338, 344
    biological, 312, 313–323, 327, 343
    hierarchy of, 412
    and personality theories, 394, 402–404, 410–412
    social, 324–330, 338–339, 344
Negative afterimage, 76, 95
Negative correlation, 608
Negative reinforcement, 224–225, 241
Negatively skewed, 605
NeoFreudians, 11, 388–389, 416
Neonate, 173
Nerve deafness, 87
Nerve fibers, 33, 59, 60, 63, 95
Nerve impulse, 48, 60, 63
Nerves, 48
Nervous system, 31–60
    autonomic, 35, 38, 59, 137, 139, 140, 316, 317, 331, 333
    central, 33–35, 59, 172, 188
    the brain, 33–46
    and neurons, 47–59
    peripheral, 33, 35, 59
    and sexual behavior, 347
    sympathetic, 35, 59, 331, 353
    wiring diagram of, 56–59
Neural coding, 63–64, 94
    of light, 77–79
    of sound, 85–86
Neural control mechanisms, 315–323, 343
Neuroglia, 51
Neurology, 462
Neuron doctrine, 47
Neurons, 47–60
    electrical activity in, 48–51
    impulse transmission between, 51–56
Neurophysiology, 128–133, 159
Neuropsychology, 14, 22, 25, 28
Neurotransmitters, 14, 25, 28, 52–56, 57, 59, 60
    and depression, 475–476, 478–479, 492, 517
    and drugs, 151, 157, 161, 516–517
    and memory, 275
    and pain reduction, 25, 28, 54–55
    and schizophrenia, 480–482, 516–517
    and sensation, 63
    and sexual behavior, 367
Newsweek, 470
Nicotine, 149, 172, 175, 488
Nightmares, 469
Nodes of Ranvier, 48, 50, 51
Noise, and behavior, 594–595, 598, 599–600
Nominal scale, 603
Nominal use of numbers, 602
Nomothetic research, 398
Nondirective therapy, 498–499, 511
Nonprofessionals in mental health field, 520, 523–526, 527
Nonverbal abilities, 428, 451

Nonverbal communications, 375
Noradrenalin, 53, 316
Norepinephrine, 151, 367, 475, 478–479, 492, 517
Normal distribution, 607–608
Normal waking state of consciousness, 126, 158
Nucleic acid (DNA), 168, 275
Nutrition
    and adaptive behavior, 323
    and development, 172, 175, 177, 208

Obedience to authority, 554–555, 563, 564, 565, 587
Obedience to Authority, 555
Obesity, 177–178, 322–323, 343, 395–396
Object permanence, 10, 181, 183, 208
Observational learning, 23, 24, 236–237, 242, 340–342, 407, 409, 417, 500, 527
Observational method, 18, 28
Obsessive-compulsive disorders, 467–468, 491
Occipital lobe, 39, 40, 41, 43, 59, 81, 95
Occupational identity, 203, 210
Oedipus complex, 387
Old age. *See* Aging
Olfactory bulbs, 88, 89, 96
Olfactory cortex, 88, 96
Olfactory tract, 88
On Aggression, 334
One Flew over the Cuckoo's Nest, 514
Operant baseline, 223
Operant behavior, 223, 241, 404–406, 417
Operant conditioning, 7, 26, 221–222, 223–224, 229, 230
Operant learning and personality, 404–406
Operant techniques,
    in therapy, 500, 502–504, 505, 527
Operational definition, 16–17
Opiate receptors, 25, 55, 517
Opiates: of the brain, 25, 28, 54–55, 60, 157, 517; and drug abuse, 148, 149, 488, 492
Opium, 148, 149
Opponent process mechanism, 75–76
Opponent process theory of acquired motivation, 338–339, 344
Opposing colors, 75–76
Optic chiasma, 41, 44, 79, 81, 95
Optic nerve, 15, 41, 44, 49, 63, 70, 71, 79, 81, 94, 95
Optic tract, 41, 44, 81
Optimization theory, 314–315, 343
Oral contraceptives, 356
Oral-genital behavior, 358
Oral personality, 387, 490
Oral-sensory stage, 190
Oral stage, 348, 378, 386, 387, 417, 490
Ordinal scale, 603
Ordinal use of numbers, 602
Organ of Corti, 85, 96
Organic disorders, 464
Organic retardation, 447, 448, 452
Organization
    in artificial intelligence, 425

    in cognitive development, 180–181
    in impression formation, 571–574
    and memory, 262–267, 269, 271, 277
Organization of Behavior, 114
Orgasmic phase of sexual response, 350
Orgasm, 349, 350, 351, 352–353, 354, 355, 357, 360, 361, 371, 374, 380
Orienting reflex, 216
Osmoreceptors, 318, 343
Osmosis, 318
Osmotic thirst, 318–319, 343
Ossicles, 84, 96
Outer ear, 85
Oval window, 84, 85, 86, 96
Ovaries, 316, 362, 363–364, 365, 379
Overjustification, 553
Overlap, 107, 123
Ovulation, 356, 362, 363, 364, 365, 368, 379
Ovum, 168, 363
Ovum stage, 171, 208

Pacing genes, 170, 208
Pain
    control of, 144, 147
    inhibited by the brain, 25, 54–55, 60
    and motivation, 332, 338–339
    sensation of, 90, 94, 96
Pair bond, 355
Pancreas, 316
Papillae, 89, 96
Parallel transmission, 283
Paranoid delusions, 138, 151
Paranoid personality, 485
Paraprofessionals, 520, 523–525, 527
Parapsychological Association, 121
Parapsychologists, 120–121
Parasympathetic nervous system, 35, 59
Parenthood, 198–200, 209
Parenting styles, 196–197, 210
Parents
    and abnormal behavior, 461, 477, 479, 482–484, 486
    and achievement, 330
    and development, 190–194, 196–197, 198, 201, 202, 204, 206, 209, 225, 461
    and needs, 328
    and socialization, 536, 556, 568
    and therapy, 502, 508–509
Parietal lobe, 39, 40, 59–60, 80, 90–91, 96
Parietal lobe syndrome, 42
Parkinson's disease, 54–55
Partial reinforcement, 225–226, 241
Partial reinforcement effect, 232, 234
Partial report technique, 245
Passive-aggressive personality, 485
Pattern recognition, 105–106, 131
Patterns of Sexual Behavior, 358
Pavlovian conditioning, 215–221, 223–224, 240. *See also* Classical conditioning
Peak experiences, 143–144, 154–155, 161, 412, 418
Pearson product-moment correlation, 610
Peer groups, 177, 194, 195–196, 197–198,

209, 489
Pegword system, 270–271
Penis and penile erection, 137, 160, 348, 350, 351, 352, 353, 361, 362, 368, 369
Penis envy, 348, 387, 388
People's Temple, 563
Perception, 8, 14, 27, 62
  auditory, 119–122
  bias in, 582, 588, 589
  of depth, 106–111, 116
  and ESP, 120–121, 124
  and language, 304–306, 307
  of motion, 111–114
  and psychedelics, 151, 161
  and schizophrenia, 476–477, 483
  of shape and form, 102–106
  social-, 570–583, 598
  and social pressure, 546–547
  of speech, 281–285
Perceptual adaptation, 99–100, 122
Perceptual constancy, 100–102, 122, 123
Performance, 212–213, 240
  and an audience, 533–535, 564
  and language, 285–286
  and memory, 249
Peripheral nervous system, 33, 35, 59
Permissive parents, 196, 210
Personal construct theory, 412–413, 418
Personal space, 596–597, 600
Personal unconscious, 389, 390
Personal zone, 596–597
Personality, 203, 381–418
  assessing, 390–391, 415
  and ''common sense,'' 390–391
  dispositional theories of, 393–404, 417
  and learning theories, 404–410
  metatheories of, 414–416
  and parenting style, 197, 210
  and phenomenological theories, 410–414
  and psychodynamic approach, 10–11, 385–393, 416
Personality disorders, 463, 484–487, 491
Personality traits, 394, 397–401, 403–404, 405, 417, 571–572, 576, 578, 579
Perspective and perception, 106–107, 123
Persuasion, 555–558, 562, 563, 564, 565
PET (positron emissions tomography), scan, 482
Peyote, 154, 489
Phagocytes, 51
Phallic stage, 348, 378, 386, 387, 416
Phase, 82, 86–87, 95
Phasic events, 137, 160
Phenomenal field, 410
Phenomenological theories of personality, 408, 410–414, 417–418
Phenothiazines, 480, 515, 516, 517
Phenotype, 169, 208
Phenylketonuria (PKU), 444
Pheromones, 88, 93, 96, 365–366
Phi phenomenon, 111, 123
Phobias, 216, 465–467, 491, 500, 504–505, 561
Phonemes, 281–283, 284, 285, 292, 298–299, 306, 307
Phonology, 280, 298–299, 306
Phosphene, 116

Photoreceptors, 63, 71, 74
Phrase structure, 288–289
Phrase structure rules, 288, 289, 307
Phrenology, 39–40
Physical attractiveness and stereotypes, 573, 581–582
Physical dependence, 150, 161
Physical development, 171–179, 208
Physiological changes
  during dreaming, 137
  during meditation, 142–143
  from noise, 594
  during sexual response, 349–351
Physiological factors. *See* Biological factors
Physiological needs, 312, 313–323, 327, 412
Physique and personality, 394–395, 403, 417
Pia mater, 33, 34, 59
Piaget's cognitive development theory, 179–186, 188, 205, 208–209
Pigeonhole effect, 433, 451, 574
Pigment epithelium, 71
Pineal gland, 37, 59
Piperidyls, 515
Pitch, 82, 85, 87, 95
Pituitary gland, 37, 38, 54–55, 59, 88
  and motivation, 343
  and puberty, 175
  and sexual behavior, 363–364, 379
Place theory of hearing, 85, 86
Plasticity of brain, 117, 118, 123, 128–129, 159
Plateau phase of sexual response, 350
Pleasure
  -center, 332, 344
  and pain, 338–339
  and personality, 387
''Pleasure centers,'' 332, 344
Pleasure principle, 461
Pluralistic ignorance, 546–547
Polarization, 48–49, 53
Polyandry, 324, 352–353, 378
Polygenetically determined systems, 170, 208
Polygyny, 352–353, 378
Pons of brain, 36–37, 39, 59
Ponzo illusion, 101
Popularity, importance of, 195–196
Population, in research, 19, 611–612
Population density, 591–592, 594, 599
Position, sense of, 92, 94, 96, 118, 123
Positive afterimage, 76, 95
Positive correlation, 608
Positively skewed, 605
Post-hypnotic suggestion, 146, 147, 161, 260, 261, 460
Postconventional level of morality, 260–207
Posthypnotic amnesia, 146, 260–261, 278
Postsynaptic element, 52, 53, 54, 56, 157
Posttraumatic stress disorders, 468–469, 491
Poverty, and behavior, 592, 599
Precognition, 120
Preconscious mental activity, 385–386
Predictability hypothesis, 231, 241
Predictive validity, 431
Predisposition, 27, 145, 167, 214

to abnormal behavior, 462, 473
to homosexuality, 372, 379
Prefrontal lobotomy, 514
Prejudices, 252–253, 573. *See also* Group stereotypes
Premarital and extramarital sex, 349, 355, 357, 359, 361, 373, 378
Premenstral syndrome, 364
Premoral level, 206, 207
Prenatal period, 171–173, 208, 369, 373, 439, 447
Preoperational stage, 181, 183–184, 185, 208
Prepotent targets, 467
Press, and behavior, 403, 417
Presynaptic element, 52, 53, 157
Preterminal fibers, 48
Preventive psychology, 521–522, 527
Primacy-recency, 574–575, 598
Primary circular reaction, 182
Primary mental abilities (PMAs), 421–422, 450–451
Primary process, 138
Primary reinforcers, 224, 241, 535, 564
Principle of encoding specificity, 257–258, 265, 267–269, 274, 277
Prior context, 299, 300–302, 305, 306, 307
Proactive interference, 272
Probe technique, 271–272
Proceptivity, 363, 379
Profound retardation, 446, 447, 448, 451
Progesterone, 175, 362–363, 379
Programmed learning, 213–215
Projection, 461
Projective tests, 390–391, 392, 416
Propanediol, 515, 517
Propinquity, 537, 564
Protanopia, 77
Prototypic feature theory, 265, 296
Proxemics, 596–597, 600
Proximity, 104, 123
Proximodistal growth, 171
Psi phenomenon, 120–121
Psilocybin, 148, 149, 151, 152, 156
Psychedelics, 148, 149, 151–157, 161–162
  and model psychosis, 483, 492
  and mystical experience, 154–157
Psychiatric social workers, 495, 526
Psychiatrists and **psychiatry,** 462, 494, 519, 526
Psychoactive drugs, 14, 148, 149, 151–157, 161–162, 494, 515–518, 527
Psychoanalysis and psychoanalysts, 11, 20, 26, 144, 494, 495–498, 511, 524–525, 526, 527
  and assessment, 390–392
  and development, 197
  dreams in, 138–139, 160, 386, 391, 461, 496
Psychodrama, 507, 524, 527
Psychodynamic approach, 5, 10–12, 27
  and abnormal behavior, 460–461, 466, 468, 472, 486, 490, 491
  and personality, 385–393, 416
  and sexual behavior, 347–348, 353, 372
  in therapy, 495–498, 510–511, 527
Psychokinesis, 120, 121
Psycholinguists, 280–281

Role playing, 507, 588
Rorschach inkblot test, 19, 98, 390–391, 392, 411, 418
Rote learning, 262
Rubella, 172, 447
Rubin vase, 103

S factor, 421
S-R psychology. *See* Behaviorism
Saccule, 92
Safety need, 412
Saltatory conduction, 50–51
Satiety and satiety center, 320–322
Saturation, 76, 95
Scale of Temperament, 394
Schedules of reinforcement, 225–227, 241
Schemata
    and depression, 474, 505
    and language, 299, 302–303, 307
    and memory, 252–253, 273, 277, 278, 306
Schemes, 180–181, 182, 183
Schizophrenia, 464, 475–484, 491–492
    determinants of, 479–484
    and model psychosis hypothesis, 483, 492
    physiological bases of, 14, 55, 480–481, 516–517, 518
    treatment of, 157, 505, 516–517, 523, 527
    vulnerability model of, 484
Schizophrenic speech, 299
Schizotypal personality, 485
Scholastic Achievement Test (SAT), 17, 603
Schwann cells, 51
Scientific method, 16–26, 27–28
Sclera, 70, 71
Scotomas, 81, 98, 99
Scratch reflex, 58
Scrotum, 350, 369
The Seasons of a Man's Life, 389
Secondary circular reaction, 182–183
Secondary reinforcers, 224, 241, 535–536, 564
Secondary traits, 397, 417
Secretin, 316
Securely attached infants, 193, 194
Security stage, 191, 194
Sedatives, 149, 150, 161, 488, 489–490, 492
Selective attention, 122, 123, 247–249, 277
Self, 6, 202–203, 399, 408, 410–414
Self-actualization, 410, 418, 498, 527
Self-awareness
    loss of, 126, 142, 158, 159, 161
    and social development, 196
Self-concept, 410–411, 412, 418, 499
Self-confidence, 191, 550, 565
Self-control procedures, 506, 527
Self-efficacy, 408, 410
Self-esteem, 195, 202, 203, 411, 472, 474
Self-fulfilling prophecy, 580–583, 588, 599
Self-hypnosis, 143, 144
Self-image, 177, 196, 210, 552
Self-perception, 551–553, 556, 565
Self-report, 413

"Self theories." *See* Phenomenological theories
Semantic categories, 263–264, 289–291
Semantic generalization, 219
Semantic memory, 259–262, 273, 277, 278, 289–291
Semantics, 280, 289–291, 295–297, 298, 299, 305, 306
Semi-circular canals, 85, 92, 93, 118
Senescence, 178–179
Senility, 251
Senoi tribe and dreams, 138–139
Sensation, 5, 61, 62–96
    characteristics of, 62–68
    skin-, 90–91
Senses
    audition, 81–87
    chemical, 87–90
    and perception, 98
    of position and motion, 91–94
    somesthesis, 90–91
    specialized, in animals, 92
    vision, 68–81
Sensitivity, 67, 68
Sensitivity training group, 507, 527
Sensorimotor learning, 238–240, 241
Sensorimotor stage, 181, 182–183, 208, 296
Sensory experience, and drugs, 151, 152, 156, 161
Sensory memory, 244, 245–246, 247, 248, 255, 276, 277
Sensory thresholds, 64–65, 94, 157
Septal region, 38, 367
Serial organization, 262–263, 277
Serialization, 181
Serotonin, 157
Set, and drugs, 154
Set-point theory, 320–322, 343
Setting, and drugs, 154
Severe retardation, 446, 447, 448, 451
Sex-change surgery, 373
Sex characteristics, 176–177, 208
Sex-differences
    and abilities, 131, 132, 175
    and abnormal behavior, 471, 485
    and aggression, 341, 376
    and cognitive skills, 374–375
    and color blindness, 77
    and communication patterns, 375–376
    and conformity, 550
    and dreams, 136
    and growth spurt, 175–176
    and identity crisis, 203, 210
    and maturation, 177
    and sexual behavior, 347, 359, 361, 371, 373–376
    and stereotypes, 584–585
Sex hormones, 175, 362–367, 373, 378–379
    and homosexuality, 373
    and human responsiveness, 356–357
    and sexual differentiation, 368–369
Sex roles, 136, 202, 367, 370, 415, 418
Sex stereotypes, 376–377, 415, 573, 582, 583, 600
Sexual behavior, 345–380, 464
    and biosocial complex, 377–378

differentiation in, 367–373;
    and educational level, 349, 359
    hormones and, 362–367
    leading researchers in, 347–351
    and sex differences, 373–376
    and sexual response, 349–351, 378
    variations in, 351–361
Sexual Behavior in the Human Female, 349
Sexual Behavior in the Human Male, 349
Sexual differentiation, 367–373
Sexual fantasizing, 349
Sexual impulses or drives, 387–388, 416, 460, 467, 496, 498
The Sexual Life of Savages in Northwestern Melanesia, 355
Sexual response, 349–351, 378
Sexual revolution, 359, 378
Sexual therapy, 351
Shadowing, 122, 247, 248–249, 254
Shape consistency, 101, 122
Shaping, 405, 407, 502
Sheep-goat effect, 120
Shock treatment, 513–514, 522, 527
Short-term memory (STM), 187, 244, 246–249, 250, 251, 254, 255, 256, 257, 269, 271–272, 275, 276, 277, 278, 286, 445
Signal detection theory, 67–68, 94
Signaling pheromones, 365
Silent areas, of brain, 41
Similarity, 104, 123
Similarity-attraction theory, 538, 564
Simple cells, 105, 123
Simultaneous conditioning, 218
Situational attribution, 576, 577, 578–579, 598
Situational specificity, 414
Size constancy, 101, 122–123
Skewed distribution, 605
Skin sensation, 90–91, 94, 96
"Skinner box," 8, 223, 229, 233
Sleep, 133–138, 146, 160
Sleep spindles, 134
Smell, 64, 87–89, 93, 94, 96, 365
Smoking, 172, 175, 177
Social behavior, sex differences in, 376
Social comparison, 544–547, 551, 556, 565
Social comparison theory, 328
Social contracts, 207
Social development, 189–205, 209
Social influence, 532–566
    and attraction, 537–541, 556, 564
    brainwashing, 561–562, 564, 565
    comformity, 547–551, 565
    dissonance, 558–561
    informational, 533, 544–547, 549, 556
    obedience to authority, 554–555
    persuasion, 555–558, 562
    reinforcement, 535–541, 543, 547, 564
    self-perception, 551–553
    social comparison, 544–547, 551, 556
Social intelligence, 450
Social interaction, 532, 567–600
    environmental effects, 591–597
    group interactions, 583–591
    and sex stereotypes, 573, 582, 583, 600
    social perception, 570–583